ENCYCLOPEDIA
OF
FRONTIER
BIOGRAPHY

ENCYCLOPEDIA

OF

FRONTIER

BIOGRAPHY

IN THREE VOLUMES
VOLUME III
P-Z
INDEX

by
DAN L. THRAPP

Published by the
University of Nebraska Press
Lincoln and London
in association with
The Arthur H. Clark Company
Spokane, Washington

First Bison Book printing: 1991
Most recent printing indicated by the last digit below:
10   9   8   7   6   5   4   3   2   1

Library of Congress Cataloging-in-Publication Data
Thrapp, Dan L.
Encyclopedia of frontier biography / by Dan L. Thrapp.
p.   cm.
Reprint. Originally published: Glendale, Calif.: A. H. Clark Co., 1988.
Includes bibliographical references and index.
Contents: v. 1. A–F—v. 2. G–O—v. 3. P–Z.
ISBN 0-8032-9417-4 (set: paper).—ISBN 0-8032-9418-2 (v. 1: paper).—ISBN
0-8032-9419-0 (v. 2: paper).—ISBN 0-8032-9420-4 (v. 3: paper)
1. Pioneers—West (U.S.)—Biography—Dictionaries.   2. West (U.S.)—
Biography—Dictionaries.   3. Frontier and pioneer life—West (U.S.)—
Encyclopedias.   4. West (U.S.)—History—Encyclopedias.   I. Title.
[F596.T515   1991]
920.078—dc20
91-15482   CIP

Reprinted by arrangement with the Arthur H. Clark Company and Dan L. Thrapp

Abbreviations used in the bibliographical citations

AHS   Arizona Historical Society.

Amelia Williams   Amelia Williams, "A Critical Study of the Siege of the Alamo and of the Personnel of Its Defenders." *Southwestern Historical Quarterly,* Vol. XXXVI, No. 4 (Apr. 1933); XXXVII, Nos. 1-4 (July, Oct. 1933, Jan., Apr. 1934).

Appleton   *Appleton's Cyclopaedia of American Biography.* N.Y., D. Appleton & Co. 1887.

BAE   Bureau of American Ethnology.

Bancroft (plus title)   Hubert Howe Bancroft, *Works,* 39+1 vols. San Francisco, The History Co., 1874-1890.

Barry, *Beginning of West*   Louise Barry, *The Beginning of the West.* Topeka, Kansas State Historical Society, 1972.

BDAC   *Biographical Directory of the American Congress 1774-1971.* Washington, Government Printing Office, 1971.

BHB   Kenneth Hammer, *Little Big Horn Biographies.* Crow Agency, Montana, Custer Battlefield Historical and Museum Assn., 1965.

Black Hawk War   *The Black Hawk War 1831-1832,* 4 vols., comp. and ed. by Ellen M. Whitney. Springfield, Ill., Collections of the Illinois State Historical Library, Vols. XXXV-XXXVIII, 1970-78.

Bourke, *On Border*   John G. Bourke, *On the Border with Crook.* N.Y., Charles Scribner's Sons, 1891; (several other editions: with Index, Glorieta, New Mex., Rio Grande Press, 1969).

Bourne, *De Soto*   *Narratives of the Career of Hernando de Soto in the Conquest of Florida, as Told by a Knight of Elvas,* 2 vols., ed. by Edward Gaylord Bourne. N.Y., Allerton Book Co., 1922 (reprint, N.Y., AMS Press, 1973).

CE   *The Columbia Encyclopedia,* 3rd edn.

Chittenden   Hiram M. Chittenden, *The American Fur Trade of the Far West,* 2 vols. Stanford, Calif., Academic Reprints, 1954.

Chronological List   *Chronological List of Actions, &c., with Indians from January 1, 1866 to January 1891.* Washington, Adjutant General Office, 1891.

Clarke, *Lewis and Clark*   Charles G. Clarke, *The Men of the Lewis and Clark Expedition.* Glendale, Calif., Arthur H. Clark Co., 1970.

Coleman, *Captives*   Emma Lewis Coleman, *New England Captives Carried to Canada between 1677 and 1760,* 2 vols. Portland, Me., Southworth Press, 1925.

Cullum   George Washington Cullum, *Biographical Register of the Officers and Graduates of the U.S. Military Academy at West Point, N.Y.,* 8 vols. Boston, Houghton, Mifflin Co., 1891-1910.

DAB   *Dictionary of American Biography,* 22 vols. plus supplements. N.Y., Charles Scribner's Sons, 1958.

DCB   *Dictionary of Canadian Biography,* vols. I-IV. University of Toronto Press, 1966-1979.

Deeds of Valor   *Deeds of Valor... How American Heroes Won the Medal of Honor,* 2 vols., ed. by W.F. Beyer, O.F. Keydel. Detroit, Perrien-Keydel Co., 1907.

De Soto Expedition Commission   *Final Report of the U.S. de Soto Expedition Commission,* John R. Swanton, chairman. House Executive Document 71, 76th Cong., 1st Sess. (Serial 10328), Washington, Government Printing Office, 1939.

Dimsdale   Thomas J. Dimsdale, *The Vigilantes of Montana.* Norman, University of Oklahoma Press, 1953.

DNB   *Dictionary of National Biography,* 21 vols. London, Oxford University Press, 1973.

Dockstader   Frederick J. Dockstader, *Great American Indians.* N.Y., Van Nostrand Reinhold Co., 1977.

EA   *Encyclopedia Americana.*

EB   *Encyclopaedia Britannica.*

EHI   *Record of Engagements with Hostile Indians within the Military Division of the Missouri, from 1868 to 1882,* compiled from official records. Washington, Government Printing Office, 1882.

Farish   Thomas Edwin Farish, *History of Arizona,* 8 vols. San Francisco, Filmer Brothers Electrotype Co., 1915-1918.

fl.   Flourished (Birth/death date not known, but subject active at dates shown).

Griswold   Gillett M. Griswold, "The Fort Sill Apaches: Their Vital Statistics, Tribal Origins, Antecedents." Unpublished manuscript courtesy of Field Artillery Museum, Fort Sill, Oklahoma, 1970.

Handbook of Indians   *Handbook of North American Indians,* 20 vols., William C. Sturtevant, general editor. Washington, Smithsonian Institution, 1978.

Heitman   Francis Bernard Heitman, *Historical Register and Dictionary of the United States Army, from 1789 to 1903,* 2 vols. Washington, Government Printing Office, 1903 (and 1965 reprint).

Hodge, HAI   *Handbook of American Indians North of Mexico,* 2 vols., ed. by Frederick Webb Hodge. Washington, Smithsonian Institution (BAE Bulletin 30), Government Printing Office, 1907, 1910.

HT   *The Handbook of Texas,* 2 vols., ed. by Walter Prescott Webb, H. Bailey Carroll. Austin, Texas State Historical Assn., 1952.

Hunter TDT   *The Trail Drivers of Texas,* 2 vols., comp. and ed. by J. Marvin Hunter. Nashville, Cokesbury Press, 1925 (reprint N.Y., Argosy-Antiquarian, 1963).

Langford   Nathaniel Pitt Langford, *Vigilante Days and Ways.* Missoula, Montana State University, 1967.

Leach, *Flintlock*   Douglas Edward Leach, *Flintlock and Tomahawk: New England in King Philip's War.* N.Y., Macmillan Co., 1958.

McWhorter, *Hear Me*   Lucullus V. McWhorter, *Hear Me, My Chiefs! Nez Perce Legend & History,* ed. by Ruth Bordin. Caldwell, Ida., Caxton Printers, 1952.

MH   *Medal of Honor Recipients — 1863-1963,* 88th Cong., 2nd Sess., Senate Subcommittee on Veterans' Affairs. Washington, Government Printing Office, 1964.

MM   *The Mountain Men and the Fur Trade of the Far West: Biographical Sketches of the Participants,* 10 vols., ed. by LeRoy R. Hafen. Glendale, Calif. Arthur H. Clark Co., 1965-1972.

Montana, Contributions   *Contributions to the Historical Society of Montana,* 10 vols. Helena, 1876-1940.

Mormonism Unveiled   *Mormonism Unveiled; or the Life and Confessions of... John D. Lee... also... Mountain Meadows Massacre.* St. Louis, Bryan, Brand & Co., 1877 (and later printings).

NARS   National Archives and Records Service, Washington, D.C.

NCAB   *National Cyclopaedia of American Biography,* 60 vols. N.Y., Clifton, N.J., James T. White & Co., 1898-1981.

O'Neal, *Gunfighters*   Bill O'Neal, *Encyclopedia of Western Gunfighters.* Norman, University of Oklahoma Press, 1979.

Orton   Richard H. Orton, *Records of California Men in the War of the Rebellion, 1861-67.* Sacramento, State Office, 1890 (Index: J. Carlyle Parker, *A Personal Name Index to Orton,* Vol. 5, Gale Genealogy and Local History Series. Detroit, Gale Research Co., 1978).

Oscar Williams   *The Personal Narrative of O(scar) W(aldo) Williams 1877-1902: Pioneer Surveyor - Frontier Lawyer,* ed. by S.D. Myres. El Paso, Texas Western Press, Univ. of Tex. at El Paso, 1968.

Parkman   Francis Parkman, *Works — Frontenac Edition,* 16 vols. Boston, Little Brown and Co., 1899.

Password   published by the El Paso Historical Society.

PCA   Roscoe G. Willson, *Pioneer and Well Known Cattlemen of Arizona.* Phoenix, McGrew Commercial Printery (for Valley National Bank), 1951, 1956.

Porrua   *Diccionario Porrua de Historia, Biografía y Geografía de Mexico,* 2nd edn. Mexico, D.F., Editorial Porrua, S.A., 1965.

Powell   William H. Powell, *Powell's Records of Living Officers of the United States Army.* Philadelphia, L.R. Hamersley Co., 1890.

Price, *Fifth Cavalry*   George F. Price, *Across the Continent with the Fifth Cavalry, 1883.* N.Y., Antiquarian Press, 1959.

REAW   *Reader's Encyclopedia of the American West,* ed. by Howard R. Lamar. N.Y., Thomas Y. Crowell Co., 1977.

Register   *Society of Montana Pioneers, Volume I, Register,* ed. by James U. Sanders. Helena, the Society, 1899.

Sand Creek Massacre   *The Sand Creek Massacre: A Documentary History,* intro. by John M. Carroll. N.Y., Sol Lewis, 1973.

Swanton, *Tribes*   John R. Swanton, *The Indian Tribes of North America.* Washington, Smithsonian Institution (BAE Bulletin 145), Government Printing Office, 1953.

Sylvester   Herbert Milton Sylvester, *Indian Wars of New England,* 3 vols. Boston, W.B. Clarke Co., 1910.

Thwaites, EWT   *Early Western Travels, 1748-1846,* 32 vols., ed. by Reuben Gold Thwaites. Cleveland, O., Arthur H. Clark Co., 1904-1907 (reprint: N.Y., AMS Press, 1966).

Thwaites, JR   *The Jesuit Relations and Allied Documents: Travels and Explorations of the Jesuit Missionaries in New France, 1610-1791,* 73 vols., ed. by Reuben Gold Thwaites. Cleveland, Burrows Bros., 1896-1901 (reprint: N.Y., Pageant Book Co., 1959).

Twitchell, *Leading Facts*   Ralph Emerson Twitchell, *The Leading Facts of New Mexican History,* 2 vols. Cedar Rapids, Ia., Torch Press, 1911, 1912 (reprint: Albuquerque, N.M., Horn & Wallace Pubrs., 1963).

Williams, Amelia   *see* Amelia

Williams, Oscar   *see* Oscar

ENCYCLOPEDIA

OF

FRONTIER

BIOGRAPHY

P

Pablo, Michel, buffalo savior, ranchman (1853-July 11, 1914). B. at Fort Benton, Montana, he was the son of a Mexican horse wrangler and a Piegan Blackfoot mother. Michel was orphaned at an early age, was illiterate but "shrewd and enterprising and very highly respected," and came to own a ranch in the Flathead Lake country where he had been raised, perhaps by his mother's people. In the spring of 1873 a young Pend d' Orielle Indian, Samuel Walking Coyote acquired eight buffalo calves that had associated themselves with the herd of horses at his camp, six of the calves, two bulls and four heifers, surviving. By 1884 they had increased to 13 head and Walking Coyote determined to sell them. Charles P. Allard, cattle rancher on the Flathead Reservation, was trying to acquire a few buffalo, and negotiated with the Indian to purchase his small herd, Pablo being interpreter. Pablo became a partner of Allard in the transaction and the two purchased the animals for $2,000 in gold. The buffalo prospered. In 1893 the owners bought 26 head from Charles J. (Buffalo) Jones along with 18 cattalo, or crosses between buffalo and cattle, and by the time Allard died in 1896 the herd numbered 300 head; half was retained by Pablo and the other half kept by Allard's heirs. Pablo refused to part with any of his animals and it is said that after 1900 about 80 percent of the American buffalo surviving originated with his herd. When he learned in 1906 that the Flathead Reservation would be partially broken up, Pablo at last offered to sell the herd, first to the American government and after it proved dilatory, to the Canadian government, which contracted for the animals at $200 a head, upon delivery to Wainright, Alberta, an arduous undertaking carried out between 1907 and 1912. Over Pablo's grave is a simple monument inscribed with his name and a replica of a bull bison, the species he was instrumental in preserving.

John Kidder, "Montana Miracle: It Saved the Buffalo." *Montana Mag.,* Vol. XV, No. 2 (Spring 1965), 52-67.

Pacheco (Fatio) Louis, black adventurer (c. 1798-January 1895). B. a slave in 1798 or 1799, he was a full-blooded Negro "or nearly so," His earliest-known master was Colonel George Mercer Brooke, founder of Fort Brooke at Tampa Bay, Florida, who sold him to Major James McIntosh who in turn sold him in 1830 to Don Antonio Pacheco from whom he took the name by which he is known to history. Pacheco, of Sarasota, Florida, died within five years, leaving Louis to his widow. By 1835 Louis was in the prime of life, "good looking—intelligent (and) able to read and write," speaking English, Spanish, Seminole and perhaps French; he was valued at $1,000. As Seminole troubles increased Major Francis Dade was directed to march a column of more than 100 men from Fort Brooke inland to Fort King and, a guide being required, Pacheco was hired at $35 a month from Mrs. Pacheco. Pacheco apparently was in touch with Negro partisans of the Seminoles, and informed them of movements of the troops; December 28 the command was attacked and destroyed, only two soldiers surviving. Louis hid in tall grass until he could identify himself to the Seminoles whom he then joined. He probably took part in several subsequent encounters with troops and in depredations upon frontier inhabitants. In April or May 1837 Louis arrived at Tampa Bay with Jumper (see entry) who claimed him because he said he had saved Pacheco's life at the Dade massacre and therefore owned him as "the spoils of war." Jesup declined to return Louis to Mrs Pacheco and sent him with many Seminoles to Fort Pike, near New Orleans from where in the spring of 1838 he was to be sent with Seminoles to Indian Territory. However white slave traders claimed him and other Negroes who were held from May 21 to June 28, 1838, until the court denied slave trader claims and Pacheco and other blacks were released to the army to continue their westward journey. Pacheco no doubt reached Indian Territory and settled in with the Seminoles. Nothing is definitely known of him for 54 years. In 1892 he was said to have returned to Florida to end his days at Jacksonville and died three years later at the age of 95.

Kenneth Wiggins Porter, "Three Fighters for Freedom:... Louis Pacheco, the Man and the Myth." *Jour. of Negro Hist.,* Vol. XXVIII, No. 1 (Jan. 1945), 65-72.

Pack, Arthur Newton, conservationist (Feb. 20, 1893-Dec. 6, 1975). B. at Cleveland, he was graduated from Williams College and the Harvard Graduate School of Business, acquired a 23,000-acre New Mexico ranch and settled finally at Tucson, Arizona. He founded *Nature Magazine,* one of the first American publications of its kind, and edited it from 1932 to 1942; later he co-founded the noted Desert Musuem at Tucson, developed in Arizona a herd of antelope from seed stock brought in his personal airplane from Wyoming, and had many business, community, and conservationist interests. He published *The Nature Almanac* (1927); *Our Vanishing Forests* (1932); *Forestry, an Economic Challenge (1933); I See 'Em at the Museum (*1954), and other works. He died at Tucson.

Arizona Daily Star, Dec. 7, 1975.

Packer, Alferd, cannibal (Jan. 21, 1842-Apr. 23, 1907). B. in Allegheny County, Pennsylvania, he was a shoemaker by trade, serving in the Union Army from April until December 1862, when he was discharged for "disability." He prospected through the west. On November 8, 1873, he left Utah for Colorado in company with 21 men, five of whom accompanied him in a search for aid after they became snowbound near present-day Montrose, Colorado. Packer reached the Los Pinos Indian Agency on April 16, 1874, and, upon questioning, confessed that he had eaten his companions, whose remains were located by searchers. Packer was imprisoned at Saguache, but escaped. He was arrested in 1883 near Fort Fetterman, Wyoming, returned to Lake City and tried, being sentenced April 13, 1883, to death. He was spirited to the Gunnison jail to avoid a lynching, and held there three years. The state supreme court reversed his conviction on a technicality; he was tried again, convicted on five counts of manslaughter and sentenced to 40 years. He remained in the Canon City penitentiary until 1901 when he was freed

through efforts of *Denver Post* publishers Frederick Gilmer Bonfils and Harry Heye Tammen, who wanted to exhibit him in a circus. As an outgrowth of the Packer affair, both publishers were shot and wounded by lawyer William W. (Plug Hat) Anderson, who was tried three times before being acquitted, the trial judge remarking to Anderson that "your motive was admirable, but your marksmanship abominable." A judge's alleged comment at Packer's first trial that "there were just seven good Democrats in this county, and you ate five of them...." is not confirmed. Yet Packer has an enduring place in the folklore of the West, perpetuated to this day by "Packer Clubs," as protests against unpopular eating establishments and in support of other worthy causes.

A good work on Packer, including many pictures and interesting asides, is Fred and Jo Mazzula, *Al Packer: A Colorado Cannibal.* Privately printed, Denver, Colo., 1968.

Padilla, Juan de, Franciscan missionary (c. 1500-Nov. 30, 1542). B. in Andalusia, Spain, he arrived in Mexico in 1528 and the next year went with Guzman to Nueva Galicia, west of Mexico City; he may have been a soldier before turning to the church (it is said that "in his youth (he) had been a warrior"). He joined the Franciscan order and was ordained a priest. In 1533 he was at Tehuantepec with Antonio Ciudad-Rodrigo and Toribio de Motolinia to take part in an expedition Cortez was organizing for the Orient, but the vessels proved unseaworthy and the effort came to nothing. Padilla had worked with Indians at Ponzitlan, Tuchpan and Zapotlan and for a time was a superior of a monastery at Tulantzingo. In 1540 he joined the Coronado expedition to explore the American southwest. Padilla seems always to have been with the advanced element of Coronado's operation. He was at the capture of Háwikuh, southwest of Zuñi, New Mexico, and was with Pedro de Tovar in discovery of the Hopi towns to the westward in July 1540. Padilla incited the storming and occupation of the first of the villages. He was with Hernando de Alvarado who left Háwikuh August 29, 1540, for a reconnaissance eastward. They reached Tiguex, a complex of pueblos centered at the site of today's Bernalillo and urged upon Coronado selection of it for winter quarters. Proceeding eastward Padilla and Alvarado discovered the buffalo plains and completed an 80-day circuit. When the Turk concocted a fable that Bigotes, a Pueblo chief possessed a bracelet of gold, a metal of intense concern to the Spanish, it was Padilla and Alvarado who were assigned to "question" the chief about it. The means were not defined, but they found out nothing, because the chief knew nothing. When the Tiguex Indians rose against the Spanish, Padilla said he would approve any steps Coronado might think appropriate against them, but added that it "was not permissible for (the Spanish) to kill anyone," an interdiction ignored in the resulting action. Padilla was a member of the select company which Coronado led to Quivira in central Kansas in the spring of 1541. While most of the Spanish were disgusted that Quivira contained none of its rumored material riches, Padilla was intrigued by the rich harvest of souls to be found there. He returned to Tiguex with Coronado, but when the leader decided to return to Mexico, Padilla opted to go back to Quivira in pursuit of missionary labors. He took with him Andrés do Campo, a Portuguese, five Indians, two blacks, two "donados," or lay brethren: Lucas and Sebastien who were Indians from Michoacan, a mestizo or half-blood boy and two other servants from Mexico. As recounted later by do Campo and perhaps others, Padilla was well-received by the Wichita Indians of Quivira, establishing himself at a village two or three days south from Tabas, the *ultima thule* attained by Coronado the previous summer. The missionary station may have been in the vicinity of today's Lyons, Kansas. After working there briefly Padilla decided to visit tribes farther east on a reconnaissance but after a day or two he and his party, consisting of do Campo, Lucas, Sebastian and perhaps some others were set upon by hostiles, possibly Kaws or Kansa Indians, and Padilla was slain. A monument to the priest has been erected at Herington, Kansas.

George Parker Winship, *The Coronado Expedition, 1540-1542.* BAE, 14th Ann. Rep., Wash., Govt. Printing Office, 1896; Herbert Eugene Bolton, *Coronado: Knight of Pueblos and Plains.* Albuquerque, Univ. of New Mex. Press, 1964; A. Grove Day, *Coronado's Quest.* Berkeley, Univ. of Calif. Press, 1964.

Padocia, Wintun chief (fl. 1852-53). This individual led a band of about 85 Cottonwood Creek (Wintun) Indians in the Sacramento River region of California. They killed some white-owned beeves for food. Whites, coming upon the scene, destroyed all but one-quarter of the butchered beef, lacing the remnant with strychnine. "The Indians returned and devoured this, from the effects of which 65 or 70 of them died. Terror-stricken, Padocia complained...of the mysterious power that swept away so many of his people.... The chief was upbraided for stealing the white man's cattle," and was warned that the whites possessed this mysterious power of retaliation. Padocia replied that his people had been starving and had found the cattle "on the Indian's own land," and believed it all right to butcher some, according to informant Ned J. Jackson, who had taken part in the incident.

Lucullus V. McWhorter, *The Border Settlers of Northwestern Virginia.* Hamilton, O., Republican Pub. Co., 1915.

Page, John Hempstead, frontiersman (1834-c. Feb. 20, 1861). B. in Maryland, he reached Arizona from California with some filibusters who had meant to join Crabb, but were too late. In 1858 he was working for the Santa Rita Mining Company at Patagonia, Arizona. At Canyon de Oro, north of Tucson, he and Alfred W. Scott were riding ahead of a freight wagon when they were ambushed by Indians. Page's wife, the former Larcena Pennington, had survived a harrowing experience when captured by Indians and left for dead in mountains near Tucson, shortly after her marriage to Page.

Sacramento *Union,* Mar. 14, 1861; Constance Wynn Altshuler, ed., *Latest from Arizona! The Hesperian Letters, 1859-1861.* Tucson, Ariz. Pioneers' Hist. Soc., 1969.

Page, Larcena Ann, frontierswoman (1837-Mar. 31, 1913). B. in Tennessee, her father was Eli Pennington who arrived in Arizona in 1857 or 1858 with four sons and eight daughters; he and his sons fought Indians frequently, and some succumbed to them. Larcena on December 24, 1859, married John Hempstead Page, killed by Indians early in 1861. Later their child was born. A month after her marriage, she was captured by Indians. Unable to keep up with her captors, she was stripped, lanced, knocked in the head and thrown over a ledge east of Helvetia in the Catalina Mountains near Tucson, and left for dead. She recovered consciousness and, after 16 days of incredible hardships, managed to regain her home, her first request upon arrival was for a chew of tobacco. After Page's death, Larcena in 1870 married William F. Scott who adopted her daughter by Page. She was survived by her husband and two children, one the wife of Robert H. Forbes.

Farish, Vol. II, 199-200; Constance Wynn Altshuler, ed., *Latest from Arizona! The Hesperian Letters, 1859-1861.* Tucson, Ariz. Pioneers' Hist. Soc., 1969.

Palla(r)day, Leon Francois, interpreter (c. 1832-post 1879). B. perhaps at St. Charles, Missouri, it is said he went to the upper Missouri River country in 1849, although he once testified that he had spoken Sioux since 1844, when he would have been 12 years of age; perhaps he acompanied his later father-in-law, Edward de Morin to the northwest, although Morin was said to have been in California in 1844. Hyde said Palladay was an "American Fur Company man" from old Fort John, on the site of Fort Laramie, closely connected by marriage and trade with the Southern Oglala Sioux and Spotted Tail's Brulés; this suggests he had another wife, perhaps an additional one, to Morin's daughter. He was supposed to have been on Harney's 1855 expedition and present at the fight at Ash Hollow. In the 1850's Palladay was clerk at Geminien Beauvais' Five Mile Ranch, that distance east of Fort Laramie, the ranch a major operation. Palladay and Todd Randall were sent out from Laramie by an 1867 commission investigating the Fetterman massacre, to try and bring hostile Indians in to testify. Palladay became a foremost interpreter for Spotted Tail's people on the Pine Ridge Reservation, but he was not universally liked. In 1870 at a conference at Pine Ridge a sharp difference of opinion among Sioux as to whether Palladay should interpret broke up the meeting. In 1875 Palladay and other interpreters accompanied Red Cloud to Washington. Arriving in May, Palladay, "that child of trouble," led the Sioux delegation to a disreputable hotel for housing and "during the whole stay . . . was hopelessly drunk," thereby losing pay for his intended services. However in 1877 when Red Cloud again went to Washington, Palladay once more was an interpreter for him at White House and other conferences, this trip probably quite sober.

James C. Olson, *Red Cloud and the Sioux Problem.* Lincoln, Univ. of Nebr. Press, 1965; George E. Hyde, *Red Cloud's Folk.* Norman, Univ. of Okla. Press, 1937; MM, VII, 40, IX, 134; J.W. Vaughn, *Indian Fights: New Facts on Seven Encounters.* Norman, 1966.

Palmer, Archibald, fur trader (d. Feb. 1840). B. probably in England, he worked under the name of James A. Hamilton for the Upper Missouri Outfit, being in charge of Fort Union occasionally in the 1830s, where he served elegantly as host for intellectual and titled guests. He died, rather well off, at St. Louis.

Ray H. Mattison article, MM Vol. III.

Palmer, Innis Newton, army officer (Mar. 30, 1824-Sept. 10, 1900). B. in Buffalo, New York, he was graduated from West Point in 1846 and assigned to the Mounted Rifles (later the 3rd Cavalry). Beginning at Vera Cruz in 1847, he fought in the Mexican War to the capture of Mexico City, winning two brevets and a serious wound. In 1849 he marched overland from Fort Leavenworth to Oregon Territory, serving at Oregon City and Fort Vancouver, then taking part in Indian campaigns in Texas from 1852-54. He transferred to the 2nd Cavalry (which became the 5th) in 1855 and returned to Texas where he served, including some Indian operations, until the Civil War. He ended the conflict a brevet Major General of Volunters and brevet Brigadier General of the army. Palmer served on the Plains with the 2nd Cavalry as lieutenant colonel and colonel, retiring March 20, 1879, whereafter he divided his time between Washington, D.C., and Denver. He died at Chevy Chase, Maryland, and was buried at Arlington National Cemetery.

Heitman; Price, *Fifth Cavalry;* Ezra J. Warner, *Generals in Blue: Lives of the Union Commanders.* Baton Rouge, La. State Univ. Press, 1964.

Palmer, Joel, Indian official, pioneer (Oct. 4, 1810-June 9, 1881). B. in Ontario, his family returned to the United States with the start of the War of 1812, and Palmer lived in New York, Pennsylvania and Indiana where he served in the state legislature two terms and left in 1845 for Oregon as an aide to the leader of the 25-wagon train from Independence. His *Journal of Travels Over the Rocky Mountains* (1847) became a standard guidebook. Palmer returned to Indiana in 1846 and took his family to Oregon in 1847. He was named commissary-general of the military forces engaged in the 1847-48 Rogue River War. However, before the army was ready to move into Indian country, Palmer, appointed by the legislature superintendent of Indian affairs for Oregon, was directed with others to prevent the Cayuses and Nez Perces from joining for hostilities. Palmer addressed the Nez Perces successfully in March 1848. In late 1848 he journeyed to California, returned to Oregon, founded the community of Dayton and built a gristmill. In 1853 he again became super-intendent of Indian affairs "and bent his enormous energy and personal magnetism to the difficult task of obtaining all their lands from the Indians without creating enough dissatisfaction among them to cause a war." This sounds harsh, like robbing the natives of their territories, and in a sense it was, but Palmer was genuinely sympathetic to the Indians and respectful of their rights to the point where he came under severe censure from white Oregonians. He negotiated 10 treaties between 1853 and 1855: with the Umpqua Cow Creek Band, September 19, 1853; Rogue Rivers, November 15, 1854; Chasta (Shasta), November 18, 1854; Umpqua and Kalapuya, November 29, 1854; Kalapuya, January 22, 1855; Wallawalla, Cayuse (with I.I. Stevens), June 9, 1855; Nez Perces (with I.I. Stevens), June 11, 1855; tribes of middle Oregon, June 25, 1855, and with the Molala, December 21, 1855. Palmer diligently sought and found reservation territories for the dispossessed peoples, not all of it worthless land by any means, for "only Palmer and Meacham (of early Oregon Indian super-intendents) had any faith that the Indians were worth much effort." Palmer's reservation program was imitated to some extent by Stevens in Washington Territory. Willamette Valley settlers objected to Palmer's activities because "he recognized illegitimate chiefs when signing treaties; he was 'bringing in thousands of Indians'" to colonize too close to white settlements, and for his political beliefs. So great was the feeling against Palmer's removal of natives to their new reservations that some of these operations were protected by strong troop elements. Bancroft, conced-ing that Palmer made "some errors," yet adjudged his efforts on the whole "humane and just. His faults were those of an over-sanguine man, driven somewhat by public clamor, and eager to accomplish his work in the shortest time.... He succeeded in his undertaking of removing to the border of the Williamette Valley about 4,000 Indians, (and) for his honesty and eminent services, he is entitled to the respect and gratitude of all good men." In 1857 Palmer was removed from office because of white impatience with his solicitude for his charges. He opened a route to the British Columbia gold fields and entered business and railroad enterprises, served as a state representative, state senator and in 1870 was defeated for governor. He died at Dayton, Oregon.

Literature abundant: Bancroft, *Oregon*, Vols. I, II; Charles J. Kappler, *Indian Treaties 1778-1883*. N.Y., Interland Pub., 1972; Stephen Dow Beckham, *Requiem for a People*. Norman, Univ. of Okla. Press, 1971; DAB; Robert Ignatius Burns, *The Jesuits and the Indian Wars of the Northwest*. New Haven, Yale Univ. Press, 1966; Palmer, *Journal of Travels Over the Rocky Mountains;* Thwaites, EWT, XXX.

Palmer, Lucien, soldier (fl. 1862-1865). A sergeant of Company C, Veteran Battalion, 1st Colorado Cavalry, he testified in April 1865 before the military commission investigating the Sand Creek Massacre in eastern Colorado November 29, 1864. He participated in the affair and believed that "if the fight had been properly managed it would have been an easy matter to take the squaws and children prisoners," noting that most killed at Sand Creek were other than warriors. In cross-examination Chivington was unable to shake his testimony. Palmer also testified to scalping and mutilation and named Sayre as one of the officers responsible for some of it.
Sand Creek Massacre.

Palmer, Richard F. (Deadwood Dick), frontiersman (d. May 31, 1906). Little is known of Palmer who sought to become accepted as the Black Hills prototype for the Deadwood Dick of dime novel fame, but he failed to make the soubriquet stick. He died in Cripple Creek, Colorado.

Wayne Gard, "The Myth of Deadwood Dick." *Frontier Times,* Vol. 43, No. 6 (Oct.-Nov. 1969), 10-11, 48-50.

Palou, Francisco, Franciscan missionary (Jan. 22, 1723-Apr. 6, 1789). B. at Palma,

Majorca, Spain, he entered the Franciscan order November 10, 1739, was ordained in 1743 and eagerly joined Junípero Serra in determination to work in Indian missions in America. They and other future missionaries reached Vera Cruz, Mexico, December 7, 1749. In July 1767 Palou accompanied Serra to the Baja California missions that the Jesuits were forced that year to leave. Palou and Serra reached Loreto, on the east coast of Lower California April 1, 1768; when Serra the next year was assigned to Upper California where he would inaugurate a mission system, Palou succeeded to the presidency of the Lower California missions, holding the position until 1773 when the Dominicans took over. Palou, wishing to work again with Serra, elected to serve in Upper California and reached San Diego August 30. He journeyed on to Monterey-Carmel, Serra's headquarters, placing friars and mission helpers at the several stations enroute and collecting historical data on them, sending his report to the new viceroy of Mexico, Antonio María Bucareli y Ursúa. From thence forward Palou worked closely with Serra and was his representative on various journeys about the mission chain. October 9, 1776, the mission at San Francisco was established, Palou was assigned there and remained until 1784 when he went to Carmel to attend the dying Serra whose confessor he had been since 1750. Palou thereupon became acting president of the California missions. In 1785, his health failing, he took ship from Monterey to Mexico where he completed his life of Serra, most of which had been written in California. He died at the college of Santa Cruz de Querétaro where it is thought he was buried. Palou's fame is second to Serra's, but he was an able missionary, good administrator and a dependable historian. In his young manhood he was of medium height, swarthy in complexion, with dark eyes and hair.

Palou's Life of Fray Junípero Serra, trans. and annot. by Maynard J. Geiger. Washington, D.C., Acad. of Amer. Franciscan Hist., 1955; Geiger, *Franciscan Missionaries in Hispanic California*. San Marino, Calif., Huntington Library, 1969.

Pambrun, Pierre Chrysologue, fur trader (Dec. 17, 1792-May 15, 1841). B. in Quebec province, he received a good education and was commissioned during the War of 1812 on the British side. He became a clerk with the Hudson's Bay Company in 1815 (and chief trader by 1839). In a defense of the Red River settlement during a dispute with North West Company agents he was one of nine men who escaped, went to England in consequence of court investigations into the feud and returned to Canada in 1819. In 1825 he was assigned to the Columbia River District, reaching Fort Vancouver the following year, remaining to become a "mainstay" on its staff, stationed at Walla Walla. He befriended the Protestant missionaries led by Marcus Whitman, though himself a faithful Roman Catholic. Pambrun is credited with leading the expedition that discovered Nisqually Pass, south of Mt. Rainier. He died following a fall from his horse, his body being removed to the Catholic cemetery at Fort Vancouver.

Kenneth L. Holmes article, MM, Vol. III; Clifford M. Drury, *Marcus and Narcissa Whitman and the Opening of Old Oregon.* Glendale, Calif., Arthur H. Clark Co., 1973.

Panton, William, Indian trader (c. 1742-Feb. 26, 1801). B. in Aberdeenshire, Scotland, he emigrated about 1770 to Charleston, South Carolina, entering commerce, moving in 1775 to East Florida where he formed an association with Thomas Forbes to trade with Indians. Panton was a Loyalist and thus incurred the enmity of Georgians and South Carolinans, confiscation of his property in those areas and identification as an outlaw at the start of the Revolution. When it became apparent the British would evacuate St. Augustine, Florida, in favor of the Spanish, Alexander McGillivray, the Creek chief and himself a trader, persuaded Panton to continue his Indian trade which he agreed to do on condition McGillivray join the company as associate and guarantee protection against Indian hostility. The pact continued as long as McGillivray lived, Panton carrying on his concern for his friend's children thereafter. When Britain and Spain concluded a treaty in 1784, Panton, by then head of the largest mercantile house in East Florida, persuaded McGillivray to transfer commercial allegiance to Spain and assure that the trade would continue to enjoy Creek protection. This was done. If Panton assisted McGillivray extend his influence among his own people, the Creeks McGillivray helped strengthen Panton's position among the Spanish as an outstanding trader to Indians whom Spain required for protection of Florida's northern border against Georgian expansionism. Panton traded not only with Creeks, but with Cherokees, Choctaw and Chickasaw Indians, his commercial empire expanding to Mobile, New Orleans, Havana, Nassau and London. Aggressive Georgian and Carolinan traders with cheaper goods and possibly more rum gradually made inroads into Panton's "empire," but his enterprises survived. He became ill in 1801 and died at sea having embarked for medical attention abroad. Panton, who never married, "influenced, perhaps more than any other one man, the course of Spanish-Indian frontier relations in the Old Southwest in the last years of the eighteenth century."

John Walton Caughey, *McGillivray of the Creeks.* Norman, Univ. of Okla. Press, 1966; Arthur Preston Whitaker, *The Spanish-American Frontier, 1783-1795.* Lincoln, Univ. of Nebr. Press, 1969; DAB.

Papin, Pierre Didier, fur trader (Mar. 7, 1798-May 1853). B. at St. Louis, he had joined the American Fur Company by 1825. In 1829 he formed his own company in opposition, but soon sold out to his rivals. Papin, as trader for the Upper Missouri Outfit, worked near the White River, South Dakota, until about 1842 when he removed to Fort Laramie, then to Fort John near Scotts Bluff, Nebraska, occasionally returning to St. Louis on business or to visit with his French wife, by whom he fathered four children. He died at Fort John and was buried near Scotts Bluff.

William A. Goff article, MM, Vol. IX.

Pardee, Julius Hayden, army officer (c. 1848-July 15, 1900). B. in New York, he went to West Point from New Mexico and was assigned to the 25th Infantry June 12, 1871, transferring to the 23rd Infantry in August. He performed frontier duty at Fort Vancouver, Washington, for a year, and at Camp Grant, Arizona from 1872 to 1874; Pardee was at Fort D.A. Russell, Wyoming, in 1874-75. Attached as a "volunteer" to the 5th Cavalry, he was a witness of the Cody-Yellow Hand duel of July 14, 1876, on Warbonnet (Hat) Creek in Nebraska, at the time acting as aide-de-camp to Merritt. Pardee was assigned to frontier duty at Fort Gibson, Indian Territory, in 1877, promoted to first lieuten-

ant, and resigned in 1885. He died near Benham, New Mexico, where he had been a rancher for some years.

Don Russell, *The Lives and Legends of Buffalo Bill.* Norman, Univ. of Okla. Press, 1960; Cullum.

Pardo, Juan, explorer, military officer (fl. 1566-67). A Spanish army officer, Pardo may have served under Menéndez (see entry) in the ousting of the French from Florida in 1556; if so he sailed with Menéndez from Cadíz in June of that year for the New World. In 1566 he accompanied Menéndez northward to the "golden islands of Guale" off the Georgia coast and to Santa Elena (St. Helena) on the South Carolina coast near present-day Beaufort-Port Royal where Fort San Felipe was established. Under Menéndez's orders Captain Pardo, in command of 125 soldiers, left San Felipe November 1, 1566 "to discover and conquer the interior country from there to Mexico." He moved northwest, probably along the Coosawhatchie River to Cofitachequi (Canos), at Silver Bluff, South Carolina, on the Savannah River just southeast of Augusta, Georgia. Pardo continued north through Ysa to Joara in the Cheraw country at the head of the Broad River where he built Fort San Juan, leaving a sergeant, Boyano (Moyano) and a small garrison there. Pardo returned to Fort San Felipe by way of the Guatari (Wateree) Indians to the east, then living on the Wateree River near the present Camden, South Carolina. He arrived at San Felipe before the end of the year. September 1, 1567, Pardo set out again, retracing his route to Joara, continuing westward for ten days through a series of Indian villages to Chiaha (Chihaque, Solameco), probably on Burn's Island in the Tennessee River of northern Alabama. Here he joined Boyano who had established a post there which he called Santa Elena (II). Pardo continued his explorations beyond Chiaha to the west and south for a few days, one of his men perhaps reaching Coosa, on the middle Coosa River, Alabama. Pardo returned, leaving small detachments at Chiaha, Cauchi, Joara and Guatari, most later destroyed by Indians. Nothing is reported of Pardo's later career. He had accurately located some of the points he visited, established the presence of the Catawba Indians in western South Carolina, and his explorations were not without lasting significance.

John R. Swanton, *Early History of the Creek Indians and Their Neighbors.* Wash., BAE Bull. 73, Govt. Printing Office, 1922; Swanton, *The Indians of the Southeastern United States.* Wash., BAE Bull 137, Smithsonian Inst. Press, 1979.

Pariseau, Pierre (Old Garnier), frontiersman (c. 1793-Jan. 21, 1892). B. perhaps in France, he had reached the Oregon country with the Hudson's Bay Company by 1832 and helped establish a fur trade post on the Umpqua River. He spent 11 years there. Pariseau settled then near Champoeg, Oregon, became an American citizen in 1864, and returned to Douglas County, Oregon, in the south were he died at his home. He was buried at Nofog.

Harriet D. Munnick aritcle, MM, Vol. VI.

Parish, Frank, desperado (d. Jan. 14, 1864). Parish was named as a horsethief and roadster by Red Yager and was a member of the Plummer gang of desperados in southwestern Montana. He was married to a Bannock woman and with Bill Bunton ran a ranch on Rattlesnake Creek, an operation which assisted in disposing of rustled cattle. Parish also took part in an occasional stage holdup. He was the first of five prisoners picked up, all hanged from a single rafter on the same day at Virginia City. Although at first protesting innocence, Parish when confronted with facts by the Vigilance Committe "confessed to more and greater offenses than were charged against him." Before his execution he "gave abundant evidence of deep contrition." He died without a struggle.

Langford; Dimsdale; Birney.

Park, George S., pioneer (Oct. 28, 1811-June 6, 1890). B. at Grafton, Vermont, he left for Ohio at 14 and three years later became the second settler of Putnam County, Illinois; subsequently he founded Parkville, Missouri. He was a Mexican War colonel at 26. Afterward he published a liberal newspaper in Missouri, had his press dumped in the river by his critics. As a Missouri state senator he was anti-slavery and pro-Union. In 1875 he removed to Magnolia, Illinois where he farmed until his death there; he was buried at Parkville. Park was married.

Vassar Views, special ed., Vol. 49 (July 1977); information from Mary B. Aker, Platte County Hist. Soc., Parkville, Mo.

Parke, Benjamin, military officer, jurist (Sept. 22, 1777-July 12, 1835). B. in New Jersey, the *Dictionary of American Biography* gives his birth date as September 2. Parke received the scant education available in his day, and went to Lexington, Kentucky, about 1797, studying law there and being admitted to the bar. He moved to Vincennes, Indiana, where he practiced law and filled various public offices including two terms with Congress as a representative from Indiana (1805-1808). For a decade he served in the militia. When Indian troubles arose culminating in the Battle of Tippecanoe, he raised a company of dragoons and joined the expedition under Harrison, participating in the Tippecanoe action, afterward being made a major, commanding the Harrison cavalry. He later served as Indian agent, and assisted in negotiating several treaties including the important ones with the Potawatomi, Miami, Wea and Delaware of October 26, 1818, signed at St. Mary's, Ohio, Parke, with Indiana governor Jonathan Jennings and Lewis Cass being the U.S. commissioners. By these agreements, central Indiana was taken over by the whites. "As a jurist Parke took high rank among the pioneer judges of Indiana," on the bench for about 27 years. He was first president of the Indiana Historical Society, serving from 1830 until his death. He married and fathered two children, but outlived them both.

BDAC; DAB; Charles J. Kappler, *Indian Treaties: 1778-1883.* N.Y., Interland Pub., 1972.

Parke, John Grubb, army officer (Sept. 22, 1827-Dec. 16, 1900). B. in Chester County, Pennsylvania, he was raised at Philadelphia, was graduated from West Point in 1849 second in his class, and joined the topographical engineers. He was second in command of the Lorenzo Sitgreaves 1851 exploration-survey from the Zuni villages of New Mexico westward to the Colorado River, down it to Yuma and thence westward to San Diego. Parke was assigned to survey passes along the 32nd and 35th Parallels in California for a future railway route and in December 1853, was ordered to find a possible route from the Pima villages on the Gila River in Arizona to El Paso, Texas. He organized an expedition of 58 men and worked westward along the route of the Cooke Wagon trail as far as the present site of Benson, Arizona, then by way of

Nugent's Pass north of the Dragoon Mountains he crossed the Sulphur Springs Valley and threaded Apache Pass, thence moving on to El Paso. Two years later he made a more detailed survey including alternate routes. In 1857-61 he was chief astronomer and surveyor establishing the boundary between Canada and the United States in their western extensions. Parke's full report on this expedition was never printed and the manuscript seems lost. By late summer of 1861 Parke was a captain. His Civil War service was good and he emerged a brevet Major General with permanent rank of major in the engineers; from 1866 until 1869 he worked with the Northwest Boundary Commission again. He served as assistant chief of engineers until appointed superintendent of West Point in 1887, retiring in 1889 as a colonel. He engaged in private pursuits of some variety until his death at Washington, D.C. Among his writings was his "Report of Explorations... Near the 32nd Parallel of Latitude, Lying Between Dona Ana, on the Rio Grande, and Pima Villages, on the Gila," in HED 129, 33rd Congress, 1st Session, 1855.

Cullum; Heitman; DAB; Jay J. Wagoner, *Early Arizona: Prehistory to Civil War.* Tucson, Univ. of Ariz. Press, 1975; John E. Parsons, *West on the 49th Parallel.* N.Y., William Morrow and Co., 1963; Andrew Wallace, "Across Arizona to the Big Colorado: The Sitgreaves Expedition of 1851," *Arizona and the West,* Vol. 26, No. 4 (Winter 1984), 325-64.

Parker, Charles, army officer (c. 1842-Dec. 12, 1890). B. in Madison County, New York, he listed his occupation as a farmer when he was mustered in as captain of the 71st Illinois Infantry in July 1862, being mustered out in October. He was commissioned a captain in the 17th Illinois Cavalry in 1864 and mustered in at St. Charles, Illinois. He joined the 9th Cavalry in 1866 and served with it on the southwestern frontier to the rank of major at the time of his death. During the Victorio and Nana campaigns, Parker was active, but has frequently been confused with Henry K. Parker who was not commissioned but a chief of scouts with the honorary title of "Captain." Parker won two brevets in 1867 for "gallant and meritorious service in battle."

Heitman; Nat. Archives, Parker's military file; William H. Leckie, *The Buffalo Soldiers.* Norman, Univ. of Okla. Press, 1967.

Parker, Ely Samuel (Hasanoanda, Donehogawa), Seneca leader, army officer (1828-Aug. 31, 1895). B. in Genesee County, New York, he was descended from Seneca chiefs and leaders, although he took his name from a white friend. He received an education but went to Washington, D.C., at 18 where for 20 years he helped promote Indian claims and became friends with such notables as President Polk. In 1852 he became a sachem of his tribe. Parker served Lewis H. Morgan as interpreter and collaborator in Iroquois research, his assistance acknowledged in the dedication to Morgan's *League of the Ho-de-no-sau-nee or Iroquois,* "still the best single volume on these Indians." Parker read law but was refused admission to the bar on citizenship grounds so he turned to civil engineering, becoming successful at that profession. At Galena, Illinois, he became acquainted with Ulysses S. Grant. In the Civil War Parker, because of his race, had difficulty becoming commissioned but eventually was named captain of engineers. September 18, 1863, he joined Grant as staff officer in the Vicksburg operation, becoming his military secretary as lieutenant colonel, August 30, 1864, and having a role in Lee's surrender. Parker was breveted up to Brigadier General in the U.S Army and in the Volunteers; after the war he served as colonel aide-de-camp to Grant from 1866 to 1869. He married a Washington woman and fathered a daughter. Parker was the first native American to become commissioner of Indian affairs as one of Grant's initial appointments as President. "His many changes in the existing system, designed to give justice to the Indians, earned him enemies," however, and he was tried for fraud by a House committee. He was fully exonerated, but resigned and went into business, making a small fortune in Wall Street, but losing it by paying the bond of a defaulter. He joined the New York City police department; Parker died at his home at Fairfield, Connecticut. He finally was buried in the Red Jacket lot of a Buffalo, New York, cemetery on land that had belonged to his tribe.

Literature abundant; *Science,* Vol. 185, No. 4156, Sept. 20, 1974.

Parker, Fleming, desperado (c. 1866-June 4, 1898). B. in Tulare County, California he became a cowboy but turned to crime and served five years at San Quentin Penitentiary for burglary. Released, he reached Arizona and on February 8, 1897, he and Jim (alias Harry) Williams of Utah held up an Atlantic and Pacific Railroad train at Peach Springs, Arizona. Williams was killed and Parker captured and jailed at Prescott. May 9 he and others broke out, killing an assistant county attorney. Parker stole Sheriff George C. Ruffner's saddle horse, Sure Shot, for his getaway, having the horse re-shod with the shoes on backwards to foil pursuit; the plan crippled the horse but didn't prevent Parker from being arrested at Tuba City, Arizona, by the sheriff. He was tried and sentenced to death. Parker was the last man hanged on the courthouse plaza at Prescott, Arizona. He was described as 5 feet, 7 1/2 inches tall, weighing 165 pounds and with light grey eyes, brown hair and regular features.

Prescott *Courier,* Centennial issue, May 15, 1964, B 1; William B. Secrest, "Tell the Boys I Died Game." *True West,* Vol. 27, No. 3 (Jan.-Feb. 1980), 28-30, 57-60.

Parker, George (or Robert) LeRoy (Butch Cassidy), desperado (Apr. 5, 1866-1909? 1911? 1937?). B. the eldest of 10 children of a Mormon family of English antecedents near Circleville, Utah, his first name is uncertain, although he himself said it was George. His father was named Robert. The boy was raised on a ranch that had been headquarters for a rustler gang among whom Mike Cassidy had stayed on as a cowhand. George became a cowboy and skilled shot. As an adult he was 5 feet, 9 inches tall, weighed 155 pounds, and had blue eyes, light brown hair, medium build. He helped drive Cassidy's cattle to Telluride, Colorado, where in company with Tom McCarty, outlaw, and Matt Warner he held up the San Miguel Valley Bank on June 24, 1889. A circuitous flight followed, Cassidy, or Parker, wintering at Lander, Wyoming, where he acquired a "horse ranch." He and others were attracted to the so-called Johnson County War, but arrived too late for the shooting and went on to Belle Fourche, South Dakota, where they attempted to rustle cattle but were dispersed by a posse. He worked on ranches in Wyoming and Utah for some time, being arrested for a misdemeanor at Rock Springs, Wyoming, but acquitted; he turned to part time rustling again and in 1892 established a "ranch" with Al Hainer in the

Wind River country near Lander, Wyoming. In June 1893, Cassidy and Hainer were arrested for horse rustling, but acquitted. The next year, in a victimless shootout Cassidy and Hainer were captured by Sheriff John H. Ward and Deputy Bob Calverly of Uintah County, Wyoming, Cassidy convicted of horse theft July 15, and sentenced to two years in the Wyoming State Prison at Laramie. He was pardoned on January 19, 1896, on his pledge, not to give up rustling, but to steal no more stock in Wyoming. He returned to Diamond Mountain in Brown's Hole, Colorado, and with Elza Lay, Bob Meeks and others organized his own gang, soon considering rustling "petty larceny," and concentrating on cash robberies. On August 13, 1896, Cassidy, Lay and Meeks robbed the Montpelier, Idaho, bank of about $7,000 to raise funds to defend colleagues charged at Vernal, Utah, with several slayings. Warner and William Wall were taken to Ogden for trial, refusing an offer from Butch to spring them, and were convicted. On April 21, 1897, Cassidy, Bob Meeks and Elza Lay stole about $8,000 in a Castle Gate, Utah, coal mine payroll holdup, and escaped to Robbers' Roost, Utah. With recruits from the Hole in the Wall gang of Wyoming, Cassidy formed a group known as the Train Robbers' Syndicate, but their first essay was thwarted by detective Charles Siringo who had penetrated the group and discovered a secret code used by its members. The syndicate included Cassidy and Lay, George Curry, Lonny and Harvey Logan, Harry Longabaugh, and others. Cassidy failed in an attempt to rob a bank at Evanston, Wyoming, being warned off by a spy. On October 19, 1896, he also was foiled when trying to rob a mine payroll at Rock Springs, Wyoming. On June 2, 1899, he probably participated with Curry, Logan and Lay in the Wilcox, Wyoming, Union Pacific train holdup, netting $30,000; he, Lay and others fled south through Arizona to Alma, New Mexico, where they worked on the WS Ranch for a time, and from which Lay took part in a Folsom, New Mexico, train robbery and was imprisoned after a shootout. Cassidy subsequently tried to reform, on one occasion meeting with the governor of Utah, but could not clear away past offenses and his tentatives came to nothing. August 29, 1900, he held up a Union Pacific train near Tipton, Wyoming, assisted by Longabaugh, Logan, and two others; the loot was inconsequential. With Longabaugh and Bill Carver he held up the First National Bank of Winnemucca, Nevada, on September 19, 1900; they got $32,640. On July 3, 1901, Cassidy, Longabaugh, Logan and Camilla Hanks held up a Great Northern train near Wagner, Montana, getting $65,000 in unsigned bank notes, easily traced. Determined to go to South America, probably to begin a new life, Cassidy, Longabaugh and a woman, Etta Place, left New York City February 20, 1902 (the date is disputed) for Buenos Aires aboard the freighter, *Soldier Prince*. They reached Argentina in March and obtained four square leagues of land in Chubut Province, working their ranch until 1906 by which time lawmen from the United States were closing in upon them. In March 1906, the trio, assisted by another American fugitive, robbed a Mercedes bank in San Luis Province, obtaining $20,000. The banker was killed. At Bahia Blanca not long afterward they took an equal amount from another bank. In Bolivia they held up a pay train at Eucalyptus. December 7, 1907, they held up a bank at Rio Gallegos, Argentina, getting $10,000. Perhaps they committed other crimes during their South American careers. After a holdup of a mine payroll near Quechisla, southern Bolivia, in early 1909, they were cornered at San Vicente, near Uyuni; legend has it that after a furious battle, Cassidy killed the mortally wounded Longabaugh and shot himself. The exact date is unknown. A photograph of the two dead bandits was reportedly identified by people who knew them well; others said the man identified as Cassidy in the picture actually was Tom Dilley, a minor Robbers Roost outlaw who also had fled to South America; that continent had more than its share of American outlaws during the years in question. According to another source the three were killed when trying to rob a bank at Mercedes, Uruguay, in December 1911. Yet another account has it that Cassidy alone, or he and Longabaugh returned to this country, Cassidy dying in July 1937, in Spokane, Washington, being buried under the alias of William K. Phillips. Other versions of his subsequent career exist. Cassidy had many redeeming qualities; acquaintances reported him good-natured, generous, truthful, and a man of some fine principles who unfortunately also possessed an uncontrollable wild streak.

Literature abundant; see: Charles Kelly, *The Outlaw Trail: The Story of Butch Cassidy and the "Wild Bunch."* N.Y., Bonanza Books, 1959; James D. Horan, *The Wild Bunch.* N.Y., Signet Books, 1958.

Parker, Henry Kinney, chief of scouts (Nov. 1854-pre 1929). B. at Corpus Christi, Texas, of a pioneer family, Parker roamed Texas, Old Mexico, New Mexico and Arizona before 1879. In January of that year he applied for a trader's license at San Carlos, Arizona, being recommended as one familiar with the Apache language, but the license was not issued despite the recommendation of San Carlos Agent Henry Lyman Hart. January 1, 1879, Hart had approved Parker's becoming chief of police at the San Carlos agency; while so employed Parker seems to have acquired a nucleus herd of beef cattle that should have been issued to the Apaches, arousing the ire of Captain Adna Romanza Chaffee, who replaced Hart as San Carlos Agent in July 1879. Late in September Parker resigned, to be succeeded by Clay Beauford (Welford C. Bridwell), Chaffee being "well pleased" with the change and reporting to the Commissioner of Indian Affairs Ezra A. Hayt that while Parker had been stealing cattle intended for issue, then trading until he "got an excellent herd," it had been impossible to prove corruption as the only people cognizant of the details were Indians involved in it, and they would not talk. Parker became a chief of scouts under Second Lieutenant James A. Maney in November 1879, retaining the position until late 1880. He was scouting for Major Albert Payson Morrow on the San Francisco River, a tributary of the Gila on the New Mexico-Arizona border when on May 17, 1880, he asked Morrow's permission to take his scouts, since the soldiers were immobilized by broken-down stock, and see what they could turn up. Morrow assented. Parker scouted southeasterly toward the Black Range for four days, then met Colonel Edward Hatch, commanding the District of New Mexico, at Ojo Caliente, where he had gone for rations. Hatch approved of Parker's mission, told him to "go out and kill one or two Indians" to pass the time. Parker continued his scout southward along the east face of the Black Range. The second day he found a camp of hostile Indians under the dread Victorio who had gone out in August

1879 and engaged in many skirmishes with troops, but was still not bested. During the night of May 23 Parker with his 59 scouts surrounded the Victorio camp, in a narrow canyon with towering cliffs about. At daylight on May 24 firing commenced, the startled Apaches being unable to break through the ring and forced to fight all day at a nearly hopeless disadvantage; Parker estimated that 30 had been killed, some estimates run as high as 55, but the chief of scouts conceded that many of the slain were women and children. Victorio himself was wounded in the leg, and no scouts were lost. The following morning Parker sent a courier to Hatch requesting ammunition and support, since the great Apache was in a death trap. No answer was received and, out of ammunition, Parker assumed his courier had been killed and pulled back, taking with him 160 captured horses. His engagement was the one clear victory over Victorio ever achieved in the United States and the decisive action in the stubborn Victorio war; from this point forward Victorio's star was in decline. He made for Mexico and never again posed any threat to New Mexico. Parker continued active in the field. June 5, 1880, he had a sharp fight with fleeing Apaches, killing three, among them Victorio's most able son, Washington, a greatly feared raider. Parker again operated with Maney from August 1 to October 21, 1880, after Victorio had been killed in Mexico; in all he reported he had had eight fights with Apaches. The Army was reluctant to bestow much credit on a civilian chief of scouts, but the people of southwestern New Mexico were not so reserved and July 16, 1880, he was presented with a $300 gold watch by the citizens of Silver City, New Mexico, in recognition of the fact that "by his brave and tireless energy, (he) not only inflicted terrible punishment upon the murderous Apaches, but...had driven them from our soil." The watch bore the inscription: "Presented to H.K. Parker, Chief of Scouts, by the citizens of Grant County, N.M., as a token of their appreciation of his bravery and success in the Indian wars of 1880." Parker settled for a time in Silver City, became a sutler at Fort Cummings, New Mexico, and in July 1882 was reported in business with Al Higbee at Chihuahua, Mexico. In 1906 upon the death of his mother at Corpus Christi, Texas, H.K.

Parker was reported living "in New Mexico," though his business and place of residence were not given. In his young manhood Parker was described as "slightly more than six feet in height, is spare in flesh, brown hair and light beard, keen gray eyes, and weighs 160 pounds. His actions are all deliberately made, yet he exhibits a nervous restlessness characteristic of frontiermen."

Information form John Bret Harte; Tucson, *Arizona Weekly Citizen,* Feb. 6, 1881; *Corpus Christi Daily Caller,* July 16, 1906, May 10, 1952; information from Susan Berry, Silver City Museum; information from Allan Radbourne; Dan L. Thrapp, *Victorio and the Mimbres Apaches.* Norman, Univ. of Okla. Press, 1974.

Parker, Isaac Charles, hanging judge (Oct. 15, 1838-Nov. 17, 1896). B. near Barnesville, Ohio, he was admitted to the bar in 1859 and began practice at St. Joseph, Missouri. He served briefly as corporal in Co. A, 61st Missouri Emergency Regiment, early in the Civil War, but soon quit the service, becoming city attorney for St. Joseph in 1862, circuit attorney in 1864, resigning in 1867. He served as a congressman from 1871-75, was appointed chief justice of Utah Territory, but declined and was appointed judge of the U.S. district court for western Arkansas March 19, 1875, serving until his death at Fort Smith. A liberal in some ways, he was an early advocate of woman's suffrage and promoted progressive measures for the Indians. At Fort Smith his jurisdiction extended over Indian Territory, a region rife with lawlessness of all kinds. One of Parker's initial acts was to appoint 200 deputy marshals; 65 were slain while he was in office. In his initial term he tried 18 murder cases with 15 convictions secured. In 31 years he passed the death sentence on 162 persons, of whom 80 were hanged. Yet he was considered "neither harsh nor cruel," his sympathies with the victims rather than the criminals. "He was well versed in the English common law, but treated the law as a growing organism" and believed that safeguards for the rights of prisoners should not protect murderers from punishment. Parker was a man of humor and was intensely interested in education. He fathered two sons. He was buried in the National Cemetery at Fort Smith.

DAB; BDAC.

Parker, James (Galloping Jim), army officer (Feb. 20, 1854-June 2, 1934). B. at Newark, New Jersey, he was graduated from West Point in 1876 and became a second lieutenant with the 4th Cavalry assigned initially to Fort Sill, Indian Territory, later to Texas. He went with Mackenzie into Mexico on a raid against Kickapoo villages in June 1878; Parker continued frontier service at Fort Hays and Fort Riley, Kansas, Fort Wingate, New Mexico, and Fort Apache, Arizona, participating in a number of scouts. He served on the Ute campaign and in Colorado in 1879-81. Parker was involved in the Geronimo campaign of 1885-86 until its conclusion, became a captain in 1888, was acting superintendent of Sequoia National Park in 1893-94 and, after Volunteer service in the Spanish American War, became a major in the 4th Cavalry in 1901, winning a Medal of Honor in 1902 for his part in the defense of Vigan in the Philippines. Parker was made a lieutenant colonel of the 13th Cavalry in 1903, colonel of the 11th Cavalry in 1907, a Brigadier General in 1913 and a Major General in 1917, but was forced by age into retirement February 20, 1918. Subsequently he was awarded three Silver Stars, one for an action during the Geronimo campaign at Devil's Creek, New Mexico, May 22, 1885, and a Distinguished Service Medal for "his unusual professional attainments, sound judgment, and devotion to duty (which were) material and important factors in the development of organizations of the American Army, and contributed in a signal way to their successful operation in action against the enemy." Joseph Dorst Patch called Parker "an original." When a Brigadier General, Patch wrote, Parker was stationed at Brownsville, Texas, and "itching for a fight with the Mexicans who had been insulting us from across the Rio Grande River. On one occasion Parker crossed the river to get at them, but he was hauled back and reprimanded by the Wilson Administration... trying to avoid a war with Mexico." Parker was considered by some the leading cavalry commander in the Army at the height of his career, and was convinced cavalry could have been used to good effect in World War I, many senior officers agreeing with him. Parker wrote *The Mounted Rifleman* (1916) and *The Old Army, Memories* (1929). He was intelligent, very able, and vigorous, but opinionated, dogmatic and his views and recollections sometimes are subject to question.

Cullum; Heitman; NCAB, XXV, 376; Parker, *The Old Army, Memories.* Phila., Dorrance & Co., 1929.

Parker, Quanah, Comanche leader (c. 1845-Feb. 23, 1911). B. among the Kwahadi band of Comanches near the later Wichita Falls, Texas, he was the son of Cynthia Ann Parker, a white woman captured by Indians and Chief Peta Nocona, who had married her. Quanah became a noted raider and participated with his kinsmen against buffalo hunters and other whites for many years, becoming widely known and feared. He was prominent in the unsuccessful June 1874, battle against about 30 white buffalo hunters at Adobe Walls, in the Texas Panhandle, but about a year later was forced to surrender at Fort Sill, accepting a reservation in southwestern Oklahoma. Here he became the tribesmen's principal spokesman and leader for the ensuing 30 years, committed to the ways of peace. He encouraged education, agriculture and, while retaining his Indian culture, became something of a businessman. He was of distinctly Indian appearance, virtually indistinguishable from his Comanche relatives. He died near Fort Sill.

Literature abundant.

Parker, Rachel T., frontierswoman (Apr. 24, 1822-July 15, 1906). B. in Green County, Illinois, she was early widowed and married Thomas R. Parker (1817-1887) a Pennsylvanian, in 1843 at Fort Gibson, Indian Territory. In 1845 they moved to Corpus Christi, Texas, which had been founded five years earlier by Henry Lawrence Kinney whose name they bestowed upon a son who became famous in the Indian wars. While Zachary Taylor's troops were camped nearby Tom Parker was granted a contract to supply them beef; the Parkers accompanied the troops to Camargo, Mexico, where they remained until the cessation of the Mexican War. Rachel Parker sewed the flag flown by Taylor at the Battle of Buena Vista. In 1848 the couple lived at Brownsville, Texas, for a few months. Here Captain Richard King, who was to found a ranching empire famed to this day, boarded with the Parkers and it was King who taught Rachel to read and write. The

Parkers returned to Corpus Christi which was their home for the remainder of their lives. They became parents of two girls and ten boys, among them Henry Kinney Parker who won fame in the Victorio War in New Mexico. Thomas and Rachel Parker died at Corpus Christi and were buried in Bayview Cemetery.

Corpus Christi Daily Caller, July 16, 1906, May 10, 1952; information from Margaret Rose, local history department, Corpus Christi Public Libraries.

Parker, Samuel, Congregational missionary (Apr. 23, 1779-Mar. 21, 1855). B. at Ashfield, Massachusetts, he was graduated from Williams College, studied theology under Theophilus Packard and after a year was licensed to preach. He served as home missionary in New York State until entering Andover Theological Seminary of Massachusetts and in 1812 was ordained. His first wife died shortly after the marriage and in 1815 he married again. Parker served New York congregations until 1835 when a call from the Nez Perce Indians of the northwest stirred him and he went with Marcus Whitman to the Pacific Northwest. When Whitman returned east, Parker went on to Oregon, arriving at Walla Walla October 6 and Fort Vancouver on the 16th. He explored the country west of the Cascades for missionary purposes, wintered at Vancouver and in April 1836 returned up the Columbia to tour the country of the Walla Walla, Cayuse, Nez Perce, Spokan, Colville and Okanogan Indians, when he returned to Vancouver. He took ship, visiting Hawaii, rounding Cape Horn and reaching the east coast May 18, 1837, after a journey in all of about 28,000 miles. Parker never returned to Oregon, although retaining an interest in it and seeking to promote missionary work there. He wrote *Parker's Exploring Tour Beyond the Rocky Mountains* (1838). He was struck by paralysis in 1849, partially recovered and died at 76. Parker had a flinty concept of his faith and as Thwaites recalls, described in his book the discovery once in the wilderness of a wooden cross over a grave; he regarded it as a form of idolatry, signifying nothing, and broke it into pieces, explaining to his Indian companions that it was more proper to place a stone at head and foot of a grave solely to mark its place, adding that "without a murmur they cheerfully acquiesced, and adopted our custom."

Thwaites, EWT, XXVII, 368n.; Myron Eells, *Marcus Whitman, Pathfinder and Patriot.* Seattle, Alice Harriman Co., 1909, Appendix A.

Parker, Theophilus, army officer (Dec. 1, 1856-May 27, 1927). B. in North Carolina he graduated from West Point and was commissioned a second lieutenant in the 8th Infantry June 15, 1877, being assigned to frontier duty against Apaches in Arizona and resigning August 27, 1879. He worked then for the Southern Railway at Danville, Virginia except for his service as major of the 4th United States Volunteers in 1898-99, for the rest of his active career. He died at Danville, Virginia, at 70.

Cullum; Heitman.

Parker, Thomas Titah, descendant (Oct. 15, 1889-July 9, 1975). B. near Cache, Oklahoma, he was the son of Quanah Parker, and when he died was the last surviving child of that noted Comanche-white leader. He had married Helen Fisher of Oklahoma City April 7, 1919, and moved to near Apache, Oklahoma, where he farmed. Quanah was son of Cynthia Ann Parker, captured in Foard County, Texas, by Comanches, and Peta Nocona, a chief of that people.

Foard County News, July 17, 1975, via Hugh O. Norman Sr., Albany, Tex.

Parkhurst, Charles Dyer, army officer (June 29, 1849-May 15, 1931). B. in Massachusetts, he went to West Point from Rhode Island and was commissioned a second lieutenant in the 5th Cavalry June 14, 1872, being sent immediately to Arizona where he was heavily engaged in operations against the Apaches. He was in fights December 14 and 20, 1872; January 19 and at Turret Mountain March 25-26, 1873; in the Aravaipa Mountains April 28 and the Mazatzal Mountains May 17-18, 1874. Parkhurst was at Fort Hays, Kansas, in 1875 and took part in Crook's Big Horn and Yellowstone Expedition of 1876, attending the action at Slim Buttes, Dakota, September 8-9. He was at Fort McPherson, Nebraska, in 1876-77, being engaged in scouting and the Wind River expedition against the Nez Perces in September-October 1877. He served at Fort McKinney, Wyoming, in 1877-78, becoming a first lieutenant August 23, 1878. Parkhurst was on the Ute operation in Colorado in 1879-80. He transferred to the 4th Artillery June 12,

1884, and became a captain in the 2nd Artillery March 8, 1898. Parkhurst retired a colonel March 9, 1909. He died at Springfield, Massachusetts.

Cullum; Heitman; Powell.

Parkhurst, Charlotte Darkey (Cockeyed Charley), stage driver (1812-Dec. 29, 1879). B. at Lebanon, New Hampshire, she was abandoned by her parents, placed in an orphanage but ran away in boys' clothing and met livery stabler Ebenezer Balch at Worchester, Massachusetts. Balch taught "Charley" to drive a team and in her teens she could manage a six-horse team and coach. With Balch she moved to Providence, Rhode Island, and, an accomplished stage driver, went to Georgia and thence in 1851 to California where, posing as a man she became one of the most prominent and ablest of all California stage drivers. Because a horse had damaged her left eye with a well-placed hoof, she wore a patch over it. She drove many routes in the Mother Lode country and along the coast, and carried on her disguise aided by a strong taste for chewing tobacco and cigars. On November 3, 1868, she was said to have become the first female to vote in the United States (while posing as a male), casting a ballot in Santa Cruz County. She sometimes worked as a logger or raised stock. She remains an enigma as a person and with respect to reasons for her lifelong disguise; apparently she was in no way a lesbian. Charley was 5 feet, 7 inches, in height, and died of cancer in her cabin near the 7 Mile House, near Watsonville, California. An autopsy disclosed her secret and also evidence that she once had given birth; a trunk disclosed a baby's red dress.

Craig MacDonald, *Cockeyed Charley Parkhurst: The West's Most Unusual Stagewhip.* Palmer Lake, Colo., Filter Press, 1973; Charles Outland, *Stagecoaching on El Camino Real.* Glendale, Calif., Arthur H. Clark Co., 1973.

Parkman, Francis, historian (Sept. 16, 1823-Nov. 8, 1893). B. at Boston, the son of a minister, he was grandson of a wealthy merchant whose estate provided him with means to carry on his historical work. Early interested in wild places and outdoor life, he nevertheless attended Harvard University and made Phi Beta Kappa. His life's work, the story of the struggle of France and Britain for America, began to take shape in his mind at this time, and was strengthened by his long wilderness journeys during vacations. In April 1846, he set out on the journey from which *The Oregon Trail* (1849) was written, the year that also saw George Ruxton and Lewis Garrard investigating the west; Parkman's aim was to study the Indians in their primitive life-style, and, although illness plagued him, he succeeded in this, living with a band of Sioux, although briefly. The last of the 15-volume work, the two-volume *History of the Conspiracy of Pontiac,* was published in 1851; the remainder followed irregularly, interrupted frequently by Parkman's continuing illnesses and near blindness which caused him to write at times with a noctograph, a device of framework and spaced wires to guide the pen so as not to cross lines. Once for five years he could neither concentrate nor see to write for more than a few minutes at a time, but he persisted and slowly the great design emerged. Although somewhat out of sequence, they were published as follows: *Pioneers of France in the New World,* 2 vols. (1865); *The Jesuits in North America in the Seventeenth Century,* 2 vols. (1867); *Discovery of the Great West* (LaSalle), 1 vol. (1869); *Old Regime in Canada,* 2 vols. (1874); *Count Frontenac and New France under Louis XIV,* 1 vol. (1877); *A Half-Century of Conflict,* 2 vols. (1892); *Montcalm and Wolfe,* 3 vols. (1884), and *History of the Conspiracy of Pontiac.* Parkman also wrote a novel of little importance, a horticultural book on roses and numerous articles on varied subjects. Perhaps America's greatest historian, at least of the narrative manner, Parkman held strong views on the preparation necessary for such work. "Faithfulness to the truth of history," he wrote, "involves far more than a research, however patient and scrupulous, into special facts.... The narrator must seek to imbue himself with the life and spirit of the time," and this he did, even to residing briefly in an Italian monastery to better understand how those of the monastic life comprehended their role. Parkman had wide interests, enjoyed people, possessed many friends and held a number of positions, not all honorary by any means. Describing him as "the greatest writer among American historians," Mason Wade pointed out that his histories have "stood the test of time, for much later research and investigation have disproved only a detail or two in the vast field in which he was a pioneer." The accuracy and judgment with which he used primary sources in English and French were remarkable for one of his physical limitations. It seems unlikely that his major work will ever be surpassed or supplanted.

Literature abundant; see *The Journals of Francis Parkman,* ed. by Mason Wade, 2 vols.   N.Y. and Lond., Harper & Bros., 1947.

Parmeter, James W., army officer (1832-c. 1906). B. at Cincinnati, Ohio, he became a carpenter and builder and worked in Bureau County, Ilinois. He then studied architecture at Niles, Michigan, and came to Olathe, Kansas, in March 1858. In April 1861 he enlisted in the 2nd Kansas Infantry and, having helped raise Company C was elected first lieutenant, serving six months. He then assisted in organizing Company H, 12th Kansas Infantry and was commissioned captain in August 1862 by General James H. Lane. In 1862 he and other volunteer officers were captured by Quantrill at Olathe, but paroled. Parmeter was stationed at Fort Larned, Kansas May 6, 1863, and assumed command of the post October 19. Larned was a key for controlling the Plains Indians, and Parmeter was reported a confirmed drunkard. Elliott Coues visited the post late in May 1864 and wrote in his journal: "We brought up at Fort Larned — mean place, built of adobe and logs, with a drunken officer in command; everybody half drunk already; and all were whole drunk by bed-time." Major T.I. McKenny, staff officer to General Samuel R. Curtis then in command of the Department of Kansas, reported confidentially: "Every officer and man that I have heard speak of (Parmeter characterize him) as a confirmed drunkard," and warned of the fragile situation with the central Plains tribes with a general war possible. In late May William Bent brought in many chiefs of various tribes to Larned to have a talk with Parmeter but said the officer and men "treated the Indians badly," and they were insulted and went away with no result. Shortly afterward, Setangya, a famous Kiowa chief was threatened when he approached the post on a friendly visit and his warriors therefore ran off 240 animals. Parmeter may have been responsible for driving some tribes to the warpath. Curtis irately ordered Chivington to get rid of Parmeter, "that

drunken captain," and Chivington placed him under arrest in July, replacing him with Captain William Backus of the 1st Colorado Cavalry. Parmeter was still at Larned until December 1864 in which month he was dismissed from the service for "habitual drunkenness." He joined L.W. Divelbias in a firm designated as "architects and builders" in 1882. He was married in 1859 and fathered a son. Parmeter was living at Olathe in 1905 and by 1908 he had died, his widow surviving him.

Information from B. William Henry, Jr., historian, Ft. Larned Nat. Historic Site; Stan Hoig, *The Sand Creek Massacre.* Norman, Univ. of Okla. Press, 1974; George Bird Grinnell, *The Fighting Cheyennes.* Norman, 1956; information from the Kan. State Hist. Soc.; A.T. Andreas, *History of the State of Kansas.* Chicago, 1883.

Parnell, William Russell, army officer (Aug. 13, 1835-Aug. 20, 1910). B. at Dublin, Ireland, McDermott gives his year of birth as 1836; his relationship if any to Irish nationalist leader Charles Stewart Parnell (1846-91) is undefined. At 18 Parnell enlisted in the 4th Hussars, transferred to the Lancers and fought in the Crimean War, being a survivor of the Charge of the Light Brigade at Balaclava. He arrived in the United States in 1860 and at the outbreak of the Civil War enlisted in the 4th New York Cavalry, served largely with the Army of the Potomac and rose to lieutenant colonel, winning two brevets. His Civil War service was excellent; he was captured once, but escaped, and was wounded several times, once severely. February 3, 1866, he was commissioned a second lieutenant in the 1st Cavalry, promoted to first lieutenant within eight months. Sent with the company to California, Parnell served under Crook; he had a prominent role in the September 26-28, 1867, Battle of Infernal Caverns near the Pit River, winning a brevet for gallantry and was wounded by an arrow March 14, 1868, in an action at Dunder and Blitzen Creek, Oregon, again under Crook. Parnell saw action with Perry in the Modoc Indian War of 1872-73. He participated in numerous other Indian campaigns and scouts in the northwest before again coming to prominence in the June 17, 1877, Nez Perce action at White Bird Canyon, Idaho. Here Parnell won a Medal of Honor (and another brevet) for saving the life of an enlisted man whose horse had been killed while crossing a marsh and whom Parnell and a few men, "in the face of a very heavy fire and at imminent peril" extricated safely. He took part in the Battle of Clearwater, Idaho, July 11-12, 1877, and in the Bannock campaign of 1878 was in the action on Birch Creek July 8 and that at John Day's River crossing, July 20. Parnell with ten men, an interpreter and guide was detailed for special duty in February 1879 to the Okanagau Pass, a severe winter journey, part of which lay through British Columbia. He became a captain April 27, 1879. He served at several northwestern posts, was on duty briefly at the Western Shoshone Indian Reservation in August 1881 and finally retired February 11, 1887, because of "wounds in line of duty." He was promoted to major on the retired list in 1904 and spent the last decade of his life as a military instructor at St. Matthew's School, San Mateo, California. He was described as a "large fleshy man" who "taxed the powers of his horse quite heavily," but was generally conceded to be a fine soldier whose career was outstanding.

Powell; John D. McDermott, *Forlorn Hope: The Battle of White Bird Canyon and the Beginning of the Nez Perce War*. Boise, Ida. State Hist. Soc., 1978; Bancroft, *Oregon*, II, 538-44, 548; Parnell, "The Battle of White Bird Canon," and "The Salmon River Expedition," in Cyrus Townsend Brady, *Northwestern Fights and Fighters*. Garden City, N.Y., Doubleday, Page & Co., 1923.

Parrilla, Diego Ortiz, military officer (fl. 1749-1780). B. in Spain, Parrilla served against the Moors, then in Cuba and at Vera Cruz as a dragoon commander. He was interim governor of Sinaloa and Sonora and successful in several Indian wars until 1756 when he became commandant of the new mission, San Sabá de la Santa Cruz for the Plains Apaches on San Sabá River, a mile north of the present Menard, Texas. He did not approve of its location, and was dubious about Apache expressions of interest in conversion and in fact the Lipan Apache never did come in because of fear of Comanche raids. Parrilla arrived at the San Sabá Presidio, established to protect the mission, in April 1757. March 16, 1758, the mission was attacked by 2,000 Comanches with ten persons, including two missionaries, killed, the other whites fleeing to the shelter of the presidio, which was besieged unsuccessfully for several days. Parrilla, who favored

abandoning the San Sabá missionary work as hopeless, offered however to lead a military operation against the northern Indians, and this notion was viewed favorably at Mexico City. A new attack by Indians in March 1759 resulted in 19 persons killed on the San Sabá and 750 horses swept off. By August 1759 Parrilla had readied a command of 380 militia and regulars, 90 mission Indians and 174 other auxiliaries, more than 600 men in all reinforced by several cannon. About 150 leagues northeast of San Sabá a Tonkawa village was surprised, 55 warriors killed and 149 persons captured. October 7 the command reached the Taovayas (Wichita) villages on the Red River 12 miles north of today's Ringgold, Texas where a large body of Indians were entrenched behind breastworks and a stockade, flying a French flag and employing French arms, as Parrilla believed. For four hours the battle raged, at the end Parrilla withdrawing having lost 52 killed with no estimate of the wounded although Parrilla himself was struck in the arm. He supposed he had inflicted equal losses upon the enemy, although there was no way to tell. Two cannon and the extra baggage were abandoned and the command sped back to San Sabá, the enemy pursuing the entire distance and the retreat becoming a rout. San Sabá was reached October 25 concluding the 17-day campaign which was "long regarded as a disgrace to Spanish arms." The cannon were not recovered for 20 years. Athanase de Mézières secured them in the spring of 1778 bringing them to Bucareli on the Trinity River in the present Madison County, Texas. Parrilla reached San Antonio in November and Mexico City in the summer of 1760 when he was reassigned to a presidio in Coahuila. He was governor of Coahuila during the last half of 1765. Late in 1766 he explored the southern Texas coast, seeking evidence of British intrusions there. He found none. He named Corpus Christi Bay and charted coastal features. By 1769 he was at San Antonio again planning another military operation against the Indians, though his activities on the frontier are not further reported. He was promoted to Brigadier General by 1780.

Herbert Eugene Bolton, *Texas in the Middle Eighteenth Century*. Austin, Univ. of Tex. Press, 1916, 1970; Noel M. Loomis, Abraham P. Nasatir, *Pedro Vial and the Roads to Santa Fe*. Norman, Univ. of Okla. Press, 1967.

Parsons, George, diarist (1850-Jan. 5, 1933). He came to Tombstone, Arizona, from San Francisco in 1880, established the mining firm of Parsons and Redfern, and became a community leader. He kept a journal from April 27, 1879, to June 27, 1882, and pocket diaries until 1929. The material was broad in scope, concerning Indians, mining, outlawry, and so on. With related documents they are at the Arizona Historical Society, Tucson, Arizona. On June 22, 1881, Parsons was injured in the great fire that swept Tombstone. He was a witness, or near-witness, to much turmoil surrounding Tombstone while the Earps were there.

Ed Bartholomew, *Wyatt Earp: The Untold Story.* Toyahvale, Tex., Frontier Book Co., 1963; Charles C. Colley, *Documents of Southwestern History.* Tucson, Ariz. Hist. Soc., 1972.

Pas-lau-tau (Pash-ten-tah, Bach-e-on-nal), bronco Apache (d. Mar. 11, 1890). An Apache probably of the San Carlos Reservation at least in his maturity, Pas-lau-tau was enlisted as an army scout and became a colleague of the Indian known as the Apache Kid. He was involved with the Kid, Hale and Say-es in the wounding of Al Sieber at San Carlos June 1, 1887, then bolted the reservation heading south; short of Mexico they swung about however and surrendered, being tried by court-martial, convicted and sentenced to death, a sentence reduced by Miles to 10 years confinement. Brought back to Arizona and retried by a civilian court upon a clarification of jurisdiction, Pas-lau-tau and the others were sentenced to seven years in the Territorial Prison at Yuma. Enroute by stagecoach driven by Eugene Middleton from Globe to the railroad at Casa Grande, Pas-lau-tau and three others, handcuffed two and two, were taken from the vehicle to lighten it moving up a sandy wash and eventually lost sight of it. The foremost two prisoners, including Pas-lau-tau overcame sheriff Glenn Reynolds who was leading the way, and Pas-lau-tau killed him with his own weapon; the rear pair disarmed Deputy William Holmes who died of a heart attack. Pas-lau-tau, catching up with the stage then wounded the driver and with keys extracted from the sheriff's pocket, freed the Kid and other prisoners, the broncos bolting for the San Carlos hinterlands. Lieutenant James Waterman Watson and a detachment including Apache scouts, ran down the band of five broncos believed responsible on the Salt River. In a sharp aciton on the Gila River Pas-lau-tau was wounded mortally by Rowdy, a scout, and Hale was killed. Hayes puts this fight in May 1890. Pas-lau-tau's head was cut off and exhibited at San Carlos by Josh, the scout instrumental in running down the broncos, according to report.

Jess G. Hayes, *Apache Vengeance.* Albuquerquee, Univ. of New Mex. Press, 1954; Dan L. Thrapp, *Al Sieber, Chief of Scouts.* Norman, Univ. of Okla. Press, 1964.

Passaconaway, Pennacook chief (c. 1570-c. 1665). A chief of the region around Pennacook on the Merrimac River, New Hampshire, he headed the Pennacook tribe, an Algonquian people related to the Abenaki of Maine. In 1829 his daughter married Winnepurget, sachem at Saugus of an allied tribe, the wedding retold by Whittier in "Bridal of Pennacook." Passaconaway was an influentual chief and medicine man, but early recognized the superior strength of the English, formally submitting to them in 1644. He was succeeded as sachem by his son, Wannalancet.

Hodge, HAI.

Patron, Juan B., pioneer (c. 1855-Apr. 9, 1884). B. at Santa Fe, he was a protege of Bishop Lamy and under his influence studied at Notre Dame University, then returned to New Mexico. In 1875 he was probate clerk to Judge L.G. Murphy, and commenced an investigation into the killing of two Mexican employees of John Copeland. He organized a citizens' posse and in a confrontation was shot in the back by John H. Riley and was not expected to live. But he recovered. Patron served in the Legislature in 1877, was speaker of the House in 1878; he sympathized with the McSween faction at Lincoln, New Mexico, and served as captain of the Lincoln County Mounted Rifles, with the Rifles when two "rustlers" were killed October 10, 1878, between Lloyd's Crossing and Fort Sumner. Patron moved to Las Vegas. He was killed in Moore's Saloon, Puerta de Luna, by M.E. Maney (alias Mike Manning), of Guadalupe County, Texas, an apparently unprovoked slaying. The jury disagreed and Maney escaped from the San Miguel County jail May 10, 1885. Maney was the son of a prominent lawyer and former probate judge at Pearsall, Texas and was working as a cowboy on the ranch of George C. Peacock at the time of the Patron shooting; Peacock was shot and killed by James C. White in 1886.

Robert N. Mullin notes; "Frank Warner Angel's Notes on New Mexico Territory 1878," ed. by Lee Scott Theisen. *Arizona and the West,* Vol. 18, No. 4 (Winter 1976).

Patterson, James, adventurer (1755-post 1832). He probably served in the Revolutionary War and reached Missouri at least by 1809 when he joined Reuben Smith and Josiah McLanahan on a somewhat mysterious expedition to Santa Fe, being imprisoned with the others by the Spanish, taken to Chihuahua, held under harsh conditions, released and returned to the St. Louis area by 1812. In 1832 he applied from St. Genevieve, Missouri, for a pension for Revolutionary War service.

W.A. Goff article, on Reuben Smith, MM, Vol. VII.

Patterson, John B., publisher (Jan. 11, 1806-Apr. 15, 1890). B. in Virginia, he became a printer at an early age and in 1828 founded the *Leesburg Observer,* advocating Andrew Jackson for President. The paper failed, as did one he founded at Washington, D.C., and in 1832 Patterson moved west, settling in northern Illinois. He served during the Black Hawk War in Captain Milton Waugh's company of Colonel James Strode's regiment, after the war working for a Rock Island merchant and American Fur Company representative, Colonel George Davenport (1783-1845). Here he became acquainted with Black Hawk and his party, returned from a tour of the East and at the Indian's request, as Patterson reported, wrote and published Black Hawk's famous "autobiography," which appeared first in 1833 and, in a somewhat revised edition, in 1882. The book's "accuracy, authenticity, and style have been both praised and damned," according to Donald Jackson, who edited one edition of it. Patterson said he compiled it from Black Hawk's narrative, as translated by Antoine LeClaire (1797-1861). Jackson concluded that at the 1833 edition, "despite the intrusive hands of interpreter and editor, is basically a tale told by an Indian from an Indian point of view." In the summer of 1834 Patterson

removed to Yellow Banks, the later Oquawka, Illinois, and in February 1848, commenced publication of the *Oquawka Spectator,* remaining connected with it for the rest of his life, during which he also held various public positions. He married twice, his first wife dying in 1886, and the second surviving him; his only son, also a newspaper editor, died in Colorado in 1880. Patterson died at Oquawka and was buried there.

Donald Jackson, ed., *Ma-Ka-Tai-Me-She-Kia-Kiak: Black Hawk, an Autobiography.* Urbana, Univ. of Ill. Press, 1956; *History of Mercer and Henderson Counties.* Chicago, 1882, 962-64; *Oquawka Spectator,* Apr. 16, 1890.

Pattie, James Ohio, mountain man (c. 1804-post 1833). B. at Augusta, Kentucky, he had some schooling and became one of the important early mountain men of the southwest. The family moved to Missouri in 1812 settling first at St. Charles, later on the Big Piney River in the northern Ozarks. James accompanied his father, Sylvester Pattie, June 20, 1825, on a trading expedition beyond the frontier (Pattie's *Personal Narrative* dates the start June 20, 1824, but Batman shows persuasively that this is in error and that the departure actually was made in 1825; the modification goes far toward solving the dating problems that plagued Pattie historians ever since the *Narrative* appeared). The Patties reached Pilcher's Fort (Council Bluffs) above the mouth of the Platte July 13 and left the 30th to join Bernard Pratte's 116-man expedition for New Mexico. They reached Santa Fe in November by way of the Pawnee villages and Taos. The Patties secured licenses to trap the Gila River, occasionally skirmished with Indians and returned to the Santa Rita copper mines in April 1826. Sylvester leased the mines while James joined a French party of beaver trappers, probably **headed by Michel Robidoux for a fresh** expedition. Near the juncture of the Salt and Gila rivers an attack, perhaps by Papago Indians, resulted in a massacre which Pattie and two companions escaped (one report said still others fled to Tucson). Pattie and his colleagues joined the Ewing Young trapping party of 29 men which he reported wreaked vengeance for the Robidoux attack, 110 hostiles being slain. The Young party trapped down the Gila and up the Colorado to Mohave country where further fighting broke out. The route they followed from there is uncertain. Pattie reported they continued into the northern Rockies reaching the Yellowstone river and Clark's Fork of the Columbia, but most students dismiss this portion of the narrative as a probable editorial insert by Pattie's editor, Timothy Flint. Rather, it is commonly supposed that from the Mohave the Young expedition trapped along the Colorado, then over the high plateau country south of Grand Canyon and up the Little Colorado to regain Santa Fe August 1, 1827. Pattie reported a brief trading trip to Guaymas on the Gulf of California, returning to the Santa Rita mines (a story Batman rejects). More probably Pattie did not go south at this time, but from Santa Fe went east to Pecos Pueblo and the Pecos River, finding trapping good but being severely wounded by Mescalero Apaches. At length he did go to Santa Rita to find that his father had been bilked of $30,000 in savings. The two were forced to return to the pursuit of beaver. They again trapped the Gila to the Colorado and floated down it to the Gulf which they reached January 18, 1828, their party now reduced to eight men. They cached their furs and made their way overland to California, enduring crushing hardships, being arrested according to James Pattie on their arrival at San Diego. He described the Anglos' treatment by Mexican authorities as harsh although in reality it appears to have been mild and for the most part considerate, their detention nominal. Sylvester Pattie died May 24, 1828 (although James reports it as April 24). Four of the trappers were issued a pass to fetch to San Diego their cached beaver, but found the furs ruined by spring flooding. After his father's death Pattie reported he was released from detention in order to vaccinate people at various mission stations against a smallpox epidemic; Batman musters evidence that this portion of the narrative too is imaginary. There was no smallpox epidemic in California at the time, and physicians were available to do what vaccinating seemed necessary. There is a suggestion that measles, rather than smallpox, may have been involved. From Monterey Pattie took ship to San Blas, visited Mexico City but was unable to secure recompense for his California losses as he had anticipated, and reached New Orleans from Vera Cruz August 1, 1830. His story was published in 1831 by Timothy Flint of Cincinnati, who embroidered it somewhat. Pattie enrolled in Augusta College. The final certain notice of him is on the June 1833, Bracken County tax rolls. Batman discounts later reports of Pattie's travels: by William Waldo asserting he probably perished from deep snow or Indians in California in the winter of 1849-50; the *History of Napa and Lake Counties, California* which reported a James Ohio Pattie living in "Rag Canyon" in March 1853; and an unnamed but "apparently trustworthy" individual who told historian Hubert Howe Bancroft in 1883 that his wife was a niece of James Pattie and that Pattie spent some time at her residence in San Diego "in late years, or at least since 1850." Batman thinks it as probable that Pattie perished in a cholera epidemic which struck Kentucky in 1832-33. However, no members of his family reported his death from any such calamity (or at all), though several continued to honor his name by bestowing it upon their children. Thus it seems possible that like many other Kentuckians he fled the epidemic, once more making his way into the West he had come to know so intimately. This would seem to support what evidence there is of his later presence in California.

James Ohio Pattie, *The Personal Narrative of James O. Pattie,* intr. by William H. Goetzmann, N.Y., J.B. Lippincott Co., 1962 (repr., Bison Books, Univ. of Nebr. Press); Joseph J. Hill, "New Light on Pattie and the Southwestern Fur Trade," *Southwestern Hist. Quar.,* Vol. XXVI, No. 4 (April 1923), 243-54; A.L. Kroeber, "The Route of James O. Pattie on the Colorado in 1826," with comments by R.C. Euler, A.H. Schroeder, ed. by Clifton B. Kroeber, *Arizona and the West,* Vol. 6, No. 2 (Summer 1964), 119-36; Rosemary K. Valle, "James Ohio Pattie and the 1827-28 Alta California Measles Epidemic," *Calif. Hist. Quar.,* Vol. LII, No. 1 (Spring 1973), 28-36; Richard Batman, *American Ecclesiastes: The Stories of James Pattie.* N.Y., Harcourt Brace Jovanovich, 1984; Ann W. Hafen article, Vol. IV, MM.

Pattie, Sylvester, frontiersman (Aug. 25, 1782-May 24, 1828). Pattie was b. at Craig's Station, Kentucky, the same day his father, John Pattie was helping bury the dead from the noted engagement at Blue Licks, Kentucky to the north. Around 1800 Sylvester moved to Bracken County on the Ohio River where he became a prominent landowner and probably studied at Bracken Academy, the forerunner of Augusta (Kentucky) College. He married Polly Hubbard in 1802 and fathered nine children, the eldest being James Ohio Pattie (see entry). In 1812 the family moved to St. Charles, Missouri, and Sylvester later established a grist mill and sawmill on Big Piney River in the northern Ozarks. Polly died of tuberculosis about 1822 and Sylvester, utterly dejected at loss of his wife according to James, sold out, sent his eight younger children to live with relatives in Kentucky, and with James in 1825 (James Pattie erroneously dates the departure in 1824) went overland to Santa Fe, arriving in November. The Patties secured licenses and trapped down the Gila River, returning at length to Santa Rita, New Mexico, where Sylvester leased the famed copper mines for the equivalent of $1,000 a year. He gathered profits of $30,000, but was bilked by an employee and joined his son in 1827, again trapping the Gila, then descending the lower Colorado River to the Gulf of Calfifornia. The party cached the furs and made their way most arduously overland to San Diego where they were initially imprisoned by Mexican authorities. Sylvester Pattie died in jail (James gives the date of death as April 24, which is in error).

James Ohio Pattie, *Personal Narrative of James O. Pattie.* N.Y., J.B. Lippincott Co., 1962 (repr. by Bison Books, Univ. of Nebr. Press); Richard Batman, *American Ecclesiastes: The Stories of James Pattie.* N.Y., Harcourt Brace Jovanovich, 1984.

Paul, Robert Havlin, lawman (1830-Mar. 26, 1901). B. at Lowell, Massachusetts, he became a cabin boy on a whaler in 1842. He reached San Francisco aboard the whaler, *Catherine,* in 1849. He remained in California 30 years as constable, deputy sheriff, sheriff and Wells Fargo agent and occasionally shotgun messenger. In 1878 the company sent him to Arizona; he arrived at Tombstone that year. In March 1881, he was riding shotgun on a stage held up near Drew's Station and the driver, Bud Philpot, was killed. The horses ran away but Paul perilously secured the reins, brought them under control and the stage into Benson. In 1881 he was elected sheriff of Pima County, Arizona, and in 1882 was sent to Colorado with the necessary papers to bring the Earps back to answer charges of murder, although they were not

returned. In 1889 Paul became a special officer for the Southern Pacific railroad. He became U.S. marshal for Arizona in 1891, serving four years. He died of cancer at Tucson. Paul was a fearless, persistent and able detective and lawman of integrity; his adventures were many.

John D. Gilchriese, "The Life of Robert Paul." *Arizona Currents,* Feb. 1966; Globe, Ariz., *Silver Belt,* Mar. 28, 1901.

Pauley, Arthur E., historical writer (Dec. 2, 1905-Aug. 8, 1984). B. in Maine, he was raised at Deer Lodge, Montana, where he became interested in the history of desperado Henry Plummer and his people through tales his grandfather and his friends told, they having been acquainted with many of the famed Montana vigilantes and their work. When Pauley retired from the construction business he commenced research in earnest and from it came his definitive *Henry Plummer: Lawman and Outlaw* (1980) and other writings. He died at Vancouver, Washington.

Information from Oneta (Mrs. Arthur E.) Pauley, Jan. 12, 1986.

Pawhuska (Teshuhimga, White Hair), Osage leader (c. 1760-Aug. 25, 1825). He was head man of the Great Osage whose village in 1806 was on the Little Osage River in today's Vernon County, Missouri. He won his nickname, White Hair when in a battle he snatched the white wig from an army officer thinking he was taking his scalp and thereafter wore it on ceremonial occasions as good "war medicine." Pawhuska met with Zebulon Pike in 1806, Pike establishing nearby Camp Independence. Pike stated that both Pawhuska and Cashesegra were created chiefs by Pierre Chouteau Jr. for trading purposes, but the tenure of both depended upon their popularity with their peers. Pawhuska was the first to sign the Osage Treaty of November 10, 1808, concluded at Fort Clark. He also signed the treaties of September 22, 1815; September 25, 1818; August 31, 1822; June 2, 1825, and August 10, 1825. He died soon after the latter date and was buried in a stone tomb on the summit of Blue Mound, Kansas. The grave was vandalized by whites, but in 1871 some Osages rebuilt the cairn which later was destroyed once more. The community of Pawhuska, Oklahoma is named for him; it is headquarters of the present Osage Agency.

Hodge, HAI, under the heading, "White Hair."

Pawnee Bill: *see* Gordon William Lillie

Pawnee Killer, Oglala Sioux war leader (fl. 1856-1870). Pawnee Killer was not a chief but a war leader of Little Wound's band of the Oglala Sioux which frequently ranged south of the Platte and lived and fought with the Southern Cheyennes; he was a close friend of Turkey Leg, a noted Cheyenne chief, and often operated with him and his people. After Sand Creek the Pawnee Killer followers were camped in the present Cheyenne County, Kansas, along with some Arapahoes and Cheyennes. Pawnee Killer was in the attack on Julesburg, Colorado, January 7, 1865. He was in the Fetterman fight of December 1866 north of Fort Phil Kearny, Wyoming, until that time the greatest white debacle in the western Indian wars. He collaborated with Red Cloud and Blue Horse, Sioux; with Strong Wolf, Little Wolf and Dull Knife, Cheyennes, and with Black Coal and Eagle Head, Arapahoes. In mid-April 1867 Pawnee Killer's people were camped with the Southern Cheyennes in central Kansas when Hancock arrived and after the Indians slipped away, burned their villages. In May Pawnee Killer and Turkey Leg conferred briefly with Custer, but with no important result, and a bit later Pawnee Killer's warriors and some Cheyenne dog soldiers attacked a Custer wagon train; no one was killed. June 24, 1867, Captain Louis Hamilton of the 7th Cavalry was engaged by Pawnee Killer and 45 of his men in a fight near the forks of the Republican River in Kansas; entrapped they would have been annihilated save that the Sioux were poorly armed while the soldiers were not; the Indians had to open the trap and let the enemy go. Pawnee Killer led the Indians who wiped out the Kidder party July 12, 1867. Whether he was in the fight at Beecher Island in September 1868 is uncertain; his village was in the vicinity. In 1869 the Sioux camps between the Arkansas and Platte twice were struck by 5th Cavalry units. Little is known of Pawnee Killer after that year. His people ultimately settled on the Red Cloud Agency of Dakota where Little Wound was a close collaborator with Red Cloud.

George E. Hyde, *Life of George Bent.* Norman, Univ. of Okla. Press, 1968; Donald J. Berthrong, *The Southern Cheyennes.* Norman, 1963; George E. Hyde, *Red Cloud's Folk.* Norman, 1957.

Paxson, Frederic Logan, historian (Feb. 23, 1877-Oct. 24, 1948). B. at Philadelphia he received his doctorate in history from the University of Pennsylvania having also studied two years at Harvard. In 1903 he accepted a position at the University of Colorado and became interested in western and frontier history. He later taught at the University of Michigan, where he completed his first book, *The Last American Frontier* (1910). In that year he became professor of history at the University of Wisconsin. Paxson wrote the *Recent History of the United States* (1921). He received the Pulitzer Prize for his *The History of the American Frontier, 1763-1893* (1924). Paxson brought out *The New Nation* (1925) and wrote *When the West Is Gone* (1930). In 1932 he went to the University of California at Berkeley where he remained until his retirement in 1947, serving the last eight years as departmental chairman. He produced the three-volume *American Democracy and the World War* (1936-48), and other works on the order of texts. Paxson also wrote 24 papers on matters related to the frontier and was said to have been numbered among the ten or twelve foremost scholars on the American west during the first half of this century. During his academic career he directed more than 60 doctoral dissertations.

Ira G. Clark, "Frederic Logan Paxson 1877-1948." *Arizona and the West,* Vol. 3, No. 2 (Summer 1961), 107-12; *Who Was Who;* REAW.

Payemingo: *see* Piomingo

Payette, Francois, fur trader (1793-post 1844). B. near Montreal, he began his career as a canoeman, was hired by Astor and shipped to Oregon aboard the *Beaver,* entering the mouth of the Columbia May 9, 1812. With sale of Astoria, Payette joined the North West Company, "accompanying numerous expeditions into the interior." A river in Idaho, and a city are named for him. In 1821 when the Hudson's Bay Company absorbed the North West Company, Payette transferred allegiance to the HBC. He took part in notable fur gathering-trading expeditions throughout the upper Rockies and was an occasional interpreter, sometimes second in command of brigades, and clerk. He was stationed at Fort Boise for his last years with the company, retiring June 1, 1844, and returning to Montreal, where he disappears. He was one of the more able and worthy HBC men in the interior of the Northwest.

Kenneth L. Holmes article, MM, Vol. VI.

Payne, David L., boomer (Dec. 30, 1836-Nov. 27, 1884). B. at Fairmont, Indiana, his mother was a first cousin of Davy Crockett. Payne went to Kansas in 1858, establishing a sawmill in Doniphan County. He became a hunter and roamer, visiting New Mexico and exploring the South Plains, occasionally operating as guide or scout. He served with the 4th Kansas in the Civil War, was elected to the Kansas Legislature, then returned to the Plains. In 1868 he became captain of Company D, 18th Kansas Cavalry and paticipated in the Custer campaign in the South Plains. In 1870 he moved to Sedgwick County, near Wichita, was elected to the Legislature the following year, and later moved to Newton, Kansas. He went back to Indiana, then returned to Kansas. He became an assistant doorkeeper at the House of Representatives at Washington in 1876, and there interested himself in Oklahoma lands. He settled at Caldwell, Kansas, and commenced agitation for the opening of unassigned Indian lands to the south. From 1879 he took an active part in the movement to settle there and became a leader of the "Oklahoma Movement," which saw as favoritism the permission granted to cattle-men to lease land from Indian tribes for grazing while settlers were kept out. He led at least eight invasions of Oklahoma, each time being arrested by U.S. soldiers and expelled. "Payne was a typical soldier of fortune, careless in his obligations, generous to a fault, frank, friendly, and having a physique which was at once robust and picturesque," and "his success as an agitator made possible the opening of Oklahoma...much sooner than it otherwise would have been." Payne County, Oklahoma, is named for him. He died at Wellington, Kansas.

NCAB, XIX, 325-26; Glenn Shirley, *Pawnee Bill: A Biography of Major Gordon W. Lillie.* Albuquerque, Univ. of New Mex. Press, 1958.

Payne, (John) Scott, army officer (Dec. 7, 1844-Dec. 16, 1895). B. of a Warrenton, Virginia fox hunting family, he was appointed from either Missouri or Tennessee to West Point, becoming a second lieutenant in the 5th

Cavalry in 1866, a first lieutenant the following year and resigning in 1868 after service in the southern States and "too many stump speeches in praise of Jefferson Davis." Payne entered the practice of law at Knoxville, Tennessee, and edited newspapers. He became a second lieutenant in the 6th Cavalry February 3, 1873, joining the regiment in Kansas, participating in field operations in Kansas and Texas and taking part in the Red River fight August 30, 1874, against Comanches and Kiowas. He was reinstated in the 5th Cavalry as first lieutenant by "special dispensation of President Grant," it was said and by act of Congress to date from 1867 and joined at Camp McDowell, Arizona in February 1875. He became a captain June 4, 1875, serving in Kansas until the following year, took part in the Big Horn and Yellowstone campaign and the battle at Slim Buttes, Dakota. In the fall of 1877 he was in the Nez Perce campaign (permanently damaging his health), and a Bannock operation in January 1878. In 1879 he joined Thornburgh's Ute campaign in Colorado and was twice wounded at Milk River after Thornburgh was killed and Payne had assumed command. The officer received high praise for his conduct during the ensuing siege and was breveted major. Payne's remaining service was in western regions until his retirement for reasons of health April 24, 1886. He died at Washington, D.C.

Powell; Heitman; Cullum; Marshall Sprague, *Massacre: The Tragedy at White River.* Boston, Little, Brown and Co., 1957.

Payne, King, Seminole chief (d. Sept. 28, 1812). Payne was probably a son of the famous Cowkeeper and the older brother of King Bowlegs, like him a chief of the Alachua Seminoles of Florida. Payne also was the grandfather, or uncle perhaps, of Micanopy, another noted Seminole chief. He first appears around 1786 when Payne's Seminoles invaded and conquered northern Florida, the chief winning a reputation as a "very sensible, discrete Indian, and well informed." His people however were blamed for raiding the Georgia settlements and in retaliation Georgia militia under Daniel Newnan in 1812 drove against the Alachua towns. Payne's people resisted successfully, driving the Georgians out of Florida, but Payne himself was wounded mortally, or died of over-

exertion. He was succeeded by King Bowlegs.
Kenneth Wiggins Porter, "The Cowkeeper Dynasty of the Seminole Nation." *Fla. Hist. Quar.*, Vol. XXX, No. 4 (Apr. 1952), 341-49; John R. Swanton, *Early History of the Creek Indians and Their Neighbors.* Wash., BAE Bull. 73, 1922.

Peabody, Endicott, clergyman (May 30, 1857-Nov. 14, 1944). B. at Salem, Massachusetts, he was a student at Cambridge Theological Seminary, Boston, in 1881 when a letter was received from Grafton Abbott of Tombstone, Arizona, inviting Peabody to take over a fledgling church there, "the rottenest place you ever saw." Although not ordained as yet, Peabody accepted, arrived at Tombstone in January 1882, held a preaching service in the courthouse, and laid the foundations for St. Paul's Episcopal Church, today the oldest still-operating non-Roman church in Arizona. Abbott never attended, himself. After six months in Arizona Peabody returned to Massachusetts, having won "the most fame for the briefest ministry of any man in the history of the Episcopal Church." He was ordained a priest in 1885, and served as headmaster of Groton School, Massachusetts, 1884-1940. He returned February 16, 1941, to preach again at St. Paul's, by then an established church, which was placed upon the National Register of Historic Places on January 29, 1972.
Jerry Wallace, "How the Episcopal Church Came to Arizona." *Journal of Ariz. Hist.,* Vol. VI, No. 3 (Autumn 1965), 101-15; *Who Was Who.*

Peaches (Tsoe, Pah-na-yo-tishn), Apache guide (c. 1853- Spring 1933). B. a member of the Canyon Creek band of the Cibecue Apaches, Peaches, as the whites called him because of his complexion had married one, or perhaps two, Chiricahua women and thus was affiliated with the Chiricahuas (one report said that a wife of his was related to Geronimo). Peaches accompanied Juh-Geronimo on the San Carlos raid which herded several hundred Warm Springs Apaches from the reservation toward the Sierra Madre of Mexico and was badly wounded on Aliso Creek, Sonora, in the hard Loco fight with Mexican Lieutenant Colonel Lorenzo Garcia; in the action Peaches' spouse(s) were slain. Peaches accompanied his friend Chatto on a devastating southwestern raid in the spring of 1883, but deserted the guerillas and was captured by Britton Davis at San Carlos in April. He was interrogated by Crook and agreed to guide the General into the Sierra Madre in May/June to contact and bring back to San Carlos the wild Apaches whose base was in the Mexican mountains. Peaches thus became a celebrated Apache; his services on the great Crook expedition were outstanding; reportedly it was he who arranged the pivotal meeting between Crook and Geronimo which climaxed the adventure. Upon Crook's return Peaches rejoined his Cibecue Apache people, abandoning his formal ties with the Chiricahuas. Thus he was not exiled to Florida when the Chiricahuas were moved there in 1886. Peaches married a Cibecue woman and fathered a daughter and three sons, including Teddy Peaches who died at Cibecue March 16, 1965. Peaches died in the spring of 1933, according to Lutheran missionary Arnold Nieman who visited with him a few days before his death and who estimated his age at the time as "some 80 years old."
Grenville Goodwin; Keith H. Basso, *Western Apache Raiding and Warfare.* Tucson, Univ. of Ariz. Press, 1971; Dan L. Thrapp, *General Crook and the Sierra Madre Adventure.* Norman, Univ. of Okla. Press, 1972; Angie Debo, *Geronimo,* Norman, 1976; H.W. Wharfield, *Cooley.* El Cajon, Calif., p.p., 1966; correspendence with Arnold Nieman, Jan. 10, 1981; Feb. 11, Mar. 2, 1983.

Peak, Junius (June), Texas Ranger (Apr. 5, 1845-Apr. 20, 1934). B. at Warsaw, Kentucky, he reached Texas with his parents at 10, settling in Dallas County. In a sketch of his early Civil War service, Peak wrote that he operated against Arapahoes, Cheyennes and Comanches in or near Indian Territory, "was in a number of hard-fought engagements, especially Round Mountain, Byrd's Creek and Chestenhla. I received three wounds, one quite severe..., during my two years service there." Later he fought at Pea Ridge and with Morgan's Raiders in Ohio, and was wounded twice at Chickamauga. After the war he served as deputy sheriff at Dallas, and by report worked for New Mexico ranchers to control rustling in 1872, although this apparently was not connected with the so-called Horrell War and details are lacking. Peak was city marshal of Dallas from 1874-78. In 1876 he led a group of Dallas friends on a successful buffalo hunt to the forks of the Wichita River. At the height of the Sam Bass uproar in the Dallas area, Peak was commissioned a lieutenant (later a captain) of a special Ranger detachment of Company B, and although he was very active, and accounted for some of Bass's colleagues, he never quite caught up with Sam. Peak was transferred to San Angelo, operating against Indians and desperadoes in West Texas; he left the Ranger service in 1880. He spent a year in Mexico working for the Mexican Central Railroad, returned to Texas in 1884 to enter cattle ranching in Shackleford County, sold out in 1899 and entered business at Dallas, where he died. He was married.

Frontier time, Vol. 4, No.11 (Aug. 1927), 6; Vol. 4, No. 12 (Sept. 1927), 4-6, has a cover portrait of Peak; HT; Robert W. Stephens, *Texas Ranger Sketches.* Dallas, p.p., 1972; Wayne Gard, *Sam Bass.* Lincoln, Univ. of Nebr. Press, 1969.

Peale, Titian Ramsay, artist, naturalist (Nov. 17, 1799-Mar. 13, 1885). B. at Philadelphia he was a son of artist Charles Willson Peale and early became attracted to natural history, as well as art. In 1818 he was on an expedition to eastern Florida and the Georgia coast with Thomas Say to study and collect fauna. In 1819 Peale became a member (as did Say) of the Stephen H. Long expedition to the Rocky Mountains. With Edwin James and others Peale attempted to penetrate the Rocky Mountains from the present site of Denver to discover the source of the South Platte, but the terrain defeated them. Peale accompanied the Long division of the expedition which sought to return to the States by the Red River, mistaking the Canadian for it, and eventually gaining the Mississippi near Cape Girardeau, Missouri. Peale's sketches were used to illustrate writings of the expedition; they show mature draftsmanship and artistic skill beyond his years and as ethnological and pictorial records they have value. In 1821 Peale became assistant manager of the Philadelphia Museum which Maximilian described as containing "the best collection of natural history in the United States," some of its wild life and ethnological artifacts collected by Peale himself. Peale drew illustrations for Charles Bonaparte's four-volume *American Ornithology* and for Say's three-volume *American Entomology* and in 1833 published *Lepidoptera Americana* for which he collected

the specimens, did the art work and the writing. Peale became manager of the Philadelphia Museum that year. He was a member of Charles Wilkes' Antarctic expedition from 1838-42, providing much of the pictorial work not only of polar aspects, but Polynesia investigations. Peale was described by Wilkes as "a person of strong and violent temper," who at one point engaged in a controversy with a naval officer until Wilkes took time to set him straight about the proper role of scientific personnel on the expedition in relationship to the naval officers directing it. On another occasion at the Tuamoto Islands Wilkes directed Peale who had a shotgun loaded with "mustard seed shot," to fire at the legs of hostile natives so that a landing could be effected. This was done, the natives fled and the expedition party safely went ashore. In 1848 Peale authored "Mammalia and Ornithology," Volume VIII of the *Reports of the United States Exploring Expedition, 1839-42,* but the work later was suppressed, for reasons unclear. When the Philadelphia Museum closed in 1848 Peale was appointed an examiner in the United States Patent Office at Washington, D.C., a position he held until retirement when he returned to his scientific and art pursuits.

Thwaites, EWT, XIV-XVII; DAB; *Autobiography of Rear Admiral Charles Wilkes.* Wash., D.C., Naval Hist. Div., Dept. of Navy, 1978.

Pearce, Harrison, Mormon pioneer (fl. 1857-1892). A man of this name was placed by *Mormonism Unveiled* at the Mountain Meadows Massacre of September 11, 1857, either consenting to or participating in the tragedy. Published in 1892, the book said he was then a resident of Washington, Utah.

Mormonism Unveiled, 380.

Pearce, James, Mormon pioneer (fl. 1857-1892). A man of this name, resident at Washington, Utah, was placed by *Mormonism Unveiled* at the Mountain Meadows Massacre of Southern Utah September 11, 1857; apparently he still was living when the book was published in 1892.

Mormonism Unveiled, 380.

Pearson, Daniel Crosby, army officer (May 19, 1845-Aug. 25, 1920). B. in Massachusetts he was graduated from West Point, a classmate of John G. Bourke, in 1870 and commissioned a second lieutenant in the 2nd

Cavalry. He was assigned to Fort Fred Steele, Wyoming and took part in Sioux expeditions in 1874 and 1875, then transferred to Fort Fetterman, Wyoming. Pearson was on the Powder River expedition of March 1876, and in the Battle of the Rosebud June 17, 1876, as he was on Crook's Big Horn expedition from May to October of that year, taking part in the Battle of Slim Buttes September 8-9. He was stationed at Montana posts: Fort Keogh from 1876-79, Fort Ellis until late 1880 and Fort Custer until 1884; at the latter station he once was presented with a pistol Tom Leforge had counted coup with, twisting it from the hand of a hostile Indian before killing him. Pearson was at various Washington and Idaho stations: Forts Walla Walla, Spokane and Sherman until 1890 when he was assigned to Arizona, being stationed at Fort Whipple, San Carlos and Fort Bowie. In 1891 he was sent east, returning to Fort Huachuca, Arizona, in 1893 and Fort Wingate, New Mexico, from 1894-95; the remainder of his career has little frontier interest. Pearson became a first lieutenant in 1879, a captain in 1889, major in 1901 and lieutenant colonel in 1904. He retired in 1905 and died at Cambridge, Massachusetts. He was married.

Powell; Cullum; J.W. Vaughn, *With Crook at the Rosebud.* Harrisburg, Pa., Stackpole Co., 1956; Thomas H. Leforge, *Memoirs of a White Crow Indian.* Lincoln, Univ. of Nebr. Press, 1974, 299-300.

Pearson (Pierson), William H., courier (c. 1818-post 1858). B. at Philadelphia, Pearson, "a small wiry man of pleasant aspect and great endurance," by report had been a Texas Ranger and Indian scout before he joined the Stevens 1853 northwestern survey expedition as expressman. On one occasion he rode 1,750 miles by the route he took, from the Bitterroot Valley of western Montana to Olympia, Washington, and back to Fort Benton on the upper Misouri River in 28 days "during some of which he did not travel. He was less than three days going from Fort Owen (in the Bitterroot Valley) to Fort Benton,...some 260 miles, which he traveled without a change of animals, having no food but the berries of the country, except a little fish." On another occasion he brought news by another swift ride of the Indian outbreak in central Washington to Stevens' camp near Fort Benton, arriving October 29, 1855. On one occasion in 1855 he was falsely reported to have been killed by Coeur d'Alene Indians, but he appeared to have a charmed life. Pearson figured in a minor way in the 1858 Indian troubles. During the Fraser River, British Columbia, gold excitement of 1858, Pearson engaged in prospecting and in mid-July reached Seattle where he contracted to take 82 gold miners to the diggings, but the party was turned back by Indian hostility.

Montana Contributions, X, 1940, 269; Robert Ignatius Burns, *The Jesuits and the Indian Wars of the Northwest.* New Haven, Yale Univ. Press, 1966; George F. Weisel, *Men and Trade on the Northwest Frontier.* Missoula, Mont. State Univ. Press, 1955.

Peary, Robert Edwin, polar explorer (May 6, 1856-Feb. 20, 1920). B. at Cresson, Pennsylvania, though raised in Maine, he was graduated in civil engineering from Bowdoin College. He worked briefly with the Coast and Geodetic Survey, then became a lieutenant in the Navy corps of engineers. He was sent to Nicaragua in 1884 with an expedition surveying the route for a possible ship's canal, and returned to Nicaragua in 1887, bringing as a valet the black, Matthew Henson, who remained with him through more than 20 years of exploration work. Becoming interested in Arctic exploration, Peary had visited Greenland briefly in 1886. He led an expedition there in 1891-92, the group including Dr. Frederick A. Cook and Mrs. Peary, the first white woman known to have wintered in the arctic in modern times. In the spring Peary sledged to the northeast coast of Greenland and return, a 1,300 mile journey overall, and made worthy scientific observations. By August 1893, he was again in Greenland, his daughter being born in September farther north, it was believed, than any other white child had been. This expedition was less than successful in its exploration, although Peary brought back to the U.S. two of three meteorites discovered. A succeeding expedition explored the west coast of Greenland. By now Peary was obsesssed with an ambition to reach the North Pole and he had devised a plan for doing so which involved staging his dog-sledge parties out on the ocean ice so that only the smallest, best conditioned and most experienced element would make the final dash. He won British support for his plans which, added to

American support, enhanced his chances. Peary wrote *Northward over the "Great Ice,"* 2 vols. (1898), and by intercession of President McKinley won five years' leave from the Navy (later extended three years) to pursue his ambition. He left New York in the summer of 1898; his ship became icebound south of his target, but he sledged supplies northward during the winter, in the course of such perilous work freezing his feet to the point that eight toes had to be amputated. Peary returned to the U.S. in 1902 after having reached 84 degrees 17' N. Latitude, farthest north in the American arctic. Peary went north again aboard the *Roosevelt,* leaving New York in the summer of 1905 and wintering on Grant Land. He left Cape Hecla for the Pole in March 1906, by April 21 had reached the farthest north until that time, 87 degrees 6', but was forced to return, reaching New York in December. He published *Nearest the Pole* (1907) about his expedition and to earn money for the next. He left once more in July 1908 (three months after his unannounced rival, Frederick A. Cook, would claim to have reached the goal), and by September the ship had reached winter quarters of North Greenland. March 1 six whites, one Negro (Henson), 17 Eskimos and their dog teams left Cape Columbia. At about 88 degrees Captain Robert Bartlett with the final support party turned back; Peary, with Henson and four Eskimos pushed on, the explorer reporting that he had reached the North Pole April 6; one of his important actions was to sound the sea, finding no depth at 9,000 feet. Peary reported he took observations and remained at the Pole 30 hours, regaining Cape Columbia in 16 days. He left aboard ship in July, reached Labrador September 6, telegraphing his success, his message reaching the outside world five days after one from Cook announced his own claim to the Pole, reached he reported, in April 1908. A resulting controversy, extending over several years, is well remembered; the result was that Peary's claim generally was accepted, and Cook's rejected, although there are those who doubt Peary and accept Cook's version. In truth some aspects of Peary's trip appear incredible as reported by him, and there remains substantial reason to doubt that either party actually reached the Pole although it is possible each man thought he had. In March 1911, Peary was placed upon the Navy retired

list with rank of Rear Admiral. Peary published *The North Pole* (1910), and received an abundance of honors, in large part deserved for his lifelong exertions in polar exploration and mapping. Peary became interested in aviation in 1913, and devoted the remaining years of his life to promoting that science. He died at Washington, D.C. Although nominally resolved, the Peary-Cook controversy surfaced from time to time, since the evidence in support of claims by either man is not conclusive nor beyond criticism and some doubt; the problem in all likelihood will never be settled finally. Peary's was not an attractive personality, particularly in his later years, while Cook's was generally persuasive, and this added complications to the controversy. Yet both were polar experts, courageous, experienced, with enviable records of accomplishment and dedication, and both probably deserve full honors.

Literature abundant; DAB; various reference works.

Peate, James Jared (Jack), scout (Nov. 29, 1847-June 23, 1932). B. in Pennsylvania, he was the son of a Methodist preacher of Pennsylvania and New York who enlisted in the Civil War but forbade his son to do so because of his youth. Peate ran away in 1866 and reached Kansas. He was employed at 18 as a scout, and "was one of the most trusted and efficient and highest paid scouts in the service." Peate was charged with enlisting scouts for duty under Forsyth and himself was of the company, but due to a mixup of orders he and seven others did not take part in the Beecher Island fight of September 1868. The group remained at Fort Wallace on escort duty, taking an occasional scout until September 21 when they were ordered to accompany Carpenter with part of the 19th Cavalry to scout the Smoky Hill stage road for hostile activity. In camp at where Sand Creek crosses the road, they learned of Forsyth's difficulty and were ordered to his relief. On September 25 the command met Jack Donovan and four others, Donovan returning from his mission to seek relief at Fort Wallace, and Donovan guided them to Beecher Island where they succored the battered Forsyth party, Peate reportedly the first to reach the island. About 20 miles toward the south fork of the Republican River, Peate and others found on their return a Cheyenne shelter entombing the remains of a man of some prominence (Peate called him a "medicine man"), who might have been Roman Nose, the great Cheyenne killed in the Beecher Island engagement. Shortly after his period as scout, Peate married Laura Page (d. June 26, 1925) and settled at Beverly, Kansas, entering business. Peate was a particular friend of Louis, or Lewis, Farley, who died on Beecher Island. He died at Beverly.

Simon E. Matson, ed., *The Battle of Beecher Island*. Wray, Colo., Beecher Island Battle Mem. Assn., 1960.

Peck, Artisan Leslie (Al, Dad), pioneer (Mar. 21, 1848-Dec. 6, 1941). B. in Chautauqua County, New York, he reached Arizona in 1884 and the next year settled in a canyon above Calabasas, some eight miles north of Nogales, raising cattle. April 27, 1886, Peck and Charley Owens were working cattle near the ranch when Geronimo and his hostiles, on their final raid north of the border attacked, killing Owens, shooting Peck's horse and , at the ranch house, killing Mrs. Peck, a 2-year-old son and kidnapping Mrs Peck's niece, Trinidad Verdun. Peck, captured, either feigned insanity or went quite mad temporarily, in either case being spared by the Apaches because of their supposed awe of one not sane. Peck made his way to Calabasas and found assistance. His family was buried at Nogales. Trinidad Verdun was rescued in Sonora about six weeks later. Peck ran a livery stable at Nogales for many years thereafter, and died at that community, being buried in the family plot.

Ariz. Hist. Soc. archives; archives of the Pimeria Alta Hist. Soc., Nogales; "Geronimo Raid on Peck Ranch," by Roscoe Willson. *Arizona Republic,* Dec. 28, 1969.

Peck, Edmund George, scout, miner (Dec. 28, 1834-Nov. 14, 1910). B. in Ontario, Peck reached Albuquerque in 1858 and left for California but his party was driven back by Arizona Indians. He reached Fort Whipple in 1863 with the Alters-Farrington party and became associated with George Banghart in ranching on a small scale. Said to be one of the finest rifle shots in the Southwest, Peck became a hunter, guide and Indian fighter, working for the army on occasion and accompanying at least one of King S.

Woolsey's Indian seeking-prospecting expeditions. He guided Lieutenant Colonel Thomas C. Devin on the first extended military reconnaissance of the Tonto Basin of Arizona in 1868. Peck participated in numerous Indian skirmishes and scouts. In 1871 he was captain of one company of prospectors in the famous Miner Expedition and had turned in earnest to prospecting by 1869. June 16, 1875, while hunting, he discovered a silver vein that became the famous Peck Mine in the Bradshaw Mountains of Arizona but, although it produced more than $1 million it was shut down in 1878 and through extended litigation and mismanagement Peck lost everything. He lived the rest of his life in comparitive obscurity as a prospector and in related activities. Peck married Ella Serena Alexander; they had three children who died young of "quick consumption." Mrs. Peck died October 13, 1887, and Peck himself died at Nogales, Arizona. He was described by acquaintences as "tall, slender, and very good looking," and was a kindly, intelligent man who did much to open and develop central Arizona.

Dan L. Thrapp, *Al Sieber, Chief of Scouts.* Norman, Univ. of Okla. Press, 1964; Patrick C. Henderson, "The Peck Mine: Silver Bonanza in the Bradshaw Mountains." *Arizona and the West,* Vol. 4, No. 3 (Aut. 1962), 227-36.

Pedro (Hacke-yanil-tli-din), White Mountain Apache chief (c. 1835-c. 1885). Originally a Carrizo Creek chief, his clan came into a feuding relationship about 1850 with one led by Miguel who drove Pedro away from the Carrizo. After two years Pedro's people were allowed by the great White Mountain chief, Esh-kel-dah-silah to settle in the region where they first came to important contact with the whites, near the later Fort Apache. Pedro was the father of Petone Sageski and also of Alchisay, both noted Apaches although they probably did not have the same mother. In 1871 two of his daughters simultaneously married Corydon Cooley, eastern Arizona frontiersman; one of them died in childbirth, leaving Cooley a monogamist. Pedro in 1872, with other Apaches including Esh-kel-dah-silah and Miguel, visited Washington, D.C.; later Crook made him, in American army fashion, chief of the White Mountain (Coyotero) Apaches. Pedro, always friendly toward the Anglos, was described in 1875 as "chief of a subtribe" (i.e., the former Carrizo Creeks), but later the nominal head of the White Mountains, most numerous of the Apaches. He held them at peace, while supplying scouts as needed to the military. Loring describes him as about 40 in 1875 and "one of the most intelligent Indians on the reservation; he is thoroughly reliable and trustworthy. He is industrious and regarded as the richest man among them. He cultivates a large piece of land, having (in 1874) sold $700 worth of corn which he raised. He has about 35 head of cattle and some mules and horses. He is desirous of having his children educated. Wants his favorite boy (Alchisay?), who is a bright, handsome lad, to be the first of the tribe, and to write a letter to the President. Pedro can boast of being able to sign his own name. Has always been friendly to the white man." In 1875 when the White Mountain Apaches were largely removed to San Carlos, Pedro and his followers were permitted to remain at Camp Apache at the insistence of Colonel August V. Kautz who argued that from them scouts could be enlisted as required. August 30, 1880, a battle occurred within sight of Fort Apache between Pedro's people and those of the militant Diablo in which Diablo himself was killed by Alchisay and Uclenny of Pedro's band. Near Forestdale, Arizona, in February, 1881, Petone was killed and Alchisay wounded, while Pedro was shot through both knees. Although at the time of the Cibecue difficulties, and occasionally perhaps at other times Pedro was alleged in some reports to have become hostile, these allegations invariably proved false. In 1882 Bourke described Pedro as "now old and decrepit (he was then 47 by Loring's calculation), and so deaf that he had to employ an ear trumpet." Pedro's date of death is not reported, although Wharfield believed it to have occurred "some years after 1882" when Alchisay became chief to succeed him.

Leonard Young Loring, "Report on Coyotero Apaches" near Camp Apache, 1875, manuscript, Bancroft Library; Lori Davisson, manuscript on White Mountain Apaches, 1978; Davisson, "New light on the Cibecue Fight: Untangling Apache Identities." *Journ. of Ariz. Hist.,* Vol. 20, No. 4 (Winter 1979), 423-44; Grenville Goodwin, *Social Organization of the Western Apache.* Tucson, Univ. of Ariz. Press, 1969; H.B. Wharfield, *Alchesay.* El Cajon, Calif., p.p., 1969; Bourke, *On Border,* 435.

Peñalosa, Diego Dionisio de, adventurer (1624-1687). B. at Lima, Peru, he was of a noble and wealthy family represented by many of the famed conquistadores of early Spanish times in the western hemisphere. He held various official positions from the age of 15 in South America but because of dissension embarked from Callao for Spain in 1652; through two shipwrecks he managed to lose most of the funds he carried with him but an uncle bishop of Nicaragua provided him with sufficient resources to take him to Mexico City. As commander of infantry he went in 1655 to Vera Cruz in response to a British threat, then proceeded to Havana on the same errand, remaining 11 months. In 1660 Peñalosa was made governor and captain general of New Mexico, where he went in 1661. There he made war on the Apaches, founded two communities and had other minor successes. While there he purportedly made a journey to Quivira, even reaching the Mississippi River, accompanied by Father Nicholas de Freytas, a Franciscan who wrote an account of the adventure, but this turned out to be spurious, the account based on those by Oñate in 1601 and his lieutenant, Vicente de Zaldívar. Peñalosa now came afoul of the Inquisition. He returned to Mexico in 1664 and was imprisoned for 32 months. After an exhaustive inquiry the inquisitors found him guilty of minor infractions, fined him all the funds they could trace to him, deprived him of his governorship and any future office of like nature, and Peñalosa left Vera Cruz in 1668 for Havana and from there in 1669 for Teneriffe in the Canary Islands, thence going to London and eventually to Paris. Here he contacted officials and sought to generate a filibustering expedition to wrest northeastern Mexico from Spanish control, that region possessing as he pointed out, wealthy silver and gold mines. La Salle returned to France in 1683 having explored the Mississippi toward its mouth. France was at a breaking point in its relations with Spain, so Peñalosa's scheme was favorably received in some quarters. Parkman reported that in January 1684 Peñalosa proposed to attack Pánuco, on the Mexican gulf coast with 1,200 buccaneers from Santo Domingo, march into the interior, conquer Durango and occupy New Mexico, proposing to combine his plans with those of La Salle for quasi-military posts in the present Louisiana and Texas. But La Salle, "who had

an interview with him, expressed distrust and
. . . reluctance to accept a colleague," although
Peñalosa's scheme may have encouraged him
to present "proposals of his own, equally
attractive." However peace between Spain
and France was concluded before Peñalosa's
adventure could be carried out. Eventually
France declined to enter into the undertaking
and the plans fell apart. Peñalosa died at
Paris in the same year that La Salle was
assassinated on the Trinity River in the
present Texas.

Nicholas de Freytas, O.S.F., *The Expedition of
Don Diego Dionisio de Peñalosa____From Santa Fe
to the River Mischipi and Quivira in 1662,* intr. by
John Gilmary Shea (1882). Albuquerque, Horn
and Wallace, 1964; Parkman, *La Salle and the
Discovery of the Great West;* Twitchell, *Leading
Facts,* I.

Penhallow, Samuel, writer (July 2, 1665-Dec.
2, 1726). B. at St. Mabon, Cornwall, England,
he came to New England in 1686, lived for a
time in Massachusetts and later at Portsmouth, New Hampshire, marrying into
wealth and holding important legislative and
other public positions; he was chief justice of
the Superior Court of Judicature at his death.
He took part in the ratification of several
treaties with Indians in the course of his
duties, but had no other significant border
experience. His renown for frontier purposes
rests upon his sole literary endeavor, *The
History of the Wars of New-England With the
Eastern Indians . . .,* printed first at Boston in
1726 and reprinted various times, most
recently in 1973. Penhallow died at Portsmouth.

Samuel Penhallow, *Penhallow's Indian Wars,* ed.
by Edward Wheelock. Williamstown, Mass.,
Corner House Pubrs., 1973.

Pennington, Eli G(reen?), pioneer (c. 1808-
June 1869). B. in South Carolina, he reached
Arizona from Texas about 1858 with his large
family, and settled in the Sonoita Creek
region south of Tucson; the Penningtons were
mainly freighters. Old Man Pennington
occupied a small cabin three miles above
Calabasas during the period of virtual
abandonment of the country by Americans
during the Civil War. "He stubbornly refused
to leave the country; said he had as much right
to it as the infernal Indians, and would live
there in spite of all the devils . . . His cattle

were stolen, his corrals burned down, his
fields devastated; yet he stood it out to the
last . . ." Frequently in his absence, it is said,
his brave daughters fought off Indians who
besieged the place. Pennington and his son,
Eli Green Pennington, were ambushed by
Indians while working their fields 14 miles
below Fort Crittenden, Eli senior succumbing
at once, and Green (b. c. 1848 in Texas)
lingering eight days. Both were buried at
Crittenden. Son James (b.c. 1833 in Tennessee) had been ambushed and killed by Indians
while freighting in the hills west of Tucson in
August 1868. John P. (Jack) Pennington (b. c.
1840 in Texas), with a party of freighters was
ambushed in Cooke's Canyon, New Mexico,
in 1861; one of the party was wounded. The
others wanted to abandon him, but Jack, at
rifle point, forced his companions to hunt up
the wounded man and rescue him from the
Apaches. In 1864 Jack was prospecting on the
Hassayampa River, Arizona. Shortly he
returned to Texas, but in 1870 reappeared in
Arizona to gather up the surviving members
of the family and take them to Texas with him.
Eli Pennington was described as "a man of
excellent sense, but rather eccentric, large and
tall, with a fine face and athletic frame." A
prominent street in Tucson is named for him.

U.S. Census for Ariz., 1870; Robert H. Forbes,
*The Penningtons, Pioneers of Early Arizona: A
Historical Sketch.* Tucson, Archaeol. and Hist.
Soc., 1919; Farish, Vol. II, pp. 199-200.

Pennington, Larcena: *see* Larcena Page

Penrose, Charles Bingham, physician (Feb. 1,
1862-Feb. 27, 1925). B. at Philadelphia, he
was graduated from the University of
Pennsylvania Medical School in 1884, and
reached Cheyenne, Wyoming, in 1891, seeking
improved health. He was persuaded by acting
Governor Amos Barber, his longtime friend,
to serve as physician for the cattlemen-
invaders of Johnson County for the Powder
River "war" of April 1892. Penrose remained
at the Tisdale Ranch and missed the fight at
the KC Ranch on Powder River when Nathan
Champion and Nick Ray were killed on April
9. The "invaders" were surrounded on the TA
Ranch on Crazy Woman Creek south of
Buffalo. The settlers' ire was thoroughly
aroused and "realizing that the game was up
we decided to hunt cover," Penrose later
wrote. Under an alias he reached Douglas.

Arrested, he narrowly missed a lynching, according to his report. His friend Barber arranged for his release under a writ of habeas corpus and he was spirited out of town on a special train. Penrose was ultimately cleared of complicity in the killings the so-called war instigated, returned to Philadelphia where he engaged in many interests until his death. He had been a friend of the novelist, Owen Wister, whose *The Virginian* has an obvious relationship to the Johnson County War.

Patrick S. McGreevy, "Amos Barber, Charles Penrose, and the War on Powder River." *Surgery Gynecology & Obstetrics,* Vol. 136, No.4 (Apr. 1973), 632-38.

Penrose, William Henry, army officer (Mar. 3, 1832-Aug. 29, 1903). The son of an officer, Penrose was b. at Madison Barracks, Sacket's Harbor, New York, and became a civil and mechanical engineer in Michigan until the Civil War when he was commissioned a second lieutenant in the 3rd Infantry, emerging from the conflict a Brigadier General of Volunteers. He was commissioned a captain in the 3rd Infantry and "languished" in that rank for 17 years, rising to colonel of the 20th Infantry however by his retirement in 1896. He performed frontier duty at Forts Niagara, Sully, North Dakota, and Douglas, Utah. Although an Infantry officer he had command of five companies of cavalry on Mile's 1868-69 Southern Plains operation through bitter cold and snow. Penrose died at Salt Lake City of typhoid fever, and was buried at Arlington National Cemetery.

Ezra Warner, *General in Blue: Lives of the Union Commanders.* Baton Rouge, La. State Univ. Press, 1964; Don Russell, *The Lives and Legends of Buffalo Bill.* Norman, Univ. of Okla. Press, 1960; Powell.

Pepoon, Silas, army officer (June 13, 1834-Oct. 16, 1874). B. at Painesville, Ohio, he moved to Illinois, then to Oregon where he enlisted in the 1st Oregon Cavalry at Jacksonville November 27, 1861, being commissioned April 8, 1863, at Fort Vancouver. In 1864 he accompanied Captain George B. Currey's extended expedition to southeast Oregon as quartermaster. He took part in an Indian skirmish February 16, 1865, near Jordan Creek, Oregon. With a cavalry detachment Pepoon accompanied Major L.H. Marshall on an Idaho expedition. A man

named Phillips was lassooed by Indians and drawn up a cliff "to be tortured and mutilated"; Pepoon sought to go to his rescue, but was forbidden by Marshall, who had a reputation for inhumanity. He sought to join the 1866 Captain J.H. Walker expedition, but Indian trouble prevented his doing so. Pepoon ended the Civil War a first lieutenant having been in seven Indian fights and many skirmishes on the Oregon-Washington-Idaho front. He was of the initial cadre for the 10th Cavalry, becoming a second lieutenant August 17, 1867, and a first lieutenant in 1872. Pepoon saw considerable active service on the Plains, commanding Indian scouts much of the time. He was with the relief forces for the Beecher Island scouts, commanding scouts on Custer's southern Plains expedition following the Washita fight in 1868-69, and with Company B, 10th Cavalry, commanded scouts on Miles' Red River campaign of 1874, acquitting himself well. But in a fit of despondency he killed himself. Surgeon Francis Laban Town said Pepoon had shot himself in the head while in his tent, about eight miles from Fort Sill, Pepoon "suffering during the past summer much from malaria and in connection with which he had exhibited great mental depression, approaching at intervals even to temporary dementia... Nothing could be discovered to indicate that this act had been premeditated." Captain Richard Jacob however reported that Pepoon was accused by fellow officers of cheating at cards and was subject to a court-martial; he pleaded for withdrawal of the charges, but was refused and then committed suicide. Pepoon was 5 feet, 10 1/2 inches tall, of light complexion with gray eyes and dark hair; he gave his profession at enlistment as a teacher. He may have been a brother to Joseph B. Pepoon, who enlisted in the 1st Oregon Cavalry November 26, 1861, serving like Silas in Company A.

A Webfoot Volunteer: The Diary of William M. Hilleary. Corvallis, Ore. State Univ. Press, 1965; Bancroft, *Oregon,* II; George A. Custer, *My Life on the Plains.* Lincoln, Univ. of Nebr. Press, 1966; William H. Leckie, *The Buffalo Soldiers.* Norman, Univ. of Okla. Press, 1967; Nat. Archives, Pepoon's military record; AGO Records: Letters Received by Appointment, Commission, and Personal Branch; "Military Reminiscences of Captain Richard T. Jacob." *Chronicles of Okla.,* Vol. 2, No. 1 (Mar. 1924), 34.

Peppin, George Warden, lawmen (Oct. 1841-Sept. 14, 1904). B. at Mountsville, Vermont, he enlisted in Company A, 5th Infantry, California Volunteers, at Allegheny, California, October 2, 1861. Peppin served at Fort Stanton from March 1863 until May 1864. A stone mason by trade, he helped build structures in the vicinity, including the jail at Lincoln, New Mexico. Peppin was appointed sheriff of Lincoln County in May 1878, succeeding Copeland who had served briefly following the slaying of Sheriff Brady; Peppin relinquished the office February 1, 1879. As deputy he had been with Brady when Brady was killed April 1, 1878, and was sheriff himself during the critical period of the Lincoln County War which included the Five Days' Battle of July in which Peppin was nominal head of the Dolan faction which won sort of a pyrrhic victory. He had been an employee of Dolan when named Sheriff and was under indictment for the murder of McNab; in April 1879, he was indicted by a grand jury (with Dudley) for arson in the burning of the McSween home at the time of the battle. Nothing came of this charge. Something of a figurehead sheriff, he was described by Angel as "Weak Murphy man — Partisan not reliable." After leaving office he became post butcher at Fort Stanton; later he was an employee of Pat Coghlan in the beef business. He died at Lincoln.

Robert N. Mullin notes; "Frank Warner Angel's Notes on New Mexico Territory 1878," ed. by Lee Scott Theisen. *Arizona and the West,* Vol. 18, No. 4 (Winter 1976).

Peralta, Miguel, miner (fl. 1860-1880). Miguel Peralta II is said to have befriended Jacob Waltz and Jacob Weiser, who later claimed to have located the lode in the Arizona Superstition Mountains which became known as the Lost Dutchman. They found it through a map Peralta reportedly gave them at Arizpe, Sonora, about 1870. Peralta reportedly told the partners that the mine had been discovered in 1847 and belonged to his grandfather Miguel Peralta, in an area known as the Peralta Land Grant, bestowed upon the family in 1748. Indians purportedly killed the grandfather and Miguel II's father, Enrico Peralta, in 1848, along with numerous associates and workmen. One son of Enrico's, Ramón Peralta y Gonzales, discovered the massacre site years later and somehow, legend has it, Miguel II obtained a map to the location. The fact of the massacre is said to be supported by numerous relics since discovered. Some support for the Peralta family history is given in Gentry. Dates of the birth and death of Miguel II or the other Peraltas are unestablished, but Miguel reportedly died in Mexico City without heirs.

Sims Ely, *The Lost Dutchman Mine.* N.Y., William Morrow and Co., 1953; Curt Gentry, *The Killer Mountains.* N.Y., Ballantine Books, 1973.

Peralta, Pedro de, Spanish official (c. 1584-1666). B. in Spain and the founder of Santa Fe, New Mexico, his best biographical treatment is Lansing B. Bloom's article in the *Dictionary of American Biography.* He reached Mexico and in 1609 was appointed third governor of New Mexico, succeeding the two Oñates, but he probably did not arrive in the territory until the following year. Santa Fe was founded in the spring of 1610, Peralta remaining there for nine years, his administration marked by disputes between himself and the Franciscans who managed mission activities. At one point Peralta was arrested by churchman as a "schismatic heretic," but Mexico City officials ordered his release. After leaving New Mexico he served the king in various capacities in Mexico and in South America. He died at Madrid.

DAB, as cited; *New Mex. Hist. Rev.,* Vol. IV, No. 2 (Apr. 1929), 178-87; 188-94.

Perceval, Don Louis, artist (Jan. 8,1908-May 13, 1979). B. at Woodford, Essex County, England, of artist parents, he moved to Hollywood, California, with his parents in 1920, studied at the Chouinard Institute of Art at Hollywood, the Heatherly School of Art and Royal College of Art at London and at various galleries of Europe, including the Prado, Madrid. From 1939 he served six years in the Royal Navy then returned to the United States, teaching art at the Chouinard Institute and at Pomona (California) College. His specialty was picturing the Indian southwest, particularly the Navaho and Hopi Indians and their country, and his work is represented in at least 50 books including his own, *The Art of Western America* and numerous *Brand Books* of the Los Angeles Corral of The Westerners. He died at Santa Barbara, California.

Los Angeles Westerners *Branding Iron,* No. 136 (Sept 1979), 3-6.

Perez Hernandez, Juan José, navigator (d. Nov. 3, 1775). A Mallorcan and already experienced navigator of Mexico's west coast (who also had served as navigator for the Manila galleon) Perez was assigned by José de Gálvez in 1769 to command the *Principe* as part of the 1769 Portolá expedition to settle Upper California. By 1774 he was a *piloto,* or mate/navigator, a non-commissioned rank although such men as Perez sometimes filled a commissioned function, commanding a ship. He was active in several voyages to California colonies before being assigned in late 1773 to take the *Santiago* northward on a voyage of discovery at least as far north as 60 degrees, and to search the coast for traces of Russian or British activities. Perez raised anchor at Monterey Bay June 6, 1774, and eight days later commenced his voyage, reaching 50 degrees north and then setting his course toward land he knew Bering and Chirikov had sighted. July 18 land was sighted near the southern end of the Alaskan panhandle. Perez was the probable discoverer of Nootka Sound on Vancouver Island, and sailed on south, on August 10 or 11 sighting a snow-covered mountain he called Santa Rosalia but believed to have been Mount Olympus on the Olympic Peninsula. Fog hampered explorations to the south but the navigator recognized Cape Mendocino, the Farallones and at last Monterey Bay was reached about August 27. Bancroft credits Perez by this voyage with having "gained the honor of having discovered practically the whole Northwest Coast," and done as much as was possible under the circumstances to fulfill his instructions; Cook is not so kind, regarding Perez as doing a cursory and slipshod job of exploration, pointing out he had even missed the Strait of Juan de Fuca and mouth of the Columbia River when he might have discovered or at least located both. In 1775 Perez was second in command to Bruno Hezeta (Heceta), again aboard the *Santiago,* their instuctions being to attain 65 degrees north latitude , if possible. They reached 42 degrees June 7, followed the coast southward to Trinidad, leaving there June 19 for the north. Hampered by adverse winds they attempted to relocate Juan de Fuca's Strait but too far to the south. The explorers got no farther north than 49 degrees 30' (although a companion ship reached 58 degrees); on the return they again missed the Strait but located the mouth of the Columbia

River though were prevented from entering by strong currents. Eventually they regained Monterey Bay. They left for Mexico November 1 and two days later Perez died at sea of a lingering disease.

Bancroft, *Northwest Coast,* I; Warren L. Cook, *Flood Tide of Empire.* New Haven, Yale Univ. Press, 1973.

Perkins, Bishop Walden, frontier lawyer, politician (Oct. 18, 1841-June 20, 1894). Perkins, whose first name was Bishop, was b. at Rochester, Ohio, graduated from Knox College, Galesburg, Illinois, prospected in California and New Mexico without much success from 1860-62, and served as sergeant of the 83rd Illinois Infantry and later as adjutant and captain of the 16th U.S. Colored Infantry. He studied law at Ottawa, Illinois, was admitted to the bar in 1867, practiced briefly in Indiana, then moved to Oswego, Labette County, Kansas, where he became prosecuting attorney, probate judge, newspaper editor, U.S. Congressman and U.S. Senator, practicing law in Washington, D.C., from 1893 until his death.

BDAC; John R. Cook, *The Border and the Buffalo.* N.Y., Citadel Press, 1967.

Perrot, Nicolas, explorer, Indian man (c. 1644-Aug. 13, 1717). B. in France, he reached Canada by 1660 as a Jesuit donné, or lay assistant, and quickly commenced learning Indian languages (he became especially proficient in Algonquin dialects) while working for the missionaries. He labored for the Jesuits until 1665 and then a year for the Sulpitians when he entered the fur trade among the Ottawas. Perrot became a most famous voyageur and widely acquainted among all the northwestern tribes, gaining their confidence and goodwill. Perrot visited the Potawatomis and the Foxes as early as 1665. Two years later he formed his first fur trading company and traveled into Wisconsin, visiting various tribes. In September of 1670 he was employed as interpreter and Indian manager for St. Lusson, who had been directed to investigate the rumor of copper deposits near Lake Superior and to formally proclaim the sovereignty of Louis XIV over the lands of the west. Perrot called deputations of many tribes to a great meeting at Sault Ste. Marie where on June 4, 1671, St. Lusson officially took possession. Perrot had traded for some furs while on this mission, but on St. Lusson's orders these were seized at Quebec. Upon his return from the St. Lusson expedition, Perrot married Madeleine Raclot, by whom he fathered eleven children, nine of whom survived him. He had obtained a land grant near Becancour, across the St. Lawrence from Three Rivers, and there made his home when back from the wilderness. In 1677 one Nicolas Perrot, alias Jolycoeur, tried to poison La Salle at Fort Frontenac (Kingston, Ontario). The attempt failed and the offender imprisoned, remaining in custody at least until January 1679. Parkman and others have assumed that this was Nicolas Perrot, the wilderness expert, but the *Dictionary of Canadian Biography,* II, 517, shows that this is not so, that the guilty man was a soldier enlisted under this alias but later confessing his real name. There is no such blemish on the record of the voyageur. "From 1684 to 1699, he was one of the chief figures in the upper lake region — exploring its rivers, trading with the savages, negotiating with them for alliance with the French, and holding them to their professions thereof." Parkman wrote that "few names are so conspicuous as that of Perrot; not because there were not others who matched him in achievement but because he could write, and left behind him a tolerable account of what he had seen." Perrot was instrumental in rallying 500 warriors of five tribes to support La Barre's futile 1684 operations against the Iroquois. In 1687 he again rallied hundreds of fighters from the upper lakes to support Denonville in his scarcely more successful operation against the Senecas, and with other *couriers du bois* commanded these irregulars. In 1685 Perrot was named commandant in chief of Green Bay, Wisconsin and neighboring regions, and in delicate negotiations established a shaky peace between the Foxes on one hand and Sioux and Chippewas on the other. He then crossed Wisconsin by the Fox and Wisconsin rivers, turned up the Mississippi and established one of his numerous trading post-forts in Sioux country. In 1689 he formally took possession of much of the upper valley of the Mississippi and tributary streams for Louis XIV, and discovered lead deposits along the big river. Perrot was entrusted in the dead of winter, 1690, with a message from Frontenac to surly tribesmen threatening to destroy the important fur post of Michilimackinac and

the outbreak was averted. Again, as late as 1696, in the face of a British threat, "Nicolas Perrot roamed among the tribes of the Mississippi, striving at the risk of his life to keep them at peace with one another, and in alliance with the French." On August 4, 1701, for a Grand Council at Montreal, 1,300 warriors of 30 tribes were summoned from a stretch of wilderness 2,000 miles in extent by Governor General Louis Hector de Calliere in pursuance of his instructions to further solidify the French western empire, seek to separate the Iroquois from alliance with Britain, better regulate the fur trade and Indian trade, and accomplish other similar ends. Perrot and the Jesuits served as interpreters, translating the governor's words in five different languages. The council in general was successful. Perrot had settled permanently after 1696 on his farm at Becancour, where hard times gradually came upon him. He had suffered severe losses in his fur trading, creditors hounded him, his post of military captain was not remunerative and the government would supply him neither a pension nor reimbursement for the heavy expenses he had incurred in purchasing presents for Indians he sought to influence for the French interest. During this period, however, he composed his memoirs, which have value, particularly as edited by the Jesuit Tailhan (they were first published in French in 1864). Perrot died at his farm. His wife, who had suffered occasionally from mental depression, became insane in 1720 and died four years later.

Thwaites, JR, LV, 320-21n5; Parkman, *La Salle and the Discovery of the Great West, Count Frontenac and New France Under Louis XIV;* DCB.

Perry, Dave, frontiersman (fl. 1869-1879). Perry with R. Rowland in 1869 was running a saloon and dance hall, the California Exchange Keg House, at North Platte, Nebraska, when Cody dropped in; both men had drinks, a quarrel started and Cody got the worst of it, judging from his appearance later. He and Perry ultimately became fast friends, but Luther North said it "looked for awhile... as though (their dispute) would end in a killing." In the winter of 1877-78 Perry scouted for Homer Wheeler of the 5th Cavalry, hunting marauding Indians which they did not come up with. In 1879 Perry often was a guest of the Cody-North ranch. When drunk he usually asked Luther North to shoot away a coin he would hold on a stick close to his fingers, Luther North said Perry operated his saloon "for many years," and "was in several gun fights, and in one he was shot through the lung, but came through it all right I think he was ordered out of the city when John Bratt was elected Mayor," Perry explaining he was run out because "the damned stranglers got after him." North never saw him again.

Man of the Plains: Recollections of Luther North 1856-1882. Lincoln, Univ. of Nebr. Press, 1961; Don Russell, *The Lives and Legends of Buffalo Bill.* Norman, Univ. of Okla. Press, 1960.

Perry, David, army officer (June 11, 1841-May 18, 1908). B. at Ridgefield, Connecticut, Perry stood a bit over 6 feet in height, held himself very erect, was pleasant of expression although one described him as "very arrogant." From Connecticut he was commissioned a second lieutenant of the 1st Cavalry March 24, 1862, becoming a first lieutenant July 27 and a captain November 12, 1864. On December 26, 1866, Perry scored a triumph over the Snakes on the Owyhee River of Idaho and won a brevet to lieutenant colonel. April 6, 1868 he had a sharp fight on the Malheur River, Oregon, killing 32 hostiles for no soldier losses and winning a brevet to colonel. Crook paid him tribute in a letter to department headquarters: "Captain Perry is an excellent officer. I assure you it is no easy matter to find an officer who is so conversant with his duty and who is so willing to do it thoroughly." Perry was in the Modoc War of northeastern California in 1872-73 and in the preliminaries to it. In the first Battle of the Stronghold, January 17, 1873, he was wounded in the upper arm, one of 39 soldier casualties that day. He recovered in time to take part in the Second Battle of the Stronghold in April. The *Chronoligical List* gives Perry credit for the capture of Captain Jack, June 1, 1873, but this was accomplished by Captain Joel Trimble. Perry was in command of troops F and H in the hard action of June 17, 1877, at Whitebird Canyon, Idaho which largely opened the Nez Perce campaign; he lost Lieutenant Theller and 33 enlisted men killed. Perry was accused by some officers of what amounted to dereliction of duty in the Whitebird action and subse-

quent Clearwater battle where he also commanded and requested a formal inquiry, which was granted. The board on November 30, 1877, exonerated him. He was further vindicated by the findings of a formal Court of Inquiry February 1, 1878. A year later, April 27, 1879, Perry became major of the 6th Cavalry and soon was posted to the Southwest. He commanded Fort Bayard, New Mexico during the Victorio campaign of 1880, but had no direct contact with that hostile, although occasionally took the field hunting him. January 20, 1882, Perry was named to command field operations in southeastern Arizona. Thus he was in overall command during the important pursuit of hostile Apaches during the Loco emeute of April 1882, his assignments being professional and effective, although most of the Indians succeeded in gaining their Sonora sanctuary. Perry became lieutenant colonel of the 10th Cavalry April 20, 1891, colonel of the 9th Cavalry December 11, 1896, and retired July 5, 1898. He was promoted to Brigadier General on the retired list April 23, 1904. He died at Washington, D.C., and was buried at Arlington Cemetery.

Heitman; *Chronological List;* Keith A. Murray, *The Modocs and Their War.* Norman, Univ. of Okla. Press, 1965; John D. McDermott, *Forlorn Hope: The Battle of White Bird Canyon and the Beginning of the Nez Perce War.* Boise, Ida., State Hist. Soc., 1978; Dan L. Thrapp, *General Crook and the Sierra Madre Adventure.* Norman, 1972.

Perry, Frank W., army officer (c. 1845-June 18, 1876). Perry was the first army officer to confer with Cochise, the noted Apache chief and war leader, after the Indian in 1861 became hostile. B. in Ohio, probably at Cleveland, Perry enlisted at 16 in the 14th Infantry, rising in less than eight months to sergeant major when on June 9, 1862, he was commissioned a second lieutenant. Before he was 21 he had taken part in 25 battles and all the actions of the Army of the Potomac through the Wilderness campaign and the Weldon Railroad affair before Petersburg except while recovering from his wounds. For Civil War service he was twice breveted, to major (and was recommended for one additional brevet) and on July 9, 1866, was promoted to captain. He served against hostile Indians in Oregon, Idaho and Arizona; commanded Camp Curry on Silver Creek in eastern Oregon, was acting assistant adjutant general of the Military District of Boise, Idaho, and after transfer to the 32nd Infantry June 9, 1867 commanded Camp Goodwin on the Gila in Arizona, a three-company post. During his nine months there he "was constantly employed in Scouting" for hostile Apaches. Lieutenant Colonel Thomas Devin, commanding the District of Arizona, had received in late 1868 word that Cochise might come in under certain conditions, and Perry, with a Coyotero Apache guide and Surgeon John Christopher Handy and Handy's wife, possibly of part Apache origin, journeyed to the Dragoon Mountains to meet the wild and dangerous Indian. Cochise at the meeting expressed a desire for peace but was adamant in his refusal to go to the post Devin had indicated he should attend. Perry remarked that he had heard Cochise often had been wounded. Cochise replied this had happened to him twice, once near Santa Cruz, Sonora in the leg, a wound which took a long time to heal, and again, two years previous to the meeting, near Fronteras, Sonora when he was shot in the neck. Cochise was given food, tobacco and a blanket "but soldiers (of Perry's escort) went hungry for three days." Perry estimated Cochise was about 50, guessed he was six feet, two inches tall, described his appearance and added that he "looks to be a man that means what he says; age is just beginning to tell on him." Perry was assigned to the 24th Infantry December 18, 1869, and stationed at Fort Duncan, Texas, at Eagle Pass on the Rio Grande. Here he must have been bored or for some other reason was discontented. He applied August 14, 1870, for a transfer to the Cavalry, a request which was denied. On June 2, 1871, he was tried by General Court-Martial at San Antonio, Texas on three charges and 20 specifications alleging he was guilty of drunkeness on duty, of conduct unbecoming an officer and of conduct prejudicial to good order and military discipline. On the latter two charges he was found not guilty; of the first he was found guilty on 13 specifications and of the charge and was sentenced to be cashiered. All members of the court, including Colonel Abner Doubleday commanding the regiment who had been president at the trial urged moderation of the sentence "in view of (Perry's) excellent record during the War of Rebellion...and of his meritorious services

subsequent thereto as shown by his record and by the testimony given at the trial." By order of the Secretary of War the sentence was mitigated to suspension of rank for 18 months and of pay except $50 a month for a like period. Perry resigned from the army February 1, 1873. He then applied for a U.S. Consul position somewhere (his request endorsed by a good friend, Harry L. Sherman of Cleveland, nephew of General of the Army William Tecumseh Sherman), but he was not appointed. He applied through an old comrade in arms and West Pointer Charles Pomeroy Stone, then chief of staff for the Egyptian army, for a position with that organization, but only engineer officers were sought. Perry called on President U.S. Grant in early 1876 for reappointment as second lieutenant to the 24th Infantry when he would immediately retire, thus winning a pension and perhaps medical attention for his troublesome wounds. Grant directed his Secretary of War Alphonso Taft to send the nomination to the Senate which was done, but before that body could act Perry died at Providence Hospital, Washington. An obituary said death came from his "wounds and disease contracted in the war." The body was buried at Cleveland where Perry's mother lived on, at least until 1885. His father, Captain John S. Perry of the 15th Infantry had died in 1850 from disease contracted during the Mexican War. Frank Perry was 5 feet, 5 1/2 inches tall, weighed around 130 pounds and was of light complexion.

Frank W. Perry Pension File, NARS; Perry Personnel File, NARS; Heitman; information from Constance Wynn Altshuler.

Peta Nocona, Comanche chief (c. 1825-1861). A leader of the Quahadi Comanche, he led the 1836 raid in which Cynthia Ann Parker, 9, was kidnapped and married her when she reached marriageable age; the couple were devoted to each other and Peta Nocona took no other wife. Several children were born to them, including the great Quanah Parker. December 18, 1860, Texas Rangers under Sul Ross and Jack Cureton struck the chief's camp, captured Cynthia Ann and mortally wounded Peta Nocona who died of an infection from his injury in the Antelope Hills shortly after the engagement.

HT; Dockstader.

Petalesharo, Skidi Pawnee chief (c. 1797-c. 1832). The son of Old Knife was b. about 1797 and grew into a man of fine physique reputed to be the most daring warrior of his tribe. At one time when his people were gathered for the sacrifice of a Comanche woman captive (the ceremony being a normal rite of the Skidi Pawnees) Petalesharo stepped forward, declared that it was his father's wish that the practice be abolished and that he would sacrifice his own life if necessary to free the victim. He then cut the thongs binding the woman, and bore her off on horseback to relative safety, gave her food and told her to make her own way to her tribe some 400 miles distant, while he returned to his village. His deed was accepted by his people because of their respect for his courage and other qualities. Petalesharo in the fall of 1821 went east with other Pawnee chiefs; the story of his rescue of the Comanche girl had preceded him and at Washington, D.C., he was presented with a silver medal to whose cost contributions had been made by students at a noted female seminary. Charles Bird King painted his portrait. Petalesharo and his father signed a September 1825 treaty with white officials, although the name does not appear on the published document. He is often confused with two others of the same name from other bands of Pawnees, but he and his father seem to have perished in a raging smallpox epidemic, perhaps started deliberately by Santa Fe traders, which caused devastating loss of life among Pawnees in 1832, a year of several disasters for the tribe.

Hodge, HAI; George E. Hyde, *The Pawnee Indians.* Norman, Univ. of Okla. Press, 1974.

Peterson, William, frontiersman (Dec. 3, 1834-Nov. 28, 1919). B. on the Bornholm Islands, Denmark, he went to sea at 15, rising at length to second mate, but after 11 years quit that profession and joined an Idaho gold rush, worked at various occupations including the operation of a pack string, and by 1865 reached Montana, eventually going to work for Charles Cook. In 1869 he joined the Folsom Yellowstone expedition, "the best-managed expedition that ever passed through the Yellowstone wilderness." In 1870 Peterson began cattle ranching in the Lemhi Valley, Montana. Later he moved to a place along the Salmon River, Idaho. He was twice mayor of the town of Salmon, where he died.

Peterson was married and fathered two children, neither of whom survived to maturity.

Aubrey L. Haines, *Yellowstone National Park: Its Exploration and Establishment.* Wash., Nat. Park Service, 1974.

Petit, Louis, army officer, priest (1629-June 3, 1709). B. in Rouen, France, he reached Quebec in June of 1665, a captain in the Carignan-Salieres regiment, and took part in the Remy de Courcelle expedition against the Mohawks in February 1666, and perhaps that of Tracy the following autumn. He studied for the priesthood, meanwhile, and was ordained by Bishop Francois de Laval late in 1670. He was chaplain at Fort Richelieu, Quebec, for more than five years, then was made vicar of Acadia, with his residence at Port Royal. When the English adventurer William Phipps demanded surrender of the place in the spring of 1690, Petit secured honorable conditions, but these were violated, Petit arrested and taken to Boston; he was exchanged in the autumn. The remainder of his career was spent in Canada and he died at Quebec.

Thwaites, JR, L, 319n8, DCB.

Peu-peu-mox-mox (Yellow Serpent, Yellow Bird). Walla Walla chief (d. Dec. 1855). "A strong and intelligent man of dignified bearing," he became leader of the Walla Walla tribe of Washington Territory and sent his son to be educated at the Methodist mission in the Willamette Valley of Oregon; this offspring became known as Elijah Hedding, named for a Methodist bishop. Peu-peu-mox-mox was related by marriage or otherwise to leading men of the Cayuse, Nez Perce and other cognate tribes, including the Yakima leader Kamaiakin and the Nez Perce, Looking Glass; thus his influence was widespread. Following the murder of his son at Sutter's Fort in 1844, great commotion swept the northwest tribes, many urging a massive retaliation against California whites and Peu-peu-mox-mox calling for extermination of the whites in the Willamette Valley of Oregon who, he felt, were somehow responsible for the crime. McLoughlin at Fort Vancouver met with the chief and warned such an adventure would prove disastrous, with no help forthcoming from the British. The matter however would remain a factor in the Whitman Massacre of

1847. In 1846 the Walla Walla chief and the Delaware Tom Hill led a mixed band of 40 Indians into California on what they promised would be a punitive raid, but the Bear Flag revolt and the Mexican War overshadowed their effort, which came to nothing. Enroute home the reduced band was struck by measles, which they blamed anew on the white man, fanning their old bitterness. Yet the Walla Walla leader took no part in the Whitman Massacre of November 29, 1847 and was regarded as friendly by whites attempting to round up the hostiles. He prospered and by 1853 had accumulated about $5,000, according to Governor Stevens, largely through sale of produce and livestock to white posts; he was reportedly generous to his neighbors, white and red. In late May and early June of 1855 Peu-peu-mox-mox attended the great council of some 5,000 Indians called by Stevens at Mill Creek, above the present Walla Walla. Its purpose was to restrict the tribes to reservations while removing from their control regions coveted by the whites. Peu-peu-mox-mox was most determined in opposition to this land grab, and many influential Indians were impressed by his stand, but in the end the chief and all the other important leaders signed the treaty. Largely because of dissatisfaction with it, however, war broke out in October. Oregon volunteers under Colonel James K. Kelly ranged the countryside; Peu-peu-mox-mox and five or six of his people approached the volunteers' camp December 4 under a truce flag, requesting a parley. The chief was seized under Kelly's orders, and when the hostiles opened a four-day engagement, the chief was murdered as were his companions, his corpse mutilated, bits cut off for souvenirs and in the words of one, "They skinned him from head to foot, and made razor-straps of his skin." Josephy concludes, "So died the descendant of Lewis and Clark's host, Yelleppit, the friend of fur traders and missionaries and the father of the slain Elijah Hedding, an Indian leader with every reason to turn with bitterness against the Americans, but a man who had remained to the end a peace chief, and not a warrior." Josephy carries a sketch-portrait of the chief as Illustration 9, following p. 705.

Alvin M. Josephy Jr., *The Nez Perce Indians and the Opening of the Northwest.* New Haven, Yale Univ. Press, 1965; Clifford M. Drury, *Marcus and Narcissa Whitman and the Opening of Old Oregon.* Glendale, Calif., Arthur H. Clark Co., 1973; Thwaites, EWT, XXX, 229n.

Pfouts, Paris Swazy, frontiersman (Jan. 9, 1829-1910). B. in Stark County, Ohio, he was raised in that state until 1843 when he and his parents moved to Missouri, settling in Oregon, Holt County. Here Pfouts concluded his education, helped out in a country store and worked as a farmer. In 1845 he went back to Ohio to learn the printing trade at which he worked for two years. He returned to Missouri in 1848. The next year he went to California, reaching Hangtown (Placerville) September 20. He spent some time in the mines, in trading, river freighting, running pack trains and other pursuits, alternately prosperous and broke. Pfouts settled for a time on the Trinity River and in the vicinity of Shasta in northern California. For a time he ranched successfully. Indian troubles concerned him in 1851-52, the prelude to the Rogue River War. Pfouts was wounded slightly by an arrow. Meanwhile he had developed a taste for whiskey which posed problems, but he conquered that form of dissipation or its worst effects, at any rate. In 1854 he returned to Missouri with funds enough to become part owner, publisher and editor of the St. Joseph *Gazette,* marrying the sister of its co-owner, James H.R. Cundiff the following year. Pfouts became a Mason in 1854, the fraternal order which became an important influence on his subsequent life. He became involved in politics as well as Masonry and other interests, and his Southern leanings led him in 1861 to quit Missouri for Denver where he arrived in July with only $7.50 to his name. He entered the commission business and was immediately successful. In September 1863 he went to Virginia City, Montana, by way of Salt Lake City and Bannack. At Alder Gulch he found "very many honest, sober, industrious men...(but) the class known as 'Roughs' far outnumbered all others... They comprised the most depraved and abandoned characters...from all the Western States." Yet Pfouts believed Virginia City was a good place to make money, and determined to remain. He was instrumental in organizing the first Masonic Lodge there because of the high positions he had held in Lodges elsewhere. "I believe, without vanity, that I may claim to be the Father of Masonry in Montana," he wrote. Desperado activity continued to plague the camps and Pfouts with four others: Nick Wall, Wilbur Fisk Sanders, Alvin V. Brookie and John Nye, met secretly to form a Vigilance Committee which rapidly grew to about 50, "all among the best and most reliable citizens of Virginia City." In his absence Pfouts was elected president "with full power to organize and control the whole," and he as much as any man was responsible for its efficiency and success in eradicating from Montana the Henry Plummer gang of criminals. More than 1,000 men took the oath in all and joined the committee "and it was difficult to find in Montana Territory a good man who was not a Vigilante." Twice Pfouts sought to resign his office with the Vigilance Committee, but each time he was outvoted. He continued to be successful in business and was elected the first mayor of Virginia City. In September 1865 he returned to the States, going as far east as New York City and Washington, D.C., where he met President Andrew Johnson. He resumed business and family affairs in Montana but in June 1867 quit the Territory for good, entering business at St. Louis. Little is known of his later years for his autobiography stops at that point. He lived his last years at Dallas, Texas with his youngest son, George and died at 81 at that place, although there is no record of his death in the archives of the Texas Department of Health. Pfouts had his ups and downs in public and private life. He was ever prepared to "tip the bottle of fellowship; to sing a few ribald songs with the other boys at the bar; to lay his gold on the table and draw three cards in a futile effort to fill an inside straight," but he was truthful and not an immodest man, and he left his mark upon the West he knew.

Your Firsts for a Modest Hero: The Autobiography of Paris Swazy Pfouts. Helena, Grand Lodge, Ancient Free & Accepted Masons of Mont., 1968.

Pfouts, William G., pioneer (Oct. 1842-June 17, 1910). B. at Mt. Eaton, Ohio, he was a younger brother of Paris Swazy Pfouts. He left Missouri for Denver in 1858 and after remaining in Colorado for some years he went to Montana where he arrived in 1864, settling initially at Virginia City. Eventually he became a merchant at Butte, where he died.

Register, pp. 236-37; *Montana Contributions,* Vol. VIII (1917), 359.

Pharo, David: *see* David Fero.

Phelps, Frederick Elisha, army officer (Oct. 8, 1847-June 10, 1923). B. at St. Mary's, Ohio, he went to West Point, was dropped after failing in mathematics the first year, but was reappointed by Secretary of War, Edwin M. Stanton, a friend of his father's, and was commissioned a second lieutenant of the 8th Cavalry June 15, 1870. He served at New Mexico posts off and on until 1876 and at Texas posts most of the time thereafter until the late 1880s when he was assigned to Fort Yates, North Dakota. In New Mexico Phelps was stationed principally at Forts Craig and Bayard, occasionally scouting from the latter post where he remained five years. He was in charge of building a military telegraph line from Las Lunas to Fort Craig, New Mexico, in 1875. In West Texas Phelps continued his scouting activities from several posts, and also served as adjutant occasionally. He was adjutant on Samuel Baldwin Marks Young's 1877 scout 200 miles into Old Mexico after errant Apaches, keeping a day-to-day itinerary and journal although characterized by Shafter as "a poor, sickly fellow, with every appearance of consumption." He outlived Shafter and many another officer who appeared healthier. In 1888 he marched with the 8th Cavalry from Fort Davis, Texas, to Dakota, a distance of 2,000 miles. The 8th was involved in the Sioux turmoil in Dakota in 1890-91, but Phelps' role is not defined. He retired April 20, 1891, for reasons of health, but rejoined in 1907 and was placed in charge of the Pittsburgh, Pennsylvania recruiting office and in 1909 appointed quartermaster. He eventually became a lieutenant colonel on the retired list and died at Urbana, Ohio. He had married three times, his first two wives dying at early ages. In his lively Memoirs, Phelps gives not only insights into army life of the late 19th century and Apache hunting, but also sharp vignettes of many notable soldiers with whom he came into contact, ranging from enlisted men to high ranking officers.

Cullum; Powell; "Frederick E. Phelps: A Soldier's Memoirs," ed. by Frank D. Reeve. *New Mex. Hist. Rev.,* Vol. XXV, Nos. 1-4 (Jan.-Oct. 1950); Barry C. Johnson, "Young's Fight on Thanksgiving Day." English Westerners' Soc., *Brand Book,* Vol. 16, Nos. 3, 4 (Apr., July 1974).

Phil, the Cannibal: *see* Charles Gardner

Philip, King, Seminole chief (c. 1776-Aug. 1839). Philip was a "good-natured, sensible Indian" of about 60 at the outbreak of the Second Seminole War of Florida. His greatest fame came because he was father of Coacoochee (Wildcat); Philip was "highly respected for his character and intelligence." He may have been active very early in the conflict, late in 1835. Around Christmas Seminoles reportedly of his band attacked sugar plantations east of the St. Johns River and south of St. Augustine. Philip, who probably was a Mikasuki, had married a sister of Micanopy and the noted black, John Caesar was his slave, as much an advisor to Philip as Abraham was to Micanopy. Philip appeared to have been quiet for a time but on February 8, 1837, with two hundred warriors he attacked a breastworks around Fort Mellon, and here Captain Charles Mellon was killed and 17 of his men wounded. Coacoochee and Pacheco probably also were in this fight. September 8-9 Brigadier General Joseph Hernandez with 170 men surrounded Philip's camp south of the Tomoka River and seized the chief, the "most important capture since the war began." The taking of Philip and 11 of his people led to the capture of Coacoochee. Philip was held at Fort Marion on the east coast of Florida along with other important Seminoles and late in December 1837 was sent with 203 others, including Osceola and Micanopy, by sea to Charleston, South Carolina, arriving January 1, 1838. They were held at Fort Moultrie where Osceola died. King Philip and the others were shipped west. King Philip died enroute and was buried 60 miles east of Fort Gibson, Indian Territory.

John T. Sprague, *The Origins...of the Florida War.* N.Y., D. Appleton & Co., 1847; John K. Mahon, *The History of the Second Seminole War.* Gainesville, Univ. of Fla. Press, 1967; Edwin C. McReynolds, *The Seminoles.* Norman, Univ. of Okla. Press, 1967.

Phillips, John (Portugee), frontiersman (Apr. 8, 1832-Nov. 18, 1883). B. Manuel Felipe Cardoso near Terra, Pico Island, The Azores, he reached California by Portuguese whaler about 1850 and became a prospector, probably taking part in a number of gold rushes and reaching the Boise basin, Idaho, in 1862. He may have participated in an Indian fight or two in Idaho and by 1863 was in Montana. He was on Jefferson Standifer's expedition of 1866, had a fight with the Sioux on Tongue River and reached Fort Kearny September 14. Phillips held no government position at the post, was not a scout but a prospector just "wintering at the fort." After the Fetterman massacre on December 21, the post was alerted but in no conceivable danger since it still had a large, well-armed garrison. Carrington hired two "citizen couriers," Phillips and Daniel Dixon, to take a report on the Fetterman disaster to the telegraph line at Horseshoe Station in the North Platte valley, 190 miles distant; each was paid $300 the following month. The two, who may have departed separately, traveled much of the way together; they stayed about 10 hours at Fort Reno and camped twice more before reaching their destination about 10 a.m. on Christmas Day. Phillips went on with a message from the commander at Reno to the commander at Fort Laramie, arriving about 11 p.m. Murray writes that "there is no indication that anyone at the time thought that the long, cold ride to Horseshoe (Station) was anything but just that. Neither Dixon nor Phillips attracted much attention nor did they seek it." It was later that accretions of myth became glued to the Phillips adventure until it emerged an enduring saga of epic proportions: a wild winter ride of a lone messenger, the savior of a beleaguered garrison carrying the news of disaster through hordes of encircling Sioux. Phillips became a mail carrier at Fort Kearny in early 1867, joined Standifer in another prospecting venture in 1869 in the Wind River country, taking part in an Indian fight August 21 near Bull Lake. He became a freighter out of Fort Laramie and Fort Fetterman from 1868 to 1878. He had a ranch on Chugwater Creek from about 1870, and in 1873 filed a claim for losses due to Indian depredations. Phillips sold out in 1878 and moved to Cheyenne, where he died. His frontier fame rests upon his long ride in December 1866 and even more on the growing and glowing fabrications others have surrounded it with, but Murray strips virtually all of these away on the basis of his research.

Robert A. Murray, *The Army on the Powder River.* Fort Collins, Colo., Old Army Press, 1972, 11-26; Grace Raymond Hebard, E.A. Brininstool, *The Bozeman Trail,* Glendale, Calif., Arthur H. Clark Co., 1960, II, pp. 15-38.

Phillips, Paul Chrisler, historian (Nov. 15, 1883-Dec. 23, 1956). B. at Bloomfield, Indiana, he was raised in Nebraska but returned to graduate from Indiana University in 1906, earning a master's degree two years later. He received his doctorate from the University of Illinois in 1911, teaching in the midwest until he became head of the history department of the University of Montana where by 1915 he was full professor. He quickly became "the historical spokesman for Montana." While his first quarter century at Montana was "a time of exceptional accomplishment," the final twenty years of his life were troubled by personal and other problems. He once resigned his faculty position until a court case exonerated him from an unfortunate allegation and he was reinstated in 1946. He died of a heart condition. Phillips left an impressive legacy of published work as well as in the students he guided and who subsequently became outstanding in their various professions. "His numerous publications...are enduring monuments to his excellence as a teacher and scholar." They included: *The West in the Diplomacy of the American Revolution* (1913); ed., with W.S. Lewis, *The Journal of John Work* (1923); ed. *Forty Years on the Frontier...Granville Stuart, Gold Miner, Trader, Merchant, Rancher and Politician* (1925); ed. with Seymour Dunbar, *The Journals and Letters of Major John Owen,* 2 vols. (1927); ed., *Scenery of the Plains, Mountains and Mines by Franklin Langworthy* (1932); ed., *Life in the Rocky Mountains* (W.A. Ferris Diary) (1940); *The Fur Trade,* 2 vols. (1961: arranged and final chapters completed after Phillips' death by John Welling Smurr); *Medicine in the Making of Montana* (1962).

Merrill G. Burlingame, "Paul Chrisler Phillips: 1883-1956." *Arizona and the West,* Vol. 24, No. 3 (Autumn 1982), 201-204.

Philpot, Eli (Bud), stagecoach driver (Apr. 1859-Mar. 15, 1881). B., it is said, in an emigrant wagon along the Platte River, Philpot became a noted California stage driver; he was the brother-in-law of Charles Foss, even better known on coach routes. Philpot went to Arizona with Bob Paul, erstwhile Wells Fargo man. Philpot was driving and Paul riding shotgun on the run between Tombstone and Benson when Bud, suffering from dysentery or influenza,

changed places with Paul. When the coach was held up after dark near Drew's Station, 15 miles north of Tombstone, Philpot was killed by an assassin obviously hoping to get Paul, and a passenger was wounded mortally. No one ever was formally charged with the crimes, but Fred Dodge said the holdup party included Doc Holliday, Billy Leonard, Luther King, Jim Crane, Harry Head and Johnny Barnes, according to Barnes; Dodge's version seems reliable. Dodge added that the holdup was planned by Holliday and Leonard.

Ed Bartholomew, *Wyatt Earp: The Man & The Myth.* Toyahvale, Texas, Frontier Book Co., 1964; Fred Dodge, *Under Cover for Wells Fargo,* ed. by Carolyn Lake. Boston, Houghton Mifflin Co., 1969; John Myers Myers, *Doc Holliday.* Lincoln, Univ. of Nebr. Press, 1973.

Piatt, Charles Carroll, scout (Apr. 12, 1848-June 9, 1910). B. in Ohio he moved to Kansas and at 20 became one of Forsyth's scouts in the famed battle of Beecher Island of September 1868 in eastern Colorado. Piatt lived in Kansas until 1881, then moved to North Dakota where he acquired 900 acres of good farm land. He died at Cooperstown, North Dakota, leaving his widow and seven children living of the 18 he had fathered. His death certificate said his demise had been hastened by "old age (he was 62) and strenuous living."

Simon E. Matson, *The Battle of Beecher Island,* Wray, Colo., Beecher Island Battle Meml. Assn., 1960, 78; Piatt's death certificate.

Pickens, Slim, rodeo clown, actor (June 29, 1919-Dec. 8, 1983). B. Louis Bert Lindley Jr. at Kingsburg, California, he became a rodeo rider and clown in the 1930s, rising to the top of that profession and acquiring his nickname when a promoter told him "slim pickin's is all you'll get in this rodeo." His motion picture career began in 1945 when he earned $25 for riding a bucking horse in a movie based on the Will James novel, *Smoky.* He became an actor fulltime in 1950 and appeared in many films, most of them westerns, including "Pat Garrett and Billy the Kid," and in such television series as "Gunsmoke" and "Bonanza." He won his greatest fame as the eccentric cowboy bomber pilot in the motion picture, "Dr. Strangelove" in 1964, in the closing scene riding an atomic bomb like a bucking horse as it fell to its target in Soviet Russia. After that memorable scene "my salary jumped five times," he recalled, and "assistant directors began calling 'Hey, Slim,' instead of 'Hey, you!'" He died at Modesto, California, and was buried at Columbia, a small gold rush town north of Sonora, California, where he had made his home.

Tucson, *Arizona Daily Star,* Dec. 10, 1983.

Pickett, Albert James, planter, historian (Aug. 13, 1810-Oct. 28, 1858). B. in Anson County, North Carolina, he was educated in Connecticut and Virginia, read law and settled in Alabama where he acquired a large farm and as an avocation wrote historical articles for newspapers. During the Creek disturbances of 1836 he was aide to Governor C.C. Clay. In 1837 he located permanently in Montgomery, Alabama, ten years later commenced his *History of Alabama* and published it in 1851; it remains a keystone for the study of Alabama and southern history. Pickett died in Montgomery County.

Information from the Ala. Dept. of Archives and Hist.; Thomas McAdory Owen, *History of Alabama and Dictionary of Alabama Biography,* 4 vols. (1921), IV. Spartanburg, So. Car., Reprint Co., 1978.

Pickett, Bill, cowboy, rodeo performer (c. 1860-Apr. 2, 1932). B. on a San Gabriel River ranch near Taylor, Texas, his mother was a Choctaw and his father mulatto. At 13 it is said he was hired by George Miller of the Oklahoma 101 Ranch, although this is disputed. There in about 1880 (the date and circumstances are uncertain) he "bulldogged" his first steer, an exasperating animal that he wrestled to the ground by twisting its neck and sinking his teeth into its upper lip to help turn its head. One of the cowboys watching was said to have remarked: "You took the bulldog's job away from him when you bulldogged that steer!" giving what became a prime arena event its name. Pickett bulldogged at fairs and shows in the southwest before the 101 Wild West Show was organized, starting in 1900 when he gave at the Arkansas Valley Fair in Rocky Ford, Colorado, the first recorded public exhibition of the feat, and this date is not agreed upon, either. When the 101 show was organized Pickett became a star attractions, as were Will Rogers and Tom Mix. In 1908 Pickett accompanied the show to Mexico City where in a tumultous incident with bull-fighting fans and vicious animals, Pickett put on a solo exhibition against an animal in the arena. Pickett performed at Madison Square Garden, New York, and in England before royalty. In the depression Pickett bought a quarter section near Chandler, Oklahoma, but returned to help out Zack Miller, the remaining son of George, who was infirm. An unbroken horse so pummeled him that he died 11 days later. Miller arranged for a lavish funeral for the "finest dirt and sweat cowboy that ever lived," and wrote a moving poetic tribute to Pickett. Bill Pickett was only 5 feet, 6 inches, tall and weighed 160 pounds at his prime. He was uncommonly agile, and was loyal, skillful and fearless.

Judy Sanders Sawicki, "Bill Pickett — Brazen Bulldogger." *True Frontier,* No. 36 (Jan. 1974), 6-8; 50-51; Don Russell, *The Wild West: A History of Wild West Shows.* Ft. Worth, Tex., Amon Carter Mus., 1970.

Pickett, Tom, desperado, lawman (c. 1856-May 14, 1934). B. at Camp Throckmorton, Wise County, Texas, he reportedly became involved with cattle rustlers in his teens, but enlisted in Co. B, Frontier Battalion, Texas Rangers, April 1, 1876, serving until August 31, 1877. He was indicted in Cooke County, Texas, for rustling in 1879, moved to New Mexico and joined the Las Vegas police force that year, then became a bartender, assistant marshal of White Oaks, New Mexico, and a cowboy on a ranch managed by Charlie Bowdre, with whom he soon was associated with Billy the Kid, joining him in horse rustling and other activities. After a ragged series of brushes with posses, in which Tom O'Folliard was killed and Pickett escaped narrowly, perhaps wounded, he with the Kid, Rudabaugh and others, surrendered December 21, 1880. Pickett, charged with rustling, was bailed out in July and disappeared. He may have participated in a stage holdup, but next certainly appears in 1882 as the marshal of Golden, New Mexico. He was run out of town by citizens who threatened to lynch him. Pickett drifted into Mexico; he was charged with others with killing four Mexicans at Seven Rivers, New Mexico, January 8, 1884, although factual support is lacking. He reported he had narrow escapes in Mexico, but appeared on the record next in Arizona, working for the Hash Knife ranch (Aztec

Land and Cattle Company). He may have been a packer with the army during the Geronimo campaign in 1886, drove the Fort Apache-Holbrook stage for some years, was a deputy sheriff from 1912 to 1914, and lived variously until his death from nephritis at Winslow, Arizona, where he was buried. Pickett was a large man, 6 feet, 2 inches, or more in height, weighed upwards of 200 pounds, was dark with dark eyes, and left-handed.

Philip J. Rasch, "He Rode With the Kid: The Life of Tom Pickett." London, *English Westerners' 10th Anniv. Pubn.*, 1964.

Pickett, Tom M., cowboy (d. post 1922). Apparently born in Texas, he reached Arizona with a trail herd for the Hash Knife ranch (Aztec Land and Cattle Company), where he was often confused with Tom Pickett the desperado-frontier character, also in Arizona at this time. Like the other, he probably had served in the Texas Rangers, and like him was employed as a Holbrook, Arizona, bartender. Tom M. Pickett fought in the Pleasant Valley War, and was wounded in 1886 or 1887 in a Holbrook gunfight. As a bartender he killed a cowboy, the Cimarron Kid, ran a gambling house at Winslow, Arizona, joined the Nevada gold rush and became inspector of Nevada police. He had his right leg amputated, but was appointed a deputy U.S. marshal, although he resigned May 6, 1922.

Philip J. Rasch, "He Rode With the Kid: The Life of Tom Pickett." London, *English Westerners' 10th Anniv. Pubn.,* 1964.

Picotte, Honore D., fur trader (fl. 1820-1848). A prominent figure in the river fur trade, he was a French-Canadian who reached the Missouri River about 1820 and entered the Columbia Fur Company. He was a member of the French Fur Company from 1827-30 and when that was merged in the American Company he became a partner in the Upper Missouri Outfit. He had a great deal of influence among the Sioux, marrying into that people, and was stationed for many years at Fort Pierre where Audubon met him in 1843. In 1846 De Smet was his guest there. About 1848 Picotte retired from active work on the upper river and moved to St. Louis. His son was Charles Picotte, also a noted figure in early Dakota history.

Thwaites, EWT, XXIV, 16n.; Annie Heloise Abel, ed., *Chardon's Journal at Fort Clark 1834-1839.* Pierre, So. Dak. Dept. of Hist., 1932.

Picotte, Joseph, frontiersman (d. 1868). B. in Canada, he was a nephew of Honore Picotte, fur trader. He was employed by the American Fur Company before 1846 when he became a partner of Harvey, Primeau and company. In 1862 he was employed by the La Barge, Harkness Company, the opposition. He died at Yankton Agency, South Dakota.

Montana, Contributions, Vol. X, 1940, 267.

Picquet, Francois, Sulpitian priest (Dec. 6, 1708-July 15, 1781). B. in Burgundy he became a Sulpitian priest and reached Canada about 1734. He worked 15 years in the vicinity of Montreal, coming to have much influence over the Iroquois. In the summer of 1749 he founded a mission and fortified post for the Iroquois whom he hoped to influence against the English, near the site of the present Ogdensburg, New York. Within two years he had about 400 Indians settled there, and ultimately 3,000. He maintained his work until 1760 when, unwilling to swear allegiance to England, he left Canada by way of New Orleans, returning to France. He died at Verjon, France.

Thwaites, JR, LXIX, 295n32.

Pierce, Abel Head (Shanghai), cattleman (June 29, 1834-Dec. 26, 1900). B. at Little Compton, Rhode Island, he stowed away when 20 on a schooner which landed him at Port Lavaca, Texas, where he secured ranch work and began to accumulate cattle on his own, livestock that then was virtually worthless. After Confederate cavalry service he continued to expand his cattle holdings, with a brother establishing the Rancho Grande on the Trespalacios River, Wharton County, by 1871. He went to Kansas for nearly two years (purportedly to escape the aftermath of the lynching of rustlers), then returned to Texas where he gradually acquired a 250,000-acre ranch and a durable reputation as an intelligent, opinionated, proud character. He and his brother were among the first to fence their range, although the two ultimately split their holdings, Shanghai taking the northern half; his brother the southern. Pierce sent thousands of longhorns up the trail to Kansas and elsewhere, though sentiment was rising against the southern cattle because of "Texas fever" they were said to bring north. Pierce became convinced the illness was caused by ticks, experimented in removing them, and toured Europe hunting a breed that would be resistant to ticks, finally settling on the Brahman as most likely to fulfill his objective. After his death his estate imported Brahman cattle, launching that valuable breed in Texas. The precise origin of his nickname is unknown although one version has it that large spurs he ordered "made him look like a Shanghai rooster," whatever a Shanghai rooster looked like. Charlie Siringo worked for him briefly as a cowboy; it is said that John Wesley Hardin once hunted unsuccessfully for him, in retaliation for Pierce's supposed role in lynching two of Hardin's friends. Toward the close of his life Shanghai employed San Antonio sculptor, Ed Teich, for $2,500 to fashion a statue of Pierce, larger than life-size, to be placed over his grave. Asked why he had done so, Pierce is said to have replied: "I knew damned well if I didn't do it, no one else would." He was buried in Hawley, Texas, near Bay City.

HT; Oran Warder Nolen, "Texas Cowman 'Shanghai' Pierce." *The West,* Vol. VII, No. 2 (July 1967), 32-33, 54-56; Mike Blakely, "Shanghai's Legacy," *True West,* Vol. 33, No. 1 (Jan. 1986), 48-53.

Pierce, Charlie, desperado (d. May 1, 1895). B. in Texas he settled at Pawnee, Oklahoma Territory, bringing along a couple of race horses and became known as a "race horse man." A particular friend of George (Bitter Creek) Newcomb, he became a member of the Bill Doolin gang. He took part in train robberies at Lillietta, September 15, 1891; Red Rock, June 1, 1892; Adair, July 14, 1892; the Southwest City, Missouri, bank robbery May 10, 1894; and the Dover, Oklahoma, train robbery, April 3-4, 1895. He was assassinated with Newcomb by Bee and John Dunn at the Bee Dunn ranch for the $5,000 reward. Pierce was buried at Summit View Cemetery, Guthrie, in a pauper's grave.

Bailey C. Hanes, *Bill Doolin, Outlaw O.T.,* Norman, Univ. of Okla. Press, 1968.

Pierce, Francis Edwin, army officer (July 6, 1833-Nov. 4, 1896). B. at New York City, he was commissioned captain in the 108th New York Infantry in 1862, and after creditable Civil War service emerged from that conflict a brevet Brigadier General of Volunteers. He became a second lieutenant in the 1st U.S. Infantry in 1866, a first lieutenant a year later and a captain in 1880. Pierce served in Arizona for several years, being recognized by Cruse as "one of the best 'Indian men' we ever had." After duty with the Hualapais in northwestern Arizona he was sent by Crook to investigate a supposedly dangerous situation among Apaches at the Fort Apache Reservation, and reported all was calm. In the spring of 1885 he succeeded Emmet Crawford as agent at San Carlos, serving until June 1, 1888. It was his mistake, based upon a faulty judgment by Al Sieber, that led to the 1885 Geronimo breakout, but he continued to merit and win the confidence of his superiors. On June 1, 1887, he figured in the breakout of Apache scouts in which Sieber was crippled and the Apache Kid earned his first notoriety. As part of "the complete house-cleaning of the Sioux Agencies," political appointees were replaced by army officers in early 1891, Pierce at Miles's insistence was named agent at Pine Ridge, South Dakota, he being a man whom the Indians "knew and trusted." He retained the post scarcely a month, however, being forced by a serious illness to resign. Pierce died at the Presidio, San Francisco of blood poisoning and internal injuries he had suffered in a fall from the balcony of his home on October 22.

Dan L. Thrapp, *Al Sieber, Chief of Scouts.* Norman, Univ. of Okla. Press, 1964; James C. Olson, *Red Cloud and the Sioux Problem.* Lincoln, Univ. of Nebr. Press, 1965; Powell.

·**Pierce, Joel,** adventurer (d. 1804). A North Carolinan, Pierce joined Philip Nolan for his 1800-1801 wild horse hunting expedition to the Trinity River of Spanish Texas and after Nolan was shot, Pierce and the others were taken as prisoners to Chihuahua where Pierce despaired of ever seeing "the honiste woman (apparently his wife) once more," and he did not. Taken ill, he died in Bean's cell, which he was permitted to share in his final extremity, at San Carlos, Chihuahua, 40 miles from Chihuahua City.

Bennett Lay, *The Lives of Ellip P. Bean.* Austin, Univ. of Tex. Press, 1960.

Pierce, Jonathan Edwards, cattleman (Dec. 6,

1839-Mar. 29, 1915). B. at Little Compton, Rhode Island, he was a younger brother of Abel (Shanghai) Pierce; reaching Texas in 1860, he served in the Confederate Army for four years, then joined his brother in establishment of Rancho Grande, Matagorda County, Texas. The two in 1880 split their holdings, Jonathan taking the southern half. When a railroad finally came through and a station was built, Pierce painted on it: "Thank God, Texas," but was persuaded to change it to Blessing, Texas, which it retains. He is buried near Hawley, Texas.

HT; Oran Warder Nolen, "Texas Cowman 'Shanghai' Pierce." *The West,* Vol. VII, No. 2 (July 1967), 32-33, 54-56.

Pierce, Robert and Thomas, Mormon pioneers (fl. 1857). Robert Pierce was probably born in Pennsylvania, and reached Utah in 1847, perhaps settling initially at Brigham City, then moving south to the Iron County country; Thomas was his son. Both were reported to have participated in the Mountain Meadows Massacre of September 11, 1857. Tom, it is said, disapproved of the butchery and started to walk from it when his father, Robert, fired at him, the bullet grazing his head and "leaving a permanent scar just above his ear."

Juanita Brooks, *The Mountain Meadows Massacre.* Norman, Univ. of Okla. Press, 1966; Frank Esshom, *Pioneers and Prominent Men of Utah.* Salt Lake City, Western Epics, 1966.

Piernas, Pedro, Spanish official (fl. 1769-1775). Piernas was directed by Ulloa to take charge in upper Louisiana in 1769. He returned to New Orleans and was appointed again by Ulloa's successor, Alexander O'Reilly. Piernas also was directed to investigate the operations of the incompetent Francisco Ríu, which he did. He became first Spanish commandant of Upper Louisiana and lieutenant governor of St. Louis, being succeeded in 1775 by Francisco Cruzat. His reports of the upper Missouri country were of value although not original. He complained that even at that early date fugitive French traders maintained themselves and had done so "for a long time" among the upper river tribes, causing legitimate traders (i.e., those with St. Louis licenses) "considerable harm and pillage by their counsel and by inciting the Indians."

Abraham P. Nasatir, *Before Lewis and Clark,* 2 vols. St. Louis, Hist. Docs. Found., 1952; Noel M. Loomis, Nasatir, *Pedro Vial and the Roads to Santa Fe.* Norman, Univ. of Okla. Press, 1967.

Pierron, Jean, Jesuit missionary (Sept. 28, 1631-Feb. 20, 1700). B. at Dun-sur-Meuse, France, he became a Jesuit and reached Canada June 27, 1667. He was assigned immediately to the Iroquois mission where he worked largely among the Mohawks and remained until 1677, returning to France the following year. Pierron had a talent for drawing and painting, and used this gift in creating pictures for the edification of his Indians; it is not known if any of these works survive, but if so they would be of interest. In 1674 after a short period in Acadia, Pierron in disguise visited New England, Maryland and Virginia; he discussed religious matters with Protestant ministers at Boston where his mask was seen through, but he was not interfered with. Pierron then spent three more years among the Iroquois, returning to France in 1678; he died in that country.

Thwaites, JR, L, 323n15; LI, 179-87; LII, 117-23; LIX, 73-75, 307n13; LXXI, 150-51.

Pierson, Philippe, Jesuit missionary (Jan. 4, 1642-c. 1688). A Belgian, Pierson was b. at Ath, in Hainault Province and was educated in France. He became a Jesuit and reached Canada September 25, 1667. He was ordained in 1669. In 1673 he was sent to the Hurons of the Mackinac mission at St. Ignace, Upper Michigan, working with them for a decade. In May of 1677 at St. Ignace he received the bones of the Jesuit, Marquette, which were brought there by Huron Christians from the original burial place near the present Ludington, Michigan. From 1683 until 1688 Pierson was a missionary among the Sioux west of Lake Superior. He died at Lorette, Quebec.

Thwaites, JR, L, 327n25; LIX, 201-205.

Pike, Albert, trapper (Dec. 29, 1809-Apr. 2, 1891). B. at Boston, he became a school teacher but in 1831 reached St. Louis and accompanied a Charles Bent wagon train to Taos, arriving November 29. In August 1832, he joined a trapping party eastward, into Comanche country, the group reaching Fort Smith, Arkansas, December 10. In the fall of 1832 he assisted in the defense of Fort

Towson, on the Red River, against a large force of Comanches. Pike, a part-time writer of poetry and prose, then quitted the West, had a varied career as newspaper publisher and lawyer in Arkansas and Louisiana. He saw cavalry service in the Mexican War, participating in the battle of Buena Vista. He reluctantly served in the Civil War as an Arkansas Brigadier General, taking part in the battle of Pea Ridge. Pike then removed to Washington, D.C., where he lived the remainder of his life. He "became the greatest scholar of the Masonic Order," and was "the best known and best loved Mason in the world." Pike had a working knowledge of seven languages, a versatile man. He died at Washington.

Literature abundant: DAB; Harvey L. Carter article, MM, Vol. II.

Pike, Zebulon Montgomery, army officer, explorer (Jan. 5, 1779-Apr. 27, 1813). B. at Lamberton, now Lamington, New Jersey, son of Zebulon Pike, an army officer and Indian fighter. Zebulon M. served at 15 in Anthony Wayne's force, although apparently he missed the battle of Fallen Timbers. He once saved his father from drowning, following a boat mishap on the Ohio River. Pike left St. Louis August 9, 1805, with 20 men to seek out the headwaters of the Mississippi. September 23 he concluded a treaty with the Sioux for the site of Fort Snelling. He built a stockade near the mouth of the Swan River and on a winter overland journey reached Cass Lake February 12, deciding it was the source of the great river, although the Mississippi actually rises near Lake Itasca. His expedition returned to St. Louis April 30, 1806. Pike left Belle Fontaine Barracks, near St. Louis July 15, 1806, under orders of General James Wilkinson, on his most famous expedition, to determine the extent of the Louisiana Territory in southwestern regions. His party of 22 men touched the Republican River, near the present Kansas-Nebraska border, then dropped to the Arkansas River, near present Larned, Kansas. He sent Lieutenant James Biddle Wilkinson with five men downstream, and with 13 others he prepared to ascend the river to its source. He discovered Pike's Peak on November 15, attempted and failed to climb it because of distance, topography, weather and shortage of provisions. He did not name it for himself; the name came into common usage and was established by

Fremont at a later date. Pike discovered the Royal Gorge December 4, upper waters of the South Platte December 13, South Park and several important passes that fall and winter. He crossed the Sangre de Cristo range in late January, reached the upper Rio Grande and wintered on the Conejo, a tributary. He was taken into custody February 26 by a 100-man Spanish force and conducted to Santa Fe from whence he left under escort March 4, 1807, for Chihuahua, arriving April 2. Governor Nemesio Salcedo y Salcedo examined Pike and ordered him returned to the United States, they reaching Louisiana July 1. Pike had been promoted to captain while away, was made major in May 1808 and journals of his expeditions with notes were published in 1810. He was promoted to lieutenant colonel about 1810 and largely trained the forces which won the battle of Tippecanoe under Harrison against the Shawnees. Pike was made a colonel in 1812 and Brigadier General in March 1813. He won a brilliant victory at York, Ontario, but was killed when an abandoned British powder magazine exploded, a rock striking him in the back. He was buried at Sackett's Harbor. Pike was a good officer, an excellent explorer although with his faults, and probably never was a spy against the Spanish possessions, as has been charged. "He was not spoiled by his achievements for he always wished to achieve still more."

Literature abundant; see Harvey L. Carter, *Zebulon Pike: Pathfinder and Patriot.* Colorado Springs, Dentan Printing Co., 1956; *The Journals of Zebulon Montgomery Pike, With Letters and Related Documents,* ed. and annot. by Donald Jackson, 2 vols. Norman, Univ. of Okla. Press, 1966.

Pilcher, Joshua, frontiersman (May 15, 1790-June 5, 1843). B. in Culpeper County, Virginia, he studied in Kentucky, entered business, and in 1819 the fur trade as a partner with Manuel Lisa and others in the Missouri Fur Company. He was initially stationed at Council Bluffs where he managed trade with the Omahas. He became president of the company when Lisa died in 1820. In 1821 he journeyed to the upper Missouri and Yellowstone rivers, but a Blackfoot attack in 1823 crippled the company, the damage enhanced by the hostility of other Indians, With an improvised force Pilcher, as an

Indian sub Agent, accompanied Leavenworth on his punitive movement upriver to attack the Arikara villages, but the engagement ended indecisively, Pilcher blaming Leavenworth for ineptness. Angry charges and bitterness erupted between the two. Although the Missouri Fur Company failure was apparent, Pilcher continued to trade at Council Bluffs until 1827 when he organized a trapping expedition for the Rocky Mountains; the trip was unsuccessful. The following season was equally so, Pilcher continuing on to Hudson's Bay Company territory, circling through Canada and returning to St. Louis in June 1830. In 1833 he was in the employ of the American Fur Company and in 1834 he was named Upper Missouri Indian Agent. He attended the 1836 Green River rendezvous; it was while he was Indian agent that smallpox devastated the northwestern Indians. Pilcher succeeded William Clark as superintendent of Indian affairs at St. Louis in 1838, serving until September 1841. He died at St. Louis.

Chittenden; DAB; Ray H. Mattison article, MM, Vol. IV.

Pinchot, Gifford, conservationist, politician (Aug. 11, 1865-Oct. 4, 1946). B. at Simsbury, Connecticut, Pinchot was one of the first major figures to see that over-grazing, extravagant lumbering methods and wasteful mining were swiftly impoverishing the country, and he demanded forceful federal action to halt these abuses. In 1898, six years after the first tentatives toward a federal forest service were begun, Pinchot, already a veteran in the field, joined the division of forestry, a forerunner of the U.S. Forest Service. He was dismissed in 1910 by President Taft for political reasons, and joined Theodore Roosevelt in forming the Progressive Party. He had helped found the Yale School of Forestry and was professor there from 1903-36, while serving on many conservation commissions. He was twice (1923-27 and 1931-35) governor of Pennsylvania. He wrote many books on forestry and timber and one, *Breaking New Ground,* on the early conservation movement. Pinchot always surrounded himself with able, intelligent men. By his progressive and sympathetic attention to their real needs, the miners, loggers and stockmen came generally to support most of his policies. Pinchot made mistakes, of course. For example he set into motion the predator

control policies which stripped the West of many of its valuable and interesting wildlife populations and led to distortions and imbalances among the non-carnivores; in this some disservice was done to the great mass of American citizenry for the benefit of the few. Yet on the whole, Pinchot's career was one of the great ones of American history; his work is enduring and largely to the benefit of the nation and posterity. He died at New York City.

Literature abundant.

Pinet, Pierre Francois, Jesuit missionary (Dec. 11, 1661-July 16, 1704). B. at Limoges, France, he became a Jesuit and reached Canada in 1694, sent initially to Michilimackinac where he came into dispute with Cadillac, and in 1696 to Illinois. He founded the mission of the Guardian Angel at Chicago among Miami bands located there; the mission was broken up the next year through Frontenac's hostility, it was alleged, but religious superiors ordered Pinet back into the field. In early 1700 he went to the Tamaroas, an Illinois tribe located near the present Cahokia. He remained with the Tamaroas despite religious disputes between the Jesuits and Seminary of Foreign Missions until 1702, then labored among the Kaskaskias until his death, which occurred at Chicago.

Thwaites, JR, LXIV, 278n22, LXXI, 158.

Pinkerton, Allan, detective (Aug. 25, 1819-July 1, 1884). B. at Glasgow, Scotland, he was founder of a detective and protection agency that became almost synonymous with the so-called "Wild West." In 1842 he migrated to America, establishing a cooper's works at Dundee, Illinois, until by chance he stumbled across a gang of counterfeiters and was instrumental in their capture. In 1846 he became deputy sheriff of Kane County, which includes Dundee, and later of Cook County, which includes Chicago. In 1850 he became the first detective with the Chicago police force, that year embarking upon his lifelong career by organizing a detective agency. His successes led to protective work for an eastern railroad where he uncovered a plot to assassinate President-elect Lincoln, and was intrumental in foiling it. Pinkerton organized a secret service for George B. McClellan, his friend, when McClellan commanded the Department of the Ohio, touring Confederate areas in disguise himself on espionage expeditions. When McClellan was made Union commander in chief, Pinkerton transferred to Washington, organizing an intelligence mechanism and conducting counter-espionage operations. After the war he concentrated on his private detective agency, expanding its operations and writing a number of autobiographical narratives stressing crime detection matters. From the frontier viewpoint, Pinkerton is chiefly remembered for the bloodhound pursuit by his agents of desperadoes from Jesse James (who once is reported to have said, "I know God some day will deliver Allan Pinkerton into my hands"), to Butch Cassidy, whom a Pinkerton man, Frank Dimaio, followed to South America. Such agents as Charles A. Siringo worked for Pinkerton whose detective abilities extended even into uncovering cattle rustling for various stockmen's organizations. Pinkerton came into some disfavor with the public for his anti-union activities. Pinkerton's employees today number about 37,000, few of whom are detectives. Upon his death his detective agency passed to his sons, Robert A. and William A. Pinkerton.

DAB; CE; *New York Times,* July 19, 1975.

Piomingo: *see* William Colbert

Piomingo, Chickasaw chief (d. 1794). A great chief of his people, he could read and write English, was friendly with the Americans and kept the Chickasaws at peace for years although one faction, in the pay of the Spanish, opposed him. He was murdered by a Chickamauga (Cherokee).

Noel M. Loomis, Abraham P. Nasatir, *Pedro Vial and the Roads to Santa Fe.* Norman, Univ. of Okla. Press, 1967.

Pipes, Sam(uel J.), desperado (c. 1857-post 1884). B. presumably in Dallas County, Texas, Pipes and his friend, Albert Herndon joined the Sam Bass outlaw gang in the spring of 1878. It may be that Pipes was an orphan, since no parents are listed for him in the census, and at 21 he was younger than Bass or others of the band. Pipes took part and was wounded in the Mesquite Station train robbery April 10, from which the loot was meager, withdrawing then to Dallas County to recover. He was arrested with Herndon by June Peak of the Texas Rangers. There

ensued a complicated series of legal maneuvers, with Rangers determined to hold the men against efforts by their Dallas friends to gain their release; this is outlined in detail by Gard. Eventually, however, the two were taken to Tyler, Texas and after indictment for mail robbery, removed to Austin. July 17, 1878, two days before the Bass debacle at Round Rock, Texas, not far from Austin, Pipes and Herndon were found guilty in a federal district court and given life sentences. They were pardoned by President Cleveland after volunteering for nursing service aboard a quarantined ship in New York harbor and "later, Pipes was killed in a street brawl." He was 5 feet, 10 inches, in height, weighed 175 pounds, had black eyes, hair and mustache.

1870 U.S. Census, Dallas County; Wayne Gard, *Sam Bass.* Lincoln, Univ. of Nebr. Press, 1969.

Pipkin, Daniel M. (Red), desperado (d. July 6, 1938). B. in Texas and raised in Apache County, Arizona, he once worked as a cowboy for John Slaughter's San Bernandino, Arizona, ranch. March 29, 1898, he joined Bill Walters and others in an inept train holdup at Grants, New Mexico; there was no loot. May 24, 1898, Walters, Pipkins and others held up a train at Belen, New Mexico, a reported $20,000 or less being taken. Pipkin and the others shot their way free from a posse, three of whose members were killed. July 29, 1898, Pipkin escaped another law ambush in eastern Arizona while Kid Johnson was mortally wounded and Walters seriously wounded and captured. Pipkin was said to be a leader of another ineffectual train robbery August 14 at Grants and may have pulled off other holdups of a minor nature. He was captured March 7, 1899, near Moab, Utah; Pipkin was returned to New Mexico, tried for horse theft in Arizona and sentenced October 25, 1900, to Yuma for 10 years; he was discharged April 24, 1907. In 1918 he was a special officer with the Gallup, New Mexico, American Coal Company and later a deputy under Sheriff Bob Roberts. He shot himself, in a note blaming cancer for his decision.

Philip J. Rasch, "An Incomplete Account of 'Bronco Bill' Walters." English Westerners' *Brand Book,* Vol. 19, No. 2 (Jan. 1977).

Pitts, Charlie: *see* Samuel Wells

Pizanthia, Greaser Joe (Frank), desperado (d. Jan. 11, 1864). Not much is known about Pizanthia except the manner of his death which was brutal. Pizanthia lived in a cabin on the outskirts of Bannack. He alone among the notorious Plummer gang of Montana desperados fought back effectively against the vigilantes who caught up with him, killing one and wounding another. When vigilantes sought to arrest him and entered his cabin he fired on them, mortally wounding George Copley and less seriously wounding Smith Ball. Attempts to shoot Pizanthia out of his retreat were futile; the mob then borrowed a small howitzer and fired into the structure, eventually wounding Pizanthia. He was dragged out, shot, hanged and his corpse cast upon the ruins of his cabin which was set afire, the remains being consumed. This was considered a step more civilized than hauling the body into the hills and leaving it for the wolves, which some vigilantes had proposed.

A Governor's Wife on the Mining Frontier, ed. by James L. Thane, Jr. Salt Lake City, Univ. of Utah Library, 1976, p. 74; Dimsdale; Langford; Birney.

Place, Etta, concubine (born c. 1878-post 1909). She was considered of "American" nationality, but the place and circumstances of her birth and early life are unknown. She has been termed a onetime school teacher. She was 5 feet, 4 inches, in height, weighed about 110 pounds, was of medium complexion with dark chestnut hair and according to a Pinkerton description, "appears to be a refined type." Picked up by Harry Longabaugh, she accompanied him and Butch Cassidy to South America in 1902 (see George LeRoy Parker entry for details), assisting them in their robberies on that continent, but was not present at the supposed San Vicente, Bolivia, shootout in 1909 when they were reported killed. One story has it that in 1907, weary of bandit life, she asked to come home. Longabaugh accompanied her to New York, where she had an appendicitis operation, then to Denver where he left her to return to South America; another version has Etta and her two male companions killed in a Mercedes, Uruguay, bank holdup attempt in 1911. She may have taken up with some other American desperado such as Tom Dilley, also from the Robbers' Roost crowd, who met Cassidy and Longabaugh in South America and participated in their escapades.

Charles Kelly, *The Outlaw Trail: The Story of Butch Cassidy and the "Wild Bunch."* N.Y., Bonanza Books, 1959; James D. Horan, *The Wild Bunch.* N.Y., Signet Books, 1958; Jay Robert Nash, *Bloodletters and Badmen: A Narrative Encyclopedia of American Criminals from the Pilgrims to the Present.* N.Y., M. Evans & Co., 1973; *English Westerners' Tally Sheet,* Vol. 19, No. 3, Pubn. 187, Jan.-Feb. 1973.

Plamondon, Simon, frontiersman (1800-1900). B. on the St. Lawrence River in Canada, he reached the Mississippi at 15, ranged the length of it, spent time on the Great Plains and in the Rockies and reached the Pacific by 1818. He joined the North West Company, becoming a voyageur, trapper and trader, explored the Columbia drainage and worked out of Fort Vancouver for the Hudson's Bay Company after it had absorbed the NWC. Following the death of his Indian wife in childbirth, about 1827, he wandered north as far as Eskimo country and the Arctic plains, before returning to the Fraser River. He eventually turned to farming on the Cowlitz prairie, Washington Territory, becoming a familiar pioneer. He was buried at Cowlitz.

Harriet D. Munnick article, MM, Vol. IX.

Plante, Antoine, frontiersman (d.c. Feb. 15, 1890). B. probably in present Montana of a French father and Gros Ventre mother, he reached Fort Vancouver in 1827 and in 1830 was with Ogden of the Hudson's Bay Company in the Snake River country; he continued to trap for several years. Plante married a Pend d'Oreille woman and later a Flathead. He settled around Spokane, Washington, in the late 1840s, went to California for the gold rush, guided a Northern Pacific Railway survey party, engaged in various occupations in the northwest and in 1878 went to the Jocko Valley of Montana. He died near Arlee, Montana.

Jerome Peltier article, MM, Vol. V.

Pleasonton, Alfred, army officer (July 7, 1824-Feb. 17, 1897). B. at Washington, D.C., he was graduated from West Point and became a brevet second lieutenant of the 1st Dragoons in 1844. He served in Florida against the Seminoles and against Indians on the western frontier, as well as in the Mexican

War. As a captain in the 2nd Dragoons (which became the 2nd Cavalry in 1861), he commanded the regiment on a march from Utah to Washington, D.C., in September and October 1861. His Civil War service was good; he became a Major General of Volunteers in 1863, being mustered out of the Volunteer service in 1866; he also was breveted Major General for his Civil War service which included operations against Sterling Price in Missouri. Pleasonton resigned in 1868 in a dispute over rank. He occupied several minor federal civilian posts and finally was placed on the retired list in 1888 as a major. He died at Washington, D.C.

Heitman; Ezra J. Warner, *General in Blue: Lives of the Union Commanders.* Baton Rouge, La. State Univ. Press, 1964.

Plenty Coups (Aleek-chea-akoosh), Mountain Crow chief (1848-May 3, 1932). B. near Billings, Montana, he was noted as a warrior and became chief of the Mountain Crows at 25. Ever friendly with the whites, he obtained Crow scouts for Custer's 1876 Sioux campaign and for the 1877 Nez Perce operations, although his role in either was not largely personal. Plenty Coups was active in negotiations for a route for the Northern Pacific Railway through the Crow country and in 1883 went to Washington, D.C., to push Crow claims for land payments. He quieted a threatened uprising among the Crows in 1887 with little bloodshed. By 1904 he had become principal chief of the Crows. In World War I he urged Crow young men to join the nation's armed forces and in 1921 was the Indian representative at dedication of the tomb of the Unknown Soldier at Arlington, Virginia. In 1928 at 80 he and his current wife deeded their home and 40 surrounding acres as a public park and museum of Crow culture and history; it is maintained as such to this day. Plenty Coups is said to have had 11 wives, but he fathered no children. He died at Pryor, Montana and as a mark of respect it was decided after his death that the term "tribal chief" would never again be conferred upon any one.

Dockstader, REAW.

Plenty Fires: *see* I-see-o

Pliley, Allison J., scout, soldier (Apr. 20, 1844-Feb. 22, 1917). B. in Ross County, Ohio,

his family moved to Iowa in 1849 and in 1858 to a farm near Topeka, Kansas. Pliley freightened in a minor way to Denver, then enlisted in 1863 in Company F, 15th Kansas Cavalry, recruited as a result of the Lawrence massacre and assigned to guard the eastern Kansas border against bushwhackers, but taking part also in operations against the Confederates in western Missouri in 1864. In 1865 the regiment guarded west Kansas overland routes against Indians, Pliley emerging as a second lieutenant. In 1866 he commenced to study law, but quit in 1867 and was employed as a scout at Fort Harker (Ellsworth) by Colonel Horace L. Moore of the 18th Kansas Cavalry. He killed an Arapaho in a curious duel. On August 21-22, 1867, as chief scout he took part in the hard fight on Beaver, or Prairie Dog, Creek, Kansas, being twice wounded. In September 1867, Pliley was at Medicine Lodge Creek for the treaty negotiations and there met Roman Nose, "the finest specimen of manhood I ever saw," became a friend of Little Raven, of the Arapahoes and on one occasion, narrowly outran Charles Bent's Cheyennes, according to Pliley. He was one of the 50 plainsmen enlisted by Forsyth and engaged with hostile Cheyennes at Beecher Island in September 1868, where Roman Nose was killed. Pliley and Jack Donovan were the second pair to slip away at night seeking relief, wearing moccasins from dead Indians, subsisting on half-rotten horse meat, after four days reaching a ranch on the Smoky Hill stage road and securing assistance at Fort Wallace. After the Forsyth affair, Pliley was named a captain in the 19th Kansas Cavalry to operate with Sheridan and Custer on the south Plains. Despite unparalleled blizzards the command reached Fort Sill, and left there March 2, 1869, on the 20th coming up with a large village of Cheyennes in the later Wheeler County, Texas, where two white women were rescued from captivity: Sarah White and Anna Belle Morgan. In May 1869 Sioux and Cheyennes raided homesteads in north central Kansas, causing casualities; a Frontier Guard was again enlisted, Pliley named captain of Company A, the organization mustered out in November. He volunteered for Custer's 1876 campaign, but was unable to accompany the command. Pliley settled at Kansas City, Kansas, engaging in supplying sand to city building contractors; in the winter he cut ice.

He was described as intelligent, modest and usually taciturn about his adventures; a photograph appears with his reminiscences. Pliley is buried in the pioneer cemetery at Quindaro, Kansas City, Kansas.

"Reminiscences of Allison J. Pliley, Indian Fighter," ed. by Alan W. Farley. Kansas City Posse of Westerners *Trail Guide*, Vol. 2, No. 2 (June 1957), 1-16; Simon E. Matson, ed., *The Battle of Beecher Island*. Wray, Colo. Beecher Island Battle Mem. Assn, 1960; information from Fred L. Lee, Westport Hist. Soc.

Plumbe, John Jr., railroad visionary, daguerreotypist (July 1809-May 29, 1857). B. in Wales, he emigrated to this country, arriving probably at Baltimore in 1821, and worked as an assistant on an Allegheny railroad survey in 1831-32. In 1836 he moved to Wisconsin, and to the embryonic Dubuque, Iowa. By 1836 he was speaking privately to nearby residents of his vision of a railroad to the Pacific, he being the first apparently to publicly address himself to the project. By March 24, 1838, the plan was formalized, calling for a "Great Atlantic and Pacific Railroad." Plumbe was named chairman of a committee to memorialize Congress on the matter. Congress appropriated $2,000 for a survey of a railroad from Milwaukee to Dubuque, the first leg of the proposed line, but Mississippi flood waters disrupted the plans. In 1839-40 Plumbe continued pushing his concept, going to Washington in 1839 to promote it, there becoming aware of the daguerreotype process, and soon establishing a chain of galleries around the country to exploit this development. He published daguerreotypes of many famous Americans of the day and otherwise entered journalism but always with a view to obtaining funds to push his transcontinental railroad project. He sold out his photographic businesses in 1849 and crossed the Plains to California, taking accurate survey notes on his six month transit for a practicable railroad route. Other promoters had seized upon the idea, which was somewhat gaining in popularity, Plumbe assailing some of the proposed schemes, while pushing his own ideas. In 1856 he returned to Dubuque, Iowa, where, ill and despondent, he committed suicide.

Cliff Krainik, "John Plumbe Jr. — Photographer with a Vision." *Westerners Brand Book,* Chicago Corral, Vol. XXX, No. 7 (Sept. 1973).

Plummer, (Amos) Henry, lawman, desperado (1832-Jan. 10, 1864). B. four miles from Houlton, Maine, he was of a family of eight children of Ed and Rial Plummer. The Plummers moved about 1845 to Sauk County, Wisconsin, where they settled on a Wisconsin River farm five miles from Portage, Henry receiving an excellent education for the times. By 1851 via Santa Fe he had reached Nevada City, California, where he became an apprentice and later part owner of a bakery. He soon developed an affinity for saloons, gambling halls and bordellos, coming to know "every bartender and madam by their first names," according to his principal biographer. December 9, 1855, Plummer was named deputy to David Johnson, an honest marshal of Nevada City. A movement by the sporting element to elect Plummer marshal with his dabbling in local Democratic politics helping resulted in victory: May 5, 1856, in a somewhat suspect election he narrowly defeated Johnson for the position. In a mixed-up shootout November 3, 1856, during an attempt to recapture an escaped prisoner, Johnson was mortally wounded and Sheriff W.W. (Boss) Wright killed, both shot apparently by mistake although Plummer's role in the affair was ambiguous. With the help of his disreputable friends Plummer was re-elected marshal in May 1857 and August 9 was re-elected to the executive committee of the county Democratic organization with assistance from politicians "as morally currupt as himself"; September 9 however he lost a bid for the state legislative assembly by a sizable margin. September 26 he killed unarmed John Vedder with whose estranged wife he had become involved. Plummer was convicted of second degree murder and sentenced to twelve years in San Quentin penitentiary; given a new trial the verdict was identical with the sentence reduced to ten years. He entered San Quentin, a relatively new and badly managed prison, February 22, 1859, was given a plush assignment in the infirmary and status of a trustee, often being sent outside the walls for medical supplies or on other errands. He acquired sufficient medical knowledge within months to feign a serious illness. July 5, caught in a heavy rainstorm he developed a cold, high fever, a wracking cough and the means to cover his pillowcase with blood so that he soon was diagnosed as a terminal consumptive with, medical petitioners stated, scarcely weeks to live. As a result of a flood of ardent requests he was released from prison August 16, 1859, and sent out to die; instead he returned to Nevada City and before the projected date of his demise was reappointed assistant marshal. February 13, 1861, Plummer savagely wounded W.J. Muldoon in a brothel brawl; Muldoon was expected to die and Plummer fled Nevada City for Carson City, Nevada, where it is alleged he took part in an abortive stage holdup, was tried but acquitted. By late spring, learning Muldoon apparently had recovered, he was back in Nevada City where oddly he struck up a friendship with his victim, terminated when Muldoon died in the summer from the injuries suffered at Plummer's hands earlier. October 27 in another bawdy-house melee Plummer killed William Riley though sustaining a deep knife slash on the forehead which left a permanent scar. He was arrested for the Riley slaying but escaped and reached Carson City once again. Plummer's friend and confidante at Carson City was Billy Mayfield who because of his relationship to Plummer came under suspicion of Sheriff John Blackburn, whom he killed. Mayfield and Plummer fled Carson City, the latter accompanied by a woman who had deserted her husband and three children to go with him. The fugitives reached Walla Walla, Washington, in the summer of 1861, sending back to California a report they had been lynched, hoping by this ruse, it is alleged, to abort any pursuit, though this is unlikely since both continued using their own names, avoiding any alias or other attempt at concealment. At Lewiston, Idaho, by 1862 Plummer deserted his mistress who, destitute, turned to prostitution, became an ·alcoholic and whose life ended in "one of the lowest dives in the town." Plummer mean-while associated with such desperado elements as Cyrus Skinner, whom he had known at Nevada City and San Quentin; Bill Bunton; Clubfoot George Lane and others whom he would boost to notoriety in Montana before very long. Mayfield was shot and killed near Placerville, Idaho. Plummer, ostensibly a gambler, actually was organizer of bandits who pillaged mining camps and miners, stealing and murdering almost at will. Affable, a good public speaker and courteous when sober, Plummer sought to derail incipient vigilante movements. But some suspected his true nature, among them Patrick Ford, a blunt and brave saloon keeper and mainstay of the

growing vigilante sentiment. In a shootout Ford was killed as was Plummer's horse while one of the desperado's colleagues was wounded. This action finally brought the Idaho vigilantes into action, and Plummer crossed the divide into Montana, reaching Deer Lodge late in 1862. Because of waxing vigilante activity and waning Idaho gold strikes, combined with flourishing gold discoveries in Montana, much of the criminal element also shifted into the fresh territory and Plummer reinstituted his crime ring, this time called "The Innocents," established to a degree attesting to his marked administrative and organizational talents. For two months Plummer was guest of J.H. Vail, superintendent of a school for Blackfoot Indians at Sun River, near the present Great Falls; here he became engaged to Electa Elizabeth (Eliza) O'Brien, innocent young sister of Vail's wife and distinctly unlike the women Plummer had associated with over the years. Seeking some worthy employment for a cover, Plummer returned to Gold Creek where he met Jack Cleveland, an old acquaintance from Nevada City and now also a fugitive. The two reached Bannack, Montana, during its gold frenzy, but quickly became estranged, Plummer fearing Cleveland would reveal his murderous background. Soon Plummer mortally wounded Cleveland in a saloon fight. Cleveland was cared for by the de facto sheriff, Henry Crawford until the former's death, leading Plummer to suspect Crawford had learned from Cleveland of Plummer's nefarious past and generating bad blood between them. Crawford badly wounded Plummer and then thought it politic to quit Bannack, since he was now a marked man. Plummer was elected sheriff of Bannack May 24, 1863, and in September became sheriff of Virginia City of the Alder Gulch placers, as well. He married Eliza O'Brien June 20, although she left him for the east on September 2 when he moved in with the Vails, now settled at Bannack. Crime rapidly increased. More than 100 citizens were reported murdered or mysteriously disappeared within a few months. Exasperated citizens were not without final recourse, however and the famous Vigilante Committee was organized by Wilbur Fisk Sanders, Paris Pfouts, James Williams (see entries) and others. From Erastus (Red) Yager, one of the outlaws, more than a score of identities of The Innocents was learned. These desperadoes, Plummer among them, were hunted down relentlessly. Plummer was hanged early Sunday morning on a Bannack gallows he had prepared for another. He was described as above medium height, slender, with mild blue or grey eyes and brown hair; he was a fastidious dresser, with good manners and spoke excellent English. Latter-day suggestions that his outlaw career in Montana was largely unproven and that he seriously intended to go straight following his marriage to Eliza need not be seriously entertained unless believable evidence is forthcoming.

Art Pauley, *Henry Plummer: Lawman and Outlaw.* White Sulphur Springs, Mont., Meagher County News, 1980, available from author at 2912 N.W. 151st St., Vancouver, Wash. 98665; Dimsdale; Langford; David Lavender, *The Rockies.* N.Y., Harper & Row, 1968; information from Ed Bartholomew.

Plummer, Satterlee Clark, army officer (c. 1844-Nov. 14, 1881). B. in Wisconsin, he was graduated from West Point in 1865, joining the 17th Infantry and, in September 1866, the 26th Infantry. He was made captain in 1868, served frontier posts in Texas and New Mexico, transferred to the 7th Cavalry in 1869 and after being assigned to Kansas was discharged December 15, 1870, at his own request. He again was commissioned, this time a second lieutenant of the 4th Infantry, in 1876 and went with the 5th Cavalry as a "volunteer" officer on the Big Horn and Yellowstone expedition. The following July he was arrested at Fort Steele, Wyoming, and dismissed from the service, but January 20, 1880, he was commissioned a second lieutenant of the 15th Infantry, dying less than two years later.

Heitman; Cullum; Don Russell, *The Lives and Legends of Buffalo Bill.* Norman, Univ. of Okla. Press, 1960.

Pocahontas, (Motoaka), Powhatan Indian woman (c. 1597-Mar. 1617). Captain John Smith said she was "a child of tenne years" in 1607 and described her as intelligent and attractive. In 1608 Smith was captured by Opechancanough and taken to Powhatan where it was apparently planned to execute him. He wrote that "two great stones were brought before *Powhatan;* then as many as could layd hands on (Smith), dragged him to them, and thereon laid his head, and being

ready with their clubs, to beate out his braines, *Pocohontas* the Kings dearest daughter, when no intreaty could prevaile, got his head in her armes, and laid her owne upon his to save him from death; whereat the Emperour (Powhatan) was contented he should live..." Historians have disputed the truth of this tale on various grounds, but there is nothing inherently improbable about it and it may be factual. In 1613 Pocahontas was taken captive by Samuel Argall with the aid of a treacherous chief and was taken to Jamestown from where authorities demanded as the price for her release, the turning over by Powhatan of English prisoners he held. The English had treated Pocahontas well; she became a Christian and was baptized as Rebecca. During her stay John Rolfe, a young widower fell in love with her and she with him, and with Governor Thomas Dale's and Powhatan's permission they were married April 5, 1614; this union had a beneficial effect upon the colonists' situation, since it brought peace with the Indians as long as Powhatan lived (he died in 1618). In 1616 the Rolfes with several Indians accompanied Dale to England where Rebecca Rolfe was received as a "princess" and proved extraordinarily popular in high circles of society. In March 1617, however while preparing to return to America she fell ill of smallpox and died at 21, being buried at Gravesend Parish church (in 1907 remains believed to be hers were unearthed at the site). She was survived by her husband and a son, Thomas Rolfe who was educated in England, returned in 1640 to America where he acquired considerable wealth and fathered a daughter, Jane who married Robert Bolling. From this union there were numerous descendants including founders of some of the distinguished families of Virginia.

Literature abundant: Hodge, HAI, CE, DAB; Dockstader; John Smith, *The Generall Historie of Virginia, New-England, and the Summer Isles.* Ann Arbor, Redex Microprint, 1966.

Poe, John William, lawman (Oct. 17, 1851-July 17, 1923). B. at Maysville, Mason County, Kentucky, he became a buffalo hunter on the South Plains in 1875, reporting he and associates had killed 20,000. Poe was town marshal of Fort Griffin, Texas, for about a year; a U.S. deputy marshal for five years. He went in 1879 to Fort Elliott, Wheeler County, Texas, working for the Canadian

River Cattle Association. Poe arrived in Lincoln County, New Mexico, early in 1881, served as deputy sheriff under Pat Garrett. He was present when Garrett killed Billy the Kid, having urged Garrett to investigate a report that the Kid was at Fort Sumner. Poe was elected sheriff of Lincoln County succeeding Garrett in 1883. Maurice G. Fulton believed Poe "made a remarkable record as sheriff as he was much more businesslike than Pat Garrett." He was "successful in rounding up criminals...due in large part to the work of Jim Brent, his chief deputy." He resigned as sheriff December 31, 1885, and turned to ranching and banking. Poe's recollections of the killing of the Kid, edited by Brininstool, were published in Wide World magazine, London, for December 1919, and issued later in booklet form as *Billy the Kid, Notorious New Mexico Outlaw.* Poe died at Roswell, New Mexico, either of pnuemonia or by suicide.

William A. Keleher, *Violence in Lincoln County 1869-1881.* Albuquerque, Univ. of New Mex. Press, 1957; Robert N. Mullin notes.

Point, Nicolas, Jesuit missionary (Apr. 10, 1799-July 4, 1868). B. at Rocroy, France, near the Belgian border he early determined to become a missionary, was accepted by the Society of Jesus in 1819 and three years later commenced his novitiate at Montrouge, being ordained in 1831. He reached the United States late in 1835 and taught at St. Mary's school near Lebanon, Kentucky until 1837 when he went to Louisiana to found a Jesuit College near Opelousas. In 1840 he transferred to St. Louis, where he was selected to accompany De Smet to the Flathead country of western Montana. Point went to Westport where, while awaiting departure he started a small church, decorating it with his own paintings of holy scenes and moral topics for the benefit of his largely illiterate congregation. When De Smet arrived the party of six Jesuits left Westport April 30, 1841, with a Bidwell and Fitzpatrick wagon train, Point as official diarist. A delegation of Flatheads met the missionaries at Fort Hall, Idaho, August 15, escorting them to the Bitterroot Valley where a mission station was built while Point occasionally exercised his artistic talent to amuse Indian converts and instruct them in things of the faith. When the Indians departed late in 1841 to hunt buffalo, Point accom-

panied them, living the arduous life of a hunting Indian through the severest weather. He worked at conversion of his native companions during that time and also met other Indians, including the Nez Perce, Pend d'Oreille, Gros Ventres and Coeur d'Alenes who particularly impressed him. October 1842 he was assigned by De Smet to open the Mission of the Sacred Heart for the Coeur d'Alenes near the Idaho lake of that name. He found many difficulties, with Indian opposition and other troubles to discourage him. By 1844 his health began to fail and he asked reassignment to Canada among French-speaking people. Meanwhile he was appointed by De Smet the intermediary between mutually hostile Blackfeet and Flatheads. August 16, 1846, he went to Fort Lewis, a fur post on the Missouri where he spent the fall and winter evangelizing the Blackfeet, before spring having baptized 600, including 30 adults. He finally arranged a lasting truce between the tribes "which made possible the rather peaceful immigration of (white) Americans to the Oregon country." Point left Fort Lewis in March 1847, reaching St. Louis in August; he departed at once for Canada. He worked among Canadian Indians so far as health permitted, but in 1859 retired to a station near Montreal and in 1865 to Quebec, where he died. He was buried in the Cathedral of Quebec. Many decades later his voluminous manuscripts were discovered and published if in part. His art work, although primitive by sophisticated standards, is colorful, innovative and instructive, offering a unique picture of missionary and Indian life in the wilderness where he worked, and picturing some of the important figures and places of his day which otherwise would have been lost to ours. His "portraits of Indians have a strength and dignity which is nothing short of amazing. Thanks to Father Point, we have a pictorial record of a people and a way of life which has vanished forever."

Wilderness Kingdom: Indian Life in the Rocky Mountains: 1840-1847. The Journals & Paintings of Nicolas Point, S.J., trans. by Joseph P. Donnelly, S.J. N.Y., Holt, Rinehart and Winston, 1967.

Poisal, John, frontiersman (1810-c. 1861). B. in Kentucky, he was jailed at Santa Fe in 1831 charged with smuggling. In 1834 he was hired by John Gantt, trader, or William Bent on the upper Arkansas River. He was married to an

Arapaho woman and fathered five children, living with his wife's people for many years. In 1849 he became father-in-law to Thomas Fitzpatrick who married his daughter. Poisal settled on Cherry Creek in 1857 and died at Denver.

Janet Lecompte article, MM, Vol. VI.

Pokagon, Leopold, Potawatomi chief (c. 1775-July 8, 1841). B. probably in southern Michigan he was by birth a Chippewa but was captured and adopted by the Potawatomi and raised as one of that people. He became in time the civil chief of the tribe, holding the position for a dozen years and signing several important treaties. Among them was that of October 26, 1832, on the Tippecanoe River of Indiana; this was the treaty by which whites secured the site of Chicago. Pokagon was ever for peace and when the Black Hawk War erupted in 1832 he held most of the tribe out of the conflict. Most of the lands of his people were obtained by the whites more or less fraudulently by treaty or other means and eventually Pokagon and his followers were settled in Cass County, Michigan, where he died, a swindled and disillusioned man.

Hodge, HAI; Dockstader.

Poker Joe (Lean Elk, Kiniknik Squalsac (Small Tobacco), Wahwookya Wasaaw (Lean Elk), Hototo), Nez Perce warrior (d. Sept. 30, 1877). Half French-Canadian and half Nez Perce, he was said to have earned his name by addiction to cards, in fact to any gambling, and was reported by some writers to have headed up from six to 18 lodges of non-conformist Nez Perce in western Montana. Others say he was merely "a good warrior" and no chief, which is more probable, although the tribal historian, Wottolen, referred to him as "Chief Hototo." He was short and voluble with a booming voice and reportedly was on his way with his family over the Lolo Trail into Idaho to visit relatives when he heard of the Chief Joseph breakout and turned back. He gashed his leg accidentally with a knife and the whites in the Bitterroot Valley accused him of having been in some Idaho fight on behalf of the Nez Perce. His own story was disbelieved to the point where he readily joined the migrating Nez Perce when they came along; his acquisition was important to them for in addition to being a brave man and bringing others with him, he had a rather thorough knowledge of trails, streams and the geography of Montana which they sorely needed. He took part in the Big Hole battle which was caused by Looking Glass's incompetence as war leader and Poker Joe thereupon became leader of the exodus across Montana as far as the Bear Paw Mountains. Wottolen said that Joe "would have the people up early in the morning, and travel till about ten o'clock. Then he ordered a stop and cooking was done while the horses filled upon grass. About two o'clock he would travel again. Kept going till about ten o'clock at night... In this way the people covered many miles each sun. They were outdistancing the soldiers, gaining on them all the time. Everybody was glad." As long as Poker Joe led them, the tribe avoided disaster. When Nez Perces encountered the Radersburg and Helena parties of vacationing whites in Yellowstone National park, Poker Joe was prominent in protecting most of them from harm (although some were shot and two killed in his absence); he saw to the safe departure of those who survived and probably saved several lives. He also served as interpreter for them on occasion, since he spoke excellent English as well as fluent Nez Perce. Joe was a capable strategist, and appears to have directed the maneuvers by which the Nez Perce avoided major contact with troops until after the crossing of the Yellowstone. Joe continued pushing the people hard to reach Canada in safety, but resentment from the increasingly wearied people grew after the skirmish with troops in Cow Creek Canyon and demands were heard that the pace be slowed. McWhorter quotes Many Wounds: "Looking Glass upbraided Poker Joe for his hurrying...told him that he was no chief, that he himself was chief and that he would be the leader. Poker Joe replied: 'Allright, Looking Glass, you can lead. I am trying to save the people, doing my best to cross into Canada before the soldiers find us. You can take command, but I think we will be caught and killed.'" So once again Looking Glass assumed leadership and once again his dilatoriness caused disaster as it had at Big Hole. He led them to a camp at the Bear Paw Mountains where they tarried until Miles and the troops caught up and much of the band ultimately was captured. Poker Joe, with many others of the best warriors, was killed on the first day of battle, shot by a Nez Perce who mistook him for an enemy.

McWhorter, *Hear Me;* L.V. Mcwhorter, *Yellow Wolf: His Own Story.* Caldwell, Ida., Caxton Printers, 1940; Helen Addison Howard, *Saga of Chief Joseph.* Lincoln, Univ. of Nebr. Press, 1978; Alvin M. Josephy Jr., *The Nez Perce Indians and the Opening of the Northwest.* New Haven, Yale Univ. Press, 1965.

Polk, (Old Polk, Polk Narraguinnep, Billy Hatch), Wiminuche Ute chief (c. 1860-c. 1924). B. possibly on Narraguinnep Creek, southwestern Colorado, his year of birth is conjecture. He became a headman or chief of a small band of recalcitrant Wiminuche (or Southern) Utes, while his sister married Old Posey, a leader among a similar bronco band of Paiutes in southeastern Utah. At times the two bands comingled, to the apprehension of white stockmen then extending their ranges in the region. Both Polk and Posey were said to be involved in the 1881 action at Castle Valley, eastern Utah, which followed two white deaths, supposedly at the hands of Indians. Ten whites were killed while no Indian losses were proven in the engagement, a disorganized affair with no troops involved. July 3, 1884, near Montezuma Canyon in eastern Utah, a roundup outfit collided with Polk's and Mancos Jim's bands of bronco Utes, with three Indians slain and several cowboys wounded. July 15 the Indians were attacked by Captain Henry Pratt Perrine of the 6th Cavalry and 80 troopers, augmented by 40 cowboys, the action occurring in rough country of eastern Utah. Jimmy (Rowdy) Higgins, a cowboy, and Joe Wormington, a government scout, were wounded mortally and the affair was broken off. Late in the century the Polk and Posey bands enrolled at the Southern Ute Reservation, their western portion of the reserve eventually becoming the Ute Mountain Reservation; they were not required to live on the reservation, however, and continued to roam the desolate regions beyond for years. A son of Polk, Tse-ne-gat, in 1914 was accused of murdering Juan Chacon, a Mexican sheep herder and his arrest was sought, Polk refusing to give him up for trial. Polk's people withdrew to a canyon near Bluff, Utah where the band was attacked late in February 1915 by a posse led by U.S. Marshal Aquila Nebeker; the posse consisted of local Indian haters and cowboys, many so drunk they could not shoot straight. Polk's following at the time consisted of about 50 individuals, including 18 males of fighting age, while Posey's camp a short distance away included about 15 people, mostly women or children. Nebeker sought to surround Polk's camp before daylight but the endeavor failed and a shootout resulted. Posey's people rushed to assist Polk and several causalties occurred on each side. The Indians withdrew to the vicinity of Navajo Mountain in southern Utah. They established contact with John and Louisa Wetherill (see entry) and were persuaded to talk with Army Chief of Staff Hugh L. Scott, who came to Mexican Hat for that purpose. Polk, Posey, Tse-ne-gat and another agreed to accompany the officer to Salt lake City, Tse-ne-gat to be taken for trial at Denver where eventually he was acquitted. Scott later reported that "my problem was to prevent those four Indians from being legally murdered." Polk and Posey, with no charges against them, were returned to their reservation. Polk became blind in his last years. Posey was wounded mortally in a clash with whites in 1923 and Polk died the following year, presumably on the Ute Mountain Reservation. He was an autocratic leader who sometimes ruled by violence; his people were afraid of him and it was said he had killed at one time or another five or six Indians while exerting his authority. He fathered at least five children.

Forbes Parkhill, *The Last of the Indian Wars.* N.Y., Crowell-Collier Press, 1961; C. Kutac, "Battle at Castle Valley." *Real West,* Vol. 22, No. 163 (May 1979), 8-11, 60-62 (includes photo of Polk); Dan Thrapp, "Polk and Posey on the Warpath." *Desert Mag.,* Vol. 5, No. 7 (May 1942), 9-13).

Pollard, Amos, surgeon (Oct. 29, 1803-Mar. 6, 1836). B. at Ashburnham, Massachusetts, he received medical training at New York City, and settled at Gonzales, Texas, about 1834. He was named surgeon of the Texas volunteer army October 23, 1835, and died at the Alamo. Several of his letters written from the Alamo are held by the University of Texas.

Amelia Williams, XXXVII, 275; HT.

Pollock, Samuel, Mormon pioneer (fl. 1857-1892). A man of this name, "of Cedar City," Utah, was placed by *Mormonism Unveiled* at the Mountain Meadows Massacre of September 11, 1857, either participating in or consenting to the tragedy. He apparently still was living when the book was published.

Mormonism Unveiled, 380.

Ponce de León, explorer, soldier (1460-1521). B. at Tierra de Campos, Palencia, Spain, he fought the Moors in Granada, then was probably a member of Columbus' second expedition to America when Puerto Rico was discovered. As captain he took part in suppressing an Indian uprising on Hispaniola (Santo Domingo), for his work being named governor of the northwestern part of the island. He received permission to attempt the conquest of Puerto Rico, from which he had heard rumors of gold, and landed there August 12, 1508, establishing a settlement and being named governor. He was ousted from his office by Diego Columbus. On March 3, 1513, he led a private expedition from Puerto Rico northward, in April discovering Florida though not realizing he was on the mainland of North America. He landed near modern San Augustine, then explored part of the west coast of the peninsula as far as Charlotte Harbor. He was named governor of Florida and "Bimini," as he called the country which was supposed to contain a "fountain of youth," in the year 1514, with authority to colonize it. First however he returned to Puerto Rico after a visit to Spain, then carried out a mission against the Carib Indians of Trinidad, and it was not until 1521 that he launched his private expedition toward Florida once more. Some believe he brought his two ships and 200 men to Sanibel Island, off the west coast near Charlotte Harbor, where he attempted a landing against fierce Indian resistance. Ponce de León was wounded by an arrow and returned to Havana, where he died. His remains were removed to San Juan, Puerto Rico. The island's second largest city, Ponce, was named in his honor.

Literature abundant; EA; EB.

Poncet de la Riviere, Joseph Antoine, Jesuit missionary (May 7, 1610-June 18, 1675). B. at Paris, he became a Jesuit and reached Canada as a missionary in 1639, working among the Hurons a year, then returned to Quebec. Most of his New France experience was in the settled parts of Canada, but in August 1653, he was captured by Iroquois and taken to their villages in the present New York State where they cruelly tortured him, leaving Poncet with a lasting aversion for that people. He was spared, however, adopted by an old woman to replace a relative lost in war, and finally freed in November 1653, after persuading the Iroquois to conclude a peace with the French. Poncet became involved in religious administrative differences in Quebec and was returned to France. In 1665 he went to Martinique, where he died.

Thwaites, JR. XV, 250n20; DCB.

Pond, Gideon H., linguist, missionary (c. 1831-Jan. 20, 1898). A brother of Samuel William Pond, he may have been born at New Preston, Connecticut, commencing work among the Dakota Indians out of Fort Snelling about 1834. The two Ponds devised an alphabet and translated much religious and secular material into the language of the Sioux, remaining with them for 44 years (see Samuel William Pond's biography for details). Gideon was ordained and a charter member of the Dakota Presbytery and the Synod of Minnesota and in addition to work among the Indians, he was pastor for many years of the Oak Grove Presbyterian Church of Bloomington, Minnesota. At his death he was a member of the Presbytery of St. Paul, Minnesota.

References to S.W. Pond biography; information from the Presby. Hist. Soc., Phila., Pa.

Pond, Peter, explorer, fur trader (Jan. 18, 1740-1807). B. at Milford, Connecticut, he enlisted in Captain David Baldwin's company of the First Connecticut in 1756 for an operation against Fort Ticonderoga; it failed and Pond returned home. In 1758 he joined his captain, now in the Second Connecticut, for a fresh attempt against Ticonderoga, but this effort too was beaten in what Pond described as "the Most Ridicklas campane Eaver Hard of." Pond in 1759 joined the Suffolk County, New York, Regiment as sergeant for an operation against Fort Niagara. He was wounded slightly in the 25-day siege of Niagara; after its success he returned to Milford and in 1760 was commissioned and joined Amherst's force before Montreal. With its fall, Pond believed there was no future in the army and turned to the sea, making a trip to the West Indies in 1761. Upon his return he found his father gone to Detroit on business and his mother had died of a fever, so Pond had to remain to take care of the family, staying at Milford three years, "the Ondlay three years of my Life I was three years in One Plase" since his maturity. He married and fathered at least two children.

He entered the fur trade, pursuing it at Detroit and in the northwest, for about 20 years. A rival trader so abused him that a duel resulted, the other being killed, but Pond was not tried for it. He made a new voyage to the West Indies in 1772. Pond made two journeys from Mackinac to the upper Mississippi country and between that stream and the Missouri in 1773 and 1774 in partnership with Felix Graham, trading with the Sioux and neighboring tribes, at length buying out Graham. From the Minnesota River country he brought a dozen important Sioux chiefs to Mackinac, to meet with Ojibways brought from Lake Superior in order to settle differences between them and bring peace where war had broken out, disrupting trade. This mission proved successful. Pond was one of the first traders to deal with the Yankton Sioux. About 1775 he made for the northwest by way of Lake Superior in the company of Alexander Henry. He spent two years on the Saskatchewan River, became one of the first traders on the Athabascan River, and probably discovered the Peace River about 1780. He also may have been the first to see the Alberta tar sands. In 1782 he killed a rival trader, Jean Etienne Waden, and two years later was ordered to Montreal for trial, but was acquitted. Pond owned one of 16 shares in the North West Company when it was organized about 1783. He revisited Milford, gave to Congress a map of his travels, which was copied for European archives, and went back to the Athabasca country in 1785. He quit the fur trading business in 1788, selling his share in the company for 800 pounds sterling, and returned to his Milford home. His last years are obscure; he is reported to have died at Boston in poverty. Pond was a paradigm of the better class of fur trader: a man of great courage and industry, a careful, judicious observor who could write with vigor and economy (although his spelling was highly original), and a man of honor and supreme competence. He was a major figure on the frontier of his day.

"The Narrative of Peter Pond," *Five Fur Traders of the Northwest*, ed. by Charles M. Gates. St. Paul, Minn. Hist. Soc., 1965; DAB.

Pond, Samuel William, missionary (Apr. 10, 1808-Dec. 12, 1891). B. at New Preston, Connecticut, he entered missionary work among the Sioux Indians with no formal training save a conversion experience. Receiving cooperation in 1834 from the Indian agent and commander at Fort Snelling, Minnesota, he and his brother, Gideon, began work at an Indian settlement at Lake Calhoun, expanding the labors to include Lake Harriet. The brothers commenced diligently studying the Dakota tongue, evolved an alphabet for it, developed a grammar, and published the first spelling book in the language. Returning to Connecticut, Pond was formally commissioned a missionary to the Sioux by a local conference of Congregational ministers, returned to Minnesota and began translating Genesis into Dakota. The Ponds moved with the Indians to Oak Grove, Minnesota, in 1843, continuing their publishing, again moved with the Indians to Shakopee, Samuel remaining there the rest of his life, continuing his researches and writing about the Sioux, which were of a basic nature and great importance. He was married twice and fathered children.

DAB; Louis H. Roddis, *The Indian Wars of Minnesota.* Cedar Rapids, Ia., Torch Press, 1956; Roy W. Meyer, *History of the Santee Sioux.* Lincoln, Univ. of Nebra. Press, 1967.

Pontiac, Ottawa chief (c. 1720-Apr. 20, 1769). B. probably in an Ottawa village on the north side of the Detroit River, there are dissenting views of the place and date of his birth. He belonged to the Ottawa nation, although one parent (which one is in doubt) may have been either Miami or Chippewa (Ojibwa). By 1747 Pontiac was a mature warrior who sided with the French during King George's War (1744-48) and perhaps raided with them into New York State. When the British threatened Fort Duquesne in 1755, the French called for Indian assistance from Great Lakes tribes. Since Ottawas were heavily involved in the ambush of the Braddock column July 9, 1755, it is assumed Pontiac was there, but there is no confirmation (or rebuttal) from any source and whether he was then leader of a war party is not stated. In July 1757 Pontiac and his Ottawas may have been with Charles Langlade (see entry) in an engagement when more than 300 English soldiers were either slain or taken prisoner. Pontiac, no doubt, with 336 Ottawas took part in the successful siege of Fort William Henry at the head of Lake George, and may have participated in the subsequent Indian assault on English prisoners, with mixed results. Later in 1757 Pontiac, described now as an "Outava chief," no doubt a war chief, delivered an oration at Fort Duquesne, reporting that George Croghan (see entry) had unsuccessfully sought to lure the Ottawas from their French alliance to one with the British. Pontiac may have been in the ambush defeat of Major James Grant near Duquesne September 14, 1758, Grant losing half his command of 842 men in dead, wounded and prisonered. The British later seized Duquesne (renaming it Fort Pitt) after its Indian defenders had withdrawn to Detroit. He may have participated in the disastrous French reverse at Niagara, and remained at Detroit thereafter until the English occupied the place on November 29, 1760 when Pontiac no doubt was of the band of Ottawas and other Indians who gathered with the French to welcome Major Robert Rogers and his command, come to take over the post; Pontiac may have been of a group that had conferred with Rogers two days earlier. The English takeover of Detroit was orderly but the Indians quickly became disaffected. Amherst's misguided strictness in avoiding what he believed "bribery," or the distribution of presents, and insistence that the Indians work to merit any largesse, generated dissatisfaction. So did the sharp contrast between other British and earlier French policies. The withholding of powder, ammunition and rum did not help. Pontiac no doubt attended the September 9, 1761, grand council at Detroit between Indians and British leaders, including Sir William Johnson (see entry), but he is not mentioned in the records and was not a principal speaker, if he was heard at all; he was swiftly becoming disillusioned with the English. During the summer of 1762 a secret Indian council in the Ottawa village on the Detroit River was attended by representatives of the Chippewas, Hurons, Potawatomis and Lake Superior tribes; Pontiac must have been a leader, perhaps instigator, of it, although surreptitious French influences too were at work. In the spring of 1763 while organizing the ensuing revolt, Pontiac reminded his allies of several wampum belts he had received from the French, urging him to war. But the principal goads to conflict were the intemperance and stupidity of Amherst and his shortsighted Indian policy. War belts, some from the Senecas, were handed about throughout

the upper Midwest in 1763. Peckham discounts the Parkman theory of a Pontiac "conspiracy" involving all phases of the great uprising, believing rather that the chief was commander only of the three villages at Fort Detroit and "a chief-to-be-consulted (with) the Chippewas and Potawatomies who came from a distance to join him." Yet it seems an odd coincidence that within weeks the uprising engulfed all of the western British-manned posts save Detroit and Fort Pitt, and both of those were under heavy siege. "In the beginning," Peckham conceded, "there was only a local conspiracy at Detroit directed by Pontiac, who, however, improvised a more general uprising after his initial tactics failed. And his second attempts almost succeeded in loosening the British hold." Pontiac with two-score followers, visited Fort Detroit on a reconnaissance May 1, 1763, and planned to seize it by ruse; on the 5th some 300 warriors entered the fort, but found the British heavily armed, Major Henry Gladwin having been informed of the plot and prepared for it. Pontiac and three chiefs once more attempted to allay British suspicions on May 8 but, not succeeding, an attack was launched the following day. It failed, Pontiac settled down to a siege that lasted until October 30, involving sometimes 1,000 warriors of Ottawa, Potawatomi, Huron and Chippewa tribes plus a scattering from others, while the Shawnees and Delawares invested Fort Pitt. Better fortune attended Indian attacks in the west: Forts St. Joseph and Miami fell to the Miamis and Illinois May 26. The Miamis, Kickapoos and Mascoutens took Fort Ouiatanon (near Lafayette, Indiana) on June 1; June 2 Chippewas seized Fort Michilimackinac and the British abandoned Green Bay, Wisconsin. The Senecas took Venango (Franklin, Pennsylvania) June 16 and later Fort de la Riviere au Boef (Waterford, Pennsylvania) and June 21 the Senecas with Ottawas, Hurons and Chippewas took Fort de la Presqu'ile (Erie, Pennsylvania). All of these posts were lightly manned and prisoners were seized at each. French assistance which had been promised was not forthcoming and Pontiac's volatile coalition commenced to fall apart as the season dragged on. The British were reinforced and although they lost skirmishes and even battles, Detroit held out, as did Fort Pitt. On October 29 news arrived that France and England had buried the hatchet, making a peace ending the seven year French and Indian War. Two days later Pontiac suggested to Gladwin a truce which was accepted. By spring Pontiac was in the Illinois country, endeavoring without much success to win support in order to renew the offensive against the British, an effort he soon realized would be futile. In 1765 George Croghan conferred with him at Fort Ouiatanon. A preliminary agreement was reached, Pontiac insisting that the British should not consider that occupying former French posts gave them the right to colonize the whole country. Pontiac and Croghan returned to Detroit where the agreement was ratified by the military and the late hostile tribesmen. In the spring of 1766 the chiefs went to Oswego, New York, where Sir William Johnson presided over a major council with them. It was reported that Pontiac would receive a British captain's pay and this alienated some of his followers; at any rate, Pontiac formally swung his allegiance from the defeated French to Britain, no doubt in part because of Johnson's blandishments. Thereafter Pontiac spurned further conspiracies against the British. Furthermore he aroused the enmity of the Ilinois for reasons unclear. March 30, 1769, he went to Cahokia, Illinois. The nearby Peorias, now thoroughly disaffected, decided in council that Pontaic must be assassinated. This was carried out by a chief's nephew with a war club and knife, as Peckham reports, or with a tomahawk as Parkman believed. His place of burial is uncertain, although the French were reported to have obtained the body and buried it at St Louis, a community then five years old. Pontiac was tall, not strikingly handsome but strongly built, light complexioned and with an air of command. He was said (by his enemies) to have been easily offended and haughty of manner. He wore his black hair short with few feathers in it, sometimes adorning himself with a necklace of white plumes or other decorative elements. He was among the greatest of all American Indians in his intelligence, vision, determination and sheer ability. He married, perhaps several times, and fathered children, none of whom rose to prominence.

Howard H. Peckham, *Pontiac and the Indian Uprising.* Univ. of Chicago Press, 1961; Parkman, *The Conspiracy of Pontiac,* 2 vols.; *Journal of Pontiac's Conspiracy 1763.* Detroit, Mich. Soc. of Colonial Wars, ed. by M. Agnes Burton, 1912.

Poole, Robert, interpreter (fl. 1610-20). B. in England, he may have been a son of Jonas Poole (d. 1612), a sea captain who reached Jamestown, Virginia, in 1607, later became a whaler in Arctic waters and who was murdered in England subsequently. Robert Poole was one of several boys sent to live with Powhatan's Indians in order to learn the language, later to become interpreters, It was he who falsely accused Henry Spelman (see entry) of betraying the English to the Indians, causing Spelman to be sentenced to seven years' servitude — a sentence soon lifted after which Poole's treachery was revealed. Officials subsequently learned Poole was "very dishonest" and even had "turned heathen." His services as interpreter however appear to have continued. His later career and the date and circumstances of his death are not reported.

Karen Ordahl Kupperman, *Settling with the Indians: the Meeting of English and Indian Cultures in America, 1580-1640.* London, J.M. Dent & Sons, 1980; DNB.

Popé, Tewa medicine man (d. c. 1690). B. probably in San Juan pueblo of New Mexico, Popé was a celebrated medicine man of the Tewa, a group of Pueblo tribes of the Tanoan linguistic family. He first appears in 1675 when he was arrested and at the orders of Governor Juan Francisco de Treviño was flogged for witchcraft at Santa Fe, this doing nothing to endear the whites or their ways to him. He settled at Taos and quietly commenced to preach a doctrine of independence of Spanish authority and restoration of the old Pueblo life. This developed into a plot to drive out the 2,400 Spanish then in New Mexico (but see the entry for Domingo Naranjo). The scheme won enthusiastic support. August 13, 1680, was set for the uprising, the news sent by runners to pueblos as distant as the Hopi of Arizona. Every precaution was taken to keep the Spanish from learning of the event; no woman was permitted to know of it, and Popé even put his own brother-in-law to death, suspecting him of treachery. Nevertheless it was feared that the news had leaked out and the date for the revolt was advanced to August 10. Four or five hundred Spanish colonists, including 21 priests were slaughtered and Santa Fe besieged; on August 20 in a sortie of 100 men the Spanish reported 200 Indians killed and 47 captured and hanged in the plaza of the community. But the following day the whites evacuated Santa Fe and began a long retreat to El Paso, or Juarez. Popé now progressed with his plan to wipe out European influence and restore the old ways of Pueblo life. Those who had received Christian baptism were washed with yucca suds; Spanish language and names were prohibited; all Christian objects and churches were destroyed, and for a time Popé, dressed in ceremonial robes, was greeted with enthusiasm as he went from pueblo to pueblo. However he became a despot. He put to death those who refused his commands and in other ways acted tyrannically. Drought afflicted the pueblos, as did the Apaches and Utes, and internal dissension arose with civil strife among the pueblos and with each other and Popé was deposed, being succeeded by Luis Tupatú of Picuris who ruled until 1688 when Popé again was elected to govern the pueblos, or some of them. Popé died before reconquest of New Mexico by Diego de Vargas. For all his weaknesses, Popé remains "the only person who successfully welded a large group of Western Indians from many tribes into a single force powerful enough to defeat their oppressors and drive them from Indian lands for such a long period of time."

Hodge, HAI; *Handbook of Indians*, 9, pp. 186-87; *Revolt of the Pueblo Indians of New Mexico and Otermín's Attempted Reconquest 1680-1682*, intr. and annot. by Charles Wilson Hackett, transl. of orig. docs. by Charmion Clair Shelby, Coronado Hist. Ser., VIII, IX. Albuquerque, Univ. of New Mex. Press, 1970; Dockstader.

Pope, George, frontiersman (fl. 1837). George Pope may have been a brother of William Pope, a Kentuckian and well-known mountain man who settled eventually in California. George Pope was a member of the ill-famed John Johnson expedition which treacherously slew Juan José Compá and 19 other Mimbres Apaches on April 22, 1837, in the Animas Mountains of southern New Mexico. Nothing else is known of him.

Rex W. Strickland, "The Birth and Death of a Legend: The Johnson 'Massacre' of 1837." *Arizona and the West*, Vol. 18, No. 3 (Autumn 1976), 257-86.

Pope, John, army officer (Mar. 16, 1822-Sept. 23, 1892). B. at Louisville, Kentucky, he was graduated from West Point and commissioned a brevet second lieutenant in the Topographical Engineers July 1, 1842, not becoming a second lieutenant until May 9, 1846. Initially he engaged in survey work in Florida and along the northeastern boundary with Canada, receiving a reprimand for misconduct and inefficiency from his superior, Lieutenant Colonel James Duncan Graham. As a second lieutenant he served with Taylor in Mexico, then returned to survey work, this time in Minnesota where in his 1849 report he "boldly plagiarized" a map and 1838 report by Joseph Nicolas Nicollet. Pope had explored the Red River Valley and made various recommendations for the political future of that country. He served the Department of New Mexico as chief topographical engineer from 1851 until 1853. Pope was a witness to the July 11, 1852 treaty with the Mimbres Apaches; years later as commander of the department concerned he would have his fill of directing military efforts to quell their persistent hostility. He was promoted to first lieutenant March 3, 1853, despite disputes with superiors over his superficial or slipshod work, and his entrance into a controversy over whether a proposed southern transcontinental railroad should follow the 35th or 38th parallel across New Mexico and Arizona. Pope had political friends however, as well as some in the army and July 1, 1856 became a captain. In 1854 he had explored the Staked Plains of Texas and became convinced that artesian wells would solve the problem of water supplies for a railroad or other travel across them. Three years of experimental drilling with mixed results limited his enthusiasm. Pope was commissioned a Brigadier General of Volunteers May 17, 1861, a Major General of Volunteers March 21, 1862, and a Brigadier General in the army July 14, 1862. After some initial successes in the Mississippi Valley he was sent east, but was soundly defeated at Second Bull Run, August 27-30, 1862. At this time the Mdewakanton Sioux were on the warpath in Minnesota, causing immense havoc and loss of life. Lincoln, desiring to have a top military man there and at the same time find a spot for the discredited Pope, gave him command of the Department of the Northwest, with headquarters at St. Paul, where he arrived September 17, 1862. He found the fury of the Sioux already spent and Henry H. Sibley advancing well against them. Pope joined the clamor for harsh punishment of the Sioux, urged the hanging of hundreds of them, and even wrote and spoke of extermination as a viable goal. He directed a military campaign be launched in 1863 and ordered Sibley to undertake it, now that the Indians had quitted Minnesota. Meanwhile Alfred Sully would move up the Missouri so that hopefully the Sioux would be crushed between two forces; the plan did not work out. After several sharp engagements Sibley withdrew leaving the Sioux defiant, and Sully was no more successful against them. Pope planned additional expeditions into the northern Plains in 1864, Sully to lead one while Sibley's subordinate, Colonel Minor T. Thomas would lead another. Again results were mixed. In late November Grant offered Pope command of the new division of the Missouri, formed of the previous Departments of the Northwest, Missouri and Kansas. Pope eagerly accepted and assumed command in January. He found the Plains aflame with Indian hostility sparked by Chivington's senseless Sand Creek Massacre and other atrocities elsewhere. Pope, with plenty now to do, oversaw operations in all areas, but he had developed beyond the simplistic extermination policy he had earlier espoused and warned such bombastic commanders as Patrick Connor that they must learn this quickly or it would cost them their commissions, "if not worse." Once more Pope's work was inconclusive and when Sherman was given command of the Division of the Missouri, Pope's was reduced to the subordinate Department of the Missouri and in 1867 of the Third District of the South. He commanded the Department of the Lakes from 1868 to 1870. He then resumed command of the Department of the Missouri, heading it until 1883 during a period of much Indian fighting which extended into the South Plains and New Mexico. Pope favored military rather than Indian Bureau control over Indian affairs, encouraged missionary activities and believed that Indians on reservations should be well treated with a view to assimilation into white culture. However, Pope had become a realist. He wished to put troops on the reservations to keep the Indians there rather than futilely chasing raiders once loose. His 13 years directing army affairs on the Plains and especially in the southwest were troubled ones. Yet he persisted. Gradually peace came about, if imperfectly. During this time Pope became a knowledgeable and hard-working commander with growing compassion and understanding of the problems of Indians — and those of border whites, as well. In 1883 Pope became commander of the Department of California and the Division of the Pacific and October 26, 1882, became a Major General; four years later, March 16, 1886, retired by reason of age. He died at Sandusky, Ohio. Pope was married and left two sons and two daughters.

Cullum; Richard N. Ellis, *General Pope and U.S. Indian Policy.* Albuquerque, Univ. of New Mex. Press, 1970; William H. Goetzmann, *Army Exploration in the American West 1803-1863.* New Haven, Yale Univ. Press, 1959; William Watts Folwell, *A History of Minnesota,* II. St. Paul, Minn. Hist. Soc., 1961.

Pope, William, trapper (d. 1842). B. in Kentucky, he joined the Patties on their 1828 expedition to California, was arrested by Mexican authorities at San Diego, released in November with Isaac Slover, and returned to New Mexico. Married and naturalized, he went back to California in 1837, lived at Los Angeles until 1841 when he moved to the Napa Valley, east of Fort Ross. He accidentally killed himself with an axe.

Andrew F. Rolle article, MM, Vol. II.

Popham, George, colonist (c. 1550-Feb. 5, 1608). The nephew of Sir John Popham was b, in Somerset County, England, and named in the 1606 patent granted the Virginia Company. With Raleigh Gilbert he set out with two ships in 1607 from Plymouth to found a colony on the New England coast, taking along as interpreter one of the Indians Waymouth had seized. They settled at the mouth of the Sagadoc (Kennebec) River at the present site of Phippsburg, Maine, erecting a palisaded position called Fort St. George. With Popham as governor the colonists settled in for a hard winter on a bleak coast, fearful of neighboring Indians who seemed hostile. Popham was described as old and honest but lacking in decisiveness and being overly discrete and cautious. He died in February and continuation of the colonial venture was impossible, the place being abandoned the following summer.

CE; DAB; *Handbook of Indians,* 15.

Portell, John, frontiersman (d. c. July 23, 1861). His age and place of birth are unknown. On May 17, 1861, he shot and wounded (not fatally) Virgil Mastin, a secessionist (who was to be killed by Apaches in 1868), at Mesilla, New Mexico. Portell was one of seven men known as the Freeman Thomas (sometimes called the Free Thompson) party, ambushed and killed by Apaches near Cooke's Spring, New Mexico. He and three others died within the breastwork they had erected, the others outside apparently seeking to escape.

W.W. Mills: *Forty Years in El Paso,* Rex W. Strickland, ed. El Paso, Carl Hertzog, pubr., 1962.

Porter, Charles, army officer (Nov. 23, 1838-Oct. 15, 1902). B. at Dublin he emigrated to this country and enlisted in 1858 in the 5th Infantry, serving in Utah and New Mexico and taking part in the Navaho Expedition in the winter of 1860-61; he operated against Confederate forces in New Mexico in 1862, was commissioned in 1863 and served against Indians on the Plains and in New Mexico in 1864 and 1865, ending the Civil War a first lieutenant. Porter transferred to the 8th Infantry in 1870 and took part in the 1872 Yellowstone Expedition, served at the Spotted Tail Agency in Dakota in 1874 and late that year was assigned to Arizona for five years. Here he led a number of scouting operations against hostile Indians, often with Al Sieber as chief of scouts. Porter won a brevet for three actions against hostiles in Arizona. He served against the Bannocks in Idaho and Oregon from July to October 1878, was sent again to Arizona in 1881 and was acting Indian Agent at the Hoopa Valley Agency, California, from 1882-85. He retired a lieutenant colonel in 1898. Martha Summerhayes reported him "charmingly witty," and described his successful seven-year campaign for the hand of "the beautiful and graceful Caroline Wilkins, the belle of the (8th) regiment." Porter was a literate man of an inquiring turn of mind.

Powell; Heitman; Dan L. Thrapp, *Al Sieber, Chief of Scouts* (which has a portrait of Porter). Norman, Univ. of Okla. Press, 1964; Martha Summerhayes, *Vanished Arizona.* Lincoln, Univ. of Nebr. Press, 1979.

Porter, David Dixon, naval officer (June 8, 1813-Feb. 13, 1891). B. at Chester, Pennsylvania, he was a famous naval officer, a son of one equally distinguished, and the frontier interest in his career rests primarily on his role in transporting camels to the U.S. for the southwestern experiment of the Army's Quartermaster Department. Porter was appointed a Navy midshipman in 1829 after he had served under his father as midshipman in the Mexican Navy. He commanded a 70-man landing party that captured a fort at Tabasco, Mexico, in 1847. From 1849 to 1855 he was an officer in merchant shipping. In 1855 Porter, who had been raised in the Middle East when his father held diplomatic posts there, was chosen to transport camels selected by Major Henry C. Wayne, and did so, employing the USS *Supply* which was modified for the endeavor under Porter's direction. The mission visited Tunis, Egypt and Turkey, selected 33 camels and sailed for this country February 11, 1856. The trip took 87 days, but was accomplished without the loss of an animal, landing them at Indianola, Texas. Porter was directed to return for a second load, leaving in late July and returning January 30, 1857, with 41 camels of various types. Porter had an outstanding Civil War record, commanding among other missions the river blockade of Vicksburg and thus assisting Grant to capture that vital Mississippi port. He was made full Admiral in 1870 after successfully reforming and expanding the U.S. Naval Academy at Annapolis. Porter died at Washington, D.C., and was buried at Arlington National Cemetery.

Literature abundant; John Shapard, "The United States Army Camel Corps: 1856-66." *Milit. Rev.. Professional Jour. of US Army,* Vol. LV, No. 8 (Aug. 1975), 77-89; *Who Was Who;* DAB.

Porter, James Ezekiel, army officer (Feb. 2, 1847-June 25, 1876). B. at Strong, Franklin County, Maine, he went to West Point and was commissioned a second lieutenant in the 7th Cavalry June 15, 1869, joining the regiment at Fort Leavenworth in October. He served at Forts Wallace and Harker, Kansas and engaged in scouting until March 1871 when he was assigned to southeastern posts until June 1873 when (having been promoted to first lieutenant March 1, 1872) he went to Fort Snelling, Minnesota. Porter was on escort duty with the Northern Boundary Survey Commission in the summers of 1873 and 1874, served at Dakota posts from 1874 until the spring of 1876 when he joined Custer's Sioux expedition with Company I. He was presumed killed in the Battle of the Little Big Horn although his remains were not identified; his coat with two bullet holes was found at the site of the Indian village.

Cullum; BHB; *Custer in 76: Walter Camp's Notes on the Custer Fight,* Provo, Utah, Brigham Young Univ. Press, 1976.

Portlock, Nathaniel, British sea captain (c. 1748-Sept. 12, 1817). Portlock entered the British navy in 1772 but previously had probably served as mate or possibly master of a merchantman. He was aboard the *Discovery* as master's mate on Cook's third voyage, transferring to the *Resolution* where he served with George Dixon in the North Pacific and Alaskan waters. In 1785 Portlock was appointed by the King George's Sound Company to command the *King George* on an expedition to the Northwest Coast of America, sailing from Gravesend August 29, 1785, in company with Dixon's *Queen Charlotte,* and commanding the expedition. They rounded Cape Horn, visited Hawaii and reached the Alaskan bight by July 19, 1786, charting the coast so far as possible, and incidentally sighting Mount St. Elias. The ships wintered in Hawaii and returned to the Alaskan coast in the spring, reaching Montague Island, east of the Kenai Peninsula, where Portlock traded for furs while Dixon worked east and south along the coast. Both ships again returned to Hawaii with winter, went on to China and England, Portlock arriving August 24, 1788. He published *A Voyage Round the World, but More Particularly to the Northwest Coast of America* (1789), the same title as one published about the Dixon voyage. Portlock's journey had significant geographical results, and also did much to open the northwest fur trade to British interests.

Bancroft, *Alaska;* Bancroft, *Northwest Coast,* I; Warren L. Cook, *Flood Tide of Empire.* New Haven, Yale Univ. Press, 1973; DNB.

Portneuf, René: *see* Robinau de Portneuf, René

Portolá, Gaspar de, military officer (1723-1784). B. at Balaguer, Cataluña, Spain, he entered the army and served in Portugal and Italy. He was captain of dragoons in the

España Regiment when he was appointed political and military governor of Baja California in 1767, assigned to carry out the expulsion of the Jesuits from their Lower California missions and oversee transfer of these to the Franciscans. In addition, Spanish authorities were somewhat alarmed by Russian incursions down the Northwest Coast of America. Wishing to assure the safety — and Spanish possession — of the coast of Upper California, Inspector General José de Gálvez in 1769 named Portolá head of an expedition which included among others, Junipero Serra on its rolls, Portolá being, in Bancroft's words, "an easy-going, popular man, but brave and honest withal." The expedition resulted in the founding of a mission at San Diego, reconnoitering Monterey Bay and discovery of San Francisco Bay. Portolá oversaw the establishment in 1770 of the presidio and mission of San Carlos at Monterey, this becoming the initial military and religious capital of the Province. Portolá remained governor of Upper California until 1770. The *Diario Histórico* of the Portolá expedition was published at Mexico City, the date undetermined precisely. In 1777 Portolá became political and military governor of the city of Puebla, Mexico, still occupying that position in 1779. The place and circumstances of his death are not reported.

Porrua; Bancroft, *California,* I; *Pioneer Register.*

Posey, Thomas, military officer, Indian agent (July 9, 1750-Mar. 19, 1818). B. in Fairfax County, Virginia, he moved at 19 to Augusta County, took part as commissary in Lord Dunmore's War of 1774 and served in other Indian affairs. March 20, 1776 he became captain of the 7th Virginia, serving under Washington, Morgan and Gates in New Jersey and New York in 1776-78. He became a major in the 2nd Virginia April 30, 1776, transferring back to the 7th on September 14. He commanded a battalion under Wayne at the storming of Stony Point and was at Yorktown, becoming a lieutenant colonel September 11, 1782, and retiring the next year. In 1793 he was appointed a Brigadier General to serve in Wayne's Indian campaign, but resigned again February 28, 1794, before the Battle of Fallen Timbers. Posey moved to Kentucky in 1794, held political positions for four years and was Major General of Kentucky levies after 1809. He moved to Louisiana and was senator from that state in

1812-13 when he became an Indian agent, removing to Shawneetown, Illinois, where he died.

Reuben Gold Thwaites, Louise Phelps Kellogg, ed., *Documentary History of Dunmore's War 1774*. Madison, Wisc. Hist. Soc., 1905; Heitman; BDAC.

Posey, William (Soorowits, Old Posey), Paiute leader (c. 1865-1923). B. on Navajo Mountain, Utah, according to Odens, or in House Rock Valley in northern Arizona as Parkhill wrote. Posey's father was one of a dozen Paiutes who had quit the main tribal body of south central Utah and struck out for themselves in eastern Utah and northern Arizona; eventually Posey came into leadership of this small fraction of his people. He was known as anti-white to the regional cowboys, miners and settlers, but how much of this originated to justify white seizure of Indian lands is unclear. Posey married Toorah, a sister of Old Polk (see entry) and his and Polk's bands ranged though the wilderness, aloof from reservations or other restrictions and a constant source of apprehension to the few scattered whites. Eventually Posey killed Toorah, generating Polk's ire until he learned that the slaying had been an accident when he insisted that Posey marry another of his sisters, Spoorka, which mollified him. Polk and Posey were reported involved in an 1881 action at Castle Valley, eastern Utah, following two white deaths, purportedly at hands of the Indians: in the engagement ten whites were killed with no proven Indian losses. Late in the century Posey's Paiutes and Polk's Wiminuche Utes enrolled at the Southern Ute Reservation in southwestern Colorado; their western portion of the reserve eventually came to be the Ute Mountain Reservation. They were not required to reside there, however, and continued to roam the Four Corners area for years. In 1914 Tse-ne-gat, Polk's son, was charged with slaying a Mexican sheep herder. Polk refused to give him up and withdrew to a secluded camp near Bluff, Utah, Posey's people camping nearby. In February 1915 a pitched battle occurred between a U.S. marshal's posse and Polk's people when Posey rushed up at a critical time with his followers and turned the tide so that the two bands could slip away; they withdrew to Navajo Mountain, south of the San Juan River.

Eventually Posey, Polk and Tse-ne-gat surrendered to Army Chief of Staff Hugh L. Scott at Mexican Hat and were taken to Salt Lake City. Tse-ne-gat was sent on to Denver for trial (he was acquitted), while Posey and Polk were not charged but sent back to their reservation. Posey's band continued to roam southeastern Utah, considered a threat by whites although rarely so in fact. In 1923 however, a warrant was issued for two young men of Posey's band, charged with robbery of a sheep herder; Posey initially refused to surrender them but at length they were tried and found guilty in a Blanding, Utah, court. In a scuffle the two narrowly missed with Sheriff Bill Oliver and broke free, the band again escaping in a hail of gunfire. A posse in an automobile chased them eight miles south until the car was ambushed and the whites turned back. A horseback posse took up the chase. Sporadically one party or the other came under fire. One of the two Indians who had been tried was shot and killed. Eventually most of the band surrendered but Posey, badly wounded in the lower back, escaped to the wilder reaches of Comb Wash to the west. Here he died of gangrene, his body buried by his people, though later dug up and photographed by whites seeking proof that Posey really was dead. The remains then were reburied in a secret place. Posey, married and father of at least 11 children, was the last "hostile" Indian killed in the United States.

Dan Thrapp, "Polk and Posey on the Warpath." *Desert Mag.*, Vol. 5, No. 7 (May 1942), 9-13; Peter Odens, *The Indians and I.* El Centro, Calif., Imperial Printers, 1971, 69-80 (with photographs); Forbes Parkhill, *The Last of the Indian Wars.* N.Y., Crowell-Collier Press, 1961; C. Kutac, "Battle at Castle Valley." *Real West*, Vol. 22, No. 163 (May 1979), 8-11, 60-62; Dale Van Atta, "Posey: Renegade and Last Warrior." *Frontier Times*, Vol. 51, No. 5 (Aug.-Sept. 1977), 26-27, 58-59.

Posey, William Hinton, trail driver (Nov. 16, 1832-Spring 1923). B. in South Carolina he moved with his father's family to Mississippi in 1839 and to Texas in 1850, settling in Burleson County and later in Brown County where he established a ranch on Indian Creek. He drove herds of cattle to Alexandria, Louisiana, in 1862, to Little Rock, Arkansas, in 1863, in 1868 to California by way of the Overland Stage route and in 1869 to Abilene, Kansas. On the California drive he lost many horses to Indians and cattle to exigencies. Posey and his only brother, John W. Posey, later of Granger, Texas, both served the Confederacy for four years. Posey died at the age of 90 from the effect of a fall from his horse while running a cow, the horse running under a low mesquite limb that swept him from the saddle.

Frontier Times, Vol. 8, No. 5 (Feb. 1931), 215-19.

Post, Christian Frederick, Moravian missionary (1710-May 1, 1785). B. in Conitz, Polish Prussia, he came to America in 1742 as a Moravian lay minister among Germans of Pennsylvania, but the following year embarked upon his lifelong missionary endeavors among the Indians, initially among the Mohicans whose language he soon learned. He married a Wampanoag Christian woman and the next year worked among the Iroquois. The missionaries came afoul of suspicious white frontiersmen and officials, however; Post, whose wife had died, married a Delaware woman, also a Christian, and settled in the Wyoming valley of Pennsylvania. Upon the death of his second wife, Post went to London, joined an expedition to Labrador and worked among the Eskimos, but a native uprising aborted his labors and Post returned to Pennsylvania. He attempted to warn the settlers against the first Wyoming massacre, but was too late; subsequently he helped arrange a conference between whites and Indians on the Ohio River to establish peace. Post had a role in the abandonment of Fort Duchesne (Pittsburgh) by the French and its occupation by the British, and later extended Moravian mission work into Ohio. Post attempted to establish a mission on the Honduran or Nicaraguan coast, later abandoning the Moravian cause for the Anglican church. He married a third time, to a white woman; she also predeceased him. Post died at Germantown, Pennsylvania. "Adventurous and fearless, he undertook . . . dangerous journeys, carrying peace belts" and seeking to further missionary and civilizing influences, but he was impatient and hard for others to work with, and although associated at various times with Zeisberger, Heckewelder and other great Moravian missionaries, he never could cooperate with them for long. Yet by helping to win Fort Duchesne, he did much to open the Ohio River valley and the Old Northwest

to the English, and his missionary labors among the Indians were enduring and of great value.

Thwaites, EWT, I, pp. 177-84; DAB; Paul A.W. Wallace, *Thirty Thousand Miles with John Heckewelder.* Univ. of Pittsburgh Press, 1958.

Poston, Charles Debrille, pioneer, "father of Arizona" (Apr. 20, 1825-June 25, 1902). B. in Kentucky, he reached California by way of Panama in 1850 and in 1854 sailed for Guaymas in a company of 25 others, including Herman Ehrenberg, aboard a British brig which was shipwrecked in the Gulf of California. The party made its way overland to the lower Colorado River, where Poston and Ehrenberg founded Colorado City, precursor of Yuma. In the east, Poston succeeded in gathering finances for the Sonora Exploring and Mining Co., and reached Tucson overland in 1856. His party prospected the Ajo mines and the Cerro Colorado and other properties near Tubac. With the Civil War he and his workmen removed to California. Poston was superintendent of Indian affairs for Arizona 1863-64, then entered political life during which he journeyed around the world. Later he returned to Arizona, held the government land office at Florence, and was a customs officer along the border. He died at Phoenix, his remains removed in 1925 to the top of "Poston Butte" near Florence. A literate man with expansionist ambitions, he was a worthy, intelligent pioneer who however proved ineffective in developing his own potential. Poston wrote volumes of indifferent verse, travel books, and notably inaccurate recollections about the building of Arizona. None of his writing is of vital importance, although it achieved a certain popularity.

Arizoniana, Vol. I, No. 1 (Spring 1960), 3-4; Benjamin Sacks, *Be It Enacted: the Creation of the Territory of Arizona.* Phoenix, Ariz. Hist. Found., 1964; A.W. Gressinger, *Charles D. Poston: Sunland Seer.* Globe, Ariz., Dale Stuart King, Pub., 1961; DAB.

Potier, Pierre, Jesuit missionary (Apr. 21, 1708-July 17, 1781). B. in Flanders he became a Jesuit and reached Canada October 1, 1743, studied Huron for a year at Lorette and was assigned to Detroit to work with La Richardie. When the latter retired, Potier became superior of the mission, remaining in charge of the mission church, which gradually became French rather than Huron, until his death.

Thwaites, JR, LXIX, 289n13, LXXI, 175.

Potter, William George, Mormon pioneer (d. Oct. 26, 1853). B. in Ohio, he reached Utah September 19, 1847, with the Daniel Spencer company, settling in the Fort Ephraim region, where Potter became a farmer and a Mormon elder. He and a brother, Gardner Godfrey Potter (b. 1820 at Essex, New York) were hired by John Williams Gunnison, an army topographical engineer, as guides during a railroad survey, and with Gunnison and others William Potter was killed, presumably by Paiute Indians, near upper Sevier Lake, Utah.

Frank Esshom, *Pioneers and Prominent Men of Utah.* Salt Lake City, Western Epics, 1966; Bancroft, *Utah;* William Wise, *Massacre at Mountain Meadows.* N.Y., Thomas Y. Crowell Co., 1976; Nolie Mumey, *John Williams Gunnison.* Denver, Artcraft Press, 1955.

Potts, Daniel T., frontiersman (c. 1796-c. 1840). B. in Pennsylvania, he was one of the Ashley men ascending the Missouri River in 1822, deserted briefly, rejoined an Ashley boat and went on up the river. He was accidentally wounded during his first winter on the Musselshell River but recovered and spent six years trapping in the northern Rockies, perhaps naming Great Salt Lake, being the first confirmed visitor and penning the first description of the later Yellowstone Park. He regained St. Louis in October 1828. Potts engaged in shipping livestock from Texas to New Orleans and reportedly was lost with his ship in the Gulf of Mexico. His interesting letters from the mountains are analyzed by Bagley.

Gerald C. Bagley article, MM, Vol. III.

Potts, Jerry, scout (1840-July 14, 1896). B. in Montana of a Scottish trader, Andrew R. Potts, and a Blackfoot woman, Potts became the ward of Alexander Harvey after his father had been killed by a Piegan; when Harvey, a very quarrelsome man, was forced to leave the country, Potts was taken care of by Andrew Dawson with whom he remained until his teens. Potts became more Indian than white; he married four times, first to a Crow, the other three wives being Blackfeet. At 23 he shot a Frenchman; later he survived skirmishes with Crows and Sioux, winning a reputation for courage, honesty and recklessness — and for a taste for whiskey. Potts was hired in 1874 as interpreter, guide and scout by assistant commissioner James F. Macleod of the new Royal North West Mounted Police, which Potts served in Alberta and thereabouts for 23 years. He was influential in the peaceful acceptance of the authority of the police force by the Blackfeet and other tribes, becoming legendary in many ways. He died of throat cancer at Fort Macleod, on the Oldman River, Alberta. Samuel B. Steele, a police officer who had worked with him for 22 years, commented: "As scout and guide I have never met his equal...in either the north west or the states to the south."

Larry L. Meyer, "The Compleat and Unlikely Plainsman." *Westways,* Vol. 66, No. 10 (Oct. 1974), 24-26, 68; for a sample of Potts' work, see "A Mid-Winter North West Mounted Patrol in 1875," from the diary of Sergt. W.D. Antrobus. Ninth Annual *Scarlet and Gold,* Vancouver, B.C., Royal North West Mounted Police Veterans' Association, n.d. (c. 1927), 44-47; William Silvester, "Whiskey Trader Jerry Potts." *Frontier Times,* Vol. 53, No. 2 (Feb.-Mar. 1979), 10-11, 38-40.

Potts, John, frontiersman (c. 1776-c. 1808). B. at Dillenburg, Germany, he was a miller who joined Lewis and Clark November 24, 1803, accompanying them to the Pacific and return. He was a friend of John Colter's and with Colter accompanied Lisa's 1807 party to the upper Missouri. Charles Clarke says that in 1810 he was a member of Andrew Henry's party to the Three Forks, but Burton Harris wrote that he was killed in 1808. In July 1808 Potts had saved Lisa from a heavy pummeling or perhaps being killed by Edward Rose, but was himself savagely beaten in the process. In the fall, according to Harris, Potts and Colter were trapping in a creek near Jefferson's Fork of the Missouri when they were surprised by Blackfeet. Potts was killed after he slew one of them, and Colter seized and loosed on his famous ordeal in which he escaped naked from the Indians, finally regaining Lisa's Fort.

Burton Harris, *John Colter.* N.Y., Charles Scribner's Sons, 1952; Clarke, *Lewis and Clark.*

Pouriére, Baptiste (Big Bat), scout (July 16, 1843-Sept. 7, 1928). B. at St. Charles, Missouri (one source asserting in 1842), Pouriére was a half-brother of Custer's scout,

Mitch Bouyer, they having the same father, but Bat's mother being a Sioux. His father died when he was 2. Bat left home at 14, went by wagon train to the present site of Casper, Wyoming, arriving in October 1858. He worked for many years hauling wood, trading with Indians, herding horses for freight outfits. He married Josephine Richaud in 1859. In the spring of 1870 he became a scout and interpreter at Fort Laramie. Bat "spent his whole life among the Plains Indians," taking part in the Hayfield Fight, near Fort C.F. Smith, August 1, 1867; Crook's fight on the Rosebud, June 17, 1876; the Sibley Scout, in July of that year, and other affairs. He was called "Big Bat" to distinguish him from "Little Bat" Garnier, with whom he was not related. Crook regarded him as most trustworthy. Vaughn gives Pouriére's version of the Hayfield fight, pp. 236-37 of *Indian Fights*, and of the Rosebud fight, pp 99-100 of *With Crook at the Rosebud*. James Cook said Bat was "a man with a reputation second to none in his particular field, and well known to every old army officer of the seventies." He signed his name Baptiste Pourier, although Vaughn gives it as Pouriére in his last book. Bat died at Manderson South Dakota, on the Pine Ridge Reservation, where he had lived for 40 years. He was survived by his wife.

J.W. Vaughn, *With Crook at the Rosebud.* Harrisburg, Pa., Stackpole Co., 1956; J.W. Vaughn, *The Reynolds Campaign on Powder River.* Norman, Univ. of Okla. Press, 1961; J.W. Vaughn, *Indian Fights: New Facts on Seven Encounters.* Norman, 1966; Pourier, Baptist, death certificate, Pierre, S.D.

Powell, Ambrose, frontiersman (fl. 1750). A member of the Thomas Walker party that officially discovered Cumberland Gap, Powell carved his name on a tree in the most westerly of several long narrow valleys holding the sources of the Tennessee River in southwestern Virginia and northeastern Tennessee. It henceforth was known as Powell's Valley, important because it was a route for Indian war parties traveling north and south, and was crossed by colonials traveling to the western country beyond the Cumberland Mountains by way of Cumberland Gap. Joseph Martin built the first cabin in the valley in 1768.

Reuben Gold Thwaites, Louise Phelps Kellogg, *Documentary History of Dunmore's War 1774.* Madison, Wisc. Hist. Soc., 1905.

Powell, (David) Frank(lin), physician, showman (1847-May 8, 1906). B. in Kentucky of largely Scot descent and one-quarter Seneca, he studied medicine at the University of Louisville and practiced "occasionally" at La Crosse, Wisconsin, where he proved to be "almost a charlatan," lining the stairway to his office with exhibits of his surgery preserved in alcohol. In addition to his practice, he was an expert shot, dealt in Indian remedies and proved a faithful drinking companion to Buffalo Bill Cody. Powell had served at Fort McPherson and North Platte Barracks, Nebraska, as an army contract surgeon, and at times at Fort Laramie and Camp Stambaugh, Wyoming. He is said to have saved a daughter of Rocky Bear, a Sioux, and been given the name of White Beaver; he had claimed membership in the Beaver clan of the Senecas through his mother. In 1876 when he pulled Wee-noo-sheik of the Winnebagos through a serious illness, he became chief medicine man of that tribe, "an asset to him during his years as a physician in Wisconsin." Powell and Cody "were in at least one Indian fight together," when the Winnebagos whom Powell was herding through an 1881 stage appearance at Chicago got drunk and went on a rampage in the green room of Chicago's Olympic Theatre; there were no reported serious casualties. Powell was the hero of some 40 dime novels and associated with Cody in many promotional schemes, including one with Schwatka for a vast colonization effort in Old Mexico; it did not work out, nor did most of the others. He died on an eastbound train near El Paso, Texas, coming from California.

Mary Hardgrove Hebberd, "Notes on Dr. David Franklin Powell, Known as 'White Beaver'." *Wisc. Mag. of Hist.,* Vol. 35, No. 4 (Summer 1952), 306-309; Don Russell, *The Lives and Legends of Buffalo Bill.* Norman, Univ. of Okla. Press, 1960; *New York Times,* May 9, 1906.

Powell, John W., frontiersman (c. 1834-May 7, 1879). B. in Virginia he joined the Isaac Stevens 1853 expedition to Puget Sound from St. Paul, Minnesota. By 1856 he was reported at Salt Lake City and with Fred H. Burr drove a small herd of cattle north to the Bitterroot Valley of present western Montana. In April 1859 he rescued from starvation Boone Helm after Helm's incredible winter lost in the mountains, Powell describing the arrival of Helm at his camp in a letter to Langford. By

1857 Powell was on Gold Creek, northwest of the present Deer Lodge, prospecting a little and following various pursuits of the frontier, being well thought of by the Stuarts and others. He married a Bannock woman and learned her language fluently; living off and on with her people he became involved in hostilities between the Bannocks and the Pend d'Oreilles, Snakes and others. Once when he was captured by Pend d'Oreilles, the Mormons at nearby Fort Lemhi reportedly refused to save him, but he escaped anyway and according to Healy, with his adopted people then made war on the Mormons to the point where they abandoned the Fort Lemhi region; Healy said the Mormons put a price of $1,000 on Powell's head, the reward never collected. To the contrary, Burns said of this incident that Powell had attempted to warn the Mormons of Indian hostility before February 25, 1858, when they attacked Lemhi, killing two Mormons and wounding five; in March the settlement was withdrawn. In 1862 Powell was credited with the discovery of gold on North Boulder River, Montana, although he apparently profited little from it. He lived in the Deer Lodge area for several years. In 1879 Powell, then about 45, was living at Dewey's Flat, 12 miles north of Glendale, Montana, which was a few miles west of the present Melrose. He had a dispute with John Reeder, or Rhoeder, and was shot and killed. Powell was said to have been of good birth and well educated.

Granville Stuart, *Prospecting for Gold*. Lincoln, Univ. of Nebr. Press, 1977; Langford; Robert Ignatius Burns, *The Jesuits and the Indian Wars of the Northwest*. New Haven, Yale Univ. Press, 1966; John Healy's statement, Mont. Hist. Soc.; *Daily Independent*, Helena, May 15, 1879; *Helena Daily Herald*, May 17, 1879.

Powell, John Wesley, explorer, geologist (Mar. 24, 1834-Sept. 23, 1902). B. at Morris, New York, he moved with his parents to Ohio, Wisconsin, and Illinois, settling at Wheaton in the latter state and attending Wheaton College, Oberlin College (Ohio), and Illinois College, Jacksonville, Illinois, but not receiving a degree. He became interested in botany and natural history generally. Powell became an artillery officer in the Civil War, lost his right arm at Shiloh, continued his service and emerged a major. He taught geology at Illinois Wesleyan College, Bloom-

ington, and in 1867 and 1868 took field trips with students across the plains to the Rockies. August 23, 1868, he and six others made the first recorded ascent of Long's Peak, a 14,255-foot landmark of the Colorado Front Range. In 1868 he first observed the canyons of the Colorado and Green rivers in Utah, conceiving the idea of exploring them by boat. May 24, 1869, funded by the Smithsonian Institution and Congress, his group of 11 men and four boats left Green River, Wyoming, and negotiated the Grand Canyon, emerging August 29. One man had quit the expedition early; three others refused to chance the perils of the final rapids, clambered up the sides of the canyon only to be slain by Indians; the remaining members reached the quiet lower Colorado safely. He made a subsequent similar journey in 1871, conducting other explorations in Arizona and Utah in 1874 and 1875. In 1875 he became director of the federal Survey of the Rocky Mountain Region (combined with others to form the U.S. Geological Survey in 1879). In 1879 he became director of the Bureau of American Ethnology by reason of his ethnological investigations along with geological work in the west, holding the ethnological post until his death. In 1881 he became director of the U.S Geological Survey, heading it until his retirement in 1894. Powell wrote *Explorations of the Colorado River of the West and Its Tributaries* (1875), which was enlarged to *Canyons of the Colorado* (1895), and many ethnological papers and other works. His impact in several directions was enduring, and he was a magnetic figure.

Literature abundant; Martin J. Anderson, "John Wesley Powell's Explorations of the Colorado River... Fact, Fiction, or Fantasy?" *Jour. of Ariz. Hist.*, Vol. 24, No.4 (Winter 1983), 363-80. Richard A. Bartlett, *Great Surveys of the American West*, Norman, Univ. of Okla. Press, 1962.

Powell, William Henry, army officer, historian (1838-Nov. 16, 1901). B. at Washington, D.C., he enlisted in the District of Columbia militia in 1861, and was commissioned in the 4th Infantry in October, eventually becoming colonel of the 9th Infantry and retiring in 1899. His writings included professional works and also: *Powell's Records of Living Officers of the United States Army* (1890); *Officers of the Army and Navy (regular) Who Served in the*

Civil War, ed. with Edward Shippen (1892); *Officers of the Army and Navy (volunteer) Who Served in the Civil War,* ed. (1893); *The Fifth Army Corps (Army of the Potomac)* (1896). *List of Officers of the Army of the United States from 1779 to 1900* (1900).
Heitman; Library of Congress Catalogue.

Power, James Buel, engineer, scientific farmer (Aug. 20, 1833-Dec. 16, 1912). B. at Stockport, New York, Power became a civil engineer, moving west with the railroads and reached St. Paul, Minnesota, in 1857. In 1861 he became head of the state land department and 10 years later joined the Northern Pacific Railroad as land commissioner. He accompanied the Custer 1874 expedition to the Black Hills as correspondent for the *St. Paul Press,* and probably in the interests of the railroad. In his official capacities with the Northern Pacific and later with the Great Northern railroad "he was very influential in the settlement of the Northwest." He resigned from the Great Northern about 1887, and removed to his large farm in Richland County, North Dakota, which with his bent for scientific agriculture he made a showplace. He became president of the North Dakota Agricultural College; after retirement he turned full attention to his farm. Greatly interested in Shorthorn cattle, he became a foremost authority on them and one of the nation's largest producers of Shorthorns. He died at his home near Fargo.
Herbert Krause, Gary D. Olson, *Prelude to Glory.* Sioux Falls, S.D., Brevet Press, 1974; *St. Paul Pioneer Press,* Dec. 17, 1912.

Powers, Bill (Joe Evans, Tom Evans), desperado (d. Oct. 5, 1892). B. probably in Texas he is said to have been a wagon boss for the Hashknife outfit of Baylor County, Texas, went to Logan County, Oklahoma, in 1889 to work for Oscar Halsell, whose ranch was a hangout of part-time outlaws. He joined the Dalton-Doolin gang, taking part in train robberies at Wharton (Perry), Oklahoma, May 8, 1891; Wagoner, September 15, 1891; Red Rock, June 1, 1892; Adair, July 14, 1892. He was killed in the Daltons' raid on Coffeyville, Kansas, banks.
Bailey C. Hanes, *Bill Doolin, Outlaw O.T.* Norman, Univ. of Okla. Press, 1968; D.S. Elliott, Ed Bartholomew, *The Dalton Gang and the*

Coffeyville Raid. Fort Davis, Tex., Frontier Book Co., 1968.

Powers, John, soldier (fl. 1876). Sergeant of Company A, 5th Cavalry, he also filed dispatches regularly on military operations against hostile Indians to the *Ellis County* (Kansas) *Star.* In this capacity he sent one of the first accounts of Cody's duel with Yellow Hand, or Yellow Hair, one of the most famous incidents in which Cody participated. It was printed August 3, 1876.
Don Russell, *The Lives and Legends of Buffalo Bill.* Norman, Univ. of Okla. Press, 1960.

Powers, William, frontiersman (Nov. 9, 1765-June 6, 1856). B. in Frederick County, Virginia, he reached the West Fork of the Monongahela River, present West Virginia, in 1781, and early became a prominent scout, enlisting in Captain Joseph Gregory's company of rangers where he served 18 months or more, scouting through half a dozen counties; he became an ensign at length. He was in the pursuit of Indians who in 1785 raided the Thomas Cunningham place, and was with Lowther's party on the Little Kanawha River in 1787, when John Bonnett was killed, taking part in numerous other border incidents. He was well educated for the day and was one of three men who largely wrote and finally brought out Withers' *Chronicles of Border Warfare.* Powers was about 5 feet, 6 inches, in height, well built, spare, light complected with dark hair. He was buried in the Broad Run Cemetery, Lewis County, West Virginia.
Lucullus V. McWhorter, *The Border Settlers of Northwestern Virginia.* Hamilton, O., Republican Pub. Co., 1915.

Poweshiek, Fox chief (c. 1813-c. 1845). Hodge believed it was Poweshiek rather than Keokuk who weakened the fighting power of Black Hawk during the Black Hawk War of 1832. The tie binding Sauks to Foxes had been weakening and when a minor Sauk chief ceded the Rock River country in Illinois without knowledge or consent of his people, the Foxes in disgust crossed the Mississippi to the present Davenport, Iowa where most sat out the war, although hospitably accepting and caring for the survivors. In 1833 he went to Washington, D.C., with Keokuk, Black Hawk and other chiefs to solicit better treatment for their peoples. He died in Kansas or at Des Moines, Iowa, the date uncertain.

Hodge, HAI.

Powhatan (Wahunsonacock), Powhatan Confederacy chief (c. 1547-Apr. 1618). John Smith said Powhatan, as he was known to the Jamestown settlers, was about 60 years of age when he first saw him in 1607 and acquired his popular name from his favorite residence at the falls of the James River (the present Richmond, Virginia). Powhatan's father was driven from the southeast, perhaps Florida, by the Spanish, migrated north and conquered five minor tribes of the Virginia Piedmont; his son, Powhatan in a loose replication of the Philip-Alexander saga, using his father's conquests as a base went on to absorb two dozen or more cognate Algonkin tribes, including some 200 villages which the chief joined in the Powhatan Confederacy. This grouping with some 9,000 people, including 2,400 warriors, confronted the Jamestown settlers in 1607 when the colony was begun, and although periodically driven to hostility by white exactions, without food and resources that the Indians from time to time supplied them the English endeavor would surely have failed. Powhatan was described as "a tall, well proportioned man, with a sower looke; his head somewhat gray, his beard so thinne that it seemeth none at al (and with) a very able and hardy body." He was considered by the colonists to be very cruel, perhaps as cruel as the English, but he also had ingratiating qualities and was a man of reason and good sense. In 1609 he was "crowned" with "royal" appurtances brought from England to impress and make subject the supposedly rude savage chieftain, but Powhatan was suspicious and insisted that as a "king" he was fully the equal of the English monarch and would be subject to no one. He would not kneel to receive the crown and two or three strong men were required to make him "stoope a little," when the crown was placed on his head, the ceremony completed. The next year the colonists tried to capture him, duplicity being more in their nature than in his. Continual demands of the English that he feed the interlopers, or colonists, irritated him, and minor hostilities developed, ceasing only when his beloved daughter, Pocahontas who had been captured by the English, was married in 1614 to John Rolfe. Then Powhatan and the whites arranged a peace that lasted until the chief's death. Upon this event in 1618, the succession was left to his brother, Opitchapan, but he soon was superceded by a younger brother, Opechancanough, who had become bitterly hostile by English mistreatment, his hatred of the whites culminating in disastrous warfare. Powhatan's Confederacy was an interesting development in Indian political evolution and made him the most powerful chieftain on the east coast south of the Iroquois.

Hodge, HAI; CE; Dockstader; REAW; DAB; John Smith, *The Generall Historie of Virginia, New-England, and the Summer Isles.* Ann Arbor, Mich. Readex Microprint, 1966.

Pratt, Parley Parker, Mormon official (Apr. 12, 1807-May 13, 1857). B. at Burlington, New York, he joined the Mormon sect in 1830; was ordained an apostle in 1835. He engaged in missions to Independence, Missouri, and to Canada, taking part in troubles between the Mormons and Missourians and being jailed on murder charges, although he escaped custody on July 4, 1839. He served missions in England, wrote nearly 50 hymns for the faithful of his sect, and reached Utah with its migration September 28, 1847, traveling first with the John Taylor company, then with the Perrigrine Sessions Company. In Utah Pratt was active in political and other public matters, and undertook a spectacular but not very rewarding mission to Chile. He was said to have been the first of the Mormons to explore southern Utah, charting the routes of later throughways in that country, was in charge of the first Indian mission, and was considered by many of his faith "a man mighty in the work of God." In non-Mormon accounts he is evaluated differently: one legend charges he attempted to trade one of his twelve or more wives to an Indian chief for ten horses. On a trip to Arkansas he made a convert of the wife of one, Hector H. McLean; she left her husband and went with Pratt. McLean then accosted him eight miles from Van Buren, Arkansas, and killed him. "Though to the church it was martyrdom, local public opinion was so strongly in sympathy with the murderer that he was not held."

Juanita Brooks, *The Mountain Meadows Massacre.* Norman, Univ. of Okla. Press, 1966; William Wise, *Massacre at Mountain Meadows.* N.Y., Thomas Y. Crowell Co., 1976; Frank Esshom, *Pioneers and Prominent Men of Utah.* Salt Lake City, Western Epics, 1966; DAB.

Pratte, Sylvester S., fur trader (Sept. 22, 1799-Oct. 1, 1827). B. at St. Louis, he may have been introduced to the fur business in one of his father's companies. He was a licensed trader on the Missouri in 1820. In 1824 he led traders to the James River, South Dakota, where they wintered. Pratte led an expedition to New Mexico in 1825, accompanied by the Patties and others, and by early 1826 was at Taos. His men trapped widely through the southern Rockies, occasionally experiencing difficulties with the Spanish when they sought to bring their furs to Santa Fe and vicinity. In the fall of 1827 Pratte led 36 trappers toward the Green River country, but died in North Park, Colorado. He was the major entrepreneur of the Taos fur business in his time, the expeditions he sent out being numerous and later-famed, but Pratte seems not to have been very competent, although he was well liked.

David J. Weber, *The Taos Trappers: The Fur Trade in the Far Southwest, 1540-1846.* Norman, Univ. of Okla. Press, 1971; Weber article, MM, Vol. VI.

Preece, Thomas William (Billy), lawman (Feb. 11, 1856-Feb. 2, 1928). B. at Salt Lake City, Utah, he worked on the Uintah Ute Indian reservation as a young man and freighted for merchants between Vernal, Utah and Rock Springs, Wyoming. He was elected sheriff of Uintah County, Utah, in 1896. He often came into confrontations with the Wild Bunch members whose Brown's Hole hangouts were not too distant from Vernal. He was instrumental in the capture of Harry Tracy, David Lant and Patrick Johnson following the slaying by Johnson of Willie Strang and shooting by Tracy of rancher Valentine Hoy in March 1898. Preece on April 17, 1900, shot and killed a rustler identified as George (Flat Nose) Curry, although there was some dispute over identity of the victim. Preece continued as sheriff until 1906. In 1909 he became a deputy U.S. marshal at Whiterocks, Utah. Later he served as city marshal at Vernal. During World War I as an excellent judge of horses he purchased animals for the British government military effort. Preece died of dropsy and was buried at Rock Point Cemetery in Ashley Valley, near Vernal. He was married, fathered five children, and was described as 5 feet, 9 inches in height and "a little on the heavy side."

Edward M. Kirby, Mary C. Preece, "Billy Preece: Frontier Lawman." *Real West,* Vol. 22, No. 164 (July 1979), 8-12, 60.

Prescott, Philander, pioneer (Sept. 17, 1801-Aug. 18, 1862). B. at Phelpstown, Ontario County, New York, he reached Fort Snelling in 1819 and remained in Minnesota most of the rest of his life. He married a Sioux woman, daughter of Kee-e-he-ie, a Mdewakanton, became fluent in Dakota and served occasionally as interpreter and translator. During the winter of 1824-25 he traded with Indians near Snelling and for three years worked for the Columbia Fur Company, spending a brief time in Louisiana but soon returning to Minnesota. Indian agent Taliaferro hired him to open a model farm for Indians at Lake Calhoun and he later became head farmer for three bands. In 1849 he laid out Prescott, near the confluence of the Mississippi and St. Croix rivers, and resided there and at Fort Snelling alternately until late in life. He was assassinated the first day of the Sioux uprising at the Lower, or Redwood Agency, initial point of attack. He had been regarded, by Indians and whites alike, a good friend of the natives.

William H.C. Folsom, *Fifty Years in the Northwest.* St. Paul, Pioneer Press Co., 1888, 214; Edward Duffield Neill, *History of Minnesota.* Minneapolis, Minn. Hist. Co., 1882, 737n.; Roy W. Meyer, *History of the Santee Sioux.* Lincoln, Univ. of Nebr. Press, 1967; *The Recollections of Philander Prescott.* Lincoln, Univ. of Nebr. Press, 1966.

Preston, William, frontiersman (Dec. 25, 1729-June 28, 1783). b. in North Ireland, his parents brought him while still a child to Augusta County, Virginia, where he was educated under care of a Presbyterian clergyman. Preston was secretary in 1751 to treaty commissioners at the important trading center of Logstown, on the Ohio River below the Forks, where a council was held with delegations from the Iroquois, Delawares, Shawnees, Hurons and Miamis. During the French and Indian War he led Rangers, serving on the 1756 Sandy Creek expedition. Preston held various public offices including that of sheriff in Augusta and Botetourt counties, Virginia. In 1773 he migrated to Draper's Meadows (the present Smithfield, Virginia) where he was commissioned county-lieutenant and took charge of frontier defense; for family reasons he could not participate in the 1774 Point Pleasant engagement with Indians, though "his services were equally important with those of the acting officers." During the Revolution he continued to protect the frontier. He defeated a 1780 Loyalist plot and sent efficient aid to the King's Mountain expedition. He led a regiment at Whitsell's Mills, March 6, 1781, where his life was saved by a neighbor and friend, Joseph Cloyd. Preston died at a regimental muster. He was described as tall, finely proportioned, with fair hair and blue eyes, easy and graceful manners, his intellect strong and well-cultivated. He left his widow and 11 children.

Reuben Gold Thwaites, Louise Phelps Kellogg, eds., *Documentary History of Dunmore's War 1774.* Madison, Wisc. Hist. Soc., 1905.

Prewitt, John and William, pioneers (d. Sept. 11, 1857). John Prewitt (b. c. 1837) and William (c. 1838), from Marion County, Arkansas, were brothers who joined the Fancher emigrant wagon train at Fort Smith, Arkansas, leaving late in March for California. With all members of the company save the infants, the Prewitts were murdered at Mountain Meadows, Utah by Mormons and Mormon-led Indians.

William Wise, *Massacre at Mountain Meadows.* N.Y., Thomas Y. Crowell Co., 1976.

Price, George Frederic, army officer (c. 1839-May 23, 1888). B. at New York City, he removed at an early age to California where he entered business. He was commissioned a first lieutenant in the 2nd California Cavalry September 3, 1861, and by November was captain of M Company. In May 1862, he commanded an expedition to the Truckee River of Nevada, seeking peace with Winnemucca of the Paiute Indians, then reconnoitred the east face of the Sierra Nevada Mountains. In the late summer he moved on to Utah, taking part in an expedition against the Shoshones on Bear River in January 1863 under General Patrick Edward Connor; this major engagement resulted in more than 224 Indian deaths, and 142 soldier casualties, including 14 killed outright, eight who died of wounds, 41 other wounded and 79 soldiers incapacitated by frostbite or other natural hazards. Price was commended in orders and

reports for courage and determination displayed at Bear River, for conspicuous gallantry in a fight at Spanish Fork Canyon, and he took part also in three fights at Cedar Fort. He was assigned to command at Fort Bridger, participating in the capture of Mopocha's Shoshone band near the Wind River Mountains. In the summer of 1864 he made a wagon road reconnaissance from Salt Lake City to El Dorado Canyon on the Colorado River, enroute rebuilding the monument erected by a previous military party at the site of the 1857 Mountain Meadows Massacre; the original monument had been torn down by Mormons, and a like fate awaited the one Price rebuilt. In March 1865, Price was named acting assistant inspector-general and acting assistant adjutant general of the military district of the Plains, serving in like capacities subsequently in the districts of Nebraska and Utah. February 23, 1866, Price was commissioned second lieutenant of the 5th U.S. Cavalry and served in the east until January 1869 when as a first lieutenant he was assigned to Fort Harker, Kansas; in April he fought Sioux and Cheyennes at Beaver and Spring creeks, participated in the Republican River expedition, for which he was adjutant, and was recommended for a brevet for his part in the decisive action at Summit Springs, July 11, 1869, against the Cheyennes. Price took a creditable part in several other Plains Indian affairs. He reached Arizona in late spring 1872, was promoted to captain, and participated in the Apache campaigns of 1872-73, taking part in a number of engagements. In June 1873, he commenced a reconnaissance and construction of a military telegraph line from San Diego to Prescott and Tucson, completing it, the first telegraph line in Arizona, by December. Price was on the 1876 Big Horn and Yellowstone Expedition and in the engagement at Slim Buttes, Dakota; he participated in the Wind River expedition against the Nez Perces in 1877. He served at a variety of Wyoming and other western posts, and in diverse duties, many of interest, until October 1, 1882, when he was assigned to New York City. He is best known, historically, for his major history of the 5th Cavalry (1883, rep. 1959), which remains a standard reference work.

Price, *Fifth Cavalry;* Orton; LeRoy R. and Ann W. Hafen, *Powder River Campaigns and Sawyers*

Expedition of 1865. Glendale, Calif., Arthur H. Clark Co., 1961; California State Archives.

Price, Hiram, Indian commissioner (Jan. 10, 1814-May 30, 1901). B. in Washington County, Pennsylvania, he became an Iowa merchant, served three terms in Congress, and was Commissioner of Indian Affairs from 1881-85. He died at Washington, D.C., and was buried at Davenport, Iowa.

DAB; BDAC.

Price, Jessie, prospector (d. July 1858). From Cache Creek, Yolo County, California, Price, with Evans and Thurley, was killed by Indians on the Okanagan River, British Columbia, near the U.S. line. The trio were of a party commanded by James McLoughlin, making for the Fraser River placers.

San Francisco, Calif., *Evening Bulletin,* Aug. 27, 1858; Bancroft, *British Columbia,* which calls this individual Rice.

Price, John Erwin, frontiersman (Aug. 11, 1857-July 31, 1928). B. in Tennessee of wealthy parents, he was educated in Germany and reached the later Shakespeare, New Mexico, a booming mining camp, by 1876, where he was junior member of a mercantile firm and division superintendent of the National Mail and Transportation Company. When the Shakespeare Guards were formed August 8, 1879, Price was named captain; the organization, composed of 32 enlisted men and expanded to include eventually more than 70, being Company C, and later Company F of the New Mexico Territorial Militia, was disbanded in 1885. Its purpose was to protect the camp against Apaches, which was unnecessary, and to fight any hostiles who came close enough, but none did. Price was described by Williams, his good friend, as "of an athletic build, and his countenance was a ruddy blond under a crown of beautiful golden-red hair... I have heard a Mexican helper describe him (as) El Dorado, 'the Gilded One'." Price later headed a railroad survey party from the Gulf of California to El Paso, was a utility operator in Jefferson City, Missouri, an irrigation developer in Colorado, and a Seattle banker, founding the Marine National Bank. He died at Seattle.

Williams; *Service Record of Men and Women of Hidalgo County.* Lordsburg, N.M., VFW Post 3099, n.d. (c. 1949), photograph of Price on p. 120;

Price death certificate, Olympia, Wash.; Emma M. Muir, "The First Militia," *New Mex. Mag.,* Vol. 30, No. 10 (Oct. 1952), 19, 41, 44-46.

Price, William Redwood, army officer (May 20, 1838-Dec. 30, 1881). B. at Cincinnati, Ohio, he was educated as a civil engineer. Commissioned a second lieutenant in the 3rd Pennsylvania Cavalry January 15, 1862, he emerged from the Civil War a major and brevet Brigadier General of Volunteers. He was commissioned a major of the 8th U.S. Cavalry July 28, 1866, and commanded much of northwestern Arizona and the eastern Mojave Desert of California and Nevada from 1867 until 1870. Price had overall direction of the so-called Hualapais War of 1867-68 as a result of which the nomadic bands of Hualapais Indians were subdued and brought onto a reservation. He was breveted colonel in the army for operations December 10 and 13, 1868, in the Aquarius Mountains of Arizona. Price was transferred to Fort Bayard, New Mexico, and led a scout against Mescalero stock thieves that initially reached Fort Stanton, New Mexico, in September, Price then holding unwilling hostage numerous Mescaleros until stolen stock should be turned over. Rather, those Mescaleros he was unable to gather dispersed in several bands, and rustling increased. Price sent out several small expeditions and himself took a command south on the trail of thieves into the Guadalupe Mountains of West Texas; he found much sign, but saw no enemy. For about a year Price commanded a "movable column" roving New Mexico and intended to police the Mimbres Apache country as well as that of other bands. During this work, which was not wholly ineffective, he added to military knowledge of the country, charted wagon roads, mapped and acquired useful information. In the summer of 1874 Price was ordered east from Fort Bascom, New Mexico, with a battalion of the 8th Cavalry to take part in Miles's Red River campaign which was to include several other columns as well. He set out August 28, met Miles in Texas September 7 and moved northeast toward the Washita. September 12 he had a fight with Kiowas and Comanches, reporting two Indians killed and six wounded. The next day his column, now acting as escort for a wagon supply, encountered the survivors of the noted Buffalo Wallow fight, almost all wounded, out of ammunition and confined to their protecting depression in the prairie. Price directed his surgeon to see to them; his men gave them raw buffalo meat, their own rations having given out, but Price left them no detail for defense, no arms with ammunition, told them he would inform Miles of their plight, and moved on. Miles, when he heard of it "severely censured Price," according to Haley, ordered the men rescued at once and recommended each for a Medal of Honor. Price's own report explains to some extent his extraordinary conduct: "The suffering of these men was extreme and their condition fearful... I detailed (Second) Lieutenant (Alfred Hibbard) Rogers and Co. 'C' to go back and notify General Miles' command of their condition, and to get an ambulance forward to their relief as soon as possible. They could not have survived the exposure of another night... An ambulance reached them and they were made comfortable between 10 and 11 o'clock that night." He might have detailed half of C Company to remain as protectors and to give them what assistance was possible, but this was not done. For what he believed Price's general incompetence, Miles assumed command of Price's four companies. After uneventful skirmishes with hostiles he again suspected Price of dereliction, placed him in arrest and planned to prefer charges against him, but if he did, nothing came of them. Price became a lieutenant colonel of the 6th Cavalry April 2, 1879, and soon was in Arizona again. Following the Cibecue affair in August 1881 he was named commander of the District of the Verde and in September was ordered to scout the Cibecue country seeking traces of the mutinous scouts who had attacked Carr's command earlier. He had with him Indian trailers under Dan O'Leary and Al Sieber, two of the best chiefs of scouts in the business, guaranteeing that the job would be thoroughly done. He found that the hostiles had drifted back to San Carlos Agency or had lost themselves in the forested back country and were unreachable. Price was forced to terminate his activities by illness October 16 and little more than two months later died at the age of 43.

Heitman; Dennis G. Casebier, *Camp Beale's Springs and the Hualpai Indians.* Norco, Calif., Tales of Mojave Pub. Co., 1980; Dan L. Thrapp, *Conquest of Apacheria.* Norman, Univ. of Okla. Press, 1967; Thrapp, *Victorio and the Mimbres*

Apaches. Norman, 1974; Lawrence L. Mehren, "Scouting for Mescaleros: the Price Campaign of 1873." *Arizona and the West,* Vol. 10, No. 2 (Summer 1968), 171-90; James L. Haley, *The Buffalo War.* Garden City, N.Y. Doubleday and Co., 1976; Ernest Wallace, ed., *Ranald S. Mackenzie's Official Correspondence...1873-1879.* Lubbock, West Tex. Mus. Assn., 1968; Thrapp, *General Crook and the Sierra Madre Adventure.* Norman, 1972.

Prigmore, Benjamin, frontiersman (fl. 1837). Prigmore was one of 18 whites who treacherously attacked the Mimbres Apache leader, Juan José Compá, on April 22, 1837 in the Animas Mountains of present New Mexico, slaying 20 and igniting extended Apache-white hostilities.

Rex W. Strickland, "The Birth and Death of a Legend: the Johnson 'Massacre' of 1837." *Arizona and the West,* Vol. 18, No. 3 (Autumn 1976), 257-86.

Primeau, Charles, frontiersman (1811-1897). B. at St Louis, he went up the Missouri River in 1831 as clerk for the American Fur Company at Fort Union. From 1846 until 1860 he was in a fur trade partnership with Alexander Harvey. He married a Sioux woman and died at Fort Yates, North Dakota.

Montana, Contributions, Vol. X, 1940, 305.

Primus, black partisan (fl. 1836-1841). A slave to Erastus Rogers, sutler at Fort King, Florida, he had a black wife among the Seminoles and early came to be fluent in that language as well as English. Rogers was killed in the Wiley Thompson assassination in late 1835, and white commanders used Primus to gather information from the Seminole camps. He was among the hostiles at the siege of Camp Izard in March 1836, bringing his talent for counting and simple mathematics to the use of the Indians. He was sent by the whites to spy on Seminoles collecting on the Withlacochee River, and remained among them, by choice or some form of imprisonment. Creek allies of the whites captured him and 60 other blacks in January 1837 near the Ocklawaha River, Primus reporting to Jesup that Osceola, a Seminole leader, was "on the Withlacoochee, sick, and that he can collect about a hundred warriors." After his capture by the Creeks, Primus became "a faithful interpreter" and his services seem to have been rewarded with freedom. He accompanied some band of Seminoles to Indian Territory where he served as interpreter on various occasions in 1841, but nothing is reported about his later years.

Kenneth W. Porter, "Negro Guides and Interpreters in the Early Stages of the Seminole War." *Jour. of Negro Hist.,* Vol. XXXV, No. 2 (Apr. 1950), 174-82.

Pring, Martin, explorer (c. 1580-1626). B. at Awliscombe, Devonshire, he may have made a 1601 reconnaissance voyage to search for the lost Roanoke settlement off North Carolina and possibly accompanied by John White (see entry), erstwhile governor of the vanished colony, but proof is lacking. Pring sailed from England April 10, 1603, in command of the *Speedwell* and *Discovery* and explored the southern Maine coast and Cape Cod, landing at Plymouth Harbor, Massachusetts, and returning to Bristol by October 2. In 1606 he touched the coast of Virginia. The rest of his life was active on many seas, but has little American frontier interest. He died at Bristol, leaving his widow and six children.

DAB; *Handbook of Indians,* 15; Paul Hulton, *America 1585: The Complete Drawings of John White,* Chapel Hill, Univ. of No. Car. Press and British Mus. Pubns., 1984, p. 16.

Pringle, John, frontiersman (c. 1728-post 1780). B. perhaps in Philadelphia, John and his brother, Samuel, were British soldiers at Fort Pitt, from which they deserted with two others in 1761, fleeing to the trans-Allegheny region of Virginia; their companions were captured, but the Pringles were employed in the wilderness by John Simpson, a trapper. The Pringles reached the Buckhannon River in 1764, taking up residence in a hollow sycamore tree until late in 1767 when, their ammunition giving out, John made his way to the eastern settlements for more. There he learned that peace had been made with the French, the brothers being free to return home. John subsequently removed to Kentucky, reportedly settling near Chaplin's Fork. He once encountered a band of Simon Girty-led Shawnees while with a convoy of three boats on the Ohio River; Pringle's craft alone escaped. Pringle married John Simpson's sister, Rebecca; some of his sons served in the War of 1812.

Lucullus V. McWhorter, *The Border Settlers of Northwestern Virginia.* Hamilton, O., Republican Pub. Co., 1915.

Pringle, Samuel, frontiersman (1731-post 1780). B. probably in Philadelphia, he and his brother served the British at Fort Pitt until they deserted in 1761 and fled to the trans-Allegheny region of Virginia, where they joined John Simpson, a trapper, and remained aloof from the settlements for about six years. They became the first known white men to enter the Buckhannon Valley of present West Virginia, as they also became the first settlers there. Learning that peace with the French had come, they returned to civilization, but came back to the Buckhannon River country about 1769 with a party that included Jesse Hughes and others. Samuel settled permanently in that area and became prominent in the border wars, being somewhat educated, energetic, a persistent scout and ruthless toward Indians. Among the incidents in which he figured was the slaughter of 13 probably Shawnee Indians living peacefully at Indian Camp Rock in the Buckhannon country about 1772. During the Revolution Pringle was captain of a company of rangers and scouts. He married Charity Cutright, sister of John Cutright Jr., of border fame.

Lucullus V. McWhorter, *The Border Settlers of Northwestern Virginia.* Hamilton, O., Republican Pub. Co., 1915.

Prophet (Sauk and Fox): *see* Wabokieshiek.

Prouville de Tracy, Alexandre de, French officer (c. 1603-Apr. 28, 1670). B. at Amiens in the cited year according to some authorities, c. 1596 in the view of the *Dictionary of Canadian Biography,* or 1601 as Parkman believed, the Marquis de Tracy was a professional soldier, a Lieutenant General of distinguished record when he was named to command troops in French Canada in 1663. He arrived at Quebec June 30, 1665, all but prostrated by fever he had contracted perhaps during Guiana service. His primary mission was to settle the Iroquois problem by war if he must, the fierce tribe not only persistently massacring the French settlers, but also diverting the rich fur trade to the English of New York. A complete Infantry regiment, the Carignan-Salieres, reached Canada that summer, quickly commencing the building of a chain of forts up the Richelieu River from the St. Lawrence to Lake Champlain. The

Iroquois, frightened by such military preparations, sent a peace tentative, but Tracy had no confidence in it; during the winter he dispatched Governor Remy de Courcelle to ravage the Mohawk River valley in present New York State, but the expedition was a virtual failure. Renewed Mohawk peace initiatives failed to convince Tracy and September 14, 1666, his expedition got under way, 600 regulars, 600 militia and 100 Indians, the whole to rendezvous September 28 at Fort Ste. Anne at the northern end of Lake Champlain. The expedition left the fort October 3 and despite hardships reached four Mohawk villages, all deserted; they were looted and burned, the land formally claimed for Louis XIV. In view of the advanced season Tracy withdrew to Canada but not without considerable difficulty due to vile weather, lack of supplies and other problems. He reached Quebec November 5. To impress the Iroquois further, Tracy hanged a prisoner and sent several from each tribe of the Five Nations back to their people to reveal to them his power and resolution. Tracy's expedition had lasting salutary effects upon the Iroquois. He left Canada August 28, 1667, after impressing everyone with his qualities: his intelligence, his martial skill, his generosity and his piety. Married twice, his only son was killed on active duty with the Army in Europe. Tracy died at Paris.

Thwaites, JR, XLIX, 274nll; DCB; Parkman, *Old Regime in Canada.*

Provost, Etienne, fur trader (1785-July 3, 1850). B. in Quebec, he was a member of the Chouteau-DeMun trading operations to the Rocky Mountains in 1815-17. The men were captured and taken to Sante Fe, imprisoned briefly, their furs confiscated, whereafter they returned to Missouri. Provost went back to New Mexico probably by 1823. The next year he worked the Green River, and crossed the Wasatch Mountains to the Great Basin, escaping a Snake Indian massacre that accounted for all but three or four of his 15-man party. After wintering on the Green, Provost contacted Ogden's party on the Weber River, present Utah, then met Ashley, traded briefly with the Utes, and attended the first rendezvous on Henry's Fork of the Green River. Provost returned to St. Louis in 1826. He went to the upper Rockies with the American Fur Company in 1828, returned to

St. Louis in 1829, and by the winter of 1829-30 was back in the Crow country. He made a number of trips between the mountains and St. Louis in the decades of the 1830s and 1840s, his final trip in 1848. He was associated at times with Thomas Fitzpatrick, William Drummond Stewart, John James Audubon and other luminaries, a man of much influence among white men and red, highly respected and well paid. Provost was "a legendary figure in his own lifetime." After him, Provo, Utah, was named.

LeRoy R. Hafen article, MM, Vol. VI; Dale L. Morgan, ed., *The West of William H. Ashley... 1822-1838.* Denver, Old West Pub. Co.,1964.

Prowers, John Wesley, frontiersman (Jan. 29, 1839-Feb. 14, 1884). B. near Westport, Missouri, he crossed the Plains at 18 in 1856 or 1857 with Indian Agent Robert C. Miller and entered William Bent's employ as clerk. In 1861 he married Amache Ochinee, 15, daughter of One Eye, Cheyenne subchief (killed at Sand Creek November 29, 1864) and became respected by Cheyennes and whites alike, learning enough of the language to serve occasionally as interpreter. That year he bought 600 head of Missouri cattle and drove them to Colorado, the first such transfer of eastern cattle to the Territory. In 1863 he bought land across from Fort Lyon, Colorado, enlarging his ranching operation to include herding government cattle, horses and mules. Because of Prowers' ties with the Cheyennes, Chivington directed Captain Samuel H. Cook to guard the ranch and allow no one to enter or leave until his contemplated attack on Sand Creek Cheyennes and Arapahoes. Prowers was a witness before the Tappan commission investigating Sand Creek, because of his experience giving background information on the Indians and their relationships with the whites. Prowers settled as a rancher near Las Animas, Colorado. He became ill late in 1883 and was taken to Kansas City, Missouri, where he died.

Portrait and Biographical Record of the State of Colorado. Chicago, Chapman Pub. Co., 1899; *Sand Creek Massacre;* Stan Hoig, *The Sand Creek Massacre.* Norman, Univ. of Okla. Press, 1974; *Colorado Livestock Record,* Denver, Col. 1, No.3 (Feb. 15, 1884).

Prudhomme, Gabriel, interpreter (d. Jan. 15,

1856). A French half-breed, he was a son of Gabriel Prudhomme who served with Ogden in 1824-25, and who settled near the mouth of the Kansas River in 1831, his 257-acre estate being the site of Westport Landing, the later genesis of Kansas City though Prudhomme was killed in a brawl with a fellow Canadian late in October or early November 1831. Young Gabriel was living among the Flatheads when Father De Smet arrived at Pierre's Hole in 1840 and secured his services as interpreter. He later was guide and interpreter for the Jesuits of St Mary's Mission, Montana, located in the Bitterroot Valley. Prudhomme accompanied De Smet east in 1846. He was an early trader, guide and interpreter out of Fort Hall, Idaho, and along the Overland Trail. In 1853 he was hired by John Mullan as not only interpreter but invaluable source of information about the surrounding country and its people. During the winter of 1853-54 Prudhomme was principal guide for Mullan on various expeditions. He died at Fort Owen, Montana.

George F. Weisel, *Men and Trade on the Northwest Frontier.* Missoula, Mont. State Univ. Press, 1955; Dale L. Morgan, *The West of William H. Ashley.* Denver, Old West Pub. Co., 1965; Barry, *Beginning of the West.*

Prud'homme, Pierre, explorer (1658-1703). B. probably at Montreal, he accompanied La Salle on a trip down the Mississippi River. A few leagues below the mouth of the Ohio Prud'homme lost his way in the woods, La Salle feared he had been killed by Indians and named a rocky prominence Fort Prud'homme after him; La Salle fortified his party on the site, believing that he would be attacked by Indians, an event that did not materialize. In 1683 La Salle gave Prud'homme a grant of land in fief in Illinois.

Thwaites, JR, LXV, 111-13; DCB, I 557.

Pryor, Nathaniel, frontiersman (c. 1772-June 1, 1831). B. in Virginia, he was a member of the Lewis and Clark expedition as sergeant, leaving St. Louis May 14, 1804, and returning September 23, 1806. Pryor was praised by the commanders for his work. In 1807, as ensign, he and his men escorted the Mandan chief, Sha-ha-ka from St. Louis toward their villages, but the Arikaras defeated and drove them back down the river. Pryor resigned from the army a second lieutenant in 1810,

traded with the Winnebagos, but in 1813 had a narrow escape from a Winnebago attack. Pryor, as a captain, fought with Jackson at New Orleans, then traded with the Osages on the lower Arkansas River. He served briefly as sub agent for the Arkansas Osages in 1830 and died at his post. Pryor, Oklahoma, is named for him.

Raymond W. Settle article, MM, Vol. II; Heitman; Charles G. Clarke, *Lewis and CLark.*

Pryor, Nathaniel Miguel, trapper (1798-1850). B. in Kentucky near the later Louisville, his relationship to Nathaniel Pryor is unknown. He joined the Glenn-Fowler party up the Arkansas River in 1821, then trapped in the Sangre de Cristo Mountains under Slover and later probably in the San Luis Valley on the upper Rio Grande; he apparently then returned to the states. In 1825 in company with three others he again set out for the mountains on a trapping expedition, spending some time in Santa Fe, accompanied the Patties to California and with them was arrested. He later worked for the San Luis Rey Mission, lived in Los Angeles from 1830, hunted sea otter, took part with the Americans against the Mexicans in 1846, and died at Los Angeles.

Raymond W. Settle article, MM, Vol. II; Bancroft, *Register of Pioneer Inhabitants of California.* Los Angeles, Dawson's Book Shop, 1964.

Pullman, John Wesley, army officer (Feb. 17, 1846-Sept. 14, 1922). B. in Michigan, he was appointed to West Point from Washington Territory, upon graduation being assigned in 1869 to the 8th Cavalry and becoming a first lieutenant in 1873. With the 8th he saw some frontier service in West Texas and perhaps New Mexico, but in 1884 he became regimental quartermaster and the rest of his service was in the Quartermaster Corps. He retired February 17, 1910, as a colonel and died at Fort Leavenworth.

Carlysle Graham Raht, *The Romance of Davis Mountains and Big Bend Country.* El Paso, Rahtbooks Co., 1919; Heitman; Cullum.

Pumpelly, Raphael, geologist, miner (Sept. 8, 1837-Aug. 10, 1923). B. at Oswego, New York, he studied science and mining engineering at Paris and Freiberg, Saxony, and conducted a geological expedition to Corsica.

In 1860 he went to Arizona, and was in charge of mines there until 1861; his writings are valuable primary sources on frontier conditions and Indian affairs as well as mining in the southern Arizona district. Pumpelly conducted scientific explorations for the Japanese government in 1861-63, led private geological expeditions through China and Mongolia in 1863-64, was in Siberia in 1864-65. He was professor of mining at Harvard from 1866-73, during which he was state geologist for Michigan in 1869-71 and director of the Missouri geological survey in 1871-73. He had charge of the New England division of the U.S. Geological Survey from 1879-81; directed the Northern Transcontinental Survey in 1881-84; and led the development of iron ore ranges in Michigan and western Ontario, and conducted an expedition to central Asia in 1903-1904. "His reputation as a mining geologist rests chiefly on his work in association with Thomas B. Brooks in the copper and iron districts of Michigan and the Lake Superior area." His writings include: *Across America and Asia* (1870); *Reminiscenes* (1918), and *Adventures of Raphael Pumpelly* (1920). He died at Newport, Rhode Island.

Who Was Who; DAB; CE; Pumpelly's writings; *Pumpelly's Arizona* ..., ed., intr., by Andrew Wallace. Tucson, Palo Verde Press, 1965.

Purington, George Augustus, army officer (July 21, 1837-May 31, 1896). B. at Athens, Ohio, he enlisted in the 19th Ohio Infantry, serving in the Potomac theater and by war's end was a brevet colonel of the 2nd Ohio Cavalry. He became a captain in the 9th Cavalry in 1866, serving with that regiment until 1883. In 1877-78, Purington, in command at Fort Stanton, New Mexico, notified his superior of the outbreak of the so-called Lincoln County War and was directed to support civil authorities in the conduct of their duties, but so confused was the situation by various factions, that Purington decided all he could do was protect women and children. He notified leaders of the factions that if they were "spoiling for a fight," they could "withdraw to the mountains and fight to their hearts' content." Directed to support Sheriff Brady's faction, Purington thereafter appeared to lean toward the Murphy-Dolan party, but probably had no alternative; he was active at several points in the "war." In August

1879, Purington reported to Colonel Hatch the bolt of Victorio from the Mescalero Reservation and start of the long drawn-out Victorio War. Purington engaged the Victorio Apaches at Lake Guzman, Chihuahua, Rio Puerco, San Mateo Mountains, San Andres Mountains, the Mescalero Agency and near Dog Canyon, all in New Mexico. In 1882 he was "in the field" in Colorado. With the 3rd Cavalry, which he joined as a major in 1883, he commanded Fort Thomas, Arizona, and Forts Stockton, Ringgold and McIntosh, Texas. He retired July 17, 1895, because of an illness which had plagued him for years, and died at Metropolis, Illinois. In the interval he had ranched in the Big Bend country of Texas. Purington was 6 feet, 2 inches in height, weighed over 200 pounds, and had snow-white hair during much of his mature life.

Robert N. Mullin notes; Philip J. Rasch, "The Men at Fort Stanton." English Westerners' *Brand Book,* No. 3, Apr. 1961, 5-6; Dan L. Thrapp, *Victorio and the Mimbres Apaches.* Norman, Univ. of Okla. Press, 1974.

Pursley, James, frontiersman (c. 1765-c. 1850). B. in Cumberland County, Pennsylvania, he joined the militia in 1780, becoming a scout and ranger. He moved to Bardstown, Kentucky, by 1792, and St. Louis in 1799, making an extended hunting trip southwesterly, then turned north and reached the Mandan villages with a trader, Regis Loisel, in 1803. Sent to trade with the Kiowas and Pawnees, he and two others were driven by Sioux into South Park, Colorado. In June 1805, they reached Santa Fe. Pursley remained in New Mexico until 1823, returned to Missouri and went back to New Mexico with trade goods, some of which he took to Chihuahua and Sonora, where he settled as a citizen of Mexico. He probably made his home at Oposura (Moctezuma), Sonora; his only son was killed by Apaches about 1848.

Janet Lecompte article, MM, Vol. VIII.

Pushmataha, Choctaw chief (c. 1765-Dec. 23 or 24, 1824). B. probably in Noxubee County, Mississippi, he early achieved notice for his roles in tribal warfare along the Mississippi, although never against the whites. He was elected chief in 1805, signed a treaty and settled near Meridian, Mississippi. The treaty provided for a major land cession in return for paltry payments to himself. When Tecumseh came south in 1811 to raise support for his confederacy, the Choctaws and some others objected to his idea of alliance with Britain. Pushmataha followed Tecumseh from camp to camp, arguing against the Shawnee's pleas, and effectively nullifying, to some degree, his mission. In the War of 1812 and accompanying white campaigns against the Creeks and other Indians, Pushmataha persuaded the Choctaws to join with the United States forces. He led a band of 500 in the Andrew Jackson forces. Afterward he signed treaties of cession in 1816 and 1820. In 1824 he visited Washington, met Lafayette, but suffering from heavy drinking and exposure to inclement weather he died about midnight of the 23-24 of December, and was buried in the Congressional Cemetery. He was about 5 feet, 9 or 10 inches tall and of portly build, fond of alcohol and probably did more for the whites than for his own people.

DAB; H.S. Halbert, T.H. Ball, *The Creek War of 1813 and 1814.* Univ. of Ala. Press, 1969; *Indian Treaties: 1778-1883,* comp. and ed. by Charles J. Kappler. N.Y., Interland Pub., 1972; Anna Lewis, *Chief Pushmataha: American Patriot.* N.Y., Exposition Press, 1959.

Q

Quaiapen: *see* Magnus

Quantrill, William Clarke, guerilla (July 31, 1837-June 6, 1865). B. at Canal Dover, Ohio, he was the oldest of eight children,and according to report a boy addicted to reckless pranks. He was sent to live with a family at Mendota, Illinois, but about 1855 killed a man and, released, commenced teaching school at 18 at Fort Wayne, Indiana, shortly removing to Kansas. He is reported by some sources to have accompanied army supply trains toward Utah in the "Mormon War," and to have operated in the Rocky Mountain west as a gambler, but if so he was back in Kansas by 1859 and taught school that winter, probably in Lawrence, where he was charged with various crimes or misdeeds, and finally fled under disgrace. He soon was involved in the slavery disputes, became pro-slavery and thus inclined toward the Southern cause. When the Civil War began he became connected, irregularly at first, with the Confederate Army. He fought at Lexington, Missouri, then developed his talent for guerilla warfare; according to some accounts he offered his services to both North and South; neither would give him a formal endorsement initially, but he drifted into the latter faction. Quantrill became a border scourge in Missouri and Kansas. He robbed mail coaches, plundered communities supposed to be Northern in sympathy, frequently murdered purported partisans or those suspected of Union leanings, and sometimes skirmished with Northern troops. In 1862 he and his band were formally declared outlaws by Union officials. Quantrill's men, or some of them, comprised part of a Confederate force capturing Independence, Missouri, in August 1862, Quantrill thereupon being mustered into the Southern service with rank of captain. A year later, leading about 300 men and with 150 or so others loosely allied to him, he descended upon Lawrence, Kansas, because it was the headquarters for James H. Lane, a prominent Free-State man and political leader. Here Quantrill perpetrated the worst atrocity of the Civil War, burning 180 or more buildings, slaughtering upwards of 150 inhabitants, most non-combatants, then withdrawing to Missouri. About two months later he defeated a small Federal body at Baxter Springs, Kansas, putting the prisoners to death. With the exception of the Lawrence raid, Quantrill's followers and associates ordinarily operated in small bands or groups, dissension naturally arising so that coopera-tion between factions often was difficult or impossible to arrange. With only 33 men in 1865, Quantrill penetrated into Kentucky, plundering and wreaking what havoc he could. On or about May 10 a Federal force of irregulars surprised the guerillas near Taylorsville, Quantrill being wounded mortally. In his own right Quantrill was a man of much evil, but the mischief he inspired far outlived him and may have been even more consequential. For example, his band and its operations served as something of a training ground for Frank and Jesse James and other noted desperadoes, and the hatred and loathing Quantrill generated far outlived him; traces of these qualities may be identified to this day in the area he ravaged. It is difficult to discover good qualities in his nature, although apologists have attempted to do so.

Literature abundant; William Elsey Connelley, *Quantrill and the Border Wars.* Cedar Rapids, Ia., Torch Press, 1909; new edition, 1956.

Queen Anne, Pamunkey woman chief (fl. 1675-1715). The name was given by the English to the woman chief of the Pamunkey tribe of Virginia about 1675. She was the widow of Totopotomoi, the chief who was killed about 1655 in English service while repelling an invasion by other Indians. During Bacon's Rebellion in 1675 the colonial government called on Anne for men to cooperate with the government forces. She scornfully rejected the appeal, observing that for 20 years since the death of her husband no reward but neglect had been meted out to her or her people, although the chief and his followers had perished in the service of the whites. Her testimony prompted pledges of better treatment, and finally she agreed to furnish the requested aid. Probably in return for this assistance she received from Charles II a silver "crown" inscribed to the "Queen of Pamunkey." She last appeared in history in 1715 as a petitioner on behalf of her oppressed people. Her crown is reportedly held by the Association for the Preservation of Virginia Antiquities at Richmond.

Hodge, HAI.

Queen Mary, Modoc woman (fl. 1872-73). The sister of Captain Jack, nominal leader of the hostile Modocs during the war of 1872-73, Mary was an unfortunate woman. She was used by whites and Indians as a courier, or messenger or point of contact during the months of hostilities and since she had lived with several Yreka, California miners at one time or another, spoke good English. Her usefulness ended with surrender of the Modocs in the late spring of 1873. She visited her brother shortly before he was hanged, and then presumably was sent into exile at the Quapaw Reservation, Oklahoma, with the other surviving Modocs.

Keith A. Murray, *The Modocs and Their War.* Norman, Univ. of Okla. Press, 1965; Richard Dillon, *Burnt-Out Fires.* Englewood Cliffs, N.J., Prentice-Hall, 1973.

Quentin, Jacques, Jesuit missionary (Feb. 1572-Apr. 18, 1647). B. at Abbeville, France, he entered the Jesuit order June 30, 1604, taught at Bourges and Rouen, and in 1609 became acting superior at the College of Eu, France. Here he became acquainted with Pierre Biard and Enemond Massé, the first Jesuits to be sent to New France as missionaries. In 1613 Quentin was named to head a new mission at Saint Sauveur (Mt. Desert Island, Maine) providing the former two priests had died, since nothing had been heard from them for some time. If they still lived, Quentin was to return to France. He reached Canada with La Saussaye's expedition which picked up Biard and Massé at Port Royal, Nova Scotia and attempted to establish a colony at Saint Sauveur. When Samuel Argall captured the place, Quentin and Biard were taken prisoner aboard his ship, remaining in captivity nearly 10 months. Quentin adventurously made his way back to France with Biard (see Biard biography), and

spent the rest of his life in the teaching ministry. The *Dictionary of Canadian Biography* gives his date of death as March 18, 1647.

Thwaites, JR, II, 307n78; DCB.

Quimby, William, victim (d. Dec. 1, 1870). Quimby, a merchant at Douglass, Butler County, Kansas, was one of four men hanged at Douglass at the same time as an extension of the lynching of four others three weeks before, all suspected of horse thievery, or of being secretly supportive of the alleged rustlers. The vigilante action was known locally as the "Butler County War," but there were no other casualties.

Butler County Hist. Soc. archives, El Dorado, Kan.

Quinn, James H., pioneer (1817-Dec. 31, 1856). B. in Maryland, he studied law and moved to Illinois where he was clerk in a district court until 1846 when he joined Weightman's company of light artillery and reached New Mexico with Clark's Battalion. Here he resumed the practice of law, became probate judge, a prosecuting attorney and filled legislative posts. In 1854 he organized a "spy company" of native New Mexicans and Taos Indians and operated against Jicarilla Apaches and perhaps others with Carleton who reported to superiors that "he never saw such wonderful trailing... as that accomplished by Captain Quinn and his Mexican Spy company." Quinn was a man of some substance in the mercantile, legislative and judicial life of New Mexico after United States occupation and until his death.

Aurora Hunt, *Major General James Henry Carleton: Western Frontier Dragoon.* Glendale, Calif., Arthur H. Clark Co., 1958; Morris P. Taylor, "Campaigns Against the Jicarilla Apache, 1854." *New Mex. Hist. Rev.,* Vol. XLIV, No. 4 (Oct. 1969), 269-91.

Quinn, Peter, interpreter (c. 1791-Aug. 18, 1862). B. probably in Ireland, he reached the Minnesota country where for the last 40 years of his life (he died at 71), he served the United States as Indian farmer and interpreter for troops in Sioux, Chippewa and French. He married a Chippewa woman who bore him seven children, only one of whom lived to advanced age: William L. Quinn of St. Paul. Charles E. Flandrau first became acquainted with Peter Quinn in 1854 when Flandrau was Indian agent, and spoke highly of him: "Never was a military expedition sent out from a post where Quinn was located that his stately and soldierly form was not prominently visible, with his cavalry saber at his belt, looking like a field marshal.... I never knew a man in the humble walks of military life who enjoyed to such an extent not only the absolute confidence but the friendship of all officers, enlisted men and citizens with whom he came in contact." Quinn was killed while interpreter for Captain Marsh's company at the Redwood Ferry on the Minnesota River at the outset of the great Sioux uprising of 1862. His body was pierced by 12 bullets. Flandrau secured his saber which "I shall continue to regard in the future, as I have in the past, as a memento of a good and brave man, whose name and fame I will defend against all assaults while I live." Flandrau's comments were in reaction to allegations by Sioux agent Thomas J. Galbraith August 5, 1862, that Quinn had proved unreliable and should be removed. These charges, Flandrau believed, arose from Galbraith's inexperience and jealousy toward Quinn of other interpreters.

Minnesota in the Civil and Indian Wars, I.   St. Paul, Pioneer Press Co., 1891, pp. 818i; William Watts Folwell, *A History of Minnesota,* II.   St. Paul, Minn. Hist. Soc., 1961; Isaac V.D. Heard, *History of the Sioux War and Massacres of 1862 and 1863.* N.Y., Harper and Bros., 1864.

Quinn, William L., interpreter (Nov. 4, 1828-Mar. 5, 1906). B. near Fort Snelling, Minnesota, his mother was a half-breed Chippewa woman and his father Peter Quinn (1791-1862); William was the only one of their seven children to reach maturity. At various times he was a sutler's clerk, a scout for the army and interpreter, being fluent in Chippewa, Sioux, English and perhaps other languages. He moved in 1875 to St. Paul, Minnesota, and lived there the remainder of his life, dying at that city.

Minnesota in the Civil and Indian Wars, I.   St. Paul, Pioneer Press Co., 1891; information from Rodney C. Loehr, Minneapolis.

Quintana, Andrés, missionary (Nov. 27, 1777-Oct. 11-12, 1812). B. at Antonorra, Spain, he joined the Franciscan order of the Roman Catholic Church at 17 and in the spring of 1804 sailed for Mexico. He reached Monterey,

California, in 1805, being assigned to the mission of Santa Cruz. Although suffering from illness in 1812, he returned from treatment at Monterey to resume his ministry because his colleague at the mission became too ill to labor. On the morning of October 12, Quintana was found dead in his bed. Poulos gives a circumstantial account which affirms that the priest was ambushed when he was journeying without a guard at night to visit an ill Indian, was hanged and then returned to his bed, the evidence of the crime concealed until an autopsy by Manuel Quix, a San Jose, California, surgeon, performed after the urging of friends of the priest, suspicious of the manner of his death. George Simpson, in his 1842 *Narrative* reporting gossip he had picked up along the coast to the effect that the priest apparently had become involved with the wife of an Indian near the mission, was mutilated "in the most brutal manner" and dispatched. Geiger, the most thorough student of California missions and missionaries, gives what facts can now be known in the most complete form. He said that a superficial examination of the priest after his death had indicated his demise had been due to natural causes; civil authorities being dissatisfied, however, an autopsy was performed during the following week; the conclusion was that "no violence had occurred." Two years later, however, an overheard conversation between two Indians resulted in a fresh investigation and the arrest and questioning of eight natives. They revealed that because of alleged cruelties by the priest they had "dispatched him in a most revolting and diabolical manner," brought him back to the mission and put the body in bed. A friar of Mission San Jose reported to a colleague that Quintana, after torture *"in pudendis,"* was murdered by suffocation "with the cloths used in administering extreme unction." Governor Pablo Solá investigated the character of the priest, reporting him zealous and kindly in his treatment of his people. Five of the Indians arrested (three others had died in prison), were sentenced to 200 lashes and to hard labor under restrictions for from two to ten years. The relative mildness of the punishment suggests that there might have been extenuating circumstances, and as Geiger points out, questions remain, unlikely ever to be satisfactorily resolved.

Thomas C. Russell, ed., *Narrative of a Voyage to*

California Ports in 1841-42. San Francisco, T.C. Russell, 1930; C. Jean Poulos, "Who Would Kill a Priest? *True West,* Vol. 24, No. 2 (Nov.-Dec. 1976), 35, 55, 58; Maynard Geiger, *Franciscan Missionaries in Hispanic California, 1769-1848.* San Marino, Calif., Huntington Library, 1969.

Quintero, Alejo J., Apache scout (1889-Nov. 3, 1969). Quintero, b. probably near Fort Apache, Arizona, served as an Apache scout from 1911 to 1941, rising to sergeant and being stationed at Fort Huachuca, Arizona, much of the time. After he left the service he became a medicine man on the Fort Apache reservation and gained a place in tribal history by recording his people's version of the creation of the world, a narration still used by them.

Fort Huachuca Scout, Mar. 3, 1977.

R

Radcliff, John, frontiersman (d. 1811). He, with his brother, William, was of the Samuel Pringle party that in 1769 established the first permanent settlement in the Buckhannon Valley of present West Virginia, being principally a hunter and scout, settling on Hacker's Creek. Radcliff was a nephew of Jesse and Elias Hughes, noted scouts. With Elias Hughes he became, in 1797, among the first settlers of Licking County, Ohio, establishing a farm four miles below Newark, Ohio. More than Hughes, Radcliff "was given to the peaceful avocations of life, and for one reared on the frontiers, had not been largely engaged in border warfare," although a noted hunter. In 1801 he joined Hughes in a punitive foray against depredating Indians, acquitting himself well.

Lucullus V. McWhorter, *Border Settlers of Northwestern Virginia.* Hamilton, O., Republican Pub. Co., 1915.

Radcliff, William, borderer (fl. 1769-1781). Radcliff was of the Samuel Pringle party that established the first settlement in the Buckhannon valley of present West Virginia, and may have resided on the West Fork of the Monongahela River subsequently . He was a nephew of Jesse and Elias Hughes, noted Indian fighters. Nothing is known of his later life.

Lucullus, V. McWhorter, *Border Settlers of Northwestern Virginia.* Hamilton, O., Republican Pub. Co., 1915.

Radisson, Pierre Esprit, explorer, fur trader (c. 1636-c. June 25, 1710). B. probably at Avignon, France, he went to Canada in his youth; his half-sister was to be widowed by the Iroquois and to remarry, this time to Médard Chouart Des Groseilliers with whom Radisson would explore and adventure for much of his grown life. In about 1651 Radisson was captured by Iroquois at three Rivers and taken to a Mohawk village near today's Schenectady, New York where instead of being burned he was adopted into an Indian family, with whom he learned much of the language. He escaped and nearly regained Three Rivers when he was taken again by the Iroquois, tortured brutally and rescued from execution by his Iroquois "family." He remained with the Mohawks until 1653 when he escaped once more and reached Fort Orange (Albany), where he served as interpreter for French-speaking Dutch, serving in that capacity when the Jesuit Joseph Antoine Poncet reached the post in November 1653. Radisson went to Europe on a Dutch ship and in 1654 returned to Three Rivers, from where he may have embarked almost immediately with Des Groseilliers for a two year expedition into the interior. Nute disbelieves that Radisson accompanied his brother-in-law on this journey, in part because of his extreme youth (she accepts a 1681 New France census suggesting he was born in 1640, rather than Radisson's own statement on two occasions that he was born in 1636), and a Quebec deed of sale dated November 7, 1655, as evidence that Radisson remained in New France rather than exploring the wilderness during those two years. Yet Radisson asserts in his reminiscences that he accompanied Des Groseilliers and there is no other manuscript extant to deny this claim; if he had been born in 1636 he would have been 18 when the expedition set out, and even if the unlikely 1640 date is accepted his two years with the Iroquois, his service as interpreter and his wild young life would have brought him enough maturity to be accepted by Des Groseilliers. There is no evidence of the date when Radisson signed the Quebec deed, or even if its date is correct — he may have signed it long after the document was drafted and dated. There is, in sum, insufficient evidence for denying him this extended adventure. The pair traversed Lake Huron, perhaps reaching Lake St. Clair, crossing overland to Lake Michigan and probably visiting Lake Superior. They collected a rich haul of beaver fur (effectually opening up the distant northwest to the trade) and returned to the St. Lawrence by the Strait of Michilimackinac and the Ottawa River. In 1657 Radisson accompanied the Jesuit Ragueneau to a mission for the Onondagas near the present Syracuse, New York; it may have been Radisson who was the key to the escape of about 60 Frenchmen from an Iroquois plot in March of 1658. In the summer of 1659 Radisson and Des Grosseilliers went again to the northwest, reaching the western end of Lake Superior and wintered at a lake in northern Wisconsin, becoming acquainted with the Sioux, learning much of the surrounding country perhaps as distant as Hudson Bay to the north and the Mississippi to the west and south. The Frenchmen traveled with the Sioux for six weeks in the spring; Parkman reports that they reached the "Forked River," which Radisson said was so named "because it has two branches, the one towards the west, the other towards the south, which, we believe, runs towards Mexico," supposing from that they had arrived at the confluence of the Mississippi and the Missouri. More likely the report describes the confluence of the Mississippi and the Minnesota rivers which meet at today's Minneapolis-St. Paul. Still early in the spring they crossed Lake Superior, visiting a band of Crees on the north shore, and Radisson affirms they journeyed on to Hudson Bay, which Nute disbelieves because of the limited time at their disposal. Still it is credible, if barely, that they journeyed overland to James Bay and returned, given the weather and swift traveling conditions. By the end of August they were back on the St. Lawrence, accompanied by 300 Indians and a flotilla of 60 canoes laden with beaver, an economic godsend to the struggling French colonies. Most of the furs were confiscated, however, both explorers fined and Des Grosseilliers jailed because they had set out without government sanction to trade for furs on their long adventure. Recovered from their mistreatment, and understandably disgruntled, the pair set out for the tip of the Gaspé Peninsula, purportedly to go from there by sea into Hudson Bay, but instead they went to New England and, well received, tried again to reach the Bay by sea, being foiled on two occasions; in 1665 they sailed for England, were captured at sea by the Dutch, landed in Spain and made their way overland to London. In 1668 the pair were sent by enterprising Britishers interested in the fur trade in separate vessels toward Hudson Bay. Des Grosseilliers arrived there, but Radisson's

vessel was forced to return, the explorer therafter penning an account of his adventures to that date at the King's command. Once more he tried to reach Hudson Bay and failed, although his partner returned with much beaver; the Hudson's Bay Company was formed as of 1670 and within a month the two Frenchmen who had inspired it set out once more for the Bay. Radisson's vessel reached the mouth of the Nelson River, the explorer then visiting the mouth of the Rupert River in James Bay where he joined Des Grosseilliers. Radisson's further activities have little bearing on American frontier history; he was active in promoting the interests of the HBC until 1675 when he was persuaded to return to France. He did not receive the treatment he expected, was shipped to Canada where French officials proved hostile, and Radisson returned to France. He took part in an expedition against Dutch colonies in Africa and the West Indies, barely surviving disaster in the Caribbean, and returned to France impoverished, went to England with little improvement in his fortunes, returned once more to France and attempted to found a French settlement at the mouth of the Nelson River in Hudson Bay, but the endeavor faltered. Furs bartered for were taken to French Canada, where Radisson attempted to avoid taxes on them, was sent back to France, then went to England and rejoined the HBC. He was dispatched to Hudson Bay and persuaded his nephew in command at the French post at the Nelson to go over to the English bringing the colony and all the furs thus far collected. Radisson remained thereafter with the British company, spending 1685-87 in Hudson Bay but the rest of his life at London. He had married three times, his first wife English and, presumably after her death, a French woman and upon her passing, another English woman. Nute's summation of his life (*Dictionary of Canadian Biography,* II) is well worth reading.

Thwaites, JR, XXVIII, 319-20n32; XL, 143; XLII, 219-23, 296n11; XLV, 235-37; Parkman, *La Salle and the Discovery of the Great West;* DCB II: CE.

Raffeix, Pierre, Jesuit missionary (Jan. 15, 1633-Aug. 29, 1724). B. in Auvergne, France, he became a Jesuit and reached Canada March 22, 1663. He was assigned to the mission among the Cayugas, in present New

York State, in 1666, but military operations prevented. It is said he accompanied both the Remy de Courcelle and the Tracy expeditions into the Iroquois country, serving as chaplain. In 1671 Raffeix was sent to the Cayuga mission, working there and among the Senecas until 1680; the rest of his career was spent in Canada and he died at Quebec. Raffeix appears to have been a cartographer of some skill, one of his works being a 1676 "Map of the westernmost parts of Canada," and another a map of "Lake Ontario, with the adjacent Regions, and especially the five Iroquois nations." A third map attributed to Raffeix represents New France from the Atlantic to Lake Erie and southerly to New England.

Thwaites, JR, XLVII, 319-20n28; LVI, 49-57; LVIII, 237-45; LXI, 225-29; LXXI, 149.

Rafferty, William Augustus (Deacon), army officer (Feb. 16, 1842-Sept. 13, 1902). B. at New Germantown, New Jersey, he went to West Point and was commissioned a second lieutenant in the 6th Cavalry June 23, 1865, becoming a first lieutenant May 1, 1866. He served in Texas from 1865 until 1871, winning a brevet October 5, 1870, for his part in an action against hostile Indians on the Little Wichita River, Texas. He had become captain May 14, 1868, after two years as regimental adjutant. Rafferty served in Kansas, Colorado and Indian Territory much of the time until 1875 and on April 6 of the latter year was engaged against Cheyenne Indians on the North Fork of the Canadian River, an action in which 19 enlisted men were wounded for 11 Indians killed. Rafferty was in Arizona from 1875 until 1884. He was cofounder of Camp (Fort) Huachuca March 3, 1877, a base still in commission as a major electronics center. In April 1882 Rafferty with Captain Tullius Tupper, also of the 6th Cavalry, led a long chase after hundreds of Apaches fleeing San Carlos Reservation for Mexico, catching up and giving them a hard fight at Sierra Enmedio, Sonora, and for this action Rafferty won a brevet. He was stationed briefly in New Mexico before moving on to Fort Leavenworth later in 1885, remaining there until November 30, 1889, when he became major of the 2nd Cavalry. He was made lieutenant colonel May 31, 1898, and colonel of the 5th Cavalry October 18, 1899. He commanded the only mounted cavalry in the Santiago campaign in Cuba during the Spanish American War. Rafferty died from injuries following a fall at San Felipe Neri, Rizal, the Philippines. He was married and fathered two children including a son who followed him into the army.

Heitman; Cullum; Rafferty's statement of his military service, AGO Records, Nat. Archives.

Ragueneau, Paul, Jesuit missionary (Mar. 18, 1608-Sept. 3, 1680). B. at Paris he became a Jesuit and reached Canada June 28, 1636, working with the Hurons almost constantly until they were all but annihilated by the Iroquois some years later. Ragueneau was superior of the Huron mission from 1645 until its end in 1649 and superior of all Canadian missions from 1650-53. In June of 1657 he and Joseph Du Peron, also a Jesuit, conducted an unsuccessful mission to the Onondagas in present New York State (the *Dictionary of Canadian Biography* suggests that it was Joseph's brother, Francois Du Peron who figured in this endeavor); the Indians proved strongly hostile to the French. The emissaries, learning of a murder plot against them, secretly fled and managed to escape; they reached Quebec April 23, 1657. Ragueneau, considered by some "the most intelligent" of all Jesuit missionaries in New France, returned to his home country in 1662 and became agent in that land for the Canadian mission. He died at Paris.

Thwaites, JR, IX, 312-13n40; DCB.

Rainbow (Wahchumyus), Nez Perce (d. Aug. 9, 1877). A famous warrior of the non-treaty Nez Perce who believed he received much of his power from the rainbow, hence the name by which he was generally known to the whites. He had come to prominence in intertribal battles before the 1877 campaign and war between Nez Perce and Anglo forces. With Five Wounds, a warrior of approximately equal fame, Rainbow just in from a buffalo hunt on the Plains joined the hostiles following the Battle of Whitebird Canyon, June 17, 1877. About July 3 Rainbow and Five Wounds led the Nez Perce who wiped out Second Lieutenant S.M. Rains of the 1st Cavalry, his ten men and a citizen scout at Craig's Mountain near the Clearwater River. There were no white survivors. Rainbow took a prominent and aggressive part in the Battle of Clearwater, Idaho, July 11-12. He was among those urging the Nez Perces at the Weippe Council in mid-July to make for the Crow country and join that tribe in either war or buffalo hunting; this the Nez Perce agreed to do. Rainbow (and Five Wounds) were among those killed on the first day of the Battle of Big Hole, Montana; he had wished to die in battle, but his loss to the Nez Perce was great.

McWhorter, *Hear Me;* John D. McDermott, *Forlorn Hope: The Battle of Whitebird Canyon and the Beginning of the Nez Perce War.* Boise, Ida. State Hist. Soc., 1978; Alvin M. Josephy, *The Nez Perce Indians and the Opening of the Northwest.* New Haven, Yale Univ. Press, 1965.

Rain in the Face, Hunkpapa Sioux warrior (c. 1835-Sept. 14, 1905). B. near the forks of the Cheyenne River, North Dakota he was of a family of six sons, one of them named Iron Horse. Shortly before his death he told Eastman, "My father was not a chief; my grandfather was not a chief, but a good hunter and a feast-maker. On my mother's side I had some noted ancestors, but they left me no chieftainship. I had to work for my reputation." He never was recognized as "chief," although he was a famous warrior. He acquired his name at 10 after a fight with a Cheyenne boy in which the Sioux's face was streaked with blood and blood-flushed paint. He is said to have again been named Rain in the Face when he joined a war party against the Gros Ventres, a hard fight resulting. Fighting all day in the rain his face again became streaked with paint. The Indian was frequently on the warpath. He first came to wider note however when he joined the December 21, 1866, attack near Fort Phil Kearny, Wyoming when Fetterman and his command of around 80 men were wiped out. Two years later near Fort Totten, near Devil's Lake, North Dakota, he was in a fight and was wounded. In August 1873 Custer led ten troops of the 7th Cavalry to the Yellowstone country as escort for railroad surveyors. A skirmish near the mouth of the Tongue River and another near the Rosebud ensued. Two civilians, Dr. John Holzinger, veterinarian for the 7th Cavalry, and a sutler named Balarian strayed from the column and were killed by Indians; Charley Reynolds, a scout with the command late in 1874 told Custer at Fort Abraham Lincoln, North Dakota, that he had heard Rain in the Face at the Standing Rock

Reservation boast of having slain the pair. Captain Tom Custer and Captain George Yates were sent to arrest the Indian. They brought him to the post where he was held for some time while George Custer closely examined him through an interpreter, at last announcing that the Sioux had confessed. A great deal of controversy over his methods arose and perhaps realizing the flimsiness of his case, Custer permitted Rain in the Face to "escape." Years later the Sioux finally was arraigned in a federal court, charged with the murders. The court agreed with arguments of the defense that prosecution was unwarranted and the case was dismissed. Nevertheless the incident contributed to the widely-held view that Rain in the Face ever afterward held a grudge against the two Custers and in the Battle of the Little Bighorn June 25, 1876, killed them both, cut out Tom Custer's heart and ate part of it to absorb virtues of a brave man. However Tom Custer's heart was not in fact cut out, and under the circumstances of the heavy action it would have been as unlikely for Rain in the Face to have recognized the Custers as they him. The story that he accounted for the brothers is generally discredited today, although stories he himself gave over the years at times claimed innocence and at others asserted that he had indeed killed the two. Some Sioux accounts on the other hand affirm that Rain in the Face was not in the engagement at all, but with the pony herd miles distant; the truth can never be known. He was however lamed by wounds he asserted he received in the engagement. He followed Sitting Bull to Canada where he remained until 1880 when he surrendered at Fort Keogh, Montana. Rain in the Face had seven wives, none of whom lived long or happily with him; the last was found in their tepee with her throat slit. He died at Standing Rock and was buried at Aberdeen, South Dakota.

Hodge, HAI; Thomas B. Marquis, *Rain-in-the-Face; Curly, the Crow.* p.p., 1934; Jay Monaghan, *Custer.* Lincoln, Univ. of Neb. Press, 1971; Edgar I. Stewart, *Custer's Luck.* Norman, Univ. of Okla. Press, 1955.

Raine, William MacLeod, writer (June 22, 1871-July 25, 1954). B. at London his widowed father brought him to America at 10, settling on a fruit and livestock farm near Searcy, Arkansas where the boy picked up the Circle-

WR brand which would adorn the covers of his 81 books. He was graduated from Oberlin College, Ohio, in 1894, settled at Seattle and did a little work as a ranch hand, became a newspaper reporter and moved to Denver. He commenced free-lancing with some success and his first novel, *The Daughter of Raasay* (1902) was set in the United Kingdom. He worked for various Denver newspapers to earn a living until his initial western novel, *Wyoming* (1908) had become a success, when he settled in to full-time writing in that genre. His formula westerns were very popular. By the 1930s his income reached about $30,000 a year. He wrote four non-fiction books: *Famous Sheriffs and Western Outlaws* (1929); with Will C. Barnes, *Cattle* (1930), reissued as *Cattle, Cowboys and Rangers; Guns of the Frontier* (1940), and *Forty-five Caliber Law: The Way of Life of the Frontier Peace Officer* (1941). His non-fiction books were carelessly written and littered with factual mistakes, but they were readable. Raine died at Denver. He had married three times, his first two wives predeceasing him. He fathered a daughter.

Lee Scamehorn, "William MacLeod Raine: 1871-1954." *Arizona and the West*, Vol. 24, No. 1 (Spring 1982), 1-4.

Rains, Sevier McClellan, army officer (c. 1851-July 3, 1877). B. in Michigan he went to West Point from Georgia and June 15, 1876 was commissioned a second lieutenant in 1st Cavalry, then stationed in the northwest. He and his detail of ten enlisted men and one civilian were wiped out to a man at a Craig's Mountain, Idaho, ambush by Nez Perce Indians led by Two Moons, Five Wounds, Rainbow and Yellow Wolf. No Indian was wounded in the fight.

Heitman; Cullum; Lucullus V. McWhorter, *Yellow Wolf: His Own Story.* Caldwell, Id., Caxton Printers, 1940; McWhorter, *Hear Me.*

Rale (Rasle), Sébastien, Jesuit missionary (Jan. 4, 1657-Aug. 23, 1724). B. at Pontarlier, France, he became a Jesuit and reached Canada October 13, 1689, studying the Abenaki language until 1691 when he was sent to Kaskaskia to work with Gravier. After two years he was sent to Acadia and in 1694 to the present Maine where he founded an Abenaki mission at Norridgewock on the Kennebec River, at the present site of Old Town. During Queen Anne's War New England officials sought to secure the neutrality of the Abenakis, and Rale said he promised to encourage this; in the summer Vaudreuil said however that Rale had promised him his Indians were ready to take up the hatchet whenever the French governor gave the word and the Abenakis took part in raids on New England settlements. Rale's reputation among the English colonists worsened and in 1705 an expedition was sent to Norridgewock to seize him; the village was burned but he escaped. After some time in Canada as missionary to Abenakis who had fled there, Rale returned to Norridgewock in 1710. With intrusion of the English into the Kennebec area, Rale supported resistance by the Indians and in 1720 the Massachusetts council offered 100 pounds for his arrest. The English sought to have the Canadian government withdraw Rale and in January 1722 a second expedition surrounded Norridgewock but Rale had fled into the forest before the noose was drawn, leaving a note warning of reprisals if his church were damaged. Abenakis attacked English settlements at the mouth of the Kennebec in reprisal for the Norridgewock raid and as a result Massachusetts declared war against the Abenakis; twice forces tried to seize Rale, but failed. In August 1724, however, a fresh expedition was fielded, Norridgewock was attacked, Rale killed and scalped, the trophy taken to Boston "to the great joy and exultation of the people of Massachusetts." Thomas Charland, O.P., concluded in his article on Rale in the *Dictionary of Canadian Biography* that "Rale shared the fate of many other missionaries of this era who, willingly or not, found themselves and their work caught up in the larger colonial struggles of France and England in the New World." Rale left a valuable Abenaki-French dictionary of his composition, the original now held by Harvard University. (See Thomas Westbrook entry.)

Literature abundant: Thwaites, JR, LXVI, 346n42, LXXI, 157; DAB; DCB; CE.

Ramezay, Claude de, colonial official (June 15, 1659-July 31, 1724). B. at La Gesse, France, of Scottish descent, he reached Canada in 1685 as an officer of colonial regular troops, being promoted to captain in 1687; by 1689 he was governor of Three Rivers and in later times was governor of Montreal and acting governor of Canada for a brief period. He commanded Canadian militia in Frontenac's 1696 expedition against the New York Onondagas and after Frontenac died became commander of the royal troops of the colony. Most of his numerous activities, in the fur trade, in colonial enterprises and in shipping, are of primarily Canadian rather than of frontier interest. In 1709 he commanded 1,500 hastily recruited men and advanced toward Lake Champlain to meet a New England colonial force; the clash did not occur, however, and both sides withdrew. Ramezay was much concerned with the infiltration into the Old Northwest of British traders, and sought by persuasive and economic means to counter the threat to French trading interests. In 1715 he organized an offensive against the Fox Indians, but it failed to produce worthwhile results; the next year he backed a second, more successful expedition against those Indians. Ramezay continued to be a leading Canadian figure and a picturesque man until his death at Quebec. He was married, fathered 14 children and was survived by two sons and six daughters.

Thwaites, JR, LXVII, 331n3; DCB, II.

Ramona, heroine (c. 1865-July 21, 1922). Ramona, part-fiction, part-genuine person originally was a Cahuilla girl of southern California, Ramona Lubo or Lugo (or as some believe Ramona Gonzaga Ortega), who lived near the Mission San Diego. She reportedly was born in a commodious cave on the Cary Ranch, Anza, California. Helen Hunt Jackson, whose *Century of Dishonor* appeared in 1881 and immediately caused a national furor, sought out Ramona and in 1884 published a novel by that name, part truth, part fiction. Mrs. Jackson gave her a romance with a man named Alessandro, wholly fictional. The true Ramona became a celebrity. She operated a souvenir stand near the mission and being a skilled basket weaver, sold her own baskets and an assortment of trinkets to tourists and other visitors. She died near Hemet, California, and was buried in the Cahuilla cemetery west of Anza near her husband, Juan Diego. The work *Ramona* has frequently been filmed, enacted as a play and honored in song; very little of the profits from all this descended upon the original Ramona.

Dockstader.

Ramsey, Alexander, lawman (c. 1847-June 5, 1875). A sheriff from 1868, when he was 21, he was serving Ellis County, Kansas, when he broke up several bands of stock thieves near Hays, Kansas, winning a local reputation. Sam Mellison, several times member of Ramsey's posses, described the sheriff's death, which he witnessed. It occurred when he accosted a horse thief encamped near Stockton, Kansas. In a gunfight the outlaw was killed and Ramsey wounded mortally. Ramsey was buried in the new Hays cemetery, begun to replace a former boot hill cemetery; in 1923 the Board of County Commissioners erected a marker over his grave.

Kansas City Star, July 5, 1953; "Ellis County Sheriff Killed By Thief." *Frontier Times,* vol. 54, No. 4 (June-July 1980), 36.

Ramsey, Joseph (Jose Ramuso), frontiersman (fl. 1840-1871). A Mexican, he was a longtime hunter at Fort Union. The bursting of a gun barrel cost him a hand, whereafter he became a horse wrangler at the post, speaking English imperfectly and dressed as an Indian. In 1871 he was associated with the Assiniboins.

Montana, Contributions, Vol. X, 1940, 294.

Ranahan, Thomas, scout, frontiersman (Nov. 28, 1839-Dec. 27, 1926). B. in Ireland, he was brought to America at 2 by his parents who settled in Vermont, moving to Kansas in 1855. In 1860 Ranahan was employed by Ben Holladay as an Overland Stage driver, continuing in that profession until 1866. He enlisted to serve with Forsyth as a civilian scout in 1868, but missed the famous Battle of Beecher Island having been assigned at the last moment to scout for Captain George Wallace Graham of the 10th Cavalry. His name appears on the monument as one present at the Beecher engagement, but this is in error. Later he scouted with Cody under Major Eugene Asa Carr of the 5th Cavalry. He moved to Idaho in 1872, where he took part in minor Indian scuffling; Ranahan located first at Boise, Idaho, then at Weiser, where he had a subcontract building the Oregon Short Line railroad. After the death of his wife in 1914, Ranahan moved permanently back to Boise, being often interviewed on frontier subjects and taking an active interest in them until his death, which occurred at Boise. He was buried at Kansas City.

Simon E. Matson, ed., *The Battle of Beecher Island*, Wray, Colo., Beecher Island Battle Meml. Assn., 1960; Ida. State Hist. Soc. Archives; *Capital News*, Boise, Ida., June 8, Dec. 27, 29, 1926; *Idaho Daily Statesman*, Boise, June 14, 1925; Dec. 28, 1926; Nov. 11, 1934.

Randall, A. Frank(lin), photographer (Mar. 2, 1854-Mar. 4, 1916). B. in Massachusetts, Randall became a newspaperman and a good photographer in the Southwest. He was for a time a correspondent for the El Paso, Texas, *Times* and perhaps for the New York *Herald*, and as such accompanied Crook on his great 1883 expedition into the Sierra Madre to bring back the hostile Apaches. An accident to the photographic equipment prevented Randall from scoring a major coup with pictures while covering the operation. He later photographed on the San Carlos, Arizona, Indian Reservation; some of his best pictures may have been appropriated and are now considered to be by Wittick, Fly and others. Randall moved to California c. 1891. His works include photographs taken in Mexico, some of California missions and certain personalities. An album he assembled is at the Huntington Library and Art Gallery, San Marino, California. Randall died at Hayward, Alameda County, California.

Dan L. Thrapp, *General Crook and the Sierra Madre Adventure*. Norman, Univ. of Okla. Press, 1972; Alameda County, Calif., Randall death certificate.

Randall, George Morton, army officer (Oct. 8, 1841-June 14, 1918). B. at Conneaut, Ohio, he enlisted in the 4th Pennsylvania Infantry April 20, 1861, was commissioned a second lieutenant in the same regiment October 24 and ended the Civil War a lieutenant colonel (as of June 1, 1865) of the 14th New York Artillery with three brevets. He became a captain in the 4th U.S. Infantry September 23, 1865, joining the 23rd Infantry December 31, 1870, assigned to Arizona. Randall was very active in Crook's Apache operations through 1874, winning two brevets for three outstanding engagements: the decisive action at Turret Peak (or perhaps the nearby Skeleton Ridge) March 27, 1873, and at Diamond Butte April 22, 1873, when Delshay, one of the most competent and feared central Arizona hostiles was captured, and for an action against Apaches March 8, 1874, which marked the

virtual end of an insurgency movement. Randall was an excellent Indian man, trusted by Indians and whites alike and called by the former the "captain-with-the-big-mustache-which-he-always-pulls." When Crook moved to the Department of the Platte Randall became his scout commander and operated effectively as such during the Battle of the Rosebud, June 17, 1876, when the Crows and Shoshones he led saved the day on critical occasions. Randall commanded 240 Indian scouts on Crook's Big Horn and Yellowstone Expedition from August to September, on the long march from Goose Creek, Wyoming, to the Black Hills. Enroute he took part in the action at Slim Buttes, September 8-9. Randall was at Fort Bennett on the Missouri River during the Wounded Knee affair in South Dakota and had no direct part in it. He became major of the 4th Infantry January 15, 1891, lieutenant colonel of the 8th Infantry March 1, 1894, colonel of the 17th Infantry August 8, 1898, and a Brigadier General February 6, 1901. He became a Major General June 19, 1905, and retired for age October 8 of that year. He died at Denver.

Heitman; Powell; Dan L. Thrapp, *The Conquest of Apacheria*. Norman, Univ. of Okla. Press, 1967; Thrapp, "Where Was the Battle of Turret Peak Fought?" *Troopers West*, ed. by Ray Brandes. San Diego, Calif., Frontier Heritage Press, 1970, 104-33; J.W. Vaughn, *With Crook at the Rosebud*. Harrisburg, Pa., Stackpole Co., 1956; Randall's death certificate.

Randall, Todd, interpreter (fl. 1851-1884). Randall was probably a partner with John Baptiste Richard in 1851 near Fort Laramie, building and operating bridges and ferries across the North Platte and Laramie rivers, but some time after 1853 Richard seems to have bought out Randall and three other partners. Randall married a daughter of Yellow Hair, a "progressive" leader of the Brulé Sioux who won some support at one time as a rival to Spotted Tail. Randall and Palladay were hired as interpreters by the Sanborn Commission in 1867 to probe the Fetterman disaster, and assigned to contact the still-hostile Sioux bands and bring them in to talk with the commission. At one time Randall and John Young Nelson ran whiskey across the Missouri for sale or barter to the Indians. John W. Wham, Red Cloud agent, considered Randall "disreputable," but he had been a trader to Spotted Tail and was in that chief's confidence to Wham's displeasure. When Francis A Walker was named special commissioner to investigate affairs at Red Cloud and Spotted Tail agencies, he put Randall in 1871 in charge of Spotted Tail's Republican River hunt in Nebraska, while admitting that Randall was "not a saint" justified his appointment as "a choice between evils." Randall, as sub-agent, wrote letters for Spotted Tail when Sheridan asked the Indian to bring some followers to put on a wild west show for the visiting Grand Duke Alexis in early 1872. When Red Cloud in 1875 planned to visit Washington the journey was delayed by Randall and Richard who apparently desired to go along and eventually did so. Randall evidently scouted for Mackenzie in 1876-77 operations against those Sioux off the reservation. In 1884 Randall was at Pine Ridge and in the summer was abruptly ordered off the reservation by Agent McGillicuddy. He was always friendly with the Sioux, but a loose interpreter, according to the record.

James C. Olson, *Red Cloud and the Sioux Problem.* Lincoln, Univ. of Nebr. Press, 1965; George E. Hyde, *Spotted Tail's Folk: A History of the Brulé Sioux.* Norman, Univ. of Okla. Press, 1961.

Ranjel, Rodrigo, chronicler (fl. 1538-1546). A native of Almendralejo, Spain, Ranjel was secretary to De Soto and chronicler, or diarist of the expedition into the southern United States, his record of great importance since it was on a day-to-day basis almost and his exact dating of events and precise information in other respects serve as a check on narrations of others. Ranjel's diary has not been found in the original, but much of it survives in the edited narration by Gonzalo Fernandez de Oviedo (1478-1557) in Book XVII of his *Historía General y Natural de las Indias.* This account Oviedo obtained some time before August 1546 on the island of Santo Domingo, where Ranjel had gone from Mexico; Ranjel's narration first was published separately at Madrid in 1851 and by Bourne in the United States in 1904. The narrative describes Ranjel (perhaps in Oviedo's words) as "a good soldier and a man of worth (who) had a good horse," and thus was a distinct asset to the expedition. Ranjel apparently had also an eye for profit; he was in the forefront among those collecting

pearls at Cofitachequi, even from the dead. And it was Ranjel who discovered in South Carolina a green item he thought an emerald, and urged De Soto not to announce it since it might be valuable; De Soto angrily rejected the suggestion, since such would be to steal from the King. It turned out to be only glass, anyway. Ranjel took a heroic part in the sanguinary battle of Mauvila, Alabama. He held back 70 furiously hostile Indians who would not face his war horse, and in the savage action more then 20 arrows stuck in his cotton-quilt armor; he had De Soto pluck them out. Ranjel's manuscript breaks off when the expedition was in Arkansas on November 2, 1541; the remainder has not been located.

Bourne, *De Soto,* II; *De Soto Expedition Commission.*

Ransom, Sam(uel), pioneer (Jan. 5, 1847-Feb. 27, 1891). Ransom was believed by the residents of Shakespeare, New Mexico, to have been a veteran of the Civil War; if so, he was an enlisted man or served in some volunteer organization whose commissioned personnel were not listed by Heitman. Ransom was said also to have been an Indian fighter, but no records of this service remain. He was "the last blacksmith who worked... as a horseshoer for the National Mail and Transportation Co.," before going to Shakespeare where he discovered the "85 Mine," named for the year of its location. The "85" proved to be "one of the most valuable mines in New Mexico." Ransom, always referred to as "captain" at Shakespeare, was married twice (both wives predeceased him), and died at White Rock, Mariposa County, California.

Service Record Book of Men and Women of Hidalgo County, Lordsburgh, N.M., VFW Post 3099, 1949.

Rath, Charles, pioneer (c. 1836-July 30, 1902). B. at Stuttgart, Germany, he came to the United States at 12 and was raised in Ohio. He ran away from home, reaching Colorado with Bent's wagon train, and worked for some time at Bent's Fort, returning to Kansas about 1855. He settled in Barton County, near Fort Zarah. Having lived long among the Cheyennes, he spoke that language, some Kiowa and perhaps other Indian languages, married a Cheyenne woman, the sister of William Bent's wife, and fathered a daughter; Rath's wife had been at one time the wife of Kit Carson (Rath divorced her in 1863 and subsequently married white women). In 1858 he took over a ranch now part of Ellinwood, Kansas, having another near the present Great Bend, Kansas. He built a trading post, stage stop, rooming house and restaurant at the junction of Walnut Creek and the Arkansas River, near Zarah. Rath freighted supplies for the building of Fort Dodge, Kansas, and continued trading with Cheyennes to the north and Comanches to the south, but during the Plains wars of 1867-68 he was forced to abandon his Kansas posts. He became interested in land transactions, railroad building and other pioneer enterprises; in September 1872 he moved to Dodge City, Kansas. From October 1871 he had become a buffalo hunter and was successful at it; in 1873 he is reported to have killed 112 buffalo from a single stand on the Canadian River. The first year the Atchison, Topeka and Santa Fe railroad reached Dodge, Rath and his partners, Robert Wright and A.J. Anthony, shipped 200,000 buffalo hides, 200 carloads of hind quarters and two cars of tongues. Sometimes he outfitted other hunters, but he became principally a hide merchant (and also later shipped millions of buffalo bones at $6 a ton). It is said that in his career he bought and sold more than 1 million hides, thousands of buffalo robes and other buffalo by-products. In 1874 Rath and Fred Leonard established a post at Adobe Walls in the Texas Panhandle, but Rath returned to Dodge City before the celebrated battle at the Walls on June 25-27 that year; the battle cost him more than $10,000 in merchandise. His hide yards were located at Fort Griffin, Hide Town (which became Sweetwater, then Mobeetie) and at Rath City, Texas. In 1876 he laid out the so-called Rath Trail from Dodge through Mobeetie, Clarendon, Matador to Rath City. He continued as late as 1877 skirmishing with Indians when he could not avoid them, but his only known wound was from a white desperado near Larned, Kansas, several years earlier. The South Plains hide business lasted little more than two years; Rath went into general merchandising at Mobeetie and elsewhere, and by 1880 had moved his headquarters back to Dodge City. He was divorced from his first white wife in 1885 and married another in 1886 (she left him after his money gave out in 1895). His business

fortunes declined and hard times came upon him. He made the 1889 Cherokee Strip run, but without any noticeable profit. Rath tried many enterprises, but was virtually broke by the time death came to him at Los Angeles, where he is buried.

Ida Ellen Rath, *The Rath Trail.* Wichita, Kan., McCormick-Armstrong Co., 1961.

Rath, Peter Paul, soldier, *see* Peter Roth

Ravalli, Antonio, Jesuit missionary (May 16, 1811-Oct. 2, 1884). B. at Ferrara, Italy, he joined the Jesuit order November 12, 1827. He taught for some years at Turin and neighboring cities, then volunteered for the Indian missions and accompanied De Smet around Cape Horn to the northwest coast, reaching Fort Vancouver, Oregon after an eight month voyage in 1844. He was assigned initially to the Kalispel Indians of present Montana, being first stationed at St. Ignatius Mission, then at St. Mary's in the Bitterroot Valley where he spent several years. In 1854 when that mission was abandoned he moved to the Sacred Heart Mission, three years later to the Coeur d'Alenes and in 1857 to the Fort Colville region of the present Washington State. In 1860 Father Ravalli retired to Santa Clara College (University), California, but was restless there and wished to get back to "his" Indians of the northwest. In 1863 he returned to Montana where he spent the remainder of his life. He had learned a number of Indian languages, was fluent in several, and his reputation as a northwestern missionary "is second only to De Smet." A monument was built over his grave, for he was much loved in Montana. His medical qualifications and interest also was of much mission value. Ravalli had much skill as a "mechanic" or craftsman, erected the first flour mill in Montana with grinding stones brought from Europe, and a saw mill made from wagon rims, hammered and filed into a saw with a crank to operate it. He also designed a church, which still is in use.

Thwaites, EWT, XXIX, 137n.; DAB.

Rawn, Charles Cotesworth, army officer (Dec. 6, 1837-Oct. 6, 1887). B. in Pennsylvania, he enlisted in the 25th Pennsylvania Infantry in May 1861, was commissioned a second lieutenant in the 7th U.S. Infantry August 5 and emerged from the Civil War a captain. He was stationed at the newly-established post, Fort Missoula in the Bitterroot Valley of Montana in the summer of 1877 when word came that the Nez Perce who had defeated U.S. troops in several Idaho engagements were coming over the Lolo Pass trail. He attempted to block their entry into the Bitterroot Valley, hastily erecting what became locally known as "Fort Fizzle." When the Nez Perce approached, he conferred with Chief Joseph, White Bird and Looking Glass, but agreement for the Indians to give up their arms could not be reached. The Indians circumvented Rawn's defenses, most of the local volunteers deserted him, and he was left with few regulars so could not bring the Indians to battle. It is possible as rumor has it that Rawn agreed to let the Indians pass if they would do so peaceably, but confirmation is lacking. Rawn with his company was with Gibbon in the Battle of Big Hole, Montana, August 9-10, 1877. Rawn became a major in the 24th Infantry April 18, 1884. He died at Lancaster, Pennsylvania.

Heitman; McWhorter, *Hear Me;* Alvin M. Josephy Jr., *The Nez Perce Indians and the Opening of the Northwest.* New Haven, Yale Univ. Press, 1965; John M. Carroll, Byron Price, *Roll Call on the Little Big Horn, 28 June 1876.* Fort Collins, Colo., Old Army Press, 1974.

Ray, Art, cowboy, buffalo handler (c. 1875-1955). A Montana cowboy, Art Ray was one of the riders who devoted years to rounding up and shipping to Canada in crates the 300 or more buffalo of the Pablo-Allard herd in 1907-12. His description of the hard and exciting work is given by Kidder.

John Kidder, "Montana Miracle: It Saved the Buffalo." *Montana Mag.,* Vol. XV, No. 2 (Spring 1965), 60-62.

Ray, Charles T. (Bill Diehl, Deal(s), Pony Diehl), desperado (1849-June 5, 1887?). B. at Rock Island, Illinois, he claimed to be a brewmaster by trade, reportedly was in Dodge City, Kansas, in the 1870s and had reached Las Cruces, New Mexico, by January 1, 1876. There, with John Kinney and others whom 8th Cavalrymen bested in a brawl, they shot through windows at the enlisted men, two soldiers and a civilian being killed, others wounded. Ray may have accompanied Kinney to Lincoln County, New Mexico, in July 1878, afterward migrating to Globe,

Arizona, becoming a bartender. Within months he was said to have joined outlaws in southeastern Arizona; it was reported on Wyatt Earp's dubious authority that Ray was with other cowboys celebrating at Tombstone, Arizona, when White was accidentally killed. Ray was a particular friend of Sherman McMasters, who was a friend of Holliday and the Earps, and with McMasters may have taken part in several stage robberies; he may also have associated with Billy the Kid Leonard and Kid Head in more or less the same pursuit; he was suspected of skirmishing with Mexicans along the border. In the late summer 1881, he was arrested for stage robbery by J.W. Evarts (or Everetts), deputy to Pima County Sheriff Bob Paul, held at Tucson, but soon escaped and quickly was back in business. February 18, 1882, Ray and two others were arrested at Cisco, Texas, charged with robbing a Bisbee, Arizona, stage, but he either was released or escaped, and was said to have been with Curly Bill at the Iron Springs, Arizona, battle with the Earps, but the presence of either Ray or Brocius in this fight is unproven. Ray associated briefly with John Ringo, suspected John O'Rourke of killing Ringo, and killed O'Rourke. It is said that Ray operated briefly in Wyoming, then returned to El Paso and fenced rustled stock for the Kinney gang. Discovered, he fled to Mexico, was extradited, tried in New Mexico and sentenced to the territorial prison at Santa Fe for five years. He escaped February 20, 1885, but was recaptured at Algodones, New Mexico, four days later. Ray was pardoned March 14, 1887. He may be the Bill Diehl who, as partner of Walapais Ed Clark in a mining venture, was killed by Gonshay-ee, one of the Apache Kid band who had fled San Carlos after shooting Al Sieber. At any rate, Ray-Diehl is not definitely reported again. He was described as 5 feet, 6 inches in height, light complected, with a heavy mustache.

Philip J. Rasch, "Ray, alias Deal." *English Westerners' Brand Book,* Vol. II, No. 4 (July 1969), 10-12; Jess G. Hayes, *And Then There Were None.* Globe, Ariz., Tyree Printing Service, 1965.

Ray, Ned, desperado (d. Jan. 10, 1864). A journeyman outlaw, Ray became a deputy to Sheriff Henry Plummer and a key figure in the band of cutthroats that ravaged Montana mining camps in 1863. He was characterized by Red Yager as "council room keeper at Bannack City," but he spent much of his time on the road and figures now and then in instances of outlawry, although rarely as a principal. Ray was picked up at Bannack with Plummer and Buck Stinson, the three being hanged from a single gallows by vigilantes. Ray loosened a hand and inserted it between the rope and his throat at his execution; thus instead of a sharp fall that would have broken his neck, he strangled to death. He had a "bunch," or knot on his foot, caused as he once explained by a shot received when escaping from the penitentiary at San Quentin, California.

Dimsdale; Langford; Birney.

Ray, Nick, cowboy, victim (1864-Apr. 9, 1892). B. in Missouri, he became a cowboy in Nebraska, probably for Bill Irvin; he may have helped Irvin bring his 40,000 head of cattle to Wyoming. Ray worked with Nate Champion on the K-C Ranch near the present town of Kaycee, Wyoming, and was killed at the outset of the famous battle which highlighted the so-called Powder River War, his body burned "beyond recognition" as the Invaders sought to force Champion into the open. Ray and Champion were buried at the Willow Grove Cemetery, Buffalo, Wyoming, "quite a commotion" being generated when their bodies were brought into the town.

Information from Anita Webb Deininger, James F. Dillinger of the Johnson County Chapter, Wyo. State Hist. Soc., Feb. 17, 1975; Helena Huntington Smith, *The War on Powder River.* N.Y., McGraw-Hill Book Co., 1966.

Raymbault, Charles, Jesuit missionary (Apr. 6, 1602-Oct. 22, 1642). B. at Senlis, France, he became a Jesuit at Rouen, reached Canada in 1637 and was stationed at Three Rivers; late in 1640 he was sent with Claude Pijart to establish Algonquin missions north of the Huron country. In 1641 the missionaries met individuals of the Sauteur (Ojibway or Chippewa) tribe, who urged them to visit their camps. Raymbault with Jogues and some Hurons left the mission station at Ste. Marie in response to the invitation. They journeyed 17 days through Lake Huron and reached the site of today's Sault Ste. Marie. Here they were welcomed by the Sauteurs and urged to remain, but were unable to do so. Hardships of his expeditions, or perhaps other causes,

weakened Raymbault's constitution, and he succumbed at Quebec, the first Jesuit to die there. Thwaites wrote that "he had not a brilliant intellect, but was a man of practical judgment and good sense, and of intense, though calm, devotion to his missionary duties."

Thwaites, JR, XI, 278-79n16.

Raymond, Henry Hubert, diarist (Feb. 21, 1848-Oct. 16, 1936). B. in Collinsville, McCoupin County, Illinois, his father's farm adjoined that of the Mastersons, who figured in his Kansas diary. Raymond worked on the railroad right-of-way near Dodge City, Kansas, later hunted buffalo with Bat and Ed Masterson. He started his diary on January 1, 1873; it became a prime source for the gossip and social events during an early year at Dodge. His last entry was for December 31, 1873. He had run out of ink toward the end and disolved gunpowder to write the final few entries, the letters turning to "a rich golden color." The diary itself is pure gold for historians. After leaving Dodge City, Raymond lived at Donbey, Oklahoma, died at 88 and was buried in Maple Grove Cemetery, Sunny Dale, Kansas.

Ed Bartholomew, *Wyatt Earp: The Untold Story.* Toyahvale, Tex., Frontier Book Co., 1963; Lola A. Harper, Fort County (Kan.) Hist. Soc.

Red Bird, Winnebago war chief (c. 1788-Feb. 16, 1828). B. near the mouth of the Wisconsin River in Wisconsin, he initially was friendly with the whites of Prairie du Chien until two Winnebagos, arrested for murder, were reported to have been turned over to Chippewas by Fort Snelling military and clubbed to death. The report was false but when it reached the Winnebago chiefs they determined upon retaliation and assigned Red Bird to carry out the decision. He directed a number of depredations and killings of whites including an attack on a Mississippi River boat in which four were killed and two wounded while the Indians lost eight men. When troops arrived, the Winnebago including Red Bird surrendered, and were imprisoned. Although they were convicted, sentence was not pronounced; Red Bird was remanded to prison to await sentencing and there he died. His companions were sentenced to death but pardoned by President John Quincy Adams in November 1828.

Hodge, HAI.

Redbuck, desperado (d. Mar. 4, 1896). Said to have been "a Plains Indian," he and George Miller teamed to depredate in western Oklahoma in the 1890's and soon had high express company prices on their heads. Redbuck was killed in a shootout with a posse which had trapped the pair in a dugout; Miller, wounded, was captured. Wanted in Texas, he was sentenced to prison there.

Tom Dale, "Oklahoma Outlaw Incident." Potomac Corral of Westerners *Corral Dust,* Vol. III, No. 4 (Dec. 1958), 29; Glenn Shirley, *West of Hell's Fringe.* Norman, Univ. of Okla. Press, 1978.

Red Cloud (Makhpiya-luta), Oglala Sioux chief (1822-Dec. 10, 1909). B. at the forks of the Platte River, Nebraska, he was a member of the Snake family, the most powerful of his tribe, and rose to eminence through his own ability, having no claim to hereditary chieftainship. He probably acquired his name after he became famous. Red Cloud took his first scalp at 16 in a raid against the Pawnees, according to Olson. In a raid on the Crows he killed a boy herding horses, ran them off and the next day killed a chief of a pursuing party. In another raid on the Pawnees he killed four men. In a raid against the Utes he pulled a drowning Ute by the hair out of a stream, then callously scalped him. He became a terror to other tribes and a man of pronounced cruelty. Red Cloud's mother was the sister of a famous chief, Smoke, leader of the Bad Faces clan. A dispute between the Smoke people and those who followed the even more famous Bull Bear arose and Hyde reported that as "some say," Red Cloud killed Bull Bear. The resulting breach between Smoke's Bad Faces and Bull Bear's Koyas (Kiyuksas), or Cut-offs created by this incident was not healed for many years. The Cut-offs gradually affiliated with the Southern Cheyennes and Smoke's people with the Northern Cheyennes, while of course retaining their own identity. Not long after the intra-tribal dispute Red Cloud was wounded dangerously by a Pawnee arrow, the injury troubling him the rest of his life. In 1854 Red Cloud with his Oglalas took part in the Grattan massacre east of Fort Larame and by the time he was 40 he was a leading warrior among the Bad Faces. He and his followers were prominent in the Plains war of 1865 and afterward. They took part in the celebrated Platte Bridge fight in July 1865. Failure of the Army's 1865 Connor North Plains operation against the Sioux served to embolden the Indians. Red Cloud and his independent-minded followers atttended a conference with government negotiators at Fort Laramie in June 1866, but on the 13th a dispute over the proposition to open up the last great Sioux hunting ground to the whites caused Red Cloud and his people to withdraw in a huff, and even more bitter warfare resulted. Red Cloud, who probably by this time was the principal leader of the hostiles, concentrated on obstructing use of the Bozeman Trail, running up the east side of the Big Horns to the Montana gold camps. His warriors harassed the whites at every opportunity and made life difficult at the three major posts the army established along the route: Forts Reno, Phil Kearny and C.F. Smith. Climax of the hostility came December 21, 1866, with annihilation of the Fetterman command of more than 80 men, the worst army debacle of the western Indian wars to that time. Red Cloud later affirmed that he had led the Indian forces; some debate the matter, but it is probable he was on the scene, since he was leader of the Bad Faces who were heavily involved. War continued, with such incidents as the Hayfield Fight and the Wagon Box Fight, both considered white victories by the whites, and Indian victories by the Indians. The Wagon Box affair was the last major action in which Red Cloud is known to have participated. November 4, 1868, he arrived at Fort Laramie with 125 chiefs and head men for a conference, coming in because the army had abandoned the Bozeman Trail posts. November 6, Red Cloud signed a treaty which had been previously signed by many other northern tribesmen beginning in May. Red Cloud's war days were over and henceforth his ways would be those of diplomacy and peace. He did not immediately surrender his people, however, but remained out all winter. March 22, 1869, he arrived at Fort Laramie with 1,000 followers, demanding and receiving food for them. He spent the summer in the Wind River Valley and the following March again appeared at Laramie to trade for goods. By May he apparently had become resigned to accepting a reservation somewhere in Dakota; in late May 1870 he was taken on the first of his several trips to Washington, D.C., with a score of other Indians. At Washington he met his chief rival,

Spotted Tail of the Brulé Sioux (long known as chief of the "friendlies," while Red Cloud was chief of the "hostiles"). Conversations with government figures were less than satisfactory, however, Red Cloud reiterating his opposition to a reservation on the Missouri, the whites unwilling to guarantee him any other. He and his party visited New York where they were treated royally and after their tour arrived back at Fort Laramie June 26; he made subsequent visits to Washington in 1872, 1875, 1877, 1881, 1889 and 1897. Red Cloud moved to a series of agencies: first at Laramie, then on the White River near Fort Robinson, Nebraska, again to one on the hated Missouri above the mouth of the White River, Dakota and finally to Pine Ridge, South Dakota, where he and his people settled permanently. He was deposed as chief by Crook in 1876. The next year he brought in the much-wanted war chief Crazy Horse in response to Crook's wish and resumed leadership of the Oglalas, finally "abdicating" formally in favor of his son, Jack on July 4, 1903. Red Cloud in his later life became something of an elder statesman among his people, at least in the eyes of whites although not so securely in the Indian view for there always was opposition to his leadership, and to Red Cloud personally. His early years at Pine Ridge were marked by a bitter, continuing feud with agent Valentine T. McGillicuddy which lasted from the latter's appointment in 1879 without let-up until he left in 1886; that was one engagement which Red Cloud seems clearly to have lost. Red Cloud came to the end of his life after 40 years journey over "the white man's road and he an unwilling traveler. It had been a tragic journey...the slow erosion of a way of life. Red Coud, more than any other of the Sioux chiefs, was associated with that erosion.... With the old guideposts gone, he made his way along the new road as best he could. As he himself said, 'I, of course, as many others have done before me, have made mistakes in not doing something I should have done and what I should not have done....' Few people have had leaders who could say more."

James C. Olson, *Red Cloud and the Sioux Problem*. Lincoln, Univ. of Nebr. Press, 1965; Goerge E. Hyde, *Red Cloud's Folk*. Norman, Univ. of Okla. Press, 1957; Hodge, HAI.

Red Fox, William, claimant (June 11, 1870?-Mar. 1, 1976). The individual who identified himself as "Chief Red Fox" said he was born on the date cited among South Dakota Sioux He came to public attention through publication of a widely-sold book, *The Memoirs of Chief Red Fox* (1971), a work largely written by Cash Asher, aged 77 in 1972, a onetime journalist and author of volumes on extrasensory perception, miracle cures and poetry. The publishers, McGraw-Hill, paid damages and made some amends for apparent plagiarism by Red Fox's book from James H. McGregor's *The Wounded Knee Massacre...* (1904). Red Fox, as he called himself, appears to have been generally unknown among the Sioux, and according to a reporter in 1972 he looked "considerably younger than 101," which the published work implied was his age at that time. Red Fox claimed he had spent 15 years with the Buffalo Bill Wild West Show, said he had served with the Navy during the Spanish American War and the Boxer Rebellion, and reported he had appeared in more than 100 motion pictures. He died at Corpus Christi, Texas, of cancer and pneumonia.

New York Times, Mar. 10, 12, 1972; *Tucson* (Ariz) *Daily Citizen*, Mar. 2, 1976.

Red Hawk, Shawnee chief (d. 1777). He was at the battle of Point Pleasant in 1774 during Lord Dunmore's War, and was killed by white treachery with Cornstalk three years later, also at Point Pleasant.

Lucullus V. McWhorter, *The Border Settlers of Northwestern Virginia*. Hamilton, O., Republican Pub. Co., 1915; *Documentary History of Dunmore's War 1774*, ed. by Reuben Gold Thwaites, Louise Phelps Kellogg. Madison, Wisc. Hist. Soc., 1905.

Red Jacket (Otetiani, Sagoyewatha), Seneca chief (c. 1756-Jan. 20, 1830). B. probably at Canoga, Seneca County, New York, he was a member of the Wolf Clan of the Seneca and in the American Revolution opposed his people's aligning themselves with the British, but when they did so he took the field with his warriors. His ability, or prominence, attracted white attention and he was given scarlet jackets from which originated the name by which he was known. Although he was on the

Wyoming Valley, Pennsylvania, raid, he was not very active as a warrior, was even reproached for cowardice and would not, for example, attack John Sullivan who invaded Seneca country in 1779, earning thereby the scorn of Cornplanter. Red Jacket was a noted orator, but not a deep thinker; he had a tenacious memory and a quick wit, but he was an egoist and of narrow mind, found it difficult to adjust to the changes brought by the whites, and "the meager measure of importance that finally attached to Red Jacket arose largely from his usefulness in communicating officially with the whites after his tribe had unfortunately lost the greater number of its leading warriors and noted chieftains." His people recognized in him a fluent speaker, if not a great leader. Whether he was present at the Treaty of Fort Stanwix in 1784 is uncertain; he was not then a chief. In 1786 at a council of Indian leaders on the Detroit River he eloquently opposed peace with the whites, Red Jacket sensing no doubt the majority opinion among his listeners. He was conservative, upholding Indian customs, and traditions and was a bitter opponent of changes dictated by the alien race; he attempted to subvert educational, industrial and missionary efforts to better his people, arguing that such instruction unfitted an Indian for "any kind of useful endeavor." Red Jacket with 50 Iroquois chiefs in 1792 visited President Washington at Philadelphia and was given a large silver medal which he thereafter wore with pride (it is held by the Buffalo & Erie County Historical Society). During the War of 1812 Red Jacket temporized but "was no more suspected of treachery than he was of courage," and remained quiet. In 1827 his wife joined the church despite Red Jacket's threat to leave her if she did so. He left but after a few months' dissipation, meekly returned and even accompanied his wife to services upon occasion. In September 1827 Red Jacket was deposed as chief by action of his people who by now had progressed beyond his brand of regression and rejected him also for other alleged offenses. Later he was reinstalled. In 1829 Catlin painted his likeness. He was buried on the Buffalo Reservation, but October 9, 1884, the remains were reburied at Fort Lawn Cemetery, Buffalo, New York, and a handsome memorial unveiled June 22, 1891.

Hodge; HAI; William L. Stone. *Life of Joseph*

Brant, II. N.Y., George Dearborn and Co., 1838; Stone, *The Life and Times of Sa-Go-Ye-Wat-Ha, or Red Jacket.* Albany, N.Y., J. Munsell, 1866; DAB.

Red Shoes (Shulush Homa), Choctaw chief (c. 1700-1748). His home village was in Jasper County, Mississippi; he quickly became war chief of a faction of the Choctaws and soon entered an alliance with the French. In 1736 he sided with the French in war but then proved "insolent," and Vaudreuil stopped supplying arms and ammunition to his party. Red Shoes became further incensed when he caught a Frenchman in adultery with his favorite wife at Fort Tombigbee, Alabama. After a period of neutrality, or relative peace, James Adair persuaded him to lead a faction of Choctaws against the French. By October 1746 De Beauchamp, among friendly (to the French) Choctaws offered a reward for the death of Red Shoes, by this time a very prominent chief. A fratricidal war broke out within the tribe, with Red Shoes steadily more closely aligned with the British. By 1747 the association was firm, he having made visits to Charlestown on the Carolina coast in its pursuit. In June 1748 Red Shoes' band with some Creeks successfully attacked a German settlement and later that year Vaudreuil's decision that Red Shoes must be eliminated was carried out. He was assassinated while bringing a train of English goods from Charlestown to his villages. English traders, seeking to nullify this setback, retrieved the goods, distributed them among the Choctaws and sought to revive the war against the French with a brother of Red Shoes to head the partisans, but the faction ran into a reverse near Fort Tombigbee.

James Adair, *History of the Amerian Indians.* N.Y., Promontory Press, 1973.

Red Spy (Seeyakoon Ilppilp), Nez Perce warrior (d. Sept. 30, 1877). A noted warrior of the non-treaty Nez Perce, Red Spy was the first hostile Indian met by Whipple's white scouts, William Foster and Charles Blewett July 3, 1877. Blewett fired first at Red Spy who then killed him; Foster escaped but was killed later in the day when scouting for the Lieutenant Rains party of ten enlisted men, all of whom were wiped out, Red Spy presumably taking part in the ambush. He had obtained the first telescope he had ever seen from the body of Blewett. Red Spy killed one of Howard's Nez Perce scouts, John Levi near Weippe before the Indians started up the Lolo Trail into Montana. At the Battle of Big Hole, Montana, Red Spy killed a canonneer and drove the other gunners away from the weapon. During the Battle of Bear Paw Mountains, Red Spy sought refuge in an Assiniboin camp but was treacherously killed by them after he had surrendered his rifle, "the Assiniboines acting under orders from... Miles."

Lucullus V. McWhorter, *Yellow Wolf: His Own Story.* Caldwell, Id., Caxton Printers, 1940.

Red Tomahawk, Teton Sioux police sergeant (c. 1853-Aug. 7, 1931). B. near the Cheyenne River of South Dakota, by the late 1880s he was a sergeant of Indian police at Standing Rock Agency, South Dakota. When as a result of the Ghost Dance unrest it was decided by Agent James McLaughlin that Sitting Bull must be arrested, his orders to that effect were carried 40 miles in four hours by Red Tomahawk to bring them into effect. He and Police Lieutenant Bull Head with 43 Indian police descended upon Sitting Bull's camp December 15, 1890. The chief at first agreed to go quietly, then held back and shooting erupted. Bull Head and other Indian police were killed; Red Tomahawk fired the mortal shot into Sitting Bull, assumed command of the detachment and in a furious hand-to-hand battle which left casualties on both sides, staved off Sitting Bull's followers until cavalry arrived. Red Tomahawk was not injured in this affair. He died at 82 at Standing Rock Agency and was buried at Bismarck, North Dakota, leaving two wives, three daughters and a son.

Robert M. Utley, *The Last Days of the Sioux Nation.* New Haven, Yale Univ. Press, 1963; Dockstader.

Red Wing, Sioux chief (c. 1750-c. 1825). There was a succession of chiefs of the Khemichan band of Mdewakanton Sioux by this name and the one cited probably was b. near the site of the present city of Red Wing, Minnesota. His Indian name was Tatanka-mani, or Walking Buffalo; like his father he was an ally of the British. He fought with them in the War of 1812 at Sandusky, Ohio, Mackinac, Michigan and Prairie du Chien, Wisconsin, but after the war sided with the Americans and was ever a friend of the whites. The name disappeared during the Sioux War

of 1862-63. His military record was said to have been exceptional, and his peace record unprecedented.

Hodge, HAI; DAB; Dockstader.

Reddy, Little, *see* Robert McKimie.

Reed, Billy (Norman Newman), outlaw (c. 1879-Oct. 7, 1899). An Oklahoman, Newman in November 1898 killed his farming partner in Greer County, Oklahoma, and shortly was jailed. He was broken out by Perry Cox, brother of William Webb Cox, a New Mexico rancher. Perry Cox gave Newman a stolen horse, instructed him to ride for his brother's San Augustine ranch where he arrived as Billy Reed. He was trailed there by Sheriff George Blalock of Greer County, who with Sheriff Pat Garrett and Deputy José Espalin of Doña Ana County, New Mexico, sought to arrest him. In a resulting fight, Newman/Reed was killed. Espalin said he had fired shots that killed the outlaw, but neither he nor Garrett, who might have shot him, was found at fault.

Robert N. Mullin, "Pat Garrett — Two Forgotten Killings." *Password,* Vol. X, No. 2 (Summer 1965), 57-62; Leon C. Metz, *Pat Garrett.* Norman, Univ. of Okla. Press, 1974.

Reed, Henry Armstrong (Autie), herder (Apr. 27, 1858-June 25, 1876). B. at Monroe, Michigan, and a nephew of George A. and Thomas Ward Custer, Autie Reed went along on the 1876 Sioux expedition at 18 for a lark; he was listed formally as a herder. He was killed in the Battle of the Little Big Horn, Montana. He is sometimes called Arthur Reed and was nicknamed "Autie" after George Custer, his uncle, who also was sometimes called Autie.

BHB; John M. Carroll, Byron Price, *Roll Call on the Little Big Horn.* Fort Collins, Colo., Old Army Press, 1974.

Reed, James Frazier, frontiersman (Nov. 14, 1800-July 24, 1874). B. in County Aramagh, Ireland, he came to America as a youth and settled in Virginia. When he was 20 he went to Galena, Illinois, a lead mining center, removing in 1831 to Springfield, Illinois. He enlisted April 21, 1832, for the Black Hawk War in the same brigade, but not the same company, as Abraham Lincoln, though it is doubtful if he saw any action. Reed engaged in furniture making at Springfield, amassed considerable wealth and was married in 1835 to Margaret Backenstoe. In April 1846 with three wagons, his wife, their four children and Mrs. Reed's mother, Mrs. Sarah Keyes, Reed joined George and Jacob Donner for California, the company known to Illinois papers as the Reed-Donner Party. They reached Independence, Missouri, early in May (see George Donner entry); Mrs. Keyes died at 80 on the Blue River near the present Manhattan, Kansas, May 30. At Weber Canyon in the Wasatch Mountains Reed, Charles Stanton and William Pike went ahead to overtake Lansford Hastings. The cutoff on the California Trail had been his idea in the first place. The Reed party sought to persuade Hastings to return and guide the Donner party over the mountains; Hastings returned part way with Reed but would only vaguely point out the route since he probably knew it as little as they. The train wasted about a month on the crossing of the range, and embarked upon the scarcely more promising transit of the Salt Lake Plains toward the Humboldt River. Reed volunteered to go forward to find water; he discovered it 20 miles ahead and hastened back to discover that his teamsters had lost his 18 oxen in the desert, leaving Reed and his nine-member party destitute, 800 miles from California. The company had moved on toward the water and finally Reed and his companions came up afoot and exhausted. A search for the lost cattle was fruitless. Finally F.W. Graves and Patrick Green loaned him a yoke of oxen to pull a single wagon. The company reached the Humboldt when a dispute arose between Reed and John Snyder, 23, a teamster for Graves who in a passion attacked Reed with his bull whip; Reed stabbed him to death. Although clearly self-defense there were those who resented Reed's prosperity, and Snyder had been popular. A council determined that Reed should be banished although his family would be permitted to remain with the train; he was to go off without even arms and ammunition, but his daughter, Virginia, 14, saw to it that he secured weapons necessary for his life and safety. George and Jacob Donner had been two days ahead at the time of the tragedy. Reed, making for California, caught up with them when he was joined by Walter Herron, 25, one of his former teamsters; they reached California though reduced almost to starvation before clearing the Sierra Nevada, and were kindly received by John Sutter. War

with Mexico had been proclaimed and Reed declined a proffered captaincy until he could get his people to safety, but accepted a lieutenancy by which he could raise recruits as he returned to the mountains, signing up 12 or 13. He borrowed horses and provisions and moved to the head of Bear Valley, finding snow deepening and no way to get through. He returned to Sutter's Fort where it was calculated that the emigrants, if they used their livestock wisely would have enough meat to survive the winter. Reed took part in Bay area operations against the Mexicans, including the fight at Santa Clara, then went to San Francisco where he asked Commodore John B. Hull for aid in succoring the 80 snowbound travelers. Hull was reluctant to commit federal funds without authority, but $1,300 was raised by public subscription including contributions from sailors aboard the Navy vessels. News was received of the safe arrival of seven of a party of 15 from the mired train, and that provided renewed incentive and hope. After further difficulties Reed made up a party laden with supplies; another relief group under Reasin P. Tucker preceded him a few days, topping the pass February 19, 1847, and descending to Donner Lake. The morning the Tucker party left the lake on the return trip, Reed departed from his base for the summit, his expedition becoming known as the Second Relief Party. He reached the snow February 25 and two days later met his wife and two of his children with Tucker's group coming out; he gave them food, sent them on into California while he continued toward Donner Lake, arriving March 1. He rescued his two remaining children and others of the starving migrants. March 3 the return was commenced with 17 emigrants escorted by the 10-man relief group. On the second day a five-day storm came upon them, making travel impossible. With provisions rapidly giving out Reed worked himself to exhaustion providing shelter; when he fell unconscious from his exertions it was only with the greatest difficulty that his life was saved; it was remarkable that any survived, but many did. His family reunited, Reed went to San Jose, then to San Francisco. He had brought considerable money from the States and bought a large tract near San Jose. When gold was discovered he went to the mines and profited. Again he invested his surplus in lands and became a wealthy San Francisco subdivider. His fortunes declined somewhat late in life, but he remained comfortably well off. His banishment from the Donner company seemed a calamity at the time, but had it not occurred the entire party might have perished in the mountains, for it was Reed who kept alive the hope of rescue and engineered its most effective efforts.

C.F. McGlashan, *History of the Donner Party*. Stanford Univ. Press, 1947; George R. Stewart, *Ordeal by Hunger*. N.Y., Ace Books, 1960; Bancroft, *Pioneer Register*.

Reed, John, mountain man (d. c. Jan. 10, 1814). Reed was "an Irishman by birth," according to Chittenden who concedes that nothing more is known of him before he joined the Astorians and went west with Hunt in the overland party. He signed on as a "clerk," although he appears to have been experienced and to have assumed more responsibility than a clerk would normally take up. It was Reed and a small party who were sent ahead to reconnoitre the Snake River, exploring its gorges. He seems to have scouted ahead from time to time as the Hunt party struggled to reach and descend the Columbia. From the new post of Astoria, Reed on March 30, 1812, was entrusted with dispatches for Astor, taking them with a small party, intending to cross the continent to New York. May 11 the group abruptly appeared back at Astoria. They had proceeded to The Dalles, Oregon, when Indians attacked them, stole provisions and snatched away Reed's dispatch box, after stunning him; the letters were not recovered. Reed explored the Willamette Valley early in 1813. In the summer he was sent to obtain provisions from the Snakes and to trap the following winter in what is now southern Idaho. He established himself along the Boise River, long known to fur trappers as Reed's River, where in January those mountain men who had survived until then were killed by the Snakes, only Pierre Dorion's wife and children left alive. They eventually escaped with the story.

Gabriel Franchere, *Adventure in Astoria*. Norman, Univ. of Okla. Press, 1967; Alexander Ross, *Adventures of the First Settlers on the Oregon*. N.Y., Citadel Press, 1969; Chittenden.

Reed, Joseph, adventurer (fl. 1800-1810). A Kentuckian, Reed was a member of Philip Nolan's 1800-1801 wild horse expedition into Spanish Texas and after Nolan was killed Reed

and the others were captured in the Trinity River country and taken to Chihuahua. Pike heard that he was somewhere in the Province of Nueva Vizcaya (Chihuahua), but could learn no particulars of his condition or prospects. Little more is known of him.

Bennett Lay, *The Lives of Ellis P. Bean*. Austin, Univ. of Tex. Press, 1960.

Reed (Read), Moses B., frontiersman (fl. 1804-1805). A member of the Lewis and Clark Expedition, he attempted to desert August 4, 1804, enroute up the Missouri and therefore was sent back to St. Louis with the 1805 return party.

History of the Expedition Under the Command of Lewis and Clark, ed. by Elliott Coues. N.Y., Dover Pubns., 1965; Clarke, *Lewis and Clark*.

Reed, Walter, physician (Sept. 13, 1851-Nov. 23, 1902). B. at Belroi, near Gloucester, Virginia, he was the youngest of five children of a Methodist minister assigned to different churches from time to time and grew up in various communities of Virginia and North Carolina. He studied medicine at the University of Virginia and received his M.D. in 1869, earning a second at Bellevue Hospital, New York in 1870. He practiced and worked at related occupations in New York until June 1875, when he was commissioned an assistant surgeon in the army and ordered to Fort Lowell, Arizona, serving there and at Camp (later Fort) Apache for several years. Reed's letters to his sister give graphic insights to his hazardous life on this still untamed frontier. In December 1878 he saved the life of an Apache girl who had accidentally stumbled into a campfire, and informally adopted her into his family. Twelve years later she was found "with child" by a soldier who had been discharged and presumably was untraceable, and Reed sent her back to her people, then prisoners of war at Mount Vernon, Alabama. She knew of no near relatives, however and was unacceptable to the Apaches by reason of her condition, so was given into the care of a "respectable negro woman," until the expected birth when it was hoped she might become a servant in some officer's family. Eventually the Reeds moved to Omaha, then were assigned to Fort Sidney and Fort Robinson, Nebraska, where Reed was stationed for three years, on one occasion treating a dangerously injured leg of Jules

Sandoz, the title character of Mari Sandoz's biography, "Old Jules." In 1887 he was assigned for three years to Mount Vernon Barracks, near Mobile, Alabama, where hundreds of Apaches still were held as prisoners of war. Reed had kept up his studies and now became interested in pathology and bacteriology, studying at Johns Hopkins Hospital at Baltimore and pointing toward an exciting new career removed from frontier interest, which led to his notable pioneering work on the causes of malaria, typhoid and yellow fever, the last of which brought him much fame and led to the control of that scourge over much of its range and eventually inoculation against it. His malaria work was never widely publicized and his typhoid investigations are less well known than those of yellow fever. In the midst of this course of study and achievement, however, Reed served on detached duty in late December 1890 and January 1891 in the Wounded Knee affair in South Dakota, the last major confrontation between Indians and army in the conquest of a continent. Reed was stationed at Fort Snelling, Minnesota, from late 1891 to September 1893, his final frontier assignment, continuing meanwhile his scientific studies at nearby St. Paul. In late 1893 he returned to Washington as curator of the Army Medical Museum and professor of bacteriology and clinical microscopy in the new Army Medical College; his brilliant later career is beyond the frontier scope. He died following surgery for a ruptured appendix and abscess of the cecum which perhaps resulted from amoebic dysentery which he may have contracted in Cuba where he did his noted yellow fever work. "He was a disciplined military physician and surgeon, a southern gentleman of a long-departed era, an upright and compassionate man, and a scientific scholar and superb investigator. His life had a grandeur born of work, character, dedication, and practical wisdom."

Literature abundant; William Bennett Bean, "Walter Reed." *Archives of Internal Medicine,* Vol 134 (Nov. 1974), 871-77.

Rees, Sol, buffalo hunter (Oct. 21, 1847-Apr 14, 1913). B. in Delaware County, Indiana, he enlisted March 5, 1865, in an Indiana regiment, too late for service in the Civil War and the next year, at 19, he went to Kansas where for a decade he homesteaded, hunted buffaloes, fought Indians and served as a government scout. In 1876 after a quick trip with Bill Kress to Philadelphia for the Sesquicentennial Exposition, Rees resumed buffalo hunting, meeting John R. Cook. The two were more or less closely associated for several seasons. Rees was a scout during the Dull Knife operation in 1878. His version of how his life was saved by Kit Carson's wife is fanciful, however, since Carson's wife was dead before he reached New Mexico, although he must have undergone some such adventure as described in Cook's *The Border and the Buffalo.* Rees homesteaded near Jennings, Decatur County, Kansas. He died at Jennings. Rees was described as 5 feet, 10 inches in height, weighing 170 pounds, with grey eyes and light brown hair. It was he who financed Cook's production of his book at $1 each for 1,000 copies of the 1907 edition; it sold for $2.

John R. Cook, *The Border and the Buffalo,* historical introduction by Milo M. Quaife. Chicago, Lakeside Press, 1938.

Reese, Tom, fur man (d. fall 1843). A black hired at Fort McKenzie on the upper Missouri River, Reese bravely started alone after Blackfeet who had stolen post cattle and was shot dead by the Indians, his murder leading indirectly to the massacre of Blackfeet by Alexander Harvey the following spring.

Montana, Contributions, Volume X, 1940, p. 248.

Reeve, Isaac Van Duzer, army officer (July 19, 1813-Dec. 31, 1890). B. in Otsego County, New York, he was graduated from West Point in 1835, joining the 4th Infantry with which he became a second lieutenant May 2, 1836, and a first lieutenant two years later. He served in Florida in 1836-37, participating in several skirmishes with the Seminoles and was on the northern frontier from 1838-40, having a role in the removal of the Winnebagos in 1840. He then returned to Florida for Seminole service from 1840-42 and remained at Key West until 1845. He participated in the military occupation of Texas in 1845 and entered the Mexican War as captain, emerging a brevet lieutenant colonel. After the war he served as a captain in Texas, New Mexico and Arizona, commanding two expeditions against the Gila Apaches in 1858. Early in 1861 he and his command were transferred from Fort

Breckenridge, Arizona, to Fort Bliss, Texas, from there moving east. Taken prisoner of war through the treachery of General David E. Twiggs near San Antonio, Reeve was not exchanged until August 20, 1862, his Civil War assignments thereafter being administrative. He became a major in 1861 and emerged from the Civil War a colonel and brevet Brigadier General. He commanded the District of the Upper Missouri and his regiment from 1865-68, retiring January 1, 1871.

Heitman; Cullum; Powell; Constance Wynn Altshuler, ed., *Latest From Arizona!* Tucson, Ariz. Pioneers' Hist. Soc., 1969.

Reger, Jacob Jr., scout, frontiersman (c. 1765-post 1800). His father emigrated from Germany, reaching Virginia about 1765, which is conjectured as the probable year of Jacob Jr.'s birth. The son reached the Buckhannon country of present West Virginia, where he became a noted scout and Indian fighter. "He often rendered valuable service to the settlements on the Upper Monongahela River." It is said to have been he who warned the Buckhannon settlement in time to fight off the last Indian raid in that country, about 1790. Although "of gigantic stature and wonderful strength," he once was savagely mauled by a wounded bear, but recovered. He is said to have died near Cincinnati, Ohio.

Lucullus V. McWhorter, *The Border Settlers of Northwestern Virginia.* Hamilton, O., Republican Pub. Co., 1915.

Reger, John, frontiersman (Jan. 15, 1769-May 14, 1844). B. in Hardy County, Virginia, he was a brother of Jacob Reger Jr., and reached the Buckhannon country where he became known as "the hercules of the frontier," being 6 feet, 2 inches, in height and of enormous physical strength. At his wedding, December 5, 1787, to a girl whose father had just been killed by Indians, his bride it is said stood upright on one of his outstretched hands. Of a kindly nature, John's feats included swimming swollen rivers, toting heavy weights of game, challenging bears in their dens, discomfitting border bullies and performing innumerable like acts. He died at his Buckhannon farm in West Virginia, and is buried there.

Lucullus V. McWhorter, *The Border Settlers of Northwestern Virginia.* Hamilton, O., Republican Pub. Co., 1915.

Reger, Philip, frontiersman (1767-c. 1856). B. in Hampshire County, Virginia, he served in the Patriot forces six months toward the close of the Revolution, being at Yorktown for the British surrender. On the western Virginia frontier he was a hunter occasionally for Henry Jackson's surveying parties, once was bitten by a rattlesnake, but recovered, if barely. He was a first official of Buckhannon, present West Virginia, the first sheriff of Lewis County and a justice of the peace for 40 years. He was a brother of Jacob Reger Jr., noted scout.

Lucullus V. McWhorter, *The Border Settlers of Northwestern Virginia.* Hamilton, O., Republican Pub. Co., 1915.

Reid, Thomas Mayne, adventurer, writer (Apr. 4, 1818-Oct. 22, 1883). B. in County Down, Ireland, his father was a Presbyterian minister, but Mayne Reid, as he was to become known, sought adventure, reaching New Orleans, Louisiana, at 19, traveling the Platte and Missouri rivers, associating with hunters, trappers and Indians. In the Mexican War he was commissioned a second lieutenant in the 1st New York Volunteers, mustered in December 3, 1846. He reached Vera Cruz in March and on September 13, 1847, he was severely wounded at Chapultepec where Mexican cadets heroically resisted the American invaders. He left the service a first lieutenant and quitted Mexico in the spring of 1848, resigning May 5. He returned to England and his true literary career commenced, Reid writing some 70 volumes of fiction and other works. He became lame in the later years from the effects of his Mexican wound. Mayne Reid's writings influenced many young men toward adventure wherever English was read. They were usually carefully backgrounded, with authentic local color and meticulous in historical and geographical settings. Among his avid readers were Theodore Roosevelt and Charles Lummis. Roosevelt wrote: "I was too young to understand much of Mayne Reid except the adventure part and the natural history part — these enthralled me." Lummis: "No other writer made the wonderland of the United States so fascinating as this fighting bantam Irishman... Reid was the very first man who taught Americans the charm of the American West; and to this day his peer has not arisen." He added that Reid's books "teach nature as no others do; ...so exciting that no sane boy alive can fail to kindle to them." Among his better known titles, some in American editions appearing after his death: *The Quadroon; or, A Lover's Adventures in Louisiana* (1856); *The Hunters' Feast; or, Conversations Around the Camp-fire* (1856); *The Young Voyageurs; or, The Boy Hunters in the North* (1857); *The Half-Breed; or, Oceola, the Seminole* (1861); *Bruin; The Grand Bear Hunt* (1864); *The Desert Home; or, The Adventures of a Lost Family* (1864); *The Bandalero; or, A Marriage Among the Mountains* (1866); *The Lone Ranch* (1884); *The Boy Hunters; or Adventures in Search of a White Buffalo* (1885); *Osceola the Seminole; or, The Red Fawn of the Flowerland* (1891); *The White Chief. A Legend of North Mexico* (1891); *The War Trail; or, The Hunt of the Wild Horse; A Romance of the Prairie* (1892); *The Wild Huntress; or, Love in the Wilderness* (1892) *The White Gauntlet* (1892); *The Rifle Rangers: A Thrilling Story of Daring Adventure and Hairbreath Escapes During the Mexican War* (1899); *The Scalp Hunters: A Thrilling Tale of Adventure and Romance in Northern Mexico* (1899); *The Boy Hunters of the Mississippi* (1912).

DAB; Library of Congress catalogue; Dudley Gordon, "Mayne Reid: Pioneer Author of the Southwest." *Corral Dust*, Potomac Corral of Westerners, Vol. III, No. 4 (Dec. 1958).

Reilly, Bernard (Ben) Jr., army officer (Sept. 12, 1843-Oct. 17, 1906). B. in Pennsylvania, he enlisted in the 25th Pennsylvania Infantry April 18, 1861, and was commissioned a second lieutenant of the 17th Pennsylvania Cavalry November 18, 1861, becoming a first lieutenant July 1, 1863. During much of his Civil War service he performed the duties of a topographical engineer. At the Battle of Chickamauga, Tennessee (September 19-20, 1863) Reilly was wounded in the left hand by a shell fragment; tooth decay also led to a rheumatic condition in his left shoulder and arm, and military leaves for health reasons. He resigned April 21, 1864. He was commissioned a second lieutenant of the 5th Cavalry May 4, 1868. He went with his regiment to Fort D.A. Russell, Wyoming, in 1870, becoming a first lieutenant March 1 of that year. In November 1871 he was with the first contingent of the regiment sent to Arizona, reaching Camp Grant in January 1872, later

being stationed at Fort Apache. From there Reilly took part in 1874 operations against hostile Apaches. April 2 with 15 Apache scouts he accompanied Lieutenant Alfred Bache and 24 soldiers up Pinal Creek under cover of night to a rancheria atop a mountain, Bache giving Reilly the honor of first strike "as we were officers of nearly the same rank, and as it was Mr. Reilly's first experience in Arizona and he was most anxious to distinguish himself." It was a very difficult approach, but the attack force reached position before daylight and struck sharply, killing 48 Indians, many of them women and children, and capturing about 50. Reilly twice was nominated for brevet to captain for his part in the fight and other scouts. In February 1875 he was assigned to Fort Lyon, Colorado, then to Fort Gibson, Indian Territory, and from June 1876 served on the Sioux campaigns in Wyoming, Montana and Dakota. He was engaged in the affairs at War Bonnet Creek and at Slim Buttes, Dakota. Reilly was court-martialed in early 1877 for an unremembered offense, was sentenced to dismissal, mitigated to suspension from rank, command and pay except $75 a month for a year; the suspension from rank and command in turn were also remitted. Following completion of his sentence, Reilly resigned June 4, 1878. He lived for a time in Kansas and Missouri with "no settled occupation," then became an attorney practicing at Washington, D.C., and Philadelphia where in 1898 he married. He died at Philadelphia and was buried at Pottsville, Pennsylvania. In his young manhood he was 5 feet, 9 inches in height, with a light complexion, light colored hair and blue eyes.

Heitman; Reilly Pension File, NARS; Price, *Fifth Cavalry;* Dan L. Thrapp, *The Conquest of Apacheria.* Norman, Univ. of Okla. Press, 1967; Wesley Merrit, "Three Indian Campaigns." *Harper's Mag.*, Vol. LXXX, No. 479 (Apr. 1890), reprint with biographical essay by Barry C. Johnson, London, Johnson-Taunton Military Press, 1972.

Reily, William Van Wyck, army officer (Dec. 12, 1853-June 25, 1876). B. at Washington, D.C., he studied two years in Germany, attended Annapolis September 1870 to October 17, 1872, when he resigned, served on a surveying expedition to Nicaragua for eight months and spent two years superintending the breakup of old monitors, or warships. Reily was commissioned a second lieutenant in the 10th Cavalry October 15, 1875, and transferred to the 7th Cavalry in January 1876. He accompanied Custer's Sioux expedition in the spring of 1876 and was killed at the Battle of the Little Big Horn while on duty with Company F. He was buried on the battlefield and reinterred at Washington, D.C., in July 1877. He was 22 at his death.

BHB; Heitman.

Remington, Frederic, artist, writer (Oct. 4, 1861-Dec. 26, 1909). B. at Canton, New York, his family shortly removed to Ogdensburg. Frederic attended the Yale School of the Fine Arts, graduating in 1880 and incidentally playing football with the great Walter Camp. His father died when he was 19, and the youth made a trip to the northwest, finding there his life's work, to record "the living, breathing end of three American centuries." At a campfire on the Yellowstone in 1880, an old freighter had pointed out that within a few years there would be no more West. Remington had not realized the end was so close. "I knew the railroad was coming... the derby hat, the smoking chimney, the cord-binder, the 30-day note... I knew the wild riders and the vacant land were about to vanish forever... Without knowing exactly how to do it, I began to try to record some facts around me, and the more I looked the more the panorama unfolded," he wrote. He visited Europe and North Africa briefly and was an artist-correspondent during the war in Cuba, but he is best known for his stirring, authentic, prolific record of the last of the wild great West. He wrote clear, honest prose, and his pictures also possessed those qualities — no one except Bodmer recorded the West in as precise detail, no one save Russell with as much heart and vivacity and enthusiasm. He neither drew nor wrote a single false scene when these things concerned what he had observed or learned first-hand; only in some of his illustration for historic works or those beyond his experience can he be faulted. Without Remington the history of much of the nation would have been less perfectly recorded and the debt owed him is immense. He worked with Eadweard Muybridge on the horse in motion, that his action pictures be authentic. His human figures have character; the equipment he drew was correct, and his landscapes, rocks, plant life and other background material true in every detail: "His Indians are Indians: his Apache is an Apache, his Sioux is a Sioux." Remington's pictures of cowboys and soldiers, the Mexicans, packers, scouts and squaw men have never been surpassed, or, for that matter, equalled. His pen-and-ink drawings are as good as his oils, and his sculptures the equal of either. His books are an authentic record of what he had seen and learned. Remington established a home at New Rochelle, New York. His collection of his own work, with the artifacts he collected, is in the Remington Art Memorial at Ogdensburg, his library at the Ogdensburg Public Library, and there are important collections of his prolific output elsewhere. In 1909 he moved to Ridgefield, Connecticut, but six months later died of appendicitis. He is buried at Canton.

Literature abundant.

Remy de Courcelle, Daniel de, French official (1626-Oct. 24, 1698). B. in France, he succeeded Saffray de Mezy as governor of Canada, reaching Quebec September 12, 1665, "breathing nothing but war" against the Iroquois. He placed himself, although superior politically, at the disposal of the Marquis de Tracy, Lieutenant General of French forces in Canada charged with ending the Iroquois menace, assisted in the building of a chain of forts between the St. Lawrence and Lake Champlain and organizing an expeditionary force. Courcelle left Canada with this 600-man command in January 1666, but misfortune attended the effort. Despite severe winter weather, the absence of guides and paucity of supplies, the expedition reached the Mohawk River where it was saved from starvation by efforts of Dutch colonials. Courcelle was surprised to learn that the English had taken over New Amsterdam. He started his return in late February, losing 60 men to the elements and other wilderness exigencies, and his campaign came "dangerously close to being a total disaster." Courcelle blamed the Jesuits for not urging the friendly tribes to supply suitable guides, opening his feud with that Catholic order. In September Courcelle joined Tracy in another, more productive campaign against the Mohawks, bringing the Indians to a more lasting peace than ever before. Courcelle was a good Indian man; in 1669 when a Seneca chief was slain by three soldiers of Montreal he had the whites arrested, tried and executed before many Iroquois come to Montreal to trade, and peace was preserved. When the western Iroquois became belligerent, convinced their remoteness put them beyond reach of the French, Courcelle took a force to Lake Ontario and forced peace upon the Indians. The governor recommended that a fur trading and military post be built at the eastern end of the lake, and he was influential and effective in assuring the bulk of the fur trade be reserved to the French. Courcelle encouraged exploration which caused vast lands to be added to the French North American empire. He was returned to France at his own request in 1672 and was governor of Toulon at his death. He was unmarried.

Thwaites, JR, XLIX, 274-75n14; Parkman, *Old Regime in Canada;* DCB.

Renault, Philippe Francois, miner (fl. 1720-1744). B. in France the son of a well-known ironmaster, he reached Fort Chartres, at the site of the present Prairie du Rocher, Illinois, in 1719 with 200 miners and artisans, and 500 black slaves purchased in Santo Domingo, it was said. From there he sent out lead prospecting parties and opened mines in the district of Ste. Genevieve, Missouri. For more than 20 years he refined ore in crude furnaces and carried lead to Fort Chartres in horse-collar molds around the necks of pack animals. The town of Ste. Genevieve was founded because of these mines c. 1735, and removed to higher ground in 1785 because of a flood. A road from it to the mines was created, suitable for two-wheeled ore carts. Lead was shipped downstream to New Orleans and thence to France. Renault in 1744 returned to France after selling his slaves to the colonists his enterprise had attracted.

Thwaites, JR, LXX, 316n39; Edwin C. McReynolds, *Missouri: A History of the Crossroads State.* Norman, Univ. of Okla. Press, 1962.

Reno, Marcus Albert, army officer (Nov. 15, 1834-Apr. 1, 1889). B. at Carrollton, Illinois, his middle name was Alfred, wrote Terrell/Walton, but Albert according to Heitman and Cullum. He went to West Point and was commissioned a brevet second lieutenant of the 1st Dragoons July 1, 1857, and a second lieutenant June 14, 1858. He did frontier duty in the northwest out of Forts Walla Walla,

Washington, and The Dalles, Oregon, until the Civil War, being promoted to first lieutenant, 1st Dragoons April 25, 1861 (it became the 1st Cavalry August 3). His civil War service was with the Army of the Potomac, his record creditable: he ended the war a brevet Brigadier General of Volunteers and brevet colonel in the army with rank of captain. After the war he briefly did frontier duty at Fort Vancouver, Washington, and was acting assistant inspector general of the Department of the Columbia from June 22, 1867, until June 15, 1869. Reno became a major of the 7th Cavalry December 26, 1868, after its fight at the Washita in which of course he had no part. He served at Fort Hays, Kansas, from December 19, 1869, to July 1871 when he was transferred east for a couple of years. Reno commanded the escort for the Northern Boundary Survey from June to October 1873 and again in the summer of 1874. He was stationed at Fort Abraham Lincoln, North Dakota, from October 30, 1875, and accompanied Custer on the Sioux expedition of 1876. His role in the Little Big Horn fight is more controversial perhaps than that of any other individual. Reno led a large scout from June 10 to 18; Terry wanted the upper reaches of the Tongue and Powder rivers reconnoitred before the main command moved farther west, Reno directed not to go so far as the Rosebud River, however. He found no Indians on the Powder or Tongue but, contrary to instructions went into the valley of the Rosebud and found a lodgpole-etched trail "half a mile wide," indicating a very large number of Indians heading up the river toward a divide between it and the Little Big Horn. Terry, Custer and some others feared that the hostiles might have seen Reno along the Rosebud and been warned away, but this proved not the case. Reno heard nothing of Crook's command to the south and west on his scout, which covered 240 miles. Custer sharply criticized him for not following the trail and having fought any Indians he found, but to do so would have been in even greater violation of his orders than penetrating the Rosebud Valley. Terry determined to send Custer, and his subordinate Reno, up the Rosebud, to penetrate the valley of the Little Big Horn where it was supposed the hostiles would be camped. This was done. The 7th Cavalry left June 22 and on the 23rd found the trail reported by Reno. At noon on June 25 the command topped the rise. Reno was assigned to command a battalion of Troops A, G and M. Later he was directed to cross the Little Big Horn and attack an Indian camp, Custer promising that "I will support you." Reno did so, found that he faced more Indians than he needed, endeavored to make a stand but was forced to retreat (a maneuver that became "a disorganized rout") back across the river to "Reno's Hill," some bluffs above the stream. Here he was besieged. He was joined about the time of his arrival by Benteen who had been on a separate mission, and later by the pack train under Mathey and McDougall. The Reno forces suffered 49 killed and 46 wounded before the Indians pulled away late June 26 before Gibbon and Terry arrived in relief. It had been "Reno's first taste of Indian fighting" and while he possessed soldierly qualities he seemed to "lack the ability to make decisions under fire (and to) have been totally lacking in the capability to command." Reno was criticized in some quarters for not charging the village instead of making a futile stand before it, for his precipitous withdrawal from the valley and for his conduct on Reno Hill, a subject of controversy for more than a century. It has been alleged that he was "cowardly in the extreme," drunk during the action, that on occasion he was in a panic according to some accounts, that he failed to go to Custer's relief or attempt to do so, and was accused of other failings, each rebutted by testimony as reliable as that by which they were leveled. The literature is voluminous and here is not the place to go into the matters raised. Reno commanded the 7th Cavalry or what was left of it from June 26 to October 18, 1876. The unfortunate officer shortly became the victim of something of a vendetta. In March and April 1877 he was court martialed at St. Paul, Minnesota, on flimsy charges that he had made improper advances to the wife of Captain James M. Bell of the 7th; she had "a rather unsavory reputation" and had been involved in affairs at other stations; she had been the aggressor, it was charged, was miffed when Reno rejected her advances, and the charges then were brought. The court found Reno guilty of conduct unbecoming an officer and gentleman, recommended that he be dismissed but President Hayes reduced the sentence to suspension without pay for two years. Immediately 7th Cavalry officers McDougall, Moylan, DeRudio and Bell

charged Reno had struck a junior officer and been drunk on duty, but Sturgis and Terry disagreed and so informed the Secretary of War who ordered the charges dropped. In 1879 because of continuing criticism over his role in the Little Big Horn action, Reno requested an official inquiry. The court, which some regarded as "a bit of a whitewash," found nothing improper in his performance. Fresh charges were leveled against Reno in 1880: striking a junior officer, being a "Peeping Tom," and being drunk at Fort Meade, Dakota. None presented a clear cut case, all were minor, but he was found guilty, dismissed from the army April 1, 1880, for "conduct to the prejudice of good order and military discipline" over the protests of Terry and Sherman, while even the court board had urged clemency. Reno tried vigorously to have his name cleared during the remainder of his life, but to no avail. He died of cancer at Providence Hospital and was buried in an unmarked grave at Glenwood Cemetery, Washington, D.C. In the mid-1960s a relative asked the army to re-examine the charges and the fatal court martial. The findings were studied and the conclusion drawn that evidence had not supported the charges, that Reno had been improperly dismissed. The 19th century charges were dismissed and he was restored to rank. In 1967 his remains were exhumed and reburied at Custer Battlefield National Cemetery, Montana with full military honors.

Literature abundant: Cullum; Heitman; John Upton Terrell, George Walton, *Faint the Trumpet Sounds.* N.Y., David McKay Co., 1966; Edgar I. Stewart, *Custer's Luck.* Norman, Univ. of Okla. Press, 1955; Barry C. Johnson, *Case of Marcus A. Reno.* London, English Westerners' Soc., Special Publn. 3, 1969; J.W. Vaughn, *Indian Fights: New Facts on Seven Encounters.* Norman, 1966; *Peter Thompson's Narrative of the Little Bighorn Campaign,* ed. by Daniel O. Magnussen. Glendale, Calif., Arthur H. Clark Co., 1974.

Renville, Joseph, fur trader, interpreter (1779-Mar. 1846). B. of a French fur trader father and a Sioux mother at Kaposia, on the site of the present St. Paul, Minnesota, his early childhood was spent among his mother's people but at 10 he was taken by his father to Canada and raised by Catholic priests, under whom he learned French. Returning to Minnesota he was hired by Robert Dickson as a *coureur des bois* and "while a mere stripling he had guided his canoe from the Falls of Pokeguma to the Falls of St. Anthony and followed the trails from Mendota to the Missouri." He identified himself with the Sioux again, marrying a woman of that people. In 1797 Renville wintered near the Sauk Rapids, Minnesota. In 1805 he was a guide and interpreter for Zebulon Pike on Pike's exploration of the upper Mississippi. Pike described him in a letter as one who "has gratuitously and willingly served as my interpreter in all my conferences with the Sioux. He is a man respected by the Indians, and I believe an honest one." At the outbreak of the War of 1812 Renville was recruited with the rank of captain by Dickson. He was present at Fort Meigs and Fort Stephenson, Ohio, "and the good conduct of the Indians there was due largely to his influence." In 1815 he attended the great council at Portage des Sioux as interpreter, resigned his British commission and thenceforth attached himself to the American interest. He organized the Columbia Fur Company with headquarters at Lake Traverse, Minnesota, recruited hardy traders left without employment by the merger of the Hudson's Bay and North West Fur companies and organized competition so able and resolute that the American Fur Company "was glad to make terms and place the Columbia Company's men in charge of its Upper Missouri Outfit." Renville meanwhile had established an independent business at Lac qui Parle which he conducted for the rest of his life. About 1834 at Prairie du Chien he met Dr. Thomas Smith Williamson, a Presbyterian physician-missionary who was interested in Sioux work and the language of that people, and arranged with him to open a mission at Lac qui Parle in 1835. That year Williamson met Renville at Fort Snelling and soon engaged in translation of the Sçriptures into Sioux. Renville translated every word of the Bible, the missionaries faithfully recording it, and he also rendered them "invaluable assistance" in constructing a grammar and dictionary of the language. In 1841 he was ordained a ruling elder of the Presbyterian mission, retaining that post until his death, which occurred at Lac qui Parle. In his advanced age he sometimes exhibited a domineering disposition, although he was ever hospitable to all who came his way. He introduced seed corn on the Upper Minnesota River. His post struck explorers and scientists alike as a rewarding place to visit since Renville's conversation was ever intelligent and informative. Renville was notably religious. He took his Indian wife to Prairie du Chien and was formally married to her by a Roman Catholic priest. He secured a large folio Bible in French and hired a clerk who could read it to him; this may have been the first Bible in Minnesota. It was printed at Geneva, Switzerland and had a Latin preface by John Calvin. Renville has many descendants among the Sisseton Sioux of South Dakota.

Hodge, HAI; Edward Duffield Neill, *History of Minnesota*. Minneapolis, Minn. Hist. Co., 1882.

Revere, Joseph Warren, adventurer (May 17, 1812-Apr. 20, 1880). B. in Boston and the grandson of Paul Revere, he entered the navy as a midshipman in 1828. He sailed for California aboard the *Portsmouth,* reaching Monterey in April 1846, and in the absence of the army he personally lowered the Bear Flag and unfurled the American standard at Sonoma, July 9, 1846, later was transferred to San Diego, participating in hoisting the American flag at La Paz, thus raised it at the most northerly and southerly points in occupied California of that day. After the war he returned to Boston, but was ordered back to California as agent for protection of naval timber lands. In 1850 he resigned from the navy as a lieutenant, became a merchant seaman and part owner of a ship. He briefly served the Mexican government as artillery instructor, returned to the U.S. in 1853 and served as military consultant to various European governments. In 1861 he was commissioned colonel of the 7th New Jersey Infantry, became a Brigadier General of Volunteers a year later, and resigned August 10, 1863. His book, *A Tour of Duty in California* (1849) included a remarkably accurate portrait of California a century in the future when "the poor Indians will have passed away; the rancheros will be remembered only as the ancient proprietors of broad lands . . . The Grizzly Bear will live only in books and tradition . . . and California . . . will she have become populous and enlightened, the seat of arts and learning, the generous rival of her elder sisters in all that is lively and of good report among men?" Francis J. Weber, "Paul Revere's Grandson Left His Mark Here." *Tidings*, Los Angeles, Calif., Feb. 15, 1974; Heitman.

Reynal, Antoine Jr., frontiersman (c. 1809-post 1872). B. at St. Charles, Missouri, he early became a trapper and trader and was captured by Pawnees while accompanying a Sioux war party. He was at Fort Laramie in 1846, had married a Sioux woman and in 1854 testified about the Grattan massacre. Reynal operated a stage station east of Laramie in 1860, then turned rancher. In 1872 he filed a claim for losses from Indian depredation.

Charles E. Hanson Jr. article, MM, Vol. IX.

Reynolds, Bainbridge, army officer (Sept. 15, 1849-July 10, 1901). B. at West Point, the son of a general officer, Reynolds himself was graduated from the Point in 1873 and joined the 3rd Cavalry at Fort McPherson, Nebraska, participating in almost continual field duty. Commanding F Company he took a conspicuous part in the June 17, 1876, battle at the Rosebud and was breveted for gallantry. Reynolds also distinguished himself in the Powder River fight March 17, 1876; Tongue River June 9 and Slim Buttes, September 8-9, 1876. He became a first lieutenant in 1879 and a captain in 1889, resigning in 1891, and dying of cancer. He never married.

Heitman; J.W. Vaughn, *With Crook at the Rosebud.* Harrisburg, Pa., Stackpole Co., 1956.

Reynolds, Charles Alexander (Lonesome Charley), scout (Mar. 20, 1842-June 25, 1876). B. on a farm in Warren County, Illinois, he attended the preparatory division of Abingdon College, Abingdon, Illinois, but moved to Pardee, Kansas, in 1859 with his parents. He was considered well educated, writing a neat hand and using good grammar, and was a sharp observer, being well thought of by George Bird Grinnell and other scientists for whom he worked. When 18 he joined a wagon train, probably for Denver, and spent a winter trapping in Middle Park. In 1861 he enlisted in the 10th Kansas regiment, engaged in border fighting on the Missouri frontier, accompanied an expedition to Indian Territory, and participated in the battle of Prairie Grove, Arkansas, then engaged in escort duty on the Santa Fe Trail to Fort

Union, New Mexico. Reynolds is supposed to have scouted against Sterling Price during his raid into Missouri in 1864. The next spring he set out on a Plains trading expedition; his partner was killed by Indians, perhaps on Rabbit's Ear Creek in northeast New Mexico. Charley wintered at Santa Fe, was a buffalo hunter on the Republican, wintered the following year at Jack Morrow's ranch on the Platte, where he wounded an Army officer who was drunk and abusive. By 1869 he had removed to Dakota Territory and for several years was a market hunter with Joe Dietrick and Peter Beauchamp. Charley helped General Sheridan entertain Grand Duke Alexis on his Plains soiree in 1872. He first scouted for the Army with Brigadier General David S. Stanley's Yellowstone expeditions of 1872 and 1873. In 1874 he guided Custer's expedition to the Black Hills, first meeting Grinnell. He helped arrest Rain in the Face for murder in 1874, though charges against the Indian were not pressed. The next year he guided Captain William Ludlow into Yellowstone Park and the Judith Basin. On the Custer 1876 operation, Reynolds was with Reno's detachment which first engaged the Indians in the valley. When the troops were ordered to withdraw, Reynolds was among the last to leave. As his horse climbed the bluff toward the prairie it fell on the scout, perhaps it had been shot, and Reynolds was pinned beneath it, where he was killed. Reynolds was about 5 feet, 8 inches tall, heavy-set and somewhat round-shouldered. He was an excellent shot. He had gray eyes, a soft voice and was abstemious, using neither tobacco nor liquor. He never married.

John S. Gray, "On the Trail of 'Lonesome Charley' Reynolds." *Westerners Brand Book,* Chicago Corral, Vol. XIV, No. 8 (Oct. 1957); E.E. Brininstool, *Troopers With Custer.* Harrisburg, Pa., Stackpole Co., 1952, 305-22.

Reynolds, Glenn, lawman (1853-Nov. 2, 1889). B. probably near Albany, Texas, he helped as a boy to protect exposed Texas settlements from Comanche raids while most adult males were serving in the Civil War; it is said he participated in trail drives afterward to Kansas railheads. Reynolds was elected sheriff of Throckmorton County, Texas, raised sheep for a time, and in 1885 with the backing of relatives who were prominent cattle raisers near Albany brought with Jess Ellison 3,000 head of cattle and 200 horses to Bowie Station, Arizona, trailing his portion of the herd 200 miles north to the Pleasant Valley region where he commenced ranching. The outbreak of the Pleasant Valley War made living conditions so unendurable, however, that Reynolds and his family moved to Globe. Here in November 1888 he was elected sheriff; as such he frequently hunted Massai and other noted bronco Apaches as well as dealing with troublesome whites. In late October 1889 Reynolds was assigned the task of conducting the Apache Kid and several other convicted men from Globe to the railroad at Casa Grande, Arizona, enroute to the territorial prison; he deputized William H. (Hunkydory) Holmes and with Eugene Middleton as stage driver the party set out November 1. The next day near the present town of Kelvin, Arizona, four of the Indians (but not including the Kid) by a ruse wrested arms from the law officers, killed Reynolds while Holmes died of a heart attack, wounded Middleton and escaped. In 1890 Mexican rurales retrieved Reynolds' watch and pistol, stolen during the melee, from a slain Apache in Sonora, although the dead Indian was not the Apache Kid. The relics were returned to Reynolds' widow at Albany, Texas.

Jess G. Hayes, *Apache Vengeance.* Albuquerque, Univ. of New Mex. Press, 1954.

Reynolds, John Purdy, surgeon (c. 1807-Mar. 6, 1836). B. at Philadelphia, he was graduated from Jefferson College of that city in 1827 and practiced medicine for seven years at Mifflin, Tennessee. He went to Texas in January 1836, with Crockett's party. He held no official position as a surgeon at the Alamo, where he perished with the defenders.

Amelia Williams, XXXVII, 275-76.

Reynolds, Joseph Jones (Joshua), army officer (Jan. 4, 1822-Feb. 25, 1899). B. at Flemingsburg, Kentucky, he was graduated from West Point in 1843, served in Texas in 1845-46, then in the 4th and 3rd artillery regiments until 1857 when he resigned to teach engineering at Washington University, St. Louis. At the outbreak of the Civil War he was a merchant at Lafayette, Indiana. He was commissioned colonel of the 10th Indiana Infantry in 1861, ended the Civil War as a

Major General of Volunteers and became colonel of the 26th Infantry in 1866. Reynolds joined the 25th Infantry in 1870 and transferred to the 3rd Cavalry late that year. He commanded the Department of the Platte from 1872 until 1876. On March 1, 1876, Crook led an expedition of ten companies of cavalry, two of infantry from Fort Fetterman, Wyoming, northward in search of Sioux hostiles. A portion of the command under Reynolds surprised a Cheyenne village (at first thought to be Crazy Horse's Sioux) on Powder River, Montana, March 17. The attack initially was successful, the village burned, but the troops were driven back and the Indians recaptured most of their horses. The affair had been unsatisfactorily handled, in the view of some, and there were charges of incompetence, cowardice and other shortcomings; Reynolds was court-martialed on charges by Crook, Reynolds in turn pressing charges resulting in court-martials of Henry E. Noyes and, with later charges by Crook, of Alexander Moore, officers with the command. Reynolds was tried from January 6 to 23, 1877, at Cheyenne, Wyoming. He was found guilty of the several charges and specifications, and sentenced to be suspended from rank and command for a year. President Grant, "in view of (his) long and faithful service" remitted the sentence, but the event "placed a stigma on Colonel Reynolds from which he never recovered." He retired from the army on account of disability June 25, 1877. Vaughn, who carefully examined the campaign and court proceedings which followed, concluded that the findings "were cruelly unjust to Colonel Reynolds." Reynolds died at Washington, D.C.

J.W. Vaughn, *The Reynolds Campaign on Powder River.* Norman, Univ. of Okla. Press, 1961; NCAB, Vol. IX, 231-32; Heitman.

Reznor, Jacob, mountain man (d. Jan. 1814). A Kentuckian, he became a trapper for the Missouri Fur Company in 1809 with Robinson and Hoback, reaching the Three Forks with Colter and trapping the upper Rockies until he was killed with the John Reed party by Indians.

Harvey L. Carter article, MM, Vol. IX.

Rhodes, Eugene Manlove, writer (Jan. 19, 1869-June 27, 1934). B. at Tecumseh,

Nebraska, his father in 1881 was named agent to the Mescalero Apaches and moved to the Fort Stanton reservation in New Mexico. Eventually they homesteaded in the San Andres Mountains east of the Rio Grande. Gene, at 13, became a cowboy, working at that trade for about 15 years, the latter part of it on his own San Andres ranch where he was visited by such notables as the Oklahoma outlaw, Bill Doolin (in his lifetime Rhodes spent a total of about 23 years in New Mexico). For two years Rhodes attended the College of the Pacific, then at San Jose, California, beginning during that period attempts at writing for publication. By correspondence he had fallen in love with a New York widow, May Louise (Davison) Purple, journeyed east and married her in 1899, fathering a son and a daughter; she had two sons by her first marriage. After three years in New Mexico the family moved to New York, remaining for 20 years while Rhodes wrote seven novels and many short stories which appeared in top magazines and were of almost uniformly high quality. In 1926 the family returned to New Mexico but after five years moved to California because of Gene's persistent illnesses. He was buried at the summit of Rhodes Pass in the San Andres; his epitaph, which he chose, was also the title of perhaps his greatest short story, "Pasó por Aquí." Among his many books, all fiction, were *Good Men and True* (1910); *Stepsons of Light* (1921); *The Trusty Knaves* (1933), *Beyond the Desert* (1934), and *The Proud Sheriff* (1935). De Voto said of his work that it was "the only body of fiction devoted to the cattle kingdom which is both true to it and written by an artist in prose," a judgment generally concurred in.

DAB; *Who Was Who;* W.H. Hutchinson, *The Life & Personal Writings of Eugene Manlove Rhodes, a Bar Cross Man.* Norman, Univ. of Okla. Press, 1956.

Rhodes, John (John Tewksbury), cowboy (c. Oct. 3, 1885-Nov. 26, 1973). Although the year of birth is given as 1887 for John Rhodes, he was the son of John Tewksbury, killed in Arizona's Pleasant Valley War September 2, 1887, and was an infant at the time of that incident; therefore he must have been born in 1885. His widowed mother married John Rhodes, a Tewksbury partisan, and the boy took his stepfather's name. John was b. at

Young, Arizona, became a cowboy and rancher, owning several places near Mammoth, Arizona, including the 60,000 acre Sacaton Ranch from 1933-53. Rhodes achieved his greatest fame and popularity, however, from his enduring skill as a rodeo performer, specializing in calf, steer and team roping, winning championships for more than 50 years. "He had that competitive spirit," said Dale Smith, one of his arena partners. "He never rode into the barrier but what he wasn't going to win." A writer said, "The man will be forever a part of rodeo in the era in which he performed." He died at Tucson.

Willard H. Porter, "John Rhodes — One of the Best." *Western Horseman,* Vol. XXXIX, No. 6 (June 1974), 50-52, 149; Earle R. Forrest, *Arizona's Dark and Bloody Ground.* Caldwell, Ida., Caxton Printers, rev. and enl. ed., 1964.

Rhodius, Charles, cowboy (c. 1860-Feb. 12, 1893). Rhodius and Matt Coffelt, cowboys with no bad reputation, were shot and killed by Oliver Lee and Bill McNew ten miles northeast of El Paso, Texas, being accused of rustling; the charge was false. Both Lee and McNew were cleared. It was suggested there was more behind the trouble than the false charge of theft. Hutchinson cites a source he labels simply "Cowman" that he had "heard lots of cow camp talk among men who knew all the parties and the consensus of opinion was that it was a wanton killing not far afield from murder."

C.L. Sonnichsen, *Tularosa: Last of the Frontier West.* Old Greenwich, Conn., Devin-Adair Co., 1972; W.H. Hutchinson, *Another Verdict for Oliver Lee.* Clarendon, Tex., Clarendon Press, 1965.

Ribaut, Jean, French adventurer (c. 1520-Oct. 12, 1565). B. at Dieppe, Ribaut was "an excellent seaman and a staunch Protestant " who on February 18, 1562, commanded an expedition from Havre to "Florida," to found a Huguenot colony. On April 30 the two or three ship flotilla entered the St. John's River, Florida, then sailed north and founded a settlement on Parris Island near Port Royal (which Ribaut named), South Carolina with 150 colonists and Rene de Laudonniere as his lieutenant. A fort was built, probably on Archer's Creek, and a friendly relationship with the Indians developed, the natives providing much of the food which kept the company from starvation. Ribaut and Laudonniere returned to France, reaching Dieppe July 20, 1562, Ribaut drawn into the Huguenot-Catholic civil war in France, rather than returning at once with aid for his colony. Upon capture of Dieppe by the Catholics, he fled to England, where he wrote a narrative of the first colonial attempt (a translation of his report to Admiral Gaspard de Coligny, who had sent out the original colonial endeavor, and entitled in English, *The Whole and True Discouerye of Terra Florida*, 1563, 1927). The colonists had by now given up after frightful hardships, killed their commander and returned to France. Queen Elizabeth suggested to Ribaut that he establish an English colony in Carolina, but Ribaut was suspicious of Catholic influences, declined, attempted to flee England and was cast into the Tower. The French colony meanwhile was restarted under Laudonniere, this time on the St. John's River, and in 1565 Ribaut, freed, took out a seven-ship reinforcement, landing in Florida August 29. A Spanish squadron approached the place September 4. After an indecisive confrontation, the Spanish moved south to where St. Augustine was being established. Ribaut, an officer of daring and much experience, moved south to attack the Spanish, while the Spaniard in command, Pedro Menéndez de Aviles marched overland and captured the French position, massacring most of the colonists found there, only a few including the wounded and ill Laudonniere escaping to France. Ribaut's fleet meanwhile was scattered by a great storm, his flagship broken up, and he and those of his followers who remained alive were captured by the Spanish who disarmed, bound them and at Menéndez's direction, "the savage soldiery, like wolves in a sheepfold, rioted in slaughter" of the hapless French. Ribaut's beard was sent in a letter to Philip II; his head was hewn into four parts, one displayed on a lance at each corner of Fort Augustine. The bodies of the murdered Frenchmen were burned. Ribaut, said Parkman, was "one far above the common stamp, — 'a distinguished man, of many high qualities,' as even the fault-finding (Jacques) Le Moyne calls him; devout after the best spirit of the Reform; and a human heart under his steel breastplate."

Literature abundant: *see* Parkman, *Pioneers of France in the New World*, I; CE.

Rice, Edmund, army officer (Dec. 2, 1841-July 20, 1906). B. in Massachusetts, he was commissioned a captain in the 19th Massachusetts Infantry in 1861 and mustered out a lieutenant colonel after the war with three brevets and a Medal of Honor for heroism in counter-charging Pickett at Gettysburg, and being severely wounded in the process. He entered the regular army's 40th Infantry and transferred in 1870 to the 5th Infantry. Rice was on duty in the East and Southwest until 1871, when he was assigned to Forts Wallace and Leavenworth, Kansas until 1873. In July of 1874 he took part in an expedition against the Utes near Spanish Peaks, Colorado; in the summer of 1876 he was in the Sioux campaign ordered to take flatboats and one 3-inch gun down the Yellowstone River in search of hostiles; when opposite Glendive Creek, Montana, he landed, threw up defense works, and was attacked by Sioux. In February 1878, he took 200 men and 35 wagons from Bismarck, North Dakota to Fort Keogh, Montana, 430 miles through the snow. In July 1879 he commanded a six-gun battery in Miles's expedition against the Sioux near the Canadian line; in one action Rice for the first time on record brought revolving breech-loading cannon into the field and used them. Rice was at various North Plains posts until 1888; he was then a captain. He became a colonel of Volunteers in the Spanish American War, was a major of the 3rd Infantry in 1898, lieutenant colonel of the 2nd Infantry in 1901, colonel of the 19th Infantry in 1902, a Brigadier General and retired in 1903. He had invented the trowel bayonet, stacking swivel and knife intrenching bayonet, long used by the army. He died at Wakefield, Massachusetts.

Don Russell, *The Lives and Legends of Buffalo Bill*. Norman, Univ. of Okla. Press, 1960; Powell; *Who Was Who; New York Times*, July 21, 1906.

Rice, William Fletcher, army officer (c. 1841-June 5, 1884). B. at Brighton, Massachusetts, he enlisted May 23, 1861, in the 1st Massachusetts Infantry, transferring to the 19th Massachusetts Infantry and rising to first sergeant by November 13, 1863, when he was commissioned a second lieutenant, a first lieutenant two days later. He was made a captain August 17, 1864, being mustered out October 4. Rice was commissioned a first lieutenant in the 26th New York Cavalry

December 30, 1864, mustered out June 30, 1865, and commissioned a second lieutenant of the 23rd U.S. Infantry July 28, 1866, and a first lieutenant July 8, 1868. He was posted to Arizona serving under Crook and taking an active part in the offensive against Apache and other hostiles in 1872 and thereafter. In December 1872 he did hard service with Dan O'Leary his chief of scouts. In early January 1873, leading Company K (because its commander, Julius Mason was taken ill) he destroyed a hostile rancheria, killing six Indians and in another attack 13, while his first sergeant killed five more the following month. Rice sought to track down the Indians who had killed A.C. Swain, George W. Taylor and John McDonald near Prescott. In January 1874 he was operating in the Tonto Basin of central Arizona. January 19, following the slaying of Jacob Almy, he arrived at the San Carlos Apache Reservation entrusted by Crook with management of the Indians. Rice was inadvertently responsible for the ocurt martial of Captain Emil Adam, the trouble arising in part over differences as to who was in command, Adam, outranking Rice although Rice had administrative authority. Principally however the charges stemmed from Adam's vacillation when he had an opportunity to attack important hostiles. Rice was stationed at Omaha Barracks in late 1875 and in 1877 was at Fort Leavenworth, Kansas. In 1884 his regiment was transferred from New Mexico to Michigan; Rice was killed in a fall from a train two miles east of Mexico, Missouri, the incident ruled accidental. His wife, two children and two sisters were on the train.

Rice's military and personnel files, Nat. Archives; Dan L. Thrapp, *The Conquest of Apacheria.* Norman, Univ. of Okla. Press, 1967; Barry C. Johnson, "Randall, Adam and Eskiminzin." *Westerners Brand Book,* Chicago Corral, Vol. XXVII, No. 8, (Oct. 1970), 57-64.

Rich, Charles Coulson, Mormon leader (Aug. 21, 1809-Nov. 17, 1883). B. in Campbell County, Kentucky, he was an early convert to Mormonism, being baptized into the sect in 1832 and ordained a high priest at Kirtland, Ohio. In 1836 he was with the Mormons in Missouri where he "rendered good service during the persecutions..., being afterward forced to flee for his life through the wilderness, and making his way to Nauvoo

(Illinois), where he was appointed a member of the high council," and for a time commanded the Nauvoo Legion. He reached Utah October 2, 1847, at the head of his own company. In 1849 he was named apostle of the church and sent on a mission to California; in 1851 he took charge of the thriving Mormon colony at San Bernardino, California, he and Amasa Lyman having purchased the ranch on which it was to be located. Rich prospered for a time, but troubles were many and in April 1857, the project, as a church endeavor, was abandoned. Probably in August 1857, Rich had a controversial contact with the ill-fated Fancher party of emigrants, then in the Salt Lake valley bound for California. Bancroft says he advised them "to take the northern route (to California) along the Bear River, but (they) decided to travel by way of southern Utah" instead. Arrington does not mention Rich's contact with the Fancher party, nor does Brooks, but Wise charges that contrary to Bancroft. the advice Rich gave was the reverse: "The church never denied that one day in early August Apostle Charles C. Rich...conferred with them about their travel plans and their itinerary." When told they preferred the northern route, he suggested there was good feed and plenty of water by the southern route instead, Wise implied, and thus set them up for their destiny with massacre at Mountain Meadows. With Daniel H. Wells, Rich reconstituted the Nauvoo Legion in Utah, and served as aide to Wells for a time. After the "Mormon War" Rich served two years in Europe from 1860, then pioneered in the Bear Lake valley of southern Idaho where he continued his public and church service and prospered as a rancher until his death at Paris, Idaho.

Leonard J. Arrington, *Charles C. Rich.* Provo, Utah, Brigham Young University Press, 1974; Bancroft, *Utah;* William Wise, *Massacre at Mountain Meadows.* N.Y., Thomas Y. Crowell Company, 1976.

Richard (Richaud, Reshaw), John Jr., frontiersman (c. 1842-July 17, 1872). B. in the North Platte River country of a St. Louis-born father and part-Oglala mother, it was reported that he was a nephew of Red Cloud and a first cousin of Spotted Tail, but the validity of these claims is not estabished. At any rate he spoke fluent Sioux and Crow, and may have been conversant in other Indian languages. The

Richard family has been described as "a hard lot," but they lived on a very rough frontier and were equipped to survive; no one to the writer's knowledge ever accused any of them of dishonesty or duplicity. Richard was settled in the Gallatin Valley near Bozeman, Montana in 1865 shortly after its founding; he soon became a freighter of supplies to Forts C.F. Smith, Montana and Phil Kearny, Wyoming, at times saving the garrisons from near-starvation. Because of his fluency in Sioux and friendship with Red Cloud and others of that people his trains rarely were molested although occasionally some of his animals were run off. In his enterprises he frequently was associated with Thomas W. Cover, Mitch Bouyer and his brother-in-law Big Bat Pouriére, and other noted frontiersmen of the region. Occasionally serving as interpreter he was criticized by one witness to a Fort Laramie treaty council who charged Richard did "not shine" as such for the Crows, translating "the eloquent speeches of the day into bad English, without regard for the genius of the Crow language." He was not accused of mistranslation, venal or otherwise, however and Blackfoot, a famous Crow chief in a speech at the same council said, "if you give us a white man for agent and trader, I wish it to be John Richard" or either of two others. "They are honest and do not lie." February 24, 1869, he appeared at Omaha with a license from the Commissioner of Indian Affairs to trade with northern Indians in the Powder River country, no doubt as a consequence of the Crow council. Instead of going to Powder River, however, he established himself at Raw Hide Creek, not far from Fort Laramie. On September 9, 1869, he mortally wounded "in a drunken rage" according to one source, or in a fight over a woman as another has it, Corporal Francis Conrad of Company E, 4th Infantry at Fort Fetterman; Conrad died September 11. A variant account said that Richard was attempting to protect his property against looting when the shooting occurred. In any event Richard fled to the Crow Reservation where he married a captive Piegan girl (and later lived with her two sisters, although one at a time), but soon moved over to Red Cloud's camp. He was indicted by a Cheyenne grand jury for the Conrad slaying, but nothing came of it. The next year Richard apparently was an influence in bringing about Red Cloud's first visit to Washington, D.C., in May and June 1870, the Oglala leader insisting

that Richard accompany him as interpreter, friend and perhaps relative. In September Richard helped bring Red Cloud in and was an interpreter at a Fort Laramie council with the Sioux. July 17, 1872, he shot and killed his former brother-in-law, Yellow Bear following an argument over one of the chief's sisters, and was knifed to death by the Indian's friends. In sum Richard was a competent frontiersman of part Indian blood who spoke the languages and had trusted friends among Crows, Sioux and perhaps Piegans; he was a good business-man, brave and self-reliant. He was married to, or at least lived with, several Indian women of various tribes.

Information from the Rev. Barry J. Hagan, C.S.C.; *Montana Post*, Aug. 27, 1865, Mar. 16, May 25, July 13, 20, 1867; James C. Olson, *Red Cloud and the Sioux Problem*. Lincoln, Univ. of Nebr. Press, 1965; Louis L. Simonin, *The Rocky Mountain West in 1867*. Lincoln, 1966; J.W. Vaughn, *The Reynolds Campaign on Powder River*. Norman, Univ. of Okla. Press, 1961; Brian Jones, "John Richard, Jr. and the Killing at Fetterman." *Annals of Wyoming*, Vol. 43, No. 2 (Fall 1971), 237-57; Jones, "Those Wild Reshaw Boys." English Westerners' Soc., *Sidelights of the Sioux Wars*, Special Pubn. No. 2, 1967, 5-46.

Richard, John Baptiste, fur trader (1810-1875). B. at St. Charles, Missouri, of French ancestry he went west before 1840 and centered his trading activities at a number of posts on the Platte River and in the western Plains. He married Mary Gardiner, part Oglala, his relationship with her people enduring all his life, the couple raising six children. Richard also farmed, built bridges across the Laramie and Platte rivers, exacting tolls from emigrants. He briefly tried the Colorado gold fields in 1858, but without much profit. He was killed while on a trading trip to the Sioux, at a crossing of the Niobrara River; the Cheyennes were blamed, but several whites also were suspected, including California Joe.

John Dishon McDermott article, MM, Vol. II.

Richard (Richaud, Reshaw), Louis, scout, interpreter (c. 1846-July 4, 1897). The son of John Baptiste Richard Sr., Louis's mother was part Oglala. He grew up in the Fort Laramie area of Wyoming, and as soon as old enough he helped his brother, John Jr., and Big Bat Pouriére operate his father's toll bridge across the Platte River near present Evansville, Wyoming. The Richard family were considered by contemporaries, a "hard lot," and Grouard's biography supports this thesis: Grouard claims Richard was very jealous of his knowledge of the country when both were working as scouts and interpreters for Crook in 1876, and that Richard tried to have Grouard murdered, only a malfunctioning pistol preventing it. Crook heard about it and fired Richard, but when he needed more scouts, Grouard hired him again, apparently bearing him no ill-will. When Richard later was fired again, Grouard hired him once more because he valued his ability as scout and interpreter. But after the 1876 fall campaign which virtually concluded with the Slim Buttes fight in September, "Richard was never hired again by the government." Vaughn adds that Richard "died one Fourth of July on Lake Creek, twenty-five miles northwest of Cody, Wyoming."

Joe DeBarthe, *Life and Adventures of Frank Grouard.* Norman, Univ. of Okla. Press, 1958; J.W. Vaughn, *The Reynolds Campaign on Powder River.* Norman, 1961.

Richards, James Russell Jr., army officer (Dec. 22, 1854-Feb. 12, 1914). B. in Virginia, he was graduated from West Point, assigned briefly to the 9th Cavalry and joined the 4th Cavalry at Fort Clark, Texas, in 1878. He commanded the escort that took the first 76 Chiricahua Apache prisoners from Arizona to their Florida exile in 1886, the noted leaders Chihuahua and Nana being of the party. Richards was made captain in 1891, retired for disability in line of duty February 25, 1896, and died at Front Royal, Virginia.

Heitman; Cullum; *Los Angeles Times,* Apr. 7, 1886.

Richards, Stephen, adventurer (fl. 1800-1807). This man's name may have been Rechert, the Spanish called him Esteban, their version of "Stephen." He was son of Mordecai Richards and with his father joined Philip Nolan for the 1800-1801 wild horse hunting expedition to the Trinity River of Spanish Texas. Mordecai deserted and made his way back to Concordia, a Spanish fort across the Mississippi River from Natchez where he and Stephen had joined Nolan at the outset. Stephen was captured by Spanish soldiery who had killed Nolan, and removed to Chihuahua City. Although illiterate, his command of Spanish became such that he was occasionally used as interpreter in court cases. He enlisted in the Spanish army, was assigned to Nacogdoches, and in 1807 was reported at Baton Rouge, Louisiana, "in the quality of a citizen." Nothing further is known of him.

Bennett Lay, *The Lives of Ellis P. Bean.* Austin, Univ. of Tex. Press, 1960.

Richardson, Albert Dane, newspaperman (Oct. 6, 1833-Dec. 2, 1869). B. at Franklin, Massachusetts, he became a Civil War correspondent for the *New York Tribune* and in 1869 described a tour of the West over the newly-completed transcontinental railroad, which appeared in the *Tribune* from May 29 to August 2. He also wrote two widely-read books, *The Secret Service* (1865) and *Beyond the Mississippi* (1866). He died at New York City.

DAB; Robert Taft, "The Pictorial Record of the Old West." *Kan. Hist. Quar.,* Vol. XVIII, No. 2 (May 1950), 116-18.

Richardson, Gladwell (Toney), (Maurice Kildare), trader, writer (September 4, 1903-June 14, 1980). B. at Alvarado, Texas, he reached northern Arizona in 1918, representing the fourth generation of his people to devote their business careers to Navaho Indian trading. Richardson began this work at the Houck Trading Post, remaining a couple of years before joining the Marines at San Francisco; he shortly was dropped because he was underage, then joined the Navy where he remained four eventful years. He returned to the Navaho Reservation to resume trading, remaining generally at that occupation until World War II when he again served in the Navy, as he did during the Korean War. In 1926 he had begun his high tempo writing career during which he wrote an estimated 300 novels (almost all published in England), and something like 1,000 articles and short stories. He used a variety of pen names (about 20, it is believed), the best known of which was Maurice Kildare; others included Calico Jones, Laramie Colson and George Blacksnake. In addition to his voluminous writings (a longtime friend calculated Richardson published around 60 million words overall) he found time for a few years to manage the annual Flagstaff Indian Pow-Wow, a popular event among native Americans and tourists alike, and in 1940 completed the U.S. census among the Navahos of the reservation, a work which resulted in compilation of perhaps the most accurate population statistics of the region to that date. Eventually he and his wife withdrew from the reservation to a Flagstaff home where they lived and worked until Richardson's death. His extensive files and thousands of photographs are held by the University of Northern Arizona library at Flagstaff. He was survived by his widow and two daughters. His *Navajo Trader,* a partial autobiography, was published posthumously.

Gladwell Richardson, *Navajo Trader,* ed. by Philip Reed Rulon, Tucson, Univ. of Ariz. Press, 1986; author's file on Richardson.

Richardson, Levi, freighter (c. 1851-Apr. 5, 1879). B. in Wisconsin, Richardson was a freighter who became enamored of a woman with whom gambler Frank Loving was living at Dodge City, Kansas. A series of differences resulted in a gunfight in which Richardson was killed by Loving in the Long Branch Saloon.

Nyle H. Miller, Joseph W. Snell, *Great Gunfighters of the Kansas Cowtowns, 1867-1886.* Lincoln, Univ. of Nebr. Press, 1967.

Richardson, Tracy, soldier of fortune (Nov. 21, 1889-Apr. 20, 1949). B. at Broken Bow, Nebraska, his parents took him at four months to Lamar, Missouri; he grew up there and considered Lamar his home. Always restless, he went to Central America in 1909 where he became acquainted with Lee Christmas and drifted into soldiering under a variety of flags, initially in Nicaragua, where he once captured its capital, Managua, single-handedly. He had advanced beyond his unit and found himself surrounded by federals. Stating that he was a messenger from the rebel leader, he demanded to be taken to the officer defending Managua, reported the city surrounded, and secured its surrender. With another soldier of fortune and two machine-guns, he once all but wiped out a federal regiment, it was reported, winning the reputation of being "the best machine gunner in the business." Richardson served as scout under Funston at Vera Cruz in 1914, later soldiered with an assortment of Mexican leaders, it was said, being the only man who ever jammed a pistol into the belly of Pancho Villa and made him publicly apologize; Villa put a price on his head and the next time they

met was in a "visit to a quack doctor in El Paso...Pancho with his pants down, being treated for the clap. The two thought it was pretty funny." Richardson was said to have been a colonel in Mexico under Diaz, a brigadier general under Madero, chief of gunnery under Carranza. He served with the Princess Pats (Canadian Light Infantry) in France in World War I, and was said to have been a British naval aviator during that war, later transferring to the American Army where one report said he served as a captain, another as a naval flyer. During World War II he was commissioned a major, ultimately promoted to colonel, and was placed in charge of an army air field. In all Richardson served under the flags of Nicaragua, Honduras, Guatemala, Mexico, Venezuela, Canada and the U.S., and was wounded 16 times. He was a man generally respected, of great courage and resourcefulness. He came upon hard times, ended his days as a house-to-house salesman in Springfield, Missouri, after minor success as a free lance-writer. He died of a heart condition.

W.K. Daetwyler article, Kansas City (Mo.) *Journal-Post,* Feb. 27, 1938; information from Daetwyler, Pleasanton, Tex.; *New York Times,* Apr. 23, 1949.

Richardson, William Antonio, pioneer (c. 1796-1856). B. in England, he reached California as mate of the whaler *Orion,* deserting in 1822 at San Francisco, and being permitted to remain providing he would teach navigation and carpentry to the settlers. He was baptized a Roman Catholic in 1823. He married a daughter of Comandante Ignacio Martinez in 1825 and was naturalized in 1830, reporting himself rather successful in various pioneering fields, also being "somewhat" engaged in smuggling in collusion with his father-in-law. Assigned to vaccinate mission Indians, he earned the title of "doctor." He resided at San Gabriel, in the south, from 1829 until 1835, then returned north to help found Sonoma and erected the first structure in San Francisco, a tent or shanty, later replaced with an adobe building. He served as captain of the port and engaged in various enterprises. Richardson went to Sausalito in 1846 to live upon a ranch he had acquired five years earlier, catering to visiting whalers against Spanish regulations and in other ways acting as a free agent. He was appointed by Stockton captain of the port and collector; he took a very minor role in the

Bear Flag revolt. He died at Sausalito, California.

Hubert Howe Bancroft, *Register of Pioneer Inhabitants of California 1542 to 1848.* Los Angeles, Dawson's Book Shop, 1964.

Richmond, Harry, actor, army officer (c. 1837-Aug. 6, 1910). B. as Louis G. Paige, Richmond was an actor from the eastern stage who reached Denver in 1860 and played leading roles with the famous and popular John S. (Jack) Langrishe Theatrical Troupe in Colorado mining camps for a dozen years. Once, in a tour de force he undertook six roles in a single production, *Nick of the Woods;* little wonder he suffered a nervous breakdown and had to withdraw from the company for a time. He was commissioned a second lieutenant in the 100-day 3rd Colorado Cavalry late in 1864 and took an active part in the massacre at Sand Creek November 29, bearing off the elaborate war bonnet of White Antelope, prominent Cheyenne chief slain on that field. Corporal James Adams testified that Richmond and others engaged in scalping the dead (two-thirds of whom were women and children) and other references support this allegation. Richmond's name appears in reviews of stage productions at New York City during the latter half of the 19th century. He visited Denver again in 1883 and in October 1902, still an actor at the age of 65. He died at a soldiers' home at Minnehaha (Minneapolis) and was buried in the family plot at Pine Island, Minnesota.

Sand Creek Massacre; Denver Post, Oct. 12, 1902, Pt. II, 6, portrait included; Alice Cochran, "Jack Langrishe and the Theater of the Mining Frontier." *Colo. Mag.,* Vol. XLVI, No. 4 (Fall 1969), 324-37; Virginia McConnell, "A Gauge of Popular Taste in Early Colorado," with portrait of Richmond c. 1860. *Colo. Mag.,* Vol. XLVI. No. 4 (Fall 1969), 338-50; *New York Dramatic Mirror,* Aug. 20, 1910.

Riddle, Frank, frontiersman (Sept. 6, 1832-Feb. 21, 1906). B. in Kentucky (one authority says as T. Frank Riddle), he went west in 1850, traveling extensively in California and taking part in three or four Indian fights. Eventually he settled at Yreka, a northern California community the Modoc Indians frequently visited. During his California years Riddle was proud of having slain 743 deer and 132 bears. In 1862 he married a 12-year-old

Modoc girl, Tobey (later Winema), whose father willingly sold her for several horses, but the coupling, commenced so casually, turned into a life-long love match, Riddle frequently expressing his admiration and affection for his wife, and Tobey for him. Living with this Modoc woman (whom he much later married in the white way), Riddle learned enough of her language to serve as interpreter for army and other white needs. Once married Riddle changed his profession from miner to stock raiser, settling 20 miles east of Yreka on Bogus Creek; in 1868 he sold out and commenced trapping in the Modoc country along Lost River, thus coming to an acquaintanceship with many leaders among those Indians. When serious trouble between Modocs and whites threatened to erupt into the Modoc War of 1872-73, the Riddles supported Old Schonchin, nominal leader of the tribe who adhered to the treaty of 1864 and lived at peace on the Klamath Reservation of Oregon. Thus the Riddles were ideologically separated from the Captain Jack faction, but retained their friendships there as best they could. They served as interpreters and confidantes for army officers engaged in trying to put down hostilities. It was during these trying years that the dedication and courage of the Riddles became ever more evident. The crisis came when the hostiles determined to assassinate Canby and other peace commissioners. Tobey learned of it and warned the whites, and the Modocs discovered that they had been alerted and threatened Tobey's life and that of her husband. Frank Riddle threatened to kill the perpetrator of the denouement, the Methodist minister Eleasar Thomas, for revealing to the hostiles that it had been Tobey who tipped them off — after swearing he would never reveal that fact. He roundly cursed the clergyman and told him that if the hostiles harmed his wife (at the moment in their power) he would shoot the clergyman "like the yellow dog you are!" At the assassination Thomas along with Canby was killed, and Meacham wounded, and the Riddles, saved from death by Scarface Charley and others who though hostile greatly respected them, were unharmed. O.C. Applegate wrote that "though his life was humble and his sphere limited, he lived an honest, temperate life, was kind and true to his family and friends, and did good and true work for all in the darkest days that ever came to the Klamath country."

He died at his home near Yainax, Oregon from a brief illness and was survived by Tobey and his son, Jeff C. Riddle.

Jeff C. Riddle, *The Indian History of the Modoc War.* Medford, Ore., Pine Cone Pubrs., 1973.

Riddle, Jefferson C. Davis, historical writer (Nov. 30, 1863-1941). The son of Frank and Tobey (Winema) Riddle, he was named either for the Confederate President or belatedly for the Army commander during the Modoc Indian War, Jefferson Columbus Davis. Jeff Riddle said he had but six months schooling in his life, three at Hawkinsville, California, and three at New York City in 1876. He was 10 at the time of the Modoc War in which his father and mother played stellar roles and Jeff himself had some first hand experiences during that conflict. Afterward he and his parents toured for a few seasons with Meacham who lectured around the country on the Modoc War. Riddle married the daughter of Old Schonchin, Modoc chief and fathered five children who survived infancy. He spent most of his life on the Klamath Reservation in Oregon where the Modocs lived. He was killed in an automobile accident in Arizona and was buried at Beatty, Oregon. His sole publication concerned the Modoc War; it appeared in a small edition in 1914 and was reissued in 1973.

Jeff C. Riddle, *The Indian History of the Modoc War.* Medford, Ore., Pine Cone Pubrs., 1973.

Riddle, Tobey (Kaitchkana, Nanooktowa, Winema), Modoc interpreter, heroine (c. 1850-Feb. 18, 1920). The daughter of Se-cot, a Modoc Indian and a cousin of Captain Jack who came to note during the Modoc War of 1872-73 in northeastern California, Tobey was born along the Link River, Oregon. She was married at 12 to Frank Riddle, a 30-year-old Kentuckian who lived east of Yreka in northern California. Although begun as a casual liaison after the Border manner, it became a true love-match, the two being devoted to each other as long as Riddle lived. They lived and trapped along Lost River, southern Oregon, when hostilities erupted between the Modocs and the whites late in 1872. The Riddles sided with Old Schonchin, nominal chief of the tribe who remained at peace on the Klamath Reservation, but retained their friendships among the dissidents and Tobey, with fathomless courage regularly made trips

to the hostiles, even under the stress of siege, when asked to do so. She was far more than interpreter, although honest and very competent in that capacity when she served the army faithfully during bloody, desperate months. Being a Modoc, her knowledge of the psychology of that people and of the personalities of their principals was invaluable to white officers, not one of whom found anything to criticize in her conduct. The most dangerous moment came in April 1873 when the Modocs overcame the reluctance of Captain Jack and determined to assassinate Canby, Thomas, Meacham and perhaps others of the white peace commissioners. Tobey learned of this at the hostile camp and warned the whites after cautioning them not to reveal how they had come by their knowledge. Thomas however, a stupid and bumbling man, immediately told an emissary from the hostiles that he had learned of the plot from Tobey. Jack then sent for her and over protestations from Canby, her husband and others she bravely rode into the enemy stronghold to confront the irate dissidents. She admitted that she had revealed their plot, but refused to tell from whom she had obtained the information and dared them to shoot her, noting that she was a Modoc too, and all she desired was peace and friendship and a halt to a senseless war. She might have been killed, but Captain Jack, impressed by her manner, came to her defense as did several other hostiles and she was escorted safely back to the peace commissioner camp. Unfortunately neither Canby nor Thomas believed the threat was real or, if so, that it should halt negotiations, and met with the hostiles the next day when the trap was sprung; Canby, Thomas and Meacham were shot (the latter recovered, after Tobey had saved his life); Scarface Charley lurked in the rocks above the camp having let it be known he would personally kill any Modoc who harmed Tobey or her husband. An assassin, Boncho, tried to take Tobey's horse and she scuffled with him until he was forced to turn away by Captain Jack himself, who confided to Tobey that he knew that by assassinating Canby he had sworn out his own death warrant, but that he could do no other. She did what she could for the fallen. At the hospital she nursed Meacham back to health and sent him off to his wife at Salem, Oregon. The Riddles were interpreters at the army court martial by which Captain Jack and three of the other ring leaders of the Canby assassinations were condemned; they were executed. The remaining Modocs then were sent to an Oklahoma reservation. Meacham, recovered, went on a lecture tour for several seasons, with Tobey Riddle and her husband its star attractions; he renamed her "Winema," by which she became generally known, although its significance has never been made quite clear, if it has any. Colonel James B. Fry said of Tobey that she possessed "more than the ordinarily personal attractions and intelligence. She loved her white husband and, Indian to the core, knew no law but his will and wish... Holding the confidence of the whites... (she was) strange to say trusted also by the Modocs." She settled late in life at Yainax, on the Klamath Reservation of Oregon, surrounded by her grand and great grand children. U.S. Senator George Hearst (1820-1891) introduced a bill to pay Tobey for her Modoc War interpretive services a pension of $25 a month; this commenced in 1890, about 17 years after the conflict concluded. She was paid nothing for the interim period. She died in Oregon.

Jeff C. Riddle, *The Indian History of the Modoc War.* Medford, Oreg., Pine Cone Pubrs., 1973; information from the Oreg. Hist. Soc.

Ridge, John, Cherokee leader (1803-June 22, 1839). The son of Major Ridge, John Ridge was educated in missionary schools, trained in Cherokee tribal politics and became a planter, merchant and writer. His father was full-blood Cherokee, his mother a mixed blood who had been named Sehoya but adopted that of Susannah. John Ridge eventually evolved into a statesman-spokesman for his people, or one faction of them at any rate. After an 1832 U.S. Supreme Court decision favorable to Cherokee retention of lands and rights in Georgia, and Jackson's refusal to honor the ruling, Ridge conferred with Jackson, verifying that "he could expect no aid from that source." At this point he became convinced that the only hope for his people lay in acquiescence to white power, abandonment of the Cherokee lands and removal west of the Mississippi. Major and John Ridge led a delegation in March 1835 to Washington to seek as favorable treaty terms as possible, aware that they represented a minority faction of Cherokees and that the majority were bitterly hostile to emigration. The Ridges

signed the emigration treaty, conscious as they did so that they had probably signed their death warrants, since tribal law, which had been drafted by John Ridge himself, called for the execution of any who signed away Cherokee lands without council sanction. In June 1837 John Ridge followed his father to the present Oklahoma, settling like the elder Ridge on Honey Creek. The disastrous "Trail of Tears" brought most of the other surviving Cherokees to the new lands and a group bitterly resentful of the course of events plotted and carried out the assassination of the Ridges and Elias Boudinot on the charge they had arranged an unsanctioned sale of Indian land. John Ridge was dragged from his bed and while his wife and children watched in horror he was stabbed repeatedly and his throat cut.

Bernard Feder, "The Ridge Family and the Death of a Nation." *Amer. West,* Vol. XV, No. 5 (Sept./Oct. 1978), 28-31, 61-63; Grace Steele Woodward, *The Cherokees.* Norman, Univ. of Okla. Press, 1963.

Ridge, Major, Cherokee leader (c. 1771-June 22, 1839). B. probably in the present Polk County, Tennessee, he was a distant cousin of Sequoyah (George Gist), was early known as The Ridge and became distinguished in war against the aggressive Anglos. He married and eventually adopted white ways partially, becoming a farmer and by 1811 a leader in the Cherokee tribal council. Ridge and most of the council sided with the Americans in the Tecumseh-Creek war of 1813-14, largely for policy reasons. He gathered a number of warriors and served under Jackson, rising to rank of major and thenceforth known as Major Ridge. Following the war he returned to a planter's life, built a white-style house on the Oostanaula River, held slaves and farmed extensively. He sent his children, John and Nancy to a missionary-school and voted for English to be adopted as the official language for the Cherokees. The Cherokees formed a republic and Ridge was prominent in its legislative councils. White pressure on the Indians continued, however. Ridge led a Cherokee delegation to Washington, conferring unsuccessfully with John C. Calhoun, secretary of war and himself a southerner imbued with that section's determination to extinguish Indian land rights as quickly as possible. Unscrupulous white maneuvering against the Indians mounted, led by the Georgian governmental apparatus. Ridge led a brief retaliatory expedition that warned white squatters off of Indian lands, then burned their shacks, but the contagion spread to Washington and some of the Cherokees began to see there was little hope of remaining in their ancestral lands. White machinations took every turn to oust the Indians and seize their lands and property, although an occasional court decision afforded some ephemeral hope of relief which however was not forthcoming; the whites had the powerful and unscrupulous President Jackson spurring them on. Major and John Ridge became convinced after John had conferred with Jackson, that the only hope for the people lay in removal west of the Mississippi; eventually, on December 29, 1835, at New Echota, Georgia, Major Ridge signed the treaty for removal affirming as he did so, "I have signed my death warrant," which was true. Cherokee law prescribed execution for ceding lands without tribal authority. March 3, 1837, Major Ridge and other emigrants left for the new lands in the present Oklahoma, establishing a farm on Honey Creek. By May 23, 1838, some 2,000 Cherokees had moved to the new region, but the others, to the number of some 15,000 refused to move voluntarily and were herded out on their "Trail of Tears" on which about one-fifth perished; about 1,000 remained in North Carolina, eventually being given a reservation there. Major and John Ridge and Elias Boudinot, another who had favored emigration as a last resort, were condemned to death for their roles, although the assassinations were "clandestinely planned and executed." Major Ridge was shot at a site across the border in Arkansas, the others also dispatched on the same day.

Bernard Feder, "The Ridge Family and the Death of a Nation." *Amer. West*, Vol. XV, No. 5 (Sept./Oct. 1978), 28-31, 61-63; Grace Steele Woodward, *The Cherokees*. Norman, Univ. of Okla. Press, 1963; DAB.

Ridgely, Charles (James Archer), desperado (d. Sept. 1866). Ridgely was a member of Henry Plummer's Lewiston, Idaho band of desperados and figured in an 1862 shooting affray on the side of Plummer in which Patrick Ford, an honest saloon keeper was killed and Ridgely wounded seriously. Ridgely did not accompany Plummer to

Bannack, Montana, perhaps because of his wound. He was killed at Austin, Nevada.

Robert G. Bailey, *River of No Return*. Lewiston, Ida., R.G. Bailey Printing Co., 1947; *Helena* (Mont.) *Weekly Herald*, Sept. 24, 1886.

Riell, Robert Barclay, pioneer (May 26, 1880-Mar. 20, 1972). B. at Newport News, Virginia, he arrived at Globe, Arizona, in March 1896. It was a rough mining town adjacent to the San Carlos Apache Reservation and Bob Riell grew up in the last days of the frontier southwest. One of his friends was Al Sieber, the noted scout and another was Bill McNelly, erstwhile cavalryman turned saloon keeper. Riell into advanced age retained a sharp mind stuffed with vivid vignettes of the frontiersmen and wild times he had known. In his later years he wrote three papers: "An Introduction to Globe," "Pioneer Days in Gila County, Arizona" and "Copper Mine Strikes in 1917." The latter was published in the *Journal of Arizona History* posthumously, but the other two, although eminently publishable have never appeared in print. Riell died at 91 at Phoenix and was buried at Globe.

Author's file on Riell; Dan L. Thrapp, *Al Sieber, Chief of Scouts*. Norman, Univ. of Okla. Press, 1964; Riell, "The 1917 Copper Strike at Globe, Arizona." *Jour. of Ariz. Hist.*, vol. 18, No. 2 (Summer 1977), 185-96.

Rigaud de Vaudreuil de Cavagnial, Pierre, de, French official (Nov. 22, 1698-Aug. 4, 1778). B. at Quebec, he was a son of Philippe de Rigaud, Marquis de Vaudreuil who had governed New France from 1703 to 1725. In 1721 the youth attended a conference with Seneca and Onondaga chiefs at Fort Niagara. As an army officer he accompanied a punitive expedition against the Foxes in 1727, though little was accomplished. He advanced steadily in rank, returned to France and in 1733 he was appointed governor of Three Rivers, holding the post for a decade. He was governor of Louisiana from May 1743 to early 1753, becoming deeply involved in tribal intrigues during a critical period. After a short stay in France he became governor of Canada in 1755, holding the office during years of extensive warfare until the surrender of Canada in 1760, after which he went to France, only to be of those tried for the loss of the French empire in North America; he spent a brief period in the Bastille, but at last was vindicated, honored and granted a generous pension. "He could not be blamed for the final defeat and loss of the colony. Rather he deserves much credit for the colony's having held out as long as it did against such heavy odds." Vaudreuil died at Paris.

Thwaites, JR, LXXI, 396n29; DCB, IV.

Rigg, Edwin Augustus, army officer (Jan. 15, 1822-Jan. 27, 1882). B. at Philadelphia, he was commissioned captain of the 1st California Infantry August 24, 1861, a major September 5, lieutenant colonel April 28, 1862, and colonel December 4, 1862. He selected the site and May 1, 1864, established the post known as Fort Goodwin on the Gila River, bringing troops from Fort Craig, New Mexico. Fort Goodwin was said to be 32 miles west of Camp Goodwin, also on the Gila and both named for Arizona's first governor; the two later were combined, and Rigg left the site August 11. He was mustered out as commander of the 1st California Infantry September 30, 1864, served as lieutenant colonel of the 1st California Veteran Infantry from March 24, 1865, until October 9, 1866, when he again was mustered out. He became a first lieutenant in the 38th U.S. Infantry January 22, 1867, joining the 25th Infantry April 6, 1870, and resigned January 1, 1871. He became a justice of the peace at Contention, south of Tombstone, Arizona, in 1881, dying a year later from pneumonia. He was married, leaving his widow and a daughter.

Heitman; Ray Brandes, *Frontier Military Posts of Arizona.* Globe, Ariz., Dale Stuart King, Pubr., 1960; Constance Wynn Altshuler, *Chains of Command.* Tucson, Ariz. Hist. Soc., 1981.

Rights, Douglas L., minister, historical writer (Sept. 11, 1891-Dec. 1, 1956). B. at Winston-Salem, North Carolina, he lived there all his life and was a graduate of the University of North Carolina and Harvard Divinity School. He was ordained to the Moravian ministry, became an army chaplain in World War I and pastored Trinity Moravian Church at Winston-Salem for 37 years before being elected bishop in 1956, though he died before being consecrated. He was an organizer of the Archaeological Society of North Carolina and its first president, and was a director of the Eastern States Archaeological Federation. Dr. Rights was a founder of the Wachovia Museum and became an outstanding author-ity on the southeastern Indians. He wrote many articles for historical publications, his major work being *The American Indian in North Carolina* (1947, 1957). He also was an authority on Moravian history and was archivist of the church's southern province. He was married and fathered three children.

Information from the Moravian Church in America: Southern Province, Winston-Salem, No. Car.

Riley, Bennet, army officer (Nov. 27, 1787-June 9, 1853). B. in St. Mary's County, Maryland, he was commissioned an ensign in the War of 1812 and ended it a second lieutenant, remaining in the army. As a captain of the 6th Infantry in 1823 Riley took part in the Leavenworth campaign against the Arikara Indians. As a brevet major in 1829 he commanded four companies of the 6th Infantry as the first military escort of a trading caravan on the Santa Fe Trail, the command leaving Leavenworth June 3 to join traders headed by Charles Bent at Round Grove, the military using the first oxen employed on the Plains until that time. The traders left the escort after crossing the Arkansas River July 10, the military to camp until their return, expected in October. However the traders were attacked by Indians only a few miles beyond and Riley went to their relief, escorting them two days deeper into the Mexican possessions, then returned to camp on the Arkansas. For several weeks his camp was enlivened by repeated Indian skirmishes and raids upon his livestock herds; four of his men were slain, the Indian losses unascertained. Riley waited until October 11 for the return of the traders from Santa Fe, a day longer than he had promised, then commenced the march east; he had not gone far when word came that the merchants were in sight, and he escorted them back to the Missouri River. The troops arrived at Fort Leavenworth November 8, where Riley soon was named to command the post. He served in the Black Hawk War of 1831-32, taking a creditable part in the battle of Bad Axe August 2, 1832; this turned out to be the decisive action of the conflict. In 1837 Riley was promoted to major, transferred to the 4th Infantry and two years later as lieutenant colonel to the 2nd Infantry. He was sent to Florida for the Second Seminole War, requesting and receiving permission to use his troops as a guerilla or partisan corps. He led a force in a sharp action June 2, 1840 at Chokachatta, destroyed an important Seminole stronghold and won a brevet of colonel for his work. Riley had a good record during the Mexican War, being brevetted up to Major General. In 1847 he took his 2nd Infantry to California, became provisional governor and in September 1849 convened at Monterey the assembly which drew up the first constitution for California and applied for its admission into the Union. Promoted to colonel of the 1st Infantry, Riley did not assume its command because of ill health. He died at Buffalo, New York, leaving a widow and five children. Fort Riley, Kansas, established May 17, 1853, was named for Riley; still operative it is one of the best known combat-training posts in the nation.

Raymond W.,and Mary Lund Settle, *War Drums and Wagon Wheels.* Lincoln, Univ. of Nebr. Press, 1966; Fred S. Perrine, "Military Escorts on the Santa Fe Trail." *New Mex. Hist. Rev.,* Vol. II, No. 3 (July 1928) 265-300; *The Black Hawk War,* Vol. II, Pt. II; John K. Mahon, *History of the Second Seminole War.* Gainesville, Univ. of Fla. Press, 1967; Heitman; DAB; Otis E Young, *The First Military Escort on the Santa Fe Trail, 1829.* Glendale, Calif., Arthur H. Clark Co., 1952.

Riley, John Henry, partisan (May 12, 1850-Feb. 10, 1916). B. on Valencia Island, Dingle Bay, Ireland, he is reported to have gone from California to New Mexico with the California Column during the Civil War, although this is disputed. He became associated with the Dolan-Murphy faction which figured in the Lincoln County War about 1874. In February 1875 he became involved in the shooting of two Mexican youths under obscure circumstances, and when his arrest was aborted by troops (those seeking to arrest him were Mexicans) he is believed to have shot their leader, probate court clerk Juan B. Patron, in the back, but was never tried. He acquired a small ranch and became a partner of J.J. Dolan in the Lincoln, New Mexico, store founded by L.G. Murphy, taking a strong, vocal and probably active part in the war, although details never fully surfaced. By 1878 the Dolan faction appeared to have lost out and Riley moved to Las Cruces, and after the Five-Days Fight of July of that year he returned to Lincoln rarely, if at all. He became associated with W.L. Rynerson, another

violent character, in cattle ventures, homesteaded east of Las Cruces, was married in 1882, then divided his time between New Mexico and Colorado. He became associated with the Walter Good faction in the Tularosa Basin's Good-Cooper range feud. He left his family about 1895 and moved permanently to Colorado, although retaining New Mexico political and economic ties and becoming associated occasionally with T.B. Catron, a controversial lawyer and politician. He established "one of the finest hog ranches" in Colorado, near Colorado Springs, where he died of pneumonia. He was considered by Fulton one of the "hotheaded Irishmen of the regular Donnybrook Fair type," and was suspected of a great deal more lawlessness than ever was proven.

Maurice G. Fulton's *History of the Lincoln County War,* ed. by Robert N. Mullin. Tucson, Univ. of Ariz. Press, 1968; Philip J. Rasch, "They Fought for the House." *Portraits in Gunsmoke,* ed. by Jeff Burton, London, English Westerners' Soc., 1971.

Riley, Sinew L., Apache scout (1891-Nov. 7, 1958). B. at Fort Apache, Arizona, Riley joined the U.S. Scouts in 1922 at Fort Huachuca, Arizona, the third generation of his family to serve in the army. He was with the Huachuca detachment until its deactivation — the last of the Apache scouts — in 1943, and retired from the army in 1947. As staff sergeant, he was the detachment's highest ranking member at the time of its deactivation. The three-story home of the Army Intelligence Center and School at Fort Huachuca, formerly a barracks, was named for Riley January 25, 1974.

Fort Huachuca Scout, Mar. 3, 1977.

Rindisbacher, Peter, artist (1806-Aug. 13, 1834). B. in Canton Bern, Switzerland, he removed to the Red River colony of the Earl of Selkirk in the future Manitoba in 1821 and for five years sold drawings and watercolors of plains life. The family moved to Wisconsin in 1826, where Rindisbacher continued painting scenes, animals and people about him. In 1829 he settled at St. Louis and was "making a considerable reputation for his pictures of Indian and animal life in the West," when he died. DeVoto calls all of his work "crude."

George C. Groce, David H. Wallace, *The New-*

York *Historical Society's Dictionary of Artists in America 1564-1860*. New Haven, Yale Univ. Press, 1957; Bernard DeVoto, *Across the Wide Missouri*. Boston, Houghton Mifflin Co., 1947.

Ringo, John Peters (Dutch John), adventurer (May 3, 1850-c. July 13, 1882). B. at Green Fork, Wayne County, Indiana, he was not related by blood to the Youngers as many believe. His maternal aunt, Augusta Peters married Coleman Younger, uncle to the Younger brothers after the death of her first husband; thus there was a tenuous relationship by marriage. Ringo was reported "a crack shot already at 12," and quit school at 14 when he, his parents and two sisters arrived at Coleman Younger's "opulent" San Jose, California estate. His activities over the next decade are not detailed. Ringo was intelligent, an avid reader of good books it was said, and appeared well educated. While reportedly involved in the Horrell War in 1873-74 in Lincoln County, New Mexico, there is no evidence of this. In the 1870s he became involved in the so-called "Hoodoo War" in Mason County, Texas. On September 25, 1875, Ringo and a companion named Williams killed a Hoodoo partisan, James Chaney. In November 1875 Ringo, Scott Cooley and others killed Charles Bader of Llano County, Texas, "by mistake," they intending to kill Bader's brother instead. December 27, 1875, Ringo and Cooley reportedly threatened the life of Sheriff A.J. Strickland, Burnett County, Texas; Ringo broke jail at Lampasas November 7, 1876. May 18, 1877 Ringo and Cooley were arrested at Moselly's Ranch in Llano County, charged with the Chaney murder and taken to Travis County jail at Austin, but Ringo was freed either through jailbreak or due to lack of evidence. He is reported to have accompanied either John or Moses Beard in 1879 to New Mexico. He may have been one of a trio including Joe Olney (Joe Hill) and another who participated in a gunbattle at Cimarron, New Mexico, killing Doc Stokes, a deputy sheriff. Eventually he reached the Safford region of Arizona where he came into dispute with Lewis (or Louis) Hancock over a drink and shot him through the left ear and neck, but did not wound him seriously, Hancock living on for many years. Ringo settled near Galeyville, on the east slope of the Chiricahua Mountains, Arizona, but occasionally was seen at Tombstone. He associated with Brocius, Diehl, the Clantons and others of the "cowboy element" in the developing feud with the Earps-Holliday in southeastern Arizona, his principal employment appearing to be as stockman-cowboy, with occasional time out for minor irruptions of boisterous play. The only major formal charge against him in Arizona was for holding up a poker game in August 1881 at Galeyville with Dave Estes, more or less as a lark. He is said to have refused to take part in a stage holdup with Holliday because of Doc's unpredictable temperament. Ringo probably had nothing to do with any smugglers' shootup in Skeleton Canyon, Arizona, as has been alleged. Ringo confronted Holliday in early 1882, well after the OK Corral incident, and tried to get Doc to fight him; both were armed, yet Holliday declined. Doc was disarmed by his faction, Ringo by Breakenridge, John paying a $30 fine for "carrying concealed weapons." Ringo's death was mysterious. On July 14, 1882, John Yoast, hauling wood for B.F. (Sorghum) Smith, noted a man apparently asleep in a grove of oaks near Smith's ranchhouse; it was Ringo, who may have committed suicide although there were disturbing factors, including one cartridge belt buckled on upside down. Yet suicide is the verdict of history, although some suspect Leslie, O'Rourke, Wyatt Earp or someone else of doing him in. He was buried on the ranch where he died. Ringo was slim, 5 feet, 11 inches tall, fair, with brown hair and blue eyes, quiet-spoken and genial when sober but unpredictable when drunk and apt to become moody and morose. In short, he was an enigma.
Ed Bartholomew, *Wyatt Earp: The Man & The Myth*. Toyahvale, Tex., Frontier Book Co., 1964; Bartholomew, *Western Hard-Cases*. Ruidoso, New Mex., Frontier Book Co., 1960; Philip J. Rasch, "The Mysterious Death of John Ringo." *Corral Dust*, Potomac Corral of Westerners, Vol. II, No. 1 (Mar. 1957), 1-2, 6; Clay Fallon, "Johnny Ringo: The Man Behind the Myth." *Real West*, Vol. 23, No. 168 (Mar. 1980), 6-9, 46-48, 53.

Risque, John P., lawyer (c. 1849-Apr. 21, 1882). B. at Washington, D.C., he was a graduate of Georgetown University and had practiced law at St. Louis before removing to Silver City, New Mexico, where he continued as an attorney. In company with John D.

Slawson, H.L. Trescott and two others he was ambushed by Apaches while enroute to examine mines near Clifton, Arizona. Risque, Slawson and Trescott were killed, the others escaping. Risque was shot through the jaw and his head smashed by rocks (this was during the Loco emeute). Risque had just been married and according to Williams had a promising future.

1880 U.S. Census, Silver City; Dan L. Thrapp, *The Conquest of Apacheria.* Norman, Univ. of Okla. Press, 1967; Oscar Williams.

Rister, Carl Coke, historian (June 30, 1889-Apr. 16, 1955). B. at Hayrick, Texas, he was graduated from Simmons University, Abilene, Texas, and earned a doctorate at George Washington University, 1925. He joined the faculty of Simmons, becoming a full professor of history, then taught at the University of Oklahoma, 1929-45, and Texas Technological College, Lubbock, Texas, until his death. Among his writings were *The Southwestern Frontier, 1865-1881* (1928); *The Greater Southwest* (with R.N. Richardson) (1934); *The Southern Plainsmen* (1938); *Border Captives* (1940); *Western America* (with L.R. Hafen) (1941); *Border Command* (1944); and, in addition to other books, numerous professional articles. His work was very competent. He lived at Lubbock until his death.

Who Was Who.

Ríu, Francisco, Spanish official (fl. 1767-1770). Sent by Louisiana governor Ulloa March 14, 1767 to build two forts near the confluence of the Missouri and Mississippi and to plant a colony of Acadians, he proved inept and incompetent and after investigation by Pedro Piernas returned to New Orleans. St. Louis merchants had demonstrated against Ríu's regulations and his administration of trade licenses.

Abraham P. Nasatir, *Before Lewis and Clark,* 2 vols. St. Louis, Historical Documents Found., 1952; Noel M. Loomis, Nasatir, *Pedro Vial and the Roads to Santa Fe.* Norman, Univ. of Okla. Press, 1967.

Rivera y Moncado, Fernando Javier de, military officer (d. July 18, 1781). A member of the Spanish military establishment, Rivera y Moncado, whose date of b. is not reported,

had been in Lower California as captain of the Loreto garrison from at least 1756. He joined the Gaspar de Portolá expedition of 1769 to Monterey, California, and northward, perhaps becoming discoverer of San Francisco Bay, or near-discoverer (although there are other claimants). He returned to his base the next year. August 17, 1773, Rivera became military commander of Upper California succeeding Pedro Fages, retaining command until February 3, 1777, when he turned it over to Neve. During this period he was very active in Indian affairs and in seeing that the missions were protected. He had differences with Anza and Serra, nothing of great significance, but culminating in a quarrel between Anza and Rivera which seems inexplicable unless Rivera was mentally unbalanced at the time. At any rate, he was returned in 1777 to Loreto to become acting lieutenant governor of Lower California. In 1778-79 he was commissioned to raise colonists for Upper California. He reached the missions for the Yumas on the Lower Colorado River early in June, bringing from northern Mexico 40 male recruits, their families and much livestock. Conditions with the Yuma Indians already were tense and the crop-ravaging Spanish animals did not help. June 19 part of Rivera's company left for the San Gabriel Mission near Los Angeles while Rivera remained on the river to recruit 257 head of stock. About 20 soldiers and laborers and some wives of these were in his company. The Spanish further exacerbated the situation by mistreatment of the Indians. On July 17th a Yuma revolt broke out. It is often stated that Rivera fell that day, but it was not until Wednesday, the 18th that he and the 12 soldiers with him were killed in their camp on the east bank of the stream, Rivera falling to arrows, many of the soldiers to clubs. Although Bancroft in one reference considered Rivera "a weak man," in his summation he wrote that Rivera was "one of the most prominent characters in early Californian annals... He was not the equal, in ability and force, of such men as Fages and Neve, but he was popular and left among the old Californian soldiers a better reputation probably than any of his contemporaries."

Bancroft, *Pioneer Register, California,* I; Jack D. Forbes, *Warriors of the Colorado.* Norman, Univ. of Okla. Press, 1965.

Rivet, Francois, frontiersman (c. 1757-Sept. 1852). B. at Montreal, he joined Lewis and Clark in Missouri, but left the party after the first winter. He subsequently worked with Manuel Lisa, formed a liaison with a Flathead woman in western Montana by 1809, and by 1813 was an interpreter for the North West Company. He served similarly for Alexander Ross on a Snake River expedition in 1823-24 of the Hudson's Bay Company. In 1829 he transferred with John Work to Fort Colville on the upper Columbia River. Rivet retired in 1838 to French Prairie on the Williamette River, Oregon, formally marrying his Flathead consort and becoming a worthy pioneer.

Harriet D. Munnick article, MM, Vol. VII.

Rivet, Louis, mountain man (June 1803-Dec. 31, 1902). B. at St. Louis, he went to work at 21 on keel boats plying between the Galena, Illinois, lead mines and St. Louis. Early in 1829 he was hired by the American Fur Company to take keel boats up the Missouri, leaving St. Louis in March and reaching Fort McKenzie, eight miles above the mouth of the Marias River, Montana, in September. The following spring he brought goods by keel boat downstream to Fort Union. From there he was sent with a trapping party up the Cheyenne River, then cross country to Fort William (Laramie). He joined Fontenelle's company across the mountains to the Snake River. He trapped that winter in the upper Rockies, and attended the Pierre's Hole rendezvous the next summer, taking part in the July battle with the Blackfeet, a celebrated fur trade incident of 1832. Rivet remained in the mountains three years, trapping the principal tributaries of the Missouri, the Deer Lodge and the Snake rivers. He came into Fort McKenzie and for 10 years served as hunter, scout and messenger out of that post. In 1843 he moved to Fort Garry, on the Red River of the North, so his three daughters could be educated in a Catholic convent; he had married Mary Arnell, a halfbreed about 1834 (she was still living in 1925). Rivet lived in Canada seven years, working for the Hudson's Bay Company and independently. For a year he had a post on Hudson Bay. He returned to Montana in 1850, serving as hunter, interpreter. In 1866 he built Fort Hawley on the Missouri and had charge of it for a year; the following year he built a post

for himself on the Milk River. Until in his eighties he hunted and trapped each winter, serving as interpreter or at other of his specialties during the off-season. He survived countless adventures with Indians, big game, and wilderness vicissitudes, and died at the home of a daughter on Milk River.

Montana Contributions, Vol. X, 1940, 250-54.

Roarke, Mike, train robber (c. 1848-post 1885). Leader of a six-man gang that bungled a train robbery January 27, 1878, at Kinsley, Kansas, Roarke, or Rourke, and Dan Dement were pursued south from Dodge City, Kansas, but were lost in the breaks of the Canadian River in Oklahoma-Texas. Roarke was captured and Dement wounded near Ellsworth, Kansas, in October 1878, Mike sentenced to 10 years. He was 6 feet tall, heavily built, sandy hair, blue eyes, wore a mustache and van dyke beard.

Ed Bartholomew, *Wyatt Earp: The Untold Story.* Toyahvale, Tex., Frontier Book Co., 1963; Nyle H. Miller, Joseph W. Snell, *Great Gunfighters of the Kansas Cowtowns 1867-1886.* Lincoln, Univ. of Nebr. Press, 1967.

Robbins, Samuel Marshall, army officer (1832-Sept. 25, 1878). B. in New York, he moved to Illinois in 1844 and to Colorado in 1860. A civil engineer he was commissioned captain of Company K, 1st Colorado Infantry (Cavalry) November 30, 1861, and took part as chief of cavalry in the battle of Apache Canyon, Pigeon Ranch and other actions in New Mexico in 1862. He was chief of cavalry on Chivington's staff at the time of the action at Sand Creek, Colorado, November 29, 1864, but was at Denver and did not participate in the engagement with Cheyenne and Arapaho Indians. He gave background information on organization of the attacking force in testimony before a panel investigating the affair at Wahington, D.C., in March 1865. His statements were impartial but generally favorable to Chivington who acted, Robbins thought, in part because of public pressure; the people "emphatically demanded that something should be done" about Plains hostilities and "they wanted some Indians killed; whether friendly or not they did not stop long to inquire." Robbins was mustered out of the Colorado service October 26, 1865. He was commissioned a first lieutenant in the 7th U.S. Cavalry July 28, 1866, and a captain

November 27, 1868, the day of the Battle of the Washita in which Robbins participated as he did in Custer's subsequent campaign on the South Plains. Robbins was "a good leader when sober, but increasingly fell under the influence of drink," according to Utley. In Kentucky in 1871 Robbins was court martialed for offenses resulting from drunkeness; the court decreed dismissal, but the Colorado delegate to Congress intervened and Robbins was allowed to resign, March 1, 1872. Described as "a good fellow and a wag," he died of yellow fever at New Orleans.

William Clarke Whitford, *Colorado Volunteers in the Civil War.* Boulder, Colo., Pruett Press, 1963; *Sand Creek Massacre;* Robert M. Utley, *Life in Custer's Cavalry.* New Haven, Yale Univ. Press, 1977; Heitman; *Denver Republican,* Sept. 13, 1883.

Robert, Henry Martyn, army officer, parliamentarian (May 2, 1837-May 11, 1923). B. at Robertville, South Carolina, he was of French Huguenot descent. He was graduated from West Point in 1857 with a brilliant record in mathematics and a taste for military engineering. Robert performed engineering duty in the Pacific Northwest for two years and was in charge of defenses for San Juan Island in the straits leading to Puget Sound. As a major in 1867, he was assigned for four years to the Military Division of the Pacific as chief engineer. He analyzed engineering problems in frontier California and Arizona, and in 1869 under his supervision was compiled an historically valuable map of Arizona. His career as a military engineer continued for 20 years during which he guided defense construction on the Great Lakes, Lake Champlain and elsewhere, becoming Brigadier General and Army Chief of Engineers. At 25 he had been called upon to preside over a meeting; discovering that no simple parliamentary guide existed, he compiled in 1876 a *Pocket Manual of Rules of Order,* which came to be called *Robert's Rules of Order.* More than a million copies are in print through its various editions and it is used universally for conduct of formal meetings, earning Robert the somewhat facetious nickname of "the great peacemaker." He married, fathered a son and four daughters, and died at Hornell, New York, being buried at Arlington National Cemetery.

DAB; *Who Was Who;* Dennis G. Casebier, *Fort Pah-Ute California.* Norco, Calif., Tales of

Mojave Road Pub. Co., 1974; Bert M. Fireman, "Order in the Wilderness: The Mapping of Southern Arizona in 1868 by Major Henry M. Robert," paper delivered at the Fort Huachuca Academic Seminar, June 1975.

Roberts, Charles Du Val, army officer (June 18, 1873-Oct. 24, 1966). B. on the Cheyenne Indian Agency in South Dakota where his father was stationed, Roberts, educated at West Point, served in the army 40 years, attaining the rank of Brigadier General. As a boy of 13 he kept a diary while his father, Cyrus S. Roberts, stationed at Fort Bowie, Arizona, was an aide to Crook, the document narrating much of interest, including the Geronimo surrender conference in March 1886, at Canyon de los Embudos, where Roberts was pictured with officers and hostiles in the famous council scene. Extracts of the diary are on file at the Arizona Historical Society, Tucson. Roberts' memory of what transpired was remarkable, even into advanced age. He won a Medal of Honor for gallantry under fire at El Caney, Cuba; the Distinguished Service Medal for conduct of combat operations of the 81st Division near Verdun; the French Croix de Guerre and the Belgian Order of Leopold for World War I service. He also saw duty in the Philippines, in Panama and at various U.S. posts. He died at Silver Spring, Maryland.

Correspondence with author; *New York Times,* Oct. 26, 1966; *Los Angeles Times,* Oct. 27, 1966.

Roberts, Cyrus Swan, army officer (Aug. 23, 1841-Mar. 18, 1917). B. at Sharon, Connecticut, Roberts enlisted in 1862 in the 22nd New York Militia and became sergeant major of the 150th New York Infantry, being commissioned February 13, 1863. He served as aide to George Crook in western Virginia and the Shenandoah Valley in 1863-64, and was breveted up to major. He became a second lieutenant of the 17th Infantry in 1866. Roberts again became aide to Crook. In 1880 he accompanied Crook who escorted Secretary of the Interior Carl Schurz on a tour of the still-remote Yellowstone National Park. He served Crook as aide in 1885-86 during the difficult months of the Geronimo campaign. With his 13-year-old son, Charles, he attended the famous conference between Crook and Geronimo in March 1886, in Sonora. Roberts assisted Crook in writing the pamphlet:

Resume of Operations against Apache Indians, 1882 to 1886, Crook's defense of his policies with reference to the Chiricahua Indians and his use of their people as scouts. Roberts rejoined Crook as a member of his staff at Chicago in 1888. He accompanied the Sioux Commission to the Dakota reservations in 1889. Roberts became a Brigadier General in 1903 and retired that year.

Heitman; *Who Was Who;* Martin F. Schmitt, ed., *General George Crook: His Autobiography.* Norman, Univ. of Okla. Press, 1960.

Roberts, Dan(iel) Webster, Texas Ranger (Oct. 10, 1841-Feb. 6, 1935). B. in Winston County, Mississippi, the son of Alexander Roberts who became known for Indian fighting, he was brought to Texas by his parents in 1843 and settled in Blanco County. Here in 1873 he and other young men joined to fight Indians who had raided into the area and "so well did young Roberts handle this small body of men," that when a Ranger force was organized in 1874 Roberts was commissioned a lieutenant and then made captain of the famed Frontier Battalion; he served in Company D., Menard County, from 1874-76, and from 1877-78, saw much service against Indians and was wounded in the left thigh on one occasion. *Frontier Times* in August 1927, carried a portrait of Dan Roberts by Warren Hunter on its cover.

Frontier Times, Vol. 4, No. 11 (Aug. 1927), 4; Robert W. Stephens, *Texas Ranger Indian War Pensions.* Quanah, Tex., Nortex Press, 1975; HT.

Roberts, James F., partisan, lawman (1858-Jan 8, 1934). B. at Bevier, Macon County, Missouri, he went west at 18, eventually reaching Arizona and settling in Pleasant Valley north of Globe where he estabished a small cattle ranch. He became friendly with the Tewksburys and considered the Grahams as rustlers, or worse, and so became involved in the 1887-88 Pleasant Valley War, in which he became a dominant figure and "the best gun fighter of them all." His partisanship commenced when his place was burned by arsonists. Mart (Old Man) Blevins disappeared late in July or early August 1887, and the first important gun battle erupted August 10 at the old Middleton Ranch, north of the Tewksbury Ranch. Which side started the action is disputed but Roberts said that Hampton Blevins reached first for his gun. Blevins and John Paine were killed, Tom Tucker seriously wounded and two other Graham riders wounded slightly. Roberts and others were indicted December 3, 1887, for the killing of Blevins (the cases were dismissed in June 1888). He may have been at the Tewksbury ranch when it was attacked by Grahams September 2, 1887, two Tewksbury facton men having already been killed nearby. Roberts had sure knowledge of the September 17 Tewksbury ambush of Harry Middleton and Joseph Underwood, and may have been present. Roberts and others were arrested by Sheriff William Mulvenon, taken to Prescott, released under bond and shortly were back in Pleasant Valley. His role in the remainder of the "war" is unclear, but at his death he was believed the last man of either side to have survived until that date. He returned to his ranch in 1888, but was broke and soon migrated to the Jerome copper camp east of Prescott. Sheriff William O. (Buckey) O'Neill appointed him deputy for Jerome December 18, 1889; January 12, 1891, he was appointed deputy by James R. Lowery, O'Neill's successor. On December 8, 1892, he was elected constable for Jerome, remaining in office 11 years. He was elected town marshal of Jerome April 4, 1904. Jerome was a rough camp, and Roberts "had to kill several bad men before... Jerome was a very peaceful mining camp." Jim Roberts then moved to nearby Clarkdale, Arizona, where he spent the remainder of his life as a special officer for the United Verde Copper Company, acting under a deputy sheriff's commission. On June 21, 1928 two would-be bank robbers, Willard J. Forrester and Earl Nelson held up the Clarkdale branch of the Bank of Arizona, and attempted to flee with $50,000. Roberts saw them leap into their car and attempt to drive off. With his single-action pistol he shot Forrester through the head, killing him instantly, the automobile crashed into a schoolhouse and Nelson was captured. Roberts six years later died of a heart attack.

Earl R. Forrest, *Arizona's Dark and Bloody Ground.* Caldwell, Ida., Caxton Printers, 1964; Clara T. Woody, Milton L. Schwartz, *Globe, Arizona.* Tucson, Ariz. Hist. Soc., 1977.

Roberts, Thomas L., army officer (d. Feb. 26, 1868). Roberts on August 26, 1861, was commissioned captain at the San Francisco Presidio of the "Washington Rifles," the first

Sacramento company to volunteer in the Civil War. It became Company E, 1st California Infantry and with it he joined the California Column moving overland to the Rio Grande valley of New Mexico, Roberts' company taking the lead, according to Carleton. July 15, 1862, after a hot dry march from Dragoon Springs, Arizona, eastward a detachment of his company was ambushed by Apaches just short of a vital spring and the celebrated battle of Apache Pass developed. After a several hours desultory fight in which two artillery pieces were used Roberts attained the spring and watered his men and animals, then withdrew because he did not have strength to hold the watering place and still send an escort back to bring Cremony's wagon train forward; it was camped 15 miles to the rear. When reached it was escorted eastward by way of the less perilous Railroad Pass to the north of Apache Pass. In his fight Roberts had two men killed and others wounded for an estimated Apache loss of ten killed. Roberts went on to the Rio Grande. He was mustered out at Los Pinos, New Mexico, September 13, 1864. Thereafter he engaged in business at Santa Fe, New Mexico, where he died following a week's illness.

Orton; Aurora Hunt, *The Army of the Pacific.* Glendale, Calif., Arthur H. Clark Co., 1951; Ariz. Hist. Soc., Hayden collection.

Robertson, Beverly H., army officer (June 5, 1826-Nov. 12, 1910). B. in Amelia County, Virginia, he was graduated from West Point in 1849 and went to the frontier with the 2nd Dragoons, seeing action against hostile Indians in Nebraska, New Mexico and Dakota from 1851 to 1859. He left the army as a captain in August 1861, to join the Confederate service where he won distinction with the Black Horse Cavalry of Turner Ashby. Robertson became a Confederate Brigadier General, engaged in business at Washington, D.C., following the war, and died there.

Army and Navy Journal, Nov. 19, 1910, 320.

Robertson, James, frontiersman (June 28, 1742-Sept. 1, 1814). B. in Brunswick County, Virginia, he was taken at a young age to Wake County, North Carolina, where as he reached manhood he probably had a part in the Regulator movement. In 1770 he visited lands to the west with a hunting party settled on the

Watauga River near the Tennessee line. He took part in Lord Dunmore's War and was at the battle of Point Pleasant in 1774 in which he fired the opening shot and saved the army from a surprise attack; he thereupon became a noted figure in the west, being described as "a man of fine appearance, about six feet high, weighing about 180 pounds, fair skinned, with blue eyes well sunk in his head." One historical writer concluded that "James Robertson was possibly the most nearly typical of the farmer-borderer-unpaid-soldier who settled the west." He did not learn to read and write until at 26 he married a 17-year-old girl, Charlotte Reeves who became his literacy instructor. Robertson was present when Richard Henderson purchased Kentucky lands from Indians and later acted as agent for the Cherokees, living some time with them. Although noted as an Indian fighter he was respected by many Indian leaders and in turn had appreciation for them and was honorable in his dealings with them, not too common a quality among border whites. In 1777 he accompanied a Virginia expedition against the Cherokees. Robertson was prominent in the defense of the border during the Revolution when many tribes were stirred up by British agents to attack the settlers. He headed an exploration party to French Lick, a Cumberland River trading post, and on January 1, 1780, brought the first settlers to the present site of Nashville, Tennessee. The next year Robertson made an unofficial treaty with the Chickasaws. As colonel of militia, he provided necessary leadership in the early days of the region. Robertson held various community positions of significance and "played an active though obscure part in the Spanish Conspiracy from 1786 to 1789," many pioneers seeing Spanish hegemony as the only economic relief for their land-locked and politically oppressed area. While he occasionally took time out to serve his community in the North Carolina Assembly, he also led expeditions against the Indians when he considered it necessary. He negotiated two treaties with the Cherokees and late in life was agent to the Chickasaws, dying at the agency at Chickasaw Bluffs, being buried at Nashville. He had "served Tennessee in various capacities for more than forty years and was paid for little of what he did." He had become the most prominent and perhaps the best-respected pioneer of the region, but when he died "it is doubtful if he had as much in money and property as when he went to Middle Tennessee in 1779."

Harriette Simpson Arnow, *Seedtime on the Cumberland.* N.Y., Macmillan Co., 1960; DAB; CE.

Robertson, John (Jack Robinson), mountain man, trader (c. 1805-1882). B. in North Carolina, he became the first permanent settler of southwestern Wyoming. He was taken by his parents to Missouri when 11, joined Fitzpatrick in 1831 and reached New Mexico; he was wounded in the famed battle of Pierre's Hole, July 18, 1832. He trapped the Rocky Mountains for several years, being associated with some of the more noted fur period figures, became financially independent, and settled near Fort Bridger, named for his good friend, in southern Wyoming. He married an Indian woman, fathered children and was buried in the post cemetery at Fort Bridger.

LeRoy R. Hafen article, MM, Vol. VII.

Robertson, John G., frontiersman (b.c. 1780). B. in New Hampshire he enlisted in Captain Amos Stoddard's artillery unit and served at Kaskaskia, Illinois from October 1, 1803. He joined the Lewis and Clark Expedition but was dismissed June 12, 1804. Nothing is known of his later life, and he is not the John (Jack) Robertson (c. 1805-1882) of Rocky Mountain fur period note.

Clarke, *Lewis and Clark;* LeRoy R. Hafen article, MM, Vol. VII.

Robidoux, Antoine, frontiersman (Sept. 24, 1794-Aug. 29, 1860). B. at Florissant, Missouri, he had reached Santa Fe by about 1823, settled there about 1825, trapping and eventually establishing a post on the Gunnison River, western Colorado, and later one in the Uinta Mountains of Utah. He returned to St. Joseph, Missouri, about 1844, but accompanied Kearny to California, receiving a lance wound at the battle of San Pasqual. He died at St. Joseph.

William S. Wallace article, MM, Vol. IV; Bancroft, *Pioneer Register.*

Robidoux, Joseph, frontiersman (1750-1809). B. in Quebec, the son of Joseph Robidoux, he and his father reached St. Louis in 1771, where Joseph Jr. married; among his children

was another Joseph. Joseph Jr. became active in fur trading and explorations, although probably not ascending the Missouri River himself, became involved in the Missouri Company, a bitter rival of Clamorgan, and came under suspicion of Clark. He died at St. Louis.

Merrill J. Mattes article, MM, Vol. VIII.

Robidoux, Joseph III, frontiersman (Aug. 10, 1783-1868). B. at St. Louis, he entered the fur trade, operating on the Missouri River initially in the vicinity of Council Bluffs, and sending his brothers, Francois, Antoine, Michel and Isadore, into the interior, Antoine as far as Santa Fe. "The independent Robidoux brothers were a force on the fur trade frontier, and had to be reckoned with," although Joseph III probably did not often lead field expeditions in person. He was a founder of St. Joseph, Missouri, named for his patron saint, and incorporated in 1845; it became a center for westward expansionists. Joseph III had several trading posts on the upper Platte River in the 1840s and 1850s. He died at St. Joseph.

Merrill J. Mattes article, MM, Vol. VIII.

Robidoux, Joseph E. (IV), mountain man, frontiersman (1801-c. 1888). The son of Joseph Robidoux III, and one of a numerous Robidoux clan, he was born at St. Louis, first appears definitely in the Rocky Mountains as an associate of Drips and Fontenelle of the American Fur Company, and "played a significant role in the historic rivalry" of the AFC and the Rocky Mountain Fur Company. He explored the Idaho fur country. He apparently operated a trading post at Bellevue, Nebraska, for a time, and a Robidoux who might be Joseph IV appears in many accounts of the western plains and upper Rockies, but the record is most confused. Joseph E. no doubt was at the Scotts Bluff "Robidoux Trading Post," as were several others of his relatives. He married a Sioux woman, raised a family — and abandoned them — by about 1857; later he married an Iowa woman, raised a second family, and died near White Cloud, northeastern Kansas.

Merrill J. Mattes article, MM, Vol. VIII.

Robidoux, Louis, frontiersman (July 7, 1796-Sept. 24, 1868). B. at Florissant, Missouri, a son of Joseph Robidoux II, he reached Taos by 1823 and became a trader between Missouri, New Mexico, and Chihuahua and Sonora. Louis married a Spanish woman, fathering eight children, and entered politics, in 1839 becoming the first alcalde of Santa Fe. He engaged in various pioneer enterprises and trapped or outfitted trappers for southwestern streams over a period of years. In late 1843 he headed toward California, arriving in March 1844, purchasing land from former pearl fisher James Johnson in the present Riverside area and farther east (Mt. Robidoux at Riverside, California, is named for him). Robidoux started one of the first grist mills in southern California. He took a minor part in the 1846 war between Mexico and the United States, was imprisoned briefly at Los Angeles, but liberated January 8, 1847, just before Americans recaptured the community. Robidoux held political office in San Bernardino County. His fortunes declined late in life, assisted by alcohol.

David J. Weber article, MM, Vol. VIII; Bancroft, *Pioneer Register.*

Robinau de Portneuf, René, army officer (Sept. 3, 1659-Oct. 4, 1726). B. at Quebec he became an officer and was active in irregular warfare against outposts of the English settlements, being particularly associated with Abenaki Indians in some of his operations. With 50 Canadians and 60 Indians he attacked Falmouth (Portland, Maine) in early 1690, and was blamed for the Indian slaughter of prisoners who had surrendered under Portneuf's pledge of quarter. In 1692 he commanded an attack on Penobscot Bay, which failed. Because of personal irregularities, Portneuf was cashiered in 1693, but continued to take part in military operations, including Frontenac's campaign against the Onandagas and Oneidas in 1696, when he was aide to the governor. He was recommissioned a lieutenant and reached the rank of captain, but most of his latter service was in Canada. He married and fathered 12 children, and died at Montreal.

Parkman, *Count Frontenac and New France Under Louis XIV;* DCB II; Coleman, *Captives.*

Robinson, Daniel, military officer (Sept. 30, 1830-Sept. 30, 1911). B. in Ireland, Robinson penned the only known eye-witness narrative of the 1861 Cochise-Bascom confrontation at Apache Pass, Arizona, aside from Bascom's official report. He emigrated to the United States at 19, enlisting in Company C, 7th Infantry September 26, 1849, and was active against the Florida Seminoles. He served on the South Plains, then on the 1858 Utah expedition, later soldiering under Canby in New Mexico. As sergeant in charge of an Army supply train he arrived at Apache Pass in 1861 from Fort McLane, New Mexico, the same day Bascom reached the Pass on his mission to rescue the Ward boy stolen by Apaches (see Bascom, Cochise and Mickey Free entries). Robinson became involved in subsequent events, was wounded in one skirmish and his graphic anecdotal account gives his recollections of significant developments thereafter. He was in the Valverde, New Mexico, battle February 21, 1862, and in operations before Albuquerque and Peralta by which time he was first sergeant, then ordnance sergeant. He was commissioned a second lieutenant August 10, 1863, and a first lieutenant May 8, 1864, being mustered out May 3, 1865. He enlisted in the 16th Infantry June 23, 1865, was commissioned a second lieutenant of the 7th Infantry again May 28, 1866, serving in various Indian campaigns in Dakota, Montana, Wyoming and Colorado. He became a first lieutenant March 1, 1872, a captain December 16, 1888, retired November 30, 1889, and was promoted to major on the retired list April 23, 1904. On his 81st birthday Robinson died at Des Moines, Iowa, where he had lived for five years; he was survived by his widow and two daughters and was buried at Fort Sheridan, Illinois.

Heitman; Powell; *Army and Navy Journal,* Oct. 7, 1911, p. 153; Des Moines *Register and Leader,* Oct. 1, 1911; information from the U.S. Army Military History Institute, Carlisle Barracks, Pa.; Daniel Robinson, "The Affair at Apache Pass," *Sports Afield,* Vol. XVII, No. 2 (Aug. 1896), 79-84.

Robinson, Edward, frontiersman (c. 1745-Jan. 1814). B. possibly in Virginia, he early settled in Kentucky where he was scalped but survived, afterward wearing a handkerchief over his head to conceal the scar. He joined Manuel Lisa in 1807; in 1809 he and others reached the Three Forks area, trapping under Colter's guidance but forced by Blackfoot hostility to abandon the region. He built a cabin on Henry's Fork of the Snake River, then set out for the settlements in the spring of

1811. Meeting Wilson Price Hunt of the overland Astorians, however, at the junction of the Missouri and Niobrara rivers, Robinson and others guided Hunt back to the Henry. He met Stuart of the returning Astorians next year but decided upon one more hunt, trapped the Snake River, joined John Reed of the Astoria trappers in late 1813, but with Reed was wiped out by Indians.

Harvey L. Carter article, MM, Vol. IX.

Robinson, Palatine, frontiersman (c. 1825-post 1864). B. in Virginia, he migrated to Kentucky where he picked up a wife and thence by way of Texas (having a fight with Lipan Apaches on the Pecos River) to Arizona, reaching Tubac by 1856, two years later moving to Tucson. He had established a store at Tubac where he dealt in "wet and dry goods," the former, according to a newspaper account, palatable alternatives to bad water. On September 10, 1859, he killed R.A. Johnson, a lawyer earlier associated in Central America with the filibuster William Walker; Robinson was acquitted. In the summer of 1860 he shot and cruelly beat Patrick Dunne, who was unarmed, and would have killed him save for a malfunctioning pistol. In 1858 Robinson abducted a 10-year-old Mexican girl, Ramona, and later sold her "along the Rio Grande," which was, of course, a felony. With the outbreak of the Civil War, Robinson attempted to confiscate property of the Sonora Exploring and Mining Company in southern Arizona for the Confederate government. On June 13, 1862, he was arrested, charged with treason and various other crimes arising from his tumultuous past, was arraigned June 30 and in July was sent to Yuma with Carleton's approval for trial. After taking the oath of allegiance to the United States and posting $5,000 bail, he was released October 20, and was still living at Yuma December 28, 1862, whereafter he disappears. Altshuler reports that six months later he was in Mexico enroute to Texas with three southerners he was taking to enlist in the Confederate army; January 20, 1864, Robinson, then at San Antonio, Texas, urged that Confederate recruiting efforts be made in California and western Arizona. Nothing more is known of his life. Robinson's wife was said to have been the most beautiful woman in the Arizona of her day.

Ariz. Hist. Soc. archives; Constance Wynn Altshuler, *Latest from Arizona! The Hesperian Letters, 1859-1861.* Tucson, Ariz. Pioneers' Hist. Soc., 1969.

Robinson, Richard, Mormon pioneer (c. 1829-post 1857). His year of birth is conjecture; he was the first born of Edward Robinson and Mary Smith who married in their native England and reached Utah, no doubt Richard with them, October 28, 1849. Richard was a member of Indian missions in southern Utah where he had settled by 1854; in 1856 he and his wife deeded their property to the Mormon church but this amounted to "just another test of loyalty," and they never were required to actually give up their effects. Robinson was placed by Albert Hamblin at the Mountain Meadows Massacre of September 11, 1857.

James Henry Carleton, "Mountain Meadows Massacre." Hse. Exec. Doc. 605, 57th Cong., 1st Sess. (Ser. 4377); Frank Esshom, *Pioneers and Prominent Men of Utah,* Salt Lake City, Western Epics, 1966; Juanita Brooks, *John Doyle Lee.* Glendale, Calif., Arthur H. Clark Co. 1962.

Robinson, William Wilcox, historian (May 1, 1891-Dec. 1, 1972). B. at Trinidad, Colorado, he moved with his parents to Riverside, California, in 1899, and later to Los Angeles. He became the pre-eminent local historian of southern California, diligent and reliable.

Jimmie Hicks, *W.W. Robinson: A Biography and Bibliography.* Los Angeles, Ward Ritchie Press, 1970.

Rockwell, Orrin Porter, Mormon Danite (June 28, 1813-June 9, 1878). B. at Belcher, Massachusetts, he was distantly related to Joseph Smith Jr., Mormon prophet. The Smith and Rockwell families became friends when both lived at Manchester, New York, and Porter Rockwell, as he was known, was one of the first baptized in the new church. He married and his family followed Mormon fortunes to Ohio and Missouri, where he first became known, whether justly or not, as a killer and militant protectionist for the young faith. He was accused of shooting from ambush and dangerously wounding former Governor Lilburn W. Boggs, but the charge was never proven. After a period of hiding, Rockwell was captured March 4, 1843, remaining a prisoner eight months before his release without trial for the shooting. When he rejoined Smith on Christmas 1843, the prophet placed his hands upon Rockwell's shoulders and prophesied that "so long as ye remain loyal and true to thy faith, need fear no enemy. Cut not thy hair and no bullet or blade can harm thee." Rockwell's long hair, worn often in a braid, became his trademark for the next 35 years. He and Bill Hickman became leaders of the Danites, the over-zealous police arm of the faith and during the 1857 "Mormon War" each was given a command of 100 men to serve as guerilla units, with which they harassed federal troops sent against the saints. Rockwell, Hickman, Brigham Young and others were subsequently indicted for treason and "wickedly, maliciously and traitorously levying war against the United States." In 1862 Rockwell was a mail contractor in Utah Territory. He was indicted for the 1858 killing of Tom Aiken and a Colonel Richard along the Sevier River, and badly wounding two others who escaped, but he died after a heart attack and "thus the gallows was cheated of one of the fittest candidates that ever cut a throat or plundered a traveler," commented the anti-Mormon *Salt Lake Tribune.* Editorially, it added that "he killed unsuspecting travelers . . . He killed fellow Saints who held secrets that menaced (others). . . . He killed Apostates who dared to wag their tongues about the wrongs they had endured. And he killed mere sojourners in Zion merely to keep his hand in. . ." None of his alleged crimes was ever proven. Nearly 1,000 attended his funeral, and Elder Joseph F. Smith, a member of the Council of Twelve Apostles delivered the eulogy: "He had his little faults, but Porter's life on earth, taken altogether, was one worthy of example, and reflected honor upon the church."

Harold Schindler, *Orrin Porter Rockwell: Man of God, Son of Thunder.* Salt Lake City, Univ. of Utah Press, 1966.

Rodgers, Andrew, lay missionary (c. 1818-Nov. 29, 1847). B. in Rockbridge County, Virginia, but raised in Monroe County, Missouri, in 1836 he moved to Warren County, Illinois, remaining until he started for Oregon in 1845. At The Dalles, Oregon, he met Marcus Whitman, returning with him to his Walla Walla, Washington, station where Rodgers taught school that winter and then determined to study for the ministry. He planned to undertake this at Tshimakain, near

the Spokane River under the Reverend Elkanah Walker. Rodgers also commenced the study of the Umatilla Indian language, among whom he planned to work as a missionary. He was killed in the Whitman Massacre.

Myron Eells, *Marcus Whitman: Pathfinder and Patriot.* Seattle, Alich Harriman Co., 1909, Appen. I.

Rodgers, Calbraith Perry, army officer (July 1, 1845-Aug. 23, 1878). A grandson of Commodore Matthew Calbraith Perry whose expedition opened Japan, Rodgers was b. in Harford County, Maryland, raised on a farm, and commissioned a second lieutenant in the 5th U.S. Cavalry November 19, 1866. In March 1869, as a first lieutenant he was assigned to frontier service, served with the Republican River expedition, was in the decisive victory at Summit Springs, July 11, 1869, over the Cheyennes, and in other actions. In 1873 he reached Arizona and in 1875 returned to the Plains. As a captain he commanded a company on the Big Horn and Yellowstone expedition and was in the fight at Slim Buttes, Dakota, September 9, 1876. He was in the field against the Nez Percé Indians in 1877. He was killed by lightning near Rock Creek Station, Wyoming, and was buried at Pittsburgh.

Price, *Fifth Cavalry.* Antiquarian Press, 1959; Heitman.

Rodgers, Harry, prospector (fl. 1863). B. at St. John's, Newfoundland, he had reached the northwest by 1862. He left Elk City, Idaho, with Bill Fairweather and four others in the fall of 1862, reaching Bannack, Montana. In February 1863, they left Bannack and on May 26 located the important Alder Gulch placers in southwestern Montana. Rodgers and Sweeney were displeased that a seventh share of the discoveries was given to George Orr, who was not in on the find, and separated from the other four for that reason. Nothing farther is known of Rodgers, but it is said he returned to Newfoundland shortly after the strike developed.

Montana, Contributions, Vol. III, 1900.

Rodgers, William, frontiersman (fl. 1849-1867). Probably b. in Missouri Rodgers was described as "an old half-breed trapper who took up trading for stock along the Emigrant

Road around 1849" (a William H. Rodgers was named captain of Company D, Andrew County, Missouri, Mounted Volunteers entlisted in 1847; his company reached the new Fort Kearny on the Oregon Trail June 6 or 7, 1848). In the fall of 1856 Rodgers abandoned trading with emigrants for their worn-out stock and became a permanent resident of the Bitterroot Valley of Montana, and apparently continued to do a little beaver trapping. He became a stockman on Willow Creek near the present town of Corvallis, Montana. Little is heard of him after that.

George F. Weisel, *Men and Trade on the Northwest Frontier.* Missoula, Mont. State Univ. Press, 1955; Barry, *Beginning of West.*

Rodriguez, Agustín, Franciscan missionary (d.c. 1582). B. at Niebla, Spain, he became a lay friar in the Franciscan Order and worked in Mexico, eventually finding himself in the southern Nueva Vizcaya community of Santa Bárbara. He worked among the Conchos Indians for a time and heard of pueblos and urban-dwelling Indians to the north. Filled with missionary zeal he applied for permission to investigate these reports, even journeying to Mexico City in November 1580 with his request, which ultimately was granted by the viceroy, Lorenzo Suarez de Mendoza, Count of Coruña. Back in Nueva Vizcaya the expedition was organized to include two other Franciscans, Padre Juan de Santa María and Padre Francisco López, a nine-man military escort headed by Francisco Sánchez Chamuscado and about a dozen Indian auxiliaries and servants. The party went down the Conchos River to the Rio Grande and up it into southern New Mexico where the Piro pueblos reported by Coronado 40 years earlier (his findings were unknown to Rodriguez) were contacted as was Puaray at the Tiguex pueblos near present Bernalillo. From Puaray explorations were undertaken in various directions, including one to the eastern buffalo plains. Snow prevented a visit to the Hopi pueblos of Arizona but other towns were visited, the expedition locating about 60 pueblos in all. Late in January Chamuscado and the military escort along with most of the auxiliaries decided to return to Mexico while Rodriguez and López determined to remain at Puaray despite entreaties and even the command of Chamuscado that they leave lest the Indians kill them. After the soldiers left the

friars went north a few leagues to the pueblos of Galisteo of the Tanos group where they labored briefly before returning to Puaray. López was killed by a solitary Indian and was buried at the pueblo with Christian rites by Rodriguez. The war captain of Puaray, in order to save Rodriguez, directed him to remove to another pueblo five miles distant for better protection, but within days the Franciscan was killed, his body thrown into the swollen Rio Grande and never recovered.

George P. Hammond, Agapito Rey, *The Rediscovery of New Mexico, 1580-1594.* Albuquerque, Univ. of New Mex. Press, 1966; Bancroft, *Arizona and New Mexico;* Twitchell, *Leading Facts,* I.

Rodriguez, Chipita, murderess (d. Nov. 13, 1863). Said to have been the only woman hanged legally in Texas, she was accused of murdering John Savage, a stock dealer, for his money. Tried before Judge Benjamin F. Neal of the 14th district court, she was sentenced to death, the execution carried out at San Patricio, Texas.

Dee Woods, "The Day Texas Hanged a Woman." *Real West,* Vol. IX, No. 50 (Nov. 1966), 9, 70-74.

Rodriquez, Men, *see* Men, R.

Roe, Frank Gilbert, buffalo specialist (Aug. 2, 1878-Apr. 11, 1973). B. at Sheffield, England, seven years before Gordon was killed at Khartoum and as long before the Northwest Rebellion in Saskatchewan, Roe's earliest reading was of the former while none of it was about Canada although the Roes migrated in 1894 to Alberta. Roe was raised on the family homestead and in 1907 at Edmonton was employed by the Grand Trunk Pacific Railway, which became the Canadian National Railway; he worked for it until his retirement in 1944, then moved to Victoria, British Columbia. Largely self-educated, he read widely and persistently. Eventually, in late middle life, he became absorbed by the history of the North American buffalo bringing to his studies his exceptional powers of analysis and criticism. In 1951 he published (University of Toronto Press) his monumental *The North American Buffalo: A Critical Study of the Species in Its Wild State,* a 957-page work that is definitive and basic to any collection on this much-written-about animal;

it is unlikely it will ever be surpassed in thoroughness, depth or usefulness for inquiry into the subject. In its scope it covers the entire continent. Four years later Roe brought out *The Indian and the Horse* (University of Oklahoma Press) which despite minor lapses remains a basic work on its subject as it was the first to deal with it in depth. In 1960 at 81 Roe became a fellow in the Royal Society of Canada. He also wrote 25 papers, five appearing in the *Transactions* of the Society and each reflecting his careful study and meticulous thought. In his spare time he wrote poetry, 700 pages of it, none for publication but rather for his own amusement. Roe died at Victoria at 94, being preceded in death a few months by his second wife.

Proceed. of the Roy. Soc. of Canada, Ser. IV, Vol. XII (1974), 62-65.

Roescher, Joseph, frontiersman (c. 1835-c. July 23, 1861). B. at Holstein, Germany, he was stagecoach driver for the Freeman Thomas (often called the Free Thompson) party of seven men ambushed by Apaches near Cooke's Spring, New Mexico. All were killed in a three-day siege. Roescher and three others were slain within the barricade they had erected for defense; the other three were killed outside as they apparently sought to escape.

W.W. Mills; Forty Years in El Paso, ed. by Rex W. Strickland. El Paso, Carl Hertzog, 1962.

Rogers, Cornelius, Presbyterian lay missionary (Sept. 24, 1815-Feb. 1, 1843). B. at Utica, New York, he became interested in religion and accompanied the 1838 missionary party that crossed the plains to Walla Walla, Washington, although not under official assignment to any mission. During the winter of 1838-39 he taught school at Lapwai, Idaho, and during 1839 lived with the Nez Perce Indians to learn their language and instruct them when they were absent from the missionary station. He proved very useful to the missionaries, worked closely with Whitman, learned the Nez Perce language well and translated scripture and hymns into Nez Perce with Asa Bowen Smith. In 1841 he resigned his connection with the mission and went to the coast where he was hired for a time as interpreter by Wilkes, then on a survey expedition to the northwest coast. September 1, 1841, Rogers married Satira Leslie, oldest daughter of a Methodist missionary. In 1842 he acompanied Dr. Elijah White, Indian agent, on a tour of tribes east of the Cascade Mountains. Rogers with his wife, her sister, another white man and two Indians drowned when their canoe accidentally was swept over the Willamette Falls at Oregon City. Rogers was widely judged "one of the most useful men" in the region and his death "wrapped the whole country in gloom."

Myron Eells, Marcus Whitman: Pathfinder and Patriot. Seattle, Alice Harriman Co., 1909, Appen. G.

Rogers, Robert, ranger (Nov. 18, 1731-May 18, 1795). B. at Methuen, Massachusetts, he grew up on a farm near Concord, New Hampshire, learned in frontier skills. When King George's War opened in 1744 Indians from the St. Lawrence raided English settlements, the family withdrawing to Rumford. In 1746 he served with the militia, but without sighting an enemy. In 1752 he joined a surveyor's party laying out a road to the Connecticut River, sharpening his woodcraft skills. When the French and Indian War broke out Rogers recruited 50 men and was made captain, purportedly to escape prosecution on a counterfeiting charge. This was in 1755, when he was 23. Rogers quickly revealed a superlative talent for scouting and gathering intelligence. In March 1756, Governor William Shirley appointed him captain of an independent company of rangers; in 1758 Sir Ralph Abercromby promoted him to major of nine such companies, the scouting branch of the British army. Rogers made countless raids in all weather, fought sharply at times, "with such dashing courage, incredible hardihood and humorous pranks, that he became famous alike in England and the colonies, the most romantic figure of the war." The high point was the raid on the Indian village of St. Francis, in October 1759, when 200 Indians were killed, five white prisoners released, the rangers then making a hazardous flight back to the colonies. Rogers did much to develop the art of scouting in wilderness country, "creating a striking force and intelligence eye" that Jeffrey Amherst was quick to appreciate. The General greatly admired Rogers, and with reason. Rogers participated in the taking of Montreal in 1760, was sent to South Carolina against a Cherokee uprising in 1761, thence to Detroit in 1763 to lift Pontiac's siege. Though a hero on two continents, he was without rank in the regular army, and found himself shortly heavily in debt. He went to London in 1765 seeking to improve his fortunes, and published two books and a play of little dramatic merit. His idea of leading an expedition to discover the Northwest Passage was rejected, but he was appointed commander of the fort at Michilimackinac. With his wife, a minister's daughter, he lived in that wilderness outpost for two years, directing Jonathan Carver to explore present-day Minnesota and was perhaps the first to use the word Ouragon (Oregon) in print. His administration of his post was a shambles; eventually he was arrested for "treason," being charged with dealings with the French. He was acquitted. In England in 1769 he failed to improve his circumstances, his obligations mounted, and he was thrown into prison for debts; his brother James paid some of them and got him out. Rogers said he served the Bey of Algiers in 1774 in a military capacity. He returned to America in 1775, having finally secured his retired pay as major. With the Revolution Rogers secretly applied to the Continental Congress for a commission; he was suspected of being a spy, however, and his proposal was rejected. He then turned to the British and was commissioned a lieutenant colonel to raise a battalion, the "Queen's Rangers." He had some successes, but was replaced in 1777 by a regular officer at the insistence of other regulars who could not brook a colonial rival. Alcohol ever was his nemesis; in 1782 he returned to England, was cast into a debtor's prison off and on and died "in miserable exile." Rogers was of remarkable physique in his youth, 6 feet in height which was very tall for those days, well muscled, of great agility and resourcefulness. He was a poor administrator, however, and his lack of self-discipline proved his undoing; his cavalier attitude toward principle and personal obligations did not help. Yet he showed many evidences of greatness and his standing as an authentic and worthy hero of the old frontier is secure.

John R. Cuneo, *Robert Rogers of the Rangers.* N.Y., Oxford Univ. Press, 1959; DAB; *Journals of Major Robert Rogers,* ed. by Elias S. Wilentz, intr. by Howard H. Peckham. N.Y., Corinth Books, 1961.

Rogers, Will(iam) Penn Adair, cowboy trick roper, humorist (Nov. 4, 1879-Aug 15. 1935). B. near present Claremore, Oklahoma, the son of a well-to-do rancher and banker, Rogers was part Cherokee on both sides of his family. As a boy he took to fine horses his father provided, and to a lariat with which he became an outstanding expert in trick as well as work roping. He briefly attended Kemper Military School at Boonville, Missouri, but quit to become a cowboy in the Texas Panhandle, sailed for Argentina in 1902 and in that same year joined Texas Jack's Wild West Circus in South Africa as "The Cherokee Kid," rope artist and bronco buster. He reached home after a tour of Australia in 1904, appeared at the St. Louis Exposition and at New York's Madison Square Garden in 1905 as a member of Zach Mulhall's show. He learned to wisecrack in a western drawl while performing his stunts and was so well received that he drifted naturally into show business, coming to stardom with the Ziegfeld Follies in 1916-18, 1922 and 1924-25. From then on his rise to a pre-eminent place in American life was steady, Rogers becoming a motion picture star, the writer of a one paragraph newspaper daily column that was syndicated to 350 outlets, and participating in other activities, all combining to produce about $600,000 annually. An aviation enthusiast, he was killed with pilot Wiley Post near Point Barrow, Alaska, when on a trip to Russia and western Europe. Although much of his "stage-presence" as an ungrammatical hick with pointed and pungent things to say about current events, mainly political, was put on, Rogers was authentically American, of keen intelligence, great durability, a careful craftsman of his writings and public appearances, and had a genuine and lasting hold on the public that was well-deserved. In his roping and riding he was a master seldom equalled; withal he was a decent family man of the finest sort.

Literature abundant.

Rolfe, John, colonist (May 1585-Mar. 22, 1622). B. probably at Heacham, Norfolk, England, he left in June 1609 accompanied by his first wife for Virginia. The company was shipwrecked, his only daughter died and Rolfe and his wife with others eventually reached Jamestown where Mrs. Rolfe died.

Rolfe, an agriculturist, was the first successful planter of tobacco. In 1613 he met and fell in love with Pocahontas who had been brought to Jamestown as a captive, and they were married April 5, 1614, the union bringing an eight-year peace with the Indians. In 1616 Rolfe took Pocahontas, who had been given the Christian name of Rebecca, to England where she proved very popular, but as the couple planned their return she died of smallpox after giving birth to a son, Thomas. John Rolfe returned to Virginia in 1617 and married again, holding various public offices and continuing his successful farming enterprise. His plantation was wiped out in the Indian uprising of March 22, 1622, and it is thought he there perished, to be survived by his third wife and one daughter. His son, Thomas, educated in England, returned to Virginia in 1640 where he founded a distinguished lineage continuing to this day.

Hodge, HAI; CE; John Smith, *Generall Historie of Virginia, New-England, and the Summer Isles.* Ann Arbor, Readex Microprint, 1966; George F. Willison, *Behold Virginia: The Fifth Crown.* N.Y., Harcourt, Brace and Co., 1952.

Roman Nose (Woquini; Sautie: The Bat), Cheyenne warrior (c. 1830-Sept. 17, 1868). Roman Nose was called a "chief of the Himoiyoquis warrior society of the Southern Cheyenne" by Hodge, but he was never a chief nor even head man of a warrior society although he was a member of the Himoiyoquis or Crooked Lance society and was the most famous fighting man of the tribe of the day. "At the time of the great wars in the 1860's he was known as a great warrior to all the Indians of the Plains, and his fame so spread to the whites that they credited him with being leader in all the fights where the Cheyennes were engaged," even when in fact he was many miles distant. The whites considered him a chief and so treated him, although he never demanded such treatment. He always wore in battle the famous war bonnet made for him in 1860 by White Buffalo Bull. As a boy Roman Nose had fasted four days on an island in a Montana lake, and dreamed of a serpent with a single horn on its head. Thus the bonnet held a single horn, rising over the center of the forehead, the bonnet with its long tail studded with eagle feathers, made with nothing that came from the whites: no cloth, thread or metal. It was very sacred. Rules that went with it forbade Roman Nose to eat anything touched by metal — if he did, he would be killed in his next battle. Roman Nose appears to have remained generally at peace with the whites until after the Sand Creek Massacre when he became one of the most effective of Cheyenne hostiles. He was at the Battle of Platte River Bridge in July 1865; in early September 1865 he was with the large party of Indians who attacked Walker's and Cole's segments of the Powder River Expedition on the Tongue River; in the spring of 1866 he moved south to the Platte, carrying out some raids along the roads and capturing some trains. In August 1866 at a council at Fort Harker (Ellsworth), Kansas, Roman Nose bitterly protested the route of the Union Pacific railroad through the buffalo country; while it was building he led sporadic attacks upon its installations and work crews. When Hancock sought to confer with the Cheyennes and others in April 1867 he demanded to know why Roman Nose "and other chiefs" did not attend; Roman Nose, not being a chief, could not attend, but Hancock did not understand this. April 14 Hancock approached the Cheyenne village, seeking Roman Nose and others; Roman Nose rode out with a deputation of chiefs and headmen to meet him. Bent affirms that Roman Nose had determined to kill Hancock, and was with difficulty turned away by other Cheyennes, but "General Hancock had a close call," unbeknown to himself. During much of the last part of his life he lived with the Cheyenne Dog Soldiers, a society to which he did not belong but whose aggressiveness he admired. In the September 1868 Battle of Beecher Island Roman Nose was present reluctantly, having learned that several days previously at a Sioux feast his medicine had been broken because he had inadvertently eaten food touched by metal — meaning he would die in his next battle, and he knew this was it. So it was. He did not take part in the first massive charge upon Forsyth and his 50 plainsmen, but being urged to lead another attack later in the day, did so, and was wounded mortally; he died early the next day, one of nine fatalities suffered by the Indians in that long siege and fight. "I knew him very well," wrote Bent, "and found him to be a man of fine character, quiet and self-contained. All the Cheyennes, both men and women, held him in the highest esteem and talk of him a great deal to this day (1906)."

George E. Hyde, *Life of George Bent Written from His Letters*, ed. by Savoie Lottinville. Norman, Univ. of Okla. Press, 1968; Hodge, HAI; Dockstader.

Romero, Diego, frontiersman (c. 1622-Oct. 23, 1678). B. in New Mexico, he became a captain in the Spanish army and agent of New Mexico Governor Bernardo López de Mendizábal. In 1660 he led a trade and perhaps political mission to the Plains Apaches from Santa Fe. Because of his father's relationship with the Indians, Romero was made "chief captain of the entire Apache nation," to the accompaniment of an elaborate ritual. Romero was condemned in a letter to Mexico City by a Franciscan Agent of the Inquisition at Santa Fe for allegedly having "married" an Apache woman, a pagan, and other "crimes" against the faith. Romero was summoned to Mexico City, and put on trial for his supposed sins. He received a comparatively light sentence on December 17, 1664, being directed to the mining district of Parral for 10 years. He sought to have his New Mexico wife join him there, but she refused, so he remarried bigamously, after declaring himself a widower. This time the Inquisition was more harsh and after public disgrace he was condemned to six years in the galleys, but died before he could begin that penance.

John L. Kessell, "A Man Caught Between Two Worlds: Diego Romero, the Plains Apaches, and the Inquisition." *Amer. West,* Vol. XV, No. 3 (May-June 1978), 12-16.

Romeyn, Henry, army officer (June 1, 1833-Feb. 21, 1913). B. at Galen, New York, he enlisted in the 105th Illinois Infantry in 1862 and was commissioned captain in the 14th U.S. Colored Infantry November 15, 1863. He became a first lieutenant in the 37th U.S. Infantry in 1867 and transferred to the 5th Infantry August 14, 1869. Romeyn was sent to Fort Larned, Kansas, in 1867 and served at various posts in Kansas, Colorado and New Mexico. In 1873 he was sent to Fort Gibson, Indian Territory and was in the field against hostile Indians in the summer of 1874. Romeyn was on the Sioux campaign in Montana in 1876 and the Nez Perce campaign in 1877. September 30, 1877, mounted on a captured Indian horse he took command of Companies A and H, 5th Infantry and launched a charge to cut the enemy off from water in the Bear Paw Mountains fight in Montana. He was struck by a bullet in the right breast which penetrated his body; another pierced his belt. The handle of his hunting knife was shot away, his field-glass case was shattered and a bullet grazed his shoulder and punctured his ear. He was carried off the field, his wounds considered mortal; he recovered consciousness the next day and seven days later was loaded into an army wagon and after a trip of seven days was taken off by a Missouri River steamer. He was awarded a Medal of Honor for "most distinguished gallantry." Romeyn became a captain July 10, 1885, and retired June 1, 1897, being promoted to major on the retired list. He died at Washington, D.C.

Heitman; *Deeds of Valor,* II, 252; Romeyn pension file, NARS.

Romo de Cardeñosa, Alonso, military officer (fl. 1538-1543). A kinsman of Hernando de Soto and Cabeza de Vaca, Romo became a captain of cavalry with De Soto's expedition to the southern United States. He often led scouting or reconnoitering parties. On one such, in northeastern Georgia in 1540 he brought in four or five Indians, none of whom would reveal the location of his tribal village although the Spanish "burnt one of them alive before the others, and all suffered that martyrdom for not revealing it." When nearing the South Carolina town of Cofitachequi, governed by a woman chief, Romo commanded the rear guard and missed two Spanish who slipped away. De Soto made him return for them and "when they arrived (a day later, De Soto) wished to hang them," but apparently was mollified. Romo seems to have survived all the vicissitudes of the four-year expedition and returned eventually to Spain.

Bourne, *De Soto,* I, II; *De Soto Expedition Commission.*

Ronan, Peter, newspaperman, Indian agent (June 1, 1838-Aug. 20, 1893). B. of Irish parentage at Antogomish, Nova Scotia, he was brought at 13 to Rhode Island and became a printer. In 1854 he worked on the Dubuque, Iowa, *Evening Times* and in 1860 joined the gold rush to Colorado, spending two years there before returning to Leavenworth where he bought an interest in the *Daily Enquirer.* With Civil War tensions growing his newspaper was destroyed by mob action, and Ronan set out for Montana, reaching Bannack in April 1863. He early went to Alder Gulch, running the *Montana Democrat* at Virginia City until August 11, 1866, when he became part owner of the Helena *Rocky Mountain Gazette,* which twice was destroyed by fire. Ronan mined briefly, then became undersheriff of Lewis and Clark County. In 1873 he had followed 21-year-old Mary C. (Mollie) Sheehan from Montana to California, and persuaded her to marry him, which she did at Mission San Juan Capistrano on January 13 of that year. April 13, 1877, Ronan was named agent of the confederated Flathead nation, holding the position for 17 years, winning praise for his work among those Indians during a difficult transition period, and respect from the Flatheads themselves. During this period he also was a factor in perpetuating the buffalo by means of the Flathead herd which did much to preserve the species and generate other significant surviving herds. Initially he was deeply concerned with the unrest caused by the Nez Perce war of 1877; later with the transition of his people from buffalo-hunting horse Indians to cultivators of the soil. Ronan took the Flathead chief Charlot to Washington, D.C., early in 1884 in an attempt to persuade him to move his people from the Bitterroot region they inhabited to the Flathead Reservation, but with mixed results, although in 1890 Charlot was forced by U.S. troops to move to the Reservation. Ronan was plagued in his final years by difficulties over white cattle-men's grazing animals on Flathead lands. Ronan attended the World's Columbian Exposition at Chicago in 1893, underwent a physical examination and was advised to live at a lower elevation. He tried Puget Sound briefly, then returned to the reservation, where he died. He was buried at Missoula, being survived by his widow. Ronan wrote, *Historical Sketch of the Flathead Indian Nation from the Year 1813 to 1890,* originally published as a series of newspaper articles but appearing in book form (Helena, Montana, Journal Publishing Company) in 1890.

Montana, Contributions, Vol. III (1900), 143-47; John Fahey, *The Flathead Indians.* Norman, Univ. of Okla. Press, 1974.

Rondin, *see* Charles Mercier

Roosevelt, Theodore, statesman, conservationist, author (Oct. 27, 1858-Jan. 6, 1919). B. at New York City, he was of distinguished lineage, graduated from Harvard in 1880 and studied law at Columbia. No attempt will be made in this sketch to summarize his many-faceted career since biographical material is available in any standard reference work. But those aspects of his busy life relating in some way to the frontier will be touched upon. This stems from his experiences as a ranchman and hunter and his pivotal role as a conservationist while holding high office when his interests could be fundamentally advanced. He engaged in an 1883 hunting trip to Dakota where he managed to kill a bull buffalo, one of the last of its species remaining in that Territory. In September 1883 Roosevelt bought a ranch known as the Chimney Butte on the Little Missouri River and the following June purchased the Elkhorn Ranch farther downstream. From 1883 until 1889 he actively pursued the profession of rancher, though without notable financial reward, while spending part of each year at New York. His ranching career helped shape his later endeavors in other directions. He also had commenced his prolific writing (about 35 books in all), reflecting his interests in history, wildlife, biography, politics and travel. Elected vice president, he became President September 14, 1901, with McKinley's assassination, serving also a second term to which he was elected by a wide majority. During his Presidency he enrolled in the public domain about 230 million acres of national forests and other lands, including more than 50 wildlife refuges (he was the first President to establish them), doubled the number of national parks to ten, including Yosemite, established the first 18 national monuments set aside under the new Antiquities Act of 1908, inaugurated the U.S. Reclamation Service, heavily promoted the national forests and in 1908 established a significant National Conservation Commission. Roosevelt did much to promote wildlife protection in Alaska, Puerto Rico and Hawaii. Throughout most of his life Roosevelt was an ardent sportsman and hunter, although enlightened about it: he never killed for its own sake, but to secure a trophy or bring some fresh experience, and he was a close, attentive and intelligent observor of wildlife in any of its manifestations; he would have become a major naturalist if his inclinations had not turned him toward politics. Following his Presidency he undertook an extended safari sponsored by the Smithsonian Institution into East Africa, biologists accompanying him and his son, Kermit, bringing back 14,000 specimens from rhinos to rodents, many new to science. In 1914 he organized an expedition to trace the River of Doubt (today's Rio Theodore Roosevelt) in central Brazil. Roosevelt wrote many books of outdoor or frontier interest. Among them were: *The Naval War of 1812* (1882); *Hunting Trips of a Ranchman* (1885); *Life of Thomas Hart Benton* (1886); *Ranch Life and the Hunting Trail* (1888); ed., *American Big Game Hunting* (1893) and *Hunting in Many Lands* (1895) for the Boone and Crockett Club; *The Wilderness Hunter* (1893); *Hunting the Grisly and Other Sketches* (1893); *The Winning of the West* (1889-96), a history of the northeastern frontier, appearing in various editions from two to six volumes; *The Rough Riders* (1898, 1899); *Hunting Trips on the Prairie and in the Mountains* (1900); with others, *The Deer Family* (1902); *Outdoor Pastimes of An American Hunter* (1903); *Stories of the Great West* (1909); *African Game Trails* (1910); with Edmund Heller, *Life Histories of African Game Animals* (1914); and his important *Theodore Roosevelt: An Autobiography* (1913). He died at Sagamore Hill, Oyster Bay, Long Island, the family home. His was one of four carvings (the others of Washington, Jefferson and Lincoln) at the Mount Rushmore National Memorial in South Dakota, dedicated in 1929 and destined to endure for millions of years. In 1947 the Theodore Roosevelt National Memorial Park was established in southwestern North Dakota. It includes 58,340 acres comprising part of Roosevelt's Elkhorn Ranch and the Dakota badlands along the Little Missouri River.

Literature abundant; John L. Eliot, "Roosevelt Country: T.R.'s Wilderness Legacy." *Nat. Geog.,* Vol. 162, No. 3 (Sept. 1982), 340-63.

Roper, Laura, captive (June 16, 1848-Mar. 11, 1930). B. in Philadelphia, she was the daughter of Joseph Roper who had a ranch on the Little Blue River about two miles from the William Eubank Ranch near the present Oak, Nebraska. She was visiting the Eubanks

August 7, 1864, when Cheyenne Indians raided the area. Nine of the Eubank clan were killed; Lucinda Eubank, her two children with a nephew and Laura Roper were captured and born off by the hostiles. Laura was given a horse to ride; the second day the horse fell into an arroyo with her and her nose was broken, the Cheyennes wiping the blood from her face and caring for her. They did not abuse her. After a month her captor traded her to the famed Arapaho chief, Neva, who spoke excellent English. Major Wynkoop at Fort Lyons, Colorado, had offered $1,000 reward for the return of any captive, but Laura said she was not ransomed, just handed over to the soldiers under Wynkoop September 11, 1864, on Hackberry Creek, a branch of the Smoky Hill River. Other captives released at this time included Isabelle Eubank, 3, Ambrose Asher and Dannie Marble, all seized at the same time as Laura. Soon after her release Laura married Elijah Soper, the couple having seven children including one daughter during their residence at Beatrice, Nebraska. Either Soper died or there was a divorce and Laura married James Vance, mothering two children by him; the couple lived at Enid, Oklahoma, in their later years. Laura Roper Vance addressed the Nebraska Historical Society in 1929 and died at Enid at 81.

The Sand Creek Massacre; information from secretary Evelyn Smart, Crawford County Clerk's Office, Girard, Kan.; *Midlands Mag.,* Omaha, Nebr., *World-Herald,* June 7, 1964; Nelson, Nebr., *Gazette,* Aug. 13, 1964; information from the Nebr. Hist. Soc.

Rosborough, A.M., lawyer (1815-Nov. 8, 1900). B. in Tennessee he reached Siskiyou County in northern California in 1853 and was in partnership with Elisha Steele in a law practice at Yreka, California, until he became county judge in 1856. He with Steele became friendly with Modoc Indians and interested in their welfare since those tribesmen were in and out of Yreka all the time during the period. Thus when the Modoc War (1872-73) broke out Rosborough and Steele did what they could to settle it peacefully. Rosborough, Steele and John Fairfield, with Frank Riddle and his Modoc wife, Tobey, made their way into the enemy stronghold February 28, 1873, and spent the night, trying to persuade the hostiles to surrender and accept white terms; through the friendship of Captain Jack and

Scarface Charley they were not harmed, although unarmed and completely at the Indians' mercy. They did persuade Jack to meet with the Peace Commission established by President Grant and of which Rosborough was briefly a member. Rosborough left the commission before the tragic attack on it by the Modocs, but he was a voice listened to until disposition of the Modoc problem. He was elected District Judge, moving eventually to Oakland, California, where he died. He was buried in a Catholic cemetery at that city.

Jeff C. Riddle, *The Indian History of the Modoc War*. Medford, Oreg., Pine Cone Pubrs., 1973.

Rose, Alexander, fur man (fl. 1850's). B. possibly in Canada, he may have reached the upper Missouri River from that country about 1851; there is an Alexander Rose listed in Ontario in 1801 who may have been his father. Alexander was of average education. He is first reported by Governor I.I. Stevens to have served in Montana in 1853 as interpreter with the Flatheads on the Musselshell River. Rose was in charge of Fort Benton in 1854, and again in 1856, perhaps in the absence of his superiors. He apparently was familiar with the Blackfoot language. One report lists a Rose's Grave on the upper Missouri which may have been his, although his son, Charley (1850-1935) said his father died at Fort Benton.

Montana, Contributions, Vol. X, 1940, 249-50.

Rose, Edward, mountain man (c. 1786-c. 1832). One of the more famous mountain men, Rose, a mulatto, became very influential among the Crows, and "no more colorful or reckless character ever roamed the trans-Mississippi wilderness." Son of a white man and a Cherokee-Negro woman, Rose grew up near Louisville and at 18 made his way to New Orleans, perhaps at this time receiving the wound that gave him the nickname, "Cut Nose." He reached St. Louis in 1806 and joined Lisa in 1807, helped build the fort on the Big Horn, and was sent to winter with the Crows. Upon his return to the fort in the spring he was principle in a grand melee after which he fled to his Crow friends, assuring his place with them by leading a war party in a savage battle against the Minnataree Sioux, securing five scalps personally. In 1809 he was interpreter for Andrew Henry among the Crows, served Wilson Price Hunt briefly in

the same capacity, then joined the Omahas for a time. His excesses led to his being arrested and taken to St. Louis in chains, after which some considered him an outlaw. Rose rejoined the Crows, remaining with them until about 1820, though living with the Arikaras periodically. Rose earned the favor of both Ashley and Leavenworth for his role during their combats with the Arikaras on the Missouri in 1823. He guided Jedediah Smith who wintered among the Crows in 1823-24, finding Rose very influential indeed among that people. Once captured by the Blackfeet, Rose escaped narrowly. He was interpreter for Atkinson who visited the Crows and was still living with that people when Zenas Leonard saw him in 1832. Rose was killed, probably by Arikaras, on the Yellowstone in 1832.

Harold W. Felton, *Edward Rose: Negro Trail Blazer.* N.Y., Dodd, Mead & Co., 1967; Willis Blenkinsop article, MM, Vol. IX; Bernard DeVoto, *Across the Wide Missouri.* Boston, Houghton Mifflin Co., 1947.

Rose, George A. (Roxie), desperado (fl. 1878-1879). Involved in the Lincoln County War in New Mexico on the Dolan side, Rose was a member of the Peppin posse that on June 27, 1878, encountered a McSween group near San Patricio, New Mexico; his horse was shot from under him by John Copeland. Rose was a member of the Peppin posse during the Five Days' Battle at Lincoln in July, 1878. In April or early May 1879 he shot a soldier at Franklin (El Paso), Texas, and wounded three bystanders.

"Frank Warner Angel's Notes on New Mexico Territory 1878," ed. by Lee Scott Theisen. *Arizona and the West,* Vol. 18, No. 4 (Winter 1976).

Rose, Isaac P., frontiersman (Feb. 18, 1815-post 1883). B. in Mercer County, Pennsylvania, he reached St. Louis by 1834 and purportedly joined Wyeth's Rocky Mountain fur trading project, although confirmation is lacking. In 1827 his right arm was crippled permanently in an Indian ambush and he returned to Pennsylvania, becoming a school teacher, administrator, and justice of the peace in Lawrence County. His book, *Four Years in the Rockies, or Adventures of Isaac P. Rose,* largely written by a hack, James B. Marsh, is unreliable and heavily plagiarized.

Aubrey L. Haines article, MM, Vol. VII.

Rose, James M., adventurer (c. 1805-Mar. 6, 1836). B. in Ohio, he went to Texas by way of Arkansas, and was at the Alamo in early 1836, not to be confused with Moses Rose, the man who escaped. James Rose died with more than 180 other defenders.

Amelia Williams, XXXVII, 276.

Rose, John, adventurer, soldier (d. 1830). B. in Livonia, a country today divided by Estonia and Latvia, he purportedly killed an opponent in a duel at St. Petersburg and fled to America. "Some time in the early part" of the Revolution, Rose, speaking German, French and English and "a fine-looking young man," well-mannered, sought a Continental commission; though already there were many foreign officers in the army, his appeal was `rejected. Having taken a brief course in surgery at Baltimore, he was named surgeon in William Irvine's 7th Pennsylvania, becoming a close friend of the commanding officer until jealousy of some American officers led him to leave the regiment in 1780. He volunteered as surgeon in the American navy, and was assigned to the ship, *Revenge,* but was captured by the British and delivered to New York that same year. Exchanged in 1781 he became an ensign in a Pennsylvania regiment and July 8, 1781, was named aide to Irvine; Rose became a "great favorite" in the general's family. He accompanied Irvine to Fort Pitt, and volunteered for the Sandusky expedition under William Crawford to whom he was assigned as "a very vigilant, active, brave young gentleman... and a surgeon." He arrived at Mingo Bottom May 22, and was heartily welcomed, being popular with various classes of soldiery. Rose gave David Williamson, the butcher of Gnadenhutten, credit for his cooperation after Crawford was named commander. Rose had a heroic role in the battle against Sandusky June 4. On one occasion, mounted on "the best horse in the army," he was pursued by mounted Indians, but coolly escaped them. The Indians were joined next day by a detachment of Butler's Rangers, and that night the withdrawal of Crawford began, according to detailed letters Rose wrote Irvine. Crawford became separated from the body of troops and Williamson took command, Rose accompanying him, exhibiting great heroism. The engagement was renewed at the eastern edge of the plains in today's Crawford County, Ohio, but the enemy was at length fought off.

The "almost superhuman efforts of Williamson and Rose" alone prevented panic, however. The retreating Continentals were harassed all the way to present Crestline. Williamson paid high tribute to Rose whose "bravery cannot be outdone." Rose returned to Fort Pitt, continuing as aide to Irvine until the end of the war. He held a civil position until February 21, 1784, sailed for Amsterdam in April after having written Irvine his true name and history. He remained in correspondence with the General and Irvine's son throughout his life, becoming Grand Marshal of Livonia. He was believed to have been the only Russian serving America during the Revolution.

C.W. Butterfield, *An Historical Account of the Expedition Against Sandusky under Col. William Crawford in 1782.* Cincinnati, Robert Clarke & Co., 1873.

Rose, Moses, frontiersman (c. 1785-c. 1850). B. in France his real name was Louis Rose and he reportedly served in Napoleon's army during invasions of Russia and Italy. He reached Texas in 1826 where he worked as a laborer until the war of independence, when he joined forces commanded by Travis. March 3, 1836, at the Alamo, learning the Texans' position was hopeless, he fled; speaking Spanish better than English he eluded Mexican forces. He worked at Nacagdoches until 1842, moved to Louisiana and died north of Logansport.

HT.

Rose, Noah H., photographer (Apr. 1874-Jan. 25, 1951). B. in Kendall County, Texas, he became a typesetter in his youth at Menardville, and traveled as a journeyman printer through southwest Texas and into Mexico. He settled for 15 years at Del Rio, learning the trade of photographer which had commenced when he won a camera and developing equipment in a magazine subscription contest. He resumed his wandering through West Texas, settling at last at San Antonio. He added constantly to his collection of pictures of outlaws, Texas Rangers and peace officers, became a friend of Emmett Dalton by correspondence and sold him pictures of his dead brothers. His collection, some he took himself and others acquired by purchase or in various ways, grew to 3,000 pictures. A flash flood at San Antonio destroyed some of his favorite negatives. He was seriously injured in an automobile accident, yet lived to be 76. His collection was purchased by the University of Oklahoma. Rose was married twice; the first ended in divorce, the second with the death of his wife.

Oran Warder Nolen, "Noah Rose — a Great Photographer." *The West*, Vol. XVI, No. 9, (Apr. 1973), 20-21, 53; J. Marvin Hunter, "Noah Rose: a Frontier Photographer," *Frontier Times*, Vol. 13, No. 2 (Nov. 1935), 101-04.

Ross, Alexander, fur trader (May 9, 1783-Oct. 23, 1856). B. in Scotland, he reached Canada in 1804, eventually joined the North West Company and in 1810 signed on with Astor for his Oregon coast project. He arrived aboard the *Tonquin* at the mouth of the Columbia in March 1811. Ross accompanied the North West Company trader-explorer David Thompson upriver to the mouth of the Okanogan, where a post was built, and Ross left in charge. When the North West Company purchased the Astoria enterprise, Ross transferred his allegiance. In 1816 he became second in command of the coast trade under James Keith, but after a year went to Fort Kamloops in present British Columbia, and later was in charge of Fort Nez Perce at the junction of the Columbia and Walla Walla rivers. When the Hudson's Bay Company absorbed the North West Company, Ross went along, directed the Snake River brigade for a year, was succeeded by Ogden, and spent his last years at the present Winnipeg, in charge of schools for the Red River settlement. His books of lasting interest included: *Adventures of the First Settlers on the Oregon or Columbia River* (1849); *The Fur Hunters of the Far West*, 2 vols. (1855), and *The Red River Settlement: Its Rise, Progress, and Present State* (1856).

Paul Chrisler Phillips, *The Fur Trade*, 2 vols. Norman, Univ. of Okla. Press, 1961; DAB; EA; Edgar I. Stewart article, MM, Vol. VI.

Ross, John (Guwisguwi), Cherokee chief (Oct. 3, 1790-Aug. 1, 1866). The son of a Scot immigrant and a woman only one-quarter Cherokee, Ross therefore was one-eighth Indian but always considered himself a Cherokee and was raised as such. He attended school at Kingston, Tennessee, went on a mission in 1809 to the Arkansas Cherokees for the Indian agent and remained in public life thereafter. He was adjutant of the Cherokee regiment under Jackson operating against the Creeks in the 1813-14 war and participated in the Battle of Horseshoe Bend. In 1817 Ross was chosen member of the national committee of the Cherokee Council, almost at once taking a stand against removal of the Cherokees to west of the Mississippi River. As president of the national committee in 1819-26 he was instrumental in the introduction of school and mechanical training and led in development of a Cherokee government. In 1827 he was associate chief with William Hicks, and president of the Cherokee constitutional convention. From 1828 until removal of the people to Indian Territory in 1839 he was principal chief of the Cherokee Nation and headed several delegations to Washington, D.C., to defend the right of the Indians to their national territory. Between 1828 and 1831 when the Georgia Legislature stripped the Cherokee of all civil rights, the Indians under Ross's leadership took their case to the Supreme Court and won, Chief Justice John Marshall delivering a scathing denunciation of Georgia's violation of treaty rights. Jackson refused to implement the decision with his un-American statement that "John Marshall has made his decision. Now let him enforce it." A minority of Cherokees under Ridge did transfer to Indian Territory, but Ross and most of the people refused to go until finally forced to do so, Ross leading them in 1838-39 on the infamous Trail of Tears when more than a fourth of them, some 4,000, perished from exposure, starvation and disease, Ross's wife among them. In the future Oklahoma Ross joined his people with the 3,000 who earlier had made the trek, helped write a constitution for the united Cherokees and was chief of the entire nation from 1839 until his death save for a temporary hiatus forced by the Federal government during Civil War dissensions. Ross counseled against a Cherokee alliance with the South during that conflict but was overruled and the people briefly joined the Confederate cause, shifting in 1863 to the Union side. In 1866 Ross, now aging, went again to Washington to work out a new treaty to protect the Cherokee and their Constitution. He died August 1, the negotiations still incomplete and was buried at Park Hill, Oklahoma. He was married twice, and fathered eight children.

Hodge, HAI; Dockstader.

Ross, Lawrence Sullivan (Sul), pioneer, educator (Sept. 27, 1838-Jan. 3, 1898). B. in Iowa, his family took him as an infant to Texas, settling in Milam County, then at Austin, and finally at Waco in 1849. He studied at Baylor University and was graduated from Wesleyan University, Florence, Alabama. During summers he returned to Texas, on one occasion being seriously wounded in an Indian fight; in 1859 he was named captain of a ranger company guarding the frontier. With about 120 men on December 18, 1860, he attacked a Comanche village on the Pease River when a chief, Peta Nocona, was killed and the legendary Cynthia Ann Parker recaptured. Ross married and in the Civil War enlisted as a private in the Confederate service, rising to Brigadier General. After the war he was elected sheriff of McLennan County, Texas, then went on to a distinguished civil career beyond frontier interest. He was a state senator, governor of Texas, and president of Texas Agricultural and Mechanical College. Ross was buried at Waco, Texas.

Literature abundant; DAB; HT.

Ross, Peter F., Texas Ranger (July 27, 1836-Mar. 26, 1909). B. in Missouri, he reached Texas with his family in 1838, was educated in New York for two years, and at 22 accompanied his father, a Texas Indian agent, to the frontier for three years. In 1858 he was named captain of a company of Texas Rangers, engaging in Indian scouts and skirmishes; the tale of a long and grueling such adventure is told by Ellison, who later joined Ross's company of the 6th Texas Cavalry for Civil War service. Ross became lieutenant colonel by the end of the Civil War, then entered the cattle business, taking trail herds to New Orleans. After four years in California he was elected sheriff of McLennan County, Texas, in 1875. He established a ranch eventually near Waco, Texas, where he died.

HT; J.W. Ellison, "Scouted on Pease River," *Frontier Times,* Vol. 5, No. 3 (Dec. 1927) 100-101.

Ross, Reuben, adventurer (c. 1782-1830). B. in Virginia he was a member of the Magee-Gutiérrez Expedition to liberate Spanish Texas, serving most heroically from May 1812 to June 16, 1813. Ross was elected a captain of the expedition. After the death of Magee at La Bahía (Matagorda Bay) in February 1813,

Kemper became colonel in command of the Anglo contingent, and Ross was promoted to major. Ross was sent east to collect recruits; he returned with 25 Anglo-Americans and 30 Coushatta Indians. When Bexar (San Antonio) was captured and the Spanish officers treacherously murdered, Kemper withdrew in disgust and Ross was made colonel in command of the American contingent. Ross either was absent or survived the August 18, 1813, disaster to the insurgents at Medina. Later he secured a colonization grant on Red River. He was murdered by a Mexican servant while enroute to Mexico City to present claims for services rendered during the Mexican Revolution, which by then had succeeded.

Harry McCorry Henderson, "The Magee-Gutiérrez Expedition." *Southwestern Hist. Quar.,* Vol. LV, No. 1 (July 1951), 43-61.

Ross, William J., army officer (c. 1846-July 28, 1907). B. in Scotland, he was raised at Hartford, Connecticut, and enlisted July 23, 1862, in Company A, 18th Connecticut Infantry, became a captain in the 29th Connecticut Infantry February 3, 1864, a major May 12, 1865, and was mustered out in October. Ross became a second lieutenant in the 32nd U.S. Infantry May 5, 1868, transferred to the 21st Infantry April 19, 1869, and was posted to Arizona. In May 1871 he commanded Fort Crittenden, southern Arizona when the survivors of the Cushing fight against Juh came in. Later he became aide to Crook and as quartermaster hired men who became famous in Arizona as scouts and at similar occupations: Al Sieber, Mickey Free and others. Ross accompanied Crook on his 1871 initial tour of Arizona; at Fort Apache the Crook group intercepted Loco, a noted Mimbres Apache chief and José Trujillo, who had been sent by Vincent Colyer to locate Cochise and bring him in. Not aware of Colyer's directive, Crook assumed the two were "spies," and threatened to shoot them until Ross intervened, having recognized Loco he spoke up for his character. Crook let the two go. The incident suggests Ross may earlier have served in New Mexico, Loco's homeland. In September 1872 Ross was with Crook at Date Creek, Arizona, when an attempt was made to arrest perpetrators of the Wickenburg massacre. A melee ensued and Ross saved Crook's life, knocking aside an assassin's weapon. Ross was very prominent in the celebrated battle of the Salt River Cave in December 1872. Ross resigned from the army October 18, 1875, and settled at Tucson. Following the April emeute of Loco and several hundred of his followers under the spur of Juh and his hostiles out of Mexico, Ross on May 10, 1882, left Tucson for Sonora. He headed a company of 50 frontiersmen determined to hunt down and exterminate the hostiles, but without Apache guides they could do nothing. Ross had been "duly commissioned as a Captain of militia of the Territory of Arizona," it was reported, although the Territory officially had nothing to do with the adventure, the company being "mounted and furnished with arms" by Pima County and Ross sworn in as a deputy sheriff, equipped with warrants for errant Apaches. May 28 near Casas Grandes, Chihuahua the Ross party ran across a Mexican troop detachment and the two groups settled down, each warily eyeing the other. Then the Ross-Mexican parties were engulfed by a regiment of infantry and squadron of cavalry, Ross and his party taken prisoners and in their view narrowly escaping execution, the Mexicans certain they were spies at best, filibusters at worst. Eventually the Mexicans disarmed the Americans, sending them on a long march back across the border with sticks across their saddles simulating rifles in the event they met hostile Indians. They returned to Tucson June 17, 1882, glad the debacle was finished. Ross later was a bookkeeper, commissary and payroll clerk for various mining companies and acquired an alcohol problem. He died at Tucson.

Heitman; John G. Bourke, *On Border;* Dan L. Thrapp, *Conquest of Apacheria.* Norman, Univ. of Okla. Press, 1967; Thrapp, *Al Sieber, Chief of Scouts.* Norman, 1964; information from Louis Menager, Tucson, Ross's step-son.

Rotchev, Alexander Gavrilovich, Russian official (1807-Aug. 20, 1873). B. in Russia, Rotchev was the last commandant of Fort Ross, California, where he was stationed from 1836-41. Cultured, he was master of Russian, French, German, English and Spanish and understood Greek and Latin, was a talented writer and a very early California booster. He befriended Sutter and assisted him in founding New Helvetia in the area of the later Sacramento, and he also befriended any stray wanderer of whatever nationality who reached Fort Ross. Rotchev sailed aboard the Constantine for his homeland and died at Saratov on the Volga at the age of 66.

A. Rotchev, "New Eldorado in California," trans. by Alexander Doll, Richard A. Pierce. *Pacific Historian,* Vol. 14, No. 1 (Winter 1970), 33-40.

Roth (Rath), Peter Paul, soldier (c. 1851-Jan. 18, 1907). B. in Wurttemberg, Germany, he enlisted at Brooklyn, New York, April 8, 1870, in Company G, 10th Infantry. July 27, 1871, he deserted, still a private, at Fort Brown, Texas. While a deserter at large he enlisted March 25, 1873, under the name of Peter Rolls in Troop A, 6th Cavalry. He surrendered as a deserter at Fort Wallace, Kansas, December 24, 1873, and was restored to duty in the 10th Infantry without trial, transferring to Troop A, 6th Cavalry May 11, 1874. In September Roth, Sergeant Zachariah T. Woodall, Privates John Harrington and George W. Smith, with scouts Amos Chapman and William Dixon were sent from Miles's headquarters on McClellan Creek, Texas to Camp Supply, Indian Territory, with dispatches. Enroute they encountered hostile Indians, mostly Kiowas, and were besieged in what became famous as the Buffalo Wallow Fight. Smith was wounded mortally, Woodall, Harrington and Chapman severely, and Roth and Dixon lightly, but they stood off the Indians while a downpour gave them drinking water. The next day the Indians departed and eventually the survivors were rescued. Each was given a Medal of Honor although the two scouts, being civilians had to turn them in again; Roth kept his which was presented November 4, 1874, for "gallantry in action with Indians." June 28, 1876, he was assigned to Camp Apache, Arizona. He was discharged June 10, 1877, at Camp Verde, Arizona, because of reduction of the army; at that time he was a wagoner. He enlisted in Company G, 11th Infantry June 19, 1879, and served until June 18, 1884, re-enlisted July 12, 1885, in the same outfit and served until March 6, 1889, when as a sergeant he was discharged for disability in line of duty. He lived at the U.S. Soldier's Home, Washington, D.C., was married to a widow in 1893, and died either at Washington or in Wurttemberg where his widow resided — the data are not clear. Roth was 5 feet, 7 inches, in height, with dark complexion, brown eyes and hair. He fathered a son who was raised in Germany.

Deeds of Valor, II; Roth Pension file, Natl. Archives.

Rotten Tail, Crow chief (fl. 1851-1864). Described by Kurz in 1851 as a middle-aged man, Rotten Tail was a well-known chief of the river Crows, heading a band of about 80 lodges. He was described as capable, shrewd, with leadership qualities engraved in his expression while his clothing, rather than of Indian origin, was "American," that is, frontier clothing, although Kurz pictured him on horseback in warrior garb, with shield and lance. He was described in 1858 as head chief of the Crows, but this role is not certain. His band was said to have robbed a wagon train on the Milk River in 1864, but most of the booty was returned.

Montana, Contributions, Vol. X, 1940, 287; *Journal of Rudolph Friederich Kurz.* Lincoln, Univ. of Neb. Press, 1970.

Roubaud, Pierre Joseph Antoine, Jesuit missionary (May 28, 1724-post 1781). B. at Avignon, France, he became a Jesuit, reached Canada in 1756 and was assigned to the Abenaki mission at St. Francis, Quebec. He was a literate man, a good writer; Thwaites prints his full report and Parkman makes use of his descriptive talents in describing 1757 military operations against Fort William Henry, New York, in which the Abenakis participated with the French command under Montcalm. Included are accounts of a war feast, cannibalism, the Indian butchery following surrender of the English garrison and observations on the Indian allies, not all of them complimentary. Following the English conquest of Canada, Roubaud supported English interests, becoming anathema thereby to most of the French, and was sent to England to supply information about American affairs. There he abjured his faith, or at least the Jesuit order, but "never became an apostate," married and became what was called a political agent of the English government. He gave contradictory accounts of documents said to have been entrusted to him for safe-keeping by Montcalm at the time of the fall of Quebec. Roubaud apparently later came on hard times. He wrote to Lord North in 1781 a memorial subsequently published under the title, *Mr. Roubaud's deplorable case,* recounting his services to the government and asking pensions for himself and wife, both in broken health. One report said that he died at St. Sulpice, in Paris, after 1781.

Thwaites, JR, LXX, 91-203, 311n25; Parkman, *Montcalm and Wolfe,* II, III.

Rouensa, Kaskaskia chief (fl. 1700-1706). A prominent chief of the Kaskaskia Indians, an Illinois tribe, their village was named for him after they had moved it to the present site of Kaskaskia in 1700, according to Gravier. Rouensa greatly assisted the work of the Jesuit missionaries, he added, and assisted in saving the life of Gravier after he was felled by a would-be assassin's arrow.

Thwaites, JR, LXV, 263n11, LXVI, 39, 57-59.

Rouleau, Hubert, frontiersman (d.c. 1890). One of several Rouleaus on the frontier, he was b. in Canada and by 1846, when Parkman met him, was a seasoned frontiersman, a literate man who fathered children by Indian women and sought to have them educated. He was a guide for the Connor Powder River expedition of 1865 and moved with the Brulé Sioux to White River, South Dakota. He died near Pine Ridge.

Charles E. Hanson Jr. article, MM, Vol. IX.

Roulleaux, de la Vente, Henri, priest (fl. 1704-1710). A secular priest, he was sent by the Seminary of Foreign Missions to Mobile, Alabama which he reached July in 1704. He quickly took sides in the internal wrangling among French in Louisiana, by his preaching developing numerous enemies, among them the governor, Bienville. Roulleaux became afflicted with ill health and returned to France in 1710.

Thwaites, JR, LXVI, 342n26.

Rouville, Jean Baptiste Hertel de, *see* Hertel de Rouville.

Rowdy Joe, Rowdy Kate, *see* Joseph Lowe

Rowland, John Albert, frontiersman (Apr. 14, 1791-Oct. 14, 1873). B. at Port Deposit, Maryland, he reached New Mexico in 1823, and trapped northward to the Green River the next year. In 1826 he began trapping the Gila, continuing in that occupation until 1833 when he withdrew to his Taos enterprises. He had married a Spanish American woman in 1825 and became a citizen of Mexico in 1829. He was peripherally engaged in trade between Santa Fe and Missouri and was suspected of involvement in the notorious Texas-Santa Fe Expedition. In 1841 he and William Workman led an emigrant party to California, settling near La Puente. He was active in California affairs, becoming a prosperous, well-known, pioneer.

David J. Weber article, MM, Vol. IV; Bancroft, *Pioneer Register.*

Rowlandson, Mary White, captive (c. 1635-c. 1688). B. probably in England, she settled with her parents, John and Joane White at Salem, Massachusetts, in 1638 and moved to Lancaster, Massachusetts, in 1653; she married the Reverend Joseph Rowlandson, first ordained minister of the community in 1656 and became the mother of four children; one died before King Philip's War. On February 10, 1675, about dawn the Indians "fell with mighty force and fury upon Lancaster," killed many and burned much of the town. Mary Rowlandson was among the 24 taken captive as were three of her children, one of whom, badly wounded, died February 18 during the long hegira the captives endured. Mrs. Rowlandson became servant to Wetamoo, Wampanoag woman sachem often referred to as the Queen of Pocasset, and the best description of whom is included in the Rowlandson narrative. She saw King Philip in early March at Coasset near South Vernon, Vermont; he treated her courteously. Mary was asked to sew for the Indians, making shirts, knitting stockings and contriving other apparel for them, sometimes being paid for her work and using payment to purchase food of which she constantly was in need. Her captors took her wandering through northern Massachusetts and into southern Vermont and New Hampshire, then brought her slowly back again to the present Princeton, Massachusetts, where ransom negotiations were begun. Mrs. Rowlandson was ransomed for 20 pounds sterling in goods on May 2, 1676, and her two surviving children were freed subsequently at different Massachusetts places, the family being reunited and residing for a time at Boston, then moving to Wethersfield, Connecticut, in the spring of 1677. The narrative of Mary Rowlandson about her captivity became a popular book, was widely read in Great Britain and the colonies, being first printed in 1682 by Samuel Green at Cambridge, Massachusetts. No copy of the first edition is extant, but the second edition, published the same year in this country and in England is known in several copies, and it has been reprinted since. The precise birth and death dates for Mary Rowlandson are unknown.

Narrative of the Captivity of Mrs. Mary Rowlandson, reprinted in *Narratives of the Indian Wars 1675-1699,* ed. by Charles H. Lincoln, N.Y., Barnes and Noble, 1959.

Roxie, *see* George A. Rose

Royal, A.J., lawman (d. Nov. 21, 1894). B. in Alabama, he migrated to Texas and operated a saloon at Junction; in 1884 he was indicted for murder of a patron, but nothing came of it. In 1889 he moved to Pecos County, West Texas, ranching near Fort Stockton and being elected sheriff in 1892. "His conduct in office aroused a great deal of opposition. Reportedly he killed at least one man, and there were rumors of others." He became overbearing. He had differences with Judge O.W. Williams and came into a feuding relationship with James and Frank Rooney. In August of 1894, Sergeant Carl Kirchner and four of his Texas Rangers were summoned to preserve order. Tension continued to mount and it is said that nine prominent men of Fort Stockton decided that elimination of the contentious lawman was called for. Someone assassinated him with a shotgun as he sat in his office; no one was arrested.

C.L. Sonnichsen, introduction to Oscar Williams.

Royall, William Bedford, army officer (Apr. 15, 1825-Dec. 31, 1895). B. in Virginia, he was commissioned from Missouri in the Mounted Volunteers July 31, 1846. He reached Santa Fe where he was assigned under Colonel Sterling Price to move upon the insurrectionists who had killed Governor Charles Bent and others. On January 23, 1847, the 500-man detachment of Mounted Volunteers and Santa Fe Infantry plus artillery moved to Taos, opposed by a force of 2,000 men. At Cañada the enemy was pushed back with little loss on either side. On the 29th the enemy was routed from strong positions in Embudo Pass with some loss. At Taos the insurrectionists were strongly positioned; eventually the enemy was defeated, Royall "distinguished for conspicuous gallantry" in the action. He served subsequently with the Santa Fe Battalion until 1848. Sent to Missouri on recruiting service he was returning with his men when at Coon Creek on the Arkansas River he was attacked June 18, 1848, by 300 Comanches; in a spectacular battle and pursuit he drove them off and for his leadership was promoted to first lieutenant. In the 2nd (which became the 5th) Cavalry, he served in Texas, participated in an expedition to the upper Concho River; won special mention for another Comanche fight May 1, 1856. Royall was engaged in "the brilliant combat with hostile Comanches" near Fort Atkinson May 13, 1859, being commended for "conspicuous gallantry." He escaped capture by the Confederates with his company in 1861, returning to the northeast for Union service. His Civil War record was good. He received six sabre wounds June 13, 1862, disabling him for some time. Royall ended the Civil War a major and brevet colonel. He served in the east until the summer of 1868 when he went to Fort Harker, Kansas, being in on the noted affair against Cheyennes at Prairie Dog Creek, October 25-26. He took part in the Republican River expedition of 1869 and was in the battle of Summit Springs. With the regiment he moved to Arizona in 1872, serving there and in California until 1875 when he marched his command to Fort Lyon, Colorado. He transferred to the 3rd Cavalry as a lieutenant colonel late in 1875. Crook assigned him to command cavalry during the Big Horn and Yellowstone expedition; Royall at the head of 15 companies of the 2nd and 3rd Cavalry regiments, "was distinguished for conspicuous gallantry" in the Rosebud battle of June 17, for which he was brevetted Brigadier General, and took part in the Slim Buttes, Dakota, affair September 9, 1876. He became acting assistant inspector general of the Department of the Platte. In September 1882, at Fort Whipple, Arizona, he assumed command of the 3rd Cavalry, and transferred to the 4th Cavalry November 1. He retired October 19, 1887, and died at Washington, D.C.

Price, *Fifth Cavalry;* J.W. Vaughn, *With Crook at the Rosebud.* Harrisburg, Pa., 1956; Heitman.

Rubí, Marques de, military officer (fl. 1764-1772). Cayetano María Pignatelli Rubí Corbera y Saint Clement, Baron of Llinas, Marquis of Rubí was a field marshal in the Spanish army when appointed by Charles III of Spain to inspect the defenses of the northern provinces of New Spain and make recommendations to revitalize and improve them. Rubí entered Texas at El Paso in August 1767 accompanied by Nicolás de Lafora, engineer and cartographer who kept a diary of the officer's travels. Rubí completed a 7,000 mile inspection of northern frontier posts from California to Louisiana. His major recommendations in a report published at Madrid in 1772 urged Spain to recognize the difference between her true and her "imaginary" dominions, and to cease attempting to garrison the latter in favor of establishing firm defenses for the former. As a result of his recommendation, all presidios in Texas north of San Antonio and Matagorda Bay and in New Mexico aside from Santa Fe should be abandoned or moved to the "real" frontier to the south. The real defenses should be strengthened. With respect to Texas he advocated reversing a policy of mercy and lenience toward the Plains Apaches who hovered about the presidios seeking shelter when the Comanches attacked them. If the Lipans were driven away, Rubí believed, the Comanche menace also would be reduced since those Indians swept in only in search of the Apaches, their prey, depredating in doing so upon garrisons in the meantime. He also advocated relocating and renovating existing presidios on the "true" frontier, making them stronger and better able to fulfill their mission. September 10, 1772 the king issued a "New Regulations of Presidios" that incorporated most of Rubí's recommendations.

Herbert Eugene Bolton, *Texas in the Middle Eighteenth Century.* Austin, Univ. of Tex. Press, 1916, 1970.

Rudabaugh, Dave, desperado (July 14, 1854-Feb. 18, 1886). B. in Illinois, he moved after the Civil War to Iowa and, about 1870, to Eureka, Greenwood County, Kansas. In about 1871 he was reported in the vicinity of Fort Smith, Arkansas, but soon made his way to the Kansas cowtowns; he is said to have been in the Fort Griffin, Texas, area about 1875, reportedly becoming a friend of Doc Holliday and other like spirits. On January 27, 1878, he with others bungled a train robbery at Kinsley, Kansas, Rudabaugh and three bandits being quickly captured, Dave turning state's evidence, thereby getting off. He appeared at Otero, New Mexico, Las Vegas, and "for awhile" drove a stage from Las Vegas to Indian Territory. When the Trinidad, Colorado-Las Vegas stagecoach was robbed August 30, 1879, Rudabaugh was charged but not convicted; when four masked men robbed the Santa Fe train November 14, 1879, he again was suspected. Rudabaugh was named a policeman of New Town, Las Vegas, under the wing of Hoodoo Brown. When J.J. Webb was under death sentence for murder, Rudabaugh on April 30, 1880, attempted to break him from county jail, but although he killed deputy sheriff Antonio Lino Valdez, he did not get Webb out. Dave then faded to the Fort Sumner, New Mexico, region and became affiliated with Billy the Kid, becoming, it was said, "the only man the Kid ever feared." On November 28, the Kid, Rudabaugh and William Wilson reached White Oaks, New Mexico, 45 miles from Lincoln, with stolen horses they endeavored to sell. The outlaws and a posse exchanged gunfire the next day, but with little effect. The Kid-Rudabaugh faction returned to White Oaks November 30, drew a posse out after them and fled to a ranch 40 miles toward Las Vegas, where they were besieged. Deputy Sheriff James Carlyle was killed. In an affray near Fort Sumner December 19, Tom O'Fol(l)iard was killed, Pickett wounded, Rudabaugh's horse killed, and the other partisans escaped to Stinking Springs (Wilcox Springs, near present-day Taiban). Here Charlie Bowdre was killed and on December 23 the others surrendered. Pat Garrett and posse took the prisoners to Fort Sumner and on to Las Vegas. Rudabaugh confessed to rifling U.S. mails in the stage and train robberies, hoping a federal case would take precedence over the Valdez murder; a mob gathered and the prisoners spirited past it to Santa Fe where Rudabaugh pleaded guilty to the mails matter and January 3, 1881, was given life, but was returned March 9 to Las Vegas to answer the murder complaint, his strategy not working well. He was sentenced to hang. On September 19, 1881, he, Webb, Thomas Duffy and H.S. Wilson tried to break out, Rudabaugh firing at a jailor, but missed; Duffy was slain. On December 3, 1881, Rudabaugh, Webb and five other desperadoes broke jail. Reaching Mexico, Rudabaugh managed a ranch for Luis Terrazas, but relationships were severed.

Dave became embroiled in a cantina fight, killing two Mexicans and wounding another before himself being killed at (Hidalgo de) Parral, Chihuahua. He was beheaded, and his head paraded on a pike through the streets.

Stanley Francis Louis Crocchiola (F. Stanley, pseud.), *Dave Rudabaugh: Border Ruffian.* Denver, World Press, 1961; Nyle H. Miller, Joseph W. Snell, *Great Gunfighters of the Kansas Cowtowns, 1867-1886.* Lincoln, Univ. of Nebr. Press, 1967; William Keleher, *Violence in Lincoln County.* Albuquerque, Univ. of New Mex. Press, 1957.

Ruelle, Baptiste, prospector (fl. 1840's). A French-Canadian onetime trapper with the Hudson's Bay Company, Ruelle reached California by way of New Mexico where he had engaged in prospecting with small success. In 1841 he discovered gold in what is now Los Angeles County, the deposits being worked for "a few years" by Mexicans from New Mexico in small numbers and not very profitably. Ruelle made his way to Sacramento, going to work for John Sutter. In 1843 he reported he had found gold on the American River (where the important discovery of James W. Marshall was made five years later), but he exhibited little of it and his find was deemed of scant significance by Sutter, Bidwell or anyone else. He died in California.

John Bidwell, *Echoes of the Past.* N.Y., Citadel Press, 1962.

Runnels, Ran(dall), adventurer (c. 1830-July 7, 1882). B. in Mississippi of a family that moved there from Georgia, Ran Runnels was a nephew of Hiram George Runnels (1796-1857), onetime governor of Mississippi and probably a brother of Hardin Richard Runnels (1820-1873), Governor of Texas. He was said to have served as a Texas Ranger and the famous Ben McCulloch referred to him as "my companion in arms in the Mexican War," reporting he had known him favorably for years. In 1850 Runnels accepted an assignment to recruit followers and put down rampant lawlessness in Panama, then used as a land-bridge by Gold Rush migrants to and from California. He entered the freighting business in Panama as a cover-up, packing by mule across the isthmus. He covertly recruited 40 men, as tough as the desperados they were pitted against. After months of under-cover work the Runnels force in January 1852, picked up 37 men they considered the worst of the outlaws and hanged them all that night. Quiet settled over the isthmus, but it was short-lived. In October 1852 Runnels and two of his men hanged another killer. When crime once again increased, he and his men picked up and hanged 41 men in a single night. In March 1854 a vigilance committee was formed and when this failed to clean up the isthmus Runnels came forward and by March 1855 it was sanitized for good. Runnels said he was present at the Panama massacre of April 15, 1856, and was "personally acquainted with all the particulars of it," although what action he took during that affair is not known. He married a niece of the governor of Panama. Ran Runnels was appointed "from Texas" U.S. Consul to San Juan del Sur, Nicaragua March 30, 1859, assumed charge May 23 and left the post October 15, 1861 (perhaps because of Confederate sympathies during the American Civil War). He became U.S. Commercial Agent at San Juan del Sur December 21, 1874, assumed charge March 31 and retired May 26, 1877. He died of consumption at Rivas, Nicaragua.

John H. Kemble, "Law and Order in the Tropics Texas Style: The Career of Ran Runnels." Los Angeles Westerners *Branding Iron* 135, June 1979, 1, 4-8; additional information from John Kemble, Jan. 4, 1980; Bancroft, *Central America*, III, 519-21 & notes 38, 43; Dept. of State Records (Record Group 59), Letters of Application and Recommendation, 1853-1861, 1869-1877, Nat. Archives.

Rush, Milum, pioneer (d. Sept. 11, 1857). Although married, Rush apparently left his family (his wife may have predeceased him) in Carroll County, Arkansas, and joined the Fancher emigrant wagon train at Fort Smith, Arkansas, in late March 1857. It departed Fort Smith for California, but was destroyed by Mormons and Mormon-led Indians at Mountain Meadows, southwestern Utah, Rush perishing with the rest of the adult company.

William Wise, *Massacre at Mountain Meadows,* N.Y., Thomas Y. Crowell Co., 1976.

Rushmore, Charles E., attorney (c. 1857-Oct. 30, 1931). B. in New York City he became an attorney specializing in business and financial law and his sole claim to frontier fame is that Mount Rushmore, South Dakota is named for him. In the 1880s he was sent to the Black Hills, to check out some mines which a large investing company planned to buy. He discovered that the mines had been salted. When walking with the then governor who congratulated him upon bringing the guilty to justice, he looked at the great bare stone mountain and asked its name. The governor replied: "It has none — it will be named for you!" A memorial to be carved on the mountain was authorized by Congress March 3, 1925, with Gutzon Borglum the sculptor, and was to consist of the enormous busts of Washington, Lincoln, Jefferson and Theodore Roosevelt, today visible from a distance of 60 miles and expected to endure for millions of years. The Mount Rushmore National Memorial of 1,670 acres was established in 1929. Borglum had almost completed the busts when he died in 1941 and his son, Lincoln Borglum finished them the following year. Charles Rushmore was invited by President Coolidge in 1929 to take part in the dedication ceremony for the memorial, but his health prevented his attendance. He died at New York City.

New York Times, Oct. 31, 1931, July 30, 1980 (Travel Sec.); CE; Rex Allen Smith, *The Carving of Mount Rushmore,* N.Y., Abbeville Press, 1985.

Rusk, Thomas Jefferson, military officer, statesman (Dec. 5, 1803-July 29, 1857). B. in Pendleton District, South Carolina, he read law, was admitted to the bar, practiced in Georgia, followed embezzlers to Texas and decided about 1833 to settle there. He became involved in the Texas revolt against Mexico and in late 1835-36 was inspector general of the army. He participated in the Battle of San Jacinto, assuming command after Houston was wounded and retaining it until October 1836 when he became Secretary of War. He served in the Texas Congress until 1838 when he helped prevent the Vicente Cordova uprising. In October 1838 he led Texas troops in a three-day battle at Kickapoo Town in Anderson County; as a result many Kickapoo agreed to leave Texas for Indian Territory. In November Rusk rounded up many Caddo Indians, delivering them to Shreveport, Louisiana. He was elected chief justice of the Texas Supreme Court in December 1838 but resigned 18 months later. In 1839 he commanded troops expelling the Cherokees from Texas. In January 1843 he became Major General of militia, then returned to law practice. Rusk was influential in organization of the Texas state government, served in the U.S. Senate, supported Polk in favoring the Mexican War, and promoted railroad construction. His wife died in the spring of 1856, Rusk becoming increasingly despondent and he committed suicide at his Nacogdoches home. Rusk County and Rusk, Texas, are named for him.

BDAC; CE; HT; DAB.

Russell, Charles Marion, artist, cowboy (Mar. 19, 1864-Oct. 24, 1926). B. at St. Louis, he was related to the Bents of fur trade fame. He made his first trip west in 1880, the same year Remington toured the wild country. Russell visited Helena and the Judith Basin, 200 miles distant, stopping briefly at a sheep ranch, then joined up with Jake Hoover, a back country prospector and hunter. He stayed with Hoover two years, roaming the wilderness and observing, learning and remembering. He returned to St. Louis in 1882, but came back to Montana in March, obtaining a job as a night-hawk in April for the 12 Z & V ranch. He took part in the 1882 Judith roundup, one of the biggest in Montana until that time, eventually becoming a full-fledged cowboy. Indians, Blackfeet mostly, roamed the country and Russell came to know them, seeing too the last of the buffalo and other integral components of the harsh northern wilderness. He established a small place of his own in Pigeye Gulch, out of Utica. For about 11 years he drifted as a cowboy, hunter, and keen-eyed observor through the cow-and-Indian country, becoming locally famed as an artist of sorts, in watercolors and clay modeling. The summer of 1886 was very dry, the following winter a disastrous time with blizzards following one another, all but destroying the range industry. Russell worked with Jesse Phelps that winter. When the owner in Helena asked in early spring for a report on his stock, Charlie sent his famous sketch of the lone steer surrounded by coyotes, with the legend, "Waiting for a Chinook." Someone added the line, "Last of the 5,000," and Russell's reputation was assured. The tiny picture has been preserved and is owned by the Historical Society of Montana at Helena. Russell wintered with the Bloods of Canada in 1888-89, then returned to Montana with a wagon freighting outfit. *Harper's Weekly* had published his "Caught

in the Act" in 1888, and *Frank Leslie's Illustrated Newspaper* on May 18, 1889, printed a full page of his drawings. A portfolio came out in 1890, and an article about him appeared in New York in 1891. His fame grew steadily from then forward, although for years his pictures were traded for drinks, given to friends, or sold for pittances. Some of them were ribald, but all were good-natured, filled with enthusiasm and life and zest. He married Nancy Cooper of Kentucky, 14 years his junior, September 9, 1896, and the following year moved from Cascade to Great Falls, where he established the studio where he would work the remainder of his life. Nancy quickly came to appreciate his unique talent. She persuaded him to reduce his drinking and by 1908 to end it, and with a sharp eye quickly caused him to place more value upon his work. After two trips to New York he was established as a major artist, if unique and specialized, and he held his first one-man show on Fifth Avenue in 1911. By 1920 he had reached the peak. He produced more than 2,600 pieces of preserved art work in all. His first Rawhide Rawlins book was published in 1921. He died of a heart attack following a goiter operation, and his body was conveyed to the cemetery in a hearse drawn by two black horses, as he had wished, driven by Ed Vance, an old-time stagecoach driver. Will Rogers remarked, "He wasn't just 'Another Artist.' He wasn't 'just another' anything..."

Harold McCracken, *The Charles M. Russell Book.* Garden City, N.Y., Doubleday & Co., 1957; *A Bibliography of the Published Works of Charles M. Russell,* comp. by Karl Yost and Frederic G. Renner. Lincoln, Univ. of Nebr. Press, 1971.

Russell, Don(ald), Westerner (Feb.1, 1899-Feb. 17, 1986). B. at Huntington, Indiana, he attended Northwestern University, Evanston, Illinois, served in the army for two years during World War I and was graduated from the University of Michigan. He was a copy reader for the Atlanta *Journal,* worked for the Chicago *Journal* and *Evening Post,* then joined the *Chicago Daily News,* of which he eventually was city editor; in the 1950s he became an associate editor of the *New Standard Encyclopedia.* An avid reader and student of the frontier, Russell was a founding member of the Chicago Westerners, a parent organization of Westerners International which now has more than 100 corrals in this country and abroad; Russell was a "Sheriff" (Chairman) of the Chicago group, later served as President of Westerners International, and was an early editor of the Chicago *Westerners Brand Book,* a periodical devoted to westerner papers and news that has been copied by other corrals in various regions. He was a foremost book reviewer, in his career assessing more than 2,000 volumes. Each of his reviews was informed, meticulously accurate and balanced, done with integrity and after a thorough reading of the work, for he never "reviewed from the jacket," a practice he abhorred. Most of his reviews were published by the Chicago *Brand Book,* but he wrote others for prominent newspapers and magazines, acquiring a national reputation for the soundness of his summaries. Russell wrote or edited books. Among those of frontier interest included: *One Hundred and Three Fights and Scrimmages: The Story of General Reuben F. Bernard* (1936), which first had appeared in *The Cavalry Journal; The Lives and Legends of Buffalo Bill* (1960); ed., *Five Years a Dragoon: And Other Adventures on the Great Plains,* by Percival G. Lowe (1965); *Custer's Last,* a work about pictorial representations of Custer's Little Big Horn fight; and *The Wild West: A History of the Wild West Shows* (1970). Russell also was a member of the Civil War Round Table and wrote on that war. He died at Grand Rapids, Michigan, and was buried at Elmhurst, Illinois, where he had made his home for many years. He was survived by his widow, Ruth, two daughters and a son.

Don Russell, "On the Reading and Reviewing of Books," Chicago *Westerners Brand Book,* Vol. XXIX, No. 12 (Feb. 1973), 89-91, 95-96; "Don Russell Night," Chicago *Westerners Brand Book,* Vol XXXV, No. 4 (Sept.-Oct. 1978), 25-32; *Chicago Tribune,* Feb. 19, 1986; *Chicago Sun-Times,* Feb. 20, 1986; author's file on Russell.

Russell, Gerald, military officer (May 1, 1832-Apr. 2, 1905). B. in Ireland, he was in his own words a "bog-trotter," then trained as a cobbler until he emigrated and July 21, 1851 enlisted in F Company, Mounted Rifles (which became the 3rd U.S. Cavalry August 3, 1861). He was first sergeant of D Company September 14, 1862, when appointed acting second lieutenant of the 3rd Cavalry, commissioned a second lieutenant July 17. He became first lieutenant August 4, 1864, and

captain November 14, 1867. Bourke gives an amusing characterization of "Jerry" Russell as he knew him in 1870 when the 3rd was enroute to Arizona. At that time Russell already was suffering from hemiplegia, or a paralysis of the left side incurred at Little Rock, Arkansas, when a fractious horse fell with him. Russell was stationed at Camp (later Fort) Bowie, Apache Pass in the heart of hostile country, and frequently scouted for and occasionally skirmished with Apaches. In April 1871 Russell took a detachment from Bowie seeking a missing mail party, found it butchered, trailed Apaches presumably of Cochise's band and had a fight with them on the 16th. October 24, 1871, in Horseshoe Canyon in the Chiricahua Mountains he had another hard fight, probably with Cochise. The 3rd Cavalry was rotated out of Arizona late in 1871 and sent to the middle Plains. In 1876 Russell and his company served under Crook against Cheyennes and Sioux. He was with Mackenzie in the November 25, 1876, attack upon Dull Knife's village on Powder River, Wyoming. Russell became major of the 5th Cavalry October 29, 1888, and retired for disability in line of duty December 17, 1890. He became lieutenant colonel on the retired list April 23, 1904 and died at New York City.

Heitman; Powell; Lansing B. Bloom, "Bourke on the Southwest II," *New Mex. Hist. Rev.,* Vol. IX, No. 1 (Jan. 1934), 48-67; Barbara Ann Tyler, *Apache Warfare under the Leadership of Cochise,* Master's Thesis, Texas Christian Univ., 1965; *Army Register,* 1906, 563; *Army and Navy Journal,* Apr. 15, 1905; information from John J. Slonaker, U.S. Army Milit. Hist. Inst., Carlisle Barracks, Pa., July 5, 1985.

Russell, Gilbert Christian, army officer (fl. 1803-1815). B. in Tennessee, he was commissioned an ensign in the 2nd U.S. Infantry November 22, 1803, became a second lieutenant September 3, 1804, and was stationed at Natchitoches, Louisiana, in 1805. He became a first lieutenant February 28, 1807, resigning the following August 17. Russell was commissioned a captain of the 7th Infantry May 3, 1808, major of the 5th Infantry May 9, 1809, and lieutenant colonel of the 3rd Infantry June 6, 1811, when he was assigned to southern Alabama and Mississippi where he took part in the Creek War of 1813-14. He was stationed at various posts during this time, and took a leading part in the

Battle of the Holy Ground December 23, 1813, which was a white success against the hostile Creeks. Russell became colonel of the 20th Infantry March 9, 1814, and transferred to the 3rd Infantry November 18, 1814. His further activities in the Creek War and possible role in Jackson's Battle of New Orleans January 8, 1815, are not reported. He was honorably discharged from the Army June 15, 1815.

H.S. Halbert, T.H. Ball, *The Creek War of 1813 and 1814.* Univ. of Ala. Press, 1969; Albert James Pickett, *History of Alabama.* Birmingham Book and Mag. Co., 1962; Heitman.

Russell, John W. (Buckskin Jack), scout (Nov. 8, 1847-post 1912). B. in Missouri he ran away from home at 15 and worked around Denver and Cheyenne until 1864 when he was employed by John Richaud Sr. at his ranch on the north fork of the Laramie River. John Richaud Jr. was attracted to Russell and adopted him as his brother in the Indian fashion. In 1865 Russell helped tend the bridge near the present Casper, Wyoming, owned by John Richaud Sr.; later he went to Deer Creek and worked for Jules Escoffee and Adolph Cuney. In the summer of 1875 Crook invited Russell to report to Big Bat Pourière and Little Bat Garnier at Red Cloud Agency, Dakota. The three as scouts joined the troops near Fort Laramie. Russell was a scout not only for the Powder River campaign, but also at the Rosebud and for the Crook summer campaign of 1876. He was at the engagement at Slim Buttes, Dakota, September 8-9. Russell toured with the Buffalo Bill Wild West Show. Apparently he still was living in 1912 near Scenic, South Dakota, but his death is unreported.

J.W. Vaughn, *The Reynolds Campaign on Powder River.* Norman, Univ. of Okla. Press, 1961; Don Russell, *The Lives and Legends of Buffalo Bill.* Norman, 1960; information from the Nebr. and So. Dak. State Hist. Socs.

Russell, Osborne, trapper, mountain man (June 12, 1814-Aug. 26, 1892). B. at Bowdoinham, Maine, he ran away to sea at 16, but a short voyage to New York City was enough and he deserted, spending three years with the North West Fur Trapping and Trading Company in Wisconsin and Minnesota. In April 1834, he joined Nathaniel J. Wyeth's second expedition to the Rocky Mountains and the Columbia River, joining at Independence and contracting for 18 months' service. When Wyeth decided to build Fort Hall, Osborne was one of a garrison of 12 left to manage it. He joined Jim Bridger's brigade of Rocky Mountain Fur Company men, then became a free trapper for several years, operating out of Fort Hall, then owned by the Hudson's Bay Company, and "experienced rather more than his share of desperate adventures" with the Blackfeet and others, including lively engagements and very narrow escapes. Russell kept a journal and, an avid reader, his was literate, accurate, observant, perhaps the finest record of mountain man life and adventures extant. It provides an early description of what became Yellowstone National Park and the Old Faithful geyser. Osborne's reading of the Bible brought him to conversion and a determination to abandon the wild rover's life, and he accompanied the Elijah White train to the Willamette River in Oregon. He was a member of the convention voting for organization of a provisional government, held at Champoeg, May 2, 1843. Russell lost an eye in a blasting accident and, while convalescing, studied law, being appointed a judge October 2, 1843, and then was elected a member of the executive committee of the embryo territory. He ran for governor unsuccessfully, and in 1847 or 1848 completed his *Journal of a Trapper,* which is so precise that his wanderings can be followed today. He became one of the original trustees of the Pacific University at Forest Grove, Oregon. Russell removed to California with the 1848 gold rush, alternately spending his time prospecting and merchandising. He also served as judge at a vigilante trial of three men, whose execution gave Hangtown (Placerville) its name. He and a colleague operated two trading vessels between San Francisco and Portland, but his partner absconded with the company funds, ruining Russell. He probably lived near Placerville for the rest of his life, never marrying, and died at the county hospital of "miner's rheumatism."

Osborne Russell, *Journal of a Trapper (1834-1843),* ed. by Aubrey L. Haines. Lincoln, Neb., Bison Books, 1966; DAB.

Russell, Richard Robertson, Texas Ranger (Oct. 8, 1858-June 28, 1922). B. in Dawson

County, Georgia, he was brought by his parents to Texas at 12 when an uncle, Peter Robertson, branded a cow for him; he was "never out of the cattle business from that time until his death." The Robertsons had settled in Menard County, then a frontier area, and Russell joined the Rangers when old enough, serving in nearby Kimble County about a year from 1879. He was elected sheriff of Menard County in 1886, serving 10 years. Russell expanded his cattle business, was a founder of a Menard bank and later entered banking at San Antonio, where he died, reportedly a millionaire. He was married and fathered two daughters.

Frontier Times, Vol. 4, No. 11 (Aug. 1927), 5; Robert W. Stephens, *Texas Ranger Sketches.* Dallas, p.p., 1972; HT; Hunter, TDT.

Russell, William, pioneer (c. 1748-1794). B. in Culpeper County, Virginia, he had removed by 1770 to the Clinch River where he became a frontier leader and justice of Fincastle County when it was organized in 1772. Russell commanded a company in Lord Dunmore's War of 1774 and took part in the important battle of Point Pleasant. He also had a leading part in the Revolutionary cause; at the outbreak of the war he was named colonel of colonial troops, took part in the capture of Stony Point and was captured at Charleston, but was exchanged. He continued his military service remaining in the army until 1783 when he was retired as a brevet Brigadier General. He married the widow of Brigadier General William Campbell who was a sister of Patrick Henry and moved to Saltville, Virginia, where he died. His son of the same name became a prominent Kentucky pioneer and a colonel in the War of 1812.

Reuben Gold Thwaites, Louise Phelps Kellogg, *Documentary History of Dunmore's War 1774.* Madison, Wisc. Hist. Soc., 1905.

Russell, William Hepburn, Pony Express pioneer (Jan. 31, 1812-Sept. 10, 1872). B. at Burlington, Vermont, Russell became a Missouri merchant and banker at Richmond, and by 1847 was engaged in government freighting with James H. Bullard. In 1850 Russell and James Brown formed a company to deliver 600,000 pounds of government supplies to Santa Fe; the same year he joined John S. Jones to deliver supplies to Fort Hall. In 1854 or 1855 he joined Alexander Majors

and W.B. Waddell in a freighting firm headquartered at Fort Leavenworth which four years later became the famous partnership of Russell, Majors & Waddell. With contracts to supply Army forces engaged in the "Mormon War" in 1857, the company prospered. In May 1859, Russell and Jones formed an independent company to operate a stage line from Leavenworth to Denver, but by February 1860, it was taken over by the partnership as the Central Overland and Pike's Peak Express Co., running coaches through to the coast. On April 3, 1860, the Pony Express came into being, largely to demonstrate the preferability of the Central Route to California over Butterfield's southern mail and stage operation; financially the Pony Express was not in business long enough to pay for itself, but as a flamboyant advertisement for the Central Route, which Russell may have intended it to be, it was a success. Russell was hailed as "the Napoleon of the West" for his triumph. The government could not pay for the service as its contract provided; however, money was found from the wrong fund, and a major Washington scandal resulted. Russell was indicted, but the case against him was dismissed and the matter forgotten in the developing Civil War. On April 26, 1861, Russell was succeeded as president of the stagecoach company; on March 21, 1862, the three-way partnership was sold to Ben Holladay, and Russell gave over his freighting interest to Majors. He withdrew to New York City where he engaged in various businesses until his death at the home of a son, John Russell, at Palmyra, Missouri. He left a wife and five children and a reputation as a towering figure of the transportation industry of the West. Public subscriptions in 1962 assembled funds for a marker for his unmarked grave at Palmyra. Russell was described as "volatile, highly temperamental, a bundle of supercharged nerves, a man who always wore carefully tailored clothes, an aristocrat by nature."

DAB; Henry Pickering Walker, *The Wagonmasters.* Norman, Univ. of Okla. Press, 1966; Barry, *Beginning of West.*

Russell, Wilson B., pioneer (June 20, 1838-Sept. 3, 1913). B. in Madison County, Indiana, he was raised in Iowa and reached Riverside, California, in 1873, in time to be virtually one of its founders. A friend of

Thomas W. Cover, he accompanied Cover in three fruitless searches for the mythical Pegleg Smith gold deposits on the Anza Borrego desert of southern California. On a fourth expedition, Cover disappeared and his body never was found. Russell at first was suspected of doing away with him, but suspicions were diverted to the Helm boys who ranched in the vicinity, cousins of the notorious Boone Helm, and no suspicion against Russell lingered. He suffered a stroke in 1893 and was partially paralyzed thereafter. Santa Fe train No. 50 struck his buggy in downtown Riverside, killing his wife instantly and injuring Russell, who expired the same day.
Los Angeles Times, Dec. 22, 1885; *Riverside (Calif.) Daily Press*, Sept. 3, 1913.

Russian Bill, *see* William Rogers Tettenborn

Ruxton, George Frederick, traveler, writer (July 24, 1821-Aug. 29, 1848). B. near Tonbridge, Kent, England, his boyhood life at school was "a succession of scrapes and schoolboy atrocities." He was sent to military school at 13, but was expelled from Sandhurst after two years and headed for a Spanish civil war, earning a medal for bravery from Queen Isabella and a good command of the Spanish language. By now something of a hero in England, he was gazetted a lieutenant in the British army, serving in Ireland and Canada. He resigned his commission, for he found army life confining, and became a hunter in the Canadian sub-Arctic, then made two trips to Africa, beginning to write hunting sketches and ethnological articles and revealing a talent for observation and recording weird dialogue and dialects. The U.S.-Mexican War having broken out in 1846, Ruxton was made a commercial attache bearing diplomatic credentials to assure British subjects in Mexico of London's solicitude and protection. He landed at Vera Cruz, performed his mission, and headed north with a guide or two, traveling by saddle animal with pack stock accompanying him. Miraculously he missed contact with raiding Comanches, bandits and irregulars. "Except for the kindness of their women, Ruxton did not like the Mexicans... (He) scorned the tight-fisted Yankee traders, the filthy, illiterate emigrants, and the American soldiers' lack of discipline. He was passionately opposed to slavery and was also anti-Mormon and pro-Indian." He

did not care for Roman Catholic priests, either, but was fond of animals, including wild game, the fabulous characters all about, and had an increasingly marvelous time. Ruxton was caustic in his descriptions of the upper families of New Mexico, of Albuquerque and Santa Fe, which struck him as akin to a "prairie dog town," although he appreciated Taos. He left there only a few days before the uprising that killed prominent Americans. Moving into Colorado Ruxton came to the area where he exerted his greatest influence: his descriptions of the trapper-mountain man which, regardless of how accurate or universally true, have been plagiarized by virtually every fiction and many fact-writers ever since. "No one was to equal him in his portrayal of the Rockies and their Mountain Men... He did for the trapper, Theodore Roosevelt said, what W.H. Hudson did for the gaucho." He wintered among the trappers in the Bayou Salado (South Park). With the spring he headed east, at Bent's Fort joining an army commissary train accompanied also by Lewis Garrard who wrote a description of the Englishman. Ruxton's papers and notes were drenched to worthlessness at a ford of the Arkansas' Pawnee Fork, but he preserved a single notebook. Probably during his Atlantic crossing he wrote much of his great *Adventures in Mexico and the Rocky Mountains*, a well-received work and often reprinted. By the following spring his equally-worthy, *Life in the Far West* began to appear in *Blackwood's Edinburgh Magazine*, a leading periodical. An old spinal injury from Colorado plagued him. He determined on a trip to the American West once more to regain his health, which was worsening; at Buffalo, New York, he ran into Garrard again. He reached St. Louis when dysentery afflicted him and although he received good medical care it was to no avail. Ruxton's books remain to mark him as one of the most colorful and influential writers to depict the Rocky Mountain country and characters in the fading days of the fur trade.
Ruxton of the Rockies: Autobiographical Writings, collected by Clyde and Mae Reed Porter, ed. by LeRoy R. Hafen. Norman, Univ. of Okla. Press, 1950; Lawrence Clark Powell, "The Adventurous Englishman." *Westways*, Vol. 65, No. 11 (Nov. 1973), 19-22, 70-71.

Ryan, Paddy, rodeo rider (c. 1896-Nov. 23, 1980). B. in Minneapolis, he served two years in France during World War I, then became a bronc rider and bulldogger from Miles City, Montana. In 1924 he won the Roosevelt Trophy, won all-round titles in 1927, 1928 and 1930 at Calgary, Alberta, and participated in rodeos around the nation for some years. At 40 he retired to his ranch near Sheridan, Wyoming, though often working as a rodeo judge. In 1978 he was inducted into the Rodeo Hall of Fame at Oklahoma City. He moved to Tucson, Arizona, in 1962 and died there.

Tucson, *Arizona Daily Star,* Nov. 25, 1980.

Ryerson, George, frontiersman (fl. 1837). Ryerson was one of 18 whites who treacherously attacked the Mimbres Apache leader, Juan José Compá on April 22, 1837, in the Animas Mountains of present New Mexico, slaying 20 and igniting extended Apache-white hostilities. Ryerson may have resided, like John Johnson, at Oposura (Moctezuma), Sonora. While there seems to be no proof, it is tempting to speculate on a possible relationship between this George Ryerson and the George Ryerson who was b. in 1830 in Texas, according to his own account, or March 10, 1832, at St. Louis by another record, fought with the Mexican army in 1847, served in the campaign against William Walker in Baja California and against the French in Mexico, attaining the rank of major. He lived all of his adult life in Mexico, in 1885 was appointed by President Diaz governor of Lower California or, according to Bancroft, commandant of the northern district of that state, and died at Sacramento, California, of Bright's disease January 24, 1896. He may have been a son of the earlier George Ryerson.

Rex W. Strickland, "The Birth and Death of a Legend: The Johnson 'Massacre' of 1837." *Arizona and the West,* Vol. 18, No. 3 (Autumn 1976), 257-86; Bancroft, *North Mexican States and Texas,* II, p. 732; information from the Bancroft Library; Ariz. Hist. Soc., Hayden File.

Rynerson, William Logan, pioneer, opportunist (Feb. 22, 1828-Sept. 26, 1893). B. in Mercer County, Kentucky, he left for California in 1852. He enlisted in the 1st California Infantry and in 1862 marched to New Mexico with the California Column, being mustered out a lieutenant colonel at Mesilla in 1866. He became interested in at least five Pinos Altos gold claims and brought from California a quartz mill to work them. He soon became involved in politics, intrigue and conflict. On December 15, 1867, he killed Chief Justice John P. Slough, a onetime Union colonel, in a Santa Fe hotel; he was acquitted on a plea of self defense. A Republican, Rynerson held various political positions, including that as territorial senator from Doña Ana County. In 1870 he became interested in silver deposits at Ralston (later Shakespeare, near Lordsburg) and others near Silver City, attacking the Mimbres and Gila River Apaches for purported depredations, attacking Charles Drew's attempt to settle the former on a reserve. Freely charged with corruption, he figured in the Mesilla riot of August 27, 1871; he was defeated for probate judge. Rynerson became involved in litigation over mining claims, dubious land title machinations and other affairs. He figured in the Lincoln County War, being generally aligned with the Dolan-Riley-Murphy faction where, as district attorney, "by undermining faith in the courts (his) partisan behavior contributed to the breakdown in law and order." He became interested in land, hogs, cattle and progressive agriculture, associated with John Riley, and was involved in mining and other enterprises. He was a booster, advocate of New Mexico statehood, the improvement of education. He died at Las Cruces.

Darlis A. Miller, "William Logan Rynerson in New Mexico, 1862-1893." *New Mex. Hist. Rev.,* Vol. XLVIII, No. 2 (Apr. 1973), 101-32.

S

Sabrevois, Jacques Charles de, army officer (c. 1667-Jan. 19, 1727). B. in France, he reached Canada about 1685 and took part in campaigns against the Iroquois in 1695 and 1696; in 1709 he was operating in the Lake Champlain area. From 1715 to 1717 he commanded at Detroit and when recalled following a dispute with Ramezay, he went to France to clear himself, and returned in 1720. He became town major of Montreal, and died there.

Thwaites, JR, LXIX, 298n43; DCB, II.

Sacajawea (Sacagawea, Bird Woman), interpreter (c. 1780-1812/1884). A Shoshone woman, she was captured by the Crows or the Minataris (Hidatsa) and won in a gambling game by Toissant Charbonneau, a voyageur-interpreter-trader in 1794 when she reportedly was 14. He married her along with another Shoshone girl. Charbonneau was hired by Lewis and Clark as interpreter and he took his wife and infant son (b. Feb. 1805 in the Mandan villages) with him as the expedition moved westward up the Missouri in 1805. Sacajawea proved of more value to the endeavor than her husband, occasionally becoming guide as well as interpreter. The first band of Shoshone encountered was headed by Cameahwait, her brother; the meeting was warm and through the relationship Lewis and Clark were enabled to obtain horses and supplies with which to cross the high mountains into the Columbia basin; they reached the Pacific coast November 7, 1805. On the return Sacajawea guided Clark's division of the expedition through the confusing mountains of Montana. Both Lewis and Clark spoke highly of her talents and character in their journals, Clark particularly taken by her and her infant son whom he called Pomp or Pompey, a leader or head man. Lewis called Sacajawea "Jenny," while Clark called her "Janey." She and her husband and son remained at the Mandan villages as the expedition returned to St. Louis, but in 1809 Clark persuaded them to come to St. Louis. In 1811, according to one version, they left their son, now named Jean Baptiste Charbonneau, with Clark to be educated, while Sacajawea and her husband joined a Manuel Lisa expedition back up the river. Lisa's clerk, John C. Luttig wrote in his journal December 20, 1812: "This evening the wife of Charbonneau, a Snake squaw, died of a putrid fever. She was the best woman in the fort, aged about twenty-five years. She left a fine infant child." Some believe that Clark accepted that as the notice that this was not Sacajawea, but the other Snake Woman whom Charbonneau had married. Eventually the child, a girl named Lizette Charbonneau also reached St. Louis and Clark became her guardian as he had offered to become for Jean Baptiste. Hebard believed that Charbonneau had taken both Shoshone wives (he also had a Mandan wife) to St. Louis and had left one there (Sacajawea) while returning upriver with Lisa and the other wife, who had died as recorded by Luttig. Sacajawea, according to this view, thereafter lived for a time among the Comanches (a Shoshone people), then rejoined her own Shoshone on the Wind River Reservation of Wyoming where she died at about 100 on April 9, 1884. This view was also accepted by Hodge and others, although today's historians are about evenly divided on the matter. By this account Sacajawea was interred at the burial ground of the Shoshone Agency where a granite monument marks the site near Fort Washakie, Wyoming. A towering cement shaft was erected in 1929 at Dakota Memorial Park, Mobridge, South Dakota, to commemorate her supposed lost grave in that vicinity. Numerous memorial plaques, statues and other permanent tributes to Sacajawea have been placed at points important to her story.

Literature abundant: Hodge, HAI; Dockstader; Grace Raymond Hebard, *Sacajawea*. Glendale, Calif., Arthur H. Clark Co., 1967.

Sadekanaktie, Onondaga chief (d. 1701). A principal chief and speaker, he is first mentioned at a council at Onondaga, New York, January 29, 1690. He was as famous as an orator as a chief. Sadekanaktie was speaker at Albany, February 25, 1693, and was prominent in the councils of 1698 and 1699. By that time he was lame and his health was failing; he removed to Albany in 1700 in fear of poisoning by his own tribesmen and died the next year; in June 1701 a successor chief was given his name.

Hodge, HAI.

Safely, Alexander F., soldier (fl. 1862-1865). In testimony before the military commission investigating the Sand Creek Massacre of November 29, 1864, Safely said he was a scout for Chivington; he was a private in the 1st Colorado Cavalry. He said his service as a scout led him to be first man on the ground. He said he had been first to wound White Antelope, one of the chiefs slain in the fight in eastern Colorado, but another soldier had finished the Indian off with a bullet in the head.

Sand Creek Massacre.

Sage, Rufus B., frontiersman (Mar. 17, 1817-Dec. 23, 1893). B. at Cromwell, Connecticut, he became an itinerant newsman. He left Independence, Missouri, in September 1841, with Lancaster P. Lupton for Fort Platte, near Fort Laramie, Wyoming, returning to Independence the following summer. He left shortly for the mountains again, living as a mountain man, journeying from Fort Hall to Texas, studiously taking notes all the while, then returning to Ohio in 1844 to write *Scenes in the Rocky Mountains* (1846; 1956), which appeared in many editions. He died at Cromwell.

Ann W. Hafen article, MM, Vol. III.

Saguanash, Potawatomi chief (c. 1780-Sept. 28, 1841). Sometimes known as Billy Caldwell, he was b. in Ontario, his father an Irish officer it is said, and his mother a Potawatomi. Saguanash was educated in Catholic schools, learned to write English and French and mastered several Indian dialects, thus was useful as interpreter. From 1807 to 1813 in the British interest he was associated closely with Tecumseh, whose secretary he may have been. After the Battle of the Thames in October 1813 he transferred his allegiance to the United States and settled at Chicago in 1820. In 1826 he was justice of the peace and during the Winnebago troubles of 1827 was of

great service in restoring order. He died at Council Bluffs, Iowa, aged about 60 years.

Hodge, HAI.

St. Castin, Jean Vincent, *see:* Abbadie de St. Castin.

St. Clair, Arthur, army officer, governor (Mar. 23, 1736-Aug. 31, 1818). B. at Thurso, Scotland, he became an ensign in the British army in 1757 and served under Amherst against the French in Canada. In 1760 he married a Boston woman and resigned the army in 1762 as a lieutenant. With funds derived from his wife's family and personal resources he settled in the Ligonier valley of western Pennsylvania and soon became an independently wealthy land owner. With the outbreak of the American Revolution he offered his services to the Continental Army; his record during the conflict was creditable, though scarcely outstanding; he became a Brigadier General August 9, 1776, and a Major General February 19, 1777. St. Clair commanded Fort Ticonderoga but withdrew in the face of Burgoyne's advance and was relieved of command after the Battle of Bennington, Vermont. He was on Washington's staff at Valley Forge; served on the jury that convicted British Major John André of spying, and helped clear North Carolina of British troops. In 1786 he was elected president of the Continental Congress and in October 1786 named governor of the Northwest Territory. He also was superintendent of Indian affairs and worked out several treaties but depredations increased due in part to expansion of white settlement. Backing the Indians were the British who held such northern border posts as Detroit, Niagara and Mackinac and whose underlying interest was solicitude for the lucrative fur trade of the northern and western country which funneled through the lake positions they sought to maintain. March 4, 1791, St. Clair was named Major General and commander of the army with the mission of defeating the powerful British-backed tribes which had previously bested Harmar. One of the most vivid descriptions of the campaign was by Theodore Roosevelt who believed St. Clair the wrong choice to lead it, as "broken in health; he was a sick, weak, elderly man, high-minded and zealous to do his duty, but totally unfit for the terrible responsibilities of such an expedition against such foes," while the troops he led were "of wretched stuff." Most were levies, or newly mustered and scantily trained troops. St. Clair led his raggedly-marching force from Fort Washington, at the present Cincinnati, Ohio, through the Ohio woods to the vicinity of the Miami villages, building two forts enroute; part of the way he was so ill he was carried on a litter by his men, and rain, hail and snow did not improve his condition. November 3 the army was about 100 miles from Fort Washington, camped on the upper Wabash River near the western border of today's Ohio. Defenses about the camp were scanty, discipline lax for all but the regulars and when the Indians attacked the following morning the militia panicked and fled, the regulars were overwhelmed and what was ordered as a retreat quickly became a rout to "blacken a full page in the future annals of America," according to a diarist. It was the worst disaster to befall an American army in the history of the frontier with a total of 918 known casualties including 647 dead, 35 of them officers, and 271 wounded of whom 29 were officers, while Indian losses were unknown but probably, in Roosevelt's view not "one-twentieth that of the whites." In addition the warriors were "rich with spoil. They got horses, tents, guns, axes, powder, clothing, and blankets... The triumph was so overwhelming and the reward so great that the war spirit received a great impetus in all the tribes. The bands of warriors that marched against the frontier were more numerous, more formidable, and bolder than ever." The chief blunder, Roosevelt wrote, "was the selection of St. Clair" to lead the effort. "He erred in many ways.... With the kind of army furnished him he could hardly have won a victory under any circumstances; but the overwhelming nature of the defeat was mainly due to his incompetence." St. Clair resigned his commission March 5, 1792. A House of Representatives committee investigated the affair, exonerated the officer and placed the blame instead on faulty preparation of the army and consequent lack of discipline and experience among the troops. St. Clair continued to have a role in political development of the Northwest Territory as a supporter of Federalist policies until 1802 when he was removed from office by Jefferson, retired to his Pennsylvania home, attempted without much success to collect money owed him for Revolutionary and Indian military campaigns and sold his property in 1810 to pay his debts. He died in poverty.

Heitman; William W. Williams, "Arthur St. Clair and the Ordinance of 1787." *Mag. of Western Hist. Illustrated* (including a portrait), Vol. I, No. 1 (Nov. 1884), 49-61; Theodore Roosevelt, "St. Clair's Defeat." *Harper's New Monthly Mag.,* Vol. XCII, No. DXLIX (Feb. 1896), 387-403; Roosevelt, *Winning of the West* (incorporating virtually the same material), V. N.Y., G.P. Putnam's Sons, 1900; Francis Paul Prucha, *The Sword of the Republic.* N.Y., Macmillan Co., 1969.

St. Cosme, Jean Francois Buisson de, *see* Buisson de St. Cosme.

St. Lusson, *see* Daumont de St. Lusson.

St. Martin, Alexis, voyageur (c. 1803-1880). B. probably at Montreal, St. Martin, a voyageur, was accidently struck in the stomach by a charge of buckshot fired from a distance of two or three feet on June 6, 1822, on Mackinac Island, Michigan. Dr. William Beaumont, an army surgeon who also conducted private practice on the island, treated him. St. Martin recovered but his wound would not heal over; the physician took advantage of the opportunity to conduct a series of 238 experiments over a period of several years at Mackinac Island, Fort Niagara, Fort Crawford, Wisconsin, Platts-burg, New York, and Washington, D.C. By them he defined the until-then mysterious workings of the stomach and its gastric juices, and compiled a study which remains useful today. St. Martin was persuaded by the enthusiastic physician to take part in the experiments, but, moody and not fully aware of the significance of the work, he proved a very contentious partner at times. Periodically St. Martin returned to Canada, from where he was lured with difficulty by Beaumont; Alexis married and eventually fathered 17 children. Having regained his health and strength he was fired by the Hudson's Bay Company, spending much time in the wilderness. Beaumont never saw him after 1834, although he made numerous attempts to lure him to St. Louis where he had established a home and private practice.

Keith R. Widder, *Dr. William Beaumont: The*

Mackinac Years. Mackinac Island, Mich., State Park Commission, 1975.

Saint-Pé, Jean Baptiste de, Jesuit missionary (Oct. 21, 1686-July 8, 1770). B. in the diocese of Oloron, France, he became a Jesuit and reached Canada in 1719 being stationed among the Miamis near the present Niles, Michigan, after a period spent at Michilimackinac. In 1724 he took part in a council held at Green Bay, Wisconsin; he worked in the upper midwest country until about 1737. The remainder of his career was spent in eastern Canada; he was superior of the Canadian mission from 1739 until 1748 and was appointed to that post again in 1754. He died at Quebec.

Thwaites, JR, LXVIII, 332n40, LXXI, 166.

St. Vrain, Cerán, frontiersman (May 5, 1802-Oct. 28, 1870). B. in St. Louis County, Missouri, he received some education. St. Vrain was raised by Bernard Pratte Sr., and in 1824 formed a partnership with Francois Guerin, with Pratte-supplied goods went to New Mexico, arriving at Taos in March 1825. St. Vrain dissolved the partnership (and soon entered another), disposed of his goods at a profit, and returned to St. Louis in 1826, bringing another supply of trading items to Taos that summer. He trapped beaver in Arizona and elsewhere, and in late 1827 reached the North Platte River at North Park, Colorado, trapping and trading; the leader of the expedition, S.S. Pratte, died from a hydrophobia dog bite and St. Vrain took over its direction. One of the party, Thomas Smith, got his pegleg that winter; a successful spring hunt preceded the return to Taos in 1828. By late 1830 St. Vrain entered a business arrangement with Charles Bent, the firm, Bent and St. Vrain, becoming one of the great establishments of frontier history, always highly respected. Their fur trade, amounting up to $40,000 annually, ranked them next to the American Fur Company. The firm erected Fort William, near present Pueblo, Colorado, in 1833, and Bent's Fort in 1834. St. Vrain, who also maintained a home and interests at Taos, spent much time at Bent's Fort, trading with a spectrum of Indian tribes and incidentally hosting countless visitors from the states, some of them notables. The company established other posts, St. Vrain visiting them all, occasionally going east as far

as Washington, D.C., on business. The influence of the firm extended from the Sioux in the north to the Comanches and Apaches in the south; Bent and St. Vrain worked well together, both highly regarded for business acumen and as gentlemen. St. Vrain became part owner of a huge land grant in New Mexico in 1844, although this led to legal difficulties after the American takeover of the southwest. With the Mexican War impending, Charles Bent and St. Vrain hurried to Missouri, visiting Kearny at Fort Leavenworth enroute, and supplying him with information about New Mexico, the personalities influential in the territory, and other matters. St. Vrain organized a force at Santa Fe to put down the Taos insurrection, becoming involved in one incident when his life was in danger, after Charles Bent's murder. Bent, St. Vrain and Company was reorganized as St. Vrain and Bent, with William Bent as junior partner, but St. Vrain withdrew in 1850, diversifying his business interests. As a lieutenant colonel of mounted volunteers he helped subdue the Utes and Jicarilla Apaches in 1855; he served briefly as colonel of the First New Mexican Cavalry in 1861. From 1855 until his death he lived at Mora, New Mexico, where he died. He had been married four times, fathering a child by each wife. An estimated 2,000 attended his funeral, St. Vrain being buried at Mora "after a life full of accomplishments, service and honors."

Literature abundant but scattered; see David Lavender, *Bent's Fort.* Garden City, N.Y., Doubleday & Co., 1954; DAB; the best resume of St. Vrain's life is Harold H. Dunham's article, MM, Vol. V; Guy L. Peterson, *Four Forts of the South Platte.* Fort Myer, V., Council on America's Military Past, 1982, including engraving of Cerán St. Vrain, 34.

St. Vrain, Marcellin, frontiersman (Oct. 17, 1815-Mar. 4, 1871). B. at Spanish Lake, Missouri, he was a younger brother of Cerán St. Vrain. Marcellin was educated and reached Bent's Fort about 1835. He managed Fort St. Vrain on the South Platte from about 1837, closing it down in 1845. He married first a Sioux woman, then a Pawnee, having children by each. St. Vrain retired from the mountains to St. Louis in 1848, where he married an Irish woman. He died a suicide, reportedly. He was short and slight and had an engaging personality.

Harvey L. Carter article, MM, Vol. III; Guy L. Peterson, *Four Forts of the South Platte.* Fort Myer, Va., Council on America's Military Past, 1982, including portrait of Marcellin St. Vrain, 41.

Salas, Juan de, Franciscan missionary (fl. 1622-1632). A Franciscan missionary, he reached New Mexico in 1622 and settled at Isleta near the present Albuquerque. In 1629 Jumano Indians from the present Texas arrived at the monastery asking religious instruction, stating they had been requested to come by the "Woman in Blue," whom some believed to be María de Jesús de Agreda of Spain. In July Salas and Friar Diego León went to the Jumanos 300 miles to the east, working among them several months. In 1632 Salas and others returned to the Jumanos, perhaps working as far east as the present San Angelo, Texas.

HT; Herbert Eugene Bolton, *Spanish Exploration in the Southwest, 1542-1706.* N.Y., Charles Scribner's Sons, 1926.

Salvívar, Juan de, *see* Zaldívar, Juan de.

Salieres, Henri de Chastelard Marquis de, *see* Chastelard, Marquis de Salieres.

Salleneuve, Jean Baptiste de, Jesuit missionary (June 14, 1708-post 1764). B. in France he became a Jesuit and reached Canada October 2, 1743. He was assigned to the Huron mission near Detroit, remaining until 1761 when disturbances between English, French and the various tribes caused him to seek refuge in Illinois. He worked particularly at Ste. Genevieve, Missouri, until expulsion of the order in 1763. With other priests he went down the river to New Orleans, leaving there for France February 6, 1764.

Thwaites, JR, LXX, 310n21, LXXI, 175.

Salvador, Francis, pioneer (1747-Aug. 1, 1776). B. in London the nephew of an English financier, he reached Charleston, South Carolina, in 1773 and became a planter and landowner with an estate of more than 6,000 acres. He shortly became a patriot, an outspoken defender of American liberties and in 1775 a representative to the First Provincial Congress; later he served in the Second Congress which became the first General Assembly of the rebel colony, making the acquaintance of such leaders as Patrick Calhoun and Edward Pinkney. Salvador did much to improve embryonic governmental processes. Leading a group of 330 men, he was killed near his plantation on the Keowee River, South Carolina, while defending the frontier settlers against a Cherokee Indian attack, believed sponsored by British elements, one of the initial engagements of the Revolutionary War.

B'nai B'rith Messenger, Los Angeles, Calif., Feb. 7, 1975.

Salvadore, Mimbres Apache (d. Feb. 12, 1871). Salvadore was a son of the great Mangas Coloradas and figured in many of the Apache-white incidents in southern New Mexico history. January 12, 1865, he and other leaders contacted the whites at Pinos Altos, seeking peace. Again he and others met with Charles Drew, a new agent, near Cañada Alamosa, New Mexico, in October of 1869, once more seeking peace. He met with Drew again at the end of the year. Despite his interest in a truce however, Salvadore apparently led a party of Apache raiders who in early February 1871, ran horses and mules off from near Silver City, New Mexico. They were pursued by Captain William Kelly of the 8th Cavalry. In a sharp fight in the Chiricahua Mountains February 12, Salvadore and 13 other Indians were killed.

Dan L. Thrapp, *Victorio and the Mimbres Apaches.* Norman, Univ. of Okla. Press, 1974; Las Cruces, New Mex., *The Borderer,* Apr. 13, 27, 1871.

Salway, Frank, frontiersman (c. 1828-post 1906). A halfbreed, he was employed by P. Chouteau Jr. & Company at their post six miles below Fort Laramie in 1854 and was an eye-witness of the Grattan affair in which about 30 whites were killed in a fight with Brulé Sioux at the Indian village below the Chouteau post. His information was accurate and McCann reproduces a modification of a sketch map Salway made of the scene. In 1868 Salway was assistant government farmer at Whitestone, South Dakota, and later on held various frontier positions. He was interviewed on the Grattan fight by Judge E.S. Ricker November 3, 1906, at Salway's home at Allen, South Dakota, when he was 78 years old.

Lloyd E. McCann, "The Grattan Massacre." *Nebr. Hist.,* Vol. XXXVII, No. 1 (Mar. 1956), 1-26.

Samoset, (Osamoset), Abenaki sachem (c. 1590-c. 1654). A native and sagamore or chief of Pemaquid on the site of Bristol, Maine, at the time of the Pilgrim landing at Plymouth, he was sachem of Moratiggon, a Maine village in Abenaki or Pennacook territory. He may have gone to the Cape Cod country with Captain Thomas Dermer and when the Pilgrims arrived he greeted them, "Welcome, Englishmen!" having learned something of their language. Samoset introduced the Pilgrims to Massasoit, who was responsible for salvation of the struggling colony in its early years, but at the outset it was the Pilgrims who befriended and fed and clothed Samoset, a kindness which he repaid by services. Two years later Samoset appeared at Capmanwogen (Southport, Maine) with Captain Christopher Levett, whom he esteemed as his special friend. He entertained Levett at Capmanwogen in 1625 and occasionally affixed his seal, a rudely-drawn bow and arrow, while someone else signed his name as John Somerset to convey land to whites, his being the earliest deeds of lands from savages to whites on this coast. Nothing further is recorded of Samoset until 1653 when, as an old man with a tremulous hand he "signed" a deed conveying 1,000 acres to William Parnell, Thomas Way and William England, also in the present Maine. He must have died soon afterward and probably was buried with his kindred on his island homestead near Round Pond in the present town of Bristol. He was described as tall and straight with hair long behind and short in front, his only native dress being a "leather" in front with a fringe, although he quickly became accustomed to such English dress as he could acquire.

Hodge, HAI; Sylvester; Dockstader; George F. Willison, *Saints and Strangers.* N.Y., Reynal & Hitchcock, 1945.

Sanaco, Penateka Comanche chief (fl. 1849-1855). It was reported that Sanaco, already a chief, succeeded Old Owl who died of cholera in 1849 as head chief of the Penatekas, but Buffalo Hump probably inherited that meaningless title, though Sanaco continued to head his own band of the Penatekas. He tried to cooperate with the whites; on one occasion he brought in a band of Wichita horse thieves, but he always had difficulty controlling his own warlike young men. In 1854 he brought his band who "must have been as prosperous as any of the southern Comanches; yet squalor and misery were in evidence everywhere," to the newly established and diminutive reservation on the Brazos River of Texas. In 1855 Sanaco and his band were told by an unscrupulous trader that a military force was enroute to kill them all and fled the Brazos Reservation for the northern Comanches dwelling along the Red River in today's Oklahoma, although some may have gone to New Mexico, at least temporarily. Little is heard of Sanaco after that period, although from time to time he is reported.

Rupert Norval Richardson, *The Comanche Barrier to South Plains Settlement.* Glendale, Calif., Arthur H. Clark Co., 1933.

Sanders, Wilbur Fiske, lawyer, vigilante, legislator (May 2, 1834-July 7, 1905). B. at Leon, New York, he studied law at Akron, Ohio, served briefly in the Civil War and moved to eastern Idaho, the later Montana where he began to practice law in Bannack in 1863. Lawlessness was everywhere. A particularly vicious murder found Sanders the only attorney daring to prosecute; despite threats to his life the criminals were convicted and executed. In view of the outlawry, hopelessly out of control, Sanders became an organizer of vigilantes who dealt summary justice to as many desperadoes as could be captured and brought a semblance of law and order to the region. Sanders became interested in mining and stock raising and had a distinguished public career, served as U.S. senator, and died at Helena.

DAB; BDAC; David Lavender, *The Rockies.* N.Y., Harper & Row, 1968.

Sandoval, Cebolla (Hastin Tlth'ohchin), Navaho chief (d. Feb. 1859). By 1830 Sandoval already was a prominent figure among the Dine Ana'aii, a militant and somewhat distinctive faction of the Navaho. McNitt wrote he was "a controversial figure... ambitious, cunning, devious, and contradictory. As he attained power he became a plotter..., an informer most often for the whites but occasionally... for the Navajos." Where trouble occurred, Sandoval was likely to be found. He would (even) buy and sell slaves among his own people." He became wealthy, his services always for hire, a dealer in Navaho scalps and by 1836 undisputed leader of the Dine Ana'aii. Believing he had become a depredator, a party of Cebolleta, New Mexico, citizens led by Juan Ramirez, attacked Sandoval's rancherias in 1840, killed no one but captured some women and children and liberated one of their own captured by the Dine Ana'aii. In March 1841 Sandoval with a number of Navaho headmen came in for a peace council; the usual treaty was agreed upon, but the Navahos became incensed over Mexican refusal to liberate captives and nullified the agreement. The Mexicans however seemed to welcome Sandoval shortly after once more into favor and he became something of an informer on Navaho thought and activities. In 1845 and later he occasionally offered his services to the governing elements in any campaign against hostile Navahos who continued raids and depredations against the settlements. He may have conducted a raid himself against wayward Navahos in September 1845. He became an agent for elements of Doniphan's command in 1846, or at least cooperated. Sandoval served as guide for some later expeditions into Navaho country. In November 1846 he was among many Navaho headmen who signed a treaty with Doniphan's representative. Sandoval was guide for John Macrea Washington's 1849 expedition into Navaho country and he figured in the clash in the Chuska Valley August 31 in which Narbona, another famous Navaho chief was slain. In 1850 it was Sandoval's turn to be suspected by Anglos as a spy, but he escaped that difficulty. Sandoval's repeated offers to guide troops caused Indians to threaten his life, but he persisted in "cooperation." He thus cooperated in 1851 with Ramón Luna, prefect of Valencia County in a retaliatory or slave raid against Navaho rancherias suspected of harboring depredators; Sandoval himself brought in captives and sold them as slaves. Part of his activity no doubt was caused by wars between Navaho factions, the Dine Ana'aii often at odds with everyone. But Sandoval was often regarded by Indians and whites alike as a trouble-maker. He was a frequent visitor at Henry Dodge's first Navaho agency at Chupadero, New Mexico. He guided and led partisans on Major Henry Lane Kendrick's exploratory sweep to the San Juan River in the summer of 1853. The next year he moved as far east as the Pecos River, threatening to raid Comanches. Sandoval and some of his warriors accompanied Bonneville on his Apache expedition of 1857 although

their performance was not noteworthy except that they took some prisoners. Sandoval one day was thrown by his horse which then kicked and badly injured him, the incident near the Rio Puerco adjacent to Red Mountain. Native healing failed and he died. Descendants of the Dine Ana'aii today called Cañoncito Navahos have a small reservation north of U.S. Highway 66, east of Laguna Pueblo.

Frank McNitt, *Navajo Wars*. Albuquerque, Univ. of New Mex. Press, 1972.

Sandoz, Marie Susetta, writer (May 11, 1896-Mar. 10, 1966). B. in Sheridan County, Nebraska, she became a country school teacher at 17, was married the next year but shortly gave up both teaching and husband, enrolled at the University of Nebraska in 1922 and spent many years there, browsing through an assortment of classes and eventually taking up writing. Her first book, *Old Jules* (1935) was published only with difficulty, but was well-received when it did appear and firmly established her as a major regional writer. It was a biography of her Swiss father and is considered by many her finest book, although there are dissenters. She dropped the "e" from her first name and devoted herself thereafter to full-time literary pursuits. She produced eight other non-fiction works: *Crazy Horse: The Strange Man of the Oglalas* (1942); *Cheyenne Autumn* (1953); *The Buffalo Hunters* (1954); *The Cattlemen* (1958); *These Were the Sioux* (1961); *Love Song to the Plains* (1961); *The Beaver Men* (1964); and *The Battle of the Little Big Horn* (1966), the least satisfactory of her works largely because as Clark reports "it was written at frantic speed in the final months of her life," and for it she borrowed heavily from already published sources and added nothing new to knowledge of the famous action. Mari Sandoz also published five full-length novels, three shorter works of fiction and four collections of briefer endeavors. In 1943 she settled in New York City, died there of cancer, and was buried on the Old Jules place in Nebraska as she had wished.

LaVerne Harrell Clark, "Mari Sandoz." *Arizona and the West,* Vol. 18, No. 4 (Winter 1976), 311-14; Bruce H. Nicoll, "Mari Sandoz: Nebraska Loner," *American West,* Vol. II, No. 2 (Spring 1965), 32-36; *New York Times,* Mar. 11, 1966.

Sanford, George Bliss, army officer (June 28, 1842-July 13, 1908). B. at New Haven,

Connecticut, Sanford was commissioned a second lieutenant of the 1st Dragoons (1st Cavalry) April 26, 1861, and a first lieutenant July 30; he became a captain October 1, 1862. His Civil record was creditable, Sanford emerging a brevet lieutenant colonel after arduous service with the Army of the Potomac. In December 1865 he went with his regiment to California and thence to Arizona, where he remained about five years, much of it in command of Fort McDowell. In September-October 1866 he led a scout and attack on an Indian rancheria, causing some casualities. June 3-4, 1869, he led a scout into the Pinal Mountains of Arizona, striking an Apache rancheria and killing about 20. He led other effective scouts December 10, 1869, and April 30 and May 25, 1870. In 1871 he moved with his company to California and from there to Idaho; he served briefly on detached duty at Sitka, Alaska. He was promoted to major June 25, 1876. In 1877 Sanford and his regiment served under Howard in the Nez Perce campaign; Sanford was in command at the scarcely glorious action at Camas Meadows August 20, 1877, the troop losses being three killed or wounded mortally, an officer and four enlisted men wounded and most of the outfit's mules swept off by Indian raiders, none of whom, was hit. Sanford also participated in the pursuit of the Nez Perce through Yellowstone Park and northeast into Montana, participating in the Battle of Canyon Creek, September 13. A year later he was involved in the Bannock War. Back in Arizona in September 1881, Sanford missed being involved in the pursuit of the Apache hostiles, Juh and Geronimo. He reported that because of recurring malaria he had turned command over to Reuben Bernard who engaged the enemy in a sharp battle (Sanford's biographer mistakenly believed Sanford had commanded this action). Sanford became lieutenant colonel of the 9th Cavalry in 1889. He commanded the Leavenworth Squadron, a mixture of troops from three cavalry regiments, in the Wounded Knee affair in 1890-91. Sanford became colonel of the 6th Cavalry in 1892. He retired July 28, 1892. He and his wife were at San Francisco during the April 18, 1906, earthquake and fire. He lived in retirement at Litchfield, Connecticut, and died at New York City.

E.R. Hagemann, *Fighting Rebels and Redskins: Experiences in Army Life of Colonel George B. Sanford, 1861-1892.* Norman, Univ. of Okla.

Press, 1969; Heitman; Powell; Oliver Otis Howard, *Chief Joseph: His Pursuit and Capture.* Boston, Lee and Shephard Pubrs, 1881; Dan L. Thrapp, *General Crook and the Sierra Madre Adventure.* Norman, 1972.

Sanford, John F.A., frontiersman (1806-May 5, 1857). B. in Virginia, he reached St. Louis in 1825 and became clerk for William Clark, as such witnessing a treaty with the Kansas Indians at St. Louis June 3. In 1826 he was appointed sub agent for the upper Missouri, remaining two years among the Mandans and contacting other upper country tribes. He returned to St. Louis briefly in 1828, and again in 1830. He went back upriver and in 1831 brought down a deputation of four Indians from as many tribes, visited Washington, and returned up the river in 1832, accompanied by Catlin. Sanford returned to St. Louis and married the daughter of Pierre Chouteau Jr., Emilie, returning up the river, this time accompanied by Prince Maximilian, and went back to St. Louis. His wife died in 1836, having mothered a son. Sanford resigned in late 1834, went to work for his father-in-law, remaining in Chouteau's employ the rest of his life. He became a partner in the firm in 1838, accumulated a fortune, lived at New York City late in life, and married once more. In 1853, owning briefly the slave, Dred Scott, he was defendant in the famous lawsuit. In December 1856, Sanford had a mental breakdown, became insane, and died in a New York asylum.

Janet Lecompete article, MM, Vol. IX.

Sanno, James Madison Johnson, army officer (Dec. 10, 1840-May 4, 1907). B. in New Jersey, he was graduated in 1863 from West Point and commissioned a second lieutenant in the 7th Infantry. After service in the east and southeast he was assigned to Fort Fred Steele, Wyoming, in 1869 and later that year to Camp Douglas, Utah, being transferred in 1870 to Fort Shaw, Montana. Here he remained except for occasional temporary duty east of the Plains until 1878. He was on the Yellowstone and Big Horn Expedition against the Sioux from March 17, until October 6, 1876, and the Nez Perce campaign in the summer of 1877, being mentioned favorably by Gibbon and winning a brevet for his part in the Battle of the Big Hole, Montana. In 1878 he was on an expedition to relocate Fort Assiniboine,

Montana, then was stationed at the Blackfoot Agency, Montana, for a year until 1879. After eastern duty, Sanno was assigned to Fort Snelling, Minnesota, in 1881 and to Forts Laramie and McKinney, Wyoming, from 1882 until 1889. In 1888 he supervised removal of bodies of victims of the Fetterman Massacre to Custer Battlefield cemetery; his remaining service has no direct frontier interest. Sanno had ended the Civil War a first lieutenant; he became a captain in 1871, a major of the 3rd Infantry in 1895, a lieutenant colonel, 4th Infantry in 1898, a colonel, 18th Infantry in 1899 and Brigadier General in 1903, the year of his retirement. He died at Fort Oglethorpe, Georgia.

Powell; Heitman; Cullum.

Santa Anna, Antonio Lopez de, Mexican leader (Feb. 21, 1792-June 221, 1876). B. at Jalapa, Vera Cruz, Mexico, his father was Spanish and his mother mixed Spanish and Indian. With a rudimentary education he enlisted in Royal forces at 14 or 15, serving the king in Texas and Tamaulipas. During the war of Mexican independence he served initially near Vera Cruz against guerilla chieftains. later he supported Iturbide (whom he subsequently opposed), occupied Vera Cruz, threw the Spanish out, and commenced to fulfill the leadership role in Mexican affairs for which he had been destined. His history is far too confused and involved for discussion here. Frontier interest in Santa Anna stems from his activities in Texas and later in permitting the Gadsden Purchase of southern Arizona and New Mexico by the United States. As president and attempted dictator of Mexico he took personal command of Mexican forces against the Texans in 1835-36, was responsible for the massacre at Goliad and the Mexican triumph at the Alamo, and also the debacle at San Jacinto where, according to rumor, instead of commanding his forces he was in a tent dallying with a woman, Emily Morgan (see entry). He was captured at San Jacinto, Houston, and on November 16, 1836, commenced a journey to Washington by way of the Mississippi and Ohio rivers, was entertained at a state dinner by President Jackson, and was returned to Mexico by Jackson aboard an American warship, or so Santa Anna recalled. The purpose of Houston, Jackson's good friend, in extricating Santa Anna from Texas fury and vengeance forces,

and arranging the singular journey to visit Jackson, and it may be, to understand United States reluctance to permit Mexico to wipe out an independent Texas, has never been satisfactorily illuminated, and many questions and problems remain. Santa Anna lost a leg at Vera Cruz two years later attempting to repulse the French; his subsequent career is most involved, with tenures as president, periods in exile and other adventures following in bewildering series. In 1853 he sold the Mesilla valley and land south of the Gila River to the United States for $10 million because Mexico — or he — needed the money; by this was added to the United States minerally-important land useful for a southern railway route. Santa Anna died in penury and squalor, a leading Mexican newspaper commenting that "his career formed a brilliant and an important part of the history of Mexico but Santa Anna outlived his usefulness and his ambitions." He was regarded in his young manhood as very handsome, 5 feet, 10 inches in height and "rather spare." His complexion was dark, hair black, and he had short black whiskers and no mustache; he could be courtly, gracious and charming of manner; he could also be ruthless, cruel and perhaps craven under some circumstances. Santa Anna was an opportunist, a man of few enduring loyalties. He characterized in his person the turbulent history of Mexico during the 19th century.

Literature abundant; *The Eagle: The Autobiography of Santa Anna,* ed. by Ann Fears Crawford. Austin, Pemberton Press, 1967; Amelia Williams, XXXVII, 111-15.

Santa María, Juan de, Franciscan missionary (d. c. 1582). B. in Catalonia, Spain, he became a Franciscan priest and was versed in astrology, as well. Juan de Santa María was one of three Franciscans accompanying the Rodriquez-Chamuscado expedition of 1581-82 from Chihuahua into New Mexico, discovering and working among more than 60 Indian pueblos. His fate is variously given but one account said that he bid goodbye to his two companions, Friar Agustín Rodriguez and Padre Francisco López, crossed the Sandia Mountains east of the Rio Grande and southeast of the pueblo at Puaray (one of the Tiguex group) where they had been working. Santa María intended to pass south by way of the salt lakes the Spanish had discovered and go on to El Paso del Norte. The third day he arrived at the Tigua pueblo of San Pablo and while resting under a tree was killed, his body burned.

George P. Hammond, Agapito Rey, *The Rediscovery of New Mexico, 1580-1594.* Albuquerque, Univ. of New Mex. Press, 1966; Twitchell, *Leading Facts.*

Santee, Ross, artist-writer (Aug. 16, 1889-June 29, 1965). B. at Thornburg, Iowa, of Swedish parents, he early showed an aptitude for art, studying four years at the Chicago Art Institute. He tried cartooning without success, and went to Globe, Arizona, becoming a horse wrangler on his uncle's ranch. He began to draw what he observed, doing it distinctively at first with a shredded match dipped in India ink. He sold a page of sketches about 1917 to the *St. Louis Post-Dispatch.* He spent a year in the Army — in Texas — during World War I, then returned to Arizona and part of each year attended the Chicago Art Institute again, studying with George Bellows and others. He managed to make it in New York with his pictures. Asked to write a short story to go with them, he did, selling it to *Boy's Life* for $25. *Leslie's* asked to see a story; he wrote one that same night and sold it to that outlet for $200. Then he returned to *Boy's Life,* bought back the first story for $25, and sold it as well to *Leslie's* for $200. "Horse trading," he called it. His first book, *Men and Horses,* appeared in 1926; he wrote and illustrated more than a dozen volumes. For years he continued to work roundups for ranches grazing on the San Carlos Apache Reservation. From 1936 to 1941 he lived at Phoenix, serving as editor of the Federal Writers Program of the WPA, bringing out a state guide of Arizona and other works. He died at Globe, two years after the death of his wife.

Lawrence Clark Powell, "How He Pictured the West." *Westways,* Vol. 65, No. 3 (Mar. 1973), 47-50, 84.

Santleben, August, stage line operator (Feb. 28, 1845-Sept. 19, 1911). B. at Hanover, Germany, he commenced carrying mail at 14 between Castroville and Bandera, Texas. During the Civil War he was a scout along the Rio Grande for the 3rd Texas Cavalry. In January 1866, he won a mail contract for service from San Antonio to Eagle Pass and on to Fort Clark, 162 miles, with about a round trip a week. Santleben operated the line throughout his two year contract despite Indian hostilities; at various times he operated lines to Monterrey, Mexico, and to Laredo. From 1867 until 1893 he operated a stage line and later a freighting business into Mexico, reporting in his memoirs that he had persisted despite many clashes with Indians and outlaws. Santleben was survived by his widow and many children.

HT; Robert H. Thonhoff, *San Antonio Stage Lines: 1847-1881.* El Paso, Univ. of Tex., Southwestern Studies 29, 1971.

Sapir, Edward, linguist, anthropologist (Jan. 26, 1884-Feb. 4, 1939). B. at Lauenburg, Pomerania, Germany, Sapir was brought to this country by his parents at 5, was graduated from Columbia University in 1904 and earned his doctorate there in 1909. He was influenced heavily by Franz Boas, as he influenced Swadesh and many other linguists and anthropologists who developed and carried on his ideas and expanded them toward fresh horizons. The bulk of Sapir's work was in American Indian languages although his restless, creative mind developed concepts which had intrigued him in various fields. One important area of interest for Sapir was that of the historical affinities among American Indian languages, frequently demonstrating his vision and wide grasp of important elements of relationships that were still obscure to slower minds. He wrote many technical papers and one book af general appeal and usefulness, *Languages* (1921, 1955). During his career he taught at the University of Pennsylvania for two years, was with the Canadian National Museum as anthropologist for 15 years, taught at the University of Chicago from 1925 to 1931, and at Yale from 1931 until his death which occurred at New Haven, Connecticut. He was an outstanding figure in several branches of science but is best known and was perhaps most influential in that of linguistics.

Who Was Who; DAB.

Sarpy, Peter A., fur trader (Nov. 3, 1805-Jan. 4, 1865). B. probably in St. Louis, as Pierre Sylvester Gregoire Sarpy, which he shortened to Peter L'Abadie Sarpy, he may have reached the Nebraska area in 1824 with the American Fur Company, for which he became an accomplished trader. He operated initially out of Fort Bellevue, north of the Platte River. He formed a partnership with Henry Fraeb, they establishing Fort Jackson in 1836 on the South Platte. It lasted two years, when the partners sold out and dissolved their association. Sarpy re-established himself at Bellevue where he remained for 26 years, expanding into various fields and living the "life of a frontier baron." He died at Plattsmouth, Nebraska.

John E. Wickman article, MM, Vol. IV; DAB.

Sarpy, Thomas L., fur trader (Mar. 7, 1810-Jan. 19, 1832). B. at St. Louis, he went up the Missouri for the American Fur Company about 1827, as a fur trader. He was killed accidentally in a gunpowder explosion on a tributary of the Cheyenne River.

George M. Platt article, MM, Vol. III.

Sassacus, Pequot chief (c. 1560-June 1637). The last chief of the Pequots "while yet in their integrity," Sassacus was b. near Groton, Connecticut, the son of Wopigwooit, first chief of the tribe whom the whites knew and who was killed about 1632 by the Dutch near Hartford, Connecticut. In October 1634 Sassacus assumed leadership of his people. He sent an emissary to Boston seeking a treaty of amity although he harbored bitter feelings against the whites. His proposal however aroused the enmity of Uncas, the Mohegan chief to whom he was related by blood and marriage. Sassacus was a powerful chief; his control extended from Narragansett Bay to the Hudson River and included much of Long Island and some 26 sachems were subordinate to him. The Puritan colonists decided in 1636 for reasons that are obscure but no doubt had to do with cupidity to make war on the Pequots. The conflict, after a horrifying massacre of several hundred Indian men, women and children near the present Mystic, Connecticut, ended within a few months, Sassacus fleeing with 20 or 30 of his people to the Mohawk country, but there he found no sanctuary; in mid-1637 his scalp and those of his brother and five other Pequot chiefs were sent by the Mohawks to the Massachusetts governor. Puritans described Sassacus as "malignant (and) furious," but to historian John De Forest he was "a renowned warrior, and a noble and high-spirited man."

Hodge, HAI; *Handbook Indians*, 15.

Sassamon, John, Indian victim (d. Jan 29, 1675). A Christian Indian of the Wampanoag people, he had studied at Harvard, returned to the wilderness and became Metacom's (King Philip's) secretary, and later came back to Natick, Massachusetts, rejoined the church, becoming a native preacher at Nemasket, Massachusetts. He warned the English that the Wampanoags were plotting an uprising, Sassamon thereafter being murdered and his body thrown into Assawompsett Pond, where ice covered it. Three Indians were executed for his slaying, the incident, a factor in the in June outbreak of King Philip's War.

Leach, *Flintlock*.

Satank, *see* Setangya.

Satanta, (Settainte), Kiowa chief (c. 1830-Oct. 11, 1878). He became a chief in his twenties because of prowess as a warrior but also was able as a diplomat, outstanding as an orator and his keen sense of humor made him a favorite with army officers and other whites although frequently he was hostile. Satanta, whose name meant White Bear, was a signer of the treaty of the Little Arkansas in 1865 and the 1867 Medicine Lodge Treaty by which the Kiowas agreed to a reservation; they delayed coming in however until Custer seized Satanta and Lone Wolf as hostages; when the Kiowas agreed to come in the leaders were freed. On May 17, 1871, Satanta with Setangya and Big Tree led a number of warriors in an attack on a wagon train belonging to Henry Warren, a government contractor, killing seven teamsters and running off 41 mules. The Indian leaders reportedly boasted of the feat too widely and were arrested at Fort Sill, Oklahoma, then sent under guard to Jacksboro, Texas, for trial, Setangya being killed enroute. Satanta and Big Tree were sentenced to be hanged, the judgments commuted to life imprisonment; Governor Edmund J. Davis in October 1873 paroled the pair in an act which was widely condemned. Shortly afterward Satanta and Big Tree were accused of leading their warriors in renewed raids, whether justifiably or not is unestablished. Satanta was rearrested, returned to the penitentiary where he committed suicide, it is said, by jumping from a second story window of the penitentiary hospital head foremost onto a brick wall below. He was "a typical Plains warrior, of fine physique, erect bearing and piercing glance... His memory is cherished by the Kiowa as that of one of their greatest men."

Hodge, HAI; HT; Dockstader; Britton Davis to Christian Albert Bach, Dec. 17, 1925.

Saunders, George W., trail driver (Feb. 12, 1854-July 3, 1933). B. in Gonzales County, Texas, he managed his father's ranch while his parent and two brothers fought in the Civil War; from 1868 he helped put trail herds together for the northern railroads, and in 1871 accompanied one to Abilene himself. In subsequent years he went up the trail with eight more herds. He had become an expert stock handler, with experience with mustangs as well as longhorns, wild as well as manageable. At 10 in 1864 he had survived his first stampede. His father drove a herd from Goliad to New Orleans in 1867. George Saunders made his first northern drive with a Monroe Choate herd, experiencing a bad stampede, much swimming water to cross, Indians and buffalo. He had adventures during his active career with Indians and other turbulent elements, some involving narrow escapes. In 1873 he joined Henry Scott's Minute Company organized to protect the border country from Mexican guerilla-bandits "and we rode with such vengeace that our company soon became a terror to the invading murderous Mexicans." For a year he was deputy under Sheriff James Burk of Goliad having "some narrow escapes and made some dangerous arrests of desperate characters." From 1880 until 1883 he ran a hack service at San Antonio; after the death of his wife he sold out, drove wild Texas mares to Missouri and Illinois, disposing of them enroute, returned to Texas and continued for a time to deal in horses. About 1885 he trailed a herd of cattle to New Mexico. In 1886 he went into the livestock commission business at San Antonio, eventually forming his own concern. He married a second time in 1889. In 1890 he introduced roping contests in stock shows, but so many cattle were crippled and killed that he petitioned the Legislature to ban the sport. Saunders was member of various stock raisers organizations; his greatest claim to historical fame was his organization of the Texas Trail Drivers Association in 1915, his service as its president, and his research and assembling of information on the old stock trails leading out of Texas to various markets and ranges. It was due to his "tenacity, foresight and unselfish labors" that *The Trail Drivers of Texas* was published under the editorship of J. Marvin Hunter, the first volume in 1920, the second in 1923, and various editions since. This massive work perpetuated the accounts of hundreds of oldtime trail men and is a lasting resource tool of immense value. "It is his monument," adjudged historical writer Harry Sinclair Drago, and a worthy one indeed. Had it not been for Saunders, much of the history of the remarkable movement of stock from Texas which, over a period of 20 years altered the face and character of the entire West, would have remained unwritten and irrecoverable.

Hunter, *Trail Drivers of Texas*, I, pp. 426-54, 959-71; HT; *Frontier Times*, Vol. 4, No. 1 (Oct. 1926), 42-43.

Saunders, John (Long John), frontiersman (fl. 1855-58). Stuart said Saunders could "throw a stone with almost the force and precision of a rifle ball." He traded with Indians in the Bitterroot Valley in 1855-56, prospected on Gold Creek, Montana, in the spring of 1856 and found some gold, and he and his companions may have been those who told James and Granville Stuart of the likely prospects on Gold Creek. Saunders was associated with Fred Burr the next season, but little is known of him thereafter.

Montana Contributions, II (1896); George F. Weisel, *Men and Trade on the Northwest Frontier.* Missoula, Mont. State Univ. Press, 1955.

Saurel, Pierre de, French officer (1628-Nov. 26, 1682). B. at Grenoble, France, he reached Canada as a captain of the Carignan-Salieres regiment and remained in that country the rest of his life. In the summer of 1666 he led an expedition of 300 French and Indians against the Mohawks, but was headed off by the Flemish Bastard. He participated in Tracy's 1666 autumn campaign, once more against the Mohawks, a successful operation. As a civilian in Canada he subsequently engaged in the fur trade; in 1682 he went to Hudson Bay with Radisson and others. Saurel died at Montreal.

Thwaites, JR, XLIX, 275n17; DCB.

Savage, James D., frontiersman (1823-Aug. 16, 1852). B. at Jacksonville, Illinois, he returned early in the 1840's to the ancestral home in Cayuga County, New York, married, and brought his wife to Peru, Illinois. In April 1846, with his wife, infant and a brother, he went to Independence, Missouri, and joined the Lilburn Boggs party for California. His wife and daughter died during the Plains crossing, his brother went on to Oregon, and James reached Sutter's Fort October 28, 1846, too late for the Bear Flag Revolt, but in time to join Fremont's California Battalion. Although "he was one of the worst malcontents in the battalion," he served until its disbandment in 1847. Thereafter he was employed by Sutter in sawmill construction on the American River. "An ignorant man of much natural shrewdness, he made many warm friends and bitter foes," according to Bancroft. By late 1848 he had commenced gold mining, using Indian labor, and pushed south to the Merced River, setting up trading posts here and there, and marrying Indian girls when possible. "He made it a point to marry a chief's daughter in every tribe," Bancroft said, and this was true. Eccleston calculated he had 33 wives, "5 or 6 only, however, of which are now living with him. They are from the ages 10 to 22 & are generally sprightly young squaws." Savage was at his post on the Fresno River when the Mariposa Indian War began, being elected major of the so-called Mariposa Battalion and capably guiding its operations during which it penetrated Yosemite Valley, rediscovered the Big Trees, and accomplished other exploration work. After the war Savage continued Indian trading and was a major factor, through his influence with the tribes, in maintaining peace between the races. On July 10, 1852, a party under Savage held the election by which Tulare County was organized. Savage was killed in a fight with newly elected county judge Walter H. Harvey at Kings River. The remains were reburied in 1855 near the Fresno River, 16 miles east of Madera, California. Eccleston described Savage as "rather small but very muscular & extremely active. His features are regular, & his hair light brown which hangs in a negligé manner over his shoulders. He, however, generally wears it tied up. His skin is dark tanned by the exposure to the sun." He had blue eyes.

Annie R. Mitchell, "Major James D. Savage and the Tulareños." *Calif. Hist. Soc. Quart.*, Vol. XXVIII, No. 4 (Dec. 1949), 323-41; *The Mariposa Indian War 1850-51; Diaries of Robert Eccleston: The California Gold Rush, Yosemite, and the High Sierra,* ed. by C. Gregory Crampton. Salt Lake City, Univ. of Utah Press, 1975; Bancroft, *Pioneer Register.*

Savage, Thomas (Thomas Newport), interpreter, Indian man (c. 1594-c. 1627). Reportedly b. to the family of Sir John Savage, first baronet of Rock Savage in Cheshire, England,

Thomas reached Jamestown, Virginia, January 2, 1608, with Captain Christopher Newport (see entry). He was left with Powhatan in exchange for an Indian lad named Nemontack whom Newport wished to take to England; Savage, whom Newport told the natives was his son (and always known to Virginia Indians thereafter as Thomas Newport), was assigned to learn the Indian language, which he quickly did. He remained with Powhatan three years, then was commissioned an ensign and appointed an interpreter for the Virginia Company. He worked with Indians for the whites for nearly 20 years, serving as guide, interpreter and scout, enjoying prestige with the natives and becoming a great favorite. In about 1618 he accompanied Thomas Hamor as interpreter on a visit to Powhatan. In 1621 he served Thomas Pory, Virginia secretary in a like capacity in a meeting with Namenacus, chief of Patuxent in the present Calvert County, Maryland. The chief Ismee Sechemea granted him a 9,000-acre tract on the eastern shore of the Potomac. Savage by his white wife fathered several children of whom two sons survived him as did his widow. The date of his death is not reported, but Willison wrote that Savage lived for about 20 years after his arrival in the colony.

DNB; George F. Willison, *Behold Virginia: The Fifth Crown.* N.Y., Harcourt, Brace and Co., 1952; Karen Ordahl Kupperman, *Settling with the Indians: The Meeting of English and Indian Cultures in America, 1580-1640.* London, J.M. Dent & Sons, 1980.

Savage, Thomas, militia officer (c. 1608-1682). B. at Taunton, Somerset County, England, he reached Boston at 27 in 1635. Savage became captain of an artillery company in 1651 and served as its officer at various times afterward. He was captain of the 2nd Boston Militia Company from 1652 until his death. In late June 1675 Savage, James Oliver and Thomas Brattle were sent to try to resolve difficulties with the Wampanoags who appeared teetering on the brink of war and already were engaged in depredations. Approaching Swansea on the 25th they came across two bodies of slain Englishmen, the opening events in King Philip's War. The emissaries returned to Boston urging military support for Plymouth Colony and war against the Indians. Boston authorities confided the military effort to Major General Daniel

Denison, with Savage, now a major, as second in command. Denison became ill and Savage took his place directing Massachusetts men in the campaign of July 1675. Following Church's defeat in an ambush, Savage and his men reached Swansea late on June 28, and two days later commenced the sweep of Mount Hope Peninsula, where it was believed Philip's men were to be found, but none were located; the Indians had decamped. During succeeding days, however the Narragansetts seemed to have been neutralized by diplomacy, and with that major threat apparently removed, Savage and the bulk of Massachusetts troops returned to Boston, arriving July 20. In February 1676 Savage was given command of a 600-man intercolonial mounted force intended to launch offensive operations against Philip's people from Brookfield, Massachusetts. The operation, into northwestern Massachusetts was however "carried out with something less than ordinary skill," and the nimble enemy easily eluded the militia. In March Savage was directed that if he failed to contact the enemy in the west, to bring his forces back to the eastern part of the colony, which he did and by mid-April had returned to Boston. He does not figure importantly in King Philip's War thereafter.

George Madison Bodge, *Soldiers in King Philip's War,* 3rd ed.   Boston, p.p., 1906; Leach, *Flintlock; Narratives of the Indian War 1675-1699,* ed. by Charles H. Lincoln.   N.Y., Barnes & Noble, 1959.

Say, Thomas, naturalist (June 27, 1787-Oct. 10, 1834). B. at Philadelphia, son of one of the "fighting Quakers" of the Revolution, he was scantily educated but of a scientific turn of mind and a founder of the Academy of Natural Sciences at Philadelphia. In 1818 with Titian Peale and others he joined a scientific expedition to the Atlantic coasts of Florida and Georgia; his monumental *American Entomology* already had been planned and a prospectus issued the year before. In 1819 Say was appointed zoologist on the Stephen H. Long Rocky Mountain expedition, which Peale also joined. Say discovered many new species of insects (in his career he discovered more new insect species than any of his predecessors). In 1823 he accompanied Long's expedition to the headwaters of the Minnesota River, also in the capacity of zoologist. At Philadelphia he became curator of the American Philosophical Society and professor of natural history at the

University of Pennsylvania. His *American Entomology,* 3 vols., appeared from 1824-28, well-received both in this country and abroad. Most of its illustrations were done by himself, others by Peale. He also was a specialist in shells, publishing *American Conchology* in six parts from 1830-34, most of the illustrations done by his wife. Say's paleontological writings also were collected. He has been the subject of many articles and books. Say's library and collections went to the Philadelphia Academy of Natural Sciences at his death.

Thwaites, EWT, XIV-XVII; DAB.

Sayenqueraghta (Old Smoke, Old King), Seneca chief (c. 1707-c. 1788). When he first comes into view he lived on Smoke Creek, a few miles south of the present Buffalo, New York. He was mentioned by Zeisberger in 1750; he figured in the Easton Treaty of 1758, the treaty of Johnson Hall, New York of April 3, 1764, and was prominent in most of the Six Nations conferences up to 1774 by which time he was the most distinguished warrior of the Iroquois Confederacy, as renowned in council as in combat and a man of "great bravery and superior intellect." In 1777 the Senecas were entitled to name the two war chiefs of the League, most of which had decided to ally with the British, and they chose Sayenqueraghta to be principle war chief and Cornplanter, only 25, the other although both had opposed breaking the treaty of amity with the Americans signed only two years previously at Albany. Sayenqueraghta was prominent in the Battle of Oriskany, August 8, 1777. With John Butler, Sayenqueraghta led the savage massacre in Wyoming Valley, Pennsylvania, in June and July 1778; Cornplanter also was present. Sayenqueraghta was in the action at Newtown in late August 1779, an engagement won by the Continental General John Sullivan. The chief continued his raiding activities until the end of the war, although so aged he must ride a horse to battle and on campaign, including the arduous Schoharie campaign in the autumn of 1780 during which he continued to exercise leadership. In 1781 there were 64 war parties out, Sayenqueraghta leading one of them toward Fort Pitt. Indian cruelties were well published, but the aged chief pointed out in 1782 council, the Americans "gave us great Reason to be revenged on them for their Cruelties to us and our Friends, and if we had the means of publishing to the World the many Acts of Treachery and Cruelty committed by them on our Women and Children, it would appear that the title of Savages wou'd with much greater justice be applied to them than to us." It was probably he, under the name of Kayenthoghke, who signed the Treaty between the Six Nations, October 22, 1784, and the United States at Fort Stanwix. Hodge said he had died "before 1788."

Hodge, HAI; Barbara Graymont, *The Iroquois in the American Revolution.* Syracuse, (N.Y.) Univ. Press, 1972.

Say-es, bronco Apache (d. Mar. 29, 1894). B. probably on the San Carlos Reservation in Arizona, Say-es became an army scout and associate of the Apache Kid who held ranks up to first sergeant. He broke out with the Kid June 1, 1887, following the melee in which Al Sieber was wounded (see Apache Kid entry for details), was retaken with the Kid and tried twice, being convicted and sentenced to seven years at the Yuma Territorial Prison. With the Kid, Pas-lau-tau and Hale, he bolted after the stagecoach affair November 2, 1889, near the present Kelvin, Arizona. Say-es missed or escaped from the fight in which Pas-lau-tau and Hale were killed and with two other bronco Apaches hid out near Mescal Creek, a tributary to the Gila. An Apache named Has-cal-te was a member of the band Say-es belonged to, and when Say-es killed a relative of Has-cal-te because of failure to provide them food, Has-cal-te, himself an outlaw, returned to San Carlos and surrendered, reporting to Sieber the whereabouts of the missing two; troops ran them down in September 1890, capturing Say-es and killing his companion, El-cahn. On October 18, 1890, Say-es was sentenced to life at Yuma Prison for killing Reynolds, which he had not done. He died there of consumption, being a cellmate of Has-cal-te, who had turned him in, who himself died of consumption three days later.

Jess G. Hayes, *Apache Vengeance.* Albuquerque, Univ. of New Mex. Press, 1954; Dan L. Thrapp, *Al Sieber, Chief of Scouts.* Norman, Univ. of Okla. Press, 1964.

Sayre, Alfred (Hal), army officer, lawyer (Mar. 10, 1834-Dec. 11, 1926). B. at Deckertown, Sussex County, New Jersey, he was raised in western New York, became a lawyer and moved in 1857 to Omaha. Two years later, in the winter of 1859-60, he walked to Denver where he engaged in mining, part of the time in the San Juan Mountains of southwestern Colorado. By 1864 he had returned to Denver and enlisted as a private in the 100-day 3rd Colorado Cavalry, shortly being commissioned a captain, then becoming a major and commanding one of five battalions under Shoup in the Sand Creek action November 29, 1864, about 40 miles northeast of Fort Lyon, Colorado. The battalion was heavily engaged from 6:30 a.m. until 1 p.m. when it broke up to pursue small bands of Indians fleeing the field, the command suffering five killed and seven wounded. Many of the soldiers took part in scalping and mutilation of the dead Indians. Witnesses testified they had seen Sayre scalp an Indian, the trophy having "a long tail of silver hanging to it." Sayre became adjutant general of Colorado. He made the first plat of Central City and was "long prominent as a mining engineer and operator," also interested in banking. He once evaluated Chivington: "I always regarded him as a good-natured, well-intentioned man... Of course his religious training forbade his use of profanity, which I always thought was something of a handicap to him." Once when Chivington had great difficulty getting his regiment into formation for inspection he directed in exasperation Sayre "to come here and cuss this regiment into line." Sayre said late in life that "I believe the conduct of the Colorado forces at Sand Creek was justified." He also attributed the murder of Jack Smith to accident, but added that "there was no mourning in our ranks over it."

Sand Creek Massacre; W.B. Vickers, *History of the City of Denver.* Chicago, O.L. Baskin and Co., 1880; Sayre, "Early Central City Theatricals and Other Reminiscences," an interview with T.F. Dawson of May 21, 1921. *Colo. Mag.,* Vol. VI, No. 2 (Mar. 1929), 47-53.

Scaggs, Henry, long hunter (c. 1725-c. 1808). Possibly a native of Virginia, he and his brothers, Charles and Richard were noted hunters "and nothing but hunters," ever working beyond the frontier; Henry Scaggs reportedly was the first white man of record to penetrate eastern Tennessee, entering along the Clinch River from Tazewell County, Virginia, the Clinch emptying into the Tennessee River. Scaggs Creek was named for the family. In 1779 Henry Scaggs, accompanied by about 20 men, left for Kentucky but was attacked by Indians in Powell's Valley, Virginia, losing some horses. Most of the men returned home, but Scaggs, his stripling son and a man named Sinclair continued toward the Green River country of Kentucky to hunt. During the following hard winter, Sinclair disappeared, perhaps drowned; young Scaggs sickened and died. His father was unable to penetrate the frozen ground to bury him, and finally interred him in a hollow log, then left alone to finish his hunt, returning afterward with the horses and peltries. Scaggs settled on Pitman's Creek in the present Taylor County, Kentucky, in 1789 "with his chldren and connections around him, sharing freely in the Indian difficulties of the times." Charles and Richard also resided in the neighborhood. Henry Scaggs died at his home in 1808 or 1809, "aged upwards of eighty years." He was of a large, bony frame, bold, enterprising and fearless.

Reuben Gold Thwaites, Louise Phelps Kellogg, *Documentary History of Dunmore's War 1774,* p. 239. Madison, Wisc. Hist. Soc., 1905.

Scammon, Charles Melville, sea captain (May 28, 1825-May 2, 1911). B. at Pittston, Maine, he became a captain of sailing vessels and reached California in 1853, engaging in the whale fishery. He discovered the haunts of the gray whale in a bay at Latitude 27 degrees 50 minutes on the Lower California peninsula since called Scammon's Lagoon. Scammon wrote the useful *Marine Mammals of the Northwestern Coast* (1874, 1970). His journal of the 1858-59 voyage on which he discovered the lagoon was published in 1970, edited by David A. Henderson, a geographer. In 1861 Scammon joined the revenue service, and during the Civil War commanded a U.S. revenue cutter; he was named captain in the revenue service, retaining connections with it until his death. He was detailed by the government to assist in the explorations of the Overland Telegraph Expedition in 1865, and commanded the flagship of their fleet for three years. He died at his home in East Oakland, California, aged 85, less than 24 hours after the death of his wife of 65 years.

NCAB; Charles Melville Scammon, *Journal Aboard the Bark Ocean Bird on a Whaling Voyage to Scammon's Lagoon, Winter of 1858-1859,* ed. and annot. by David A. Henderson. Los Angeles,

Dawson's Book Shop, 1970; *Science,* June 9, 1911, p. 887.

Scammon, Eliakim Parker, army officer (Dec. 27, 1816-Dec. 7, 1894). B. at Whitefield, Maine, he was graduated from West Point in 1837 and the next year was appointed to the topographical engineers. Scammon was active in the Seminole War in Florida, performed astronomical work at Oswego, N.Y., in 1840, and in 1846 was aide to Winfield Scott in the Mexican War, being commended for gallantry at the battle of Vera Cruz. From 1847-54 he was engaged in the survey of the Great Lakes. Dismissed from the army in 1856 for disobedience, he taught mathematics at St. Mary's College, Cincinnati, Ohio. He became a Brigadier General in the Civil War, was captured in 1864, exchanged, and commanded the district of Florida at war's end. His professional life continued after the conflict, and he died at New York City.

NCAB.

Scarborough, George A., gunman (Oct. 2, 1859-Apr. 6, 1900). B. in Louisiana he arrived in Texas as a child and grew up in McLennan County, becoming a cowboy. In 1885 he was sheriff for Jones County and later was a deputy U.S. marshal at El Paso, Texas, under Marshal Dick Ware. June 21, 1895 he was one of three lawmen killing Martin Morose, a Mexican citizen and suspected Texas rustler; the other two were Jeff Milton and Texas Ranger Frank McMahon. April 6, 1896, Scarborough killed John Selman (the slayer of Wes Hardin) in an El Paso alley, the evidence showing it to be probable murder. Scarborough was acquitted but resigned his deputy's commission. At Deming, New Mexico, he became a detective for the Grant County Cattlemen's Association. He recaptured stagecoach bandit Pearl Hart after she had escaped from a Tucson jail. July 29, 1898, near Solomonville, Arizona, he and Jeff Milton encountered train robber Bronco Bill Walters. Walter's companion Bill (Kid) Johnson was wounded mortally, Red Pipkin escaped although his horse was killed, and Walters was wounded seriously but recovered to serve a prison term. April 5, 1900, Scarborough and rancher Walter Birchfield were tracking purported cattle rustlers George Stevenson and James Brooks (supposed to have been one time affiliates of Butch Cassidy's Wild Bunch). In a canyon in the

Chiricahua Mountains of southeastern Arizona a bullet punctured Scarborough's leg and killed his horse. Scarborough was returned to Deming where his leg was amputated, but he died, four years to the day after he had killed John Selman. Stevenson and Brooks were captured near Pilares de Terres, Sonora, by Silver City, New Mexico, Sheriff W.D. Johnson and deputy Miles Marshall, jailed at Silver City but escaped May 28 and were not retaken.

Ed Bartholomew, *Biographical Album of Western Gunfighters.* Houston, Frontier Press of Tex., 1958; Robert N. Mullin notes; O'Neal, *Gunfighters.*

Scarface Charley (Chic-chack-am, Lul-al-kuel-atko), Modoc chief (c. 1851- Dec. 3, 1896). Little is known of his earlier life. Various stories are told of how he got the scar from which derived his nickname; Murray said it was when as a boy he fell from the Yreka stagecoach while hitching a ride. While a child he saw his father murdered in a particularly cruel manner by whites, near the present town of Malin, on Tule Lake, Oregon. Scarface Charley became a noted warrior and fired the first shot in the Modoc War of 1872-73 in northeastern California. This was on November 29, 1872, when Second Lieutenant Frazier Boutelle, 1st Cavalry, tried to arrest him, a step Charley resisted. The two fired almost simultaneously, neither hitting the other although their bullets penetrated the garb of each other. The incident launched the Battle of Lost River in which there were casualties on both sides. The Indians raided settlers, killing about 14 of them, then faded into the Lava Beds south of Tule Lake, not all quite convinced that war was the proper course but being gradually pressed into it by their peers and events. Charley took part in the first Stronghold Battle, gradually becoming known as a leader. In February he and other Modocs were indicted by a Jacksonville, Oregon, grand jury for the settlers' murders of November 30, but were never tried. Scarface Charley took part in preliminary conversations with Canby early in 1873; it was he who saved the lives of Elisha Steele and H.W. Atwell who had penetrated the Stronghold alone to sound the hostiles about peace sentiment; other Indians wanted to kill them, but Charley saw that they escaped. When it was decided to assassinate Canby and Thomas, Scarface Charley said he would take no part but not interfere; he would be nearby and if any attempt were made to injure Riddle or his wife, Tobey, he personally would kill the offenders; the Riddles were interpreters, Mrs. Riddle being a Modoc and respected by most of the hostiles as well as the whites. In the second Stronghold Battle, April 26, it was Scarface Charley who laid the ambush which all but wiped out the Evan Thomas command and did most damage to the whites, four officers being killed along with 18 enlisted men and as many wounded. Charley hollered at the survivors: "All you fellows that ain't dead better go home. We don't want to kill you all in one day!" The whites pulled out, agreeing that they had "suffered a frightful beating." At the disintegration of the Modoc force following this battle, Charley stuck with Jack until the end but at last surrendered. "Scarface Charley had done all his fighting in the open," he was highly respected by the whites and "it was believed no one had been killed by him except in fair fight. He was not treated as a 'war criminal' and had nothing to fear for his life." Immediately after the execution of Captain Jack, Colonel Wheaton appointed Charley "chief" over the surrendered Modocs. He acted as such for about a year. During that time the Indians were moved to the Quapaw Agency of Oklahoma, but despite the agent's request he could not or would not keep his people from gambling and was deposed in favor of Bogus Charley. In the early 1880s Scarface Charley was converted to Christianity by a Quaker missionary; the Indian died of tuberculosis at the Quapaw Agency. He was considered the wisest and best strategist among the Modocs.

Keith A. Murray, *The Modocs and Their Way.* Norman, Univ. of Okla. Press, 1965; Jeff C. Riddle, *The Indian History of the Modoc War.* Medford, Oregon, Pine Cone Pubrs., 1973; Richard Dillon, *Burnt-Out Fires.* Englewood Cliffs, N.J., Prentice-Hall, 1973; Dockstader.

Schaaf, Olga, *see* Olga Schaaf Little

Schellie, Don(ald) Robert, writer (Mar. 8, 1932-Feb. 15, 1983). B. at Chicago, he was graduated from the University of Illinois, served in the Air Force for three years, worked for the Champaign-Urbana, Illinois *News Gazette,* the *Douglas* (Arizona) *Dispatch* and in

1958 joined the Tucson *Citizen* for which he worked 23 years, becoming a widely-known columnist. In 1968 he wrote *Vast Domain of Blood,* until his death the definitive work on the Camp Grant Massacre of 1871 (see Williams S. Oury entry), although fictionalized in part. Schellie wrote a history of the *Citizen* and four western-oriented novels for teen-agers. He died of cancer, being survived by his widow, Coralee and three daughters.

Tucson, *Arizona Daily Star,* Feb. 16, 1983; personal acquaintance with author.

Schenofsky, Jules C.A., army officer (fl. 1862-1876). B. in Belgium, he was the son of a General of the Belgian army and was educated at Paris with a view to serving in the French army. He came to the United States at the start of the Civil War, was commissioned a captain June 11, 1862, serving from Antietam to the surrender of the Confederacy. He was appointed a second lieutenant from Missouri in the 7th Infantry May 11, 1866, transferred to the 5th Cavalry March 30, 1867, and became a first lieutenant September 22, 1868. On frontier duty, he saw action against Indians in Kansas at Shuter Creek, on the north branch of the Solomon River, participated in the Canadian River expedition, and in the spring of 1869 against Sioux and Cheyennes on Beaver Creek, where he was cited for gallantry, and Spring Creek. Schenofsky saw action later with the Republican River expedition, at Spring Creek again and Prairie Dog Creek. He was honorably discharged at his own request in 1870, returned to France and served in the Franco-German War as major of cavalry; Schenofsky was captured by the Commune of Paris late in the war, and narrowly escaped execution. He returned to his father's estate in Belgium where he was living in 1876.

Price, *Fifth Cavalry.*

Scheurich, Teresina Bent, pioneer (Oct. 25, 1841-Feb. 25, 1920). The daughter of Charles Bent, governor of New Mexico who was killed in the Taos uprising of January 19, 1847, and although only 6 at the time, Teresina well remembered the terror of that day. Kit Carson took her to live in his home, his wife being an aunt of Teresina's. Carson removed his family to Rayado, New Mexico and here Teresina grew up. A visiting Cheyenne chief once threatened to take her by force if the whites did not permit him to buy her, but he was thwarted. Teresina's education was completed at a convent at Sante Fe. In about 1860 she married an American named Locke who as a Confederate disappeared forever in the war. June 24, 1865, she married a wagon trader, Aloysius Scheurich of Bavaria, the couple raising five children, her husband prospering and holding public positions. She became a grande dame of pioneer and local history at Taos and a community institution before her death; she was buried in Kit Carson Cemetery.

Jean M. Burroughs, "Grande Dame of Taos." *Frontier Times,* Vol. 53, No. 1 (Apr.-May 1979), 14-18.

Schiefflin Albert E., prospector (Aug. 27, 1849-Oct. 15, 1885). B. in Tioga County, Pennsylvania, he went with the family to California in 1856, then to Oregon about 1857. He joined his brother, Ed, at Austin, Nevada, about 1873, and later removed to Arizona where he was working at a mine on the Bill Williams River, when Ed sought him out in 1877 to get support in developing interesting ore samples he had found near the future Tombstone, Arizona. Al took the samples to Dick Gird for assay. The report was promising and Al, somewhat reluctantly, agreed to accompany the other two to the San Pedro River country where the samples originated. The three, starting in January 1878, made their big strike before spring; the town of Tombstone sprang up and their mine proved very rich. The brothers sold out in 1880 for $600,000, later evening up their portion with Gird, who sold his share in 1881, so each received the same. Al Schiefflin was the first of the trio to die, succumbing to tuberculosis before he could fully enjoy his wealth. He died at his brother, Ed's home at Los Angeles, California.

Odie B. Faulk, *Tombstone: Myth and Reality.* N.Y., Oxford Univ. Press, 1972; Ariz. Hist. Soc. Archives.

Schiefflin, Edward Lawrence, prospector (Oct. 8, 1847-May 14, 1897). B. in Tioga County, Pennsylvania, he reached California, then the Rogue River country of Oregon with his parents in 1856. He became a prospector, wandering through the West with indifferent success. An abstemious man, he did not drink, gamble, nor spend wildly, even when he had funds. He was at Eureka, California, in 1874, at Austin, Nevada, in 1874-75, thence to Idaho, back to Oregon, and went on to Arizona. He arrived at Fort Huachuca, about April 1, 1877, with Hualapai Indian scouts and Chief of Scouts Dan O'Leary. When he determined to prospect the hills beyond the San Pedro River, he was warned, presumably by O'Leary, that all he would find there would be his tombstone, so the name of the community that grew up to serve his great strike logically became Tombstone, Arizona. Schiefflin had made some interesting finds starting August 1, 1877, tried to get support for further prospecting, went to work on the Silver King, near Globe, and in Mohave County, Arizona. Finally, with his brother, Albert, and Richard Gird, in January 1878, he set out. Before spring they had discovered what became the Lucky Cuss, richest of Tombstone lodes. Always a prospector, Ed wandered off hunting new mines in 1879; he and Al sold out for $600,000 in March 1880. Gird sold out in 1881 for reportedly the same figure, then hunted up the Schiefflins and with no obligation to do so, shared with them until each of the three had received exactly the same for their great strike. Ed Schiefflin continued the life of a prospector thenceforth, wandering as far as Alaska, where he spent two years along the Yukon. He also prospected in South America. Ed died in the doorway of his cabin, 20 miles east of Canyonville, Oregon, his body removed to the site he had selected three miles west of Tombstone for burial under "a monument such as prospectors build when locating a mining claim," as read his instructions. In 1876 Schiefflin was described as "about the queerest specimen of human flesh ever seen, about 6 feet, 2 inches, in height, with black curly hair that hung several inches below his shoulders. His long, untrimmed beard was a mass of unkempt knots and mats.... Although only 27...he looked at least 40."

Odie B. Faulk, *Tombstone: Myth and Reality.* N.Y., Oxford Univ Press, 1972; Ed Bartholomew, *Wyatt Earp: The Man & the Myth.* Toyahvale, Tex., Frontier Book Co., 1964.

Schiel, Jacob H., scientist surgeon (1813-post 1860). B. at Stromberg, he attended the University of Heidelberg where he studied geology, chemistry and perhaps medicine. He came to the United States toward the end of the 1840s, and returned to Heidelberg in 1859, settling at Baden-Baden, where he lived the rest of his life; Schiel published articles and possibly other works on chemical and geological subjects. He was a surgeon-scientist with the Gunnison expedition of 1853, exploring for a railroad route through the middle Rocky Mountains; Schiel avoided the massacre of Gunnison and seven others on October 26 near Sevier Lake, Utah. His account of the expedition, originally published in Germany, has been translated and printed in this country at least three times.

Jacob H. Schiel, *Journal Through the Rocky Mountains and the Humboldt Mountains to the Pacific Ocean,* trans. and ed. by Thomas N. Bonner. Norman, Univ. of Okla. Press, 1959; Nolie Mumey, *John Williams Gunnison.* Denver, Artcraft Press, 1955.

Schlesinger, Sigmund, *see* Sigmund Shlesinger.

Schmidt, Jacob, pioneer (Aug. 8, 1832-Mar. 1, 1907). B. at Etlinger, near Heidelberg, Germany, he reached New York as a tailor at 16, then migrated to St. Louis, journeyed by steamer up the Missouri River, reaching Fort Benton in 1854. He engaged in a number of pioneering enterprises in Montana until his death at Chouteau. He was married and fathered 11 children.

Montana Contributions, Vol. X, 1940, 278-79.

Schnitzer, John, soldier (fl. 1885). A private of H Company, 23rd Infantry, he was cited for heroism in an engagement with Chiricahua Apaches in Guadalupe Canyon, on the New Mexico-Arizona border June 8, 1885. Hostiles had surprised a small detachment guarding a supply wagon train, killed three and captured a welcome hoard of ammunition and rations. Schnitzer carried a mortally wounded sergeant out of the canyon "under heavy fire within a short distance of the hostile Indians concealed in the rocks" and was awarded a certificate of merit for his deed.

"The Reluctant Corporal: The Autobiography of William Bladen Jett," ed. by Henry P. Walker. *Jour. of Ariz. Hist.,* Vol. XII, No. 1 (Spring 1971), 34, 48n49.

Schonchin John, Modoc war leader (c. 1828-Oct. 3, 1873). A younger brother of Old Schonchin, head chief of the Modocs, John was called by Bancroft striking in appearance and with a sensitive face, although he was among the most militant of the irreconcilable

Modocs whose nominal leader was Captain Jack. Schonchin John was second in command. He survived the Wright massacre of the Modocs in November 1852, one of five among 46 Indians, and because of this incident perhaps he became an outstanding militant, urging Captain Jack to go to war even before the latter had determined upon hostilities. He was grey-headed by this time, but prominent in the actions in the Lava Bed Stronghold of northeastern California during the 1872-73 Modoc war. Schonchin John had a major role in the council that decided upon the murder of Canby and other peace commissioners. He was detailed to shoot Alfred B. Meacham as part of the plot, but muffed his role, Meacham surviving if sorely wounded; Schonchin John obtained some of his clothes, however. Although "among the most vociferous of the war party and . . .credited with numerous crimes," Schonchin John surrendered May 31, 1873, as the Modoc war party broke up; he was shackled to Captain Jack and by late June they with other prisoners had been moved to Fort Klamath, Oregon. These two with four others involved in the assassinations were court martialed and condemned to death, four actually being hanged. Schonchin John stated on the gallows that he "took no active part" in the Modoc War, which was untrue, adding that "My heart tells me I should not die — that you do me a great wrong in taking my life. . . ."

Bancroft, *Oregon,* II; Keith A. Murray, *The Modocs and Their War.* Norman, Univ. of Okla. Press, 1965; Jeff C. Riddle, *The Indian History of the Modoc War.* Medford, Ore., Pine Cone Pubrs., 1973; Hodge, HAI.

Schonchin (Skonches), Old, Modoc chief (c. 1797-Aug. 10, 1892). B. at Tule Lake, California, Old Schonchin (to distinguish him from Schonchin John, his younger brother) was not an hereditary chief of the Modocs but attained the chieftainship by his own ability and effort. His early record is shadowy, but he was head chief over perhaps 600 warriors (an over-estimate, probably) by 1846, took an early part in hostilities between Modocs and whites, and said he had done all he could to exterminate the interlopers. By the 1860s however he had become convinced that to continue to fight the immigrants courted annihilation; thus he was a signatory to the treaty of October 14, 1864, by which the

Modocs were assigned to the Klamath Reservation of Oregon and from that time forward lived at peace with the whites. He held his followers on the Klamath Reservation when Captain Jack and his portion of the tribe abandoned the reserve to resume their former life on the Lost River and Tule Lake and eventually to become involved in the Modoc War. On October 3, 1873, when four of the leaders of the Modoc uprising, including Schonchin John, were hanged, Old Schonchin attended the execution, coming he told his brother on the gallows, "not to bid you farewell, but to see if you die like a man. I see you lack courage, I see tears in your eyes. You would not and did not listen to me, so now I say I cast you to the four winds. You are no brother of mine. . ., so now die. I cast you away." He turned then and rode away. Old Schonchin, who was the father-in-law of Jeff Riddle, died at 95 on the Klamath Reservation.

Jeff C. Riddle, *The Indian History of the Modoc War.* Medford, Ore., Pine Cone Pubrs., 1973; Hodge, HAI.

Schoolcraft, Henry Rowe, ethnologist (Mar. 28, 1793-Dec. 10, 1864). B. in Albany County, New York, he studied natural sciences at Middlebury College and in 1817-18 accompanied as a geologist an expedition to Missouri and Arkansas; he took part in a Lewis Cass expedition to the upper Mississippi and Lake Superior area in 1820, following that with another expedition in 1832. In 1822 he became Indian agent to Lake Superior tribes, the following year married a part-Chippewa woman (who died in 1842; Schoolcraft married again in 1847). Schoolcraft became superintendent of Indian affairs for Michigan in 1836, negotiating treaties with the Chippewa and other tribes. Deeply interested in Indian ethnology, he continued this pursuit after leaving the Indian Department in 1841. He published widely but paralysis and other ailments curtailed his production from 1857. Among his many writings were: *Journal of a Tour into the Interior of Missouri and Arkansas. . . in the Years 1818 and 1819* (1821); *Narrative Journal of Travels Through the Northwestern regions of the United States. . . in the Year 1820* (1821); *Travels in the Central Portions of the Mississippi Valley . . . .* (1825); *Narrative of an Expedition Through the Upper Mississippi to Itasca Lake . . . .* (1834); *Algic Researches, Comprising Inquiries Respecting* *the Mental Characteristics of the North American Indians* (1839); *Notes on the Iroquois....* (1846); *The Red Race in America* (1847); *Outline of the Life and Character of Gen. Lewis Cass* (1848); *The Indian in His Wigwam, or Characteristics of the Red Race of America* (1848); *A Bibliographical Catalogue of Books, Translations of the Scriptures and other Publications in the Indian Tongues of the United States* (1849); *Personal Memoires of a Residence of Thirty Years with the Indian Tribes on the American Frontier....* (1851); *The American Indians....* (1851); *Western Scenes and Reminiscences....* (1853); *The Myth of Hiawatha* (1856); and his most memorable work, the six-volume *Historical and Statistical Information Respecting the History, Condition, and Prospects of the Indian Tribes of the United States* (1851-57). The sixth part of this monumental work, which was subsidized by the federal government, was republished about 1970 as *History of the Indian Tribes of the United States.* "Schoolcraft may be regarded as the chief pioneer in study of the Indians."

Literature abundant; DAB; CE.

Schoolcraft, Leonard, renegade (b. 1763). Raised on the western Virginia frontier, he was captured by Indians (probably Shawnees) near Buckhannon Fort at 16 (in 1779), turned renegade as did two of the four brothers also taken. His ill-fated family of 16 including his parents was broken up by Indian forays, nine in all being killed, including his mother. Schoolcraft led a party of Indian raiders in an attack on the Hacker's Creek settlement of present West Virginia in September 1787. He "always remained with the Indians," as did brothers Simon and Michael, although two others, John and Jacob, ultimately escaped back to the Virginia border.

Lucullus V. McWhorter, *The Border Settlers of Northwestern Virginia.* Hamilton, O., Republican Pub. Co., 1915.

Schreiber, Edmund, soldier (c. 1840-post 1891). Schreiber served during the Civil War in the 3rd and 4th Maryland Infantry regiments, was wounded August 21, 1862, at Second Bull Run; during his war service he was promoted up to first sergeant at one time, and variously held the grade of sergeant or was reduced to the ranks. He re-enlisted in 1866, serving then until his retirement in 1891.

With the 5th Cavalry he saw considerable Indian action against hostiles. In 1873 he was on several Arizona scouts with Walter Schuyler and became a good friend of scout Al Sieber. In 1876 he was a witness to Buffalo Bill Cody's "duel" with Yellow Hand, or Yellow Hair on Warbonnet Creek in Nebraska. Schreiber was severely wounded at Slim Buttes, Dakota, September 9. He re-enlisted in 1884 at Fort Niobrara, Nebraska, and in 1889 at Fort Supply, Indian Territory. When he retired at Fort Supply he was an ordnance sergeant.

Dan L. Thrapp, *Al Sieber, Chief of Scouts* (includes a photograph of Schreiber). Norman, Univ. of Okla. Press, 1964; Don Russell, *The Lives and Legends of Buffalo Bill.* Norman, 1960.

Schuchard, Carl, artist, mining engineer (1827-May 4, 1883). B. in Hesse-Cassel, he was a graduate of the German school of mines at Freiberg who joined the 1849 gold rush to California. Later he drifted to Texas, where he became a surveyor. Schuchard joined the Gray Reconnaissance in 1854 for a southern route for a railway to the Pacific coast; he made many original sketches of the survey and relating to it; they were stored for some years at the Smithsonian Institution at Washington, but were destroyed by fire about 1865. Schuchard returned to southern Arizona as a mining engineer and investor in the Sonora Exploration and Mining Company, but early sold his shares and, according to Brady, "like a sensible man...went back to Texas" and raised sheep. After the Civil War his attention was drawn to mining once more, and he spent most of the remainder of his life in Mexico, where he died.

A.B. Gray Report, ed. by L.R. Bailey. Los Angeles, Westernlore Press, 1963; Robert Taft, *Artists and Illustrators of the Old West: 1850-1900.* N.Y., Bonanza Books, 1953.

Schultz, James Willard, writer (Aug. 26, 1859-June 11, 1947). B. at Boonville, New York, he was educated by private tutor and spent four years at the Peekskill Military Academy, from which he hoped to go to West Point. At St. Louis, however he heard stories of the Northwest, borrowed $500 from his parents for a "brief" trip there and reached Fort Benton in 1877. Schultz became a trading partner of Joe Kipp (see entry), settled in the region which would become Glacier National

Park, married a Blackfoot girl, Musti Ahwaton Ahki (Pretty Shield) and was accepted into the tribe where he lived some years and where was born his son, Hart Merriam Schultz (Lone Wolf), who became a noted Arizona artist and sculptor. James Schultz's life as an Indian ended with the death of his wife in 1903. He turned to writing, became book critic for the *Los Angeles Times*, returning each summer to Glacier Park. He married twice more, to white women, and died at 87 at Lander, Wyoming. His many books included *My Life as an Indian* (1906, 1935); *With the Indians in the Rockies* (1912); *An Indian Winter* (1913); *Sinopah, the Indian Boy* (1913); *On the Warpath* (1914); *Apauk, Caller of Buffalo* (1916); *Blackfeet Tales of Glacier National Park* (1916); *Bird Woman (Sacajawea), the Guide of Lewis and Clark* (1918); *Rising Wolf, the White Blackfoot* (1919); *The Trail of the Spanish Horse* (1922); *William Jackson, Indian Scout* (1926); *Red Crow's Brother* (1927); *Alder Gulch Gold* (1931), and *Signposts of Adventure: Glacier National Park as the Indians Know It* (1940).

Library of Congress Union Catalogue; *Who Was Who;* Michael S. Kennedy, ed., *The Red Man's West*, N.Y., Hasting House, 1965.

Schulz, Julius, soldier (May 17, 1858-Nov. 9, 1944). B. at Neudorf, Wagrowiec, Posen, Germany (now Poland), he emigrated to this country and enlisted August 9, 1882, in Company I, 6th Cavalry and was sent to Fort McDowell, Arizona. By way of indoctrination Sergeant Zachariah T. Woodall, a Medal of Honor winner, had him box Sergeant Tom Silvan and when Schulz knocked Silvan out, Woodall took him on himself and was flattened, which concluded the "indoctrination." In the spring of 1883 Schulz went into the Sierra Madre with Crook, Captain Adna Romanza Chaffee in command of his troop. After that expedition Schulz's company was posted to southern New Mexico. Near Lake Palomas he was kicked in the knee by a mule, the kneecap injured and as a result of that and a subsequent accident he was lamed for life, although he participated in the full Geronimo campaign. He was discharged August 8, 1887, at Fort Wingate, New Mexico. Schulz was a brick mason by trade. He died at the Sawtelle Veterans Hospital, Los Angeles.

Schulz's memoirs, dictated to Lois Springman Carmesan in 1930, copy supplied by Harriette Ayres, Duarte, Calif.

Schurtz, Don Carlos, Mormon pioneer (July 27, 1836-post 1892). Schurtz, or "Dan C. Shirts, of Harmony, now of Potatoe Valley, Utah," was for a time a son-in-law of John D. Lee and an Indian interpreter who was placed at the Mountain Meadows Massacre of September 11, 1857, by *Mormonism Unveiled*. He was a son of Peter Schurtz (Shirts). Wise reports that Schurtz was sent by Lee to round up Indians for the original attack on the Fancher train, and William H. Rogers reported in 1860 that Schurtz had met the emigrants at the north end of Mountain Meadows and in reply to their request for advice, told them to water and recruit their stock at the lower end, where the massacre occurred. Schurtz told Rogers he had heard the firing of "a great many guns" from the direction of their camp, and supposed they were under attack by Indians, but did nothing about it. His date of death and its circumstances are not reported.

Mormonism Unveiled, 380; Juanita Brooks, *John D. Lee.* Glendale, Calif., Arthur H. Clark Co., 1962; William Wise, *Massacre at Mountain Meadows.* N.Y., Thomas Y. Crowell Co., 1976.

Schurtz (Shirts), Peter, Mormon frontiersman (b. Apr. 23, 1808). B. at St. Clair, Ohio, he was married, fathered five children including (Don) Carlos Schurtz, joined the Mormon faith in 1833 and reached Utah in 1850. He was of the first group to settle Parowan, Utah, first to move to Pariah Creek, and among the first to move farther east to the little known San Juan River country in southeastern Utah. According to Brooks "different stories are told as to the time and place of his death."

Juanita Brooks, ed., *Journal of the Southern Indian Mission.* Logan, Utah State Univ. Press, 1972.

Schuyler, Peter, colonial official (Sept. 17, 1657-Feb. 19, 1724). B. at the present Albany, New York, he was a lieutenant in the mounted forces in the Albany militia by 1684 and two years later became mayor of Albany and head of its board of Indian commissioners, the first of his many public positions. On February 9, 1690, during King William's War came the French and Indian massacre of 60 and capture of 25 Dutch settlers at Schenectady, near Albany, led by the brothers Jacques Le Moyne de Sainte Hélène and Pierre Le Moyne d'Iberville. Schuyler, the son of Dutch immigrants himself, wrote officials requesting help and cooperation for a spring campaign against the French in retaliation. The operation was delayed for one reason or another, but August 1, 1691, Schuyler led a mixed force of Indians and whites in an attack on the French at La Prairie de la Magdeleine south of Montreal, causing the enemy heavy casualties. However as his fast-moving column withdrew, it was intercepted by Philippe Clement Du Vault de Valrennes and a mixed command and broke free only with difficulty and suffering losses in its own right. W.J. Eccles wrote that "both sides greatly exaggerated the losses they had inflicted," Schuyler conceding he had lost only 37 killed and 31 wounded, the French admitting but 45 killed and 60 wounded. It was the last attempt of the Albany militia to raid into Canada. Schuyler always held considerable influence over the Iroquois and as often counseled as campaigned with them; in 1693 he routed a French party near Schenectady. Upon conclusion of the war, he was dispatched to Quebec to meet with Frontenac and arrange for the return of war prisoners. He was an influence in preparing operations of 1709 and 1711 against Canada during Queen Anne's War, tentatives that came to little, and in 1710 he was at London where he was received with several Mohawk chiefs at the Court. He frequently held important public offices and was acting governor of New York in 1719 and 1720. Schuyler, who was a major land holder, married twice and fathered eight children.

Parkman, *Count Frontenac and New France Under Louis XIV;* DAB; DCB, II, 148.

Schuyler, Walter Scribner, army officer (Apr. 26, 1850-Feb. 17, 1932). B. at Ithaca, New York, he was graduated from West Point in 1870 and commissioned a second lieutenant in the 5th Cavalry, being posted to Wyoming initially, then to Arizona. From June 1872 until May 1873 he engaged in scouting and from February 1873 until February 1875 commanded scout companies taking part in numerous engagements and for them being breveted first lieutenant. His chief of scouts most often was Al Sieber and they made an effective team, Schuyler enjoying the complete confidence of Crook, then commanding the department of Arizona. On leave from February 1875 to February 1876 he visited Finland and European Russia. Schuyler was

aide to Crook from May 30, 1876, until 1877, becoming a first lieutenant and taking part in the "Starvation March" and the fight at Slim Buttes, Dakota, September 9-10, 1876. He was with Mackenzie in the attack on the Cheyenne village on Bates Creek, Wyoming, November 25, 1876. He was aide to Merritt during the relief expedition to save the Thornburg command on Milk River, Colorado, in October 1879. Schuyler was professor of military science at Cornell University from 1883-86 and from 1896-98; he became a captain in 1887. During the Spanish American War he served as colonel of volunteer regiments, became major of the 2nd Cavalry in 1899 and lieutenant colonel in 1903. He was a military observer with the Russian army during the war with Japan in 1904, attending several major battles and upon conclusion of hostilities traveled by the trans-Siberian railroad to St. Petersburg and returned to the United States. He became colonel of the 5th Cavalry in 1906, a Brigadier General in 1911 and retired April 26, 1913, by reason of age. He then became president and general manager of the Sierra-Alaska Mining Company of California. Schuyler's retirement home was at Carmel, California, and he died at San Francisco. Schuyler was one of the better, more dependable and intelligent officers in the Indian-fighting army and was widely esteemed. He was described in 1875 as 5 feet, 7 1/2 inches tall, with medium forehead, brown eyes, straight nose, medium mouth, round chin, black hair, fair complexion and round face.

Schuyler file, Huntington Library, San Marino, Calif; *Who Was Who;* Heitman; Cullum; Dan L. Thrapp, *Al Sieber, Chief of Scouts.* Norman, Univ. of Okla. Press, 1964.

Schwatka, Frederick, army officer, explorer (Sept. 29, 1849-Nov. 2, 1892). B. at Galena, Illinois, he moved with his parents to Oregon at 10, eventually attending Willamette University, then going to West Point. He was commissioned a second lieutenant of the 3rd Cavalry June 12, 1871, and took part against hostile Yavapai and Apache Indians in Arizona out of Camp McDowell, but not for long. He went to Fort McPherson, Nebraska, May 1, 1872, took part in a Big Horn expedition August through October that year and served at Nebraska and Wyoming posts until May 1876 when he joined Crook for Sioux operations. Schwatka served in M Company of the 3rd Cavalry under Anson Mills who wrote of him that Schwatka was "one of the most interesting officers...I ever met." The lieutenant took part in the Rosebud battle against Crazy Horse June 17 and was a member of Crook's Big Horn and Yellowstone expedition and the "starvation march" until September, being also a participant of the action at Slim Buttes, Dakota September 8-9, he leading a drive of wildly stampeding enemy horses right through the hostile camp. Schwatka did Plains scouting for a time and was assigned to the Spotted Tail Agency, Dakota, for a few months. On a leave of absence he led an Arctic expedition from March 6, 1878, to October 1, 1880, searching for the remains of the Sir John Franklin vanished polar expedition of 1847-48. Some 40 expeditions had sought the lost explorer who finally was determined to have perished after his two ships had been caught and crushed in polar ice and not one of his 129 men had survived. Remains of some of the men and one of the ships had been discovered earlier, but Schwatka on and near King William Island unearthed evidence clearing the last questions, located the remains of the only previously unreported ship and of many of the perished, giving them burial, bringing back relics and evidence that Franklin's records were lost. During their long search the Schwatka party had completed the lengthiest sledge journey on record, of 3,251 miles, Schwatka completing the exploration and returning home without a scratch only to slip on some sidewalk ice and break a leg. He became a first lieutenant March 20, 1879. After completing frontier duty in Wyoming and serving as aide to Miles he led an expedition in 1883-84 to Alaska where he traced the course of the Yukon River, resigned from the army January 31, 1885, commanded a *New York Times* financed expedition to the Arctic in 1886 and visited the Tarahumare Indians of Sonora and Chihuahua. At 43 he died at Portland, Oregon. Schwatka had become a popular lecturer and had written a good deal for popular publications. His books included *Along Alaska's Great River* (1885); *Nimrod of the North* (1885); *The Children of the Cold* (n.d.); and *In the Land of Cave and Cliff Dwellers* (1893), appearing posthumously. During his final years he had suffered acutely from a stomach ailment which necessitated his use of laudanum; his death occurred from an overdose of that drug.

Heitman; Cullum; CE; DAB; J.W. Vaughn, *With Crook at the Rosebud.* Harrisburg, Pa., Stackpole Co., 1956; Bourke, *On Border.*

Scott, Albert Blackstone, army officer (c. 1858-January 10, 1906). B. in Texas, he was graduated from West Point in 1880 becoming a second lieutenant in the 13th Infantry, with which he saw frontier service including operations against the Geronimo hostiles in 1885-86, for a time commanding Navaho scouts. Scott was made a captain in 1898 and in the charge up San Juan Hill in Cuba during the Spanish American War was wounded so severely that he never recovered, succumbing to his injuries almost a decade later.

Cullum; Dan L. Thrapp, ed., *Dateline Fort Bowie: Charles Fletcher Lummis Reports on an Apache War.* Norman, Univ. of Okla. Press, 1979.

Scott, Charles, army officer (c. 1739-Oct. 22, 1813). B. in what is now Powhatan County, Virginia, he served as a noncommissioned officer in the Braddock campaign, raised forces and became a Brigadier General in the Revolution, seeing hard service in several actions and enduring Valley Forge with Washington. Scott became brevet Major General in 1783. He moved to Kentucky in 1785, settling in the later Woodford County, representing that area for two terms in the Virginia Assembly. He took part in heavy frontier fighting, being a member of the "inconclusive" 1790 expedition of General Josiah Harmar against the Shawnee and Miami Indians along the Scioto and Maumee rivers in Ohio. The whites lost in an action September 30, 1790, 183 killed and 31 wounded; the Indians lost 120 killed and 300 wigwams burned. In the spring of 1791 he led an expedition against Indians on the Wabash River in present Indiana, pressing the campaign relentlessly, but with slight results; Scott took part in Arthur St. Clair's debacle at the hands of Little Turtle of the Miami Village, Ohio, November 4, 1791, when the Americans lost 631 killed and 263 wounded, the Indian loss unknown. On October 24, 1793, with 1,000 mounted Kentuckians, Scott joined Major General Anthony Wayne and on August 20, 1794, took part in the battle of Fallen Timbers, a decisive white victory. In 1808 Scott was elected governor of Kentucky, commissioning William Henry Harrison in 1812 a Major General of militia in addition to his

U.S. Army rank of Brigadier General, in order to have undoubted command over the turbulent Kentuckians in the forthcoming war. Scott married twice. He died in Clark County, Kentucky, his body now resting in the State Cemetery, Frankfort.

DAB; CE; *Indianapolis Gazette,* Sept. 5, 1826; *Alphabetical List of Battles 1754-1900.* Wash., D.C., Govt. Printing Office, 1900.

Scott, Henry Dalton, pioneer (fl. 1857). Scott, his wife, Malinda Cameron Scott (b. 1829), and their children, Joel, Martha and George, joined the Fancher emigrant wagon train at Fort Smith, Arkansas. It left late in March 1857, for California. En route Malinda gave birth to a fourth child, whose name is unknown. At Salt Lake City the Fancher train turned south, to be destroyed by Mormons and Mormon-led Indians at Mountain Meadows, Utah, but Scott and perhaps other families continued on the main road to California. In subsequent years Malinda Scott gave a statement of the journey of the Fancher train until she and her husband parted from it.

William Wise, *Massacre at Mountain Meadows.* N.Y., Thomas Y. Crowell Co., 1976.

Scott, Hiram, mountain man (c. 1805-c. 1828). B. in St. Charles County, Missouri, he joined Ashley for the 1822-23 expedition up the Missouri. A large and powerful man of dark complexion, Scott took part in the disastrous battle at the Arikara villages. He probably became an experienced mountain man, by 1827 was clerk and a leader to some degree, and brought valuable furs to Chouteau at St. Louis, leaving the same fall for the mountains again. He probably perished in 1828, the circumstances widely reported but no two accounts in agreement. Apparently, too ill to travel, he was abandoned by his companions and died near the great Scott's Bluff landmark named for him, his bones found the following season many miles from where he had been deserted.

Merrill J. Mattes article, which examines the sources, MM, Vol. I.

Scott, Hugh Lennox, army officer (Sept. 22, 1853-Apr. 30, 1934). B. at Danville, Kentucky, he went to West Point and was commissioned a second lieutenant of the 7th Cavalry the day after the Custer fight on the Little Big Horn, which he learned about July 6, 1876, while attending the Philadelphia Centennial Exposition. He reported immediately for duty to Major Reno at Fort Abraham Lincoln, Dakota (from which Custer had marched to his fatal battle). Scott was on a Sioux expedition from Lincoln in October 1876 and the next year was sent with others of Company I of the 7th to rebury exposed remains of officers and enlisted men on the field, although time and circumstances prevented more than superficial covering of the bones. Later, in 1877 Scott was on the Nez Perce campaign, scouting after the Indians who had crossed Yellowstone Park and moved northeast, but failing to contact them. Scott was on the Black Hills and Cheyenne Indian expedition of 1878 and was on post and garrison duty with many scouts to his credit until 1888, during which he mastered Indian sign language and much ethnological material and became a foremost army expert on the upper Plains tribes. In 1888 he was sent to Fort Sill, where he was in charge of monitoring any ghost dance disturbances on the southern Plains coincidental with the Messiah craze in the north that led to Wounded Knee. No such occurrence developed in the south, in part perhaps due to Scott's influence. In 1892 he enlisted Company L, 7th Cavalry, composed of Kiowa, Comanche and Apache Indians, and commanded it for the five years it endured. From 1894 until 1897 he had charge of the Chiricahua prisoners at Fort Sill, Oklahoma. He had gone to Alabama to confer with the Apaches in 1894, recording the proceedings of the resulting council at which some of the more prominent Apaches spoke. When these Indians reached Sill, Scott was instrumental in thwarting the commander's ill-conceived plans for them which might have resulted in an outbreak. Scott was intrigued by reports of wild Apaches still living in the Sierra Madre of Old Mexico and devised a plan for luring them out, but the government of Mexico refused to allow the attempt. In 1911 Scott returned to the Apaches to help make arrangements for them to move to the Mescalero Reservation of New Mexico. Scott became a first lieutenant in 1878, a captain in 1895 and a major of the 3rd Cavalry in 1903, shortly transferring to the 14th Cavalry. He was adjutant general of Cuba from 1898 to 1903, when he became commander of troops and governor of the Sulu Archipelago of the Philippines where he abolished the slave trade. He was superintendent of West Point from 1906-10, headed a

Texas border patrol in 1913-14 and was Chief of Staff from 1914-17; he saw action in France in World War I and retired in 1919, then becoming a member of the Board of Indian Commissioners. In 1919 he visited the Custer battle ground again, interviewing many Crow scouts and Sioux and other veterans of the engagement, retaining a lively interest in such matters for the rest of his life. He died at Washington, D.C.

Cullum; Heitman; Hugh Lennox Scott, *Some Memories of a Soldier.* N.Y., Century Co., 1928; W.A. Graham, *The Custer Myth.* Harrisburg, Pa., Stackpole Co., 1953; McWhorter, *Hear Me;* Angie Debo, *Geronimo: The Man, His Time, His Place.* Norman, Univ. of Okla. Press, 1976; DAB.

Scott, Richard, pioneer (fl. 1857). A brother of Henry Dalton Scott, Richard Scott and his wife, whose name and age are unknown, and their children, also of unknown ages and names, joined the Fancher emigrant wagon train at Fort Smith, Arkansas. It left for California late in March 1857. Whether Scott continued with the Fancher element to Mountain Meadows, where it was destroyed by Mormons and Mormon-led Indians, or accompanied his brother Henry, and family to California by the northern route is undetermined.

William Wise, *Massacre at Mountain Meadows.* N.Y., Thomas Y. Crowell Co., 1976.

Scott, Richard W., army officer (d. Nov. 30, 1817). B. in Virginia he was commissioned an ensign in the 35th Infantry March 31, 1813, became a third lieutenant March 3, 1814, a second lieutenant October 1, transferred to the 7th Infantry May 17, 1815, and became a first lieutenant April 30, 1817. Assigned to Georgia and the Florida frontier he commanded 40 soldiers in a large open boat traveling up the Apalachicola River; with them were seven soldiers' wives and four small children. Due to the swift current the boat avoided midstream and proceeded slowly along the heavily timbered shore where it fell into a Seminole ambush a mile below the mouth of the Flint River. At the first volley Scott and most of his men fell dead or wounded. One woman, not hit, was captured, and six soldiers dove over the side and swam to the farther shore, all but two of them wounded. Everyone else of the party not slain outright, was later killed by the Indians. April 1, 1818, Jackson stormed the

Mikasuki towns; in one was found erected a red-painted pole, symbol of the Red Sticks, or militant Indians, and hanging from it were 44 scalps, identified as belonging to Scott and his party.

Heitman; Edwin C. McReynolds, *The Seminoles.* Norman, Univ. of Okla. Press, 1967.

Scott, Robert, borderer (1764-post 1833). B. in Pennsylvania, he was taken with the family to the Wheeling, western Virginia area, about 1777, where as a boy Robert took part in defense of the place against Indians; he moved from Wheeling in the spring of 1781 to Jefferson County, Kentucky, where he engaged as scout and militiaman against Indians. Scott served under George Rogers Clark in an expedition to Vincennes, and scouted and skirmished with Indians frequently through 1783. After 10 years in Jefferson County he removed to Henry County, Kentucky, where he lived six years, then to Gallatin County, Kentucky, where he resided the remainder of his life.

Lucullus V. McWhorter, *The Border Settlers of Northwestern Virginia.* Hamilton, O., Republican Pub. Co., 1915.

Scott, Walter Edward (Death Valley Scotty), adventurer (Sept. 20, 1872-Jan. 5, 1954). B. near Cynthiana, Kentucky, the youngest of six children, he ran away at 14, reaching Wells, Nevada, where his two brothers were cowboys. Scotty became a skilled bronco rider and in the early 1890s toured with Buffalo Bill's Wild West Show where "he learned the tricks of the showman and the huckster." About 1903 he established himself in the Death Valley region, purportedly as a prospector. In 1905 he chartered a special three-car train on the Santa Fe railroad for a record trip from Los Angeles to Chicago — 2,265 miles in 44 hours, 54 minutes. By this he achieved national notoriety. Subsequently was built in northern Death Valley the $2.5 million "Scotty's Castle" with resources provided by wealthy insurance man Albert M. Johnson who with such eastern financiers as Julian Gerard and E. Burdon Gaylord had earlier been fleeced unmercifully by Scotty, whose con man talents were spectacular. Johnson however had come to appreciate the laughs Scotty had given him and funded the never-completed castle as his own part-time residence, to be shared by Scotty when he wished. Today it is a prime tourist attraction. Scott was a hearty, friendly, outrageous confidence man, always controversial but often popular.

Richard E. Lingenfelter, *Death Valley & the Amargosa: A Land of Illusion*, Berkeley, Univ. of Calif. Press, 1986; Donald Duke, "Fastest Cowpuncher on Rails: Death Valley Scotty's $5,500 Santa Fe Ride," *Branding Iron*, Los Angeles Westerners, No. 107 (Sept. 1972).

Scurlock, Josiah Gordon, partisan (Jan. 11, 1849-July 25, 1929). B. at Talaposa, Alabama, he probably studied medicine and in 1869 went to Tampico, Mexico, but returned to Eagle Pass two years later and went to work for John Chisum, cattleman. By 1875 he had arrived in New Mexico, charged with stealing horses and with his front teeth missing, according to report lost in a card game dispute which his opponent did not survive. He became a partner of Charles Bowdre in a ranch on the Rio Ruidoso and served as physician and school teacher for the neighborhood. He became involved in the Lincoln County War as a McSween faction partisan. On September 2, 1876, he accidentally shot and killed a friend, Mike G. Harkins. He was married October 19 of that year to Antonia Miguela Herrera (June 13, 1850-1912). Scurlock had a solid role in the swirling fighting and turbulence of the "war," and was a participant in various killings and escapes, as one of the so-called Regulators. A party including him killed Morris J. Bernstein, Indian agency clerk, while stealing horses from the Mescaleros. He worked briefly for Pete Maxwell, but in the fall of 1879 broke with his turbulent past, gave away his guns, sold a gold mine which brought the purchaser a fortune, and returned to Texas. He lived in Potter County, then near Vernon, then Cleburn, Granbury, Mabank, Athens and Eastland, writing fair poetry and pursuing intellectual pasttimes while farming and following other pursuits. He had brown eyes, dark brown hair, a quick temper, was 5 feet, 8 inches in height and weighed about 150 pounds, and was a member of the Theosophical Society. He died following a heart attack.

"Man of Many Parts," by Philip J. Rasch, Joseph E. Buckbee, Karl K. Klein. *English Westerners' Brand Book* No. 85, Vol. V, No. 2 (Jan. 1963), 9-12.

Scurlock, Mial, adventurer (1809-Mar. 6, 1836). B. in Chatham County, North Carolina, he moved to Tennessee, then to Mississippi

and finally Texas, which was reached in 1834. He joined the Texas army October 17, 1835, and took part in the siege of Bexar (San Antonio). He was killed at the Alamo.

Amelia Williams, XXXVII, 277;HT.

Sears, George Washington (Nessmuk), woodsman, canoe expert (Dec. 2, 1821-May 1, 1890). B. at Oxford Plains, Massachusetts, he moved to Wellsboro, Pennsylvania, and became a cobbler. His boyhood friend had been an Indian, Nessmuk, and through him he learned to love and enjoy the wilderness. "Almost single-handedly he changed what the outdoors could mean to people," instructing them to learn woodland skills, be their own guides. He was the first to demand lightweight canoes of Henry Rushton, a Canton, New York, manufacturer of these fine craft, and with them he made long trips through the Adirondaks, paving the way for modern canoeing. Sears was 5 feet, 3 inches, in height 110 pounds, was active and a man of fine good humor; he wrote woodcraft literature under the name "Nessmuk." He died at Wellsboro.

Zack Taylor, "Canoeing's Little Giants." *Sports Afield*, Vol. 166, No. 1 (July 1971), 42-43, 96.

Seattle, (Seathl), Duwamish chief (c. 1790-June 7, 1866). Seattle was a chief of the Duwamish and Suquamish tribes of the Puget Sound region, Washington, and probably was b. near the present city named for him. He was son of a Suquamish father and a Duwamish mother and seems always to have been friendly toward the whites. His name was first to be signed to an 1855 treaty negotiated by Isaac Stevens. By this treaty he and his people agreed to restrictions, moving to the Post Madison Reservation in Kitsap County near Bremerton. From the beginning he had welcomed the whites, earning the friendship of many of them in return. In the general outbreak of 1855-56 Seattle remained friendly, while believing that the Indian faced extinction, for he saw no reason to hasten their doom. Through efforts of Jesuit missionaries he became a Catholic and inaugurated regular morning and evening prayers, the practice continuing throughout his life. Seattle, believing with his people that mention of a dead man's name disturbs his rest, levied a small tax upon citizens of the town of Seattle as pre-payment for the difficulties naming the town Seattle would mean to his spirit after he had gone. He died at Seattle and was buried in the Suquamish Indian Cemetery near that city. He had married twice, his first wife, a Duwamish woman, dying after the birth of their daughter; the second gave birth to three daughters, all of whom died young, and two sons. In appearance Seattle was dignified and venerable, somewhat resembling the famous Senator Benton. A monument was erected over his grave in 1890 by the people of Seattle.

Hodge, HAI; Bancroft, *Washington, Idaho & Montana.*

Seekaboo, Creek interpreter (c. 1771-c. 1815). Seekaboo was a gifted linguist fluent in Muskogee (Creek), Choctaw, Shawnee and English and knew a little Spanish and French. He was Tecumseh's chief interpreter when the great Shawnee toured the Creek and Choctaw country in 1811, seeking recruits for his confederacy, and became something of Tecumseh's southern representative as he was his cousin (Tecumseh's Creek mother and Seekaboo's mother were sisters). Seekaboo had gone north with Tecumseh following the September 30, 1792, attack on John Buchanan's station near Nashville, Tennessee, the assault repulsed with losses to the hostiles. Seekaboo remained with Tecumseh during the following two decades and returned to his own people with the Shawnee on his southern mission, remaining thereafter with the Creeks. He doubtless took part in the Creek War of 1813-14, for upon its failure he and about 1,000 other Creeks withdrew deep into Florida to join their Seminole kinsmen. Around 1816 Pushmataha and 12 of his Choctaw warriors went to Florida on some tribal matter, the details unremembered. But Pushmataha, the noted Choctaw chief, sought to obtain Seekaboo's services as interpreter. He found upon reaching Seminole country that Seekaboo had died and, finding no other satisfactory interpreter, brought his delegation back to Mississippi.

Glenn Tucker, *Tecumseh: Vision of Glory.* N.Y., Bobbs-Merrill Co., 1956; H.S. Halbert, T.H. Ball, *The Creek War of 1813 and 1814.* University of Ala. Press, 1969; Anna Lewis, *Chief Pushmataha: American Patriot.* N.Y., Exposition Press, 1959.

Seeskomkee, *see* No Feet.

Seeyakoon Ilppilp, *see* Red Spy.

Segundo, Navaho chief (fl. 1804-1855). Segundo was reported to be "an influential Navaho leader" when he appeared in April 1804 at Laguna, New Mexico, requesting peace between his people and the Spanish; it was to no avail. He was seized January 17, 1805, in a trememdous Spanish victory over the Navahos in the vicinity of Canyon de Chelly, Arizona, in which about 115 of his people were slain and more than 30 captured. Segundo with other prisoners was brought to Zuñi, New Mexico, and released May 12, 1805, on the signing of a "treaty" at Jemez. Segundo grew in Spanish esteem after that event. In 1822 Governor Facundo Melgares approved the appointment of Segundo as "president" of the Navahos, if his tribesmen would accept him as such; nothing more is heard of that idea. On May 20, 1848, Segundo signed the Colonel Edward Newby Treaty, which never was ratified. July 17, 1855, he was a signer of the Treaty of Laguna Negra, New Mexico, negotiated by Governor David Meriwether.

Frank McNitt, *Navajo Wars.* Albuquerque, Univ. of New Mex. Press, 1972.

Seldom Seen Slim, *see* Ferge, Charles.

Selman, John Henry (John Gunter), gunman (Nov. 16, 1839-Apr. 6, 1896). B. in Madison County, Arkansas, he was credited by his biographer, Leon Metz, with killing at least 12, perhaps 25 or 30 men and, as a leader of vigilantes, may have participated in a score of lynchings, although he never was spectacular nor sought publicity. The family moved to Grayson County, Texas, John receiving a fair schooling. On December 15, 1861, he enlisted in the 22nd Texas Cavalry, deserting April 25, 1863. He moved to the vicinity of Fort Davis on the Clear Fork of the Brazos in Stephens County (not the Fort Davis in West Texas), enlisting in the State Militia February 8, 1864, being elected a lieutenant April 15, 1865. Arrested for Confederate desertion in late April, he escaped or was released and returned to Fort Davis, June 5, 1865, married Edna de Graffenreid August 17, fathered his first son in 1869, and moved with his family to Colfax County, N.M., by 1870. He returned to Texas within a year or two, and killed Indians in one or two skirmishes. In the almost lawless Clear Fork of the Brazos area, Selman apparently became affiliated with extra-legal law enforcement groups which disposed of numerous trouble-makers. At even more lawless Fort Griffin, Selman is said to have killed a white who had slain one of Selman's Tonkawa friends. Selman came under the influence of John Larn, a neighbor and a "deadly" character who may have been John's "evil genius." Selman and Larn in Shackelford County, organized in 1874, became leaders of a vigilante committee. When Larn was elected sheriff, Selman may have unofficially acted as deputy on occasion. Selman killed one, Shorty Collins, a purported badman, but this was only one of many shooting which rumor credited him with but for which proof naturally is lacking. Selman and Larn apparently had turned to parttime rustling which continued even after they were appointed deputy inspectors of hides and animals for the county. Their activities took on the characteristics of a feud with grangers. Several attempts to bushwhack Selman proved fruitless although Larn, arrested and jailed, was lynched. Selman fled westward (his abandoned wife soon died in childbirth), and by mid-1878 was in the center of Lincoln County, New Mexico, troubles. On July 8 he, his brother Tom (Tom Cat) Selman, John Gross and a few others raided the George Coe ranch on the Hondo River, burned it and melded gradually into the so-called Seven Rivers gang, or Warriors, Selman reaching for its control, assuming it after he had killed his rival, Edward (Little) Hart, a veteran of the Horrell War. The gang killed two Mexicans needlessly on the Hondo River in mid-September; three more on the Bonito river, another elsewhere; looted a store, and settled in near Fort Stanton where the dwindling band picked up fresh recruits, among them Gus Gildea. They drifted to the Pecos and back again, aroused citizens accounting for several and intra-gang disputes for others. By March 1879, Selman and some of his followers were in West Texas, continuing their lawless ways. His band disintegrated or was decimated, by external or internal means. Selman contracted and nearly died of smallpox, and settled down in Fort Davis, West Texas, maintaining his contacts with outlaw elements and rustlers. He was arrested before the Evans shootout with Rangers, but Shackelford County didn't want him and although returned to Albany, he was spirited away before a trial where "his testimony might

have been embarrassing to many people." He had married a Mexican woman and probably spent some time in southern Chihuahua, being reported variously back and forth across the border, taking part in one escapade or another. In the spring of 1888 he moved to El Paso, Texas. On November 3, 1891, he was attacked by assassins, but escaped though seriously wounded. In November 1892, he was elected a constable at El Paso. April 5, 1894, he killed Bass Outlaw who had mortally-wounded another officer. August 19, 1895, he killed John Wesley Hardin in the Acme Saloon. On April 5, 1896, he was shot and mortally wounded by Deputy U.S. Marshal George Scarborough in a private fight; Scarborough was found not guilty of murder. In his prime Selman was 5 feet, 10 inches tall, with dark hair, dark complexion and eyes blue, though so pale it was hard to tell where the pupil left off and the white began; he was very intelligent, very cunning, a skillful talker, persuasive and logical, and expert gambler, but his death was no loss to anyone.

Leon Claire Metz, *John Selman: Texas Gunfighter.* N.Y., Hastings House, 1966.

Selman, Tom (Tom Cat), desperado (1849-c. June 1880). B. probably in Madison County, Arkansas, he was 10 years younger than his brother, John, and was taken as a boy by his family to Grayson County, Texas. He moved with some of the family, including John, to Fort Davis on the Clear Fork of the Brazos River, about 1863. Tom enlisted April 20, 1872, in Company C of the Montague County Minute Men, being discharged August 20, when he joined his brother in the Fort Griffin area, both becoming notorious for extra-legal activities. The Selmans escaped the Shackelford County, Texas, vigilantes after John Larn was executed, and reached Lincoln County, New Mexico in 1878, becoming involved in its "war." The pair worked briefly for John Slaughter but soon were in west Texas "blazing a path of terror...from the Panhandle to the presidio on the Rio Grande." It is probable that Tom was arrested, taken back to Shackelford County, and lynched. Tom was described as small-boned and usually in frail health.

Galveston *News,* Aug. 21, 1880; Leon C. Metz, *John Selman: Texas Gunfighter.* N.Y., Hastings House, 1966.

Semig, Bernard Gustave, surgeon (d. Aug. 1, 1883). B. in Hungary he enlisted from California in the 9th New York Infantry May 4,1861. May 20, 1863, he became a hospital steward and on July 2, 1864, a medical cadet. He served as a contract surgeon with the army in the Modoc War of 1872-73. He assisted Cabaniss in treating Meacham after the assassination of the peace commissioners, and served nobly attending the wounded in the Thomas-Wright debacle April 26, 1873, until he was wounded so severely that he lost a leg and was temporarily paralyzed. He became an assistant surgeon with the regular army November 10, 1874, serving until his death.

Heitman; Keith A. Murray, *The Modocs and Their War.* Norman, Univ. of Okla. Press, 1973.

Senat, Antoine, Jesuit missionary (d. Mar. 25, 1736). B. in the province of Toulouse, France, he reached America in 1734 and was assigned to the Illinois mission where in 18 months he became skilled in the language. In 1736 he was chaplain to d'Artaguette's punitive expedition against the Chickasaws. When the French force was routed, Senat "might, as many had done, have sought safety in flight; but refusing a horse that was offered him, he preferred to yield to the fury of the barbarians, rather than leave without Spiritual succor the brave head of the army and the French, whom he saw Stretched on the ground through their wounds, or carried off by the enemy." Senat was burned at the stake on Palm Sunday with his commander and other captured officers. The site was near the present Fulton, Mississippi.

Thwaites, JR, LXVIII, 309-11, LXIX, 29-31, LXXI, 171.

Sequoyah, Indian intellectual (c. 1760-Aug. 1843). B. in the Cherokee town of Taskigi, Tennessee, he was the son of Nathaniel Gist (whose father was the famed Christopher Gist) and a mixed-blood Cherokee woman, Wurteh, daughter of a chief of Echota. His native name was Sikwayi, corrupted by white usage to Sequoyah, and he also was known as George Gist. Sequoyah grew up among his mother's people, unlettered but adept at hunting, trapping and fur-trading. In early youth he became involved with alcohol, but soon discovered that it did him no good and abstained thereafter. On a hunting trip he injured a leg and arthritis set in, making him a permanent cripple so he turned to metal craftsmanship, becoming an outstanding silver worker. Sequoyah also was "an ingenious natural mechanic" with pronounced inventive powers. He became intrigued with writing systems, initially so he could engrave his name on his silver artifacts, and became aware of the system's usefulness to whites. Around 1809 he commenced to experiment with picture symbols for use among his people, but soon gave that up as impractical. Undismayed by the discouragement and ridicule of his peers, he continued to experiment, drawing symbols from English, Greek and Hebrew until he had devised an alphabet of 86 characters to express the various sounds of the Cherokee language. Despite his physical handicap Sequoyah and other Cherokees fought with Jackson against the Creeks in 1813-14. In 1821 he submitted his syllabary to the chief men of his nation. To demonstrate its practicality he composed a message with his alphabet which was turned over to his 6-year-old daughter. She read and understood it and replied in kind. The Tribal Council forthwith adopted the system. Cherokees of all ages immediately set about to learn and use this novel alphabet; within months thousands were able to read and write their own language. In 1822 Sequoyah visited Arkansas to introduce his system to the Western division of the Cherokees, and he settled among them permanently in 1823. By 1824 parts of the Bible were translated into Cherokee, and by doing this Sequoyah won over missionaries who previously had been cool to his new system. In 1828 the *Cherokee Phoenix,* a weekly newspaper appeared and flourished for seven years until it began to advocate Cherokee rights to their lands when it was shut down by Georgia authorities. In 1828 Sequoyah was sent to Washington to represent the Arkansas band, and when the Eastern Cherokees joined the Western, Sequoyah's influence and counsel became important in the organization of the newly united nation in Indian Territory. In his declining years he withdrew from political affairs and turned to more theoretical pursuits. He sought among many tribes elements of a universal speech and grammar, but found few. He had heard that one band of Cherokees had crossed the Mississippi long before and disappeared in the Southwest, and he tried to seek out descendants of those people. Accompanied by his son, Tessee and seven devoted followers he reached the Mexican Border where he heard that farther south there was a mysterious band of Indians who had migrated from the north and spoke a tongue unintelligible to others. After Chief Bowles had been killed in Texas many of his people had indeed fled into Mexico and settled in a village near San Fernando, southwest of Matamoros in Tamaulipas State. Sequoyah and his little band contacted these folk (one of Chief Bowles's daughters had married a son of Sequoyah). In this village Sequoyah became ill with dysentery; his followers went to find food for him. When they returned they found him in his final extremities and he died near San Fernando, to be buried in a hidden grave along with his treasured papers. Sequoyah was the only American Indian north of Mexico to invent a system of writing fully adequate for the needs and understandings of his people, and which could be universally learned and used by them. His bust has been placed in the nation's Capitol Statuary Hall by the state of Oklahoma, but his most memorable monument no doubt are the great California trees named in his honor: *Sequoia sempervirens* and *Sequoia Washingtoniana* or *gigantea* are named for him, the tallest and among the oldest living things on earth and the grandest forest trees of the continent.

Hodge, HAI; Dockstader; Grace Steele Woodward, *The Cherokees.* Norman, Univ. of Okla. Press, 1963; Grant Foreman, "The Story of Sequoyah's Last Days." *Chronicles of Okla.,* Vol. XII (Mar.-Dec. 1934), 25-41; Mary Whatley Clarke, *Chief Bowles and the Texas Cherokees.* Norman, 1971.

Sergeant, John, missionary (1710-July 27, 1749). B. at Newark, New Jersey, he was graduated from Yale and a tutor there until an offer came to provide a ministry for Indians of Berkshire County, Massachusetts. He was inspired, as he himself once wrote, by the example of missionary endeavors of the "Romish Church." In 1735 he entered permanently upon his missionary work among the Housatonic (Stockbridge) Indians, a tribe of the Mahican group which a century later removed to Wisconsin where descendants live still. Sergeant was ordained a Congregational minister in 1735. He learned the language of his congregation "better than they (knew it) themselves," and translated into it Bible portions, prayers and a catechism. He was interested particularly in education of Indian

youth, publishing a paper on the subject. He was married.

Thwaites, JR, XXVI, 316n4; DAB.

Serigny, Joseph le Moyne de, *see* Le Moyne de Serigny, Joseph.

Serra, Junípero, Franciscan missionary (Nov. 14, 1713-Aug. 28, 1784). B. at Petra, Majorca, Spain, he was baptized as Miguel José Serra. September 14, 1730, he became a Franciscan novice at Palma and the next year chose the name of Junípero in memory of a companion of St. Francis. He was ordained probably in December 1738, taught philosophy and theology for several years and determined to become a missionary to American Indians. He sailed from Spain April 13, 1749, landing at Vera Cruz, Mexico, December 7 and walked to Mexico City, 250 miles distant, arriving January 1, 1750. Shortly he was assigned to the mission at Jalpán, in northern Puebla, where he remained, at Jalpán and other stations of the Sierra Gorda group, until 1758. He briefly was assigned that year as a replacement for missionaries killed by Indians at San Sabá, Texas, but never actually went there, continuing his work and preaching in central Mexico until 1767 when he was to assume presidency of the missions of Lower California, the Franciscans replacing the ousted Jesuits. He arrived at Loreto on the east coast of Lower California April 1, 1768, making his headquarters there, from which he supervised work at the 15 Lower California missions the Jesuits had established. Serra eagerly volunteered for the work of extending missions into Upper California, leaving Loreto on muleback, joining the Portolá expedition and arriving with it at the future site of San Diego, California, July 1, 1769 despite an infirmity of his legs and feet which necessitated his being conveyed by stretcher some of the time. He established at San Diego the mission San Diego de Alcalá July 16. Serra devoted the next 15 years of his work to Upper California where he inaugurated the mission system and established nine of them in a network that eventually numbered 21; while their impact and influence is controversial, Serra's indefatigable zeal and energetic labors are beyond question. He remained at San Diego until mid-April 1770 when he sailed to Monterey, midway between Los Angeles and San Francisco. Near Carmel on June 3 the

Mission of San Carlos was established and here he maintained his headquarters until his death at 70. Other California missions Serra established included San Antonio, July 14, 1771; San Gabriel, near Los Angeles, September 8, 1771; San Luis Obispo, September 1, 1772; San Francisco, October 9, 1776; San Juan Capistrano, November 1, 1776; Santa Clara, January 2, 1777, and San Buenaventura at Ventura March 31, 1782. Serra also was present at the founding of the presidio at Santa Barbara in 1782. During his California years he made four trips by land between Monterey and San Francisco, and five from Monterey to San Diego. By the time of his death there had been 6,736 Indian baptisms at the nine missions and 4,646 Indians were living in them, all Christianized according to mission records. Serra died at Mission San Carlos. He was described as 5 feet 2 inches, in height with a swarthy skin, dark hair and eyes, a resonant voice and an initially robust constitution, although he was afflicted late in life with asthma. He sometimes quarreled with civilian governors, and he was not averse to using corporal punishment, sometimes roughly, on Indians he believed had misbehaved, but in general he was sympathetic to Indian converts and the race. He has become the most famous of the California missionaries and the cause for his beatification (a step toward possible recognition of sainthood) is underway. He has been the subject of numerous books and other writings, virtually all based upon the biography written by his lifelong friend and colleague, Francisco Palou. It first was published in 1787 and rendered into English initially in 1884, the best edition appearing in 1955.

Literature abundant: *Palou's Life of Fray Junipero Serra,* trans. & annot. by Maynard J. Greiger, Wash., D.C., Acad. of Amer. Franciscan Hist., 1955; Geiger, *Franciscan Missionaries in Hispanic California.* San Marino, Calif., Huntington Library, 1969.

Service, Robert William, poet (Jan. 16, 1874-Sept. 11, 1958). B. at Preston, England, he was raised at Glasgow, Scotland, where he became apprenticed as a bank clerk but soon emigrated to western Canada. For a decade he roamed the western part of Canada and the U.S., working at a variety of jobs and writing verse. In 1905 he became teller of a Canadian bank at Vancouver, British Columbia, and

soon was transferred to branch banks at Whitehorse and Dawson in the Yukon country. His most vivid poems began to appear, focusing on gold, saloons, and prospectors and trappers, two of the most famous being "The Shooting of Dan McGrew" and "The Cremation of Sam McGee." Service left Canada to become a war correspondent in the Balkans in 1912, was an ambulance driver in World War I and an intelligence officer with the Canadian Army. He lived in France for most of the remainder of his life. He died at Lancieux, in that country. Many of his later writings have little frontier interest, but his better known works included: *Songs of a Sourdough* (1907), reprinted in 1908 as *The Spell of the Yukon; Ballads of a Cheechako* (1909); *Rhymes of A Rolling Stone* (1912); *Rhymes of a Red-Cross Man* (1916); *Ballads of a Bohemian* (1912); *Bar-room Ballads* (1940); and two autobiographical volumes: *Ploughman of the Moon* (1945), and *Harper of Heaven* (1948).

EA;CE.

Setangya (Satank), Kiowa chief (c. 1810-June 6, 1871). Setangya, whose name meant Sitting Bear, was b. in the Black Hills region, became an important medicine man and also a war chief of the Kiowas. He is credited with having been a principal agent in negotiating the important peace about 1840 between the Kiowas and Cheyennes, from which time they frequently were allies against the whites. In 1867 Setangya was a signer of the Medicine Lodge Treaty. three years later his son was killed while raiding in Texas. Setangya himself went to Texas, gathered up the bones and thereafter carried the bundle about with him upon a special horse until his own death. On May 17, 1871, Setangya with Satanta and Big Tree attacked a wagon train owned by Henry Warren near the present town of Graham in Young County, Texas, seven teamsters being killed and 41 mules run off. Setangya made the mistake of boasting of this deed in the vicinity of Fort Sill and he and the two other leaders were arrested and sent to Texas for trial. En route Setangya who may have feared he was to be executed anyway, sang his death song, tore the handcuffs from his wrists, injured a guard with a knife and captured his carbine, which apparently jammed. While he was trying to clear it he was shot to death by Corporal John B. Charlton.

He was buried at Fort Sill Cemetery.

Hodge, HAI; HT; Dockstader; R.G. Carter, *On the Border With Mackenzie*. N.Y., Antiquarian Press, 1961; Mildred P. Mayhall, *The Kiowas*. Norman, Univ. of Okla. Press, 1962.

Seton, Ernest Thompson (*also:* **Ernest Seton Thompson**), naturalist, writer (Aug. 14, 1860-Oct. 23, 1946). B. at South Shields, Durham, England, he was raised and educated in Canada, living part of the time on the frontier and western plains in that country and the U.S. He studied art at the Royal Academy of London and in Paris from 1890 to 1896. He illustrated many of his own books with pen and ink sketches. Most of his works were popularizations of nature subjects (Theodore Roosevelt called him a "nature faker," though that was before some of his enduring work appeared), but he also produced writing of lasting worth. Seton was a founder of the Woodcraft League of America and of the Boy Scouts, serving as chief scout from 1910 to 1915. He died at Santa Fe, New Mexico. Among his many writings were: *A List of Mammals of Manitoba* (1886); *Birds of Manitoba* (1891); *Wild Animals I Have Known* (1898); *The Trail of the Sandhill Stag* (1899); *Biography of a Grizzly* (1900); *Lives of the Hunted* (1901); *Two Little Savages* (1903); *The Arctic Prairies* (1911;) *Rolf in the Woods* (1911); *Forester's Manual; or, The Forest Trees of Eastern North America* (1912); *Book of Woodcraft and Indian Lore* (1912); *Wild Animal Ways* (1916); *Lives of the Game Animals*, 4 vols. (1925-28); *Trail of an Artist-Naturalist* (autobiographical) (1940).

EA; CE; M.J. Rohrbough, "Ernest Thompson Seton, 1860-1946," *Ariz. and West*, Vol. 28, No. 1 (Spring 1986), 1-4.

Severiano (Sibi-ya-na), Gracias, interpreter (c. 1841-post 1883). Of Mexican parentage he was born, Gatewood reported, in Sonora and was captured as a child by Apaches, growing up among the White Mountain branch of that people and at length marrying a White Mountain woman, by 1869 living with Miguel's branch of Apaches. Since he remembered Spanish well and came to know Apache very fluently he commonly served as interpreter, but whether finally into English is uncertain — it may have been from Apache into Spanish. He enlisted as a scout August 23, 1871, the record showing he was of

dark complexion, 5 feet, 7 inches tall, and appeared about 30. Severiano may have been his Mexican name, and Sibi-ya-na an Apache approximation of it. Gatewood said he was "excitable, nervous, with a lively imagination, rather poetic temperament and consequently considerable oratorical ability," adding that "his services have been valuable, and (he) earned every dollar of his pay." In 1883 Severiano was one of two interpreters taken by Crook on his great expedition into the Sierra Madre to locate a sizable pool of hostile Apaches and talk them into returning to the Arizona reservation. As the culmination of this adventure, Crook was encircled by belligerent Indians and sent for Severiano and Mickey Free, the other interpreter to come and translate for him. The two went, the only persons from the military side except for Crook to attend the two-hour conversation on a stony hillside. Crook's intrepidity and the equal bravery of the two interpreters suggests that Severiano indeed may have translated from Apache to English, since Free probably could not do it and Crook understood little Spanish. Not much is learned about Severiano after that period except that he returned with the expedition to Arizona and his wife and family.

Dan L. Thrapp, *General Crook and the Sierra Madre Adventure*. Norman, Univ. of Okla. Press, 1972; Allan Radbourne to author, June 21, 1972.

Sevier, John (Nolichucky Jack), frontiersman (Sept. 23, 1745-Sept. 24, 1815). B. in Rockingham County, Virginia, he was of a family whose French Huguenot name was Xavier. He penetrated Watauga County, North Carolina, then on the frontier, in 1772 and two years later was a captain of Virginia troops in Lord Dunmore's War against the Ohio Indians; he took part in the battle of Point Pleasant. Sevier "had the qualities of a frontier leader and Indian fighter. He (was) tall, muscular, fair haired, blue eyed, daring and resourceful." He was a leader at the Revolutionary War battle of King's Mountain. With James Robertson he became a founder of the state of Tennessee and first governor of the abortive state of Franklin, a political entity which did not survive. Because of political turmoil accompanying settlement of the west, Sevier was arrested and taken to North Carolina, charged with treason, but was freed by Watauga horsemen who spirited him from a log courthouse. He became first a political rival, then a bitter enemy of Andrew Jackson. Sevier was made a Brigadier General in "the Territory South of the River Ohio," resigning his commission in 1800. He was elected governor of the new state of Tennessee in 1796 and served three terms, until 1809. He was one of the War Hawks who promoted the notion of war with Britain in 1812. He died near Fort Decatur, Georgia.

Literature abundant.

Seymour, Samuel, artist (1796-1823). B. probably in England, he was draftsman with the Stephen H. Long expedition to the Rocky Mountains in 1819-20 and in 1823 with Long's expedition to the upper Mississippi, illustrating James' and Keating's narratives of the events. Seymour is said to have sketched 150 views during Long's first expedition, 60 at least being "finished." They were the first paintings of the Rockies and far western life known to have been made by an accomplished artist.

George C. Groce, David H. Wallace, *The New-York Historical Society's Dictionary of Artists in America 1564-1860.* New Haven, Yale Univ. Press, 1957; Bernard DeVoto, *Across the Wide Missouri.* Boston, Houghton Mifflin Co., 1947.

Shabonee, Potawatomi chief (1775-July 17, 1859). A grand-nephew of Pontiac, he was b. on the Maumee River, Indiana, his father an Ottawa who had fought under Pontiac. Shabonee emigrated at an early age with some of his tribe to Michigan and became a Tecumseh lieutenant, fighting with him until Tecumseh was killed in the Battle of the Thames in 1813. Incensed at the treatment of the Indian allies by the British commander he transferred allegiance to the Americans, joining the Potawatomi; he was chosen peace chief of the tribe and spokesman for them at various councils. In the 1827 Winnebago and 1832 Black Hawk troubles he performed valuable services for th whites. The Sauk and Foxes in retaliation tried several times to murder him and did kill his son and nephew. Shabonee went with the Potawatomi across the Mississippi when they emigrated, but soon returned to two sections of land in DeKalb County, Illinois, given him by the government for his services in the Black Hawk War. His tribe urged him to rejoin them, which he did, but in 1855 returned once more to DeKalb County only to learn that "speculators" had disposed of his two sections on the grounds that he had

abandoned them. Citizens of Ottawa, Illinois, then bought him a small farm on the Illinois River in Grundy County, where he spent the rest of his life with a small annuity and contributions from friends. He was buried at Morris, Illinois, a granite marker erected in 1903 over his grave in Evergreen Cemetery.

Hodge, HAI.

Shacknasty, Jim (Ski-et-tete-ko), Modoc subchief (fl. 1872-1876). Leader of a small band of Hot Creek Modocs, Jim was the brother of Shacknasty Jake (their first name originating, Murray said, because "their mother was a sloppy housekeeper") and was called "only a youth" like Boston Charley, 19, or Bogus Charley, 21. The band was reluctant to move to the Klamath Reservation of Oregon, but not enthusiastic about joining Captain Jack's militants since initially "they were more eager to avoid killing than to start trouble." Nonetheless they were absorbed into the hostile company because of a lynching threat against them (they had been peaceful until that time) by a drunken and irresponsible set of whites of Linkville (now Klamath Falls, Oregon). Their 14 warriors, and 45 people overall gave welcome strength to the Captain Jack faction in the Lava Beds of northeastern California where the Indians carried on their courageous war with white troops for several months. Shacknasty Jim's following remained loyal to him and were a faction among the Modocs. He was always more belligerent than Captain Jack. In early April when Jack was willing to surrender, Shacknasty Jim and others not only refused to go along, but threatened to shoot those who capitulated. Jim accompanied the assassination party that killed Canby and Thomas; he fired his rifle but apparently hit no one, although it was he who stripped the clothing from the wounded Meacham, thinking him dead. He and others chased Riddle away, but with no intent to harm him. Shacknasty Jim and the rest of the Hot Creeks blamed Captain Jack for the death of Ellen's Man, killed by soldiers; although they had been most vocal in supporting the war and against concessions, they now turned against the main body of Modocs and split off, dooming the resistance. May 22, 1873, about a dozen Modoc warriors including Jim surrendered to the soldiers. Shacknasty Jim and three others agreed to try to find Captain Jack and the bulk of the Modocs and bring them in, so were dispatched by themselves to attempt this. They contacted the hostiles and caused disintegration of them and their eventual piecemeal surrender. For this they received a kind of reprieve for themselves although they had been the most guilty of hostility and murder. During the imprisonment and court martial at Fort Klamath, Shacknasty Jim and the other "bloodhounds" were permitted to remain outside of both prison and stockade, and were not tried for any crime. October 12, 1873, Shacknasty Jim with 152 other Modoc men , women and children, were sent to Redding, California, and from there by railroad to the Quapaw Agency, Oklahoma, where they remained many years, some by choice permanently. Shacknasty Jim and others occasionally accompanied Meacham on lecture tours, as evidence of his Modoc experiences. Some of the Modocs turned Christian and adopted English names; whether Shacknasty Jim did this is not reported, but he fades from view in Oklahoma.

Keith A. Murray, *The Modocs and Their War.* Norman, Univ. of Okla. Press, 1965; Richard Dillon, *Burnt-Out Fires.* Englewood Cliffs, N.J., Prentice-Hall, 1973; Jeff C. Davis, *The Indian History of the Modoc War.* Medford, Ore., Pine Cone Pubrs., 1973.

Shafter, William Rufus (Pecos Bill), army officer (Oct. 16, 1835-Nov. 12, 1906). The first white boy b. in Kalamazoo County, Michigan, according to report, he was commissioned a first lieutenant in the 7th Michigan Infantry in 1861, ending in the Civil War a brevet Brigadier General, and earning a Medal of Honor, bestowed much later. In 1866 he was commissioned a lieutenant colonel. Assigned to the black 24th Infantry in 1869, he saw much service in West Texas. In 1875 he commanded a major scouting expedition from Fort Concho (San Angelo) across the Staked Plains to the Pecos River in New Mexico and return, an operation involving great hardship, the exploration of new country, and some skirmishing with Indians. In 1876 he led another large operation involving infantry and cavalry units against Lipan and Kickapoo Indians living in Mexico but depredating upon Texas. The raid was successful, but "the whole Mexican population rose against them and they had to make good time getting back." Shafter was active during most of his time in Texas in scouting and operations against

Indians, and to keep the frontier pacified, or at least patrolled. "In person Shafter, was not *distingué,*" wrote Parker, an 1878 colleague, "being short and corpulent. His language, too, at times was. . . inelegant. But he was a soldier, energetic and thorough. Officially his manner was vigorous, nervous, abrupt. In this he somewhat resembled Mackenzie, whom he greatly admired. In return Mackenzie had great confidence in Shafter." Parker added, however, that Shafter "was greatly disliked by many officers. He hated a slacker. A private letter of his to General Ord, freely commenting on the failings of a number of officers in his command," inadvertently was published by Congress and "was bitterly resented. From that time on Shafter was more or less in hot water," though his progress in his profession continued. He was promoted to colonel of the 1st Infantry in 1879, but remained in command of the 24th until it was transferred to Indian Territory in 1880. Shafter, because of his soldierly qualities, was given command as a Brigadier General of the expedition against Santiago, Cuba, in 1898; he succeeded, but was criticized for the operation's shortcomings, none of them his fault. He was made a Major General on the retired list July 1, 1901, living at Bakersfield, California, until his death; he was buried at the Presidio of San Francisco. A town and various geographical features are named for him in Texas, where he was much admired by frontiersmen for his Indian-fighting abilities.

Heitman; James Parker, *The Old Army Memories.* Phila., Dorrance & Co., 1929; William G. Muller, *The Twenty Fourth Infantry.* Ft. Collins, Colo., Old Army Press, 1972; HT.

Shanks, George (Jack Williams), desperado (d. May 15, 1866). B. probably in New York state, Shanks reportedly had been a pressman for the New York *Tribune* before going to California in the middle 1850s and settling at Nevada City. He tried mining without profit, worked as a ranch hand, cook and writer, was fired by a stage company after trying to rob a passenger and was sentenced to San Quentin for stage robbery. He enlisted in Company G, 4th California Infantry at Auburn, California, October 25, 1861, deserted at Camp Sigel, California, December 18 but was apprehended and deserted again at Camp Union, California, March 5, 1862. In 1864 he worked as a cook at Nevada City under the name of Billy Smith.

He tried to assassinate his employer, William Barton, but failed. After a shooting at Colfax, California, Shanks drifted into Grass Valley a few miles south of Nevada City, got into more trouble and adopted the name of Jack Williams, a desperado hanged a decade before and whose "ghost" Shanks obviously became. Shanks concentrated thereafter on stage robbery, sometimes in concert with Robert Finn and George Moore, both ex-convicts and hard cases. May 15, 1866, the trio robbed a Wells Fargo stage a few miles west of Grass Valley of some $8,000 in gold dust, were tracked down by lawman Stephen Venard and all three killed with four shots from Venard's Henry rifle, and all within five minutes.

William B. Secrest, "When the Ghost Met Steve Venard." *Old West.* (Fall 1968), 20-23; Orton.

Shannon, George Jr. (Peg Leg), frontiersman (1784-Aug. 30, 1836). B. near Washington, in Washington County, Pennsylvania, he later lived near Barnesville, Ohio, where his father froze to death in an 1803 snowstorm. At 18 at Maysville, Kentucky, George Jr. joined the Lewis and Clark expedition and made the trip to the Pacific and return, becoming a good hunter, experienced in dealing with Indians. In 1807 he was of a party under Nathaniel Pryor attempting to return the Mandan chief, Shahaka up the Missouri to his home. Near the present Bismarck, North Dakota, the company was attacked by Arikara Indians, Shannon being wounded in the leg which eventually was amputated at St. Charles, Missouri. Shannon was fitted with a wooden leg whence came his nickname; in 1813 he was pensioned. In 1810 William Clark sent him to Philadelphia to assist Nicholas Biddle in preparing for publication the Lewis and Clark journals, and while there Shannon took up the study of law. He married in 1813, studied at Transylvania University of Kentucky, was admitted to the bar, practiced at Lexington and was a circuit judge for a time. He was a member of the Kentucky House of Representatives in 1820 and 1822, then moved to Missouri where he practiced at Hannibal and later at St. Charles and became a state senator and U.S. Attorney for Missouri. He died at Palmyra (one report says he died in court) and was buried in the Massey Hill Cemetery a mile north of the community; a century later a marker was erected to his memory, but it was removed for later highway expansion and if not destroyed

its present whereabouts are unknown. Shannon County, Missouri, was named for him.

Information from Corbyn Jacobs, Palmyra, Mo.; and Katherine Rawlings, Carmichael, Calif.; Ruth Cooper, Warsaw, Mo.; *History of the Expedition Under the Command of Lewis and Clark,* ed. by Elliott Coues. N.Y., Dover Pubns., 1965; Clarke, *Lewis and Clark.*

Shaver, Paul, frontiersman (1759-post July 1834). B. in Pendleton County, Virginia, he served as scout in Randolph County, Virginia, in 1776, and the following year joined Stuart's company "for defense of the Western Waters," in Lewis County, trans-Allegheny. In 1778 he removed to near Louisville, Kentucky, scouted the Illinois country under Captain Andrew Kincaid, took part in Clark's expedition against Kaskaskia and the operation to recapture Vincennes, serving until November 1780; he was wounded at Andersontown, Indiana, and never fully recovered. There is some confusion over whether he took part in the "flight of 1770" from Buckhannon country of western Virginia before Indian raids; it may have been another of the same or similar name. Shaver, who was illiterate, was granted a pension for a few years, but then denied it as having been "too young" for Revolutionary service, a judgment that was unjust.

Lucullus V. McWhorter, *The Border Settlers of Northwestern Virginia.* Hamilton, O., Republican Pub. Co., 1915.

Shaw, Alston Knox, soldier (1833-post 1908). B. in Norfolk County, Ontario, he went to Chicago in his twenties and traversed the upper Mississippi River country. After a brief visit home he went to Colorado where in 1864 he enlisted in the 100-day 3rd Colorado Cavalry. September 1, 1864, Shaw, by now a sergeant, was assigned to guard five guerillas or desperadoes, part of the Jim Reynolds band, captured after assorted holdups, purportedly for the Confederate cause. They were to be taken to Fort Lyon for a court-martial, according to Hoig, or were enroute to Fort Leavenworth having already been court martialed, by Shaw's account. At any rate, no rations were drawn for them for the nine-day transit and on the fourth morning out a soldier detachment including Shaw, Abe Williamson who before his enlistment had been a stage driver and a robbery victim of the gang, A.

Neiland, Oscar Packard, Isaac Beckman and Frank Parks took the five away from the line of march and executed them. Hoig said that Williamson killed four and Shaw one, the other soldiers refusing to perform as a firing squad. Shaw's less than convincing account says he directed the execution of all five, Williamson giving each the coup de grace. It was all done, Shaw reported, at the implied instance of Captain Theodore G. Cree. After his service Shaw became a freighter, making thirteen trips between Fort Leavenworth and Denver. Later he entered ranching, became a sheepman and lived late in life around Hotchkiss, Colorado.

Stan Hoig, *The Sand Creek Massacre.* Norman, Univ. of Okla. Press, 1974; Luella Shaw, "Jim Reynolds and His Gang." *Frontier Times,* Vol. 37, No. 4 (June-July 1963), 15, 69-70.

Shaw, Jim, outlaw, informer (d. Oct. 14, 1897). An Arizona cowboy, Shaw linked up with the Christian gang (see William Christian biography for details), but soon turned traitor, cuckolding his host, and fled after learning the Christians suspected him of betraying them. Later he made peace with them, but again double-crossed the gang, leading the posse which killed Black Jack Christian. August 13-14, 1897, surviving members of the gang tried to dynamite the house near Deming, New Mexico, in which Shaw and his friends were staying; Shaw escaped a later ambush, as well, but was shot to death within five miles of where Black Jack had died.

Jeff Burton, *Black Jack Christian: Outlaw.* Santa Fe, Press of Territorian, 1967.

Shaw, Joshua, artist (c. 1777-Sept. 8, 1860). B. at Bellingborough, Lincolnshire, England, he migrated as an artist to America in 1817, traveled widely through the country, sketching and painting, and may have gone up the Missouri River with some party in 1820. Robert Taft said that one painting by Shaw of "Indians Hunting Buffalo" existed, but there is little other evidence that he painted one. He died at Burlington, New Jersey.

George C. Groce, David H. Wallace, *The New-York Historical Society's Dictionary of Artists in America 1564-1860.* New Haven, Yale Univ. Press, 1957; Bernard DeVoto, *Across the Wide Missouri.* Boston, Houghton Mifflin Co., 1947.

Shears, George, desperado (d. Jan. 24, 1864). Listed by Red Yager as a roadster and

horsethief, Shears seems to have been an outlaw long before he reached southwestern Montana in 1862. He affiliated himself with the notorious Henry Plummer band of desperadoes. Vigilantes caught up with him at Frenchtown, Montana, in the winter of 1864 and Shears quietly accepted his fate, remarking that "I knew I should come to this sometime, but I thought I could run another season." He willingly confessed crimes he was asked about, cooperated with his executioners, and with a rope around his neck at the top of a ladder, said: "Gentlemen, I am not used to this business, never having been hung before. Shall I jump off, or slide off?" "Jump!" he was advised. "All right," George replied, "good-bye!" and he sprang into space, got a good drop and died without a struggle. His phrase, "Shall I jump off or slide off?" became a Vigilante by-word.

Dimsdale; Langford; Birney.

Shedd, Warren Fay, frontiersman (Nov. 6, 1829-Apr. 19, 1904). B. at Sardinia, New York, he was the seventh generation of Massachusetts Bay settlers; April 1, 1848, he married, but his wife died a few years later, and they had no children. In 1852 Shedd moved to Winnebago, later to Malta, Illinois; in 1855 he married again, fathered three children, but early in the Civil War abandoned his family and disappeared. He visited briefly St. Joseph, Missouri, Denver and Leadville, Colorado, and El Paso, Texas. By the end of 1861 he was located at San Augustin Springs, in the foothills of New Mexico's Organ Mountains, a place he made notorious. He purchased it from Thomas J. Bull, onetime member of Doniphan's column who had settled at the springs and acquired title to 160 acres which Shedd took over (Shedd may or may not have been related to Joshua Shedd, who operated the first Anglo saloon at Mesilla). Warren Shedd's place became a community, rather than an isolated ranch. He operated the general store; a dance hall with accommodating women; an inn where according to legend the price was double if the visitor was on the dodge, but which became a prosperous sideline because the place was rather secure from the law; corrals where stolen livestock could be held securely, and two miles of stone fences to keep animals from straying. "Shedd's ranch was generally known in the 1870's as a harbor for stolen livestock (though) Shedd was never arrested but one time, the charge: conducting business without a license." Shedd was friendly with Rynerson, district attorney, and Warren Bristol, district judge, and these friendships did him no harm. He was justice of the peace and postmaster at San Augustin Springs until tripped by a postal inspector in 1886 for certain offenses and fined. Shedd also was interested in mining ore in a small way and mining guests in a big way: he charged extra for water and kept the springs padlocked to prevent anyone from getting a free drink. At length Shedd over-extended himself: he planned to build a resort-type hotel but ran out of money and lost his property through a judgment on a mechanics' lien. A son visited him in 1891. In 1897 a "younger daughter" took him with her from El Paso to her home in Arkansas City, Arkansas, where he was reunited with his wife, Mary, after 36 years. She died in 1899 when Shedd went to live with other relatives at Elgin, Illinois, where he died. He had had some legitimate brushes with Indians in and about the springs, mainly with Apache stock raiders, and "Indians were blamed on some occasions when corpses were found near Shedd's ranch. Even if such accusations were true, they were doubtless few in comparison with the number of unrecorded deaths of Anglos at the hands of other Anglos at the springs between 1865 and 1885." Shedd never had his picture taken; he was described only as "well built," and "well set up."

Robert N. Mullin notes and collected information.

Sheldon, Charles, hunter, naturalist (Oct. 17, 1867-Sept. 21, 1928). B. at Rutland, Vermont, he was graduated from Yale in 1890 and became affiliated with an Ohio railroad; he was associated with the Chihuahua and Pacific Railway of Mexico from 1898 to 1902. During this period he supervised construction of a line from El Paso to Chihuahua City, invested in mining property and within five years had accumulated enough capital to retire. He spent the last quarter century of his life exploring in North America from Old Mexico to the Yukon, hunting, collecting museum specimens and helping preserve the continent's wildlife and wild lands. The Charles Sheldon Antelope Range in Nevada and Mount Sheldon in the Mount McKinley National Park of Alaska were named for him. He hunted with the Seri Indians of Tiburon Island in the Gulf of California and with Alaskan natives in many

areas. He wrote two books during his lifetime: *The Wilderness of the Upper Yukon* (1911) and *The Wilderness of the North Pacific Islands* (1912); a later book, *The Wilderness of Desert Bighorns and Seri Indians* was published in 1980 from his field notes and photographs. It was produced under auspices of the Arizona Desert Bighorn Sheep Society of Phoenix, Arizona. Sheldon's collection of 7,000 volumes was acquired by the Yale University library.

Who Was Who; Tucson, *Arizona Daily Star,* Apr. 20, 1980.

Shephard, "Mam" (Old Mother Feather Legs), character (d. 1879). Born possibly in northern Louisiana, she first appears inhabiting a dugout on Demmon Hill between Raw Hide Buttes and Running Water, near the present town of Jay Em, south of Lusk, Wyoming. She won her nickname because the long red pantalettes she wore tied to her ankles, fluttered in the breeze "like a feather-legged chicken in a high wind." Said to be a go-between for road agents and other desperadoes, she harbored gamblers and dispensed whiskey and perhaps services to "travelers." About a year after her arrival she was shot by Dick (Terrapin) Davis, a hanger-on, and robbed of more than $1,000. It was later learned that she was mother of Tom and Bill Shephard, outlaws with Davis of the Tensas swamps, northern Louisiana. Both sons were lynched. Davis returned to the swamps where he, too, was lynched, on the scaffold confessing the murder. A monument has been erected over her grave, 15 miles north of Jay Em, between the graves of Ike Diapert and George McFadden, both said to have been killed.

Agnes Wright Spring, *The Cheyenne and Black Hills Stage and Express Routes.* Lincoln, Univ. of Nebr. Press, 1965; *Los Angeles Times,* Feb. 25, 1973.

Shepherd, William M., physician, adventurer (fl. 1835-1858). A Virginian, Shepherd became a surgeon in the Texas army in 1837 and served as Secretary of the Navy for a year beginning December 5, 1837. He, with Edward Weyman and others, plotted the conquest of California, Shepherd to take a land party west while Weyman brought their single ship around South America with a view to combining forces for an assault on San Francisco; the plan was aborted by Houston. Shepherd served as a private in the Mier Expedition in 1842, was captured, released in 1844 and was still living in Texas in 1858.

HT; Hunter Anderson, "Texan Plotted Conquest of California." *Frontier Times,* Vol. 4, No. 1 (Oct. 1926), 1-3.

Sheridan, Philip Henry, military officer (Mar. 6, 1831-Aug. 5, 1888). Sheridan's place of birth is unknown; his own statements give Boston, Somerset, Ohio or Albany while there is some reason to suppose he was b. in Ireland, or at sea while his parents were emigrating to the United States. He went to West Point from Ohio, was commissioned a brevet second lieutenant of the 1st Infantry July 1, 1853, and a second lieutenant of the 4th Infantry November 22, 1894. In Oregon in October 1855 he took part in a lengthy but fruitless campaign against the Yakima Indians; no contact was made. Sheridan wintered at Fort Vancouver. March 26, 1856, Yakimas and other Indians captured a blockhouse at the Cascades, near The Dalles on the Columbia River; Sheridan and 40 dragoons helped retake the position, the officer narrowly escaping death in the action. He later captured 13 men of the Cascade (Watlala) Indians, nine of whom were executed by order of Colonel George Wright although at least some were clearly innocent of any wrongdoing. Sheridan spent his remaining years in the Northwest on the Grande Ronde Indian Reservation of northeast Oregon, living with a Rogue River Indian girl, gaining from her a knowledge of one native tongue but no empathy whatever for Indians as a people. He became a first lieutenant March 1, 1861, and went east to join the 13th Infantry. His Civil War record was outstanding; he emerged a Major General and one of the most famous Union cavalry commanders. Immediately following the conflict Grant sent Sheridan to command 52,000 men along the Rio Grande, the action widely interpreted as a threat to the French position in Mexico. Sheridan always felt, with some justification, that this move persuaded the French to abandon the Emperor Maximilian, who was executed by Mexico in 1867. Sheridan commanded the Fifth Military District (Texas and Louisiana) until he took over the Department of the Missouri at Fort Leavenworth February 29, 1868. Indian hostility and turbulence on the Plains mounted. August 29 Sheridan ordered Colonel George A. Forsyth into the field with about 50 frontiersmen to see if they could find and fight any Indians. In eastern Colorado they located some and the disastrous engagement at Beecher Island resulted (see entries for Forsyth and his personnel). Sheridan organized and directed the involved South Plains campaign of November 1868, the major result of which was Custer's attack on Black Kettle's camp on the Washita River of Indian Territory; the peace-minded Black Kettle and about 100 of his people were killed, more than 50 women and children captured and Custer withdrew rather than face more militant Indians camped just below the Cheyenne village. Sheridan was elated at Custer's preliminary report and assured Sherman, commanding the Division of the Missouri, that "if we can get one or two more good blows there will be no more Indian troubles in my Department." History would not second his enthusiasm for the Custer "victory." Sheridan personally accompanied the troops that in December under Custer embarked upon a sweep to complete the earlier action on the Washita. The expedition set out December 7 from Camp Supply near the present Fort Supply, Oklahoma, reached Fort Cobb December 18 and went on to the future site of Fort Sill in early January, herding in erstwhile hostile Indians as it progressed. Sheridan returned to Camp Supply to arrange supplies for Custer's column, intending to rejoin later, but March 2, 1869, received orders to hurry to Washington and learned March 6 at Fort Hays, Kansas, that he had been named Lieutenant General by the newly elected President Grant and would command the Division of the Missouri succeeding Sherman, now commander-in-chief of the Army. The Division included the Departments of Dakota, the Platte, the Missouri, Texas and the Gulf, a million square miles extending from Canada to Mexico and from Chicago, where Sheridan made his headquarters, to Utah. He was to administer this military domain until late 1883. This gave much wider scope to his operations but severely limited opportunities for taking the field in person, to such an active man a distinct disadvantage. Yet in his new office, as in the former one, he had a profound influence on military, Indian and civil developments of a vast frontier, and one that on the whole he administered ably. He and Belknap on a trip to Texas "directed" Mackenzie (without written orders) to push into Mexico illegally in 1873 and punish Kickapoo Indians who had been raiding Texas stockmen, this instruction without the knowledge, let alone authority, of Sherman or anyone else. It was a perilous action for a military officer to undertake, but Sheridan came out of it well, winning *ex post facto* approval of Grant, although Sherman did not conceal his displeasure over an event unsanctified by international law. Of more moment was Sheridan's direction and coordination of the Red River War of 1874-75, conducted in the field by Mackenzie, Miles, Davidson, Buell, and Price leading separate columns; it resulted in skirmishes but no major battles, yet drove recalcitrant Kiowas, Comanches, Cheyennes and others onto reservations and brought something resembling a peace to the South Plains. Sheridan also did much of the planning for the great Sioux wars of 1876-77, the most important single action of which was the Little Bighorn fight of Custer, Sheridan's veritable protégé, and related developments. Sheridan oversaw the closing phases of the Nez Perce movement toward Canada since their hegira brought them into Montana, a segment of the Division of the Missouri. How much he was responsible for the eventual establishment of peace on the Plains is problematical; any worthy officer might have done as well, but the fact remains that he was in the director's chair and credit must be given him for its being brought about. Sheridan's impulsiveness often led him into cul de sacs of his own making, as when he enthusiastically lauded Major E.M. Baker for the bloody action against a peaceful Piegan camp in Montana January 23, 1870, before the full facts of this virtual replication of Sand Creek were learned, and in his eager endorsement of the earlier Washita affair under like circumstances. It is paradoxical that Sheridan's support of Baker as much as anything else turned back an almost sure Congressional approval of transfer of the management of Indian affairs from Interior to War Departments, a step Sheridan and many other officers ardently championed. Upon Sherman's resignation preparatory to retirement Sheridan became commander-in-chief of the Army November 1, 1883. Among his accomplishments in this position was the salvation through army control of Yellowstone National Park and by projeciton of the whole concept of national parks for the benefit of future generations. Sheridan held the postion of Army commander until his death at Nonquitt, Massachusetts, a few days before

which he was made a four-star General. He was married and fathered one son and three daughters. He had formed strong friendships and many enemies. He was intelligent and his mind was agile, but it was not profound and in many ways he was a one-sided man. Sheridan was something of a sycophant, not markedly original in thought, found it difficult to correct his own erroneous views, was often harshly inflexible when compromise might effectively accomplish desired ends and on the whole, while attractive to many was less appealing to others. As a combat commander he had been superb, as an administrator satisfactory, but in some departments he was occasionally found wanting.

Literature abundant; Paul Andrew Hutton, *Phil Sheridan and His Army*. Lincoln, Univer. of Nebr. Press, 1985; Carl Coke Rister, *Border Command: General Phil Sheridan in the West*. Norman, Univ. of Okla. Press, 1944; De B. Randolph Keim, *Sheridan's Troopers on the Borders: A Winter Campaign on the Plains* (1870), Williamstown, Mass., Corner House Pubrs., 1973.

Sherman, Tom, gunman (fl. 1873). Sherman, "a killer of the most vicious type," ran a dancehall at Dodge City, Kansas, at the formation of the town. On March 11, 1873, at Dodge City he brutally murdered Charles Burns, who had killed a friend of Sherman. Sherman was described as "a big, lubberly fellow, who ran with a limp."

Ed Bartholomew, *Wyatt Earp: The Untold Story*. Toyahvale, Tex., Frontier Book Co., 1963.

Sherman, William Tecumseh, military officer (feb. 8, 1820-Feb. 14, 1891). B. at Lancaster, Ohio, he went to West Point and was commissioned a second lieutenant, 3rd Artillery July 1, 1840. He served in the Second Seminole War in 1840-42 becoming a first lieutenant November 30, 1841. He was stationed in California for an uneventful three years from 1847-50, part of the time as aide to Stephen Watts Kearny. He became a captain September 27, 1850, and resigned from the Army September 6, 1853, when he returned to San Francisco (and later New York) for an unsuccessful essay into banking, then to Fort Leavenworth for an equally disappointing attempt to practice law. He became the successful head of a small Louisiana college in 1859. May 14, 1861, Sherman was commissioned colonel of the 13th Infantry. His Civil

War career was spectacular. He emerged one of famous officers of the Union Army, although with an undeserved reputation for harshness and ruthlessness, traits never a part of his complex character. Grant characterized him as "the most brilliant but the least understood of our Generals," adding that "a more unmanageable man there is not in America," although Sherman was utterly loyal to his concept of the Constitution and the national spirit and served both with all his being throughout his distinguished career. He became Lieutenant General July 25, 1866. He commanded at his own request the Military Division of the Mississippi until August 5, 1866, when it became the Division of the Missouri. That year he was sent on a brief diplomatic mission to President Benito Juarez of Mexico, then attempting to overthrow the Emperor Maximilian; Sherman soon returned to his St. Louis headquarters. His impact on the trans-Missouri frontier was profound. He was an enthusiastic expansionist and did as much as anyone to promote railroad construction into the west as a great national enterprise and the "solution of our Indian affairs." Sherman made countless inspection trips into the west; once the railroads were completed some of these excursions extended as far as San Francisco and Boise, Idaho. Most were undertaken with minimal escorts and while Sherman never saw a hostile Indian on the loose, three times he narrowly averted catastrophe. In May 1871 he drove over a road near Fort Richardson, Texas, a few hours before Kiowa warriors under Satanta (see entry) and others destroyed on that route the Henry Warren wagon train; Sherman at Fort Sill was instrumental in the arrest of the leaders of this attack. In August 1877 he narrowly missed a collision with the militant Nez Perce then on their famous hegira from Idaho toward Canada. And in April 1882 Sherman's small party "missed the Chiricahuas by the narrowest of margins" during the Loco emeute from San Carlos, Arizona. None of these affairs ruffled Sherman's composure very much. He was never an Indian hater, nor was he anti-Indian by philosophy although he was anti-hostile whether the enemy be Indian or white. Sherman was ever a close friend and confidante of Grant and Sheridan. He was sufficiently misled by the latter's overblown enthusiasm to endorse Custer's unfortunate attack on the friendly Cheyenne camp of Black

Kettle on the Washita River November 27, 1868, and the even more atrocious attack by Major E.M. Baker (see entry) on a friendly Piegan camp in Montana January 23, 1870; he would have approved neither incident had he been in full possession of the facts. Sherman was capable of penning the most ferocious viewpoints, instructions and advisements but, his rhetoric aside — and often on mature consideration he did brush it away — he was just, reasonable and considerate toward people of any race or status. He had no faith in the work of the post-Civil War Peace Commission toward settling Indian difficulties and found to his "horror" that he had been named to the Board of Peace Commissioners himself by the Act of July 20, 1867, though he worked with it conscientiously while cordially detesting some members (see Samuel F. Tappan entry). He did not attend the significant Medicine Lodge Treaty council of October 1867, sending Augur in his place, nor the Fort Laramie council of November 1867, Augur again standing in for him. But Sherman, as a member of the Peace Commission, signed the important Fort Laramie Treaty of April 1868 vacating the Bozeman Trail military posts (rendered obsolete anyway in his view because railroad construction had progressed westward of that route). He signed the Crow Treaty of May 7, 1868, the Cheyenne and Arapaho Treaty, May 10, 1868, the important Navaho Treaty, June 1, 1868, unravelling the misbegotten Bosque Redondo Reservation of Carleton and allowing the Navahos to return to their ancestral lands. He also signed the Shoshone-Bannock Treaty of July 3, 1868. With Grant's election to the Presidency Sherman became a four-star General March 4, 1869, succeeded Grant as commander-in-chief of the Army and was "banished" from his comfortable St. Louis headquarters to the political jungle of Washington. Grant disappointed Sherman in not bucking the importunities of his political secretaries of war John Rawlins and W.W. Belknap who sought, and received, tight control over the Army Sherman was supposed to command, even to inconsequential management details. In disgust Sherman moved his headquarters back to St. Louis from 1874 to 1876. With the appointment of Alphonso Taft as Secretary of War however his line of command was re-established and Sherman returned to Washington to continue serving as Army commander until November 1, 1883, when he resigned preparatory to retirement because of age February 8, 1884. Sheridan succeeded him as commander-in-chief. "Although his judgments were crisp and his methods often blunt, (Sherman) was sensitive and even artistic in temperament. His mind was an orderly one, and his constitutional leanings guided him unerringly and without deviation in the direction of just ends," concluded Athearn. Sherman was married to the daughter of his boyhood guardian. He died at New York City.

Literature abundant; Robert G. Athearn, *William Tecumseh Sherman and the Settlement of the West.* Norman, Univ. of Okla. Press, 1956; Paul Andrew Hutton, *Phil Sheridan and His Army.* Lincoln, Univ. of Nebr. Press, 1985.

Shibell, Charles Alexander, frontiersman (Aug. 14, 1841-Oct. 21, 1908). B. at St. Louis, Missouri, he attended high school and college in Iowa, crossed the plains with his father in 60 days, reaching California in 1860. As a teamster he reached Fort Yuma, Arizona, February 15, 1862, and with the California 1st and 5th Infantry and 1st Cavalry, crossed Arizona, returning to settle at Tucson January 1, 1863, engaging in mining, ranching and freighting. In 1863 he returned to Los Angeles, California, and from there to Camp Mojave on the Colorado River, and down the river by "canoe" to Yuma. His ranching activities were centered on Sonoita, Arizona, during which he had many brushes with Indians and lost much stock to them. Shibell from 1867-69 was inspector of customs at El Paso, Texas. He participated in the Camp Grant massacre, in Arizona, when more than 100 Apache noncombatants were killed in the spring of 1871. From 1876 to 1880 he was sheriff of Pima County, Arizona, operated the Palace Hotel at Tucson until 1883, was a merchant and deputy sheriff and in 1889 became county recorder, a position he held until 1902. He was president of the Arizona Society of Pioneers. He died at Tucson.

Farish, IV; Ed Bartholomew, *Wyatt Earp: The Man & the Myth.* Toyahvale, Tex., Frontier Book Co., 1964.

Shield, Gerome W., lawman (Mar. 23, 1862-Jan. 3, 1932). B. in Panola County, Mississippi, he went to Texas with his parents in 1869, settling in Hunt County and in 1874 at Trickham, Coleman County. Shield in 1884 went to work on the William Hewitt ranch in Tom Green County and in 1888 was elected hide and animal inspector. In 1892 he was elected sheriff, serving four consecutive terms. He was "a terror to violators of the law, and when he went after a man...he always brought him in dead or alive. He was absolutely fearless..." It was said that he stamped out cattle thievery in the Concho county. Shield died at San Angelo, Texas.

Frontier Times, Vol. 9, No. 5 (Feb. 1932), 233-35; Vol. 9, No. 6 (Mar. 1932), 241-42 (portrait on cover).

Shields, John, frontiersman (1769-Dec. 1809. A kinsman of Daniel Boone, he was b. near Harrisburg, Augusta County, Virginia, and at 35 was the oldest man of the Lewis and Clark Pacific party. He joined the expedition October 19, 1803, in Kentucky where he had moved by way of Tennessee; he was married and had a daughter. Shields was praised highly by Lewis and others, Lewis writing "nothing was more peculiarly useful to us in various situations than the skill and ingenuity of this man as an artist in repairing our guns and accountrements," and he also earned corn and meat from the Indians for doing their iron work during the winter of 1804-1805. After the return Shields spent a year trapping with Boone in Missouri and the following year with Squire Boone, a brother of Daniel, in Indiana. He died in Indiana and may be buried near Corydon, Harrison County.

History of the Expedition Under the Command of Lewis and Clark, ed. by Elliott Coues. N.Y., Dover Pubns., 1965; Clarke, *Lewis and Clark.*

Shikellamy, Oneida chief (d. Dec. 6, 1748). His origins are obscure. He was said by one account to have been French, b. in Montreal, captured and adopted by the Oneida although he claimed to be a Cayuga. He was emissary from the Iroquois Confederacy to the forks of the Susquehanna in 1728 to oversee Iroquois interests and keep an eye on Delawares and Shawnees, Of great dignity, sobriety and prudence, he was a firm friend of the whites, particularly of missionaries. In serving his post he conducted many important embassies between the Pennsylvanian government and the Iroquois council at Onondaga; the area he oversaw was of prime importance to the Iroquois after subjugation of the Conestoga Indians. Settled at Shamokin (Sunbury), Pennsylvania, Shikellamy was promoted in

1745 to full vice-regency over tributary tribes in the Susquehanna Valley. He was instrumental in formation of the important 1736 council at Philadelphia attended by chiefs of the Six Nations of Iroquois by which they deeded their Susquehanna lands, or some of them, to the Pennsylvania government, and some weeks later after almost all of the Indians had departed, by a second deed added the drainage of the Delaware River. Thus the Iroquois gave up their claims to lands in southeastern Pennsylvania. By this move Pennsylvania brought on herself a Delaware war, but escaped an Iroquois war and perhaps a French alliance with the Iroquois which, if it had come about, might have proven even more disastrous. From 1742 onward Shikellamy was influenced by the Moravians who were working in Pennsylvania, although he was not baptized by them since he explained he had been baptized as a child by a Catholic missionary. The chief often associated with Conrad Weiser (see entry), and sometimes appeared to represent Pennsylvania interests as much as those of the Iroquois, although he never forgot to whom he owed primary allegiance. In 1748 he fell ill of malaria and barely had strength enough to reach his home. David Zeisberger, Moravian missionary, ministered to him until death. The facts about Shikellamy are very confusing and contradictory, but he was a major figure on the eastern frontier.

Hodge, HAI; DCB; Dockstader.

Shipp, William Ewen, army officer (c. 1861-July 1, 1898). B. in North Carolina, he was graduated from West Point and named second lieutenant in the 10th Cavalry in the summer of 1883. He soon reached the Apache theatre and performed good service during the Geronimo campaign. Shipp accompanied Crawford's November 1885, expedition into the Sierra Madre and was present when the commander was wounded mortally by Mexican irregulars, giving a full statement of his knowledge of that incident for the official report. He continued to serve at Forts Apache, Grant and elsewhere until 1893 when posted to Fort Buford, North Dakota. He was at Fort Assinniboine, Montana, in 1898 when he went to Cuba. Shipp was killed in the battle of San Juan, Santiago.

Heitman, Cullum; U.S. Milit. Acad. at West Point, *Annual Reunion of the Association of Graduates, 1899.*

Shirley, Dame, *see* Louisa Amelia Knapp Smith.

Shirts, Don Carlos, *see* Schurtz, Don Carlos.

Shively, John S., frontiersman (c. 1833-Feb. 15, 1889). B. in Pennsylvania he went west in 1852 and became a prospector, eventually reaching the Black Hills and from there making his way into Montana. He became familiar with the rugged wilderness of the Absaroka Mountains north of Yellowstone Park. August 23, 1877, he was captured at his camp in northern Yellowstone Park by Nez Perce under Chief Joseph on their long march from Idaho toward Canada, having already fought and won several engagements with U.S. troops. Now they were bewildered and impressed Shively as guide to Clark's Fork of the Yellowstone. Shively, "an altogether honest and reliable man," guided them briefly before the Nez Perce rejected him for a Snake chief who thought he knew the trail, but did not. Hopelessly confused the Nez Perce turned once more to Shively who set them straight and guided them to within reach of Clark's Fork. Having been with the hostiles 13 days (by his count), Shively escaped (although the Indians seemed ready to let him go in any event), and made his way to Bozeman where he arrived September 5. His narrative of his adventures appeared in several Montana newspapers. Shively died at Philipsburg, Montana, apparently of apoplexy.

Daniel Goodenough, Jr., "Lost on Cold Creek." *Montana: Mag. of West. Hist.,* Vol. XXIV, No. 4 (Autumn 1974), 16-29; Deer Lodge, Mont., *New North-West,* Sept. 14, 1877; *Helena Daily Independent,* Sept. 12, 1877; *Bozeman Times,* Sept. 13, 1877; *Philipsburg* (Mont.) *Mail,* Feb. 21, 1889; information from Mont. Hist. Soc.

Shlesinger, Sigmund, scout (1848-Apr. 20, 1928). B. in Hungary, he came to this country at 15, moving to Kansas where he held a variety of jobs including a winter of hunting coyotes. In 1868 he joined the company of frontiersmen with which Forsyth was besieged in September on Beecher Island on the North Fork of the Arickaree River in eastern Colorado. In the engagement five scouts were killed and 16 wounded by Cheyenne Indians under Roman Nose and other leaders, one of the celebrated actions of Plains history Shlesinger's diary is a valuable first-person account of that incident.

Shlesinger himself shot a coyote which fed some of the besieged, and scalped three Indians, none of whom he had killed. In his later life Shlesinger lived at New York and later at Cleveland, being engaged in mercantile pursuits.

Merrill J. Mattes, "The Beecher Island Battlefield: Diary of Sigmund Shlesinger." *Colo. Mag.,* Vol. XXIX, No. 3 (July 1952), 161-69; George A. Forsyth, *Thrilling Days in Army Life.* N.Y., Harper & Bros., 1900; Simon E. Matson, ed., *The Battle of Beecher Island.* Wray, Colo., Beecher Island Battle Mem. Assn., 1960.

Shonsey (Shaughnessy), Mike, partisan, cowman (c. 1867-Aug. 6, 1954). B. in Canada of Irish parentage, Shonsey's name probably was Shaughnessy, but was spelled phonetically in Wyoming which he reached at 14 in 1881 from Marion County, Ohio. At 17 he became a cowboy, working for some years for W.E. Guthrie who was appreciative of his talents, and later becoming foreman for other outfits. It is said that he won several steer roping championships at Cheyenne, perhaps at Frontier Days affairs which commenced in 1898. With Johnson County, Wyoming, big cattlemen vs. small settlers difficulties mounting in 1891, Shonsey became a key man, assigned in addition to his regular work, Guthrie later reported, to gathering information to funnel to the cattle interests; he proved adept at this activity, "confirming" rustling and other illegal actions underway. On November 1, 1891, Nate Champion and his partner, Ross Gilbertson were attacked in their bunk by four would-be assassins whom they ran off. At that time Shonsey was foreman of the nearby NH Ranch and was suspected of knowing who the assailants had been. Champion accosted Shonsey and forced him to reveal their names. When the invasion of Johnson County by cattlemen's gunmen actually began in April 1892, Shonsey directed them to the KC Ranch where, he reported fourteen "rustlers" were housed; when the invaders arrived however only two they believed to be such were there: Champion and Nick Ray. Both were killed. Like the other invaders once their project failed, Shonsey was arrested but ultimately went free. May 23, 1893 he shot and killed Nate Champion's twin brother, Dudley in what he reported was self defense and others thought murder. A cattleman friend advised Shonsey to leave the

country and sent him on a scout to locate cattle-feeding sites in Nebraska. He settled at Central City and later at Clarks, Nebraska, where he lived most of the rest of his life. By his friends he was described as competent, honest, fearless and loyal, and by his enemies as something less than that; everyone agreed he had an explosive temper. He was portrayed late in life as a small man, erect and with snow-white hair parted in the middle. He died at Council Bluffs, Iowa.

Virginia Cole Tenholm, "Last of the Invaders." *True West,* Vol. 9, No. 3 (Jan.-Feb. 1962), 18-20, 59-60; Helena Huntington Smith, *The War on Powder River.* N.Y., McGraw-Hill Book, Co., 1966.

Shoot, Littlebury (Littleberry, Berry), victim (July 27, 1824-Sept. 14, 1851). B. in Kentucky he was raised in Monroe County, Missouri, where in July 1839 upon the death of his father he was apprenticed to a tailor with the consent of his brother, William, his official guardian. Whether he practiced the new profession is unknown, but the apprenticeship lasted until 1843. In July 1846 he was mustered into Captain N.B. Giddings company at Fort Leavenworth for service in the Mexican War. Other members of the Monroe County organization included three Helm boys: David, Frank and their cousin, Turner. The company was engaged in the battles of Taos and Morotown, New Mexico, but casualties were slight and it was mustered out at Fort Leavenworth in September 1847. A particular friend of Boone Helm, Littlebury, to mollify Helm when the other was drunk agreed to accompany him to Texas, but when Helm came to get him at his home, refused to go, whereupon Helm killed him with a bowie knife; this Paris, Missouri affair was the first murder attributed to Boone Helm. Shoot was survived by his widow, Dorothea, who died in November 1853.

U.S. Census for Monroe County, Mo., 1850; *History of Monroe and Shelby Counties, Missouri.* St. Louis, Nat. Hist. Co., 1884, 222-23; Colin Rickards, "Boone Helm - Man Eater!" *True West,* Vol. 20, No. 4 (Mar.-Apr. 1973), 6ff.

Shoot, William, avenger (1810-post 1874). B. in Kentucky, perhaps in Fayette County, he was raised in Missouri and January 17, 1836, married Mary Jane Pavey, 13 years his junior; they became parents of at least six children. In July, 1839 upon death of his father, William was named guardian for Littlebury (Berry) Shoot, his younger brother. Around 1850 William was settled at Hannibal, Missouri, where he ran a livery stable with a man named Davis. March 29, 1852, a fire cost them between 25 and 30 head of horses. September 14, 1851, Littlebury Shoot was murdered by Boone Helm, incipient desperado. William Shoot trailed Helm southward across Missouri at length losing him beyond Boonville and returning then to Paris, Missouri, where the murder had taken place. He hired Joel Mappen and Samuel Querry, experienced man-hunters, to take up the chase, offering $200 reward (added to the state's similar offer) and eventually Helm was brought back from Indian Territory. Legal delays and changes of venue resulted in Helm's being held to the limit allowed by law for bringing an accused to trial, and he was released, vastly frustrating Shoot though Bill never forgot it. At Hannibal, Missouri, in 1854 Shoot was in the hotel business, managing the Monroe House, and later was connected in some way with the Planter's House at Hannibal, although neither owner nor manager of it. He entered other businesses, and seems to have been a responsible citizen. Eventually he went to Virginia City, then a gold camp of the first order in southwestern Montana. The precise date of his arrival is unknown, but there are hints he was there by late in 1863 or very early in 1864. Here the vigilantes around January 13, 1864, arrested Boone Helm with other members of the Plummer gang, and investigated his case as thoroughly as it could be done in a single night and day. Although it cannot be proven that Shoot was in Virginia City at this time, evidence given which could only have originated with him, and many additional clues strongly suggest that he *was* there and his evidence was instrumental in the decision to execute Helm whose true nemesis Shoot at long last had become, although it is possible that verdict would have been reached in any event. Shoot seems also to have been a primary source for Dimsdale and Langford providing background information on Helm, who was lynched January 14, 1864, with four other desperadoes. September 17, 1864, it was announced that Shoot and his son, John A. Shoot, had taken over management of the Planter's House Hotel at Virginia City which they had had "enlarged and refitted." This would indicate that they had been in town

some months previously seeing to the construction work. Shoot remained at the camp about a year, held civic office, speculated a bit on mining property, and at length sold out and took the stage east where he all but disappears. Only in a real estate matter in February 1874 and as executor of a will in July of that year does his name again appear in any public or private document thus far uncovered. Nothing is known of his further life.

Dan L. Thrapp, *Vengeance: The Saga of Poor Tom Cover,* manuscript in preparation; information from a variety of county, state and federal sources in Missouri from Marilyn J. Gross, Jefferson City, Mo.; information from Colin Rickards, Toronto, biographer of Boone Helm; information from Dick Pace, Virginia City, Mont.

Short Bull, Brulé Sioux medicine man (c. 1845-c. 1915). One of the leaders of the Ghost Dance movement among the Sioux he had been chosen in 1890 one of a delegation of three to visit Wovoka (see entry) at Pyramid Lake, Nevada. On his return Short Bull represented himself as the special vicar of Wovoka and later, before his imprisonment, considered himself the "Messiah" in person. He was of great popularity during the height of the Ghost Dance enthusiasm but after the murder of Sitting Bull, the disaster at Wounded Knee and other sad events support dwindled and he cooled on the cause. In 1891, although imprisoned at Fort Sheridan, Illinois, he was permitted to join the Buffalo Bill Wild West Show and went to Europe. Short Bull remained with Cody for several years and continued off and on in show business as late as 1913. He became a Congregationalist and died peacefully on the Rosebud Reservation, South Dakota, around 1915.

Hodge, HAI; Dockstader; Don Russell, *The Lives and Legends of Buffalo Bill.*   Norman, Univ. of Okla. Press, 1960.

Short, Luke writer, *see* Frederick D. Glidden.

Short, Luke L., gambler, character (1854-Sept. 8, 1893). B. in Mississippi, he was brought at 2 to Grayson County, Texas, uncertain authority affirming he killed several Indians in his teens, and went up the trail to Abilene, Kansas, in 1870, becoming a gambler. He reportedly was a whiskey seller at Dodge City in 1873. It is reported, again shakily, that he was in Nebraska in 1876 stealing Indian ponies and scouting for Crook; there is no confirmation of the claims, nor that Short "killed five Indians" in the Black Hills in 1876. He reportedly sold whiskey to Sioux in northern Nebraska, south of their reservation, for 18 months, killing several who, drunk, became disorderly. He was at Denver in 1878, then visited Leadville, Colorado, Cheyenne, Deadwood, Laramie, and finally Dodge City again. He reportedly was hired briefly by the Army as scout or dispatch-bearer in the 1878-79 Cheyenne Indian affair. By 1880 he was at Tombstone; on February 25, 1881, he shot and killed Charlie Storms at the Oriental Saloon there. Acquitted, Short returned to Dodge City, buying Chalkley Beeson's interest in the Long Branch Saloon. His partner, W.H. Harris, was defeated for mayor. The new mayor, L.E. Deger and his administration adopted resolutions against prostitution, gambling and kindred activities, enforcement being generally against the Short-Harris faction. Arrested and forced to leave town, Luke moved to Kansas City, but kept a wary eye on Dodge. In June, he, Wyatt Earp, Bat Masterson, W.F. Petillon and others descended upon Dodge City, had a famous photograph taken, but the threatened confrontation with the Deger faction never came off. Short sold his interest in the saloon to Harris in November 1883, and went to Fort Worth. Here on February 8, 1887, he killed Jim Courtright, a dangerous man, after luckily shooting off his thumb initially, hampering Courtright's return fire. Short died of dropsy at Geuda Springs, Kansas, and was buried at Fort Worth.

Nyle H. Miller, Joseph W. Snell, *Great Gunfighters of the Kansas Cowtowns, 1867-1886.* Lincoln, Univ. of Nebr. Press, 1967; William R. Cox, *Luke Short and His Era.* Garden City, N.Y., Doubleday & Co., 1961.

Shoup, George Laird, army officer, politician (June 15, 1836-Dec. 21, 1904). B. at Kittaning, Pennsylvania, he went with his parents at 16 to Galesburg, Illinois, and in 1859 to Colorado to mine and enter the mercantile field. During the Civil War he enlisted in Captain Henry Backus's independent scout company in September 1861, soon was commissioned a second lieutenant and ordered to Fort Union, New Mexico, in 1862. He served on the staff of Colonel John P. Slough operating against the Confederates at

Glorieta Pass, Pigeon's Ranch and Apache Pass and coming to the attention of John M. Chivington, who took over from Slough and was largely responsible for turning back the Sibley Confederate thrust. Promoted to first lieutenant Shoup was assigned in 1862 to the 2nd Colorado Infantry but remained on duty with the cavalry; in May 1863 he was formally assigned to the 1st Colorado Cavalry, Chivington's outfit. As a lieutenant he was instrumental in mid-1864 in the destruction of a small group of Texas guerillas under Jim Reynolds, bringing five of them to Denver; they were taken into military custody by Chivington and later shot "trying to escape," although Shoup had nothing to do with their impromptu execution. He was a member of the 1864 convention to draft a constitution for the proposed state of Colorado. Upon Chivington's recommendation he was commissioned colonel September 21, 1864, of the newly organized 3rd Colorado Cavalry (a 100-days outfit), and was mustered out December 28, 1864. Shoup commanded the 3rd Colorado as the principal element of the Chivington operation at Sand Creek November 29, 1864, and thus must share the blame for that bloody massacre in which neither Chivington, Shoup nor most of the other officers did anything to restrain their men and witnessed barbarous acts with no reproof, if they did not actually incite their commission. Chivington had directed that no prisoners be taken and Shoup did nothing to temper that barbaric directive, nor halt the horrifying mutilation of the dead who numbered around 150, mostly women and children. Chivington said the 600 men of the 3rd Colorado (700 men in all were in the operation) were "well commanded by their gallant young Colonel...," and in the testimony taken by various investigating committees thereafter, Shoup offered not a word of censure of Chivington nor regret for his own part in the affair, even terming it a "great victory." He lost nine men killed, one missing and 44 wounded. After being mustered out he resumed his mercantile career at Denver and in 1866 went to Virginia City, Montana, operating a store for a short time, then moving on to Salmon, Idaho, a community he helped found. He was married there and fathered six children. In 1874 he was elected to the territorial legislature. In the 1877 Nez Perce campaign Shoup raised an informal company of volunteers, fortified to some extent the Lemhi Valley but made it a point not to engage in overt hostilities against the able Nez Perce. August 15, 1877, an eight wagon, three team train supplying Shoup and C.A. Woods was burned and five whites slain, the incident known as the "Birch Creek Massacre," although it resulted more from a whiskey barrel being tapped than from evil intent. Shoup expanded his political activities and interests and was territorial governor of Idaho in 1889-90 and the first governor of the new state in 1890, resigning to become one of the first senators from Idaho, serving at Washington, D.C., from December 18, 1890, until March 3, 1901. He died at Boise, Idaho, and is buried there.

BDAC; *The Sand Creek Massacre;* Stan Hoig, *The Sand Creek Massacre.* Norman, Univ. of Okla. Press, 1974; Merrill D. Beal, *"I Will Fight No More Forever," Chief Joseph and the Nez Perce War.* Seattle, Univ. of Wash. Press, 1980.

Shull, Sarah Louisa, frontierswoman (Oct. 3, 1833-June 1, 1932). B. at Watauga River, Ashe County, North Carolina, she went west with David McCanles, although he was married to another, in 1859, settling at Rock Springs stage station, Nebraska. Her affections, it was reported, later shifted to James Butler (Wild Bill) Hickok, and she may have been a factor in the dispute which led to the McCanles shooting of July 11, 1861. She was put on a westbound stage the day after the affair; she returned to Shull Mill, North Carolina, in 1897, remaining there until her death.

Joseph G. Rosa, *They Called Him Wild Bill,* 2nd ed. Norman Univ. of Okla. Press, 1974.

Shumway, Charles, Mormon pioneer (Aug. 1, 1806-May 21, 1898). B. at Oxford, Massachusetts, he became a Mormon convert in 1840 in Illinois, soon moved to Nauvoo where he became a city policeman and helped fend off mob violence against his people. He was first to cross the Mississippi River with the exodus from Nauvoo in February 1846, and with his son, Andrew (Feb. 20, 1833-June 12, 1909), went on to Utah, Shumway becoming an adopted son of Brigham Young. Shumway was a pioneer of Manti, Utah, and was one of the first settlers of Mendon in north Utah in 1859. He also helped found settlements in southern Utah and in 1880 built a grist mill at Shumway (named for him) near Taylor, Arizona, being

described by Peterson as "tough old Charles Shumway." He died at Johnson, Kane County, Utah.

Andrew Jenson, *Latter-day Saint Biographical Encyclopedia,* 1. Salt Lake City, Deseret News Press, 1901; Charles S. Peterson, *Take Up Your Mission: Mormon Colonizing Along the Little Colorado River 1870-1900.* Tucson, Univ. of Ariz. Press, 1973.

Shunk, William Alexander, army officer (Dec. 23, 1857-Dec. 23, 1921). B. at Westville, Indiana, he was a West Point graduate and attended various army professional schools. He became a second lieutenant with the 8th Cavalry in 1879, a first lieutenant in 1885 and a captain in 1892. With the 8th he saw considerable frontier service. He operated against Victorio in Texas and New Mexico in 1879-80, and in 1880 was with a cavalry detachment escorting Livermore on his West Texas road survey. In 1885 Shunk was active in New Mexico during the Geronimo operations. He said that he took part also in "many minor Indian operations." After volunteer service during the Spanish American War he rejoined the 8th Cavalry as major in 1902. He had helped put down the Philippine Insurrection in 1899-1901 and was in Cuba in 1901-1902. Shunk became a lieutenant colonel with the 1st Cavalry in 1908, colonel in 1912, and transferred to the 15th Cavalry in 1915. He made his home in retirement at Fort Leavenworth, Kansas.

Heitman; *Who Was Who;* Carlysle Graham Raht, *Romance of Davis Mountains and Big Bend Country.* El Paso, Rahtbooks Co., 1919.

Sibley, Frederick William, army officer (Oct. 17, 1852-Feb. 17, 1918). B. in Texas, the son of Caleb Chase Sibley (1806-1875), a Brigadier General, Frederick Sibley was graduated from West Point in 1874 and joined the 2nd Cavalry, much of it then with Crook on the North Plains. He took a creditable part in the March 17, 1876, attack on a hostile village on the Powder River, at first thought to be Crazy Horse's camp. July 5, 1876, Sibley, with scouts Frank Grouard and Big Bat Pouriére, 25 troopers, a correspondent, Finerty, and a packer, left the Crook camp on a scout toward the Tongue River, reaching the stream the next day but having been seen meanwhile by a Sioux Indian scout who alarmed his village. By daylight on the 7th Grouard and Pouríere detected an advance upon the party by masses of Sioux and Cheyenne hostiles. The whites withdrew toward the mountains, but soon were encircled by Indians. The Sibley scout pulled back into the timber under heavy fire to make a stand, miraculously losing no men in doing so. Grouard claimed to have killed two Indians with one shot; this so disconcerted the enemy that the Sibley party managed to slip away on foot. Keeping to rough country, and blessed with a terrific lightning and thunderstorm to wash out their trail, they made good their escape, but it was a harrowing trip back to Crook's camp and some of the men barely made it. "The 'Sibley scout' is famous among Indian fighters as being one of the narrowest escapes from savages now on record," wrote Finerty, and his assessment remains true today. Sibley won a brevet for gallantry. He also took part in the Big Horn and Yellowstone expedition to follow. Sibley was promoted to first lieutenant in 1881, captain in 1893, major of the 11th Cavalry in 1902, served in the Far East for a time; from October 25 to December 14, 1907, he was on detached service commanding an expedition against unruly Ute Indians. He became lieutenant colonel of the 4th Cavalry in 1909 and colonel of the 14th Cavalry in 1911, served with the Mexican punitive expedition in 1916 and was promoted to Brigadier General, retiring that year. He died at Rockford, Illinois.

Joe DeBarthe, *Life and Adventures of Frank Grourard.* Norman, Univ. of Okla. Press, 1958; John F. Finerty, *War-Path and Bivouac.* Lincoln, Univ. of Nebr. Press, 1961.

Sibley, George Champl(a)in, frontiersman (Apr. 1, 1782-Jan. 31, 1863). B. at Great Barrington, Massachusetts, he was raised at Fayetteville, North Carolina, received an appointment as clerk by the Indian Bureau and in 1805 was assistant factor at Belle Fontaine Barracks, Missouri. In 1808 he accompanied the military party that constructed Fort Osage on the Missouri River, 40 miles below the mouth of the Kansas; it was named November 10 and Sibley became the first factor, holding the post for about 20 years, "a man of character, a surveyor and a dilettante scientist," according to Mathews. On September 27 he had counciled with the Osages, effecting what proved to be a permanent peace between that powerful nation and the whites. May 11, 1811, Sibley, 11 Osages and a few others left Fort Osage for the Kansa and Pawnee villages, one of his duties according to Mathewes, "to effect an amity among the tribes of the area and make of them a happy family of American allies in the face of British activity in the area covered by his authority as a factor," this in anticipation of hostilities to become known as the War of 1812. Sibley had successful meetings wherever he went, and returned to the fort July 11 after a 1,000-mile trip. He was married in 1815, taking his wife to Fort Osage. He was named in 1825 one of three commissioners to mark out a trail from Council Grove (which he named) to Santa Fe. Sibley, Benjamin H. Reeves and Thomas Mather, the other two commissioners and their 40-man expedition left Fort Osage July 17, the party including Benjamin Jones, onetime Astorian, Joseph Reddeford Walker and Benjamin Majors, father of Alexander Majors, and later William S. (Old Bill) Williams. By September 11 the party reached the 100th meridian and the Arkansas River (the boundary of Mexican territory) and after a futile wait for Mexican permission to proceed, half the group returned to Missouri and Sibley with the remainder reached Taos October 30, and Santa Fe in November. The commissioners filed their report on the Santa Fe road October 27, 1827 (it was not published until 1952). In 1827 Sibley traveled into Kansas again, correcting part of his earlier survey and shortening the road distance and naming landmarks. He aroused some controversy during his career by his charges that free traders were swindling and corrupting the Indians, while he himself was "generally praised for his honesty and good judgment...and his tactful relations with his savage wards." Sibley retired from government employment and settled at St. Charles, Missouri, where his estate ultimately became Lindenwood College. He died at his home.

Berry, *Beginning of West;* John Joseph Mathews, *The Osages.* Norman, Univ. of Okla. Press, 1961; Ora Brooks Peake, *A History of the United States Indian Factory System 1795-1822.* Denver, Sage Books, 1954; DAB.

Sibley, Henry Hastings, fur trader, soldier, pioneer (Feb. 20, 1811-Feb. 18, 1891). B. in Detroit, he studied law and in 1828 worked for the sutler at Fort Brady, Sault Ste. Marie, Michigan, the next year joining the American Fur Company at Mackinac Island, being clerk for five years. In 1834 he joined Hercules L. Dousman and Joseph Rolette in an AFC trading venture between Lake Pepin and the Rocky Mountains. At Mendota, now in Minnesota but then Wisconsin, he built a stone house said to be the first residence in the later Minnesota, and now managed by the Daughters of the American Revolution. His place became a center for frontiersmen of all kinds; Sibley became influential among the Sioux. He was elected to Congress, a delegate first from Wisconsin, then from Minnesota serving from 1848-53, then declining reelection. He was governor of Minnesota from 1858-60. "As territorial delegate he had urged on Congress a change in Indian policy but in vain, and in the Sioux uprising in Minnesota of 1862 he led the military forces of the state against the Indians." As a colonel he lifted the siege at Birch Coulee "after a brisk action" September 2, and defeated warriors of the several bands at Wood Lake on September 23 in "a long and well-contested battle." Three days later he captured the hostiles' main camp of about 2,500 Indians, freed 150 female captives and 250 mixed bloods also held by the Sioux. September 29, 1862, he was commissioned a Brigadier General of Volunteers for his Wood Lake victory, placed in command of the military district of Minnesota and ordered to organize an expedition against refugee Sioux on the upper prairies. He left Camp Pope June 16, 1863, located the hostiles on the Cheyenne River of South Dakota, and routed them "in three separate engagements, July 24th, 26th and 28th...with a heavy loss of warriors... Many of the enemy were drowned in their haste to cross the turbulent Missouri". and their demoralization was reported complete. The 4,000-man command returned to Fort Snelling, Minnesota, September 13. Sibley was made a member of the mixed commission to negotiate treaties with the Sioux and other tribes. He was promoted to Major General of Volunteers November 29, 1865. Sibley moved to St. Paul, Minnesota, where he engaged in public and private affairs and was president of the Minnesota Historical Society from 1879-91. In 1883 he was president of a commission to settle damages claimed by the Ojibway Indians resulting from construction of reservoirs. He died at St. Paul and was buried in Oakland Cemetery.

Literature abundant; BDAC; DAB; CE; *Minnesota in the Civil and Indian Wars 1861-65.* St. Paul, Minn., Pioneer Press Co., 1891.

Sibley, Henry Hopkins, army officer (May 25, 1816-Aug. 23, 1886). B. at Natchitoches, Louisiana, he was graduated from West Point and in 1838 joined the 2nd Dragoons and served in Florida against the Seminoles in 1838-39. He fought in the Mexican War as a captain, winning a brevet at Medelin, March 25, 1847. Sibley served in the Mormon War from 1857-59, and was on the 1860 campaign against the Navahos, commanded by Canby. In May 1861 he was commissioned a colonel in the Confederate army, becoming Brigadier General on June 17, and was commander of an expedition to seize New Mexico and Arizona for the Confederacy. He moved up the Rio Grande with 2,000 men, won the battle of Valverde February 21, 1862, but lost at Glorieta Pass, and was forced into retreat. His regiment re-entered Texas by July 6, 1862, with 500 fewer effectives than when he had moved north. His later service in the Civil War was in a subordinate capacity. Charges twice were filed against him, but he survived them. After the Civil War Sibley went abroad, from 1869 until 1873 was general of artillery in the Egyptian army and, returning to the United States, lectured on the Egyptian experience. His last years were spent in poverty and ill health; he died at Fredericksburg, Virginia. Sibley's name was associated with the Sibley Tent, similar to an Indian tepee, which he patented and which was used initially by both North and South, but later was supplanted. His alleged predilection for the bottle was widely publicized.

Heitman; Ezra J. Warner, *Generals in Gray: Lives of the Confederate Commanders.* Baton Rouge, La. State Univ. Press, 1959; HT.

Sieber, Al(bert), scout (Feb. 29, 1844-Feb. 19, 1907). B. at Mingolsheim, not far from Heidelberg, Germany, the ninth child of a miller-farmer family, Sieber as a young boy emigrated with his mother and several siblings to Lancaster, Pennsylvania where they remained for several years before Sieber and his mother moved to Minnesota. He enlisted March 3, 1862, in Company B, 1st Minnesota Infantry, fought in the Peninsula campaign and at Antietam, Fredericksburg and Gettysburg where he was badly wounded; when recovered he transferred to the 1st Regiment, Veteran Reserve Corps. After the Civil War he went to California, then to Nevada where he joined the White Pine silver rush, returned to southern California and drove horses from San Bernardino to Prescott, Arizona, which he reached about 1868. As a foreman for the well-known Curtis Coe Bean, Sieber managed a Williamson Valley ranch, participating in two Indian-hunting expeditions to control depredations. In 1871-72 when Crook began organizing a force for his initial "offensive" against hostile Yavapai and Apache Indians, Sieber was signed on as a packer and shortly became a chief of scouts. In the summer of 1871 he had taken part in the celebrated, and futile, so-called Miner expedition hunting gold in east central Arizona, but no profit resulted. In the spring of 1872 he doubtless accompanied Crook as a packer in Crook's confrontation with Apache Mohaves believed responsible for the Wickenburg Massacre in which several persons riding a coach westward from Wickenburg had been slain. In a resulting melee the General barely escaped with his life and several of the Indians were slain. Sieber was an important figure in the September 25, 1872, Muchas Cañones fight on the Santa Maria River in which several rancherias of hostile Indians were surprised and destroyed; Sieber led more than 80 Hualapais scouts and was commended in Crook's General Orders 32 for his role. Sieber continued his scouting for Crook during the officer's offensive operations of 1872-73, being again commended upon their conclusion in Crook's General Orders 14 of April 9, 1873. He then was assigned to Camp Verde, east of Prescott where he worked for several years with Lieutenant Walter Schuyler. The most active recalcitrant among Indians of that region was Delshay (see entry) and Schuyler and Sieber frequently scouted for him or his band. On one occasion after Delshay had been brought in, he and some of his followers determined to break out again, surrounded Schuyler and his subordinates, and Sieber no doubt was instrumental in effecting their release from a most perilous situation. In late winter of 1875 when it was determined to move the 1,500 Indians from the Camp Verde Reservation to San Carlos, Arizona, Sieber led Indian scouts making up the escort; at one point when fighting broke out between elements of the people being transferred, it was Sieber, according to Dudley (see entry) who rushed between the warring factions and by his personal force alone settled the difficulty, an intrepid act. He continued to

scout for the army throughout the decade of the 1870s and after, becoming ever better known and respected by military officers, Indians and white frontiersmen as the years progressed. In 1876 when the Chiricahuas were removed from their reservation in southeastern Arizona to San Carlos, Sieber under Captain Brayton was charged with scouting through the Sulphur Springs Valley and around the southern end of the Chiricahua mountains to make sure none of the Indians escaped into Mexico by that route; he ably fulfilled this function, the Chiricahuas who fled leaving by terrain that had been left to others to cover. Sieber had no immediate role in the pursuit of Juh and Geronimo who fled San Carlos for Mexico late in 1881 after the Cibecue affair in which again he had no role except that afterward he and his friend, Dan O'Leary were chiefs of scouts for two companies of Indians sent to determine what had become of the hostiles, their work being performed efficiently, as always. Sieber often was sent with scouts on independent missions as army officers became increasingly appreciative of his efforts and as their confidence in his judgment and capacity strengthened. Thus it was Sieber alone who discovered the trail of Juh and his partisans in the early spring of 1882 slipping north out of Mexico for San Carlos; Sieber sent word to the military authorities but it was received too late to head off Juh under whose direction several hundred Mimbres Apaches under Loco were herded out of the giant reservation and south toward Mexico in the most spectacular feat of Apache arms. Sieber was attached as chief of scouts to the Tupper-Rafferty command which pursued the fleeing enemy into Sonora, fought them in a sharp engagement at Sierra Enmedio and caused them casualties. Again, in the summer of 1882 Sieber accompanied troops which converged on Big Dry Wash in central Arizona for a spectacular engagement brought on when Sieber ferreted out an ambush and guided the troops to spring the trap on the hostiles who had laid it. His work in that engagement was highly praised by Cruse and Britton Davis, as well as by others. When Crook resumed command of the Department of Arizona he occasionally sent Sieber on spy missions into Sonora to learn something of the hostile positions and attitudes, the scout performing this dangerous work satisfactorily. When Crook organized his great Sierra Madre Expedition in the spring of 1883 he selected Sieber as his chief of scouts, with other scouts subordinate to him. At one of the most dangerous points during this most hazardous operation it was Sieber who thwarted a planned Chiricahua uprising that might well have endangered the entire command, one of the many occasions when his intelligence, knowledge of Indians and intrepidity made the difference between success and disaster for some operation in which, according to some he had no "book authority" at all. Sieber was largely responsible for the Geronimo outbreak of 1885 through a miscalculation. Britton Davis, at a focal point in this tumultuous episode conceded that Sieber had made a "disastrous mistake," but added "we should remember him by the many critical situations he handled successfully over a period of nearly fifteen years, risking his life repeatedly that others might be saved. If there ever was a man who actually did not know physical fear, that man was Al Sieber!" Sieber accompanied one expedition into Mexico early in the Geronimo campaign, then was stationed at San Carlos where he continued to perform scouting and police duties. He was badly wounded in the leg June 1, 1887, during the Apache Kid outbreak (although not by the Kid, but by Pas-lau-tau-or Curley) and was permanently crippled. He was naturalized at Globe, Arizona, October 30, 1889. Sieber was fired from his San Carlos chief of scouts position in December 1890 by Major John L. Bullis (see entry), whose motives were clouded, Sieber having been peripherally involved in a dispute between Bullis and another civilian. Thereafter the former scout engaged in prospecting and assorted frontier activities until he was killed by a falling boulder during construction near Roosevelt Dam, Arizona; the incident is unclear and there are rumors that the rock was pushed down upon him by Apache workers who held a grudge against him, although this is unproven. Sieber never married. His education was rudimentary he was highly intelligent, honest, intrepid, loyal and worthy of the many encomiums from army officers for whom he had worked. He was buried at Globe.

Dan L. Thrapp, *Al Sieber, Chief of Scouts*. Norman, Univ. of Okla. Press, 1964; Thrapp, *General Crook and the Sierra Madre Adventure*. Norman, 1972; Britton Davis, *The Truth About Geronimo*. New Haven, Yale Univ. Press, 1929.

Sieker, Edward Armon Jr., Texas Ranger (1853-Apr. 17, 1901). B. at Baltimore, Sieker was one of four brothers serving with distinction in the Texas Rangers, Ed having come to the state, according to legend, in order to join the organization. He enlisted in Captain Cicero R. (Rufus) Perry's Company D, Frontier Battalion, at Blanco in 1874, serving subsequently under F.M. Moore and Dan Roberts, eventually reaching the rank of sergeant. One of his most famous actions was in July 1880, in the Big Bend country of Texas when Sieker's Rangers were in pursuit of an outlaw band headed by Jesse Evans. The bandits had robbed a Fort Davis store and were heading for Mexico. In a hard fight, one Ranger, George (Red) Bingham and George Davis, an outlaw (said to have been Evans's brother) were killed (Metz calls this man Charles Graham, alias Charlie Groves), and others involved had narrow escapes, Sieker shooting the desperado and reporting he would have killed them all had he known that they had shot Bingham. When Sieker resigned August 31, 1881, "he was regarded as one of (his company's) most experienced and efficient members." Sieker settled at Menard, Texas, married, served as a justice of the peace, raised cattle and became an oil inspector for the state. He died at Menard.

Frontier Times, Vol. 4, No. 11 (Aug. 1927), 1-4, including a photograph of Sieker; *Maurice G. Fulton's History of the Lincoln County War,* ed. by Robert N. Mullin. Tucson, Univ. of Ariz. Press, 1968; Robert W. Stephens, *Texas Ranger Sketches,* Dallas, p.p., 1972; Leon Claire Metz, *John Selman: Texas Gunfighter.* N.Y., Hastings House, 1966.

Sieker, Lamar(tine) Pemberton, Texas Ranger (Apr. 8, 1848-Nov. 13, 1914). B. at Baltimore, he was a brother of Ed, Frank and Tom Sieker, all famed Texas Rangers. When only 15 he joined Captain W.W. Parker's company of Longstreet's corps, and throughout the Civil War was noted for bravery and the fact he always wore a conspicuous red flannel shirt. He reached Texas about 1873 and in 1874 enlisted in Captain C.R. Perry's Company D, Texas Rangers, saw much service against Indians, Mexicans and outlaws from the Red River to the Rio Grande, and by 1882 was a captain. He was named quartermaster of the force at Austin in

1885 and four years later assistant adjutant general. He resigned in 1905 and operated a hotel at Brazoria, dying at Houston, where he is buried.

Frontier Times, Vol. 5, No. 2 (Nov. 1927), 56 (which includes a photograph of Lamar Sieker); Robert W. Stephens, *Texas Ranger Sketches.* Dallas, Tex., p.p., 1972.

Silver Heels, Shawnee chief (d. c. 1775). A noted leader of the Shawnees, Silver Heels took part in Lord Dunmore's War, incidentally rescuing several Pennsylvania traders at its outset, at the risk of his life escorting them to Pittsburgh. He participated on the Indian side in the Battle of Point Pleasant, West Virginia, October 10, 1774. July 16, 1775, with Cornstalk, Bluejacket and other famous chiefs he arrived at Fort Pitt to sign a peace treaty and with the other Indians proceeded at once to get drunk. While intoxicated either on this occasion or another he was killed by Indians.

Reuben Gold Thwaites, Louis Phelps Kellogg, *The Revolution on the Upper Ohio, 1775-1777.* Madison, Wisc. Hist. Soc., 1908.

Silverthorne, John, frontiersman (1816-Dec. 16, 1887). B. probably at Pittsburgh, Pennsylvania, he may have reached Montana from Salt Salke City. According to James H. Bradley, he appeared at Fort Benton in October 1856 and sought to purchase supplies with gold dust, the source of which he declined to state but which when later evaluated was found to be worth $1,525. From this reported incident came the suppostition by some that he had been first to find gold in any quantity in Montana, and that he had a secret "mine", or placer somewhere. Granville Stuart; who knew Silverthorne well however, said that the gold had come from John Owen of Fort Owen in the Bitterroot Valley of Montana who had sent Silverthorne with it to buy supplies at Fort Benton, the metal having come originally from Oregon and Owen obtaining it by trade. Silverthorne and his Indian wife had a number of children at their place on Silverthorne Creek west of Stevensville, Montana; he had formally staked out a homestead there of 160 acres by 1870. He died at Stevensville, and was buried there.

George F. Weisel, *Men and Trade on the Northwest Frontier.* Missoula, Mont. State Univ. Press, 1955; *Helena* (Mont.) *Herald,* Sept. 21, 1875; *Montana Contributions,* X (1940).

Silvestre, Gonzalo, explorer (fl. 1538-1587). A Portuguese from Elvas, he was not mentioned by the Gentleman of Elvas as a member of the De Soto expedition to southern United States, 1538-43, but he was there and the omission seems curious unless by chance Silvestre himself was the "Gentleman of Elvas" who wrote the most famous account of the endeavor and whose modesty may have forbid mentioning his own name or role. Silvestre endured all the vicissitudes of the four-year trek, after which he went to Peru as did many other De Soto veterans, to recoup his fortune. In this he was unsuccessful. About 1555 he returned to Spain in poverty (the Gentleman of Elvas published his chronicle in 1557). Garcilaso first met Silvestre in 1567 and in 1587 persuaded him to relate his experiences on the expedition of 44 years earlier. Garcilaso does not reveal Silvestre's name as his informant, but Silvestre figures in it more prominently than anyone but De Soto, Moscoso or Juan de Añasco, and in Bourne's view is the likeliest candidate for Garcilaso's informant.

Bourne, *De Soto,* I, Introduction.

Silvy, Antoine, Jesuit missionary (Oct. 16, 1638-Sept. 24, 1711). B. at Aix-en-Provence, France, he became a Jesuit and arrived in Canada in 1673. He was assigned the following year to the mission for the Ottawas, centered on Michilimackinac. For the succeeding four years he worked among tribes of the region as far south as the Illinois, among the Sauks, Foxes and Winnebagos, the Crees of the north and the Chippewas, learning to speak a number of related Indian tongues. He then was transferred to the Saguenay mission and spent the rest of his 40 years as a missionary in eastern Canada, writing intelligently and in detail of the Eskimos and other peoples as far north as Hudson Bay. He died at Quebec.

Thwaites, JR, LIX, 306-307n11; DCB, II.

Simmons, Luther W. (Louy, Lewis, Lew), frontiersman (1817-Apr. 22, 1894). B. in Kentucky, he reached the central Rockies by 1833, when he was reported at Brown's Hole on Green River; he was trapping the upper mountain country about 1839. In 1847 he brought the news of Charles Bent's death at Taos to William Bent on the Arkansas River and was of the jury that convicted the insurrectionists. He accompanied Kit Carson to California about 1848, and was in Chihuahua about 1850. In 1852 he married Adaline, Carson's daughter. He drove sheep to California in 1853. When an emigrant to California stole Adaline, Simmons was reported to have followed them to the coast, killed the man, brought Adaline back and returned her to Carson, grumbling, "She is no good to me; she won't stay with me." Simmons had reached Montana by 1860 where he not only trapped, but commenced to prospect a little. February 4, 1863, he left Bannack, Montana, as guide for a party of prospectors, including Bill Fairweather, Henry Edgar, Tom Cover and four others; one of the group, George Orr, dropped out at LaBarge City (Deer Lodge), but the others worked south, intending to join the expedition of James Stuart, prospecting the Yellowstone country. May 2 the party was captured by Crow Indians and Simmons, who spoke some Crow, guided the whites through a hazardous period when they might have been wiped out, until the Indians let them go; they went on to make the immensely rich Alder Creek gold strike on May 26 but Simmons, who remained with the Crows, got no share of it, although Orr was granted a share equal to those of the six others. In the 1870s Simmons was trapping in Brown's Hole; he and Gus Lankin were said to have been the last trappers in the Snake and Bear River valleys of northwestern Colorado. Simmons spent his final years in the Uintah Mountains and Vernal region of Utah, and died at Provo of "senile dementia."

LeRoy R. Hafen article, MM, Vol. V; Hafen correspondence with author, Nov. 10, 1976; "Journal of Henry Edgar." *Montana Contributions,* Vol. III, 1900, 124-42.

Simms, Harry Thomas (Pink), gunman authority (Nov. 20, 1876-Dec. 6, 1943). B. perhaps in New Mexico or possibly Texas, his year of birth probably was 1876 rather than 1886 which he once gave for reasons given below. He was a cousin of William H. (Billy) Sim(m)s, silent partner with Jack Harris in a San Antonio, Texas, saloon and after Harris was killed by Ben Thompson, Billy Simms had figured in the killing of Thompson and King Fisher, but to what extent is unknown. Pink Simms in the early 1880s moved with a relative to Tombstone, Arizona, thence to Meade, Kansas, at which time he went to work as a

"chore boy" on the Jingle Bob outfit on the Cimarron River near Liberal, Kansas, the place owned by one, James Summers, or Sommers. He returned to New Mexico "still in my early teens" after Summers had been killed by a railroad switch engine and Asa Roberts, John Chisum's brother-in-law, had taken over the outfit. Subseqently Simms "ranged the frontier from Honduras to Nome," and at various times reportedly was a cowboy, guard, sheriff, deputy U.S. marshal and it is said worked for Pinkerton's detective agency for a time. "For awhile he worked with Charlie Siringo after Butch Casssidy and the Hole-in-the-Wall gang." He wrote that "I was a lawman at the time the Wild Bunch were being hunted all over the west, and I was with Charles Siringo when he came north looking for (George) Curry, at the same time I went down into the Black Hills country to investigate a report that the Sundance Kid (Harry Longbaugh) was hiding at a ranch there." He considered the Clementses of Texas "just a salty bunch of Texas boys and that was all thousands of us were." He became well versed in outlaw history and once wrote, "I knew Wyatt Earp, and have seen him shoot a revolver and he was not a peerless performer with one by a long shot and I never knew a man I was less afraid of." Simms contributed quite a few photographs to Noah Rose for his great collection, "was an avid fan of what Rose was doing and wrote often to give information..., identified many of these unknown individuals for Rose captions." He helped Rose correctly identify the men in the famous Wild Bunch photograph taken at Fort Worth, Texas. Simms "knew many of the desperate men," and "his comments...have been a valuable contribution to factual history of the West." On January 17, 1912, he was hired by the Rocky Mountain Division of the Chicago, Milwaukee and St. Paul Railroad Company as a fireman. When employed he gave his birth year as 1886, an obvious and not infrequent fabrication in those pre-Social Security records days to obtain a position; in a letter to Maurice G. Fulton in 1932 Simms wrote that "I am not yet 60 years of age," suggesting a birthdate in the mid-1870s. He entered military service in January 1917, and returned to the railroad in June of 1919, a decade later becoming a locomotive engineer; he left his employment, probably because of physical disability, April 3, 1937. During his years with the railroad he worked out of Lewistown, and perhaps at times Miles City, Montana. He may later have gone into the construction business, if his health permitted. Married, he had fathered a son and daughter; they, with his widow, survived him. His place of death has not been ascertained.

Robert N. Mullin notes; Ed Bartholomew collection of letters from Simms to Rose; Bartholomew, *Biographical Album of Western Gunfighters.* Houston Frontier Press of Tex., 1958; John L. Ihde, Lewistown, Mont., to author, June 13, 1975; F.G. McGinn, vice president, Chicago, Milwaukee, St. Paul and Pacific Railroad Co., to author, Feb. 27, 1976; a photograph of Simms is included in the 1934 catalogue of the S.D. Myres Saddle Co., El Paso, and another in Bartholomew's *Biographical Album.*

Simms, Jeptha Root, historical writer (Dec. 31, 1807-May 31, 1883). B. at Canterbury, Connecticut, he became a school teacher, then entered business and at Schoharie, New York, became interested in local history. Later he moved to Fultonville, New York. Among his writings were *History of Schoharie County* and *Border Wars of New York* (1845); *The American Spy* (1846); *Trappers of New York* (1850), and *Frontiersmen of New York*, 2 vols. (1883, 1884); in addition he wrote many newspaper articles on Mohawk Valley history.

Harry V. Bush article, in 1935 edition of *Trappers of New York.* St. Johnsville, N.Y., *Enterprise and News.*

Sim(m)s, William Henry (Billy), gambler (Nov. 16, 1845-Nov. 24, 1907). If the William H. Sim(m)s of Texas fame was the William Henry Sims who died at San Luis Obispo, California, his birth and death dates are as given. William H. Sim(m)s' name was spelled Sims by Gillett, who knew him, and by many contemporary Texas newspapers. Bartholomew gives Billy Sim(m)s' year of birth as 1856, but Gillett, who reported Sims was born and raised at Austin, Texas, said he was a boyhood chum of Ben Thompson (see entry), who was born in 1842 so that 1845 is a more probable date. The death certificate said Sims was born at Charleston, possibly South Carolina although there was a Charleston in Delta County, northeast Texas, and the state of birth is not decipherable on the document. Sims possibly learned gambling from Thompson,

though later there were differences between them. In young adult life Sims and Thompson ran competitive keno games at Austin. The rivalry grew into animosity and Thompson ran Sims out of town, the latter settling at San Antonio where he associated with Jack Harris (see entry), conducted gambling in the Harris saloon and Bartholomew reports him to have been Harris's silent partner. Harris was killed by Thompson in 1882. Thereafter Sims was reported by some to have set up Thompson and King Fisher (see entry) for their assassinations at San Antonio in March 1884; the death report shows William Henry Sims to have reached California in 1884, also. Sims was reported by Bartholomew to have been prominent earlier in San Antonio public affairs, to have been a cousin of Pink Simms (see entry), and to have "died in California some years ago." No William H. Simms was recorded to have died in California after 1905, but William Henry Sims was listed, as here cited. He had resided in San Luis Obispo County one month at the date of his death from "cerebral hemorrhage." His occupation was listed as "paper hanger," a calling Billy Sims might have learned from his Irish-born father whom Gillett reported was a plasterer by trade. William Henry Sims was married.

San Luis Obispo County, Calif., death records; O.C. Fisher, J.C. Dykes, *King Fisher: His Life and Times.* Norman, Univ. of Okla. Press, 1966; Ed Bartholomew, *The Biographical Album of Western Gunfighters.* Houston, Frontier Press of Tex., 1958; James B. Gillett, "Ben Thompson and Billy Sims." *Frontier Times,* Vol. 12, No. 1 (Oct. 1934), 1-3.

Simonds, Jim, Delaware hunter (fl. 1843-post 1877). Probably one of the Delawares from the Kansas Reservation, Jim and his brother, Ben possibly were with Fremont on one or more of his explorations, leaving Fremont at St. Vrain's Fort on the last occasion. Sometime in 1849 or 1850 they commenced trading along the Oregon Trail and wintering in southwestern Montana, eventually becoming associated with the Flathead Indians. Jim became a hunter for John Owen of Fort Owen in the Bitterroot Valley, sometimes carrying out missions for Owen as distant as to The Dalles of the Columbia River. He was reported to be a reliable interpreter and a good hunter and guide by Isaac Stevens at the Blackfoot Council near Fort Benton in 1855. Jim married a Nez Perce woman. In July 1877 when the Nez Perces came over Lolo Pass on their trek toward Canada, Jim was interpreter for Captain Charles C. Rawn who sought to stop the Nez Perce at the pass from what was nicknamed Fort Fizzle; Jim interpreted at the futile talk between Rawn and Looking Glass. Jim does not appear after that incident in published reports checked by this writer.

George F. Weisel, *Men and Trade on the Northwest Frontier.* Missoula, Mont. State Univ. Press, 1955; McWhorter, *Hear Me.*

Simpson, Edward, scout (fl. 1868). Simpson enlisted August 19 in the "First Independent Company of the Kansas State Militia" at Hays City, Kansas, but soon left to join George A. Forsyth's company of about 50 scouts and plainsmen and with them fought in the Beecher Island battle near the present Wray, Colorado, in mid-September 1868.

Blaine Burkey, *Custer, Come at Once!* Hays, Kan., Thomas More Pre, 1976; Simon E. Matson, ed., *Battle of Beecher Island.* Wray, Colo. Beecher Island Battle Mem. Assn., 1960.

Simpson, George, fur trader (1792-Sept. 7, 1860). B. in Ross-shire, Scotland he was employed in a merchant's office at London in 1809 and in 1820 went to Montreal, that year joining the Hudson's Bay Company and being stationed at Lake Athabasca. The next year, following coalition of the Hudson's Bay and the North West Fur companies Simpson was named governor of its northern department (Rupert's Land), a position he filled until his death, it having been enlarged by that time to include full control of the company's Canadian affairs. In 1828 he crossed the continent by canoe, reaching the British Columbia coast. In 1837 he sponsored the charting of the Arctic coast from the Mackenzie delta to Point Barrow, Alaska. Simpson was knighted in 1841 and in that and the following year traveled around the world. He left Liverpool in March, reached Fort Garry in the Red River country (today's Winnipeg) in May and traveled by horse across the plains and mountains to Fort Colville on the Columbia River in today's Washington State. He continued downstream to Fort Vancouver at its mouth. From there he visited California, then went north to Alaska, returning to London overland through Siberia after an absence of 19 months. He published *A Narrative of a Journey Around the World, 1841-42* (1847). Simpson died in Canada.

Thwaites, EWT, XXIX, 132n.; DNB.

Simpson, George Semmes, pioneer (May 7, 1818-Sept. 7, 1885). B. at St. Louis, he may have studied law briefly, but reached the Rocky Mountains in 1838. He joined several free trappers including Bill Williams, attending the 1839 rendezvous on Horse Creek, then worked with other trapping parties. He returned to St. Louis in 1840, joined the Bidwell-Bartleson California party next year but left it at Fort Laramie, and settled for a time as a trader at Bent's Fort. He helped build El Pueblo, or Old Pueblo on the Arkansas River, and later Hardscrabble, to the west. He later circulated in the Taos-Santa Fe area. Simpson went to California in 1850, returning to New Mexico about 1852. He believed he was responsible for instigating the Pikes Peak gold rush, though probably he was not. He died at Trinidad, Colorado, and is buried in a special tomb at Simpson's Rest.

Harvey L. Carter, Janet S. Lecompte article, MM, Vol. III.

Simpson, James Hervey, army officer (March 9, 1813-Mar. 2, 1883). B. at New Brunswick, New Jersey, he was graduated from West Point and commissioned a brevet second lieutenant in the 3rd Artillery July 1, 1832, and a second lieutenant November 30, 1833, serving at Fort Preble, Maine, Fort Monroe, Virginia and Fort King, Florida. He became a first lieutenant April 30, 1837, and was aide to brevet Brigadier General Abram Eustis during part of the Second Seminole War, being involved in the fight at Loche-Hachee, Florida January 24, 1838, when the troops lost seven killed and 32 wounded for an unknown Indian loss. Simpson transferred to the new Topographical Corps July 7, 1838, working at harbor improvements and roads in the east until March 1847 when ordered to accompany Marcy and an emigrant train out of Fort Smith, Arkansas, and to explore, survey and direct construction of a wagon road to Santa Fe along the south bank of the Canadian River. Simpson kept a journal. The column reached Santa Fe June 28. Simpson became chief of Topographical Engineers for the Department of New Mexico and was attached to the staff of Lieutenant Colonel John Macrae Washington, military governor of

New Mexico. Simpson accompanied him on an expedition into Navaho country; it left Fort Marcy (Santa Fe) August 16, 1849, reached Canyon de Chelly, Arizona, and returned to base September 26 after negotiating a treaty September 9 with some Navahos, Simpson being the last of the Anglos to sign it as witness. He wrote up his journal for publication early in 1850 (it has been published), then surveyed a site for Fort Union, New Mexico, near the base of the Gallinas Mountains. Illness caused his return to his Buffalo, New York, home for six months in mid-1850 and in 1851 he was sent for five years to Minnesota to lay out roads through the wilderness, and make surveys. He was promoted to captain March 3, 1853. Simpson spent two years on a coast survey, then was assigned in 1858 chief of Topographical Engineers under Albert Sidney Johnston in Utah. He explored and charted new roads and new routes to California from Great Salt Lake; he found a route, already traveled in part and used later by the Pony Express, while a more southerly route he surveyed was used by various mail and freight outfits. He returned east the year before the Civil War, and had no further frontier experiences in the West. Simpson served briefly as colonel in a New Jersey Volunteers organization but resigned in 1862. He became a major in the Topographical Engineers August 6, 1861, a lieutenant colonel of engineers June 1, 1863, colonel March 7, 1867, and retired March 31, 1880, a brevet Brigadier General. He died of pneumonia at his St. Paul, Minnesota, home. He was married. Simpson wrote *The Shortest Route to California* (1869), and *Coronado's March in Search of the Seven Cities of Cibola* (1871).

Cullum; Frank McNitt, ed., *Navaho Expedition: Journal of a Military Reconnaissance From Santa Fe, New Mexico, to the Navaho Country, Made in 1849 by Lieutenant James H. Simpson.* Norman, Univ. of Okla. Press, 1964; *Who Was Who.*

Simpson, John, trapper, frontiersman (d.c. 1825). A western Virginia borderer, he sheltered the Pringles after they had deserted British arms in 1761 until 1764, erected the first camp at the site of Clarksburg, present West Virginia, then disappeared "in all probability going to Kentucky," perhaps settling near Chaplin's Fork. He was "a man of fierce temperament," killing one, Cottrell,

in an altercation over two gallons of salt, despite Cottrell's "great fighting qualities." Simpson apparently became a man of some means, owning slaves, and willing them to his sister, Rebecca, who married John Pringle.

Lucullus V. McWhorter, *Border Settlers of Northwestern Viriginia.* Hamilton, O., Republican Pub. Co., 1915.

Simpson, Lewis, wagonmaster (fl. 1857-60). Simpson became a wagonmaster for his father-in-law, Alexander Majors, the firm, of Majors and Russell holding contracts to transport army supplies for the Mormon War of 1857-59. Mary Ann Cody, Buffalo Bill's mother, heard that Simpson "was a desperate character and that on nearly every trip he had made across the plains he had killed some one," but freighter William H. Russell assured her this was an exaggeration, that Simpson was regarded as one of the most reliable of wagonmasters. In 1857 Simpson was in charge of a 25 wagon outfit, train Number 26, which was come upon by Lot Smith and his Mormon guerillas. Simpson stood up to Smith until his men were captured, Lot Smith affirming that Simpson was "the bravest man I met during the campaign," and according to Smith was given two wagons to transport his men and supplies back to Leavenworth which they reached "late in the year," wrote the Settles, or took on to Fort Bridger for the winter, as Don Russell believed. Smith destroyed the remainder of the train. Simpson apparently went back on the plains for in January 1859, he traveled from Bridger back to Leavenworth as a brigade trainmaster of three wagon trains moving a day apart. On this trip Simpson, Bill Cody and George Woods were trapped by Indians, but fought them off. In 1858 or 1859 Simpson insisted that a carefully selected bull train could beat any mule outfit; his employers gave him a chance to demonstrate it, which he did on a trip from Leavenworth to beyond the crossing of the North Platte, but his oxen were exceptional animals. In mid-1860 Simpson took a wagon train from Leavenworth to Fort Laramie.

Don Russell, *The Lives and Legends of Buffalo Bill.* Norman, Univ. of Okla. Press, 1960; LeRoy R. and Ann W. Hafen, *The Utah Expedition 1857-1858.* Glendale, Calif., Arthur H. Clark Co., 1958; Raymond W. and Mary Lund Settle, *War Drums and Wagon Wheels.* Lincoln, Univ. of Nebr.

Press, 1966; Henry Pickering Walker, *The Wagonmasters*. Norman, Univ. of Okla. Press, 1966.

Sinclair, Alexander, mountain man (c. 1790-July 18, 1832). B. probably in Tennessee, he, George Nidever and others joined the so-called Bean-Sinclair trapping party in 1830 at Fort Smith, Arkansas, Alexander Sinclair becoming the leader by default. After two seasons trapping they reached Pierre's Hole for the annual rendezvous, Sinclair being killed by Blackfeet in the celebrated battle that occurred there.

LeRoy R. Hafen article, MM, Vol. IV.

Sinclair, Prewett Fuller, mountain man (c. 1803-c. 1882). B. probably in Tennessee, he was a younger brother of Alexander Sinclair and with him joined the Bean party at Fort Smith, Arkansas, in 1830 for a Rocky Mountain trapping expedition. Prewett apparently remained in the mountains until 1837 when he became a partner in Fort Davy Crockett, Brown's Hole, Colorado. He went to California in 1843, joined Fremont briefly in 1846, then settled at Corralitos, Santa Cruz County becoming a fairly prominent pioneer and businessman. There he died.

LeRoy R. Hafen article, MM, Vol. IV.

Sippy, Ben, lawman (fl. 1881). Texas records indicate a Ben Sippy was wanted in Parker County, where he was indicted for theft. On January 4, 1881, Sippy was elected marshal of Tombstone, Arizona, serving until about June 4. During his time as marshal, Sippy figured importantly in saving Johnny-Behind-the-Deuce (O'Rourke) from a mob, arrested Luke Short for killing Charlie Storms, and as a partisan of the Earp crowd, in some way became involved in Doc Holliday's stagecoach holdup troubles. Sippy left town mysteriously.

Ed Bartholomew, *Wyatt Earp: the Man & the Myth*. Toyahvale, Tex., Frontier Book, Co., 1964.

Siringo, Charles A. (or Angelo), cowboy, detective, author (Feb. 7, 1855-Oct. 19, 1928). B. in Matagorda County, Texas, Siringo was a cowboy from 11 until he was 26 or so, accompanying trail herds north and west, living a rollicking life that he recorded in his widely-read books. He was a detective for the

Pinkerton's National Detective Agency for 22 years, then spent the rest of his life living mainly in New Mexico and California, "some of it in writing, perhaps more of it spent in contesting a power that suppressed what he had written." He sold many thousands of his own privately printed books. The first was *A Texas Cowboy or Fifteen Years on the Hurricane Deck of a Spanish Pony* (1885); then came *A Cowboy Detective* (1912); *Two Evil Isms: Pinkertonism and Anarchism* (1915); *A Lone Star Cowboy* (1919); *Billy the Kid* (1920), and *Riata and Spurs* (1927). Dobie called him "the first authentic cowboy to publish an autobiography," adding that "no record of cowboy life has supplanted his rollicky, reckless, realistic chronicle." Will Rogers called his first book, "the Cowboy's Bible when I was growing up." Siringo was described as slender, wiry, dark-eyed, dark-mustached, modest, a quick and dead shot, shrewdly intelligent, infallible in judgment of others, and a man of great resourcefulness, courage and quick good humor while "in a critical moment, or an emergency cold and steady as a rock." He died at Hollywood, California.

Literature abundant; see J. Frank Dobie's introduction to *A Texas Cowboy*. Lincoln, Univ. of Nebr. Press, 1966.

Sitgreaves, Lorenzo, military officer (c. 1810-May 14, 1888). B. at Easton, Pennsylvania he went to West Point and was commissioned a brevet second lieutenant, 1st Artillery, July 1, 1832, becoming a second lieutenant September 30, 1833. He served without coming to much prominence in the Black Hawk War of 1832, later in the Creek Nation, and resigned August 31, 1836, to work as a civil engineer for two years. July 7, 1838, he was appointed again as second lieutenant, this time in the Corps of Topographical Engineers. He became a first lieutenant July 18, 1840. Sitgreaves constructed roads in Wisconsin, surveyed Sault Ste. Marie, was on a Texas boundary survey and helped survey the Florida reefs. He won a brevet to captain at the Battle of Buena Vista, during the Mexican War. September 24, 1851, Sitgreaves led a small party from Zuñi, New Mexico on a survey to find a suitable route to California, reaching Yuma November 30; his second in command was brevet Second Lieutenant John G. Parke and Antoine

Leroux was guide. The 10-week expedition was successful in that Sitgreaves reported on a 700-mile stretch of country little known and returned with general observations, but it was less successful in that its rather sketchy report was published too late to assist in selection of a railroad route across northern Arizona. Sitgreaves became a captain March 3, 1853, a major August 6, 1861, and a lieutenant colonel of engineers April 22, 1864. He retired July 10, 1866, living at Washington, D.C. for the remainder of his life.

Heitman; Cullum; *Annual Reunion of West Point Graduates,* June 11, 1888; Andrew Wallace, "Across Arizona to the Big Colorado: The Sitgreaves Expedition of 1851," *Arizona and the West,* Vol. 26, No. 4 (Winter 1984), 325-64; Andrew Wallace correspondence, March 18, 1983.

Sitting Bull (Tatanka Yotanka), Hunkpapa Sioux medicine man and chief (Mar. 1834-Dec. 15, 1890). B. on Grand River, South Dakota he was, according to Hodge "a chief by inheritance" and according to Marquis "all of the Uncpapas...looked upon Sitting Bull as their principal chief." At the time of the Little Big Horn battle Sitting Bull was generally regarded by the Sioux as the most able chief of all those in the five Dakota tribes present, but he had no authority beyond the Hunkpapas. Marquis added, "That he was a genuine chief is the testimony of all the old Indians of that time — and they know. That he was a great chief...is shown by the high regard all of the plains Indians had for him." Vestal, Sitting Bull's principal biographer (who believed he was b. in 1831) regarded him as the leading chief, perhaps the head chief of the Teton Sioux, although conceding that some elements of the Tetons did not recognize him as such. At any rate, the notion that Sitting Bull was a medicine man only, and not a chief or a true chief, is fiction, for indeed he was by inheritance and by selection. The denigration of him to a subsidiary and less-reputable role was the work of James McLaughlin and whites who wished to subvert his intractability and work with more malleable leaders such as Gall, who might be persuaded to accept the white cause and blandishments. As a boy he was known as Jumping Badger; he hunted buffalo calves at 10 and at 14 accompanied his father on the warpath against the Crows, counting coup on an enemy. On the return of the party his father, also named Sitting Bull

(or Four Horn) gave a feast and announced that the boy was entitled to bear his name: Four Horn, which was changed to Sitting Bull in 1857, when he first "made medicine." Sitting Bull took an active part in the plains wars of the 1860s and led a raid aginst Fort Buford December 24-25, 1866. Sitting Bull was on the warpath with his band from 1869 to 1876, especially against the Crows but also against Shoshones and others, and raided white posts and installations. In 1876 he refused — or was ignorant of — the demand that he bring his people to a reservation and this led to extended military operations against the Sioux, culminating in the Custer fight on the Little Big Horn June 25, 1876, in which Sioux and Cheyennes destroyed the bulk of Custer's command and decimated what was left. During the engagement Sitting Bull was in the hills "making medicine"; he took no part in the fighting. But his accurate predictions of the battle led him, according to McLaughlin "to come out of the affair with higher honor (among his people) than he possessed when he went into it." After the fight the great Indian encampment broke up, because it was impossible to gather food enough for so many people. Sitting Bull, in command of the western party, ravaged the North Plains and harassed troop operations in Montana, although never in a major confrontation. October 21, 1876, Miles had an inconclusive conference with Sitting Bull, the Indian stating that he would trade for ammunition but wanted to live free, and Miles insisting that he come into an agency and surrender. In an ensuing fight on Clear Creek, Montana, two soldiers were wounded and five Indians killed; on the 27th 400 lodges, or about 2,000 Sioux surrendered, while Sitting Bull, later joined by Gall and others, escaped northward. Sitting Bull hovered around the upper Missouri River and its tributaries for some time, but eventually withdrew to Canada. In 1881 under a pledge of amnesty, he returned to Fort Buford, Dakota, and was held at Fort Randall, the present Gregory County, South Dakota, until 1883. He remained largely unreconciled, and refused to go along with white demands. He had become one of the most famous Indians however, and June 6, 1885, signed a contract to appear with Buffalo Bill's Wild West Show for four months; he received $50 a week, a bonus of $125, the rights to sell his photographs and painfully traced autographs. He frequently was hissed as a villain at appearances in the United States, but was royally treated in Canada and appeared to enjoy the attention and miss it when it was lacking. He met President Cleveland and some of the army officers against whom he had fought. "It was Sitting Bull's only season in show business, but there is no indication that he was dissatisfied." Yet he continued to reject white overtures designed to persuade him to agree to the sale of Sioux lands and for that he was considered "unfriendly" at best, a rascal at worst by some white officials. It was through his influence that the Sioux in 1888 rejected a new offer to sell their land. It was at his camp at Standing Rock agency, and at his invitation that Kicking Bear organized the first ghost dance on the reservation although the extent to which Sitting Bull was influenced by the movement is unestablished. The attempt to arrest Sitting Bull, said Vestal, "had nothing to do with the Ghost Dance," but the ghost dance was the pretext. The real reason for his arrest may have been that he was regarded by McLaughlin and others as an obstacle to management of the Sioux, largely because of his unwillingness to bend to their importunities. At any rate, he was shot and killed by Lieutenant Bullhead and Sergeant Red Tomahawk of the Indian police in the course of the arrest ordered by the military months after McLaughlin requested it. His son, Crow Foot, 17, and several others, with six of the Indian police also were killed, Bullhead being wounded mortally. Out of the ensuing turmoil developed the Wounded Knee affair, another debacle for the Sioux. McLaughlin, in an obituary writing quoted by Vestal said, "The shot that killed (Sitting Bull) put a stop forever to the domination of the ancient regime among the Sioux of the Standing Rock Reservation," and that was the true reason for his slaying. Sitting Bull had been married several times (one report counts nine) and fathered nine children.

Hodge, HAI; Stanley Vestal, *Sitting Bull: Champion of the Sioux*. Norman, Univ. of Okla. Press, 1969; Edgar I. Stewart, *Custer's Luck*. Norman, 1955; Thomas B. Marquis, *Sitting Bull: Gall, the Warrior*. p.p., n.p., 1934; Don Russell, *The Lives and Legends of Buffalo Bill*. Norman, 1960.

Sitting Bull (Tatanka Iotanka), Oglala leader

(1841-Dec. 17, 1876). B. near Deer Creek, north of Fort Laramie, Wyoming, he was ten years younger than Sitting Bull, the famous Hunkpapa medicine man and chief and no relation to him. He learned to read and write from an Overland Trail telegrapher, Oscar Collister, learned to use the telegraph and became fluent in English. With the Sand Creek outrage he became hostile, fought at Julesburg, Colorado, scourged the Overland Trail stations, took part in the Fetterman fight in Wyoming and eventually joined Red Cloud, famed Oglala chief. With the chief he settled at the Red Cloud Agency, Dakota, and at 29 was of a delegation of 20 going to Washington, D.C., returning again with Red Cloud to the capital in early 1875. There he was presented with a Winchester carbine June 7, engraved as a gift from the President, in remembrance of help he had given a beleaguered army contingent near Camp Robinson earlier. Late in 1876 he was sent with four chiefs and a small party bearing a white flag to contact Crazy Horse and persuade him to come in to the agency. Enroute the party was attacked without warning by a dozen Crows, Sitting Bull and four of his companions being killed.
Dockstader.

Sitting Woman, Gros Ventre chief (fl. 1855-1868). The son of a father who bore the same name and who had been killed by Assiniboins at the Cypress Mountains before 1853, Sitting Woman signed the treaties of October 17, 1855, and November 16, 1865, at Fort Benton, and on July 13, 1868, at Fort Hawley. White Eagle was second chief under Sitting Woman.
Montana Contributions, Vol. X, 1940, 274-75.

Six-Shooter Bill, see: James W. Smith.

Skillman, Henry, stageline operator (c. 1814-Apr. 15, 1864). B. in New Jersey and raised in Kentucky, he was described variously as a "renowned Indian fighter," a Mexican War veteran, and "an old frontier man." Skillman in 1850 was awarded the first contract for transporting mail between San Antonio and El Paso, Texas. He had "distinguished himself for bravery" while a volunteer with the Doniphan expedition during the war with Mexico and it is said carried mails horseback in 1849, presumably before winning his initial contract, from San Antonio to El Paso. His advertising notices in the *Western Texan* of

San Antonio described his later service in "four horse coaches." Big Foot Wallace was one of his drivers. In 1857 I.C. Woods, general superintendent for the San Antonio-San Diego line authorized that year, hired Skillman as one of his key men. Skillman was killed near Presidio, Texas while attempting, it is said, to carry Confederate mail into Texas. His party was surrounded by a Union soldier detachment and called upon to surrender; Skillman retorted he would rather die, and so he did, being shot by Captain Albert H. French, Company A, 1st California Cavalry. Skillman was described by Ormsby in 1858 as "resembling the portraits of the Wandering Jew, with the exception that he carried several revolvers and bowie knives, dresses in buckskin, and has a sandy head of hair and beard. He loves hard work and adventures, hates 'Injuns,' and knows the country...."

Waterman L. Ormsby, *The Butterfield Overland Mail.* San Marino, Calif., Huntington Library, 1942; Robert H. Thonhoff, *San Antonio Stage Lines: 1847-1881.* El Paso, Univ. of Tex. at El Paso, Southwestern Studies 29, 1971; Twitchell *Leading Facts,* II, 390; Robert N. Mullin notes; Wayne R. Austerman, *Sharp Rifles and Spanish Mules,* College Station, Tex. A & M Univ. Press, 1985.

Skinner, Cyrus, desperado (1829-Jan. 25, 1864). B. probably in Ohio, he reached Texas with a younger brother, George and promptly got into trouble for they left Texas for California in 1850 under the aliases of Cyrus and George Williamson. They were arrested at Coloma, El Dorado County, in August, 1851, charged with burglary and grand larceny. George escaped but Cyrus went to San Quentin penitentiary August 18, 1851, for two years, being released August 18, 1853; George was picked up in November 1852 and did his two years starting the 20th of that month. Cyrus was arrested as Cyrus Peters in Yuba County, California, on another grand larceny charge, given three years and began serving this sentence June 14, 1854, escaping October 24. He reached Nevada County and became a close friend and follower of Henry Plummer (see entry) before commencing a new 14 year term at San Quentin on five grand larceny counts May 29, 1856. When Plummer arrived in early 1859, Skinner showed him the prison ropes; Plummer was released within months and Skinner escaped May 11, 1860,

surfacing next at Lewiston, Idaho, where he opened a saloon catering to Plummer-type brigands preying upon gold rush miners and others. Skinner either joined or at least cooperated with Plummer's organized crime ring, but shortly went over the mountains to the new Montana goldfields, opening a saloon at Bannack in 1862. He was there to welcome Plummer to the camp; shortly after the discovery of the rich Alder Gulch placers, Skinner opened a saloon at Virginia City. At Bannack he had quickly come to the fore through careless gunplay and strongarm tactics against those he deemed hostile. His brutality was directed at nearby Indians as well as white men. Dimsdale wrote that Skinner "always bore a bad character. His reputation for dishonesty was well known..., he was a blood-thirsty and malignant outlaw, without a redeeming quality." Skinner was believed principal architect of the murder of Lloyd Magruder, an Elk City, Idaho, merchant who was slain in the Bitterroot Mountains when returning to Idaho from Virginia City late in 1863. Skinner was arrested at Hellgate, Montana, by vigilantes. Before his execution he broke away and ran, urging his nemeses to shoot him down; they pursued and recaptured him rather, and hanged him.

Art Pauley, *Henry Plummer: Lawman and Outlaw.* White Sulphur Springs, Mont., Meagher County News, 1980; Dimsdale; Langford; Birney.

Skinner, John Oscar, surgeon (May 1845-post 1903). B. in Maryland he served as a contract surgeon with the army at Fort Vancouver, Washington, from March 1871 to January 1872 and then went south with the 23rd Infantry reaching Fort Yuma in April, arriving back at Fort Vancouver in May 1872. He served at northwestern posts until the Modoc War, 1872-73 when he served in the field. He was at Mason's camp on April 11 when Sherwood was wounded mortally as part of the Modoc assassination campaign against the Peace Commissioners. He wrote that Sherwood as officer of the day went out to see what was wanted by Indians who had approached under a white flag; they persuaded him to leave his weapons on the ground as he advanced "but this magnanimity on his part cost him his life.... It was the basest sort of treachery on the part of the Modocs. I got Sherwood off the field after he was mortally wounded. He died shortly afterward." Skinner went to Fort Augustine, Florida, in 1875 and was stationed there and at other southeastern and eastern posts until 1878 when he was posted to Arizona, serving in the field during the 1881 Apache campaign. In 1883 he was sent east and was stationed at various eastern posts until he retired a major October 26, 1893.

Heitman; Powell; Jeff C. Riddle, *The Indian History of the Modoc War.* Medford, Ore., Pine Cone Pubrs., 1973.

Skull, Sally, character (fl. c. 1870). Sally Skull was "quite a character," according to George W. Saunders. He said she traded horses throughout the Texas brush country along the Rio Grande, assisted by Mexican helpers, operating well into Mexico. She "had a record of being the most fearless woman ever known."

Hunter, *Trail Drivers of Texas,* Vol, I, p. 438.

Slacum, William A., naval officer (d. Nov. 1, 1839). A purser in the Navy from June 8, 1829, Slacum was commissioned by John A. Forsyth, President Jackson's secretary of state, to visit Oregon and ascertain the truth of Hall Jackson Kelley's charge that American settlers were being oppressed by the Hudson's Bay Company, and that the HBC was in flagrant violation of the 1818 Treaty of Joint Occupation, charges that were false in substance. Slacum began his journey June 1, 1836, crossed Mexico and sailed from La Paz October 10 for Honolulu. He might have shipped for the Columbia aboard a Hudson's Bay vessel, but instead chartered the brig, *Loriot* for $700 a month, left October 24 and reached Fort Vancouver January 2, 1837. John McLoughlin believed him a U.S. spy, as in a sense he was since information-gathering was his purpose, although there was nothing sinister about it. Slacum remained with McLoughlin until January 10, then went up the Willamette Valley where he stayed with missionary Jason Lee for two weeks. He organized the settlers into a company, they contributing funds (added to by McLoughlin) to buy Spanish cattle in California since HBC rules precluded the company's selling cattle to settlers — another bone of contention. Slacum took a party to San Francisco Bay aboard the *Loriot,* they purchasing cattle and driving them overland to Oregon. In his report,

Slacum pointed out the desirability of Puget Sound as a deep water port, and thus was a strong influence in the eventual American determination to fix a northern boundary on the 49th Parallel. "In a military point of view," Slacum's report said, Puget Sound "is of the highest importance to the United States." Slacum urged a large colony of American settlers in Oregon to assist in bringing about such an end. There is evidence that Slacum assured Lee secretly that the U.S. government would subsidize the cost of chartering a ship to bring settlers, ostensibly as missionaries, to Oregon. Slacum subsequently met often with Lee at New York, from the fall of 1838 onward, sometimes sharing speaking platforms with him. Slacum also was an influence in sending the five-ship expedition of Lieutenant Charles Wilkes as far northward as Oregon, the party arriving at the Columbia river mouth in April 1841. Slacum died at St. Augustine, Florida.

Clifford M. Drury, *Marcus and Narcissa Whitman and the Opening of Old Oregon,* 2 vols. Glendale, Calif., Arthur H. Clark Co., 1973; Bancroft, *Oregon,* 2 vols.; "William A. Slacum's Report on Oregon 1836-7." *Quart. of Ore. Hist. Soc.,* Vol. XIII, No. 2 (June 1912), 175-224; Nat. Archives RG 45, Naval Records Collection, Office of Naval Records and Library, Acceptances 1829-30, p. 77; RG 24, Records of the Bureau of Naval Personnel, "Records of Officers," M-330, Roll 4, Vol. G, No. 825; M-330, Roll 5, Vol. H, No. 1228.

Slade, Joseph Alfred (Jack), frontiersman (1829-Mar. 10, 1864). B. at Carlyle, a community founded by his father in Clinton County, Illinois, Jack was one of five children of Charles Slade (d. July 26, 1834), onetime U.S. marshal for Illinois, businessman, legislator and Congresssman who died in office. Jack enlisted May 4 or 22, 1847 in Company A, 1st Illinois Infantry, went with it to New Mexico and was mustered out at Alton, Illinois October 16, 1848, still a private. Around 1850 Slade is reported to have killed with a rock an older man and fled to the West. What he did during the several years following is not known with certainty (much of his career is unestablished with any precision), although he spent some time in California. During the late 1850s he was engaged as a wagon boss freighting on the Overland Trail. About 1860, according to the reliable Granville Stuart, Slade while drunk killed one of his teamsters west of Green River, Wyoming, the name of the victim not recorded. Callaway concluded Slade "came through his freighting experience a seasoned frontiersman, with the reputation of a first-class fighting man." He became a stage driver, then was agent at Kearney, Nebraska, for the Overland stage line and shortly was selected by Benjamin F. Ficklin (see entry) as district superintendent for the Sweetwater division from Julesburg, Colorado to South Pass, Wyoming. This was reputedly the roughest segment of the line, exposed to hostile Indians and rampant white lawlessness. Slade, fearless, cool and with excellent executive ability, was the proper man to clean it up. He was ruthless and dictatorial, thoroughly honest with his employers and single-minded as to his mission. He arbitrarily ran off crooked ranchers, executed stage robbers as he could catch them, treated horse thieves similarly and left bodies hanging as warnings to others, "would fight with fist, knife, or pistol," according to Langford although evidence that he personally killed people is sparse, while he may have presided over several multi-executions. He could be kind. On one occasion his men, in shooting up an alleged rustler's hangout, orphaned a small boy named Jimmy Savoie whom Slade adopted and treated as his own son. The boy, who eventually went to Denver with his widowed foster mother, was known to have lived for some years subsequently around Fort Bridger, Wyoming and Brown's Hole, Colorado. Among the better-known of Jack Slade's legendary actions was the killing of Jules Reni, or Beni, though even here facts are scant and controversial. Slade came into dispute with Jules who was suspected of crooked activities. Reni heavily wounded Slade, reportedly unarmed at the time. Recovered, Slade by one circumstance or another had Reni captured and lashed to a corral snubbing-post and slowly shot him to death in a most cruel manner, although there are discrepancies and disputes about virtually every aspect of this celebrated incident. What is known with certainty is that Slade cut off Jule's ears and carried them about for the rest of his life, the mementoes becoming naturally tanned to a deep and leathery brown. Having cleaned up the Sweetwater division, Slade was given charge also of the Rocky Ridge division immediately to the west, to which many

outlaws had fled. In his abrupt, ruthless way he sanitized that region, in sum terminating lawlessness over 600 miles of the stage route. On one occasion he was captured by outlaws but was rescued by his beauteous and resourceful wife, the former Maria Virginia Dale whom he had married around 1858. An amusing description of Slade is given by Mark Twain in *Roughing It* (1872), Twain while staging westward in 1861 having met Slade although the writer's comments owed much to Dimsdale's *Vigilantes of Montana,* published in 1866. At his enlistment Slade had been described as 5 feet, 6 inches in height with a dark complexion, black eyes and light hair; Callaway's informants said that by 1860 he weighed some 150 pounds, was very muscular, his form "round rather than square of build," that he was usually clean-shaven, his complexion "ruddy," his hair reddish-brown. Callaway records a number of legends about Slade and his peace-making activities, though few are undisputed. In 1862 Slade left the Overland's employ, said to have been fired after a drunken spree at Fort Halleck. The next year he returned briefly to Carlyle, then made for Virginia City, Montana, where a gold strike had generated a monstrous rush by those in pursuit of wealth by fair means or foul. Enroute he had a brief run-in with James Williams (see entry) over captaincy of a wagon train, losing the position but ever afterward respecting Williams, a man as hard-bitten as himself. At Virginia City Slade established a freighting business and a Madison River valley ranch. He asserted he had become one of Montana's famed vigilantes, though confirmation is lacking. Slade when sober was peaceful and unassuming; when drunk he became boisterous and a menace. Several times he was accused of rowdyism after he shot up saloons and places of business (although invariably paying for damages after sobering up), and on occasion he wildly threatened law-abiding citizens. The long-suffering Vigilante Executive Committee at last determined upon Slade's execution. He was picked up at the direction of Jim Williams, now the executive officer of the Vigilantes, informed of his fate, given a few minutes to pen a letter to his wife and was hanged before she could interfere. The execution was not because of criminal activity but because of Slade's blind refusal to behave himself despite repeated admonishments, and because in the general view he had become a dangerous nuisance. His distraught widow had the body placed in a zinc-lined coffin filled with whiskey or alcohol, planning to return it to Carlyle, but she had it buried July 20, 1864, in the City Cemetery, Salt Lake City, that interment expected to be temporary. However Maria Slade married James Henry Kiskadden, a Montana vigilante who had witnessed Slade's demise (the second marriage lasted but two years) and never returned to Carlyle. The grave was believed lost until relocated in 1975 by Boren in Block B, Lot 6, Grave 7, and part of the original headstone uncovered. Little is known of Slade's widow in later years. She remained for a time at Denver and was living at Chicago in 1890.

Lew. L. Callaway, *Montana's Righteous Hangmen: The Vigilantes in Action.* Norman, Univ. of Okla. Press, 1982; Dimsdale; Langford; Jack DeMattos, "Jack Slade," *Real West,* Vol. 28, No. 203 (June 1985), 46-48, 58; Kerry Ross Boren, "Jack Slade's Grave Located," *Frontier Times,* Vol. 50, No. 3 (Apr.-May 1976), 24-25, 56; Granville Stuart, *Forty Years on the Frontier.* Glendale, Calif., Arthur H. Clark Co., 1925, I, 151.

Slade, William Sr., Mormon pioneer (fl. 1857). B. probably in Washington County, New York, he settled at Cedar City, Utah, and is placed by *Mormonism Unveiled* at the Mountain Meadows Massacre of September 11, 1857, either participating in or consenting to the tragedy. He had died before appearance of the book in 1892.

Mormonism Unveiled, 380.

Slade, William Jr., Mormon pioneer (fl. 1857-1892). A resident of Cedar City, Utah, *Mormonism Unveiled* places him at the Mountain Meadows Massacre of September 11, 1857, with his father, both either participants in or consenting to the tragedy. He apparently still was alive when the book was published.

Mormonism Unveiled, 380.

Sladen, Joseph Alton, army officer (Apr. 9, 1841-Jan. 25, 1911). B. at Rochdale, England, he emigrated to this country and August 6, 1862, enrolled in the 33rd Massachusetts Infantry being commissioned a second lieutenant in the 14th U.S. Infantry late in 1864 and ending the Civil War a first lieutenant; he had won two brevets and a Medal of Honor for distinguished gallantry in

the battle of Resaca, Georgia, May 14, 1864, before being commissioned. Sladen became a second lieutenant in the 1st Infantry in 1866, transferring to the 26th Infantry in September and rejoining the 14th Infantry as a first lieutenant in 1870, becoming a captain in 1888. He had been a clerk in Brigadier General O.O. Howard's headquarters from May 21 1863, and may have come to the General's attention at that time; he was aide to Howard for most of the remainder of his army career. Sladen was officially quartermaster but actually aide and confidante of Howard on his memorable visit with Cochise in 1872 and in 1896 wrote an extended resume of that expedition which includes many details, incidents and insights unobtainable elsewhere. Sladen was a special Indian commissioner from April to June of 1873, and transferred with Howard to the Department of the Columbia in August 1874. He was adjutant general of the department during the Nez Perce campaign in the summer of 1877 and in the field during the Bannock campaign, August 21 to September 15, 1878. In 1879 he transferred to West Point as aide to Howard, and accompanied him to the Department of the Platte in 1883. On October 12, 1875, Sladen's right leg was broken in a fall from a horse against a tree; gangrene set in and the leg was amputated above the ankle on October 25. On August 18, 1876, while enroute to Astoria, Oregon, on the steamer *John L. Stephens,* Sladen fell and broke his right leg again, this time above the knee which may have led to a fresh amputation, the record not being clear on this point. At any rate, he was retired April 8, 1889, incapacitated because of the loss of his leg, the injury being considered in line of duty. Sladen was advanced to major on the retired list May 12, 1908. He died of a coronary condition at Portland, Oregon, where he had lived in retirement. Sladen was married, and was survived by his widow. At his enlistment he was 5 feet, 6 inches, in height with light hair and complexion and hazel eyes, his occupation given as a student. He reported that in his youth he had studied medicine which adds weight to his descriptions of the physical and health conditions of the Indians with whom he came into contact. He was a careful observer and a good writer.

Sladen's pension file, Nat. Archives; Sladen Family Papers, U.S. Army Milit. Hist. Research Collec., Carlisle Barracks, Pa.

Slaughter, Christopher Columbus (Lum),
cattleman (Feb. 9, 1837-Jan. 26, 1919). B. in
Sabine County, Texas, by 12 he was a cowboy
helping drive a herd of Freestone County,
Texas, cattle to a point about 250 miles distant.
At 17 he went on a trading expedition, clearing
$520 in three months; by 18 he had more than
70 head of cattle. In 1855 he and his father,
George Webb Slaughter made a trip to West
Texas and a new base was selected in Palo
Pinto County, five miles north of the present
Palo Pinto. The next year Lum drove 1,500
head of cattle 300 miles to the new ranch,
selling beef to Fort Belknap and various Indian
agents. An unprovoked attack by whites on a
peaceful Indian camp in 1857 launched an
Indian war that lasted off and on for 15 years.
During the Civil War federal troops were
withdrawn and the frontier remained virtually
defenceless; Slaughter was chosen captain of
an impromptu ranger company patrolling the
region. He was in many Indian engagements.
In 1860 he was with Captain Sul P. Ross when
Cynthia Ann Parker was recaptured from the
Comanches. Slaughter bought cattle from
settlers withdrawing from the exposed frontier
during Civil War turbulence and expanded his
holdings. In 1867 he drove 300 steers to a
Jefferson, Texas, packing plant, receiving a
good price. By 1868 he was trailing cattle north
to Kansas railheads; that year he sold a herd
for $32,000. Another in 1869 brought a like
price; in 1870 3,000 head of his cattle sold for
$105,000 and others for lesser amounts in suc-
ceeding years, but still for substantial sums. In
1887 he established the Long S Ranch and at
one time claimed a section of West Texas
plains representing millions of acres. He
brought in Shorthorn and Hereford bulls to
upgrade his herds, was an organizer of the
Northwest Texas Cattle Raisers Association
and was a civic leader at Dallas where he died.
He was married twice, his first wife dying in
1876.

Frontier Times, Vol. 8, No. 10 (July 1931), 433-37
with portrait; HT.

Slaughter, John H. (Johnny, or Johnnie),
stagecoach driver (c. 1850-Mar. 25, 1877). The
son of city marshal J.N. Slaughter of
Cheyenne, Wyoming, Johnny had lived at
that city for some years before becoming a
stage driver on the Cheyenne-Deadwood
route. He was killed by a shotgun purportedly fired by Robert McKemie (Little Reddy)
during a Sam Bass-Joel Collins holdup
attempt; McKemie was said to have been run
out of the gang because of the killing.
Slaughter was buried at Cheyenne on April 4.

Agnes Wright Spring, *The Cheyenne and Black
Hills Stage and Express Routes.*   Lincoln, Univ. of
Nebr. Press, 1965.

Slaughter, John Horton, cattleman, lawman
(Oct. 2, 1841-Feb. 16, 1922). B. in Louisiana,
he was brought as an infant to the Republic of
Texas by his parents and received a rudimentary education at Lockhart, Texas, becoming a
cowboy as quickly as he could. His father, Ben
Slaughter, was a cattleman engaged in
gathering wild longhorns from the brush
country and later would hire such future
frontiersmen as James H. Cook to ride for
him. John Slaughter had brushes with
Comanches, served the Confederacy during
the Civil War more against Indians than
Yankees and subsequently briefly joined the
Texas Rangers. He was married in 1871 to
Eliza Harris. John Slaughter went into
partnership with his brothers, William and
Charles, establishing a stock ranch and
driving cattle to what markets they could find:
east to Gulf posts, south into Mexico or
eventually north to the railroad in Kansas. In
the late 1870s Slaughter moved his cattle
operation to New Mexico where he flourished,
never being too careful exactly how his herds
grew, so long as they did so. In 1876 he killed a
Texan, Barney Gallagher, who had planned
to kill Slaughter because of a grudge over a
gambling game. Lew Wallace, later governor
of New Mexico considered the act murder; in
1879 Slaughter was arrested but soon
released. His first wife died and in 1879 he
married again, to Cora Viola Howell. He
moved shortly to the Tombstone, Arizona,
region he had visited two years earlier, taking
with him his cattle minus 500 head that range
inspectors considered not properly Slaughter's, although whose they were was not
stated. Slaughter remained in Arizona for the
rest of his life save for a brief excursion to
Oregon to see if the change of climate would
benefit his persistently tubercular condition.
He felt it would not and returned and in 1884
bought the famed San Bernardino Ranch in
the southeast corner of Arizona, including
much acreage in Sonora. Here he had the
usual Apache troubles if nothing serious,
though he did sit in on the surrender council

between Miles and Geronimo in early September 1886 in Skeleton Canyon on his range. In November he was elected sheriff of Cochise County, Arizona, then considered beridden with outlaws, rustlers and their ilk. He held the job until 1890, shot people when he had to, but would rather arrest a man than kill him. "His name is Slaughter, all right," said one Tombstone observor, "but he wasn't in any way the sort of a man we used to call a 'killer.' He didn't like to shoot people. He did it simply because it was in the day's work, was his duty, and was for a good purpose." Slaughter became one of the famous Arizona sheriffs, but two terms were enough for him. His successor, noted photographer C.S. Fly in 1895 named Slaughter a deputy sheriff, a position of honor he held until his death in 1922. In 1907 Slaughter was elected to the Arizona Legislature from Cochise County; he served a single term. He died at Douglas, Arizona, a town he had helped establish, and was buried there. Slaughter had fathered children and had made his mark on the Southwest. Diminutive in size, he was great in frontier stature. His life had been pretty much a mosaic: cattleman, gambler, sharp dealer, a bit careless about some legal niceties, lawman, gunman, pioneer and empire builder. He was all of that and more, too; his name will long be remembered.

Allen A. Erwin, *The Southwest of John Horton Slaughter.* Glendale, Calif., Arthur H. Clark Co., 1965.

Sleeth, David W., scout, borderer (May 18, 1762-post 1834). B. in Frederick County, Virginia, he enlisted as scout and ranger in 1777 from Hacker's Creek, Lewis County, present West Virginia, and served until late 1780, thereafter continuing as scout and Indian fighter as long as border hostilities continued. He was in several Indian skirmishes, was known by John Cutright, Elias Hughes and others as an able and qualified scout. In 1834 he was living on Leading Creek, Lewis County.

Lucullus V. McWhorter, *The Border Settlers of Northwestern Virginia.* Hamilton, O., Republican Pub. Co., 1915.

Slolux (Elulk-salt-ako, George Denny), Modoc warrior (d. July 22, 1899). One of the dissident Modocs who followed Captain Jack, Slolux first appears as a member of Hooker Jim's faction which killed about 14 white settlers above Tule Lake in northeastern California following the Lost River battle of November 29, 1872. He then faded into the Lava Bed country to the south with Jack and took part in the Modoc War of 1873. Slolux and Boncho (Barncho)were assigned to take weapons to a spot near the peace conference April 11, 1873 to arm the assassins who were to kill Canby and Thomas. This they did, although they took no part in the actual slayings though Slolux joined other Modocs in "wildly" shooting after the killings had taken place. Slolux was tried with Captain Jack and five others at Fort Klamath, Oregon, for the murders, was convicted and sentenced to hang. However his and Boncho's sentences were commuted to life imprisonment at Alcatraz Island, then a military prison. After five or six years Slolux was pardoned and joined his fellow Modocs in Oklahoma, taking the name, George Denny. He died at Quapaw Agency, Oklahoma.

Jeff C. Riddle, *The Indian History of the Modoc.* Medord, Ore., Pine Cone Pubrs., 1973; Keith A. Murray, *The Modocs and Their War.* Norman, Univ. of Okla. Press, 1965.

Slover, Isaac, mountain man (1780-Oct. 14, 1854). B. probably in Pennsylvania, he reached Arkansas by 1819, and in 1821 was with the Glenn-Fowler party trapping in the Rockies. Later he trapped with Ewing Young, then joined the James Ohio Pattie expedition to California. He returned to California about 1840, settling at Colton, near San Bernardino, but continuing to trap the Sierra Nevada. An avid foe of grizzlies, he was fatally mauled by one on Mt. San Antonio near Cajon Pass. The mountain at his ranch he named Mt. Slover; long a landmark for highway travelers, it has been demolished by the Portland Cement, Co., for its valuable rock.

Andrew F. Rolle article, MM, Vol. I; Arthur Woodward, "Notes on Don Cristobal Slover." Los Angeles Westerners' *Branding Iron,* No. 73, (June 1965), 6-8; Richard Batman, *American Ecclesiates: An Epic Journey through the Early American West.* N.Y., Harcourt Brace Jovanovich, 1984.

Slover, John (Mannucothe), frontiersman (c. 1753-post 1782). B. in Virginia, he was captured at 8 by Miami Indians from his father's farm on New River, other members of the family being also captured, or killed. Slover remained six years with the Miamis in

Ohio, then was obtained by a white trader with whom he lived among the Shawnees on the Scioto River, Ohio for an additional six years. In 1773 at 20 he was brought to Fort Pitt by the Shawnees for a treaty council. There he met some of his relatives and reluctantly agreed to leave the Indians to live among whites once more. At the start of the American Revolution he enlisted in the Continental army, served 15 months and was discharged. He married, settled in Westmoreland (Fayette) County, Pennsylvania, where he became a member of an Episcopal church. He had achieved local fame as a frontier scout by reason of his knowledge of Indians and their customs, and of the Ohio country, and was signed on as scout for the William Crawford (see entry) expedition against Sandusky, Ohio, in 1782. He was captured and taken to a Shawnee town on the Scioto River where it was decided he should be burned (as Crawford himself was executed in a celebrated frontier incident). Slover was painted black, tied to a stake, but as the wood about him was kindled, a sudden heavy rainstorm extinguished the blaze and his execution was postponed to a later day. Slover escaped, stole a horse and at length through his superb knowledge of the country and wilderness expedients, reached the Ohio River; he was the last survivor of the Crawford expedition to regain Fort Pitt where he arrived July 10. Illiterate but highly intelligent, Slover dictated a narrative of his adventures to Hugh H. Brackenridge, a Pittsburgh attorney and later Pennsylvania Supreme Court judge. Slover remained in Fayette County for some years after the Crawford expedition, then moved to Kentucky. The date and circumstances of his death are not reported, and it is not known what relationship, if any, he held to Isaac Slover, although he may have been his father.

Consul W. Butterfield, *An Historical Account of the Expedition Against Sandusky Under Col. William Crawford in 1782.* Cincinnati, Robert Clarke & Co., 1873; Joseph Doddridge, *Notes on the Settlement and Indian Wars.* Parsons, W. Va., McClain Printing Co., 1960; Alexander Scott Withers, *Chronicles of Border Warfare.* Cincinnati, Robert Clarke Co., 1895.

Smith, pioneers (d. Sept. 11, 1857). A family of this name, composition unknown, perished

with the Fancher emigrant wagon train, wiped out by Mormons and Mormon-led Indians at Mountains Meadows, southwestern Utah.

William Wise, *Massacre at Mountain Meadows.* N.Y., Thomas Y. Crowell Co., 1976.

Smith, A. Sidney, army officer (c. 1844-post 1871). B. in Missouri he enlisted in the 5th Kentucky Infantry September 9, 1861, was commissioned a second lieutenant February 1, 1862, and a first lieutenant March 1, 1863. Having an opportunity to go into business he resigned March 25, 1864. On June 18, 1867, he was commissioned a second lieutenant in the 37th U.S. Infantry, transferring to the 3rd Cavalry July 30, 1868, and being assigned to Arizona. In April 1870 he accompanied Captain Patrick Collins, 21st Infantry on a central Arizona scout in which 11 Indians were killed, five captured and rancherias destroyed, Smith being praised by Collins in his report for "energy and spirit." Smith took part in other scouting operations before resigning his commission January 31, 1871. His further history is unreported.

Smith's military file, NARS; Heitman.

Smith, Abiel Leonard, army officer (July 14, 1857-Apr. 24, 1946). B. at Fayette, Missouri, he was graduated from West Point in 1878, became a second lieutenant with the 19th Infantry and transferred the following February to the 4th Cavalry; he became a first lieutenant in 1883. Smith did frontier duty in Indian Territory in 1878 and said he had participated in Indian campaigns until the end of the Geronimo campaign in 1886. He received a brevet for "gallant and meritorious service" in the latter affair, during which he served with Lawton. Later he was posted to Fort Lowell, Arizona, and Walla Walla, Washington, in 1890, which effectively ended his frontier service. The remainder of his distinguished career was largely with the Quartermaster Corps, Smith becoming a Brigadier General in 1916 and retiring January 3, 1918. He lived in retirement on his Carmel, New York, farm and died at New York City.

Cullum; Heitman; *Who Was Who.*

Smith, Adam, pioneer (1838-June 28, 1864). B. in Germany, he emigrated to Nebraska where he became a freighter, farmer and

acquaintance of Frank and Luther North. Smith was killed by Spotted Tail's Brulé Sioux in a raid on Pawnees at the reservation centered on the present Fullerton, Nebraska.
Man of the Plains: Recollections of Luther North 1856-1882, ed. by Donald F. Danker. Lincoln, Univ. of Nebr. Press, 1961.

Smith, Allen, army officer (Apr. 21, 1849-Oct. 30, 1927). B. at Fort Marion, St. Augustine, Florida, the son of a Major General, Smith was a cadet at the U.S. Naval Academy, Annapolis, from 1863 to 1866, then became an Infantry officer and later served in the Cavalry. He became a second lieutenant of the 1st Infantry in 1866, a first lieutenant two years later and a captain in 1880, transferring that year to the 4th Cavalry. With this regiment he took part in the 1885-86 Geronimo campaign from the start, being stationed at Fort Apache at the time of the emeute. Smith rose to lieutenant colonel of the 1st Cavalry by 1901, became colonel of the 6th Cavalry in 1902 and was made a Brigadier General in the year of his retirement, 1905. He then settled at Spokane, Washington.
Heitman; Dan L. Thrapp, ed., *Dateline Fort Bowie: Charles Fletcher Lummis Reports on an Apache War*. Norman, Univ. of Okla. Press, 1979.

Smith, Algernon Emory, army officer (Sept. 17, 1842-June 25, 1876). B. at Newport, New York, he enlisted in the 7th Infantry in June of 1862 but was commissioned a second lieutenant August 20 in the 117th New York Infantry, emerging from the Civil War a captain and brevet major having been severely wounded at Fort Fisher in 1865. He was commissioned a second lieutenant in the 7th Cavalry August 9, 1867, and became a first lieutenant December 5, 1868. Utley said he was a member of the Custer clique of the 7th. Smith was in the Washita fight November 27, 1868; he was on the David Stanley Yellowstone expedition of 1873 and quartermaster on Custer's Black Hills Expedition of 1874. He commanded Company E at the Battle of the Little Big Horn and fell on the slope below Custer. His remains were buried at the battlefield, but in August 1877 were reburied at the Fort Leavenworth National Cemetery.
BHB; Robert M. Utley, *Life in Custer's Cavalry*. New Haven, Yale Univ. Press, 1977; Heitman.

Smith, Asa Bowen, Congregational missionary (July 16, 1809-Feb. 10, 1886). B. at Williamstown, Massachusetts, he was graduated from Middlebury College, Vermont and theological seminaries at Andover, Massachusetts and New Haven, Connecticut, being ordained November 1, 1837. He married Sarah Gilbert White (Sept. 14, 1813-May 1855) on March 15, 1838, and shortly they left for the Oregon missions. He so quickly mastered the Nez Perce language that he and Andrew Rodgers, with the aid of Lawyer, a Nez Perce, were soon engaged in translating scripture and hymns into the Nez Perce language, also completing a vocabulary and grammar of the tongue. Because of problems of health the Smiths went to Hawaii where they arrived in January 1842 and transferred their activities to the mission station of Waialua, on Oahu, until 1845 when Smith's health again failed and they returned to the States by way of China. Mrs. Smith died of tuberculosis and Smith married again. His further religious activities were carried out in the northeastern States until late in life when he undertook pastoral work at Sherwood, Tennessee, where he died.
Myron Eels, *Marcus Whitman: Pathfinder and Patriot*. Seattle, Alice Harriman Co., 1909, Appen. D.

Smith, Ben F., cattleman (d. c. 1882). Probably born in Texas, he had a ranch in Turkey Canyon, Chiricahua Mountains, Arizona. On July 11, 1882, he was charged at Tombstone with robbery, but settlement of the case is unclear. On July 14, a short distance from the Smith ranchhouse, desperado John Ringo was found shot to death. A coroner's jury on which Smith sat decided it was suicide. Smith later was "found in his livery stable at Pearce, Arizona, seriously wounded, and... died from these wounds." It was reported to be suicide, although he may have been murdered.
Ed Bartholomew, *Wyatt Earp: The Man & the Myth*. Toyahvale, Tex., Frontier Book Co., 1964; Ed Bartholomew, *Western Hard-Cases*. Ruidoso, N.M., Frontier Book Co., 1960.

Smith, Buckingham: *see* Thomas Buckingham Smith.

Smith, Chalmers, scout (July 27, 1847-Mar. 31, 1919). B. in Mercer County, Kentucky, Smith was a Civil War soldier and reached Lincoln County, Kansas, about 1866. One of Forsyth's scouts, he took part in the Beecher Island battle of September 1868, and survived the hard action. Afterward he settled at Beverly, Lincoln County, Kansas, where he farmed. With H.H. Tucker and James J. Peate, in 1898 Smith journeyed to the Arickaree Fork of the Republican River and relocated the Beecher site, marking it in a preliminary way. He became one of the well-known veterans of the Indian wars in his region. Smith died at Beverly. He was described as "plain and unassuming, noted more for his unfailing good nature and cheerfulness than anything else (but) he had nerve and courage."

Simon E. Matson, *The Battle of Beecher Island*. Wray, Colorado, Beecher Island Battle Mem. Assn., 1960; death record, State of Kan; *Salina* (Kan.) *Evening Journal*, Apr. 1, 1919.

Smith, Charles C. (Hairlip Charley), lawman, gambler (c. 1854-post 1886). Probably the Smith b. in Indiana, he surfaced at Tombstone, A. T. , during the Earp-Holliday period as "an efficient officer of the law," and a gambler. In 1882 he was informally named U.S. deputy marshal by Crawley Dake. Smith was considered a friend of Earp, served on his posses, if any, and one report said he fled Arizona with the Earps; if so, he shortly returned. In February 1886, he still was there, indicted on an attempt to murder one, Charles Cunningham, said to have been a former brother-in-law of Nellie Cashman. One report said "each shot the other, but not fatally," while Smith was attempting to make an arrest. The case was dismissed. Cunningham lived at Douglas, Arizona, in 1935.

Ed Bartholomew, *Wyatt Earp: The Man & the Myth*. Toyahvale, Tex., Frontier Book Co., 1964; Ed Bartholomew, *Western Hard-Cases or, Gunfighters Named Smith*. Ruisoso, N.M., Frontier Book Co., 1960.

Smith, Cornelius Cole, army officer (Apr. 7, 1869-Jan. 10, 1936). B. at Tucson, Arizona, the son of Gilbert Cole Smith, an army quartermaster, young Smith traveled with his father to various posts in Arizona and New Mexico until December 1882 when the family moved to Vancouver Barracks, Washington. The boy was sent east, to the community of Louisiana, Missouri, and in 1884 to Baltimore. In 1888 a move was made to Helena,

Montana, and May 22, 1889, Smith joined the Montana National Guard and April 9, 1890, enlisted in the 6th U.S. Cavalry, rising to sergeant of K Troop by November 22, 1892. January 1, 1891, Smith with others of K Troop were escorting a supply train on a bitterly cold day along White River in South Dakota when a sharp fight developed with hostile Sioux. Smith with four men held their position despite attacks by a superior force and subsequently pursued them for some distance. He won a Medal of Honor on this occasion. Smith was commissioned second lieutenant of the 2nd Cavalry November 19, 1892. He served in Cuba, became a first lieutenant March 2, 1899, captain February 2, 1901, served in the Philippines 1903-1905, and in 1908 was superintendent of Sequoia and Grant National parks, California. He served again in the Philippines in 1910, joined the 5th Cavalry in 1912 and March 13, 1913, accepted the surrender of the famed Emilio Kosterlitzky and 209 followers at Nogales, Arizona. He joined the 10th Cavalry in 1914, became a major July 1, 1916, lieutenant colonel June 23, 1917, and a colonel August 5. Smith died at Riverside, California. He wrote many articles on frontier life and soldiering and engaged at times in heated disputes with other writers over questions of accuracy on frontier subjects.

Cornelius C. Smith, Jr., *Don't Settle for Second*. San Raphael, Calif., Presidio Press, 1977; *Deeds of Valor, II*.

Smith, Daniel, pioneer (Oct. 28, 1748-June 6, 1818). B. in Stafford County, Virginia, he was educated at William and Mary College and became a surveyor, moving to Augusta County, Virginia, in 1773. He aided in defending the frontier during the Revolution. He moved to Tennessee upon its conclusion, settling in Sumner County. Smith became first secretary of the territory south of the Ohio River from 1790 to 1796 and drafted the first map of Tennessee. Twice he served as United States senator from his adopted state and served as Major General of militia. He was one of the most prominent of the early pioneers, his estate famous for its hospitality. Smith died at his home near Hendersonville, being interred in the family burial grounds on the homesite.

BDAC; Thwaites, EWT, III, pp. 255-56; Reuben Gold Thwaites, Louise Phelps Kellogg, *Documen-*

tary History of Dunmore's War 1774. Madison, Wisc. Hist. Soc., 1905.

Smith, Deaf: *see* Erastus Smith.

Smith, Erastus (Deaf), frontiersman (Apr. 19, 1787-Nov. 29, 1837). B. in Duchess County, New York, he was taken at 11 by his parents to near Natchez, Mississippi. At 30, in 1817 he went to Texas but did not remain long, soon returning to Mississippi, although by 1821 he was in Texas for good, settling near San Antonio but wandering widely enough to acquire an intimate knowledge of the geography and aboriginal inhabitants, as well as of the Spanish/Mexican and Anglo residents of the region. In 1822 he married Guadalupe Ruiz Duran and fathered four children. He became deaf and acquired his lifelong nickname, it is said while hunting along the Guadalupe River; his gun fell into deep water and Smith, who could not swim, searched for it aided by a long rope he had tied to a tree, the underwater labors resulting in his permanent affliction. He was said to have been a guide for the Green C. DeWitt Colony which developed in Texas in the 1820s. At the outset of the Texas Revolution Smith was neutral, but had a difference with Mexican soldiery and so joined the Texas side, quickly becoming prominent as a scout. He was in the Battle of Concepción October 25, 1835; he was prominent in the Grass Fight and the defeat of Cos at Bexar (San Antonio), where he was wounded. In December he guided Francis W. Johnson's troops into San Antonio. He heard of the fall of the Alamo after the event and was sent by Houston to obtain particulars; it is said that he went to·Santa Anna himself and obtained the release of Mrs. Almeron Dickerson and her child who had been spared when the Alamo fell. In March 1836 Houston made Smith captain of a scout company, covering the withdrawal of Houston from Gonzales to San Jacinto. April 19, 1836, Smith learned that Santa Anna was nearby and on the 21st destroyed a bridge the Mexican wished to use, a stroke that many believed decided the course of the Revolution. Deaf Smith ended the war one of Texas's heroes, although he never held much rank if among the most active of the revolutionary combatants. He captained a party of Rangers briefly after conclusion of hostilities but soon withdrew into retirement at Richmond,

Texas, in Fort Bend County, where he died. A portrait of Smith, painted at Houston's request, hangs in the Houston Public Library. Deaf Smith County, organized in 1890, was named for him.

Frontier Times, Vol. 9, No. 5 (Feb. 1932), 236-40; HT.

Smith, F.H., adventurer (fl. 1899). B. either in Chicago or New York City, Smith reportedly had gone south from Colorado into New Mexico with Sheriff Ed Farr, and was engaged "as a lark" in a gunfight with the Carver-Lay band of train robbers at Turkey Canyon, near Cimarron, July 16, 1899. Smith received a "serious but not dangerous wound" in the leg. He recovered. Smith returned to his eastern home immediately and did not testify at the Elza Lay (Bill McGinnis) trial.

Ed Bartholomew, *Western Hard-Cases.* Ruidoso, N.M., Frontier Book Co., 1960; Jeff Burton, "Suddenly in a Secluded and Rugged Place." London, English Westerner' Soc., *Brand Book,* Apr., July 1972.

Smith, George Albert Sr., Mormon leader (June 26, 1817-Sept. 1, 1875). B. at Potsdam, New York, he was a cousin of Joseph Smith, Mormon prophet and founder of the Church of Jesus Christ of Latter-day Saints, and early joined the movement. In 1833 he was with the saints at Kirtland, Ohio, and worked on the Kirtland temple. "He was one of those who went up to redeem Zion in Jackson County, Missouri (where the Mormons came into difficulties with their gentile neighbors),... traveling some 2,000 miles, most of the way on foot." Smith was ordained in 1839 an apostle of the church, one of the 12-man guiding board of the faith. In 1846-47 he migrated from Nauvoo, Illinois, to the Salt Lake basin, walking, he said, 1,700 miles and riding horseback 800; he claimed to have planted the first potato in the valley. He became a foremost pioneer of the Mormon endeavor, laying out Parowan, Utah, in 1850, with Ezra Taft Benson; Pleasant Grove, Utah, in 1853, and other communities. In 1857 Smith may have had some involvement in the notorious Mountain Meadows Massacre, although he took no direct part in the atrocity; Wise considered him a principal architect and plotter of the affair, although Brooks is more temperate in her assessment, conceding however, in passages she reprints, that he helped through his eloquence and personality to whip up the sentiment and emotion which made the crime possible. Certainly he knew of it shortly after it was committed, visited the site July 29, 1858, almost a year afterward, and sent two reports on it to Brigham Young, one August 6, 1858, and another on August 17. The first was a whitewash of the Mormon role in the affair, and the second laid all the blame on the Indians. In a deposition in 1875 Smith swore that "he never directly or indirectly aided, abetted, or assisted in perpetration (of the massacre), or had any knowledge thereof, except by heresay..." Bancroft said that "almost until the day of his death (he) took a prominent part in settling and redeeming the vales of Deseret (Utah)." He was appointed church historian and in 1868 first counsellor to Brigham Young, holding from time to time other high offices. In 1860 a son was killed by Navaho Indians.

Bancroft, *Utah;* Juanita Brooks, *The Mountain Meadows Massacre.* Norman, Univ. of Okla. Press, 1966; William Wise, *Massacre at Mountain Meadows.* N.Y., Thomas Y. Crowell Co., 1976.

Smith, George Albert Jr., Mormon pioneer (July 7, 1843-Nov. 2, 1860). The son of the apostle, George Jr. was fond of horses and good equipment, having spent $319 for two animals and an outfit to accompany Jacob Hamblin on a missionary expedition to northern Arizona; he had taught his gray mare numerous tricks, legend reports. His mare ran away to join Indian horses at a camp east of the Colorado River; George Smith found her in possession of a Navaho, and in a resulting fracas was mortally wounded.

Frank Esshom, *Pioneers and Prominent Men of Utah.* Salt Lake City, Western Epics, 1966; Juanita Brooks, *John D. Lee.* Glendale, Calif., Arthur H. Clark Co., 1962.

Smith, George W., soldier (c. 1848-Sept. 13, 1874). B. at Greenfield, New York, he enlisted at Green Point, New York, for five years from January 31, 1870, in Company M, 6th Cavalry. Smith was of a detachment of four enlisted men and two scouts assigned in September 1874 to carry dispatches from Miles's headquarters on McClellan Creek, Texas to Camp Supply, Indian Territory. Near the Dry Fork of the Washita River they were attacked by Kiowas and Smith was wounded

mortally at first fire. He was left for dead as the others withdrew to a buffalo wallow for defense, but later found to be alive and was brought to the depression by Amos Chapman and perhaps others. He died early on September 13. November 4, 1874, Smith posthumously was awarded the Medal of Honor as were the survivors of the famous Buffalo Wallow Fight.

William H. Leckie, *The Military Conquest of the Southern Plains.* Norman, Univ. of Okla. Press, 1963; MH; *Deeds of Valor, II;* Smith Military Record, Natl. Archives.

Smith, George Washington, army officer (Mar. 11, 1837-Aug. 19, 1881). B. in Virginia, Smith was commissioned from Kansas in the 18th Infantry in 1861, being breveted to lieutenant colonel in the Civil War and becoming a friend of Lew Wallace's. Smith resigned in 1866. In 1873 he accepted a commission as second lieutenant in the 9th Cavalry, serving in New Mexico where he saw some action against the Apaches. At Fort Stanton he was peripherally involved in the Lincoln County War policing and peace-keeping activities. In August 1878, Smith accompanied Captain Henry Carroll on a scout to Dog Canyon, was injured when his horse fell on him, and was sent to the Mescalero Reservation or Stanton, to recuperate. He was there when McSween's faction killed the clerk, Morris Bernstein. When Victorio fled the Mescalero reserve in August of 1879, Smith first took up the pursuit, chasing the hostiles toward the Rio Grande and perhaps beyond. In 1880 his rapid movements were credited with saving the Mescalero Agency from attack by Apaches. In August of 1881 Nana's finale of his great southern New Mexico raid occurred near McEver's Ranch (Lake Valley); Smith and 19 troopers, with civilian George Daly and other non-Army personnel, collided with Nana; Smith was killed as were five others, including Daly, and at least three were wounded in the fight in Gavilan Canyon. The command lost 30 horses and about 1,000 rounds of ammunition to the hostiles as well. Smith's body was mutilated and partially burned; he was interred at Fort Bayard, New Mexico. Two years later the body was disinterred and "shipped east."

Philip J. Rasch, "The Men at Fort Stanton," English Westerners Soc., *Brand Book,* No. 3, Apr.

1961, p. 6; Dan L. Thrapp, *Victorio and the Mimbres Apaches,* Norman, Univ. of Okla. Press, 1974.

Smith, Henry, politician (May 20, 1788-Mar. 4, 1851). B. in Kentucky he reached Texas in 1827, settling in the present Brazoria County where he taught school and did some surveying. He was in the 1832 battle of Velasco, Texas, an engagement between Texans and Mexicans preliminary to the Texas move toward independence. Smith was wounded but recovered. He was elected alcalde for Brazoria and held other public offices, becoming one of the so-called independence party and the first American governor of Texas, later serving as secretory of the treasury under Houston. He continued to be prominent politically, although never diplomatic in or out of office. In 1849 he joined the gold rush to California and died at a mining camp in Los Angeles County. He had married three times and fathered nine children.

Frontier Times, Vol. 8, No. 6 (Mar. 1931), 241-42; HT.

Smith, Henry Clay (Hank), frontiersman (Aug. 15, 1836-May 1912). B. in Bavaria, Smith was orphaned at 12, and came to this country, serving briefly as a Lake Erie sailor. He was a member of the Captain Innis N. Palmer surveying party up the Missouri River in 1855-56. He went to California in 1858, observing enroute the ruins of the Fancher train at the site of the Mountain Meadow Massacre which had occurred in September 1857. After a time at San Bernardino, he went to the Gila mines of Arizona, probably late in 1858. He claimed to have seen the "desert shipwreck" enroute to Yuma. The mines played out and Smith worked variously as a teamster, market hunter, prospector, engaged in skirmishes with Indians and herded stock, taking 1,200 cattle eastward through Apache Pass toward the Rio Grande, contacting the Chiricahuas and then the Mimbres Apaches enroute, but finding them peaceful. He turned the herd over to the army at Fort Bliss. With others he made a gold strike at Pinos Altos in 1859, almost a full year before the official discovery of those important deposits. He was there as Pinos Altos developed boom proportions. He was in on considerable Indian fighting as the Mimbres, abused by the whites, retaliated with vigor. Smith with others

prospected up into the White Mountains, located some gold sign on the upper Gila, then returned to Pinos Altos. He was in the fight resulting in the killing of Elías, a Chiricahua or Mimbres chief. After more Indian skirmishes, Smith with others joined Confederate Lieutenant Colonel John R. Baylor after he reached Mesilla in July 1861. He continued to serve the Confederate cause, more or less in the capacity of scout, or irregular, who thoroughly knew the country. Smith was the only witness to the shooting of Mesilla editor Robert P. Kelley by Baylor in December 1862. Smith reportedly was captured by Union forces, briefly joined them, deserted and returned to the Confederate side. After the war he was a government contractor at El Paso and Fort Quitman, and a freighter between San Antonio and Fort Griffin. In 1878 he established a ranch in Crawfish Canyon, becoming the first permanent settler of Crosby County, Texas, filling several county government positions. Part of his ranch, including the rock house in which he and his wife lived, is a Texas state park.

Panhandle Plains Hist. Rev., Vol. I, No. 1 (1928), 67-115; Vol. II, No. 1 (1929), 65-97; HT.

Smith, Henry Percival Adams, attorney (Feb. 4, 1820-Dec. 20, 1868). B. at Franconia, New Hampshire, he studied law and was admitted to the bar in Maine in 1848. In 1858 or 1859 he joined the Colorado gold rush, taking part in political maneuvers preliminary to organization of Colorado as a Territory; it was he who suggested naming the new community for James William Denver, governor of Kansas of which Colorado then was a part. Smith was named probate judge of Arapahoe County, in which Denver was located. One Sunday morning in a card game he lost thirty town lots in less than ten minutes. Smith lived mainly in Gilpin County, Colorado. In addition to his law activities he was an amateur actor, Iago being his favorite character. He reached the Montana gold fields in 1862 in the party of Samuel McLean, George Washington Stapleton and Tom Cover, settling initially at Bannack. Eventually he moved to Virginia City where his professional talents were called upon to defend Charley Forbes (Edward Richardson) and Hayes Lyons, who had shot to death John Dillingham, an honest deputy sheriff in June 1863. The pair got off. Smith also defended George Hilderman and George

Ives who was first of the Plummer gang to be executed by Montana vigilantes. This time Smith's talents were not enough. For his defense of the Plummer people, however Smith was banished for two years which he spent for the most part in Arizona, then returned to Montana, practicing law at Helena until his death. He was a "man of remarkable ability in his profession, and of correct and generous impulses. To a clear and logical mind, and thorough knowledge of his profession, he added fine powers as an orator; and it was these qualities, more than any sympathy he indulged for his clients, that rendered him obnoxious to public censure and suspicion." A noted tippler, it was universally felt that dissipation was the primary cause of his demise. He left a widow, son and two daughters, residents of Maine.

Langford; Dimsdale, 77-82; *Montana Contributions*, Vol. IV, 233; Stanley W. Zamonski, Teddy Keller, *The Fifty-Niners.* Denver, Sage Books, 1961, p. 39; *Helena Weekly Herald,* Dec. 21, 1868; *Rocky Mountain News,* Denver, Dec. 7, 1870.

Smith, Henry Street (Billy the Kid), pioneer (c. 1860-Oct. 17, 1955). Smith was believed by some to be Henry McCarty, alias Billy the Kid, who, they said, was not killed by Pat Garrett as history records, after all. Typical of many suspected to be the genuine articles rather than the notorious figures supposedly demised, Smith's credentials are better than most. By 1943 Smith had moved from El Paso, Texas, to Duncan, Arizona, where a specialist on the Kid, Leslie Traylor, interviewed him at length. Smith himself never claimed to be the Kid, but from a variety of clues Traylor believed him to have been. He died at the Arizona Pioneers Home, Prescott, and is buried in its cemetery.

Ed Bartholomew, *Western Hard-Cases.* Ruidoso, N.M. Frontier Book Co., 1960.

Smith, Hugh Dickson (Shine), Presbyterian missionary (Aug. 24, 1882-Dec. 18, 1966). B. at Rome, Georgia, he was graduated from the Presbyterian Theological Seminary, Austin, Texas, in 1912, ordained and assigned to a church at Coleman, Texas, where he spent four years as a cowboy preacher, learning the cattle trade as well as minding his flock. June 5, 1917 he commenced a work among the Arizona Navahos, mastering their language and pastoring a church at Chinlee on the Navaho Reservation. After three years he resigned and spent his remaining 45 years on the Reservation as a freelance missionary, coming to widespread prominence as one of the respected and best known Christian workers of the Southwest. Early in his career he taught Indian children a hymn which repeatedly included the word "shine"; they dubbed the minister "Shine," and from that time forward he was known everywhere as Shine Smith. He had an adventurous, rewarding career among the Navahos and occasional Paiutes, serving them in sickness and in health, burying their dead, roaming the reservation on horseback and in later years by pickup truck or other vehicle. He frequently penetrated the wilder, more remote areas of the region, serving equally outlaws, renegades and solitary families of Indians. Smith operated mainly out of Tuba City, Arizona. He became acquainted with such noted figures as writer Zane Grey and traders S.I. and Hubert Richardson among others. Because of failing health he retired to Flagstaff in his early 80s, entered a rest home at Winslow, Arizona, a month before his death and at his request his body was buried "in a plain, unadorned pine box," at Tuba City on the Reservation. He never married.

Maurice Kildare, "The Indians Named Him Shine," *Frontier Times,* Vol. 40, No. 6 (Oct. -Nov. 1966), 20-23, 50-51; Ariz. Hist. Soc. Archives.

Smith, I.C., physician, linguist (d. Aug. 21, 1884). According to Montana Supreme Court Justice Llewellyn L. Callaway, Smith "was a famous man in Alder Gulch (Virginia City, Montana); an unusual man, a genius." Smith reached Virginia City in June 1863, the first week after founding of the camp, and in 1863-64 he served "with distinction" in the Idaho Legislature (Montana then being part of Idaho). His place and date of birth are unreported. His wife and children were killed by Indians according to Callaway who said "it occurred when they were passengers in a stagecoach coming west," no doubt to join Smith. An able and inventive physician, Smith "performed acts as a surgeon which made eastern surgeons famous years afterward. I am sure he was the originator of the cardiagraph in the (18)70s — long before the discovery was assigned to another. He drank too much whiskey, but was a hero when sober," Callaway added. In 1877 Callaway's father, James

E. Callaway organized a company of volunteers to help Howard in his fight against the Nez Perces, Smith being a member of the company. When the Indians under Looking Glass attacked the joint encampment at Camas Meadows, Idaho, August 20, 1877, Dr. Smith who understood the Nez Perce tongue "told the officers of Howard's command the orders given (by Looking Glass); they said his tactics were as perfect as if he were a graduate of West Point." From Virginia City Dr. Smith left August 21, 1884, in answer to a sick call from a rancher in the Madison Valley, 20 miles distant. Searchers on Saturday found him lying under his upset wagon, his neck broken and "death must have been instantaneous."

L.L. Callaway letter to Mrs. Ralph Ortel, Nov. 2, 1950, copy in Mont. Hist. Soc. archives; Deer Lodge, Mont. *New North-West,* Aug. 29, 1884.

Smith, J.B., justice of the peace (c. 1827-c. 1886). B. in Missouri, he was appointed justice of the peace February 1, 1882, at Charleston and Contention, Arizona, and issued arrest warrants for Holliday and two Earps, charging them with murder in the OK Corral affair at Tombstone, Arizona. The cases were transferred to Tombstone, and disposed of. Smith, in 1886, killed George (Crazy Horse) Thompson, a onetime Kansas lawman and Earp friend, in Jerry Barton's saloon at Fairbank, Arizona, but was freed. He dropped dead in a Tombstone restaurant.

Ed Bartholomew, *Wyatt Earp: The Man & the Myth.* Toyahvale, Tex., Frontier Book Co., 1964.

Smith, Jacob Ward, pioneer (1830-Jan.23, 1897). B. at New York City, he learned the butcher's trade and removed to Virginia City, Nevada, in 1859. Smith gradually worked into stock brokering and silver speculation, but he went bankrupt and moved to Montana in 1866. He took part in the 1870 Washburn expedition to the Yellowstone country where his ready good humor, wit and ebullient spirits gave much lift to the expedition, although he irritated Langford, as is revealed in the latter's book. In 1872 Jake returned to San Francisco, became a broker again, soon was a millionaire and almost as quickly broke once more; his wife divorced him in 1892 and Smith married again. He died of apoplexy at San Francisco.

Aubrey L. Haines, *Yellowstone National Park: Its Exploration and Establishment.* Wash., Nat. Park Service, 1974.

Smith, James, pioneer (1737-1812). B. in Franklin County, Pennsylvania, he was captured by Indians in 1755, remaining in captivity for four years. He was at Fort Duquesne at the time of Braddock's defeat obtaining first hand information of the French and Indians who assailed the British expedition. Smith escaped near Montreal after obtaining much primary data about border warfare from the Indian side and a knowledge of their character and principal men. He served as an ensign in 1763 and was a lieutenant under Henry Bouquet in 1764. For several years he was a leader of the Black Boys, a regulator type of organization for border tranquility, including in their activities the policing of traders who, the Black Boys suspected, supplied the Indians with arms; the band was so-named because of the members' custom of painting their faces black and red after the Indian manner. In 1766-67 with a small party Smith explored into Tennessee, believed to have been the first whites of record other than the hunter, Henry Scaggs, to probe into eastern Tennessee. As troubles with Britain mounted Smith was chosen for frontier service. He was a captain in the Pennsylvania border country, then in 1777 a major under Washington and in 1778 as a colonel of militia led an expedition against an Indian town on French Creek. After the Revolution he went to Kentucky, moving there permanently in 1788, settling at Cane Ridge, Bourbon County, near the town of Paris. He filled public offices and preached among the Indians, also performing Presbyterian missionary labors in Kentucky and Tennessee. Smith is remembered historically for his book, *An Account of the Remarkable Occurrences in the Life and Travels of Col. James Smith...*(1799), a work of much value which has been reprinted several times. He also published *A Treatise on the Mode and Manner of Indian War...*(1812), drawn largely from his earlier volume. He was married twice, fathered seven children, and died in Washington County, Kentucky.

Alexander Scott Withers, *Chronicles of Border Warfare,* ed. by Reuben Gold Thwaites, Lyman Copeland Draper. Parsons, W. Va., McClain Printing Co., 1970; Harriette Simpson Arnow, *Seedtime on the Cumberland.* N.Y., Macmillan Co., 1960.

Smith, James, victim (d. Nov. 10, 1870). Smith, whose name "obviously was an alias," was shot down by vigilantes who suspected him of horse thievery in the incident which eliminated four Butler County, Kansas, suspected rustlers, including Jack Corbin, scout for Custer.

Butler County Hist. Soc. Archives, El Dorado, Kan.

Smith, James W. (Six-Shooter Bill, John Henry Jankins) desperado (c. 1856-Aug. 1882). B. probably in Texas, he was first reported around Gainesville, Texas. A Bill Smith was wanted for murder in Cooke County, Texas, in 1878; about this time Six-Shooter Smith showed up in Kansas. August 17, 1878, Bat Masterson arrested Six-Shooter for horse theft near Dodge City, Kansas. In 1879 Smith went west with the "Dodge City gang," worked Las Vegas, New Mexico, where he knew most of the underworld, then moved on to Deming, New Mexico, and Tombstone, Arizona. As a rustler he was wounded in the San Simon valley in a fight with ranchers in November 1881. He was a master of small-time rackets, such as hijacking railroad hoboes for $2 a division for their rides, and as a "caricature of Hoodoo Brown," reigned over the "vice town" of Mimbres, 10 miles east of Deming, New Mexico, but was hustled on and settled next at Benson, Arizona, where he was involved in at least one shooting scrape. Eventually he again was run out, made San Marcial, New Mexico, then headed for Laredo, Texas, where he was known as California Jim. Working at a Laredo cafe, he quarreled with his boss and with his pistol made him dance a jig, and when the chief of police arrived, mortally wounded the officer. He hiked up the railroad tracks toward San Antonio, and at Cactus, Texas, robbed the station agent. At Cibolo, Texas, he was accosted by two cowboys, Charles Smith and Wesley de Spain. Wesley was wounded and Six-Shooter mortally shot, dying at 3 a.m. the next day. Much of his life is obscure, but he was colorful.

Ed Bartholomew, *Wyatt Earp: The Unknown Story, Wyatt Earp: The Man & the Myth.* Toyahvale, Tex., Frontier Book Co., 1963, 1964; Ed Bartholomew, *Western Hard-Cases.* Ruidoso, N.M., Frontier Book Co., 1960.

Smith Jedediah, mountain man (Jan. 6, 1799-May 27, 1831). B. at Bainbridge, New York, he was raised in Erie County, Pennsylvania,

and the Western Reserve of Ohio, receiving some education and strong religious (Methodist) motivation. He reached St. Louis in 1822, determined to become a trapper in the Oregon country. Joining Ashley, he went up the Missouri to the mouth of the Yellowstone, remaining under Andrew Henry and wintering on the Musselshell River. In the spring he was sent with a message to Ashley, encountering him below the Arikara villages, and distinguished himself for bravery in the fight against those Indians June 1, 1823. He then volunteered to cross the plains, contact Henry and bring back reinforcements, which he did, rejoining Ashley at the mouth of the Cheyenne River. After Leavenworth's indecisive operation against the Arikaras, Smith with a group of a dozen men, among whom were Clyman and Fitzpatrick, crossed the plains south of the Yellowstone to open up new trapping grounds. Before they reached the Powder River Smith was mauled by a grizzly, scarred for life, and wore long hair thereafter to conceal the evidence. The party wintered with the Crows, then crossed by way of South Pass to the Green River. In September 1824, Smith contacted Hudson's Bay Company trappers in Idaho. With Ashley he brought nearly 9,000 pounds of beaver to St. Louis late in 1825, returning to the mountains within a month, now a partner in the business. With Ashley he pioneered the Oregon Trail to the mountains. The next summer Smith joined Jackson and Sublette in a partnership succeeding the Ashley enterprise. Smith, about August 15, 1826, took a party from Cache Valley south by way of Utah Lake, the Sevier River, Virgin River and the Colorado River to the Mohave villages, thence across southern California to San Gabriel Mission. After some difficulty with Spanish authorities, Smith worked up the San Joaquin River to the American River. With three men he crossed the Sierra Nevada in May and June by way of Ebbetts pass to Walker Lake and by July 2 had regained Cache Valley and the rendezvous at Bear Lake. With 18 men on July 13, 1827, Smith left the rendezvous and headed for California again. At the Mohave villages half of his men were killed by Indians at the Colorado River crossing. Smith and the others retraced their earlier route to the San Gabriel Mission, then north to the old camp on the Stanislaus River, arriving September 18. He became embroiled in difficulties with the Mexican-Spanish officials, but sold his furs to a sea captain, John Bradshaw, bought horses for later sale in the Rocky Mountains, trapped central and northern California, reached the Klamath River, Oregon, May 3, 1828, and the ocean May 19 after great difficulties. The group worked up the coast, reaching the Rogue River June 27 and the Umpqua July 12; two days later 14 of Smith's men and an Indian boy were massacred by the Kalawatset Indians; Smith and three others, being away from camp, escaped, reaching Fort Vancouver August 8 and 10. Smith with another left Vancouver March 12, 1829, and returned to the upper Rockies. He trapped the Blackfoot country with Bridger. At the 1830 rendezvous at the Wind and Popo Agie rivers, Smith and his partners sold out to five famous mountain men who formed the Rocky Mountain Fur Company, and Smith returned to St. Louis. He bought a house but shortly organized a caravan to Santa Fe, 74 men with 22 wagons, half belonging to himself. They left St. Louis April 10, 1831. By late May they had been three days without water in the dry country between the Arkansas and Cimarron rivers. Smith and Fitzpatrick went ahead searching for water, separated, Smith rode on and disappeared. Indians, having reached Santa Fe with some of Smith's equipment, reported that 20 Comanches had been concealed at a water hole awaiting buffalo when Smith rode up. In a fight Smith killed the leader of the party, but was himself slain. Smith was perhaps the greatest of the mountain men, and one of the strongest characters among them. He was abstemious, did not smoke, was clean shaven, ever carried a Bible and read from it, was habituated to command and was referred to as Mister Smith or Captain Smith by others. He figures in the three most disastrous battles mountain men engaged in, although he was not to blame for any of them; his contributions to geographical knowledge of the west, and his pioneering expeditions were of great value; his journals and records suggest that he intended at some time to publish his findings, but his early and lamented death aborted that plan, if he held it. Smith was more than 6 feet tall, spare, a man of great courage, vision, dedication and persistence; so far as the record shows he was not a man of much humor, but that is guesswork since there is no way for those unacquainted with him in person to judge. "Among the mountain men...he stands alone, and it was alone that he died."

Literature abundant: Maurice S. Sullivan, *Jedediah Smith: Trader & Trailbreaker*. N.Y., Press of Pioneers, 1936; Dale Morgan, *Jedediah Smith and the Opening of the West*. Indianapolis, Bobbs-Merrill Co., 1953; D.W. Garber, *Jedediah Strong Smith: Fur Trader from Ohio*. Stockton, Calif., Univ. of Pacific, 1973; Harvey L. Carter article, MM, Vol. VIII.

Smith, Jefferson Randolph (Soapy), confidence man (1860-July 8, 1898). B. in Georgia, he became a cowboy in Karnes County, Texas, went north with trail herds, and then became a confidence man, working a variety of games in Texas, New Mexico, Colorado, Kansas and Old Mexico. For example at Creede, Colorado, he caused to be secretly buried and openly uncovered a 10-foot statue of a "prehistoric man," on which he collected from gullible sight-seers. He won his nickname, it is reported, by selling bars of soap for $5 under the illusion that some lucky purchaser would find a $20 bill wrapped around his purchase, although none but shills were apt to make the discovery. In 1897 he joined the Alaska gold rush, but found his wealth running the underworld in Skagway where he and his crooks fleeced thousands. When the honest citizens organized a "Committee of 101" to enforce the law, Soapy and his people formed a "Committee of 303" to oppose them. He offered President McKinley a privately-raised company of men for the Spanish-American War. The offer was not accepted. In an odd confrontation, Smith had a three-hour conference with the Salvation Army's attractive Evangeline Booth, who had taken a party to Skagway to save souls; the meeting ending with a prayer session in which Smith participated. Whether he was converted will never be known, however, for six weeks later when Soapy tried to crash a vigilante meeting on the wharf there was a shoot-out between Smith and Frank Reid, the city engineer. Smith was killed outright and Reid died 12 days later. Funeral services were held for Soapy in a church he had helped build, the minister's text, from Proverbs xiii, 15, "The way of transgressors is hard."

Ed Bartholomew, *Western Hard-Cases: or, Gunfighters Named Smith*. Ruidoso, N.M., Frontier Book Co., 1960; *Decision*, July 1965.

Smith, Jim, renegade (fl. 1869). Smith, a member of Jack Swilling's party to locate Phoenix, on August 2, 1869, shot to death James Nelson, another member and fled, presumably to the Indians. On December 3, 1870, a man presumed to be Smith, dressed in buckskin and carrying a Henry rifle, visited a ranch on the upper Hassayampa River, in central Arizona, secured food and was tracked to where his trail joined that of Indians and disappeared. No more was ever heard certainly of him.

Farish, VI.

Smith, Jim (Limpy), buffalo hunter (fl. 1877). In March 1877, Smith was second in command of a party of about 45 buffalo hunters engaged in a punitive expedition against the Comanches of the Staked Plains region. At Rath's Store later Smith killed Tom Lumpkins in a duel; he surrendered himself at Fort Griffin later that year and was "tried," the verdict being "justifiable homicide." Although Bartholomew called this Smith "Hog" Smith, Hog Smith in fact was a different man. Bartholomew also dates the Lumpkins duel 1876, which is in error.

John R. Cook, *The Border and the Buffalo.* Chicago, Lakeside Press, 1938; Ed Bartholomew, *Western Hard-Cases.* Ruidoso, N.M., Frontier Book Co., 1960.

Smith, John, adventurer, explorer (Jan. 1579/80-June 21, 1631). B. at Willoughby, Lincolnshire, England, he quickly discovered that merchandizing had little charm for him and went soldiering on the continent. At length he found himself in Transylvania fighting the Turks, was captured, sent to Constantinople and eventually became a slave but killed his master and escaped. He again roved Europe where he recounted having numerous adventures, some unverifiable today, but his account substantiated in a number of particulars. Smith returned to England about 1604 and soon engaged in preparations for the colonization program of the Virginia Company. He sailed for Virginia in late 1606 and was among the 105 colonists who debarked May 24, 1607, at the site of Jamestown where he was a member of the seven-man council although not at first permitted to sit with it. He immediately engaged in exploration of the vicinity, revealing qualities of courage, resourcefulness and energy which led him to become in a

broad sense a savior of the enterprise. The colonists were sickly, had little idea of agriculture or what was required to survive in a pristine wilderness; the Indians, while friendly at first, were soon disenchanted by the persistent demands upon them for food to feed these strangers who seemed to produce little for themselves, and it was John Smith's enterprise almost alone that brought in the trickles of grain and game that enabled them to endure the first years. When Smith, after two companions had been slain by the Powhatan Indians, fell into their hands and according to his account was condemned to death only to be saved by Pocahontas, the chief's daughter, the two became friends. In the summer of 1608 Smith explored the Potomac and Rappahanock rivers and went up Chesapeake Bay to its head; he drafted a useful map of Virginia including the Bay and the rivers he had traversed. Smith had little faith in the existence of gold deposits in Virginia and resisted demands from the Company officials at London that he divert resources and personnel to hunt for them. He became president of the Council and against opposition from some quarters "carried the colony through periods of intense suffering, hunger, and want, remaining firm, tactful, and resourceful." Injured by an explosion in 1609 he sailed for England in October. In 1614 he went to New England for London merchants, returning with a valuable cargo of fish and furs, a good map of the coast and the conviction that New England was a favorable site for future colonization. He also argued the great value of such resources as fish and furs, both readily marketable in Europe. The following year he started on another voyage to the New World, financed this time by Ferdinando Gorges, but was captured by pirates and then by the French, eventually returning to England. His several writings and maps added to the importance of his discoveries and adventures, and made permanent much of the record; his writings are summarized fairly well in his *Generall Historie of Virginia, New-England and the Summer Isles* (1624, often reprinted), and his work has inspired an extensive bibliography. "Apparently he had gained, as he deserved, high repute among those engaged in American colonization," while his career has been of interest to historians until this day. He died in England.

Literature abundant.

Smith, John (Jack, O-toz-vout-si, Wo-pe-kon-ne), victim (c. 1842-Nov. 30, 1864). The son of John Simpson Smith and Wapoola, his Cheyenne wife, Jack grew up as a Cheyenne, subject to the solicitude of an affectionate mother and the harsh discipline of a stern father. Although Cheyenne was his native tongue, he also was fluent in English and occasionally was used as an interpreter. Lewis Garrard met him when he was 3 or 4 years of age, "plainly showing in his complexion and features the mingling of American and Indian blood." In October 1858 Jack Smith was panning gold in Colorado, making $14 a week, it was reported. By the Treaty of February 18, 1861, with the Arapaho and Cheyenne, Jack was granted 649 acres of land on the north side of the Arkansas river above Bent's Old Fort. In his majority Jack Smith looked "far more white than Indian," but associated largely with the bands of Black Kettle, White Antelope, Left Hand and others. He was with them at their Denver Council September 28, 1864, and accompanied them back to Fort Lyon where, under the impression they would be protected by the military, they were advised to camp at Sand Creek, Colorado, Smith residing with them. At the November 29, 1864, Chivington-led Sand Creek Massacre, Jack Smith was captured while his father was protected by Chivington himself. The elder Smith, knowing Jack was to be shot, muttered "I can't help it," as he could not. Smith was murdered in a Cheyenne lodge by a soldier of Company E, 1st Colorado Cavalry, after Chivington, asked by First Lieutenant Clark Dunn if he objected to Jack's being killed, said he need not be asked about it, he had already directed that no prisoners were to be taken.

The Sand Creek Massacre; Stan Hoig, *The Western Odyssey of John Simpson Smith.* Glendale, Calif., Arthur H. Clark Co., 1974; Lewis H. Garrard, *Wah-to-yah and the Taos Trail.* Norman, Univ. of Okla. Press, 1955.

Smith, John Simpson, trader, frontiersman (1810-June 29, 1871). B. at Frankfort, Kentucky, he was an upper Rockies trapper by 1830, on one occasion doing in seven Blackfeet by trickery and earning the nickname Blackfoot Smith. By 1843 he was at Fort Laramie and by 1846 at Bent's Fort, being host, incidentally, to Lewis Garrard who wrote of him, Smith assisting him in his study of the Cheyenne language. As a Cheyenne trader, Smith also met Ruxton, one theory being that he was the prototype for "Killbuck" in the Englishman's classic, *Life in the Far West.* Smith was an interpreter for the important Fort Laramie treaty council in 1851 which Thomas Fitzpatrick managed, and as interpreter accompanied a Sioux, Cheyenne and Arapaho peace mission to Washington, D.C. Smith briefly was a guide for the army's Utah Expedition of 1857, but did not go all the way to Salt Lake. He was a pioneer founder of Denver and neighboring communities; by 1862 he was living at Fort Lyon, Colorado. In 1864 he, as interpreter, had helped persuade the Cheyennes under Black Kettle to camp at Sand Creek, Colorado, and when the Chivington massacre occurred there November 29, Smith tried vainly to prevent it; his son, Jack, was murdered and Smith narrowly escaped death. He gave testimony to an investigating committee on the disaster, and when the Cheyennes settled down after the resulting war, Smith served as interpreter at the Little Arkansas council, then accompanied the Cheyennes to their new reservation in Indian Territory. He remained with them as friend, counselor and, through his Cheyenne wife, kinsman, until he died.

Ann W. Hafen article, MM, Vol. V; Lewis H. Garrard, *Wah-To-Yah and the Taos Trail.* Norman, Univ. of Okla. Press, 1955; George Frederick Ruxton, *Life in the Far West.* Norman, 1951; *The Sand Creek Massacre: A Documentary History.* N.Y., Sol Lewis, 1973, reprinting government documents thereon, first series, 5-12; 84-88; second series, 58-61; third series, 125-28; Stan Hoig, *The Western Odyssey of John Simpson Smith.* Glendale, Calif., Arthur H. Clark Co., 1974.

Smith, Joseph, Mormon pioneer (fl. 1857-1892). A resident of Cedar City, Utah, a man of this name was placed by *Mormonism Unveiled* at the Mountain Meadows Massacre of September 11, 1857, either participating in or consenting to the tragedy. He appears to have been still alive when the book was published.

Mormonism Unveiled, 380.

Smith, Lot, Mormon soldier (May 15, 1830-June 21, 1892). B. in Oswego County, New York, Smith at 16 marched to California with the Mormon Battalion, then moved on to Utah where he achieved note as an Indian fighter in several campaigns. He became an influential major of the Utah militia and achieved prominence during the 1857-58 so-called "Mormon War," operating against Albert Sidney Johnston's forces approaching Utah, capturing and burning two provision trains of 52 freight wagons east of Green River, Wyoming, and driving off oxen and beef cattle (Smith's lengthy narrative describing his operations in some detail is reprinted by the Hafens). Smith and his men "did what they could to impede (the United States forces) progress, but they were not much more effective than a swarm of mosquitos trying to stop a buffalo." In 1876 Mormon church leaders determined to effect the settlement of the Little Colorado country of northern Arizona, and Lot Smith was chosen by Brigham Young as the "strong hand needed to make the Arizona mission succeed," although he was autocratic and a difficult man to work with in many ways. Smith led the vanguard of settlers to the area between present-day Holbrook and Winslow, Arizona, he and his colleagues initiating "an era of Mormon colonization that extended well into the 1890's." With his full red beard, volatile manner and absolute dedication to the cause, Smith "was the most forceful character involved" in the project and "must be acknowledged as one of its most colorful and interesting figures. Unfortunately he was also over-bearing, intolerant, and hot-headed in the extreme. Assuming that his call to 'general overview' of the Arizona mission and later to the position of stake president gave him total command, he badgered, threatened, and fumed to make his denomination a reality... No real authority existed except as it related to the person of Smith...." Smith's Circle S Ranch extended from Mormon Lake to Tuba City; he built one home in a canyon near Tuba City and another within the community. In 1892 he became involved in an altercation with Navahos over their grazing of sheep on Mormon land; he shot several of the animals and was shot mortally by the Indians. He was buried as he requested in a canyon near his house, but later the body was exhumed and sent to Farmington, Utah, for final interment. Smith had at least eight wives.

Leroy R. and Ann W. Hafen, eds., *The Utah Expedition 1857-1858.* Glendale, Calif., Arthur H. Clark Co., 1958; Charles S. Peterson, *Take Up Your Mission: Mormon Colonizing Along the Little Colorado River 1870-1900.* Tucson, Univ. of Ariz. Press, 1973; Frank Esshom, *Pioneers and Prominent Men of Utah.* Salt Lake City, Western Epics, 1966.

Smith, (Origen) Charlie (Hairlip Charlie), frontiersman (c. 1849-c. 1890). Smith reached Arizona apparently from Texas where he had been seriously wounded at one time, and became "an efficient officer of the law, and a gambler as well." In Tombstone he resided for a time with Bob Winders, a sometimes associate of the Earps. Following a Benson to Tombstone stage robbery January 7, 1882, Smith and Fred Dodge joined Wyatt and Morgan Earp in a sweep after the desperadoes, but did not get them. In December 1883, Dodge and Smith searched for the perpetrators of the Bisbee Massacre of the 8th, but Charlie became ill while the roundup of suspects was still incomplete. Smith later made the arrest of Barney Riggs who had shot a man named Hudson, later being sentenced to life. Charlie Smith was a key member of the Fred Dodge crew that solved a train robbery which occurred April 27, 1887, at Pantano, Arizona, and a repeat at the same place August 10 by the same bandits. Shortly afterward, Smith and his erstwhile friend, Charley Cunningham (whom Smith had wounded in the leg in February 1886) got into a scrape and Cunningham shot Smith, shattering his leg near the hip after which "he was a cripple and could hardly get around and a couple of years later Died from the Effects of this wound."

Great Register of Cochise County, 1881; Ed Bartholomew, *Western Hard Cases or, Gunfighters Named Smith.* Ruidoso, N.M., Frontier Book Co., 1960, 32-34; Bartholomew, *Wyatt Earp: The Man & The Myth.* Toyahvale, Tex., Frontier Book Co., 1964; Fred Dodge, *Under Cover for Wells Fargo.* Boston, Houghton Mifflin Co., 1969.

Smith, Reuben, frontiersman (c. 1775-July 1828). B. probably in Bedford County, Virginia, and raised in Georgia, he received some education. He removed to Tennessee about 1795 and joined the army as an artillery officer by 1803. He resigned in 1806. Two years later he had reached the St. Genevieve district of Missouri. He was leader of one of the first expeditions to Santa Fe, leaving Missouri about November 20, 1809, the motives of the group uncertain, although the Burr-Wilkinson schemes may have been a factor (Reuben was brother of later Brigadier General Thomas Adams Smith and Colonel John Smith, the latter quite interested in the Burr project). Ostensibly the Reuben Smith undertaking was commercial in purpose. Early in 1810 the party was arrested by Spanish authorities among the Comanches, brought to Santa Fe, and sent to Chihuahua. After some harsh treatment, Smith and his colleagues were released in early 1812 and made their way to the Mississippi, arriving in April. Reuben Smith settled in Missouri again, farming and mining (at Bellefontaine). In 1825 at the age of 50 he married a teen-ager, Susan Caroline Horine, fathered two sons, and died comparatively well off.

W.A. Goff article, MM, Vol. VII.

Smith, Shine: *see* Hugh Dickson Smith.

Smith, Solomon Howard, pioneer (1809-1876). B. in New Hampshire, he became a Grand Banks fisherman, but joined Nathaniel Wyeth for his northwestern fur expedition. In 1832 the party joined a William Sublette brigade for the Rockies, attending the Pierre's Hole rendezvous, continuing on with Milton Sublette to the Columbia, Smith accompanying Wyeth to Fort Vancouver. Here he became a school teacher, starting the first educational institution in Oregon and settled at Chehalem Creek, later on the Clatsop Plains, near Astoria. Smith became a worthy pioneer and eventually state senator.

Harriet D. Munnick article, MM, Vol. VI.

Smith, (Thomas) Buckingham, historian (Oct. 31, 1810-Jan. 5, 1871). B. on Cumberland Island, Georgia, he in 1824-25 was with his father in Mexico where the elder Smith was U.S. Consul, and later was graduated from Harvard Law School, eventually practicing at St. Augustine, Florida. He became secretary of the U.S. consulate at Mexico City where he served from 1850-52 and of the consulate in Spain, 1855-58. Here he became acquainted with specialists in the Spanish archives and famed historians, continuing the archival research he had commenced in Mexico. Although a slaveholder, he sided with the North in the Civil War. His most important literary works included: *The Narrative of Alvar Nuñez*

Cabeza de Vaca (1851, 1871); *Narratives of the Career of Hernando de Soto in the Conquest of Florida, as told by a Knight of Elvas* (1866); *Letter of Hernando de Soto and Memoir of Hernando de Escalante Fontaneda* (1854), and *Collección de Varios Documentos para la Historia de la Florida y Tierras Adyacentes* (1857). His writings were many and varied. Smith suffered a stroke in New York City and a policeman, thinking him a drunk, locked him in a cell; he was taken the next morning to Bellevue Hospital where he died. He was about to be buried in a pauper's plot when his body was recognized and burial was at St. Augustine, Florida. Smith left his papers to the New York Historical Society and his property for the benefit of St. Augustine negroes.

DAB; *Who Was Who.*

Smith, Thomas James (Bear River Tom), lawman (June 12, 1840-Nov. 2, 1870). B. at New York City, Smith became a professional boxer. He joined the city police force; he was exonerated in the accidental shooting of a 14-year-old boy, but resigned the force and went west. Smith reportedly served in the army in Arizona, then joined the Union Pacific railroad in Wyoming, where he became a teamster at short-lived Bear River City, 12 miles southeast of present Evanston, Wyoming. Because of his fearlessness and dexterity with his fists, he was named the first law officer at the camp, assisting in putting down endless disturbances. He served similarly at Greeley, Colorado, and on June 4, 1870, because marshal at Abilene. A lawman who did not use a weapon, although he carried two pistols, Smith disarmed Abilene, making it an offense to carry guns within the city limits. Although this edict aroused resistance, Smith was backed by law-abiding members of the community. An assassination attempt against him failed. He continued to enforce the law with his fists, by August reportedly earning $225 a month. Apparently he killed no one during his career at Abilene. He went to Ellis, near the Kansas-Colorado border, where an assassination attempt against him also failed. He returned to Abilene, resumed his law enforcement duties, was appointed deputy and under sheriff of the county in addition to his job as marshal. Sent with an assistant to arrest Andrew McConnell, charged with murder at Detroit, a small settlement 10 miles from Abilene, Smith was shot but subdued McConnell when the latter's partner, Moses Miles, bludgeoned Smith to the ground and all but decapitated him with an axe. Miles and McConnell were captured three days later, Miles receiving 16 years and McConnell 12.

Carl W. Breihan, *Great Lawmen of the West.* N.Y., Bonanza Books, 1963; Joseph G. Rosa, *The Gunfighter: Man or Myth?* Norman, Univ. of Okla. Press, 1969; Ramon F. Adams, *Six-Guns and Saddle Leather.* Norman, 1969.

Smith, Thomas L (Pegleg), mountain man (Oct. 10, 1801-Oct. 15, 1866). B. in Garrard County, Kentucky, he left Missouri in 1820 for a two year trapping-trading expedition with Antoine Robidoux to the Sioux and Osage Indians. Smith went to Taos in 1824 and as a free trapper worked up the Rio Grande River and down the Grand River into Utah, then south to the San Juan River, and back to Taos by way of the Hopi and Navaho country. He trapped the eastern Great Basin the next year (1825), and in 1826 worked southeastern Colorado; in the fall he joined Ewing Young, working the Salt and Gila rivers; the outfit was joined by James Ohio Pattie and two other survivors of a Papago massacre of the Robidoux party. Skirmishing from time to time with various Indian tribes, sometimes perpetrating their own massacres, the whites worked up the Colorado. Smith and a small group left Young at the mouth of the Virgin River and trapped it and perhaps the Sevier River, but without much fortune, eventually, after hardships, regaining New Mexico. In the fall of 1827, in North Park, Colorado, Smith was wounded by Indians in the left leg; with Milton Sublette's help he amputated his foot, recovered and was taken by companions to the Green River where during the winter he was fitted with a wooden leg from which his nickname came. He reached Taos May 23, 1828. Smith attended the Bear Valley rendezvous in 1828 and reached Los Angeles, California, early in 1829, stealing more than 300 horses which he drove to Taos. He trapped the mountains until 1836 when he associated with the Ute chief, Walkara and Jim Beckwourth, burying and stealing horses from southern California. In 1839 he and Walkara made away with 3,000 California horses by theft. Smith established a trading post on the Oregon Trail in Bear

Valley, where he remained until 1850, being of great assistance to emigrants and others. He removed to Sacramento late in 1850. In 1854 he led an expedition from Los Angeles to the mouth of the Virgin River, searching for gold, but, according to report, finding only disappointment. He remained until his death in the San Francisco area. Pegleg Smith's greatest claim to fame for succeeding generations was in the probably mythical "Pegleg Smith gold" discovery, which he reportedly located by accident atop a hill in the California desert region while Smith was with a party enroute from the Colorado River to the coast. He apparently had little faith in the discovery himself, since aside from the 1854 expedition he spent no time hunting it up, but countless later treasure hunters have proved more enthusiastic. No one ever proven conclusively that it has been found.

Sardis Templeton, *The Lame Captain.* Los Angeles, Westernlore Press, 1965; Alfred Glen Humphreys article, MM, Vol. IV.

Smith, Tom (Three-Shooter Bill), minor desperado (fl. 1880s). So nicknamed because he was "only half as bad" as his buddy, Six Shooter Smith, Three-Shooter was of the same ilk, pursuing his little rackets in Las Vegas and other New Mexico railroad towns, being reported at Deming, San Marcial and elsewhere. His beginning and his end are lost in obscurity, which is just as well.

Ed Bartholomew, *Wyatt Earp: The Man & The Myth.* Toyahvale, Tex., Frontier Book Co., 1964.

Smith, Tom, gunman (d. Nov. 5, 1892). B. in Texas, he was a deputy U.S. marshal in Indian Territory and elsewhere in the West was a stock detective and partisan. He came to prominence during the Jaybird-Woodpecker War of Fort Bend County, Texas in 1888-90. The Jaybirds represented about 90 percent of the white population while the Woodpeckers counted about forty officials and former officials who were beneficiaries of black votes. Following various shootings, the Woodpeckers retained control after the 1888 election. The county became an armed camp and violence came to a head in the "battle of Richmond" August 16, 1889. Leaders on both sides were killed and others wounded. Smith, as deputy to Sheriff James Garvey of the Woodpecker faction swept up the officer's carbine after Garvey had been wounded mortally and killed Henry Forst, Jaybird leader, and wounded several others including Volney Gibson, another leader of the opposing faction. Smith was working as a stock detective in Wyoming when he was directed to recruit gunmen to assist the cattlemen's faction in a planned invasion of Johnson County, Wyoming, attacking small ranchers and others there. At Paris, Lamar County, Texas, he had no trouble picking up 22 young fighters who were told their job was merely to serve warrants on "dangerous outlaws," although there never were any warrants. Pay was to be $5 a day with a $50 bonus for each man killed. He chose men who as deputies or U.S. deputy marshals had fought against organized outlaws and thieves infesting the Brazos, Pecos and Panhandle counties of Texas, men who were not "of small or mean calibre." Smith named as his lieutenants G.R. Tucker (Booker), later chief of police and deputy U.S. marshal at Ardmore, Indian Territory, and Buck Garrett "who in later years was to write such pages of flaming heroism while serving as the sheriff of Ardmore." In April the invaders killed at the KC Ranch house Nick Ray and Nate Champion. When settlers became aroused by the assault the invaders withdrew toward the TA Ranch, although urged by Smith to go ahead and fight, which he believed they had come for. He was overruled and the besieged invasion party faced annihilation when U.S. Cavalry forces rescued and took them into custody. Eventually the Texans were released on their own recognizance and returned home, never having come to trial. Smith was killed by a black aboard a train in the Indian Territory; he was one of the last of the leaders of the Jaybird-Woodpecker feud to perish.

Helena Huntington Smith, *The War on Powder River*. N.Y., McGraw-Hill Book Co., 1966; Robert B. David, *Malcolm Campbell: Sheriff.* Casper, Wyo., Wyomingana, 1932; Ed Bartholomew, *Western Hard-Cases.* Ruidoso, N.M., Frontier Book Co., 1960, 149-50.

Smith, Van Ness Cummings, pioneer (July 12, 1837-Aug. 29, 1914). Known to southwesterners as Van C. Smith, he was b. at Ludlow, Windsor County, Vermont, and reached Arizona in 1863 by way of California, selecting a ranch and donating the initial acreage for the settlement of Prescott, of

which he was an original commissioner. Appointed by Governor John N. Goodwin on May 26, 1864, the first sheriff of Yavapai County, he served two months. Smith founded Roswell, New Mexico around 1871, naming it for his father Roswell Smith. He visited Tombstone shortly after the camp was established in 1879 and was named first deputy sheriff by John H. Behan. In 1882 Smith served as chief of scouts out of Fort Cummings, New Mexico. Later he prospected and ranched in Mexico and was a spy for Colonels Luther P. Bradley and Ranald Mackenzie, watching over activities of that nation's Apaches who periodically raided into the United States. At various times Smith held beef contracts for the army, traded, was a gambler for a time and roamed the southwest from Zuñi and Navaho country to below Janos and Corralitos in Mexico. He never married and died at Prescott. "He was of gentle disposition, but on the line of duty a more courageous man never lived." He was always popular and had a wide acquaintanceship throughout the region.

Ariz. Hist. Soc., Hayden Collec.; Dan L. Thrapp, *General Crook and the Sierra Madre Adventure.* Norman, Univ. of Okla. Press, 1972.

Smith, William (Bill), lawman (Apr. 24, 1848-Apr. 1908). B. in Leicestershire, England, his father brought the family to Utica, New York, in 1853, the next year to Lawrence, Kansas. During the Civil War Bill Smith served in the 11th Kansas (Infantry?), was stationed at Ft. Riley for a time. He and his brother, John, went to Wichita, Kansas, in 1869 when but eight families lived there, establishing a sawmill. Bill was defeated for sheriff of Sedgwick County, Kansas, in 1870, but served a month as city marshal. He served as deputy sheriff in 1873, was appointed sheriff in September 1873, and later was a deputy U.S. marshal. Bill was appointed marshal of Wichita, Kansas, where he also was constable, on April 15, 1874. Mike Meagher was elected April 8, 1875, to succeed him, although Smith apparently continued as constable for a time. In 1877 he moved to Galena, Kansas, where he became one of the first mayors, serving in 1895-96.

Ed Bartholomew, *Wyatt Earp: The Untold Story.* Toyahvale, Tex., Frontier Book Co., 1963; Kan. Hist. Soc. Archives .

Smith, William, desperado (1856-April 30, 1884). B. at Vernon, Texas, he was a ranch foreman in Kansas when with Henry Brown and others he attempted to rob the Medicine Lodge, Kansas, bank, was captured and lynched.

Nyle H. Miller, Joseph W. Snell, *Great Gunfighters of the Kansas Cowtowns, 1867-1886.* Lincoln, Univ. of Nebr. Press, 1967.

Smith, William Densley (Seco), frontiersman (Oct. 21, 1836-May 24, 1927). B. in Franklin County, Mississippi, he went with his parents to California during the gold rush and returned to Texas in 1856. He settled near San Antonio, later moving to the Seco River in Bandera County. "He engaged in many Indian fights, and made many scouts with Big Foot Wallace, and other noted frontiersmen." He was married three times and left 14 children. He died near Medina, Texas.

Frontier Times, Vol. 4, No. 10 (July 1927), 39.

Smohalla, Indian prophet (c. 1818-1907). His name, also given as Shmoquala, means "The Preacher" and was bestowed upon him after he attained fame through his religious activities. He was a chief of the Sokulk, a small tribe of between 150 to 200 members cognate to the Nez Perce and centering about Priest rapids on the Columbia in eastern Washington. In his boyhood Smohalla, a hunchback, frequented a Roman Catholic mission and absorbed some of its ritual and teachings. Despite his infirmity he became a noted warrior, around 1850 commenced to preach and acquired a reputation as a medicine man and visionary. His fame aroused the enmity of Moses, chief of the nearby Sinkiuse-Columbia; in a battle Smohalla was left for dead, but recovered enough to secretly leave his home and absent himself for a long time, roaming as far south as Mexico. Upon his return he said he had been to the spirit land and had been sent back to deliver a message to Indians: that they must return to their primitive mode of life, refuse teachings or articles of the white man, and in all things be guided by the dreams and visions of Smohalla and his priests. He acquired many followers, known as "Dreamers," among them Chief Joseph, Olikut and many Nez Perce leaders. For long after his death the new faith continued to flourish and may have adherents even today. Smohalla was married

ten times, his last wife surviving him, and he died and was buried in Washington State.

Hodge, HAI; Dockstader.

Smyth, Constantine, army officer (d. Dec. 28, 1835). B. in Ireland, he was commissioned from New York a second lieutenant in the Marine Corps August 27, 1825, transferred to the 2nd Artillery November 20, 1830, and became a first lieutenant May 30, 1832. He was a friend of Seminole Indian Agent Wiley Thompson, who had earned the fierce hostility of many Indians and was slain with Thompson in an ambush/assassination near Fort King, in central Florida.

Heitman; Edwin C. McReynolds, *The Seminoles.* Norman, Univ. of Okla. Press, 1967.

Snelling, Josiah, army officer (1782-Aug. 20, 1828). B. at Boston, Snelling was commissioned first lieutenant of the 4th Infantry May 3, 1808, and captain June 12, 1809. He fought at the Battle of Tippecanoe in 1811 as a company commander. Stationed at Detroit, he was taken prisoner at the outset of the War of 1812 when Hull capitulated, but was soon exchanged. He became major inspector general April 25, 1813, ended the War of 1812 a colonel inspector general and was retained as a lieutenant colonel of the 6th Infantry as of May 17, 1815. He became colonel of the 5th Infantry June 1, 1819. That year the regiment was sent to select sites and build three posts on the northwest frontier, the principal one becoming Fort St. Anthony near the present Minneapolis, Minnesota. Snelling laid the cornerstone for it in 1820, shifting its location slightly to the mouth of the Minnesota River; in 1825 it was renamed Fort Snelling. During construction Snelling was virtual ruler of a vast extent of wilderness into which few whites except fur men had penetrated. He was harsh in discipline and could be harsh in action. In May 1827 a party of Chippewas camped before the fort with Snelling's permission. Nine Sioux were entertained hospitably by the Chippewa and on leaving wheeled and fired on their hosts, killing two, mortally wounding a child among others. Snelling ordered the assailants brought to him, turned the principal offenders over to the Chippewa who executed four of them (another report said that the two Chippewa were only wounded and criticized Snelling for his over-reaction). When not drinking heavily

Snelling was admired by his men who had considerable respect for him. He remained in command until January 1828 and died at Washington, D.C. He was twice married.

Heitman; William Watts Folwell, *A History of Minnesota,* I. St. Paul, Minn. Hist. Soc., 1956.

Snively, Jacob, adventurer (c. 1815-Mar. 18, 1871). B. in Pennsylvania, the *Handbook of Texas* gives his year of birth as "about 1809," but the U.S. Census for 1870 states his age that year as 55 according to information he presumably supplied. He was educated, became a civil engineer and reached Texas around April 1835 as surveyor for the Mexican government. He settled at Nacogdoches. Snively served to colonel in the revolt against Mexico in 1836-37, was briefly Texas secretary of war, performed such missions for Houston as dealing with Shawnee and Caddo Indians and occasionally was army paymaster general. He petitioned the Texas government in early 1843 for permission to lead an expedition against Mexican traders on the Santa Fe Trail, largely in retaliation for humiliations Texans had suffered through their ill-fated Santa Fe and Mier expeditions and Adrian Woll's 1842 Mexican campaign against San Antonio, although loot was also an objective. The endeavor was authorized in February, Snively's expedition to include no more than 300 men and gains to be divided equally between his personnel and the Texas government. The party, which originally numbered about 190 although more were added later, left Georgetown, south of the Red River, late in April; May 27 it reached the Santa Fe Trail and Arkansas River in present Edwards County, Kansas. June 20 a Snively force under a Captain Ribon ambushed a Mexican military unit, killing 17 soldiers and capturing 82 for no Texas losses. A week later the so-called Battalion of Invincibles split into two bands, one of about 100 men commanded by Snively, the other headed by Eli Chandler. The Snively party on June 30 was taken prisoner by Captain Philip St. George Cooke of the 1st U.S. Dragoons, but released shortly whereafter some went to Independence, Missouri with Cooke and others joined Chandler. Snively temporarily resigned his command, eventually resuming it, his reduced body of hapless adventurers disbanding August 6 at Bird's Fort on the Trinity River in Texas. The expedition was sharply criticized by non-Texans everywhere, from President Andrew Jackson down, and Walker concludes that at best it was "a blunder" and "truly a Texas gamble" that luckily failed, for repercussions had it succeeded would have been unfortunate for all parties concerned. Snively joined the California Gold Rush of 1848 and went to Arizona in 1857. In 1858 he made a good gold discovery on the Gila River; later he settled at the boom town of La Paz on the Colorado River, still largely concerned with mining. In 1860 with Henry Birch (see entry), a reported killer, and prospector James W. Hicks, Snively located the important Pinos Altos gold find which attracted a major rush to that southern New Mexico region although Snively himself apparently never profited much from it. He was back in Texas by late 1866, undertook various prospecting endeavors but these either failed to locate anything or were turned back by Indian hostility. He was in Arizona again in 1870 and became a surveyor out of Wickenburg though still primarily a prospector. Snively was killed by Tonto Apaches or Yavapai Indians 20 miles east of Wickenburg in the White Picacho (Hieroglyphic) Mountains. He was buried at nearby Snively Holes but in 1878 his remains were disinterred by his friend Jack Swilling (see entry) and reburied at Gillett(e), today a ghost town. Hayden gives the date of Snively's death as March 27, 1871 and said his slayers were Tonto Apaches.

HT; Stephen B. Oates, "The Hard Luck Story of the Snively Expedition," *Amer. West,* Vol. IV, No. 3 (Aug. 1967), 52-58, 77-79; Henry P. Walker, "A Texas Gamble: The Snively Expedition of 1843," Tucson Westerners, *Smoke Signal* 42 (Fall 1981), 17-31; Farish, I, p. 296, II, pp. 254, 300; James H. Tevis, *Arizona in the 50's.* Albuquerque, Univ. of New Mex. Press, 1954, 190; Dan L. Thrapp, *Victorio and the Mimbres Apaches.* Norman, Univ. of Okla. Press, 1974; Carl Trumbull Hayden, *Charles Trumbell Hayden: Pioneer.* Tucson, Ariz. Hist. Soc., 1972, 15.

Snook, Joseph Francis (Esnuco), sea captain, pioneer (d. c. Apr. 1847). B. in England, he arrived on the California coast either in 1824 or 1830, and engaged in coastal shipping, legal or illegal, between Callao, Honolulu and California ports for many years. He was naturalized in 1833, married the daughter of J.B. Alvarado of San Diego, California, purchased a 20,000-acre ranch at Point Reyes or Tomales, and was granted the San Bernardino rancho in 1842. He died in either 1847 or 1848 and was buried in the later Presidio Park, San Diego, where his grave was identified in 1974.

Bancroft, *Pioneer Register;* Associated Press, San Diego, Nov. 28, 1974.

Snorri Karlsefnisson (Thorfinnsson), Norseman (b. c. 1005). The son of Thorfinnr Karlsefni, Snorri was the first white child known to have been born in America. His father was leader of a Vinland colonization attempt and his mother, Gudrid, a notable pioneer woman. Snorri was three when the colonization attempt (whose location is uncertain, although it may have been on Newfoundland) was abandoned. He returned with his parents to Greenland and thence to Iceland, where he matured, married and founded a distinguished lineage which included within three or four generations at least three bishops and other noteworthy citizens of Iceland.

Magnus Magnusson, Hermann Palsson, *The Vinland Sagas: The Norse Discovery of America.* Baltimore, Penguin Books, 1965; Gwyn Jones, *The Norse Atlantic Saga.* N.Y., Oxford Univ. Press, 1964; Farley Mowat, *Westviking.* Toronto, McClelland and Stewart, 1965; DCB.

Snorri Thorbrandsson, Norseman (fl. 980-1003). A son of Thorbrand of Alptafjord, Iceland, he sided with Eirik the Red in a feud preceding Eirik's banishment for three years. Around 1000 Snorri joined Karlsefni, a successful Iceland merchant, in a voyage to Greenland, spending the winter with Eirik at Brattahlid. Karlsefni and Snorri determined to try to find Vinland, sighted by Bjarni Herjolfsson and visited by Leifr, the son of Eirik in years past. The expedition formed, it visited Helluland, Markland and probably Newfoundland, establishing a base perhaps at L'Anse aux Meadows or some similar site. Later the expedition sailed southward "for a long time," and wintered, in the spring surviving a sharp fight with the "Skraelings," or natives, although Snorri's son and one other Norseman were killed. Little more is known of Snorri Thorbrandsson.

Magnus Magnusson, Hermann Palsson, *The Vinland Saga: The Norse Discovery of America.* Baltimore, Penguin Books, 1965.

Snyder, Roy, lion hunter (Jan. 1, 1893-Nov. 14, 1974). B. at Paducah, Texas, he was taken with his family to eastern Arizona but in 1920 the Synders took up a ranch west of Reserve, New Mexico. On March 1, 1944, Roy Snyder joined the New Mexico Department of Game and Fish, and became the "premiere lion hunter" of the state.

William S. Huey, "In Memoriam." *New Mex. Wildlife,* Vol. XV, No. 6 (Nov.-Dec 1974), 30-31.

Solis, Juan Mendez, explorer (d. Oct. 18, 1540). B. at La Lisena of Seville, he joined the De Soto expedition to the southern United States in 1538 and was killed "for his sins" at Mauvila in southern Alabama where De Soto fought a disastrous battle with the Chickasaw Indians.

Bourne, *De Soto,* II; *De Soto Expedition Commission.*

Somerby, Rufus, army officer (d. Dec. 26, 1882). B. in Kentucky, Somerby seems to have been a talented soldier who served in the army for 20 years alternately as officer and enlisted man and who lost a lifelong battle with alcohol. He enlisted in Company A., 9th Kentucky Infantry May 10, 1862, was commissioned a first lieutenant and a captain August 1, but resigned June 10, 1863. He enlisted in the 11th Kentucky Cavalry November 27, 1863, and rose to sergeant major by March 25, 1864, when he was commissioned a second lieutenant, being mustered out July 6, 1865. He enlisted in the 1st U.S. Cavalry October 9, 1865, and rose to sergeant major before being commissioned a second lieutenant in the 8th Cavalry June 18, 1867 and was posted to Arizona. He was engaged in scouting, often with Ed Peck as guide during the summer of 1868, reporting successes against hostiles in October and December. He became a first lieutenant September 7, 1869, and won two brevets (to captain) for work in the field against Indians. Early in 1870 he obtained leave and went east but "while there entered upon a life of dissipation" which took him to Boston where, broke, ill and desperate he enlisted (while still an officer of the 8th Cavalry) in the artillery. When this came to the attention of Washington, he was given the choice of resigning his commission or standing a court martial; he resigned March 1, 1870, and two days later enlisted in the 5th Artillery, rising steadily to first sergeant of Battery E by July 1, 1874. He then either transferred or enlisted in B Company, 1st Cavalry on December 4, 1874, rising to sergeant by December 3, 1879, much of his service in Indian country. Somerby transferred to Troop E of the 6th Cavalry March 16, 1881, and became a sergeant August 1. He may have taken part in the battles of Cibecue and Big Dry Wash, in Arizona. During the Christmas season of 1882, while stationed at Fort Lowell, Arizona, he commenced anew drinking heavily. He had applied to Senator David Davis of Illinois for help in obtaining the position of commissary sergeant, and was "sharply rebuked," which lowered his spirits. The day after Christmas, in the presence of men of his company in the barracks, he loaded his carbine, rested the butt upon the floor and leaned over the weapon and pulled the trigger. Death was instantaneous. He was buried at Fort Lowell with military honors, being generally esteemed and well liked.

Heitman; *Arizona Miner,* Aug. 22, 29, Oct. 17, 1868; Tucson *Star,* Dec. 27, 1882.

Sopete, Plains Indian slave: *see* Ysopete.

Sosa, Gaspar Castaño de: *see* Castaño de Sosa, Gaspar.

Souel, Jean, Jesuit missionary (c. 1693-Dec. 11, 1729). B. in Champagne Province, France, he became a Jesuit and reached Louisiana in 1726, being asssigned to work among the Yazoo Indians of Mississippi. The Yazoos, instigated by the Natchez, joined in the Indian uprising of late 1729 and a warrior party shot Souel not far from the present Vicksburg, Mississippi.

Thwaites, JR, LXVII, 341n39, LXXI, 168.

Soule, Silas S., army officer (c. 1843-Apr. 23, 1865). B. probably at Boston the son of Amasa Soule, he accompanied his father in 1854 to Kansas, the elder sent by the Emigrant Aid Society ostensibly to represent the group but actually to operate the Underground Railway and in other ways to further the abolitionist cause. Amasa Soule took up a homestead on Coal Creek, ten miles south of the later Lawrence, Kansas, and headed up Underground Railway work for Kansas, Missouri and Arkansas. Silas became an active Jayhawker while in his teens and soon was attracted to the cause of John Brown. In July 1859 at St. Joseph, Missouri, Soule was instrumental in the daring release from jail of Dr. John Doy, a leader in the abolitionist cause. Four months later Soule was involved in an attempt to release John Brown, sentenced to hang after his Harper's Ferry raid and in jail at Charlestown, Virginia. Brown however would not cooperate, asserting that his execution would mean more to the cause of abolition than his escape. Soule then attempted to rescue two other abolitionists arrested with Brown, but the case was hopeless and abandoned. He returned to Kansas by way of Boston where he was feted by "the abolitionist leadership of the country," including Walt Whitman. At the start of the Civil War Soule enlisted as a private in the first contingent of volunteers at Lawrence. Shortly afterward, at the request of Kit Carson who was a friend of his father's, Soule became a member of Carson's scouts at Raton, New Mexico, and was commissioned a second, then a first lieutenant. Eventually Soule transferred to the 1st Colorado Cavalry, becoming captain of D Company in the outfit known as Chivington's regiment. Soule, with a sharp sense of humor and a warm manner was a very popular officer and the tales told of him are numerous. On one occasion he walked from La Junta, Colorado, to Lawrence, Kansas, and back just to see his mother. He explained that the Indians were quiet, there was nothing to do, so he got a furlough, walked 550 miles, stayed overnight and walked back to pick up his army duties. When the 1st Colorado returned to Colorado in the fall of 1862 from its New Mexico triumphs Soule became adjutant at Colonel Chivington's headquarters at Denver where he remained until 1864 when he became second in command to Wynkoop at Fort Lyon, east of Denver. From there he helped escort seven chiefs of Cheyennes and Arapahoes to Denver for a peace council with Governor Evans and Chivington; the Indians, believing they had secured a peace, were directed to camp at Sand Creek, Colorado. Soule and other officers strongly protested to Chivington against his planned attack upon the Indians at Sand Creek, although the colonel threatened to place Soule in irons if he persisted in obstructing the design. Soule and his company went with Chivington to Sand

Creek; Soule refused to order his men to attack the camp, but read to it the order with the comment that the directive was contrary to military law and the principles of civilized warfare; he refused to order his men to fire. Despite threats against his life Soule testified for several days before a board examining into the affair and "told the truth about one of the most brutal episodes in Indian-white history." Two or three attempts on his life were made. Soule was appointed provost marshal of Denver. He was married April 1, 1865, to Theresa Coberly. About three weeks later shots were heard in the night and Soule armed himself and rushed to investigate. His assassin, Charles W. Squiers of the 2nd Colorado Cavalry met him and the two fired simultaneously, Squiers being wounded in the arm and Soule struck in the head and killed instantly. Squiers fled Denver, was arrested at Las Vegas, New Mexico and returned by Lieutenant James D. Cannon. He was allegedly court martialed in August 1865, although the record has not been found. He escaped custody and fled to California. Cannon three days after bringing Squiers to Denver was found dead in his hotel bedroom, whether from poison or otherwise has not been ascertained. Soule, in addition to being a very brave man, was one of principle, honesty and sobriety; his life was positive. Posthumously he was promoted to major.

Sand Creek Massacre; C.A. Prentice, "Captain Silas S. Soule, a Pioneer Martyr." *Colo. Mag.,* Vol. 12, No. 6 (Nov. 1935), 224-28; Stan Hoig, "Silas S. Soule: Partizan of the Frontier." *Montana,* Vol. XXVI, No. 1 (Jan. 1976), 70-77; Lonnie J. White, *Hostiles & Horse Soldiers.* Boulder, Colo., Pruett Pub. Co., 1972.

Soule, William Stinson, photographer (Aug. 28, 1836-Aug. 12, 1908). B. at Turner, Maine, he was brought up on a farm and enlisted in 1861 in Company A, 13th Massachusetts Infantry, was wounded at Antietam, served out the Civil War in the Invalid Corps and in 1865 set up a photography studio at Chambersburg, Pennsylvania. He did a good business but when fire destroyed his studio in early 1867 he went west, becoming a clerk in the sutler's store at Fort Dodge, Kansas. In late 1868 or early the next year he went to Camp Supply, Indian Territory, as a trader and settled at Fort Sill, Indian Territory; he had continued taking photographs during his

peregrination and kept up that practice at Sill, concentrating on Indian subjects. He became official photographer at Sill, recording construction of the post and for six years operated a studio in connection with the post trader's store. "Soule was one of the best photographers of his day, although he never became famous," wrote Nye. "His pictures are in sharp focus, and are well composed. His contrast and tone values are as good as those of... Matthew Brady," or noted photographers of the frontier. Soule sent some negatives to his brother's art store at Boston. At Fort Sill he mounted prints of his pictures in large albums, a few of which are still in existence. It was reported that someone had sold many of his negatives to an unknown party in the Far West; 69 negatives were discovered at the Los Angeles County Museum and Nye himself did much to identify Indians and others pictured on as many Fort Sill prints as possible. In 1875 Soule returned to Washington with a delegation of Indians; he there married, lived for a time at Philadelphia, then moved to Vermont and in 1882 to Boston where he ran a small business until his retirement in 1900. He died at Brookline, Massachusetts.

Wilbur Sturtevant Nye, *Plains Indian Raiders.* Norman, Univ. of Okla. Press, 1968; Russell E. Belous, Robert A. Weinstein, "The Man Who Photographed Indians." *Quarterly,* Los Angeles County Mus. of Nat. Hist., Vol. 7, No. 4 (Spring 1969), 5-21; Weinstein, Belous, *Will Soule, Indian Photographer at Fort Sill, Oklahoma, 1869-1874.* Los Angeles, Ward Ritchie Press, 1969; Soule's death certificate.

Sousouquee (Cecushcecue, Brown), Nez Perce (d. c. 1865). An older brother of Chief Joseph, he was described as a little past middle-age at the time of his death in the Wallowa Valley, well-formed and handsome, "a man everybody liked." He and Wayouhyuch (Blue Leg) were both drunk; Wayouhyuch apparently believed Sousouquee intended to kill him and fired an arrow into his leg; from the wound he bled to death. Joseph tried twice to avenge his brother, but eventually became reconciled to the slayer and they developed a close friendship.

McWhorter, *Hear Me.*

Spalding, Eliza, missionary wife (Aug. 11, 1807-Jan. 7, 1851). B. as Eliza Hart at

Kensington (Berlin), Connecticut, she met Henry Harmon Spalding, her future husband, in 1831; after teaching school for a time, she married Henry October 13, 1833, and accompanied him to seminary at Cincinnati. Henceforth her life was shared with him (see his biography). Eliza, one of the first two white women to cross the Rocky Mountains (the other was Narcissa Whitman), was the best educated of the six women in the Oregon Mission, had some artistic ability, was attracted to languages, and had a quick, accurate ear for them. She was described as "above medium height, slender in form, with coarse features, dark brown hair, blue eyes, rather dark complexion, coarse voice, of a serious turn of mind." Bancroft wrote that she had, "excellent attainments for a new country," was an "apt linguist, and something of an artist in water-colors, both of which acquirements proved of use in the missionary work, the first in catching the native tongues, the second in teaching by rude but vigorous pictures what could not be conveyed with force in language." He termed her "sagacious, decided, sympathizing, and faithful..., fitted by nature for the work of a missionary." She died near Brownsville, Oregon, her remains moved in 1913 to Lapwai to be reburied beside her husband.

See Henry Harmon Spalding references.

Spalding, Henry Harmon, missionary (Nov. 26, 1803-Aug. 3, 1874). B. out of wedlock at Wheeler, New York, he was "bound out" to a local family until about 17, apparently knowing some hardships. He joined a local Presbyterian church in 1825, studied for the ministry, was ordained in 1835 and with his wife, Eliza, went to the Osages for the American Board of Commissioners for Foreign Missions. Spalding was offered a post in the Oregon missions, initially rejecting it because he had been turned down in a marriage proposal by Narcissa Prentiss, who had become Mrs. Marcus Whitman, the Whitmans also assigned to Oregon. After a meeting with Whitman, however, he reconsidered since the two missionaries would have separate stations. Nevertheless, for some time little love was lost between the two families, although the differences eventually were smoothed over. Spalding began work among the Nez Perces at Lapwai, near present Lewiston, Idaho. The Spaldings were

warmly received by the Nez Perces, already eager for Christian missionaries, and from the start his work was successful and developed well. Spalding shortly learned enough Nez Perce to preach in that tongue; he was named pastor of the first Presbyterian church organized in the Oregon Territory, established in the Whitman home at Waiilatpu (near present Walla Walla) August 13, 1838, but concentrated his work at Lapwai. One of the secrets of his success was that he cultivated the important chiefs, among them Teutakas, or Old Joseph, the father of Chief Joseph of the 1877 Nez Perce uprising. Although criticized frequently by other white missionaries with whom he came into contact, and always suspicious of Catholic missionaries, Spalding's main work flourished. About 1845 he translated and had printed the Gospel of Matthew in Nez Perce. The Spaldings narrowly escaped the Whitman massacre at Waiilatpu in 1847, yet within a month they had to abandon Lapwai where they had worked for 11 years, quitting a thriving, healthy mission station, and "no Protestant missionaries in all of Old Oregon were as successful in their work of Christianizing and civilizing the natives as were Henry and Eliza Spalding." The Spaldings settled in the Willamette Valley, Oregon, where Eliza died January 7, 1851, Spalding marrying Rachel Smith of a missionary family in 1853. Spalding returned to the Nez Perces in 1871, representing the Presbyterian Board of Foreign Missions, being welcomed by the Indians "with enthusiasm... (and) drawing great crowds," and claiming during his tour there to have baptized 1,000 persons. He also visited the ruins of Waiilatpu. At his home at Kamiah, Idaho, he baptized a Cayuse chief, Umhawalish with the name of Marcus Whitman, of whom the Indian had been an early pupil, and his wife later was baptized, at Spalding's direction, Narcissa Whitman, his final tribute to the Whitmans and admonition to Marcus's Christian Indians to carry on. Spalding's work was enduring in its effects, and his influence toward making the Nez Perces outstanding Chrisitan Indians of sophistication and honor, can scarcely be over-emphasized, although he never won the acclaim accorded his less-successful colleague. Spalding died at Lapwai.

Clifford M. Drury, *The Diaries and Letters of Henry H. Spalding and Asa Bowen Smith Relating to the Nez Perce Mission 1838-1842.* Glendale, Calif., Arthur H. Clark Co., 1958; *Marcus and Narcissa Whitman and the Opening of Old Oregon,* 2 vols. Glendale, 1973.

Sparks, Isaac, frontiersman (c. 1804-June 16, 1867). B. in Bowdoin, Maine, he joined Jedediah Smith's party in 1831 at St. Louis for Santa Fe; one man was killed by Pawnees and Smith perished at the hands of Comanches. In the fall Sparks enlisted with Ewing Young for a beaver-trapping expedition to California, reaching Los Angeles February 10, 1832. He tried sea otter hunting, reluctantly took part in the Mexican War on the side of the Americans, and became a rancher in present San Luis Obispo County. He died at Santa Barbara.

John E. Baur aritcle, MM, Vol. II.

Sparks, William (Timberline Bill), cowman, Arizona Ranger, writer (c. 1861-c. Dec. 15, 1928). B. in Iowa, Sparks became a prospector, professional hunter, peace officer and packer. He arrived on the Blue River in eastern Arizona about 1878, was a line rider on the Fort Apache Indian Reservation, Arizona, coming into close contact with many noted Indians, including the Apache Kid. He had a "full and creditable part" in mining activities at Tombstone, Globe and Clifton, Arizona. In June of 1888 on Eagle Creek he was badly mauled by a grizzly bear, which he nonetheless killed. Sparks went to Cuba as a packer with the "Carter P. Johnson Expedition which took arms and ammunition to the Cuban insurgents," and later to the Philippines, also as a packer. He was first sergeant of the Arizona Rangers from 1901-1907, under Thomas Rynning. In 1906 he saved the life of Ranger Jeff P. Kidder at Naco, Arizona, shooting a "hobo" who sought to kill his partner. The man recovered. Sparks became a "politician of sorts," ran unsuccessfully for sheriff, but was "trigger-happy" in the words of one who knew him, shooting down Frank Thompson, his mining partner, in June 1916. Convicted of second degree murder, Sparks went to prison, was paroled in the "mid-1920s." He had started to write his book of recollections and poetry while in the penitentiary, later finished it. Exhausted physically and financially, he was assisted by his friend, Governor Hunt, to a job with the Arizona Highway Department at Springerville, where

he contracted pneumonia and died at Fort Apache. Sparks was described by Bud Ming as a "great and good man, honorable, tall, straight, never drank, never smoked, never gambled and wasn't married; he would weigh about 185 pounds."

Jess G. Hayes correspondence; Bud Ming notes; William Sparks, *The Apache Kid, a Bear Fight and Other True Stories of the Old West.* Los Angeles, Skelton Pub. Co., 1926; *Arizona Rangers,* ed. by Joseph Miller. N.Y., Hastings House, 1972.

Sparrow, Joseph J., cattleman, killer (d. May 23, 1924). The son of a onetime justice of the peace, Josephus Sparrow, Joe Sparrow was b. at Goliad, Texas, and became a cowboy, businessman and "small-time desperado" who worked for Print Olive in Kansas briefly, borrowed money from him, refused to repay it all and after a dispute assassinated Olive August 16, 1886, at Trail City, Colorado. His first two trials ended with hung juries; the third saw him freed at Pueblo, Colorado, in 1888. Joe returned to Texas, married Lulu May Wiggington at Victoria in 1889, later raised cattle in Brooks County, Texas, and died at Tampico, Mexico.

Harry E. Chrisman, *The Ladder of Rivers: The Story of I.P. (Print) Olive.* Denver, Sage Books, 1962.

Spelman, Henry, interpreter, military officer (1595-Mar. 23, 1623). The third son of Sir Henry Spelman (c. 1564-1641), an historian and antiquarian of Congham, Norfolk, England, young Henry "in displeasure of his friends and desirous to see other country" shipped to Jamestown, Virginia where he arrived with other youths in 1609. He was directed to live with Powhatan's Indians in order to learn the language and remained with them until December 1610 when he was brought back to the colony by Captain Samuel Argall. He remained popular with Indians and whites alike, though he and other interpreters never were properly recompensed for their work. Spelman returned to England on brief visits in 1611 and 1618. On occasion misunderstandings arose. Spelman in his twenties was accused of ridiculing Sir George Yeardley, the current governor, before the powerful chief Opechancanough, a serious offense. He was demoted from captain of the Virginia militia to interpreter and sentenced to seven years' servitude. The judgment quickly was lifted and his captaincy restored however, while it was afterward learned that the charge had been false. It was concocted against Spelman through the treachery of another interpreter, Robert Poole (see entry). Spelman survived the Jamestown massacre of 1622 perpetrated by Opechancanough. In the famine times that followed, Spelman offered to lead an expedition up the Potomac to barter with the Anacostan Indians for corn. At the mouth of Anacostia River, the site of the present Washington, D.C., while Spelman was ashore, Indians attacked his boats, hacked a shallop to pieces, almost captured the *Tiger*, his command vessel which with survivors then fled, leaving Spelman and about 30 of his men ashore. They were swiftly slain. An old planter conceded that the assault had been justified because of earlier English duplicity, adding that the death of Spelman was "a great loss to us, for that Captain was the best linguist of the Indian tongue in this countrye."

Karen Ordahl Kupperman, *Settling with the Indians: the Meeting of English and Indian Cultures in America, 1580-1640.* London, J.M. Dent & Sons, 1980; George F. Willison, *Behold Virginia: The Fifth Crown.* N.Y., Harcourt, Brace and Co., 1952; DNB.

Spencer, Charley, scout (c. 1840-Nov. 26, 1886). B. in New York State, he reached Arizona and became a mail rider between Prescott and Hardyville on the Colorado River by the mid-1860s. He participated in several skirmishes with the Hualapais and perhaps other Indians, being wounded six or seven times. In 1867 he rode for rancher George Banghart, a noted pioneer. Spencer's most serious brush with Indians occurred March 21, 1868, when he was besieged all day by a considerable party of Hualapais near the Willows, Arizona, eventually escaping them, though very badly wounded. An able scout by this time, he guided Lieutenant George M. Wheeler's survey party across Arizona in 1871. He was associated with Dan O'Leary (see entry) briefly in a mining operation, but soon severed business relations, the mine never of much profit anyway. In 1880 Spencer guided Colonel Orlando B. Willcox, Arizona Department commander into the Havasupai country along the Colorado River. Spencer married into the Hualapais tribe, learned to speak that language fluently and became influential with that people. He never blamed the Hualapais or other Indians for hostilities, asserting they had been frequently abused by whites and resulting depredations and warfare were not their fault. Spencer became involved in a dispute with his neighbor and partner, Charles Cohen of Prescott and was killed by Cohen in Truxton Canyon, Arizona. Spencer was an able frontiersman and early in life was congenial and popular; later he grew increasingly irascible, ill-temper leading to his slaying.

Arizona Miner, frequent references; Dan L. Thrapp, *Al Sieber, Chief of Scouts.* Norman, Univ. of Okla. Press, 1964; Thrapp, *The Conquest of Apacheria.* Norman, 1967.

Spencer, Pete (Spence), frontiersman (c. 1852-1903). B. in Texas, Spencer has been painted "as a very bad man, a robber and a killer" by the Earp partisans, but the extent to which the characterization is just is unclear. He and his Mexican wife and their family lived near the Earps at Tombstone, Arizona, about 1880. Later, at his place in South Pass of the Dragoon Mountains, Arizona, the so-called Indian Charley (Florentino Cruz) worked as a wood-cutter; he was murdered by the Earps in supposed retaliation for Morgan Earp's assassination. Spencer, a man of some means, was a friend of Frank Stilwell, also murdered in reaction to Morgan's death. Spencer and Stilwell were arrested for stagecoach robbery in September 1881, but the evidence against them was not conclusive, and both were cleared by a federal court. The Earp faction charged Spencer and others with being involved in a stage holdup January 6, 1882, south of Benson, Arizona, but again there was no substantial evidence. A coroner's jury charged Spencer and others with the murder of Morgan Earp, but he had been identified by no witness; no record of a murder charge against Spencer is known. Yet Earp suspicion of, and hatred for, Spencer apparently was lasting. In 1886 he was deputy sheriff and constable at Georgetown, New Mexico, a very rough community which Spencer, called by the *Silver City Enterprise* "one of the best peace officers in the west" was fully equipped to tame. Spencer in August 1886 pistol-whipped to death Rodney O'Hara, a killing regarded by many as "unnecessary." Spencer, described as about 6 feet in height and very slender was conceded to be a man of violent temper, if otherwise dependable. The *Enterprise* definitely identified this Spencer as "one of the combination who broke up the Earp gang in Arizona." About June 20, 1888, Spencer shot and killed "Curley" Martinez in Henry Longmore's saloon at Morenci, Arizona and was himself wounded but recovered. When Warren Earp was killed by John Boyett, a "cowboy" at Willcox, Arizona, July 7, 1900, Virgil and probably Wyatt were convinced Boyett was merely the agent and probably suspected Spencer of being behind it. One report said that Spencer was the subject of a prolonged search by the Earps which led Virgil to China under the name of Joe Prae (Earp spelled backwards). It is said Virgil located Spencer "just south of Nogales," that he and Wyatt sought him and another out, and killed them, Wyatt doing in Spencer. It is certain that Virgil later wrote in his diary: "Warren may rest in peace. His assassin is just resting permanently."

Ed Bartholomew, *Wyatt Earp: The Man & the Myth.* Toyahvale, Tex., Frontier Book Co., 1964; Robert N. Mullin notes; *Silver City Enterprise,* Apr. 30, July 30, Aug. 13, 1886.

Sperry, Lyman Beecher, scientist, explorer (Feb. 19, 1841-July 1, 1923). B. at Sherman, New York, he studied medicine at the University of Michigan and practiced from 1867-68, but soon drifted into other fields. He was agent for the Arikaras, Gros Ventres and Mandans from 1873-75; professor of geology, chemistry and physiology at Carleton College, Minnesota, from 1875-84, and taught parttime elsewhere for several years. During the summers from 1894 to 1906 he explored, camped and climbed mountains in Montana, particularly in the later Glacier National Park where Sperry Glacier and Sperry Glacier Basin were named for him. He had become a public lecturer and writer and pursued those vocations until his death. Sperry made his home at Los Angeles late in life.

Who Was Who.

Spicer, Edward H., anthropologist (Nov. 29, 1906-Apr. 5, 1983). B. at Cheltenham, Pennsylvania, he became a seaman, studied economics at Johns Hopkins University and earned a degree in economics from the University of Arizona in 1932, his master's degree in archeology the following year and a doctorate in anthropology from the University

of Chicago in 1939. He had done exploratory archeology among Tuzigoot ruins in the Verde Valley of Arizona and helped establish the site as a national monument. He and his wife, Rosamond spent a yearlong honeymoon among Yaquí Indians near Tucson and from this study came Spicer's doctoral thesis on the tribe's social and ceremonial organization, and his wife's master's thesis on its Easter ceremonies. From this work was published *Pascua, a Yaqui Village in Arizona* (1940). In all Spicer wrote nearly a dozen books based upon studies of the Indians of the southwest and northern Mexico; in 1964 he also visited Peru for research purposes. Among his volumes were *Potam, a Yaqui Village in Sonora* (1954); ed.; *Perspectives in American Indian Culture Change* (1962); *Cycles of Conquest: The Impact of Spain, Mexico, and the United States on the Indians of the Southwest, 1533-1960* (1963), and *A Short History of the Indians of the United States* (1969). Spicer taught at the University of Arizona from 1939-41, and from 1946-78. In 1972 he was president of the American Anthropological Association, receiving its distinguished service award in 1979 and its distinguished scholarship award in 1980. He died at Tucson, survived by his widow and three children.

Reference Encyclopedia of the American Indian, 2nd Ed., II, ed. by Dan Icolari. Rye, N.Y., Todd Pubns., 1974; *Arizona Daily Star,* Apr. 6, 1983.

Spicer, Peter, renegade (d. 1815). Captured by Shawnee Indians with several brothers and sisters when his family was attacked in Virginia in 1777, he was raised by Indians and "became a cruel tyrant to other (white) prisoners." He was very active with Indian raiding parties, often seen riding stolen horses, and with white prisoners and scalps. On one such raid the George Tush family was murderously assaulted on September 3, 1794, one of the last attacks by Indians on Wheeling Creek settlements, Virginia. The father escaped, wounded, but the mother and five of six children were butchered, the other being wounded. Spicer died on the Sandusky River.

C.B. Allman, *Lewis Wetzel, Indian Fighter.* N.Y., Devin-Adair Co., 1961,

Spicer, Wells, judge (1832-post 1884). B. probably near Monmouth, Illinois, he may have been related to the Earps by marriage, and at Tombstone, Arizona, Spicer, Wyatt Earp, and Wells Fargo agent Marshall Williams became friends. An attorney and mining engineer at Salt Lake City, he had run unsuccessfully for the Utah Legislature in 1874. Spicer was a defense lawyer in 1875 for John D. Lee at the Beaver, Utah, trial wherein Lee was charged with the Mountain Meadows Massacre of 1857. Spicer's description of Lee suggests his respect for the man, but he lost the case. By 1878 Spicer was at Tombstone, Arizona, as attorney, mining broker, and U.S. Commissioner for Deeds, among many other things. Soon he became a justice of the peace and a central figure in the turbulence surrounding the Earp-Holliday operations in Arizona; his actions are controversial. When Kate Holliday drunkenly charged Doc with stage robbery and murder, Spicer acted as her attorney to get her released from other charges against her, and hustled Kate out of town for good. Spicer was an obvious partisan of the Earps and Holliday, and it was in his court they were cleared December 1, 1881, following the OK Corral shooting of October 26, but this seems to have been Spicer's eventual undoing as a justice. The last mention of Spicer found was in 1884 when Tombstone and Phoenix newspapers referred to his mining activities in Mexico.

Ed Bartholomew, *Wyatt Earp: The Man & The Myth.* Toyahvale, Tex., Frontier Book Co., 1964; Robert N. Mullin notes.

Spillman, C.W., horse thief (c. 1837-Aug. 26, 1862). Spillman, with B.F. Jermagin and William Arnett reached Gold Creek, Montana, August 21, 1862, with six good horses and little outfit. They showed themselves experts at monte and with cash to spend. August 25 two men arrived from Elk City, Idaho, who had trailed them, alleging they were horse thieves. Arnett was killed when he resisted; Jermagin was freed on his testimony, supported by Spillman that he had been picked up afoot by the other two in the mountains and given a horse to ride to the Montana camp. Spillman, whom Stuart considered a "rather quiet reserved pleasant young man" was tried and found guilty. "He made no defense and seemed to take little interest in the proceedings," Stuart said, asking only writing materials to compose a letter to his father. In it he said bad company had brought him to his fate, begged his father's forgiveness and hoped his fate would be a warning to others. Then he quietly said he was ready and "walked to his death with a step as firm and countenance as unchanged as if he had been the nearest spectator instead of the principal actor in the tragedy. It was evident that he was not a hardened criminal and there was no reckless bravado in his calmness. It was the firmness of a brave man, who saw that death was inevitable, and nerved himself to meet it." He was hanged at 2:22 p.m., the first people's tribunal execution in Montana. Stuart always regretted the incident and believed if Spillman had pleaded for his life, it would have been granted him. James Stuart destroyed the letter Spillman had written, believing it better that his father remain in doubt about the fate of his son, rather than have evidence that he had been executed for criminal activity.

Granville Stuart, *Forty Years on the Frontier.* Glendale, Calif., Arthur H. Clark Co., 1925, Vol. I, pp. 218-21 and n.

Spinner, Phillip, soldier (d. Aug. 13, 1895). A private in Company B, 7th Cavalry, he probably was in the hill fight at the Custer battle, and survived it. He died, still a private, from a gunshot wound and was buried at Fort Sheridan, Illinois.

Chicago *Westerners Brand Book,* Vol. XXXIII, No. 9 (Jan. 1977), 72.

Splawn, Andrew Jackson, pioneer (July 31, 1845-Mar. 2, 1917). B. in Holt County, Missouri, his father died there and in 1851 the family was taken by the mother to Linn County, Oregon, where he remained until he was 15. He then accompanied his oldest brother, Charles into the Klickitat Valley, Washington, and the next year to the Yakima Valley where he entered the cattle business, remaining with it for 35 years. He worked for a Major John Thorn in 1861, driving cattle to the British Columbia gold fields where he had a series of bloodless encounters with Boone Helm, a noted desperado. In 1867 Splawn and others drove cattle from Yakima to the Deer Lodge Valley of Montana. Occasionally he drove horses or cattle to British Columbia in later years. Splawn became interested in the history of the Northwest, gathered countless bits of information and included them in his privately printed book, a collection of personal experiences and miscellaneous essays on historical subjects of the region; it is of considerable interest. In 1887 Splawn established a herd of purebred Hereford cattle, winning prizes with them. He helped organize an early packing plant at Tacoma, Washington and at various times headed livestock associations in the state of Washington. He also held various public offices. He died at North Yakima, Washington, leaving a widow, two sons and a daughter.

Andrew Jackson Splawn, *Ka-mi-akin: The Last Hero of the Yakimas.* Portland, Ore., Kilham Staty. & Printing Co., 1917, 1944.

Spokan, Garry, Salish or Spokan leader (1813-Jan. 14, 1892). B. near the confluence of Latah Creek and the Spokane River, Washington, he was son of a chief and in 1825 he and Kootenai Pelly were selected to attend an Anglican missionary settlement on the Red River of Canada; there they would be educated. In 1829 he returned to his people, fluent in English with the ability to read and write it, and imbued with Christian teachings. Among the many he influenced was Lawyer, a noted Nez Perce chief who was so impressed that he caused a delegation of six of his people to journey to St. Louis to obtain missionaries for the Nez Perce. Two of the delegates turned back before leaving the Rockies; four went on to St. Louis where two died and were buried. A fifth died on the return and only one survived to reach his people again. But the delegation had achieved its purpose and the Pacific Northwest thenceforth became a primary region for missionary endeavor. Garry himself never went to St. Louis. In 1830 he took four Indian boys to the Red River settlement where they were baptized, but in 1831 Kootenai Pelly died, and Garry was left alone to carry on as he might with his *Book of Common Prayer.* He taught his people as well as he could until he became a subject of ridicule to them and in frustration and injured embarrassment he desisted, even refusing on occasion to lend assistance to formal missionaries when they reached neighboring tribes. He felt that Christian leaders neglected him and the needs of his people, sending no missionary to them despite his requests. He turned his attention to tribal matters, having been chosen a chief. Indian lands were taken up by increasing numbers of whites. Garry was driven from his home in 1888 and in 1890 the city of Spokane was incorporated on the

Spokan tribal lands. Garry died bitter and impoverished at his home in Indian Canyon, near Spokane. He was married twice and fathered two sons and two daughters.

Clifford M. Drury, *Marcus and Narcissa Whitman and the Opening of Old Oregon.* Glendale, Calif., Arthur H. Clark Co., 1973; Alvin M. Josephy Jr., *The Nez Perce Indians and the Opening of the Northwest.* New Haven, Yale Univ. Press, 1965; Robert Ignatius Burns, S.J., *The Jesuits and the Indian Wars of the Northwest.* New Haven, 1966.

Spotted Crow (Ok-uki-wo-woaists), Southern Cheyenne chief (d. Nov. 29, 1864). A prominent leader of the Southern Cheyenne he was killed at Sand Creek, Colorado, by Chivington's men.

George Bird Grinnell, *The Fighting Cheyennes.* Norman, Univ. of Okla. Press, 1956.

Spotted Tail, Brulé Sioux chief (1823-Aug. 5, 1881). B. (in 1833, according to Hodge based on Eastman; Hyde says 1823 with sound reasons) on the White River in southern South Dakota, he was not a chief by birth, but rose by reason of his fighting qualities, winning his name from a raccoon tail given him as a child. It is said he won his first wife by a knife-duel with a subchief, was battle tested, and when a head chief died, Spotted Tail became his successor. Crazy Horse, the great Oglala, was a nephew of Spotted Tail's, being the son of his sister. Spotted Tail first distinguished himself in fights with the Pawnees, great enemies of the Brulé Sioux. He was a key figure in the killing of Lieutenant John L. Grattan and his men August 19, 1854, near Fort Laramie. Because a chief, Brave Bear, had been killed in the Grattan affair, Spotted Tail and two others had to seek revenge; they destroyed a mail wagon and its personnel enroute to Salt Lake City. William S. Harney led a major force that caught the Spotted Tail people at Ash Hollow, Nebraska, September 3, 1855; in the resulting battle Spotted Tail performed well, but received two bullet wounds and two sabre cuts in return. Harney had thoroughly cowed the Brulé Sioux; he demanded surrender of those who had attacked the mail wagon and on October 18 Spotted Tail and his several companions, dressed in war finery and singing their death songs, rode into Fort Laramie and surrendered. They reached Leavenworth December

11; they were pardoned January 16, but remained at Leavenworth through the winter, Spotted Tail learning much of the whites and their power. He had been noted in war when he surrendered, but came back to his people late in 1856 "very greatly changed by what he had seen and learned, looking to the future and ready to take up the load of responsibility which any true leader must bear." By then he had four wives. There is little mention of him between 1856 and 1863, but gradually he was coming to be identified with the peace faction of the Sioux, convinced it would be suicidal to attempt to stave off the white encroachments by arms, and compensating for this by unrelenting war on the Pawnees. Spotted Tail appeared at several Plains councils in 1863 and 1864, talking vigorously of Sioux rights, but still inclined toward peace if it could be maintained. He may have led the raid on Julesburg, Colorado, January 6-7, 1865, however, in retaliation perhaps for the Sand Creek affair which had involved Cheyennes, rather than Sioux, but came in to Fort Laramie April 14, 1865, with sixty lodges and was permitted to join the friendlies camped near the post. Spotted Tail and other Sioux were arrested and sent down the Platte toward Fort Kearny as prisoners. At Horse Creek the warriors managed to hold off the troops while their families forded the North Platte, and the whole assembly of Indians escaped to the north, Spotted Tail with them. He apparently remained aloof from subsequent hostilities, and said he wintered on the Powder River. He was persuaded to come in to Fort Laramie again and March 9, 1866 brought his people in. By then he was thought of as the head chief of the Brulés, his predecessor, Little Thunder, being now in retirement. The wilder Sioux, under Red Cloud and others, were also persuaded to come in for a treaty talk, but they refused to sign while the whites held posts along the Bozeman Trail in their country and broke off, Spotted Tail and some other peaceably-inclined Indians remaining to sign for their particular bands on June 27, 1866. Spotted Tail with his people continued to hunt their Republican River country; he as head chief met constantly with peace commissioners and high army officers. He went to Fort McPherson on several occasions where he was found "dignified but affable, and his friendliness had nothing of servility about it. He was no orator,

but he spoke effectively..., had good sense, was witty," and understood something of the ways of the whites. In the spring of 1868 the Brulés and Spotted Tail signed another treaty at Fort Laramie and, unbeknown to them, by trickery were persuaded to sign away their lands along the Republican and Platte. They were forced to remove to Whetstone Creek, 23 miles above Fort Randall in South Dakota, although Spotted Tail himself settled on White River, 30 or more miles to the west. Conditions were miserable for the Sioux at the agency, and their hardships led to dissensions among them. During one of these a drunken chief, Big Mouth, attempted to kill Spotted Tail October 29, 1869, and was killed by the other in turn. In the spring of 1870 Spotted Tail, Red Cloud and other chiefs visited Washington, D.C., Spotted Tail winning the right to remove his people from their hated Missouri River agency to a new agency on the upper White River. In January 1872, he and some of his men put on Indian shows for the Grand Duke Alexis, then touring the Plains on a sporting trip. In 1872 Spotted Tail made another trip to Washington to discuss a new agency where more farm land was available. August 5, 1873, large numbers of Spotted Tail's Sioux, buffalo hunting along the Republican, ran into a sizable camp of Pawnees also hunting, attacked their traditional enemies and killed about 100 of them; this was Spotted Tail's last fight and a great triumph for the Sioux. Despite his leaning toward peace with the whites, he maintained his exalted position among his people, even among the war-inclined. Spotted Tail was much concerned over Custer's expedition in 1874 into the Black Hills and subsequent invasion of that region by white gold hunters; the Indian even made his own reconnaissance of the Hills, and came to understand their great value to Sioux and white alike; the Sioux refused to sell the land. In June 1876, at the peak of the Sioux warfare around the Little Big Horn, Spotted Tail went on a visit to Fort Larned and Denver, then returned to his agency and managed to keep his people quiet. In 1876, under great duress, Spotted Tail signed the treaty giving away the Black Hills of which "the praying (white) men of the 1876 (treaty) commission robbed them." He was sent to talk Crazy Horse and the rest of the hostiles into surrender, and in the spring they came in. In the summer Spotted Tail went to Washington and was persuaded once more to move his agency to the Missouri River, to an area which his people detested. But in 1878 they were moved back to the Rosebud Reservation, while Red Cloud's Oglalas went to the Pine Ridge reserve. The venerable chief came into a dispute with Crow Dog and on August 5, 1881, Crow Dog killed him, a "wanton murder of the ablest chief the Sioux ever had."

George E. Hyde, *Spotted Tail's Folk: A History of the Brulé Sioux.* Norman, Univ. of Okla. Press, 1961; Hodge, II, pp. 626-27.

Sprague, John Titcomb, army officer (July 3, 1810-Sept. 6, 1878). B. at Newburyport, Massachusetts, he was commissioned a second lieutenant in the Marine Corps October 17, 1834. In September 1836 he directed a removal of a final contingent of Creeks from Tallassee, Alabama, to the trans-Mississippi lands allotted to them. Sprague resigned July 3, 1837, as a Marine and became a second lieutenant in the 5th Infantry, tranferring to the 8th Infantry July 7, 1838, and becoming a first lieutenant May 1, 1839. Sprague was aide to brevet Major General Alexander Macomb, sent to Florida in 1839 charged with ending the interminable Second Seminole War. Sprague remained in Florida for some time. A good officer, he yet was sympathetic to the Seminoles, remarking that "Their sin is patriotism, as true as ever burned in the heart of the most civilized." When Colonel William Jenkins Worth brought his 8th Infantry to Florida in 1840, Sprague, as regimental adjutant, became his aide and eventually his son-in-law. He won a brevet March 15, 1842 for "meritorious and successful conduct" in the Seminole campaigns and became a captain September 21, 1846. The next year he published his important work on the Second Seminole War, for more than a century the only full-scale history of that seven year conflict and still an indispensable source. Sprague emerged from the Civil War colonel of the 7th Infantry and retired December 15, 1870. He died at New York City.

Sprague, *The Origins, Purposes and Conclusion of the Florida War.* N.Y., D. Appleton & Co., 1847 (1964); John K. Mahon, *The History of the Second Seminole War.* Gainesville, Univ. of Fla. Press., 1967.

Sprague, Joseph, soldier (1803-post 1839). B. at Washington, Vermont, he enlisted in Company B, 3rd Artillery and was of the command of Major Francis Dade which was destroyed December 28, 1835, by Seminole Indians between Forts Brooke and King, Florida. Three men survived; Sprague, Ransom Clarke and John Thomas, although Thomas had left the column with an injured back before it was engaged by Indians. Both Sprague and Clarke were badly wounded, Clarke hiking the 60 miles back to Fort Brooke by December 31, and Sprague coming in on January 1, 1836. Sprague was discharged on expiration of his fourth enlistment at Micanopy, Florida August 22. Three months later he enlisted from Sackett's Harbor, New York for his fifth three-year hitch, this time in the 2nd Infantry. He was discharged November 12, 1839, upon its fulfillment and left Fort Gilmer, Georgia. Nothing further is reported of him.

Frank Laumer, *Massacre!* Gainseville, Univ. of Fla. Press, 1968.

Squando (sometimes: Squanto), Sokoki chief (fl. 1670s). Known generally as "the Sagamore of Saco," he headed his band, an Abenaki people, on the Saco River of Maine. He was believed to see visions, and Mather called him "a strange, enthusiastical sagamore." His enmity toward the English was aroused when off Indian Island his wife and child were drowned when their canoe was intentionally rammed by a boatload of English sailors, "a senseless outrage." Squando led his people into war against the English, burning their settlement at Saco September 18, 1675. He signed a peace at Cocheco in 1676 and eventually his band with most of the Abenakis moved to Canada.

Hodge, HAI, II, pp. 629; Thwaites, JR, XXIV, 311n15; Sylvester, II, pp. 273-74n, 295, 377.

Squanto (Tisquantum), Wampanoag Indian (d. 1622). Squanto (a shortening of his true name, Tisquantum), is famed as friend and virtual savior of the Plymouth colony during its early, crucial period. He belonged to a band of Indians living at "the little fall" called Patuxet, on the site of Plymouth, Massachusetts. He may have been one of the Maine Indians taken to England in 1605 by Captain George Waymouth; he was returned to Cape

Cod by Captain John Smith in 1614. Captain Thomas Hunt then seized a score of Indians, including Tisquantum, selling them as slaves in Spain. The future Squanto either was released or escaped to England, where he lived two years with John Slaney, treasurer of the Newfoundland Company, being sent to Cupid's Cove, on Conception Bay, Newfoundland. From there Thomas Dermer took him back to England in 1618, then brought him to the Massachusetts coast the following year, fortunately after the great smallpox pestilence of 1617 had wiped out his people. In March 1621, Squanto as the English now called him, visited the Pilgrims at Plymouth Bay, becoming their invaluable interpreter and instructor in wilderness survival arts, though Sylvester believed that "he was a born mischief-maker, a self-constituted ward heeler in the crude politics of his race." Squanto introduced Winslow to Massasoit and assisted in drafting a treaty between that Wampanoag chief and the Pilgrims. Squanto came to earn Massasoit's enmity, however, the latter seeking to obtain his enemy from the colonists in order to execute him or so it was supposed. At one time Squanto was seized by Corbitant, a Massachuset sachem and foe of the English, but was freed by Myles Standish in an endeavor that led to Corbitant and the English signing a peace in 1621. Later Squanto was suspected of acting in league with Corbitant to the detriment of the English; he often was accused of double-dealing, but his invaluable assistance and interpretive skill made necessary to the English his preservation. Squanto died at the present Chatham, Massachusetts, "of an Indean feavor...desiring the Govr to pray for him, that he might goe to the Englishmans God in heaven." His death was regarded as a great loss to the colonists.

Literature abundant: Hodge, HAI, II; Sylvester, I; DAB; DCB.

Standifer, Jefferson J., frontiersman (d. Sept. 30, 1874). Standifer was reported to have gone to California in 1849. In 1862 he was in Idaho, engaged in mining. In March of 1863 he led a party of prospectors in pursuit of Indians, locating some in the vicinity of Salmon Falls where the whites killed 15 and wounded about the same number. Leading about 200 volunteers a short time later, Standifer struck

Indians in the present Elmore County, Idaho, all the men being killed and the women taken prisoner. Meanwhile it was learned that a "fortified village" of Indians had been located some distance to the northwest. After a night march the village on the Malheur River was surrounded. One day's siege failed to reduce the place although the whites by one artifice or another managed to work closer to it. A woman was sent out to treat with them and Standifer was permitted to enter the fort; by subterfuge he opened the way for his men when they indiscriminately shot down men, women and children, only three of the latter escaping. One boy of about 4 was adopted by John Kelly, an Idaho City violinist who taught him to play the instrument and do tumbling acts; he was taken to London and Australia subsequently, being a popular performer. Standifer led still another expedition against the Indians with similarly conclusive results. Orick Jackson alleges that "Jeff Standefer" and followers brought their "Montana gang" to Arizona where a gold strike was in progress around 1864, behaving more like outlaws than pioneers. Standifer was faced down by King S. Woolsey, Jackson reported, and he believed him to have been killed later in southern Arizona, obviously an error. Late in July 1866 Standifer led about 100 men to Rock Creek of Clark Fork of the Columbia, then took part of his expedition south into the Big Horn Basin and eventually to the Sweetwater, prospecting as they went but finding nothing of importance. For a time Standifer worked for railway construction crews in Wyoming; in 1868 he suffered a broken leg and kept his pet grizzly bear in his room while recuperating at Bear River or Green River. Reportedly he was hired as scout for an 1874 Big Horn expedition, but was compelled by sickness to abandon the enterprise. He died after a lengthy illness at Fort Fred Steele, Wyoming and was buried there. Standifer was described as 6 feet in height, with broad shoulders, fine features, black hair, eyes and mustache, and "brave as a lion."

Bancroft, *Washington, Idaho & Montana; Helena* (Mont.) *Independent,* Nov. 15, 1874; information from Robert A. Murray; Orick Jackson, *The White Conquest of Arizona.* Los Angeles, West Coast Mag., 1908, 34; Farish, II, 223-24.

Standing Bear, Ponca chief (c. 1829-Sept. 1908). The Poncas were longtime residents at the mouth of the Niobrara River in Nebraska, but their lands were inadvertently included in an 1868 treaty on Sioux lands, the others periodically depredating upon these "interlopers on Sioux lands." In a lame attempt to correct the situation in 1875, Washington, rather than establishing a recognized Ponca reservation, merely appropriated money to compensate them in part for past Sioux attacks, leaving the situation muddled. After the 1876 Sioux war Congress decided to move the northern tribes to Indian Territory. In February 1877 Standing Bear and eight other chiefs went to Indian Territory ostensibly to select lands. They were dismayed at the prospects and refused to choose any site, desiring only to return home. Indian Inspector Edward C. Kemble told them if they wanted to go back they would have to walk so they did, covering 500 miles to the Niobrara in 40 days with only a blanket apiece and a few dollars. The government remained intransigent, and 170 Poncas were persuaded to move south in April but the adamant Standing Bear was imprisoned. A new agent released him. The official then called in soldiers to move the Poncas and 500 were taken on a 50-day emigration to Indian Territory where a fourth died in the first year and more later, including Standing Bear's son. In January Standing Bear, wishing to bury his son on the Ponca home range, set out for Niobrara with 66 followers. There they were arrested by Crook, under orders from higher authority, and held at Fort Omaha where Crook himself and newspaperman Thomas H. Tibbles interviewed them, appalled at the Indians' condition and history. Newspaper accounts roused intense public interest; Standing Bear was allowed to tell his story in a packed local church. Attorneys A.J. Poppleton and John L. Webster volunteered their services and Judge Elmer S. Dundy issued a writ of habeas corpus to determine by what authority Crook was holding the Poncas prisoner. The United States attorney argued that Indians were not "persons within the meaning of the law" and thus a habeas corpus writ was not legal. The great civil rights case, *Standing Bear vs. Crook* commenced April 18, 1879. It was a short trial. Standing Bear's eloquent statement was overwhelming in its appeal. Dundy ruled that not only was an Indian truly a person within the meaning of the law, but in peacetime there was no authority to force them to move or be confined against their will. Crook was the first to congratulate Standing Bear on his victory. The chief and his immediate band of followers were allotted land on the Niobrara, but the Oklahoma Poncas were not permitted to join them. In the winter of 1879-80 the chief went on a lecture tour of the East, accompanied by Tibbles and Susette and Francis La Flesche who tranlated for him. He died in 1908 at about 80, "remembered as one of the first leaders to advocate nonviolent resistence to military force, to fight illegal acts through the courts, and to use the power of an informed and aroused public opinion to achieve some element of justice for his people."

Hodge, HAI; Dockstader; James W. Howard, *The Ponca Tribe.* Smithsonian Inst., BAE Bull. 195, Wash., Gov. Printing Office, 1965; Thomas Henry Tibbles, *The Poncas Chiefs: An Account of the Trial of Standing Bear.* Lincoln, Univ. of Nebr. Press, 1972.

Standing in Water (Map-eva-ni-ists), Cheyenne chief (d. Nov. 29, 1864). With Lean Bear, War Bonnet and other chiefs, Standing in Water in March of 1863 visited Washington, D.C., and conferred with Lincoln, then went to New York and met P.T. Barnum, the showman before returning home. Standing in Water was active in Plains affairs in the summer of 1864 and was killed at Sand Creek, Colorado, by Chivington's men.

George E. Hyde, *Life of George Bent.* Norman, Univ. of Okla. Press, 1968; Stan Hoig, *The Western Odyssey of John Simpson Smith.* Glendale, Calif., Arthur H. Clark Co., 1974.

Standish, Myles, (Miles), military officer (c. 1584-Oct. 3, 1656). B. probably in Lancashire, England, he early became a professional soldier and served as mercenary in the Low Countries. Although not a Puritan, or Separatist, he was enlisted for his military skills by the *Mayflower* company and reached the Massachusetts coast in late autumn 1620. December 6 Standish with 17 others set out in the ship's boat to explore Cape Cod, seeking a place for settlement. Two days later, near the present Eastham, there occurred the initial clash of Indians and English on this coast. No whites were injured and so far as determined no Indians either though the whites pursued them some distance. Plymouth Harbor was selected as site for a landing, effected by Standish and others December 21. The Pilgrims made friends with Indians Samoset, Squanto and Massasoit (see entries), assuring the survival of their colony. Standish who had been acting captain officially became captain of the colonial military in February 1621. That year he came to Squanto's defense in an inter-tribal dispute, several Indians being wounded by "mistake," and were "kindly cared for" by the English until recovery. Standish laid out and oversaw building of a fort, which also became a house of worship at Plymouth. In 1623, hearing of an Indian - threatened Weymouth, to the north, Captain Standish with Edward Winslow and a detachment of only seven men (not to excite Indian suspicions with a larger company) marched there. The party soon was surrounded by turbulent natives believed of hostile intent; the captain lured several ring-leaders into a room where they were swiftly killed, Standish himself knifing the foremost suspect. "Winslow and Standish have been blamed for this sanguinary performance, but it was probably a question of killing or being killed, with them," adjudged Bodge. Standish's wife, Rose had died January 29, 1621, during the general sickness of the first winter; by his second wife, Barbara, whom he married in 1624, he had six children, his widow and four sons surviving him. Standish was commander-in-chief of the Plymouth military throughout his life in America; he also was treasurer of the colony for some years, assistant for 18 years, held other civil posts and was a significant figure in the settlement's development. In 1625-26 he visited London for the purpose of negotiating new loans and securing assistance for Plymouth from the Merchant Adventurers and Council for New England, as well as to secure Pilgrim rights to land and property in the New World. He was partially successful. In 1628, with a small force, Standish broke up Merry Mount (the present Quincy, Massachusetts), the settlement of the Anglican, Thomas Morton (see entry). There were no further Indian troubles closely affecting Plymouth during Standish's lifetime except the Pequot War of 1637 in neighboring Connecticut. In 1653 Standish was a member of a Council of War preparing an expedition against the New York Dutch, the captain to command a two-vessel party of 60 men. His commission was dated June 20, 1654, but a peace was arranged between the two colonies and war averted. Standish was a founder of Duxbury, Massachusetts (1631, incorporated in 1637). There he died, the noted monument erected to his memory in 1872. He apparently was a well-read man, his library among the largest in Plymouth Colony. Intellectually alert, he mastered several Indian dialects. Standish was short of temper and stature, heavy-set but active and intrepid. The legend that John Alden was asked to propose for Standish marriage to Priscilla Mullens was a Henry Wadsworth Longfellow fable, no more.

Literature abundant; George Madison Bodge, *Soldiers of King Philip's War...*, Leominster, Mass., p.p., 1896.

Stanley, David (Little Whirlwind's Voice), Cheyenne (d. Oct. 19, 1899). The son of Badger, he became known as David Stanley when he enlisted with Indian scouts at Fort Keogh, Montana. May 23, 1897 he with other young Cheyennes killed a white sheep herder, John Hoover, on or near the Northern Cheyenne Reservation at Lame Deer, Montana. Initially refusing to give himself up, he dressed in war paraphernalia and paint and declared himself ready to die in battle rather than surrender. Agent George W.H. Stouch refused him a hero's death however, and eventually persuaded Stanley to give himself up. Tried, he pleaded guilty to second degree murder and was sentenced to prison, dying in confinement within 15 months. The incident caused much tension between whites and Indians and for a time a breakout was feared but was avoided through the tact and smooth handling of Agent Stouch.

Lonnie E. Underhill, Daniel F. Littlefield Jr., "The Cheyenne 'Outbreak' of 1897 as Reported by Hamlin Garland." *Arizona and the West,* Vol. 15, No. 3 (Autumn 1973), 257-74; Underhill, Littlefield, "Cheyenne 'Outbreak' of 1897." *Montana, Mag. of Western Hist.,* Vol. XXIV, No. 4 (Autumn 1974), 30-41.

Stanley, David Sloane, army officer (June 1, 1828-Mar. 13, 1902). B. at Cedar Valley, Ohio, he entered West Point in 1848 and was commissioned in the Dragoons in 1852. He was quartermaster and commissary for Lieutenant A.W. Whipple's 1853-54 survey for a railway route from Fort Smith, Arkansas, to Los Angeles. As first lieutenant in the new 1st Cavalry he engaged in 1857 under Colonel Edwin Vose Sumner in a battle with Cheyennes on the Solomon River, about nine Indians and two whites being killed, ten soldiers wounded. At the outbreak of the Civil War he rejected a Confederate commission, narrowly escaped from Fort Smith to Kansas. His Civil War record was good and he became Major General of volunteers. After the war he became colonel of the 22nd Infantry and returned to the frontier. He took a detachment to Texas to support diplomatic moves against the French in Mexico. In 1872 and 1873 he led survey expeditions to the Yellowstone; between 1879 and 1882 he settled minor Indian issues in Texas. "His great service was his 34 years spent in opening of the West. He was a master in handling Indians." He retired a Brigadier General and died at Washington.

DAB; HT; *Relations with the Plains Indians: 1857-1861,* ed. by LeRoy R. and Ann W. Hafen. Glendale Calif., Arthur H. Clark Co., 1959.

Stanley, Ebin, scout, frontiersman (Feb. 1843-Nov. 19, 1904). Stanley, whose first name sometimes is given as Eben although he invariably spelled it Ebin, was b. at Leon, Decatur County, Iowa, enlisted August 13, 1861, in Company C, 5th Kansas Cavalry and was mustered out September 13, 1864, by reason of physical disability. That autumn he accompanied a drove of longhorns to Fort Sumner, New Mexico, and went on to San Diego, California, before returning to Texas for another longhorn herd which was driven in 1866 to Fort Sumner. Stanley enlisted November 22, 1866, in D Company, 3rd Cavalry at Fort Marcy, Santa Fe. The next year he accompanied a scout after Mescalero Apaches from Fort Union, New Mexico, to the Davis Mountains of West Texas. For a time he was farrier and briefly was first sergeant of his company; at his honorable discharge at Camp McDowell, Arizona, November 22, 1871, he was sergeant. February 1, 1872, he enlisted in Company A, 5th Cavalry, taking part in several scouts and some Apache fighting, notably March 25 and 27, 1873, at and near Turret Mountain, Arizona. For this work Stanley was awarded April 12, 1875, a Medal of Honor, but by then he was out of service. He had been mustered out at Fort Whipple for illness May 10, 1873, still a private. Much of his work in the 5th had been with Indian scouts, and he continued as civilian

chief of scouts and post guide at Camp (later Fort) Apache in eastern Arizona. January 9, 1876, it was Stanley who detected and reported that Diablo (see entry) was generating trouble near the post; this was followed by a light foray against Camp Apache by hostiles, one of the few times in western history where a military establishment was openly attacked by Indians. March 27-28 that year in a hard fight in the Tonto Basin Stanley's 40-man Company A, Indian Scouts killed 16 hostiles. During these years Stanley became one of the best-known guides and scouts in Arizona. October 31, 1877, he left that calling and settled in the St. Johns and Springerville area where he raised cattle and followed frontier pursuits. On one occasion he saved the life of James G.H. Colter, local rancher and deputy sheriff who while unarmed had tried to arrest a man with a knife, and was badly slashed before Stanley rescued him, being cut in the hand but subduing the assailant. Stanley, who had been married twice before, wed Sarah or Mary Strickland, 14, July 1, 1877, having by her three children. He was divorced July 10, 1882, and September 3 married a widow, Mary Clanton Slinkard, daughter of Newman Haynes Clanton. Stanley was mixed up in eastern Arizona lawlessness to some degree although not himself a desperado of any sort. In 1887 his brother-in-law, Phin Clanton (see entry) was sentenced to ten years in prison; at the same time Stanley "who has been heretofore of good reputation...was held on a smaller charge, but was not prosecuted on condition that he leave the Territory within 60 days," reported the *Phoenix Herald* of September 22. He crossed into New Mexico, going first to Eagle, east of the Rio Grande where he was postmaster for some years, then settling at Las Palomas and later at Kingston, both west of the river. One of his New Mexico friends was Andrew Kelley (see entry), a very good Indian man. Stanley died at Hillsboro, New Mexico. In his last years he had been all but incapacitated by rheumatism or arthritis. He was described in his young manhood as 5 feet, 8 inches tall with light hair, blue eyes and a fair complexion; during his Camp Apache scouting days he wore a heavy beard.

Stanley Pension File, NARS; information from Sara D. Jackson; Price, *Fifth Cavalry* (where name is erroneously given as William Stanley, there being no William Stanley in A Company at that date); Clara T. Woody to author, Aug. 10, Sept. 2, 1964;

Farish, VI, 298; Bancroft Library, Ebin Stanley biographical statement, Arizona Dictations, Apache County; information from Sue C. Van Slyke.

Stanley, John Mix, artist (Jan. 17, 1814-Apr. 10, 1872). B. at Canandaigua, New York, he was orphaned and apprenticed to a wagon maker. He went to Detroit at 20 and turned to art, first painting Indians at Fort Snelling, Minnesota. "No early Western artist had more intimate knowledge by personal experience of the American West than did Stanley." In 1842 he entered the daguerreotype business briefly at Washington, using this art on at least one of his subsequent western expeditions. In the fall of that year he established himself at Fort Gibson (present Oklahoma) with Sumner Dickerman, painting Indians and western scenes; the next year he attended a Cherokee council, doing portraits of John Ross and numerous other leading men, then visiting a Comanche council on the plains. In 1846 he painted Keokuk, a Sauk chief, before journeying to Santa Fe where in the autumn he joined the Kearny expedition to California, serving as artist. Enroute he painted from life a picture he labeled "Black Knife" who was the famed Apache chief Cuchillo Negro (see entry), the painting now with the National Collection of Fine Arts, Smithsonian Institution. He reached Oregon from California July 1847. That November he started for the famous Whitman mission in eastern Washington to do portraits of Dr. and Mrs. Whitman, but short of his goal was informed that they had been massacred. He was one of the first to report the tragedy to Walla Walla. On his return from the west coast by sea, Stanley remained a year on Hawaii; his protraits of King Kamehameha III and his queen are still in existence. His collection of more than 200 pictures from 43 Indian tribes, all done from life, was deposited in the Smithsonian Institution in 1852; all but five were destroyed by fire, although a catalogue of them remains. The next year he was artist for a railroad exploration from St. Paul to Puget Sound. Stanley, whose work sometimes was adjudged superior to Catlin's was "by far the best equipped both by ability and experience of any of the artists that accompanied the Pacific Railroad Surveys." He made daguerreotypes and paintings of many of the 30 Piegan chiefs he had brought to a council at Fort Benton. Stanley's most elaborate surviving work was "The Trial of Red Jacket," a picture containing about 100 figures. His work was skilled and professional; the loss of much of it was tragic. He died at Detroit.

Robert Taft, *Artists and Illustrators of the Old West 1850-1900.* N.Y., Charles Scribner's Sons, 1953; DAB.

Stanley, Steph(en), teamster, hard-case (1828-post 1878). B. in Arkansas, he was a half-brother of A(lexander) Ham(ilton) Mills; the family reached Lincoln County, New Mexico, about 1868, the half brothers already hard characters. As they pistol practiced one day, it is said, Mills stuck out a forefinger and urged the other to shoot it off; when this was done Mills complained, "You took too much. Now give me a chance," whereupon he shot off a joint of Stanley's finger. Mills was sheriff of Lincoln County during the so-called Horrell War, but both were involved; Stanley's wife may have been killed in one incident. In January 1875, Stanley was wounded in the leg by Mescalero Apaches, and by July had been crippled for life by a cinnamon bear he had wounded; one side of his face had been torn away, an arm and both legs broken by the animal. On February 18, 1876, he dueled with S.W. Lloyd over property rights, took unfair advantage and seriously wounded Lloyd. In the spring Stanley became a teamster for L.G. Murphy & Co., economic monopolists of the county, and was engaged in hauling goods between the Murphy store at Lincoln and the Mescalero Agency, Stanley purportedly later being paid $300 to testify against Godfroy that he had hauled goods of the poorest quality to the agency, and smuggled goods from it to the Murphy store. He was with the group that killed Bernstein at the Mescalero Agency August 5, 1878; shortly afterward he disappeared. McSween had filed an affidavit that Murphy had wanted to organize a vigilance committee to do away with Patron, Stanley and Brewer, and this may have had something to do with Stanley's fadeout. Stanley was said to have been mentally immature or feeble minded. Indian Inspector E.C. Warkins in an affidavit to Angel said: "This man Stanley is a hard case in every respect. It is said & generally believed that he has killed at least four men in this Ty. one of whom was a Zuni Indian..."

"Frank Warner Angel's Notes on New Mexico Territory 1878," ed. by Lee Scott Theisen. *Arizona and the West*, Vol. 18, No. 4 (Winter 1976); Robert N. Mullin notes: Philip J. Rasch, "A. Ham Mills — Sheriff of Lincoln County." *English Westerners' Brand Book*, Vol. 4, (Apr. 1962), 11-12.

Stansbury, Howard, army officer (Feb. 8, 1806-Apr. 17, 1863). B. at New York City, he was trained as a civil engineer and conducted railroad and canal surveys in the Great Lakes and upper middle west regions, being engaged in 1838 on a survey of a rail route from Milwaukee to the Mississippi River. That year he entered the army as a first lieutenant of topographical engineers, being promoted to captain within two years. In service he continued with Great Lakes surveys until 1849 when he was directed to explore the Great Salt Lake basin with John Williams Gunnison as his assistant. The expedition reached Fort Bridger August 11, hiring Bridger as guide to Salt Lake. Gunnison was sent by the well-traveled road to the Mormon settlements while Stansbury and Bridger explored for a better route around the Wasatch Range to the north. Stansbury concluded that a good road could be found through Cache Valley. Before reaching Salt Lake City Stansbury was informed of Mormon suspicion and hostility, that no survey of the basin would be permitted and his life perhaps was in danger. Stansbury had a long conference with Brigham Young and Mormon unease was allayed. October 19, 1849, Stansbury commenced an exploration around the western side of Great Salt Lake where few had ventured; his difficult journey completely around the lake was concluded successfully, although suffering was endured. He was the first to understand that Great Salt Lake was residuary from Lake Bonneville, a huge inland sea that once covered a great deal of the basin. Gunnison, meanwhile, surveyed the Utah Lake region to the south. The next spring a more precise survey of Great Salt Lake was completed. "It was a thorough job, and the bounderies (and islands) of the long-mysterious lake now stood revealed." Enroute home Stansbury discovered and rudimentarily surveyed a central overland route south of the main trail through South Pass, but on the Chugwater River he was injured by a fall from a horse, effectively ending the study; yet this new survey "was one of (his) most important achievements, for it was the most direct and

efficient route located thus far to the Salt Lake... The lasting effects on the history of transportation wrought by Stansbury's survey were thus considerable," and the Union Pacific railroad later followed the course he laid out. Stansbury's *Report* which included much material from other western survey expeditions, "for its time gathered...a respectable amount of geographical data of all descriptions...and provided a matchless picture of the Mormon community and the environmental conditions which governed its existence." For a decade following, Stansbury conducted surveys of the Great Lakes and of Minnesota military roads. He retired a major in 1861, later re-entered service, and died at Madison, Wisconsin, survived by a widow and two children.

Heitman; Bancroft, *Utah;* DAB; William H. Goetzmann, *Army Exploration in the American West 1803-1863*. New Haven, Yale Univ. Press, 1959; Howard Stansbury, *Exploration of the Valley of the Great Salt Lake of Utah*, Sen. Exec. Doc. 3, 32nd Cong., Spec. Sess., Wash., 1853.

Stanton, Charles Tyler, pioneer (Mar. 11, 1811-Dec. 24, 1846). B. at Pompey, Onondaga County, New York, he was a store clerk in his youth but studied natural history and read widely, becoming knowledgeable in botany, geology and other branches of learning. When his widowed mother died in 1835 he moved to Chicago; Stanton wrote well and was something of a poet. He joined the Donner company in 1846 for California (see George Donner entry). With Reed, Stanton was sent ahead through the Wasatch Mountains in an attempt to overtake Lansford Hastings who had suggested the near-impossible "cut off" for California-bound emigrants, to persuade him to return and pilot the Donner party through the maze of mountains. Reed-Stanton were only partially successful. As the train lagged far behind its schedule, it became apparent troubles would increase and Stanton and William McCutchen were sent ahead around September 18 to California to purchase provisions and bring them back to help the Donner train reach its goal. Stanton arrived at Sutter's Fort, obtained five mule loads of dried beef and flour and recrossed the Sierra Nevada to meet the train October 19 near the present Wadsworth, Nevada. He brought two Indian guides. November 12 with a party of 14 Stanton tried to make it through the snow to the pass and over it into California, but barely reached the head of Donner Lake, the group forced by drifts to turn back. Stanton joined the group of 15 that in December made a supreme effort to surmount the pass. He died on Christmas Eve, the fourth day, due to exposure added to starvation and hardship. His body was found in May 1847 by W.C. Graves with a relief party. Seven of the 15 had reached Bear Valley, aided by the meat from the two Indian guides whom William Foster shot.

C.F. McGlashan, *History of the Donner Party*. Stanford Univ. Press, 1947; Bancroft, *Pioneer Register*.

Stanton, Henry Whiting, army officer (c. 1823-Jan. 19, 1855). B. in New York State, he was graduated from West Point and became a second lieutenant in the 1st Dragoons in 1842, assigned to frontier duty at Fort Leavenworth. In 1843 he went to Fort Gibson, Indian Territory, and took part in Plains scouting operations; he also served at Fort Towson, Indian Territory, in 1844 and at Leavenworth again from 1844-46, during which he was a member of a South Pass expedition of 1845 under Stephen Watts Kearny. After the Mexican War he returned to Leavenworth, then was assigned to frontier duty at Sonora, California, in 1850-51, Fort Orford, Oregon, 1852-53, and to Fort Fillmore, New Mexico, in 1854. With Richard Stoddert Ewell and about 100 dragoons in January 1855, Stanton engaged in a pursuit of Mescalero Apaches, the command being attacked in camp on the Peñasco River in the Sacramento Mountains on the 17th. In a hard fight several of Stanton's men were killed or wounded; he was shot in the head and killed instantly. Fort Stanton, New Mexico, is named for him.

Cullum; Heitman; Aurora Hunt, *James Henry Carleton... Frontier Dragoon*. Glendale, Calif., Arthur H. Clark Co., 1958.

Stanton, Thaddeus Harlan, army officer (Jan. 30, 1835-Jan. 23, 1900). B. in Indiana, Stanton enlisted in the 3rd Washington, D.C., Infantry in 1861, was commissioned captain in the 18th Iowa Infantry in 1862, but on October 3 he began his long career as paymaster which culminated in 1895 when he was made paymaster of the army and Brigadier General. In his professional capacity he was paying troops at Fort Fetterman, Wyoming, in 1876 when Crook was assembling his expedition

for a strike at Crazy Horse's village believed to be on the Powder River. Crook had been seeking a correspondent for the New York *Tribune* to go along as "he wanted someone along who would present all the facts... to the country." Editor Whitlaw Reid wired he had no one to send and urged that Stanton go as special correspondent. Crook accepted this arrangement and appointed Stanton chief of scouts, although he had had little combat experience. Crook was reprimanded for this action, but Stanton won a brevet for his part in the March 17 fight, an honor which he apparently deserved. Alex Moore's "second report," reproduced by Vaughn, appears to have been written by Stanton and oddly is condemnatory of Moore, although Moore signed it. Stanton testified at court-martials that grew out of the expedition, later commanded citizens and irregulars on the Big Horn and Yellowstone expedition; he had no further frontier service.

J.W. Vaughn, *The Reynolds Campaign on Powder River*. Norman, Univ. of Okla. Press, 1961.

Stanwood, Frank, army officer (c. 1842-Dec. 20, 1872). B. in Maine, he was commissioned from Massachusetts a second lieutenant in the 3rd Cavalry August 5, 1861 and a first lieutenant February 21, 1862, ending the Civil War in that rank but with brevets to lieutenant colonel. He became a captain July 28, 1866. Stanwood arrived at Camp Goodwin, Arizona in March of 1870, went on leave and returned to Camp Grant, Arizona in April 1871, when he assumed command. He was on a scout at the time of the murderous Camp Grant Massacre, the worst atrocity in Arizona history, perpetrated by certain Tucson whites using Mexicans and nearby Indian enemies of the Apaches on the flimsiest and most unconvincing of pretexts. Stanwood, with other active officers, accompanied Crook on his initial tour of southeastern Arizona, leaving Tucson July 11, 1871, and proceeding by Camp Bowie, and Camp Apache and back to Camp Verde and Prescott. Stanwood was active throughout his Arizona career in scouting, and was universally popular with his men, officers and civilians. He died at Brighton, Massachusetts of tuberculosis.

Heitman; Bourke, *On Border;* Constance Wynn Altshuler, *Chains of Command*. Tucson, Ariz. Hist. Soc., 1981; Dan L. Thrapp, *The Conquest of Apacheria*. Norman, Univ. of Okla. Press, 1967.

Stapleton, George Washington (Wash), pioneer (Nov. 28, 1834-Apr. 25, 1910). B. at Knightstown, Rush County, Indiana, he left Colorado for Montana, arriving at Grasshopper Creek (Bannack), Montana, July 10, 1862, with the first stampeders, and took a prominent part in development of the Territory and state. He often held elective positions and in 1889 was a member of the Montana constitutional convention. One well acquainted with him considered Stapleton "a charming fellow. Whenever he spoke he was listened to." He died at Butte.

Montana Contributions, VIII (1917), 363; *Register;* Herbert M. Peet Collec., Box 10, Folder 9, Mont. Hist. Soc.

Stark, John, ranger, army officer (Aug. 28, 1728-May 8, 1822). B. at Londonderry, New Hampshire, he was raised on the frontier where Indian scuffling vied with hunting as a principal occupation. Twice he was captured by Indians in his youth, once on Baker's River, New Hampshire, in the spring of 1752, returning home in the summer, and again on Stark's River, named for him but the name since changed to John's River, a tributary of the Connecticut; the second captivity was in 1754. Stark served as guide for exploring parties into the Coos Valley, New Hampshire, and other areas. During the latter French and Indian wars, Stark served with Rogers Rangers, earning a field captaincy for gallantry; actions in which he participated included the defeat of Dieskau in 1755, the attack upon Fort William Henry, July 6, 1757; Fort Ticonderoga, July 6 and 8, 1758, and the reduction of Crown Point and Ticonderoga the next year. In the Revolution he fought at Bunker Hill, escorted the American retreat southward from Canada in 1776, participated in the battles of Trenton and Princeton, and had a distinguished role in the triumph over Burgoyne. He was on the board of officers which tried British Major John André. Stark was made a Brigadier General October 4, 1777, and breveted a Major General in 1783. He was described as of medium height, of robust physique, with light blue eyes and strong features. He was married and fathered eleven children.

Grant Powers, *Historical Sketches of the ...Coos Country and Vicinity.* Haverhill, N.H., J.F.C. Hayes, 1841; DAB; William H. Powell, *List of Officers of the Army of the United States from 1779 to 1900.* N.Y., L.R. Hamersly & Co., 1900.

Stark, John, pioneer (1817-1875). B. in Wayne County, Indiana, his mother was a cousin of Daniel Boone. He started for California from Monmouth County, Illinois, with M.D. Ritchie whose daughter was Stark's wife. Taking the Fort Hall road they arrived in California safely. John Stark was a powerful man, weighing 220 pounds, and of considerable endurance. He was a member of the Third Relief Party for the Donner company, snowbound on the east side of the Sierra Nevada and, with Charles Stone and Howard Oakley came upon the Breen family, three Graves children and Mary Donner forlornly camped near the summit of the pass into California where they had been left with other stronger people pushed ahead. His companions decided to leave the hapless people and go for further help, but Stark would not. He alone remained and herded them into California, carrying as many as he could on his back, depositing those ahead and returning for the others. To him, wrote John Breen, "myself and others owe our lives." It was a heroic deed, and successful. Stark settled in Knights Valley, was sheriff of Napa County for six years, county judge in 1850-51, and a member of the State Legislature in 1851 and 1855-56. He lived near Calistoga, California, from 1851-68, and in Lake County from 1868 until his death of a heart attack which occurred while he was pitching hay. He fathered 11 children, eight of whom with his widow survived him.

C.F. McGlashan, *History of the Donner Party.* Stanford Univ. Press, 1947; Bancroft, *Pioneer Register.*

Starr, Belle (Myra Maybelle Shirley), character (Feb. 3, 1846-Feb. 3, 1889). B. at Carthage, Missouri, she had four brothers and one sister, one of her brothers, Ed, purportedly being her twin; he has been called a captain under Quantrill. Belle, or Bella, as she often referred to herself, served as courier, it is said for Confederate guerillas during the early part of the Civil War. On her birthday in 1862, she was captured by Union Major Herbert M. Enos near Newtonia, Missouri. Released, she sped to Carthage to warn her brother, Ed, who escaped but shortly was killed by Union Troops. In 1866 Belle married James Reed in Texas despite her father's disapproval, and mothered a daughter, Pearl, in 1869. Reed became a fugitive after a killing about 1870; with his family he went to Los

Angeles where in 1871 a son was born, and returned to Texas, settling near Dallas. Reed continued in outlawry in Indian Territory, on November 19, 1873, reportedly participating in a $30,000 robbery of Watt Grayson of the Creek nation, much of it said to have been tribal funds. Reed was killed in 1875 for the reward by an associate and another. Belle drifted into outlawry herself, being arrested at Dallas for horse theft, associating with Jack Spaniard, Jim French and Blue Duck, each of whom was more than a friend, it is said. She spent two years in Nebraska and about 1880 married Sam Starr, Cherokee in part. In 1883 she and Sam did minor time at Detroit. Starr was killed about 1886 in Oklahoma. Belle was shot by an unknown assassin, for reasons not clear.

S.W. Harman, *Belle Starr: The Female Desperado*, 1898, repr. in Ed Bartholomew, *Some Western Gun Fighters*. Houston, Frontier Press of Tex., 1954; Jeff Burton book review, English Westerners' *Tally Sheet*, Oct. 1973, Vol. 20, No. 1, Pub. No. 192.

Starr, Henry George, desperado (Dec. 2, 1873-Feb. 22, 1921). B. near Fort Gibson, Indian Territory, Henry was three-eighths Cherokee and at 15 became a cowboy. February 13, 1892, he was arrested for horse theft, but the charges were dropped. He got into more trouble on one minor charge after another, held up several stores and when tracked down by two detectives, Henry C. Dickey and Floyd Wilson, Starr on December 13, 1892, shot Wilson, the only man he ever killed. He committed more robberies, acquired a reputation and March 27, 1893, he and Frank Cheney robbed Starr's first bank, at Caney, Kansas, getting $4,900 by Starr's account. Within a month he had organized a small gang. Six of them held up an M.K. & T. train on Pryor Creek, Indian Territory, May 2, 1893, getting an estimated $6,000. June 5, 1893, they robbed a Bentonville, Arkansas bank of $11,000, Starr by now becoming one of the most notorious regional bandits. The gang split up and Starr and Kid Wilson went to Colorado Springs where July 3, 1893, they were arrested and returned to Fort Smith, each indicted on 15 counts. Wilson drew 24 years; Starr, convicted, had to stand trial for three additional counts on which Wilson was not indicted; and convicted of those he stood trial for the murder of Floyd Wilson. He was found guilty,

sentenced by Isaac Charles Parker to hang, but the Supreme Court directed a new trial. His second trial, also before Judge Parker in September 1895, resulted in a second death sentence; the Supreme Court once more demanded a new trial. Starr pleaded guilty to a charge of manslaughter and January 15, 1898, was sentenced to three years, plus 12 years for various robberies. The Cherokee National Council later called for his release; his mother took testimónials to President Theodore Roosevelt who recalled that a Starr relative had been a Rough Rider and upon Starr's pledge to reform, pardoned him January 16, 1903. Starr married and named his first child Theodore Roosevelt Starr. He went straight for several years until Arkansas requested his extradition for the 14-year-old robbery of a Bentonville bank June 5, 1893. Not knowing what Oklahoma's response would be, Starr fled, teamed up again with Kid Wilson, who had been paroled, and robbed a bank at Tyro, Kansas March 13, 1908. Again large rewards were offered for the two. They went to Colorado, robbed a bank at Amity, but soon separated, Starr convinced that Wilson was "going nutty." Wilson never was seen again. Starr was arrested in Arizona, tried for the Amity, Colorado, robbery, and November 30, 1909, was given a seven to 25 years sentence. In prison Starr studied law, wrote an autobiography and September 24, 1913, was paroled. His wife had divorced him and Starr and a female companion returned to Oklahoma where between September 8, 1914, and January 13, 1915, he was credited with robbing 14 banks before he settled in Tulsa. He wanted to cap his career by robbing two banks at one time and again selected six riders to accompany him. He entered Stroud, Oklahoma, March 27, 1915, and with three men entered the Stroud State Bank while the other three took on the First National Bank. A 17 year-old boy, Paul Curry wounded Starr and Lewis Estes and the two were captured. Starr pleaded guilty to the two robberies and on August 2, 1915, was given 25 years in the Oklahoma State Penitentiary, again becoming a model prisoner. He was paroled March 15, 1919, and decided to enter the motion picture business. He acquired a quarter interest in the Pan-American Motion Picture Company of Tulsa, returned to Stroud and filmed the attempted double robbery of five years before, getting Curry to re-enact his crucial role. He made a couple of other pictures, but reported he was cheated out of his share of the proceeds. In 1920 he married a woman half his age and gradually found himself in debt, returning to his old profession. February 18, 1921, Starr attempted to rob the People's National Bank of Harrison, Arkansas, but was wounded mortally by W.J. Myers, former president and large stockholder of the bank; he was buried at Dewey, Oklahoma. Starr had lived up to his boast he would "rob more banks than any man in America," although he spent 18 years of his life in custody for his bent. Henry Starr was a reader of the classics, a literate man, and one who could not turn from the high adventure of his perilous calling. He wrote of his decision to become a holdup man, how it "all came to me in a flash. There was the road for me; it stretched out before me, and I could see its turnings, its high and low places, and, in a dim sort of way, its ending, and I knew it was what I had been longing for and I took to it right gladly, feeling the spirit of exultation and freedom surge within me as my resolve was made. It was to answer the voice of the prairies and the mountains, and the blood of my ancestors was to have full play at last...."

Glenn Shirley, *Henry Starr: Last of the Real Badmen.* N.Y., David McKay Co., 1965.

Stauffer, Rudolph, soldier (Nov. 27, 1836-June 8, 1918). B. at Bern, Switzerland, Stauffer enlisted in Company K, 2nd Cavalry (later 5th Cavalry) at Cincinnati, June 24, 1855, becoming eventually first sergeant. He served in the same outfit until December 11, 1878. His Arizona service was worthy. He won a Medal of Honor for an action July 30, 1872, near Camp Verde. A butte which Stauffer and soldiers under his direction cleared of hostiles was named Stauffer's Butte, although the name has since been lost. Writer-officer Charles King called him, "grim old Stauffer, the first sergeant." He never married and died at 81 at the Old Soldier's Home, Washington, D.C.

Pension record, Nat. Archives; Dan L. Thrapp, *Al Sieber, Chief of Scouts.* Norman, Univ. of Okla. Press, 1964.

Steamboat, bucking horse (c. 1896-Oct. 14, 1914). Steamboat was the first truly great bucking horse of rodeo history and in the view of riders who saw most of the outstanding ones for half a century or more, the greatest of them all, particularly since he bucked before the use of the flanking strap and other goads became common. He was named by Jimmy Danks, bronc rider, because, having broken a bone in his nose at 3 he whistled while breathing hard and "sounds just like a steamboat." Steamboat stood 15 hands high, weighed 1,100 pounds, was coal black save for a white star on his forehead and three white feet, was mixed mustang and Morgan and had breeding, stamina, strength, speed and a heart to go with his original and hard-to-master movements in the arena. He performed for 15 years. Jake Manning said: "I never rode a horse that was any comparison to him." Jimmy Danks: "He was the hardest bucking horse I have ever rode, and he became worse as he grew older." Joe Cahill: "Old Steamboat was in a class by himself." Clayton Danks, twice winner of the world championship on Steamboat: "I have rode all the great buckers of my day. None compared to Steamboat." Dunk Clark obtained Steamboat for his Denver stock show and for many years he was king of the rough string. In the fall of 1914 he was injured at Salt Lake City, shipped to Cheyenne where he was again injured in a box stall during a thunderstorm. He was shot with the .30-40 Winchester 93 which had belonged to Tom Horn, and was buried at the Frontier Days rodeo grounds at Cheyenne.

Art Fee, "Steamboat King of All Buckers." *Real West,* Vol. XVI, No. 116 (June 1973), 8-10, 65.

Steamboat Frank (Slat-us-locks), Modoc warrior (d. June 1886). So named by Yreka whites because his fat mother huffed and puffed as she walked, Frank was a member of the Hot Creek band of Indians and had a role in the Modoc War of 1872-73 in northeastern California. With the other Hot Creeks he was driven to war by white stupidity and entered the Lava Beds with Captain Jack's band of hostiles. He with other Hot Creeks denounced Jack for the death of the popular Ellen's Man, asserting the leader had placed him where he would be killed, although this probably was not true. Anyway, the Hot Creeks split off from Captain Jack's force in May, thus dooming Modoc resistance, and surrendered May 22, Frank thereafter becoming one of the "Modoc bloodhounds" dedicated to rooting out his former colleagues, the remaining hostiles. Thus he was spared a court martial. Sent with the survivors to the Quapaw Agency in Oklahoma, Frank was converted to Christianity, changed his name to Frank Modoc, and attended the Oak Grove Seminary at Vassalboro, Maine, where he died of tuberculosis before being ordained.

Keith A. Murray, *The Modocs and Their War.* Norman, Univ. of Okla. Press, 1973; Jeff C. Riddle, *The Indian History of the Modoc War.* Medford, Ore., Pine Cone Pubrs., 1973; Richard Dillon, *Burnt-Out Fires.* Englewood Cliffs, N.J., Prentice-Hall, 1973.

Stearns, Abel, pioneer (Feb. 9, 1798-Aug. 23, 1871). B. at Lunenburg, Massachusetts, he journeyed to Mexico in 1826 and was naturalized in 1828, reaching Monterey, California, in July of 1829. He expected to receive a land grant; instead he aroused the enmity of Governor Manuel Victoria and was banished to the frontier, but returned as one of the leading instigators of a revolution in 1831. By 1833 he had become a trader at Los Angeles, dealing in hides, liquor and smuggling for which he came into difficulties in 1835 though he perhaps "was not more addicted to contraband trade" than others more fortunate in keeping such peccadilloes under cover. In 1835 he was involved in a dispute over a barrel of wine with one William Day, a trapper and a bad man to provoke. Stearns began the fight, but Day stabbed him severely, one cut nearly severing Stearn's tongue and leaving him with a speech impediment the rest of his life. In 1836 Stearns was made fiscal agent for Los Angeles, but perhaps for vigilante activity came into disfavor with Governor Mariano Chico and was ordered to leave the country. Instead, Stearns joined in a revolution by which Juan Bautista Alvarado came to power and California for two brief years was an independent republic. In 1839 Stearns again was involved in political tumult. In 1842, six years before the discovery at Sutter's Fort, Stearns sent 20 ounces of gold taken from placers near the present Newhall, California, to the Philadelphia mint, but little notice was taken of this find which, in any event, was minor. He entered stock raising and ranching and by 1846 was perhaps the wealthiest man in California; Stearns was "somewhat active" in a movement against Micheltorena in 1845, took Larkin's side in the struggle for California freedom from Mexico, although as a Mexican official remained as neutral as possible. He held many

public and private offices and despite droughts and other natural hazards, his wealth grew until his death, which occurred at San Francisco. "Don Abel was shrewd..., somewhat tricky in petty transactions...but apparently honorable..., a man of quick temper and strong prejudices, but ...a good friend, and kind husband. He hated Mexico and the Mexicans, but liked the Californians.... In person he was very ugly (known sometimes as) Cara de Caballo.... His wife was... daughter of Juan Bandini, as beautiful as her husband was ugly..., who survived him without children."

Bancroft, *Pioneer Register.*

Steck, Michael, Indian official (Oct. 6, 1818-Oct. 6, 1883). B. at Hughesville, Pennsylvania, he was graduated from Jefferson Medical College at Philadelphia about 1843 and practiced medicine at Miffenville, Pennsylvania, for six years. He went to New Mexico in 1849 as contract surgeon with the army, remaining two years and returning to Washington in 1852. Upon the recommendation of Schoolcraft, Director Joseph Henry of the Smithsonian Institution, and Luke Lea, commissioner of Indian affairs, he was appointed by Fillmore Indian agent to New Mexico, being reappointed by Presidents Pierce and Buchanan. Steck became agent for the Mimbres Apaches May 9, 1854, with an added duty overseeing the Mescalero Apaches as well, his headquarters at Fort Thorn, New Mexico. He was not only among the earliest, but was one of the best agents ever assigned to those peoples; much of his work in the new field required ingenuity, improvisation and vision to be properly fulfilled. He was interested in his charges, and reports detailing their manner of living and related matters are of historical and ethnological interest. In 1858-59 he made the first significant contacts of an agent with the Chiricahuas, the Coyoteros and Pinals, all Apache peoples living in present Arizona, then administratively part of New Mexico. In the autumn of 1859 he again visited the Chiricahuas, through whose lands the Butterfield stage route now was operating, and met Cochise and other leaders. Steck visited Washington briefly in 1860, returned to his New Mexico post, but with the Civil War in 1861 he left the Southern Apaches as agent for good. In 1863 Steck was named by Lincoln superintendent of Indian affairs for New Mexico, serving until May 1, 1865. His relationship with the military commander, James Carleton, was occasionally strained during this period, Steck disapproving of the Bosque Redondo experiment and other Carleton notions, and war conditions made his tenure not as effective as he wished. He became interested in mining operations in New Mexico, ran unsuccessfully on the Greenback ticket for lieutenant governor of Pennsylvania, and died at Winchester, Virginia, on his birthday. Steck, as a trained physician, had an opportunity to assess and better understand the Indians' problems of health and resettlement, and he was "genuinely interested in the Indians' welfare," a concern which was manifest in all his reports. He was a man of good judgment and apparent integrity.

Dan L. Thrapp, *Victorio and the Mimbres Apaches.* Norman, Univ. of Okla. Press, 1974; Steck Papers, Zimmerman Library, Univ. of New Mex., Albuquerque.

Steele, Elijah (Elisha), pioneer (Nov. 13, 1817-June 17, 1883). B. near Albany, New York, he was educated at Oswego, New York, where he read law and in 1840 was admitted to the bar. He moved to Wisconsin, practicing law until 1850 when he crossed the plains to California. He mined in northern California and settled eventually at Yreka where he became respected for fair dealing by the Shasta and other Indians, traded for a time, prospected and eventually established a ranch, operating it for a few years and then settling to the practice of law. He served in the Legislature one year and was made superintendent of northern California Indians in 1863, but although his work was first rate he aroused local opposition and soon was deposed. When Captain Jack who wished with his Modocs to remain in their ancestral lands along Lost River questioned Steele as to how this might be arranged, the lawyer suggested that they dissolve the tribe, take up claims and pay taxes; no law permitted an Indian to do this, but Steele believed that the Constitution would give them that right if tested. Steele visited the Modocs during the war of 1872-73, on occasion in the Lava Beds, and most of them trusted him, but on his last visit in the winter of 1873 he found them savagely divided and barely escaped with his life. He retained the friendship of Jack and the influential Scarface Charley; but he would go back no more, and

returned to Yreka. After the court martial verdict demanding execution of Jack and three other Modoc leaders, Steele, by then sheriff of Siskiyou County, filed a formal appeal for clemency; the appeal was not granted. In 1879 Steele was elected Superior Court judge for the county. He was married three times, and fathered children. Steele died at Yreka.

Jeff C. Riddle, *The Indian History of the Modoc War.* Medford, Ore., Pine Cone Pubrs., 1973; Keith A. Murray, *The Modocs and Their War.* Norman, Univ. of Okla. Press, 1965.

Steele, Frederick, army officer (Jan. 14, 1819-Jan. 12, 1868). B. at Delhi, Delaware County, New York, he was graduated from West Point in 1843 and assigned to the 2nd Infantry, serving with it throughout the Mexican War, winning two brevets for gallantry and becoming a first lieutenant in 1848. The next year he was sent to California and from 1853 to 1860 served in the Pacific Northwest. Steele was promoted to captain in 1855 and major in May 1861 at the start of the Civil War from which he emerged a brevet Major General, most of his service being west of the Mississippi although he had a role in the Vicksburg campaign and in the early winter of 1864 assisted Canby in the reduction of Mobile. In 1865 he was sent to Texas, then was given command of the Department of the Columbia. In 1866 he was promoted to colonel commanding the 20th Infantry. Indian Superintendent J.W. Perit Huntington in the summer of 1867 said that he had conversed with Steele on the subject of using Indian scouts from the Warm Springs, Oregon, agency in a campaign against the Snakes, suggesting that the officer desired the war to be one of "extermination." Steele afterward reported officially that "The Indian scouts have done most valuable service.... In late expeditions, they have done most of the fighting and killing.... It is my opinion that one hundred, in addition to those now employed, would exterminate the hostile bands before next spring..." His attitude apparently encouraged subordinates to insist upon the summary execution of all prisoners, regardless of age or sex. Steele died at San Mateo, California. Fort Fred Steele, Wyoming, established June 30, 1868, was named for him.

NCAB, IV, 51; Heitman; Keith and Donna

Clark, eds., "William McKay's Journal, 1866-67: Indian Scouts," pt. 1. *Ore. Hist. Quar.,* Vol. 89, No. 3 (Fall 1978), 328-33.

Steen, Enoch, army officer (Feb. 22, 1800-Jan. 22, 1880). B. in Kentucky, he early moved to Missouri from where he became a second lieutenant of the Mounted Rangers July 16, 1832, transferring to the 1st United States Dragoons the following year, "the last of that class of men like Bonneville, Boone and Martin Scott, who were the mighty hunters and woodsmen of our little Army.... He was a man of splendid physique, of the most temperate habits, and he had the endurance of old Daniel Boone himself. He was, in woodcraft, the equal of any Delaware Indian...." Steen became a first lieutenant in 1836 and a captain in 1840. In 1834 he was stationed at Fort Leavenworth, 1st Dragoon headquarters. In 1835 he was in charge of ordnance for a 1st Dragoon expedition under Colonel Henry Dodge up the Platte River and its south fork to the Rocky Mountains, and back by way of Bent's Fort, the Arkansas River and Santa Fe Trail. From September 5 to 25 Steen was of a command of Stephen W. Kearny northwest to the Platte, east to the Missouri and a meeting with Potawatomi Indians at Council Bluffs and back to Leavenworth. He apparently was stationed at Fort Gibson, Indian Territory, in 1843 for he supplied dragoons to cooperate with Philip St. George Cooke in escorting a Santa Fe wagon train in August or September of that year, although Steen himself was too ill to accompany the party. Steen took part in the Mexican War, earning a brevet of major in the battle of Buena Vista, February 22-23, 1847. He accompanied Dragoon Captain Croghan Ker and a civilian party under James Collier to New Mexico, leaving Leavenworth May 17, 1849, and reaching Santa Fe July 11. He was assigned to command Doña Ana, a post he established in southern New Mexico. Steen, with 50 Dragoons, tracked a band of Mimbres Apache raiders to the Santa Rita coppermines and in a hard fight August 16, 1849, defeated them, being badly wounded in this engagement. It was reported that he had been shot by the white renegade Jack Gordon, this version confirmed by Steen's subsequent verbal admission, and by Gordon's statement as recorded by John Nugent. February 5, 1850, he wrote his Santa Fe headquarters that Apaches raided and seized captives within sight

of the post in broad daylight and that he had led several unsuccessful expeditions against them. In June 1850 he commanded an exploring expedition from his post over the Organ Mountains, around the southern edge of the White Sands, New Mexico, and into Mescalero Apache country, but ran into a superior force of Indians and withdrew. Steen was the first to suggest on the basis of his reconnaissances that a post near the Santa Rita mines be established to control the Mimbres; it was created in 1852 and named Fort Webster with Steen in command. During 1852 he went east briefly and brought recruits back to New Mexico; of a party of 183 men, 20 died of cholera enroute. April 7, 1853, Steen as commander at Fort Webster, was the first Anglo witness to sign a compact or treaty with Mimbres Apaches, including Delgadito, Cuchillo Negro, Victorio and nine other leaders. It was never ratified by the United States, however. In May 1853, Steen, "that excellent officer," escorted William Carr Lane to the Gila River from Fort Webster. It is probable that Steins Peak and Steins Pass in southwestern New Mexico, both important points in frontier history, were so-called for Steen, whose name sometimes was spelled Stein. He was promoted to major July 15, 1853, and by 1860 he was in Oregon Territory. General Harney ordered him to command a joint exploring expedition to find a route from Harney Lake, Oregon, to Salt Lake City, and from Crooked River westward to the head of the Willamette River. On August 8 Steen struck a hand of hostiles and had a fight and pursuit over a lofty butte which today bears the name of Steen Mountain, a landmark in southeastern Oregon. Late in 1860 Steen was in command of Fort Walla Walla, Washington Territory. Returned east for the Civil War, he was assigned to the 1st Cavalry, then became lieutenant colonel of the 2nd Cavalry by autumn 1861. He was assigned to Cantonment Holt, near Washington, D.C., until June of 1862 when he went to Fort Craig, New Mexico. In March 1863, he was at Benton Barracks, Missouri; he retired officially September 23, 1863, probably for reasons of age, but continued to serve actively at his own request in various capacities. He commanded the fort at Sandy Hook, New York Harbor, September 30, 1863, through May 1864 and perhaps longer; he commanded Fort Lyon, Colorado Territory, early in 1866.

"Here he was near his old friend, Col. (Nathan) Boone (a son of Daniel with whom he had originally joined the army) who had a fine ranch on the Purgatoire River, and they were not crowded by civilization.... When the law was passed prohibiting retired officers from being placed on duty, (Steen) retired to his farm in Missouri where he remained the remainder of his days." He died at his residence in Jackson County, Missouri, and was buried at Mt. St. Mary's Cemetery, Kansas City. A son was Alexander Early Steen, who became a Confederate Brigadier General and was killed at the battle of Kane Hill, Arkansas, November 27, 1862.

Heitman; Steen's military file, Nat. Archives; Barry, *Beginning of West;* Dan L. Thrapp, *Victorio and the Mimbres Apaches.* Norman, Univ. of Okla. Press, 1974; Lee Myers, "Military Establishments in Southwestern New Mexico." *New Mex. Hist. Rev.,* Vol. XLIII, No. 1 (Jan. 1968), 5-48; Bancroft, *Oregon,* II; information from Msgr. Henry G. Bauer, director, Catholic Cemeteries Associated, Roman Catholic Diocese of Kansas City-St. Joseph, Mo; information from Wayne R. Austerman.

Stefansson, Vilhjalmur, Arctic explorer (Nov. 3, 1879-Aug. 26, 1962). B. at Arnes, Manitoba, of Icelander parentage he was taken to Pembina County, North Dakota at 2, later attending the University of North Dakota and graduating from the University of Iowa in 1903. He attended Harvard Divinity School for a year and studied anthropology for two years at Harvard Graduate School. Stefansson conducted archeological research in Iceland in 1904 and 1905 for Harvard's Peabody Musuem. As an ethnologist he accompanied the 1906-1907 polar expedition led by Ernest de Koven Leffingwell and Ejnar Mikkelson, sponsored by Harvard and the University of Toronto. He lived with the Mackenzie Delta Eskimo learning the language and customs, and convincing himself that civilized man could survive in the Arctic by adopting Eskimo methodology. From 1908-12 under auspices of the American Museum of Natural History of New York City and the Canadian government, Stefansson spent 53 months in the Arctic living with Eskimos and by the chase, as well as exploring the archipelago north of the continent. His successes revolutionized thinking about cultured man's ability to live off the country under harsh conditions. Among his discoveries on this expedition was the 500-mile Horton River, emptying into Franklin Bay east of the Mackenzie delta; out of his experiences came *My Life With the Eskimo* (1913). Around Prince Albert Sound on Victoria Island he found and wrote about the so-called "blond Eskimos," a few individuals with no known white ancestry but with eyes lighter than most Eskimos (sometimes even blue or grayish) and hair lighter in color and texture than that of the typical native. Stefansson speculated that these might reveal traces of Norse blood resulting from intermingling of Greenland Norse and Eskimos in the 15th century or earlier. The theory was disputed, but Stefansson never shunned controversy. From 1913-18 he led the Canadian Arctic Expedition, spending five years north of the Arctic Circle, again demonstrating his ability to live almost exclusively by hunting as the Eskimos did, and as a diversion once more seeking out and studying blond Eskimos. From this final polar expedition came his widely-read *The Friendly Arctic* (1921) which went through 10 printings before being reissued in an enlarged edition in 1943. On the Canadian Arctic Expedition Stefansson discovered several islands, including Borden, Brock, Lougheed and Meighen and explored widely on the polar sea. In 1924 he visited the interior of Australia to make warm latitude observations to compare with his polar experience. Stefansson possessed an active, inquiring mind. He rarely accepted the findings or beliefs of earlier explorers without investigating the facts for himself and applying logic and common sense to the solution of Arctic problems as they arose. He disclaimed any heroics during his years of exploration, saying "everything you add to an explorer's heroism you have to subtract from his intelligence," and when sometimes asked if he had ever visited the North Pole would retort, "I'm a scientist, not a tourist!" His interests were wide. He tried to promote establishment of Canadian sovereignty over Wrangel Island in 1921-22 with tragic results (see Ada Blackjack entry); from this came *The Adventure of Wrangel Island* (1925). He urged domestication of musk oxen and colonization of the north polar regions, as well as their use for air routes and submarine navigation. During World War II he was advisor to the United States government on defense matters in Alaska and Arctic survival methods for military personnel and downed airmen; from this came the two volume *Arctic Manual* (1940), compiled under direction of the Chief of the Army Air Corps. A one-volume condensation was prepared for ground forces and a single volume commercial edition was published (1944) for the general public. Stefansson was consultant to Pan American Airways on northern operations from 1932-45. He was Arctic consultant to Dartmouth's Northern Studies Program from 1947 until his death, and served as advisor to other organizations and institutions. He received numerous honors and awards. He ever was convinced of the value of meat as a sufficient food for the human body. In an experiment sponsored by the Russell Sage Institute of Pathology, he and Karsten Andersen lived for a year on meat alone, being regularly tested by specialists who found they suffered no ill effects (the explorer insisted that plenty of fat with the lean was the secret of maintaining health on such a diet, for without fat one lacked the necessary vitamin intake). He concluded that man is very adaptable and "can be healthy on meat without vegetables, or vegetables without meat, or on a mixed diet." He was a prolific writer. Among his 24 books, in addition to those mentioned were: *Hunters of the Great North* (1922); *The Northward Course of Empire* (1922); *The Three Voyages of Martin Frobisher* (1938); *Unsolved Mysteries of the Arctic* (1938); *Iceland: The First American Republic* (1939); *The Problem of Meighen Island* (1939); *Ultima Thule* (1940); *Greenland* (1942); *Arctic in Fact and Fable* (1945); ed., *Great Adventures and Explorations* (1947, 1952); wrote *Northwest to Fortune* (1958), and an autobiography, *Discovery* (1964), published posthumously. Stefansson died at Hanover, New Hampshire. He was married.

Literature abundant: EA; CE; *Current Biography*, 1942, 801-804.

Steptoe, Edward Jenner, army officer (c. 1816-Apr. 1, 1865). B. in Virginia, he was graduated from West Point in 1837, becoming a second lieutenant in the 3rd Artillery. He served in Florida against the Seminoles in 1838, took part in the Cherokee removal to Indian Territory that year and returned to Florida where he again served in the Seminole War until 1842, then continued service in the east until the Mexican War. His experience in that conflict was extensive up to the capture of Mexico City in 1847. Steptoe returned to Florida for another bout with the Seminoles in 1849-50, and served at eastern stations until 1854. He led a march to Washington Territory via Great Salt Lake in 1854-55 (having been offered the governorship of Utah and declined). Steptoe performed frontier duty at Forts Vancouver, Cascades and Dalles and took part in the Yakima Expedition of 1856; he was at Fort Walla Walla from 1856-58, and on the Spokane Expedition of 1858, "being engaged in the desperate combat of To-hots-nim-me, Washington," on May 17, 1858. Here he was "routed," with the loss of 18 men in dead and wounded including two officers, and was forced to abandon his howitzers and other equipment to the enemy. Steptoe was on sick leave of absence from 1858 until 1861, resigning November 1 of that year. He died at Lynchburg, Virginia.

Cullum; Heitman; Robert M. Utley, *Frontiersmen in Blue: the United States Army and the Indian, 1848-1865.* N.Y., Macmillan Co., 1967; Robert Ignatius Burns, *The Jesuits and the Indian Wars of the Northwest.* New Haven, Yale Univ. Press, 1966

Sterling, Albert D., Indian police chief (c. 1853-Apr. 19, 1882). B. in Ohio, probably at Cincinnati, he was a "spendid young fellow...who was fascinated with Indian life," according to George A. Forsyth. Ranald Mackenzie reported that Sterling had been a chief of scouts at Fort Cummings, New Mexico from which post he resigned to go to San Carlos, Arizona, where he became Chief of Indian Police, serving from August 8, 1880, to June 30, 1881, was discharged (at the end of the fiscal year) and rehired July 1, 1881, to serve until his death. Jason Betzinez, an Apache who was his good friend said that "sometimes I visited his quarters, in turn he come to our teep(ee)...so he could talk a little Apache," adding that the "Warm Spring and San Carlos Indians all liked him so well; he was also a great friend of Indians." Burnham said Sterling "had under his command about twenty Indians who were employed in scouting...I was appointed to assist Sterling (who) always took great chances with his Indian scouts," but earned their respect by his honesty and bravery. His adventures were numerous in fulfilling his duties. In the summer of 1881 he was sent to the Cibecue to investigate Indian unrest there and reported the situation very serious. In early September he interviewed Mickey Free who had been at the site of the late-August Cibecue engagement but had not joined in the fighting. Free had hastened to the Agency with the premature report that Carr's command had been massacred. Sterling reported this version which attained wide publicity before the true story was revealed when Carr returned to Fort Apache with his command. On February 4, 1882, Sterling broke up a tiswin drunk among the Apaches as no doubt he often had done before, bringing in prisoners. April 19, 1882, when the Juh band of Sierra Madre hostiles raided San Carlos and the subagency at Fort Thomas, Arizona, to herd Loco and the balance of the Warm Springs Apaches to Mexico, Sterling and one of his policemen, Sagotal, hastened to intercept the raiders. Sterling was killed at the outset, and Sagotal somewhat later; according to one report, Sterling's head was severed and played with like a football by the hostile raiders. He was unmarried.

Record of Employees, San Carlos Agency, Vols. 9, 10, RG 75, Nat. Archives; James H. McClintock, *Arizona___.* Chicago, S.J. Clarke Pub. Co., 1916, I, pp. 232, 235; Frederick Russell Burnham, *Scouting on Two Continents.* Garden City, N.Y., Doubleday & Co., 1926, 54-55; Mackenzie to F.J. Sterling, Letters Sent, Dist. of New Mex., 1881-83; RG 393, 112, Apr. 14, 1883; Dan L. Thrapp, *Conquest of Apacheria, General Crook and the Sierra Madre Adventure.* Norman, Univ. of Okla. Press, 1967, 1972.

Sternberg, Sigismund, army officer (d. Aug. 1, 1867). B. in Prussia, he was commissioned a first lieutenant in the 175th New York Infantry September 26, 1862, resigned February 13, 1864, was commissioned a captain in the 7th New York Infantry October 22, 1864, and was mustered out August 4, 1865. He became a first lieutenant in the 82nd U.S. Colored Infantry September 10, 1865, a captain June 30, 1866 and mustered out September 10. Sternberg became a second lieutenant of the 27th U.S. Infantry March 7, 1867, and immediatley was assigned to Fort C.F. Smith, Montana, on the Bozeman Trail. He was killed in the so-called Hayfield Fight with Sioux Indians. He was shot in the head while "ordering his men to stand up and fight like soldiers," having until then acted "with

great coolness and gallantry," according to his companions.

J.W. Vaughn, *Indian Fights: New Facts on Seven Encounters.* Norman, Univ. of Okla. Press, 1966.

Stevens, Fannie A., pioneer (c. 1831-c. 1908). B. at New Harmony, Illinois, she followed her husband, Lewis A. Stevens to the Prescott, Arizona, region after 1864. In September 1867, she and a hired man stood off about 20 Yavapais Indians attacking the Stevens' ranch at Point of Rocks, near Prescott; when she had the opportunity to contact her husband attending a session of the territorial legislature at the capital, she asked not for rescue, but for more ammunition, winning plaudits from frontiersmen for her pluck. Lewis Stevens died in March 1878. Mrs. Stevens never remarried, but became "the first successful school teacher in Prescott." She died at Los Angeles, California.

Arizona Miner, Sept. 21, 1867; archives of the Sharlot Hall Hist. Mus., Prescott.

Stevens, George H., frontiersman (1844-post 1906). B. at Southwick, Massachusetts, he reached Arizona in 1866, married an Apache woman, apparently the daughter of a chief, and became a scout for Crook. Stevens owned a series of ranches, one, a sheep outfit, being heavily raided by Juh in 1882. The rancher became a sheriff of Graham County, Arizona, and was elected to the territorial legislature. In 1906 he was reported running a gambling house in Victoria, British Columbia. Stevens often was used as an interpreter by Apache agents, army officers and others; his knowledge of the Apache tongue was considerable. He fathered several children.

Dan L. Thrapp, *The Conquest of Apacheria.* Norman, Univ. of Okla. Press, 1967.

Stevens, Isaac Ingalls, legislator (Mar. 25, 1818-Sept. 1, 1862). B. at Andover, Massachusetts, he was graduated from West Point the head of his class in 1839 and entered the Corps of Engineers. He served on Scott's staff in Mexico, winning brevets for gallantry in three battles, then was assistant in charge of the Coast Survey Office at Washington, D.C. In 1853 he was named governor of Washington Territory and organized the northern Pacific exploration party which charted a route for a railway from St. Paul, Minnesota, to Puget Sound, upon his arrival in Washington Territory resigning his commission as major in the Engineers to become Governor. He served from 1853 until 1857. He had conducted several councils with Indians in 1853, and elements of his command had conducted important surveys and explorations enroute to the coast. In his dual capacity as governor and superintendent of Indian affairs for Washington, Stevens concluded a number of treaties in 1855-56 with separate Indian peoples: December 26, 1854, with the Nisqualli and Puyallup; January 22, 1855, with the Duwamish, Suquamish and others; January 26 with the S'klallam; January 31 with the Makah (all the preceding to clear Puget Sound for white settlement); a treaty June 9, 1855, in the Walla Walla Valley with the Wallawalla, Cayuse and other tribes, the same day one with the Yakima, and June 11, another with the Nez Perce. July 1, 1855, he concluded a treaty with the Quinaielt and other peoples; July 16 a treaty with the Flatheads and others in the Bitterroot Valley of western Montana, and October 17 in the Judith Valley of Montana with the Blackfeet and other tribes. His treaty policy was alleged to have generated a number of serious Indian uprisings in the territory, and his reign as governor therefore was highly controversial, particularly because of his declaration of martial law, the reasons therefore and his actions under the edict. In 1857 he was elected to Congress for two terms as a Democrat and during the Civil War he was appointed colonel of the Highlanders, the 79th New York Infantry, being assigned to the defense of Washington, D.C. He was appointed a Brigadier General of Volunteers and commanded a brigade in the Port Royal expeditionary force, and was appointed a Major General, but Congress did not confirm the promotion, although he continued to command a division. At the battle of Chantilly, Virginia, he was killed, "but his courage and devotion had saved the city of Washington." According to Bancroft, Stevens was a brilliant man, of small stature, and a positive influence in the settlement of Washington Territory.

BDAC; *Montana, Contributions,* Vol. X, 1940, 267-68; Bancroft, *Washington, Idaho & Montana.*

Stevens, Roswell, Mormon pioneer (Oct. 17, 1809-May 4, 1880). B. at Grand River, Upper Canada, he joined the Mormon sect in 1834,

removing to Nauvoo, Illinois, where he became a member of the police force. He enlisted in the Mormon Battalion and reached Santa Fe with it, then was directed to go to "Winter Quarters," Iowa, with funds for the Mormon exodus to Utah. He was of the pioneer company reaching the Great Salt Lake valley in July 1847. Stevens died at Bluff City, Utah.

Andrew Jenson, *Latter-day Saint Biographical Encyclopedia,* I. Salt Lake City, Deseret News Pub. Co., 1901.

Stevenson, pioneers (d. Sept. 11, 1857). A family of this name, composition unknown, perished as part of the Fancher emigrant wagon train at ,Mountain Meadows, southwestern Utah, destroyed by Mormons and Mormon-led Indians.

William Wise, *Massacre at Mountain Meadows.* N.Y., Thomas Y. Crowell Co., 1976.

Stevenson, James, geologist (Dec. 24, 1840-July 25, 1888). B. at Maysville, Kentucky, he went west at 16, joined the surveys of Lieutenant G.K. Warren and Captain W.F. Raynolds and became acquainted with Ferdinand V. Hayden and Jim Bridger. He wintered at times with the Sioux and Blackfeet, acquiring their languages and assisting his later ethnological studies. In the Civil War he rose from an enlistment to the rank of lieutenant, it is said, although he is not included in Heitman. In 1866 he accompanied Hayden into the Dakota badlands, and participated in each subsequent Hayden expedition until creation of the U.S. Geological Survey in 1879. Stevenson was supremely competent at managing and directing expeditions as well as in accomplishing their intended purpose. He made the first ascent of the Grand Teton July 29, 1872, accompanied by Nathaniel P. Langford. A 10,300-foot peak in the Absaroka Range east of Yellowstone Lake and an island in the lake were named for him. When the Geological Survey was founded, Stevenson became its executive director; because of his interest in the American Indian, however, he was detailed to the Bureau of Ethnology to do southwestern research. He explored cliff and cave dwellings, and lived among the Zuñi and Hopi tribes collecting artifacts. He contracted Rocky Mountain spotted fever in 1885, and never fully recovered; he died at New York City. His

Indian collections "constitute a valuable and, in most respects, unique contribution to science."

Aubrey L. Haines, *Yellowstone National Park: Its Exploration and Establishment.* Wash., Nat. Park Service, 1974; DAB.

Stevenson, Jonathan D., army officer (Feb. 27, 1846-Oct. 9, 1882). B. in New York City, his possible relationship to Jonathan Drake Stevenson, who took the 1st New York Volunteers to California in 1847 and went on to become a prominent pioneer, is unknown. The younger Jonathan enlisted in the 102nd New York Infantry in 1861, was mustered out because of illness in 1862; he enlisted in the 25th New York Cavalry in 1864 and was commissioned that same year. He took part in the first battle of Winchester, Virginia; Bank's retreat in the Shenandoah Valley; the engagements at Harper's Ferry; White House Landing; Cedar Creek; Fisher's Hill; and Newtown, Virginia, in the latter action commanding a cavalry squadron. In 1866 he became a second lieutenant in the 8th Cavalry, moving with his regiment to Arizona. May 30, 1867, he had a sharp fight with hostiles near Beale's Springs. On January 14, 1868, he was severely wounded in action with the Huala-pais Indians in the Cerbat Mountains, being shot in six places, once through the body and again through the groin, while his carbine was shattered by a hostile bullet; his command killed five of the enemy. After a further harrowing experience he reached Fort Mojave for recuperation. In 1869 he moved with the regiment to New Mexico where on May 6, 1872, near Tierra Amarilla he had an engagement with the Utes, losing a man killed and causing the enemy light casualties. January 20, 1873, he had a slight brush with Mimbres Apaches, reporting killing one of them. In 1877 he was transferred to West Texas, but increasingly severe bouts of illness prevented any great amount of field duty, although he was promoted to captain in 1879. Stevenson was plagued with what was diagnosed as consumption (tuberculosis) and only his spirit kept him active as long as he remained so. He died at Detroit. Stevenson was 5 feet, 8 inches, tall, light complected with blue eyes and brown hair.

Stevenson Military File, Nat. Archives; Dan L. Thrapp, *The Conquest of Apacheria.* Norman, Univ. of Okla. Press, 1967; *Chronological List.*

Stewart, Benjamin Franklin, Mormon pioneer (Oct. 22, 1817-June 22, 1885). B. in Jackson Township, Missouri, he joined the Mormon sect in 1844 and was of the first migration to Utah. Stewart was one of ten men left at the Upper Platte Ferry to bring Mormons across the river, then went on to Utah. He was a founder and two-term mayor of Payson, Utah County, and was a founder of Benjamin, named for him, in Utah County where he was killed by lightning. He left a widow and children.

Andrew Jackson, *Latter-day Saint Biographical Encyclopedia,* I. Salt Lake City, Deseret News Press, 1901.

Stewart, Edgar Irving, historian (June 27, 1900-Nov. 24, 1971). B. in Michigan, he was professor of history at Eastern Washington State College, Cheney, Washington, until his retirement in 1967. He wrote *Custer's Luck* (1965), and edited *The Field Diary of Lt. Edward Settle Godfrey,* etc. (1957), along with several articles in professional journals relative to the Custer affair. His first book has been termed justly "the best single narrative volume on the Little Big Horn campaign and its prelude." Stewart died at Vancouver, British Columbia.

Barry C. Johnson, "Death of Edgar I. Stewart." *English Westerners' Talley Sheet,* Vol. 18, No. 3, Pub. No. 176 (Jan.-Feb. 1972), 1-2.

Stewart, Reid T., army officer (1850-Aug. 27, 1872). B. in Pennsylvania, probably at Erie, he was graduated from West Point and commissioned a second lieutenant of the 5th Cavalry June 12, 1871. He joined the regiment at Fort McPherson, Nebraska, accompanying the first detachment in November by way of San Francisco and the Gulf of California for Arizona and was stationed at Camps McDowell, Lowell and Crittenden until August 1872. He left Crittenden for Tucson, Arizona, the morning of August 27, 1872 and in Davidson Canyon was ambushed by Indians; he was killed instantly. His driver, Corporal Joseph P.G. Black, more experienced in Indian warfare, was captured and tortured to death. Stewart's remains were buried at Erie, Pennsylvania. General Howard later saw Stewart's "beautiful rifle" in Cochise's camp in the Dragoon Mountains, Arizona.

Price, *Fifth Cavalry,* 568-69; Dan L. Thrapp, *The*

Conquest of Apacheria. Norman, Univ. of Okla. Press, 1967; Cullum; O.O. Howard, *My Life and Experiences Among Our Hostiles Indians.* Hartford, Conn., A.D. Worthington & Co., 1907, 221-22.

Stewart, William, scout (fl. 1868). Stewart served with about 50 other frontiersmen under George A. Forsyth on the Middle Plains and fought in the battle of Beecher Island against hostile Cheyennes and others from mid-September 1868. In 1905 he was living at Cripple Creek, Colorado.

Simon E. Matson, ed., *The Battle of Beecher Island.* Wray, Colo., Beecher Island Battle Mem. Assn., 1960.

Stewart, William C., Mormon official (fl. 1857-1875). A Mormon high priest and member of the Cedar City, Utah, council, Stewart was a participant in the Mountain Meadows Massacre of September 11, 1857. On September 9 he had shot and killed William Aden (Aiden), a member of the besieged Fancher wagon train, while Aden was seeking Mormon help to break the Indian attack, believing he would be befriended by the Mormons as his father had befriended the sect. He was mistaken. Stewart was a participant in the massacre, although his exact role has not been defined. Afterward he fled with others of the guilty to a hideout they called Balleguard, perhaps in the Henry Mountains of Utah. He was indicted, but as late as 1875 was still hiding. Arrested at last, he hired John Ward Christian of Beaver, Utah, to defend him and "has often told me he did not think the Church ordered (the massacre) or knew of it until after it occurred but he considered it a natural result of doctrines that had been promulgated."

Juanita Brooks, *The Mountain Meadows Massacre.* Norman, Univ. of Okla. Press, 1966; William Wise, *Massacre at Mountain Meadows.* N.Y., Thomas Y. Crowell Co., 1976.

Stewart, William Drummond, Scottish adventurer (Dec. 26, 1795-Apr. 28, 1871). B. at Murthly Castle, Perthshire, Scotland, he was the second son and one of seven children of Sir George Stewart, 17th lord of Grandtully, fifth baronet of Murthly. William joined the 6th Dragoon Guards, was three months in Spain and Portugal and as a lieutenant served under Wellington at Waterloo, five years later becoming a captain in the 15th King's Hussars

and soon retiring on half pay. Seeking adventure he visited St. Louis in 1832, contacted William Clark, Pierre Chouteau Jr., William Ashley and other luminaries and arranged to accompany Robert Campbell who was taking a Sublette pack train to the 1833 rendezvous of mountain men. The party left St. Louis April 13 and attended the Horse Creek Rendezvous in the Green River Valley of Wyoming. Here Stewart met Jim Bridger, Antoine Clement, Bonneville, Tom Fitzpatrick and others. With some of these people Stewart visited the Big Horn Mountains, wintered at Taos, and attended the next rendezvous at Ham's Fork of the Green, later that year journeying on to Fort Vancouver, Washington. He attended the 1835 rendezvous at the mouth of New Fork River on the Green and reached St. Louis in November. Stewart's income from Murthly had sadly declined so he went to New Orleans, speculated in cotton to recoup, wintered in Cuba and in May joined Fitzpatrick's train to the Rockies once more for another rendezvous on Horse Creek. He wintered in 1836-37 at New Orleans, speculating in cotton again; he learned that his son-less older brother was dying of cancer, which would make William the seventh baronet of Murthly with plenty of money. For the rendezvous of 1837 he took along an artist, Alfred Jacob Miller, who painted a notable series of works on Mountain Man life, the rendezvous, Indians and Rocky Mountain scenes, some of which done as oils would later grace Murthly Castle. Again Stewart accompanied Fitzpatrick's train to the rendezvous on the Green and later visited the Wind River Mountains. Stewart attended the following rendezvous on the Popo Agie River and enroute back to St. Louis learned that his brother John had died. Stewart leisurely returned to Scotland and Murthly Castle in July 1838 with Clement and some Indians and his many trophies, Miller arriving later with his sketches. Homesick for the American West Stewart returned to this continent in late 1842. Stewart and his entourage joined the Sublette train to the 1843 rendezvous — the last the Rockies would see — and afterward visited the area that would become Yellowstone Park, returning to St. Louis in October and going back to Scotland for good. His later life was generally tranquil; his son George survived the Charge of the Light Brigade in the Crimea, but died before his father. William Stewart's parenthood, if it was that, of the mysterious Francis Nichols was never proven, although Nichols migrated to Texas and called himself Lord Stewart until the English House of Lords insisted he stop it, whereafter he was known merely as Mr. Stewart. He married but was soon divorced and died at San Antonio November 23, 1913, aged 67.

Mae Reed Porter, Odessa Davenport, *Scotsman in Buckskin*. N.Y., Hastings House, 1963; Marshall Sprague, *A Gallery of Dudes*. Lincoln, Univ. of Nebr. Press, 1979.

Stickney, Benjamin F., pioneer (Oct. 23, 1838-Feb. 1912). B. in Monroe County, New York, he was raised in Illinois and hired out as a teamster in 1860 for a trip to Central City, Colorado, then engaged in prospecting until 1863 with fair success. He bought a team and hauled provisions to Virginia City, Montana, that year, combined freighting with mining for a time, selling his freight interests in 1872. He was a member of the 1870 Washburn Expedition to the Yellowstone. Subsequently he took up ranching near Craig, Montana, expanding from cattle into sheep raising, undertaking various business enterprises. He died in Florida.

Aubrey L. Haines, *Yellowstone National Park: Its Exploration and Establishment*. Wash., Nat. Park Service, 1974.

Stiles, William (Bill Chadwell), desperado (1857-Sept. 7, 1876). B. in Missouri but raised in Minnesota, Stiles there became an accomplished horse thief and minor desperado. He joined the James gang in Missouri in time to take part in the Otterville, Missouri, train robbery July 7, 1876, in which it was reported $15,000 was taken. It is said that it was Chadwell, as he then was known, who persuaded a somewhat reluctant Jesse James and others to attempt to rob the Northfield, Minnesota bank. In the resulting fiasco Chadwell/Stiles was killed in the town; his corpse was secured by the young medical student, Henry M. Wheeler who had shot two others of the bandits. Later Chadwell's skeleton adorned Wheeler's office when he went into practice.

William A. Settle Jr., *Jesse James Was His Name*. Columbia, Univ. of Mo. Press, 1967; Homer Croy, *Jesse James Was My Neighbor*. N.Y., Dell Pub. Co., 1960; Colin Rickards, "Bones

of the Northfield Robbers." *Real West*, Vol. 22, No. 161 (Jan. 1979), 28-31, 60.

Stilwell, F.C. (Frank), frontiersman (1855-Mar. 20, 1882). B. in Texas, he was a younger brother of Simpson E. (Jack) Stilwell, a noted scout. Frank moved west, worked as a cowboy and got into occasional trouble. In October 1877, he shot Jesus Bega through the lung near Miller's Ranch outside of Prescott, Arizona, because the newly hired cook had served him tea instead of coffee. At Tombstone Stilwell and Jack Cassidy escaped a grand jury indictment for "lack of evidence" in a brutal clubbing death of J. Van Houten near the old Brunckow Mine on November 9, 1879. Stilwell was a gambler and sometimes miner, appointed a deputy under Sheriff John Behan of Cochise County, Arizona, and was charged with a September 1881 Bisbee stage robbery, but the case never reached court. He was suspected (whether with cause is not apparent) in the murder of Morgan Earp at Tombstone. Stilwell was assassinated in the railroad yards at Tucson by the Earp faction, including Wyatt and Warren Earp, Doc Holliday and a couple of others.

William B. Shillingberg, *Wyatt Earp & the 'Buntline Special' Myth*. Tucson, Ariz., Blaine Pub. Co., 1976, 48n; Ed Bartholomew, *The Biographical Album of Western Gunfighters*. Houston, Frontier Press of Tex., 1958; Odie B. Faulk, *Tombstone: Myth and Reality*. N.Y., Oxford Univ. Press, 1972.

Stilwell, Simpson Everett (Jack), scout (Aug. 25, 1849-Feb. 17, 1903). B. in Tennessee he moved with his family to Missouri, then Kansas and at 14 joined a wagon party for Santa Fe, remaining in New Mexico for nearly 10 years. He became a scout for the Army in 1867 and on August 28, 1868, he joined Major George A. Forsyth's company of 50 scouts out of Forts Harker and Hays, seeking hostile Cheyennes. Camping near an island in the then-dry Arickaree fork of the Republican River, the Forsyth party was attacked by Cheyennes under Roman Nose and besieged. On the first night Stilwell and Pierre Trudeau slipped away, seeking aid. At one point, concealed in a buffalo wallow under cover of darkness, according to legend, an Indian party came almost within touch of them while a rattlesnake buzzed in their faces. Either Stilwell or Trudeau (reports differ) is said to have discouraged the reptile with a well-aimed spray of tobacco juice. Stilwell became widely known for securing relief for Forsyth on this occasion. He served as scout under Custer, Miles and Mackenzie over the next 13 years. In March 1882, hearing that his brother, Frank, had been murdered by Wyatt Earp and others at Tucson, he started for Arizona to avenge the killing, but returned without doing so. He was a U.S. deputy marshal in Oklahoma, settled at El Reno where he became a police judge, then a U.S. commissioner at Anadarko and, having studied law, was admitted to the bar. In 1898 he moved to William F. Cody's ranch near Cody, Wyoming, where he died (Carter says he died of Bright's disease near Eagle Mountain, Kansas). He was highly respected for his intelligence, courage and loyalty.

DAB; George A. Forsyth, *Thrilling Days of Army Life.* N.Y., Harper & Bros., 1900; Robert G. Carter, *On the Border With Mackenzie.* N.Y., Antiquarian Press, 1961.

Stinson, I.N. (Buck), desperado (d. Jan. 10, 1864). B. at Greencastle, Indiana, his parents took him at the age of 14 to Andrew County, Missouri. He was bright, studious, devoted to books, reading almost constantly and "gave promise of genius." His family was highly respectable and many prophesied a bright future for the boy, but he drifted west, reaching Montana, came under bad influences and ended up as a deputy under the notorious Sheriff Henry Plummer, a murderer and desperado. In the spring of 1863 Stinson murdered a friendly Bannock chief for no apparent reason. Stinson, Hayes Lyons and Charley Forbes killed a fellow deputy, Dillingham, on a main street of Virginia City in June 1863, and got off through blundering of a "miners' court." Stinson was involved in several robberies or attempted robberies of stage coaches and assorted attempted killings as well as murders of record. He was arrested with Plummer and Ned Ray by vigilantes at Bannack and hanged with them. Like Ray, his execution rope slipped and he strangled to death. Stinson was buried at Bannack, the grave identification now lost. Toponce's recollections of Stinson are mostly in error.

Langford; Dimsdale; Birney; Alexander Toponce, *Reminiscences.* Norman, Univ. of Okla. Press, 1971.

Stitt, Merle E., National Park figure (Aug. 8, 1920-June 8, 1980). B. at Gettysburg, Pennsylvania, he was graduated in forestry and wildlife management from the University of Michigan, and served in the Korean War as a survival training officer. In 1953 he was appointed a ranger at Grand Teton National Park, was transferred to Yellowstone National Park and then as supervisory ranger to Rocky Mountain National Park. In 1957 he became chief ranger at Lassen Volcanic National Park and in 1961 of Craters of the Moon National Monument, Idaho. He was transferred to Washington, D.C., in 1962 and served five years as wildlife management biologist for northeast and southeast regions of the National Park Service; in 1967 he was appointed regional chief of resources management in the National Park Service regional office at San Francisco, in 1971 becoming assistant director of operations in that region. In 1972 he was appointed the 15th superintendent of Grand Canyon National Park. He initiated and completed the Grand Canyon National Park Master Plan, the Wilderness Proposal, the Feral Burro Management Plan and the Colorado River Management Plan, and believed he had succeeded in the face of great odds in preserving the character of the Grand Canyon for future generations. He died at Tucson, survived by his widow. Stitt was buried at Grand Canyon cemetery.

Flagstaff, *Arizona Daily Sun,* June 10, 1980.

Stobie, Charles Stewart, westerner, artist (Mar. 18, 1845-Aug. 18, 1931). B. at Baltimore, his family moved to Chicago in 1860. Stobie studied architecture in Scotland and in 1865 headed west to see the country. At St. Joseph, Missouri, he met Moses E. (California Joe) Milner and with Milner was in three Indian skirmishes while crossing the Plains with a wagon party. He had made sketches along the way and on the basis of his art was employed by a Denver decorating firm. In 1866 Stobie befriended Ute Indians and reported he had accompanied a Ute war party against the Arapahoes and Cheyennes, later scouting for Major Jacob Downing (see entry) of the Colorado Volunteers against the same tribes. Stobie settled at Chicago and took up art seriously, using memory and field sketches as the basis for paintings of Indian and frontier scenes and people. He also collected Indian artifacts. Many of them and some of his paintings are held by the Colorado Historical Society. Stobie died at Chicago.

"Charles S. Stobie Exhibition," *Colo. Heritage News,* Nov. 1983; Don Russell, *Life and Legends of Buffalo Bill.* Norman, Univ. of Okla. Press, 1960; information from Don Russell; *Denver Post,* Aug. 19, 1931.

Stockton, Isaac T. (Ike), gunman, rancher (1852-Sept. 27, 1881). B. near Cleburne, Texas, he was an older brother of William Porter (Port) Stockton, and twice broke Port out of jail in New Mexico. In 1874 Ike Stockton was a saloon keeper at Lincoln, New Mexico, but with his family left Lincoln that year. He was involved to some extent in the so-called Colfax County (New Mexico) War of 1875-76. He removed in 1878 to the Animas Valley of San Juan County, Colorado, where he became a stockman and soon a partisan once more. Stockton became heavily involved in feuding between factions at Durango, Colorado, and Farmington, New Mexico (sometimes called the San Juan County War), with a great deal of shooting, lynching and general devilment going on in 1880-81. In June 1881 Stockton and others helped ranchers repel Paiutes depredating in the Grand River valley of Colorado, with ten Anglos reported killed. August 24 an erstwhile Stockton partisan, Burt Wilkinson, resisting arrest killed D.C. (Clate) Ogsbury, marshal of Silverton, Colorado. A large reward (one source said $2,500) was offered for Wilkinson's arrest. Stockton and Bud Galbreth, alias M.C. Cook secured appointments as deputy sheriffs, arrested Wilkinson and won the reward money. Wilkinson was jailed at Silverton and lynched September 4. Barney Watson was named sheriff at Durango and swore to serve his warrants, a novel situation for the time and place. He and Deputy Sheriff James J. Sullivan on September 26 arrested Galbreth at Durango on Texas requisitions charging him with murder, rape, arson and stock stealing. Then they went looking for Stockton, wanted on a New Mexico requisition for the murder of Aaron Barker, a stockman, in March 1881. Stockton resisted and was shot in the thigh, taken to a nearby building where physicians decided amputation was necessary. Six headed by Dr. H.A. Clay severed his leg, but Stockton died about 2 a.m. next day. He was described as 5 feet, 4 inches in height, weighing 164 pounds and with grayish-blue eyes. He and Port Stockton were considered by Ramon Adams "bad men of the first order."

F. Stanley, *The Private War of Ike Stockton.* Denver, World Press, 1959; Philip J. Rasch, "Feuding at Farmington." *New Mex. Hist. Rev.,* Vol. XL, No 3 (July 1965), 215-32.

Stockton, (William) Port(er), gunman (c. 1854-Jan. 10, 1881). B. at Cleburne, Texas, he was a younger brother of Ike Stockton and was said at 12 with a shotgun to have killed a man. At 17 Port assaulted another and was charged with attempted murder but Ike got him off. After a brief stay at Dodge City, Kansas, Port arrived in New Mexico in 1874, Ike having opened a saloon in the county seat of Lincoln. Port killed Juan Gonzales in Colfax County, New Mexico in October 1876 and got off on a plea of self defense (one story relates that Ike broke him out of jail in a predawn escapade). He and Ike moved to Trinidad, Colorado, where in December Port killed another man in a saloon fight; he was captured by a posse and once more Ike helped him escape. In 1879 Port was marshal of Animas City, Colorado. In June 1879 he killed William or Ed Withers at Otero, New Mexico, but escaped with no charges to hold him. He was involved in assorted other shootings and mayhem. Eventually he got restless and joined an alleged rustler gang on the La Plata River, New Mexico. He had a difference with a rancher, Alfred Graves of Farmington, New Mexico, and was killed by Graves outside Stockton's home. Ramon Adams considered the Stocktons "bad men of the first order."

Robert N. Mullin Notes; Ed Bartholomew, *Wyatt Earp: The Man & The Myth.* Toyahvale, Tex., Frontier Book Co., 1964, 25; Philip J. Rasch, "Feuding at Farmington." *New Mex. Hist. Rev.,* Vol. XL, No 3 (July 1965), 215-32; Ramon F. Adams, *Six Guns and Saddle Leather.* Norman, Univ. of Okla. Press, 1969, 611.

Stokes, Joe, desperado (1854-Apr. 1881). B. near San Antonio, Texas, reportedly the son of a wealthy cattleman, he was disowned by his father, removed to Dodge City, Kansas, where he is said to have murdered a man, escaped jail and in 1875 appeared at Otero, New Mexico. Here he joined his brothers, Bill and Doc Stokes, in a dancehall operation.

Doc was killed at Cimarron, New Mexico, March 27, 1879, as a deputy sheriff in a gunbattle possibly with Joe Olney (Joe Hill) and others. Joe Stokes moved on to Las Vegas, New Mexico, cutting the throat of a poker playing associate. Joe and Bill, with another were charged with stage and train robbery. Joe escaped jail, but was recaptured. He was released after 16 months when Rudabaugh confessed committing the crimes for which the Stokes brothers were charged. Joe became a cattle rustler near El Paso, where he was lynched. He was described as 5 feet, 9 inches tall, weighed 165 pounds, "was rated as a desperado, and is said to have killed at least half a dozen men."

Philip J. Rasch, "R.I.P., Joe Stokes." *Corral Dust,* Potomac Corral of Westerners, Vol. III, No. 4 (Dec. 1958), 27-28; Ed Bartholomew, *Wyatt Earp: The Man & the Myth.* Toyahvale, Tex., Frontier Books Co., 1964.

Stone, John, adventurer (d. Jan. 1633/34). An English sea captain, he established his base on St. Kitts (Christopher), which had been settled by the English only a few years before he appeared on the New England coast, already with a reputation for piracy, hard drinking and roguery. During some early voyage according to David de Vries, Stone's boat "met with a misfortune so that his men ate each other," although the details and explanation of that sad event are not given. Stone spent some time in Virginia, then loaded cattle for New England; he was forced to put in at Manhattan Island to water his stock, but did not know the anchorage and lay off Sandy Hook until David de Vries, bound for Holland, signalled him and coming up recognized Stone as an old acquaintance. De Vries gave him a pilot who brought him to anchor near Fort Amsterdam. Stone met the governor, Wouter van Twiller, and got him so drunk that he permitted Stone to board a Plymouth pinnace that was loaded with 500 pounds sterling worth of New Amsterdam fur for New England. Stone hijacked the vessel in the absence of its master and crew who were ashore. With the drunken acquiescence of Van Twiller he sailed her away for Virginia intending to dispose of the valuable cargo to his own rich profit. But some Dutch seamen who had "been often at Plymouth and kindly entertained there" pursued Stone, overtook and captured him and his vessel, and brought them safely back to Fort Amsterdam when the ship and its cargo were returned to its rightful captain. Stone afterwards went to Massachusetts, arriving at Boston June 2, 1633, was charged by Plymouth Colony with piracy and was to be tried by the Admiralty Court in England. But the Plymouth people finally were persuaded they did not have a very good case and the matter was dropped. Stone's quick temper and lawless inclinations soon brought him into fresh difficulties in the colony however (Jennings says he was found "rolling in bed with another man's wife") and in September he was fined heavily and forbade again to enter Massachusetts Colony on pain of death, so he departed hastily for Plymouth. Stone seemed predestined for endless troubles. In Plymouth Colony, despite his peccadilloes he was well entertained, but revenge "boyled in his brest" for the original insult — the indictment against him — and he was thought to plan the assassination of Governor Edward Winslow "but by God's providence and the vigilence of some was prevented" from carrying it out. With a kindred spirit, Captain Walter Norton, Stone put out for Virginia in a pinnace but for some reason detoured up the Connecticut River; not knowing the way to their obscure destination they kidnapped two Western Niantic Indians for guides. On anchoring for the night, Stone and his men asleep, other Indians boarded the pinnace, killed Stone, Norton and their crew and liberated the two captives. Stone's death, which seems very good riddance, was used two years later as a clumsy pretext for the brutal English war of extermination against the Pequots, a tribe loosely allied with the Niantics.

Of Plymouth Plantation 1620-1647, by William Bradford, ed. by Samuel Eliot Morison. N.Y., Modern Library, 1967; William Bradford, *History of Plymouth Plantation 1620-1647,* 2 vols., Vol. II. New York, Russell & Russell, 1968; John Winthrop, *The History of New England from 1630-1649,* ed. by James Savage, 2nd ed., 2 vols. Boston, Little, Brown & Co., 1853; Francis Jennings, *Invasion of America.* Chapel Hill, Univ. of No. Car. Press, 1978; *Narratives of New Netherland 1609-1664,* ed. by J. Franklin Jameson. N.Y., Barnes and Noble, 1967.

Stone, John Finkel, frontiersman (1836-Oct. 5, 1869). B. near Griffin Corners (Fleischmanns), Delaware County, New York,

Stone in 1859 went to Utah with Albert Sidney Johnston, and remained there until 1862. He went then to Colorado and by 1863 was in New Mexico where it is said he served as a deputy U.S. marshal until April 1867. He was appointed deputy collector of customs for the District of El Paso del Norte and shortly moved to the Chiricahua Mountains where he established the Apache Pass Mining Company, based upon his several gold claims, the principal being 1,500 yards east of the old stage station. He also had some kind of business arrangement with miners at the Pinos Altos works of New Mexico. Indians sporadically harassed his work, equipment and laborers. The stage on which he was journeying to Tucson was ambushed near Dragoon Springs and Stone, a driver named Kaler, and four soldiers were killed; the Indians then attacked a nearby herd of Texas cattle enroute to California, killed a herder and ran off the animals, the five remaining herders escaping. They reported seeing three white men operating with the hostiles. Stone was buried at the Fort Bowie graveyard in Apache Pass. In early February Reuben Bernard attacked a rancheria near Apache Pass, recovering from the body of a victim a bar of Stone's gold; the scalp of the Indian was exhibited at Charlie Brown's saloon at Tucson. Stone Avenue, a principal Tucson thoroughfare, was named for John Stone. He was unmarried at the time of his death.

Ariz. Hist. Rev., Vol. VI, No. 3 (July 1935), 74-80; AHS Archives; *Los Angeles Times,* Apr. 18, 1886.

Stone, Milburn, actor (July 5, 1904-June 12, 1980). The nephew of famed stage actor Fred Stone, Milburn Stone was born at Burrton, Kansas, and turned down an appointment to Annapolis to pursue an acting career. He appeared on Broadway and in about 150 films but achieved greatest renown for his role as Dr. Adams in the 20-year television run of *Gunsmoke.* He was married and fathered a daughter.

Tucson, *Arizona Daily Star,* June 13, 1980.

Stoneman, George, army officer (Aug. 8, 1822-Sept. 5, 1894). B. in Chatauqua County, New York, he went to West Point and was commissioned a brevet second lieutenant, 1st Dragoons, July 1, 1846, served in the Mexican War as a quartermaster of the Mormon Battalion in its march from Fort Leavenworth

to San Diego, California. He became a second lieutenant July 12, 1847. He participated in several skirmishes with Indians in California and was on frontier duty from the Presidio of San Francisco and Sonoma from 1848-50, scouting much of the time. He was on the Gila River expedition of 1851-52, skirmishing occasionally with Yuma Indians. Stoneman escorted Second Lieutenant Robert S. Williamson's topographical party in the Sierra Nevada and Second Lieutenant John Grubb Parke's railroad surveying party through Arizona and Texas in 1853-54. He became a first lieutenant July 25, 1854, and was on frontier duty in Texas until the Civil War, becoming a captain of the 2nd Cavalry March 3, 1855. He refused to surrender to his superior, Brigadier General D.E. Twiggs who had cast his lot with the Confederacy; Stoneman escaped with part of his command and gained Union territory. His Civil War record was excellent, Stoneman becoming Major General of Volunteers and brevet Major General in the army. He became colonel of the 21st Infantry July 28, 1866, joining the regiment in Arizona and commanding it and the District (later the Department) of Arizona until August 16, 1871, when he retired for disability in line of duty. He was not too effective in Arizona and was inadvertently partially responsible for the Camp Grant Massacre of April 30, 1871, a contributing factor in his decision to retire. He had implied, Arizonans believed, that they should handle their own Indian problems and minor depredations, and they took that to be a signal to resort to arms, which they did in the ill-advised and senseless slaughter of scores of Aravaipa Apaches, principally non-combatants. Stoneman established himself on a lavish estate near Los Angeles, California. He became a railway commissioner, a member of the Board of Indian Commissioners and was governor of California from January 10, 1883, to January 10, 1887. He died at Buffalo, New York, survived by his widow and their four children.

Cullum; Buffalo *Courier,* Sept. 6, 1894; Dan L. Thrapp, *Conquest of Apacheria.* Norman, Univ. of Okla. Press, 1967.

Storms, Charles, gunman (c. 1854-Feb. 25, 1881). A gambler who was known in Kansas, Nebraska, Deadwood, South Dakota, and Colorado, Storms reached Tombstone,

Arizona, about 1880 where he reopened an ancient grudge-dispute with gambler Luke Short. The two met on the street in front of the Oriental Saloon and Short killed Storms. Bat Masterson, a friend of both men, unsuccessfully tried to prevent their encounter. Storms was described as "gritty," and "had been in a number of shooting affairs, in all of which he showed plenty of nerve."

Ed Bartholomew, *Wyatt Earp: The Man & the Myth.* Toyahvale, Tex., Frontier Book Co., 1964; William R. Cox, *Luke Short and His Era.* Garden City, N.Y., Doubleday & Co., 1961.

Story, Nelson, frontiersman (Apr. 4, 1838-Mar. 10, 1926). B. in Meigs County, Ohio, he attended college briefly and went west at 20, accompanying the military columns toward Utah in 1858, but became ill at Fort Laramie and, not being a soldier, was left behind. Story eventually reached Montana, profited from Alder Gulch gold mines, and turned to stock raising. He went to Fort Worth in 1866, bought longhorns, and drove them north. He reached Fort Leavenworth, then turned west up the Platte, gaining Fort Laramie and, despite Sioux hostility, took his wagon train and trail herd north into Montana, skirmishing with Indians enroute. One rider was killed by Indians on Clark's Fork of the Columbia, but Story reached the site of present Livingston, Montana. He sold the beef at a rich profit to Alder Gulch miners, but kept out his breeding stock, adding to it where he could, and within four years was a leading stockman of Montana, centering his activities, which had broadened into other fields, at Bozeman. In 1874 he led a party of armed citizens and fought three battles with Sioux toward the southeast, defeating them each time. Story became interested in steamboating on the Missouri, operating a fleet between St. Louis and Montana. He branched out into horse raising, beginning with 200 California mares in 1876, soon having a herd of 1,300 animals which he found readily marketable. By the 1880's Story had become "one of the fabled entrepreneurs of the Northern Plains," had entered the fields of finance and business, and was a millionaire with palatial homes at Bozeman and Los Angeles. In 1892 he sold 13,000 head of beef for delivery within three years, "one of the largest single transactions in livestock recorded in the history of northwest ranching." Story became something of a philanthropist before his death at Los Angeles.

Cowboys and Cattlemen, ed. by Michael S. Kennedy. N.Y., Hastings House, 1964; Dorothy M. Johnson, *The Bloody Bozeman.* N.Y., McGraw-Hill Book Co., 1971.

Stouch, George Wesley Hancock, army officer (Mar. 3, 1842-Nov. 11, 1906). B. at Gettysburg, Pennsylvania, he enlisted November 30, 1861, in the 11th Infantry rising to sergeant major by 1864 when he was commissioned a second lieutenant in the 3rd Infantry shortly becoming a first lieutenant. He retired as major of the 20th Infantry in 1898 for disability in line of duty, and was made a lieutenant colonel on the retired list in 1904. February 28, 1894, he was appointed agent at the Northern Cheyenne Reservation at Lame Deer, Montana, proving himself a dedicated friend of the Cheyennes and a good agent. May 23, 1897, a white sheepherder, John Hoover, was murdered by Indians north of the agency. White unrest led to dispatch of two troops of the black 10th Cavalry to the agency for protection of the law-abiding Indians there, the force later supported by additional units. Through all the tension and turmoil that followed Stouch proved a calm, mediating influence and his actions no doubt prevented considerable bloodshed. In November 1897 he was transferred to the adjacent Crow Agency but with the outbreak of the Spanish American War he returned to strictly military duties. After his retirement from the army he became for a time agent for the Southern Cheyennes and Arapahoes in Oklahoma. He died at Washington, D.C.

Lonnie E. Underhill, Daniel F. Littlefield Jr., "Cheyenne 'Outbreak' of 1897." *Montana: Mag. of West. Hist.,* Vol. XXIV, No. 4 (Autumn 1974), 30-41; Stouch Pension file, Nat. Archives; Heitman.

Stoudenmire, Dallas, lawman (1845-Sept. 18, 1882). B. in Macon County, Alabama, he served in the Confederate army and then went west. He won note as a gunman at Columbus, Texas, and later was named city marshal of El Paso, Texas. On April 14, 1881, Stoudenmire took part in a wild El Paso gunbattle that followed an Anglo-Mexican killing affair near town, Dallas killing three of the four city victims. This brought him into a feuding relationship with the three Manning brothers, influential in El Paso, and their satellites. April 17, 1881, he killed Bill Johnson, whom he had succeeded as marshal, after Johnson tried to ambush him, Stoudenmire himself shot in the heel by another hidden assassin. Dallas's brother-in-law, Samuel M. (Doc) Cummings, was killed by Jim Manning and perhaps others, Cummings having precipitated the fight. After awhile Stoudenmire and the Mannings signed a "peace treaty," having it published locally, but bad blood continued. After well splitting El Paso into pro- and anti-Stoudenmire factions, Dallas resigned May 29 as marshal, but July 13 became a U.S. deputy marshal. A ferocious and unpredictable man when drunk, Stoudenmire continued his bouts with the bottle. On September 18 he was badly wounded but also wounded Doc Manning and wrestled with him in the street outside a saloon. While so engaged he was killed by Doc's brother, Jim, who was acquitted of murder. Stoudenmire was 6 feet, 4 inches in height, with dark brown hair and green eyes.

Leon Claire Metz, *Dallas Stoudenmire: El Paso Marshal.* Austin, Tex., Pemberton Press, 1969; Metz, *The Shooters.* El Paso, Mangan Books, 1976.

Strahorn, Robert Edmund (Alter Ego), newspaperman, railroad builder (May 15, 1852-Mar. 31, 1944). B. in Center County, Pennsylvania, he was a newspaperman from 1866 until 1877 and during this time a correspondent for the *Rocky Mountain News, Chicago Tribune* and other papers during the Sioux wars of 1876-77. Finerty described him as a correspondent "who in every situation proved himself as fearless as he was talented." Strahorn attended the Reynolds Campaign of early 1876, was with Crook at the Rosebud, and Bourke reported that he "remained throughout the entire campaign, winter and summer, until the last of the hostiles surrendered." He also testified at court-martial proceedings following the Reynolds campaign. Strahorn joined the Union Pacific railroad, handling its publicity department from 1877 until 1883, then worked at a variety of promotional, industrial, agricultural and railroad enterprises, of little frontier interest. He wrote: *Wyoming, Black Hills and Big Horn Regions: To the Rockies and Beyond; The Enchanted Land; Where Rolls the Oregon,* and other works. He was a founder of the College of Idaho at Caldwell and made his home late in life at Boise. He married twice, both wives predeceasing him.

J.W. Vaughn, *With Crook at the Rosebud.* Harrisburg, Pa., Stackpole Co., 1956; Vaughn, *The Reynolds Campaign on Powder River.* Norman, Univ. of Okla. Press, 1961; John F. Finerty, *War-Path and Bivouac.* Lincoln, Univ. of Nebr. Press, 1961; *Who Was Who.*

Strange, William, borderer (c. 1764-1795). B. in Fauquier County, Virginia, his birth date is conjecture. He was "an indifferent woodsman," who accompanied Jacob Reger Sr. and others on a western Virginia hunt, and disappeared. His bones were found years later with his gun, ramrod and shot pouch near a beech tree on which, purportedly, was carved: "William Strange is my name, And in these strange woods I must remain." He apparently had become lost or accidentally wounded, and perished in the wilderness.

Lucullus V. McWhorter, *The Border Settlers of Northwestern Virginia.* Hamilton, O., Republican Pub. Co., 1915.

Stratton, Arthur, Mormon pioneer (fl. 1857-1892). A man of this name is placed by *Mormonism Unveiled* at the Mountain Meadows Massacre of September 11, 1857, either participating in or consenting to the tragedy. The book made no mention of his death before its publication, but said he was from Virgin City, Utah. *Journal of the Southern Indian Mission* mentions an A.J. Stratton in southern Utah about the time of the affair, but this may refer to Anthony Johnson Stratton (Jan. 11, 1824-Nov. 29, 1887), b. in Tennessee and who died at Snowflake, Arizona. He was a bishop's counselor at Virgin City, a school teacher and farmer, and first lieutenant in Company C, battalion of Infantry.

Mormonism Unveiled, 380; Frank Esshom, *Pioneers and Prominent Men of Utah.* Salt Lake City, Western Epics, 1966; *Journal of the Southern Indian Mission,* ed. by Juanita Brooks. Logan, Utah State Univ. Press, 1972.

Strauss, Levi, clothier (Feb. 28, 1829-Sept. 28, 1902). B. at Buttenheim, Bavaria, he emigrated to the United States in 1847, becoming a dry goods merchant. In late 1852 he sailed around Cape Horn for San Francisco to join a brother-in-law, David Stern, again in dry-goods merchandising. The firm prospered and expanded. In 1872 it received a letter from a tailor-customer, Jacob Davis of Reno,

Nevada, who had hit upon the fabrication of durable men's workwear of canvas, with pocket seams and other weak points strengthened by copper rivets; the product had proven popular but Davis needed a patent to protect his invention. Levi and his partners secured the necessary patent May 20, 1873, and Davis agreed to become production manager for what became known as "blue jeans" and much later as "Levi's." More than 200 million pair have been sold until now. Levi Strauss & Company (incorporated in 1890) was left to Strauss's four nephews. It branched out into other fields, but the famed Levi's remain its best known product.

Ed Cray, *Levi's*, Boston, Houghton Mifflin Co., 1978; Alvin M. Josephy Jr., "Those Pants that Levi Gave Us," *American West*, Vol. XXII, No. 4 (July/Aug. 1985), 30-37.

Strawhun, Samuel O., frontiersman (Oct. 10, 1845-Sept. 27, 1869). B. in southern Missouri, he may have moved to Illinois as a young man. He was hired as a plains teamster November 1, 1868, became a courier between Hays City and Fort Dodge, Kansas, and in late March was jailed at Dodge by a deputy marshal on a federal warrant, the charge being unknown today. In an altercation in the Leavenworth Beer Saloon on S. Fort St., Hays City, he was killed by James Butler (Wild Bill) Hickok with whom he reportedly had previously had difficulties.

Joseph G. Rosa, *They Called Him Wild Bill*, 2nd ed. Norman, Univ. of Okla. Press, 1974.

Streeter, Floyd Benjamin historian (Dec. 5, 1888-Jan. 1, 1956). B. on a farm near Hesston, Kansas, he was graduated from the University of Kansas, became an archivist for the Michigan Historical Society and in 1926 head librarian at Kansas State College, Fort Hays, retiring in 1953. A meticulous, honest historian, he became over 40 years a leading expert on the history of early cow towns, outlaws, gunmen and characters. He published many articles on his specialties as well as: *Tragedies of a Kansas Cow Town* (1934); *Prairie Trails & Cow Towns* (1936); *The Kaw: the Heart of a Nation* (1941); *Ben Thompson: Man With a Gun* (1957). He also edited George G. Thompson's *Bat Masterson: The Dodge City Years* (1943). His books are reliable.

"A Note on Dr. Floyd Benjamin Streeter 1888-

1956," in Streeter, *Ben Thompson: Man With a Gun*. N.Y., Frederick Fell, 1957.

Streeter, (William) Charles, frontiersman (1851-Apr. 5, 1919). B. at Santa Barbara, California, he was a half-brother of Zebina Nathaniel Streeter and a son of William Adams Streeter and Josefa Valdez, his wife and third generation descendant of José Francisco Ortega, founder of Santa Barbara. In his youth he went south to Ventura, California, where he married, had difficulty with his wife, left her and went to New Mexico and Arizona, never marrying again. He returned to Santa Barbara twice to see his aging mother, but otherwise did not again visit California. Charles met Zebina Streeter again and was associated with him off and on as long as his half-brother lived, many of the news stories of Zebina's activities apparently originating with Charley Streeter, as he usually was called, most of them fairly accurate. About 1884 Zebina's full brother, William Crandel (Crandall) Streeter (1837-1920) of St. Louis, came to Silver City and worked in the drug store/post office of O.L. Scott. Whether he contacted the half-brother or Zebina during that period is unknown. From St. Louis he wrote later that he already was "homesick" for the Southwest. He lived in and about Tombstone, Arizona, for a time, but drifted into Sonora and with others located what developed into one of the richest copper mines in Mexico at Nacozari Viejo. "He got several thousand dollars in stock in the (Moctezuma Concentrating) company that was formed by eastern capitalists to develop the mine, and started for New York, but never got farther than El Paso. After his money was gone he returned to Nacozari...," broke once more. Phelps Dodge took over, developed and now operates the mine. It was at Nacozari that Charley's brother, Zebina, was shot from ambush and killed in 1889 and apparently Charley never forgot it. He always carried a gun, but was a quiet man, generally well-liked. He enjoyed poker and at Nacozari one day in 1911 or thereabouts, he killed Antonio Montaño with whom he was playing cards, by shooting him from under the table; he was jailed at Moctezuma, but in a few months came the Mexican Revolution, the jail doors were opened and he lost no time getting across the Border to Douglas, where he lived the remainder of his life. One wonders whether there was some connection between the shooting of Zebina and the shooting by his brother Charley, of the Mexican, both at Nacozari where the town was well policed and murders extremely rare. His newspaper obituary concluded that Charley was "a kind-hearted old man and his passing will be regretted by many" He was described by acquaintances as short, in good condition, weighing about 160 pounds and with grey hair. They added that he "spoke very good Spanish and the Mexicans liked him."

Interviews with Fernando Ortiz, Francisco Andrade, Antonio Montaño (the son of Streeter's victim); interview with George Clare Streeter, Mrs. Ynez Josephine Davis, Carmelita Martine Freeman; Streeter probate file; *Tombstone Prospector,* Apr. 8, 1919; information from Susan Berry, Silver City Museum.

Streeter, Zebina Nathaniel, renegade (Oct. 8, 1838-c. June 26, 1889). B. at Genoa, New York, the son of William Adams Streeter (1811-1902) and William's first wife and cousin, Hannah C. Day. Zebina at the age of 8 started off to school one day and did not return for six months; at 11 he went to sea. He followed the sea until 1856, making four voyages. In that year he sought to desert his ship at Panama, but was pursued with bloodhounds, shot and recaptured. Apparently his wound prevented him from being taken back aboard the vessel however, for he is next heard from during Albert Sidney Johnston's campaign in the Mormon War of 1857 when he served with the quartermaster as a clerk, teamster or something similar. While out hunting for the mess one day he narrowly escaped capture by the Cheyennes, then hostile. He went on to California from Salt Lake City, stopping with his father now married to Josefa Valdez, a third generation descendant of José Francisco Ortega, founder of Santa Barbara, the family residing there; here he met the oldest son of the couple, William Charles Streeter (1851-1919) with whom he would closely associate later in life. Zebina was commissioned a second lieutenant in Company B, 1st Battalion of Native Cavalry May 9, 1864, was court-martialed for drunkenness and dismissed October 21. On December 5 he enlisted as a private in Company C, 1st Battalion of Native Cavalry for one year during which he was now and then made sergeant but each time quickly dropped

back to private again. He was mustered out at San Francisco December 5, 1865, on expiration of his term of service having served "honestly and faithfully" according to his discharge. He was described at that time as 5 feet, 5 inches, in height, of light complexion, grey eyes with auburn hair. Streeter went to Mexico as he later reported, was commissioned under the name of Don Casimero to serve under Juarez and emerged a colonel; no evidence has been found to substantiate the claim, but it is not improbable. He was fluent in Spanish and had learned something of the Apache tongue and served as an interpreter and scout at Fort Craig, New Mexico; here he became a friend of Tom Jeffords, and acquainted with such noteworthy Apaches as Loco, Victorio, Juh, Geronimo and perhaps Cochise; this report is confirmed by numerous dispatches and communications from Fort Craig files of the day. Occasionally Streeter was sent on delicate missions to or with the Indians, and so far as the record shows performed them satisfactorily. His knowledge of the Apache tongue increased (it is said he later married into the tribe, although this lacks confirmation). In 1872 Streeter said he accompanied Howard on the General's celebrated mission to Cochise. No official account confirms his presence, but Joseph Sladen in a lengthy private communication does so, asserting that Howard's party picked up Streeter (then living with a Mexican "wife") at Cañada Alamosa (Monticello), New Mexico and took him along to the Dragoon Mountains for the lengthy conference with Cochise. Later Streeter was in Grant County where he said he became a deputy to Sheriff Harvey Whitehill, who was elected in 1874. There is no confirmation of Streeter's service as deputy but records for the period are virtually non-existent so that proves little. Several reports have Streeter working as a clerk at the San Carlos Apache Agency, Arizona although once more confirmation is lacking. He reported that he came to cross-purposes with the so-called "Indian ring," and was run out of Arizona as an outlaw with a $5,000 price on his head; this basic assertion is supported by contemporary newspaper stories, but efforts to check it out in detail have been unavailing. At any rate he apparently then joined Juh's band of Southern Apaches and thereafter until the death of Juh traveled and raided with them, it being reported that "since that time he has taken an active part in every campaign made by Juh in Mexico and Arizona." If true this would put him in the 1882 raid by Juh to San Carlos where Loco and his band of some 700 Apaches were herded out to Mexico, the most spectacular feat of Apache arms on record; Geronimo also was along on this foray, as a subordinate to Juh. There are confirmed reports of a few of Streeter's activities during subsequent years. In 1880 he may have attempted to assist the "poet-scout" Jack Crawford when the latter tried to contact Victorio and bring that great war leader in, but the mission was unsuccessful. At some time Streeter had a broken leg attended to at Tombstone. In April 1883 Streeter, then according to Mexican newspapers "leading a band of Apaches," was wounded in a fight between Apaches and Mexicans, captured and taken to Hermosillo, where for some reason he was later released. Henry Flipper reported meeting him in Sonora. In June 1886 he joined Leonard Wood who was hunting Geronimo in northern Mexico as Wood reports in his diary which calls him "old man Streeter," although Zebina was but 48 at the time. Dobie in *Apache Gold and Yaqui Silver* refers to "Casimero Streeter," relates his career in a somewhat imaginary way, and in correspondence said he could not recall where he had picked up the story. Streeter was shot and killed at Nacozari, Sonora by the brother of a girl to whom he had been paying attention. An official investigation was held into the incident, but with results unreported. He was buried informally at Nacozari, an Anglo "making a few remarks over the grave," the site of which is now a small community plaza.

Dan L. Thrapp, *The White Apache: Adventures of Zebina Nathaniel Streeter,* manuscript in preparation.

Stringer, Sam, frontiersman (d. 1912). A teamster at Fort Phil Kearny, Wyoming, he helped haul in the bodies from the Fetterman Massacre of December 1866. Stringer said he had been a Pony Express rider and in later years rode the mail in Johnson County, Wyoming, sometimes through rigorous weather. He died at Buffalo, Wyoming.

Archives and photograph, Gatchell Mus., Buffalo, Wyo.

Stuart, David, fur trader (Dec. 22, 1765-Oct. 18, 1853). B. in Perthshire, Scotland, he migrated to Canada before 1800, becoming a fisherman and fur trader. He joined the North West Company in 1807 but shortly associated with Astor for his Oregon coast enterprise, leaving New York aboard the *Tonquin* September 6, 1810. He went up the Columbia River in 1811, helped build Fort Okanogan and explored the interior, returning to Astoria in the summer of 1813; Stuart opposed the sale of Astoria to the North West Company, then reluctantly agreed to it, although he declined to join the British concern. He reached Montreal September 1, 1814, went on to New York and joined Astor's American Fur Company. Eventually he was assigned to Michilimackinac, on the Great Lakes. In 1834 he retired, settling eventually at Detroit, where he died.

Jerome Peltier article, MM, Vol. VII.

Stuart, Granville, frontiersman (Aug. 27, 1834-Oct. 2, 1918). B. at Clarksburg in the present West Virginia, he was taken with his older brother, James, by their parents to Muscatine County, Iowa. His early life and until he reached Montana parallels that of James. The Stuarts are generally credited with touching off the Montana gold rush by writing to a third brother, Thomas in Colorado describing their finds and urging him to join them. Word of the letter got about and scores of Colorado gold miners flocked to the northern country, as well as others from Idaho and the Pacific coast. The Stuarts never profited much from the great gold discoveries for which they paved the way, however. Granville did not join James on his Yellowstone expeditions of 1863 and 1864; with James he moved to Bannack in 1862 and to Virginia City, Montana, in 1863. His role in the vigilante activities that wiped out the Plummer gang in the winter of 1863-64 are unclear, but he may well have had something to do with it in view of his heavy involvement in later vigilante activities and his praise of his close friend Dimsdale's *The Vigilantes of Montana* as "an absolutely correct narrative of the operations" of that organization, information he would be unlikely to possess unless he had a role in it. Granville Stuart settled at Deer Lodge in 1867 opening a store and lumberyard and always took a responsible part in public affairs; he was elected to the territorial council twice, in 1883 serving as its president. He had ever been interested in the cattle business; in 1860 he and his brother and others brought in 60 head from Oregon Trail trading and their purchase of trailworn and footsore oxes which would quickly recuperate on lush Montana ranges. In 1879 Granville and three others formed a partnership, purchased 2,000 head of cattle and rode the grasslands of central Montana looking for a good range on which to settle and raise stock. Stuart visited the Tongue River at this time, picked up relics on the site of the Custer fight, checked still-legible inscriptions left by his brother's exploring expedition on the Big Horn River 17 years earlier, and finally settled on a site on Ford's Creek in the Judith Basin, about 20 miles northeast of the present Lewistown, Montana. Here he established a headquarters ranch and near it the army later established Fort Maginnis. The range was good but cattle losses were heavy due to Indian raids, white rustlers, hard winters and attrition. In 1883 stockmen considered their condition desperate and vigilantes again were organized, Granville Stuart reportedly the leader, or at any rate very prominent among them. In one battle July 8, 1884, a band of alleged rustlers was attacked at their hideout and many killed or wounded. Patrick Francis (Frank) Burke, a soldier who with a small detachment took part, said that 16 were killed, but the figure may have included wounded as well as slain, and perhaps other vigilante victims executed in various places. At any rate the popular activity eliminated major rustling in Montana for years to come. Adverse market conditions and the notorious winter of 1886-87 all but wiped out the Montana cattle industry. Granville Stuart determined to quit that business. "I never wanted to own again an animal that I could not feed and shelter," he wrote. In 1891 he was appointed state land agent. President Cleveland named him Minister to Uruguay and Paraguay in 1894 and he remained in South America until 1899 when he returned to Montana. In 1904 Stuart was named librarian of the Butte Public Library and in 1916 was commissioned by Montana to write a history of the state, although he did not live to complete it. He died in Montana. Stuart was an intellectual, a fine writer and a wise man with an engaging sense of humor. He was a bit

of a philosopher and an excellent artist, though without formal training. His sketches were in no sense crude. They reveal a mathematical or architectural mind and are devoid of extraneous detail but with a good sense of proportion and perspective, delineating clearly what he wished to convey. He wrote three major works: *Montana As It Is* (1865), a geographical description of the Territory, its resources and communications; *Forty Years on the Frontier,* two volumes (1925) presenting perhaps the best, clearest, most readable and most graphic narration of the settlement and early history of Montana; and *Diary and Sketchbook of a Journey to "America" in 1866* (1963), more than casually interesting because of Stuart's frequently amusing style; it relates an overland trip to the States and return up the Missouri River by steamboat, illustrated by his sketches of river scenes, fortifications, trading posts and other points of interest. The late Paul C. Phillips who edited *Forty Years on the Frontier,* believed Stuart's writings were "of real historical importance. He has given us the fullest description of life in Montana before and during the gold rush. He has sketched the last days of the old Hudson's Bay Company in the Northwest. He has given us glimpses of the Catholic Indian Missions... He has... presented the pioneer's views of the hostile redskins. The history of the cattle business in the Northwest is his most important contribution...." Stuart was married initially to Aubony (Ellen), a Snake woman, May 2, 1862, and fathered nine children; Aubony died in 1887 at Maiden, Montana; about 1890 he married a white woman, Isabel Alice Brown, with whom he lived the remainder of his life.

Granville Stuart, *Forty Years on the Frontier,* 2 vols. Glendale, Calif., Arthur H. Clark Co., 1925 (rep. by Bison Books, Lincoln, Nebr., 1977); "Letters From the Wild West," ed. by Charles T. Burke. *Montana Mag.,* Vol. XIX, No. 1 (Winter 1969), 17-19; REAW; DAB.

Stuart, James, frontiersman (Mar. 14, 1832-Sept. 30, 1873). B. in Harrison County, Virginia, he was the older brother of Granville Stuart; their parents took them to Bureau County, Illinois, and later to Muscatine County, Iowa, in 1838, then a frontier region where they matured. James Stuart's education was rudimentary although he attended a high school at Iowa City in 1847-48. His father made one trip to California gold fields in 1849-51 and in 1852 set out again, James and Granville accompanying him, reaching the Sacramento Valley on September 28. The father returned east and the boys remained in California, mining, herding stock and engaging in other occupations. In 1855 they narrowly escaped death on the Klamath River, Oregon, at the outbreak of the second Rogue River War. The Stuarts joined the California Volunteers at this time. Once James with a companion ran across two Indians they suspected of horse stealing and killed both, returning the animals to the Shasta Valley. In 1857 James and Granville, with Rezin Anderson, their cousin, and eight others left Yreka, California, for the States; the three separated from the others and because of Mormon hostility veered northeast to the present Montana, spending the winter of 1857-58 in the Beaverhead Valley and on the Big Hole River where then there were only the bare rudiments of white settlement. They had heard rumors of an 1852 gold find of undetermined magnitude in the Deer Lodge Valley and in 1858 found good color on what is now Gold Creek, northwest of Deer Lodge. James Stuart that spring suffered a concussion while roping a wild horse, but recovered. June 14, 1858, he and three others drove some horses to Fort Bridger on the overland trail in present Wyoming, arriving on the 28th, then to Camp Floyd, Utah, where Johnston's army was encamped, selling the horses there at a good profit. The Stuarts returned to Green River, buying trailworn oxen from wagon trains and wintering on Henry's Fork. The next summer, their cattle fat and healthy, they continued trading for livestock and returned in early 1861 to Gold Creek. Here they mined, again finding good prospects, Gold Creek becoming in a small way the first mining settlement of any significance in western Montana. Word of their discoveries spread and with the strike at the Bannack placers on Grasshopper Creek, a real rush began. Stuart sent east for medical books and supplies, read medicine and studied surgery assiduously. He never practiced except without compensation among friends and associates, but became "very successful, and rarely failed to cure any case." He was elected first sheriff of Missoula County in 1862. There was virtually no law apparatus in the Montana of the day, and Stuart and others provided common-sense

methods of solving crime and dispensing what justice appeared appropriate. The Stuarts engaged in the butchering business at Bannack briefly late in 1862 and early 1863, but James left that enterprise and in April 1863 with about 15 companions set out to explore the Yellowstone country for gold or other profit. It was a long and adventurous trip. Samuel T. Hauser, one of the party, spoke for all when he said anent one very severe fight with Indians that the white lives were saved largely by Stuart's "wisdom and heroic bearing" and in that engagement and afterward "his nobleness of soul and heroic courage shone more brilliantly than ever before." Stuart at this period had little but derision, if not contempt for any Indian, and would happily have shot them all had that been possible, but he was basically a man of generous and amiable inclinations, of great intellectual power and perfect honesty and well deserved to be considered, as he was, a foremost pioneer of Montana. The expedition finally dropped down to Fort Bridger and returned by way of Bear River, reaching Bannack on June 24, 1863. Stuart moved to Virginia City, Montana, endured a severe attack of typhoid fever and in September formed a business partnership with Walter B. Dance that was "very successful" and which he continued for seven years. His role if any in the famous vigilante movement that wiped out the Plummer gang in the winter of 1863-64 is undefined but given his leadership, courage and occasional ferocity in battling for what he considered right he may well have been involved in some way. In the spring of 1864 he organized a second Yellowstone expedition of 73 men with the joint objective of discovering gold and killing as many Indians as possible in retribution for sufferings at native hands on the previous trip; they found no Indians, nor any gold, and Stuart and 14 others returned about May 18, the remainder in the summer. Late in 1864 Stuart was elected to the legislature; in 1865 he was commissioned a lieutenant colonel of the Montana Militia, but nothing came of that enterprise; in 1867 he was named general manager and superintendent of a silver mining company at Phillipsburg, Montana, and in 1871 was appointed post trader at Fort Browning, Montana, retaining the position until 1873. He then removed to a Fort Peck Sioux agency, his earlier antipathy toward natives apparently outgrown. "He was eminently fitted by nature to deal with the Indian tribes, for he easily and quickly acquired their languages, and had that peculiar tact so necessary in dealing with them. He was a good judge of human nature, either civilized or savage," and he freely treated their wounds and diseases, thus winning influence among them. Stuart died of a liver ailment. His body was brought back to Deer Lodge where he was given the Masonic funeral he had requested.

Montana, Contributions, Vol. I (1876), 36-79.

Stuart, James Ewell Brown, army officer (Feb. 6, 1833-May 12, 1864). B. in Patrick County, Virginia, he attended Emory and Henry College for two years before going to West Point; he was commisioned a brevet second lieutenant of the Mounted Rifles July 1, 1854, and a second lieutenant October 31. Stuart spent most of the ensuing six years in Kansas where he quickly won a reputation as a superior officer. He transferred to the 1st Cavalry March 3, 1855. After a swift courtship he married the daughter of Philip St. George Cooke and became a first lieutenant December 20, 1855. Stuart was with Colonel E. V. Sumner in July 1857 and on the 29th, for perhaps the only time in the history of Indian warfare, the soldiers launched a sabre attack upon the mounted Cheyennes, an estimated 300 of them. Several Indians were slain, Sumner's command losing two soldiers killed and ten wounded while Stuart received a pistol ball in his chest, the surgeon heroically saving him "for a more illustrious death seven years later." Stuart was in several Indian campaigns and combats. He took an active part in the Kansas Border troubles of the 1850s and was on Colonel Albert Sidney Johnston's Utah expedition in 1858. He became a captain April 22, 1861, but resigned May 14 to join the Confederacy with which he became a Major General and a distinguished cavalry leader. He was wounded mortally May 10, 1864 at Yellow Tavern, Virginia, and died at Richmond.

Cullum; Heitman; Percival G. Love, *Five Years a Dragoon*. Norman, Univ. of Okla. Press, 1965; Robert M. Utley, *Frontiersmen in Blue*. N.Y., Macmillan Co., 1967.

Stuart, John, Indian agent (c. 1700-Mar. 21, 1779). B. in Scotland, he arrived in America

perhaps with the Highlanders under Oglethorpe; he is reported to have campaigned against the Spanish in Florida in 1740 and in 1757 was commissioned captain in the South Carolina Provincial militia. Stuart was active in the Cherokee troubles of 1760 which were, it was suspected, engineered by the French and which resulted in the capture of Fort Loudon (where Stuart was second in command) in eastern Tennessee, with all but three of the garrison and refugees massacred. One of the chiefs, Attakullaculla, purchased Stuart, his longtime friend, from his captor by putting up his rifle, clothes and everything else the Indian possessed. Attakullaculla then delivered Stuart safely to Virginia; through the Cherokee's influence Stuart was accepted as British agent for the southern tribes, his title being Indian Superintendent in the South. In 1764 he held a great council for the southern bands at Mobile, persuading most of them to rally from the French to the British interest. In 1769 he was appointed to the king's council for South Carolina, building a mansion at Charleston on his not inconsiderable salary of 1,000 pounds sterling with 3,000 pounds sterling expense money annually. He was suspected of Loyalist sympathies as the Revolution approached and in 1775 escaped Charleston to Florida, where he lived the rest of his life, at first trying to keep the Indians out of the war which, he explained to them, was a dispute between whites who would settle it themselves. When Gage urged that he incite the Indians to pro-British activity, Stuart argued that they should be used in concert with troops and no good would come from indiscriminate attacks or sporadic hostilities. Stuart believed his Indians were loyal to him and that it was necessary to settle disputes between the tribes before they could be used effectually in the white men's war. Later however Stuart gave in and in early 1776 began to encourage the Cherokees and others to pick up the tomahawk. Stuart conferred with Henry Clinton in the spring of 1776 and in the fall, after Cherokee activities against the Americans had collapsed, tried to settle the Creek-Choctaw dispute in order to muster new forces for use on the southern frontier. His Indians proved unenthusiastic however about war in the absence of any important British support. By 1777 Stuart's health began giving him problems. The Indian frontier was disorganized and largely ineffectual as a drain upon colonial strength. He came into dispute with Patrick Tonyn, governor of East Florida who thought Stuart indolent and vain and not as effective as he might be, being largely unaware of the very real difficulties under which Stuart worked with his mercurial charges, In May 1777 Stuart again conferred with some 2,800 tribesmen at Mobile, Creeks, Chickasaws, Choctaws. But American rum and agents wrecked any accomplishments. Stuart punished the Creeks by cutting off trade goods until they begged for resumption, the trade being renewed in early 1778. Again Tonyn demanded Indian assistance against what he feared would be a Georgian invasion; it was not forthcoming. In early 1779 a few Creeks were mustered, but they accomplished little. Stuart died at Pensascola "after a tedious and painful illness, which he bore with resignation for several months," his death a blow to British southern hopes which were never realized. At the time of his death Stuart was under criticism for the great expenses he incurred in fulfilling his mission, and by the non-understanding Tonyn for his inability to rally and maintain effective support for the Crown.

Reuben Gold Thwaites, Louise Phelps Kellogg, *Documentary History of Dunmore's War 1774.* Madison, Wisc. Hisc. Soc., 1905; James H. O'Donnell III, *Southern Indians in the American Revolution.* Knoxville, Univ. of Tenn. Press, 1973.

Stuart, Robert, fur trader (Feb. 18, 1785-Oct. 29, 1848). A nephew of David Stuart, he migrated to Canada in 1807, joined the North West Company and in 1810 with his uncle went with Astor's Pacific Fur Company as a partner. He and David shipped for Oregon aboard the *Tonquin,* whose irascible captain, Jonathan Thorn, Robert once threatened with a pistol to save his uncle. The Stuarts had a creditable role in founding Astoria, Robert taking on missions of increasing responsibility. June 29, 1812, he headed the Astorian party returning overland with dispatches, discovered South Pass, reaching St. Louis April 20, 1813, "after a most remarkable journey." Stuart married Elizabeth Sullivan at New York, continued with Astor, in 1822 was placed in charge of the American Fur Company's Great Lakes Division at Michilimackinac, retaining its direction until Crooks bought out Astor in 1834. He then moved to

Detroit, held public office, prospered in business, was superintendent of Indian Affairs for Michigan from 1841 to 1845, and fathered a family of nine children. Stuart was intensely loyal to his comrades and employers, intelligent, honest, and while sometimes imperious, won respect from white and Indian alike. His influence was distinctly positive.

Harvey L. Carter article, MM, Vol. IX; Gabriel Franchere, *Adventure at Astoria 1810-1814.* Norman, Univ. of Okla. Press, 1967; Washington Irving, *Astoria,* ed. by Edgeley W. Todd. Norman, 1964.

Stuart, Thomas, frontiersman (1839-May 23, 1915). A younger brother of James and Granville Stuart, famed Montana pioneers, Thomas was b. in Iowa where his brothers who had been born in the present West Virginia, grew to manhood. Thomas Stuart joined the Colorado gold rush and in 1861 was in the vicinity of Cripple Creek. His brothers wrote him there, urging that he join them in the Deer Lodge region of Montana where they had discovered promising gold placers. Thomas showed the letter to friends which sparked the rush to Montana of 1862, augmented by the discovery of a rich strike at Bannack, and thus Thomas Stuart was of moment in Montana history although he did not reach that Territory until 1864. He never attained the prominence of his brothers, but was a respected pioneer. He died at Deer Lodge, Montana.

Montana Contributions, Vol. I (1876), 64; II (1896), 122; VIII (1917), 364.

Stuck, Hudson, clergyman, arctic traveler (Nov. 11, 1863-Oct. 10, 1920). B. at London, England, he emigrated to the U.S. in 1885, taught school at San Angelo, Texas, studied for the ministry at the University of the South and was ordained into the Episcopal priesthood in 1892, serving initially at Cuero, Texas. He became dean of the cathedral at Dallas but resigned to become archdeacon on the Yukon in 1904 under Bishop Peter Trimble Rowe, and spent the rest of his life in the North. An inveterate traveler, he became more intimately acquainted with central and arctic Alaska than perhaps any other of his time, most of his journeying in the service of his church, visiting countless missions and religious workers in the field, winter and summer, year after year. Stuck was a careful observer, an eloquent champion of the rights and potential of Indians and Eskimos, and a spokesman for the magnificence of the Alaskan wilderness, although he always insisted that the Territory comprised "at least five countries," and that he was intimate with but one or two of these vast sections. He made the second confirmed ascent of Mt. McKinley, and the first of the south, its highest peak, June 7, 1913, with Harry Karstens, later superintendent of Mt. McKinley National Park, and two others. This fulfilled his dream: "I would far rather climb that mountain than own the richest gold-mine in Alaska." He had laid plans over nine years before the attempt (the five-man Lloyd party of miners in 1910 had attempted McKinley's more difficult and slightly lower north peak — 300 feet less in elevation — not knowing which was higher, and two attained it (see Pete Anderson, William R. Taylor entries), planting a spruce trunk as a flagpole upon it, doing that task so well that it still was erect and visible to Stuck as he stood upon the higher elevation several miles distant). Stuck's great love for the wilderness land, and his eloquent understanding and comments about it, are supremely evident in his writings: *The Ascent of Denali* (or McKinley) (1914); *Ten Thousand Miles With a Dog Sled* (1914); *Voyages on the Yukon and Its Tributaries* (1917); *A Winter Circuit of Our Arctic Coast* (1920), which last, it has been said, "deserves a place among belles-lettres," and described an outstanding winter journey along the coast of the Arctic Ocean. Stuck, who was unmarried, died at Fort Yukon.

Stuck's writings; *Who Was Who; DAB.*

Stumbling Bear (Setimkia), Kiowa chief (1832-1903). A cousin of Kicking Bird, Stumbling Bear was in a disastrous (for the Kiowas) battle with the Sauks and Foxes in 1854 and "his bravery there won him a chieftainship" at the age of 22. Two years later he and Big Bow led a raid against the Navahos, returning with horses, and in the winter of 1858-59 he and Satanta led a war party against the Utes on which scalps were taken; this was a revenge raid for the Utes having killed several Kiowas in an earlier affray. In Kit Carson's battle of Adobe Walls in 1865 it was Stumbling Bear and Do-hauson who led heroic charges against the soldiers that caused Carson to withdraw. From 1850

until 1872 Stumbling Bear was in nearly every battle the Kiowas fought and his prowess was universally recognized. With Big Tree, Big Bow, Satanta and Setangya (Satank) he was a scourge of the lower Plains as far south as Chihuahua. Stumbling Bear signed the Little Arkansas Treaty October 17, 1865, and two years later the famous Medicine Lodge Treaty. Soon he joined his cousin, Kicking Bird in leaning toward peaceful accomoda-tion with the whites, aided it is said by a doctor at one of the army posts who saved the life of a desperately ill small son. In the summer of 1872 Stumbling Bear and seven other chiefs and leading men traveled to Washington, D.C. In the fall of 1877 the government built a home for him on the reservation in which he lived until his death at Fort Sill, Oklahoma, among the last Kiowa chiefs of the old Plains days.

Mildred P. Mayhall, *The Kiowas.* Norman, Univ. of Okla. Press, 1962; Wilbur Sturtevant Nye, *Plains Indian Raiders.* Norman, 1968; Nye, *Bad Medicine & Good: Tales of the Kiowas.* Norman, 1980; Dockstader.

Sturgis, James Garland, army officer (Jan. 24, 1854-June 25, 1876). B. at Albuquerque the son of Samuel Davis Sturgis, he went to West Point and was commissioned a second lieutenant June 16, 1875, in the 7th Cavalry of which his father was commanding colonel. He joined Company M at Fort Rice, Dakota, October 29 and was a member of Custer's Sioux expedition with Company E. He was missing at the Battle of the Little Big Horn and presumed killed at the age of 22. Camp James G. Sturgis, a short-lived military post at Bear Butte, Dakota, was named for him July 1, 1878.

Cullum; BHB.

Sturgis, Samuel Davis, army officer (June 11, 1833-Sept. 28, 1889). B. at Shippensburg, Pennsylvania, he was graduated from West Point in time for the Mexican War. He was captured and held for eight days before the Battle of Buena Vista, then released. He served with the 1st Dragoons in New Mexico in the early 1850's, taking part in operations against the Jicarilla Apaches following the March 30, 1854, disaster in which Davidson had lost about 22 men killed. The next year he was engaged in operations against the Mescalero. Sturgis took part in the Mormon "war" of

1857-58, and a campaign against the Kiowas and Comanches in 1860. Although many of his soldiers deserted to the Confederacy and hostile militia surrounded Fort Smith, Arkansas, where he was stationed in 1861, Sturgis brought out some of his troops and most of the property. His heroism at Wilson's Creek led to his appointment as a Brigadier General of Volunteers, and after a good Civil War record in the east he emerged a brevet Major General. As lieutenant colonel of the 6th Cavalry and later colonel of the 7th he saw some Indian service, although he was on detached service most of the time, while effective command of the 7th through Sheridan's influence was exercised by Custer, for whom Sturgis had little use. After the Little Big Horn fight Sturgis said Custer was a brave though very selfish man, one "insanely ambitious for glory and the phrase 'Custer's luck' a good clue to his ruling passion." He also termed Custer's Indian fighting experience "exceedingly limited." It was Sturgis who, in 1878, ordered that special attention and care be given to Comanche, Keogh's horse, the only living survivor on the army's side of the battle, according to legend. Sturgis retired in 1886 and died at St. Paul, Minnesota.

DAB; *New Mex. Hist. Rev.,* Vol. XLIV, No. 4 (Oct. 1969), 275, 277; Edgar I. Stewart, *Custer's Luck.* Norman, Univ. of Okla. Press, 1955; Robert M. Utley, *Custer and the Great Controversy.* Los Angeles, Westernlore Press, 1962.

Sublette, Andrew Whitley, mountain man (1808-Dec. 18, 1853). B. at Somerset, Kentucky, he reached St. Charles, Missouri, by 1817, one of five brothers to become famous in the Rocky Mountains. Andrew entered the fur trade in 1830, accompanying William Sublette, his older brother, to the Wind River rendezvous, went to Santa Fe and in 1832 returned to the upper Rockies, a trader. He was a participant in the rivalry with the American Fur Company on the upper Missouri, and the division between the AFC and the Rocky Mountain Fur Company of the beaver area that followed. Andrew became a partner of Louis Vasquez in 1835, they establishing a post at the later Platteville, Colorado, in the South Platte River. The partnership was dissolved in 1840. Sublette farmed in Missouri for two years. In 1844 he guided a party to Fort Laramie. With his brother, Solomon, he journeyed to Taos and

returned to St. Louis in 1845. He served with Missouri volunteers from 1846 to 1848 at Fort Kearny, then accompanied Beale to California where he remained. He died from injuries received from a grizzly in Malibu Canyon, near present Santa Monica; he had been injured by another the preceding May.

Doyce B. Nunis Jr. article, MM, Vol. VIII; Dale L. Morgan, Eleanor Towles Harris, eds., *The Rocky Mountain Journals of William Marshall Anderson.* San Marino, Calif., Huntington Library, 1967.

Sublette, Milton Green, trapper, fur trader (c. 1801-Apr. 5, 1837). B. at Somerset, Kentucky, his family settled at St. Charles, Missouri, in 1817 and by 1823 he was in the employ of Ashley and Henry as trapper and trader on the upper Missouri River and northern Rocky Mountains. In September 1826, he became one of a Ewing Young party to trap the Gila River in the southwest, being wounded by an Apache. He was on the Young great circle operation of 1826-27, by way of the Gila and Colorado rivers, central Rockies and Arkansas and Rio Grande rivers to Santa Fe once more. In the fall of 1827 he trapped with Pratte and St. Vrain into the Colorado Rockies, at North Park assisting Thomas L. Smith in amputating Smith's leg, shattered by an Indian weapon. Sublette went back to St. Louis in 1828, shortly returning to Santa Fe with the Meredith Marmaduke party, enroute saving the outfit during a Comanche attack. He joined his brother, William Sublette, in forming the Rocky Mountain Fur Company in 1830, becoming a partner with Bridger, Fitzpatrick and others. He worked with the firm four years in the northern Rockies country. He took part in the Blackfoot fight at Pierre's Hole July 18, 1832, and joined Nathaniel Wyeth for a year, becoming increasingly involved in the intricate maneuvering between the old Rocky Mountain Fur Company, the American Fur Company and other short-lived firms. Milton Sublette traveled east in late 1833, seeking financial help, visiting Philadelphia, New York City and Boston, but his old Apache wound troubled him increasingly. He set out from St. Louis with a mountain caravan, but was forced by illness to turn back. In 1835 his leg was amputated. With a cork substitute he made the 1836 rendezvous. He died at Fort William, on the upper Platte River. His death may have been from cancer, according to medical opinion.

Doyce B. Nunis Jr., article, MM, Vol. IV; Dale L. Morgan, Eleanor Towles Harris, eds., *The Rocky Mountain Journals of William Marshall Anderson*. San Marino, Calif., Huntington Library, 1967.

Sublette, Pinckney W., mountain man (c. 1812-Mar. 1828). B. in Lincoln County, Kentucky, he joined his brother, William, in 1827 on a fur expedition to the northern Rocky Mountains, where he was killed by Blackfeet.

John E. Sunder article, MM, Vol. I.

Sublette, Solomon P., frontiersman (c. 1815-1857). B. in Lincoln County, Kentucky, but raised in Missouri, he entered business at Independence, but abandoned it during the Panic of 1837, and two years later went to Santa Fe. He traded on the upper Platte and Arkansas rivers. In 1843 he joined his brother, William, on an expedition to the Green River of Wyoming, resumed trading on the upper Arkansas and visited California for a few months. He roamed the west and southwest, briefly was agent for the Sauks and Foxes, resumed trading to points as distant as Chihuahua. Sublette tried his hand at many things but was generally improvident rather than incompetent, and he died with few resources at his Missouri farm.

John E. Sunder article, MM, Vol. I.

Sublette, William Lewis, frontiersman (Sept. 21, 1799-July 23, 1845). B. near Stanford, Kentucky, he moved in 1817 with his parents to St. Charles, Missouri. He joined Ashley in 1823 and escaped death in the Arikara fight on the upper Missouri River, accompanying Jedediah Smith and others on a cross-country expedition toward the Crow region, trapping in the spring of 1824 on the Green River and tributaries. Sublette accompanied Smith in 1824-25 to the far northwest, reaching Hudson's Bay Company territory; he continued trapping through the mountains until 1826 when he joined Smith and David E. Jackson in acquiring the Ashley interests. Sublette went to St. Louis in early 1827, bringing supplies out for the rendezvous that summer, trapped the Snake-Salmon country and returned to St. Louis in mid-1828, returning with supplies in 1829. He again obtained supplies in St. Louis in 1830, bringing them in wagons to the Green River,

the first appearance of the vehicles in the Rockies. The partnership was dissolved in favor of a new company and Sublette returned to St. Louis in the fall of 1830. He tentatively entered the Santa Fe trade in 1831, but Smith was killed enroute and Sublette abandoned that business. He took a supply train to the mountains in 1832, being accompanied by Nathaniel Wyeth; Sublette was wounded in the Blackfoot battle at Pierre's Hole July 18. He then entered the upper Missouri fur trade with Robert Campbell but soon sold out to the American Fur Company. Sublette took still another supply train to the Rockies in 1834. He then entered business at St. Louis, became interested in politics, established a progressive stock farm, and accompanied William Drummond Stewart to the Rockies on a pleasure trip in 1843. He died at Pittsburgh and was buried at St. Louis.

Literature abundant; John E. Sunder, *Bill Sublette, Mountain Man*. Norman, Univ. of Okla. Press, 1959; DAB; Sunder article, MM, Vol. V.

Sugarfoot, bandit (d. Dec. 1858). A road agent focusing upon stagecoaches, "Sugarfoot," whose title arose from his foot wrappings to disguise his tracks, with his band held up Charley Parkhurst's stage on the Calaveras run in California in February 1858; in December when he tried it again, Charley (who was a woman) mortally wounded him with a shotgun.

Craig MacDonald, *Cockeyed Charley Parkhurst*. Palmer Lake, Colo., Filter Press, 1973.

Sugarfoot Jack, frontiersman (c. 1842-c. 1870). B. probably in England, he was sent to Tasmania as a convict, escaped and found his way to San Francisco. He joined the California column about 1862, but was discharged, either for thievery or for striking an officer and came to Arizona about 1863, reportedly as a bullwhacker. Among the first settlers of central Arizona, he was, according to Banta, "brave as a lion," and once, Banta wrote, "saved the lives of the whole party (except one) by making a fight and driving off the red devils single-handed." In this fight George Goodhue was killed. Daniel Conner wrote that Jack was "one of the handsomest young men I ever saw. As a dare-devil he proved that he had few equals — brave, reckless and cruel to the last extent," and gives examples of his savagery and sadism. "I considered Sugarfoot Jack the most hardened, indifferent wretch I ever met," he added. Conner reported Jack was stabbed fatally "at a Mexican Fandango on the Rio Grande." Banta wrote that he "had his brains blown out while sitting at a gambling table in Taos, New Mexico." His date of death, given above, is conjecture.

Daniel Ellis Conner, *Joseph Reddeford Walker and the Arizona Adventure.* Norman, Univ. of Okla. Press, 1956; *Albert Franklin Banta: Arizona Pioneer,* ed. by Frank D. Reeve. Albuquerque, Hist. Soc. of New Mex., 1953; C.A. Franklin, "Old Timers." *Prescott Weekly Courier,* Dec. 29, 1883.

Sughrue, Michael, lawman (1844-Jan. 2, 1901). B. in County Kerry, Ireland, he was a twin brother of Pat Sughrue and, like him, a Kansas sheriff. He came to Kansas from Quincy, Illinois. In August 1861, Mike enlisted in the 7th Kansas Cavalry, serving until 1865. A deputy under Pat, who became sheriff of Ford County Kansas, in 1884, Mike was sent to Ashland, Kansas, to settle a disturbance caused by Joe Mitchell and Nels Mathews who had murdered two men, and held the town in a tumultuous uproar. Mike arrested Mitchell, who was lynched in his absence, and chased Mathews but without seizing him. Because of his intrepid work, Sughrue was named in December 1884, town marshal of Ashland at a salary of $175 a month. He became the first sheriff of Clark County when it was organized in May 1885, and was elected to a full term that November, serving until 1890 and again from 1899 to 1900. He died at Ashland and is buried there.

See Pat Sughrue entry for references; Clark County (Kan.) Hist. Soc.

Sughrue, Patrick F., lawman (1844-1906). B. in County Kerry, Ireland, he was a twin brother of Mike Sughrue, also a Kansas lawman. He had lived at Leavenworth, Kansas, and became a blacksmith. In March 1877, he became a policeman at Dodge City and on November 6, 1878, was elected constable of the township. He captured Charles Trask, a horsethief in January 1879, and later that year went to Leadville, Colorado briefly. He was elected sheriff of Ford County, Kansas in 1883, being sworn in January 14, 1884, and served as such until 1888. On July 21, 1884, he arrested Mysterious Dave Mather who had killed assistant marshal

Tom Nixon, presumably in a difficulty over a woman. On May 10, 1885, Sughrue arrested Mather for murder a second time after Dave Barnes was killed in the Junction Saloon; Mather never came to trial and the shooting apparently was done by his brother, Josiah W. (Cy) Mather. Sughrue was a cool, courageous officer of intelligence, journeying on occasion as far as New York or Fort Worth to pick up prisoners. He presided over Dodge City as trail driving to that point ceased, state prohibition shut down its saloons, and the city moved from frontier ways into those settled and more peaceable.

Wayne T. Walker, "The Twin Sheriffs of Western Kansas." *The West,* Vol. 10, No. 5 (Apr. 1969), 28-31, 50-53; Nyle H. Miller, Joseph W. Snell, "Some Notes on Kansas Cowtown Police Officers and Gun Fighters." *Kan. Hist. Quar.,* Vol. XXVIII, No. 2 (Summer 1962), 214-32.

Sullivan, John, army officer (Feb. 17, 1740-Jan. 23, 1795). B. at Somersworth, New Hampshire, he became a lawyer and after his marriage in 1760 moved to Durham, New Hampshire, where he made his home the rest of his life. He early was attracted to the independence movement and at the second Continental Congress of 1775 at Philadelphia was made a Brigadier General. After initial successes he came upon adverse fortunes, but was chosen to command the 1779 expedition against Indians in the Finger Lakes region of New York, and in that lies the frontier interest in his career. Washington assigned him the task of neutralizing the Iroquois who as allies of the British had ravaged the northern border throughout the Revolutionary War. Washington planned a two-part invasion of Iroquois country: Sullivan with three brigades plus artillery was to come up the Susquehanna River while Brigadier General James Clinton would move along the Mohawk River and turn south toward Sullivan. The two commanders would then combine for a united drive. Washington directed them to destroy what Indian villages they could, capture as many prisoners as possible and if the tribes sued for peace, tell them to attack Fort Niagara as evidence of their change of heart. Sullivan and Clinton joined forces at Tioga (Athens, Pennsylvania) and in late August set out for Newtown near the present-day Elmira, New York, where the Iroquois made their principal stand, but were repulsed. Sullivan razed the settlement, destroyed crops and moved on to destroy the stronghold at Genesee, near Cuylerville, New York. In all he burned more than 40 villages and thoroughly devastated their country, returning to Pennsylania and reported back to Washington October 8. The expedition had neither broken Indian power nor made the frontier safe; it had chastised the Indians but not subdued them, in Graymont's view. She added that "it was indeed ironic that an expedition so carefully planned and so perfectly and successfully carried out in every detail should have had such negligible results." It did push the Iroquois west of the Genesee River, made them more dependent upon the British, but it also introduced thousands of soldiers to the lush Iroquois lands for the first time, and this was to have a negative impact upon the Indians in years to come. Sullivan, citing failing health, retired late in 1779 and returned to Durham. He served as delegate to the Continental Congress for one year, became involved in New Hampshire politics and served three terms as president of the state. He helped put down New Hampshire's reflection of Shays' Rebellion. His health worsened however, and alcohol became a problem. He died at 55.

Journals of the Military Expedition of Major General John Sullivan Against the Six Nations of Indians in 1779. Glendale, N.Y., Benchmark Pub. Co., 1970; Charles P. Whittemore, "John Sullivan: Luckless Irishman," *George Washington's Generals,* ed. by George Athan Billias. N.Y., William Morrow and Co., 1964; Barbara Graymont, *The Iroquois in the American Revolution.* Syracuse, N.Y., University Press, 1972.

Sullivan, John, soldier, prospector (1839?-c. 1885). A soldier under Col. George Stoneman engaged in construction of the "Stoneman Grade" up the Pinal Mountains of central Arizona, in 1870 he found chunks of ore capable of being flattened by a hammer and proving to be silver. If the detachments constructing the road came from Camp Goodwin, which seems probable, John Sullivan, born in Ireland, would appear to be the individual listed here, according to the 1870 federal census. When his enlistment expired he showed the lumps to Charles G. Mason, a Gila River rancher, without revealing precisely where they had been found. Sullivan disappeared and Mason and others prospecting in the general location they supposed the ore to lie, discovered the

deposit which became the Silver King mine northwest of present-day Superior, Arizona. Between 1875 and 1889 it produced upwards of $17 million in ore. In 1882 Sullivan, then an aging man, returned from California, penniless, having lost out on his great strike; he was given light work by the mine operators and cared for until his death.

Farish, VI; *Arizoniana,* Vol. I, No. 2 (Summer 1960), 3-4.

Sullivan, W.F., Texas Ranger (Mar. 8, 1854-Dec. 8, 1926). B. at Moorsville, Mississippi, he reached Texas at 16 and served as a Texas Ranger on the frontier, doing "well his part in ridding the country of savage foes." He lived in San Saba County, entered the hardware business, married and fathered 12 children. He died at San Saba, Texas.

Frontier Times, Vol. IV, No. 5 (Feb. 1927), 64.

Sully, Alfred, army officer (1821-Apr. 27, 1879). B. in Philadelphia, he was a son of Thomas Sully, artist, and was graduated from West Point in 1841. He served in the Seminole War in Florida in 1841-42, taking part in the attack on Hawe Creek camp, January 25, 1842. He accompanied the 2nd Infantry to Mexico, participating in the siege of Vera Cruz. Sully served as captain in the 1853 campaign against the Rogue River Indians of Oregon, and in a Cheyenne operation in 1860-61. He served early in the Civil War in Missouri and at Washington, D.C., taking command of the 1st Minnesota Volunteers in 1862, served conspicuously in the Peninsula campaign, receiving two brevets and attended the battles of South Mountain, Antietam Fredericksburg, and Chancellorsville, then was assigned to the district of Dakota to control the restless Sioux. In a battle at White Stone Hill, Dakota Territory, September 3-5, 1863, his units caused some 300 Sioux casualties, capturing 300 as well, at a cost of 30 men killed and 38 wounded. He led an expedition of some 3,400 men into Sioux country to finally pacify the Indians in the summer of 1864, the operation for which he is best remembered in frontier history. The operation began and ended at Fort Sully, near Fort Pierre, and reached the Missouri above the Big Bend, and the Yellowstone. In the battle of Killdeer Mountain, the troops lost two killed and some wounded; the Indian loss was uncertain, they reporting 31 killed, and the whites reporting up to 150 killed. A Badlands skirmish followed in August. The 1,600-mile, four month expedition was inconclusive, Sully acknowledging that "it will be exceedingly difficult to bring all the Sioux bands to a complete subjection," but claiming his operation succeeded "as far as it was in the power of ...any body of troops to make it so." Sully led 7th Cavalry and 3rd Infantry contingents in a Sand Hills engagement, Indian Territory, September 11-15, 1868, in which he lost three men killed and five wounded for Indian casualties of 34. He initially had commanded the expedition Custer eventually took to the Washita in 1868, but leadership was given his rival and Sully withdrew. Sully was breveted up to Major General of Volunteers and Brigadier General of the Army. He served on boards until 1869 when he was again ordered west, becoming colonel of the 21st Infantry in late 1873. He took part in several Indian operations and died at Fort Vancouver, Washington. Sully was a frequently irascible, short-tempered man who disliked intensely a wide spectrum of people and verbally tilted with many, including Custer and Fremont; his language was strong ("some ranked him with General William S, Harney in the language department"). He had inherited some artistic talent from his father and enjoyed painting, even creating a self-portrait alongside his favorite horse, and at other times producing water colors of Indians, forts, and Spanish California. He married a Spanish-Mexican woman at Monterey and fathered a child; both died tragically.

NCAB, Vol. XII, 285-86; Langdon Sully, *No Tears for the General: The Life of Alfred Sully, 1821-1879.* Palo Alto, Calif., Amer. West Pub. Co., 1974; Louis Pfaller, "The Sully Expedition of 1864 featuring the Killdeer Mountain and Badlands Battles." *No. Dak. Hist.,* Vol. XXXI, No. 1 (Jan. 1964), 1-54.

Summerhayes, John Wyer, army officer (Jan. 6, 1835-Mar. 8, 1911). B. on Nantucket Island, he made several voyages aboard whalers and spent a brief period probably on the upper Missouri River as a trapper before enlisting in the 20th Massachusetts Infantry September 9, 1861; he was commissioned a second lieutenant in 1863. Wounded three times in action and winning a brevet for his part in the campaign terminating with the surrender of Lee, Summerhayes emerged from the war a captain; he was demobilized in 1865. Two years later he was commissioned a second lieutenant in the 33rd Infantry, transferring in 1869 to the 8th Infantry with which he served 20 years, most of it in Arizona, California, Nevada and Nebraska and often in a quartermaster capacity; he was on the Cibecue punitive expedition of William Redwood Price in 1881 in a quartermaster capacity, winning praise from the commander. Summerhayes became a captain with a staff position in the Army Quartermaster Department in 1889, was retired for age in 1900 as a major, and was appointed in 1904 a lieutenant colonel. He died at Nantucket and was buried at Arlington Cemetery. His wife, Martha Dunham Summerhayes, authored *Vanished Arizona,* the near-classic autobiographical account of an army officer's wife on the frontier.

Heitman; Nat. Archives military, pension records for Summerhayes; introduction to Martha Summerhayes, *Vanished Arizona.* Lincoln, Univ. of Nebr. Press, 1979.

Summerhayes, Martha Dunham, army wife, writer (Oct. 21, 1846-May 12, 1911). B. at Nantucket, she was a descendant of Jonathan Edwards. She studied two years in Germany. She married Second Lieutenant John Wyer Summerhayes, also a Nantucket islander, and set out in 1874 for Wyoming Territory. He had been briefly a whaler and a trapper on the upper Missouri or upper Mississippi River. After a short time at Fort D.A. Russell, near Cheyenne, she went with her husband's 8th Infantry regiment to Arizona, where they were stationed four years, until 1878. Her experiences were incorporated into her book, *Vanished Arizona,* first published at Philadelphia in 1908 and since appearing in several editions. Subsequently John Summerhayes served in Nevada, Nebraska, Texas and New Mexico, rising to the rank of major, and retiring January 6, 1900. He died at Nantucket in March 1911, and Martha two months later at Schenectady, New York. Her book is not quite the classic it has been labeled, for it lacks precision, information and depth. Yet as the nostalgic recollections of a young army wife on a turbulent frontier it is not without value.

Martha Summerhayes, *Vanished Arizona: Recollections of My Army Life.* Lakeside Classics, ed., with intro. by M.M. Quaife. Chicago,

R.R. Donnelley & Sons, 1939; Lawrence Clark Powell, "Martha Summerhayes' Vanished Arizona." *Westways,* Vol. 63, No. 7, (June 1971), 16-19, 60-61.

Sumner, Edwin Vose, army officer (Jan. 30, 1797-Mar. 21, 1863). B. at Boston he was commissioned a second lieutenant in the 2nd Infantry March 3, 1819, became a first lieutenant in 1823 and captain of the 1st Dragoons March 4, 1833, his service principally on the frontier. June 30, 1846, at the outbreak of the Mexican War, Sumner became major of the 2nd Dragoons. He accompanied Kearny to New Mexico, later joined Winfield Scott in Mexico; his abilities were recognized by Scott and he was detached to command the regiment of Mounted Riflemen (later the 3rd Cavalry) just organized but without military training and requiring a strong hand to mold it. A musket ball glanced off his skull at Cerro Gordo, winning Sumner the nickname "Bull," which his men embroidered to "Bull of the Woods," in view of his booming voice and harsh reputation. Ewell in 1847, a captain in the 1st Dragoons, considered Sumner "the greatest martinet in the service, who for our sins has got command of us...We are in perfect Purgatory here, and Major Sumner would be chief devil anywhere (but he) has had one good effect on us — he has taught some of us to pray who never prayed before, for we all put up daily petitions to get rid of him." Sumner became lieutenant colonel of the 1st Dragoons July 13, 1848, and in 1851 was assigned to command the 9th Military Department with headquarters in New Mexico, leaving Leavenworth May 26. His command suffered some losses from cholera and reached Santa Fe July 19. His directions were to withdraw garrisons from the territory's communities and establish a series of posts as well as directing or conducting scouts and military operations against Navahos, Utes and Apaches, his activity to be unceasing. He was an efficient officer and his influence was positive: he was responsible for founding such New Mexico posts as Forts Union, Fillmore, Conrad and Webster, Cantonment Burgwin and Fort Massachusetts. In August 1851 he led seven companies into the Navaho country and selected the site for Fort Defiance, although his contact with the Indians was fleeting. Sumner was often at odds with James

S. Calhoun, governor of New Mexico, and when Calhoun, mortally ill, left for the States in mid-1852 Sumner became acting governor, presuming himself to be also, by reason of that office, superintendent of Indian affairs for the Territory; thus he came into conflict with John Greiner, the actual superintendent of Indian affairs. Upon the arrival of Calhoun's successor, William Carr Lane, he quickly came into a feuding relationship with that official as well at the height of which Lane challenged him to a duel, the offer declined. Sumner, in part because of the difficulties with Calhoun, Greiner and Lane was relieved of command of the 9th Department and left Santa Fe June 26, 1853, although not in disgrace. He became colonel of the newly organized 1st Cavalry March 3, 1855, and operated with it on the Plains. He left Fort Leavenworth in 1855 for Fort Laramie and a spring Indian campaign, but his horse proved unfit and he returned to Leavenworth which he commanded in 1856 during Kansas turmoil between pro- and anti-slavery factions. Sumner attempted to maintain order, and dispersed partisans of both sides. "With white hair and beard and a large, powerful frame, he was a tough old frontier dragoon who loved a fight," and on July 29, 1857, he had his chance against hostile Cheyennes. About 300 of them, by Sumner's estimate, offered battle on Solomon's Fork of the Kansas River. He ordered a sabre charge and "for the first and last time in the annals of Indian warfare a large force of cavalry swept forward to attack a body of mounted Indians with the steel." The Cheyennes scattered, only about four of them and two Dragoons being killed (Sumner claimed nine hostiles slain), but "it was a psychological victory of major proportions," and had a salutary effect upon the Indians. In 1858 Sumner became commander of the Military Department of the West, with headquarters at St. Louis, becoming Brigadier General March 16, 1861. He served in the east early in the Civil War, commanding the II Corps in the Peninsular campaign, at South Mountain and at Antietam and becoming Major General of Volunteers July 4, 1862. He was relieved from duty at his own request and died at his home at Syracuse, New York. Married, his son Edwin Vose Sumner Jr. became a Brigadier General and another son, Samuel Storrow Sumner, a Major General; none of the Sumners were West Pointers.

Heitman; Robert M. Utley, *Frontiersmen in Blue*. N.Y., Macmillam Co., 1967; *The Making of a Soldier: Letters of General R.S. Ewell*, ed. by Percy Gatling Hamlin. Richmond, Va., Whittet & Shepperson, 1935; *Official Correspondence of James S. Calhoun*, ed. by Annie Heloise Abel. Wash., Govt Printing Office, 1915; Frank McNitt, *Navajo Wars*. Albuquerque, Univ. of New Mex. Press, 1972; Percival G. Lowe, *Five Years a Dragoon*. Norman, Univ. of Okla. Press, 1965; George E. Hyde, *Life of George Bent*. Norman, 1968.

Sumner, Edwin Vose, army officer (Aug. 16, 1835-Aug. 24, 1912). B. at Carlisle, Pennsylvania, the son of Edwin Vose Sumner the elder, he was commissioned a second lieutenant of the 1st Cavalry August 5, 1861, and ended the Civil War a captain with a brevet rank of Brigadier General of Volunteers. In 1866 he joined his company on the Pacific coast where he served (except for two years recruiting duty in the East) nearly 14 years. Sumner was stationed at Drum Barracks, Camp Independence and the Presidio of San Francisco in California, and at Fort Lapwai, Idaho. He participated in the Modoc War of 1872-73 as an acting assistant adjutant general and aide de camp for brevet Major General Jefferson C. Davis and afterward for a year as acting assistant inspector general on the staff of Howard. During the 1877 Nez Perce campaign Sumner operated near Mt. Idaho with Major John Green and during the Bannock War of 1878 was in the fight at Blue Mountain, Idaho. Sumner became a major with the 5th Cavalry March 4, 1879, joining the regiment at Fort D.A. Russell, Wyoming. October 1 he was on the relief expedition to Milk River, Colorado, to raise the Ute siege of troops and was in the action of October 5, then commanding a battalion at White River, Colorado, the rest of the year. In 1880 he commanded Fort Robinson, Nebraska. Sumner became lieutenant colonel of the 8th Cavalry in 1890, colonel of the 7th Cavalry in 1894 and a Brigadier General March 27, 1899, three days before his retirement to his home at Syracuse, New York.

Heitman; Powell; Price, *Fifth Cavalry; Who Was Who.*

Sumner, Samuel Storrow, army officer (Feb. 6, 1842-July 26, 1937). The son of Edwin Vose Sumner, he was b. in Pennsylvania, commissioned a second lieutenant of the 5th Cavalry

June 11, 1861, serving in the East, mainly on the staff of his father, during the Civil War until the elder Sumner's death, ending the conflict a captain, with brevet of major. Sumner was ordered to the frontier service in 1869, was on the Republican River expedition, received a brevet of lieutenant colonel for his part in the decisive victory over the Cheyennes at Summit Springs, July 11, 1869, was in Arizona from 1872-75. As commander of Fort Bowie, he reported in October 1872, on O.O. Howard's important visit with Cochise, the Chiricahua Apache, and in 1874 assisted Dudley in his journey to visit Cochise. In 1876 he participated in the Sioux campaign, was engaged in a skirmish at War Bonnet (Hat) Creek, Wyoming, continued service with the Big Horn and Yellowstone expedition and was in the fight at Slim Buttes, Dakota. In 1877 he served with the Wind River expedition as battalion commander. He became a major in the 8th Cavalry in 1879, lieutenant colonel of the 6th Cavalry in 1891 and its colonel in 1896. He became a Major General of Volunteers and a Brigadier General in the army during the Spanish American War. He was made Major General in 1903 after service in the Far East. Sumner commanded the Department of the Missouri 1903-1904, the Southwest Division 1904-1905, and the Division of the Pacific in 1905-1906; he retired February 6, 1906.

Price, *Fifth Cavalry;* Heitman.

Sun, Tom, scout, cattleman (c. 1841-1909). Of French Canadian parentage with the christening name of Thomas Debeausoliel, Sun probably was b. at Montreal. He ran away from home at 11, reached the Missouri River and met a French trapper named LeFever; with him he trapped and eventually reached St. Louis. During the Civil War he worked on railroad construction for the Union army, then resumed the trapper's life and reached Wyoming where he became a guide and scout out of Fort Fred Steele. Sun was "one of the earliest, if not the earliest settler in the Sweetwater Valley," establishing a ranch near Devil's Gate. He had guided an English sportsman, Sir John Rae Reid, and became his close friend. In 1877 Reid sent Sun funds and a partnership was formed, but hard conditions wiped them out. The next year Sun went into partnership with Edwin C. Johnson of Connecticut, buying his partner out in

1893. Meanwhile he had continued his other activities. In 1874 he scouted for Anson Mills out of Rawlins to the Powder River, then through the Big Horn Mountains and back to Rawlins without sighting hostiles. Sun and five others, on July 20, 1889, hanged Ella Watson and James Averell, alleging they were cattle thieves, the incident one of the most notorious of the so-called Powder River War which it did much to precipitate. Warrants were served on the six, Sun "cooly accepted arrest, admitted his part in the hanging and named the others." They were arraigned at Rawlins, on October 14; the Grand Jury failed to indict them and they went free. Sun was named to the executive committee of the Wyoming Stock Growers' Association in 1889 and served until his death. Tom Sun Jr., b. at Omaha November 5, 1884, d. February 12, 1975, succeeded his father in ownership of the ranch properties.

Don Russell, *The Lives and Legends of Buffalo Bill*. Norman, Univ. of Okla. Press, 1960; Helena Huntington Smith, *The War on Powder River*. N.Y., McGraw-Hill Book Co., 1966; information from the Wyo. State Archives and Hist. Dept; *Rawlins Daily Times*, Feb. 13, 1975.

Sundance Kid: *see* Harry Longabaugh.

Sutter, John Augustus, pioneer (Feb. 1803-June 18, 1880). B. at Kandern, Baden, of probable Swiss ancestry, he became, it is said, a captain in the Swiss army, emigrated and reached St. Louis in 1834. He made trading trips to Santa Fe in 1835 and 1836, and in 1838 migrated to Oregon. He sailed from Fort Vancouver, Washington, to Honolulu, thence to Sitka and from there to San Francisco, his goal, arriving July 1, 1839. He persuaded Mexican authorities that he could build a fort to "protect" the northern limits of Mexican occupation and was encouraged to select a site on the American River at its junction with the Sacramento, where the future capital of California would arise. Here his fortified post and extensive plantation-like developments were undertaken. His success was "phenomenal." He fulfilled his pledge of loyalty to Mexican officialdom, his grant was enlarged, and he came to be called "General" Sutter, the overlord of Nueva Helvetia, as he called his establishment. He aided immigrants from the states though in June 1846. Fremont seized his

fort temporarily; it later was restored. In 1849 he was a delegate to the convention drafting the state constitution and was a candidate for governor. Gold was discovered on his place January 24, 1848, however (see biography of James W. Marshall), his workmen deserted him to join the mad rush for wealth, squatters pre-empted his lands, his herds disappeared to feed hungry prospectors and rovers, and by 1852 he was bankrupt. The California legislature for 14 years granted him a sizable monthly pension. His second homestead burned and he removed to Lititz, Lancaster County, Pennsylvania, where he died, petitions for redress from Congress unacted upon. A generous man, he was highly controversial for other perplexing qualities. In appearance he was a "typical" Swiss short, fat, bald-headed, and lively. "He remains one of the most appealing figures in American history."

Literature abundant.

Swadesh, Morris, linguist (Jan. 22, 1909-July 20, 1967). Swadesh was trained in linguistics at the University of Chicago under Leonard Bloomfield and Edward Sapir. He went in 1931 to Yale University to continue work under Sapir, the strongest influence on his life. "The many-sided interests and vigorous originality of Swadesh's thinking made him a unique figure in linguistics. Because of his bold and venturesome mind, he became at times a controversial figure," occasionally in fields far removed from his specialty. Swadesh was a very prolific writer. Stanley Newman, in an obituary article, wrote that "from the beginning (Swadesh) displayed a two-pronged interest in empirical research and in studies of broad theoretical problems." He commenced his work with several Indian languages and continued his interest in American Indian languages and proto-languages throughout his career. He became associate professor of anthropology at the University of Wisconsin in 1937, worked and taught in Mexico, particularly in the Tarascan language, holding several public positions as well as university-level teaching posts. With World War II he returned to the United States, was commissioned in the Signal Corps and from 1942-46 directed the preparation of much linguistic material for the Armed Forces; partly as a result of this he developed a desire to make linguistics "useful" and comprehensible to the layman, and many of his publications attest that interest, which for him was a lasting one. He continued his work in the United States for some years after his military service, turning increasingly to comparative studies. Swadesh was a prime force in the development of the glottochronological method which has to do with the chronology of language. Although his ideas generated bitter controversy, he "was not one to shrink" from such and remained "convinced that the method was useful, not only for measuring the time depths of languages known to be genetically related, but also for demonstrating more remote and previously unsuspected relationships. As time went on, he became increasingly intrigued with the possibility of finding broader linguistic relationships, continental and even global in scope." He began to suspect a fundamental relationship, for example, between proto-Indo-European and some proto-American Indian languages, perhaps through a distant common ancestral tongue, and described his ideas and work in writings. Because of his championing of student demonstrations he was labeled a "leftist" during the McCarthy era and returned to Mexico where he became professor at the Universidad Nacional Autónoma de Mexico and at the Escuela Nacional de Antropología e Historia, besides holding a number of other responsible positions. But he continued to swim in the mainstream of linguistics, writing as fluently in Spanish as in English and publishing widely in both languages. He taught from time to time for brief periods in universities of this country and abroad during the last decade of his life. "It is tragic that he should have been cut off at a time when he had reached the crest of his powers and was enjoying the most rewarding satisfactions in his professional work and his personal associations." He died at Mexico City. Swadesh had been married.

Language: Jour. of Linguistic Soc. of Amer., Vol. 43, No. 4 (Dec. 1967), 948-57, including a bibliography of his writings; Swadesh, "On Interhemispheric Linguistic Connections," S. Diamond, ed. *Culture in History: Essays in Honor of Paul Radin.* N.Y., Columbia Univ. Press, 1960, 894-924.

Swanock, Jim (Shawanock and variations), Delaware hunter (d. post 1849). A son of William Anderson, head chief of the Delawares, Swanock himself became a principal chief, settling on a reservation in northeastern Kansas. In 1833 he led Delawares in a punitive raid against the Pawnees, then signed a treaty with them and other tribes November 12, 1833, at Fort Leavenworth. He became a Rocky Mountain beaver trapper and hunter at least by 1834, a well-regarded associate of frontiersmen and a wise and courageous leader. He may have attempted in 1844 to avenge the murder of a Delaware trapping party by Plains Indians but, if so, the attempt was unsuccessful. Swanock joined Fremont in 1845; he often frequented the Bent's Fort region.

Harvey L. Carter article, MM, Vol. VII.

Swanton, John Reed, ethnologist (Feb. 19, 1873-May 2, 1958). B. at Gardiner, Maine, he was graduated from Harvard in 1896 where he received his master's degree in 1897 and doctorate in 1900. Swanton was an ethnologist for the Bureau of American Ethnology at Washington, D.C., from 1900 to 1944, when he retired. He was a member of many scientific societies including the National Academy of Sciences and was interested in anthropology and linguistics as well as ethnology. His publications included: *Contributions to the Ethnology of the Haida* (1905); *Haida Texts and Myths* (1908); *Social Conditions, Beliefs, and Linguistic Relationship of the Tlingit Indians* (1908); *Tlingit Myths and Texts* (1909); *Indian Tribes of the Lower Mississippi Valley and Adjacent Coast of the Gulf of Mexico* (1911); with J.O. Dorsey, *A Dictionary of the Biloxi and Ofo Languages* (1912); *Early History of the Creek Indians and Their Neighbors* (1922); *Social Organization and Social Usages of the Creek Indians* (1928); *Religious Beliefs and Medical Practices of the Creek Indians* (1928); *Social Conditions and Religious Beliefs of the Chickasaw Indians* (1928); *Myths and Tales of the Southeastern Indians* (1929); *Source Material for the Social and Ceremonial Life of the Choctaw Indians* (1931); *Linguistic Material from the Tribes of Southern Texas and Northeastern Mexico* (1940); *Source Material for the History and Ethnology of the Caddo Indians* (1942); *Indians of the Southeastern United States* (1946); *The Wineland Voyages* (1947), and *The Indian Tribes of North America* (1952). Swanton was chairman of the U.S. De Soto Expedition Committee and under his supervision was

published its *Final Report* (1939) which he
personally wrote, the definitive history of that
great Spanish endeavor into southeastern
United States. Swanton lived in retirement at
Newton, Massachusetts.

Who Was Who; William C. Sturtevant, "Fore-
ward" for *De Soto Expedition Commission,* Wash.,
D.C., 1985, a facsimile reproduction of the original
Final Report.

Sweeney, Michael, prospector (fl. 1863) B. at
Frederickstown, St. John's River, New
Brunswick, he reached the northwest as a
prospector by 1862. With Bill Fairweather,
Henry Edgar and three others he left Elk City,
Idaho, and in the fall of 1862 reached
Bannack, Montana. They left there in
February 1863 and on May 26 the party of six
located the important Alder Gulch placers in
southwestern Montana. Sweeney and Rodgers were unhappy when a seventh share of the
discoveries was given to George Orr, who was
not in on the discovery; they separated from
the other four for that reason, according to
Edgar. Nothing definite is known of Sweeney
further, but it is said he returned to New
Brunswick.

Montana Contributions, Vol. III, 1900.

Swetnam, James Manoah, physician (Nov. 11,
1841-Feb. 4, 1921). B. in Lawrence County,
Kentucky, he went west in 1858, driving an ox
team from the Missouri River to Colorado,
eventually drifting on to Prescott, Arizona.
Here he fell in with a party planning to settle
the Tonto Apache-ridden Verde Valley of
central Arizona. It left Prescott in January
1865, contructed a stone fort at the confluence
of the Verde River and Clear Creek, and
determinedly stuck out bad weather, Indian
hostility and other pioneer hazards, until the
settlement was effected and farms begun.
Swetnam's journal is the only primary record
of this pioneering effort. Swetnam left the
Verde Valley in 1866, attended school at
Denver, was graduated from the University of
Michigan in 1870, attended lectures at the
Ohio Medical College, Cincinnati, for two
years, practiced medicine at various middle
western cities and in 1894 moved to Phoenix,
Arizona, where he practiced until his death.
He married three times, his first two wives
predeceased him. Swetnam's Verde Valley
record in the form of a letter is printed in
Farish.

Farish, IV, 215-46; AHS Archives, Hayden File;
Robert W. Munson, "The Clear Creek Settlers'
Fort," manuscript.

Swift, William Henry, army officer, engineer
(Nov. 6, 1800-Apr. 7, 1879). B. at Taunton,
Massachusetts, he entered West Point at
almost 13 and left before graduation in
December 1818, to accompany Stephen
Long's expedition to the Rocky Mountains,
becoming one of the first three white men to
scale Pike's Peak. With the other two, Dr.
Edwin James, botanist, and Joe Bissonette,
guide, they struggled upward to bivouac
perilously on a steep pitch, and reached the
summit at 4 p.m. next day; Pike's Peak since
has become "the most famous single mountain
within the United States." Commissioned an
artillery lieutenant in 1819, Swift had an
aptitude for engineering and was instrumental
in developing the embryonic railroad network
in the east. He transferred to the topographical
engineers in 1832 (they were organized as an
independent corps in 1838), and his skills were
well employed until 1849 when he resigned
from the army to pursue in civilian life his
profession, broadened to include the fields of
finance and business administration. He
became successful in many areas. He died at
New York City.

DAB; David Lavender, *The Rockies.* N.Y.,
Harper & Row, 1968; Chicago Hist. Soc., which has
several hundred Swift papers.

Swilling, John W., adventurer (1831-Aug. 12,
1878). B. in Georgia, he moved with his family
to Missouri in about 1853, married and
became a farmer, but when his wife died he left
his daughter and went about 1857 to Texas,
worked for the Butterfield Overland Mail Co.,
in southern New Mexico, and enlisted in the
Confederate force that overran southern New
Mexico in 1861. He became a lieutenant in the
2nd Texas Mounted Rifles battalion of Capt.
Sherod Hunter. With it he reached Tucson
February 28, 1862, and on April 15, defeated a
Union scouting force at Picacho Pass, to the
northwest. When the Confederates retired
from New Mexico, Swilling deserted and
remained, carrying expresses, perhaps serving
as guide, for the Union forces. He was present,
may have had a role in, the capture and
execution of Mangas Coloradas at Fort
McLane, then accompanied the Joe Walker

expedition back to Arizona and north to the Hassayampa River. Swilling was reputed to be one of the discoverers of Rich Hill and other profitable placers, being active in the Wickenburg area. In 1867 he began the project to construct and operate irrigation works based on the Salt River, but in 1871 or 1872 moved north to the Black Canyon and resumed mining. He married again, his mining and farming ventures were successful, he founded the town of Gillett, Arizona, but Swilling had a taste for liquor and had become a drug addict through use of morphine to relieve recurring headaches. When sober he was a steady, reliable courageous man, but when under the influence of liquor or drugs he became unmanageable. He was charged in an April 1878 stage holdup near Wickenburg, boasting while not himself that he had done the deed, which he may not have, and died in the Yuma prison while under investigation. He was one of the founders and true pioneers of Arizona.

Andrew Wallace, "John W. Swilling." *Arizoniana,* Vol. II, No. 1 (Spring 1961), 16-19

T

Tacket(t), Cynth(i)a, pioneer (d. Sept. 11, 1957). From Johnson County, Arkansas, Mrs. Tackett, whose husband, Martin, may have predeceased her, joined the Fancher emigrant wagon train at Fort Smith, Arkansas. With her were her children: Pleasant Tackett, 25, who was married; William H., 23; Marian, 20; Sabbyrd, 18; Matilda, 16; James M., 14 and Jones M., 12. Leaving Fort Smith late in March bound for California, the company was wiped out at Mountain Meadows, Utah, by Mormons and Mormon-led Indians and all members above the age of infancy murdered.

William Wise, *Massacre at Mountain Meadows.* N.Y., Thomas Y. Crowell Co., 1976.

Tackett, Pleasant, pioneer (c. 1832-Sept. 11, 1857). With his wife whose name is unknown and two children: Milum, aged 7, and William, about 3, Tackett, from Johnson County, Arkansas, joined the Fancher emigrant wagon train in March 1857, bound for California. The elder Tacketts were killed in the Mountain Meadows, Utah, Massacre by Mormons and Mormon-led Indians; the two children were recovered by United States agents subsequently and returned to Arkansas.

William Wise, *Massacre at Mountain Meadows.* N.Y., Thomas Y. Crowell Co., 1976.

Tafoya, José, comanchero and scout (pre 1859-post 1893). Tafoya, whose name is sometimes given as José Piedad Tofoya, was on the Staked Plains with his father at least as early as 1859, for the elder in that year was scout for soldiers and surveyors marking the Texas-New Mexico border, and José was present. Bergmann, commander at Fort Bascom, in 1864 reportedly furnished Tafoya with supplies to pursue the *comanchero* trade he was pledged to terminate. So did Lieutenant Charles J. Jennings in 1876, but that year, Tafoya later testified, he had stopped the trade because the troops "got after" the comancheros. By then he had become, according to Kenner, the "prince of the *Comancheros.*" Yet he must have resumed the trade. José Tafoya became a noted scout on the Staked Plains after Mackenzie's men caught him as a *comanchero* (presumably from New Mexico) and purportedly hanged him from a wagon tongue until he agreed to scout for the army against his erstwhile customers, although Kenner considers that story probably mythical. Tafoya is said to have guided Mackenzie's forces to a Tule Canyon Comanche camp in September 1874. According to Haley, Quanah Parker learned Tafoya had guided Mackenzie to the Comanche retreat and growled to Goodnight that if he ever caught him he would "broil him alive." Tafoya thereafter "found the genial New Mexico climate preferable" to that of Texas and the Staked Plains, Haley wrote. However Tafoya, called "Hosea" by John R. Cook, had a significant scouting role against the Comanches or Plains Apaches in the so-called Hunters' War of 1877 by buffalo hunters of the Staked Plains.

Oscar Williams, 45, 78-79; J. Evetts Haley, *The XIT Ranch of Texas.* Norman, Univ. of Okla. Press, 1967; Charles L. Kenner, *A History of New Mexican-Plains Indian Relations.* Norman, 1969; John R. Cook, *The Border and the Buffalo.* Chicago, Lakeside Edition, 1938.

Taggart, Frank, cowboy, train robber (c. 1861-Mar. 10, 1884). Described as "the type of regulation cowboy," he may have been born in Texas, but worked in eastern Arizona and western New Mexico where, November 24, 1883, with Kit Joy and others he held up a Southern Pacific train near Gage, west of Deming, New Mexico. He was arrested January 14, 1884, in Apache County, Arizona, by Sheriff Harvey Whitehill and assistants of Grant County, New Mexico, and taken to Silver City, New Mexico. On March 10, several train robbers and others broke jail, were pursued some miles, Taggart and others taken; he and Mitch Lee, another train robber, were lynched. Taggart was 5 feet, 8 1/2 inches tall, weighed 150 pounds, had light hair and mustache, blue eyes, a large mouth and ready smile. His hanging was unjust.

Ed Bartholomew, *Wyatt Earp: The Man & the Myth.* Toyahvale, Tex., Frontier Book Co., 1964; *This Is Silver City 1882, 1883, 1884.* Silver City, N.M., *The Enterprise,* 1963.

Tahchee (Dutch, Captain William Dutch), Cherokee chief (d. Nov. 12, 1848). One of the most prominent of the Western Cherokee, he was among the first to take up residence west of the Mississippi. In 1820 at the head of Cherokee warriors, he sought out his friend, the Osage trader Nathaniel Pryor (1772-1831) a mile above the mouth of the Verdigris River. He was in pursuit of Mad Buffalo, an Osage warrior whose men had killed three Cherokees, and Tahchee wanted three Osages to sacrifice in recompense, but Mad Buffalo eluded him. Tahchee's men ransacked Pryor's post, stealing 150 pounds of beaver fur, as consolation. Tahchee settled south of the Arkansas River and when the government in 1824 demanded that he move north of the stream he indignantly refused, vowed he would go to the Spanish territories and never return. Late in 1825 he announced to a Cherokee council his intention to separate, and moved to the Red River, settling above the mouth of the Kiamichi, extending his fame as a fearless leader of his lawless band of Cherokee and Kickapoo, making war on other tribes. He reportedly had married an Osage woman while living for a time among them; his wife for some offense was put to death by her people and this enraged Tahchee, making him an inveterate enemy of that people. He killed and scalped a number of Osage (the total unknown even to himself), performing some of his most daring feats against them and becoming a terror to the Osage. July 18, 1826, he led a particularly bold raid against Osages camped near Fort Gibson. He stole horses from white people on this occasion, and two of his men were killed. Tahchee joined Bowles shortly after that chief had moved to Texas. He opposed the Washington Treaty of May 6, 1828, between the United States and the Western Cherokee, and did not sign it. With the help of the Arkansas branch of the tribe, Tahchee's band was moved from Texas to the mouth of the Canadian River in 1831 where Tahchee built "a handsome plantation," surrounded by an extensive settlement of Cherokee. "His great force of character, his extensive knowledge of the frontier and resourcefulness made him a valuable guide and hunter on numerous missions performed for the Government. The Cherokee living in the West long held him in the highest respect for his service as a warrior and leader..." In 1834 his portrait was painted by Catlin (reproduced by Foreman, *Indians and Pioneers,* paperback: 1975). In 1840 Tahchee was a delegate from the Western Cherokees to Washington, D.C., having late in life made peace with the government. He died in Flint District of the Cherokee Nation, in the present Oklahoma. At that time he was a member of the Cherokee National Council.

Hodge, HAI; Grant Foreman, *The Five Civilized Tribes.* Norman, Univ. of Okla. Press, 1966; Foreman, *Indians and Pioneers.* Norman, 1975.

Taimah, Fox chief (c. 1790-c. 1830). A subordinate chief of the Fox tribe, he also was a prominent medicine man, ever friendly toward the whites and on one occasion saved the life of an Indian agent at Prairie du Chien, Wisconsin, whom an assassin had threatened. He was a signer of the Sauk and Fox Treaty at Washington, D.C., August 4, 1824. He died in Iowa and the town and county of Tama are named for him.

Hodge, HAI.

Tait, (Tate), David, frontiersman (c. 1769-1829). the son of British Indian agent and later Colonel John Tait who was stationed at the Hickory Ground (the present Wetumpka, Alabama) in 1778, and Sehoy, daughter of Alexander McGillivray, David Tait was half-brother to William Weatherford, noted Creek war leader of the Red Sticks, or hostile faction prominent in the 1813-14 Creek War. While still a boy David Tait was taken north by McGillivray where he remained five years at school under the supervision it is said of George Washington. Following the death of McGillivray in 1793 Tait was sent to Scotland with McGillivray's son, Panton. He finished his education, returned to the Creek Nation at 22 and took possession of his property which had been cared for by McGillivray while he lived. Tait was a man of "stern character, reserved manners, classical education and was said to have been a wonderful judge of human nature." He had a large fortune which he dispensed liberally to those in need. Tait was at Fort Pierce when Fort Mims was captured by Creeks. Unlike Weatherford, Tait remained friendly with the whites, while retaining amicable relations with Weatherford and many hostiles. In the summer of 1813 Peter McQueen and other Red Sticks went to Pensacola for Spanish munitions and Tait and William Pierce were sent by Colonel Joseph Carson to check on whether arms actually had been sold the Creeks. The spies succeeded in their mission, returning with detailed information on negotiations and the intentions of the Red Sticks. Tait remained aloof from such military operations as the Battle of Burnt Corn and the Fort Mims massacre of August 30, 1813, which had been initiated by Weatherford, but met the latter 12 miles from Mims after the first phase of the attack, Weatherford telling him of the early stages and how he had tried to prevent the massacre. Occasionally Tait and other neutrals hunted up militiamen lost in the wilderness, sparing them a slow and agonizing death from starvation or wounds. Tait lived at Montpelier, in Baldwin County for many years and died there. He was survived by four daughters.

H.S. Halbert, T.H. Ball, *The Creek War of 1813-1814.* Univ. of Ala. Press, 1969; Albert James Pickett, *History of Alabama.* Birmingham Book and Mag. Co., 1962; James D. Dreisback, "Weatherford — 'The Red Eagle'." *Ala. Historical Reporter,* Vol. 2, No. 4 (Mar. 1884), n.p.; information from the Ala. Dept. of Archives and Hist.

Talbot, Levi, trapper (d. c. Aug. 25, 1823). One who responded to Ashley's call for "one hundred young men" to ascend the Missouri River to trap beaver, Talbot became associated with Mike Fink and Bill Carpenter, wintered with them and others on the Musselshell River and returned to Fort Henry in the spring of 1823. Here Fink killed, probably deliberately, Carpenter in a shooting contest supposedly aimed at perforating a cup of whiskey on the other's head. When, some weeks after, Fink conceded that the killing had been done purposefully, Talbot with a pistol shot Fink through the heart. Talbot took a courageous part in Leavenworth's operation against the Arikara villages, August 9-14, but drowned 10 days later attempting to swim the Teton (Bad) River, a Missouri tributary in South Dakota.

Walter Blair, Franklin J. Meine, *Half Horse Half Alligator: the Growth of the Mike Fink Legend.* Univ. of Chicago Press, 1956; Dale L. Morgan, *The West of William H. Ashley.* Denver, Old West Pub. Co., 1964; this gives Talbot's first name.

Talbot(t), Pres(s)ly, army officer (fl. 1859-1865). A Kentuckian, Talbot reached Colorado in 1859 and became "pretty well acquainted with Indian affairs." In the late summer of 1864 he was commissioned a captain of Company M of the 100-day 3rd Colorado Cavalry and as such fought at Sand Creek, Colorado, November 29, 1864. Half an hour after the engagement commenced he was wounded by a bullet through the body and removed from the field. Louderback was detailed as his nurse. Chivington sought to extract from Talbot (a witness favorable to the colonel) information usable in an attempt to impeach Louderback's testimony but was not permitted to do so and his reasoning therefore was not clear nor his purpose in seeking to destroy Louderback's testimony.

Sand Creek Massacre.

Tall Bull, Cheyenne Dog Soldier chief (c. 1830-July 11, 1869). His name was hereditary among the Cheyenne, borne at different times by distinguished men the most noted of whom to the whites was the Tall Bull killed by Carr's forces at Summit Springs, Colorado (King says this man was the fourth to bear the name). His Indian name was Hotoa-qa-ihoois. In April and May 1864, Lieutenant George S. Eayre, commanding the Independent Battery of Colorado Volunteer Artillery attacked the relatively peaceful camps of the Cheyenne on the Plains east of Denver and across the Kansas line, harming them little but stirring them up, which in George Bent's view was the reason for the activity. Tall Bull, as a chief of one of the most militant of the Cheyenne warrior societies, was active in Plains hostilities but in 1867 he with others signed the Medicine Lodge Creek Treaty of October 28. In the Plains wars of 1868-69 Tall Bull was active; he took part in the Battle of Beecher Island, and it was he with White Horse and other Dog Soldier leaders who talked Roman Nose into leading his fatal charge. As Bent wrote, "The whites give this fight much importance, but the Indians take it as an ordinary incident," and contrary to white reports, they suffered few losses, although Roman Nose was among the leaders who fell. In May 1869 Tall Bull led his Dog Soldiers in actions against the soldiers who were scouring the region for him, without suffering serious losses. Tall Bull intended to make for the Black Hills when his camp was surprised by Carr and the Indians roundly defeated, Tall Bull among the slain. Bent wrote that "Bill Cody and Frank North claim they killed Tall Bull, but the Pawnees say no one knows who killed him, as they were all shooting at him." One of Tall Bull's wives escaped on horseback before the fight; one was killed with the chief and the other, White Buffalo Woman, was captured, and lived on the Tongue River Reservation of Montana for many years. With Tall Bull's death the power of the Dog Soldiers was broken.

Hodge, HAI; Dockstader; George E. Hyde, *Life of George Bent.* Norman, Univ. of Okla. Press, 1968; George Bird Grinnell, *Fighting Cheyennes.* Norman, 1956; James T. King, *War Eagle: A Life of General Eugene A. Carr.* Lincoln, Univ. of Nebr. Press, 1963; Don Russell, *The Lives and Legends of Buffalo Bill.* Norman, 1960.

Tallman, W.A. (Al), pioneer (fl. 1855-1865). Tallman with Louis Robouin and Henri M. Chase was living on the Clearwater River, Idaho, when the 1855-56 Nez Perce disturbances forced them to flee and they settled in the Bitterroot Valley of western Montana, near Fort Owen. Here Tallman worked at any occupation he could find and occasionally being an "old hunter" was sent by Owen on a mission of some sort to the Indians. In 1865 it was suspected he and others were selling whiskey to the Indians. Tallman escaped two deputy U.S. Marshals (J.X. Beidler was one of them), his stock was confiscated as bond but the outcome of the affair was not recorded.

Montana Contributions, II (1896); VII (1910); George F. Weisel, *Men and Trade on the Northwest Frontier.* Missoula, Mont. State Univ. Press, 1955.

Talon, Jean Baptiste, intendant of New France (c. Jan. 1626-Nov. 24, 1694). B. at Chalons-sur-Marne, France, he was educated in Paris by the Jesuits and as intendant of New France served from 1665-68 and from 1670-72. He was most vigorous, intelligent and honest and his accomplishments for France in Canada were of the first magnitude, the population almost doubling during his

administration and its economic well-being greatly enhanced in many directions. For American frontier interest his greatest impact was in the encouragement of exploration. He sent Albanel to Hudson Bay, St. Lusson to the upper Great Lakes, and opened the way for expansion of the fur trade and other activities beyond the frontier. "Again and again he urged upon (Jean Baptiste) Colbert (chief minister) and the King a measure from which, had it taken effect, momentous consequences must have sprung. This was the purchase or seizure of New York, — involving the isolation of New England, the subjection of the Iroquois, and the undisputed control of half the continent," but his recommendations were not pursued. Talon was one of the most able French officials in Canadian history, and his influence was more extensive and lasted longer than many others. A lengthy essay on his work in New France may be found in *Dictionary of Canadian Biography,* I. He died in France.

Literature abundant; Thwaites, JR, XLIX, 275n14; CE; Parkman, *Old Regime in Canada,* I, pp. 188, 215-36; II, pp. 3-251; Parkman, *Count Frontenac and New France Under Louis XIV,* 18-43.

Tammany, Delaware chief (c. 1625-c. 1701). A noted and influential Delaware chief he lived in the present Bucks County, Pennsylvania and while few facts are remembered of his life there are plenty of legends about him. He is said to have welcomed William Penn to America October 27, 1682, and his name in one of its variants appears as a signer of deed to Penn in 1683. Heckewelder said he was the greatest and best chief known to Delaware tradition and "although many fabulous stories are circulated about him among the whites, but little of his real history is known.... He was in the highest degree endowed with wisdom, virtue, prudence, charity, affability, meekness, hospitality, in short with every good and noble qualification that a human being may possess ...He was a stranger to everything that was bad." To some he became known as St. Tammany, patron saint of America. Many organizations incorporated his name in their title, two to them enduring for a long time: "The Improved Order of Red Men," and "The Society of St. Tammany," founded in 1789 and which eventually became the Democratic party organization of New York, its most famous label being Tammany Hall, representing the party in some of its urban manifestations. Tammany died in Pennsylvania and was buried in the Tammany Burial Grounds, near Chalfonte.

Hodge, HAI.

Tanner, Sidney, Mormon pioneer (April 1, 1809-Dec. 5, 1895). B. at Bolton, Warren County, New York, he joined the Mormon sect and by 1849 was in Utah. He was sent then to San Bernardino, California, where the church was engaged in establishing a settlement and where he remained until 1857. In company with William Matthews he engaged in freighting between Salt Lake City and San Bernardino. On a trip to California their train was delayed by the turmoil coincident with the Mountain Meadows Massacre of September 11, 1857, being held first at Parowan, then at Cedar City, Utah, until after the event. They saw loot from the slaughter arriving at Cedar City. A week afterward they started anew for California "but saw nothing of the scene of carnage because they were guided past it in the night and ordered to stay with their wagons and keep moving." Tanner demanded that Ira Hatch accompany them as guide and protector of the train from restless Indians; they reached San Bernardino safely October 1. In late 1857 Tanner was recalled to Utah and settled at Beaver, where he died.

Frank Esshom, *Pioneers and Prominent Men of Utah.* Salt Lake City, Western Epics, 1966; Juanita Brooks, *The Mountain Meadows Massacre.* Norman, Univ. of Okla. Press, 1966.

Tappan, Benjamin Jr., army surgeon (Nov. 18, 1840-Mar. 22, 1866). B. at Steubenville, Ohio, his father was a physician and his uncle Edwin M. Stanton, Lincoln's secretary of war. Tappan began the study of medicine under his father, continued it at San Francisco under Dr. A.J. Bowie, and returned to Ohio in 1861. He enlisted in the Ohio Volunteers, shortly became an acting hospital steward, continued his medical studies at Philadelphia and returned to Ohio where, still an enlisted man, he assisted in the capture of the Confederate guerilla, John Morgan. Tappan studied at Bellevue Hospital Medical College, New York, in 1863-64. Graduated, he was named acting assistant surgeon in the army's Department of the Pacific. In 1865, he was named purveyor of the District of Arizona, assigned to Fort Yuma, performing his duties well enough, but becoming involved in continued disputes with Lieutenant Colonel Madison Boulware, commanding. Tappan was the subject of court-martial charges for what appear minor offenses; they were dropped. On March 7, 1866, he left Yuma for Camp Grant Arizona, the party commanded by brevet Major James Franklin Millar, who also had served in the Ohio Volunteers. On March 22, 35 miles west of Grant in the vicinity of Cottonwood Springs, the party was attacked by an estimated 75 or more Indians described as Tonto or Pinal Apaches. Millar and three soldiers were killed outright, Tappan wounded twice, in body and foot. Survivors left him in care of a teamster named Sumner, went for water, lost their bearings and could not find their way back. A party under Captain Jonathan B. Hager returned to the site March 26, found the bodies of the four initial victims but best efforts failed to locate Tappan although tracks showed he had wandered off, "evidently deranged." There is a report that he suffered periodically from epilepsy. There is no report on the fate of Sumner.

Arizona Miner, Prescott, Apr. 11, 1866; Edward S. Peterson, "Abandoned Near Cottonwood Springs." *Westerners Brand Book,* Chicago Corral, Vol. XXXII, No. 8 (Dec. 1975), 57-58, 64.

Tappan, Samuel Forster, military officer, newspaperman (1830-Jan. 6, 1913). B. at Manchester, Massachusetts, he became a newspaperman and firm friend of such strong abolitionists and social activists as William Lloyd Garrison, Theodore Parker and Wendell Phillips, seconding to some extent their views on issues of the day. Tappan also became acquainted with Horace Greeley of the *New York Tribune* and when the slavery issue arose in Kansas was sent by Greeley as correspondent to cover developments. Tappan, a man of principle and undoubted courage spent several years not only reporting on, but participating in events of that turbulent period. He became acquainted with John Brown. He was of the party that rescued Jacob Branson of Lawrence, a Free-State man, from the pro-slavery faction in a celebrated incident of 1855 and in a subsequent confrontation beat off a pro-slavery sheriff who tried to arrest him. Tappan became involved politically and was assistant clerk in the 1855 constitutional convention of Kansas and of the House of

Representatives thereafter. In September 1856 after a visit to Washington, D.C., Tappan and others brought to Kansas arms and munitions for the anti-slavery forces, for they were as militant as the forces they supported. With the turmoil abating, Tappan moved to Colorado in 1858 by one account, or in July 1860 by another to join in the gold rush, settling first at Denver where he became assistant editor of the *Denver Herald,* and then at Central City in the gold mining district of Gilpin to the west. He still corresponded for the *Tribune,* but as a sideline operated a print shop. With the outbreak of the Civil War Tappan as captain recruited Company B of the 1st Colorado Volunteers and was named lieutenant colonel of the regiment that left March 3, 1862, for New Mexico. He had a creditable part in the battle of Pigeon's Ranch on March 26 and at Apache Pass two days later. When the regimental commander, Colonel John Slough resigned in a huff, command was turned over to Tappan, but the men preferred Chivington who was named to the post April 14, and enmity between Tappan and Chivington may have been generated at that time. When the 1st was reassigned back to Colorado, Tappan became commander of Fort Lyon. Against Chivington's instructions he sent reinforcements to Fort Larned in Kansas when he learned of Indian disturbances there. Chivington angrily removed him from command at Lyon, replacing him with Major Scott J. Anthony, a Chivington man, while Tappan moved to Fort Garland, Colorado. Tappan took no part in the Sand Creek massacre of November 29, 1864, directed by Chivington, although he adopted an Indian girl orphaned there; she died while attending a New York girls' school, where she was an excellent student. Tappan was detailed to sit as president of a commission to ascertain the facts of the massacre and whether civilized rules of warfare had been violated during it. Tappan's presence on the board was bitterly contested by Chivington, (who had resigned his commission), the latter considering Tappan "an open and avowed enemy," prejudiced and unable to divest himself of such views. Tappan defended his objectivity and remained as chairman of the commission which commenced hearings February 1, 1865, at Denver, moved to Fort Lyon March 10, returned to Denver April 8 and continued until May 30, 1865. No conclusion was

reached or sought, its purpose merely to uncover the facts of the tragedy; the record shows that Tappan was indeed scrupulously fair to Chivington throughout, giving him every opportunity to present his case. In 1867 Tappan, by now a civilian, was named by President Grant to the Peace Commission intended to further settlement of Indian difficulties, other civilian members being Senator J.B. Henderson, chairman of the Senate Committee on Indian Affairs; Indian Commissioner N.G. Taylor and John B. Sanborn; military members included Generals W.T. Sherman, W.S. Harney, A.H. Terry and C.C. Augur. The commission arranged at Fort Laramie a treaty with the Sioux April 29, 1868; with the Crows May 7 and with the Northern Cheyenne and Arapaho May 10. Sherman and Tappan then went to Fort Sumner, New Mexico, where on June 1 they concluded a treaty with the much-abused Navaho, unraveling the disastrous Bosque Redondo experiment and providing for the Indians to return to their ancestral homeland. On July 2 Tappan with Sherman and others arranged a treaty at Fort Bridger, Wyoming, with the eastern Shoshone and Bannock. Tappan had signed all the agreements as had Sherman, although Sherman did not like Tappan and had told him so on occasion. When Custer attacked friendly Cheyenne on the Washita November 27, 1868, Tappan lashed out with his newsman's pen against what he believed an unjustified provocation which could only result in more bloodshed, although Sherman defended Custer. During his work with the peace commission in the west, Tappan had become acquainted with correspondent Henry M. Stanley; it was through Tappan's introduction that Stanley was employed by James Gordon Bennett of the *New York Herald* who sent him in 1870-71 to Africa to find the missionary explorer, David Livingstone. Tappan spent the last 26 years of his life at Washington, D.C., where he died in his 83rd year. He was buried at Arlington National Cemetery.

Tappan death certificate; *Collecs. of the Kan. State Hist. Soc., 1913-1914,* Vol. XIII. Topeka, Kan. State Printing Plant, 1915; Stanley W. Zamonski, Teddy Keller, *The Fifty-Niners.* Denver, Sage Books, 1961; William Clarke Whitford, *Colorado Volunteers in the Civil War.* Boulder, Colo., Pruett Press, 1963; *Sand Creek Massacre;* Stan Hoig, *The Sand Creek Massacre.* Norman,

Univ. of Okla. Press, 1974; Robert G. Athearn, *William Tecumseh Sherman and the Settlement of the West.* Norman, 1956; Charles J. Kappler, *Indian Treaties, 1778-1883.* N.Y., Interland Pub. Inc., 1972; information from the Kan. State Hist. Soc.

Tarhe (The Crane), Wyandot (Huron) chief (1742-Nov. 1818). B. at Detroit he was known to the whites as The Crane and first came to public attention in 1774 at the Battle of Point Pleasant, the climax of the Lord Dunmore War when he fought with Cornstalk. Of the 13 chiefs who participated in the Battle of Fallen Timbers in 1794, Tarhe was the only one who escaped, though badly wounded. It was largely through his influence and in the face of strong opposition that the Treaty of Greenville in 1796 was made possible; he ever after considered its terms inviolate and held to them, even to opposing Tecumseh from 1808 until the latter's death. Tarhe remained faithful to the American cause during the War of 1812. Although more than 70 he led his warriors through the whole of Harrison's campaign into Canada and participated in the Battle of the Thames (in which Tecumseh was slain) October 5, 1813. From the end of the war until his own death, Tarhe became well known to settlers of central Ohio. Harrison described him in 1814 as a "venerable, intelligent, and upright man." Tarhe was the keeper of the calumet for his tribe, an article which bound the tribes of northern Ohio into a confederation for their mutual benefit and protection. The place of his burial is unknown.

Hodge, HAI.

Tartarin, René, Jesuit missionary (Jan. 22, 1695-Sept. 24, 1745). B. in France, he became a Jesuit and reached Canada or Louisiana July 23, 1727, being assigned to the Illinois missions; he remained at Kaskaskia two or three years. The rest of his service is unreported. He died in the Louisiana missions, at a site unspecified.

Thwaites, JR, LXVII, 342n43, LXXI, 169.

Tasker, Charles P., rancher (c. 1849-post 1877). B. at Philadelphia, he was a man of some means who suffered from tuberculosis. He employed Hank Smith to locate a ranch for him in Blanco Canyon of the Staked Plains of Texas, becoming the first settler of the vicinity. He was however, more fond of "cards and drink" than ranching, accumulated considerable debts, and disappeared. Smith, who held a lien on the ranch, took it over.

Oscar Williams; J. Evetts Haley, *The XIT Ranch of Texas.* Norman, Univ. of Okla. Press, 1967.

Tassin, Augustus Gabriel de Vivier, army officer, writer (Oct. 12, 1842-Oct. 19, 1893). B. in France, he apparently received some military training, perhaps abroad, and was commissioned a first lieutenant of the 35th Indiana Infantry October 9, 1861, serving throughout the Civil War and rising to colonel. He then joined the 12th Infantry as a captain July 28, 1866. On December 1, 1870, he was discharged at his own request, went back to France and served in the Franco-Prussian War, after which he returned to the U.S. and re-entered the American army as a private in the Signal Corps, June 18, 1872. He was commissioned a second lieutenant in the 12th Infantry March 19, 1873, and at his death was a captain, having received brevets through colonel for Civil War gallantry. A son, Algeron de Vivier Tassin, writer and actor, received after his father's death an award to him of the French Legion of Honor for his service in the Franco-Prussian War. Another son was a noted geologist and metallurgist. Tassin, posted to several frontier establishments in Arizona, wrote articles of historical interest on his service; they appeared in the *Overland Monthly.* Among them were "Reminiscences of Indian Scouting," Vol. XIV, No. 80 (Aug. 1889), 151-69; and "Among the Apaches," Vol. XIV, Nos. 81, 82 (Sept., Oct. 1889, 311-20; 374-79.

Heitman; Dennis G. Casebier correspondence with author, Jan. 22, 1975; *Overland Monthly.*

Tate, Mormon pioneer (fl. 1857-1892). A man of this name, of Cedar City, Utah, was placed by *Mormonism Unveiled* at the Mountain Meadows Massacre of September 11, 1857, either participating in or consenting to the tragedy. He was reported to have "since been a Captain of militia."

Mormonism Unveiled, 380.

Tatum, Lawrie, Indian agent (May 22, 1822-Jan. 22, 1900). B. at Mullica Hill, New Jersey, of Quaker parentage he was taken to Ohio at 6 and after a meager education went to Iowa in 1844 where he taught school and commenced farming. He married in 1848 and eventually settled at Springdale, Iowa. In the spring of 1869 Tatum, prominent for his Quaker work, was named first agent for the Kiowas and reached Fort Sill, Oklahoma, July 1 with little knowledge of wild Indians but the firm intention to tame them by honesty, industry, patience and kindness. There were to be 2,000 Kiowas, 2,500 Comanches and several hundred other Indians under his supervision. Tatum's relations with the army were excellent and at first the Indians responded well to his encouragement of agriculture, other industries, and the school he began. Tatum was innovative and energetic, but his many problems included propensity of the Indians to depredate, mainly into Texas; political corruption which hampered his work and authority; disinclination of the Kiowas to take up farming; and increasing confrontations with Indians who followed the war trails. This led Tatum to closer dependence upon firmness and discipline for his charges and policing of their conduct. Tatum suspected Satanta and other Kiowa chiefs of having led the 1871 Warren wagon train raid in Texas, and managed to win a boasting confession from him. The agent hurried a message to Sherman, visiting at Fort Sill, requesting that three chiefs, Satanta, Setangya and Big Tree be arrested, which Sherman directed be done; these arrests stunned the Kiowas and the chiefs were hustled off for disposition according to legal procedures. In July 1871 Tatum went to Jacksboro, Texas to testify in the trial of Satanta and Big Tree (Setangya had been killed by his captors), and when the two were sentenced to hang Tatum, fearing a blood bath if that were done, successfully persuaded Governor Davis of Texas to commute the sentences to life imprisonment, thus holding the chiefs hostage for the good conduct of their people. Tatum increasingly viewed force as necessary to control his turbulent charges, thereby coming into opposition with his Quaker superiors, including Superintendent Enoch Hoag who still believed that mildness, kindness and tolerance could tame the wildest of Indians. Eventually Tatum lost confidence in Grant's Peace Policy which the Quakers had instigated. When he learned that Satanta and Big Tree were to be pardoned, he realized that his light hold over the Kiowas would evaporate. In December 1872 he submitted his resigna-

tion, and early in 1873 returned to Iowa. Tatum had been a good agent faced with impossible situations and came to depend more upon military force than his superiors would endorse. He was one of the best-known Indian agents of his day, and his book has become a standby for historians and "classic in the literature of the Southern Plains." Tatum also wrote religious works of Quaker interest. He was active in promoting in Iowa a mutual fire insurance company and establishment of a bank for which he was a director for many years; he also was ever interested in education matters. In late life he was appointed guardian for the infant Herbert Hoover, future President of the United States. Tatum died at Springdale.

Lawrie Tatum, *Our Red Brothers and the Peace Policy of President Ulysses S. Grant.* Lincoln, Univ. of Nebr., 1970; Lee Cutler, "Lawrie Tatum and the Kiowa Agency 1869-1873." *Arizona and the West,* Vol. 13, No. 3 (Autumn 1971), 221-44; information from David Kinnett, manuscript librarian, State Hist. Soc. of Iowa; *A Topical History of Cedar County, Iowa,* 1, ed. by C. Ray Aurner. Chicago, S.J. Clarke Pub. Co., 1910, p. 491.

Tavibo, Paiute chief and medicine man (c. 1810-c. 1870). The father of Wovoka, he was b. near Walker Lake, Esmeralda County, Nevada, and won fame as a medicine man. When the whites crowded the Indians out of their valleys and settlements he was interrogated as to what hope remained. Having gone into the mountains to receive a revelation, Tavibo prophesied that the earth would swallow the whites and the Indians would repossess their land once more. Devotees flocked to him from Nevada, Idaho and Oregon. As his forecasts failed to materialize his faithful became fewer and hastily assembled later revelations that only the true believers would be saved did little to stem the tide of defections. Tavibo died at about 60 around 1870 before his son's great role in the Ghost Dance enthusiasm became apparent.

Hodge, HAI.

Taxous, Abenaki chief (d. c. 1720). A noted chief of his people, he captured Groton, Massachusetts, in 1694. He was seized with others by the English at Pemaquid in present day Maine, in 1696, but killed his guards and escaped. Following the treaty of Utrecht ending Queen Anne's War in 1713, Taxous and other prominent chiefs on July 11-13, 1713, concluded a peace with New England at Portsmouth, New Hampshire. He died in 1720 or 1721.

Thwaites, JR, LXVII, 334n10.

Taylor, Bernard, soldier (fl. 1874). B. at St. Louis, Taylor was sergeant of Company A, 5th Cavalry and accompanied First Lieutenant Charles King in advance of the unit November 1, 1874, falling into an ambush in Sunset Pass in eastern Arizona. King was severely wounded, his arm broken by an Indian bullet and was pinned down. Taylor, a "big, strapping powerful fellow" rejected King's order to leave him and save himself. Instead he picked up King and through heavy fire from Tonto Apaches carried him half a mile to safety. For his conduct Taylor was awarded a Medal of Honor and won King's lasting gratitude. King made the incident an exciting part of his novel, *Starlight Ranch,* in which he calls Taylor, O'Grady and himself, Lieutenant Billings, with other names of actual persons changed to suit his fictional purposes.

Price, *Fifth Cavalry,* 677; MH; *Deeds of Valor,* II, 195-96; Oliver Knight, *Life and Manners in the Frontier Army.* Norman, Univ. of Okla. Press, 1978, 208-13; King to George O. Eaton, Aug. 9, 1924, copy of letter in author's collection.

Taylor, Edward Griffith (Griff), army officer (Dec. 23, 1828-Sept. 17, 1908). B. at Leesburg, Virginia, he was educated in Ohio and Iowa and from Wisconsin went in 1852 to California. He was mustered in August 16, 1861, as a second lieutenant of Company F, 1st California Infantry and promoted to first lieutenant June 23, 1862, serving three years in all. He reached Fort Yuma in December 1861 and Old Fort Gaston near the Colorado River 60 miles north of Yuma January 15, 1862. He commanded a detachment immediately following that of Lieutenant James Barrett, ambushed at Picacho Pass in the only engagement between California Volunteers and Confederates within Arizona. Taylor arrived at Tucson June 27 and Mesilla, New Mexico, August 15, 1862, reaching Fort Wingate, New Mexico, in October 1863. From there he was active protecting emigrants on the northern road into Arizona and California and scouting for hostile Navahos and other Indians. He left November 7, 1863,

for the new gold fields of central Arizona and helped establish Fort Whipple, near Prescott December 23. Taylor was discharged at Los Pinos, New Mexico, August 31, 1864, returned to Prescott and settled permanently in Yavapais County where he became a prominent citizen, active in mining and other pursuits. He retired to the old soldier's home at Sawtelle, California June 1, 1901, and died at Beaver City, Nebraska, where he was buried.

Arizona Historical Society, Hayden file; Farish, *History of Arizona,* III, 44-45; Orton.

Taylor, Elizabeth, lynching victim (c. 1854-Mar. 15, 1885). B. in Wales as Elizabeth Jones, she was a twin of Thomas Jones, who was hanged with her. The Jones family migrated to the United States about 1860 and Elizabeth married James A. Taylor in Missouri in 1869, settling on a farm in Spring Ranche Precinct, Clay County, Nebraska. Trouble soon arose with neighbors over the grazing of loose stock and similar matters. A domineering woman who became mother of three children, Elizabeth was suspected in some quarters of poisoning her husband, who died May 27, 1882. Her father died and Ben Bethlemer, hired man, disappeared, both under somewhat mysterious circumstances. Soon it was suspected she and her brother headed a band of cattle rustlers, but there was no proof. Edwin Roberts, a neighbor, was shot presumably by one of Elizabeth's sons in a timber dispute. Mrs. Taylor and Jones, with others, moved into a sod house on the Blue River, from which they were taken near midnight by about 50 vigilantes, some masked, others not, to a bridge half a mile from their home, from which they were hanged. They were buried in the Spring Ranche Cemetery.

Jean Williams, *The Lynching of Elizabeth Taylor.* Sante Fe, Press of Territorian, (c. 1966).

Taylor, William Levi (Buck), cowboy (Nov. 1857-1924). The "first and original 'King of the Cowboys'" was b. at Fredericksburg, Texas, and his father, a cavalryman, was killed in the Civil War. Young Taylor became a cowboy, and by 14 was "able to ride and rope with some of the best of them." He drifted north and arrived at Cody's Nebraska ranch where he learned to read and write and was in the first widely-read publication with a

cowboy hero, a dime novel written by
Ingraham, *Buck Taylor, King of the Cowboys,* appearing in 1887 and followed by a
handful of other books of the type. Taylor
suffered a broken leg at London in an 1887
performance of the Wild West and Cody gave
him a gambling concession while he recovered.
Taylor bought a ranch in the Sweetwater
valley of Wyoming in 1890. He superintended
a cowboy tournament and wild west show at
Denver in 1892, and organized his own show,
which failed in 1894. He died at Downing-
town, Pennsylvania.

Don Russell, *The Lives and Legends of Buffalo
Bill.* Norman, Univ. of Okla. Press, 1960.

Taylor, William R. (Billy), sourdough,
mountain climber (Mar. 15, 1888-post 1937).
One of two men who made the first confirmed
ascent of Mt. McKinley, he reached the
summit of its more difficult (and slightly lower)
North Peak May 17, 1910. Taylor was born in
Ontario and reached Alaska about 1901
following the death of his parents. He drove
teams, located at Kantishna where he operated
pack horses, then dog teams and became a
prospector. Recruited late in 1909 by Tom
Lloyd who determined to make the McKinley
climb on a $5,000 bet after Fairbanks people
disbelieved that Cook had done so as he
publicly claimed. Taylor, Pete Anderson,
Charley McGonogal with Lloyd and three
others, left Fairbanks before Christmas and
made their camp first on Cache Creek, then
their initial mountain camp February 27,
realizing that the upper Muldrow Glacier was
the route to the top. Although Lloyd reported
that he, Taylor, Anderson and McGonogal
reached the top April 3, 1910, Taylor said
that Lloyd never got above 11,000 feet. The
others climbed to within about "four hours of
the top," saw a storm approaching and descended, Lloyd returning to Fairbanks and the
other three to their employment at Kantishna.
When Lloyd's initial story, sent around the
world, aroused doubts, he communicated with
the three and urged them to make a fresh try,
taking photographic equipment to prove the
feat, and raising a flag atop the peak. They
took with them a 14-foot spruce pole, 4 inches
thick at the butt and 2 1/2 inches at the top,
carrying it part of the way and dragging it the
rest. Leaving their 11,000-foot camp at 3 a.m.,
Taylor and Anderson gained the summit,
erected the pole and raised a flag (see Hudson

Stuck entry), left a board with their names and
the date, and regained their camp about dark.
McGonogal did not make it quite to the top.
Taylor remained at Diamond, Alaska.
Norman Bright interviewed him in 1937,
describing him in the *American Alpine Journal*
(Summer 1939) as "affable," a fine man, big
and "strong as a horse," weighing then about
250 pounds. He seems to have been unmarried.

Terris Moore, *Mt. McKinley: The Pioneer
Climbs.* College, Univ. of Alaska Press, 1967.

Taza (Tahza), Apache chief (c. 1843-Sept. 26,
1876). The older son of Cochise, chief of the
Chiricahua Apaches, Taza's mother was
Dos-teh-seh, daughter of Mangas Colorados,
the great chief of the Mimbres Apaches.
Cochise died in 1874 and Taza succeeded as
chief. When the Chiricahua Reservation in
southeastern Arizona was broken up in 1876
in order to concentrate the Apaches at San
Carlos, Arizona, Taza had a fight with Skinya,
Pionsenay and other recalcitrants opposed to
the move. Skinya was killed and the Taza
faction triumphed, then were transfered by
John Clum (see entry) to the San Carlos
Reservation. In September Taza was of a
delegation of Apaches taken to Washington,
D.C., for an official visit; while there he
contracted pneumonia, died and was buried in
the Congressional Cemetery, Site 125, Range
2 (a headstone was not emplaced until September 26, 1971, when the American Indian
Society sponsored its installation with
appropriate ceremony). Brigadier General
O.O. Howard, who had arranged for the
Chiricahua Reservation in 1872, attended the
funeral. Taza, who never married and fathered
no children, was succeeded as principal chief
by his younger brother, Naiche (Natchez), the
last chief the Central Chiricahuas ever had.

Griswold; Dan L. Thrapp, *Conquest of Apach-
eria.* Norman, Univ. of Okla. Press, 1967; Howard,
*My Life and Experience among Our Hostile
Indians.* Hartford, Conn., A.D. Worthington &
Co., 1907, p. 224.

Tecumseh, Shawnee chief, strategist (Mar.
1768?-Oct. 5, 1813). Supposedly born near
Old Chillicothe, Ohio, but the date is
uncertain. He was a brother, perhaps the twin
brother, of Tenskwatawa, the Prophet. His
father, Pucksinwa, a Shawnee chief, was killed
at Point Pleasant in 1774. Tecumseh early
became distinguished as a warrior, although

he shunned torture, and his word was inviolate. He and his people were forced by white pressure into Indiana, the band settling on the Wabash River below the mouth of the Tippecanoe River, near present-day Lafayette. The place became known as the Prophet's Town. Tecumseh early saw the necessity for Indian bands to unite to stop the white onrush. He argued that no sale or cession of Indian land was valid without consent of all tribes concerned, although the whites naturally sought to deal with them separately. Tecumseh visited various tribes seeking to form a confederacy, and to develop Indian resistance to white blandishments, He taught sobriety and encouraged the practice of agriculture, in order to avoid destruction of his people and to adapt them to civilization. He sought British support to achieve his goals, finding them sympathetic and apparently eager to establish an Indian buffer state north of the Ohio. From the British Tecumseh received arms, ammunition, clothing and encouragement. He hesitated going to war with the Americans without actual British military support. Tecumseh journeyed south to visit the Creeks and other tribes, and in his absence the Prophet disastrously engaged in the battle of Tippecanoe, November 7, 1811, which ended in a draw, or perhaps even a white defeat, since General William Henry Harrison abandoned the field, though effectively destroying any hopes for an Indian confederacy. Tecumseh had cautioned his brother on no account to be drawn into battle and had he been present the action might never have taken place or its outcome might have differed. With the War of 1812 Tecumseh was made a Brigadier General in the British Army and helped rally his warriors to the cause. He fought valiantly in several actions, scathingly castigated the British for withdrawing from lands Tecumseh believed his though he covered their withdrawal. Tecumseh was killed reportedly by Colonel Richard Mentor Johnson (see entry) in the Battle of the Thames in Ontario, October 5, 1813, a British defeat, remaining for long afterward an Indian hero and an American political football. "Tall, straight, and lean, with a light copper complexion, he was a magnificent figure of a man...," and among the most noteworthy, if not the greatest, of his race of whom we have record; although Edmunds concluded that he was "in many respects, a 'white man's Indian.'"

Literature abundant: DAB; Glenn Tucker, *Tecumseh: Vision of Glory.* Indianapolis, Bobbs-Merrill Co., 1956, which includes an assessment of source materials; R. David Edmunds, "Tecumseh, The Shawnee Prophet, and American History: A Reassessment." *Western Hist. Quar.,* Vol. XIV, No. 3 (July 1983), 261-76; *Tecumseh: Fact and Fiction in Early Records,* ed. by Carl F. Klinck. Englewood Cliffs, N.J., Prentice-Hall, Inc. 1961.

Tedro, Philip (Hadji Ali, Hi Jolly), camel driver (1828-Dec. 16, 1903). Called by some Arizonans the "happy little Turk," Tedro, whose Asia Minor name was Hadji Ali, corrupted in southwesternese to Hi Jolly, was said to have been a Syrian who reached the United States in 1856 or 1857 with a shipment of camels for use by the army. He first crossed the desert with Edward Fitzgerald Beale, reaching California where he prospected for some time. He became a part-time scout with the Arizona army and was naturalized as Philip Tedro in 1880 at Tucson, shortly marrying in that community (Wagoner includes a photograph of Tedro and his bride), and fathering two daughters. About 1889 Tedro resumed prospecting, lived in the desert near Quartzsite, Arizona, visited California on occasion, but died at Quartzsite where there is a monument to him, erected in 1935 and including the ashes of the last of his camels.

Jay J. Wagoner, *Early Arizona: Prehistory to Civil War.* Tucson, Univ. of Ariz. Press, 1975.

Tefft (Tift, Teffe), Joshua, renegade (d. Jan. 18, 1676). He was usually described as "an Englishman," suggesting he was probably b. in England. A one time resident of Pettaquamscut, Rhode Island, he seems to have come into disfavor with his father who by his will cut him off with a shilling, and he went to live with the Narragansett Indians. He was described by Captain James Oliver as "a sad wretch he never heard a sermon but once these 14 years." January 14, 1676, Tefft was captured when accompanying depredating Indians. He admitted he had been with the Narragansetts during the Great Swamp Fight of December 19, 1675, in which the Indians were soundly defeated; he claimed that the Mohegans and Pequots, supposed to be helping the English, purposely fired high to avoid killing the trapped Narragansetts. Tefft also described the situation of the hostiles, and attitudes of their leading chiefs. Leach believes that "whether Tefft was actually as much of a traitor as he was thought to be may now be open to doubt." but he was taken from Providence to Wickford, Rhode Island, tried by a military court, convicted of treason, hanged and quartered.

George Madison Bodge, *Soldiers in King Philip's War*. Leominster, Mass., 1896; Leach, *Flintlock*.

Teganissorens (Decanesora), Onondaga chief, (fl c. 1675-1725). For approximately 50 years Teganissorens was prominent in the rivalries and wars between French and English, and in diplomatic maneuvers influenced by war, the fur trade, jealousies and sometimes strained relationship among the three powers: French, British and Indian. He was an eloquent, persuasive orator, a man of fine physical appearance, able to hold his own in any setting. He was a warm friend of Frontenac, though after the death of the governor (1698) he turned toward the English. He is described by Norton as "one of the greatest leaders in Iroqouis history and a strong advocate of temperance," although the latter point is disputed since he once asked for a ban on liquor being used by traders to the Iroquois, and a short time later asked that the ban be lifted. Teganissorens was a man of vision who clearly saw the peril for his people of the pressure from two great white powers and warned against becoming too closely bound to either. He apparently died about 1725, "an old man" and probably peacefully. The best account of his life and the stressful times in which he lived is in W.J. Eccles' essay in the *Dictionary of Canadian Biography*, II.

Thwaites, JR, LXII, 273n11; Thomas Elliot Norton, *The Fur Trade in Colonial New York 1686-1776*. Madison, Univ. of Wisc. Press, 1974; DCB, II.

Tekakwitha, Kateri, Mohawk Christian (1656-Apr. 17, 1680). B. near the present Auriesville, New York, her mother was a Christian Algonquin captured near Three Rivers, Quebec, and her father Mohawk. She nearly perished of smallpox at 4, the disease leaving her an orphan, and she was raised by an anti-Christian uncle. She had shown an inclination toward Christianity and was converted by the Jesuit Jacques de Lamberville in 1675, being baptized on Easter Sunday the following year, and receiving the name of Kateri. She fled persecution in her native village and settled with Christian Iroquois and others near the Lachine Rapids on the St. Lawrence above Montreal. Her faith deepened. She desired to found a community of Indian nuns, but Lamberville persuaded her to abandon that idea since he was convinced it was not practical. Yet she took the vow of perpetual chastity, submitted herself to painful mortifications and after her death a strong devotion to her developed, and has continued. About 50 biographies of her have appeared. Thwaites published a photograph of a Joseph Sibbel statue of her as a frontispiece to *Jesuit Relations* LXII, and a photograph of a painting of her by the Jesuit Chauchetière facing page 176 of that volume.

Literature abundant: Thwaites, JR, LXII, 275-76n18; DCB, I.

Tekwerimat, Noel: *see* Noel Nagabamat.

Templeton, George M., army officer (Nov. 1841-May 4, 1870). B. at Canonsburg, Pennsylvania, he enlisted as a corporal in Company D, 149th Pennsylvania Infantry August 23, 1862, and was commissioned a captain in the 32nd U.S. Colored Infantry in 1864, being mustered out in August 1865. He became a first lieutenant in the 18th Infantry in 1866, transferred to the 27th Infantry that year and became a captain October 19, 1867. In July 1866, already afflicted with tuberculosis, he commanded a small wagon train moving up the Bozeman Trail, Wyoming Territory. July 21 the company was attacked by a large party of Sioux at Crazy Woman's Fork in present Johnson County, Wyoming. Two other trains joined the Templeton group and also came under attack. Two men were killed, Second Lieutenant Napoleon H. Daniels and Lance Sergeant Terrence Callery. Templeton was assigned to Fort C.F. Smith on the Bozeman Trail for two years. He participated in skirmishing associated with the famed Hayfield Fight of August 1 and 2, 1867. On another occasion he drove off a raiding party of Sioux, saving a mule herd and several white people, including the commanding officer's wife. Templeton left Fort Smith a captain in 1868, commanded Fort Reno, Wyoming briefly, campaigned against hostiles south of the Platte and eventually was stationed at the Cheyenne, Wyoming ordnance depot. He was unassigned, probably because of illness, from

June 14, 1869, until his death from diabetes. He was described as 6 feet, 1 inch in height with a light complexion, black eyes and dark hair.

Heitman; information from the Newberry Library. Chicago; Barry J. Hagan, "I Never Before Thought Death So Near." *Periodical* 35, Vol. X, No. 1 (Spring 1978), 3-13; William Gardner Bell, "Portrait for a Western Album," *Amer. West,* Vol. XV, No. 4 (July/Aug. 1978), 22-23, with portrait.

Ten Bears (Parra-wa-semen), Yamparika Comanche chief (c. 1792-c. 1873). B. of a Ute mother and a Comanche father he was considered a Comanche, but when his mother was allowed to visit her people among the Utes, he determined to become a Ute. A chief adopted him. The chief's son became incurably ill and the chief did not want him to waste away, but to die the glorious death of a warrior. Acceding to the chief's wish, Ten Bears and a friend dressed in their war clothing as did the sick boy. In a battle pantomime Ten Bears and his friend killed the youth. The Ute chief gave the boy's horse and clothing to them and advised Ten Bears to return to the Comanches (no doubt because young Utes might try to "avenge" the death). Ten Bears rose to prominence as much by his intelligence and skill as orator and negotiator as by his warrior prowess, In 1863 he was selected by Agent Samuel Colley to go to Washington, D.C., with a delegation that included Arapaho, Cheyenne, Kiowa and Plains Apache chiefs as well as Comanches. At Washington they agreed to stay away from the Santa Fe Trail and to reinforce a Fort Atkinson treaty of July 27, 1853; it had been signed by Ten Bears, among others. Ten Bears also signed the Little Arkansas Treaty of 1865 and that at Medicine Lodge in October 1867. At that famous council Ten Bears delivered an eloquent address that frequently has been reproduced "since it presents the Indians' case so forcefully" (it is printed in full in Richardson and in Wallace and Hoebel). In 1872 he addressed a council south of Fort Dodge and that year again went to Washington. Ten Bears upon hs return became ill. "His people deserted him," wrote Nye, "so the agent gave him a bed in the agency office (at Fort Sill). Here Ten Bears died, a pathetic figure, alone in the midst of an alien people, in an age he did not understand.... In his old age he had taken the whites man's road. His people cast him off. The white man's road did not bring him happiness."

Rupert Norval Richardson, *The Comanche Barrier to South Plains Settlement.* Glendale, Calif., Arthur H. Clark Co., 1933; Ernest Wallace, E. Adamson Hoebel, *The Comanches: Lords of the South Plains.* Norman, Univ. of Okla. Press, 1952; Wilbur Sturtevant Nye, *Carbine & Lance.* Norman, 1951; Dockstader.

Ten Eyck, William Burgen, saddler (Apr. 30, 1858-July 29/30, 1922). B. at Lumber City, Pennsylvania, he reached Montana probably before the 1876 Custer fight and in the 1880s established a saddlery and harness shop at Billings. Curly, the Crow scout, reportedly wore a Ten Eyck ammunition belt at the Custer fight as did the scout Bloody Knife and some of the hostiles. Ten Eyck was deeply interested in Indians, learned to speak Crow fluently, and collected Indian artifacts as far distant as Arizona and New Mexico. He was most famous for his saddles, maintained a working force of 15 men at his shop and his carefully tooled saddles were widely known and used in the Northwest as late as the 1920s; perhaps some still are, although his saddle business failed as the cattle industry waned. Ten Eyck married and fathered two daughters who survived. Because of financial and perhaps health problems he shot himself on the courthouse lawn at Billings.

Lelia La Vine Quihuis, "The Legacy of a Saddle Maker." *True West,* Vol. 28, No. 4 (Mar.-Apr. 1981), 14-20.

Tennille, George Culver, feudist (Dec. 29, 1825-July 8, 1874). B. in Sabine County, Missouri, he was taken to Texas as an infant with his parents who migrated as part of Stephen Austin's third colony. In 1846 George married but the arrangement did not last and in 1853 he married again. He became a lawyer. He enlisted in the 2nd Texas Infantry in the Civil War, was charged with desertion but explained the circumstances satisfactorily and probably was reinstated. Tennille somehow became involved in the Taylor-Sutton feud on the Taylor side. He appears to have been a friend of Wes Hardin and Mannen Clements and probably was an accomplice in at least some of the bloodshed that followed, for Hardin spoke of him as a trusted friend and companion. Tennille, upon Hardin's departure, apparently planned withdrawal to Mexico, but a Gonzales County posse of 25 men shot him down 14 miles from Gonzales near John Runnels' house. He left six children, two of his daughters marrying Clements men.

Chuck Parsons, "Forgotten Feudist." *Frontier Times, Vol. 50, No. 1 (Jan. 1976), 28-29, 44-45.*

Tenskwatawa, Shawnee prophet (Mar. 1768?-c. 1836). B. probably at Old Chillicothe, Ohio, he was a brother, perhaps twin brother, of Tecumseh, and long eclipsed him in fame. His mother, said by some to be a Creek, probably was Shawnee like his father. About November 1805, he proclaimed himself a Prophet, and was referred to as such thereafter by the whites. He foretold an eclipse in 1806, achieving great renown. Through witch burnings he rid himself of rivals and enemies. Like his brother he reached abstinence and self-reliance, forbade intermarriage with the whites, urged the recovery of earlier customs. Eventually the Prophet's teachings merged with Tecumseh's political vision, and the brothers worked together, although to the whites the greater responsibility for increasing Indian resistance lay with the Prophet. In 1811, when Tecumseh went south to the Creeks, he enjoined upon his brother the necessity of avoiding a clash with the whites, but the Prophet, perhaps because of bravado or for other reasons, was maneuvered by William Henry Harrison into the battle of Tippecanoe, although the Prophet himself remained aloof from the fighting, "making medicine." The Indian loss was 170 killed, 100 wounded; white loss, 62 killed, 126 wounded. The battle was a draw, but the whites withdrew, although the developing Indian confederacy was broken, its objectives ruined. The Prophet's prestige also waned. He took no part in the War of 1812, lived upon a British pension in Canada until 1826 when he returned to Ohio, then removed to Cape Girardeau, Missouri, and thence to Kansas, where George Catlin painted his portrait in 1832.

Literature, by way of Tecumseh, abundant; R. David Edmunds, "Tecumseh, The Shawnee Prophet, and American History: A Reassessment." *Western Hist. Quar.,* Vol. XIV, No. 3 (July 1983), 261-76.

Terrell, Edward, S., frontiersman (May 24, 1812-Nov. 1, 1905). B. either in Maury County,

Tennessee, or Madison County, Kentucky, Terrell went to Texas where he was said to have been the first white man to have camped on the site of Fort Worth. After the Indian treaty of 1843 Terrell became an Indian trader and a trapper at the mouth of Clear Fork on Trinity River, the present Fort Worth. He was captured by Indians and held for more than a year. Terrell became city marshal of Fort Worth in 1873 and later that year its first chief of police. Later he became a railroad contractor and finally settled at Graham, Young County, Texas, where he died.

Frontier Times, Vol. 52, No. 5 (Aug.-Sept. 1978), p. 1.

Terreros, Alonso Giraldo de, Franciscan missionary (d. Mar. 16, 1758). From the College of Santa Cruz of Querétero, Father Terreros reached Texas in 1748 as superior of the San Xavier missions and four years later was named president of missions on the Rio Grande where he became interested in work among the Apaches, principally Lipans. In 1756 he became superior of Apache mission work financed by his cousin, Pedro Romero de Terreros who had become wealthy from Mexican mines and who supported the proposed Apache work providing his cousin would direct it. Stationed at the mission of San Sabá de la Santa Cruz near the present Menard, Texas, Father Terreros was killed in an attack by an estimated 2,000 Comanches; nine other persons also died.

Herbert Eugene Bolton, *Texas in the Middle Eighteenth Century.* Austin, Univ. of Tex. Press, 1916, 1970.

Terry, Alfred Howe, army officer (Nov. 10, 1827-Dec. 16, 1890). B. at Hartford, Connecticut, he was commissioned colonel of the 2nd Connecticut Infantry May 7, 1861, ended the Civil War a Major General of Volunteers and was commissioned Brigadier General of the army January 15, 1865. Utley wrote that he was a "wealthy bachelor...whose cultural and professional attainments earned him wide respect." He commanded the Department of Dakota from 1866-68 and from 1873-86 although Terry himself said he commanded that department from September 1866 until his retirement April 5, 1888. Thus he was in overall command of the theater of major Sioux wars and much of his frontier fame derives from that circumstance. Although inexperienced in Indian fighting, he came into command of the Sioux operation of mid-1876 and personally supported Custer's request that Custer go along in command of the 7th Cavalry, supposedly upon the earnest entreaty of the Civil War hero. Custer went. Terry's actual field role in the Little Big Horn campaign was secondary to Custer, as it turned out, for Custer first came upon the Indians and his command was wiped out except for troops under Reno who were besieged until shortly before Terry arrived on the scene with the bulk of the Dakota Column. The Indians had gone and left the field a ghastly spectacle of dead men and horses; the clean-up and re-ordering of the commands was a difficult job but was efficiently completed by Terry. In October 1877 he headed a commission to Canada to confer with Sitting Bull and try to persuade him to return to a United States reservation, but the angry Sioux would barely speak to him, advising him only to "go home," which he shortly did. Terry became a Major General March 3, 1886, came into command of the Division of the Missouri with headquarters at Chicago. He retired to New Haven, Connecticut, where as a young man he had studied law at Yale University, and he died in that community. He was 6 feet tall, straight, vigorous and active. He never married. Terry generally was highly regarded.

Literature abundant; Robert M. Utley, *Frontier Regulars.* N.Y., Macmillan Co., 1973; Edgar I. Stewart, *Custer's Luck.* Norman, Univ. of Okla. Press, 1955; John S. Gray, *Centennial Campaign,* Fort Collins, Colo., Old Army Press, 1976.

Tettenborn, William Rogers (Waldemar Tethenborn, Russian Bill), desperado (c. 1850-Nov. 7-8, 1881). B. a Russian subject in a Baltic Sea port, he purportedly was the son of a "Teuton" subject of the Czar and the daughter of William Rogers, a Scot sea captain. Bill took to the sea and wound up in the U.S., going inland from San Francisco to Fort Worth, Texas, where he was wounded in a gunfight and thereafter was slightly lame. At Denver, Colorado, he was slashed in the shoulder during a knife fight. He surfaced again in the southwest New Mexico-southeast Arizona region with the "cowboy element," which included many rustlers and desperadoes. He became friendly with Sandy King, according to report, taking part in numerous

escapades and minor outlawry. The two were arrested at Deming, New Mexico, by Deputy Sheriff Dan Tucker, removed to Shakespeare, New Mexico, and lynched by hanging from the rafters of the bar room of the Shakespeare Hotel, King for his deeds and Bill, according to local gossip, "because he was a damned nuisance," although some printed accounts erroneously attribute that characterization to King instead of Tettenborn. The bodies were left hanging until the morning stage arrived, to show the way Shakespeare people handled evil-doers, and a passenger appropriated Bill's new boots, it is said. Later, according to a Silver City newspaper, Sheriff Harvey Whitehill received an inquiry from an "American consul in Russia," on behalf of "a lady of means," asking about her son. Again local gossip is the source for the report that the citizens, not wishing to distress her with the facts, replied that Bill had come to his end "from a shortage of breath due to a sudden change in altitude," and that ended the case of Russian Bill. He was a "gangling man of blonde complexion," reportedly 6 feet, 2 inches or more in height.

Emma Marble Muir, "Shakespeare Becomes a Ghost Town," *Service Book...of Hidalgo County.* Lordsburg, N.M., VFW Post 3099, (c. 1949); Philip J. Rasch, "AKA 'Russian Bill.'" *Branding Iron,* Los Angeles Corral of Westerners, No. 86 (Mar. 1968), 12-31; U.S. Census 1980, Shakespeare.

Tevanitagon, Pierre (the Iroquois), mountain man (d. 1828). B. probably in New York State, by 1804 he was a North West Company voyageur on Lake Superior and in 1816 he went to the Rockies with Donald Mackenzie. He bequeathed his name to Pierre's Hole and with other Iroquois trappers explored and worked much of the northwestern country, scuffling with Blackfeet and other Indians, having many adventures coincident to working in a rough country. He was killed by Blackfeet on Red Rock Creek, tributary to the Jefferson River.

Merle Wells article, MM, Vol. IV.

Tevis, James Henry, frontiersman (July 11, 1835-Aug. 29, 1905). B. at Wheeling, present West Virginia, Tevis served a year in Central America under the filibuster William Walker, then returned to Iowa where he had moved from the east. With 24 other young men he went overland to Arizona, reaching Tucson, September 28, 1857. He went on a trapping, Indian-fighting trip with Moses Carson to the San Francisco River, skirmishing with Mangas Coloradas' Apaches, then joined other adventurers visiting the Sonoita Valley of southern Arizona, where they scuffled with Chiricahuas. Tevis eventually reached Apache Pass where he was hired by Anthony Elder, in charge of the Butterfield Stage Station then under construction. When Elder came afoul of the Indians and was promoted out of harm's way, Tevis succeeded him, completing construction and operating the station. Here he became acquainted with Cochise and other noted Chiricahua Apaches. By Tevis's account, he not only took care of the mail company's business, but accompanied at least one raiding party into Old Mexico, and planned another into the Navaho country; his recollections were not always above reproach, however. Tevis's adventures with the Chiricahuas and disreputable whites were many, but about 1859 he left the Overland Mail Company and entered into a ranching partnership with Elder at Canutillo, New Mexico, near Mesilla. Tevis was commissioned to raise a company of rangers, attacked a Mimbres rancheria above the Overland Mail crossing of the Mimbres River, then heard of the gold strike at Pinos Altos and joined the rush. He mined for six months, he reported. The California Column confiscated his property long after he departed, and he never returned to Pinos Altos. While still in the vicinity, however, on December 4, 1860, Tevis led a group of Texans in an attack on a peaceful Mimbres camp in which Elías, an Apache chief, was killed and lasting enmity between Indians and whites engendered; he conducted the raid against his better judgment, but he did it, and the incident was not to his credit. Later Tevis and two companions were captured by Cochise; he reported his companions were tortured to death, but he escaped through friendship with one of the Chiricahua chiefs. Tevis joined the Confederate forces moving up the Rio Grande, reporting that eventually he came to command the "Arizona Scouts," which served the Confederate cause until the end of the Civil War. He then went to St. Louis, married and engaged in business. He moved to Austin, Texas, in 1879 and in 1880 to Arizona. He settled on a San Simon Valley ranch where a

community called Teviston arose; it is today's Bowie. Many gold and silver claims in the Dos Cabezas Mountains were incorporated into the Tevis Mining District, and mining and merchandising provided him a livelihood; he also operated hotels at Bowie and Tucson, where he moved in 1897, until his death. He and his wife are buried at Bowie, Arizona.

James H. Tevis, *Arizona in the '50's*. Albuquerque, Univ. of New Mex. Press, 1954; Dan L. Thrapp, *Victorio and the Mimbres Apaches*. Norman, Univ. of Okla. Press, 1974.

Tevis, John C., businessman (fl. 1842-55). From St. Louis, he made a trip up the Missouri River to Fort Benton late in 1852 and returned next year with Second Lieutenant Rufus Saxton of the Stevens survey party in a mackinaw boat. Tevis made a second trip to Benton in 1854 and planned to continue weather observations by the Stevens party at Benton, but instead returned to St. Louis that winter. He may have died on the return trip or shortly after.

Montana Contributions, Vol. X, 1940, 254.

Tewksbury, Edwin, partisan (d. Apr. 4, 1904). B. probably in Humboldt County, California, around 1852 (conjecture), he was the son of the Pit Indian wife of Maine-born John D. Tewksbury Sr., and had three full brothers: John Jr., James and Frank. John D. Sr. had reached California from Massachusetts by sailing vessel around Cape Horn early in Gold Rush days. The family moved to Oregon and then Nevada; the mother died in 1878 and her husband, lured by tales of silver strikes, brought his boys to Globe, Arizona where he married a widow, Lydia Crigler Shultes, an Englishwoman. By her he had two more sons and a daughter. In 1879 the Tewksbury boys moved to Pleasant Valley, north of Globe, establishing a horse and cattle ranch at Canyon and Rock Creeks. By 1882 Tom Graham and his brothers from Iowa settled on a ranch not far distant and at first the two families were friendly (some said rustling partners, although Mrs. Woody, on the basis of her exhaustive research believed the Tewkburys were innocent of stock thefts or other important wrong-doing). January 11, 1883, Ed Tewksbury was accosted by John Gilliland, foreman for the nearby James Stinson ranch and a dispute over stock ownership arose. Shots were fired, Tewksbury wounding slightly Gilliland and his young brother, Elisha. Charges were filed at Prescott but the the case was dismissed on grounds that Tewksbury had acted in self defense. Frank Tewksbury, youngest of the brothers, who went to Prescott for the trial contracted measles and pnuemonia on his return and died. A falling out eventually occurred between the Tewksburys and the Grahams, this leading by 1887 to the sanguinary Pleasant Valley War, one of the notable feuds of the West; according to Woody it was not generated by any sheep and cattle dispute as Forrest believed, but had other, subtler causes. First blood was drawn in July 1887 when Mart Blevins, patriarch of an unruly family of Graham partisans, disappeared, slain as the Grahams believed by Tewksburys or their faction. Ed Tewksbury was at the Newton (Middleton) Ranch house in Pleasant Valley with three of his faction when Hampton Blevins, John Paine, Tom Tucker and two others rode up August 9, 1887, seeking a fight. They got it. When the smoke cleared Blevins and Paine were dead, Tucker seriously wounded and the other two lightly wounded. No man of the Tewksbury faction was hit, but the ranch house later was burned to the ground by somebody. Ed was at the Tewksbury Ranch house September 2 when his brother John and a man named William Jacobs were shot from ambush within view. Although siege was laid to the cabin no further casualities occurred although the men inside were forced to watch half-wild hogs devouring parts of the bodies of the fallen. About September 18, after other shooting affairs in which Ed did not take part, he, his brother Jim and Jim Roberts (see entry) were camped along Canyon Creek below their ranch when partisans surrounded the bed-grounds and fighting erupted, the attackers losing one man mortally wounded, another seriously shot and perhaps others also wounded for no Tewksbury losses. September 21 Sheriff William Mulvenon arrested Ed and Jim Tewksbury and five of their faction, taking them to Payson, Arizona, for a preliminary hearing and then to Prescott where they were indicted for the murders of Hampton Blevins and John Paine; shortly they were released on bond and returned to Pleasant Valley, the cases the following June being dismissed. Principals of the Graham faction at length were reduced to one, Tom

Graham. Tom married and settled at Tempe in the Salt River Valley. Ed Tewksbury retained his ranch holdings in Pleasant Valley. For some reason he apparently felt that his life was insecure while Tom Graham lived, and on August 2, 1892, he and John Rhodes, who had moved to the Salt River Valley, waited in ambush for Graham who came along driving a grain wagon. A shot was fired and the Pleasant Valley War was over. Ed Tewksbury was arrested, charged with murder and not allowed bond, spending two and one-half years in jail during his two trials, the first ending in a conviction, the second in a hung jury when the case finally was dismissed. His ranch had deteriorated while he was in custody and he sold out and moved to Globe where he became constable, served as deputy under Sheriff Dan Williamson in 1898-99 and eventually died of tuberculosis, leaving his widow and four children. His father, John D. Tewksbury, Sr., outlived Ed by several years, also dying in Pleasant Valley and was buried near the old ranch; he had taken no part in the vendetta although occasionally finding himself in the vortexes of its explosive events.

Earle R. Forrest, *Arizona's Dark and Bloody Ground.* Caldwell, Ida., Caxton Press, 1964; Clara T. Woody, Milton L. Schwartz, *Globe Arizona.* Tucson, Ariz. Hist. Soc., 1977; Will C. Barnes, "The Pleasant Valley War of 1887." *Ariz. Hist. Rev.,* Vol. IV, Nos. 3, 4 (Oct 1931; Jan. 1932), 5-34; 32-40.

Tewksbury, James, partisan (d. Dec. 4, 1888). B. in Humboldt County, California, the third son of John D. Tewksbury Sr., Jim came with the family to Globe, Arizona, in 1879 settling eventually on a horse and cattle ranch with his brothers in Pleasant Valley north of the mining camp (see Edwin Tewksbury entry for details). Jim hired out as cowboy to the Graham brothers who reached the valley in 1882. When he learned the Grahams were careless about what stock they branded, how-ever, he quit his $50 a month job, if reluctantly. In 1883 Jim, with Ed and John, another brother, were arrested and taken to Prescott on an assault charge evolving out of a shooting of neighboring stockmen, but the case was dismissed — self defense — and Jim had had no part in it anyway. He was involved in aspects of the subsequent Pleasant Valley War however including the Newton (Middle-ton) Ranch shootout of August 9, 1887, with a Graham faction which had come seeking a fight. Whether Jim Tewksbury fired the first shot is unknown, but as a result of the affair two Graham men were killed, one badly wounded and two slightly wounded with none of the Tewskbury faction injured. Jim was at the Tewksbury cabin September 2, 1887, when his brother, John Tewksbury and William Jacobs were killed outside from ambush, their bodies partially devoured by hogs while the brothers were held inside the structure by a Graham siege. This incident added bitterness, if that were possible, to the vendetta. Murder warrants had been issued for the Tewksburys and others of their party in connection with the Newton Ranch battle and Jim with Ed and others surrendered and were indicted at Prescott; the case ultimately was dismissed. Jim Tewksbury died at Prescott of consumption in 1888 according to Woody (183) or on March 18, 1891 according to Woody (252); other authorities believe the 1888 date is correct.

See Edwin Tewksbury entry for sources.

Tewksbury, John Jr., partisan (d. Sept. 2, 1887). the second son of John D. Tewksbury Sr., he came with his father and brothers in 1879 to Globe, Arizona, and shortly settled on a horse and cattle ranch with the others in Pleasant Valley, north of Globe (see Edwin Tewksbury entry for details). With the others he was involved in the Pleasant Valley War of 1887-88 and was the only one of his family to die violently. He and William Jacobs were killed from ambush by Andy Cooper and others of the Tom Graham faction outside the Tewksbury ranch house, the bodies partially consumed by hogs while the Grahams held the remaining Tewksbury under siege for several days; the incident is one of the most famous of the spectacular feud.

See Edwin Tewksbury entry sources.

Tewksbury, John III: *see John Rhodes.*

Texas Jack: *see* John Burwell Omohundro Jr.

Thaovenhosen, Huron chief (fl. 1710). A warrior chief of great courage and effectiveness, he became a Christian of equally profound piety and conviction who resided in 1710 at the Huron settlement of Lorette, near Quebec. The Jesuit Louis d'Avaugour in a letter to his superior October 7, 1710, said of

Thaovenhosen that "there is nothing barbarous in him, save his origin," and continued with a warm tribute to the Huron. In the course of it he told how Thaovenhosen argued desperately against the time-honored and virtually universal custom of burning captives to avenge relatives lost in battle in order to save from torture a prisoner. Thaovenhosen had fought at Deerfield, Massachusetts on the great raid against that community. Because the head chief of the Lorette Christians had fallen in that engagement, it was determined to execute by torture a captive. Thaovenhosen however "prays, he entreats them to remember that they are Christians...; that dire cruelty is unbecoming to the Christian name." He won his point. "Thus," concluded d'Avaugour, "does this remarkable man make use of his authority for the welfare of the unfortunate." Other circumstances of his life are unreported.

Thwaites, JR, LXVI, 165-71.

Tharp, Edward, frontiersman (Apr. 5, 1824-Feb. 2, 1848). B. at St. Louis and a brother of William Tharp, he was a man of bad temperament and was killed at the store of his brother, Louis Tharp, at Pueblo, Colorado, by Jim Waters in a fight over the latter's wife.

Janet Lecompte article, MM, Vol. III.

Tharp, Hale Dixon, pioneer (1830-Nov. 5, 1912). B. in Michigan, he reached California during the Gold Rush period, settling initially at Placerville and then becoming a stockman and pioneer resident of the Three Rivers region. He is recognized as the discoverer of Giant Forest; it is now a prime attraction of Sequoia National Park. He first visited the forest in 1858, accompanied by two Yokuts Indians, revisiting it in 1860 and determining to occupy it in 1861. Tharp lived in a rustic cabin, part of which was a hollowed-out Sequoia log, each summer from then until the park was established in 1890, and ranged his livestock in nearby meadows. Alta Peak (11, 204 ft.) nearby once was named for him, but was renamed to its present title in 1876. Tharp died at his Three Rivers ranch home.

Information from Sequoia Nat. Park; Richard H. Dillon, "Hale Tharp's Noble Den." *Westways,* Vol. 56, No.6 (June 1964), 39-40.

Tharp, Louis, frontiersman (1808-post 1853). B. at St. Louis he was a brother of William Tharp and opened a trading post at Pueblo,

Colorado, about 1847; his place was robbed and three of his men killed by Indians. He quitted Pueblo by February 1848. In 1853 he drove sheep to California where it is presumed he remained.

Janet Lecompte article, MM, Vol. III.

Tharp, William, fur trader (July 20, 1817-May 28, 1847). B. at St. Louis, he was related to Cerán St. Vrain and commenced trading with the Cheyennes for Bent and St. Vrain by 1841, working for the firm on the western Plains and at St. Louis. In 1844 he removed to Pueblo, Colorado, where he centered his trading activities thereafter. He married a woman from Taos, and fathered two children; both died at an early age. Freighting his robes and peltries east, he was cut off, probably by Comanches, when hunting and was killed near Walnut Creek on the Arkansas River.

Janet Lacompte article, MM, Vol. III.

Thayendanegea: *see* Joseph Brant

Thayer, Isaac, scout (1821-Oct. 13, 1905). B. at Boston, he went to sea at 16, making four trips around the world in 12 years. In 1849 he went overland to California, three of the party supposedly killed by Indians enroute. Thayer reportedly had good fortune in the gold fields. He went to Colorado during its gold rush. He enlisted in the artillery during the Civil War. Thayer was one of Forsyth's scouts at the affair at Beecher Island in September 1868. In the early 1870's he went to Hays City, Kansas, and contracted to haul mail between there and Central City, Colorado, driving a stagecoach in connection with that occupation. He had some adventures with hostile Indians and desperadoes. Thayer was elected sheriff at Hays City, later moved to Wichita, then to Leavenworth, and finally to Kansas City. He left his widow and a daughter.

Simon E. Matson, ed., *The Battle of Beecher Island.* Wray, Colorado, Beecher Island Battle Mem. Assn., 1960.

Theller, Edward Russell, army officer (c. 1831-June 17, 1877). B. in Vermont, he migrated to California where on October 25, 1861, he was commissioned captain of the 2nd California Infantry with which he served throughout the Civil War, being breveted major. With his Company I, Theller was

stationed mainly in northern California during the war, and briefly afterward on the San Pedro River of Arizona and at Camp Grant. He was mustered out in 1866, commissioned a second lieutenant in the 9th U.S. Infantry in 1867 and transferred to the 21st Infantry later that year, becoming a first lieutenant in 1871. Theller had a creditable role in the Modoc Indian war in northern California in 1873. In 1877, attached to the 1st Cavalry, he took part in actions against the Nez Perce. Near the mouth of White Bird Creek, Idaho, he and his command of 18 men were trapped in a box canyon by hostiles and wiped out to a man. General O.O. Howard called him "a generous, brave man, with a warm heart." Theller's body was said to have been reburied at San Francisco, but its whereabouts have not been ascertained, He was married and left his widow but no children.

Helen Addison Howard, Dan L. McGrath, *War Chief Joseph.* Lincoln, Univ. of Nebr. Press, 1964; Heitman; Nat. Archives, Theller's military and pension records; O.O. Howard, *Nez Perce Joseph.* Boston, Lee and Shepard Pubrs., 1881; Bancroft, *California Inter Pocula.*

Thing, Joseph, sea captain, frontiersman (c. Jan, 25, 1790-post 1849). Probably by birth a southerner he became a ship's captain out of Boston. Thing joined Wyeth in 1834 and accompanied him to the upper Rockies; when Fort Hall was commenced, he went on to the Pacific and explored the Willamette River with Wyeth. Thing returned to Fort Hall, reaching there December 24, 1834, skirmished with Blackfeet that winter and in March 1836, was placed in charge of the post. He sold the fort and its goods to the Hudson's Bay Company at the 1837 rendezvous for around $8,000. He returned to Fort Vancouver, then shipped to Oahu, came back to Monterey, boarding another ship at Santa Barbara for Boston where he arrived in 1839. In May 1849 Thing captained a packmule train for California composed of two groups organized at Boston as the "Granite State and California Mining and Trading Company," comprised of 69 men; several died of cholera at Independence. The company crossed the Missouri line May 26 or 27. June 12 it was met by Captain Howard Stansbury who noted it included 140 pack and riding mules besides horses and cattle and was "badly conducted," the mules overloaded and poorly packed. Once in California Thing disappears from the records.

Judith Austin article, MM, Vol. IX; Bernard DeVoto, *Across the Wide Missouri.* Boston, Houghton Mifflin Co., 1947; Thwaites, EWT, XXI; Barry, *Beginning of West.*

Thoen, Louis, stone mason (1850-June 8, 1919). B. in Bergen, Norway, Thoen reached the Black Hills, South Dakota, in 1876 where he pursued his profession of stone mason. He settled at Gayville, then removed to Spearfish, South Dakota. Thoen married in 1880. In 1887 he found a flat sandstone on the west side of Lookout Mountain. It was engraved on one side with the message: "Came to these hills in 1833 seven of us DeLacompt, Ezra Kind, G.W. Wood,T. Brown, R. Kent, Wm. King, Indian Crow. All died but me Ezra Kind. Killed by Ind. beyond the high hill got our gold in 1834." On the other side was scratched: "Got all the gold we could carry our ponys all got by the Indians I have lost my gun and nothing to eat and Indians hunting me." Thoen was an honest man and there are no doubts he found the stone as reported; some of the names can be traced in part, but the absolute authenticity of the inscription of course cannot be proven, although the evidence in favor of it is "fairly strong." Thoen died following a stroke which came after he was thrown from his buggy when traveling from Whitewood to Spearfish.

Wi-iyohi, So. Dak. Hist. Soc., Vol. V, No. 8 (Nov. 1, 1951); *Queen City Mail.* Spearfish, Apr. 17, 1889; correspondence with Jane Carlstrom, *Queen City Mail,* Aug. 15, 1974; Frank Thomson, *The Thoen Stone: A Saga of the Black Hills.* Detroit, Harlo Press, 1966.

Thomas, Benjamin Morris, Indian agent (July 25, 1843-Oct. 2, 1892). B. in Warren County, Indiana, he was by profession a dentist who journeyed to New Mexico in 1870 for health reasons. In 1871 he entered the U.S. Indian service, holding offices at one reservation or another until 1883; he served initially as agent for the Southern Apaches (Victorio's people), then for the New Mexico Pueblos, and at the Cimarron and Tierra Amarilla agencies of Utes and Jicarilla Apaches. He was with Agent James H. Miller of the Navahos when Miller was killed by them in September 1872, Thomas receiving an arrow through a blanket he was wearing at the time. Thomas was one

of the better agents to serve the Mimbres Apaches, but because he was inflexible and could not be intimidated, the Indians never liked him as they did some of the weaker agents. Recollections of today's descendants of the Mimbres reflect such attitudes. Thomas was called "the father of education" for the Pueblos, establishing a system of schools for them. In 1883 Thomas was appointed register of the land office at Tucson, Arizona, where he served nearly five years. In 1889 Harrison named him secretary of New Mexico, an office he fulfilled until his death. Twitchell called him "a man of forceful character and high ideals; he was possessed of some administrative ability, with a conscience that never permitted him to swerve from what he deemed right." A Presbyterian, he "gave valuable aid to the cause of Presbyterianism in New Mexico."

Dan L. Thrapp, *Victorio and the Mimbres Apaches.* Norman, Univ. of Okla. Press, 1974; Twitchell, *Leading Facts,* II, 503-04.

Thomas, Earl Denison, army officer (Jan. 4, 1847-Feb. 17, 1921). B. at McHenry, Illinois, he served in the Civil War from private to sergeant major of the 8th Illinois Cavalry, taking part in many hard fights with the Army of the Potomac. Appointed then to West Point, upon his graduation he joined the 5th Cavalry at Fort McPherson, Nebraska, in 1869, winning a brevet when he led a detachment June 8, 1870, in pursuit of Indians who had depredated near the fort, killing three and destroying a camp. Thomas reached Camp McDowell, Arizona, in August 1871, and participated in a number of actions in Crook's offensive operations of 1872-74. He commanded Pima scouts at the battle of Skeleton Cave on Salt River December 28, 1872, earning another brevet, took part in an action near Four Peaks and one on Pinto Creek, and others in northwestern Arizona at Music Mountain and in the Cerbat Mountains against the Hualapais. He earned a third brevet for his Hualapais work. From 1875 until 1878 he was aide to Kautz, then commanding the Department of Arizona, also serving as engineer officer and sometimes as quartermaster, laying out several important military roads. He was stationed at Fort Washakie, Wyoming, from 1878, commanding a company and again constructing wagon roads. In September 1879, he escorted a U.S. surveying party in Yellowstone National Park. He was a captain when the Spanish American War broke out. Thomas served subsequently in the 8th, 5th, 13th, and 11th Cavalry regiments, in Puerto Rico, Cuba and the Philippine Islands; he was made a Brigadier General in 1907 and was in charge of operations on the Arizona and New Mexico border with Mexico during 1910 troubles. Thomas retired January 4, 1911, and made his home at Laurel, Maryland.

Heitman; *Who Was Who;* Price, *Fifth Cavalry; Winners of the West,* Nov. 1924.

Thomas, Eleazer, clergyman (Jan. 16, 1814-Apr. 11, 1873). B. at Chatham Four Corners, New York, he became a Methodist and migrated to western New York at 17, was ordained and joined the Genessee Methodist Conference, then transferred to California where initially he served the Powell Street Church at San Francisco. He was editor of the *California Christian Advocate* from 1856 to 1865. In 1873 he was appointed to the Peace Commission to settle Modoc hostilities in northeastern California. In this work he served under Canby. Thomas was an unthinking, even a stupid man although immersed in a genuine submission to his faith, and with a sincere desire to end the Modoc confrontation peaceably. When Tobey Riddle at the risk of her life brought word from the Stronghold that the Modocs planned to assassinate the peace commissioners, she pledged them each before she told her story never to reveal that it had come from her, otherwise her life would be in the gravest jeopardy. Thomas swore he would never reveal it. Yet subsequently he confronted Bogus Charley, one of the hostiles, with their plot to murder the commissioners and when Bogus demanded who had told him, Thomas instantly blurted "Tobey." For this Tobey's husband, Frank Riddle accosted the minister and threatened to shoot him if any harm came to his wife who had again gone to the Stronghold with a Canby message. Fortunately she outfaced the hostiles, Captain Jack came to her rescue and she was escorted safely back to the soldier camp. Thomas attended the fateful council, outwardly positive that God would protect him and the other commissioners. He was shot by Boston Charley and wounded mortally and stripped of his clothing by the Modocs. He left a widow and three children. He was buried first at the

Lone Mountain Masonic Cemetery, his remains removed in 1910 to a cemetery at Woodlawn, near San Francisco.

Jeff C. Riddle, *The Indian History of the Modoc War.* Medford, Ore., Pine Cone Pubrs., 1973.

Thomas, Evan, army officer (Dec. 1843-Apr. 26, 1873). B. in Washington, D.C., the son of Brigadier General Lorenzo Thomas who at one time was Adjutant General of the Army, Evan Thomas was commissioned a second lieutenant of the 4th Artillery April 9, 1861, and emerged from the Civil War a captain with two brevets for battlefield gallantry. In November 1865 he was charged with wounding a civilian at Georgetown, D.C. (part of Washington), and together with fellow officers of the 4th Artillery Howard Cushing and Rufus King, who tried to spring him from jail, was convicted by a general court martial and sentenced to suspension from rank and pay for a year. By 1873 he and his battery were in the Lava Beds of northeastern California for the Modoc Indian War. On April 26, 1873, he advanced against strong hostile positions with a sizable force which worked its way into a trap laid by Scarface Charley, one of Captain Jack's more effective warrior-leaders. When the Indians opened fire, many of the soldiers panicked, the officers having great difficulty keeping them together in the face of numerous casualties. Thomas said at last, "Men, we are surrounded. We must fight and die like men and soldiers." Heavily wounded he added, "I will not retreat a step farther. This is as good a place to die as any." And there he perished, along with three of his four officers, the other being wounded mortally, and much of his command in the worst disaster in the sanguinary history of the Modoc War. In all five officers were killed or fatally wounded along with eighteen soldiers slain and about as many wounded.

Heitman; Richard Dillon, *Burnt-Out Fires.* Englewood Cliffs, N. J., Prentice-Hall, 1973; Keith A. Murray, *The Modocs and Their War.* Norman, Univ. of Okla. Press, 1965; Thomas personnel records, Nat. Archives.

Thomas, Freeman, frontiersman (c. 1832-c. July 23, 1861). B. in Ohio, he was listed in the 1860 U.S. Census of El Paso, Texas, as a "grocer," but he was a conductor on the Overland Mail Company coach westward that left Mesilla, New Mexico, July 20, 1861.

The seven-man party, widely known as the Free Thompson group, included, in addition to Thomas; Joseph Roeschler, driver; Emmett Mills; John Wilson; John Portell; Robert Avaline and Matthew Champion. The coach was ambushed by Apaches led by Mangas Coloradas and Cochise a mile west of Cooke's Spring, New Mexico. The seven made their way half a mile south to a small knoll, where they erected a breastwork and a three-day siege began. Four were killed within their breastwork; three, including Thomas, apparently sought to escape, Thomas and Champion being killed about 60 yards outside the barricade, and Wilson 150 yards. Janos residents later said they had heard from the Indians that Mangas, having lost some 40 men in killed and wounded, withdrew after two days, leaving Cochise to mop up.

W.W. Mills: Forty Years in El Paso. Rex W. Strickland, ed. El Paso, Carl Hertzog, publisher, 1962.

Thomas, George Henry, army officer (July 31, 1816-Mar. 28, 1870). B. in Virginia he went to West Point and was commissioned a second lieutenant of the 3rd Artillery July 1, 1840, and a first lieutenant April 30, 1844, having served in the Second Seminole War in Florida, where he earned a brevet. Thomas served under Taylor in the Mexican War winning two more brevets, became a captain December 24, 1853, and took command of Fort Yuma, California in July 1854. He became major of the 2nd Cavalry, stationed in Texas, May 12, 1855. The regiment was called "Jeff Davis's Own," and Davis, Secretary of War and foreseeing an eventual conflict between North and South according to some historians, purposely staffed it with West Point-trained Southern officers with a view to incorporating the regiment bodily into a Southern military force should occasion arise. Thomas, born in Virginia, suited his specifications, but Thomas was one of the four Virginia officers to opt for the Union when the Civil War erupted. In 1856 Thomas commanded Fort Mason, on Comanche Creek near the Llano River, Texas. He assumed command of the regiment October 24, 1857, in the absence of Robert E. Lee and would continue to lead it until November 12, 1860, longer than any other officer while the regiment was in Texas. In the summer of 1859 Thomas commanded the escort for the movement of

reservation Indians out of Texas and into Indian Territory; he had nothing to do with initiating the unfortunate undertaking, merely following his orders. the operation was completed without serious incident. In October and November 1859 Thomas led a long reconnaissance to the headwaters of the Red and Canadian rivers and into New Mexico. In mid-1860 he led a major scouting expedition to the headwaters of the Concho and Colorado rivers, leaving Camp Cooper July 23. On August 26 in a fight with Comanches he took two arrows, in the chin and in the chest, both superficial wounds, though painful. The command arrived back at Cooper August 30. Thomas entered the Civil War a lieutenant colonel, won fame as the "Rock of Chickamauga," and emerged a Major General. He took command of the Division of the Pacific June 1, 1869. He died of apoplexy at San Francisco, universally esteemed by his peers and regarded with affection by those who served under him.

Heitman; Cullum; Harold B. Simpson, *Cry Comanche: The 2nd U.S. Calvary in Texas, 1855-1861.* Hillsboro, Tex., Hill Junior Coll. Press, 1979; Constance Wynn Altshuler, *Chains of Command.* Tucson, Ariz. Hist. Soc., 1981.

Thomas, Henry Andrew (Heck), lawman (Jan. 3, 1850-Aug. 15, 1912). B. at Oxford, Georgia, near Atlanta, Thomas, who became one of the great lawmen of the southwest, was a policeman at 18 at Atlanta. He was an express messenger in Texas, operated his own detective agency at Fort Worth, and eliminated Jim and Pink Lee of the "notorious Lee gang" of Texas outlaws. From 1886 to 1892 he worked out of the court of Isaac Charles Parker, the "hanging judge" of Fort Smith, Arkansas, and from 1893 to 1900 served under successive U.S. marshals in Oklahoma. During this time he worked with Bill Tilghman and Chris Madsen, the trio becoming known as the "three guardsmen" of the territory. A better set of lawmen never lived, and it is difficult to say one should be ranked above the other. All remained friends until their deaths. Thomas was something of a dandy, once dubbed "Scissors-tails" by Madsen after appearing in a Prince Albert coat. He "invariably picked the most dangerous desperadoes" to go after, in part, of course, because the largest rewards were paid for them, and was wounded half a dozen times in gun-fights. It was Thomas who headed the posse which killed Bill Doolin, although his precise role in that affair is disputed, and it is held that, armed with a rifle, he inflicted only a minor wound on Doolin who fell before shotgun blasts of the Dunns. Thomas called the Jennings crowd the "most comic band of robbers" in the Territory, a judgment concurred in by those who had to wipe out the tough professional outlaws. He served as chief of police at Lawton, Oklahoma, and as deputy U.S. marshal for the western district of Oklahoma. Thomas died of Bright's disease at his Lawton home, a few days after writing to Madsen that he and Tilghman were not to attend the funeral and there should be "no flowers."

Glenn Shirley, *Heck Thomas, Frontier Marshal: The Story of a Real Gunfighters.* Phila. and N.Y., Chilton Co., 1962.

Thomas, Minor T., army officer (1830-Oct. 2, 1897). B. probably at Galveston, Indiana, he reached Minnesota in 1854. A civil engineer by training, Thomas was commissioned a second lieutenant in the 1st Minnesota Infantry April 29, 1861, was wounded in the first Battle of Bull Run and promoted to first lieutenant. He became lieutenant colonel of the 4th Minnesota Infantry October 18, 1861, and colonel of the 8th Minnesota Infantry August 24, 1862. During the great Sioux uprising in Minnesota he took command of Fort Ripley during the winter of 1862-63 and then was transferred to St. Cloud. In the summer of 1864 the 8th Infantry was mounted in order to participate in the Sully expedition against the Sioux. Thomas commanded a brigade including his regiment plus six companies of the 2nd Minnesota Cavalry, two sections of artillery and a company of white and Indian scouts. By June 5 the command was readied: 2,100 men, 106 mule teams, two 6-pounder cannon, two mountain howitzers. It left for Swan Lake, Dakota, turned south and met Sully, then crossed the Missouri and located Fort Rice July 9. On July 28 hostiles were found near the Knife River and the Battle of Killdeer Mountain occurred, decided in Thomas's view by the artillery which laced into the 1,600 Sioux lodges and eventually routed the hostiles with undetermined losses. White casualties were minor. August 8 another action occurred in the South Dakota Badlands, Thomas commanding in this affair because of Sully's illness. Indian losses were reported heavy, while white casualties included nine killed and about 100 wounded. Scattered bands of hostiles were pursued and the command eventually reached the Yellowstone, arriving at Fort Union August 18. From there the expedition returned by way of Fort Berthold, the only notable further adventure being an invasion of the camp by a buffalo stampede, 100 of the animals being killed. Fort Snelling was reached October 15. Thomas and his command were sent downstream to the Civil War theatre, taking up station in Tennessee. He commanded a brigade at Murfreesboro and until the end of the war, being breveted Brigadier General March 13, 1865. Thomas practiced civil engineering at St. Paul after the war, primarily affiliated with the St. Paul and Pacific Railroad. He died at St. Paul and was buried at Galveston, Indiana. He was married and fathered children.

Minnesota in the Civil War and Indian War, 2 vols. St. Paul, Pioneer Press Co., 1891, 1899; *Collecs. of the Minn. Hist. Soc.,* XIV, *Minnesota Biographies 1655-1912,* comp. by Warren Upham, Rose Barteau Dunlap. St. Paul, 1912; *St. Paul Pioneer Press,* Oct. 4, 1897.

Thompson, Ben(jamin), gunman (Nov. 2, 1843-Mar. 11, 1884). B. at Knottingley, Yorkshire, England, he and his brother, William (Billy) Thompson (see entry), were brought by their parents to America in 1851, settling near relatives at Austin, Texas. Ben continued his education until about 15, including two years at a private school, and became a printer, enhancing his ability to communicate. He early learned to handle firearms, reportedly wounding an acquaintance at 13 and killing an Indian when 16. He went to New Orleans in 1860, may have engaged in blood-letting fights, but the evidence is scarce and unenlightening. In any event Thompson soon returned to Austin where he commenced gambling, a profession that engaged him off and on the rest of his life. Under Col. John S. (Rip) Ford, Ben in May 1861, fought Juan Nepomuceno Cortina; despite rumors to the contrary, he never rode with Cortina. On June 12 Thompson enrolled in the 2nd Texas Cavalry for Confederate service. In about 1863 according to report he killed a lieutenant and wounded a sergeant, then surrendered to a superior officer asserting they had tried to kill rather than arrest him. Streeter's research does not confirm this episode, nor does it absolutely preclude it. Thompson took part in several Civil War engagements within Texas; then obtained a transfer to Rip Ford's regiment patrolling the Rio Grande. He had several adventures along the river, including shooting affrays, some of his escapes being narrow. Federal officers reaching Austin in 1865 issued an order for Thompson's arrest, presumably for killing Union soldiers. Thompson escaped jail and went to Mexico, joining the forces of Maximilian, becoming a devoted follower of the outstanding General Tomas Mejia. Thompson was commissioned and wound up a major; he had many adventures, finally was downed at Vera Cruz by fever and returned to Texas in 1866 after he heard that civil government had been restored. The report was premature, Thompson's hairbreadth escapes continued; at length he was tried for a Texas killing, acquitted, became associated with Phil Coe and Tom Bowles in a saloon-gambling operation at Austin, and by 1868 began to branch out to other communities. He came afoul of the law again, was sentenced to Huntsville, Texas, penitentiary, and served half of a four-year term, being released in 1870. He returned to Austin, then took his gambling proceeds to Abilene, Kansas, where he became associated with Coe once more in an enterprise, the Bull's Head Saloon, Thompson bringing his wife and son there from Texas. Ben may have come to dislike Hickok, but gunfire did not occur between them although Bill on October 5, 1871, mortally shot Coe. Thompson then was enroute back to Texas to recuperate, he and his family having been injured in a buggy mishap. He returned to Ellsworth, Kansas, June 1, 1873, being joined by his brother. In a mid-August affair, Billy Thompson shot Sheriff Chauncey B. Whitney. Ben subsequently was arrested on a minor charge; Billy escaped. Ben returned to Texas. On Christmas night 1876, he shot and killed Mark Wilson, theatre owner, and severely wounded Charles Mathews. He was acquitted. In 1877 he and Billy went to Dodge City, Ben becoming a friend of Bat Masterson. In 1879 he followed the silver boom to Colorado, enlisting on the side of the Santa Fe Railway in its "war" with the Denver and Rio Grande, earning a reported fee of $5,000 for his role in the bloodless conflict. He returned to Austin and resumed his gambling career. He is said to have joined in a final pursuit of hostile Indians, but the report is dubious on several grounds. Thompson ran for city marshal of Austin, was defeated, ran again and was elected. While he was in office, it was reported, "crime dropped to an all-time low." In July 1882 at San Antonio, he killed Jack Harris, was acquitted, and returned to Austin in triumph. On a visit with King Fisher to San Antonio the two were involved in an affair at the Vaudeville Theatre and shot, apparently from ambush. Thompson, 5 feet, 9 inches, in height, with black hair and blue eyes, was a fine dresser. He was highly respected and had a host of friends to whom he was invariably loyal, but when drunk or in a playful mood could be deadly and had an unpredictable temper. Streeter said eight killings on his record could be confirmed; estimates of his total ran from 10 to 21 or even more. He had unquestioned courage.

Floyd Benjamin Streeter, *The Complete and Authentic Life of Ben Thompson: Man With a Gun.* N.Y., Frederick Fell, 1957.

Thompson, David, fur trader (Apr. 30, 1770-Feb. 10, 1857). B. at Westminster, England, he became "one of the greatest practical land geographers the world has ever known," as much interested in mapping and exploration as he was in fur trading, his ostensible occupation. Much of his finest work was in Canada, but he also traveled and explored in the northwest of what is now the U.S., erecting establishments, tracing the course of the Columbia and other major bodies of water and rivers of the north and west; "he laid the foundation for much of the great fur trade" of the Northwest. At 14 he was bound to the Hudson's Bay Company and shipped to Fort Churchill on Hudson Bay. There and elsewhere he became a wilderness man, highly intelligent, curious, able and swiftly seasoned. He accompanied a party that opened trade with the Blackfeet in 1787-88, learned surveying, explored and opened routes between Canadian posts, and in 1797 joined the North West Company, conducting a major mapping tour west of Lake Superior, and accurately charting the boundaries of the lake itself. He married a Scot-Cree woman in 1799, fathering five children and remaining loyal to her all his life. After repeated attempts, he managed to cross the Rockies in 1807 south of Alexander McKenzie's crossing, though he was not the first to accomplish this. He wintered at Windermere Lake, building a post, the first on the upper Columbia. In the spring he voyaged by canoe part way down the stream, and later that summer traced almost its entire route. He gave the name, via his French Canadians, to the Nez Perces, introduced firearms among the various tribes, and was very active for several seasons as trader as well as explorer. He reached the mouth of the Columbia July 15, 1811, after the Astorians had commenced construction of their post, although his arrival at that point was never his principal aim, for his business was trading and locating new fur country. He returned to Fort William on Lake Superior July 12, 1812, and never went back to the west. At Montreal he completed a great map of the western lands he had explored and surveyed. Thompson settled in Quebec, later in Ontario. From 1817 to 1827 he worked for the British Boundary Commission surveying the U.S. boundary as far west as Lake of the Woods; from 1834 to 1840 he surveyed lands in eastern Canada. He died, impoverished and in poor health, virtually blind, at Montreal, where he is buried. He was all but forgotten for many years, but his accurate maps and notes were widely used anonymously until Joseph B. Tyrrell uncovered Thompson's notebooks, his huge manuscript map, and his narrative in the 1800s. In 1916 he published Thompson's narrative, and publication of his field journals was accomplished piecemeal later, so that Thompson gradually is coming into the widespread recognition he deserves.

Alvin M. Josephy Jr.'s extended article, MM, Vol. III; DAB; Bancroft, *History of the Northwest Coast.*

Thompson, Free: *see* Freeman Thomas.

Thompson, John Albert (Snowshoe Thompson), ski expert, mountaineer (Apr. 30, 1827-May 15, 1876). B. at Upper Tins, Prestijeld, Norway, he was brought to Illinois in 1837 and lived in the midwest until 1851 when he crossed the Plains to California, settling at Hangtown (Placerville). Thompson became a rancher in 1856 on Putah Creek, in the Sacramento Valley. He heard of the great difficulty in transporting mail across the Sierra Nevada in winter, made snowshoes

(actually skis), as he and known them in Norway, 10 feet long, 4 1/2 inches wide, and undertook to carry the mail from Placerville to Carson City, 90 miles distant, and return, a feat he easily accomplished. He transported the mail all winter, 60 to 80 pounds per pack, and once more than 100 pounds. Thompson carried no weapon, no overcoat nor blanket, no liquor and no food that required cooking. It is reported that he continued to carry mail, express and other items between various camps about the Sierra for some 20 years, occasionally under government contract. He rescued James Sisson about Christmastime 1856, who was freezing in a mountain cabin, then made a hurried trip across the Sierra from Genoa, Nevada, to Sacramento for chloroform with which a surgeon prepared Sisson for a double foot-amputation. Sisson survived. Thompson was at Pyramid Lake May 12, 1860, when 105 men, in a battle with Paiutes, suffered 76 killed. He was "in the thick of the fight," near Major William Ormsby when the officer fell. Thompson, become a legend in his own time by amazing ski journeys about the Sierra, often on errands of mercy, petitioned the federal government for $6,000 compensation for his many years' work, but received nothing although he visited Washington in 1874; when his train became stuck in the snow 35 miles west of Laramie he plunged ahead on foot, finally reaching Cheyenne and boarding another train for the east. He often ski-jumped for pleasure, once, it is said, sailing 186 feet through the air. Late in life he became a mine superintendent and was a member of the board of supervisors for Alpine County at his death, at Genoa, Nevada.

Dan deQuille (William Wright), *Snow-shoe Thompson,* preface by Carroll D. Hall. Los Angeles, Glen Dawson, 1954, reprinted from *Overland Monthly,* Oct. 1886.

Thompson, John B., explorer (fl. 1804-1806). A member of the Lewis and Clark Expedition, he was a onetime surveyor at Vincennes, Indiana. He was dead by 1828.

History of the Expedition Under the Command of Lewis and Clark, ed. by Elliott Coues. N.Y., Dover Pubns., 1965; Clarke, *Lewis and Clark.*

Thompson, John Charles, army officer (c. 1846-Aug. 31, 1889). B. in Maryland, he was graduated from West Point in 1866, commissioned a second lieutenant in the 3rd Cavalry. Thompson was stationed at Fort Craig, new Mexico, remaining there two years. He was at Camp Halleck, Nevada in 1870-71, Camp Verde, Arizona in 1871-72 and went to Fort McPherson, Nebraska in 1872, remaining until 1874 when as regimental quartermaster one of his employees was William F. Cody, the celebrated Buffalo Bill who served as scout. Thompson was on a Big Horn expedition in 1874 and remained at Wyoming posts until 1878. He became captain August 10, 1879, a decade before he died at 43.

Cullum; Heitman; Don Russell, *The Lives and Legends of Buffalo Bill.* Norman, Univ. of Okla. Press, 1960.

Thompson, Lewis, army officer (c. 1839-July 19, 1876). B. in Pennsylvania he enlisted from Maine April 21, 1861, in the 71st New York State Militia, serving three months. February 19, 1862, he was commissioned a second lieutenant in the 2nd U.S. Cavalry, becoming a first lieutenant October 28, 1862, and ending the Civil War with two brevets. He became a captain July 28, 1866. He was sent to the north plains. January 19, 1870, under Major Eugene M. Baker, Thompson's command and others left Fort Shaw, Montana, the temperature around 30 below zero, and on January 23 struck a Piegan village on the Marias River. The result: 173 Indian men, women and children killed and others, many suffering from smallpox, captured. Baker praised his officers for their work in this celebrated — and frequently condemned — action. In August 1872 Thompson and his Company L, 2nd Cavalry, were part of Baker's force escorting the western surveying party for the Northern Pacific railway and thus operating against the Sioux and Cheyennes in the Yellowstone valley. At dawn on the 14th the camp was nearly overrun by large numbers of Sioux while Baker was sleeping off some heavy drinking, and only strenuous efforts by Thompson and other junior officers prevented a debacle. Fights with large numbers of hostiles were had on several other occasions, Thompson himself in command of an action August 17. In the 1876 Sioux war James Brisbin's battalion of the 2nd Cavalry, including Thompson's company, operated as part of Gibbon's Montana column. In May Thompson performed much scouting duty; on the 18th his and another company scouted

down the Yellowstone to the Tongue River, an operation requiring four days. He had one narrow escape, but returned without important incident. Later he repeated the scout. June 15-19 Thompson scouted as far as the Big Horn, finding little Indian sign. No doubt Thompson and his company were with Gibbon when the site of the Custer engagement was reached, and helped clean up the battleground. On July 18 a post trader arrived with a good supply of an intoxicant called Jamaica ginger, Thompson and others imbibing freely. Carroll reported Thompson as "very sick" that night and at 4 a.m. the officer shot himself through the heart, living about ten minutes. "This has cast a gloom over the whole camp," wrote Carroll in his diary. "Can only say that he was talented and noble," concluding: "Alas! poor Thompson; good, generous, noble soul."

Heitman; Robert J. Ege, *"Strike Them Hard!"* Bellevue, Nebr., Old Army Press, 1970; *Montana Contributions,* II (1896); Thomas B. Marquis, *Keep the Last Bullet For Yourself.* N.Y., Two Continents Pub. Group, 1976.

Thompson, Philip F., frontiersman (c. 1810-Jan. 22, 1854). B. in Tennessee, he reached Fort Vasquez on the South Platte in 1837, and two years later was operating Fort Davy Crockett in Brown's Hole, Colorado. Thompson went to Independence Missouri, for supplies in 1839, and returned to the mountains, where he took part in suspect activities, including horse stealing and a massive raid on California ranchos. Thompson arrived in Oregon in 1842. He served as captain during the Cayuse Indian War, was appointed an Indian agent in 1853, but soon died at Wapato Lake of tuberculosis.

LeRoy R. Hafen article, MM, Vol. III.

Thompson, Wiley, Indian agent (Sept. 23, 1781-Dec. 28, 1835). B. in Amelia County, Virginia, he moved to Elberton, Georgia, served in the Creek War of 1813-14, then in the Georgia state senate and was commissioned Major General of the 4th Division, Georgia Militia, in November 1817. He served under Jackson in the First Seminole War, 1817-18, resigning his commission in 1824; he already was a Representative to Congress where he served from 1821 to 1833. Thompson was a tall, powerful man, although inclined to ill health; he held forthright views, but was not insensitive to those of others. On August 29, 1833, he was named an Indian agent in Florida becoming, in McReynolds' view "the best agent who had been sent to the Seminoles." As a Jackson man he supported the general idea of removal of the Indians to the trans-Mississippi, but he had some principle about it. He was directed by Governor Duval to prepare the chiefs for removal, a difficult thing to do with plenty of obstacles: reluctance of the Indians to go; the problem of what to do about their slaves, and standing off rapacious white slave traders and such powerful figures as Jackson himself who supported their greed; Creek claims upon Seminole slaves; pressure from assorted white interests to speed the opening of Indian lands to them, and many others. Thompson soon came to understand the Seminoles better than his superiors, and feared resistance to removal might become violent, as it did. Inevitably he came to seem to the Seminoles the agent of removal, the symbol of their distrust, then their enmity. He insisted that signatures to the Payne's Landing Treaty of 1832 and the supplementary Fort Gibson Treaty of 1833 had signified their agreement to removal; some of the chiefs argued that they either had not known what the ambiguous documents meant, or had not signed them but their names had been affixed without their knowledge. Thompson foolishly "removed" as chiefs those leaders most adamantly opposed to emigration and that fueled their hatred, although it did little to damage their standing with their own people. For a time he felt obliged to imprison Osceola, one of the most important leaders, but when friendly chiefs interceded, he turned him loose. Directed at last to formulate a plan for removal, Thompson completed it August 27, 1835, with every detail taken care of, as he believed. But resistance on the part of the Indians mounted. There were scattered depredations, violence, murders and the assassination of Charley Emathla, a chief who had favored emigration. December 28, 1835, Thompson and his dinner companion, Lieutenant Constantine Smyth were taking a stroll near Thompson's office when they were killed from ambush by a number of disaffected Seminoles, Thompson with 14 bullet wounds, Smyth with two. The Indians scalped them both, killed Erastus Rogers the sutler and his two clerks, and escaped. That same day a 100-man military column commanded by Major Francis Dade was wiped out enroute from Fort Brooke to Fort King; only two men escaped, both badly wounded, and the Second Seminole War was underway. Thompson was buried at Elberton.

Edwin C. McReynolds, *The Seminoles.* Norman, Univ. of Okla. Press, 1967; John K. Mahon, *The History of the Second Seminole War.* Gainesville, Univ. of Fla. Press, 1967; BDAC.

Thompson, William, army officer (Nov. 10, 1813-Oct. 6, 1897). B. in Fayette County, Pennsylvania, he was admitted to the bar at Mount Vernon, Ohio, in 1837, moved to Iowa, became chief clerk in the territorial legislature and a Congressman (1847-50) and for five years edited the *Iowa State Gazette.* July 31, 1861, he was commissioned captain of the 1st Iowa Cavalry and emerged from the Civil War a colonel and brevet Brigadier General of Volunteers. He became a captain of the 7th U.S. Cavalry July 28, 1866, the oldest officer of the regiment. He served with Custer on the Plains and was in the Battle of the Washita and Custer's later campaign into Texas in search of hostile Cheyennes and Kiowas. Having reached the age of 62 Thompson retired December 15, 1875 and died at Tacoma, Washington.

Heitman; BDAC; Robert. M. Utley, *Life in Custer's Cavalry.* New Haven, Yale Univ. Press, 1977.

Thompson, William (Texas Billy), gunman (July 12, 1841-post 1892). B. at Wakefield, England, he was the older brother of Ben Thompson rather than the younger, as is often stated (Schoenberger attributes the foregoing date to a birth certificate in his possession. John Thorpe, on the basis of *his* certified copy of a birth certificate, gives Billy's date of birth as August 28, 1845 at Knottingley, Yorkshire, England). Billy, Ben and one sister were brought by their parents to Austin, Texas, in 1851 where the children, with another sister born in Texas, matured. Billy enlisted in the 2nd Texas Cavalry in time to take part in a Louisiana campaign, then transferred as had Ben to Rip Ford's regiment patrolling the Rio Grande. The brothers met at Laredo in the summer of 1863, engaging in several adventures along the rough border. March 31, 1868 Billy in a bordello fight mortally wounded Private William Burk, chief clerk in the office of the Texas Adjutant General and fled, Ben Thompson assisting him in his difficult escape.

In June 1873 Billy went north with a trail herd, joining Ben at Ellsworth, Kansas. August 15 as the result of an involved ruckus, Billy Thompson shotgunned to death Chauncey B. Whitney the sheriff whom Ben is reported to have cried was "our best friend!" Billy is said to have retorted, "I do not give a ————; I would have shot if it had been Jesus Christ!" Billy fled Ellsworth with a $500 price on his head, made his way back to Texas and lived as a fugitive for three years, was arrested, returned to Kansas for trial and September 14, 1877, was acquitted. In the summer of 1880 Billy was at Ogallala, Nebraska, where he engaged in a shooting affray with Jim Tucker, another Texan who was wounded in the hand while Thompson received five buckshot wounds, although none dangerous. Ben's friend, Bat Masterson volunteered from Dodge City; "I'll go and bring him out, but he doesn't deserve it." Masterson did so, escaping with Thompson by a ruse from Ogallala and bringing him to Dodge City in July. It is rumored that Billy Thompson killed a man at Corpus Christi, Texas in 1882. He was at San Antonio when Ben Thompson and King Fisher where assassinated and claimed Ben's body. His subsequent movements are obscure. Schoenberger reports that about 1886 Thompson got into an argument with Mexicans at a fandango in Nuevo Laredo, Mexico. Two of the Mexicans trailed Billy back across the border to Laredo, Texas and on the old military road between Laredo and Zapata occurred "a wild shoot-out (in which) all three men were killed." Schoenberger attributed this account to Catherine Thompson, widow of Ben. However detective Fred Dodge asserts that Billy Thompson was of material help to him at Houston in January 1892 in solving a difficult criminal case, and Dodge's statement is not to be lightly dismissed; perhaps the gunfight which Catherine Thompson reported occurred after January 1892.

Floyd Benjamin Streeter, *The Complete and Authentic LIfe of Ben Thompson: Man With a Gun.* N.Y., Frederick Fell, 1957; Ed Bartholomew, *The Biographical Album of Western Gunfighters.* Houston, Tex., Frontier Press, 1958; Dale T. Schoenberger, "Whatever Happened to Texas Billy Thompson?" *Real West,* Vol. 25, No 183 (Mar. 1982), 6; Fred Dodge, *Under Cover for Wells Fargo,* ed. by Carolyn Lake. Boston, Houghton Mifflin Co., 1969; John Thorpe, "Ben and Billy Thompson: Their Documented Origins," English Westerner' Soc. *Brand Book,* Vol. 23, No. 1 (Winter 1984), 9-10.

Thorbrand Snorrason, Norseman (d. c. 1003). The son of Snorri Thorbrandsson, co-leader of the Karlsefni expedition to the New World from Greenland, Thorbrand was one of two whites killed by the Skraeling attack on Karlsefni's camp. He was struck in the head by a flint-tipped arrow or atlatl dart, Freydis snatching up his sword to defend herself from the natives.

Magnus Magnusson, Hermann Palsson, *The Vinland Sagas: The Norse Discovery of America.* Baltimore, Penguin Books, 1965.

Thorhall, Gamlason, merchant (fl. c. 1005). An Icelandic merchant, he went to Greenland with Bjarni Grimolfsson and joined Karlsefni's expedition to Vinland, a place they did not find. Little is known of him thereafter except that *Grettir's Saga* refers to him as "the Vinlander."

Magnus Magnusson, Hermann Palsson, *The Vinland Sagas: The Norse Discovery of America.* Baltimore, Penguin Books, 1965.

Thorhall, the Hunter, frontiersman (fl. c. 986-1005). A member of Eirik the Red's household he was reported about 1005 to have been in Eirik's service "for a long time, acting as his huntsman in summer, and had many responsibilities. He was a huge man, swarthy and uncouth." At this date he was said to be getting old and becoming "bad-tempered and cunning, taciturn as a rule but abusive when he spoke, and always a trouble-maker." He was a pagan, rejecting Christianity, and was not popular although "Eirik and he had always been close friends." Thus he accompanied Thorvald Eiriksson, Eirik's son, to the New World with the Karlsefni expedition largely because "he had considerable experience with wild regions." Eventually he differed with Karlsefni about where Vinland lay, became disgruntled and with his crew left, intending to return to Greenland. However they were blown east to Ireland where "they were brutally beaten and enslaved; and there Thorhall died."

Magnus Magnusson, Hermann Palsson, *The Vineland Sagas: the Norse Discovery of America.* Baltimore, Penguin Books, 1965.

Thorn, Jonathan, sea captain (c. June 15, 1811). B. at Schenectady, New York, his year of birth is conjecture. He was the short-fused captain of Astor's Oregon ship, the *Tonquin.* He was appointed a midshipman in the U.S. Navy April 28, 1800, served on the *New York* during the quasi war with France, was acting lieutenant in the *Adams, Enterprize* and *Congress* in the Mediterranean from 1802 to 1805, was in several attacks on Tripoli and was a member of the famous expedition under Stephen Decatur to destroy the captured *Philadelphia* in Tripoli harbor February 16, 1804. He was promoted to lieutenant May 18, 1804. Thorn was in command of the New York Navy Yard and the gunboats there from June 1806, until May 1807. He was furloughed for two years from May 1810, to command the *Tonquin* for the northwest coast fur venture, leaving New York September 8, 1810. He engaged in endless bickerings with the Scot and Canadian fur men aboard. At the Falklands Islands where the ship put in for water, Thorn abandoned a number of Astor's men until a brother of one of them, who had remained aboard, threatened the captain with a pistol unless he hove to, which the officer did, permitting the stranded party to come aboard. The *Tonquin* touched Hawaii February 12, 1811, reaching the dangerous bar across the mouth of the Columbia River March 22 when Thorn ordered a boat put over amidst a frightful storm to sound for the channel. Commanded by the first mate, E.D. Fox, the boat was manned largely by non-sailors and with all five men was lost; another boat lost three more seamen, but the ship finally negotiated the passage and anchored in Baker Bay. The construction of Astoria was commenced April 12. Thorn and the *Tonquin* left Astoria June 1, crossing the bar on the 5th, and bore northward in compliance with Astor's instructions to trade and explore for fur-gathering regions, reaching Nootka Sound on Vancouver Island about June 12, and anchoring in Newettee Inlet on the northwestern promontory of Vancouver Island. Here Indians swarmed aboard the ship to trade; Thorn at one point became incensed and slapped a ranking chief across the face with an otter pelt. The Indian, insulted and enraged, may have organized the attack which resulted in the capture and subsequent blowing up of the *Tonquin* (the

explosion contrived by a wounded seaman) and the loss of all of its party of 30 except a Gray's Harbor interpreter (Lamanse), who later told of the disaster. Thorn was a most controversial and enigmatic figure. Raised in the iron discipline of the Navy, he had little patience with those not so cultured; he was imperious, demanding to the point of being tyrannical, contentious and stiff-necked. He also was meticulous in attention to his duties and for the welfare of his ship and crew, wholly brave and thoroughly honest and his rise in the Navy structure and selection to command the *Tonquin* attests to his ability. According to Bancroft the "gods had... made him mad," while Irving treats him more indulgently, perhaps because he had known him in his youth. The most balanced description of him and his performance is in Chittenden.

Gabriel Franchere, *Adventure at Astoria, 1810-1814.* Norman, Univ. of Okla. Press, 1967; Alexander Ross, *Adventures of the First Settlers on the Oregon.* N.Y., Citadel Press, 1969; Bancroft, *Northwest Coast,* Vol. II; Chittenden; *Register of Officer Personnel United States Navy and Marine Corps and Ships' Data 1801-1807.* Wash., U.S. Printing Office, 1945; information from Operational Archives Branch, Naval Historical Center.

Thornburgh, Thomas Tipton, army officer (1843-Sept. 29, 1879). B. at New Market, Tennessee, of Virginia parents who opposed slavery, he joined the 6th Tennessee in the Civil War and fought under Sheridan at Stone River. Appointed to West Point in 1863, he was assigned upon graduation to an artillery outfit at San Francisco. He was named major over many officers with greater longevity and transferred to the Paymaster's Corps, the promotion coming through influence of his father-in-law, Robert D. Clarke. An excellent shot, he narrowly lost a match to Dr. Frank Carver, rifle expert and self-proclaimed frontiersman, at Omaha. Thornburgh was named commander at Fort Fred Steele, east of present Rawlins, Wyoming, through George Crook's influence, and tranferred to the 4th Infantry. He failed to intercept Dull Knife's fleeing Cheyennes working north from Indian Territory. In September 1879, he was sent to the White River Agency, northwest Colorado, because of Ute unrest. His command included a company of the 4th Infantry, two of the 5th Cavalry and one of the 3rd, about 200 men in all. Thornburgh was killed at the outset of an engagement on Milk Creek, north of the Agency, toward which he was enroute.

Marshall Sprague, *Massacre: The Tragedy at White River.* Boston, Little, Brown and Co., 1957; EHI.

Thorne, Abraham D., physician, legend generator (1826-1895). B. in New York State, he was graduated from a medical college in Philadelphia, practiced briefly in East St. Louis, and went west. He was reported in California in 1852, and in 1859 in Arizona. He reached New Mexico shortly after the outbreak of the Civil War, and settled at Lemitar, four miles north of Socorro. Reportedly he became a friend of Kit Carson. He went to Fort McDowell, Arizona, about 1864 as contract surgeon, and befriended Indians, treating them for various ailments. He reported they had secretly led him blindfolded to a cache of gold, assumed to be in the Superstition Mountains. The legend of the Doc Thorne Mine generated excitement among southwesterners for 40 years, and may have been related to the so-called Lost Dutchman, as it may have inspired the Miner Expedition to the Gila River County several years later. Thorne practiced at Lemitar and Belen, New Mexico, for some years, returned in 1883 to attempt to relocate the gold area in company with Robert Groom and others, believed he found the right canyon, but not the gold.

Sims Ely, *The Lost Dutchman Mine.* N.Y., William Morrow and Co., 1953; *John Spring's Arizona,* ed. by A.M. Gustafson. Tucson, Univ. of Ariz. Press, 1966; U.S. Census returns for New Mex.

Thornton, Amos G., Mormon pioneer (Dec. 30, 1832-Apr. 5, 1901). B. at Pickering, Ontario, he reached Utah and took part in the so-called Walker War against the Ute chief Walkara which continued from July 1853 until the spring of 1854. He settled at Cedar City and Pinto, southern Utah, from 1854, marrying late in 1856. He was placed by Albert Hamblin in the Mountain Meadows Massacre of September 11, 1857. Thornton was a presiding elder of the Pinto Ward of his church for several years.

James Henry Carleton, "Mountain Meadows Massacre." Hse. Exec. Doc. 605, 57th Cong., 1st Sess., (Ser. 4377); Frank Esshom, *Pioneers and Prominent Men of Utah.* Salt Lake City, Western Epics, 1966.

Thoroughman, Thomas H., pioneer (1832-Dec. 24, 1896). Thoroughman studied law and was admitted to the Missouri Bar in 1858, being appointed city attorney of St. Joseph and then being elected circuit attorney. He was commissioned in the Confederate forces in 1862 with rank of colonel. In 1863 he was captured, imprisoned at Quincy, Illinois, then paroled, when he went to Montana, forming a law partnership with Alex C. Davis at Virginia City. The firm later relocated at Helena. Thoroughman was commissioned a Brigadier General in the Montana Militia by acting governor Thomas Francis Meagher in 1867, but after Meagher's death was demoted to colonel by Governor Green Clay Smith; his principal responsibility was the Gallatin Valley, although there was no fighting against Indians. In 1870 Thoroughman went to St. Louis where he practiced law until his death. He was married twice; the first marriage was before he went to Montana and by it he fathered three daughters. He married again at Virginia City and fathered five children, including two sons.

White Sulphur Springs, Mont., *Meagher County News,* Jan. 16, 1897.

Thorpe, James Francis (Jim), athlete (May 28, 1888-Mar. 28, 1953). B. at Prague, Oklahoma, Thorpe said he was five-eighths Indian: three-eighths Potawatomi on his mother's side, and two-eighths Sauk and Fox on his father's side; he was a member of the latter tribe. His father was part Irish; his mother a grand-daughter of the famous Black Hawk, and Jim was one of twins, his brother dying at 9. Thorpe was sent to the government Indian school at Carlisle, Pennsylvania, in 1904, becoming probably America's greatest all-around athlete. His feats at football are legendary. At the 1912 Olympic Games he won the decathlon and pentathlon and King Gustav of Sweden told him, "Sir, you are the greatest athlete in the world," which was no overstatement. His honors were stripped from him when it was learned he once had played semi-professional baseball in the Eastern Carolina League for $15 a week, apparently not realizing this would jeopardize his amateur standing. Thorpe played professional baseball from 1913-19, professional football, and in 1920 became first president of the American Professional Football Association. In 1950 he was voted the best athlete of the half-century, but he ended his life an alcoholic and in near-poverty. He died at Lomita, California. A borough made up of the former communities of Mauch Chunk and East Mauch Chunk, Pennsylvania, was named Jim Thorpe in 1954. Thorpe was a genial, friendly man, one of the permanent luminaries of the American story.

Personal interview with author; Gene Schook with Henry Gilfond, *The Jim Thorpe Story: America's Greatest Athlete.* N.Y., Julian Messner, 1951; EA.

Thorstein Eiriksson, Norseman (d. c. 1000). A son of Eirik the Red, he married Gudrid and led an abortive expedition to the New World seeking the body of his brother, Thorvald, who had been killed there; according to one *Saga* Eirik accompanied him, but this probably is untrue, if Thorstein even made the trip. The chronology is very confusing. Thorstein returned to his farm at Lysufjord, Greenland, where he died of plague.

Magnus Magnusson, Hermann Palsson, *The Vinland Sagas: The Norse Discovery of America.* Baltimore, Penguin Books, 1965.

Thorvald Eiriksson, Norseman (d. c. 1003). The middle son of Eirik the Red, Thorvald led an expedition to the New World in search of Vinland, probably before the Karlsefni expedition. He is reported to have relocated Leif's Vinland, but this is uncertain. On an exploratory voyage north he was killed by a Skraeling (Eskimo or Indian) arrow. One *Saga* account has him put away by a Uniped, which adds a fanciful dimension to the story. Some students believe the incident occurred on or near Lake Melville, Labrador, and believe he was buried there.

Magnus Magnusson, Hermann Palsson, *The Vinland Sagas: The Norse Discovery of America.* Baltimore, Penguin Books, 1965.

Thrapp, William Harrison (Harry), frontiersman (Sept. 30, 1836-Sept. 27, 1928). B. in Ohio, he went west as a young man and reported that he had made several trips across the Plains before the transcontinental railroad was built. He was in Colorado during the gold fever years and is mentioned by Bancroft as being one of a party which reached the Bitterroot Valley of Montana in 1862, uncertain whether to make for the Idaho or Montana placers (Bancroft by error spells the

first name Henry). Thrapp was in Alaska before the Gold Rush of 1898, and finally settled in the Puget Sound area. He died at Tacoma, Washington, three days short of his 92nd birthday.

Thrapp death certificate; family reminiscences; Bancroft, *Washington, Idaho & Montana,* 618n.

Three-Shooter Bill: *see* Tom Smith

Thurley, Joseph, prospector (d. July 1858). From Horsetown, Shasta County, California, Thurley with Evans and Price was killed by Indians on the Okanagan River, British Columbia, near the U.S. line. The party, under James McLoughlin, was making for the Fraser River placers.

San Francisco, Calif., *Evening Bulletin,* Aug. 27, 1858; Bancroft, *British Columbia,* which calls this individual Hurley.

Thurston, George Alva, army officer (Feb. 22, 1834-July 13, 1892). B. in New York City he was appointed from civil life in Nevada first lieutenant of the 1st Nevada Infantry April 10, 1864, being mustered out December 15 of the following year. He became a second lieutenant of the 4th Cavalry March 7, 1867, a first lieutenant in 1868, transferred to the 3rd Artillery January 13, 1874, and became a captain late in 1889. Thurston was officer of the day (in charge of the military escort) when Satanta, Big Tree and Setangya were being moved under arrest for their part in killing seven teamsters in Texas. Setangya was killed while attacking the guard. Thurston was not a witness to the shooting, although he immediately rode up and took charge. Thurston was in command of the mule packs during Mackenzie's lightning raid across the Rio Grande in May 1873 against the Kickapoos in northern Mexico; the mules could not keep up with the fast-moving column, but this was not Thurston's fault, and he was praised by Mackenzie for having "acted handsomely" in the operation. June 22, 1873, Thurston and his 40-man 4th Cavalry detachment discovered a herd of stolen cattle across the Rio Grande in Old Mexico, the officer reporting that the rustlers voluntarily brought them back to Texas soil but news accounts of the operation stating he had crossed the river, captured the thieves and returned the animals.

R.G. Carter, *On the Border with Mackenzie.* N.Y., Antiquarian Press, 1961; Ernest Wallace,

Ranald S. Mackenzie on the Texas Frontier. Lubbock, Tex., West Tex. Mus. Assn., 1964; "Ranald S. Mackenzie's Official Correspondence Relating to Texas, 1871-1873," ed. by Ernest Wallace. Mus. Jour., Vol. IX, 1965, 169.

Thwaites, Reuben Gold, historian (May 15, 1853-Oct. 22, 1913). B. at Dorchester, Massachusetts, he moved with his parents to a Wisconsin farm and by 20 had entered journalism, working on the Oshkosh Times, and becoming managing editor of the Wisconsin State Journal, Madison, by 1876. He became acquainted with Lyman C. Draper, secretary of the State Historical Society and was selected by Draper in 1886 to succeed him as secretary, becoming "Draper's most important contribution to the Society." Thwaites became "one of the outstanding historical editors of his generation," a man of boundless energy, determined that the historical society should open its doors to the public and "anyone interested in history," and a driving force in improving local historical societies, bringing libraries to the communities of the state, and in other ways advancing the appreciation of personalized learning and research. He also did much to enlarge the collections of the state society and broaden its acceptance and impact. He was an active Unitarian and prominent in many professional societies. He died suddenly "at the height of his career," holding the respect of professional historians of that day and this. His works included: Down Historic Waterways: Six Hundred Miles of Canoeing upon Illinois and Wisconsin Rivers (1888); The Story of Wisconsin (1890); The Colonies, 1492-1750 (1891); Chronicles of Border Warfare, ed. (1895); The Jesuit Relations and Allied Documents of Travels and Explorations of Jesuit Missionaries in New France, 1610-1791, ed., 73 vols. (1896-1901); On the Storied Ohio (1897); Father Marquette (1902); Hennepin's "New Discovery" (1903); Daniel Boone (1903); How George Rogers Clark Won the Northwest, and Other Essays in Western History (1903); A Brief History of Rocky Mountain Exploration, With Especial Reference to the Expedition of Lewis and Clark (1904); Early Western Travels, 1748-1846, ed., 32 vols. (1904-1907); Original Journals of the Lewis and Clark Expedition, 1804-1806, ed., 8 vols. (1904-1905); France in America, 1497-1763 (1905); Lahontan's New Voyages to North America (1905); Documentary History of Dunmore's War, ed. (1905); Wisconsin: The Americanization of a French Settlement (1908); Revolution on the Upper Ohio, ed. (1908); Frontier Defenses on the Upper Ohio ed. (1908).

Clifford L. Lord, "A Dedication to the Memory of Reuben Gold Thwaites 1853-1913." Arizona and the West, Vol. IX, No. 1 (Spring 1967), 1-4; Who Was Who.

Tibaud, Pierre, sailor, pilot (fl. 1651). The Jesuit Gabriel Druillettes on his mission to Boston came upon Tibaud and hired him; the sailor had shipped on a privateer which had captured a French ship off the Cape Breton coast. The priest described him: "He is a young sailor from Saint Nazaire, on the river of Nante; is a good interpreter of english, flemish, dutch, and spanish; can serve as pilot for the coast of new england, as far as Virginia." It was not explained how he came to serve the English privateer against the French.

Thwaites, JR, XXXVI, 97.

Tibbles, Thomas Henry, newspaperman (May 22, 1838-May 14, 1928). B. in Washington County, Ohio, he was educated at Mt. Union College, Ohio and reached Kansas City in 1856 when he joined John Brown's company of Free Staters, later serving as guide and scout on the Plains. He was in the Secret Service and a correspondent during the Civil War, afterward entering the newspaper field at Omaha, working for the Omaha Bee in 1873-74 and the Omaha Herald and World-Herald from 1876-79. It was while with the latter that Tibbles according to his own statement, was asked by Crook to intercede for Standing Bear of the Poncas and his followers who were forced to give up their hereditary lands and move to Indian Territory, and when they returned were to be made to go back once again. Tibbles became the keystone in Standing Bear's defense and for the court decision, which affirmed that an Indian, after all, was a person in the legal sense of the word (a tenet heretofore denied) and could not be moved or transferred without his assent or due process. It was a landmark in reform and America's treatment of its native population (see Standing Bear entry). Thereafter Tibbles took up his cudgels for the reformist movement. In 1882 he married Susette La Flesche (see entry) for his second wife, the first having died, and together they embarked upon lecture and writing endeavors that awakened the American conscience to a marked degree. Tibbles was Washington correspondent for the *Nonconformist,* 1893-94; founded a newspaper at Lincoln, Nebraska, in 1895, was candidate for Vice President of the United States on the People's ticket of 1904 and continued newspaper work and writing throughout his life. Among his books were *The Ponca Chiefs* (1881), the story of Standing Bear's trial, and *Buckskin and Blanket Days* (1957), an autobiography. He lived the rest of his life in Omaha and after the death of his second wife in 1903 married again in 1907; his widow survived him.

Thomas Henry Tibbles, *The Ponca Chiefs.* Lincoln, Univ. of Nebr. Press, 1972; Tibbles, *Buckskin and Blanket Days.* Lincoln, 1969.

Tidball, John Caldwell, army officer (Jan. 25, 1825-May 15, 1906). B. in Ohio County of present West Virginia he went to West Point and became a brevet second lieutenant of the 3rd Artillery July 1, 1848, and a second lieutenant of the 2nd Artillery February 14, 1849. He served in Florida against the Seminole Indians in 1849-50 and then at various southeastern posts becoming a first lieutenant March 31, 1853, in which year he was sent to Fort Defiance, New Mexico (Arizona) and spent the next year exploring a route to California. He returned east and remained there save for the period of 1860-61 at Fort Leavenworth, throughout the Civil War from which he emerged a captain and brevet Major General of Volunteers. He commanded the District of Astoria from Fort Stevens, Oregon in 1867-68 and the District of Kenai and District of Alaska from Kodiak and Sitka until 1871, his last frontier post. Tidball wrote the *Manual of Heavy Artillery Service for the U.S. Army* (1880). He retired in January 1889.

Heitman; Cullum; Powell.

Tidball, Thomas Theodore, army officer (Oct. 2, 1826-Jan. 28, 1913). B. at Pittsburgh, Pennsylvania, he enrolled at 19 in the 3rd Ohio Infantry, went with his company to the Rio Grande and took part in the defense of Camargo, a hundred miles above Matamoras. He was discharged at New Orleans June 18, 1847, and returned to Ohio. Tidball went via Cape Horn to California in 1849-50, engaged

in mining, returned east in 1854, married, resided in Indiana, and in 1857 went back to California to farm in the Salinas valley. In 1861 he became captain in the 5th California Infantry, marching overland with it to Tucson, Arizona, which he reached in April 1863. He commanded an expedition against the Aravaipa Apaches in May 1863, killing 50 Indians while losing one man. Tidball commanded at Fort Bowie in the Chiricahua Mountains of Arizona from late May 1863 until September 1864, during that time operating against the Apaches, destroying rancherias on the San Carlos River, at Dripping Springs Wash, and elsewhere killing in all 51 Indians and capturing booty. In August 1864, in the Chiricahua Mountains he killed a chief named Old Plume. Tidball was mustered out at Las Cruces, New Mexico, November 30, 1864. He returned to California, became county clerk of Santa Cruz County, collector of internal revenue and entered business at Jolon, a stage station between San Francisco and Los Angeles, about 20 miles South of King City. He died at Monterey, California.

AHS Archives, Hayden file.

Tiffany, Joseph Capron, Indian agent (Dec. 13, 1828-July 14, 1889). A first cousin of Charles Lewis Tiffany (1812-1902) who founded the New York jewelry firm, he was b. at Baltimore and became a contractor to the government during the Civil War. He was investigated for malpractice, but nothing came of it, and continued in construction and other businesses at New York. A layman of the Dutch Reformed Church he was named agent at the San Carlos Apache Reservation of Arizona in 1880, holding the position for about two controversial years. During this time he directed the "arrest or killing" of an Apache medicine man with a large following, Noch-ay-del-klinne, thus precipitating the Cibecue affair which had far-reaching consequences over the next several years. Tiffany also was interested in settling the Victorio outbreak and in the spring of 1881 confirmed the death of that Apache. Tiffany's San Carlos administration was roundly condemned by an 1882 grand jury after he had left the Territory, but he was never brought to trial for alleged corruption in Arizona, although he figured in an investigation of the charges at Washington by the Attorney General. Afterward Tiffany settled near

Deming, New Mexico, where he died after "driving a silver spike" to launch construction of a minor railroad. Nicknamed "Big Belly" by the Apaches, he was considered brutal and overbearing by them, but he had strong white supporters as well as opponents. He was a man of intelligence and vigor whose corruption, if any, was never proved.

Information from Sidney B. Brinckerhoff, Ariz. Hist. Soc.; Dan L. Thrapp, *General Crook and the Sierra Madre Adventure.* Norman, Univ. of Okla. Press, 1972; *Victorio and the Mimbres Apaches.* Norman, 1974.

Tilghman, William Matthew, lawman (July 4, 1854-Nov. 1, 1924). B. at Fort Dodge, Iowa, his father briefly became sutler at Fort Ridgely, Minnesota, then homesteaded near Atchison, Kansas where Bill was raised. As a boy he casually met James Butler Hickok and in 1871 commenced hide hunting, claiming that in five years he killed 12,000 buffalo. In September 1872 he killed four of seven Cheyennes pilfering his camp. At Kit Carson, Colorado in 1873 he began a lifelong friendship with horse rustler Dutch Henry Born (see entry). Another close friend was William A. (Hurricane Bill) Martin (see entry). Tilghman had many frontier adventures. In 1874 he narrowly escaped lynching at Granada, Colorado on a false charge of murder. In early 1875 he settled at Dodge City where he operated a saloon for a time as he later did elsewhere, although himself a teetotaler. In 1877 he married a widow, Flora Kendall (d. 1900). He was charged with train robbery in February, 1878, but it was mistaken identity, case dismissed. For most of his life Tilghman was a lawman, perhaps the greatest of frontier record, holding positions ranging from city marshal to deputy U.S. marshal, working in Kansas until 1889. July 3, 1888 he killed a longtime friend, Ed Prather in Wichita County after Prather left him no option; his only other white killing noted by his principal biographer was at Perry, Oklahoma September 17, 1893 when he shot a drifter, Crescent Sam who insisted upon a gunfight. Tilghman, of absolute courage, ever resorted to gunplay only under extreme provocation. He joined the 1889 rush to the Guthrie region and thereafter made Oklahoma his base. His principal concern during the 1890s was destruction of the notorious train robbery band of Bill Doolin. Shirley does not accept the pervasive legend that

Doolin once saved his life when Tilghman blundered into an outlaw hangout. September 1, 1895 Tilghman and Heck Thomas wounded Little Bill Raidler, a Doolin man, capturing him. Tilghman took Doolin at Eureka Springs, Arkansas, although the outlaw later escaped jail and eventually was shot by Thomas. Tilghman, Chris Madsen and Thomas, "the Three Guardsmen," were largely responsible for wiping out organized outlawry in Oklahoma. In 1903 Tilghman married Zoe Agnes Stratton, who survived him. In 1910 he became a state senator and in 1911 chief of police of Oklahoma City. He supervised filming of a motion picture, *The Passing of the Oklahoma Outlaws,* in 1915, exhibiting it around the country for a few years. In 1924 Tilghman, 70, became marshal of rowdy Cromwell, an oil boom town 70 miles east of Oklahoma City. He was treacherously killed by Wiley Lynn (see entry), a boozing prohibition officer who died in a shootout in 1932. Masterson, also a onetime lawman, characterized Tilghman as "the greatest of us all," a judgment widely shared. He was said to have been paid more reward money than any other law officer.

Glenn Shirley, *Guardian of the Law: The Life and Times of William Matthew Tilghman,* Austin, Texas, Eakin Press, 1988; Zoe A. Tilghman, *Marshal of the Last Frontier: Life and Services of William Matthew (Bill) Tilghman,* Glendale, Calif., Arthur H. Clark Co., 1964.

Tiloukaikt, Cayuse chief (d. June 3, 1850). A Cayuse chief, he became head chief of the Waiilatpu band of his tribe upon the death of Cut Lip, or Umtippe in the winter of 1840-41. He early came under the influence of missionary Marcus Whitman, though unstable in his professions of Christianity, and proving treacherous. In 1843 with some reluctance he entered into a treaty. In 1847 he was one of the principals involved in the Whitman Massacre of November 29. The following year he was one of five chiefs who surrendered and was hanged with the four others: Tomahas, Ish-ish-kais-kais, Clokamas and Kia-ma-sump-kin. Each of the five had been baptized as Catholics before their execution.

Thwaites, EWT, XXX, 106n.; Clifford M. Drury, *Marcus and Narcissa Whitman and the Opening of Old Oregon,* 2 vols. Glendale, Calif., Arthur H. Clark Co., 1973.

Tilton, Henry Remsen, army surgeon (Feb. 1, 1836-June 25, 1906). B. at Barnegate, New Jersey, he graduated in medicine from the University of Pennsylvania in 1859 and became an assistant surgeon with the army August 26, 1861, later becoming surgeon. Tilton was post surgeon at Fort Lyon, Colorado, from 1866-70 and participated in skirmishes with Cheyenne Indians September 8 and October 7, 1868. He was on Stanley's Yellowstone expedition in the early 1870s and was stationed at North Plains posts for some years thereafter. He became a major in 1876. Tilton was in a skirmish with hostile Indians January 8, 1877, at Wolf Mountain, Montana and was on Miles' expedition against the Nez Perce which resulted in the battle at Bear Paw Mountains, Montana where on September 30, 1877, Tilton won a Medal of Honor for "fearlessly exposing his life and displaying great gallantry in rescuing and protecting the wounded men," of whom there were many. He retired a lieutenant colonel February 2, 1900, and was promoted to colonel on the retired list. He died at Sackett Harbor, New York. Tilton was married.

Powell; Heitman; *Deeds of Valor,* II, 252; Tilton's pension file, NARS.

Tinoco, Arías, military officer (fl. 1538-1543). Arías and his probable brother, Diego Tinoco were related to Hernando de Soto and accompanied his expedition to the southern United States, Arías as captain of cavalry. Both survived the undertaking and returned to Spain around 1543 or later.

Bourne, *De Soto,* I, II; *De Soto Expedition Commission.*

Tisdale, John A., cattleman, victim (c. 1849-Dec. 1, 1891). B. in Williamson County, Texas, and educated at a small college in that state, he may have known Frank M. Canton in Jack County, and it was rumored that Canton (then named Joe Horner) had killed two of his friends, generating bad blood between them. Tisdale had bossed three longhorn herds up the trails to Kansas. He established himself for a few years in North Dakota where he worked for and became a friend of Theodore Roosevelt; later he was in charge of the Northern Pacific railroad stockyards at Mandan, North Dakota. Married and with two children, he migrated to Wyoming in 1889, settling on a place at the head of Red Fork in Johnson County. It is reported that he quickly had a fresh run-in with Canton and faced him down; at any rate there was little love lost between them. Tisdale was a friend of Nate Champion's (they had come from the same Texas county) and with him was a partisan in the growing tension between big cattle outfits and small cattlemen and homesteaders. Tisdale left Buffalo, Wyoming November 30, 1891, for the 60-mile wagon drive to his place, spent the night at the Cross H Ranch, and the next day continued after expressing forebodings of an attempt to be made on his life. He was shot in the back by an assassin in Haywood's Gulch, about nine miles south of Buffalo. Frank Canton was identified by an eye-witness, Charles Franklin Basch who knew him well, as the killer, but Canton whose alibi was shaky, never was tried although he later fled the county only to come back the following spring with the big cattlemen's army of hired gunmen; the Tisdale murder never was solved officially.

Helena Huntington Smith, *The War on Powder River.* N.Y., McGraw-Hill Book Co., 1966; Daisy F. Baber, *The Longest Rope.* Caldwell, Ida., Caxton Printers, 1940, 33-40.

Tobin, Tom Tate, frontiersman (c. Mar. 15, 1823-May 16, 1904). B. at St. Louis, he was a half-brother of Charles Autobees and used Autobees as his name for some years. Tobin reached Taos in 1837 and trapped for Lancaster Lupton in the early 1840s. He narrowly escaped death in the Taos insurrection in January 1847. Recognized as a superior mountain man, in 1853 he guided the Beale expedition from the Gunnison River to California. Ten years later, on September 7, 1863, Tobin and a detachment of soldiers tracked down two bandits named Espinosa for whom $2,500 reward had been offered, Tobin killed both, cut off their heads to bring back so he could claim the reward — which he never received in full. He was buried at Fort Garland, Colorado.

Harvey L. Carter article, MM, Vol. IV.

Toclanny, Roger, Apache scout (Aug. 14, 1863-Jan. 3, 1947). A Mimbres Apache, Toclanny was reported to have the longest period of service with the U.S. Army of any Apache, and never took up arms against the Anglos. Toclanny enlisted as scout several times during the Victorio War of 1879-80. He served with Crook on the 1883 expedition into the Sierra Madre, and two years later when Geronimo went out he served with Lieutenant Britton Davis's command which penetrated the Sierra Madre and returned from Chihuahua via El Paso in late 1885. In November as a scout he went again into Mexico with Capt. Emmet Crawford; in 1886 he was with Lawton. He was married three times; two of his sons were named Britton and Lawton for the officers under whom he worked. Despite his long record of faithful service, Toclanny was sent into Florida exile with the hostile and other Chiricahua-Warm Springs (or Mimbres). At Mt. Vernon Barracks, Alabama, he enlisted in Co. I, 12th Infantry, and at Fort Sill in Troop L, 7th Cavalry, an all-Indian organization. When the Apaches in 1913 were freed as prisoners of war, he returned to the Mescalero Reservation of New Mexico, where he died. His grandson, Peter D. Kazhe on July 5, 1967 was commissioned a second lieutenant in the U.S. Artillery. His home was on the Mescalero Reservation.

Griswold.

Todd, John Blair Smith, army officer (Apr. 4, 1814-Jan. 5, 1872). B. at Lexington, Kentucky, he moved with his parents to Illinois in 1827, went to West Point and was commissioned a second lieutenant in the 6th Infantry July 1, 1837, a first lieutenant December 10 of that year and served in the Florida war against the Seminoles from 1837-42. He became a captain November 22, 1843, and served in the Mexican War. Todd was on frontier duty at Fort Snelling and Gaines, Minnesota from 1849-50 and at Fort Ripley, Minnesota, from 1850-54. He was on garrison duty at Jefferson Barracks, Missouri, from 1854-55 when, commanding Company A, 6th Infantry, he was dispatched to Fort Leavenworth to take part in the William S. Harney expedition against the Sioux (see Harney entry). His informative journal of the expedition has been reprinted, including the engagement at Ash Hollow, Nebraska, in which the Sioux suffered a severe reverse. Todd resigned from the army September 16, 1856, and became an Indian trader at Fort Randall, Dakota

Territory. He studied law, was admitted to the bar and served as Brigadier General of Volunteers from September 19, 1861, until July 17, 1862. When the Territory of Dakota was formed he was elected delegate to Congress and thereafter served in public life in various capacities while continuing his mercantile and legal activities. He died in Yankton County, South Dakota, and was buried in Yankton Cemetery.

Cullum; BDAC; Ray H. Mattison, ed., "The Harney Expedition Against the Sioux: The Journal of Capt. John B.S. Todd." *Nebr. Hist.,* Vol. 43, No. 2 (June 1962), 89-130.

Tofft, Peter, artist (1825-1901). B. at Kolding, Jutland, Denmark, Tofft was one of the earliest painters of western Montana scenes "and an artist of some attainment." He accompanied Acting Governor Thomas Meagher on a tour through western Montana and illustrated Meagher's article which appeared in *Harper's Magazine* in October 1867. A riding accident so injured Tofft that he was forced to confine his movements for a time, but later he traveled and painted in South America, Africa and Asia. Eventually he settled at London, where he died.

George F. Weisel, *Men and Trade on the Northwest Frontier.* Missoula, Mont. State Univ. Press, 1955.

Tomahas, Cayuse chief (d. June 3, 1850). A chief of the Cayuse tribe of Washington State, he first met Whitman September 25, 1841. Tomahas never was a follower of the missionary and grew increasingly hostile toward him. In the Whitman Massacre of November 29, 1847, Tomahas dealt Whitman the first, and perhaps mortal, blow on the head with a tomahawk. He subsequently took part in the fatal attack on Judge L.W. Saunders. Tomahas, christened Peter, baptized and confirmed into the Roman Catholic Church the day of his execution, was hanged at Oregon City with four others for the murders.

Clifford M. Drury, *Marcus and Narcissa Whitman and the Opening of Old Oregon,* 2 vols. Glendale, Calif., Arthur H. Clark Co., 1973.

Tomau (Tomah), Menominee chief (c. 1752-July 8, 1818). His name in Engish was Thomas Carron, his father a half-French, half-Menominee acting head chief, and his mother an Abenaki; he was b. near Green Bay, Wisconsin. While not a hereditary chief, he became one by merit since the hereditary chief himself was incapable of ruling. In 1805 he met the explorer, Zebulon Pike who hired him as guide and believed him a friend of Americans, although subsequent developments did not fully bear that out. When Tecumseh was mustering support for his war against the whites, Tomau counciled peace and only a few of his followers opted for the war party. During the War of 1812 Tomau joined the British under Robert Dickson; he was present at the occupation of Fort Mackinac, the attack on Fort Sandusky and the 1814 battle at Mackinac. In 1816 Tomau gave the Americans permission to build a fort in Menominee country and two years later he died, either at Mackinac Island or the present Mackinaw City, Michigan. He had married three times and fathered children.

Hodge, HAI.

Tomochichi, Creek chief (c. 1650-Oct. 5, 1739). B. at Apalachukla, a Lower Creek town on the Chattahoochee River, Alabama, his name appears on behalf of this settlement in a 1721 treaty between the Creeks and South Carolina. Shortly afterward for an unremembered reason he was outlawed and with a few followers withdrew to the Savannah River where he established himself in a new town, Yamacraw at the site of today's Savannah, Georgia. He became friendly with Oglethorpe upon the establishment of the English colony of Georgia in 1733 and was instrumental in developing a treaty of alliance between that colony and the Lower Creeks that year; at the same time a reconciliation was effected between himself and his tribe. In 1734 with family members and others he accompanied Oglethorpe to England where his portrait was painted. He continued to be of assistance to the colonists for the rest of his life, his death occurring at the age of 75 in his town. A monument was erected to his memory at Savannah in 1899 by the Colonial Dames of America.

Hodge, HAI.

Tompkins, William, Indian sign language specialist (1867-Feb. 3, 1955). B. at Kingston, Ontario, he left Canada about 1878 following the death of his parents and joined a brother at Fort Sully, about 35 miles north of Pierre,

South Dakota. He became a cowboy on his brother's ranch at Okoboji Creek and from 1886-88 was foreman. Many Sioux visited the place, and Tompkins began to pick up their tongue, including sign language. Meanwhile he roamed the range country from Pierre to Rapid City, and from the Nebraska line northward to the Northern Pacific Railroad; it was said he scouted for a time for the army. He continued his study of sign language, eventually learning 700 or 800 gestures. In 1889 he moved to Pierre, organized a band, helped secure for Pierre the site of the new state capitol, and became manager of the community's Opera House. He married and in 1906 settled at San Diego, California, maintaining his interest in Indian sign talk and his friendships with Theodore Roosevelt and many other Dakota pioneer figures. In 1926 he published his book, *Universal American Indian Sign Language*, the work eventually being taken over by the Boy Scouts of America, Tompkins adding the Scouts to his lasting enthusiasms and attending a world jamboree in 1929 at Bickenhead, England. He sold about 100,000 copies of his book and lectured widely, traveling some 95,000 miles in ten years in America and Europe, lecturing 3,200 times and believed he had taught more than 1 million Scouts and others something of his subject. He died at San Diego but his wife (Grace Goodwin Tompkins, Feb. 27, 1872-Oct. 16, 1978), who lived to 106 carried his book on through eight more editions (19 in all), and it still is in print.

Charles S. McCammon, "The Sign Talker." *Frontier Times,* Vol. 54, No. 4 (June-July 1980), 22-25.

Tonty, Alphonse de, colonial official (c. 1659-Nov. 10, 1727). A younger brother of Henri de Tonty, he was b. in France and agreed to ship with La Salle's ill-fated expedition to colonize the Gulf coast of the Mississippi valley, but a dispute over wages prevented his actually departing with the squadron, and he reached Canada in 1685. In personality he was the direct opposite of his famous brother: discourteous where the other was considerate; frequently accused of peculations where Henri was completely honest; the center of controversy while his older brother was ever a mediating force. Alphonse settled initially at Montreal, becoming involved in the fur trade and for a year from 1697-98 was commandant at Michilimackinac. He became a friend of Rigaud de Vaudreuil (governor of Montreal from 1698 to 1703 and of New France from 1703 to 1725) who frequently shielded Tonty from charges of excesses in his various positions, some said because Tonty secretly was paying Vaudreuil a percentage. Alphonse de Tonty was second in command to Cadillac when the latter founded Detroit and often was de facto governor there, proving able enough in military and Indian affairs. He was removed on Paris instructions in 1705 whereafter for two years he was commandant at Fort Frontenac (Kingston, Ontario) on Lake Ontario, but again was removed for cause by French officials, although he had not lost Vaudreuil's favor. In 1717 under the governor's sponsorship he was named commandant of Detroit, holding the post for the last decade of his life although "detested by everyone." A new governor had determined to withdraw his appointment, but Tonty died before word reached him. He had married twice and fathered 13 children.

The best brief biographical treatment of Alphonse de Tonty is in DCB, II; see also references included therein.

Tonty, Henri, de, explorer, fur trader (c. 1650-Sept. 1704). B. at Gaeta, Italy, he was a cousin of Pierre de Liette and of Daniel Greysolon Du Luth (Du Lhut). He served two years as a cadet in the French army and four years as a midshipman in the navy; Tonty was said to have been on four warship and three galley sea operations. On service in Sicily his right hand was blasted off by a Spanish granade. Tonty was taken prisoner, later exchanged and fitted with an iron hand and volunteered for further duty in the Mediterranean; his artificial hand was to become his trade mark among New World natives. About 1678 Tonty met La Salle and became his loyal and trusted lieutenant in La Salle's grand scheme for discovery in the valley of the Mississippi and for creating a gigantic French realm in the valley. Tonty journeyed with La Salle to Canada and by the end of 1678 had reached Niagara where he put his naval experience to use during the winter supervising construction of the 45-ton *Griffon,* first sailing vessel to appear on the upper lakes. On August 27 of 1679 Tonty with La Salle brought the vessel to Michilimackinac at the Strait of Mackinac; they then moved by lighter craft to the St.

Joseph River where Fort Miami was constructed, and in January 1680 commenced building Fort Crevecoeur near the present Peoria, Illinois. La Salle left Tonty in charge of this post and went off to the northeast to seek word of the missing *Griffon,* laden with a valuable cargo of furs; the ship was lost in the lakes and never again heard from. La Salle directed Tonty to plan construction of another post at Starved Rock, near the present Utica, Illinois, and while Tonty was inspecting that site, the men he had left at Crevecoeur mutinied, destroyed the fort and most of them deserted. With five loyal men, Tonty settled in at an Illinois village where he staved off an Iroquois attack — no small feat — and then completed an arduous, perilous overland trek to Green Bay, later continuing to Michilimackinac where he once again met La Salle in June 1681. Tonty accompanied La Salle to Montreal, returned to Fort Miami collecting men for La Salle's projected expedition down the Mississippi to its mouth. The endeavor was completed in the first half of 1682 and the Mississippi valley claimed for the king of France, an historical event of far-reaching proportions. Tonty and La Salle went back up-river, reaching Michilimackinac in midsummer, from where Tonty returned to the Illinois country to trade, commencing construction of the fort at Starved Rock on the Illinois River and scouring the region about for Indians willing to bring in their furs. Tonty's command of the post was interrupted briefly by an order from the French governor, La Barre, who hated La Salle, but the directive was overturned and by June of 1685 Tonty was back once more in the Illinois country. Here he learned that La Salle had returned to the Gulf coast and set out to find and assist him, but was unsuccessful in contacting the other and returned to Illinois. The Iroquois were a perennial problem to the French posts, frequently hostile, often committing acts of war against them, and Tonty upon invitation joined Denonville's 1687 expedition against the Senecas, but this was without decisive results through no fault of Tonty's; he returned to the Illinois country again. Late in 1689 Tonty at Starved Rock learned of the death of La Salle, and two months later went south with seven others including four Frenchmen, to try to succor the hapless colony La Salle had founded, but after great hardships was obliged to give up the effort in the present Houston County, Texas, and regained the Illinois country. Here he traded for two years or more, making one trip to Michilimackinac and another to Quebec. He tried to persuade French officials that the interior trade should be routed by way of the mouth of the Mississippi, but Canadian officials opposed this. He secured permission to trade with the Assiniboins to the northwest, and later was granted special privileges to continue his Illinois trade when most other fur men had been called in by the French king in the face of a serious oversupply of beaver. By 1698 he was ordered to work with Iberville, who had been assigned the task of founding colonies on the Gulf coast to bulwark French interests against Spanish and English. During the last four years of his life he worked in the south, trading into the interior, helping make peace with the Chickasaws and fighting the Alabamas. He died of yellow fever at Mobile. "There are very few names in French-American history mentioned with such unanimity of praise as that of Henri de Tonty," wrote Parkman. "Hennepin finds some fault with him; but his censure is commendation. The despatches of the governor...speak in strong terms of his services in the Iroquois war, praise his character, and declare that he is fit for any bold enterprise... The missionary, St. Cosme, who travelled under his escort in 1699, says of him: 'He is beloved by all the *voyageurs*....he is loved and feared everywhere.'" The *Dictionary of American Biography* summed up his career: "A great explorer and an able (and honest) administrator, he succeeded where La Salle failed, was respected and trusted by the Indians and by the settlers, and was particularly noted for his courtesy and consideration," and Thwaites believed him "one of the most courageous, loyal, and far-sighted among the pioneers of New France."

Literature abundant: Parkman, *La Salle and the Discovery of the Great West;* Thwaites, JR, LXIII, 304-305n25; DAB; DCB; HT; CE.

Toohoolhoolzote, Nez Perce chief: *see* Tuhulhulzote.

Toponce, Alexander, pioneer (Nov. 10, 1839-May 13, 1923). B. at Belfort, France, his family brought him to this country at 7; he ran away at 10 and at 15 was in Missouri where he worked briefly at lumbering. In 1855 he made two trips as a bullwhacker for Majors and Russell, one to Santa Fe and the other to Walnut Creek at the Arkansas River (today's Great Bend, Kansas). He also made a couple of passages down the Mississippi to New Orleans for a man dealing in mules and slaves. He drove stage from Westport to Santa Fe and briefly rode for the Pony Express in Nebraska. Toponce was an assistant wagon boss during the Mormon War of 1857 campaign, and spent much of the rest of his life in and out of Utah. He always got on well with Mormons, although not one himself, was a friend of Porter Rockwell and considered Brigham Young "the squarest man to do business with in Utah, barring none." After a brief return to Missouri he took part in the Colorado gold rush, reaching the Territory in 1860. In 1863 he left Denver for the Montana gold fields, reaching Bannack May 14; a member of his party was Jack Gallagher, later hanged by vigilantes. He secured a claim in Alder Gulch, profiting from it as he did from several of his enterprises, although none of his gain seemed to remain long. Toponce had contacts with Buck Stinson and others of the "roughs" who were dispatched by vigilantes. He also was a friend of John X. Beidler, a prominent vigilante, and of Jim Williams, its chief executive officer, and Toponce figured in a minor way in the demise of Joseph Slade. He continued trading between the Salt Lake valley and the Montana gold camps, and claimed he took the first wagon freight train into Helena over a road he cut out himself. He also freighted between Forts Union and Benton when steamers could not be had for the trip, occasionally skirmishing with Blackfoot or Sioux. In 1867 Toponce went to the Nevada silver camps, continuing his freighting and merchandising affairs. The next year he supplied beef for the Union Pacific railroad crews in Wyoming. At Beartown, Wyoming, he managed to get a beleaguered editor out of town just as the famous battle erupted in which Toponce estimated 17 men were killed outright. Some people, he conceded, "called it a massacre, but it had a good effect and just as in the case of the 'Vigilantes' in Montana there was an end to the rough stuff on the Union Pacific." In 1868 Toponce bought from Wells Fargo 79 surplus wagons and nearly 500 head of oxen transporting 100,000 ties to various railheads, but was never paid for this work. He attended the "Golden Spike" ceremony at Promontory Point, Utah, in 1869. Toponce went into the cattle business in Idaho for some years and also ran short stage lines to mining towns, built roads on the side, sometimes raised sheep or engaged in assorted other enterprises. He died at Ogden, Utah; his book, written by him was completed on his 80th birthday, but was published posthumously. He married and his widow survived him.

Remininscences of Alexander Toponce: Written by Himself. Norman, Univ. of Okla. Press, 1971.

Torontisati, Mohawk chief (d. 1652). The *Jesuit Relation* of 1654 said following peace negotiations of 1654 that the Mohawks "cannot forget the death of their great Captain Torontisati, whom we burned at Three Rivers only two years ago, when he saw himself betrayed while plotting to betray us... They regard us as criminals for having escaped death at their hands when they planned it."

Thwaites, JR, XLI, 57.

Torsvan, Berick Traven (B. Traven), writer (May 3, 1890-Mar. 26, 1969). According to Traven's will the writer's date of b. was as given, his birthplace Chicago, he the son of Burton Torsvan and Dorothy Groves, given the name of Traven Torsvan Groves, which Johnson believed might actually have been Berick Traven Torsvan; there remain dissenters to all of these understandings. Johnson believed the Norwegian-American boy was taken to Germany at an early age, maturing to a life in which he mastered eight languages and some Indian dialects, wrote widely-read fiction in German, English and Spanish, and retained a German accent in his spoken English and Spanish. He went to sea for some time, but eventually returned to Germany where he became a writer and political activist under the name of Ret Marut, later using more than 20 other aliases. Sentenced to death in Bavaria for radical activities, he escaped and found his way as a fugitive to Mexico which became his adopted country. However, Will Wyatt, a British Broadcasting Company producer, after extended research believed Traven had been born Hermann Albert Otto Maximilian in Swiebodzin, Poland, in February 1882, his parents being Hormina Wienecke, a mill worker, and Adolf Rudolf Feige, a brick and tile maker. He did military service, became a radical and evolved into the

man of many names, best known as B. Traven. He first became known as Ret Marut, Wyatt maintains, then changed his name again while a fugitive, at length reaching Mexico. There are other theories about Traven's identity, origins and early years. His first significant novel was *The Death Ship* (1926). He traveled widely in Mexico, Central and perhaps North America, researched archeological ruins including those of the Mayas, studied photography under Edward Weston, and continued his writing, authoring such novels as *The Rebellion of the Hanged* and *Bridge in the Jungle,* while developing a marked secretiveness about himself so that his actual life and the man himself became enveloped in a virtually impenetrable fog of myth, half-truths and tales, good and bad, told as fact. His greatest literary success, *The Treasure of the Sierra Madre,* was made into a superior motion picture, winning him much presumably unwelcome fame. He retired from Acapulco when he learned his identity was being seriously probed, and lived thereafter at Mexico City and in Chiapas. Despite his protective shroud of myth, he had many warm friends with whom he was convivial. His work was translated into as many as 34 languages and was read by millions. Esperanza Lopez Mateos, whose brother later became president of Mexico, was his secretary and general assistant until she committed suicide in 1951 to terminate a difficult illness. Rosa Elena Luján, a friend of both, succeeded Esperanza and married the writer in 1957; she survived him. Traven died at Mexico City.

William Weber Johnson, "A Noted Novelist Who Lived and Died in Obscurity." *Los Angeles Times,* Apr. 13, 1969; *Los Angeles Times,* July 23, 1967; *New York Times,* Mar. 28, 1969; Johnson, "Trying to Solve the Enigma of the *Sierra Madre." Smithsonian,* Vol. 13, No. 12 (Mar. 1983), 156-75; Will Wyatt, *The Secret of the Sierra Madre: The Man Who Was B. Traven.* Garden City, N.Y., Doubleday and Co., 1980.

Touey, Timothy Arthur, army officer (c. 1850-Sept. 28, 1887). B. in New York he was graduated from West Point and commissioned a second lieutenant in the 6th Cavalry June 16, 1875, being shortly posted to Arizona. In the late spring of 1877 his command was defeated by hostiles in the Animas Mountains of southwestern New Mexico. He was cited for gallantry in the important fight of Curwen McLellan in Hembrillo Canyon of the San Andres Mountains, New Mexico, April 7, 1880; in this action Touey received a bullet through his coat, but was uninjured. He was promoted to first lieutenant June 3, 1880. Touey was in the hard fight of Tupper and Rafferty with Loco's Apaches April 28, 1882, at Enmedio Mountain, Chihuahua. Touey apparently became addicted to drugs and died of an apparent overdose at Fort Stanton.

Dan L. Thrapp, *Al Sieber, Chief of Scouts.* Norman, Univ. of Okla. Press, 1964; Thrapp, *Victorio and the Mimbres Apaches.* Norman, 1974; Cullum; information from David Perry Perrine.

Tough, William Sloan, scout (May 19, 1840-May 24, 1904). B. at Baltimore, after receiving a good education he went west at 17, trapping in the Rocky Mountains. Finding this unprofitable since the fur decline had set in, he returned to Leavenworth. At 19 in 1859, a born horseman he signed on as rider for the Pony Express according to four of six rosters extant. After a year he gave that up and went to work for wagon freighters supplying military posts in Nebraska and Kansas, soon becoming a wagon boss, having grown in height and weight since his Pony Express days. He was captured by bushwhackers in the border guerilla fighting of the time, knifed the man guarding him and escaped. Tough joined the Red Legged (later the Red Legs) Scouts, a free-state faction in Kansas. One of his subordinates was Willy Cody, the later Buffalo Bill. When Major General James G. Blunt, a founder of the Red Leggeds, became commander of the Department of Kansas at Fort Scott he named Tough his chief of scouts; Tough brought along many of his onetime companions in the Red Leggeds and Pony Express, as well as his younger brother, Littleton. Tough was sent on many missions into Missouri and Indian Territory and won the respect of his officers and men. On one occasion he was with Blunt when the column was attacked by Quantrill and his guerillas, the Northern force decimated although Tough and a few others escaped. Following the Civil War he married and settled at Leavenworth. March 23, 1873, he was appointed U.S. Marshal for Kansas, retaining the post until 1876, a turbulent time when some of the Plains notables served under him

as deputies. A lover of fine horses, he was a race enthusiast, and later in life with his two sons operated the largest horse and mule market at the Kansas City stockyards, selling many animals for use in the Boer War in Africa. He died peacefully at his home.

Wayne T. Walker, "A Man Called Tough." *Real West Special,* Spring 1882, 48-51.

Tovar, Pedro de, military officer, explorer (fl. 1531-1549). One of the first settlers of Guadalajara, Mexico, he arrived there in 1531 with Nuño de Guzman; later he was a founder of Culiacán, Sinaloa. As second in field command of the expedition of Coronado in 1540, Tovar was ensign or standard bearer and a captain of cavalry. He brought along savage dogs which precipitated one of the crises of the operation. With Coronado's advance upon Cibola, the first Pueblo southwest of Zuñi, New Mexico, Tovar brought in prisoners whom Coronado indoctrinated into the purposes of his endeavor and released to carry word into the settlement. But the place still offered resistance and Coronado stormed it, Tovar being well bruised in the process although not "wounded." From Cibola Coronado heard of Indian towns to the west and sent Tovar with 17 mounted Spanish and several afoot to explore in that direction, developing any discoveries he might make. Thus Tovar on July 15, 1540 left Cibola on his reconnaissance, led by Zuñi guides to Hopi land, of which he was the European discoverer. The Hopis lived on four mesas in seven towns, archeological research showing that five were occupied by Spanish at the time, no doubt by Tovar. The five were Walpi and Awatobi on the East Mesa, Shongopovi and Mishongnovi on the next, and Oraibi, still in existence on the West Mesa. Tovar encountered only slight resistance. He heard there of the great river and canyon to north and west: the Colorado River and Grand Canyon, but did not himself visit them. Tovar and his dogs accompanied Coronado to Tiguex, on the Rio Grande River about where Bernalillo, New Mexico is today, and his dogs were used to attack captive chiefs in an endeavor to extract information from them, although whether set on them by Tovar or another is uncertain, the incident however helping to precipitate the Tiguex War. In early 1541 Coronado received word of unrest and Indian hostility in northern Sonora, and sent Tovar to restore order and return with reinforcements. Tovar arrived back at Tiguex in the fall, about when Coronado returned from his trip to Quivira (central Kansas). Tovar brought important dispatches from Mexico. He had intended going on to Quivira had Coronado remained there. He was bitterly disappointed to learn there would be no more Spanish treks to that area of disillusionment, and accompanied the Coronado expedition back to Mexico. Tovar settled at Culiacán where he lived for many years. In 1549 he was named alcalde mayor of Nueva Galicia for a period of two years. Tovar married well and became known as "the most virtuous and accomplished gentleman in that kingdom." The date of his death is unknown, but he died at Culiacán and was buried there.

George Parker Winship, *The Coronado Expedition, 1540-1542.* BAE, 14th Ann. Rept., Wash., Govt. Printing Office, 1896; Herbert Eugene Bolton, *Coronado: Knight of Pueblos and Plains.* Albuquerque, Univ. of New Mex. Press, 1964; A. Grove Day, *Coronado's Quest.* Berkeley, Univ. of Calif. Press, 1964; George P. Hammond, Agapito Rey, *Narratives of the Coronado Expedition.* Albuquerque, 1940.

Town, Charles, trader (d. June 20, 1848). B. probably at St. Louis, he had reached the Rocky Mountains about 1840, and perhaps became a beaver trapper. He was at Bent's Fort and Taos in 1841, and at Fort Pueblo, Colorado, in 1842 and 1843, accompanying Fremont to California in the latter year. Returning to Pueblo in 1844, he married a Mexican woman and settled at Taos in 1845, apparently trading with the Utes. On January 19, 1847, he escaped the massacre of Charles Bent and other Americans, joined Cerán St. Vrain's volunteers who defeated the insurgents at Taos. In 1848 Town joined Lucien Maxwell and others to trade with Utes in southern Colorado and was killed at Manco de Burro Pass, near Raton.

Janet Lecompte article, MM, Vol. I.

Townsend, John Benjamin, Indian killer (June 28, 1835-Sept. 16, 1873). B. in Tennessee by his own statement, Townsend was raised in Texas and served briefly in the Confederate forces during the Civil War, enlisting December 10, 1861, in Captain Bernard Timmons Company, Nichols' Regiment of Texas Infantry and being discharged

at Houston April 17, 1862, upon expiration of his term of service. Half Cherokee, Townsend had several of his relatives killed by Comanches in Texas, engendering an "undying hatred" of the red race whose members he killed at every opportunity. He reached Arizona in 1863, settling on a small farm in the Prescott area and delighting in tracking down and killing any Indian intruders. By 1871 he had slain 26 that he knew of, and in the spring took part in Lieutenant Charles Morton's scout to the East Fork of the Verde River on which endeavor he added eight more to his total. For his work he was presented June 22, 1871, by the citizens of Prescott with a brand new Henry rifle, latest design, a silver plate on it engraved, "Honor to the Brave!" He also was given 1,000 rounds of ammunition to shoot at Indians. Townsend was named one of eight white chiefs of scouts to work with troops during Crook's initial operations in central Arizona. In late September 1872 he accompanied First Lieutenant Max Wesendorff on a scout, having a hard fight September 30 at Squaw Peak when 17 hostiles were killed and a girl captured. It may have been on this occasion that Townsend took 15 scalps; when Crook heard about it, the report goes, he instantly ordered Townsend dropped from the army rolls. At any rate Jack Townsend was dismissed by March. September 16, 1873, while trailing half a dozen Indians who had raided his ranch he suddenly came upon them at Dripping Springs, about 16 miles south of the present Mayer, Arizona. In an exchange of gunfire he was mortally shot. He was buried at Prescott before a large turnout. Townsend left his widow and six children.

James M. Barney, "The Townsend Expedition." *Ariz. Highways,* Vol. XIII, No. 3 (Mar. 1937), 12, 23-25; Dan L. Thrapp, *Al Sieber, Chief of Scouts.* Norman, Univ. of Okla. Press, 1964; author's collection on Townsend.

Townsend, John Kirk, ornithologist, physician (Aug. 10, 1809-Feb. 6, 1851). B. at Philadelphia, he became a physician and surgeon and at the same time pursued his avocation of naturalist. He was eager to explore the western country and joined Nathaniel Wyeth's second expedition to Oregon, leaving Independence, Missouri, April 28, 1834, with the annual fur trade caravan and by June arriving at the Green

River rendezvous, from there going on to Fort Vancouver, Washington. Townsend became post surgeon until 1836, after a few months in Hawaii. He explored the lower Columbia River, visited Walla Walla and the Blue Mountains completing his bird collection and left by way of Cape Horn November 30, 1836, arriving home a year later. His book, *Narrative of a Journey across the Rocky Mountains to the Columbia River...*, appeared in 1839. He also published *Ornithology of the United States of America* a year later. Townsend died at Washington, D.C.

Thwaites, EWT, XXI; Townsend, *Narrative of a Journey.* Lincoln, Univ. of Nebr. Press, 1979.

Tracy, Alexandre de Prouville: *see* Prouville de Tracy

Tracy, Harry, desperado (Jan. 1, 1869-Aug. 5, 1902). B. near Newburg, New York, he ran away from home at an early age, reaching Chicago where he worked about the stock-yards, migrated to the Colorado gold fields, then to Billings, Montana, where he secured a ranch job, taking up rustling as a sideline. He killed Deputy Sheriff Arly Grimes and fled to the Cripple Creek area of Colorado. Tracy reportedly killed two more men and pursued a criminal career in and about the Hole in the Wall, Wyoming, and Brown's Hole, Color-ado, regions, associating at times with remnants of the so-called Wild Bunch. His career was punctuated by more shootings, and he was imprisoned at Aspen, Colorado, but escaped. Eventually he reached Portland, Oregon, where he continued his life of crime and killing, was arrested February 6, 1899, at Portland where his colleague, David Merrill, had been arrested the day before. Both were sentenced in March to the Salem, Oregon, penitentiary, Tracy for 20 years, Merrill for a somewhat shorter term. With the aid of a female accomplice, Tracy and Merrill escaped June 9, 1902, killing three men and wounding another in doing so. Tracy murdered Merrill near Chehalis, Washington, on June 28, believing that he was "weakening." In all Tracy killed seven men in his flight. He was cornered on the G.E. Goldfinch Ranch, 11 miles southeast of Creston, Washington, shot twice in the right leg, crippled, and committed suicide.

Literature abundant; see John Cody, "Gunsmoke Payoff." *True Frontier,* No. 41 (Feb. 1975), 42-44,

60-61; *Los Angeles Times,* June 10, 11, 12, etc., Aug. 6, 7, 1902.

Trask, Elbridge, pioneer (July 15, 1815-June 22, 1863)). B. at Beverly, Massachusetts, he shipped as a seaman in 1833 for Oregon, reaching the Pacific coast the following summer. Trask joined Nathaniel Wyeth at Fort Hall in December 1835, later working for the American Fur Company, usually with Osborne Russell. He weathered many adventures coincident to years of trapping in the northern Rockies. He and Russell migrated to Oregon in 1842, Trask marrying a widow emigrant, Hannah Abel, settling near Astoria and later near Tillamook. He died of fever.

Jo Tuthill article, MM, Vol. IV.

Traven B., writer: *see* Torsvan, Berick Traven

Travis, William Barret, Alamo commander (Aug. 9, 1809-Mar. 6, 1836). B. in the Edgefield District, South Carolina, the Travis family moved to Alabama in 1818 where Travis received a good education, taught school and studied law. He married, fathered a son and daughter but, believing his wife unfaithful, left his family and went to Texas, setting up a law office at Anahuac. A subsequent attempt at a marital reconciliation failed. Travis leaned toward Texas indepen-dence, was imprisoned briefly, and became a leader in the so-called "war party"; he strongly disliked Mexicans and Mexican rule. In 1832 he moved to San Felipe, capital of Austin's colony. On June 29, 1835, Travis raised a company of 25 volunteers and the next day captured Captain Antonio Tenorio at Anahuac where Tenorio had been sent by Santa Anna to restore order. Many Texans resented Travis's apparent attempt to precipitate war, but conflict became inevitable and Travis joined the Texas army as soon as it was called up. He was given important commands in the scouting service and in November captured 200 Mexican horses within 40 miles of San Antonio. By December, with Houston the commander in chief, Travis had been named major of artillery and on Christmas Eve was commissioned lieutenant colonel of cavalry. In January Travis was ordered to Bexar (San Antonio) with only 30 men to join a garrison of 120 and Bowie; Travis had strong forebodings, and pleaded with Governor Henry Smith for some other assignment, but Smith did not rescind the order and, a good soldier, Travis obeyed. "It is probable that no man in Texas did more...to initiate the revolution, certainly none fought more bravely, served more faithfully, or died more heroically." Travis and Bowie were to share command at the Alamo, their selected stronghold at Bexar; there had been some discord between the two, the result being that Travis was to command the "regulars" and Bowie the "volunteers." Then Bowie became hopelessly ill with typhoid-pneumonia and full command fell to Travis. His heroic and stirring communications from the Alamo, whose siege commenced February 24, 1836, moved not only Texans but others wherever they were read. According to legend he was shot in the head during the early stages of the Mexican final assault. Travis was 6 feet tall, weighed about 175 pounds, was of fair complexion, with auburn hair and blue or gray eyes. With intimates he was good humored, but to others appeared austere. His temper was quick and not under perfect control, and he was ambitious. No satisfactory likeness of him exists; Williams discusses the existing portraits.

Literature abundant; Amelia Williams, XXXVII, 80-90.

Trespalacios, José Felix, revolutionist (1781-Aug. 4, 1835). B. at Chihuahua City, he took part in early revolutionary movements; a member of the militia, he was tried in 1814 for conspiracy to provoke a rebellion, sentenced to death, but that was commuted to 10 years imprisonment. He escaped, joined a revolutionary band, was recaptured, escaped again and made his way to New Orleans where he associated with James Long in his filibustering expedition. After Long's capture Trespalacios helped secure his release and became governor of Texas for nearly a year. He was accused by some of having engineered the assassination of Long at Mexico City, but this was never proven. With independence Trespalacios was recognized as one of Mexico's minor heroes, served briefly as a senator from Chihuahua, and retired shortly before his death at Allende, Chihuahua.

HT; *Porrua.*

Tribolet, Albrecht (Albert, Abe), pioneer (c. 1845-Jan. 1895). B. in Switzerland, he was a

brother or half-brother of Robert (Bob) Tribolet and with him and six or seven other brothers or near relatives came to the Tombstone, Arizona area. In the 1880 Census he was listed as a miner in the Empire Ranch vicinity of southeastern Arizona. He was sometimes referred to as a butcher. Another reference said that he was a brewer in the Eagle Brewery and Saloon at Tombstone. Married, he and his family later moved to Phoenix, Arizona, where he worked on a ranch and engaged in the butcher business. He apparently joined the trek to California and was shot and killed at Bakersfield by a painter, George Giovannoni "in a quarrel over a woman."

Undated, unidentified Tombstone newspaper clipping from Jan. 1955; information from Robert N. Mullin; 1880 Census, Cochise County, Ariz.

Tribolet, Charles, pioneer (c. 1842-c. 1900). Probably a half-brother of Robert (Bob) Tribolet, Charles was a butcher or in the meat retailing business at Tombstone, Arizona, in 1880 and thereafter and probably died at Phoenix, Arizona, between 1893 and 1907, although his death was not officially recorded there. He was survived by his widow (d. 1920), but left no children. Daly asserts it was Charles Tribolet who sold Geronimo the whiskey in 1886 which sent him back onto the warpath after his conference with Crook, but this is no doubt in error. Bob Tribolet was the man generally credited with selling the liquor.

Henry W. Daly, "Geronimo." *Jour. of U.S. Cavalry Assn.,* Vol. XIX, No. 9 (July 1908).

Tribolet, Robert (Bob), frontiersman (June 22, 1861-June 28, 1895). B. at Zurich, Switzerland, he and seven or eight brothers, half-brothers or other close relatives migrated to Tombstone, Arizona, where in the 1880s they pursued various occupations including those of brewers, butchers and miners. Bob appears to have been at times a rancher or butcher doing some bootlegging on the side and was said by Crook to have had meat contracts with the army. He apparently had a ranch or bootlegging operation near Guadalupe Canyon, Sonora, in March-April 1886; when Crook and Geronimo agreed to the latter's surrender, Crook returned to Fort Bowie and Geronimo and his followers were sold whiskey and fed frightening yarns about their probable fate by Tribolet, leading to their being flushed out on the warpath once again, nullifying months of hard work which had led to their abortive surrender. Tribolet later established a ranch or farm near Fronteras, Sonora; here according to McClintock he was arrested for a stage robbery and "shot while trying to escape." Tribolet family memories are that he was "lynched" by mistake after a cattle or horse robbery. "Then the state of Mexico (paid) a lifelong 'rent' to his widow for this terrible mistake." A variant family recollection is that Mexico paid $50,000 American for the error of causing his demise. The facts of the case have never been researched out. Tribolet left a widow and children.

Dan L. Thrapp, *Conquest of Apacheria.* Norman, Univ. of Okla. Press, 1967; Thrapp, ed., *Dateline Fort Bowie: Charles Fletcher Lummis Reports on an Apache War.* Norman, 1979; James H. McClintock, *Arizona,* I, 255; Dan King, "The 13 Graves." *True West,* Vol. 7, No. 2 (Nov.-Dec. 1959), 24-26, 50-51.

Trimble, Joel Graham, army officer (Sept. 15, 1832-Nov. 16, 1911). B. at Philadelphia his family took him as a child to Cincinnati where at 17 he entered Kenyon College. Before graduation however gold was discovered in California and Trimble, employed as a herder for the Mounted Riflemen, went to Oregon in 1849 and in 1851 as a civilian accompanied the 1st Dragoons to California, taking part in two engagements of the initial Rogue River War, being wounded in the head in one of them. February 5, 1855, he enlisted in the 1st Dragoons and on October 31 participated in an action against Indians at Hungry Hill, Oregon, later taking part in the Steptoe and Wright campaigns in Washington Territory. His enlistment expired in 1860 and Trimble for a few months was a Pony Express rider, then re-enlisted, this time in the 2nd Dragoons (2nd Cavalry). With his outfit he went east where he fought through the Civil War, being twice wounded. He was commissioned a second lieutenant in the 1st Cavalry in 1863 and ended the war a first lieutenant with two brevets. He accompanied his regiment to Texas, thence back to Oregon, becoming a captain December 26, 1868. He took part in the Modoc War in California in 1873, receiving the surrender of Captain Jack, an Indian leader in that conflict. Trimble commanded Camps Warner and Harney in

Oregon and in May 1877 reached Fort Lapwai, Idaho, in time for the Nez Perce campaign. As commander of Company H, 1st Cavalry he was in at the start of the Indian exodus, took part in the disastrous Perry fight June 17 at White Bird Canyon and the hard fight on the Clearwater River, Idaho, July 11-12; thereafter the Nez Perce migrated east and Trimble remained on scout duty in Idaho. He went on sick leave in the spring of 1878 and retired for disability in line of duty August 21, 1879, having lost the sight of his right eye and most of the vision of his left. Married, he fathered three sons and two daughters and died at Berkeley, California.

Heitman; Powell; John D. McDermott, *Forlorn Hope: the Battle of White Bird Canyon and the Beginning of the Nez Perce War.* Boise, Ida. State Hist. Soc., 1978; Trimble, "The Country They Marched and Fought Over," "The Killing of the Commissioners," and "Carrying a Stretcher Through the Lava Beds" (all relating to the Modoc War), and "The Battle of Clearwater," in Cyrus Townsend Brady, *Northwestern Fights and Fighters.* Garden City, N.Y., Doubleday, Page & Co., 1923.

Tripp, Milan, frontiersman (Jan. 18, 1845-Mar. 25, 1930). The man who allegedly shot Looking Glass, the noted Nez Perce chief in the Battle of Bear Paw Mountain, Montana, was b. in Wisconsin at Milwaukee joined the 17th Wisconsin Infantry October 28, 1864. Tripp was attached to Company H, 15th Connecticut Infantry and was captured March 8, 1865, at Southwest Creek, near Kinston, North Carolina, confined at Libby Prison, Richmond, Virginia, on March 23 and was paroled three days later, being mustered out June 5, 1865. Tripp lived at Fort Benton, Montana, following the war, remaining in Montana from 1869 to 1884, engaging in various frontier activities. During the Nez Perce campaign of 1877 he was hired as a scout and was present at the Bear Paw battle from September 30 to October 5, 1877. The only man to be killed after the first day's heavy casualties was Chief Looking Glass who was shot in the head by Tripp October 5. In 1887 Tripp married Mary Boudry, 20 years his junior, and lived for some years as a farmer at Badoura, Hubbard County, Minnesota, where their five children, all daughters, were born. Mrs. Tripp died January 18, 1927, and Tripp moved to Long Beach, California where he died at 85. He was described at 18 as 5 feet, 5 inches in height, of dark complexion with brown hair and blue eyes. Charles A. Smith Sr., who had served with him in Montana, wrote McWhorter that he remembered Tripp from 1877 as "a little round shouldered and light hair and complexion."

Tripp pension file, Nat. Archives; McWhorter, *Hear Me,* 495n.; Charles A. Smith Sr. to McWhorter, Nov. 28, 1937, McWhorter archives, Wash. State Univ. Library, Pullman, Wash.

Truckee, Captain: *see* Captain Truckee

Trudeau, Pierre (Old Pet), frontiersman (d. 1869). Described by Carter as "an old frontiersman," he achieved fame during Forsyth's besiegement on the Arickaree fork of the Republican River when he and Jack Stilwell slipped through Cheyenne positions on a five-day hunt for assistance. The mission was successful, but Trudeau apparently broke under the strain, never fully recovered, and died the next spring, being buried at Fort Sill, Oklahoma.

Robert G. Carter, *On the Border With Mackenzie.* N.Y., Antiquarian Press, 1961.

Truteau, Jean Baptiste, frontiersman (Dec. 11, 1748-1827). B. at Montreal, he received a good education. He reached St. Louis in 1774, already experienced as an Indian trader in the Illinois country. He settled down as a school teacher, but in 1794 led the first expedition of the Missouri Company, an organization headed by Clamorgan and designed to oust the British from Spanish territory, open trade with Indians, discover a route to the Pacific, and defend the Spanish Empire. Truteau left St. Louis for the Mandan villages June 7. Stopped by the Teton Sioux, Truteau wintered in what is now Charles Mix County, South Dakota, and in 1795 reached the Arikara country where he contacted various tribes, collected information, and awaited a second expedition to be sent up the river that year by the company. This party, however, was badly led and got no farther than the Poncas. Sioux attacked the Arikaras in 1796, forcing Truteau to withdraw to the Omaha country. He reached St. Louis once more June 4, 1796, resuming his teaching profession. His work in the upper country was of value, and Truteau was a worthy explorer and trader.

Abraham P. Nasatir article, MM, Vol. IV;

Nasatir, *Before Lewis and Clark,* 2 vols.   St. Louis, Mo., Hist. Docs. Found., 1952.

Tse-ne-gat (Everett Hatch), Wiminuche Ute (1888-Jan. 11, 1922). The son of Wiminuche chief Old Polk (see entry), Tse-ne-gat was born somewhere between the Ute reservation in southwestern Colorado and Navajo Mountain a hundred miles to the west. His father was sometimes known to the whites as Billy Hatch, and the son as Everett Hatch. Tse-ne-gat learned little English but became fluent in Paiute, Navaho and could speak some Spanish. A Mexican herder, Juan Chacon, was killed March 27, 1914, in the western part of the Southern Ute Reservation and three Indians asserted Tse-ne-gat committed the crime although he claimed Chacon was his friend. A warrant charged Tse-ne-gat with murder, but he refused to surrender, his arrest made difficult by Polk's disinclination to turn him over. October 14, 1914, Tse-ne-gat was indicted for murder by a federal grand jury at Denver. A large posse under U.S. Marshal Aquila Nebeker attacked Polk's camp near Bluff, Utah, late in February 1915 and was driven off after a gunfight in which Indians and whites alike suffered casualties. Tse-ne-gat, Polk, Posey and another Indian subsequently surrendered to Army Chief of Staff Hugh L. Scott at Mexican Hat, Utah, and Tse-ne-gat was sent to Denver for a widely publicized trial which began July 6, 1915. A handsome man, he won wide popular support and was aquitted. Tse-ne-gat ignored motion picture and circus offers, and eventually was appointed a mounted policeman of the Navaho Reservation but did not serve because he lacked equipment. He died of tuberculosis.

Forbes Parkhill, *The Last of the Indian Wars.* N.Y., Crowell-Collier Press, 1961; Dan Thrapp, "Polk and Posey on the Warpath." *Desert Mag.,* Vol. 5, No. 7 (May 1942), 9-13.

Tsoe (Tzoe): *see* Peaches

Tucker, Dan, lawman (fl. 1875-1892). Dan Tucker was an able, adventurous lawman of whose origins and ending little has turned up. *The Silver City Book, I,* says he arrived in 1875 at Silver City, New Mexico from Colorado where it was rumored he "got his man" and went on to say that he had killed 17 men in all; C.M. Chase, in *New Mexico and Colorado in 1881* reported that by 1882 Tucker had killed eleven men. Both summaries may have been saloon gossip, but they suggest the mettle of the man. August 4, 1877, Tucker was named county jailer at Silver City and January 5, 1878, was chosen captain of the Silver City men heading for El Paso, Texas, and its salt war. In April he became the first town marshal of Silver City and by July had put a stop to the discharging of firearms on the city streets. He resigned as marshal in November but became deputy sheriff under Harvey Whitehill and again was appointed city marshal May 2, 1879. January 2, 1880, he had a narrow escape when a Mexican, Carpio Rodriquez, drunk and resisting arrest, shot at him but missed, although the bullet pierced Tucker's clothing. By the end of the month Tucker had been appointed deputy sheriff for the mining boom town of Shakespeare, near the present Lordsburg, New Mexico, and thereafter spent much time in Shakespeare or at Deming, east of Lordsburg. One early visitor to Deming found that Deputy Tucker had quickly brought order to what had been a wild railroad town. "He was certainly the right man," he wrote, "for if he wanted to arrest a desperado he was sure to either arrest or kill him." In 1881 Tucker arrested 13 members of the "cowboy gang" of desperados within 20 days and few ever returned to Deming while Tucker was the law there. Chase wrote that early in November 1881 Tucker killed a cowboy roisterer who had sought to ride his horse into the hotel dining room. In March 1882 the Earp crowd in their hasty exit from Tombstone toward Colorado, rather than take the train through Deming — Tucker's Territory — went on horseback the long way around. Apparently they were reluctant to test Tucker's ability to make the arrests Arizona officials desired. In August 1882 Tucker was involved in the killing of James Burns, a deputy sheriff of Paschal, then a town in Grant County, New Mexico. He was cleared. Tucker put a quick damper on the desperado-rambunctiousness of Russian Bill Tettenborn and Sandy King, arresting both without trouble and lodging them November 6 in the Shakespeare jail. He was not present when they were extracted by masked men the night of November 7-8 and lynched from rafters of the hotel dining room — the only timber lofty enough in that desert town to be useful as a gallows. By late in the year Tucker was Silver City-Deming express messenger and December 14 at

Deming experienced an adventure far from the line of duty. He "entered a house" in the Mexican section and two women instantly "threw their arms around him." Tucker, hopefully believing "they were playing,... struggled gently to release himself but...a man jumped behind him, and pulled (Tucker's) revolver from the scabbard on his belt. Tucker at once threw himself upon the man and a hand to hand fight ensued." Dan retrieved his weapon and fired but missed the man, slightly wounding a woman. Other Mexicans then flung themselves into the fray, one secured the weapon and shot Tucker in the shoulder, "shattering the bone and inflicting a very painful wound." Several Anglos, hearing the commotion, plunged into the room and rescued Tucker. By 1884 Tucker had opened a saloon across from the railroad depot in Deming. In 1885, early in the Geronimo outbreak, Tucker and a partner were prospecting a few miles from Deming when Indians jumped them; the whites found an empty boxcar and within it made their stand, the Indians eventually departing. The El Paso *Lone Star* reported October 3, 1885, that Tucker had been appointed U.S. deputy marshal for Grant County. As deputy still on October 2, 1887, Tucker arrested a dangerous rustler, Dave Thurman, jailing him at Hillsboro, New Mexico. Tucker, "one of the best peace officers Grant County ever had," left New Mexico for California from where in May 1892 he returned for a visit although he had "grown so fleshy that his friends hardly knew him." Nothing further is reported of him. Tucker was described early in his Silver City residence as 5 feet, 7 inches in height, "slim built, blue eyes and light hair and of a shy and retiring disposition."

Silver City Book, Vol. I, "Wild and Wooly Days," Susan and David Nelson, eds. Silver City, Silver Star Pubns., 1978, 19; C.M. Chase, *New Mexico and Colorado in 1881* (The Editor's Run...) Fort Davis, Texas, Frontier Book, Co., 1968, 127-28; information from Ed Bartholomew, Fort Davis, Tex; information from Susan Berry, Silver City Mus.; information from Mrs. Helen Lundwell, librarian, Silver City Public Library; various references from *Silver City Enterprise,* 1882-1892, *Grant County Herald, New Southwest, Southwest Sentinel.*

Tucker, H.H., scout (c. 1841-Mar. 6, 1908). B. near Mansfield, Ohio, he served with the 20th and 31st Ohio Infantry regiments during the Civil War, was wounded and discharged for disability, and subsequently served as first lieutenant, breveted to captain, in the 143rd Illinois Volunteers. He then moved to Ottawa, Kansas. One of Forsyth's scouts, he took part in the Battle of Beecher Island in September 1868. Early in the engagement he was ordered to the north bank of the riverbed as sharpshooter but his left arm was broken by a bullet; he returned to the island where John Haley sought to bandage the injury, but was himself wounded. Eli Ziegler then attempted to apply a tourniquet when Tucker was wounded again by an arrow that was removed only with difficulty. After the rescue Tucker walked part of the way to Fort Wallace because the jouncing of the government wagon was too painful. In 1869 he was first lieutenant of Company C, second battalion, Kansas State Militia. Thirty years after the Beecher Island affair, with Chalmers Smith and James J. Peate, he relocated and preliminarily marked the site. At that time he was living in Oklahoma. He died at his Oklahoma City home, and was buried at Hobart Cemetery.

Simon E. Matson, ed., *The Battle of Beecher Island.* Wray, Colo., Beecher Island Battle Mem. Assn., 1960.

Tucker, Reasin P. (Dan), pioneer (fl. 1846-1881). A migrant to California he and his family had joined the immense wagon train of 1846 that included also the Donner company as far as Fort Bridger. The Donner group sheered off to follow the Hastings Cut-off while the Tuckers with others continued on the old road to Fort Hall, Idaho, and thence to California, arriving safely. They remained at Johnson's Ranch that winter. In January Tucker encountered a survivor of the Donner party staggering in from the snow-covered Sierra Nevada and learned of the distress of the others. He brought in the seven "Forlorn Hope" survivors of 17 who had sought to make it over the mountains in mid-winter. Tucker became captain of the First Relief Party which crossed the pass February 19, 1847, and descended to Donner Lake. On February 22 the rescuers left with 23 persons able to travel, but some died or turned back and the rest faced starvation anew from the loss to wild animals of food cached for their return; the Second Relief Party under Reed

however came to their rescue at the last moment and saved their lives, 18 being brought to the settlement. Tucker also accompanied the Fourth Relief Party which reached the cabins near Donner Lake April 17, finding with the snow gone a sight that "beggars all description...Human bodies, terribly mutilated, legs, arms, skulls, and portions of remains, were scattered in every direction and strewn about the camp." They rescued Lewis Keseberg, arch-cannibal and some believe arch-criminal of the camp whom a few of the relief party wished to hang but Tucker prevented this. The fourth party brought Keseberg out alive. Tucker settled with his sons in the Napa Valley. By 1879 he was living at Goleta near Santa Barbara.

C.F. McGlashan, *History of the Donner Party.* Stanford Univ. Press, 1947; Bancroft, *Pioneer Register.*

Tuhulhulzote (Sound), Nez Perce chief (c. 1810-Spet. 30, 1877). The approximate year of his birth is as given by Dockstader; Mc-Whorter said that he was in "his declining years" in 1877. Howard's sour description of him was as a "cross-grained growler." He believed Tuhulhulzote was an obstructionist seeking to derail Howard's intent to place all five of the non-treaty Nez Perce chiefs and their bands upon the Lapwai Reservation in Idaho. Yet Tuhulhulzote had been charged by the others as their spokesman; he was an orator and he was determined to deliver his speech regardless of how restive it made the impatient whites. As a result Howard and David Perry led the old man out and had him imprisoned so that the council could terminate. Tuhulhulzote was freed before the Nez Perce War of 1877 commenced and with his Pikunanmo band which included about 30 fighting men took an active part in the great campaign. Tuhulhulzote was a very powerful man, tall and heavy but neither fat "nor was he ugly-looking." Once he carried two black-tailed buck deer at once out of the mountains where he had killed them, the only man of the tribe powerful enough to do so. On another occasion eight men were not sufficient to control him when he was drunk. Tuhulhulzote probably was present at the Whitebird Canyon fight which opened the 1877 Nez Perce campaign, but he was not a leader there and personally did not favor war, nor did the other four non-treaty chiefs. He had a leadership role in the Clearwater battle of July 11-12, however, and his war capacity was demonstrated clearly. A week later he attended the Weippe Valley council at which it was determined that the Nez Perce would leave Idaho by the Lolo Trail and seek to join the Crows in the buffalo country to the east. Tuhulhulzote was in the Big Hole fight, but few details are preserved. He was killed on the first day of the Battle of Bear Paw Mountain, his body, being between the Indian and Anglo forces lying unburied, at least until the surrender.

McWhorter, *Hear Me;* Alvin M. Josephy, *The Nez Perce Indians and the Opening of the Northwest.* New Haven, Yale Univ. Press, 1965; Helena Addison Howard, Dan L. McGrath, *War Chief Joseph.* Lincoln, Univ. of Nebr. Press, 1964; Dockstader.

Tully, Pinckney Randolph, merchant (Mar. 25, 1824-Nov. 10, 1903). B. at Port Gibson, Mississippi, he was of a large family that started for Oregon in 1845, but his father died in western Missouri and the trip was abandoned. Tully reached Santa Fe in 1846 and California in 1849. Returning through Arizona the party was attacked by Indians, Tully carrying a head scar from the incident until his death. In 1858 he helped save Mimbres Apaches near Fort Thorn from an unprovoked Mexican attack. As acting Southern Apache agent in 1861 he sought to resolve trouble between Mimbres Apaches and miners at Pinos Altos, New Mexico, charging that the whites were "the principal cause" of the difficulties. His work in southern New Mexico was terminated by the Bascom affair at Apache Pass and military movements coincident with the Civil War. In 1864 the firm, Tully, Ochoa & Co., was formed with S.R. DeLong as junior member. It became the largest mercantile organization in southern Arizona, with outlets at Tubac, Tucson and other settlements, employing hundreds in freighting, farming and various pursuits. When the Southern Pacific reached Tucson in 1880, it spelled doom for wagon freighting enterprises and the firm, although not bankrupt, closed out with heavy losses. Tully engaged in stock raising in southern Pima County. He was treasurer of the Territory for four years, twice mayor of Tucson, and held other public offices. Tully Peak in the Rincon Mountains is named for him. He removed to California and died near Healdsburg, Sonoma County. He was a worthy pioneer.

Hayden files, AHS; Dan L. Thrapp, *Victorio and the Mimbres Apaches.* Norman, Univ. of Okla. Press, 1974.

Tunstall, John Henry, cattleman, investor (Mar. 6, 1853-Feb. 18, 1878). B. at Dalston, Middlesex, England, Tunstall in 1876 with capital to invest visited British Columbia and California before reaching Santa Fe where he met Alexander McSween and was persuaded to inspect Lincoln County, New Mexico, which he reached in November 1876. Tunstall under McSween's guidance looked over land properties in the area and turned down a ranch nominally owned by Lawrence G. Murphy and James J. Dolan because, McSween cautioned him, the title was defective; Tunstall and McSween thereby earned the enmity of the Murphy-Dolan faction, a fatal development. Dolan and his new partner, John H. Riley also noted with dismay the Tunstall-McSween determination to finance and operate a rival mercantile business at Lincoln; McSween came under fire from various directions including the courts which were heavily influenced by the Dolan interests and their friends, few of the court actions appearing based on valid grounds. But they were symptoms of the growing tension. "Feuding and fighting between the Dolan-Riley and McSween (Tunstall) factions expanding in scope and intensity during the last months of 1877 and first months of 1878." Dolan claimed he attempted to goad Tunstall into a gunfight, but the Englishman, averse to violence, declined. McSween's property was attached by court action and since Tunstall was his partner in certain ventures, an effort was made to attach his cattle, also. This was temporarily avoided. But Tunstall was shot down by members of a Mathews posse on the road to Lincoln for reasons that are most murky and ill-defined. The most credible account of the shooting comes from George Kitt who was not with the advance element that killed Tunstall, but with the main body of the posse which shortly reached the scene. He was told that Tunstall, becoming aware of the oncoming party, turned and rode toward the foremost trio: William Morton, Jesse Evans and Tom Hill. One of the three assured Tunstall he would not be harmed, but when he had come close enough Morton fired his rifle, the bullet striking Tunstall in the chest and causing his body to pitch off the horse. Evans then snatched Tunstall's revolver and fired a shot into the back of his head, then killed Tunstall's horse. Attempts were made to suggest that Tunstall had fired at the trio, which was absurd; there were reports that Tunstall's skull was smashed by Morton with the butt of his rifle. John Newcomb brought the body to Lincoln in a wagon afterward. Dr. Taylor F. Ealy, a Presbyterian medical missionary, examined and embalmed the body, assisted by Dr. D.M. Appel, post surgeon of Fort Stanton who was paid the exhorbitant amount of $100 for a post-mortem, which he did to the satisfaction of the Dolan partisans whom, in company with most Fort officers, he favored. Tunstall was buried February 22 at Lincoln.

Maurice G. Fulton's History of the Lincoln County War, ed. by Robert N. Mullin. Tucson, Univ. of Ariz. Press, 1968; William A. Keleher, *Violence in Lincoln County 1869-1881.* Albuquerque, Univ. of New Mex. Press, 1957; Frederick W. Nolan, *The Life & Death of John Henry Tunstall.*Albuquerque, 1965.

Tupatú, Luis, Picurís chief, insurrectionist (d. Dec. 30, 1693?). Tupatú was chief of the Picurís (San Lorenzo) Pueblo about 40 miles north of Santa Fe and 16 miles southwest of Taos; an exaggerated report gives it a population of 3,000 in 1680. He was an important leader in the 1680 Pueblo Uprising which ejected the Spanish for a dozen years from New Mexico. When Popé, nominal leader of the insurrection, lost control over the pueblos, Tupatú succeeded him in ruling the Tewa and Tanos peoples until 1688 when Popé came back into power. When Vargas recaptured Santa Fe in September 1692 and accepted surrender of the Tanos, Tupatú appeared on horseback garbed in Spanish dress (to indicate his willingness to submit) and tendered his allegiance. As the most powerful of all Indian chieftains Tupatú offered to assist the Spaniards in reconquest of New Mexico and supplied 300 warriors for an expedition against the Pecos Pueblo of the east. While the Spaniards conducted a western expedition against still hostile pueblos, Vargas appointed Tupatú "governor" of the reduced pueblos and he no doubt retained that position when Vargas returned to El Paso for the winter. On

his permanent reoccupation of New Mexico in 1693 Vargas approached Santa Fe in mid-December. Tupatú appeared depressed, explaining that it had been reported that Vargas intended to execute all who had taken part in the revolt. Vargas reassured him although warning against a second uprising. Tupatú was sent into Santa Fe ahead of Vargas to pave the way and took trade goods, returning with corn the whites badly needed. Vargas entered Santa Fe himself December 16, initially welcomed, but strains developed as Spanish demands for sustenance and housing became heavy. December 29 a battle ensued. After two days of fighting the insurgents surrendered after "their governor hanged himself," and harsh punishment was exacted. Whether the "governor" who committed suicide was Luis Tupatú is uncertain, but Tupatú is not mentioned as alive in any further record examined. In 1696 when the Picurís fled New Mexico for eastern Colorado they were under Lorenzo Tupatú, brother of Luis, and Juan Tupatú, nephew either of Luis or Lorenzo; obviously Luis Tupatú did not then accompany the Picurís and therefore apparently was dead. Lorenzo became head chief of the Picurís and remained such for a number of years.

Charles Wilson Hackett, Charmion Clair Shelby, *Revolt of the Pueblo Indians of New Mexico,* 2 vols. Albuquerque, Univ. of New Mex. Press, 1970; Twitchell, *Leading Facts,* 1; Bancroft, *Arizona and New Mexico;* Oakah L. Jones Jr., *Pueblo Warriors & Spanish Conquest.* Norman, Univ. of Okla. Press, 1966; *Handbook of Indians,* 9.

Tupper, Tullius Cicero, army officer (Sept. 23, 1838-Sept. 1, 1898). B. at Strongsville, Ohio, he enlisted at 22 in Company E, 6th Cavalry and rose to first sergeant and sergeant-major of the regiment by July 7, 1862, when he was commissioned a second lieutenant. He won a brevet at Gettysburg and ended the war a first lieutenant, being promoted to captain September 17, 1867. July 21, 1867, at Buffalo Springs, Texas, he had a fight with hostiles; October 6, 1871, another near the Little Wichita River, Texas. April 11, 1874, he took part in a skirmish with hostiles at Bull Bear Creek, Indian Territory and August 30 near the Red River he led a cavalry charge in an action under Nelson Miles against Comanches and Kiowas. Tupper was engaged in the pursuit of Victorio in

September 1877 after the Apache's bustout from San Carlos Reservation in Arizona. During this dogged, difficult operation along the San Francisco River of New Mexico, Tupper or scouts or detachments under his command killed a dozen hostiles and captured 13. In April 1882 he led the very difficult and lengthy pursuit of Loco's band of Apaches fleeing the San Carlos Reserve, pursuing them from southeastern Arizona into northwestern Chihuahua where a hard fight at Enmedio Mountain resulted in a standoff; for this action combined with the Red River operation eight years earlier he won a brevet to lieutenant colonel. Tupper at various times commanded Fort Huachuca, Arizona. January 1, 1891, with two troops of the 6th Cavalry he routed Sioux attacking the regimental wagon train near Wounded Knee Creek in South Dakota. Tupper had been promoted to major in 1887. He retired July 26, 1893, and died five years later at Cleveland, Ohio.

Heitman; Powell; *Chronological List;* Dan L. Thrapp, *Al Sieber, Chief of Scouts.* Norman, Univ. of Okla. Press, 1964; Thrapp, *Victorio and the Mimbres Apaches.* Norman, 1974; Robert M. Utley, *The Last Days of the Sioux Nation.* New Haven, Yale Univ. Press, 1963.

Turk, The (El Turco), Indian slave (d. c. Aug. 15, 1541). Called by some a Pawnee, The Turk, so named "because he looked like one," was a slave at the Pueblo of Cicúique (Pecos), New Mexico when he was taken as guide by Hernando de Alvarado on a 1540 exploration of the buffalo plains to the east. The Turk was keen-witted and soon discovered the passion of the Spanish for gold, a metal of which until then he probably was ignorant. He fabricated a monstrous myth of the gold-rich "kingdom" of Quivira on the central Plains, his yarns instrumental in Coronado's leading an expedition there in the summer of 1541. How much of what The Turk reportedly told was actually related by him, and what was owed to Spanish avidity for such tales is unknown, but he spoke only a bit of "Mexican," and the Spanish less of his tongue. Though in chains The Turk was guide for Coronado who left the Tiguex pueblos on the Rio Grande April 23, 1541, and arrived at Quivira with 30 horsemen in July. He explored the Quiviran (Wichita) towns as far as Lindsborg, Kansas, found no gold and before return of the expedition in mid-August The Turk's doom was sealed. The

Turk said he was from the land of Harahey beyond Quivira and before his death reportedly confessed he had been directed by pueblo dwellers to lead the Spanish on to the Plains where they might become lost, their horses die of starvation and the whites so weakened they would be easy prey upon their return. The Turk was garroted at Tabás, northernmost Quiviran town visited, the deed reportedly done by Francisco Martín, a butcher from Mexico City. Coronado personally did not favor the execution, but acceded to general clamor.

George Parker Winship, *The Coronado Expedition, 1540-1542.* BAE 14th Ann. Rept., Wash., Govt. Printing Office, 1896; Herbert Eugene Bolton, *Coronado: Knight of Pueblos and Plains.* Albuquerque, Univ. of New Mex. Press, 1964; A. Grove Day, *Coronado's Quest.* Berkeley, Univ. of Calif. Press, 1964.

Turley, Simeon, frontiersman (1806-Jan. 21, 1847). B. in Madison County, Kentucky, he reached Missouri about 1816, learned distilling and other frontier arts, and arrived in New Mexico in 1830. He erected a flour mill, and distillery in Arroyo Hondo, near Taos, informally "married" a Spanish woman, fathered seven children, and worked a minor gold deposit. He was crippled in one leg, but active as a trader and businessman, open-handed to Mexican and Anglo alike. His mill was burned and Turley murdered during the Taos insurrection.

Janet Lecompte article, MM, Vol. VII.

Turnell, William, sea captain (fl. 1613-14). A lieutenant of Samuel Argall at the capture of the French colony at Saint Sauveur, Maine, July 3, 1613, Turnell was described by Parkman as "an officer of merit, a scholar, and linguist," and apparently a man of conscience and honor. He was placed in command of the *Jonas,* a vessel captured from the French. Returned to Jamestown, Argall and the three-ship flotilla were ordered north again to complete destruction of Saint Sauveur, wipe out any other French settlements in Maine or Canada, and send back to France prisoners they took, other than those slated to be hanged. After Port Royal, Nova Scotia, was burned the three English vessels turned toward Virginia; Argall's reached there safely; another was lost at sea, and the third, under Turnell and bearing two Jesuits and another

Frenchman, was blown toward the Azores. Turnell dreaded putting into port for supplies and having the Catholic Portuguese discover his Jesuit prisoners; he might have cast them into the sea to obviate that possibility, but instead persuaded them to hide from authorities while in port, which they did in the hold of the ship for many days. The *Jonas* then reached England, where Turnell was suspected of being a pirate, but was cleared of suspicion by testimony of the priests, and was freed. He thereupon disappears from view.

Thwaites, JR, I—IV.

Turner, Ben, gunman (d. Dec. 1873). A brother-in-law of the fighting Horrell brothers, though related to a wife of whom is uncertain, Ben Turner, "very conspicous in lawlessness" participated in many of their fights with the law and other opponents. He was at Jerry Scott's Matador Saloon at Lampasas, Texas, when Captain Thomas Williams of the State Police tried to arrest Bill Bowen, another Horrell partisan, and shooting erupted. The result: Williams and three other State Police killed and Mart and Tom Horrell wounded. Mart was lodged in the Georgetown, Williamson County, jail from which Turner, the other Horrells and partisans broke him out, migrating with them to Lincoln County, New Mexico. Here Ben Horrell was killed when resisting arrest by a Mexican constable; the Horrells, with Turner and others in retaliation attacked a peaceful Mexican wedding dance, killing four and wounding two. Several gun battles followed, when the Horrells determined to leave New Mexico for Texas again. Enroute Turner was shot from ambush, "presumably by some Mexican glad to inflict at least some degree of vengeance for the ruthlessness of the *Tejanos.*"

James B. Gillett, *Six Years with the Texas Rangers.* New Haven, Yale Univ. Press, 1925; Robert N. Mullin, ed., *Maurice G. Fulton's History of the Lincoln County War.* Tucson, University of Ariz. Press, 1968; O'Neal, *Gunfighters.*

Turner, Frederick Jackson, historian (Nov. 12, 1861-Mar. 14, 1932). B. at Portage, Wisconsin, he was graduated from the University of Wisconsin at Madison in 1884 intending to become a journalist but heavily influenced by William Francis Allen, an historian who pressed for scientific methods of evaluation. He convinced Turner that social institutions and events are partially formed by "powerful forces and evolutionary changes." After briefly working as a newspaperman, Turner returned to the university and Allen for his master's degree in history, his thesis the Wisconsin fur trade. In 1888 he went to Johns Hopkins University for his doctorate under Herbert Baxter Adams, reworking his master's thesis for his advanced dissertation. It was last reprinted as *The Character and Influence of the Indian Trade in Wisconsin: A Study of the Trading Post as a Institution* (1977). In 1889 Turner became assistant professor of history at Madison, remaining there until 1910. In 1893 he read at the meeting of the American Historical Association at Chicago a paper, "The Significance of the Frontier in American History," advancing a thesis little noted at the time but which came to have seminal significance in American historiography and responsible for Turner's elevation to the very small circle of major figures in the field and probably the founder of the New History, so-called. His Frontier Thesis was a landmark in the approach of professional historians to the study of America's singularity of past, present and future, although his thesis was not accepted at face value by all historians and has endured periods of rejection as well as popularity. "For more than half a century the most useful — and controversial — concept employed in interpreting American history has been the 'frontier hypothesis'," observed Billington, however. Turner's belief was that the Frontier was determinative in the evolution of the American character, which differed and was divorced from the European character. The ever-westering frontier, and co-advancing edge of settlement, and the beckoning lure of free land led to a stripping away of the baggage of social and political restrictions. Cultural niceties were sacrificed but in their place evolved by necessity a self-reliance and basic democracy that has endured as a lasting American characteristic. "To the frontier the American intellect owes its striking characteristics," he wrote. "That coarseness and strength combined with acuteness and inquisitiveness; that practical, inventive turn of mind, quick to find expedients; that masterful grasp of material things, lacking in the artistic but powerful to effect great ends; that restless, nervous energy." Even when the settlement, formerly on the frontier, at last matured differing from European communities for it had engendered fundamental democracy; thus the frontier was a powerful and lasting force for generating and delineating the democratic character which makes the nation unique. Turner's thesis quickly won wide support, and disciples by the score. During the 1920s and 1930s it came under increasingly critical examination and re-evaluation however and, to some degree, modification, although in its essentials, and at core, its acceptance seemed assured. Under the vigorous fresh support of historians like Billington and Jacobs it has had something of a resurgence, and it seems likely to continue as a pivotal concept in elucidating the origin, development and durability of the Americn character. Turner accepted a professorship at Harvard in 1910 and remained there until his retirement in 1924. He intended then to settle at Madison, but failing health ruled otherwise and in 1927 he became a research associate at the Huntington Library of San Marino, California where he spent his final years in research and writing. Turner was not a prolific writer. His "Frontier Thesis" paper was published in 1894 in the *Proceedings of the State Historical Society of Wisconsin* and reprinted that year in the *Annual Report of the American Historical Association. The Rise of the New West* (1906) was his initial book length effort; *The Frontier in American History* (1920), and *The Significance of Sections in American History* (1932) completed the lengthy works (although the latter two were collections of essays) published during his lifetime, but his *The United States, 1830-1850: The Nation and Its Sections* (1935) appeared posthumously. His influence spread not only through the work of historians intrigued by his thesis, but through the many graduate students who worked with him and reflected his thought.

Ray Allen Billington, *Frederick Jackson Turner: Historian, Scholar, Teacher.* N.Y., Oxford Univ. Press, 1973; Wilbur R. Jacobs, *The Historical World of Frederick Jackson Turner.* New Haven, Yale Univ. Press, 1968; Billington, *The American Frontier Thesis: Attack and Defense.* Wash., Amer. Hist. Assn. pamphlet, 1971; Walter Rundell, Jr., "Concepts of the 'Frontier' and the West." *Arizona and the West,* Vol. I, No. 1 (Spring 1959), 13-41.

Turner, George, cattleman (d. May 13, 1881). In southwestern New Mexico he was associated with the Ringo-Curly Bill people, working principally as a cowboy and small rancher. In July 1880, he and others were in the vicinity of Maxey, Arizona, having supposedly delivered beef to the San Carlos Apache Reservation, Arizona, giving them money to spend. In late 1880 he and a "posse" he had called together, had a gunbattle with "rustlers" in the San Simon Valley, killing one and wounding another. Turner and three others were killed when their camp near Fronteras, Sonora, was attacked by Mexicans while the cattleman were asleep. Turner lived long enough to kill José Juan Vasquez, leader of the assailants.

Ed Bartholomew, *Wyatt Earp: The Man & the Myth.* Toyahvale, Tex., Frontier Book Co., 1964.

Turner, John Sr., frontiersman (d. Aug. 1756). Living with the Simon Girty Sr. family, Turner avenged the 1751 death of Girty by killing his murderer, an Indian called The Fish. Having married the widowed Mrs. Girty he removed with her and her four sons, along with his own son by her, John Jr., into the vicinity of Girty's former home in Sherman Valley, Perry County, Pennsylvania. After Braddock's defeat, Turner, his family and other settlers withdrew under French-Indian threat, into Fort Granville, on the Juniata River, near present Lewistown, Pennsylvania, but surrendered upon a French pledge of quarter. Turner then was savagely tortured and burned at the stake by Indians with his wife and the children as witnesses.

Consul W. Butterfield, *History of the Girtys.* Cincinnati, Robert Clarke & Co., 1890.

Turner, John Jr., borderer (1754-May 20, 1840). A half-brother of Simon Girty, Turner was the son of the man who avenged Simon's father's murder; his mother was the wife of both. He was born near present Harrisburg, Pennsylvania. Turner was captured with the family at Fort Granville, near present Lewistown, Pennsylvania, in the summer of 1756, and his mother taken to live with the Delawares. Mrs. Turner still was alive in 1759. That year she, Turner and three Girty children were brought in to Pittsburgh, the former Fort Duquesne, where Turner settled and later married. In 1774 with Simon Girty he enlisted in Lord Dunmore's forces, entertaining Dunmore himself with Indian dances which he performed with Girty. The two were not at the battle of Point Pleasant, but accompanied the force against the Shawnee towns in Ohio. In 1783 Turner and Thomas Girty visited Simon at Detroit; both had been suspected of Tory sympathies although they escaped reprisal, and apparently sought employment by the British. Both returned to western Pennsylvania and "became loyal and good citizens." Simon Girty, the noted partisan, is said to have visited them near Pittsburgh in 1811, but on uncertain authority. Turner survived the last of the Girtys by 20 years, dying at Squirrel Hill, four miles from the confluence of the Monongahela and the Allegheny; according to his will he was comparatively well off.

Consul W. Butterfield, *History of the Girtys.* Cincinnati, Robert Clarke & Co., 1890.

Turner, John S., mountain man (d. Spring 1847). A mountain man of great experience and durability, he accompanied Jedediah Smith in 1827 on his second expedition to California and survived the Colorado River Môhave massacre in which ten trappers died. Turner continued with Smith into the Umpqua River country of southern Oregon where another Indian massacre on July 13, 1828, took 14 white lives, and only four, Turner and Smith among them, escaped, being absent from camp at the time of the attack. Turner guided the Alexander McLeod party of Hudson's Bay Company men who later in 1828 found and buried the victims of the Umpqua affair, dropping into California on that expedition. He went again to California with a Michel Laframboise Hudson's Bay brigade out of Oregon in 1832 when he transferred to the Ewing Young party, but first "paid his debt & delivered up his traps and horses" to leave Laframboise free and clear. Turner settled shortly in the Willamette Valley of Oregon, well apart from other settlers. Again he went to California, this time in 1837 on behalf of the mission settlement to purchase cattle to be driven back to Oregon. The company of eight was attacked in south Oregon on their return by Indians; four whites were killed and the others barely got away, Turner, a giant of a man, laying about him "like a madman" with a flail until the assailants left him alone. He and his three surviving companions, one very badly

wounded, made it to the Willamette settlements. Some time later Turner once more removed to California. He was near Clear Lake in 1846 and the next year was a member of the Second Relief Party seeking to rescue the snowbound Donner emigrants from the Sierra Nevada in February and March 1847, bringing out 15 survivors although several had perished enroute. Turner died that spring in Yolo County, cause of death not stated.

Bancroft, *Pioneer Register, California* III-V, Oregon, I, II; Thwaites, EWT, XXI; Dale L. Morgan, *Jedediah Smith and the Opening of the West.* N.Y., Bobbs-Merrill Co., 1953; Kenneth L. Holmes, *Ewing Young.* Portland, Ore., Binfords & Mort, 1967.

Turner, Thomas Elwyn, army officer (d. Aug. 1, 1862). B. in Pennsylvania he was commissioned from California a second lieutenant in the 2nd Artillery May 20, 1857, transferring to the 4th Infantry the following March. In this organization he was based at Fort Ter-waw, near the present Crescent City and served with Crook in northern California operations against Indians. In 1858 he went with Crook to Washington Territory to take part in Garnett's operations against hostiles who had bested troops at Steptoe's Butte May 17. The 4th reached Fort Simcoe on the present Yakima Reservation on August 2. In a succeeding operation a village was taken and some Indian men, suspected of having killed several whites earlier, were captured, bound and executed in accordance with orders. "This whole business was exceedingly distasteful to me," wrote Crook, "and as ...Lt. Turner rather enjoyed that kind of thing, I detailed him to execute them, which was done...." Turner became a first lieutenant May 14, 1861 and a captain November 25, 1861. He won a brevet of major at the battle of Gaines Mill, Virginia, June 27, 1862 about a month before he died.

Heitman; *General George Crook: His Autobiography,* ed. by Martin F. Schmitt. Norman, Univ. of Okla. Press, 1960, 58, 64.

Turner, Timothy Gilman, newspaperman (July 9, 1885, April 7, 1961). B. at Independence, Missouri, he was a cowboy on the Kansas-Colorado border and in western Texas, before becoming a reporter in Grand Rapids, Michigan, in 1906. He removed to El Paso, Texas, in 1910 and as an Associated

Press correspondent covered the Mexican Revolution with the Madero, Orozco, Villa and Carranza forces to 1915, writing a superior book on the affair, *Bullets, Bottles and Gardenias* (1915). He worked as a newsman in New York City until 1924, then joined the *Los Angeles Times,* retiring a few years before his death at Los Angeles.

Los Angeles Times, Aug. 23, 1948; Apr. 8, 12, 1961.

Turrill, Henry Stuart, army physician (Sept. 8, 1842-Apr. 24, 1907). B. in Connecticut, he became an assistant surgeon of the 17th Connecticut Infantry in 1864, was mustered out at the end of the Civil War, rejoining the army afterwards and rising to the rank of Brigadier General by 1905. He claimed to have been in numerous Indian fights, but support is not available. He was a member of the party under Colonel Gordon Granger which conferred with Cochise in 1872 near Cañada Alamosa, New Mexico, and reported a speech by the Indian, sometimes quoted but dubious on several counts. Turrill claimed to have selected the site of the abortive Tularosa Reservation to which the Mimbres Apaches were removed for two years. It failed.

Henry Stuart Turrill, *Vanished Race of Aboriginal Founders.* N. Y. Soc. of the Order of Founders and Patriots of Amer., 1907; Powell; Heitman.

Tuski Hadjo, Seminole chief (d. pre-1832). An Apalachicola chief of the Seminoles, Tuski Hadjo signed the Camp Moultrie Treaty of September 18, 1823, which limited the Florida Indians to reservations and opened 5 million acres to white occupation. He also signed the additional article which provided that he and four other Seminoles who had served the American cause in the Creek War and First Seminole War would have small reservations near their homeland along the Apalachicola River, where he already had commenced farming and completed "improvements." Even then Tuski Hadjo was considered an "old chief," and it is not reported how long thereafter he lived, but he had died before 1832.

James W. Covington, "Federal Relations with the Apalachicola Indians: 1823-1838." *Fla. Hist. Quar.,* Vol. XLII, No 2 (Oct. 1963), 126; John K. Mahon, "Treaty of Moultrie Creek, 1823." *Florida Hist. Quar.,* Vol. XXXX, No. 4 (Apr. 1962), 350-72.

Tutt, Davis K., frontiersman (c. 1839-July 21 1865). B. at Yellville, Arkansas, his father had a role in the pre-Civil War Tutt-Everett feud of Marion County, Arkansas. Dave Tutt may have met Wild Bill Hickok in 1863 when the latter was quartered at Yellville, and there are rumors of some sort of affair between Hickok and one of Tutt's sisters. Tutt may have served in the 27th Arkansas Infantry on the Confederate side, reportedly at times was a scout and "spy," and with conclusion of hostilities moved to Springfield, Missouri, where his family temporarily lived. There was trouble over a card game, and Hickok killed Tutt on the public square at 6 p.m. Hickok was acquitted by a jury.

Joseph G. Rosa, *They Called Him Wild Bill,* 2nd ed. Norman, Univ. of Okla. Press, 1974.

Tuttle, Daniel Sylvester, bishop (Jan. 26, 1837-Apr. 17, 1923). B. at Windham, New York, the son of a village blacksmith although his ancestors had served in the French and Indian War and American Revolution, Tuttle was graduated from Columbia College and General Theological Seminary being ordained a deacon in the Episcopal Church in 1862 and a priest in 1863. Assigned to Morris, New York, he married the daughter of the man he succeeded and before he was 30 was elected missionary bishop of Montana with jurisdiction in Utah and Idaho; he had to wait at Morris until his birthday before he could accept and May 1, 1867, moved to the field where he would work for 19 years, in the first 13 of which he baptized 268 children and 33 adults, married 21 couples, buried 23 and confirmed 240. Of a large, powerful physique and possessed of a finely tuned sense of humor he became very popular in Montana, then as rough a frontier as America could boast. Toponce reported (p. 210) on a stage ride from Helena to Salt Lake City with the bishop and eight other passengers including two dance-hall girls "tough as hickory and hard as bull quartz." The bishop talked to them "as if they had been queens in disguise, not a word of preaching, no 'holier than thou' talk, just plain every-day American... When we reached Salt Lake one of them asked me, 'Where is the church where he preaches? I am going to hear him next Sunday, if I have to crawl on my hands and knees to get there.'" One editor called him, "the great hearted and lovable champion of Christianity whose hand was as firm to chastise a rowdy as it was gentle to baptize a babe." In 1868 Tuttle was elected bishop of Missouri but turned the selection down because he felt he was needed more on the frontier. The following year he brought his wife and children to Salt Lake City from the east where he had left them when taking up his duties in Montana. He and the Mormons respected one another despite religious differences. In 1886 Tuttle received a second call to Missouri and this time accepted, settling at St. Louis. In 1903 he became presiding bishop of the Episcopal Church, his popularity becoming nationwide. The bishop retained his vigor into advanced age, cutting wood and swimming until in his 80s. He died at 86 from the flu, contracted while conducting a funeral; he had been a bishop for 56 years and had helped consecrate 89 other bishops; he was buried in a St. Louis cemetery under a tombstone engraved, as he had requested: "God be merciful to me a sinner."

Daniel Sylvester Tuttle, *Reminiscences of a Missionary Bishop.* N.Y., Thomas Whittaker, 1906; *Montana Contributions,* V (1904), 283, 289-324; Alexander Toponce, *Reminiscences.* Norman, Univ. of Okla. Press, 1971; DAB.

Twain, Mark: *see* Clemens, Samuel Langhorne.

Twaddle (Twaddell), Harvey, frontiersman (c. 1837-Aug. 5, 1867). B. and raised in South Hanover, Indiana, he was by 1862 in Valencia County, New Mexico. On October 10 near Polvadera he killed Juan Jaramillo, a private of Company I, 1st New Mexico Volunteers who with other soldiers was raiding an apple orchard Twaddle had been hired to guard. The case was investigated by a three-man board, including First Lieutenant William H. Brady (see entry). Twaddle was indicted for murder, released on $1,000 bond, and there the surviving record closes. Shortly he was prospecting near Prescott, Arizona, the 1864 census showing he had been in the Territory four months. By 1866 he was working for King Woolsey, a noted pioneer, and narrowly escaped an Indian ambush November 8 when his three companions were slain. July 27, 1867 Twaddle, hunting strayed mules four miles from Walnut Grove, was shot in the heart by an Indian arrow. With his Henry rifle he killed his assailant and a second Indian and wounded a third, then chased the two mules back to camp where he

arrived delirious and fevered. After some hours he recovered sufficiently to relate what had occurred, but succumbed nine days later. "An examination after death showed that he was wounded by a headless arrow, but that the reed had actually penetrated the heart, and it is wonderful that he survived so long. He was well known as a pioneer and fearless man, a good citizen."

New Mex. State Records Center & Archives, Valencia County Dist. Court Rec., Criminal Cause 212; Donald R. Lavash, *Sherriff William Brady: Tragic Hero of the Lincoln County War,* Santa Fe, Sunstone Press, 1986; U.S. Census, Ariz., 1864, p. 116; Daniel Ellis Conner, *Joseph Reddeford Walker and the Arizona Adventure,* Norman Univ., of Okla. Press, 1956; *Arizona Miner,* Prescott, Nov., 10, 1866, Aug 10, 1867.

Twiggs, David Emanuel, army officer (1790-July 15, 1862). B. in Richmond County, Georgia, he was commissioned a captain in the 8th Infantry March 12, 1812, and ended the War of 1812 a major of the 28th Infantry. Within a few months of turning civilian he was commissioned captain of the 7th Infantry on December 2, 1815. Serving under Edmund Pendleton Gaines in Florida in the First Seminole War, on November 20, 1817, he was directed to bring in the belligerent chief Neamathla of Fowl Town, an Indian village 14 miles east of Fort Scott on the Apalachicola River. The Indians fled so Twiggs destroyed the village and its stores. He transferred to the 1st Infantry December 14, 1821, and became a major May 24, 1825. In 1828 Twiggs commanded Fort Howard at Green Bay, Wisconsin, and troops under his direction built Fort Winnebago at the portage between the Fox and Wisconsin rivers, it becoming an important link in the chain of northwest posts. Twiggs commanded there until he became a lieutenant colonel of the 4th Infantry July 15, 1831. During the Black Hawk War of 1832 he arrived at Fort Gratiot, Michigan, with cholera threatening his command, the officer himself falling victim of the dread disease, but recovering. His role in the Black Hawk War was not major, nor did he see combat. In the Second Seminole War Twiggs served in Florida under Gaines, now commanding the Western District of the Army. Gaines with 1,100 men reached Florida February 10, 1836, but Twiggs remained there only briefly. He became colonel of the 2nd Dragoons June 8,

1836, and later returned to Florida with his mounted command. March 21, 1838, he took prisoner more than 500 Indians, 151 of them warriors. Twiggs' service in the Mexican War under Zachary Taylor was tempestuous, highlighted by great gallantry and monumental quarrels with his fellow officers, notably brevet Brigadier General William J. Worth, but is outside the field of frontier interest. Twiggs became a Brigadier General June 30, 1846, and after the Mexican conflict came into command of the Western Division of the Army. In still another attempt to persuade those Seminoles remaining in Florida to remove to the west, Twiggs on January 19, 1850, met with the chiefs, but to no avail and later contacts were scarcely more fruitful. Twiggs became commander of the Department of Texas before the Civil War. Because of Southern sympathies he surrendered Union forces and stores to the Confederacy, was dismissed by the Army, became a Major General in Confederate forces but retired within months and died about ten miles from Augusta, Georgia.

Heitman; Francis Paul Prucha, *The Sword of the Republic.* N.Y., Macmillan Co., 1969; *Black Hawk War,* Vol. II, Pts, 1, 2; John K. Mahon, *The History of the Second Seminole War.* Gainesville, Univ. of Fla. Press, 1967; Edwin C. McReynolds, *The Seminoles.* Norman, Univ. of Okla. Press, 1967.

Twiss, Thomas S., Indian agent (c. Sept. 1802-c. Spring 1871). B. in New York, he went to West Point from Vermont and became a brevet second lieutenant of engineers July 1, 1826. He taught mathematics and other subjects at West Point for two years then resigned his commission June 30, 1829, and became professor of mathematics, astronomy and natural philosophy at South Carolina College where he remained from 1829 until 1847. He held various positions in industry until March 3, 1855, when he was named Indian agent for the upper Platte; it was a time of turmoil among the Sioux. Twiss reached Fort Laramie August 10 and became a kind of "dictator in control of the Sioux" until he ran afoul of Harney (a dictator in his own right). Harney suspended Twiss as Indian agent in 1856, although he had no authority to do so; Twiss went to Washington and maneuvered himself into reappointment for another five years. He was instrumental in securing the surrender of Spotted Tail, Red Leaf and Long Chin whom the army wanted to answer for depredations. Twiss was energetic and tried to promote farming among his charges, but was not above nepotism and sometimes was suspected of corruption in small or large measure. In 1856-57 he moved his agency from Rawhide Butte Creek, 30 miles east of Fort Laramie, to Deer Creek, 100 miles west of the post on the North Platte. He had married an Oglala girl and eventually fathered four boys and perhaps some daughters. Twiss abandoned his notion of persuading the Sioux to settle and farm and allied himself with the wildest bands of Oglalas, to the discomfiture of more friendly bands. He became associated with John Richards Sr. and Joe Bissonette, traders and bootleggers, and was charged by some influential Sioux with stealing their annuity goods and other nefarious undertakings. Occasionally Twiss sought additional appropriations for opening additional agencies or for presents to far-ranging Sioux who, he argued, might thus be lured to come under agency control, although it was charged that his real purpose was to fatten his own resources. Twiss was removed from office by Lincoln in 1861 and took his Oglala wife to Powder River to join her people. In 1864 he came to Fort Laramie with the Indians, Eugene Ware describing him as "an old gentleman whose hair, long, white and curly, hung down over his shoulders and down his back. He had a very venerable white beard and mustache. His beard had been trimmed with scissors so that it was rather long, but pointed, Van Dyke fashion... He was dressed thoroughly as an Indian," but when officers gathered about commenced arguing about Grant's operations around Vicksburg, Twiss took a learned part in the conversation, comparing Grant's moves with Napoleon's at Borodino and sketching in the dust at his feet diagrams to illustrate his points. By the next day he had "disappeared to the north." Hyde reports that Louis Twiss, a grandson, said that Twiss about 1870 took up 40 acres of land near Rulo, Richardson County, Nebraska, but soon died, a sister from the east settling his affairs. She took back one son, William to be educated, but he returned and joined his three happier brothers being brought up in the Indian way and "wild as young wolves." The two oldest boys, Charles and James (?) scouted for Crook in 1876. The youngest was named Frank. There are many

descendants among the Sioux today.
Burton S. Hill, "Thomas S. Twiss, Indian
Agent." *Great Plains Jour.,* Vol. 6, No. 2 (Spring
1967), 85-96; Alban W. Hoopes, "Thomas S. Twiss,
Indian Agent on the Upper Platte, 1855-1861."
Miss. Valley Hist. Rev., Vol. XX, No. 3 (Dec. 1933),
353-64; George E. Hyde, *Spotted Tail's Folk.*
Norman, Univ. of Okla. Press, 1961; Eugene F.
Ware, *The Indian War of 1864.* N.Y., St. Martin's
Press, 1960; Robert M. Utley, *Frontiersmen in
Blue.* N.Y., Macmillan Co., 1967.

Twitchell, Ralph Emerson, historian (Nov.
29, 1859-Aug. 26, 1925). B. at Ann Arbor,
Michigan, he attended schools in Missouri,
was graduated from the University of Kansas
and in 1882 from the University of Michigan
Law School. He reached Santa Fe, New
Mexico, that year and worked for a representative of the Atchison, Topeka and Santa Fe
Railroad, retaining his affiliation with that
company until his death, although he formally
retired in 1915. He was elected president of the
New Mexico Bar Association in 1888. In 1897
Governor Miguel A. Otero appointed him
colonel and judge-advocate of the Territorial
Militia, and he was called "colonel" the rest of
his life. He held various social, political and
Republican Party offices. Ever interested in
history he focused on the origins of Santa Fe
and New Mexico. He wrote many important
works: *History of the Military Occupation of
New Mexico, 1846-1851* (1909); *Leading
Facts of New Mexican History,* 5 volumes
(1911-1917), first two volumes rep., 1963; *The
Spanish Archives of New Mexico,* 2 volumes
(1914); *Historical Sketch of Governor
William Carr Lane* (1917); *Col. Juan Bautista
de Anza: Diary of His Expedition to the
Moquis in 1780* (1918); *Spanish Colonization
in New Mexico in the Oñate and De Vargas
Periods* (1919); *The Story of the Conquest of
Santa Fe... and... Old Fort Marcy...*
(1923); *Dr. Josiah Gregg, Historian of the
Santa Fe Trail* (1924); *Captain Don Gaspar de
Villagrá...* (1924); *Old Santa Fe: The Story
of New Mexico's Ancient Capital* (1925). He
died at Los Angeles and was buried at Santa
Fe. He was survived by a widow and a son.
Myra Ellen Jenkins, "Ralph Emerson Twitchell."
Arizona and the West, Vol. 8, No. 2 (Summer 1966),
102-06.

Two Face, Oglala chief (d. May 1865).
Described as a "very friendly" chief, he and his

band were met with in 1864 on the Platte by
Brigadier General Robert B. Mitchell and sent
under guard to Camp Cottonwood, but ran
away. In 1865 he and Black Foot, another
Oglala chief, decided to come in to Fort
Laramie. They purchased at heavy expense a
white captive of the Cheyennes, Mrs. Lucinda
Eubanks and child, intending to turn her over
at Laramie as evidence of their good
intentions. However they were accused of
themselves capturing and mistreating the
woman by Colonel Thomas Moonlight and
Lieutenant Colonel William Baumer, who
reportedly were drunk at the time, and
Two Face was hanged. The punishment was
not warranted by the facts.
George E. Hyde, *Red Cloud's Folk.* Norman,
Univ. of Okla. Press, 1957; Hyde, *Life of George
Bent.* Norman, 1968; Robert M. Utley, *Frontiersmen in Blue.* N.Y., Macmillan Co., 1967.

Two Guns White Calf (John Two Guns),
Blackfoot chief (c. 1872-Mar. 12, 1934). His
face became familiar to countless white
Americans early in the 20th century, and was
used in designing the Indian head on the
famed "buffalo nickel" issued in 1913. He was
b. near Fort Benton, Montana, and had the
customary upbringing of Indian boys of the
period. His face was selected as one of three
James Earl Fraser used in preparation for
the design of the buffalo nickel, the other two
being John Big Tree, a Seneca, and Iron Tail, a
Sioux. Two Guns White Calf posed for
thousands of tourists at the Glacier Park
Hotel where he was a major attraction. He
also traveled for the publicity department of
the Great Northern Railroad, the agency
bestowing upon him the name of Two Guns
White Calf, which otherwise was meaningless.
He died of pneumonia at 63 at the Blackfoot
Indian Hospital, Browning, Montana, and
was buried in the Catholic Cemetery at
Browning.
Dockstader.

Two Leggings, Crow war chief (1844-Apr. 23,
1923). A River Crow Indian, he was b. on the
Big Horn River, Montana, and participated as
a youth in horse stealing expeditions against
the Sioux, but otherwise was undistinguished
in war or raiding. He was married but fathered
no children. Two Leggings was the subject of a
book by William Wildschut, edited by Peter
Navokov, *Two Leggings: The Making of a*

Crow Warrior (1967). He died at his home south of Hardin, Montana.
Dockstader.

Two Moon, Northern Cheyenne chief (1847-c. 1917). Grinnell said that Two Moon was b. in 1847; Dockstader reported he died at home "around 1917." Vaughn wrote that Two Moon, so-called because Cheyennes never pronounced the plural (Two Moons) was one of the nine little chiefs of the Fox Warrior Society until in 1877 he surrendered to General Miles when Miles made him head chief of the Northern Cheyennes, a position he was eminently equipped to fill. Two Moon was a nephew of a noted Northern Cheyenne warrior chief of the same name who won fame in many battles and who is sometimes confused with the younger man. Young Two Moon was present at the hostile village attacked by Renolds under Crook March 17, 1876, and escaped unhurt, having led his people to recapture the pony herd which the whites had seized at the outset of the engagement. Two Moon was in the exhilarating fight with Crook on June 17, 1876, on the Rosebud, a fight in which he said "many soldiers were killed — few Indians. It was a great fight, much smoke and dust." He and his people then camped along the Little Big Horn with the Sioux and Two Moon had a role in the fight against Custer, although how significant a part is debated. Two Moon told his story of the fight to Hamlin Garland (reprinted in Graham), but in it did not claim any role or authority more than that his Indian position would make probable. After the fight Two Moon brought his people down the Tongue River to Fort Keogh where he surrendered about April 22, 1877, to Miles; he later enlisted as an Indian scout. When Little Wolf brought his Northern Cheyennes to Montana from Oklahoma following the long exodus undertaken with Dull Knife, Two Moon was first to contact them. Once surrendered, Two Moon lived in peace the rest of his life, interested in the progress of the Cheyennes toward the white notion of civilization. In 1914 he met President Wilson at Washington, and was said to have made several trips to the capital. Garland described him in 1898 as "a tall old man, of a fine, clear brown complexion, big-chested, erect, and martial of bearing (with) manners courteous and manly."

George Bird Grinnell, *The Cheyenne Indians,* 2 vols. Lincoln, Univ. of Nebr. Press, 1972; Grinnell, *The Fighting Cheyennes.* Norman, Univ. of Okla. Press, 1956; J.W. Vaughn, *The Reynolds Campaign on Powder River.* Norman, 1961; Dockstader; W.A. Graham, *The Custer Myth.* Harrisburg, Pa., Stackpole Co., 1957.

Two Moons, Nez Perce chief (c. 1835-post 1911). Of a Nez Perce mother and a Salish father, Two Moons was considered a full Nez Perce; he was named for a grandfather. At 13 he had his first brush with the Crows, barely escaping with his life. On a later occasion he killed a Snake chief near the later Old Crow Agency, Montana. In a subsequent battle he tauntingly put on the elaborate headdress of a slain Crow chief and rode back and forth through Crow positions three times while they fired at him, always missing because, he felt, of the security of his "power" which always prevented him from being wounded. Once he took a key part in a great victory over the Blackfeet. Two Moons said that the Nez Perce wanted no trouble at the time of the 1877 outbreak, and the war was caused by General Howard "who showed us the rifle," i.e., delivered an unacceptable ultimatum. Young Indian men, vastly irritated, then committed depredations so that war must inevitably follow. At the initial battle, that of White Bird Canyon, Two Moons conceded he had fired the second shot from the Indian side, "but did not kill" with it. He was in charge of 16 Indians who ravaged Perry's left flank in the action. He figured importantly in the attack that wiped out Lieutenant Rains and his party of ten enlisted men July 3, 1877. He was in the Clearwater action July 11-12 and at the Weippe Council in mid-July opposed the decision that the Nez Perce seek an alliance with the Crows over in the buffalo country; his position lost. His narrative of the great fight at Big Hole, Montana, August 9-10 is one of the most graphic from the Indian side. Two Moons was in the Camas Meadows, Idaho action August 20 and with others stole the horses while the bulk of the Nez Perce ran off the soldiers' mules. He was in the Canyon Creek fight in Montana, September 13. Two Moons took a prominent part in the Bear Paw battle, September 30-October 5. After the engagement, Two Moons said, "I stopped one snow with the Sioux (in Canada). From there I came to the Flathead reservation and stayed with that tribe two snows. Then I wandered to the Lemhi in southern Idaho, and remained there one snow. From the Lemhi I drifted to the Spokanes and visited them one snow." Later he met the returning exiles of Joseph's band at Lapwai and was transferred to the Colville Reservation of Washington with them. He became a principal informant for McWhorter and thus may well have lived into the 1930s, although confirmation is lacking. There is no notice of his death among the McWhorter papers.

McWhorter, *Hear Me;* Lucullus V. McWhorter, *Yellow Wolf: His Own Story.* Caldwell, Ida., Caxton Printers, 1940; information from the Library, Wash. State Univ.

Two Strike, Brulé Sioux war leader (c. 1821-1914). A Brulé Sioux war leader, he was said by Charles Eastman to have won his name when he knocked from a horse two Ute warriors, counted coup and killed them, but the Sioux were not fighting the Utes at that time, according to Hyde, and Two Strike himself said he won his name by killing two buffalo cows with a single arrow which passed through one and struck the other in the heart. He was a lifelong comrade of Spotted Tail. Two Strike in the mid-1800s took part in actions against the Pawnees and Omahas and in the 1860s in several raids including an attack on a Union Pacific railroad train at Plum Creek, Nebraska, according to Dockstader. In 1872 he accompanied Spotted Tail to Washington, D.C., and the two again went with others to the capital in 1880. Two Strike was within view when Crow Dog killed Spotted Tail August 5, 1881, and thereafter led a portion of Spotted Tail's following of Brulé Sioux, endeavoring to hold them to tradition and avoid contamination by the whites. He was strongly supportive of the Ghost Dance movement, taking his people to the camp of Short Bull, a leader in it. However he finally decided that the Ghost Dance was dangerous for the Sioux and took his people to the Pine Ridge agency, beyond trouble. After the Wounded Knee disaster his warriors quitted Pine Ridge and went out in a frenzy of grief and anger; Miles quickly sent a warning that white power was overwhelming while amnesty would be granted to those who came in, and January 15, 1891 Two Strike surrendered. Shortly he went to Washington, D.C., once more with a delegation seeking

better conditions for his people. Thereafter he lived quietly on the reservation. He was buried on the Pine Ridge Reservation of South Dakota.

George E. Hyde, *Spotted Tail's Folk: A History of the Brulé Sioux.* Norman, Univ. of Okla. Press, 1961; Dockstader.

Two Thighs (Two Buttes, Nishi-no-mah, Nissom-o-min). Cheyenne chief (d. Nov. 29, 1864). The father of the chief known as Little Coyote or Little Wolf, he was a chief of the Fox Soldier band of the Southern Cheyennes at least by 1853. He was killed in the Chivington attack upon a peaceful village at Sand Creek, Colorado.

George Bird Grinnell, *The Fighting Cheyennes.* Norman, Univ. of Okla. Press, 1956.

Ty-gee (Ti-gee, Tagie), Bannock chief (d. c. 1872). Described by Stanton G. Fisher as "an old Bannock chief who died at or near the Crow Agency (Montana) in the winter of '71-'72," his name was given to a low pass in the Rocky Mountains between the North Fork of the Snake River and South Fork of the Madison River, a little south of east of Henry's Lake.

"Journal of S.G. Fisher," *Montana Contributions,* II, 1896, 270n.

Tyrkir, the Southerner, explorer (fl. c. 1001). Probably a German from the Rhine or other vineyard country, he associated with Eirik the Red and became foster father (a title of honor) to Eirik's son, Leifr. He accompanied Leifr on his memorable voyage to Vinland. Leifr thought highly of him, noting that he had been with Eirik's family "for long time, and when Leifr was a child had been devoted to him." On one occasion Tyrker was missing and when found revealed to Leifr that he had discovered an abundance of grapes and grapevines for which the place would be called Vinland. Little more is known of Tyrkir, who was described by the *Greenlanders Saga* as with "a prominent forehead and shifty eyes, and not much more of a face besides; he was short and puny-looking but very clever with his hands."

Magnus Magnusson, Hermann Palsson, *The Vinland Sagas: The Norse Discovery of America.* Baltimore, Penguin Books, 1965.

Tzi-kal-tza (William Clark's son), Nez Perce (c. 1807-c. 1878). The reputed son of explorer

William Clark, Tzi-kal-tza apparently was conceived between early May and June 10, 1806 when Clark was guest of a Nez Perce band led by Chief Broken Arm in the Kamiah Valley of present Idaho. Great hospitality was shown the white explorers during that period while snow-bound passes prevented their crossing the higher mountains. Tzi-kal-tza matured in the eastern Nez Perce country, then married a Flathead woman and lived among her people for many years, his best-known name being the Flathead version of the Nez Perce Tsa-ya-hah. In 1867 Nathaniel Pitt Langford persuaded the Indian to have his photograph taken and Granville Stuart, who knew him well, affirmed that the likeness was genuinely his; he added that Tzi-kal-tza, who was proud of his parentage, had yellow hair. In 1877 Tzi-kal-tza joined the Nez Perces on the epic peregrination from their western homelands toward Canada and with two of his wives was captured following the Bear Paw Mountains engagement in September. He was sent to Oklahoma with others of the surrendered Nez Perce, and died there in late 1878 or early 1879, aged about 72 years. He was buried in an unmarked grave. Gulick's article includes the photograph of Tzi-kal-tza and related pictures.

Bill Gulick, "William Clark's Indian 'Love' Child." *True West,* Vol. 31, No. 2 (Feb. 1984), 12-16.

U

Uemura, Naomi, adventurer (Feb. 12, 1941-c. Feb. 16, 1984). B. in Hyogo Prefecture, near Kobe, island of Honshu, Japan, Uemura early became attracted to adventure in the earth's lonely places, explaining he wanted "to meet the challenge of doing something for the first time in history." In 1968 he rafted alone down 3,782 miles of the Amazon River in South America. In 1970, again alone, he climbed Mt. McKinley, the tallest peak in North America. He lived with Greenland Eskimos for a year in 1973 to learn their language and ways before starting a 17-month, 7,440-mile dogsled journey from northern Greenland to Kotzebue, Alaska. April 30, 1978, he became the first to attain the North Pole alone; his feat involved a 54-day, 600-mile dogsled trek from Cape Columbia, Ellesmere Island, Uemura reporting adventures with a polar bear and dangerous ice conditions enroute. He was technologically assisted by the National Aeronautics and Space Administration enabling him to satellite-check his position regularly and confirming by independent means his attainment of his objective. Because of the spring movement of Arctic ice he then was airlifted to Greenland. With his dogs he traversed the 1,600-mile length of Greenland from north to south, the first such accomplishment on record. Uemura and a companion climbed Mt. Everest, at 29,028 feet the world's tallest peak. He scaled alone the highest mountains of four other continents: in addition to McKinley he climbed Kilimanjaro in Africa, Mt. Blanc in Europe and Aconcagua in South America. He wished to complete his conquest of the loftiest spots on earth with the 1982 scaling of the 16,868-foot Vinson massif, the tallest mountain of Antarctica, but the Falkland Island War forced him to postpone that endeavor, so he chose in February 1984 to attempt the first solo wintertime climb of Mt. McKinley, duplicating his earlier feat of a more opportune season. He completed the record-breaking climb (McKinley had been scaled in winter twice before, but only by teams of climbers) on his 43rd birthday, February 12, by way of the West Buttress route, radioing of his success the following day. Jim Pennington, an experienced mountain airplane pilot of Talkeetna, Alaska, reported he spotted Uemura in descent at the 16,600-foot level on February 16, the adventurer waving that he was all right. He was not seen again. Uemura's colleagues of the Robata-kai (Fireside Club), the alumni association of Meiji University's Alpine Club at once sent two rescue missions, the first of four, the second of 14 climbers, who persisted in the search until April. They found that Uemura had established base camp in a snow cave at 17,200 feet where he left much gear, and that he actually had reached the summit of McKinley, emplacing there the Hinomaru flag (the Sun Flag), with a handkerchief (identified by his wife as Uemura's) attached to it. But no trace of the body was found. "We are not at all sure," said a summary, "whether he went into a crevasse to escape from fierce wind and was buried in it, or was blown away by a fierce blast." Others speculate he may have been killed in a fall while descending an almost vertical face between the 14,000 and 16,000-foot levels of the mountain. In any event it is not unlikely that some such fate would have been his choice for an ending to his adventurous life, had he it to make.

New York Times, Mar. 7, May 2, 7, 1968; Tucson, *Arizona Daily Star,* Feb. 17, 22, 24, 27, 28, 1984; information from the National Geographic Society; *Disappearance in the Far North: Naomi Uemura Search Report and Memorial,* ed. by Masatake Nakao. Tokyo, Meiji Univ. Alpine Club — Fireside Group, publ. by Yana to Keikokushi, 1985 (this book is in Japanese except two pages in English which give a good summary of Uemura's life and accomplishments; it is illustrated with a map and photographs, many in color, showing Uemura's route up McKinley and related scenes); price not stated.

Ulibarri, Juan de, military officer (fl. 1696-c. 1710). A Spaniard of intelligence and courage, Ulibarri may have accompanied Vargas on the reconquest of New Mexico but is first reported in 1696 on a campaign against Picurís fleeing their pueblo for the northeast in fear of retribution for their role in uprisings. About midnight on October 25 Ulibarri fired an arquebus at a hostile Picurí setting signal fires; he killed the Indian and "there were no more warning signals that night." Ulibarri is variously described as "captain," his probable actual rank; a "general" which referred to occasional function rather than military rank; and as "sergeant major," a commissioned and high rank. He went as captain in 1702 to the Moqui villages of northern Arizona to investigate unrest. In 1706 Ulibarri was sent northeast of Santa Fe in response to pleas from Picurís Indians who had fled in 1696 that they were being held as virtual slaves by Plains Indians of eastern Colorado. They wished to be granted Spanish assistance in returning to their pueblo. With 28 presidio soldiers, a dozen militiamen and about 100 Indian auxiliaries, Ulibarra, by now a man of "excellent experience...and prudent resolution," set out upon his expedition, part of which was into unknown territory. The effort was a success. He reached a site later known as El Cuartelejo in eastern Colorado (perhaps the present Kiowa County), located the Picurís and their leaders, Don Lorenzo Tupatú, son or nephew of Luis Tupatú, a leader in the great 1680 uprising which and ousted the Spanish from New Mexico, and Juan Tupatú, and brought 62 safely back to New Mexico where Lorenzo continued as their chief for many years. Because of these excellent results, Governor Francisco Cuerbó y Valdés suggested thanks to Ulibarri in the name of the king. Later Ulibarri led expeditions against the Faraon (Mescalero) Apaches, though results are not reported.

Alfred B. Thomas, *After Coronado*. Norman, Univ. of Okla. Press, 1969; Oakah L. Jones Jr., *Pueblo Warriors & Spanish Conquest*. Norman, 1966; Bancroft, *Arizona and New Mexico;* Herbert Eugene Bolton, *Texas in the Middle Eighteenth Century.* Austin, Univ. of Tex. Press, 1916, 1970.

Ulloa, Antonio de, governor (Jan. 12, 1716-July 5, 1795). B. at Seville, in 1766 he became the first Spanish governor of Louisiana. He had entered the Spanish Navy in 1733 and, being an intellectual, wrote a popular narrative of his experiences in South America from 1736-44 and later a confidential report on conditions in the Peruvian Viceroyalty, subsequently translated and published in England; both works won acclaim. When Louisiana was ceded by France to Spain Ulloa was named governor, arriving at New Orleans in March 1766. He found the administration impoverished, conditions tumultuous and himself unable to find the resources or the iron will to set them aright. In October 1768 a Creole uprising ousted him, and Alexander O'Reilly was sent with 2,000 troops to restore order, which was promptly done. Ulloa commanded a naval squadron in a war with Great Britain in 1779, was court-martialed for his conduct of it but was vindicated.

Noel M. Loomis, Abraham P. Nasatir, *Pedro Vial and the Roads to Santa Fe.* Norman, Univ. of Okla. Press, 1967; DAB; CE.

Ulzan(n)a: *see* Josanie

Uncas, (Woncas), Mohegan chief (c. 1606-1683). A controversial chief in early Pilgrim days, in 1626 he married the daughter of Sassacus, chief of the Pequods and for a time affiliated with that tribe. A rebellion against Sassacus however led to his defeat and banishment, when he went to the nearby Narragansetts but soon made peace and returned to the Pequods. Sometimes he warred as a Mohegan against both Pequod and Narragansett. When the Narragansett, Miantonomo was taken prisoner and handed over to the English only to prove an embarrasment to them, he was returned to Uncas his deadly rival, for execution in 1643, solidifying the hatred against Uncas of the many supporters of Miantonomo who regarded his death as a prime example of English treachery for which Uncas was the implement. In 1656 in another war between the Narragansetts and Mohegans the English came to Uncas's assistance. During King Philip's War of 1675-76 Uncas sided with the English but was not prominent in the fighting. Yet his participation may have meant the difference between defeat and victory. Uncas developed an alcohol problem before his death, which occurred in 1682 or 1683, and by that time he had lost almost all of the affection the whites earlier had had for him. A monument was erected to his memory by the citizens of Norwich, Connecticut, the cornerstone laid by President Jackson 1833 and the structure completed by July 1847. He was the (highly fictionalized) subject of James Fenimore Cooper's novel, *Last of the Mohicans*.

Hodge, HAI; Francis Jennings, *The Invasion of America: Indians, Colonialism, and the Cant of Conquest.* Chapel Hill, Univ. of No. Car. Press, 1978.

Underhill, John, military officer (c. 1597-Sept. 21, 1672). B. in England, he followed his soldier of fortune father into service in the Netherlands and later was an officer in Ireland and at Cádiz, Spain. He married a Dutch woman and came to America June 12, 1630, with Daniel Patrick, another noted soldier, in the company of John Winthrop who became Massachusetts governor. Named captains, Underhill and Patrick were assigned to instruct men of the Massachusetts Bay colony in military skills and to direct any war operations that became necessary. When John Oldham, adventurer-trader, was killed in July 1636 by Narragansett Indians off Block Island, Underhill became one of four captains of a 90-man expedition under John Endecott to exact retribution from the Block Island Indians. The force sailed August 24, 1636, in three pinnaces and two shallops. It largely failed, only one Indian being killed although the whites did what depredations they could to deserted villages. Lightly reinforced the militia pursued raids against the mainland Pequods (who had had little to do with the Oldham slaying) with no better luck, returning to Boston in September without loss of a man. However the Pequods were now aroused against the English and heavy depredations commenced, leading to the 1637 Pequod War. April 10, 1637, Underhill with 20 men was sent to reinforce Saybrook Fort at the mouth of the Connecticut River. In May 1637 with his picked force he joined Captain John Mason (see entry) at Saybrook for a campaign against the Pequods. May 26 the white soldiers, supported by about 500 Narragansett Indians, attacked a principal Pequod palisaded town near the present Groton, Connecticut, Mason commanding one element and Underhill the other. The place was shot up, burned and fugitives slain as they fled, with between 600 and 700 men, women and children killed, decimating the Pequod tribe, which never recovered. Two English were killed and about 20 wounded, among them Underhill, struck in the left hip

by an arrow. A nominal Puritan, Underhill was impatient with civil or ecclesiastical authority and too outspoken to be long tolerated in the Massachusetts theocracy. He became a follower of the liberal Anne Hutchinson, was accused of antinomianism, and periodically came under fire from church authorities He was banished to Dover, New Hampshire, where he became governor for two years, then was reinstated by the Massachusetts church. Underhill moved to Stamford, Connecticut, held public office, then accepted an offer from New Netherland governor William Kieft (see entry) to fight for the Dutch against Indians Kieft had stirred up, Underhill because of his marriage being fluent in Dutch. He was a leader of the force that in March 1644 attacked a populous Indian village near the present Pound Ridge in eastern Westchester County, New York. It was a replica of the Pequod massacre, with from 500 to 700 Indians killed. Underhill settled on Long Island where he became a member of the governor's council of New Amsterdam (New York City) and sheriff of Flushing. He spoke out against Governor Petrus Stuyvesant's Indian policies and attitude toward the English and came into disfavor when the conflict with the British opened in 1664. He helped bring about English control of New Netherland and also served successfully as a privateer on occasion. He held various public offices, moved to Oyster Bay, Long Island, married once more after death of his first wife and fathered children by both. Underhill was described by Bodge as "a handsome and somewhat dashing officer, making much of his soldierly appearance and abilities. He was popular, and of winning address," but somewhat dissolute and, in Jameson's view, an "amusing reprobate."

George M. Bodge, *Soldiers in King Philip's War,* Leominster, Mass., p.p., 1896; *Narratives of New Netherland, 1609-1661,* ed. by J. Franklin Jameson. N.Y., Barnes & Noble, 1967; Francis Jennings, *The Invasion of America: Indians, Colonialism and the Cant of Conquest.* Chapel Hill, Univ. of No. Car. Press, 1978; John Underhill, "Newes from America: or, A New and Experimentall Discoverie of New England," Mass. Hist. Soc. Collecs., 3 ser., Vol. VI, 1837.

Underwood, Henry, desperado (b. c. 1846). B. in Indiana, Underwood had served on the

Union side in the Civil War, reached Kansas where he was married, and arrived at Denton County, Texas, about 1871. He worked as a freighter to Dallas. In 1847 he joined Sam Bass in a race-horse project; some of their escapades were outside the law. Underwood shot two men in a saloon scrape in southwestern Texas and was wounded himself, fled and returned to his wife and two children in Denton County. He was indicted but not prosecuted for burning a church that temporarily held records of persons awaiting trials. He was in and out of jail on various minor charges and was considered mean to blacks. After Bass returned from the Black Hills with holdup profits, Underwood joined him in stage robberies in Texas. On Christmas Day he was arrested at Denton on a Kearney, Nebraska, charge that he was really Tom Nixon, who had assisted Bass in a celebrated Union Pacific railroad holdup in that state. He soon escaped from the Kearney jail, however, returned to Texas with one Arkansas Johnson, and together they joined the Bass gang March 31, 1878. April 10 he was with Bass in a train holdup at Mesquite Station, near Dallas. Underwood was wounded in the arm during the Jackson farm skirmish with the law, eight miles south of Denton, on June 9. He escaped from the Salt Creek fight with officers June 13, and never rejoined the Bass gang. His fate has not been certainly ascertained: Gard reports various Underwood legends: that he lived out his life in Illinois, or in Mexico, or in New Mexico. Walker identifies Underwood with Dr. Henri Stewart (c. 1844-Aug. 29, 1879), an interesting if enigmatic figure who was hanged at Fort Smith, Arkansas, for murder. Ramon Adams (*Burs Under the Saddle,* 166, 459) denies that anyone named Stewart rode with Bass, but apparently failed to consider Stewart's possible alias at the time.

Wayne Gard, *Sam Bass.* Lincoln, Univ. of Nebr. Press, 1969; Wayne T. Walker, "The Doctor Who Rode With Sam Bass." *True West,* Vol. 30, No. 4 (Apr. 1983), 12-15; Glenn Shirley, *Law West of Fort Smith.* Lincoln, 1968, 214.

Unruh, John David Jr., historian (Oct. 4, 1937-Jan. 18, 1976). B. on a farm near Marion, South Dakota, he was graduated from Bethel College, a Mennonite school of North Newton, Kansas, with a major in history. He undertook church related work for two years at Akron, Pennsylvania. Unruh then turned to study for his doctorate in history at the University of Kansas, teaching (to associate professor) at Bluffton (Ohio) College, at intervals. His degree was awarded in October 1975 and his dissertation, eight years in formation, was published posthumously as *The Plains Across....* It was a magisterial, 565-page widely-acclaimed study of enduring value which Doyce B. Nunis Jr. described as "an exciting narrative clothed in flawless style, exhaustively researched, laced with brilliant insights... It will become required reading for any serious student and scholar of the history of the American West and the westward movement." Nunis added that "No historian and scholar could ask for a more fitting epitaph." Unruh died two days after an operation upon a malignant brain tumor. He was 38.

John David Unruh Jr., *The Plains Across: The Overland Emigrants and the Trans-Mississippi West, 1840-60.* Urbana, Univ. of Ill. Press, 1979.

Upham, John Jaques, army officer (July 25, 1837-Oct. 21, 1898). B. in Delaware he was graduated from West Point in 1859, became a second lieutenant of the 6th Infantry and by September 1861, a captain. He ws assigned to California, serving at Fort Crook and Benicia Barracks, and returned to the East for the remainder of the Civil War, winning a brevet at Gettysburg and ending the war as a brevet major. He served in the southeast until 1869 when he was ordered to the frontier, serving at Fort Gibson, Indian Territory, and at Kansas posts until he was transferred to the 6th Cavalry about January 1, 1871. He saw "considerable field service" on the Plains, in 1874 transferred to the 5th Cavalry as a major. He was on the Big Horn and Yellowstone expedition, engaged in the fights at Warbonnet (Hat) Creek and Slim Buttes, then served at Wyoming and Nebraska Posts. Upham became lieutenant colonel of the 3rd Cavalry in 1888, colonel of the 8th Cavalry in 1892 and shortly retired.

Price, *Fifth Cavalry;* Heitman.

Upson, Marshall Ashmun (Ash), writer (Nov. 23, 1829-Oct. 6, 1894). B. at Wolcott, Connecticut, he once worked as reporter for the *New York Herald,* but by 1874 had reached Silver City, New Mexico, where he is said to have boarded with the mother of the later Billy the Kid, and was stagecoach agent at various stations in New Mexico. He worked on newspapers at Central City, Ft. Stanton, Elizabethtown, Las Vegas and Mesilla, New Mexico, and established the Albuquerque *Press*, but his reported alcoholism prevented success anywhere. In 1876 he was reported a justice of the peace at Roswell, New Mexico, and became peripherally involved in the Lincoln County War. In 1880 he became a "clerical deputy" for Pat Garrett, newly elected sheriff of Lincoln County, retaining Garrett's friendship for the rest of his life. He moved to Uvalde, Texas, with Garrett, and died there. Upson is generally credited with ghost-writing Garrett's *Authentic Life of Billy the Kid*... (1892), in which he fattened up his scant knowledge of the Kid's early years by imagination and "supplied incidents from the Kid's boyhood which one finds hard to believe yet difficult to disprove." It is said that "the whole book can be picked to pieces from beginning to end," but it made the reputations of the Kid and Garrett.

Sam Henderson, "Ash Upson — Pat Garrett's Sidekick...and Ghost Writer!" *Golden West*, Vol. X, No. 4 (Mar. 1974), 26-27, 52-55; Ramon F. Adams, *Six-Guns and Saddle Leather*. Norman, Univ. of Okla. Press, 1969.

Urban, Gustavus, army officer (c. 1834-Jan. 11, 1871). B. in Prussia he emigrated as a youth to the United States, enlisted in the old 2nd Cavalry (which became the 5th Cavalry) in 1855 and served in Texas where he took part in several Indian fights including a sharp action May 13, 1859, at Small Creek. When Texas was surrendered to the insurgents in 1861, he sailed with a detachment for New York, was commissioned in the 5th Cavalry, becoming captain and brevet major by war's end, compiling a good combat record, and being twice wounded. In May 1865, he was named aide to Merritt and served in the Division of the Southwest and Texas until November, then in the East until 1868, when he was transferred to Kansas. He was engaged in fights on Prairie Dog Creek, Shuter Creek and the Solomon River, Kansas; participated in the Canadian River expedition of 1868-69, and was engaged in actions at Beaver and Spring creeks. He served on the Republican River expedition of 1869. Urban died at Fort McPherson, Nebraska, and was buried at Morganton, North Carolina.

Heitman; Price, *Fifth Cavalry*.

Ur(i)e, John Mormon pioneer (fl. 1857-1892). A man of this name is placed by *Mormonism Unveiled* at the Mountain Meadows Massacre of September 11, 1857, either participating in or consenting to the tragedy. The book says that Ure, as it spells the name, was of Cedar City. Philip Klingonsmith testified at Lee's first trial that Urie with others had branded all the emigrant cattle they could round up after the event with the church brand, a cross. Ure or Urie apparently was living at the time *Mormonism Unveiled* appeared.

Mormonism Unveiled, 380; Juanita Brooks, *John D. Lee*. Glendale, Calif. Arthur H. Clark Co., 1962.

Urrea, José Cosme de, Mexican army officer (c. Sept. 30, 1797-Aug. 1, 1849). B. possibly, but not certainly, in the presidio of Tucson, Arizona, he at any rate was baptized there on the cited date (in one of his papers he mentioned that his birth date was in April which might mean the event took place in the northern part of present Sonora). Urrea became a cadet in the presidial company of San Rafael Buenavista in 1809 and two years later operated against insurgents in Sinaloa. He was made lieutenant in 1816, fought in Jalisco and Michoacán, took part in various restless movements on the eve of Mexican independence and became associated with Santa Anna by 1829. By 1831 he was a lieutenant colonel and by 1835 a colonel fighting against the Comanche Indians. He was made governor and commander in chief of Durango, then was ordered to participate in Santa Anna's expedition against insurgent Texas. Urrea took part in the actions at San Patricio, Bexar (San Antonio), the Alamo and Goliad before reaching the field at San Jacinto. Urrea was ordered by Santa Anna to comply with the decree of December 30, 1835, of the Mexican Parliament which called for execution of all prisoneres taken, and thus was the instrument of the massacre at Goliad; Urrea personally "was not blood thirsty and when not overruled by orders of a superior, or stirred by irritation, was disposed to treat prisoners with leniency," and he recom-mended clemency for Fannin and the other Texas prisoners taken at Goliad and nearby, but Santa Anna, who had sought the decree of December 30, was adamant, and probably 342 of the prisoners were executed, 48 escaping that fate one way or another. Urrea was not generally blamed for the tragedy. At the Battle of San Jacinto, lost through Santa Anna's weaknesses, Urrea alone held his forces in fairly good order, and withdrew to Guadalupe Victoria in Mexico. In 1837 he was named comandante general of Sonora, his command extending later to Sinaloa. He was a good governor but became enmeshed in Mexican politics, and in 1845 was forced to flee; in 1846 he fought against the Anglo-Americans.

Henry F. Dobyns, Tucson, Ariz., Dec. 9, 1976; HT; *Porrua.*

Urrutia, José, frontiersman (1678-July 16, 1740). B. at Guipúscoa, Spain, his year of birth may have been earlier than given. He came to America in 1691, joined the Domingo Terán de los Ríos expedition into Texas and was left at a post established on the Neches River; when the soldiers withdrew in 1693 he remained with the Indians, living for several years among the Kanohatino on the Brazos, Xarame near the present San Antonio and other tribes. Urrutia became a leader among tribes hostile to the Plains Apache and led extensive campaigns against them. He had had some 40 years of experience among the Texas Indians when he became captain of the presidio at San Antonio July 23, 1733, "and was probably the best informed of all Spaniards on Indian affairs in Texas." Upon his death his son, Toribio de Urrutia succeeded him as captain of the San Antonio presidio, and later José Urrutia, possibly a grandson, was a draftsman in the Spanish army executing valuable drafts of Spanish presidios.

HT; Noel M. Loomis, Abraham P. Nasatir, *Pedro Vial and the Roads to Santa Fe.* Norman, Univ. of Okla. Press, 1967; Max L. Moorhead, *The Presidio.* Norman, 1975.

Ursine, Marc Antoine de la Loire des, French colonial (d. Nov. 28, 1729). Ursine reached Louisiana about 1713 and afterwards was an official in the Company of the Indies (the Mississippi Company). In 1722 he was in Illinois. Later he owned a concession near Natchez and was killed in the Indian uprising at that place.

Thwaites, JR, LXVIII, 165, 327n18.

Utter, Colorado Charley, frontiersman (1838-post 1913). A friend of such frontier notables as Wild Bill Hickok, Utter was b. near Niagara

Falls in New York state and raised on a farm in Illinois. Adjacent resided William L. Bross, later a noted Chicago journalist, lieutenant governor and the unacknowledged brother of Stephen Decatur Bross (see entry) who in Colorado also became Utter's friend. Charley may first have met Hickok in Kansas. He reached Middle Park of the Rockies by 1858, lived among the Utes and trapped for a year or two, then became recorder for the Illinois Central District of the gold fields. He filed claims and was employed occasionally as Ute interpreter, following other frontier occupations as well. In July 1866 he accidentally shot himself while pursuing a bear, but recovered. Utter bought a small ranch near Empire, west of Denver and married a 15-year-old girl (who had left him by the 1880s), still spending much time hunting, guiding and roaming the mountains. For some years his mule trains packed ore in from the mines. Only 5 ft., 5 in., in height Utter often wore two revolvers, buckskin clothing, long hair and was fastidious in person, considered a likeable dandy by most acquaintances. At some point he took up gambling, becoming in time a professional. In 1868 he guided into the Rockies a party including Vice President Schuyler Colfax and William Bross, by now part-owner of the *Chicago Tribune.* Around 1872 Hickok arrived in Colorado and stayed with Utter for some weeks. By September 1874 Utter was at Cheyenne, contemplating a horseback express service between Laramie and the Black Hills, if the incipient gold rush there warranted it. Hickok also came to Cheyenne about that time. When the Black Hills boom matured Utter, in March 1876, with Richard (Bloody Dick) Seymour and another got the mail service underway and in June, with Hickok and his brother Steve Utter, he set out for Deadwood, arriving about July 12. Hickok and others shared his camp, Utter frequently introducing Wild Bill as his "pardner," which in western parlance was acceptable, if never technically accurate. On August 2 Utter reached the No. 10 Saloon shortly after Wild Bill's assassination. The funeral was held at his camp and sometime later Charley supplied a headstone for the grave, its legend concluding: "Pard, we shall meet in the Happy Hunting ground to part no more." In 1879 Utter was indicted at Lead, South Dakota, for maintaining a "nuisance," i.e. a dancehall; found guilty, he was jailed for an hour and fined $50. That fall he removed to Gunnison, Colorado, bringing along "complete gambling equipment" which he promptly put into use. Thereafter for some years gambling was his established calling. He practiced it in Colorado, at Socorro, New Mexico, and El Paso. Later Utter moved to Panama, acquiring drugstores at Colón and Panama City. He was last reported there around 1913, by which time he was graying and had become blind. The date and place of his demise are unreported but it may have occurred in Panama.

Agnes Wright Spring, *Good Little Bad Man: the Life of Colorado Charley Utter,* Boulder, Co., Pruett Publishing Co., 1987; Joseph G. Rosa, *They Called Him Wild Bill,* Norman, Univ., of Okla. Press, 2nd ed., 1974; Upton Lorentz, " 'Colorado Charley,' Friend of 'Wild Bill,' " *Frontier Times,* Vol. 13, No. 8 (May 1936), 374-75.

V

Vaillant, de Gueslis, Francois, Jesuit missionary (July 20, 1646-Sept. 24, 1718). B. at Orleans, France, he entered the Jesuit novitiate in 1665, went to Canada in 1670 and was ordained in 1675. In 1678 he was assigned to the Mohawk mission in present New York State, working there seven years when Iroquois hostilities forced his return to Quebec. He accompanied Denonville on the expedition against the Senecas in 1687 and later that year went to New York to meet with Governor Thomas Dongan in fruitless attempts to gain his mediation between the French and Iroquois. Vaillant remained in Quebec until 1701 when he was assigned to Detroit to establish an Indian mission, but the hostility of Cadillac toward the Jesuits cancelled out that project. From 1702 until 1706 he worked among the Senecas. He then was stationed at Montreal until illness forced his return to France in 1717. He died at Moulins, France.

Thwaites, JR, LX 315n1.

Valentine, John J., express man (Nov. 12, 1840-Dec. 21, 1901). B. at Bowling Green, Kentucky, he removed to California in 1861. At Strawberry Valley, he became agent for Wells Fargo and Co.'s express, and the Pioneer Stage Telegraph Co. He transferred to Virginia City, Nevada, as agent of Wells Fargo and the Overland Mail Co., and superintendent of the Pioneer Stage Co. He became superintendent of the Pacific division of the express line. In 1869 Wells Fargo appointed him general superintendent of its express with headquarters at New York City, which transferred the following year to San Francisco when Valentine became general manager. In 1882 he was elected vice president and in 1892 president of Wells Fargo. He died at Oakland, California. During his early years with the company he often dealt with train and stage robberies. About 6 feet, 4 inches in height, full bearded, he was a relentless pursuer of outlaws.

Ed Bartholomew, *Wyatt Earp: The Man & the Myth.* Toyahvale, Tex., Frontier Book Co., 1964; *Herringshaw's Library of American Biography.* Chicago, Amer. Pubrs. Assn., 1909.

Valois, Gustavus, military officer (d. Dec. 20, 1891). Valois, whose proper name was Gustavus Haenel, was b. in Prussia, enlisted in the 3rd Maryland Infantry April 12, 1862, was commissioned a first lieutenant April 27, 1864 and was mustered out a captain May 29, 1865. He enlisted in Company I, 5th U.S. Cavalry December 11, 1865 and July 18, 1868, was commissioned a second lieutenant in the 9th Cavalry. With a troop detachment and eight Indian scouts he skirmished with a small band of Kickapoo Indians on Pendencia Creek, Dimmitt County, Texas, May 20, 1872, with no reported losses on either side. Valois became a first lieutenant Auguat 25, 1872. With Troop I, 9th Cavalry he had a hard fight August 16, 1881, with Nana (see entry) and his raiders in the Cuchillo Negro Mountains of New Mexico, losing two enlisted men killed and Second Lieutenant George R. Burnett wounded. Valois became a captain November 22, 1884, and retired February 11, 1887.

Heitman; *Chronological List;* EHI; *Deeds of Valor,* II, 277-81.

Valverde y Cos(s)io, Antonio de, governor (1671-post 1726). B. in Villa Presente, Burgos, Castile, he reached Mexico and in 1693 at 21 campaigned as an officer with Vargas in the reconquest of New Mexico. In 1696 he was made a captain for life of the presidio at El Paso and shortly afterward was attached to the presidio of Santa Fe. That year he commanded presidio soldiers in a Vargas pursuit of Picurís who had fled their pueblo for the plains. Following the reconquest, Valverde returned to El Paso where he engaged in various enterprises until 1716 when he was named interim governor of New Mexico, becoming governor by royal title two years later and continuing as such until 1722, when he was succeeded by his nephew and son-in-law, Juan Domingo de Bustamente. In 1719 Valverde led a major reconnaissance northeastward of Santa Fe into Colorado ostensibly to counter hostile Utes and Comanches. He left Santa Fe with 100 Spaniards including 60 presidial soldiers and 40 settlers, and 200 Pueblo Indians, being joined at Taos by about 265 more Pueblos. The great expedition left Taos September 20, 1719 and proceeded to the present Cimarron, New Mexico, where it was joined by a few Jicarilla Apaches. Valverde then turned north, threading Raton Pass and reaching the present Trinidad, Colorado, where Chief Carlana of the Sierra Blanca (Sangre de Cristo) Apaches offered some of his warriors as auxiliaries. The expedition reached the Arkansas River near the present Pueblo, Colorado, worked downstream to the site of today's Las Animas where it met Plains Apaches of Cuartelejo in the present Kiowa County, among them a man or two exhibiting wounds received they said from Frenchmen among the Pawnees and Jumanos. This alarmed Valverde who withdrew to Santa Fe having encountered neither Utes nor Comanches and "nothing more formidable than poison-oak, which attacked the officers as well as the private of (the) command." Valverde, according to Thomas undertook several other expeditions against the Plains Apaches and Comanches, but results are unreported. Since Spanish authorities desired a scapegoat for the Villasur disaster of 1720, Valverde was tried at Santa Fe in 1726 for having sent an "inexperienced" officer on that mission rather than heading it in person. He defended himself point by point, and although convicted was fined but lightly. Valverde was living at El Paso in 1726, though nothing is known of his later life.

Alfred B. Thomas, *After Coronado.* Norman, Univ. of Okla. Press, 1969; Oakah L. Jones Jr., *Pueblo Warriors & Spanish Conquest.* Norman, 1966; Dolores A. Gunnerson, *The Jicarilla Apaches.* DeKalb, Ill., Northern Ill. Univ. Press, 1974; Bancroft, *Arizona and New Mexico.*

Van Camp, Cornelius, army officer (1834-Oct. 1, 1858). B. in Pennsylvania, perhaps at Lancaster, he went to West Point and was commissioned a brevet second lieutenant with the 1st Cavalry July 1, 1855, becoming a second lieutenant in the 2nd Cavalry the same day. He was stationed at Jefferson Barracks, Missouri, until October, then served at Forts Mason and Belknap and Camp Verde, Texas, becoming one of the best riders of the regiment. His first fight with hostile Indians was on the Verde River, Texas,

October 30, 1857, when he conducted a successful pursuit of Indians, with his small command covering 200 miles in five days. September 15, 1858, he was named adjutant and topographical officer of Van Dorn's Wichita expedition, participating in the hard fight October 1 at the Wichita Village. Leading a charge he was struck in the heart by an arrow, but managed to extract it before his immediate death. In the spring of 1859 his remains were reburied at Lancaster, Pennsylvania.

Price, *Fifth Cavalry,* 546-47; Harold B. Simpson, *Cry Comanche: The 2nd U.S. Cavalry in Texas.* Hillsboro, Tex., Hill Junior Coll. Press, 1979.

Van Curler, Arendt, Dutch official (1620-July 1667). B. at Nykerk, The Netherlands, he was baptized in February 1620, and was a grand nephew of Kiliaen van Rensselaer, a patroon on the middle Hudson River, New York. Van Curler came to New Netherlands at 17, becoming in addition to other functions, secretary of the colony until 1642, ruling the region with firmness, justice and honesty and achieving some status in the fur trade. He early learned an Iroquois dialect, made a study of the Indians and their customs his particular interest, and "during nearly forty years...won their esteem and confidence by his unvarying fairness." Van Curler often visited Iroquois villages to ransom Christian captives or negotiate agreements. "It was through his good offices that peace was maintained between New Netherlands and the Five Nations." It has been said that he was the originator of the Dutch policy of peace with the Indians, a program afterward followed by the English. As colonial secretary and through his hostility to the liquor traffic, he won the enmity of traders "in the bush," and was nearly assassinated, but his honesty and firmness brought him through. He assisted the Jesuit, Isaac Jogues, in September 1642, make his escape from Mohawk captivity and helped him reach Europe in safety. Married in 1644, Van Curler revisited Holland the next year, then returned to settle about four miles north of Fort Orange (Albany) on the Hudson. Then in 1661 he purchased from the Iroquois a tract on the Mohawk River and led the first settlement where the later Schenectady arose. Van Curler frequently assisted Petrus Stuyvesant in negotiations with the Iroquois and formation of his Indian policy, and after the

English takeover of New Netherlands helped counsel the British on Indian matters. In the winter of 1666 when the French governor of Canada, Remy de Courcelle, led his ill-managed expedition into the Mohawk country, Van Curler saved it from starvation by organizing relief supplies from Dutch settlers. Van Curler was invited by French Lieutenant General Alexandre Prouville de Tracy to visit Canada in the course of Tracy's preparations for renewed action against the Mohawks. Van Curler set out with several Indians, but their craft was upset in a gale and the Dutch leader was drowned in Lake Champlain's Perou Bay, often thereafter called Corlaer's Bay after him. The esteem of the Iroquois for Van Curler was demonstrated by their naming subsequent English governors Corlaer in tribute to his "courage and human understanding," a name which in one variant is still used by them.

Thwaites, JR, XXV, 287-88n2; DAB; NCAB, Vol. IV, 507; Francis Parkman, *The Jesuits in North America, Vol. II.*

Vanderburgh, William Henry, fur trader, mountain man (Dec. 6, 1800-Oct. 14, 1832). B. at Vincennes, Indiana, of a good family, he attended West Point for four years from 1813, but did not graduate. He worked for the Missouri Fur Company near Council Bluffs, serving under Manuel Lisa and Joshua Pilcher, and short-lived Fort Vanderburgh, North Dakota, was named for him in 1821. Made an officer in an informal legion of fur men by Colonel Henry Leavenworth, he took part in an attack on the Arikara villages August 9-15, 1823. In 1826 Vanderburgh and others formed a fur trading company to succeed the Missouri Fur Company; he wintered on the Green River in 1827-28, and traded with the Poncas in Nebraska the following winter. He served under Kenneth McKenzie of the American Fur Company at Fort Union, at the mouth of the Yellowstone, then led 50 men to Green River in the summer of 1830. Vanderburgh traded through the mountains, took part in the battle of Pierre's Hole July 18, 1832; he and Andrew Drips followed up a Rocky Mountain Fur Company brigade into Blackfoot country to the vicinity of Alder Gulch, where he and a trapper, Alexis Pilou, were killed in an Indian ambush. His body was not recovered. Vanderburgh was one of the more intelligent mountain men,

fearless and well regarded, and his loss was a major one.

DAB; Chittenden; Harvey L. Carter, "William H. Vanderburgh," MM, Vol. VII.

Van Derslice, Joseph Henry, army officer (June 29, 1828-Feb. 27, 1894). B. at Philadelphia he enlisted in Company A, Engineers January 30, 1851, serving to sergeant by August 28, 1861. He worked on military surveys in Texas, was on the 1857 Mormon Expedition to Utah and served in the south until the Civil War. He was commissioned a second lieutenant in the 14th Infantry May 14, 1861, emerging from the Civil War a first lieutenant and becoming a captain March 22, 1866. Assigned to Camp McDowell, Arizona, he performed scouting duty until May 1869. The next year he was stationed at the Spotted Tail Agency, Dakota, and at the Whetstone Agency nearby. Van Derslice was at Fort Fetterman, Wyoming from 1871 to 1874 and in the next two years also served at Fort Cameron, Utah, and the Red Cloud Agency as well as being on an 1876 expedition against the Sioux. In 1877 he was at the Bannock Reservation, Idaho, and until 1879 at Camp Douglass, Utah. He retired April 23, 1879, for disability in line of duty, and died at Peekskill, New York.

Heitman; Powell.

Vandever, William, soldier, Indian inspector (Mar. 31, 1817-July 23, 1893). B. at Baltimore, he moved to Illinois in 1839 and to Iowa in 1851, studying law and being admitted to the bar at Dubuque where he established a practice. Vandever served in Congress from 1859 to 1861 when, having raised a regiment he was mustered in September 24, 1861, as colonel of the 9th Iowa Infantry, served with distinction at Pea Ridge and under Sherman and emerged from the Civil War as a Brigadier General of Volunteers and brevet Major General. He resumed the practice of law at Dubuque when he was appointed a United States Indian Inspector in 1873, serving until 1877. He is said to have conferred with Cochise in 1874 (the chief died June 8), studied and commented upon Jeffords' rationing procedures in which he found little to criticize. He investigated charges that San Carlos Agent John Clum had been profiteering, cleared the official and urged his superiors not to be so credulous where army charges of corruption were concerned and added "I only wish that (those officers) themselves could be called to account for the numerous frauds and rascalities they are known to commit with impunity." Needless to say this attitude did little to endear Vandever to the army. Vandever also charged Jeffords with malpractice in his services as agent later, however, charging him with having a malignant influence over the Chiricahuas. Vandever moved to Ventura, California, in 1884, served in Congress from that state from 1887 to 1891 and died and was buried at Ventura.

BDAC; Dan L. Thrapp, *Victorio and the Mimbres Apaches.* Norman, Univ. of Okla. Press, 1974.

Van Dorn, Earl, army officer (Sept. 17, 1820-May 8, 1863). B. near Port Gibson, Mississippi, he was graduated from West Point in 1842 and commissioned a brevet second lieutenant in the 7th Infantry, becoming a second lieutenant November 30, 1844. He served at Louisiana, Alabama and Florida posts until 1845, then with the army of occupation in Texas and saw much service in the Mexican War, being breveted to major for gallantry and meritorious service. He was at Pilatka, Florida, during operations against the Seminoles from September 1849 until February 1850. He was appointed senior captain of the 2nd (which became the 5th) Cavalry in 1855 being stationed at Camp Cooper, Texas, later serving at other posts in that state. Van Dorn accompanied Lieutenant Colonel Robert E. Lee in an expedition against the Comanches in the summer of 1856 and in July routed a party of hostiles on the headwaters of the Brazos. From September 1858 until January 1859 he commanded the Wichita Expedition. In one hard fight October 1 near Rush Spring with four companies and Indian allies he attacked a village of Comanches and claimed an enemy loss of 56 hostile warriors killed outright and another 25 wounded mortally, while Van Dorn was dangerously wounded with an arrow in his stomach and another in his wrist, Texas Ranger Sul Ross badly wounded, four white soldiers dead and nine soldiers and one white civilian with serious injuries. Although Van Dorn's wound was believed fatal, he was on horseback again within five weeks. On May 13, 1859, he won another sharp victory over Comanches who were trapped in a brush-

choked defile. The fight occurred in a heavy rain adding to difficulties, but 49 hostiles were killed while Van Dorn had six killed or wounded mortally while two officers were badly wounded as were nine soldiers. Van Dorn by this time "enjoyed... greater distinction than any other mounted officer of his grade in the service. He was one of the most daring men in the army. His courage was excessive and he seemed to court danger for the excitement it afforded." On June 28, 1860, he was promoted to major. Van Dorn was an ardent secessionist and resigned his commission January 31, 1861, to join the Confederacy in which he became a Major General. His Civil War record in the beginning matched his slashing reputation, but as a general officer he was less fortunate; he was the losing commander at the important battle of Pea Ridge and was relieved from command. He was at Vicksburg in June and July 1862 but was again relieved of command after a defeat at the battle of Corinth and once more was defeated April 10, 1863, at Franklin, Tennessee. Van Dorn was murdered by a Dr. Peters who had requested a pass to go through the lines. The officer placed his signature to the requested document when the doctor shot him in the head, picked up the pass, with it got through the lines and was never brought to justice. Price in summary said that Van Dorn "was a good cavalry officer, capable of accomplishing valuable results under the direction of others, lacking, however, in the essentials necessary to successfully maneuver large bodies of troops." The *Dictionary of American Biography* said "His death was a serious loss to the service, for his was an excellent cavalry commander. As he was defeated in both the important battles in which he was in chief command, his real merits have been generally overlooked."

Cullum; Heitman; DAB; *Fifth Cavalry;* Robert M. Utley, *Frontiersmen in Blue.* N.Y., Macmillan Co., 1967.

Van Dyke, John Charles, desert conservationist, writer (Apr. 21, 1856-Dec. 5, 1932). A university professor and expert on the history of art, he was born at New Brunswick, New Jersey, and wrote on his specialty, but gradually he became aware of and interested in the southwest, its deserts and mountains. Most writers of the desert admit their debt to Van Dyke who initially focused upon the beauty of arid land and the need for preserving it. His outstanding books on the area include *The Desert* (1901), in many editions; *The Opal Sea* (1906); *The Mountain* (1916); *Grand Canyon of the Colorado* (1920); *The Open Spaces* (1922), and *The Meadows* (1926). He was opposed to all desert development, writing: "The deserts should never be reclaimed. They are the breathing spaces of the West and should be preserved forever."

Lawrence Clark Powell, "The Desert by John C. Van Dyke." *Westways,* Vol. 64, No. 3 (Mar. 1972), 29-31, 70-71.

Van Horn, James Judson, army officer (c. 1834-Aug. 30, 1898). B. in Ohio, he was graduated from West Point in 1858 and posted to west Texas, being stationed at Fort Davis from 1859 to 1861, commanding Company F, 8th Infantry. Part of the time he was stationed at what became known as Van Horn Wells, near Lobo, Texas, to protect the California Trail. The community of Van Horn, Texas, the Van Horn Mountains and Van Horn Creek also were named for him. Van Horn was taken prisoner at the outbreak of the Civil War and held until April 4, 1862. He was promoted to Captain in 1862. After the Civil War with F Company of the 8th Infantry he was sent to Arizona where he served at Forts Whipple, Prescott, Apache and Lowell. He was made major of the 13th Infantry in 1879; lieutenant colonel of the 25th Infantry in 1885 and colonel of the 8th Infantry in 1891. In 1892, commanding at Fort McKinney, Wyoming, Van Horn was called upon to quell the Johnson County "war" in Wyoming and on April 13 took 45 nominal prisoners and what munitions they possessed to the post, ending the conflict. He displayed coolness and mature judgment throughout. In early July 1898, Van Horn commanded one of three "brigades" under Lawton at the siege of El Caney at Santiago, but shortly was succeeded by William Ludlow. Van Horn went on sick leave and died within six weeks.

Heitman; HT; Helena Huntington Smith, *The War on Powder River.* N.Y., McGraw-Hill Book Co., 1966.

Van Vliet, Frederick, army officer (Sept. 28, 1841-Mar. 8, 1891). B. in New York, he was commissioned a second lieutenant of the 3rd Cavalry August 5, 1861, a first lieutenant July 17, 1863, and became a captain July 28, 1866,

having emerged from the Civil War breveted to lieutenant colonel. Van Vliet was sent to Arizona where he commanded Camp Hualpai in 1870. He took part in the Reynolds campaign of March 1876 against hostiles on the Powder River, Wyoming, and testified at the court-martial of Captain Alexander Moore following it. Van Vliet commanded Company C of the 3rd Cavalry on Crook's Big Horn and Yellowstone Expedition. At the Battle of the Rosebud June 17, 1876, he and Emmet Crawford succeeded in thwarting a Sioux attempt to surround part of the command and held bluffs to the south. In his official report Crook lists no casualties for Van Vliet's squadron of two troops but Crook stated verbally that Van Vliet's unit along with Henry's squadron and Andrews' company had suffered the most severe losses in the action. June 26, 1882, Van Vliet became major of the 10th Cavalry and took part in operations against Geronimo in 1885 and 1886, principally in New Mexico, although later in Arizona. Van Vliet died at the age of 49 at Hooker's Ranch in Arizona.

Heitman; John M. Carroll, Byron Price, *Roll Call on the Little Big Horn.* Ft. Collins, Colo., Old Army Press, 1974; J.W. Vaughn, *The Reynolds Campaign on Powder River.* Norman, Univ. of Okla. Press, 1961; Vaughn, *With Crook at the Rosebud.* Harrisburg, Pa., Stackpole Co., 1956; Dan L. Thrapp, *Al Sieber, Chief of Scouts.* Norman, 1964; Thrapp, *The Conquest of Apacheria.* Norman, 1967.

Van Vliet, Stewart, army officer (July 21, 1815-Mar. 28, 1901). B. at Ferrisburg, Vermont, he was graduated from West Point in 1840 and became a second lieutenant of the 3rd Artillery. He served against the Seminoles in Florida and was stationed at various southeastern posts until 1846, then was in the Mexican War, taking part in the battles of Monterrey and Vera Cruz. Van Vliet directed construction of Fort Laramie, Wyoming, Fort Kearny, Nebraska, and other frontier posts from 1847-51. He took part under Philip St. George Cooke in the battle of Blue Water Creek, Nebraska, against the Brulé Sioux September 3, 1855, when 160 Indians were killed, wounded or taken prisoner while the whites lost 13 in dead, wounded and missing. In a quartermaster capacity Van Vliet was engaged in fitting out the Utah Expedition of 1857-58, and reached Salt Lake City months in advance of the troops, when Brigham Young sought to impress upon him the determination of the Mormons to fight any takeover by U.S. forces. Van Vliet served largely in the quartermaster department in the Civil War, emerging as a brevet Major General; his regular army rank would rise by 1872 to colonel. He was chief quartermaster of the Department of the Missouri from 1872-75, and retired January 22, 1881.

Cullum; Heitman; Appleton; Juanita Brooks, *The Mountain Meadows Massacre.* Norman, Univ. of Okla. Press, 1966.

Vargas Zapata y Lujan Ponce de Léon, Diego de, military officer (c. Oct. 29, 1643-Apr. 8, 1704). B. at Madrid he was married, fathered three daughters and two sons, and in the summer of 1672 left Spain for Mexico, returning to his homeland but once (in 1677 upon death of his wife). Of his youth little is known although in view of his ancient and powerful family Bloom thought it probable Vargas had served as a queen's page and later as an officer. He was alcalde mayor at various points in Mexico and in 1686 or 1687 requested the post of governor of New Mexico, then in control of Pueblo Indians who had engineered a 1680 uprising. Authorities had not decided how to reconquer the north, but Vargas won out, by February 22, 1691 was at El Paso del Norte and left there August 21, 1692, with around 200 men, Indian auxiliaries and three Franciscan friars. He went up the Rio Grande finding pueblos in ruins and September 13 reached Santa Fe, surrounding the heavily fortified town. The Tanos inhabitants were fiercely defiant, but Vargas parleyed with them, the defenders surrendered without a fight and the place became Spanish once again. Tupatú, the Pueblo Indian who had inherited the command from the late Popé, appeared at Santa Fe in Spanish dress to show his penitence, tendering his allegiance and offering to accompany Vargas to other pueblos and help talk them into surrender. Vargas went to the great pueblo of Pecos to the east and in five days talked its residents into submission. September 29 Vargas left on a tour of the north, accepting the surrender of pueblos everywhere, some prepared for war but easily talked into giving up. By October 15 Vargas could report to the viceroy that all pueblos for 36 leagues around Santa Fe had

submitted, the friars had baptized 1,000 children and surrenders continued from distant towns. October 30 Vargas with 89 men marched on Acoma to the west where resistance was anticipated but which surrendered. At Zuñi the inhabitants fled, the Spanish camped at the town and were attacked by Apaches who stole livestock but caused no major damage. Vargas succeeded in luring the inhabitants back and accepted their submission, about 300 children being baptized. He went on to the Moqui country, accepting submission of towns. Vargas now returned to El Paso, being attacked by Apaches enroute; the hostiles wounded a man and captured horses while Vargas in turn captured an Apache man who was baptized and shot. Vargas reached El Paso December 20, his entrada having cost "not a single drop of blood, except in the conflicts with Apaches." He now assembled people and means for a permanent reoccupation of New Mexico. The viceroy, enthused, agreed to supply him with people and supplies requested but Vargas, not awaiting them, assembled 800 colonists and with 100 soldiers left El Paso October 13, 1693, for Santa Fe. With him went 18 churchmen. As the column progressed, disquieting rumors of Indian resistance were heard and hunger weakened his company, 30 perishing from want. Vargas proceeded cautiously and having reassured Tupatú and others of his good intentions but warning against a fresh uprising, entered Santa Fe December 16, 1693. His want of provisions, dependence upon the natives for sustenance and harsh weather contributed to a new revolt which the Spanish quickly put down while the native governor (Tupatú, perhaps) committed suicide, 70 Indian insurgents were executed, 400 women and children sold into slavery and about 3,000 bushels of corn confiscated and divided among the whites. Vargas's hold upon Santa Fe was secure but the countryside was in an uproar: stock raids were frequent, Spaniards were attacked when they ventured beyond the walls and while some pueblos remained friendly others were hostile or abandoned by rebellious Indians. Organized expeditions against the hostiles had mixed results with casualties on both sides. During 1694 fighting was commonplace. The final major action was at San Ildefonso, reduced after a several days' engagement. By the end of the year the friars had been distributed and were at work and Spanish control again was secure. A crop failure in 1695-96 caused severe hardships and Vargas was blamed for poor management of existing stores. Native unrest alarmed the missionaries and some retired to Santa Fe. June 4, 1696, the explosion came when the Taos, Picurís, Tahuas and the Keres of Santo Domingo, Cochití and the Jemes arose, killed 26 Spaniards including five missionaries, abandoned their pueblos and fled to the mountains. Vargas toured the evacuated towns, executing any rebels who could be caught, enslaving the noncombatants and by November all seemed quiet except at Acoma and the pueblos of the west. Vargas's five-year term as governor expired in 1696 and although he had applied for a second term, the request reached the king too late and Pedro Rodriquez Cubero succeeded him at Santa Fe. Vargas was complimented and honored by the king and promised a new term when Cubero's would expire in 1702. Nevertheless, Vargas was charged at Mexico City with various offenses: embezzlement; provoking hostilities of 1695-96; mismanagement and so on, his guilt determined by the new governor who lacked authority to do so but had become Vargas's bitter personal enemy. Vargas was jailed for three years, fined 4,000 pesos and his property was confiscated. News of his harsh treatment reached Mexico City and he was ordered released without condition; he left for Mexico in July 1700. In August 1703, Cubero, learning that Vargas was enroute to reassume the governorship and fearing retaliation fled and Vargas, by now a marquis by royal edict reassumed the governorship November 10, 1703. On a campaign against the Apaches he became ill, died at Bernalillo and was buried at Santa Fe, the date of his demise often mistakenly given as April 4.

Bancroft, *Arizona and New Mexico;* Twitchell, *Leading Facts;* Alfred B. Thomas, *After Coronado.* Norman, Univ. of Okla. Press, 1969; John Francis Bannon, *The Spanish Borderlands Frontier 1513-1821.* N.Y., Holt Rinehart and Winston, 1970; Lansing B. Bloom, "The Vargas Encomienda." *New Mex. Hist. Rev.,* Vol. XIV, No. 4 (Oct. 1939), 366-417; John L. Kessell, "Diego de Vargas: Another Look," *New Mex. Hist. Rev.,* Vol. 60, No. 1 (Jan. 1985), 10-28.

Varnum, Charles Albert, army officer (June 21, 1849-Feb. 26, 1936). B. at Troy, New York, he went to West Point from Florida and was commissioned a second lieutenant in the 7th Cavalry June 14, 1872. After service at eastern posts he was assigned to frontier duty at Yankton, Dakota Territory, in 1873 and that summer was on David Stanley's Yellowstone expedition, being in engagements with the Sioux at Tongue River August 4 and the mouth of the Big Horn August 11. Varnum was on Custer's 1874 Black Hills expedition and was engaged in scouting out of Fort Randall, Dakota, in 1875. He commanded Arikara scouts on the Custer Sioux expedition of 1876 and was wounded in the leg in the Battle of the Little Big Horn June 25, 1876, the same day he was promoted to first lieutenant. Varnum was with the Reno command. He served against the Nez Perce in 1877, operating in Montana, though with no reported contact with hostiles. He was regimental quartermaster until 1879 and engaged in scouting activities for several years from northern Plains posts. Varnum was promoted to captain July 22, 1890, and was in the Sioux campaign from late 1890 until 1891, participating in the Battle of Wounded Knee, December 29, 1890, and winning a Medal of Honor at White Clay Creek December 30: when ordered to withdraw his command he noted that to do so would be to expose another command and despite orders reoccupied a commanding position, enabling both commands to safely pull back. Varnum served in Cuba, became a major in the 7th Cavalry in 1901, lieutenant colonel of the 4th Cavalry in 1905 and was retired for disability after Philippine service October 31, 1907, being promoted to colonel during his recall to active duty on July 9, 1918. He was awarded a Silver Star for gallantry in action and died at San Francisco, aged 86.

Heitman; Cullum; *Deeds of Valor,* II; BHB; *I, Varnum: Autobiographical Reminiscences of Custer's Chief of Scouts,* ed. by John M. Carroll, Charles K. Mills. Glendale, Calif., Arthur H. Clark Co., 1982.

Vasco Porcallo de Figueroa, military officer (fl. 1538-1539). A resident of Cuba, he was made Captain-General and lieutenant-governor of Florida by De Soto before the expedition for the southern United States left Havana on its exploration mission. Vasco Porcallo succeeded Nuño de Tobár in the exalted position after Tobár had gotten into trouble a young woman who was waiting-maid to De Soto's wife (he later married the girl). Vasco Porcallo led several scouts into Florida near Tampa Bay, demonstrating that he had some military skill and the necessary bravery, as well as cruelty. On one occasion an Indian guide failed or misunderstood him, he casually "threw him to the dogs"—i.e., had the Irish greyhounds, "very bold, savage dogs," tear him to pieces. At another time an Indian woman advised a messenger not to return to the Spanish and for this she, too was thrown to the dogs. Such tragedies were not uncommon during the history of the De Soto expedition. Vasco Porcallo's principal object in coming to Florida was to seize Indian slaves for his plantation. In this he was not overly successful and determined to return to Cuba. As the Gentleman of Elvas reported, some harsh words were exchanged between Vasco Porcallo and De Soto, but "with words of courtesy, he asked permission... to return (to Cuba), and took his leave." Ranjel said the parting came because of a clash between Vasco Porcallo and De Soto, the origin of which was known only to them and "the departure of this cavalier was regretted by many." He pledged to attend to affairs of state at Cuba (where De Soto was nominally governor), and to provision the expedition when necessary.

Bourne, *De Soto,* I, II.

Vasconcelos, André de, military officer (d. c. Jan. 1543). From Elvas, he was leader of the Portuguese contingent of the De Soto expedition into southern United States, enlisting in 1538 at Seville and was soon named a captain of cavalry. Vasconcelos commanded a ship of the fleet De Soto took from San Lucár to Havana. The captain served faithfully through all the vicissitudes of the four-year trek only to die at Aminoya, a Siouian village on the west bank of the Mississippi below the mouth of the Arkansas River in the winter of 1542-43.

Bourne, *De Soto,* I; *De Soto Expedition Commission.*

Vasquez, Antoine Francois (Baronet), frontiersman (Sept. 11, 1783-Aug. 5, 1828). B. at St. Louis, he visited the Kansas and perhaps Pawnees with his father, a trader, beginning in 1796. He joined Pike's expedition in 1806 as interpreter and hunter, reached Santa Fe (though not with Pike himself) in April 1807, and was arrested, taken to Chihuahua, and

reached Natchitoches in October 1809, St. Louis in 1810. He was married there. Vasquez had joined the army as an officer, eventually serving with the 1st Infantry. He took part in the Battle of Tippecanoe under Harrison. At Fort Madison, Iowa, he endured a brief attack by Winnebago Indians, took part in actions at Niagara, Lundy's Lane, and Fort Erie, but resigned from the army October 1, 1814, and returned to St. Louis. He became a Rocky Mountain trader, although his movements are obscure, then associated with Sylvestre Pratte and operated a trading post near the present town of Onawa, Iowa, occasionally being the victim of Indian hostility. In 1822 he was named interpreter and acting sub agent to the Iowa Indians, being praised by William Clark, on one occasion taking Indian leaders to Washington, D.C. Later he was assigned to the Kansas Indians. He died of cholera.

Janet Lecompte article, MM, Vol. VII; *Journals of Zebulon Montgomery Pike,* ed. by Donald Jackson, 2 vols. Norman, Univ. of Okla. Press, 1966, II, 353n.

Vasquez, (Auguste) Pike, frontiersman (1813-Jan. 19, 1869). B. in Missouri, he was the son of Antoine Vasquez. In 1835 he left for the Rocky Mountains with Louis Vasquez (his uncle) and Andrew Sublette, centering his activities for several years at Fort Vasquez on the South Platte, north of present Denver. In about 1840 he joined the Upper Missouri Outfit of the American Fur Company, occasionally visiting St. Louis. In 1854 he guided an elaborate hunting party of Sir George Gore, became an early merchant in Denver c. 1859, and died, broke, at the present La Veta, Colorado.

Janet Lecompte article, MM, Vol. VII.

Vasquez, (Pierre) Louis, mountain man, trader (Oct. 3, 1798-c. Sept. 5, 1868). B. at St. Louis, he early became a fur man, receiving his first license (to trade with the Pawnees), in 1823. By the early 1830s he had shifted his operations to the mountains, a popular and very active mountain man and trader. Vasquez became a partner of Andrew Sublette, perhaps in 1834, returned to St. Louis in 1835, and went back to trade on the South Platte that winter. He traveled back and forth between the mountains and St. Louis almost yearly, his reputation growing. He sold out about 1841 and became associated with Jim Bridger. By 1843 they had built Fort Bridger on Black Fork of the Green River, which became as much an emigrant station as trading post. At St. Louis in 1846 Vasquez married a widow, Mrs. Narcissa Land Ashcraft and took his new family to Fort Bridger. Vasquez opened a store at Salt Lake City in 1855, and he and Bridger sold their fort in 1858, but Vasquez already had retired to Missouri. He died at his Westport home, and was buried at St. Mary's Church cemetery.

LeRoy R. Hafen article, MM, Vol. II; Dale L. Morgan, Eleanor Towles Harris, eds., *The Rocky Mountain Journals of William Marshall Anderson.* San Marino, Calif., Huntington Library, 1967.

Vasquez, Tiburcio, desperado (Aug. 11, 1835-Mar. 19, 1875). B. of a respectable Monterey, California, family, he was well educated but at 17 in 1852 commenced a career of crime. At a dance which he attended with brigand Anastacio Garcia, Constable William Hardmount was slain and Vasquez implicated. He fled with Garcia, launching a 23-year career in outlawry. By 1856 Vasquez had his own gang and was on the way to becoming California's major outlaw. For horse theft near Newhall, California, he was sentenced to five years in San Quentin Penitentiary. Once out he resumed stage holdups, robberies, rustling and other deviltry interspersed with half-hearted attempts at earning an honest living, all in central California. Twice more he served time in San Quentin. In 1873 in a raid at Tres Pinos south of Hollister, San Benito County, three citizens were slain and a small amount of gold taken; heavy rewards were offered for the bandit. Vasquez fled south, holing up in the San Gabriel Mountains near Los Angeles. An amorous adventure with the wife of one of his men, Abdon Leiva, led to Leiva's confiding to authorities the site of the hideout, but in a shootout Vasquez and his chief lieutenant Clodovio Chavez escaped. By December 26, 1873, Vasquez with a new band resumed raiding in central California, attacking Kingston, in Fresno County, and seizing some $2,500; the bounty rose to $8,000 for Vasquez alive, $6,000 dead. Noted lawmen from all over California including Sheriff Harry Morse of Alameda County, joined in the hunt, but after several spectacular stage holdups, Vasquez, Chavez and their men disappeared in the San Gabriels once more. In April 1874

Vasquez drifted furtively west, holing up at the adobe home of Greek George Caralambo (see entry), or George Allen, in the present West Hollywood. Vasquez attempted a raid on a sheep ranch but Sheriff William Rowland of Los Angeles took up the chase, losing the bandit in heavy brush and difficult terrain. On a tip supplied by Morse, Rowland learned Vasquez had returned to Greek George's place and on May 14, 1874, Undersheriff Albert Johnson with a posse of picked lawmen arrested the outlaw, wounding him six times in the process. He was jailed at Los Angeles until May 23, taken by steamship to San Francisco and thence to Salinas where he was held on murder charges growing out of the Tres Pinos affair. Vasquez was tried at San Jose in January 1875 and hanged in March. Clodovio Chavez fled to Arizona after Vasquez's capture and November 25, 1875, was killed near Yuma by deputies seeking his arrest. Ben Truman, Los Angeles newsman who interviewed Vasquez following his capture described him as quite unremarkable in appearance: "Take away the expression of his eyes, furtive, snaky and cunning, and he would pass unnoticed in a crowd. Not more than five feet seven inches in height, perhaps 130 pounds in weight, of very spare build, he looks little like a man who could create a reign of terror." But he did. Vasquez Canyon, a tributary to Tujunga Wash, and Vasquez Rocks, a Los Angeles County park, are named for him.

John W. Robinson, "Tiburcio Vasquez in Southern California." Los Angeles Westerners *Branding Iron*, Sept, Dec. 1882, Nos. 148, 149, with map and photographs of personalities involved in his pursuit and capture.

Vaudreuil, Philippe de Rigaud de, French official (c. 1643-Oct. 10, 1725). B. near Revel, France, he arrived in Canada in 1687 with a military background, a rudimentary education and a thirst for advancement. He was acting governor of Montreal at the time of the Lachine massacre and "his errors of judgment ...were at least partly responsible for the disaster." During the 1690's he was active in combatting persistent Iroquois raiders harassing Canada and took part in Frontenac's 1696 offensive against the Iroquois in the present New York State. He was passed over in his endeavor to succeed Frontenac following the governor's death in 1698 but was named governor of Montreal where he served capably and in 1703 upon the death of governor Louis Hector de Calliere he finally became governor of Canada, serving until his own demise. Even while New France was nominally at peace with New England, Vaudreuil encouraged continued raiding by the Abenakis and mission Iroquois of eastern Canada upon the frontier English settlements in order to prevent the Abenakis from being won over by England and turning against the French, while the Iroquois thus acquired by booty what the faltering beaver trade would have made it impossible for them to obtain by other means. He also had deep concerns over frontier matters in the west, where the building of Detroit caused unforeseen difficulties for the French in their relationships with the tribes, and where Iroquois hostilities were always to be averted or contained. His conduct of Canadian affairs during Queen Anne's War (1701-1713) was creditable and fortunate; his hostility to Cadillac at Detroit resulted in the other's removal, to the benefit of New France, and in most of his several disputes with his countrymen Vaudreuil seems to have bettered his position and name. Aside from his involvement in affairs purely of Canadian or French interest, he entered the fur trade to strengthen his financial position by 1715 and after temporary defeat of the Fox nation in 1716 he directed the building of trading and military posts in the Great Lakes-Mississippi country to further a resurgence of French economic interests there. Vaudreuil engaged in a dispute with Louisiana over division of the Mississippi valley for military and economic purposes, while renewal of Fox hostilities complicated affairs in that region. Expansion of English influence into the upper Mississippi valley also concerned him. Relationships with the English were becoming markedly more strained at the time of his death, but Vaudreuil had managed to check their expansionist ambitions to some extent while defending Canada from a number of threats against its economic and physical health.

Thwaites, JR, LXIII, 303-304n23; DCB, II; Parkman, *A Half Century of Conflict;* Douglas Edward Leach, *Arms for Empire.* N.Y., Macmillan Co., 1973.

Vaughan, Alfred J., Indian agent (1801-June 1871). B. in Virginia, he entered the Indian service probably in 1842; he was agent at the Osage agency in 1845, and sub-agent for the Iowas, Sauks and Foxes in 1848-49. He succeeded James H. Norwood as agent for the Upper Missouri Indians in 1852 and five years later became agent for the Blackfoot Indians, holding the office until 1861. Vaughan had an Indian wife who came from the vicinity of Fort Pierre, South Dakota. Larpenteur reported sourly that Vaughan was "a jovial old fellow, who had a very fine paunch for brandy, and... would take almost anything which would make him drunk.... As he received many favors from the (American Fur) Company, his reports must have been in their favor." But Larpenteur was sour about everyone, and his report of Vaughan is quite inaccurate. Ewers reports that in 1858, far from favoring the AFC, Vaughan recommended prohibition of trade in buffalo robes to prevent ruthless slaughter of the animals the Blackfeet needed for food; had his recommendation been followed "it would have ruined the AFC's business in the entire Upper Missouri region." Ewers added that Vaughan was an experienced and able agent who tried hard to civilize his charges; although a Protestant he urged the Jesuits to establish missions in the Blackfoot country to help settle the tribesmen. He encouraged farming and urged that a deputation of Blackfeet be sent each year to Washington, D.C., to impress upon them the power of the whites; this was not implemented. As a southerner, Vaughan was replaced in 1861, with outbreak of the Civil War, but he returned eight years later to help conclude treaties with Blackfeet, Gros Ventres and Crows. Vaughan's influence was most apparent with Little Dog, head chief of the Piegans. Vaughan died in Marshall County, Mississippi.

Montana, Contributions, Vol. X, 1940, 272-73; John C. Ewers, *The Blackfeet: Raiders on the Northwestern Plains.* Norman, Univ. of Okla. Press, 1958.

Vaughn, J. Wendel, writer (Mar. 4, 1906-Sept. 29, 1968). B. at Dadeville, Missouri, he was graduated from the University of Missouri in 1925 and took a law degree from Denver University, practicing in Windsor, Colorado, for 39 years. He served briefly in the army in World War II, but was discharged in 1943. He died at Greeley, Colorado. Vaughn wrote four superior books on Indian-white combat: *With Crook at the Rosebud* (1956); *The Reynolds Campaign on Powder River* (1961); *The Battle of Platte Bridge* (1963), and *Indian Fights: New Facts on Seven Encounters* (1966). His books were all honest, reliable, thoroughly researched, original and probably definitive within their scope. They rank at the peak of writings in their field. Vaughn left no works in progress, affirming after publication of his fourth book that, "I've made my contribution," and was apparently satisfied with that.

Correspondence with Blair Macy, pub. of *Windsor Beacon*, Windsor, Colo.

Vázquez de Coronado, Francisco: *see* Coronado, Francisco Vázquez de

Veil, Charles Henry, army officer (Feb. 14, 1842-Jan. 1, 1910). B. near Johnstown, Pennsylvania, he enlisted in the 9th Pennsylvania Reserves July 29, 1861, and became a second lieutenant in the 1st U.S. Cavalry April 7, 1864, a first lieutenant July 1 and ending the Civil War a brevet major. Veil reached Arizona with C Company of the 1st in July 1866, and for a time commanded it in the absence of its commanding officer who was persistently ill. Veil was discharged honorably January 1, 1871, farmed for a time near Phoenix, Arizona, where his wife died in 1891, and returned to Pennsylvania. He died at Blackwell.

Heitman; Constance Wynn Altshuler, *Chains of Command*, Tucson, Ariz. Hist. Soc., 1981.

Velasco, Luis de, Powhatan (?) Indian (fl. 1559-1571). The brother of a chief of a Virginia region known to the Spanish as Axacan and probably a Powhatan village or area west of Chesapeake Bay, Luis was seized about 1559 by Spanish explorers perhaps accompanied by Dominican clergymen. They took the boy to Mexico where Don Luis de Velasco, viceroy from 1550-1564 caused him to be baptized and bestowed his name upon the boy. At Havana in 1566 the young Luis embarked with a company of 30 Spanish soldiers and two Dominicans for his home country where they planned to establish a mission, but it failed; they took their Indian protege with them to Spain where he became a favorite of King Philip II until he re-embarked for Havana with some Dominicans intending to establish a mission in Florida. This endeavor failed also, and Luis joined Jesuits in 1570 who arrived September 10 at Chesapeake Bay. A mission was established at a river settlement ruled by a younger brother of Luis. A chapel was erected and Luis served as interpreter until after the first of the year when he quitted the whites and returned to his Indian people. Early in February 1571 he was urged to come back to the mission by a messenger from the Jesuits who apparently did not yet know the Indian tongue and were virtually helpless without Luis's assistance. He promised to return the following day, but that same night with support of warriors of his tribe overtook the returning emissaries and slew them. On February 8, the remaining missionaries at their settlement were disarmed by a ruse when the Indians fell upon and killed them all, except a little boy, Alonso. He was rescued by Pedro Aviles de Menendez later in 1571 when he sought to wreak vengeance upon the natives for their murders, although how he obtained word of them and the details of their fate is not reported.

Hodge, HAI.

Velo, (Belleau, Bellot), Jacques, adventurer (fl. 1744). Velo deserted in 1744 from the French service in Illinois, wandered across the Great Plains and reached Pecos on the Pecos River, east of Santa Fe. He was escorted to Santa Fe, and sent south to Nueva Vizcaya (Chihuahua).

Noel M. Loomis, Abraham P. Nasatir, *Pedro Vial and the Roads to Santa Fe.* Norman, Univ. of Okla. Press, 1967.

Venard, Stephen, lawman (c. 1823-May 20, 1891). B. at Lebanon, Ohio, he went to California in the early 1850s, settled at Nevada City and when mining failed to profit him, engaged in storekeeping and freighting. He became city marshal of Nevada City in 1864 and was highly regarded as an officer and for proficiency with his 16-shot Henry rifle. May 15, 1866, the Wells Fargo stagecoach was robbed several miles from Nevada City by three men: George Shanks, Robert Finn and George Moore, who seized nearly $8,000 in gold dust for the effort. Venard became separated from the posse in pursuit, and trailed the three to near the headwaters of Myer's Creek, a tributary of the South Yuba River. In a swift series of duels Venard killed all three with a total of four shots and by 2 p.m. had returned the gold to the Wells Fargo agent at Nevada City. Venard was much honored for his great feat and went to work for Wells Fargo as guard and special officer. During construction of the transcontinental railroad he guarded the pay cars and later saw extended service as detective. He had an important role in the capture of the John Houx desperado gang in 1871. He died of complications from a kidney ailment. Venard never married. He was buried at Nevada City.

William B. Secrest, "When the Ghost Met Steve Venard." *Old West*, Fall 1968, 20-23; information from William B. Secrest.

Verendrye, Louis Joseph Gaultier de la, explorer (Nov. 9, 1717-Nov. 15, 1761). B. at Lac St. Pierre, Quebec, he learned something of map making and left Montreal in 1735 with his father, Pierre, the party reaching Fort Charles on the Lake of the Woods where they wintered. In the fall of 1736 he was sent to re-establish Fort Maurepas on the Red River of the North where his father joined him for a March council with Cree and Assiniboin Indians. He made a short exploration trip toward Lake Winnipeg, then withdrew to Fort Charles. In 1738 he accompanied his father to the Mandan villages of the present North Dakota, reached the Missouri River and returned with the expedition to Fort La Reine, at the present Portage la Prairie, Manitoba. The next year he continued exploration around Winnipeg. On April 29, 1742 he left with his brother, Francois Gaultier Du Tremblay and others for the Mandan country and eventually, he hoped the "western sea." He reached the Mandans May 19, remaining among them until July 23, awaiting the Gens des Chevaux, or Horse Indians, probably Cheyennes. These Indians did not appear, and Verendrye obtained two guides and marched 20 days west southwest, arriving August 11 at the mountain of the Gens des Chevaux, where his guides quit. September 14 he saw smoke to the southwest and sent his one remaining Mandan and a Frenchman to investigate. They found a village of Beax Hommes, perhaps Crows, who welcomed them and told them by signs there were three Frenchmen established nearby, but contact with these strangers could not be made. Verendrye's remaining Mandan now left and with Crow guides the expedition left November 9 and on the second day came to a

village of the Petits Renards, or Little Foxes, who may have been a band of Cheyennes; they conducted the party to "a populous village of the same tribe," whose members proved friendly and guided the expedition to a village of the Pioya (perhaps Kiowa) which was reached on the 15th. They also being friendly, the party was conducted past another village until the 19th when the Frenchmen finally reached a camp of the Gens des Chevaux which they found in disarray, "all their village having been destroyed by the Gens du Serpent, or Snake Indians" (Shoshone), a people who were considered "very brave," very warlike and very numerous, being "friendly to no tribe" in 1741 having destroyed 17 villages and taken many slaves. The Gens des Chevaux told Verendrye that no member of their tribe had ever been to the sea, since the way was blocked by the Snakes, but by a long detour he might meet tribes "who traded with white men at the sea." He found guides to take him to the Gens de l'Arc, who might have been another band of Cheyennes or of their linguistic stock, who did not fear the Snakes and who were friendly with tribes that traded with the coast people. They found this people hospitable, being received by the "great chief," noting that this tribe and others of the Plains possessed "a large number of horses, asses and mules," and had become true horse Indians. The French were persuaded to join the band which was headed toward "the great mountains which are near the sea," and learned of whites along the coast whom they judged to be Spaniards, since the Indians spoke a few words of that tongue. The band moved southwest or sometimes northwest until on January 1, 1743, "we were in sight of the mountains." The search continued until on January 8 they had reached the range, thickly wooded and very high. On the return there was a slight skirmish with unknown Indians who were frightened off by gunfire. The return continued until February 9 when the village of the Bows was regained. On March 15 they reached the "Little Cherry" tribe near the Missouri, arriving at the river on the 19th. Here Verendrye found an Indian who had been raised by Spaniards, spoke their language perfectly and said that the Spanish country was "very far and there were many dangers to be met" enroute, and "it took at least twenty days to make the trip on horseback." The Spanish, he added, made articles of iron and carried on a large trade in buffalo skins and slaves, giving horses and merchandise, but no guns or ammunition, in exchange. Again Verendrye heard of a Frenchman who had settled several years before not far distant, but although he wrote him a note, received no reply and they did not meet. Then he buried on a hill near the place (at the present Fort Pierre, South Dakota) a lead plate (which was discovered February 16, 1913, and is now held by the South Dakota Historical Society). Verendrye left the camp April 2, on the 9th encountered a village of Prairie Sioux and reached the Mandans once more May 18. On the 26th his expedition joined a party of Assiniboins and reached Fort La Reine July 2nd. The explorers had "added considerably to the geographical knowledge of the period, (and) ensured for the Canadians and French the friendship and loyalty of... Indian tribes until then unknown ...(and it demonstrated) that the route to the western sea was not to be sought to the southwest, but to the northwest..." In 1747 Louis Joseph returned to Quebec. In early 1748 he took part in an expedition against the Mohawks. For political reasons the Verendryes were removed from positions of responsibility in the far west and in 1752 Louis Joseph reentered the fur trade. In 1758 he was trading on Lake Superior; in 1759 he took Indians from Michilimackinac to Montreal to fight against the English and their allies on Lake Champlain. Following the peace, Louis Joseph announced his intention to remain in Canada, but determined first to visit France to conclude some personal business. He sailed from Quebec October 15, 1761, but a month later the vessel was broken up on Cape Breton island during a gale and Verendrye was lost along with most of the passengers and crew. His widow died in great poverty in 1825 at Montreal. He was an energetic, practical and very honest man, and had won the esteem and respect of virtually everyone with whom he had dealt.

Anne H. Blegen, trans., "Journal of the Voyage Made by Chevalier de la Verendrye with One of His Brothers in Search of the Western Sea, Addressed to the Marquis de Beauharnois," *The Verendrye Overland Quest of the Pacific. Quar.* of Ore. Hist. Soc., Vol. XXVI, No. 2 (June 1925), 51-64; Jan M. Dykshorn, "The Verendrye Plate." *Dakota Highlights,* Pierre, S.D., State Hist. Soc., Leaflet 1, 1973; DCB, III; G. Hubert Smith, *The Explorations of La Verendryes in the Northern Plains, 1738-43,* ed. by W. Raymond Wood. Lincoln, Univ. of Nebr. Press, 1980.

Verendrye, Pierre Gaultier de Varennes et de la, explorer, fur trader (Nov. 17, 1685-Dec. 5, 1749). B. at Three Rivers, Quebec, he studied briefly at the Quebec seminary, was commissioned in the colonial regulars in 1696 and was a member of Hertel de Rouville's force which attacked Deerfield, Massachusetts, in 1704. He campaigned briefly in Newfoundland, went to France in 1708 and was commissioned in the Bretagne Regiment, being seriously wounded and captured by the British on September 11, 1709; he returned to Canada in 1712. He married, fathered six children, and lived quietly for 15 years, entering meanwhile into the fur trade in a small way. In 1726 a brother, Jacques René Gaultier de Varennes came into command of a wilderness area north of Lake Superior, with headquarters at Kaministiquia (the present Fort William, Ontario), and Verendrye was taken into the company as second in command; he became commander in 1728 when his brother left to take part in a campaign against the Fox Indians. Verendrye became interested in the perennial French preoccupation with the "western sea," as a theoretical pathway to the Orient, and questioned Indians about the lands and peoples to the west. In 1730 he went to Quebec, conferred with governor Charles de la Boische, the Marquis de Beauharnois, who became his friend and longtime supporter. Beauharnois determined to send Verendrye the next summer to Lake Winnipeg to build a post; in 1731 Verendrye journeyed with his party to the western end of Lake Superior and went on to Rainy Lake where Fort St. Pierre was built, the first of eight posts he constructed in the northwest. Fort St. Charles was built on Lake of the Woods the next year, it serving for some time as Verendrye's principal base. In 1734 he again returned to Montreal, received some financial assistance from Beauharnois and the next year went west again, eventually reaching Lake Winnipeg and the Red River of the North, then returned to Quebec in 1737, still seeking substantial backing for further exploration to the west. Thus far his probing the frontier and pushing it northwestward had benefitted the beaver trade, but had not fulfilled his ambitions and his mission to explore a route to the western sea. He argued however that employment to large numbers of French, the capture of considerable numbers of slaves and the harvest of great quantities of beaver had all been of benefit to France. He returned to the west in 1738, reaching Fort Maurepas on the Red River September 22 and building Fort La Reine on the site of the present Portage la Prairie on the Assiniboin River south of Lake Winnipeg. On October 18, with two sons, 20 other whites and 25 Assiniboins he struck off for the southwest, on the third day being joined by an additional 40 lodges of Assiniboins. He reached the Mandan villages on the Missouri River in present North Dakota December 3, the site about 20 miles from the present town of Sanish. He found that "This nation is mixed white and black (meaning perhaps, fair-skinned and red-brown skinned). The women are fairly good-looking, especially the white, many with blonde and fair hair. . . . The men are stout and tall, generally very active, fairly good looking with a good physiognomy and very affable. The women have not the Indian physiognomy. . ." He said also that their forts were well built, "the palisade supported on cross-pieces mortised into posts of fifteen feet," surrounded by a moat 15 feet deep and 18 feet wide. "Their fort can only be gained by steps or posts which can be removed when threatened by an enemy. If all their forts are alike they may be called impregnable to Indians. Their fortifications are not Indian." Since Verendrye was the first white of record to visit the Mandans, his report is of particular interest; he did not describe what tools they used to "mortise" the joints in their log fortifications. He and his expedition were well treated during their visit to the several Mandan villages. Verendrye regained Fort La Reine in January 1739, and went on the next year to Quebec where Beauharnois received him as warmly as ever and granted him a fur trade monopoly at the posts he had founded. He reached Fort La Reine once more in 1741, sent out on another exploration with his son Louis Joseph Gaultier de la Verendrye that took the expedition in 1742-43 perhaps to the Big Horn Mountains of Wyoming because of which Louis Joseph is considered by some to have "discovered" the Rockies, or at least the northern extension of them. Verendrye resigned his position as commandant of the northwest in 1743, realizing that support for him was wanting in Paris, although he won a confortable retirement and maintained his economic interests in the west. He died at Montreal. Verendrye was one of the great figures of the frontier of New France, although not sufficiently appreciated by the officials of his own day, a fate not rare among enterprising Frenchmen of the time.

Literature abundant: Thwaites, JR, LXVIII, 334-35n46; Russell Reid, "Verendrye's Journey to North Dakota in 1738." *No. Dak. Hist.,* Vol. 32, No. 2 (Apr. 1965), 117-29 (this presents a detailed study and map of Verendrye's route on his 1738-39 exploration journey); *The Verendrye Overland Quest of the Pacific.* Repr. from *Quar.* of Ore. Hist. Soc., Vol. XXVI, No. 2 (June 1925); DCB, III DAB; G. Hubert Smith, *The Exploration of La Verendryes in the Northern Plains, 1738-43,* ed. by Raymond Wood. Lincoln Univ. of Nebr. Press, 1980.

Vermillion, Jack (Texas Jack; Shoot-Your-Eye-Out Jack), desperado (fl. c. 1870-1889). Not from Texas, Vermillion was at Dodge City, Kansas in the 1870s, and made most of the camps from there into the Southwest. He was at Leadville, Colorado, about 1878, but with others was run out and reached Las Vegas, New Mexico, the following year, there meeting Wyatt Earp, Doc Holliday and similar types, with whom he associated. He followed the Earps-Holliday through Deming, New Mexico, to Benson and Tombstone, Arizona, reaching the latter place about 1880. Jack claimed he had been in Arizona before, had lived in a cave in the Dragoon Mountains of Chiricahua fame, his place called Vermillion's Stronghold, and had "often" fought Indians from it when he was the only white man in the region. He fled Arizona with the Earps after joining them in the murders of Frank Stilwell, Florentino Cruz, and the skirmish with Curly Bill or another at the Whetstone Mountains spring. He was reported working with a confidence gang at Denver, and was with the "Kansas gang" at Guthrie, Oklahoma, in 1889. He was reported, without confirmation, to have killed the "cowtown comic," Robert Gilmore (Bobby Gill) among others in Arizona.

Ed Bartholomew, *Wyatt Earp: The Man & the Myth.* Toyahvale, Tex., Frontier Book, Co., 1964.

Verrazzano, Giovanni, explorer (c. 1485-c. 1528). B. near or in Florence, Italy, Verrazzano received a classical education judging from his famous letter, lived in Cairo for a time, and may have learned seamanship in the Mediterranean. Thwaites said he was a corsair in French employ by 1521 harassing Spanish commerce under the name of Juan Florin or Florentin, but William F.E. Morley, in the *Dictionary of Canadian Biography*, judged this a confusion of personalities, finding no evidence of such activity at the time on Verrazzano's part. He may have been on Aubert's voyage to Newfoundland in 1508, but there is no proof. He was commisioned by Francis I of France and made an important voyage to the New World in 1523-24, coasting Spain and incidentally harrassing commerce enroute, touching the Madeiras, and sailing a little north of west, making a landfall on the North American continent above Florida (perhaps in North Carolina) in March 1524. He followed the continent northward to Cape Breton Island, visiting New York Harbor (perhaps the first European to do so), Narragansett Bay, missing the Bay of Fundy, and eventually reached Newfoundland, having abducted an Indian boy enroute to exhibit to the king on his return. "His six-month voyage is one of the most important in North American exploration. . . . Verrazzano had, in fact, joined Canada to the rest of America," proving there was no central route to Cathay, and demonstrating the existence of an expansive, hitherto unknown continent of great potential. His voyage was reflected in the maps drawn after his time, and the place names he gave to features of the new land. The account of the exploration was given in a Letter he wrote to Francis I who had commissioned this first journey to America under official French auspices. His next voyage to the New World was commissioned in 1526 and he set out in 1528 for Florida, the Bahamas, the Lesser Antilles and probably Darien. On an island of the Lesser Antilles, Verrazzano was captured with a party, killed by Caribs and eaten within sight of his crew. His ship returned to France in 1530.

Thwaites, JR, III, 291-92n5; DCB; CE.

Vestal, Stanley: *see* Campbell, Walter Stanley

Vial, Pedro (Pierre), explorer, frontiersman (c. 1746-c. Oct. 1814). B. in Lyons, France, he may have been on the Missouri as a trapper before the American Revolution. Loomis speculates that "Vial must have spent considerable time in Canada and on the headwaters of the Missouri, and then gone to Spanish Illinois," although there are objections to this theory. In the early 1770s Vial was

said to have been in the Illinois country. In the spring of 1779 he ransomed a captive of the Indians and had gone to New Orleans. A governor of Louisiana, Bernardo Vicente Polinarde, referred to him in that year as a gunsmith who frequently lived among the Indians, repairing their firearms. He had spent several years among tribesmen of the southern Plains; it was reported he had been a Comanche captive "for many years," and also had lived among the Jumanos. In 1786 he was commissioned by Texas Governor Domingo Cabello to explore a direct route between San Antonio de Bexar, in south Texas and Santa Fe. He set out October 4 with Cristóbal de los Santos and a packhorse, proceeding north until he came to the Colorado River which he ascended for a distance. He was injured in a fall from a horse and turned eastward toward the Brazos to recuperate for six weeks with the Tawakoni, a Caddoan tribe of Wichita affiliations. Vial left December 15 and ascended the Brazos 62 leagues, then turned northeast to the Taovayas villages on the Red River; he left them January 8, going west up the Red River. Following a brief stay among the Comanches, with whom he was well acquainted, Vial resumed his trek February 18 and reached Santa Fe May 26, 1787, the first known to have made the journey from San Antonio if scarcely by a direct route. José Mares was sent to straighten out the course, if that were possible, and Vial was sent by Governor Concha to chart a route to Natchitoches, Louisiana, then to return by way of San Antonio. Vial left Santa Fe June 24, 1788 accompanied by Francisco Xavier Fragosa and three soldiers: José María Romero, Gregorio Leyva and Juan Lucero along with a Comanche interpreter, two Indians and an escort of four cavalrymen headed by Santiago Fernández who kept a diary of the journey as far as the Taovaya villages on the Red River where they arrived July 20. From there the military escort returned to Santa Fe and Vial went directly to Natchitoches, being familiar with the route. He arrived August 20, 1788. He remained at Natchitoches ten days, then followed the Camino Real, a familiar road by way of Nacogdoches to San Antonio, arriving November 18, 1788. June 25, 1789, Vial left San Antonio for Santa Fe, going north to the Brazos River, then northwestward and reaching Santa Fe August 20, 1879. He had gone to Natchitoches about as directly as it could be done, and from there directly to San Antonio. From there his return to Santa Fe also was as geographically economical as Mares's journey had proven to be. For three years Vial does not figure in important surviving documents, but in 1792 he was commissioned by New Mexico Governor Fernando de la Concha to open a direct route from Santa Fe to St. Louis. He left May 21 with José Vicente Villanueva and Vicente Espinosa; since he could not write Spanish well, he was instructed to keep a diary in French. He and his companions were captured and almost killed by Kaw (Kansa) Indians June 29, being stripped and held naked until August 16; they were taken to the Kansa village at the confluence of the Kansas and Missouri rivers, remaining until September 11 when a French trader rescued and transported them down the Missouri by pirogue to St. Louis where they arrived October 3. Vial remained at St. Louis until June 14, 1793, when he went up the Missouri to near the Nebraska line, tarrying at the mouth of the Little Nemaha River (near Nemaha, Nebraska) until September 12 when his party cut west in company with Pawnee guides, reaching a Pawnee village September 20. They bought ten horses and left October 4, narrowly escaping a night attack on the North Canadian River by other Pawnees who mistook them for Comanches, and reached Santa Fe November 15. In 1795 Vial was commissioned to make a peace between the Pawnees and the Comanches, no doubt to facilitate plains travel, and fulfilled his undertaking satisfactorily. Spanish suspicions of Frenchmen increased about that time due to international events, and he secured a license to trap beaver on the Rio Arriba, but drifted east and was reported living in 1799 at Portage des Sioux, north of St. Louis and in 1801 at Florissant, west of St. Louis. For a time he operated a lead mine in the Missouri country. Relations between France and Spain eased once more and Vial returned to Santa Fe. In succeeding years he fulfilled various missions for the government: he went to the Pawnees again in 1804 and in 1805 to Taos to pick up two Frenchmen and an American (James Purcell), in New Mexico illegally. In October he again went to the Pawnees on a Spanish errand: he was to winter with them and learn what he could of the activities of

Lewis and Clark. But his party ran into Kiowas of greater strength and returned to Santa Fe November 19. April 24, 1806, Vial left once more on a mission to the Pawnees but his men deserted and he returned to Santa Fe by May 30. By 1808 he was on the Missouri again. September 14, 1808, William Clark, governor of Louisiana Territory issued him a license to trap up the river, but by late 1809 he was back in New Mexico, where apparently he remained the rest of his life. He signed his will October 2, 1814, stating that he was ill, no doubt with his final ailment. The date of his death is not recorded. Vial never married. He may have fathered illegitimate children, but nothing is said of them in his will. In 1787 Vial at the prompting of the New Mexico governor drew a map of the west he knew and some of which he personally had seen. This map interestingly shows the three-fork origin of the Missouri River, a feature until then unreported elsewhere. However the map does not show the correct course of the Missouri, its great bend, nor the fact that the Three Forks flow from south to north but rather depicts them as flowing from northwest to southeast; thus it appears that while Vial had heard of the nature of the origin of the Missouri River he had not actually visited its headwaters but relied for his information upon tales of *coureurs du bois* or other wilderness wanderers, or perhaps from Indian sources. Nevertheless, Vial was a major frontier figure and traveler, a literate man, intelligent, forceful, courageous and a supreme master of wilderness.

Noel M. Loomis, Abraham P. Nasatir, *Pedro Vial and the Roads to Santa Fe.* Norman, Univ. of Okla. Press, 1967; Herbert Eugene Bolton, *Texas in the Middle Eighteenth Century.* Austin, Univ. of Tex. Press, 1916, 1970.

Victor, Frances Fuller, historian (May 23, 1826-Nov. 14, 1902). B. in Rome township, New York she lived at Erie, Pennsylvania, and Wooster, Ohio, where her first writing was published — poetry. She moved subsequently to Monroeville, Ohio, and to New York. In 1850 she went to Michigan, married Jackson Barritt in 1853 and moved to Omaha. She left her husband shortly, however, and returned to New York. She wrote two dime novels for her brother-in-law, an editor of the House of Beadle, was divorced and married Henry Clay Victor, a brother of Orville Victor, her sister's husband. She and Henry, a navy engineer, sailed to California in 1863 where he joined his ship and Frances settled at San Francisco, continuing her writing. Henry left the navy within a year and they moved to Portland, Oregon. Mrs. Victor immediately became interested in Oregon history and began collecting material on it. She and her second husband separated in 1868. She had met onetime mountain man Joseph L. Meek and in 1870 published a book, *The River of the West*, largely a biography of Meek. Bret Harte published her first historical article, "Manifest Destiny in the West" in the *Overland Monthly* in August 1869. In 1872 she published *All Over Oregon and Washington*. In 1878 Mrs. Victor accepted a position with Hubert Howe Bancroft. She largely wrote his *History of Oregon*, 2 vols., *History of Washington, Idaho and Montana; History of Nevada, Colorado and Wyoming*, and parts of the seven-volume *History of California; California Inter Pocula; History of the Northwest Coast*, 2 vols., and *Chronicles of the Builders of the Commonwealth*, all of which are cited by Bancroft as being of his own authorship which they were not. She was one of the authorities consulted by Hiram Martin Chittenden for his *American Fur Trade in the Far West*. She was commissioned by the Oregon Secretary of State in 1892 to compile an Indian wars history; the definitive *Early Indian Wars of Oregon, Compiled from the Oregon Archives and Other Original Sources, with Muster Rolls*, appeared in 1894 and remains a much sought-after work. Mrs. Victor took an active part in the controversy over whether Marcus Whitman "saved" Oregon in the dispute with Britain, she taking the negative side. A biographical article by Hazel Emery Mills in *Arizona and the West* includes a selected bibliography of Frances Fuller Victor's historical works. Mrs. Victor died at Portland.

Hazel Emery Mills, "Frances Fuller Victor, 1826-1902." *Arizona and the West*, Vol. 12, No. 2 (Summer 1970), 111-14 (with portrait); *Reader's Encyclopedia of the American West*, this also by Hazel Mills.

Victorio, (Lucero, Bidu-ya, Beduiat), Mimbres chief Apache (c. 1825-Oct. 15, 1880). B. in the southwestern part of present New Mexico, Victorio almost certainly was a full-blood Apache despite legends that he was a Mexican

captive who developed into chieftainship. He became leader of the Chihennes band, which was incorporated into what whites called the Mimbres people of the Eastern Chiricahuas. Victorio first came to public attention when he put his "X" to an 1853 "provisional compact." He appears also to have been known subsequently as "Lucero," but under either name he became an outstandingly successful warrior-leader. Among the great raids he probably led was that in the summer of 1855 against Sonora and Chihuahua when the Apaches returned with large numbers of captives and stock. During that summer a considerable battle was fought with Mexicans at Namiquipa, Chihuahua, and Victorio may have participated, although Juh appears to have been the Indian hero of the day. Probably abstemious, he escaped the wave of arsenic poisoning that accompanied 1857 Mexican gifts of whiskey and rations to his people. Victorio, or Lucero, was no doubt involved in the scuffling that went on in the vicinity of Pinos Altos, New Mexico, coincident to the gold strike there, and it is reported that with Mangas and Cochise he took part in the Apache Pass battle with the California Column in July 1862; he must have been involved in the numerous skirmishes and depredations that occurred between whites and Indians with the Civil War. He and his people (Victorio at this time shared the Mimbres leadership with Loco), were settled near Cañada Alamosa, New Mexico (today's Monticello), within a few years after that war by Agent Charles E. Drew and his successors. In 1872 the Mimbres were moved to a reservation at Tularosa, New Mexico (today's Aragon), but after two years of mounting distaste for it as remote and cold, they were returned to Ojo Caliente, above Cañada Alamosa. Victorio in 1876 was described by Indian Inspector John Kimball as "short and stout, with a heavy, firm-set lower jaw, and an eye [of a] politician. He was dressed in a grimy calico shirt and coarse trousers, and was without paint, feathers or ornament of any kind." In another place he said the Indian was "burly," and a fine horseman. Kimball's description would fit a typical Apache as being not tall, but very strong and robust. The agent at that time was John M. Shaw, to be fired shortly upon Kimball's finding he was thoroughly intimidated by his charges to the point of regularly allowing them three times their normal rations, and covering by claiming he had three times the Indians to ration than were at the agency. The Indian concentration policy being in full flower, they were removed by Agent John Philip Clum in the spring of 1877 to San Carlos, Arizona, where, settled among their enemies, they soon became restive. On September 2, 1877, about 300 Mimbres led by Victorio and Loco broke out, eventually coming in at Fort Wingate, New Mexico, from where they were ultimately returned to Ojo Caliente to await a decision on their final settlement. The decision was to return them to San Carlos; Loco and some others were transferred, but Victorio and his most dedicated followers once more broke out, committing only a few depredations, and filtering eventually into the Mescalero Reservation near Fort Stanton, New Mexico, where they were permitted to remain and ration themselves. Mistaking a chance visit by officials as a plot to arrest and imprison them, however, Victorio, on August 21, 1879, bolted for the last time, leading his people to the Black Range west of the Rio Grande where he fought a number of successful skirmishes with troops, eventually plunging south across the border into Old Mexico, assisted in his exit by a Juh-led diversionary operation. Pursued even across the international line by Major Albert Payson Morrow, Victorio and Juh were caught up with northeast of Janos and, in a grim moonlight battle, turned back the soldiers. Victorio then moved east to the Candelaria Range, Chihuahua, where he ambushed two parties of Mexican militia, killing an estimated 30 of them with no losses to himself. By January 1880, he had returned to New Mexico. Skirmishes followed with troops in the Black Range and across the Rio Grande eastward in the San Andres mountains, ending indecisively or sometimes disastrously for the troops. In April Victorio was located again in the San Andres canyon called Hembrillo. A major effort failed to destroy him, Victorio escaping to the Black Range, while the troops went on to disarm the Mescaleros whom Department Commander Edward Hatch was convinced had been supporting the hostiles with arms and recruits. His action merely strengthened the Victorio band however, by frightening many Mescaleros from their reserve and into the hostile camp. Bands from Victorio's Black Moutain retreat raided as far as Arizona, but Victorio

himself remained elusive, until he was trappped in a canyon at the head of the Palomas River on the east face of the range by Henry K. Parker and several score of his Apache scouts, and suffered his initial outright defeat. Lack of ammunition and support kept Parker from terminating Victorio's career, and once more the elusive hostile gained Old Mexico, by late August being securely lodged anew in the Candelaria Range. From here he twice attempted to penetrate West Texas, perhaps seeking to reach the Mescalero Reservation from the south, in each case being turned back by troops, although never defeated outright and suffering little loss, even if the hostiles were becoming very wearied and worn down. Lieutenant Colonel Joaquin Terrazas, meanwhile, had been directed by his cousin, Chihuahua Governor Luis Terrazas, to hunt down the Indians and after a long campaign laid a successful ambush for them in the Tres Castillos upthrust in Chihuahua. Juan Mata Ortiz was his effective second in command. The Apaches, or their main body, were trapped finally, practically out of ammunition, and the warriors slain to the last man at a cost of three Mexican militia killed and 10 wounded. The Apaches lost 78 killed, 68 taken prisoner, all of them women and children, and two boy prisoners freed. Terrazas, promoted to full colonel for his feat, was said to have earned $17,250 for the scalps he had taken and $10,200 for his prisoners, though of course this had to be divided among his command. The death of Victorio was certified by Loco, at Tiffany's request at San Carlos, and in various other ways. Victorio, who has some claim to the title of America's greatest guerilla leader, understood strategy and tactics very well, although he had no teacher but experience. One veteran officer "considered Victorio the greatest Indian general who had ever appeared on the American continent." He was notably self-disciplined, married but once according to the record, probably abstained from alcohol, remained aloof from whites, and possessed many admirable qualities but was driven into hostility by obtuse policies of distant agencies and individuals. He earned the respect of those who fought him and retained that of his large band of followers even to the end. Victorio had one daughter and four sons, three of them killed in the Victorio campaigns. The youngest son, Istee, about 10 in 1880, survived because he was at San Carlos and did not go out when his father bolted in 1879. Istee went east with other prisoners of war, attended Carlisle Indian School, returned to Fort Sill and married, eventually moving to Mescalero where Istee died about 1946. Victorio's descendants, through marriages, brought into the families relationships with Mangas Coloradas and other great Apaches. His descendants live today at Mescalero, New Mexico, near Fort Sill, Oklahoma, at New York City, and elsewhere.

Dan L. Thrapp, *Victorio and the Mimbres Apaches.* Norman, Univ. of Okla. Press, 1974; Griswold; unsigned article apparently written by Kimball, "Victorio and His Young Men," *New York Times,* Nov. 28, 1880, p. 8.

Viele, Charles Delavan, army officer (Feb. 7, 1841-Oct. 6. 1916). B. at Albany, New York, he served in the Civil War as an officer of the 1st Infantry, taking part in the Vicksburg and Red River operations. Viele became a captain in 1868, joining the 10th Cavalry at the end of 1870. He served in Indian Territory, Arizona, Texas and Montana, participating in numerous Indian campaigns and much scouting activity, particularly on the South Plains against Cheyennes, Comaches and westward against Mescalero Apaches. He was with Grierson in the hard fight against Victorio's Apaches at Rattlesnake Springs, Texas, in August of 1880 and in 1885 participated in campaigns after the Geronimo hostiles. Viele commanded the 1st Cavalry in the Spanish American War, became colonel of the 4th Cavalry in 1899 and retired for disability in line of duty in 1900, being advanced to Brigadier General in 1904.

Heitman; William H. Leckie, *The Buffalo Soldiers.* Norman, Univ. of Okla. Press, 1967; Dan L. Thrapp, *Victorio and the Mimbres Apaches.* Norman, 1974; *Who Was Who.*

Vigo, Francis, patriot (1740-Mar. 22, 1836). B. at Mondovi, Sardinia, probably of Spanish parentage, he joined a Spanish regiment and served at Havana and New Orleans. He entered the fur trade, working gradually up the Mississippi until 1772, when he reached embryonic St. Louis, where Lieutenant Governor Francisco de Leyba became his silent partner. For several years he made long journeys on the Mississippi River, Missouri

River, and other northernwestern streams in pursuit of trade. He met George Rogers Clark at Kaskaskia, became his financial backer and, "without the semblance of selfish motive, he came forward and cast himself and his fortune into the scale of American freedom." Sent to Vincennes by Clark to help secure it for the Americans Vigo was captured by Hamilton's forces which had retaken the place, but argued that he was a simple Spanish trader. He spied out the situation about Vincennes, journeyed to St. Louis and then contacted Clark once more, urging a military effort in late winter when the British might be surprised. He assisted Clark in rebuilding his force and financing it, and on February 25, 1779, Vincennes was taken again by Americans. After the Revolution he continued to advance funds and perform sevices for the fledgling country for more than a generation, during which he was heavily engaged in the Indian trade. He obtained intelligence about British dispositions at the request of Anthony Wayne and others. Vigo became a friend of Wayne, William Henry Harrison and numerous other important figures. Harrison, acquainted with Vigo for 39 years, said he was "utterly incapable of misrepresentation, however great his interest." Vigo, ruined by sharpsters in his advanced age, died at Vincennes. His claim on the U.S. for funds advanced at various times, was finally paid 98 years after the deeds were performed. The conquest of the Old Northwest was "as much owing to the councils and services of Vigo as to the bravery and enterprise of Clark."

John T. Faris, *The Romance of Forgotten Men.* N.Y., Harper & Bros., 1928.

Villa, Pancho (Doroteo Arango), Mexican insurrectionist (June 6, 1878-July 20, 1923). B. of peasant stock on the Hacienda Rio Grande, northern Durango, he early became a bandit and, when opportunity afforded, a revolutionist of considerable talent; he was largely responsible for the triumph of Francisco Madero over Porfirio Diaz in the revolt of 1910-11. In the confused fighting that followed his reputation spread, although he was virtually uneducated and without formal training. He is best known north of the border for his raid against Columbus, New Mexico, of March 9, 1916, which led to the Pershing Punitive Expedition that drove deep into

Mexico. The reasons for the raid are obscure and disputed. As a result of it 125 were killed, including 17 Americans, eight soldiers, nine civilians. One week later John J. Pershing entered Mexico with 10,000 men, remaining nearly a year but without cornering the elusive Villa. Villa was assassinated at Parral; his grave was desecrated three years later and his head reportedly stolen, possibly for a rumored reward. A soldier of fortune, Emil L. Holmdahl, (see entry) was suspected of the theft. Villa's wife, Luz Corral, was living as late as 1968 at Chihuahua City. She was then 75.

Literature abundant; see John L. Sinclair, "When Villa Visited Columbus." *Westways,* Vol. 56, No. 10 (Oct. 1964), 4-7; *Los Angeles Times,* Feb. 19, 26, Mar. 26, 1967; Apr. 14, 1968.

Villagrá, Gaspar Pérez de, military officer (c. 1555-spring 1620). B. at Puebla de los Angeles, Spain, he left for New Spain (Mexico) probably around 1580; he was related to Francisco de Villagrá who achieved distinction fighting against the Araucanian Indians in Chile. When in 1596 Juan de Oñate was recruiting and organizing his force for the conquest and colonization of New Mexico, he appointed Villagrá procurador general (quartermaster) of the expedition, he being "a person of character and qualified for said post." On the same day he commissioned him a captain and appointed him to the council of war of the operation. Villagrá was described at the time as well-built, of medium height, with a gray beard and he may have been losing his hair since by 1604 he was bald. Villagrá, to his dismay, initially was ordered to remain in Mexico taking care of administrative details while Oñate proceeded to New Mexico, but he fulfilled his duty meticulously and, so long were the delays the expedition encountered he was after all a member of the first phase of the party to set out. Oñate and others held Villagrá in very high regard: his efforts assisted the army in leaving earlier than it otherwise would; with Vicente de Zaldívar he discovered the pass where today's El Paso is situated and which opened the way to New Mexico; he accompanied Oñate to the various pueblos visited, and Zaldívar to discover the salt lakes of so great interest to the Spaniards. Shortly after establishment of the colonial headquarters at San Juan-San Gabriel north of today's Santa Fe, Villagrá with a party was

sent in pursuit of deserters. They captured and executed two. He had further adventures, some of them harrowing. When Juan de Zaldívar was killed with some of his men at Acoma pueblo, Villagrá was sent with Zaldívar's brother, Vicente, to avenge the slayings, this leading to the celebrated battle of Acoma of which Villagrá is the principal narrator and primary source. Villagrá was of the heroic party of 11 who under cover of darkness gained a vantage point at one end of the pueblo which is situated on a sharp butte, difficult of access. Meanwhile Zaldívar with his principal command assaulted Acoma from the opposite direction. The distraction provided by the secondary attack from the rear is what turned the tide of battle in favor of the Spaniards. Villagrá's epic poem, *Historía de la Nueva Mexico* (1610) has been lavishly praised by historians as the primary source for a study of the Oñate expedition and "has the distinction of being the first published history of any American commonwealth," and in Bancroft's view "little, if at all, the less useful for being in verse." It has also been written that this work, "while of extreme value to the student . . . cannot be regarded as of poetical merit," but Villagrá was a soldier, not primarily an author as he himself concedes. Villagrá headed a party from New Mexico to Mexico City in 1599 to report on Oñate's discoveries and recruit more soldiers. By August 1600 the reinforcements were assembled at Santa Barbara, Nueva Vizcaya, and arrived at San Gabriel nearly two years after Villagrá had gone south. Villagrá was honored for his part in the conquest and became alcalde mayor of Guanacevi in the present Durango. He returned to Spain early in the 17th century and was with a fleet that went to Mexico in 1608 and returned in 1609, the year in which he completed his *Historía.* Four years later he still was in Spain, reporting he had served in an expedition under Lope Diáz de Almendariz, the nature of which is not reported. By 1613 the leisurely Spanish legal machinery had taken up allegations of misdeeds on the Oñate expedition into New Mexico 15 years earlier and Villagrá at Mexico City was called upon to answer charges that he had beheaded two deserters without trial and without permitting them to confess; that he had let the other two deserters go; that he had written the viceroy praising the resources of New Mexico when in fact that realm had very few indeed. Found guilty, Villagrá on May 13, 1614 was sentenced to banishment from New Mexico for six years, exile from the environs of Mexico City for two years, and to pay the costs of the trial. He returned to Spain in 1615 where he probably remained until February 20, 1620, when he was appointed alcalde mayor of Zapotitlan, Guatemala. While enroute to assume the post he died at sea. He left a widow and two children.

Gaspar Pérez de Villagrá, *A History of New Mexico*, trans. by Gilberto Espinosa, foreword by Frederick W. Hodge. Chicago, Rio Grande Press, 1962; Twitchell, *Leading Facts*.

Villantray, Sauvole de, army officer (d. c. 1701). A lieutenant under Iberville, some have claimed he was a brother of his commander, although Thwaites thought this unlikely. He was commandant at Fort Maurepas at Biloxi, Mississippi, where he died in August 1701, according to one report, or in April 1702, as another asserts.

Thwaites, JR, LXV, 167, 270n31.

Villard, Henry, journalist, promoter (Apr. 10, 1835-Nov. 12, 1900). B. in Bavaria he reached New York in 1853, quickly learned English and became a journalist. In 1859 he journeyed to Colorado and published a good guidebook for emigrants: *The Past and Present of the Pike's Peak Gold Regions* (1860). His subsequent activities were many, Villard becoming a major figure in the railroad and transportation development field, particularly in Oregon; he was associated with many prominent men, retained his interest in journalism, and died at Dobbs Ferry, New York.

DAB; EB; EA.

Villasur, Pedro de, explorer (d. Aug. 13, 1720). B. in Castile, he must have reached Mexico by the early 18th century. He became a sublieutenant at El Paso, alcalde and a war captain at Santa Bárbara, Nueva Vizcaya, and reached Santa Fe by 1719 where he became lieutenant governor under Valverde who left him in charge of New Mexico while the governor carried out a reconnaissance against Utes and Comanches to the northeast. In 1720 Villasur was given command of an expedition onto the plains, seeking French rumored to be among Indian tribes there. The Villasur

expedition left Santa Fe June 16, 1720, crossed the Sangre de Cristo Mountains and turned north, reaching the site of today's Pueblo, Colorado. They bore easterly down the Arkansas River to El Cuartelejo in the present Kiowa County, Colorado, near the confluence of Adobe and Mustang creeks. From there the expedition turned north to the Rio Jesús María (South Platte) and followed it downstream to its junction with the San Lorenzo, which Thomas believes to have been the North Platte. At a point near the confluence of the North and South Platte (some authorities believe the site to be at the junction of the Platte and Loup rivers) near the present North Platte, Nebraska, the Villasur party encountered a Panane (Pawnee) camp. Villasur sought to establish contact with the Indians, but results were discouraging. No evidence was found that Frenchmen were among the Pawnees, though some Indians carried what appeared to be French arms. The Indians retained the Pawnee interpreter Villasur sent as messenger into their village, and in other ways appeared hostile, so the Spanish withdrew to camp in tall grass on the south bank of the North Platte. August 13, shortly after daybreak the Spanish were attacked by Pawnees and perhaps some Otos. Villasur was killed early, one of 36 Spaniards and 11 Indian auxiliaries, of 60 taken along, were slain while an officer, a corporal, 11 soldiers, a white settler and 49 Indians escaped. Included among the dead were the priest-chaplain Juan Minguez, José Naranjo and Jean l'Archévèque. Valverde was tried six years later for having sent Villasur instead of himself leading the expedition; he was found guilty of negligence and lightly fined.

Alfred B. Thomas, *After Coronado*. Norman, Univ. of Okla. Press, 1969; Thomas, "The Massacre of the Villasur Expedition at the Forks of the Platte River August 12 (sic), 1720." *Nebr. Hist.,* Vol. VII (1924), No. 3 (Nov. 1925), 66-81; Oakah L. Jones Jr., *Pueblo Warriors & Spanish Conquest.* Norman, 1966.

Ville(s), Jean Marie de, Jesuit missionary (Sept. 8, 1672-June 15, 1720). B. at Auxerre, France, he became a Jesuit, reached Quebec in 1706 and the next year was sent to Illinois; upon the death of Mermet in 1716 he became superior of the Jesuit mission in that region. Early in 1719 he went down the Mississippi to

Mobile to seek from Bienville restrictions upon French traders and *coureurs de bois* in Illinois as well as measures against English traders from the Atlantic seaboard. While in Louisiana he accompanied the French forces as chaplain during their attack on Spanish Pensacola, Florida. Become seriously ill, he wintered at Natchez, Mississippi, where he died, possibly of dysentery.

Thwaites, JR, LXVI, 341-42n25, LXXI, 162.

Villiers, Balthazard de, military officer (d. 1782). In 1778 Captain Villiers said that in 20 years he had commanded virtually every post in French Louisiana including Natchitoches. In 1778, since he was forever in debt, he asked Louisiana Governor Bernardo de Galvez to permit him to remain at that "most disagreeable post in the universe," Arkansas Post, so he could become solvent. In 1780 he captured Concordia, a Spanish post across the Mississippi from Natchez, from the British. Two years later he fell ill and went to New Orleans where died following an operation.

Noel M. Loomis, Abraham P. Nasatir, *Pedro Vial and the Roads to Santa Fe.* Norman, Univ. of Okla. Press, 1967.

Vilott, Fletcher, scout (Nov. 3, 1831-Feb. 15, 1912). B. in Indiana, Vilott was one of Forsyth's scouts at the affair at Beecher Island in September 1868. In the early 1870's he settled in Jewell County, Kansas, where he married in 1873 and fathered eight children, six surviving him. Vilott suffered a stroke and was bed-ridden the last few years of his life.

Simon E. Matson, ed., *The Battle of Beecher Island.* Wray, Colo., Beecher Island Battle Meml. Assn., 1960; information from Mrs. Jessie Chandler, Vilott's daughter, Apr. 6, 1977.

Vincennes, Francois Margane (Morgan) Bissot de, army officer (June 17, 1700-Mar. 25, 1736). B. at Montreal, he became an officer of the colonial regular troops. He had accompanied his father at 13 on a visit to the Miami Indians of present southern Michigan and Indiana, and by 1718 was assigned to a French post on the upper Wabash River. In 1730 Vincennes moved down the Wabash and the next summer began construction of a post 80 miles up the Wabash from its confluence with the Ohio River, approximately at the site of today's Vincennes, Indiana. Vincennes' situation was complicated by too few troops

to control the many Indians in the vicinity, and growing pressure by British traders from the east. In 1736 he joined forces with Pierre d'Artaguiette from Fort de Chartres on the Mississippi in an expedition against the Chickasaw Indians. On March 25 a Chickasaw complex of villages was attacked; after initial success the Indians destroyed the attacking force and about 20 French officers and men were captured, including Vincennes. Most of them were burned at the stake the same day, near the present Fulton, Mississippi. Vincennes was survived by his half-Indian wife, daughter of a settler of Kaskaskia, by whom he had two daughters. "His memory... was long revered by the Miamis."

Thwaites, JR, LXX, 316-17n40; DCB, II.

Vincent, Charles Thomas, bear hunter (fl. 1866-1888). Considered the "all-time champion bear hunter of San Gabriel Canyon" in the San Gabriel Mountains of southern California, he discovered the Big Horn Mine (probably gold mine) on the East Fork of the San Gabriel River in 1866. He was a noted hunter whose outstanding feat was the 1888 slaying of three grizzlies within a few minutes. Two of the charging animals he shot at close range; the third he killed with a knife just as it reached him. Grizzlies were extinct in the canyon by 1903.

Los Angeles Times, Oct. 6, 1888; *Mt. San Antonio Historian,* Vol. XIV, No. 2 (Spring 1978), 64.

Virgin Mary: *see* Mary Brown

Vislavki, Deza, soldier (d. June 8, 1885). A private of C Troop, 4th Cavalry, he was one of a detachment guarding an important supply train in Guadalupe Canyon between Arizona and New Mexico. It was struck by an Apache raiding party led by Chihuahua, and Vislavki and two other soldiers were killed, the Indians coming across loot including 10,000 rounds of ammunition and a plentiful supply of rations, a notable boost for them in war against the whites.

"The Reluctant Corporal: The Autobiography of William Bladen Jett," ed. by Henry P. Walker. *Jour. of Ariz. Hist.,* Vol. XII, No. 1 (Spring 1971), 33, 48n45.

Vitry, Pierre de, Jesuit missionary (May 2, 1700-Apr. 5, 1749). B. in France he became a

Jesuit and arrived at Louisiana in 1732, spending within that mission the remainder of his life. He was superior of the mission from 1739 until his death at New Orleans.

Thwaites, JR, LXIX, 300n50.

Vivier, Louis, Jesuit missionary (Oct. 6, 1714-Oct. 2, 1756). B. at Issoudun, France, he became a Jesuit and arrived in Canada in 1749, being sent at once to the Illinois mission. He was stationed at Kaskaskia for four years and about 1753 was transferred to Vincennes, where he died.

Thwaites, JR, LXIX, 288n16, LXXI, 177.

Vizcaino, Sebastian, navigator, trader (c. 1550-c. 1629). B. in Spain he took part in expeditions to the Philippines from 1586-1589, being with the Manila galleon, *Santa Ana,* plundered by Cavendish. He explored and traded with Baja California from 1596-97, establishing a short-lived colony at La Paz, his men exploring many leagues up the eastern coast of the peninsula and locating promising pearl waters, though an Indian attack and other difficulties caused termination of that enterprise. The Count of Monterrey, viceroy, found in him "more ability than he had expected in a mere merchant," and by royal cedula he was commissioned captain-general to lead an expedition up the western coast of North America, seeking a harbor where Manila galleons might be recruited, and the elusive Strait of Anian, or Northwest Passage. With two ships and a frigate, he left Acapulco May 5, 1602, with difficulty made Magdalena Bay. He left there September 9, reaching and renaming San Diego Bay in November and Santa Catalina Island in December. On the 15th he discovered Monterey Bay which Vizcaino praised so lavishly it was relocated certainly only with difficulty by later arrivals. On January 9, 1603, the fleet anchored in Drake's Bay. The vessels were repeatedly separated by terrible weather, one reaching Cape Blanco in latitude 43 degrees, but its discoveries are difficult to locate positively. The Vizcaino expedition, like that of Cabrillo earlier, missed San Francisco Bay. Scurvy caused great havoc and the expedition returned to Mexico in grave distress, having accomplished little more than Cabrillo, except to rename many of his discoveries. Not for a century and one-half would his route be seriously retraced by explorers, and the

expedition's misapprehension that the longed-for Anian Strait entered the Pacific about Latitude 43 degrees persisted for a long time, influencing others. Vizcaino sought, in Mexico and Spain, to gain assent for a settlement to serve the Manila galleons in Monterey Bay. He sailed from Acapulco in March 1611, for Japan, a disastrous trip for him. He fought Dutch pirates in 1616. Vizcaino died probably in New Spain.

EA; Bancroft, *North Mexican States & Texas; Spanish Exploration in the Southwest 1542-1706,* ed. by Herbert Eugene Bolton. N.Y., Barnes & Noble, 1963.

Vizcarra, José Antonio, army officer, governor (d. c. 1833). Probably b. in Durango, Mexico, for his parents lived at Cuencame (although Twitchell says he was b. in Chihuahua), Vizcarra early entered the army. In 1820 David Meriwether, then a trader but later governor of New Mexico, was captured on the Plains while with Pawnees by Mexicans possibly under command of Vizcarra. He was taken prisoner to Santa Fe and later released. By 1822 Vizcarra was lieutenant colonel and commanding troops in New Mexico, having arrived during the Spanish period and remained under Mexican rule. He was its first governor after its independence from Spain, beginning in 1822. At times before 1839 New Mexico had a single individual both as military and political chief or "governor" while at other times the offices were separate. Thus in addition to military governor, Vizcarra was political chief of state until June 1823 when he was succeeded in the latter position by Francisco Javier Chavez, who shortly was succeeded by Bartólome Baca, but Vizcarra continued as military chief until 1825. He was political and military governor again briefly in 1828. Vizcarra was famed as a soldier and Indian fighter. Twitchell said he was of "commanding appearance, dignified, with perfect manners. His horsemanship, extraordinary (even) for a Spaniard," was demonstrated before Philip St. George Cooke and other officers; he also was an excellent roper and adept with bow and arrow. The treacherous murder of Navaho chiefs and warriors in 1822 at Cochiti Pueblo, New Mexico, probably occurred during the administration of Governor Melgares, rather than Vizcarra; it led to severe Navaho reprisals. Vizcarra presented a four-point ultimatum to the Navahos in council at Laguna Pueblo in February 1823. The "agreement" reached served only to widen the gap between the races. In June 1823 Vizcarra left Santa Fe leading a 1,500-man 74-day punitive expedition into Navaho country. He went as far as Canyon de Chelly and three Hopi Mesas to the west, skirmishing now and then with Navahos or even Utes, and returned to Santa Fe August 31, reporting 33 Navahos including eight women, killed, 30 others captured and livestock taken for five Mexicans reported killed, four dead of sickness and 13 more wounded. April 14, 1824, Vizcarra married a widow at Santa Fe, becoming foster father of Ramón Ortiz, later a priest who won fame for his kindnesses to prisoners from the Texan-Santa Fe expedition of 1841. Vizcarra undertook another, and not so lengthy expedition against persistent Navaho raiders in the early spring of 1825, returning in April with 22 captives and the report that 14 Indians had been killed. He suggested that the captives be sent to Vera Cruz, believing that if the Navahos saw them "disappear, it may serve to stimulate (peace) and they will do no more evil." He was succeeded as military governor by Antonio Narbona in 1825, Vizcarra becoming assistant inspector general of troops in New Mexico. As such he commanded forces patrolling the Santa Fe Trail from the Arkansas River crossing to Santa Fe; his relationships with Americans patrolling eastern reaches of the Trail were good. In 1829 his command had a fight with Gros Ventres on the Cimarron. By surprise the northern Indians fired on the Mexicans then in camp and Vizcarra narrowly escaped with his life. A Mexican captive and two or three privates were killed. In 1830 Vizcarra was promoted to Inspector General for New Mexico which office he held until his death from cholera at Santa Fe.

Twitchell, *Leading Facts,* II; Josiah Gregg, *Commerce of the Prairies.* Norman, Univ. of Okla. Press, 1954; Frank McNitt, *Navajo Wars.* Albuquerque, Univ. of New Mex. Press, 1972; Fidelia Miller Puckett, "Ramón Ortiz: Priest and Patriot." *New Mex. Hist. Rev.,* Vol. XXV, No. 4 (Oct. 1950) 265-95; John P. Wilson, *Military Campaigns in the Navajo Country.* Santa Fe, Mus. of New Mex., Research Records 5, 1967; *NMHR* Vol. II, No. 2 (Apr. 1927) 190 n.

Volkmar, William Jefferson, army officer (June 29, 1847-Mar. 4, 1901). B. in Pennsylvania, he enlisted and served as sergeant in the 33rd Pennsylvania Infantry during the Confederate invasion of his state, June 19 to August 4, 1863; his captain and colonel recommended him for gallant conduct during the Gettysburg campaign to West Point, from which he was graduated in 1868, being commissioned in the 5th Cavalry and reporting to Fort Harker, Kansas. He was engaged in a fight with Cheyenne Indians near Fort Larned almost at once, then served with the Canadian River expedition. In May 1869, he took part in fights with Sioux and Cheyennes at Beaver and Spring creeks, narrowly escaping death in the latter and being recommended for a brevet. Volkmar was on the Republican River expedition, participated in the decisive victory over the Cheyennes at Summit Springs being recommended for another brevet, and in several subsequent skirmishes. He reached Arizona in 1872, commanded the post at Date Creek briefly and returned to the Middle West where he performed staff functions and other duties (he often was an engineers officer) until 1879 when as a captain he joined his company at Fort D.A. Russell, Wyoming. He was to take part with Major Thornburgh in an operation against the Utes, but was recalled to Chicago where he served as aide to Pope, then to Sheridan until 1885; by 1898 he had become a colonel and he retired in 1900.

Price, *Fifth Cavalry;* Heitman.

Vollum, Edward P., physician, surgeon (Sept. 11, 1827-May 31, 1902). B. at New York he was commissioned an assistant surgeon in the army May 31, 1853, and assigned to Fort Belknap, on the Red Fork of the Brazos River, Texas. At the request of the Indian department he became medical attendant to three tribes of Comanches under Chiefs Katumse, Buffalo Hump and Sanaco as a pacific measure; he also attended to medical needs at Fort Phantom Hill on Clear Fork of the Brazos as well as those at Belknap. He was accosted twice by hostile Comanches and robbed, then released because of his profession. He returned to New York on leave in 1856 and in a yellow fever emergency was assigned to Fort Hamilton until the disease subsided. On September 1, 1856, he was ordered to Fort Umpqua, Oregon, as post surgeon. Enroute he*was shipwrecked and rescued by Coast Indians. About 1860 he was ordered to Fort Crook, Shasta County, California, but in October 1861 accompanied elements of the 1st Dragoons and 4th and 6th Infantry by way of Panama to New York. During the Civil War he served in eastern theaters. July 5, 1870, he was assigned to Camp Douglas, Utah, as post surgeon, went east in 1876 and January 30, 1883, was commissioned Surgeon with rank of lieutenant colonel, becoming a colonel in 1889. He retired September 11, 1891.

Heitman; Powell.

Volsay, Pierre Francois de, army officer (c. 1730-Sept. 28, 1795). B. at Paris, he entered the army and came to Canada at some unascertained date. As a captain he was stationed at Fort de Chartres on the Mississippi River above Kaskaskia, where he married the daughter of the last French governor of Illinois. The Jesuit Watrin recounts how he conducted a party including English captives of the Indians, slaves and others down the Mississippi to deliver them safely to New Orleans. Upon the cession of his fort to the English in 1765 he moved to St. Louis, under the Spanish flag, where he died.

Thwaites, JR, LXX, 318n47.

Von Schmidt, Harold, artist (May 19, 1893-June 3, 1982). B. at Alameda, California he studied at San Francisco Art Institute and under such noted artists as Maynard Dixon and Harvey Dunn. He served as an artist-illustrator in both World Wars and his work appeared in countless books and popular magazines. His paintings are held by a variety of museums although not more than a few hundred are extant because Von Schmidt routinely destroyed those he did not regard as his best work after appearance in publications. He was an illustrator who worked in oil and his subjects ran the gamut from sailing days of fighting ships to western themes. "He was the grand-daddy of the present day Western art," his son, Eric, said following the artist's death, noting that one of his works had brought $50,000 and another $40,000 shortly before his passing. Ill health forced Von Schmidt to give up painting around 1960. He died at

Westport, Connecticut, where he had lived in retirement.

New York Times, June 6, 1982.

Von Schrader, Frederick, army officer (Feb. 12, 1851-Apr. 7, 1916). B. in Illinois, he was a great grandson of Brigadier General Daniel Bissell of the War of 1812 and was educated at the University of Michigan, being commissioned a second lieutenant of the 12th Infantry in 1873. Von Schrader served at Fort Hall, Idaho; in California; at Camp McDermit, Nevada, and then was assigned to Arizona, having taken part in various Indian campaigns in Idaho, Nevada, Oregon and Washington. He remained in Arizona until 1882, commanding Indian scouts from 1879 until 1882. June 25, 1879, he caught up with hostiles supposedly guilty of killing Frank Kearney near Baker's Springs and killed six, capturing a woman. In April 1880 he took Apache scouts to put down unrest on the Papago Reservation in Arizona, then moved them by rail (the first time troops were carried by train in Arizona) eastward to join Carr's abortive drive against Victorio. Following the Cibecue affair in Arizona, Von Schrader with Dan O'Leary as chief and Hualapais Indian scouts joined William Redwood Price for a long scout southward to the Mexican Line. They found no hostiles but determined that most had fled into Mexico and Von Schrader was complimented by Price in General Order 1, January 3, 1881, for rendering "valuable assistance" during the operation. Von Schrader later was trained as a Signal Corps officer and placed in charge of U.S. military telegraph lines in Arizona and New Mexico. He became a first lieutenant in 1878, captain in 1893 and major in the Quartermaster Department in 1901. He retired April 13, 1910 as a colonel, and died at San Francisco.

Powell; Dan L. Thrapp, *General Crook and the Sierra Madre Adventure.* Norman, Univ. of Okla. Press, 1972; Heitman; 1916 *Army Register.*

Voorhees, Luke, frontiersman (1835-Jan. 16, 1925). B. at Belvidere, New Jersey, he moved with his parents to Michigan at 2 and was educated at Pontiac. In 1857 he headed west, hunted buffalo on the Kansas plains, went to Colorado with the Pike's Peak gold rush, mined until 1863 when he went to Alder Gulch (Virginia City), Montana, and prospected north into Saskatchewan and in British Columbia where it is said he discovered the Kootenai strike in 1863-64. He returned after a few months to Virginia City, Montana, then mined in Utah and Nevada; he is said to have attended the Golden Spike ceremony completing the trans-west railroad May 10, 1869. Voorhees in 1871 went to Texas, bought a herd of longhorns and trailed them to a Utah ranch. About 1876 he became superintendent of the Cheyenne and Black Hills stage line, continuing in that occupation until 1883 when he embarked on a cattle ranching enterprise near Raw Hide Buttes, south of Lusk, Wyoming. He suffered heavy losses, and returned to mining. Voorhees became territorial treasurer of Wyoming and served the U.S. Land Office at Cheyenne. He died at 90, "a pioneer in every sense of the word." He was married.

Agnes Wright Spring, *The Cheyenne and Black Hills Stage and Express Routes.* Lincoln, Univ. of Nebr. Press, 1965

Vroom, Peter Dumont, army officer (Apr. 18, 1842-Mar. 19, 1926). Son and namesake of a New Jersey governor (1791-1873), Vroom was b. at Trenton, New Jersey, commissioned in the 1st New Jersey Infantry August 13, 1862,

became major of the 2nd New Jersey Cavalry in 1863, received two brevets during the Civil War and afterward joined the 3rd Cavalry with which he served until 1889. He had an important role in Crook's fight on the Rosebud, June 16, 1876; his company, L of the 3rd, was ordered to occupy a ridge far in advance, was surrounded by hostiles and became the worst cut up of any unit in the engagement, losing more men than any other. Vroom also participated in Apache operations in 1883. As a major he became inspector general in 1889 and was promoted steadily to Brigadier General April 11, 1903, retiring next day. Finerty described him in 1876: "A magnificent specimen of the human race, tall, well-built and good-looking. He has since grown much stouter, the result, doubtless, of the absence of Indian campaigns." He wrote also that Vroom was one of the "literary men of the outfit," whose small paperback library was constantly circulating around the encampment. Vroom's home in retirement was at Trenton.

Who Was Who; Heitman; J.W. Vaughn, *With Crook at the Rosebud.* Harrisburg, Pa., Stackpole Co., 1956; John F. Finerty, *War-Path and Bivouac.* Chicago, Lakeside Press, 1955.

W

Wabokieshiek (White Cloud, the Prophet), Sauk and Fox medicine man, leader (c. 1794-c. 1841). A friend and adviser to Black Hawk, celebrated war chief of the tribe(s), Wabokieshiek presided over the "Prophet's Village," on the Rock River, Illinois, about 35 miles above its mouth. Half Winnebago and half Sauk, he was well acquainted in both tribes and was considered by some cruel and aloof toward Anglo Americans. By his prophesy of substantial assistance from somewhere he inclined Black Hawk toward war after 1830. Following the Indian debacle at Bad Axe, Wisconsin, the Prophet and Black Hawk were captured by Winnebagos and delivered to Agent Joseph Montfort Street August 27, 1832. They were taken to Jefferson Barracks, Missouri, where the Prophet's portrait was painted by Catlin (it is now at the National Museum); another portrait by R.M. Sully, made while the Prophet was held at Fortress Monroe, Virginia, is reproduced in HAI, ii, 886. In April 1833, the leaders of the tribe, including Black Hawk and Wabokieshiek were taken to Washington, D.C., where they met President Jackson. "Having lost his prestige as a prophet, Wabokieshiek lived in obscurity among the Sauk in Iowa until their removal to Kansas, and died among the Winnebago." He was described by one student as "gloomy," and "a man of ardor and cunning...who stood more than six feet tall and was inclined...to be rather fat. His face was full and his eyes set deep, and most of the time he frowned," He was said to wear his hair long and to have had a black mustache, and by many white contemporaries was considered "a scoundrel..." Such was the opinion of his enemies, but Major Thomas Forsyth, long the agent of the Sauks, recited many good and generous qualities of the Prophet, and this Indian assuredly saved the life of Colonel Henry Gratiot, who had entered the hostile camp to persuade the Indians to return to Iowa and was threatened with death by incensed tribesmen. Wabokieshiek listened to Gratiot, guarded him in the Prophet's house, and subsequently permitted him to "escape."

HAI; *Ma-Ka-Tai-Me-She-Kia-Kiak: Black Hawk: An Autobiography,* ed. by Donald Jackson. Urbana, Univ. of Ill. Press, 1956; William T. Hagan, *The Sac and Fox Indians.* Norman, Univ. of Okla. Press, 1958.

Wade, James Franklin, army officer (Apr. 14, 1843-Aug. 23, 1921). B. at Jefferson, Ohio he was commissioned a first lieutenant in the 6th Cavalry in 1861 and emerged from the Civil War a colonel and brevet Brigadier General. In 1866 he was commissioned a captain in the 6th Cavalry and later that year a major in the 9th Cavalry with which he saw much frontier service in the southwest. Wade commanded the military escort that made possible John Clum's evacuation of the Mimbres Apaches from Ojo Caliente, New Mexico, to San Carlos, Arizona, in 1877, and later that year was the commanding officer at Fort Bayard, southwestern New Mexico. He was active in trying to corral the Mimbres who with Victorio soon fled the Arizona reserve in late 1877; Wade scouted the Mogollon and Black ranges so actively as to force the hostiles northward to surrender to Fort Wingate authorities. He became lieutenant colonel of the 10th Cavalry in 1879 and was in command at Fort Apache, Arizona, in September 1886 when the Chiricahua Apaches were removed to Florida, Wade telling them to assemble disarmed because they were going to visit the President at Washington where no firearms were allowed; thus the deplorable operation went off peacefully. Wade became colonel of the 5th Cavalry in 1887 and a Brigadier General a decade later, becoming a Major General in 1903 and retiring in 1907. He commanded the Cuban Evacuation Commission in 1898, the Division of the Philippines in 1903-1904, and the Atlantic Division, 1904-1907. He retired in 1907 to his home at Jefferson, Ohio.

Heitman; Powell; Dan L. Thrapp, *Victorio and the Mimbres Apaches.* Norman, Univ. of Okla. Press, 1974; Odie B. Faulk, *The Geronimo Campaign.* N.Y., Oxford Univ. Press, 1969; *Who Was Who.*

Wadsworth, Samuel, militia officer (d. Apr. 20, 1676). Wadsworth came with his father from England to Duxbury, Massachusetts in 1632 and moved to Milton, Massachusetts, in 1656. He married and fathered children. When King Philip's War broke out in mid-1675 Wadsworth became a militia captain. With his men he reached Wickford, Rhode Island, to reinforce militia elements January 10, 1676 and then was placed in command at Marlborough, Massachusetts. In early February he heard of an impending attack upon Lancaster, Massachusetts, and forced his way into the town which was under fierce assault, helping at the last moment to turn the tide and forcing the Indians to withdraw. The last week in February he was ordered to the southern shore of Boston Bay to help clear the area of hostiles. April 20 Indians heavily attacked Sudbury, 17 miles west of Boston, and Wadsworth, hurrying in from Marlborough, contacted an enemy force about a mile west of town but was led by it into an ambush and withdrew to nearby Green Hill, to a better defense position. When Indians fired dry grass and brush the choking smoke caused the Wadsworth force to rush down from the hill in a disorganized mob whereupon the Indians fell on them "like so many tigers" and upwards of 30 were killed, including Wadsworth and Captain Samuel Brocklebank.

George Madison Bodge, *Soldiers in King Philip's War,* 3rd ed., Boston, p.p., 1906; Leach, *Flintrock; Narratives of the Indian Wars 1675-1699,* ed. by Charles H. Lincoln. N.Y., Barnes & Noble, 1959.

Waggoner, Peter, Indian captive (c. 1786-Feb. 26, 1879). B. in the Buckhannon country of western Virginia, he was captured when 6 by Shawnees in 1792, taken to the Scioto River, Ohio, area and remained with them 20 years, becoming an Indian in all but ancestry. He was cajoled into returning home, leaving (temporarily, he thought) his Indian wife and children, but never was allowed to return to Ohio. He always regretted having left the Indians, although he married a white woman in 1814 and fathered a family. "He never lost his Indian mode of speech. His words were few, but expressive..., he was simple, honest and upright," becoming a renowned hunter. He died on Hacker's Creek, Lewis County, West Virginia, and was buried near Jane Lew. Two sisters captured with him remained with the Indians for varying periods, both eventually returning to Lewis County.

Lucullus V. McWhorter, *The Border Settlers of Northwestern Virginia.* Hamilton, O., Republican Pub. Co., 1915.

Waggoner, Tom, rancher (c. 1856-June 4, 1891). A German horse breaker and rancher from Nebraska City, Nebraska, Waggoner established a prosperous horse ranch in Weston County, northeastern Wyoming. He was married April 11, 1891, to Mrs. Rosa Chuler, his common-law wife who earlier had given birth to his infant son and a daughter. Waggoner was taken from his home June 4, 1891, for alleged rustling by three disguised men claiming to have a warrant for him. Eleven days later his body was found where he had been lynched about two miles north of his cabin. Bill Walker alleged that Waggoner's slayers had been "Tom Smith," a former deputy marshal; "Schock" Hall and Fred W. Coates. However Roger Hawthorne, whose research on the crime seems persuasive, places the blame not on the Texas Tom Smith of Johnson County War fame who was not in Wyoming at the time, but on Thomas G. Smith, also a former U.S. deputy marshal; Joe Elliott, deputy sheriff of Weston County and detective of the Wyoming Stock Growers Association, and George Burns, a horse thief nominally under arrest and in Elliott's custody. A coroner's jury found that Waggoner had been lynched by parties unknown and no one was charged with the killing. Waggoner left about 1,000 horses in his pastures and his estate was estimated variously at from $17,000 to $70,000. Coates, one of the inquest jurors, was named administrator of the estate.

D.F. Baber, as told by Bill Walker, *The Longest Rope: The Truth About the Johnson County War.* Caldwell, Ida., Caxton Printers, 1959; Robert Hawthorne, "Conflict and Conspiracy:... The Lynching of Tom Waggoner." *True West,* Vol. 31, No. 6 (June 1984), 12-17; Helena Huntington Smith, *The War on Powder River.* N.Y., McGraw-Hill Book Co., 1966; Western History Research Center, Univ. of Wyo.

Wagner, Henry Raup, historian (Sept. 27, 1862-Mar. 27, 1957). B. at Philadelphia he was graduated from Yale in 1884 and from Yale Law School in 1886, engaging in business in the west, particularily mining. He went to

Mexico in 1892, and for several years thereafter and in 1898 as ore buyer for the Guggenheim interests went to Chile for four years, later going to London where he became infected with the book-collecting fever. He built up a collection on Irish economics, later presented to Yale, and gathered extensively in the fields of mining, metallurgy and Chilean and Peruvian history. Wagner spent the next decade in Mexico and in addition to pursuing his business interests collected books and manuscripts on Spanish and Mexican history, pursuing his Latin American enthusiasms with a further two years at Santiago, Chile. In 1921, after his 59th birthday, he determined to retire from business and devote himself to study and the writing of historical works. He sold his Mexican collection to Yale in 1915, his Midwestern books, including those on Texas, in 1919, donated his Irish collection to Yale in 1936, sold his California collection to the Huntington Library of San Marino, California, in 1922 and after that devoted himself to research and writing rather than the mere collecting of books. He wrote prolifically for historical journals while among his books were *The Plains and Rockies; A Contribution to the Bibliography of Original Narratives of Travel and Adventure, 1800-1865* (1921); *The Spanish Southwest: 1542-1794: an Annotated Bibliography* (1924); *Sir Francis Drake's Voyage Around the World* (1926); *The Portolan Atlases of American Interest in the Henry E. Huntington Library and Art Gallery* (1929); *Spanish Voyages to the Northwest Coast of America in the Sixteenth Century* (1929); *Apocryphal Voyages to the Northwest Coast of America* (1931); *Spanish Explorations in the Strait of Juan de Fuca* (1933); *The Fages-Serra Letters* (1936); *Henry R. Wagner's The Plains and Rockies: A Bibliography* ... (1937); *The Cartography of the Northwest Coast of America to the Year 1900*, 2 vols. (1937); *The Spanish Southwest, 1542-1794: An Annotated Bibliography*, 2 vols. (1937); *Juan Rodriguez Cabrillo* ... (1941); *The Discovery of Yucatan by Francisco Hernández de Córdoba* (1942), and with Helen Rand Parish, *The Life and Writings of Bartólome de las Casas* (1967).

Wagner and Parish, *The Life and Writings of Bartólome de las Casas,* with preliminary notes. Albuquerque, Univ. of New Mex. Press, 1967;

Wagner, *Bullion to Books.* Los Angeles, Zamorano Club, 1942.

Wagner, John (Dutch John) desperado (d. Jan. 11, 1864). B. in Germany, he spoke English with a thick accent, hence his nickname. He said he had come from the Pacific slope into southwestern Montana to trade for horses, then fell under the malignant influence of Henry Plummer and joined his band of desperados, a man purposeful and relentless (Langford wrote however that he "had been a murderer and highwayman for years" before his vigilante execution). In the fall of 1863 Wagner and been wounded in an inept attempt with Stephen Marshland to rob a Milton S. Moody train of wagons and pack animals bound from Bannack, Montana, to Salt Lake City. Dutch John was captured single-handedly by the intrepid Neil Howie and returned to Bannack. Here he was guarded by John Fetherstun and on one occasion rejected an opportunity to escape custody. The vigilantes in discussing his case might have voted for his banishment had that been possible under the rules of the organization; instead his execution was decreed. He wrote to his mother in Germany, telling her the sentence was just, and was hanged, dying bravely. This occurred at Bannack, where he was buried.

Langford; Dimsdale; Birney.

Wagner, John, cowboy (c. 1850-Apr. 10, 1877). He was thrown from a horse, perhaps rendered "partially insane," as a result sometime in the 1870s. On April 9, 1877, Marshal Ed Masterson attempted to disarm him at Dodge City, Kansas, while Wagner was drunk; in the resulting fight both Masterson and Wagner were wounded mortally and another man seriously.

Nyle H. Miller, Joseph W. Snell, *Great Gunfighters of the Kansas Cowtowns, 1867-1886.* Lincoln, Univ. of Nebr. Press, 1967.

Waightman or Weight(s)man, George (Red Buck), desperado (d. Mar. 4, 1896). Believed to be from Kansas, he was a notorious horsethief, regarded by some law officers as the most dangerous of the Doolin gang. He killed at least four men and reportedly would kill for $50 a head. He was powerful, heavy-set, weighing 180 pounds and 5 feet, 10 inches tall, wore a full mustache; his hair was deep red. He was arrested in 1889 by Heck Thomas, sentenced to nine years in 1890 for mule theft, but escaped from a train near Lebanon, Missouri. He made his way back to the Cherokee Strip where he hid out until Doolin formed his gang. He operated with Doolin, escaped in the big gun fight at Ingalls, September 1, 1893, and took part in a train robbery at Dover, Oklahoma, April 3, 1895. In January 1895, he reportedly attempted to shoot Bill Tilghman, lawman, in the back, but was forcibly dissuaded by Doolin. It was probably Waightman who killed a "harmless old preacher" and was criticized even by the outlaw element for it. Waightman was killed near Arapaho, Oklahoma, by peace officers including Chris Madsen.

Bailey C. Hanes, *Bill Doolin, Outlaw O.T.* Norman, Univ. of Okla. Press, 1968; Richard S. Graves, *Oklahoma Outlaws.* Fort Davis, Tex., Frontier Press, 1968.

Walden, Elisha, frontiersman (c. 1734-post 1800). A "rough frontiersman and a noted hunter," Walden in 1761 penetrated into Powell's Valley, southwestern Virginia, named Walden's Mountain and Walden's Creek, penetrated Cumberland Gap to the Cumberland River and went on to the Laurel Mountains where some Indians turned the party back. In 1774 he lived near today's Martinsville, Henry County, Virginia. Later he settled on the Holston River about 18 miles above Knoxville, Tennessee, where he was living in 1796. A few years afterward he migrated to Missouri "where he lived hunting up to an extreme old age."

Alexander Withers, *Chronicles of Border Warfare,* ed. by Reuben Gold Thwaites. Parsons, W. Va., McClain Printing Co., 1970, incorporating information from Lyman C. Draper, 59-60n.

Walderne, Richard: *see* Richard Waldron

Waldron, (Walderne), Richard, pioneer (c. Jan. 5, 1615-June 27-28, 1689). B. at Alchester, Warwickshire, England, he reached New England in 1640, settling at Dover, New Hampshire, and acquired lands at Cocheco (now part of Dover) and Penacook, now Concord, 40 miles to the west. He engaged in lumbering and Indian trade, holding public office and served often as representative to the General Court at Boston, sometimes as speaker. He could be harsh, as when he sentenced at Dover three Quaker women to be whipped as vagabonds at the tail of a cart through 13 towns. As major of county militia his service was uneventful except once when he managed to take by treachery some 200 hostile Indians and hanged six or seven of them, selling most of the rest into slavery. This incident was remembered grimly by tribes about and was the ultimate cause of Waldron's death. In 1680 when a separate provincial government was established for New Hampshire Waldron was appointed to the president's council and for a time served as acting president. Despite his prominence he was not always successful at court and in one case lost much real estate and was fined for "mutinous and seditious words," an easy thing to fall afoul of in the New England of his day. In King William's War (1688-97) the Abenaki tribes, stirred up by the French, savagely attacked the frontier outposts including those in New Hampshire. June 27, 1689, they planned to attack Cocheco. Indians invaded the town and entered Waldron's house, capturing him and, sitting him at his trading table commenced "crossing out their accounts" by slashing him with their knives. They cut off his hand, the one with which they alleged he had weighted the scales against their furs; "they cut off his ears and his nose and crammed them into his mouth. Then, spent with loss of blood, and tottering from his chair, one held the major's sword under him, and he was spitted upon his own weapon. So died Major Waldron, and so the savages, one by one, had settled their accounts." Their cruelty was in repayment in large measure for his cruelty to the Indians he had captured, mistreated or hanged years earlier. Waldron was twice married; his descendants were politically prominent in New Hampshire for many years.

Charles H. Lincoln, editor, *Narratives of the Indian Wars 1675-1699.* N.Y., Barnes & Noble, 1959; Sylvester; DAB; George Madison Bodge, *Soldiers in King's Philip's War,* 3rd ed. Boston, p.p., 1906.

Walkara (Walker), Ute chief (c. 1808-Jan. 29, 1855). B. at Spanish Forks, Utah, he was a son of a chief and became one himself in the Sevier region of Utah. As a young man and expert rider he took part in the great horse stealing raids on California in association with such supreme rustlers as Pegleg Smith, Jim Beckwourth and other opportunists. Because of his name he was often confused in reports of these capers with Joseph Reddeford Walker who never took part in them, so far as the record shows. In 1840 Walkara and his people ran off 3,000 horses from the California ranchos, was angrily pursued but defeated his opponents at Cajon Pass, California. Brigham Young established friendly relations with Walkara who could converse in English and was fluent in Spanish, and the Ute was baptized into the Mormon faith in 1850. However when the Mormons failed to assist him against his enemies, the Shoshones, Walkara became disenchanted with his new friends; to compound his displeasure they would not sell him liquor and a Mormon girl refused his marriage proposal. Around 1853 the Walkara Utes became hostile to the Mormon settlers; Brigham Young showed great restraint in the face of depredations however, visited the Indian camps in person and eventually won Walkara back to peace. The chief was once more disillusioned and became restive, but died at Meadow Creek near Fillmore, Utah, without becoming actively hostile again.

Bancroft, *Utah,* with references; Paul Bailey, *Walkara: Hawk of the Mountains.* Los Angeles, Westernlore Press, 1954.

Walker, Courtney Meade, fur trader, pioneer (Apr. 14, 1812-1887). B. at Nicholasville, Kentucky, he went to the northwest with Jason Lee and other missionaries in 1834 and became a clerk for Nathaniel Wyeth at Fort William, on Wappatoo Island, Oregon. He hired out to John McLoughlin of the Hudson's Bay Company in a confused situation, and spent two years at Fort Hall, a noted host to travelers. He then became an Oregon pioneer, served against the Rogue River Indians in 1851, and died near Blaine, Oregon.

Jo Tuthill article, MM, Vol. III.

Walker, Elkanah, Congregational missionary (Aug. 7, 1805-Nov. 21, 1877). B. at North Yarmouth, Maine, he began studying for the ministry at 26, entered Bangor Theological Seminary in 1834 and was graduated three years later. He intended to serve in Africa, but tribal wars discouraged those plans and he chose Oregon as his field. He was ordained at Brewster, Maine, in 1838, married shortly to Mary Richardson (Apr. 1, 1811-Dec. 4, 1897)

who had been appointed a missionary to Siam until her marriage ended those plans. The day after their marriage they started west, arriving in due course at Whitman's mission, Washington, spending a decade working with Indians, particularly the Spokans. After the Whitman Massacre, November 29, 1847, the Walkers remained at their station until March, then removed to Fort Colville for safety until June when they moved once more, to the Willamette Valley of Oregon. He assisted in founding Tualatin Academy, which developed into Pacific University. The Walkers were parents of eight children. Walker compiled a booklet on the Spokan language, on which he had become an authority.

Thwaites; EWT, XXVII, 367n; Myron Eells, *Marcus Whitman: Pathfinder and Patriot.* Seattle, Alice Harriman Co., 1909, Appen. E.

Walker, Henry Pickering (Pick), historian (Feb. 8, 1911-Aug. 22, 1984). B. at Schenectady, New York, raised on a farm near Hudson, Massachusetts, he graduated from Harvard in 1933, two years later receiving a master's degree in mining geology. After business experience Walker in 1940 went on Army active duty, serving in Panama and in Italy, where he was liaison officer between American, British, South African and French divisions and earned the *Croix de Guerre.* He later served in Korea and Germany, retiring in 1960 as a lieutenant colonel. Walker then earned a master's degree in history at Texas Western College, his thesis, "William McLane's Narrative of the Magee-Gutierrez Expedition" published in the *Southwestern Historical Quarterly.* He earned a doctorate at the University of Colorado, his thesis on Great Plains wagon freighting, published by the University of Oklahoma Press as *The Wagonmasters* (1966), still definitive in its field. In 1965 Walker became assistant editor, and sometimes acting editor, of *Arizona and the West* at Tucson. With cartographer Don Bufkin he produced the *Historical Atlas of Arizona* (1979). His shorter works appeared in *Arizona and the West, Montana, Journal of Arizona History, Military Review* and elsewhere, all of permanent value. Notable were "Soldier in the California Column: The Diary of John W. Teal," *Arizona and the West,* Volume XIII, No 1 (Spring 1971), 33-82, and "The Enlisted Soldier on the Frontier," *The American Military on the*

Frontier, Proceedings of the Seventh Military History Symposium, United States Air Force Academy, 1976. At his death he was completing a biography of Commodore John Grimes Walker (1835-1907), an ancestor and significant 19th century naval officer. Married, Walker fathered two sons and a daughter. He died at Tucson.

Walker, "Wagon Freighting in Arizona," Tucson Corral of Westerners *Smoke Signal,* No. 28 (Fall 1973), 181-204; author's file on Walker.

Walker, Jacob, adventurer (c. 1805-Mar. 6, 1836). A resident of Nacogdoches, he joined the struggle for Texas independence and was killed at the Alamo as a gunner. Mrs. Almaron Dickerson, a survivor of the holocaust, said that Walker was the last Texan slain, being shot down at her side.

Amelia Williams, XXXVII, 282.

Walker, Joel P., frontiersman (1797-post 1878). B. in Goochland County, Virginia, he was an older brother of Joseph Reddeford Walker and volunteered for the 1814 Jackson campaign against the Creeks, later fighting Seminoles in Florida. With the other Walkers he eventually settled at Independence, Missouri, and became one of the earliest Santa Fe traders. In May 1823 Walker with Stephen Cooper led a 31-man expedition from Missouri, each man with two pack horses and about $200 in goods to trade in Santa Fe. June 1 Indians ran off all but six of their horses; Walker, Cooper and two others returned to Missouri for more animals and the trek continued. Later on the Arkansas they met Joseph R. Walker and a trapping party, also Santa Fe bound. The combined company of 55 men and 200 animals suffered so from thirst that at one point they killed buffalo and drank the blood. On their return to Missouri in November they brought 400 mules in addition to beaver and "a considerable sum in specie." In 1825 the Walker brothers accompanied commissioners appointed to mark out the Santa Fe Trail as far as New Mexico, when Joel and Joe went on to Santa Fe. In 1827 Joel was hired by a party to complete the survey to the New Mexico capital. Joel married and fathered four children by 1840 when he took his family and two wagons from Westport, Missouri, with a 40-man fur trading caravan, including the Jesuit missionary, Pierre-Jean De Smet, the

Walkers the first true immigrant family to enter Oregon. They settled on the Willamette, but Joel didn't care for the climate and conditions and the next year went to California where he worked for Sutter, returning at length to Oregon with a herd of cattle for sale. He remained in Oregon for five years, becoming a justice of the peace for Yamhill County in 1845. In 1848 the Walkers returned to California and lived at Napa until 1853, Joel being a member of the Constitutional Convention of 1849. About 1853 he moved once more, to Sonoma County where he lived until his death. His wife, the former Mary Young, was the first Anglo woman to reach California overland, or to settle north of San Francisco Bay; the Walkers had one additional child, born in Oregon in 1841.

Thwaites, EWT, XXX, 190n.; Bancroft, *Pioneer Register;* Barry, *Beginning of West.*

Walker, John, Indian agent (Jan. 18, 1800-1873). B. in Boyle County, Kentucky, he was a grandson of Felix Walker, a founder of Boonesboro; at an early age he removed to Rogersville, Tennessee. Walker served as colonel of a Tennessee militia regiment in the Mexican War, while his son, Francis Marion Walker was lieutenant in the same outfit. As a political appointment, Walker was named in 1857 first agent to the Papagos, Pimas, and Maricopas, with his base at Tucson, Arizona. He reached Santa Fe in June and Tucson in December. With a troop escort he visited the Papagos in January and the Pimas and Maricopas in February. In financial and administrative areas Walker left something to be desired, but he turned out to be a fine agent otherwise, and not only got his office to a firm start, but won the approval and friendship of his charges and of the settlers at Tucson. His principal difficulties were administrative, the Commissioner of Indian Affairs occasionally appointing special agents among the distant Pimas and Maricopas without notifying Walker, their presumed "official" agent. Having Southern sympathies, Walker returned to Tennessee in 1862, although he was too old for active duty. His son, Francis, was killed in the battle of Atlanta as a Brigadier General; another son also was killed in the Civil War, and a third son drowned. Walker himself was taken prisoner but was freed through intervention of a friend, a Union officer. Walker had brought back from

Arizona with him a 12-year-old Apache boy, William Francisco, whom he raised; Billy married, fathered four sons, and disappeared in the Spanish-American War. Walker married Talitha Taylor, niece of Zachary Taylor and, after her death, he wed Mrs. Mary Givens Wheat. His once-sizable fortune vanished, Walker died at Rogersville.

Frank C. Lockwood, "Who Was Who in Arizona." *Ariz. Star*, Jan. 19, 1941; Edward E. Hill, "The Tucson Agency." *Prologue*, Vol. 4, No. 2 (Summer 1972), 77-82.

Walker, John D., frontiersman, miner (1840-Sept. 2, 1891). B. at Warsaw, Illinois, reportedly part Wyandot in ancestry, Walker was taken as an infant to Nauvoo where he received some education and afterwards taught school. In 1861 he moved with his parents to California, enlisting at Oroville November 22 in Company L, 5th California Infantry, being discharged at Mesilla, New Mexico, November 30, 1864, and finding his way back to Tucson. He worked for a trader to the Pimas at Sacaton and, having studied medicine under an army surgeon at Fort McDowell, became agency physician. A "natural linguist," he soon mastered Pima and was said to be the first to reduce it to writing, originating a grammar of the language. "To all intents and purposes, Walker became an Indian and was one of the big chiefs of the Pima tribe. He was a leader in all their councils and big talks," as well as an important medicine man, because of his training. Walker was "a man of extraordinary intelligence, somewhat of a scientist," and a self-taught intellectual. He raised Company C, Arizona Volunteers, among the Pimas to fight Apaches in 1865-66. "It is said that when in the field you could not tell him from the other Indians. He dressed like them, with nothing on but a breechclout, and whooped and yelled like his Indian comrades." He led his company in one famous victory over the Tonto Apaches at the Picacho, south of Pinal, where an entire community of 75 was slaughtered or driven over a perpendicular cliff to their deaths. Walker became surveyor of Pinal County, a justice of the peace and probate judge. About 1878 he became interested in mining, working first at the Jessie Benton Mine at the Owls Head, 45 miles south of Florence, Arizona. In 1879 or 1880 he was shown the Vekol Mine on the Papago Reservation by Indians; he and Peter R. Brady began operations, Walker

eventually buying Brady out and taking in his brother, Lucien Walker, as partner; it is said the mine yielded about $2 million in silver, "most of which Walker spent among the Pima Indians." It was while working the mine that Walker suffered a paralysis attack and slipped into insanity. Walker had married a Pima woman under Indian practices, and fathered a daughter. While in failing health "a woman came out from Illinois and became his nurse, and conceived the idea of marrying him, which she did." Upon his death in an insane asylum at Napa, California, his estate became involved in extensive litigation involving, on one side, Walker's three brothers and four sisters; on another the Illinois wife; and on a third, Juana, his half-Pima daughter. Ultimately the estate went to his brothers and sisters; the U.S. Supreme Court denied Juana anything, upholding a Territorial law that prohibited a white from marrying an Indian. Walker, in sum, was "a man of fine attainments, generous to a fault; the best type of the Western man."

Hayden Collection, Ariz. Hist. Soc.; Farish, IV, 117-20.

Walker, John George, army officer (July 22, 1822-July 20, 1893). B. in Cole County, Missouri, he attended a Jesuit college at St. Louis and from 1846 fought in the Mexican War with the 1st Mounted Rifles, afterward joining the regular army as a captain, which rank he attained in 1851. At Eagle Springs, Texas, he and Eugene Asa Carr, then a lieutenant, were directed to pursue some Apache stock thieves, and on October 6, 1854, from the site of the future Camp Davis, Walker penned a long and interesting report of the pursuit. After a gruelling chase, the command had a hard fight with numerous Apaches of whom six or seven were believed killed, and others wounded on the Indian side, one soldier killed, Carr and others wounded on the army side. Apparently the stock was not recovered. Walker resigned as captain in 1861 and joined the Confederacy, taking part in such engagements as Second Bull Run, Antietam and other battles of the East, soon being appointed Brigadier General, then Major General. He led a Texas Infantry division in the Red River campaign of 1864, and in June that year took over command of the Confederate district of Texas, New Mexico and Arizona. After hostilities ceased he went to Mexico without waiting for his personal parole. He subsequently served

as United States consul at Bogotá, Colombia, and as special commissioner to South America Republics on behalf of the Pan-American Union. He died at Washington, D.C., and was buried at Winchester, Virginia.
Robert M. Utley, "Action on the Texas Frontier," (Walker's report of his Apache fight). *Potomac Corral of Westerners Corral Dust*, Vol. V, No. 4 (Oct. 1960), 25-26, 28; Ezra J. Warner, *Generals in Gray: Lives of the Confederate Commanders*. Baton Rouge, La. State Univ. Press, 1959; Walker's military file, Nat. Archives.

Walker, Joseph Reddeford, mountain man (Dec. 13, 1798-Nov. 13, 1872). B. in Tennessee, Joe Walker, who became one of the great mountain men, moved with the family to Missouri in 1819 and journeyed with a party of hunters and trappers to New Mexico in a year or two. Arrested, he was soon released to help the Spaniards in an Indian campaign. He accompanied a U.S. survey party, charting and marking the Santa Fe Trail as far as the Mexican border. He entered western Missouri politics briefly, reportedly giving the name to Independence, seat of Jackson County, Walker being elected its first sheriff. He served two terms of two years each. In February 1831, he embarked upon a trading venture to the Cherokee country, and at Fort Gibson encountered B.L.E. Bonneville, an army officer planning a fur-trading operation in the Rocky Mountains. Walker became Bonneville's subordinate, the party of about 110 men leaving Fort Osage May 1, 1832, reaching the Green River, then moving on to winter on the Salmon River. Walker, leaving Green River July 24, 1833, embarked upon his controversial exploration trip to California, uncertain because the instructions given him by Bonneville are not precisely known, nor is the ultimate objective and motive of the expedition entirely clear. But the expedition itself was an outstanding success. The party of 40 men, with perhaps a score of free trappers along in addition for the adventure of it, gained the Humboldt by a course later to be followed by countless emigrants and Forty-niners, engaged in a murderous attack upon Digger Indians, accused of theft of traps and being general nuisances about the camp, and from Carson Lake accomplished a very difficult three-week crossing of the Sierra Nevada, descending between the Merced and

Tuolumne rivers. On November 13 Walker discovered Yosemite Valley and the giant sequoia trees. Walker's party reached the coast and wintered at Mission San Juan Bautista. Well supplied by Mexican stockmen, Walker's men moved up the San Joaquin Valley, crossed the Sierra by Walker's Pass, followed the Owens Valley north until they struck their former trail and followed it back to the rendezvous having added much exact geographical knowledge that would be incorporated in future maps of the West. Walker trapped next season in the upper Rockies, then since Bonneville had returned to the states, joined the American Fur Company as a brigade leader. Painter Alfred Jacob Miller completed two pictures of Walker while accompanying William Drummond Stewart to the 1837 rendezvous. Walker is reported to have visited Arizona about 1837-38, where he may have made a gold discovery, and in 1839 was at Fort Davy Crockett in Brown's Hole, Colorado. Here he and other noted mountain men stole back horses that less-principled trappers had stolen from Snake Indians to recoup losses from horse thieves of some other tribe, and returned the animals to the Snakes. Walker, following the demise of large-scale Rocky Mountain fur operations, engaged in horse and mule trading trips to California, trapped and traded out of Fort Bridger, sometimes guided California-bound parties, worked for Fremont on his second expedition, and then on the first part of his third (when Walker Lake was named in Joe's honor). He engaged in numerous other frontier activities. In 1850 he headed an expedition to the Upper Virgin River and in 1851 took New Mexico sheep to California. Walker ranched in California for several years, was interested in railroad surveys of the west, explored the Mono Lake region of California, and in 1859 guided troops in a campaign against the Mohaves along the Colorado River, and in 1861 organized the group that would open up central Arizona. It left the Kern River by way of Walker Pass, touched southern Colorado, dropped down into New Mexico and moved west, being instrumental in the capture of the noted Apache chief, Mangas Coloradas (who subsequently was assassinated) enroute. Walker's group entered southern Arizona and moved up the Hassayampa River to Granite Creek in the vicinity of later Prescott,

Arizona. Gold was struck on Lynx Creek. There and in the vicinity "Walker diggings" a rush developed swiftly, leading to a nucleus of settlement that shortly would incorporate the first major capital for the new Territory of Arizona. Joe returned to California in 1867, to live the rest of his life with his nephew, James T. Walker, on a Contra Costa County ranch, where he died. His impact on the west was immense, his life replete with significant deeds, and Walker was a man with integrity, vision, intelligence, fortitude and great worth. He was buried at Martinez.

Douglas Sloane Watson, *West Wind: The Life of Joseph Reddeford Walker.* Los Angeles, p.p. by Percy H. Booth, 1934, reprint by *Old West,* Vol. III, No. 2 (Winter 1966), 72-96; Daniel Ellis Conner, *Joseph Reddeford Walker and the Arizona Adventure.* Norman, Univ. of Okla. Press, 1956; Conner, *A Confederate in the Colorado Gold Fields.* Norman, 1970; DAB; Ardis M. Walker article, MM, Vol. V.

Walker, Joseph Rutherford "Jr.", pioneer (Apr. 3, 1832-Feb. 26, 1897). B. in Jackson County, Missouri, he reached California in 1850 and joined the prospecting,expedition of his uncle, Joseph Reddeford Walker, leaving California in May 1861, traveling through Colorado, New Mexico, and Arizona where it made the strike resulting in the founding of Prescott, about 1863. An Indian fighter, miner, lawman for many years, he was sheriff of Yavapai County, Arizona, from 1878-82. In late 1879 he and a posse tracked down a pair of stagecoach holdup artists, and in a shootout one was killed, the other taken. Walker also was a rancher and Prescott businessman. He died at his homestead on Beaver Creek, in the Prescott area, and was buried at Prescott in the Masonic Cemetery.

Bancroft Library records; Sharlot Hall Historical Mus. of Ariz., Prescott; Dan L. Thrapp, *Al Sieber, Chief of Scouts.* Norman, Univ. of Okla. Press, 1964.

Walker, Juan Pedro, adventurer (c. 1776-c. 1822). A native of New Orleans, Walker apparently was well educated and of a scientific turn of mind. He had been associated with Andrew Ellicott in running a boundary line between the United States and Spain from 1796 to 1800; in 1803, then living at Nacogdoches, he applied to remain in Spanish territory and surveyed for the Spanish government on the Rio Grande and

Guadalupe River. As an ensign, or second lieutenant, he was stationed at Janos, Chihuahua, and when Pike was sent to the city of Chihuahua, he was quartered with Walker who also served as interpreter and translator in communications between Pike and Governor Nemesio Salcedo. Walker was a cartographer of some skill, his map of 1805 of the Internal Provinces being "remarkably detailed." He also was interested in rocks and mining and other scientific subjects. He became involved in independence movements, was arrested and confined at Encinillas, Chihuahua, and died shortly after Mexican independence was won.

Porrua; Donald Jackson, ed., *Journals of Zebulon Montgomery Pike,* 2 vols. Norman, Univ. of Okla. Press, 1966; Bennett Lay, *The Lives of Ellis P. Bean.* Austin, Univ. of Tex. Press, 1960.

Walker, Samuel, army officer (Oct. 19, 1822, Feb. 6, 1893). B. in Franklin County, Pennsylvania, he served with Free-state forces in Kansas in 1855. He was commissioned captain in the 1st Kansas Infantry in 1861, became a major in the 5th Kansas Cavalry the following year and lieutenant colonel of the 16th Kansas Cavalry in 1864. Walker commanded the central of three columns of the Connor 1865 Powder River expedition against the Sioux, leaving Fort Laramie August 5 with ten squadrons of the 16th Kansas Cavalry with a detachment of the 15th Kansas Cavalry, two mountain howitzers and a supply train. He was to move northeast to the Black Hills, north along their western front to the head of the Little Missouri, then northwest to the Rosebud, where he was to meet Connor and Cole, who commanded the right column. His 16th at first refused to march because their enlistments would expire before their return, but Connor outbluffed them and the movement commenced. Walker's column did not suffer quite the hardships endured by Cole's element, nor did it see the action which attended both Connor's and Cole's commands, but he was at one point surrounded by hostile Sioux. On August 18 Walker and Cole met and thereafter remained in loose contact as they progressed northwestward from the Little Missouri. On September 8 there was some indecisive skirmishing. Savage weather and other exigencies cost Walker at least 250 of his animals, with another 150 broken down, and his men were reduced to eating horseflesh when they could get it. The two commands were contacted by Connor's Pawnee scouts who guided them to Fort Connor, 80 miles up the Powder River where they arrived September 20. Walker acknowledged that he did not know positively that his men had killed a single Indian, though "I saw a number fall." Walker was mustered out December 6, 1865. In 1866 he was made a brevet Brigadier General of Volunteers for his work on the Sioux campaign. His last public office was when he was elected in 1872 to the Kansas State Senate. He died at Lawrence, Kansas.

LeRoy R. and Ann W. Hafen, eds., *Powder River Campaigns and Sawyers Expedition of 1865.* Glendale, Calif., Arthur H. Clark Co., 1961; Robert M. Utley, *Frontiersmen in Blue; The United States Army and the Indian, 1848-1865.* N.Y., Macmillan Co., 1967.

Walker, Tandy, blacksmith, frontiersman (d. 1842). B. in Virginia, he reached the Tombigbee country of Alabama in 1801 as a government blacksmith, stationed first at St. Stephens on the Tombigbee River, then assigned to assist Creek Indians develop modern farming methods and maintain their metal appurtenances. He became fluent in Creek (perhaps having married a Creek woman) and was a trusted friend of some of their leaders. Tandy Walker in 1812 was the hero of a thrilling border incident: he learned from a Creek that a white woman, Mrs. Crawley, had been captured in Tennessee and brought to Great Falls, at the present Tuscaloosa, Alabama, by a party under Little Warrior, returning from a visit to the northern Shawnees. Walker agreed at the risk of his life to try to rescue the woman although she then was in the hostile camp. Within two weeks he brought Mrs. Crawley by canoe to the settlements on the lower Tombigbee where she was restored to good health by the wife of George Strother Gaines; Walker received formal thanks and a monetary award from the Tennessee legislature, although he had not expected either. He was an experienced and daring backwoodsman and fearless Indian fighter. In a private Indian hunting trip in November 1813 he was severely wounded, shot in the side and his arm broken but although reported killed, he outran his enemies, lay out all of a cold autumn night, made a raft of reeds to cross the Alabama River and in a day and

one-half made it afoot to Fort Madison between the Alabama and Tombigbee rivers. Walker died either in Alabama or in Texas. He had fathered two daughters.

H.S. Halbert, T.H. Ball, *The Creek War of 1813 and 1814.* Univ. of Ala. Press, 1969; Thomas McAdory Owen, *History of Alabama and Dictionary of Alabama Biography,* 4 vols. (1921). Spartanburg, So. Car., Reprint Co., 1978.

Walker, Thomas, physician, explorer (Jan. 25, 1715-Nov. 9, 1794). B. in King and Queen County, Virginia, he was educated as a physician and practiced for some years in Fredericksburg. In 1784 already in comfortable circumstances, he became interested in western lands and accompanied James Patton and John Buchanan on a two-year expedition into southwest Virginia. Further explorations were made beyond the Alleghenies when Cumberland Gap (discovered April 13, 1750), the Cumberland River and Cumberland mountains were named for the English duke of that title, and the Kentucky River officially discovered and named. Walker had a narrow escape at Braddock's defeat. He was a friend of Peter Jefferson and in 1757 was appointed guardian of young Thomas Jefferson with whom he maintained a lifelong friendship and may have exerted some influence, although evidence is lacking, in favor of the Louisiana Purchase even though it occurred seven years after Walker's death. Ever interested in lands and expansion Walker was said to have been active in pushing George Rogers Clark's undertaking in the Ohio country. Walker acted as commissary with rank of major in the French and Indian War. Walker was charged with fraud in connection with his commissary accounts in 1759, but was absolved. Occasionally he served in the Virginia House of Burgesses. In 1768 Walker represented Virginia in the Indian treaty negotiations at Fort Stanwix, New York. He had a role in Revolutionary activities although not in military events, and served in various public offices. He died at Castle Hill, Albemarle County, Virginia, and is buried there. Walker was married twice and fathered twelve children.

Reuben Gold Thwaites, Louise Phelps Kellogg, *Documentary History of Dunmore's War 1774.* Madison, Wisc. Hist. Soc., 1905; Harriette Simpson Arnow, *Seedtime on the Cumberland.* N.Y., Macmillan Co., 1960; DAB.

Walker, William filibuster (May 8, 1824-Sept. 12, 1860). B. at Nashville, Tennessee, he was well educated; by 20 he was a graduate of the University of Pennsylvania Medical College and had traveled in Europe two years, studying at Paris, Edinburgh and Heidelberg. He now studied law at New Orleans for two years and practiced briefly, only to give it up to become editor of the New Orleans *Crescent.* At this time he was 5 feet, 5 inches in height, weighed 120 pounds and had gray eyes and blond hair. In 1850 he went to California, working initially for the San Francisco *Herald;* he soon became embroiled in the tribulations that accompanied newspapering in a wild, crime-ridden and politically volatile community and January 12, 1851, fought one of the four duels of his career, on this occasion with William Hicks Graham who wounded him in the arm. Walker himself never hit anyone in his gunfights. He took up the practice of law at Marysville, north of Sacramento. It was an age of filibustering, and his ambitions turned toward a freebooting expedition to northern Mexico; he considered Sonora, then Lower California. October 8, 1853, he left San Francisco by sea with 45 men, landed at La Paz, Lower California, seized the place without firing a shot and proclaimed a new republic with himself as president. He withdrew to Ensenada, farther north, was reinforced by Henry Watkins with some 230 men, but although he beat off a Mexican attack, Walker's strength for various reasons dwindled and he was forced to pull back into the United States, where he was tried for violation of the neutrality laws, and acquitted. He became editor of the San Francisco *Commercial-Advertiser* for a publisher who believed thoroughly in Manifest Destiny and felt at home in this environment. In June 1855 he turned his attention toward Nicaragua. In Central America British overt and covert activities were confronted by American financial and political interests and hapless entities like Nicaragua seemed ripe for such adventurism as attracted Walker, who also was something of an idealist, an ascetic and a romanticist. Limited by available funds he could ship only 58 of the hundreds who applied when he left California and at the invitation of the political faction at León, landed in Nicaragua. He captured Granada, avoided tying himself to either of the major parties struggling for

domination and had himself elected president in July 1856. But his triumph was short-lived. He came to cross-purposes with the powerful Cornelius Vanderbilt and his Accessory Transit Company upon which Walker depended for his supplies; defeated militarily, he was forced to surrender in May 1857 to the U.S. Navy at Rivas. He attempted a fresh invasion later that year, but was arrested immediately, again by the U.S. Navy and shipped back to the United States. Walker had strong support from American public opinion but the government feared recognizing his "republic" and its possible admission as a slave state in the Union would antagonize Britain perhaps to the point of war, and gave him no real support. Again Walker was acquitted of violating his homeland's neutrality. In 1860 he made a final attempt to win over and cement the Central American states into a single political entity, seeking now to invade Honduras, but was taken prisoner by the British Navy, turned over to Honduras and shot by a firing squad at Trujillo. The English part in his demise is unclear but there is little doubt that Walker's elimination was viewed by the British as removing an obstacle to its own vigorous ambitions in the area. Walker was intelligent, reserved, imaginative and notably courageous and he won fierce loyalty from his partisans and often enmity from others. For many he was an outstanding American hero of his times.

William Walker, *The War in Nicaragua.* Mobile, S.H. Goetzel & Co., 1860; Albert Z. Carr, *The World and William Walker.* N.Y., Harper and Row, 1963; CE.

Walker, William W., frontiersman (c. 1866-c. 1940). B. in Iowa, Walker claimed that Kit Carson was his great uncle. Walker was taken as a child by his parents to Loveland, Colorado. He began cowboying at 17, working around 1882-83 for the Erie Cattle Company of Arizona, a well-known ranch on the Sonora border where Walker said he had shot two Mexicans rustlers or perhaps, rurales. By 1886 he had reached the Sweet-water country of Wyoming and became a top hand for various big outfits; wounded by rustlers he was taken in by Ben Jones, an old frontiersman-trapper and thereafter a partnership developed. Walker in 1888 became a freighter with an eight-horse outfit for several years between Casper, old Fort

Fetterman, Douglas and Buffalo, Wyoming, often spending the off-season either trapping or cowboying. In the winter of 1891-92 he and Jones trapped coyotes for their fur. Acquainted with Nate Champion and Nick Ray they spent the night of April 8-9, 1892 at their KC Ranch, Wyoming, and thus became eyewitnesses of the Johnson County War's initial action: the murder of Champion and Ray. The hapless Walker and Jones were spirited about by big cattle interest agents, living hand to mouth and wary of threats to kill them if they did not quit the country. At last they were escorted away, extricating themselves with monumental difficulties from one legal entanglement after another in Wyoming and Nebraska until they reached Kansas City and were shipped by rail to Westerly, Rhode Island, where they remained more than a year at the Windsor Hotel, their bills grudgingly paid by the cattlemen through the Stock Growers' Association of Cheyenne. Each had been promised $2,500 after the legal dust had settled, but the checks bounced: "no funds." Thus they were the ultimate victims of the ultimate double-cross. Jones disappeared perhaps, Walker thought, done in by cattlemen for his insistence upon payment. Walker wandered back west, stopping off to see the 1893 World's Columbian Exposition at Chicago, left the railroad at Niobrara, Nebraska, bought a wagon and camp outfit and trailed on home. He interested an attorney of Longmont, Colorado, in reopening the cattlemen's murder case in which the bogus check was to be a prime bit of evidence, but it was stolen with other papers from his belongings and the effort collapsed. Walker said he became a game warden in the present Rocky Mountain National Park of Colorado. He lived the latter part of his life at Lyons, Colorado. His wife predeceased him, but he was survived by four children and ten grandchildren, "mostly red-headed." In his advanced age Walker narrated his adventures to Daisy F. Baber (d. Mar. 26, 1947) and from them Mrs. Baber wrote two books, so highly fictionalized as to be of less value than they ought to have been. For example, Walker's physical description of Tom Horn, whom he claims to have known well, is all wrong, although he may have met Horn in Arizona as well as in Wyoming. Yet his book on his Wyoming experiences (which includes a portrait photograph of Walker as a young

man) does possess insights available nowhere else and despite the many errors and lapses, it is a primary account. His year of death is conjecture.

Baber, as told by Bill Walker, *The Longest Rope: The Truth About the Johnson County Cattle War.* Caldwell, Ida., Caxton Printers, 1940; Baber, as told by Bill Walker, *Injun Summer: An Old Cowhand Rides the Ghost Trails.* Caxton, 1952; Robert B. David, *Malcolm Campbell: Sheriff.* Casper, Wyomingana, 1932.

Walking Coyote, Samuel, buffalo conserver (d. 1884). A young Pend d'Oreille Indian who lived with the Flatheads, while hunting on the Milk River of present Montana in 1872-73 Walking Coyote somehow came into possession of eight buffalo calves and decided to save them. Why he did so is not known although there are several suggeestions, as imaginative as they are unlikely. Six of the orphaned animals survived, two bulls and four heifers and by 1884 when the Northern Herd had been all but destroyed, had increased to 13 head. Walking Coyote determined to sell them and according to one account took them to the ranch of Jake Schmidt, at the foot of Haystack Butte. Schmidt suggested he take them to Michel Pablo in Mission Valley. Walking Coyote sold the little herd to Pablo and Charles Allard, another rancher for a reported $2,000. With the money he went on a prolonged drunk and died under a bridge in a nearby town.

John Kidder, "Montana Miracle: It Saved the Buffalo." *Mont. Mag.,* Vol. XV, No. 2 (Spring 1965), 57-58.

Wall, Nicholas, riverboat captain, frontiersman (1820-Oct. 2, 1880). B. near Alexandria, Virginia, he settled at Galena, Illinois, about 1836 and shortly began a steamboat career. He built and commanded "many popular steamers" plying the Mississippi, Missouri and Illinois rivers; the last boat built and commanded by him was the *Prairie Bird,* an Illinois River packet. In 1850 Wall left the river and entered the steamboat agency business with Captain Joseph Widen of St. Louis. In 1862 he removed to Montana Territory where he followed various occupations, including operating a general store at Deer Lodge where he was a pioneer resident. In 1862 he grubstaked Thomas W. Cover and others who on August 15, 1862, were involved in the first important gold strike in the Territory at the later (East) Bannack. Wall was one of five men who founded the famed Montana Vigilance Committee in late 1863. He with Paris S. Pfouts, president, Alvin W. Brookie, John A. Nye and Wilbur F. Sanders guided the dread group which wiped out the Plummer gang of desperadoes and in all was responsible, directly or indirectly, for perhaps 34 executions. Although drastic, the organization effectively cleaned up Montana and its effect on the whole was beneficial. Early in 1876 Wall left Montana, returning to St. Louis where he resided until his death. He was married in 1851; his widow, a son and daughter survived him. Wall died at St. Louis and was buried there.

Helena (Mont.) *Herald,* Oct. 11, 1880; information from the Mont. Hist. Soc.

Wallace, George Daniel, army officer (June 29, 1849-Dec. 29, 1890). B. in York County, South Carolina, he was graduated from West Point in 1872, joined the 7th Cavalry, took part in the 1873 Yellowstone Expedition and commanded Indian scouts on Custer's 1874 Black Hills Expedition. Wallace was on the Sioux Expedition of May 17-September 26, 1876, being promoted to first lieutenant the day after the Custer debacle to succeed slain Lieutenant William Winer Cooke. Wallace had confided to Godfrey and Gibson following an unusual officers' council at a late stage of the Custer operation "his belief that Custer was going to be killed and had a premonition of disaster" because of the odd way in which the commander spoke. Wallace was in Reno's detachment, and fought with the others in the valley and on the hill, escaping unwounded. He was on a Nez Perce expedition in the summer of 1877 and served generally at upper Plains frontier posts for more than a decade thereafter, being promoted to captain September 23, 1885. Wallace was killed December 29, 1890, in the Wounded Knee affair in South Dakota. He was described as a "tall, gaunt fatherly looking" individual. His body was interred at Yorkville, South Carolina, January 6, 1891.

Heitman; Edgar I. Stewart, *Custer's Luck.* Norman, Univ. of Okla. Press, 1955; Kenneth Hammer, *Little Big Horn Biographies.* Custer Battlefield Hist. and Mus. Assn., 1965; John M. Carroll, Byron Price, *Roll Call on the Little Big*

Horn, 28 June 1876. Ft. Collins, Colo., Old Army Press, 1974; Robert M. Utley, *Last Days of the Sioux Nation.* New Haven, Yale Univ. Press, 1963.

Wallace, Jim (or Jake), cowboy, gunman (fl. 1880s). At Galeyville, Arizona, he accosted deputy sheriff William Breakenridge, playfully drew a gun on him and made him stand for drinks for the boys. Curly Bill Brocius later upbraided Wallace for "rudeness" to the law officer and was shot in the neck, not fatally, by the other, who, learning Brocius would recover, borrowed $10 from Breakenridge and took the stage for Las Vegas, New Mexico. He was reported killed at Roswell, New Mexico, several years later.

Ed Bartholomew, *Wyatt Earp: The Man & the Myth.* Toyahvale, Tex., Frontier Book Co.,1964.

Wallace, Lew(is), soldier, writer, executive (Apr. 10, 1827-Feb. 15, 1905). B. at Brookville, Indiana, he was early attracted to reading and to outdoor life, becoming a newspaper writer, then studying law. He served in the Mexican War, practiced law in Indiana, was elected a state senator and with the Civil War was named adjutant general for the state, raising 130 companies, being made colonel of the 11th Indiana Infantry and ending the war a Major General of Volunteers, being highly commended by Grant for his work in averting a Confederate threat to Washington, D.C. After the war he spent time in Galveston and other places in Texas investigating reports that Texas Confederates and Mexican imperialists wanted to re-annex Texas to Mexico. He then served on the court martial trying suspects in Lincoln's assassination conspiracy. Wallace, in northern Mexico, attempted to muster support for Mexico's liberals fighting the Maximilian regime. In 1878 he was named governor of New Mexico, serving until 1881 and coming to frontier prominence by his statehouse role in the Lincoln County War and the Victorio War. On the night of March 17, 1879, Wallace had his celebrated meeting with Billy the Kid which resulted in the Kid's surrender March 23. There is much confusion surrounding the matter in turbulent Lincoln County, however, and the roles of both men are somewhat ambiguous. Despite his guarantee to the Kid of immunity, Wallace later was "obliged to write out with his own hand and sign his name to a paper which authorized the outlaw's death by hanging." Wallace left New Mexico May 30, 1881, having accepted the position of minister to Turkey. While at Santa Fe, despite all distractions, he had written the last third of his great novel, *Ben-Hur: A Tale of Christ,* and seen it published and well received. Even the Santa Fe *New Mexican,* "always a bitter critic" of Wallace, said as he left: "Wallace made hosts of friends here, and was as good a governor as the Territory has had." Although he wrote other works, nothing specifically was of the frontier experience; his *Lew Wallace, An Autobiography,* he brought down to 1864, but it was completed sketchily by his wife and another woman and referred only in passing to New Mexico. Wallace, who always wrote his first name as "Lew." with a period, died at Crawfordsville, Indiana.

Literature abundant; William A. Keleher, *Violence in Lincoln County 1869-1881.* Albuquerque, Univ. of New Mex. Press, 1957.

Wallace, William Alexander Anderson (Big Foot), frontiersman (Apr. 3, 1817-Jan. 7, 1899). B. at Lexington, Rockbridge County, Virginia, he learned in 1836 that his brother, Samuel and a cousin, Major Benjamin C. Wallace had been shot by Mexicans at Goliad and with others determined to join the War of Independence; the Battle of San Jacinto had been fought before they departed, but some of them went anyway, reaching Texas October 5. He had come he said to take some "pay out of the Mexicans" for the shooting of his kinfolk and later believed "accounts with them are now about square." In 1837 he hired out to a surveying party reconnoitering beyond the frontier, and here he received his introduction to wilderness life, saw buffalo, killed his first deer, first bear, first Indian and became in fact a Texan. He was an immense man for the day, 6 feet, 2 inches tall, weighing 240 pounds and with a reach of 6 feet, 6 inches, with courage to match. Nevertheless he was captured by Comanches, saved from execution as he believed by adoption, learned something of the Indian tongue and after a few months escaped back to the settlements. He tried farming near La Grange, Texas, then in 1840 moved to Austin where, he later said he saw the last of the wild buffalo run down Congress Avenue, and moved to San Antonio which he considered less populated, and thus more attractive. He made numerous scouts for

Indians and his adventures with them were many. In 1842 he with other Texans fought the Mexican General Adrian Woll and the expedition that captured San Antonio and then retreated into Mexico again. Wallace volunteered for the Somervell and Mier expeditions, the Texans in their turn invading Mexico. Mexicans captured the Texans at Mier December 26, 1842, Wallace enduring their harrowing ordeal and imprisonment at Perote Prison in the Mexican state of Vera Cruz. While a captive he came by his nickname, Big Foot (he wore number 12 shoes) when it proved impossible to purchase for him in that part of Mexico footwear large enough. He was released November 22, 1844, with five or six others and returned to Texas, immediately joining the Texas Rangers under Jack Hays, serving with them in the Mexican War. In the 1850s he commanded a Ranger company, fighting Indians and Mexican bandits. For a time he drove a mail wagon from San Antonio to El Paso, and during the Civil War he served in frontier defense forces against marauding Indians. He ranched from time to time and lived the latter part of his life at Bigfoot, in Frio County. One of his friends was John C. Duval, who chronicled the early part of his life from tales he told and from his diary on occasion. Dobie wrote that Wallace "was as honest as daylight but liked to stretch the blanket and embroider his stories. He read and was no illiterate frontiersman, but he summed up in himself all the frontiers of the Southwest. His picturesqueness, humor, vitality, and representativeness of old-time free days, free ways and free land have broken down the literalness of every writer who has treated of him," and he became one of Texas's outstanding folk heroes. He never married. The Texas Legislature provided for his burial in the State Cemetery at Austin.

John C. Duval, *The Adventures of Big-Foot Wallace.* Lincoln, Univ. of Nebr. Press, 1966; HT.

Wallace, William Miller, army officer (Jan. 9, 1844-Nov. 5, 1924). B. at Prairie du Chien, Wisconsin, he was the son of an army officer and educated at Washington, D.C., Georgetown, Maryland and a military school at Sing Sing, New York. He was commissioned a first lieutenant in the 13th New York Artillery in 1864, but was mustered out within two months. In 1866 he was commissioned a second lieutenant in the 8th Infantry and, as a first lieutenant, then a captain served with the 6th Cavalry from late in 1870 until 1894 during which he saw considerable Indian service in Arizona. Wallace was commander of Fort Bowie, Arizona, during the transfer of Apaches from Ojo Caliente, New Mexico, to San Carlos, Arizona, in 1877, and was involved briefly in a dispute with Agent John Clum, but nothing came of it. He served in the field under William Redwood Price following the Cibecue Apache fight in Arizona in 1881. Commanding Troop H of the 6th in the summer of 1882 he had a role in the Big Dry Wash campaign, although he was not present at the engagement which culminated it. Wallace, as a major transferred to the 2nd Cavalry in 1894 and as a colonel to the 15th Cavalry in 1901. He became a Brigadier General and was retired in 1906.

Who Was Who; Heitman; Dan L. Thrapp, *General Crook and the Sierra Madre Adventure.* Norman, Univ. of Okla. Press, 1972.

Wallen, Henry Davies, army officer (Apr. 19, 1819-Dec. 2, 1886). B. at Savannah, Georgia, he was graduated from West Point and commissioned a brevet second lieutenant of the 3rd Infantry July 1, 1840, and a second lieutenant of the 4th Infantry October 4, serving with it in the Second Seminole War in Florida and later in the Mexican War; he became a first lieutenant September 9, 1846, Wallen was made a captain January 31, 1850. He became a major of the 7th Infantry November 25, 1861, went to Sante Fe, New Mexico, in 1862, served on Carleton's staff and was named to command Fort Sumner, the post on the Pecos at the Bosque Redondo Navaho Reservation. December 18, 1863, he reported a successful pursuit of Navaho stock thieves and return of the animals after a sharp fight in which a dozen Indians were killed. Wallen became lieutenant colonel of the 14th Infantry July 30, 1865, and went to Tucson, Arizona, and April 28, 1866, was given command of the subdistrict south of the Gila and east of Tucson. The subdistrict, however was never activated and June 10, on transfer of John Mason, Wallen came into command of the District of Arizona. He was not very effective, and not greatly interested in the position or anything else, went on leave shortly to the east from where he did not return and was succeeded August 11 by Colonel Charles S. Lovell. Camp Wallen on the Babocomari

Creek was named for him; it was a short-lived post. December 15, 1870 Wallen joined the 8th Infantry, became colonel of the 2nd Infantry February 19, 1873, and retired almost exactly a year later. He died at New York City.

Heitman; Cullum; Orton; Constance Wynn Altshuler, *Chains of Command.* Tucson, Arizona Hist. Soc., 1981.

Waller, Reuben, soldier (Jan. 5, 1840-post 1929). B. a slave in the deep south, he was taken by his master, a Confederate general officer, as servant during the Civil War, participating in 29 battles. While with Stonewall Jackson's cavalry, Waller absorbed an appreciation for that arm of the service and on July 16, 1867, he enlisted at Fort Leavenworth in H Company of the 10th Cavalry under Captain Louis H. Carpenter, "for the Indian war that was then raging in Kansas and Colorado." He said he fought at Beaver Creek, Sand Creek, Cheyenne Wells, and in other actions, and helped rescue the Forsyth scouts from Beecher Island in September 1868. Waller claimed to have special knowledge that Sharp Grover killed Will Comstock and himself was killed in a sod saloon "by one of the boys who was in the Beecher fight with him," but this is at variance with the record on both counts. Waller went with Company H to Fort Supply, Indian Territory, in 1870, engaged in a winter campaign against hostiles, campaigned again after Satank, Lone Wolf, Big Tree and others, and was in on the killing of Satank, which he considered justifiable. Waller received an honorable discharge in 1877 and settled at Eldorado, Kansas.

Simon E. Matson, ed., *The Battle of Beecher Island.* Wray, Colo., Beecher Island Battle Mem. Assn., 1960.

Wallingford, David W., army officer (1837-July 11, 1883). B. in Vermont he enlisted as a corporal June 20, 1861, and served briefly in the 2nd Kansas Infantry; he was commissioned a second lieutenant August 29 1863, in the 15th Kansas Cavalry, being mustered out with no advancement April 29, 1865, a year in which a court martial convicted him of pillage upon civilians of Arkansas and Kansas. Endorsed by numerous politicians his court-martial was overlooked and the War Department gave him an honorable discharge. He failed an examination for a regular army commission, but on a second try passed and was commissioned second lieutenant in the 7th Cavalry July 28, 1866, becoming a first lieutenant June 8, 1867. He participated in the Battle of the Washita and Kansas governor Samuel J. Crawford urged he be breveted for gallantry, but he was court-martialed again, this time for associating with enlisted men and "prostitutes and lewd women." Found guilty he was ordered dismissed, but high authority reversed the court; he was court-martialed again for consorting with "a notorious prostitute or lewd woman" and disgracing the service and was finally dismissed May 10, 1870. He died in the Kansas Penitentiary, according to Benteen, where Wallingford was serving time for horse rustling.

Heitman; Robert M. Utley, *Life in Custer's Cavalry.* New Haven, Yale Univ. Press, 1977.

Walsh, Robert Douglas, army officer (Oct. 14, 1860-Aug. 15, 1928). B. in California he was graduated from West Point and joined the 4th Cavalry in 1883. He saw duty at Fort Bowie, Arizona, participating in long Wirt Davis scouts into the Sierra Madre of Old Mexico after the Geronimo hostiles. He won a brevet for gallantry in actions in the Teras Mountains of Sonora, September 22, 1885, and the Patagonia Mountains, Arizona, June 6, 1886. He also served at Fort Walla Walla and Vancouver Barracks, Washington, and Boise Barracks, Idaho. Walsh saw service in France in World War I, winning the DSM and the French Legion of Honor, and was made a National Guard Brigadier General in 1917. He retired in 1919.

Heitman; *Who Was Who.*

Walters, William (Bronco Bill), desperado (Oct. 1860-June 16, 1921). B. probably at Austin, Texas, he apparently reached New Mexico as a youth. According to one report he was a painter at Sante Fe; another has him fighting with the Higgins faction against the Horrells in Lampasas, Texas, in 1877. He may have worked for John Chisum in 1878, and he stated in an 1889 newspaper interview that he had been a cowboy since 1877, many of that trade entering it at 16 or 17. If he had any role in the Lincoln County War it is not remembered. Perhaps he held up a bank at San Marcial, New Mexico, in 1888. He was arrested at Separ, New Mexico, for horse theft

in 1889, and later at the same place for general deviltry, taken to Silver City by Whitehill, escaped jail, was rearrested April 20, 1892. Several escapades of Walters were reported subsequently, involving some shootings, another jailbreak, this time from Socorro, and an incident at Deming, New Mexico, in which he may have been wounded. He and others on October 2, 1896, attempted to hold up an Atlantic and Pacific passenger train west of Albuquerque, but incompetence led to abandonment of the effort with one would-be bandit (Cole Young, or Estes) killed. The same gang later reportedly robbed two stagecoaches between White Oaks and San Antonio, New Mexico. He may have been at times with the Black Jack Ketchum gang; with it, according to Tom Ketchum, Walters took part in another abortive train holdup, this one December 9, 1897, near Steins, New Mexico, and still another March 29, 1898, near Grants, New Mexico. A more successful effort occurred May 24, 1898, near Belen, New Mexico, in which up to $20,000 reportedly was taken. Bill and his gang shot their way out of an ambush the next day, three of the law party being killed one assertedly by Walters. Walters was shot and wounded seriously at a hideout in eastern Arizona July 29, 1898, and his close companion, Kid Johnson, wounded mortally by a posse headed by George A. Scarborough, Jeff D. Milton and Eugene J. Thacker. By August 17 Walters was back in the Santa Fe penitentiary. He was indicted for three killings, finally pleaded guilty to one charge of second degree murder and was sentenced to life; he escaped April 16, 1911, was quickly returned, but pardoned April 17, 1917, when he went to work for the Diamond A ranch near Hachita, New Mexico. He died following a fall from a windmill.

Philip J. Rasch, "An Incomplete Account of 'Bronco Bill' Walters." London, English Westerners' *Brand Book,* Vol. 19, No. 2 (Jan. 1977); *Los Angeles Times,* Aug. 8, 9, 1898.

Waltz, Jacob (Walz, Walsz, Walzer, von Walzer), prospector (1810-Oct. 25, 1891). B. in Prussia, he may have studied mining engineering at Heidelberg University, and perhaps had some German military experience. He came to the U.S. coincidentally with the 1848 Rhineland Revolution, in company with the Weiser family, of whom Jacob was to become his partner in the southwest. If he served as a soldier (reportedly Confederate) in the Civil War it was very briefly; Waltz was naturalized at Los Angeles July 19, 1861. With Weiser he reached Prescott, Arizona, in 1863. He reportedly saved one Miguel Peralta in a brawl at Arizpe, Sonora, in gratitude for which Peralta gave him a map to a mine in the Superstition Mountains of Arizona, said to have been worked by his family. According to legend, the Waltz-Weiser party found the deposit with little trouble. It was very rich, the pair bringing to Tucson $60,000 in gold, of which Peralta took half. On their return to the mine the partners surprised and killed two Mexicans working it. After some time at the mine, Waltz reported that he went to a Gila River settlement for supplies, returned to find Weiser slain, apparently by Indians. Waltz then carefully covered the mine's entrance and quitted the place. He lived with an Indian woman for a time at the Pima villages, it is said, and in 1875 bought land in Phoenix and settled there. He reported he made one more trip to the mine, to recover additional ore that had been extracted, then concealed the opening again. Other reports have him working the mine and transporting ore until about 1884. He lived thenceforth with Julia (Helena) Thomas, a mulatto, until his death, Waltz denying to her that he had· killed Weiser, and confiding details about his mine. Within five years after his death prospectors were searching the Superstitions for the "Dutch Jacob mine," and the "Lost Dutchman," fable or fact, has become one of the great lost-mine legends of the West. It may not have been all fiction in the beginning, but it is surrounded by fiction today.

Literature abundant; Sims Ely,*The Lost Dutchman Mine.* N.Y., William Morrow and Co., 1953; Curt Gentry, *The Killer Mountains.* N.Y., Ballantine Books, 1973; Robert Blair, *Tales of the Superstitions: The Origins of the Lost Dutchman Legend.* Tempe, Ariz. Hist. Found., 1975.

Wamsutta, (Alexander), Wampanoag chief (c. 1635-c. 1662). An elder son of Massasoit, Wamsutta succeeded his father as chief of the Wampanoags, but died a few months after he took over in 1661. His younger brother, who became King Philip, succeeded to the chieftainship.

Famous Indians: A Collection of Short Biographies. Wash., D.C., Govt. Printing Office, 1974.

Wandell, Charles W. (Argus), Mormon pioneer (fl. 1844-c. 1875). First mentioned at Nauvoo, Illinois, he joined the Mormon emigration to the Salt Lake Valley. About 1851 he and John Murdock (July 15, 1792-Dec. 23, 1871) were sent to Australia as first Mormon missionaries there, in March 1852, organizing the initial church at Sydney; it had 36 charter members. Wandell returned to San Francisco September 1, 1853, with a small number of recruits, "the first fruits of the mission." For a time he worked in the church historian's office at Salt Lake City. Wandell is supposed by Brooks to be the "Argus" who wrote an open letter to Brigham Young which appeared as a series of articles in the Corinne *Utah Reporter,* demanding that the mystery of the Mountain Meadows Massacre of September 11, 1857, be cleared up, that the guilty he brought to justice "and that the shame of this deed be lifted from the shoulders of innocent members of the church." The open letter "drew an instant reaction wherever it was read." In court at John Doyle Lee's first trial Philip Klingensmith testified he had told the facts of the massacre to Wandell.

Juanita Brooks, *The Mountain Meadows Massacre.* Norman, Univ. of Okla. Press, 1966.

Waneta, Yanktonai chief (c. 1795-1848). A Sioux of the Cuthead band, he was b. on the Elm River in Brown County, South Dakota, and enlisted with his father, Shappa (Red Thunder) in English service in the War of 1812. He fought valiantly at Fort Meigs and Fort Sandusky, Ohio, being seriously wounded in the latter engagement. After the war, with a captain's commission in the British army, he visited England. He continued to favor the British until 1820 when he sought by stealth to destroy Fort St. Anthony (Snelling), Minnesota; he was thwarted by Colonel Josiah Snelling and thereafter was persuaded to support American interests. Waneta was a dominant chief of the Sioux and very active in warlike operations. He signed a treaty at Fort Pierre July 5, 1825, and August 25 of that year another treaty at Prairie du Chien, Wisconsin, fixing the boundaries of Sioux territory. He died on Beaver Creek, Emmons County North Dakota.

Hodge, HAI.

Wannalancet, Pennacook sachem (c. 1625-c. 1700). A son of Passaconaway and successor as sachem of the Pennacook on the Merrimac, New Hampshire, the Pennacook being most closely related to the Abenaki, another Algonquian people. During most of his life he was friendly with the English, but it was not easy. In 1659 he was imprisoned for debt. In King Philip's War of 1675-76 the greater part of the Pennacook remained on friendly terms with the English until the treacherous seizure of 200 of Wannalancet's people and exiling them into slavery abroad. Wannalancet then abandoned the country for Canada where his people joined the Abenaki and other Indians of St. Francis. Wannalancet died in Canada late in the 17th Century.

Hodge, HAI, Swanton, *Tribes,* 18.

Wapasha (Wabasha), several Mdewakanton Sioux chiefs. The first Wapasha of record (although there were predecessors) was born on Rum River, Minnesota, in 1718, his father a chief of the same name, his mother a Chippewa. In 1747 through relatives of his mother Wapasha negotiated a peace between the Chippewa and his people. In 1763 an English trader was killed at his St. Anthony Falls store by a Sioux named Ixatape in retaliation for which the English cut off the trade upon which the Sioux had become dependent. To alleviate the destitution of his people Wapasha determined to take the murderer to Quebec and deliver him to the English. With many tribesmen he started, but defections occurred, finally the prisoner escaped, and Wapasha went on almost alone to offer himself as a vicarious sacrifice for the murder of the trader. The English were deeply impressed by his intent and he was accorded much honor. War broke out anew between his people and the Chippewa and in 1778 he scored some victories in an effort to recover former Sioux land around Spirit Lake, but his party was ambushed and many of his men slain. Two years later he avenged his loss in a notable battle near Elk River, Minnesota. Wapasha sided with the English in the American Revolution; he served in the west with Charles Langlade. He established his band near the present Winona, Minnesota, where he died about 1799. Wapasha II, b. about 1773, succeeded his father as chief. He met Zebulon Pike in 1806 at Prairie du Chien, Wisconsin, and advised him to make Little

Crow the American chief of the Sioux. Although nominally with the English in the War of 1812, his sentiments were mainly with the Americans; after the conflict he was prominent in relations between the whites and the Sioux. He died of smallpox in 1836. Wapasha III, or Joseph Wapasha succeeded as chief of the old Red Leaf band and took his people to the reservation on the upper Minnesota River. He was opposed to the 1862 Great Sioux Uprising, but mildly assisted in it, afterward removing to the Missouri with his followers and locating ultimately at Santee, Nebraska. He signed the Treaty of 1868 which formally ended the Red Cloud War and died at the Santee Agency in Nebraska April 23, 1876. Wapasha IV (Napoleon Wapasha) succeeded his father as chief of the Santee Sioux on the Santee Reservation, Niobrara, Nebraska, where he still was living in 1909.

Hodge, HAI; Roy W. Meyer, *History of the Santee Sioux.* Lincoln, Univ. of Nebr. Press, 1967.

War Bonnet (Ka-ko-yui-si-nih), Southern Cheyenne chief (d. Nov. 29, 1864). Head of the Oivimana Clan, he was a prominent chief in the Plains activities of the Southern Cheyennes and in March 1863 visited Washington, D.C., and with other Indian leaders conferred with Lincoln, then went to New York where they visited showman P.T. Barnum. War Bonnet and about half his clan died at Sand Creek, Colorado, in the Chivington attack.

George Bird Grinnell, *The Fighting Cheyennes.* Norman, Univ. of Okla. Press, 1956; Stan Hoig, *The Western Odyssey of John Simpson Smith.* Glendale, Calif., Arthur H. Clark, 1974; George E. Hyde, *Life of George Bent.* Norman, 1968.

Ward, Edward Wilkerson, army officer (d. Dec. 13, 1897). B. in Kentucky, he served in Twyman's company of Kentucky Scouts from 1861 until 1863, then in the 3rd Kentucky Cavalry until the close of the Civil War. July 22, 1867, he was commissioned a second lieutenant in the 5th Cavalry, becoming captain by 1878. He was transferred to the Kansas frontier in 1868, taking part in actions at Prairie Dog Creek, Shuter Creek and the Solomon River, was adjutant on the Canadian River expedition of 1868-69, fought Sioux and Cheyennes at Beaver and Spring creeks in 1869, was on the Republican River expedition and in the fight on Prairie Dog

Creek. He reached Arizona in 1873, was in an Apache fight at Santa Teresa Mountains, commanded Indian scouts at Camp Apache, and returned to Fort Wallace, Kansas, in 1875. After an extended sick leave, one of many, he took part in the Powder River expedition and the fight on Bates Creek, Wyoming; he retired because of disability in line of duty May 1, 1879, living subsequently at Lincolnton, North Carolina, where he died.

Price, *Fifth Cavalry;* Heitman.

Ward, Elijah Barney, frontiersman (Mar. 29, 1813-Apr. 10, 1865). B. at Richmond, Virginia, he reportedly left home at 15, became an Indian trader, and joined Wyeth in 1834, helping build Fort Hall, Idaho, that summer. In 1837 he and John W. Patrick established a trading post at the later site of Provo, Utah, operating it until 1848. He was a mountain man, survivor of Indian skirmishes, reportedly served in the Mexican War, visited California at least once, became a Mormon and friend of Brigham Young. He often served as interpreter. He was killed in the Black Hawk War in Salina Canyon, near Gunnison, Utah.

LeRoy R. Hafen article, MM, Vol VII.

Ward, Jerome, L., lawman (May 6, 1833-Sept. 26, 1913). B. at Vernon, New York, he moved to Jefferson County, Wisconsin, about 1843 and married in 1853. In 1862 he became a wagoner for the 1st Wisconsin Cavalry, but was discharged for disability in the line of duty February 9, 1863, at Cape Girardeau, Missouri. He moved to California, then to Arizona where he was elected sheriff of Cochise County in 1882, succeeding John Behan. Like Behan he was interested in fast horses, once paying his predecessor $1,000 for a mare Behan had purchased for $20 in California. Ward's deputy, D.T. Smith, was killed in the "Bisbee Massacre" of December 6, 1883. Ward was instrumental in apprehending the outlaws and ran the public execution March 8, 1884, at which five were hanged (a sixth man had been lynched). Ward was killed by a truck in a San Diego, California, parade. He had fathered four children.

AHS Archives; Ed Bartholomew, *Wyatt Earp: The Man & The Myth.* Toyahvale, Tex., Frontier Book Co., 1964.

Ward, Nancy, Cherokee woman (c. 1738-c. 1824). Her father was said to have been a British army officer and her mother a sister of Attakullaculla, principal chief of the nation at the time of the first Cherokee War. She may have been related, perhaps by marriage, to Brian Ward, oldtime trader among the Cherokees. During the Revolution she lived at Echota, Georgia, where she held title of "Beloved Woman" or "Pretty Woman," by virtue of which she was entitled to speak in councils and decide the fate of captives. She was a determined friend of the white Americans, always seeking peace and, in time of trouble bringing warnings of impending raids as on the occasion of the great invasion of the Watauga and Holston settlements in 1776. A Mrs. Bean, perhaps of the famous Watauga Bean family, captured during this incursion was saved by Nancy's intervention after being condemned and bound to the stake. In 1780 during another Cherokee outbreak she assisted traders to escape; the next year she was sent by the chiefs to make peace with John Sevier and Arthur Campbell, advancing against the Cherokee towns. Peace was not then granted but her relatives brought in with other prisoners were treated with consideration due to her good offices. She was described by Robertson at this time as "queenly and commanding" in appearance and manner, her house furnished in keeping with her position. Nuttall was told when among the Arkansas Cherokee in 1819 that she had introduced the first cows into the nation and greatly elevated the Cherokee condition. He was also told that her advice and counsel bordered upon the supreme, and her intervention was decisive even in affairs of life and death. She was described as tall, erect and beautiful with a prominent nose, regular features, clear complexion, long silken black hair, large piercing black eyes, and an imperious yet kindly air. Her descendants are still living in the nation.

Hodge, HAI; Thwaites, EWT, XIII, 183-84 and 183n.

Ward, Seth E., frontiersman (Mar. 4, 1820-Dec. 9, 1903). B. in Campbell County, Virginia, he reached St. Louis by 1836, Independence, Missouri, two years later, and was hired by Lancaster P. Lupton, trader on the South Platte. He continued to Fort Davy Crockett, Brown's Hole, Colorado, remaining three years trading and occasionally trapping. By 1845 he was associated with Ceran St.

Vrain on the South Platte, later with William Le Guerrier (killed in a gunpowder explosion in 1858) in the Fort Laramie region, occupying himself with various pioneering enterprises. In 1857 he became sutler at Fort Laramie, a central figure in many stirring events. In 1871 he removed to Westport, Missouri, reportedly a millionaire. He became one of the most prominent builders of Kansas City, where he died.

Merrill J. Mattes article, MM, Vol. III.

Ware, Eugene Fitch, soldier, historical writer (May 29, 1841-July 1, 1911). B. at Hartford, Connecticut, he moved as a youth with his family to Burlington, Iowa. Ware enlisted in a couple of short-lived volunteer outfits from Iowa in 1861, then joined the 4th Iowa Cavalry November 23, 1861, to be mustered out October 25, 1862, at Helena, Arkansas. He enlisted again, this time in Company A, 7th Iowa Cavalry February 14, 1863, was commissioned a second lieutenant September 4, and eventually became captain before being mustered out in May 1866. He had spent his years in the 7th on the Plains, the organization charged with others with keeping the overland routes open and free from Indian attack; from this service came his most noted book, *The Indian War of 1864.* It was written long after the events it describes, but was based upon "a daily journal. While in the service I frequently wrote to my mother long letters. Upon her death...I found that she had saved them. So, the journal and letters and the company field-desk enable me to write more fully and accurately than I otherwise might." His book contains "a vivid description of the frontier during the Civil War and of the hard, dangerous, mononous role played by the Civil War soldier who was sent west rather than south," and Ware generally is accurate, although afflicted with heated prejudices. In his peacetime career he was a newspaperman, was admitted to the Kansas bar in 1871, served in the Kansas Senate, was active in the state Historical Society, an erstwhile poet and died at Cascade, Colorado. He wrote a book of verse and one on the Civil War, *The Lyon Campaign.* He married and was the father of four children.

Ware, *The Indian War of 1864,* intr. by Clyde C. Walton. N.Y., St. Martin's Press, 1960; *Collecs. of the Kan. State Hist. Soc., 1913-1914,* Vol. XIII, 19-71.

Ware, William M., Texas Ranger (c. 1855-1930). B. at Uvalde, Texas, he became a Ranger under Lieutenant Pat Dolan. He reported he had taken part in "numerous skirmishes" with Comanches. In 1885 he was deputy sheriff at Pecos, Texas "during the stormy days of a feud," the sheriff being killed. In 1918 he was running a sheep ranch for James G. McNary. During his career he was reported to have killed five men "without counting Indians." He suffered from cancer in his later years and shot himself at El Paso. Ware was married and left his widow and a son, Robert, at San Angelo, Texas.

Frontier Times, Vol. 7, No. 12 (Sept. 1930), 555-56.

Warfield, Charles Alexander, frontiersman (c. 1810-post 1863). B. probably at New Orleans, his date of birth is conjecture. He had reached the Rocky Mountains by about 1832, becoming a trapper with Bridger and others, occasionally skirmishing with Blackfeet and other Indians. He resided in Brown's Hole, Colorado, about 1839, visited California, lived for a time in New Mexico and reached Texas. He was commissioned a colonel August 16, 1842, to head an expedition against Santa Fe. Warfield traveled to New Orleans, Arkansas, and the Plains fur-trading posts seeking recruits and in March 1843, formally enrolled them on the south bank of the Arkansas River, eventually moving closer to New Mexico with his tiny band. Everything went wrong, a raid on Mora, New Mexico, was of no lasting benefit, and on May 29 Warfield disbanded most of his organization. Meanwhile, Snively, with a larger formation of Texans, had moved to the Santa Fe Trail and Warfield joined him. Warfield attacked and defeated a New Mexico force under Armijo June 19, 1843, but the Snively-Warfield expedition was defused by Philip St. George Cooke. Warfield became acquainted with William Drummond Stewart and accompanied the Scotsman to Europe in 1844; he was back in New Orleans by 1845. He lived in Arkansas and Missouri for some years, associating in trading ventures with Albert Gallatin Boone, moved to Santa Fe with the Civil War, and eventually to California where his trail dims in the middle 1860s.

Nicholas P. Hardeman article, MM Vol. VII; Barry, *The Beginning of West;* Josiah Gregg,

Commerce of the Prairies. Norman, Univ. of Okla. Press, 1954.

Warfield, John C.A., soldier (Nov. 26, 1842-Aug. 2, 1937). B. in Carroll County, Maryland, he enlisted at Louisiana, Missouri, on February 1, 1862, in Company A, 3rd Missouri Cavalry, and re-enlisted in the fall of 1864 in the 14th Missouri Volunteer Cavalry, where he was commissioned a second lieutenant, being mustered out in November 1865 as a first lieutenant. On April 20, 1863, at the battle of Patterson, Missouri, he was captured and paroled; at the time he was a sergeant. In September 1865, Warfield was found "perfectly justified" in shooting Private Phil Door (or Dorr) of Company F, 14th Missouri Cavalry, after ordering Door's arrest for being drunk and disorderly in a Junction City, Kansas, saloon. Door was severely but apparently not mortally, wounded; he had threatened Warfield with a "hevy knife." On January 23, 1868, Warfield enlisted in the 3rd U.S. Cavalry, serving in F Company for 10 years, usually with grade of sergeant, but several times being reduced to private. Posted to Arizona, F Troop was one of the most active Apache-hunting outfits of the army of the day, and Warfield saw much service against hostiles; he was considered by Bourke one of the most powerful men of the company, and with "Big Dan" Miller once saved the life of the legendary Lieutenant Howard Bass Cushing when the officer was swept from his feet by a flash flood on Pinal Creek. Warfield was not present in the fight in which Cushing was killed. The sergeant had a prominent role in Reynolds' Powder River fight with the Cheyennes March 17, 1876, and led one of the first parties into the enemy village. He was slightly wounded in a June 9 skirmish with the Sioux, and won warm praise of Bourke and others for his role in the battle of the Rosebud, June 17, 1876. After his second 3rd Cavalry enlistment, Warfield lived for a time in Wyoming and for many years in the Salt Lake Valley of Utah. He married twice. His first wife, Anna Cramer, was wed in 1872 at Tucson. By her he had three children, but never kept in touch with them after his divorce, which came in 1876 after "infidelity on her part," in adddition to Warfield's discovery she had never been properly divorced by her previous husband, making the second marriage invalid. He married Emma

Clark in 1882 at Granger, Wyoming, this marriage enduring. Warfield died at Los Angeles, California. Although described as "powerful" by Bourke, Warfield in his young manhood was 5 feet, 9 inches in height, and weighed less than 160 pounds; he had eyes variously described as gray or blue, light or auburn hair and a complexion either "light" or ruddy. In his declining years he suffered from various ailments.

Warfield's service and pension records, Nat. Archives; John G. Bourke, *On Border;* J.W. Vaughn, *The Reynolds Campaign on Powder River.* Norman, Univ. of Okla. Press, 1961; J.W. Vaughn, *With Crook at the Rosebud.* Harrisburg, Stackpole Co., 1956.

Warfington (Worthington, etc.), Richard, soldier (b. 1777). B. at Louisburg, North Carolina, he enlisted in Captain John Campbell's company of the 2nd Infantry and became a corporal, his enlistment due to expire August 4, 1804. Nevertheless he went up the Missouri with Lewis and Clark and wintered with them at the Mandan villages after arranging with Lewis to continue in service beyond the expiration date as though still actively enrolled; Lewis needed him to take a detachment south to St. Louis in the spring of 1805 with dispatches and a collection of articles. He had great confidence in Warfington, writing that "the duties assigned him on this occasion were performed with a punctuality which (uniformly characterized) his conduct while under my command," and recommended special consideration for the corporal from the government. He reached St. Louis June 1, 1805, Clarke affirming that he returned to his original military company and was formally discharged. Nothing further is known of him.

History of the Expedition Under Command of Lewis and Clark, ed. by Elliott Coues. N.Y., Dover Pubns., 1965; Clarke, *Lewis and Clark.*

Warnell (Wornell), Henry, adventurer (c. 1812-c. June 1836). B. probably in Arkansas, when his wife died in 1834 he moved to Texas and settled at Bastrop; it was reported that Warnell, a slight man, had been a "jockey and a great hunter" in Arkansas. He was at the Alamo under Travis and volunteered for courier service. According to one report he left the Alamo early in March 1836, carrying a message to Houston that arrived at San Felipe

March 4, although Warnell was wounded, dying within a few weeks of the incident (one account said three years afterward); other sources believed he died at the Alamo. He was described as weighing 118 pounds, was blue-eyed, red-haired, freckled and "an incessant tobacco chewer."

Amelia Williams, XXXVII, 282-83.

Warner, Dave, gunman (d. Dec. 1, 1873). Warner apparently sided with Ben Horrell and Jack Gylam in their dispute with lawman Juan Martinez at Lincoln, New Mexico, in the first episode of the so-called Horrell War. Warner was killed with the other two Anglos and Martinez in the gun battle which erupted.

Robert N. Mullin notes.

Warner, Jonathan Trumbull, ranchman, pioneer (Nov. 20, 1807-Apr. 22, 1895). B. at Lyme, Connecticut, he reached St. Louis in 1830. He was hired by Jedediah Strong Smith in the spring of 1831 as clerk for a trading expedition to New Mexico, the party eventually numbering 83 men, well equipped with wagons, goods, and even a cannon. Smith was killed by Comanches, but the remainder of the group reached Santa Fe in July, Warner continuing to Los Angeles with the David E. Jackson expedition, arriving December 5. Warner beaver trapped in the California valleys 1832-33, settled in Los Angeles in 1834, was one of the vigilantes two years later putting to death a woman and her accomplice for a savage murder. Occasionally he became embroiled in political tumults. He returned to the States in 1839 via Vera Cruz, and in a lecture at Rochester, New York, spoke for a transcontinental railroad. He returned to California by sea in 1841, becoming briefly a seal hunter off the coast. Being naturalized in 1844 he obtained the Agua Caliente rancho, a vast area extending to Mt. Palomar in present San Diego County where he lived for a dozen years, the place acquiring the name of the Warner Rancho. It became famous as a stopping place for travelers and for other reasons. General Kearny's force camped there just before the battle of San Pasqual, and the Mormon Battalion visited it. Warner endured passing Indian troubles, one uprising driving him and his family from their home in 1851, though they soon returned. He moved to Los Angeles in 1855, and the ranch was out of his control by 1861. He wrote much about early California. Because he was a tall man, 6 feet, 3 inches, in height, he was known as Don Juan Largo (Long John). He married (his wife died in 1859), and fathered several children.

Bancroft, *Pioneer Register;* DAB; Dale Morgan, *Jedediah Smith and the Opening of the West.* Indianapolis, Bobbs-Merrill Co., 1953.

Warner, Solomon, merchant (Feb. 8, 1811-Nov. 14, 1899). B. near Warnersville, New York, he made for the Mississippi River at 26 and worked river boats for a time, then migrated to California during the gold rush. In 1851 he sailed to Panama, worked in Nicaragua briefly, and returned to San Francisco in 1853. A mason by trade he laid foundations for Fort Yuma in 1855, then became associated with merchants George F. Hooper and Francis Hinton. He took a pack string of mules to Tucson, reaching it February 29, 1856, with goods to open the first Anglo-supplied store there, which commenced operations March 10. He formed a partnership with Mark Aldrich, later a mayor of the town, and prospered until the Confederates confiscated his stock, he removing to Santa Cruz, Sonora, just ahead of their patrols. When the war ended he returned and reopened his business. He was wounded seriously by Apaches January 28, 1870, when enroute from Santa Cruz to Tucson; his companion was killed. His enterprises continued to prosper until he became too old to care for them properly, and he died from cancer in somewhat strained circumstances.

Donald N. Bentz, "Tucson's First Merchant." *Best of the West,* (1973), 13, 65-66.

Warren, George, prospector (c. 1845-1892). B. in Massachusetts, some sources, apparently erroneously, give his year of birth as about 1835. His mother died when he was a child and he was sent to New Mexico, about 1855, to live with his teamster father. Apaches killed the parent and captured the boy; he lived with them for "several years." He was traded for by prospectors for a 15-pound sack of sugar and freed, to become a prospector himself. Warren had very little schooling. In about 1877 he was grubstaked at Fort Bowie by chief of scouts Jack Dunn and perhaps others, given the location in the Mule Mountains of southeastern Arizona where Dunn earlier had found silver ore, and sent to hunt it up. Alcohol got the better of him, and he brought others in to found the future Bisbee, Arizona, a fabulously rich copper camp. Warren let millions slip through his fingers because of his addiction to whiskey and because he was eccentric, so much so that he was adjudged insane about March 2, 1881, and sent to a Phoenix asylum. Upon his release, he tried prospecting in Mexico from 1885, returning to Bisbee, worked at odd jobs and, while drunk, contracted pneumonia from which he died. He was buried in Brewery Gulch, Bisbee, in the Evergreen Cemetery, his remains reinterred in 1917 and an imposing monument placed over them.

Opie Rundle Burgess, *Bisbee Not So Long Ago.* San Antonio, Tex., Naylor Co., 1967; brief manuscript by James M. Hart, "History of George Warren." AHS, 1926.

Warren, Gouverneur Kemble, army officer (Jan. 8, 1830-Aug. 8, 1882). B. at Cold Spring, New York, he was graduated from West Point second in his class in 1850 and joined the Corps of Topographical Engineers. He worked on river surveys in middle America and in 1854 took part in western railroad surveys. He joined Harney for the Sioux expedition, taking part in the September 3, 1855, battle of Blue Water. He explored the upper Missouri and Yellowstone river basins for suitable sites for military posts and later conducted numerous river and seashore surveys as well as studies of means of bridging streams for railroads; his many writings as portions of books or of article length, included descriptions of the results of his work (see list in *Centennial of the United States Military Academy at West Point, New York 1802-1902.* Vol. II). Warren taught mathematics at West Point until the Civil War in which his record was brilliant; he had a decisive role at Gettysburg and an important part in the climactic battle of Five Forks until Sheridan unjustly and rudely removed him. Warren was completely exonerated by a Board of Inquiry although the results were not published until after his death. Following the war he completed maps and reports of his campaigns and early explorations, particularly in Dakota and Nebraska, his work always distinguished. He belonged to a number of scientific and professional organizations. He married and fathered a son and a daughter. Warren died a lieutenant colonel of engineers at Newport, Rhode Island.

Montana Contributions, Vol. X, 1940, 297; DAB; Heitman; Cullum; CE.

Warren, William Whipple, Ojibway historian (May 27, 1825-June 1, 1853). B. at LaPointe, Minnesota, the son of fur trader Lyman M. Warren and Mary Cadotte, French-Chippewa woman, he was well educated and traveled to New York to further his studies at Clarkson and the Oneida Institute. Returned home he determined to study the history of the Chippewas, further perfected himself in the language until he understood and spoke it more fluently than old Chippewas themselves. He married in 1842 but commenced to suffer from tuberculosis. He moved in 1845 to Crow Wing, Minnesota, and in 1850 was elected to the Minnesota Legislature, quickly becoming known for ability and hard work. He wrote sketches of the Chippewa for newspapers, in 1852 completed a manuscript, *History of the Ojibways, Based Upon Traditions and Oral Statements,* and took it to New York, but failed to interest a publisher. He returned home, got as far as St. Paul where he died of his affliction at the age of 28 and was buried in a local cemetery. His work was published posthumously.

William W. Warren, *History of the Ojibways.* St. Paul, *Minn. Hist. Collecs.,* 5 (1885), pp. 21-394; for sketch of Warren, see ibid., 9-20.

Washakie, Shoshone chief (c. 1804-Feb. 20, 1900). Said to be of mixed Shoshone and Umatilla blood (and some believed him part white), he left the Umatilla before maturing and joined his mother's people, the Shoshone. While a noted warrior against his tribal enemies, he was a firm friend of the whites. He became chief of the eastern band of Shoshone, which came to be known as Washakie's band; it is said that when 70, younger men sought to depose him as too elderly to lead his people. Washakie disappeared and returned two months later to present the council with six scalps he had taken on a lone warpath, thus affirming his vigor. When in the 1850's numbers of emigrants traversed his country, he and his people avoided friction, aided overland travelers, helped them recover stock or ford streams. So friendly and helpful were they that it was said 9,000 emigrants signed a paper commending the tribe. Washakie owed his popularity among his followers to his warpath feats, especially against Blackfeet and Crows. He was for years hired by the Hudson's Bay and American Fur companies, and was a valued companion of white trappers. Before Connor's battle in 1863 on the Bear River with the Bannocks and hostile Shoshones who refused to follow Washakie, the chief took most of his tribe to Fort Bridger, Wyoming, saving them from destruction. Washakie frequently served as scout or irregular in white operations against neighboring warlike tribes. At his death he was a devout Episcopalian and a friend of missionaries. He was buried with military honors at Fort Washakie, Wyoming, where his grave is marked with a monument. Washakie was described as light in color, of commanding figure, tall, powerfully built, dignified and of great endurance.

Hodge, II, p. 919; Virginia Cole Trenholm, Maurine Carley, *The Shoshonis: Sentinels of the Rockies.* Norman, Univ. of Okla. Press, 1964; Grace R. Hebard, *Washakie.* Cleveland, Arthur H. Clark Co., 1930.

Washburn, Henry Dana, explorer (Mar. 28, 1832-Jan. 26, 1871). B. at Windsor, Vermont, his parents moved the year of his birth to Wayne County, Ohio, where Washburn lived until 1850. He was a school teacher for a time, then studied law and opened an office at Newport, Indiana, in 1854, being married late that year. He raised a company which became Co. C., 18th Indiana Infantry, for Civil War service, taking part in actions west of the Mississippi, including Pea Ridge, then at Vicksburg and later in the Shenandoah Valley, Washburn emerging as a brevet Major General. He was elected U.S. representative, but after two terms in the House, requested appointment as surveyor general of Montana Territory, in the hope that life in the west would improve his health, ravaged during Civil War campaigns. He was appointed April 17, 1869. One 70-day voyage up the Missouri failed to deposit Washburn and his family in Montana because of a mishap to the craft, and Washburn went overland to Helena, sending his family back to Indiana. In 1870 he led an important expedition into the Yellowstone country, proving himself an ideal commander for such an enterprise. However, a cold caught while searching for the lost Truman Everts south of Lake Yellowstone advanced his

tendency toward tuberculosis and he returned to Indiana. Here, although ill, he wrote an account of the Yellowstone adventure which was highly praised. He died at Clinton, Indiana.

Aubrey L. Haines, *Yellowstone National Park: Its Exploration and Establishment.* Wash., Nat. Park Service, 1974.

Washburn, Hiram Starrs, frontiersman (Feb. 7, 1820-Feb 16, 1889). B. at Randolph, Vermont, he was trained as a surveyor and reached the Gila River in Arizona as early as 1857. He was resident in the Pima villages on the stream in 1860; later he appears to have engaged in mining in the Santa Rita Mountain area south of Tucson. In the summer of 1865 he was commissioned to raise elements of the so-called Arizona Volunteers to fight Apaches and for other purposes; July 15 he wrote Governor John N. Goodwin that he had recruited more than 80 men, more were expected; Oscar Hutton, an old Apache fighter, had been named first lieutenant and Manuel Gallegos would be named second lieutenant. Washburn thought enlistment of Mexican recruits "opportune" on several counts: "It promotes amity and mutual confidence between the two nations"; he believed them superior in Indian fighting, and besides, "they would be the most desirable auxiliaries in checking French aspirations and intentions (in Mexico), which have now progressed as far as Hermosill(o), with nothing to obstruct the progress to the line.... It has long been openly asserted among the Mexicans that the French intend, as soon as they have put down all opposition in Sonora, to cross the line and capture all the country ceded to the United States by Santa Anna.... But what we want first is to wipe out the Apaches and restore our own Arizona to that condition wherein emigrants and capitalists...can come here and mine, manufacture and cultivate the soil in security...." On September 1, 1865, Washburn wrote from Fort Mason, acknowledging the willingness of military authorities of the California command to continue the Arizona Volunteers "in active service," and reported preliminary success in taking an Apache scalp: his men captured an Apache and "took him down to where the Apaches had killed a Mexican fiddler in June last, where his spirit followed that of the poor fiddler's." Washburn was not averse to treachery to best the Apaches, as his communications make clear; how effective he was as commander the record does not reveal. January 4, 1866, as a captain he was ordered to take command at Camp Lincoln on the Verde River, Arizona, the post later designated as Camp or Fort Verde. His command dwindled by sickness, desertion and other factors, and was made inept by lack of supplies from any source, and no pay; by August 29 he was forced by lack of manpower to abandon Camp Lincoln and in November his last remaining command, Company E, was deactivated to Washburn's relief. He returned to the East. Washburn settled at Washington, D.C., for the remainder of his life, married, and died.

AHS Archives, Hayden File; Robert W. Munson, "The Clear Creek Settlers' Fort," manuscript.

Washington, George, soldier, partisan (c. 1841-c. June 8, 1882). B. in Texas he enlisted in Company B of the black 9th Cavalry and on July 8, 1869 was riding guard on the mail-carrying stagecoach in outlaw country near Lipan Springs, west of San Antonio. In the gloom of night he heard a shout and saw a figure clambering into the slow-moving vehicle. The soldier fired blindly, mortally wounding David M. Mason, who was seeking to hitch a ride as an employee of mail contractor Ben Ficklin. An investigation cleared Washington, since it was felt he had only done his duty. Later he deserted, it is said, but if he had signed up when the regiment was formed in 1866 his enlistment would have expired when he next was reported, a laborer at Fort Stanton, New Mexico, garrisoned by 9th Cavalry troops. He subsequently became a "servant" in the home of Alexander McSween of Lincoln. Thus he was involved in the Lincoln County turmoil on the McSween side, but the extent of his activities is not certainly known. His involvement in the five days battle of July 1878 was peripheral. On July 20, 1879, he reportedly killed his wife and child "while trying to shoot a dog." According to Lincoln County tradition, Washington taught Josefina Baca to play the guitar, they eloped and the girl's father, Saturnino Baca overtook the couple, returned them to Lincoln where Washington was hanged in Baca's barn.

Wayne R. Austerman, *Sharps Rifles and Spanish Mules: The San Antonio-El Paso Mail, 1851-1881.* College Station, Texas A & M Univ. Press, 1985; Robert N. Mullin notes; Philip J. Rasch, "George Washington of Lincoln County," Potomac Corral of Westerners *Corral Dust,* Vol. VI, No. 6 (Dec. 1961), 45-46.

Washington, John Macrea, army officer, governor (Oct. 1797-Dec. 24, 1853). His father was a second cousin of George Washington, and John Washington was b. in Safford County, Virginia. He was graduated from West Point and July 17, 1817, was commissioned a third lieutenant of artillery, a second lieutenant March 20, 1818, and a first lieutenant May 23, 1820. He joined the 4th Artillery June 1, 1821, and became a captain May 30, 1832, all of his service until then being at southeastern posts. From 1833-38 he was engaged in Florida against Seminole and Creek Indians; January 24, 1838, he participated in the battle of Loche-Hachee, Florida, under Brigadier General Thomas Sidney Jesup. In the action there were seven soldiers killed and 32 wounded, while Indian losses were unknown. He assisted Winfield Scott's transfer of the Cherokees in 1838-39 to Oklahoma. Washington then helped quell Canadian border troubles until 1842. He commanded a battery in John E. Wool's column in the Mexican War, becoming a major in the 3rd Artillery February 16, 1847, and winning a brevet to lieutenant colonel at Buena Vista. Washington was placed in command of an expedition to Santa Fe and served as civil and military governor of New Mexico for a year from October 1848. Indian hostility in March 1849 led him to call up militia and August 16 he led an elaborate expedition into Navaho country. During a skirmish August 30 the important Navaho chief Narbona was killed. The command went to the Canyon de Chelly where September 9 Washington arranged a "treaty" with Mariano Martinez, a chief and Chapitone, a headman of a northerly band of Navahos. Washington returned by way of Zuñi, Laguna and Albuquerque. He recommended military posts in Navaho country. His treaty was short-lived since it was signed by the Navahos as "an empty gesture to satisfy the American intruders and induce them to leave as quickly as possible. Terms of the treaty...were impossibly one-sided and opposed to Navaho interests." Washington soon was moved to a New Hampshire post where he served until December 1853 when he embarked aboard the steamer *San Francisco* for the west coast. In a violent storm off the mouth of the Delaware a giant wave flushed the ship, sweeping Washington, three other officers and 178 men into the sea to their deaths. He had married and fathered three children.

Cullum; Heitman; Frank McNitt, *Navajo Wars.* Albuquerque, Univ. of New Mex. Press, 1972; Twitchell, *Leading Facts,* II.

Wasson, John, editor (1833-Jan. 16, 1909). B. in Ohio, he was editor and publisher of the *Tucson Citizen* from 1870 to 1874, and during that time was largely responsible for instigating and promoting the Camp Grant massacre of more than 100 peaceful Apaches by a mixed crowd of whites and Papago Indians. He had taught schools in Ohio and Utah, published newspapers in Idaho and California, remained at Tucson 12 years where in addition to editing he was surveyor-general of the Territory, was prominent in Republican politics in Arizona and California. He died at Pomona, California.

Farish, VI; Estelle Lutrell, *Newspapers and Periodicals of Arizona 1859-1911.* Tucson, Univ. of Ariz. Press, 1949.

Waters, James Wesley, mountain man, pioneer (Jan. 30, 1813-Sept. 20, 1889). B. at Brainard's Bridge, Rensselaer County, New York, he left home at 16, drove mules on the Erie Canal towpath, in the early 1830s was at St. Louis and by 18 or 20 was trapping in the Rockies. He associated with Jim Bridger, Kit Carson, Bill Williams, Rube Herring and other mountain greats for several years. On one occasion in Ute country on the Upper Arkansas, Waters was wounded by an Indian; his companions, Bill Williams and Dick Wootton cut out the bullet with a butcher knife, doused the wound with "Taos lightning," bandaged it with a blanket piece and got Waters to Fort Bent where he ultimately recovered. Around 1842 he made his first trip to California, journeying with Jim Beckwourth and a dozen others, and in January 1844 again reached California with Beckwourth. In the fall Waters and a party chartered a sailboat, coasted to Lower California and returned to Los Angeles with a cargo of abalone shells which one report said

they packed to Fort Laramie, although it did not explain why this was done or the disposition of the shells. While in California Jim had become slightly involved in turbulence surrounding the 1845 revolt of Castro and Alvarado against Governor Manuel Micheltorena, but soon he regained the Rockies, continued on to St. Louis and guided the Washburn emigrant family back to Pueblo, Colorado. On February 2, 1848, Ed Tharp, a brother of William Tharp quarreled with Waters over Jim's wife, the half-Indian Candelaría, and the Ed was killed. There were no repercussions, but the affair may have convinced Waters that his mountain days were played out and he determined to remove permanently to California. With his lifelong friend John Brown and others he arrived at Salt Lake City July 4, 1849. Here the party separated, Waters piloting an emigrant wagon train to southern California, arriving at Chino Ranch near present-day Pomona October 29, all 114 of the travelers "in good health." Jim went north to the mines, rejoined Brown, Alexis Godey and Rube Herring for fruitless gold prospecting, then settled at San Juan Bautista, northeast of Monterey, operating a hotel and livery stable until 1852. He went south to San Bernardino and purchased lots in the heart of the new community. In 1853 he drove cattle north to the San Francisco region and bought a ranch in Mariposa County, but never lived on it for extended periods. In February 1856 at San Bernardino he married an English woman (no report of what happened to Candelaría!), taking his bride and a flock of sheep to his Mariposa County place where a son was born later that year. Two years afterward he purchased the Rancho del Yucaipa near San Bernardino. Waters entered local politics, developed stock raising on properties as widely apart as San Diego County, California and Montana; his economic interests steadily expanded. He died at San Bernardino, respected and a comparatively wealthy man, leaving a son and six daughters.

Arthur Woodward, *Trapper Jim Waters,* Los Angeles Westerners *Keepsake 23,* 1954; Janet S. Lecompte, "William Tharp," MM, III; Dale L. Morgan, *The West of William H. Ashley.* Denver, Old West Pub. Co., 1964.

Waters, Jonah, adventurer (fl. 1800-1807). B. at Winchester, Virginia, he was a hatter by trade. He joined Philip Nolan for his 1800-1801 wild horse hunting expedition to the Trinity River of Spanish Texas and after Nolan was killed he and others were taken prisoner to Chihuahua City. Here he turned against his prisoner comrades, informed on them to authorities, foiled their attempts at escape, resumed his trade in the city and did what he could to win the confidence and support of his captors. Ellis Bean severely mauled him with a club for his duplicity, leaving him "with two women" of the house where he lived to care for him. Waters rolled a high turn of the dice thus avoiding hanging under a Spanish edict that one of the prisoners must die to atone for Nolan's having fired at the Spanish soldiery that accosted his party in Texas. Nothing further is known of Waters.

Bennett Lay, *The Lives of Ellis P. Bean.* Austin, Univ. of Tex. Press, 1960.

Waters, Joseph, desperado (d. Dec. 18, 1881). With Bill Campbell he engaged in a savage shootout at a Joseph H. Breed trading post at Sunset Crossing, Arizona, killing Joe Barrett and William Blanchard, Waters being slightly wounded. Captured, Campbell and Waters were lodged in the county jail at St. Johns, Arizona, from which they were taken by a mob and lynched.

Maurice Kildare, "Murder at Sunset Crossing." *Old Timers Old West,* 1975, 38-41, 60-61.

Waters, T.J., sporting man (c. 1840-July 1880). A 6 foot, 200 pound, individual, he boasted while drunk that he would assail anyone who joshed him about his gaudy new shirt; his friend, inoffensive E.L. Bradshaw, commented upon it later, a fight developed and Bradshaw shot Waters dead on a Tombstone, Arizona, street.

Ed Bartholomew, *Wyatt Earp: The Man & the Myth.* Toyahvale, Tex., Frontier Book Co., 1964.

Watie, Stand, Cherokee leader (Dec. 12, 1806-Sept. 9, 1871). B. at Coosawalee, near Rome, Georgia, he was more than half Cherokee, well educated and early assumed a role in tribal affairs. He signed the removal treaty of New Echota favored by Major Ridge and thus was among the first of the Cherokee to move west of the Mississippi River, but in doing so came to cross-purposes with the conservative faction headed by John Ross. Stand Watie was warned of the assassination attempt upon Elias Boudinot and the Ridges and escaped, but opposed Ross the rest of his life as consequence. He was a member of the Cherokee Tribal Council from 1845 to 1861 and its speaker from 1857-59. At the outbreak of the Civil War he with many Cherokees sided with the South and in time he commanded two regiments of the Cherokee Mounted Rifles, in 1862 leading his units at the Battle of Pea Ridge, Arkansas; May 10, 1864 he was commissioned a Brigadier General and was the last Confederate General to surrender following the war, giving up June 23, 1865. In 1864 he had been elected principal chief of the Southern Band of Cherokees. Stand Watie was a principal source for Henry Schoolcraft on the ethnology and history of the Cherokees. He died in Delaware County, Oklahoma, and was buried in Ridge Cemetery.

Hodge, HAI; Grace Steele Woodward, *The Cherokees.* Norman, Univ. of Okla. Press, 1963.

Watkins, Solomon, pioneer (d. May 12, 1853). B. in Indiana or Illinois he was at Fort Hall in 1851 and journeyed that year to The Dalles, Oregon, with John Owen, later working at the latter's famous Fort Owen in western Montana. He drowned at Hell Gate on the Missoula River.

George F. Weisel, *Men and Trade on the Northwest Frontier.* Missoula, Mont. State Univ. Press, 1955.

Watrin, Philibert, Jesuit missionary (Apr. 1, 1697-post 1764). B. at Metz, he became a Jesuit, reached North America in 1732 and spent 30 years of his life in the Louisiana mission. His lengthy, detailed summary of Jesuit work in the interior of North America, the trials and triumphs and sometimes heroic deaths of Jesuit missionaries, and a defense of their manner of conducting their missions, was reproduced by Thwaites, the authorship inferred because only he could be described as having lived "about thirty years in Louisiana." He left for France February 6, 1764, from New Orleans as the Jesuits were expelled from the French colonial possessions.

Thwaites, JR, LXX, 213-301, 313n36, LXXI, 170.

Watson, Douglas Sloan, historical writer (Apr. 2, 1875-Dec. 18, 1948). B. at New York City, Watson lived most of his life in the San Francisco Bay area, being interested professionally in real estate, oil developement and geology. His daughter, Margaret, married Herbert Hoover Jr., bringing Watson into contact with the future President. When Hoover was inaugurated, Watson noted that the White House library contained only dry reference works. He interested the American Booksellers Assn. in sprucing up the collection with 500 titles of current and lasting value, he and Alice Roosevelt Longworth being the arbiters of the collection. A writer by avocation, for some years Watson was a director of the California Historical Society and edited a number of publications. His most original work perhaps was *West Wind: The Life Story of Joseph Reddeford Walker, Knight of the Golden Horseshoe,* printed in 1934 by P.H. Booth who purportedly interested Watson in the project initially. In addition Watson produced: (ed.) William Heath Davis, *Seventy-five Years in California* (1929); (ed.) *The Santa Fe Trail to California 1849-1852: The Journal of H.M.T. Powell* (1931); (intr.) *Diary of Johann Augustus Sutter* (1932); (ed.) *Diary of Philip Leget Edwards: The Great Cattle Drive from California to Oregon in 1837* (1932); (ed.) *John Henry Brown: Reminiscences and Incidents of Early Days of San Francisco* (1933); (ed.) *The Spanish Occupation of California* (1934); (ed., trans.) *Francisco Palou, Founding of the First California Missions* (1934); (intr. and exp. text) *California in the Fifties* (1936).

New York Times, Dec. 19, 1948; information from Herbert Hoover III in correspondence with author, Sept. 9, 1975.

Watson, Ella, victim (c. 1862-July 20, 1889). B. probably at Lebanon, Kansas, Ella had gone as far west as Wyoming and become a prostitute, or so it was alleged, by 1886. On May 17, under the name of Ellen Liddy Andrews she was issued a license to wed James Averell (c. 1855-July 20, 1889), an army veteran and part-time surveyor who had a homestead near Independence Rock on the Sweetwater River where he also was store and saloon keeper, postmaster and justice of the peace. The marriage either was not finalized or was kept secret so Ella could file on a second homestead a mile west of Averell's; here it was alleged, she continued in her profession, sometimes accepting stolen cattle in payment, although that charge never was proven. The two homesteads were in the center of lands claimed for grazing by Albert J. Bothwell,

"most arrogant" of bigtime cattlemen of the region who soon came to cross-purposes with Averell who wrote letters to newspapers and in other ways charged Bothwell with imperiousness and related faults. Watson and Averell were accused of rustling and lynched by six men including, according to warrants issued on the testimony of eye-witnesses, Bothwell, Tom Sun, Ernest McLean, Robert B. Connor, Robert M. Galbraith and John Durbin. She was the only woman executed, legally or illegally, in Wyoming, the affair called "probably the most revolting crime in the entire annals of the West" and a key incident leading to the so-called Powder River War between cattlemen and small ranchers. Ella was described by pro-cattlemen newspapers as a virago and "the equal of any man on the range. Of robust physique, she was a dare devil in the saddle, handy with a six shooter and an adept with the lariat and branding iron," some of which can be discounted.

Helena Huntington Smith, *The War on Powder River.* N.Y., McGraw-Hill Book Co., 1966; Charles Hall, *Documents of Wyoming Heritage.* Cheyenne, Wyo. Bicentennial Commis., 1976.

Watson, Elmo Scott, newspaperman (Apr. 2, 1892-May 5, 1951). B. on a farm near Colfax, Illinois, he was one of two founders (the other was Leland Case) at Chicago in 1944 of the Westerners, an organization which today numbers scores of "corrals" in cities around the globe constituting associations of those interested in some way in the frontier and pursuing enthusiams related to it. Watson was graduated from Colorado College at Colorado Springs, Colorado, in 1916; he taught journalism at the University of Illinois from 1918 and at the Medill School of Journalism, Northwestern University, from 1925. He was editor of the *Publishers' Auxiliary* for 20 years. Watson, whose interests were wide enough to permit him on one occasion to manage a Colorado Springs rodeo, was intrigued by western history and the Indian wars, and had a particular enthusiasm for pioneer photographs and early newspaper coverage of the West. He was married and fathered two children. He died at Denver.

Publishers' Auxiliary, May 12, 1951; Leland D. Case, "The Westerners: Twenty-five Years of Riding the Range." *Western Hist. Quar.,* Vol. I, No. 1 (Jan. 1970), 63-76.

Watson, James Waterman, army officer (Oct. 3, 1854-May 12, 1920). B. in Mississippi he was a West Point graduate, commissioned a second lieutenant in the 10th Cavalry June 12, 1880, and became first lieutenant in 1887. In the late 1880's Watson saw a much arduous field service commanding Arizona Indian scouts in pursuit of the Apache Kid and other bronco Apaches. He won a brevet as captain for his role in a fight along the Salt River in March 1890, in which the Kid's band of renegades was largely destroyed. On January 27, 1891, Watson was assigned to Fort Bayard, New Mexico, and in March 1892 he was sent east. In 1893 he was posted to Fort Assiniboine, Montana, and was acting agent at the Crow Agency, Montana, from February 1894 to January 1, 1898, becoming a captain January 11. During the Spanish American War he served in Cuba. Watson was retired as a major February 21, 1906, because of disability incurred in line of duty. He became a planter at Port Gibson, Mississippi, but later resided for health reasons at Holguin, Cuba, although keeping up his plantation work.

Cullum; Dan L. Thrapp, *Al Sieber, Chief of Scouts.* Norman, Univ. of Okla. Press, 1964.

Watson, Thomas B., cattle buyer (Apr. 15, 1838-Sept. 24, 1903). His place of birth is unreported. Watson became the best-known cattle buyer of northwestern Colorado along the Yampa, Elk, Snake and White rivers, and the friend and confidante of its pioneer ranchmen. He owned a general store at Meeker, Colorado, for a time, but spent most of his life in the saddle, and his adventures were many. He also did some freighting from Rawlins, Wyoming, to Colorado. He died at Yampa and is buried there.

Reuben Squire, "Tom Watson: Long-time Cattle Buyer." *True West,* Vol. 24, No. 2 (Nov.-Dec. 1976), 21, 49, 52-53; John Rolfe Burroughs, *Where the Old West Stayed Young.* N.Y., William Morrow and Co., 1962.

Watts, Charles Henry, army officer (Oct. 4, 1849-Oct.26, 1917). B. in New York he was graduated from West Point and commissioned a second lieutenant in the 5th Cavalry June 14, 1872, assigned to Arizona. He served in the field in 1873 and was present at San Carlos Reservation May 27 when Lieutenant Almy was assassinated, being involved in the subsequent affairs in the Santa Teresa

Mountains and near San Carlos. Twice Watts was nominated for a brevet for his conduct during the 1874 closing campaign against the Tonto Apaches. In 1875 he was at Fort Lyon, Colorado. He participated in Crook's Big Horn and Yellowstone operation against the Sioux until July 7, 1876 when he was wounded by the accidental discharge of a pistol. Watts was on the Wind River expedition against the Nez Perces in September-October 1877, serving at upper Plains posts for some time thereafter. He became a first lieutenant April 2, 1879, captain March 8, 1891, major February 28, 1901, lieutenant colonel of the 9th Cavalry October 1, 1906, and a colonel of cavalry March 3, 1911, retiring May 23, 1911, for disability in line of duty. He died at Washington, D.C.

Cullum; Price, *Fifth Cavalry,* 538-39; Heitman.

Waymouth (Weymouth), George, navigator (fl. 1585-1612). B. in Devonshire, England, he wrote in 1605 that he had been "for twenty years" engaged in the study of ship-building and mathematics, but nothing definite is known of his early life except that he was better educated than the run of sea captains of his day. He was widely traveled in his early life and in 1601 suggested to the East India Company that an attempt be made to locate the fabled Northwest Passage to the Indies. He sailed in May 1602, rounded southern Greenland, discovered Hudson Strait but his crew mutinied (the revolt not led by his chaplain, John Cartwright, as alleged) and put back to England again. He wrote a manuscript on the arts of navigation, ship-building and instruments of war, sending it to the king and although it was preserved, it was not published. March 5, 1605, as commander of the *Archangel* he left England and sighted Nantucket May 14 but made no landing. He went north to Monhegan, ten miles east of Bothbay Harbor, Maine, traded with Indians near the Georges Islands and explored the St. George's River a short distance. Waymouth captured five Indians, among them reportedly Tisquantum (Squanto), taking them to England with "two Canoas, with all their bowes and arrowes" when he "quit the land" on June 16; the Indians later were used as guides by Martin Pring, George Popham and Raleigh Gilbert. In 1607 two of these Indians accompanied 120 English who attempted a colony on the Kennebec River of Maine, but it failed; many of the Indians they met spoke some French, picked up from fishermen or traders who left no other record. Waymouth made no further recorded voyages to the New World, but was granted a pension in 1607 and in 1610 took part in the siege of Jülich in northwest Germany. His pension last was paid in 1612.

DCB; DAB; Sylvester; *Handbook of Indians,* 15.

Wayne, Anthony, army officer (Jan. 1, 1745-Dec. 15, 1796). B. at East Town, Chester County, Pennsylvania, he attended Philadelphia Academy and became a surveyor, employed for a time in Nova Scotia, returned, married and was left by his father a business which gave him a comfortable income. He was prominent in affairs leading up to the Revolutionary War, had a distinguished career in the fighting, and because of his marked victory over the British at Stony Point on the Hudson July 16, 1779, where he was wounded, he was given a special gold medal and the thanks of the Continental Congress. He ended the Revolution a brevet Major General with a reputation for impetuosity and arrogance but recognition as one who could "fight as well as brag." He won the nickname of "Mad Anthony," it was said because of his impetuous battle tactics. Rankin observed that while some biographers believe Wayne was not called "Mad" until after the Revolution, "it appears that the nickname was already associated with him" by 1780, André's poem brought out in that year referring to "mad Anthony's fierce eye." After Yorktown Wayne was sent to oppose British, Loyalists and Indians in Georgia. He bested the Creeks in May 1782, negotiated treaties with the Creeks and Cherokees that year, but shortly retired since the Revolution was won. He had shown himself able to adapt to Indian warfare and comprehend and bend the Indian mind in the brief period he spent in the south. After the defeats north of the Ohio of Josiah Harmar September 30, 1790, with a loss of 214 men in killed and wounded, and St. Clair November 4, 1791, with 918 casualties, President Washington sought a commander with verve and effectiveness to crush the looming Indian threat in the northwest. He evaluated 16 officers as possible candidates. Of Wayne he wrote in his memorandum: "More active and enterprising than Judicious and cautious... Open to flattery; vain, easily imposed upon; and able to

be drawn into scrapes. Too indulgent...to his Officer and men. Whether sober or a little addicted to the bottle, I know not." But he chose Wayne as the best of the lot for the purpose, commissioning him Major General and commander of the army March 5, 1792. Wayne had often quarreled with other officers, but in times of action he was superb. Peace commissions to the Indians north of the Ohio proved ineffective, the tribesmen after their great victories over Harmar and St. Clair remained convinced of their power and sure, too of British aid although this was less preordained than they supposed. Wayne commenced gathering his people and supplies from his Pittsburgh headquarters and disciplining and training them, meting out harsh punishments when he deemed it necessary (malingerers and deserters were subject to penalties ranging from death by hanging or firing squad to branding of the forehead with the word "Coward"). Peace attempts had definitely collapsed by the late summer of 1793 and Wayne determined upon a campaign the following year. July 28 his army of 3,500 men moved out from Fort Green(e)ville, west of Pittsburgh. By August 8 it reached the confluence of the Maumee and the Auglaize where he built Fort Defiance. He continued his march on the 15th down the Maumee, and by the 18th was within ten miles of the British Fort Miami. He started again on August 20 and shortly was confronted by about 500 Indians, most of the enemy having deserted the coming action to hunt food and because Wayne, deliberately no doubt, withheld his attack for 48 hours after they expected it, their mercurial natures not adequate for such a suspenseful pause. The action came amidst a maze of timber downed by a tornado some time previously, and the affair thus was known as that at Fallen Timbers. A bayonet charge routed the enemy within 45 minutes and the engagement, in which the troops suffered 107 losses in killed and wounded, was over. The Ohio country was won. Wayne strengthened Fort Defiance, moved on to the Wabash and built Fort Wayne. The British withdrew their support from the Indians who agreed to negotiate and August 3, 1795, a treaty was signed by Wayne on the one hand, and chiefs and sachems of the Wyandots, Delawares, Shawnees, Ottawas, Chippewas, Potowatomis, Miamis, Kickapoos and minor groupings on the other, putting "an end to a destructive war," seeking to establish a perpetual peace and all the rest of it. Wayne turned over command of his army to James Wilkinson December 14 and returned east. The next year he completed an inspection tour but died at Presque Isle, Lake Erie, on his return. He was buried at the foot of the flagpole at Presque Isle as he had requested, but the remains were exhumed in 1809 and reinterred at St. David's Episcopal Church cemetery, Radnor, Pennsylvania.

Heitman; BDAC; Hugh F. Rankin, "Anthony Wayne: Military Romanticist," *George Washington's Generals,* ed. by George Athan Billias. N.Y., William Morrow and Co., 1964, 260-90; Theodore Roosevelt, "Mad Anthony Wayne's Victory." *Harper's New Monthly Mag.,* Vol. XCII, No. DLI (Apr. 1896), 702-16 (reprinted virtually intact in Roosevelt's *Winning of the West.* N.Y., G.P. Putnam's Sons, 1900, V, 175-230); Francis Paul Prucha, *The Sword of the Republic.* N.Y., Macmillan Co., 1969.

Wayne, Henry Constantine, army officer (Sept. 8, 1815-Mar. 16, 1883). A camel specialist, he was born at Savannah, Georgia, graduated from West Point in 1838, served as an artillery officer on the northern border until 1841 and took part with some distinction in the Mexican War. During his southwestern service, Wayne conceived the idea of using camels for tranportation purposes, although the suggestion had been advanced by Crosman some 20 years earlier. Wayne mentioned the idea to Jefferson Davis who, as senator from Mississippi, took the proposal to Congress and finally, as Secretary of War about 1855, a secured a $30,000 appropriation and named Wayne to select animals in the Middle East. With naval officer David Dixon Porter to manage transportation, Wayne purchased 33 head (làter increased by 41 more) in Tunis, Egypt and Turkey, bringing them without important mishap to Indianola, Texas, by May 11, 1856. He conducted extensive tests of the animals which initially were based at Camp Verde, Texas, 60 miles north of San Antonio. His work was successful, the camels demonstrating an uncommon usefulness as transportation animals, easily adaptable to American conditions and being used experimentally to cross the continent to California. However there was a lack of proper indoctrination of Army personnel assigned to handle them, and of the public which was the ultimate support for the endeavor, and so it failed — through no fault of the camels or of Wayne, their most enthusiastic promoter. Wayne received a gold medal, first class, from the Societe Imperiale Zoologique d'Acclimatation of Paris for his work. In 1857 he predicted it would take a decade to establish camels in this country and prove their value, but the Civil War intervened and the effort was lost. Wayne resigned from the Army December 31, 1860, joined the Confederate forces and served as a Brigadier General. He died at Savannah.

Appleton; John Shapard, "The United States Army Camel Corps: 1856-66." *Military Rev: Professional Jour. of US Army,* Vol. LV, No. 8 (Aug. 1975) 77-89.

Wayne, John, actor (May 26, 1907-June 11, 1979). B. Marion Michael Morrison at Winterset, Iowa, he studied and played football from 1925-27 at the University of Southern California, but did not graduate. His first film role was *The Big Trail* (1929) intended to be Fox Studios' talking picture remake of the *Covered Wagon.* Among the 200 films (which grossed a total of $700 million) in which Wayne appeared were, of frontier interest, *Stagecoach* (1939), *Red River* (1946), *The Alamo* (1959) which he also directed and *True Grit* (1968), for which he won an Oscar award. Wayne died of cancer at Westwood, California. He was married three times and fathered seven children

Who's Who; Arizona Daily Star, June 12, 1979.

Wayouhyuch (Blue Leg), Nez Perce warrior (d. post 1880). One of Chief Joseph's non-treaty Nez Perce, Wayouhyuch about 1865 killed Sousouquee, Joseph's older brother, in the Wallowa Valley of northeastern Oregon when both were drunk. Wayouhyuch apparently believed the other was about to slay him and fired an arrow into Sousouquee's leg, from which he bled to death. Wayouhyuch then fled to the Spokane Reservation, returning after a time. Joseph twice tried to kill him, but the two became reconciled and close friends, going through the 1877 war together. Wayouhyuch escaped from the Bear Paw Mountains, Montana, to Canada, joined Sitting Bull and finally died at Stites, Idaho.

McWhorter, *Hear Me.*

Weatherford, William (Lamochattee, Red Eagle) Creek chief (c. 1780-March 9, 1824). Son probably of a Scot or English trader, Charles Weatherford, and a Creek woman, half-sister of Alexander McGillivray, Billy Weatherford was b. in the present southern Alabama and grew to 6 feet, 2 inches in height with a fair complexion, light brown hair and black eyes according to his grandson, Charles Weatherford, Jr. Billy Weatherford's first wife, Mary Moniac, an Indian woman, died in 1804; among their children was Charles Weatherford (c. 1795-c. 1890). His second wife, Sapoth Thlanie, also was an Indian woman who died sometime before 1817 when Weatherford married a third time, to Mary Stiggins, a white woman who died near Mount Pleasant, Monroe County, Alabama, in 1832. When Tecumseh visited the Creeks in 1811 in furtherance of his plan for a united uprising, Weatherford joined the Red Sticks, or war faction with which he quickly rose to prominence. He apparently had no part in the Battle of Burnt Corn Creek, July 24 1813, which opened the Creek War, but was a leader in the August 30, 1813, massacre at Fort Mims, near Tensaw, Alabama, in which, according to one of the best authorities, 517 people were slain while only 36 escaped of the 553 at the post including 265 soldiers, of whom 70 were home militia, 175 Mississippi volunteeers under Major Daniel Beasley, commanding Fort Mims, and sixteen from Fort Stodderd under Lieutenant S.M. Osborn. Weatherford, considered by Halbert and Ball "an influential leader but not a real chief," led the initial assault upon Mims, where discipline was very lax, no guard established and one of the two principal gates wide open. Various reports assert the Creeks attacked with 1,000 men in two phases, Weatherford taking part in the first action only, then leaving because, he reportedly afterward said, he did not approve of the indiscriminate slaughter that soon developed. This statement is disputed. At any rate he was generally credited with directing the successful assault, resulting in one of the worst massacres in frontier history. He participated in a number of small actions of which little record remains. He was in the engagement at Autossee (Calabee) November 29, 1813, on the south bank of the Tallapoosa River, 20 miles above the confluence with the Coosa River. The Creeks were surprised by Georgia militia General John Floyd with 950 troops and 400 friendly Indians, many Creeks being slain in their lodges before they could rally to the defense, the toll being 200 Creeks killed to 50 killed and wounded among the whites and their allies. Weatherford escaped unhurt. He was a leader in the Battle of Holy Ground, or Eccanachaca, about two miles north of the present White Hall, Lowndes County, Alabama, December 23, 1813. Mississippi Volunteers Brigadier General Ferdinand Leigh Claiborne was the white commander, the troops winning the engagement with one man killed and 20 wounded for a Creek loss of 33 killed, including 12 blacks. Holy Ground had been Weatherford's headquarters after the Fort Mims affair. He conducted the defense of the town "with judgment and courage," and was the last to escape after the rest of the Creeks had withdrawn across the Alabama River. Mounted upon a fine horse, he jumped the animal from a 12-foot bluff into the water and successfully negotiated the crossing under a hail of bullets, escaping to the other side with neither himself nor his mount wounded. Most of the loot from Holy Ground town was given to Pushmataha's Choctaws who had assisted in the attack. Weatherford was not present at the decisive Battle of Horseshoe Bend March 27, 1814, which completed destruction of the hostile Creeks, although Hodge and others place him there. Some time after this event Weatherford surrendered to Jackson under circumstances variously defined. Jackson reportedly described Weatherford as possessing "in a most preeminent degree the elements of true greatness, and for reckless personal courage was the Marshal Ney of the Southern Indians." Apparently Jackson was convinced that his opponent was a truthful man of positive impulses, and accepted the surrender on condition Weatherford work for peace and the Creek, although he had anticipated execution, agreed. Because of white hostility toward him as the destroyer of Fort Mims, Weatherford was sent secretly by Jackson to a place of safety and later accompanied the future President to the "Hermitage," Jackson's Tennessee estate, remaining there several months while David Tate, his half-brother, alone among Alabamans, knew of his whereabouts. Following conclusion of the Creek war, Weatherford returned to settle in lower Monroe County, Alabama. He became a dignified, industrious and sober plantation owner, his children intermarrying freely with the whites. Weatherford died and was buried a short distance west of Little River, Alabama, east of the Alabama River, a stone monument constructed over his grave.

George Cary Eggleston, *Red Eagle and the Wars with the Creek Indians of Alabama.* N.Y., Dodd, Mead Co., 1878; H.S. Halbert, T.H. Ball, *The Creek War of 1813 and 1814.* University of Ala. Press, 1969; James W. Holland, *Andrew Jackson and the Creek War: Victory at the Horseshoe.* Univ. of Ala. Press, 1968; Hodge, HAI; James D. Dreisback, "Weatherford — 'The Red Eagle.'" *Ala. Hist. Reporter, vol. 2, nos. 4, 5, 6 (Mar., Apr., May 1884) n.p.*

Weaver, Pauline, mountain man (1800-June 21, 1867). B. in the later White County, Tennessee, his father was white, his mother Cherokee, and he was named Paulino, soon changed by custom to Pauline. He reached St. Louis at an early age and continued west, working for some time it is said for the Hudson's Bay Co. as trapper. He left that employment and is reported to have reached Arizona by 1830; his name is scratched on the walls of the Casa Grande ruins, dated 1832, but Weaver was illiterate. He continued on eventually to California. For his services in negotiating a treaty with Indians, he was granted 2,800 acres at present Banning, California, in San Gorgonio Pass. He lived there occasionally, but continued trapping in Arizona. In 1846 Kearny moved into California and sent Weaver to guide the Mormon Battalion westward, joining that organization November 28, 1846. In 1853 Weaver gave much of his San Gorgonio tract to Dr. William Isaac Smith who had treated him for illness, the mountain man continuing to make his intermittent headquarters with the Smiths. An occasional prospector, he guided A.H. Peeples and others to Rich Hill, Arizona, and Weaver Diggings, Arizona, where important gold strikes were made, negotiating vital treaties with various Indian bands to keep peace in the region. He was early in the Prescott area, and moved on to the Verde Valley, Arizona, acting as guide, scout and interpreter for Army units in their pacifying missions. He had suffered an arrow wound a year or two before he died; he was buried with military honors at Camp Lincoln (later Camp Verde) Arizona. His remains were removed to San Francisco and returned

in 1929 to Prescott where they lie under a marked monument to one of the true founders of the present state.

Sharlot M. Hall, *First Citizen of Prescott: Pauline Weaver, Trapper and Mountain Man.* Prescott, Ariz., (c. 1929).

Webb, John Joshua, lawman, desperado (Feb. 13, 1847-Apr. 12, 1882?). B. in Keokuk County, Iowa, he was hunter and teamster for a surveying party which in January 1870, left Missouri for Indian Territory, reaching Arkansas City in the spring of 1871. Webb was a onetime resident of Deadwood, South Dakota, and Cheyenne, Wyoming, reaching Dodge City, Kansas, in 1877, where he sometimes was deputized by Sheriffs Charlie Bassett and Bat Masterson for posse work. In September 1877, he accompanied both in a fruitless search for train robber Sam Bass. In 1878 he filled in during the absence of Jim Masterson of the Dodge City police force. Webb was one of many gunmen hired for the prospective "war" between the Santa Fe and Denver & Rio Grande railroads for control of the Royal Gorge of the Arkansas River in the Rockies, but little action developed. He became an occasional special officer at Las Vegas, New Mexico, and in 1880 was named city marshal. While serving as such, on March 2, 1880, he and another killed Michael Keliher for purposes of robbery. Tried for murder, he was sentenced April 9 to hang. In an attempt to free him, Dave Rudabaugh killed a jailer, but Webb remained incarcerated. His death sentence was commuted by Governor Lew. Wallace to life imprisonment three weeks before the date of execution. On September 19, 1881, Webb, Rudabaugh, who had been convicted of murder, and two others attempted to break out of the San Miguel County, New Mexico, jail. One prisoner was killed, the break thwarted. December 3, 1881, Webb, Rudabaugh and five others escaped, making their way to Texas and Mexico. Here, according to Keleher, Webb "disappeared." Hertzog, however, said he died at Winslow, Arizona, of smallpox.

Nyle H. Miller, Joseph W. Snell, *Great Gunfighters of the Kansas Cowtowns, 1867-1886.* Lincoln, Univ. of Nebr. Press, 1967; William A. Keleher, *Violence in Lincoln County 1869-1881.* Albuquerque, Univ. of New Mex. Press, 1957; Peter Hertzog, *A Directory of New Mexico Desperadoes.* Santa Fe, Press of Territorian, 1965; Kan. State Hist. Soc. records.

Webb, Walter Prescott, historian (Apr. 3, 1888-Mar. 8, 1963). B. in Panola County, Texas, he was raised in Stephens County, West Texas, and became a Phi Beta Kappa graduate of the University of Texas in 1915. He taught school for three years, then returned to the university for graduate degrees and to teach, remaining on its staff to full professor for 40 years. He was a lecturer in American history at the University of London in 1938 and professor of American history at Oxford in 1942-43. Although not a particularly prolific writer, he became "one of the most challenging historians of the century," and the broad themes he outlined and promoted will no doubt continue to stimulate generations of historians and intellectuals. In his major works he was controversial and frequently criticized for not attending to scholarly minutiae, but he was a vivid, moving writer (who sometimes referred to his works as "art" rather than "history"), and such criticism rarely stirred him. His reputation rested largely on two books: *The Great Plains* (1931) and *The Great Frontier* (1952); he published four other books: *The Texas Rangers* (1935), a thankfully detailed account of that law enforcement body; *Divided We Stand* (1937); *More Water for Texas* (1954), and a collection of papers, *An Honest Preface* (1959). Another of his great legacies is the two-volume (recently increased by a third volume) *Handbook of Texas,* a reference work of thorough scope and permanent value for which he was editor-in-chief and primary originator. It appeared in its basic form in 1952. Webb also wrote an abridged narrative of his ranger book, *The Story of the Texas Rangers* (1957) intended primarily for younger readers. Webb, wrote Rundell, "made a fundamental impact on American historiography." He added that "Those for whom the American West has meaning will always care about Walter Prescott Webb for he explained some of that meaning in luminous terms that have become basic in our thinking." In *The Great Plains* Webb declared that the 98th Longitude split the United States by geographic reality, and that this had a profound impact upon the cultural adaptations required to dominate each environment. This in turn had continous, visceral impact upon the two societies welded into the one nation. In *The Great Frontier* he sought to extend Frederick Jackson Turner's Frontier Thesis to global

dimensions and lamented that with the passing of the world geographical frontier must come a subduing of exhilarating human challenges and opportunities, leading to all sorts of individual, social and political modifications. There was considerable criticism of this thesis but, as Webb believed, it would take several centuries to assess fairly the observations and conclusions it drew. Webb died in a traffic accident at Austin, Texas. His first wife, Jane Elizabeth Oliphant, died in 1960; his second wife, widow of United States Representative Maury Maverick Sr., was injured in the accident that killed her husband of one year.

Walter Rundell Jr., "Walter Prescott Webb 1888-1963," and "Walter Prescott Webb: Product of Environment." *Arizona and the West,* Vol. 5, No. 1 (Spring 1963), 1-28.

Webb, William Edward, pioneer (c. 1839-Aug. 19, 1915?). B. at New York City, he went to the Plains for a short time in 1867 and was the effective founder of Hays City, Kansas. The first community in the neighborhood, after the military post, had been called Rome. Webb was rebuffed in his attempt to join Cody and William Rose in their effort to found Rome, so "moved on a mile or so and laid out Hays City," whereupon Rome collapsed. Cody and Webb later became friends, went buffalo hunting and Indian skirmishing together, and Webb gave Cody his first "book publicity" in his *Buffalo Land...1872).* Webb also was a friend and admirer of Hickok: "To the people of Hays he was a valuable officer, making arrests when and where none other dare attempt it. His power lies in the wonderful quickness with which he draws a pistol and takes his aim," although he debunked legends of Bill's miraculous marksmanship as exaggerated. "Living as he does by the pistol Bill will certainly die by it unless he abandons the frontier." A photograph of Webb is in Burkey's *Wild Bill Hickok: The Law in Hays City,* p. 21. Webb died at Chicago, according to one report; a William Edward Webb died on the date given above at Slasconset, Massachusetts, his age not given. This Webb was vice president and a director of the J.H. Dunham and Company dry goods merchandising firm of New York City at the time of his death.

Don Russell, *The Lives and Legends of Buffalo Bill.* Norman, Univ. of Okla. Press, 1960; Joseph

G. Rosa, *They Called Him Wild Bill.* Norman, 1974; Blaine Burkey, *Wild Bill Hickok: The Law in Hays City.* Hays, Kan., Thomas More Prep, 1975; *New York Times,* Aug. 20, 1915.

Weber, John H., frontiersman (1779-Feb. 1859). B. in Denmark, he was educated, ran away to sea, became a captain before he was 21, and commanded ships for five years. By 1807 he had reached Ste. Genevieve, Missouri, probably served in the War of 1812, and joined Ashley in 1822. He most likely led Alexander Henry's party up the Yellowstone as far as the Powder River, where he turned to trapping and trading. In 1824 with others he crossed into the Green River valley, trapping with good success. In further explorations he and others reached Bear Lake, Great Salt Lake and Weber Canyon and Weber River, Utah. The latter two were named for him, as was Bear Lake originally. Weber probably returned from the mountains in 1827, moved to Galena, Illinois, in 1832 and in 1834 to Bellevue, Iowa, where he lived until his death. He was large of frame, fearless, intelligent, somewhat mercurial in temperament, and cut his own throat when plagued by illness, ending his life.

LeRoy R. Hafen article, MM, Vol. IX; Dale L. Morgan, Eleanor Towles Harris, eds., *The Rocky Mountain Journals of William Marshall Anderson.* San Marino, Calif., Huntington Library, 1967.

Week(e)s, Stephen, ship's armorer (d. c. June 15, 1811). An armorer aboard the ship *Tonquin,* Weeks was an experienced and resourceful sailor. In the perilous approach to the treacherous bar across the mouth of the Columbia in March 1811, he was one of a party of five, including two Hawaiians , who sounded for the passage aboard the ship's boat; two were swept off to sea and lost. Weeks and the Hawaiians struggled desperately for their lives, one of the latter succumbing to exposure and Weeks being rescued after severe hardships. He was a member of the crew which sailed the *Tonquin* to Vancouver Island in June. The ship was overrun and seized by Indians in Newettee Inlet and most of her company murdered, Weeks alone, badly wounded, remaining aboard. He lured great numbers of Indians onto the ship, then presumably set off a train to her magazine which contained 4 1/2 tons of powder, blowing up the ship and causing an estimated 200 Indians and himself to lose their lives.

Gabriel Franchere, *Adventure at Astoria 1810-1814.* Norman, Univ. of Okla. Press, 1967; Chittenden.

Weichel(l), Maria (Mrs. George), captive (fl. 1869). B. at Luneberg, Hanover, Germany, she had been in the United States two months, settling with her husband on the Solomon River, Kansas, when Tall Bull's Cheyenne Dog Soldiers raided on May 30, 1869, killed George Weichel and took Maria captive, she becoming, it is said, the "wife" of the Indian leader. Captured at the same time was Mrs. Thomas Alderdice whose baby was strangled. This incident led to the 5th Cavalry expedition under Eugene Asa Carr which resulted in the decisive battle of Summit Springs, July 11, and destruction of the Tall Bull people. Of $1,300 in money (taken as loot by the Indians) found in the village, $900 was given to Mrs. Weichel (Mrs. Alderdice having been killed in the fight). Mrs. Weichel was taken to Fort Sedgwick, Colorado, to recuperate, and married the hospital steward who took care of her there.

Don Russell, *The Lives and Legends of Buffalo Bill.* Norman, Univ. of Okla. Press, 1960.

Weightman, Richard Hanson, frontiersman (Dec. 28, 1816-Aug. 10, 1861). B. at Washington, D.C., he was graduated from the University of Virginia in 1834, and went to West Point; it was reported that he was expelled for slashing a fellow cadet with a knife. From St. Louis in 1846 he was made captain of Battery A, Missouri Light Artillery. He saw Mexican War action at Sacramento, Chihuahua, February 28, 1847, and was mustered out in June 1847 at New Orleans, serving the regular army as paymaster until 1849, moving to Santa Fe in August, practicing law and becoming involved in politics; he was appointed Indian agent for New Mexico in July 1851. Weightman was elected New Mexico's first delegate to Congress (1851-53). He was "a gentleman with a temper," with a proclivity for dueling: in 1849 he bloodlessly duelled Territorial Judge Joab Houghton, who had felt himself insulted. In 1853 he entered the newspaper business, starting *Amigo del Pais* at Albuquerque, shortly removing it to Santa Fe where he became acquainted with the famous frontiers-man, Francois X. Aubry, first as a friend, then as a bitter enemy. August 18, 1854, he killed Aubry with a bowie knife in a cantina fight. Weightman was tried September 20-21, 1854 before Judge Kirby Benedict and was found innocent on his plea of self defense. The case had received nationwide publicity because of the prominence of Weightman and Aubry. On October 1 Weightman left for Missouri. In 1858 he moved to Kickapoo and Atchison, Kansas, and in 1861 to Independence, Missouri. He was named colonel of the 1st Cavalry, 8th Division, Missouri State Guard of the Confederate forces in 1861, soon came to command the 1st Brigade of the division, and was killed at Wilson Creek, Missouri; he was buried on the battlefield near Springfield, Missouri.

BDAC; Donald Chaput, *Francois X. Aubry.* Glendale, Calif., Arthur H. Clark Co., 1975.

Weippert, George, fur trader (1820-Jan. 12, 1888). B. in Quebec of Holland-French ancestry, he clerked in a St. Louis store until 1839 when he ascended the Missouri to Fort Union where he became a clerk for the American Fur Company, remaining in its employ for 27 years and never leaving Montana. After a year at Union he moved to Fort McKenzie (Fort Brulé), and later to Fort Benton. He was at Fort McKenzie in 1843 when the incident occurred that led Alexander Harvey the following February to perpetrate the famous Blackfoot massacre. Weippert worked for the North West Fur Company for a year after it bought out the AFC, then in 1876 entered the restaurant and saloon business at Fort Benton. He lost his eyesight in an 1888 accident and was cared for by his half-Blackfoot daughter and her husband, Dan O. Blevins, until his death at their home at Highwood Creek, near Fort Benton.

Montana Contributions, Vol. X, 1940, 247-49.

Weir, Thomas Benton, army officer (Sept. 28, 1838-Dec. 9, 1876). B. in Ohio, he was commissioned a second lieutenant of the 3rd Michigan Cavalry in 1861 and ended the Civil War a lieutenant colonel with two brevets, one for gallantry in an engagement with Forrest near Ripley, Mississippi. He became a first lieutenant of the 7th Cavalry in 1866 and a captain a year later. Weir was witness at the court-martial of Custer in 1867. He was in the

battle of the Washita under Custer, and when Hamilton was killed took command of A Company. At the Little Big Horn Weir commanded a battalion under Benteen and fought well on Reno Hill. He had a bitter wrangle with Reno, trying to persuade the senior officer to move out to Custer's relief, finally broke off and gained Weir's Peak a mile or more distant, from where he could see the dust, smoke and some of the Indian activity where Custer's command no doubt already had been wiped out. Weir died a few months later in New York and was buried on Governor's Island the same day.

Heitman; Lawrence A. Frost, *The Court-Martial of General George Armstrong Custer.* Norman, Univ. of Okla. Press, 1968; Edgar I. Stewart, *Custer's Luck.* Norman, 1955.

Weisel, Daniel, surgeon (1838-Oct. 30, 1888). B. at Williamsport, Maryland, he became assistant surgeon for the army October 9, 1867, and reported at Fort Davis, Texas, December 18, 1868, bringing his bride of a year with him. He was transferred May 18, 1872, to Fort Richardson, Texas, serving thereafter a succession of posts and rising to rank of captain assistant surgeon. He died at Fort Sill, Oklahoma.

David A. Clary, "The Role of the Army Surgeon in the West: Daniel Weisel at Fort Davis, Texas, 1868-1872." *Western Hist. Quart.,* Vol. III, No. 1 (Jan. 1972), 53-66.

Weiser, Conrad (Johann), Indian interpreter (Nov. 2, 1696-July 13, 1760). B. in Wurtemberg, he migrated with his father in 1710 to New York, in 1714 settling at Schoharie where Weiser came into contact with the Mohawks, became fluent in their language and was adopted into the tribe. In 1729 with his wife and five children Weiser moved to the present Berks county, Pennsylvania, settling near Womelsdorf and later becoming a founder of Reading. He first was employed as an interpreter in 1731 and for 30 years was official interpreter for Pennsylvania, employed in every important Indian transaction. He worked at times also for interests in Virginia and New York. Throughout King George's War (1745-48) he was occupied with negotiations with the Iroquois, seeking successfully to detach them from the French interest and later to deflect them from the New York influence of Sir William Johnson to that of

Pennsylvania; in this, too, he was effective. Weiser also kept the Pennsylvania Delawares quiet. August 11 to October 2, 1748, he undertook an important tour of the Ohio country. This mission was the first official approach to the trans-Allegheny Indians on the part of Pennsylvania; it was designed to strengthen the British cause among the Indians at the expense of the French; to settle the matter of a recent attack upon Carolina settlements by northern Indians, and Weiser had other matters of significance on his agenda. His mission was carried out successfully. In 1755 Weiser raised a company of soldiers for a Canadian expedition and eventually became lieutenant colonel with supervision of several frontier forts. He became in time the most influential German perhaps of the colony. "His sincerity, honesty, and trustworthiness made him greatly respected...and his death was considered a public calamity." He died at Womesldorf.

Thwaites, EWT, I; DAB; CE.

Weiser (Wiser, Wisner), Jacob, prospector (c. 1810-1871). B. in Germany, he became a carpenter and emigrated to this country before the Civil War. If he served in the Confederate Army, as has been suggested, it was very briefly. He reached Arizona probably in the mid-1860s, and was with Jacob Waltz at Arizpe, Sonora, according to legend, in time to save Miguel Peralta II in a brawl. In return Peralta gave the two a map to a Superstition Mountains mine purportedly worked by his family for nearly a generation. Weiser and Waltz located the Arizona mine, extracted considerable gold, later killed two Mexicans found poaching ore, and Weiser was slain, by Indians, as his partner reported, or by Waltz as persistent rumor has it. The alleged ore body became the famous Lost Dutchman "mine" of Southwestern legend.

Literature abundant; Sims Ely, *The Lost Dutchman Mine.* N.Y., William Morrow and Co., 1953; Curt Gentry, *The Killer Mountains.* N.Y., Ballantine Books, 1973; Robert Blair, *Tales of the Superstitions: The Origins of the Lost Dutchman Legend.* Tempe, Ariz. Hist. Found., 1975.

Weiser, Peter M., mountain man (Oct. 3, 1781-c. 1810). B. in Berks County, Pennsylvania, he joined the Lewis and Clark expedition probably late in 1803, accompany-ing it to the Pacific and return. In 1807 he signed on with Lisa, reached the Three Forks area and ascended the Madison River. Weiser may have guided Henry to Henry's Fork of the Snake River in 1810. He presumably was killed by Blackfeet about that time; he assuredly was dead by 1825. Weiser, Idaho, and the Weiser River are named for him.

Clarke, *Lewis and Clark;* Clarke article, MM, Vol. IX.

Weium, (Weuim, William Faithful), Modoc warrior (d. Nov. 1911). Not much is known of this man until the middle of the Modoc War of 1872-73 in the Lava Beds of northeastern California when he appears as a staunch supporter of Captain Jack against the turbulent Hot Creek Indians and, like him, leaning toward a peaceful settlement of their conflict with the whites. When the Hot Creeks insisted upon massacring Canby and other peace commissioners, it was Weium who came to the support of Captain Jack who tried to find another way. It was Weium who told the admirable woman interpreter, Tobey Riddle, his cousin, that the Modocs planned to assassinate the commissioners, and she warned the whites; when her admonition was revealed to the hostiles, she stoutly refused to identify Weium as the source, thus saving his life and he hers. After the murders Weium, a brave man, kept Black Jim from shooting Captain Jack. Weium probably was sent to Oklahoma with the rest of the Modocs who were permitted in 1909 to return if they wished to the Klamath Reservation, Oregon. He died on that reservation. He was a reliable and generally peaceful man.

Jeff C. Riddle, *The Indian History of the Modoc War.* Medford, Ore., Pine Cone Pubrs., 1973; Keith A. Murray, *The Modocs and Their War.* Norman, Univ. of Okla. Press, 1965.

Wellammootkin (Tuekakas, Old Chief Joseph), Nez Perce chief (c. 1790-Aug. 1871). Of the Cayuse tribe of Washington by birth, he married a Nez Perce woman of the Grand Ronde Valley, and fathered four children, including Joseph and Olikut of Nez Perce war fame. Wellammootkin was prominent at the coming of the missionaries Whitman and Spalding and it was the latter who baptized and gave him the name of Joseph. The chief apparently received some mission education and could read, although whether in English or a native tongue is not stated. In 1843 at the Spalding mission station at Lapwai, Idaho, Joseph and some 700 warriors staged a mock battle for the education of visiting missionaries. Joseph was among the first of his tribe to embrace Christianity but he turned his back on the new faith when he saw his country overrun with godless immigrants whom he assumed had been drawn in by the missionaries. Although he quitted the Lapwai country for the Grand Ronde and Wallowa valleys of northeastern Oregon, he never had any part in the despoiling of the mission stations or hostilities against them. Late in life Joseph took up the Smohalla "dream" religion. He was married twice. He was blind at the time of his death, and was buried finally at the foot of Lake Wallowa, Oregon.

McWhorter, *Hear Me;* Dockstader.

Wellman, George A., cowman (c. 1859-May 9, 1892). B. in Canada he went to Johnson County, Wyoming, from Bay City, Michigan, in 1880, working as a cowboy for Henry A. Blair's Hoe Ranch. When Frank Laberteaux, foreman, was jailed as a result of the Johnson County invasion in early 1892 Wellman, described as well-educated, intelligent, honest and popular was named foreman. He piloted correspondent Ed Towse safely to Gillette, Wyoming, to escape the country, then entrained to Martha, Wisconsin, where on April 12 he was married. He returned to Wyoming to be named deputy U.S. marshal in addition to his duties as foreman for the Hoe outfit. He and another deputy, Bob Gibson were directed to go from Cheyenne to Buffalo, Wyoming, to serve papers. About 16 miles east of the Crazy Woman stage crossing between the Hoe Ranch and Buffalo Wellman was shot from ambush. The murder never was solved officially, although it was widely believed that Henry Smith, Charlie Taylor and Ed Starr were guilty of it. The killing was believed the last important act of violence of the so-called Johnson County War.

Robert B. David, *Malcolm Campbell: Sheriff.* Casper, Wyomingana, 1932.

Wellman, Paul I., writer (Oct. 14, 1898-Sept. 16, 1966). B. at Enid, Oklahoma, Wellman wrote 27 books in addition to numerous screen plays and other material. He is best known as a popular historical writer of the West. He was taken as an infant of six months by his father, an expert on tropical diseases, to Angola for 10 years. He worked as a cowboy out of Vernal, Utah, from 18, migrating to western Kansas and Oklahoma, and served one year in the Army during World War I. He then became a reporter for the Wichita (Kansas) *Beacon,* and the paper's city editor, moving to the *Kansas City Star,* where he worked until 1944, becoming a widely-read feature writer on Old West subjects. Here he published seven works, including *Death on the Prairie* and *Death on the Desert,* his chronicles of the Plains Indians wars, *Bronco Apache,* a fictionalized life of the Apache broncho, Massai, and others among them *The Trampling Herd,* a general history of the longhorn cattle business. He also wrote novels of the early west. He became a partner in an Oregon ranch. Wellman after 1944 began writing plays for motion pictures. He died at Los Angeles. Wellman's histories have been superseded, but he was among the first to seriously research his subjects and with a newsman's training, substituting fact for hearsay and conjecture, and frequently plumbing original sources. His books, particularly his earlier ones, are generally reliable if a tendency to romanticize or fictionalize did permeate them to some degree and subject them to later revision and correction. Wellman's proclivity for the apt phrase and readability sometimes impaired their overall accuracy, but his best works have enduring value.

New York Times, Sept. 19, 1966; *Los Angeles Times,* Sept. 18, 1966.

Wells, Almond Brown, army officer (June 61, 1842-Sept. 7, 1912). B. in New York he reached Nevada by 1863. It was decided there that a battalion of six companies of volunteer cavalry would be formed with an equal number of infantry units. The companies were mustered, said Bancroft "with the promise of being sent to fight the battles of the Union," but instead were detailed to operate against hostile Indians or suppress civil disturbances. Wells was commissioned a first lieutenant July 13, 1863 and captain of D Company on May 1, 1864; he reportedly saw some Indian fighting, being mustered out November 18, 1865, and becoming a second lieutenant of the 8th U.S. Cavalry July 28, 1866, a first lieutenant a year later. In October 1867 Wells led one of three columns of the 8th Cavalry in the so-called Hualapais War of northwestern Arizona; he scouted for 12 days through the mountains and had a fight on the 6th, killing seven Indians with no loss to the soldiers, followed by another brief skirmish. Wells led many scouts in central Arizona in 1868 including one in November when 17 Indians were reported killed and 40 wounded out of 100 attacked. He became a captain May 23, 1870, his first command being Fort Craig, New Mexico, where Frederick E. Phelps found him "a man of good education but (with) a peculiarity...and that was his exceeding jealousy of the officers of his troop. He expected us to obey his orders absolutely, and, of course, that was right; but the slightest variation...made him savage in a moment, and this peculiarity made him a hard man to get along with. He was a magnificent drill master, very proud of his troop, but knew little how to manage money matters," although ever ready to advance personal funds to supplement his men's rations. He became major of the 4th Cavalry July 1, 1891, transferred back to the 8th a week later, became lieutenant colonel of the 9th Cavalry February 14, 1899, colonel of the 1st Cavalry February 2, 1901, and Brigadier General on his retirement August 6, 1903. He died at Geneva, New York, leaving his widow and four offspring.

Heitman; Bancroft, *Nevada, Colorado & Wyoming,* 181-82 and n.; Prescott, Ariz., *Miner,* Aug. 22, Sept. 5, Oct. 3, Nov. 14, 1868; Frank D. Reeve, ed., "Frederick E. Phelps: A Soldier's Memoirs." *New Mex. Hist. Rev.,* Vol. XXV, No. 1 (Jan 1950), 43-47; Constance Wynn Altshuler, *Chains of Command.* Tucson, Ariz. Hist. Soc., 1981.

Wells, Daniel Hanmer, Mormon leader (Oct. 27. 1814-Mar. 24, 1891). B. at Trenton, New York, he settled at Commerce (Nauvoo), Illinois, about 1833, welcomed the Mormons, donated land for their temple, and "indignation at their maltreatment, rather than sympathy with their sect," caused him to join them shortly before they commenced their exodus to the Salt Lake Valley. He reached Utah September 20, 1848, commander of a division in the Brigham Young Company. With the organization of the provisional government Wells was made attorney general and later chief justice of "Deseret," holding many other public and responsible positions. With Charles C. Rich, Wells reorganized in Utah in 1849 the Nauvoo Legion, a state armed militia, became Major General and was associated with it, along with other duties, until its disbandment September 15, 1870. He was accused by Ettie Smith of plotting, with Young and others, the murder of an American trader in 1853. Although he had no role in the Mountain Meadows Massacre personally, Wells testified at John D. Lee's second trial, merely commenting on Lee's lack of status with the Legion, said that he was a man of influence among the Indians, understanding something of their language. In 1871 Wells was indicted for murder and under the national 1862 antipolygamy law, but nothing came of these charges. In 1857, commanding 1,250 men, Wells defended Echo Canyon, northeast of Salt Lake City, against the supposed threat of U.S. regulars, ordered Lot Smith to take up guerilla operations against Johnston's forces, which was about all the active hostility that the so-called "Mormon War" generated between opposing elements. Wells was one of the 12 apostles of the church and second counselor to Brigham Young for 20 years. He took the field against Indians in southern Utah on occasion, presided over the European mission of his church at times, directed organization of settlements in Utah and Arizona and did much to develop Utah economically. He died at Salt Lake City. He had seven wives and produced many offspring.

Bancroft, *Utah;* Frank Esshom, *Pioneers and Prominent Men of Utah.* Salt Lake City, Western Epics, 1966; William Wise, *Massacre at Mountain Meadows.* N.Y., Thomas Y. Crowell Co., 1976.

Wells, Richard W., soldier (c. 1835-May 23, 1863). Wells enlisted at San Francisco, August 14, 1861, in Company E, 1st California Cavalry and with it reached Camp Bowie, Arizona, where on May 23, 1863, he died of "fever." His gravestone is the only original marker still legible in the Fort Bowie cemetery, although it had made an extended peregrination among nearby ranches in the intervening years and is not now placed on the original gravesite, which is unknown.

Gravestone, Fort Bowie Cemetery; Orton.

Wells, Samuel (Charlie Pitts), desperado (d. Sept. 21, 1876). B. at Independence, Missouri, Wells joined the James gang in time to participate in the Otterville, Missouri, train robbery of July 7, 1876, and the Northfield, Minnesota, attempted bank robbery of September 7, 1876. He escaped from the town and when the fugitive band split up, went with the Youngers. When they were at last surrounded by a posse, Wells was killed in the ensuing gunfight. His body was sent to St. Paul, although not until some grisly souvenir hunter had cut off an ear (now on exhibit at Northfield). The body was given to a student from Chicago's Rush Medical College but it was in such a condition that he turned it over to Dr. Henry F. Hoyt (later an army surgeon) who had the skeleton rearticulated and used it in his physician's office at Chicago.

Homer Croy, *Jesse James Was My Neighbor.* N.Y., Dell Pub. Co., 1969; Colin Rickards, "Bones of the Northfield Robbers." *Real West,* Vol. 22, No. 161 (Jan. 1979), 28-31, 60.

Wells, William, adventurer (c. 1766- Aug. 15, 1812). Wells as a child lived in the home of Nathaniel Pope near Louisville, Kentucky, and in 1774 at 8 (Griswold says 12) he was stolen by a band of Eel River (Miami) Indians and brought to Little Turtle's village in northern Indiana. Little Turtle adopted him, their friendship enduring as long as they lived. Wells became an excellent shot, mastered several languages which later gave him great influence among the Indians, and became adept in their wild pasttimes. Heckewelder relates that Wells once wounded and incapacitated a large black bear which then, helpless, whined piteously; Wells approached, stroked its nose with his ramrod, and talked earnestly to it in the Miami tongue. A white companion asked what he had said, and Wells replied he had told the bear that its injury had been the fortunes of war, that it should not be a coward, that if the reverse had been true, had Wells been injured mortally, he would never cry about it but accept his fate bravely and "died with firmness and courage, as becomes a true warrior." Wells married first Little Turtle's sister, Anahquah, and when she died, he married Wahmangopath, daughter of the chief; his third wife he met in Kentucky. Wells fought valiantly with the Indians in their great victories over John Hardin and Josiah Harmar, and Arthur St. Clair. However, he came to regret his warfare against his own people and in the spring of 1792 Little Turtle gave Wells his formal freedom, for despite his

qualities he had been considered nominally a prisoner until that time. He went to Louisville to visit a brother, from there was summoned to Fort Washington (Cincinnati, Ohio), by General Rufus Putman who required his services as interpreter. When Anthony Wayne arrived with his army in April 1793, Wells was placed in command of a unit of scouts, Griswold commenting that Wells "was glad of a situation in which he could influence Wayne to a more conciliatory attitude toward the Indians and hoped that actual warfare could be avoided." That however was not possible. Wells's intimate knowledge of the terrain, the Indians and their leaders was more extensive than that of anyone else, and he was considered reliable. Little Turtle found it impossible to stop, although he could hamper, Wayne's advance upon the Maumee towns and Wells's heroism at the decisive battle of Fallen Timbers was notable. The action concluded he went on to Fort Wayne. He assisted in building the fort, was appointed Indian agent and won the recognition of Congress in the form of a tract of good land near the post. At Fort Wayne he effected a reunion with Little Turtle and the bond between them resumed. Both signed the Treaty of Greenville August 3, 1795, and together they visited the east in 1796-97, conferring with George Washington at Philadelphia. Wells became Indian agent at Fort Wayne in 1799 and continued in that capacity with interruptions until 1809 when he was dismissed "apparently for distrust of his integrity," although details are lacking. In August 1805 Wells and the chiefs of the Delawares, Miami, Eel River and Potawatomi met for a council at Vincennes with Governor William Henry Harrison, the official reporting he had agreed to "a general amnesty and act of oblivion for the past," and arranged for purchase of 3 million acres of "some of the finest land in the Western country." July 14, 1812, Little Turtle died at Wells's home. Word came on August 7 from Hull at Detroit that he had ordered Fort Dearborn (Chicago) dismantled, Captain Nathan Heald, its commandant to move his command to Detroit, the War of 1812 being underway, with a consequent effect upon Indians in contact with the British expected along the frontier, this as an aftermath of the still-rippling excitement over the Tecumseh affair. Wells felt the evacuation unwise and in an attempt to avert it took 30 Miami warriors to Dearborn, leaving Wayne August 8 and reaching Dearborn the 13th. He found it too late to halt the evacuation, and "good soldier that he was, joined heartily with his escort" in plans to effect it. At 9 a.m. August 15 Heald marched out of Dearborn with his soldiers, noncombatants and Indians, Wells and half of his escort leading the way. Wells detected an ambush, rode back to alert Heald and shortly the Dearborn Massacre commenced. Heald was wounded and Wells shot through the lungs. He rushed to his niece, the wife of Nathan Heald to say, "Farewell, my child; tell my wife, if you live to get there, I died at my post doing the best I could." His horse was shot down and hostiles swarmed over his body, according to a contemporary account cutting out his heart and dividing it among them. More than 50 in all were slain, most of the rest captured. Wells had three daughters and two sons by his first marriage; the girls all married white men. Of his two daughters by his second marriage, only one survived infancy, and she also married a white man. A son of his third wife, Yelberton Wells, went to West Point but did not graduate, nor did he become an officer in the army.

Fort Wayne, Gateway of the West 1802-1813, ed. by Bert J. Griswold. Indianapolis, Historical Bureau of the Indian Library and Hist. Dept., 1927 (pub. as Vol. 15, Indiana Hist. Collecs.); Bert Anson, *The Miami Indians*. Norman, Univ. of Okla. Press, 1970; John Heckewelder, *History, Manners, and Customs of the Indian Nations*. N.Y., Arno Press, 1971; *Trans. of Ill. State Hist. Soc.* (1904), Springfield, Ill. State Hist. Library.

Werner, William, frontiersman (fl. 1804-1828). Probably b. in Kentucky he was a member of the Lewis and Clark Expedition, going to the Pacific and return. Later he assisted Clark in Missouri at the Indian agent's office and in 1828 was reported in Virginia.

Clarke, *Lewis and Clark*.

Wesley, John, desperado (1853-Apr. 30, 1884). B. at Paris, Texas, he lived near Vernon, Texas, and was a Kansas cowboy when with Henry Brown and others he attempted to rob a Medicine Lodge, Kansas, bank, was captured and lynched.

Nyle H. Miller, Joseph W. Snell, *Great Gunfighters of the Kansas Cowtowns, 1867-1886*. Lincoln, Univ. of Nebr. Press, 1967.

Wessells, Henry Walton Jr., army officer (Dec. 24, 1846-Nov. 9, 1929). B. at Sacketts Harbor, New York, he enlisted in the 7th Infantry March 1, 1865, and was commissioned a first lieutenant July 21, 1865. Wessells transferred to the 3rd Cavalry January 1, 1871, and became a captain December 20, 1872. He was wounded January 22, 1879, near Fort Robinson, Nebraska, as the Cheyenne Indians broke out in an effort to reach their Montana homeland. Wessells came upon some of the Indians holding positions in a gully and when they refused to surrender charged and killed or captured the entire party; three enlisted men were killed and besides Wessells two were wounded while the Cheyenne loss was 23 killed and nine captured, including three wounded. He took part in the Battle of Big Dry Wash, Arizona, in July 1882. Wessells became a major August 16, 1892, a lieutenant colonel May 8, 1899, a colonel February 2, 1901, retiring for disability in line of duty. He was advanced to Brigadier General on the retired list in 1904. He had served in the Philippines.

Heitman; *Who Was Who*.

West, Alexander, scout (Aug. 11, 1760-June 1834). B. in Accomack County, Virginia, he reached Hacker's Creek, Lewis County, in the trans-Allegheny country, with his father just before Lord Dunmore's War. At 16 in May 1777, he enlisted in Captain Boothe's company of rangers and scouts, serving 13 months in Monongalia County, W. Virginia. In May 1781, he journeyed to Fort Pitt, Pennsylvania, joining Clark's projected expedition against Detroit, but received a discharge at Louisville, Kentucky, in December. On December 5, 1787, his father, brother and brother's wife were killed by Indians. He took part in many Indian skirmishes and was one of the more prominent trans-Allegheny scouts. He claimed that often on scouting expeditions or in times of peril he would have a premonition, or warning of danger by seeing a red doe pass before him in a dream; invariably, he said, this was followed by the slaying of a companion. Those who knew him said he was of a religious, or devotional turn of mind. He lived most of his life in Lewis County, and died there. West was "a tall, spare-built man, very erect, strong, lithe, and active; dark-skinned, prominent Roman nose, black hair, very keen eyes; not handsome, rather raw-boned, but with an air and mien that commanded the attention and respect" of others. He wore a "plain blue linsey hunting shirt," cape and belt, a black-wool hat and moccasins. West was "very fleet-footed."

Lucullus V. McWhorter, *The Border Settlers of Northwestern Virginia.* Hamilton, O., Republican Pub. Co., 1915.

West, Barrington King, army officer (Aug. 31, 1856-Apr. 24, 1906). B. in Kentucky he was graduated from West Point and commissioned a second lieutenant of the 6th Cavalry June 13, 1882, being posted to Arizona. From Fort Apache he scouted and campaigned against Chiricahua Apaches from October 1, 1882, until May 19, 1884. He transferred then to Fort Lewis, Colorado, scouting in Ute country. West was engaged with Ute Indians in the Blue Mountains, Utah, July 15, 1884. After mid-1887 he was transferred to Virginia. He became a first lieutenant of the 9th Cavalry February 20, 1891, but April 27 transferred back to the 6th where he became a captain February 4, 1898, and a major February 2, 1901. Most of his later service in the Commissary Department, West becoming a lieutenant colonel. He died at Denver, aged 49.

Heitman; Cullum.

West, Benjamin, artist (Oct. 10, 1738-Mar. 11, 1820). B. near Springfield, Pennsylvania, he was of Quaker background but not a member of the Society of Friends, He early became attracted to art and developed a taste for historical subjects. West went to New York about 1759, then abroad, studying in Italy and settling for the rest of his life in England. Here he painted his "Death of Wolfe," now at Grosvenor House, London, and his famous "Penn's Treaty with the Indians," at Independence Hall, Philadelphia. His other work had little frontier interest, although West was important to American painting for the encouragment and help he gave young American artists.

Literature abundant; CE; DAB.

West, Frank, army officer (Sept. 26, 1850-Aug. 26, 1923). B. at Mohawk, N.Y., he was descended from Roger Williams. A West Point graduate, he was commissioned in 1872, joined the 6th Cavalry at Oxford, Mississippi, accompanied it to Ft. Harker, Kansas, and Camp Supply, Indian Territory. From the

latter post he was sent as escort to a wagon train on a four month 1,400-mile mission to supply southwestern posts. West joined Miles' 1874 campaign against the South Plains Indians, being breveted first lieutenant for "gallant services in action" on the Washita River, Texas, where his escort and wagons were besieged by 300 Kiowa and Comanche Indians September 9-11. In 1875 West was stationed at Fort Verde, Arizona, and for about nine years served against the Apaches and other hostile Indians, occasionally commanding Indian scouts. He was made first lieutenant in 1876. In the spring of 1882 he was with Forsyth's command which chased Juh, Loco and other hostiles into Old Mexico; West won a Medal of Honor in July 1882, for his outstanding role at the Battle of Big Dry Wash, Arizona, where he led an attack against a "fortified position" and carried it. In the spring of 1883 he was with Crook during the General's very important operation into the Sierra Madre of Sonora to bring hostiles back to Arizona reservations. West served at Forts Craig and Wingate, New Mexico, and in 1885-86 took part in the Geronimo campaigns. He was promoted to captain in 1889, participated in Pine Ridge, South Dakota, operations against the Sioux in 1890-91, was stationed at Fort Niobrara, Nebraska, and sent to Wyoming in 1892 to help police feuding cattlemen during the Powder River "war." West was sent to Chicago during the 1894 strike riots. His role in the Spanish American War was commendable; he won a brevet as major for "gallantry in battle" at San Juan, Cuba, July 1, 1898. From 1900-1901 he was acting superintendent of Sequoia National Park, California. As a major he went to the Philippines in 1901; his subsequent military service was worthy. In 1914 he retired by reason of age, a colonel of the 2nd Cavalry. He settled at Mohawk, N.Y. West married twice, his first wife, whom he wed in 1880, died in 1912; his second survived him. He fathered a son, Arthur, who also survived him.

U.S. Military Academy, *Ann. Report,* June 11, 1924; Heitman; Cullum; communication from David Perry Perrine to author, Oct. 16, 1975.

West, Joseph Rodman, army officer (Sept. 19, 1822-Oct. 31, 1898). B. at New Orleans, he was taken as an infant to Philadelphia, attended the University of Pennsylvania two years, returned to New Orleans in 1841, and served in the Mexican War as a captain of Mounted Volunteers. In 1849 he went to California where he was engaged in newspaper work at San Francisco until the Civil War. He was named lieutenant colonel of the 1st California Infantry August 5, 1861, and became colonel the following June when he was subordinate to Carleton as the California Column moved east toward the Rio Grande; he was named Brigadier General of Volunteers October 25. On October 12 Carleton from Santa Fe had ordered that all Indian men, because of hostility, were to be killed whenever found. West, in command of a district that included southwestern New Mexico, was directed to "immediately organize a suitable expedition to chastise what is known as Mangus Colorado's Band of Gila Alpaches. The campaign . . . must be a vigorous one and the punishment (of the Indians) must be thorough and sharp." West instantly perceived the link between this directive and the previous; a band of civilian prospectors under Joseph Reddeford Walker captured Mangas Coloradas, the great chieftain of the southern Apaches and southwestern history, and turned him over to West's forces at Fort McLane, New Mexico. Here on the night of January 18, 1863, Mangas was murdered while under control of the troops after West had clearly implied that he wanted him shot. West's official report of the affair seems to be a fabric of lies from beginning to end. He was breveted a Major General January 4, 1866, "for faithful and meritorious services." He was mustered out at San Antonio, Texas, on that date, returned to New Orleans where he became deputy United States marshal and served in the United States Senate from 1871-77. He retired from public life in 1885, died at Washington, D.C., and was buried at Arlington National Cemetery.

BDAC; Heitman; Dan L. Thrapp, *Victorio and the Mimbres Apaches.* Norman, Univ. of Okla. Press, 1974; Darlis A. Miller, "The Role of the Army Inspector in the Southwest: Nelson H. Davis in New Mexico and Arizona, 1863-1873." *New Mex. Hist. Rev.,* Vol. 59, No. 2 (Apr. 1984), 137-64; Constance Wynn Altshuler, *Chains of Command.* Tucson, Ariz. Hist. Soc., 1981.

West, Parker Whitney, army officer (Aug. 21, 1858-Jan. 20, 1947). B. in California he was appointed from Louisiana to West Point and commissioned a second lieutenant in the 3rd

Cavalry June 26, 1881, being assigned to Arizona. He served at the San Carlos Apache Reservation under Captain Emmet Crawford and with Crawford received and interviewed noted Apache leaders who came in from Mexico after Crook's 1883 Sierra Madre expedition, witnessing for example the lengthy statement of Chihuahua as to his residence and activities in Old Mexico. West became a first lieutenant in 1887, serving at Texas posts and from December 1892 until June 1893 was active suppressing disturbances along the Rio Grande. He became a captain in the 8th Cavalry in 1898, transferring to the 5th Cavalry in 1899. West served in Cuba and the Philippines during and after the Spanish American War, was an observor in the Russo-Japanese War in Manchuria in 1904-1905. He became a major in the 14th Cavalry in 1906 and retired November 29, 1909, for disability in line of duty. He died at 88 at Washington, D.C.

Cullum; Heitman; Powell.

West, Richard (Little Dick, Dick Weston), outlaw (1865-Apr. 7, 1898). B. in Texas, he went to Oklahoma with an Oscar Halsell trail herd, working on Halsell's Logan County ranch until 1889, and was considered a good, reliable hand. Here he met Bill Doolin, later a prominent outlaw, whose gang he joined in 1892. West was said to have been singular in his ability to use two guns, one in each hand, with equal accuracy and became known as a "savage gunfighter and dead game." He helped Doolin rob the Southwest City, (Missouri) bank May 10, 1894, a bloody affair in which West seriously wounded Oscar Seaborn and fatally wounded former state Senator J.C. Seaborn, West being wounded himself. West was at Dunn's Rock Fort when Bill Tilghman accidentally blundered in, but there was no shooting. West helped Doolin rob a train at Dover, Oklahoma, April 3, 1985. He went to New Mexico with Doolin in 1895, hired out as a cowboy and remained there until 1897 when he returned to Oklahoma to help organize the so-called Jennings band of outlaws. This was done at Tecumseh, the gang initially attempting without success to rob a train August 18 at Edmond, Oklahoma, and two weeks later failed equally to take one at Bond Switch, south of Muskogee. The inept gang was frightened off from another train robbery attempt and one against a bank at Minco, Oklahoma. A fumbled attempt against a Rock Island train October 1, 1897, north of Chickasha netted only an inconsequential sum, and robbery of a store at Cushing, Oklahoma, also was unproductive. West was killed by a posse headed by Bill Tilghman and Heck Thomas five miles southwest of Guthrie.

Bailey C. Hanes, *Bill Doolin, Outlaw O.T.* Norman, Univ. of Okla. Press, 1968; Richard S. Graves, *Oklahoma Outlaws.* Fort Davis, Tex., Frontier Book Co., 1968.

Westbrook, Thomas, colonial officer (d. Feb. 11, 1744). The date of his b. is not known, but it must have been about 1684 because in 1704 "as a young man," he applied for a commission as scout and Indian fighter. He was son of John Westbrook, a farmer of Portsmouth, New Hampshire. When commissioned in Queen Anne's War (1701-13), he was given three men to accompany him on scouting forays; his adventures may have been many and surely were successful for he steadily assumed greater responsibilities until given command of all military operations in the "eastern district," i.e., Maine. In 1710 he was a member of the Provincial Council of New Hampshire. Following Queen Anne's War Westbrook returned briefly to Portsmouth and became King's Mast Agent, assigned to select tall and perfect pines to be harvested for masts for His Majesty's warships. Westbrook made his headquarters at Stroudwater, near Falmouth, Maine, living in a house stockaded against the ever-present Indian threat. In 1721 as a militia colonel the general court of Massachusetts directed him to organize an expedition against Norridgewock, Maine, to capture the Jesuit missionary, Sebastien Rale (see entry), and convey him to Boston to answer for the priest's alleged role in Border depredations. Norridgewock was attacked early in 1722; Rale escaped but a box of his papers and his manucript-dictionary of the Abenaki tongue was brought back by the expedition; the Maine Historical Society holds the papers and Harvard University's Houghton Library the dictionary, which was published in 1833. February 11, 1723, Westbrook again left Kennebec, Maine, for Norridgewock with 230 men, several armed vessels and escorting whaleboats. The party ascended the Penobscot River and left their boats above the present Bucksport, Maine; Norridgewock was found deserted. Passadumkeag Fort and surrounding huts, constituting a French post believed headquarters for the Jesuit Etienne Lauverjat (see entry), were burned. Westbrook did not directly command the August 1724 assault a third time on Norridgewock when Rale finally was killed. In the fall of that year however, he led still another expedition into the Penobscot country, but no significant results were reported. His final appearance as a military officer was at a great council with Indians in 1725 at Falmouth. In 1733 Westbrook built a paper mill and two years later a dam and sawmill at the falls on the Presumpscot River. He associated with Brigadier General Samuel Waldo in many business ventures and became quite wealthy until a falling out occurred. Waldo by unscrupulous or ruthless means divested Westbrook of his lands and much of his wealth by 1743 and he died heavily in debt. A legend reports that a custom of the time permitted the seizure of a dead body for debt, so Westbrook was buried secretly by friends in an unmarked grave, the location of which was never revealed. The city of Westbrook, Maine, was named for him. He was survived by his widow who died at 75 at Portsmouth in 1748, and two daughters, one of whom married the grandson and namesake of Richard Waldron (see entry).

Ernest R. Rowe, *Highlights of Westbrook History.* Westbrook Women's Club, c. 1952; information from the Maine Hist. Soc.; Thwaites, JR, LXVII, 337-38n27; Sylvester, III; Parkman, *Half Century of Conflict,* I.

Westfall, Jacob, army officer, frontiersman (Oct. 10, 1755-Mar. 5, 1835). B. probably in Virginia, he was commissioned first lieutenant under George Rogers Clark June 20, 1781, at Morgantown, Virginia, for the projected Detroit expedition, being discharged at Louisville, Kentucky. He was the builder of Westfall's Fort, Randolph County, Virginia, and "was an active partisan during the border wars." He removed to Indiana, living first in Montgomery County, and dying in Putnam County.

Lucullus V. McWhorter, *The Border Settlers of Northwestern Virginia.* Hamilton, O., Republican Pub. Co., 1915.

Weston, John, Mormon pioneer (fl. 1854-1857). An individual of this name, resident of Cedar City, Utah, was placed by *Mormonism Unveiled* at the Mountain Meadows Massacre of September 11, 1857, either participating in or consenting to the tragedy. He had died before appearance of the book.

Mormonism Unveiled, 380.

Wetamoo (Namumpam), Wampanoag woman chief (c. 1650-Aug. 6, 1676). She was the female chief of the Pocasset, a portion of the Wampanoag, and generally known during King Philip's War as the Squaw Sachem of her people. She had been wife of Philip's older brother, Alexander (Wamsutta), was sister of Philip's wife Wootonekauske and went under the name of Namumpam until Alexander's death in 1662. Around July 1, 1675, she espoused Philip's cause in the war with the British in Rhode Island, Massachusetts, Plymouth Colony and Connecticut and sent her warriors to aid him. By this time she had married again, to Quinnapin (Peter Nunuit), son of Ninigret, chief of the Niantics, a Narragansett tribe which remained aloof from the hostilities. On August 6, 1676, the colonials clashed with hostile Indians and defeated them. Wetamoo escaped; however her body was found shortly, floating in the Taunton River in which she had drowned while attempting to cross. Her head was cut off and set on a pole within view of her followers, now prisoners. Wetamoo was tall, well-built and attractive, with considerable charm and a spectacular dresser. Mary Rowlandson described her as garbed for a dance: "She had a kersey coat covered with girdles of wampum from the loins upward. Her arms from her elbows to her hands were covered with bracelets. There were handfuls of necklaces about her neck, and several sorts of jewels in her ears. She had fine, red, stockings, and white shoes, her hair powdered, and her face painted red."

Hodge, HAI; Leach, *Flintlock;* Dockstader.

Wetherill, (Benjamin) Alfred, discoverer of Mesa Verde's Cliff Palace (June 25, 1861-Jan. 5, 1950). B. of Quaker parentage at Fort Leavenworth, Kansas, he had four brothers: Richard, John, Clayton and Winslow and a sister, Anna. Around 1875 the family migrated to Mancos, Colorado, where they homesteaded, their place becoming the Alamo Ranch, eventually including 1,000 acres. It bore a heavy mortgage and there was little cash, but the boys ran wild horses and learned ranch arts, and eventually commenced to explore the canyons and breaks of the little-known country to the south. The region was visited by a Hayden survey team in 1874-79, but while the government expeditions explored the mesa above the great ruins now the feature attraction of Mesa Verde National Park, Hayden missed the important cluster of dwellings themselves. In 1882 a trapper told the Wetherills of great buildings up some of the defiles and the boys commenced seeking these out, making a number of remarkable discoveries. Pot hunters had preceded them to a few of the more available sites, but the truly grand ruins were undisturbed and the Wetherill finds were sensational. Al and his brothers, while amateurs, became careful lay archeologists and learned to record where they had found unusual artifacts and to preserve them. They opened a museum at Durango, Colorado, but public interest did not support it, and they fared little better at Pueblo and Denver. Part of their collection was sold to a promoter and exhibited at the Chicago Columbian Exposition in 1893 with Richard, oldest of the boys and "the most fluent talker" helping dramatize it. Around 1887 Al Wetherill, with Richard and Byron Cummings went exploring through the canyons and on this trip Al Wetherill alone discovered the now-famous Cliff Palace: it was late afternoon and "I looked up and saw the towers and tops of the buildings of Cliff Palace. In the blue dusk and the silence, it had all the appearance of a mirage. The solemn grandeur of those outlines was breathtaking. I walked in close and stood looking up at the ruins in surprised awe...This discovery surpassed my wildest dreams." He rejoined Cummings and Richard Wetherill and told them of what he had seen, but they had to postpone exploration of them for several months when they were "rediscovered." Richard named the ruins Cliff Palace. The Wetherills found everything inside "arranged in the rooms just as if the people were out visiting somewhere and might return at any moment. Perfect specimens of pottery on the floors" and other artifacts lay everywhere; the finds seemed too rich for reality. The Wetherills, said Alfred, tried to interest the government in protecting the ruins but with little luck; the Smithsonian was not impressed either, although it would "accept" any collection the boys decided to send it. They continued their exploration of the great community, and word of it gradually spread. They took visitors to it, including Alex Hrdlika and Baron Gustav Nordenskjold who took a collection from Mesa Verde back to his native Sweden in 1890 and wrote a book about the ruins. The Wetherills continued their ranch, but it was hard going and eventually all the brothers, by now married, sold out to Al, returning to Alamo Ranch as they could to help run the place. Eventually however the mortgage was foreclosed and Al Wetherill and his wife in 1901 left the place for good, the contents of their private museum given to the Colorado Historical Society. Under public pressure the Mesa Verde area became a 52,000-acre National Park June 19, 1906. Al Wetherill moved to Farmington, New Mexico, then to Atchison, Kansas, returning to operate a trading post at Thoreau, New Mexico, then to Gallup where he became postmaster for several years, and eventually moving to Arkansas and at last to Sand Springs, Oklahoma. He died at Tulsa at 88 and was buried at Sand Springs.

Arthur H. Seigfried, "Al Wetherill of the Mesa Verde." *True West,* Vol. 13, No. 1 (Sept.-Oct. 1965), 22-25, 52-56; Wetherill death certificate.

Wetherill, John, Indian trader (Sept. 24, 1866-Nov. 30, 1944). B. at Leavenworth, Kansas, his family moved in 1880 to Mancos, Colorado, where John matured. With his brothers, Al, Richard, Clayton and Winslow and Charlie Mason he explored the southwestern Colorado country for cliff dwelling and other archeological sites, discovering a great number and exploring many of them. Among these were Cliff Palace of Mesa Verde, discovered by Al and Richard and Charlie Mason, with John soon on the scene. The Wetherills became famous for their work in making known the scores of until then unknown or little known ruins in the pine and mesa country (see Alfred and Richard Wetherill entries for details). John and his wife, Louisa, settled at length at Kayenta, Arizona, where they became known as "traders to the Navajos," remaining at that occupation virtually all their lives although from 1924 onward for some years they operated the La Osa dude ranch south of Tucson before returning to Kayenta full time. Clyde Kluckhohn wrote of John Wetherill in the 1930s that his "knowledge of cowboy and Indian is equalled by few living persons. And the role which John Wetherill played in the discovery of the antiquities of the Southwest is overwhelming.... For frontiersmanship in that region I don't think anyone can be compared with him.... He is the first citizen of the Four Corners country...." John Wetherill died at Ash Fork, Arizona, enroute from Kayenta to Needles, California, for medical treatment of a long-standing ailment. He was buried at Kayenta.

Mary Apolline Comfort, *Rainbow to Yesterday: The John and Louisa Wetherill Story.* N.Y., Vantage Press, 1980; Clyde Kluckhohn, *Beyond the Rainbow.* Boston, Christopher Pub. House, 1933; archives of Ariz. Hist. Soc.

Wetherill, Richard (Anasazi), rancher, lay archeologist (June 12, 1858-June 22, 1910). B. at Chester, Pennsylvania, he was raised at Fort Leavenworth, Kansas, by his Quaker parents. In 1876 the Wetherills moved to Joplin, Missouri, and in 1879 to Colorado. They lived briefly at Bluff City, Utah, and moved in 1880 to the Mancos Valley of southwestern Colorado, establishing the Alamo Ranch three miles southwest of the town of Mancos. As the ranch was built up the five Wetherill boys in addition to routine work developed an interest in cliff dwellings and commenced to explore the surrounding country. In the winter of 1887 Al Wetherill discovered Cliff Palace of Mesa Verde (or rediscovered it, if W.H. Jackson had seen it in 1874) and told Richard and others about it. The account given by Jesse Fewkes of the Smithsonian Institution, that Cliff Palace had been sighted in 1881 by James Frink of Mancos was refuted later by Fewkes himself. December 18, 1888, Richard Wetherill and Charlie Mason again saw Cliff Palace, the most spectacular ruin of the Mesa Verde country, and explored it for the first time. "Before this exploring had been a pasttime. Now it was to become a passion.... He had discovered a lost civilization." From that time forward he devoted several months of each year, usually in the winter to exploration, excavation and study of countless previously unknown (to white men) prehistoric ruins. The public remained uninterested for years, although the Wetherill boys arranged exhibits of their finds at Durango and Denver, where one collection was sold to the Colorado Historical Society for $3,000. The money was used to further explore and excavate around Mesa Verde which by March 1890 had extended to identification of 182 ruins. Discoveries were recorded as carefully as the boys could do it for the benefit of future scientific studies. Richard Wetherill coined the term, "Basket Makers," for the unknown creators of the buildings and culture. In 1891 Richard and his brothers Al and John assisted the Swedish Baron Gustav Nordenskjold to assemble a collection to take to Sweden (acquired at length by the National Museum at Helsinki, Finland). Another collection was bought in 1892 for exhibition at the Chicago Columbian Exposition and ultimately went to the Museum of the University of Pennsylvania. A fourth collection also shown at the Chicago World's Fair ultimately was acquired by the Colorado Historical Society to add to the original collection bought from the Wetherills. While at first he sold relics to casual visitors, by 1895 Richard had come to see that this was inadvisable and ceased to market the items. In his later years what he excavated remained intact and eventually reached the American Museum of Natural History at New York. Richard Wetherill's attempts to interest the Smithsonian Institution, Harvard's Peabody Museum and other repositories in his finds were not favorably received and although he and his brothers later were accused of vandalism and worse, they were a cut above the "pot hunters" of the times; they did have a feel for the scientific testimony they were uncovering and they were as solicitous of the integrity of their work as could be expected in that era. Incidental charges that Richard by avocation even was a cattle rustler were refuted by McNitt's search for records of such activity at five county seats. In the fall of 1893 Richard went to Chicago to attend the exhibit at the World's Fair and answer questions from visitors. There he met Talbot and Fred Hyde Jr., who were eager to finance an exploring expedition into Grand Gulch, in southeastern Utah, above the San Juan River. Out of this association, came "pioneering which may be called the cornerstone of Southwestern archaeology." The association endured from 1893 until 1903. In November 1893 Richard

Wetherill commenced the actual exploration of Grand Gulch where more than 80 prehistoric sites have been located. Concurrently with his several years' work there his interests extended south of the San Juan into Navaho country and eventually as far as Canyon de Chelly, although this was never a major interest for him. He discovered Kiet Siel (Keet Seel) west of Kayenta, the largest cliff dwelling in Arizona. Pueblo Bonito had not attracted archeologists to any extent until Richard Wetherill dug there and he also worked extensively in Chaco Canyon, in prehistoric times a heavily populated area. He and the Hydes pioneered its first scientific excavations. In the late 1890s Wetherill opened a trading post at Pueblo Bonito. He got on well with most of the Navahos but had differences with some, among them Chischilling-begay, who lived nearby. Charges filed against Wetherill and the Hyde brothers alleging vandalizing and selling artifacts for profit were investigated and found baseless; the area eventually became a National Monument. Richard attended the St. Louis World's Fair of 1904. Excavation at Pueblo Bonito was discontinued by government edict, and Wetherill thereafter concentrated on ranching and Indian trading. He was shot and killed by Chis-chilling-begay for reasons unclear but possibly because of trouble between his cowboy, Bill Finn, and another Navaho; Chis-chilling-begay said he had fired at Finn but killed Wetherill instead. Ultimately the Navaho was convicted of voluntary manslaughter and sentenced to 5 to 10 years. Wetherill was married and survived by his widow and several children. In reviewing McNitt's biography, Watson Smith, curator of archaeology in the American Southwest at Harvard's Peabody Museum concluded: "It is clear that Richard Wetherill was not a saintly character, that he was aggressive and self-assertive and possibly not above dissimulation. But equally clear must be the fact that he was a man of strength, resourcefulness, and dedication who made history in a dual sense: by being himself an actor in the rough and ready drama of a troublesome time, and by serving as the discoverer and reporter of much of the prehistory that we know today."

Frank McNitt, *Richard Wetherill Anasazi.* Albuquerque, Univ. of New Mex. Press, 1966; *Arizona and the West,* Vol. 1, No. 3 (Autumn 1959) 295-96.

Wetzel, George, frontiersman (1761-June 1786). B. in Lancaster County, Pennsylvania, he was a brother of Lewis Wetzel, noted Indian slayer. George was killed in an ambush with his father when his party was returning by canoe on the Ohio River, two miles above Fish Creek, Virginia.

C.B. Allman, *Lewis Wetzel, Indian Fighter.* N.Y., Devin-Adair Co., 1961.

Wetzel, Jacob, Indian fighter (Sept. 16, 1765-July 27, 1827). A brother of Lewis Wetzel, he was b. in Lancaster County, Pennsylvania, and took an active part in the Indian wars of Virginia, Pennsylvania and Ohio. With Simon Kenton he killed five Indians near the mouth of the Kentucky River, but the date of this incident was not recorded. In October 1790 at Fort Washington (Cincinnati), Ohio, Jacob killed a chief with a knife in a hand-to-hand struggle. On one occasion he carved a man's head from a stump, using it to lure two hostile Indians whom he slew. In 1803 Jacob Wetzel became a magistrate and sheriff of Ohio County, Virginia; he moved to Boone County, Kentucky, in 1808; to Laurel, Franklin County, Indiana, in 1811, and finally to Morgan County, Indiana, in 1818. He is said to have ably served as scout under Generals William Henry Harrison, Arthur St. Clair and others. Wetzel was 5 feet, 11 inches in height, weighed 250 pounds and was a square-built, broad-shouldered, powerful man. He died and was buried at McKinsey Cemetery, Waverly, Indiana.

C.B. Allman, *Lewis Wetzel, Indian Fighter.* N.Y., Devin-Adair Co., 1961; Patricia Jahns, *The Violent Years: Simon Kenton and the Ohio-Kentucky Frontier.* N.Y., Hastings House, 1962.

Wetzel, Lewis, Indian fighter (Aug. 1763-Summer 1808). B. in Lancaster County, Pennsylvania, the son of a Holland-born immigrant, he moved with his family in 1764 to Big Wheeling Creek, Marshall County, present West Virginia. At 13 he and a younger brother were captured by Indians and taken to Ohio where, thanks to Lewis's courage they effected a hairbreadth escape. Later he killed his first three Indians near Wetzel's spring, St. Clairsville, Ohio. By 17 Wetzel was a veteran scout, devoted to killing Indians who ravaged the country during the Revolutionary War. He had taken part in the battle of Captina in

May 1778 when seven Indians and three whites were killed; about that time in another incident he killed two of three Indians and grumbled because he didn't get them all. He was said to be friendly with the Hurons, but deadly to Delawares and others. Once he killed two Indians with one bullet near Wheeling Creek. Wetzel was a member of the disastrous Crawford punitive expedition of 1782, and participated in the defense of Fort Henry at Wheeling on September 11 of that year. He helped construct Fort Harmar at Marietta, Ohio, killed an Indian who had come in to make peace there and was outlawed by brevet Brigadier General Josiah Harmar; he was captured and handcuffed but escaped, hid out four days, swam the Ohio River and found a friend to saw off the manacles after which Harmar placed a price on his head. Wetzel is said once to have trapped six Indians by a ruse, and toma-hawked them all. After his father and brother, George were killed in a June 1786 ambush which Wetzel escaped he roamed up and down the Ohio, seeking out and killing Indians relentlessly; one report said he had killed 27 Indians in all. Once he was captured, condemned to be burned at the stake when an aged chief saved his life by "adopting" him, led him to the Ohio, gave him his horse and weapons and told him he was free — and Wetzel shot him dead. "He made me walk, and he was nothing but an Indian," he explained. Ostracized for that and similar atrocities he went to Kentucky for further adventures, which were countless, many seemingly unbelievable or by now forgotten. Captured by soldiers he was returned to Fort Harmar, tried for murdering the Indian who had sought peace and was sentenced to hang but popular pressure forced reversal of the verdict. He resumed his vendetta, once slaughtering three of four sleeping men. He and Albert Maywood once fought off a large party of Wyandots (Hurons) near present day Belpre, Ohio, rescuing Rose Forester whom Maywood then married. In about 1787 Wetzel killed Canipsico, an important Mingo chief. He journeyed by flatboat to New Orleans where he was convicted, possibly falsely of counterfeiting and served a two-year term; arrested again at New Orleans for a like offense he spent five years in the Spanish prison, escaped by a ruse, took a ship for New York and perhaps he met George Washington at Philadelphia before returning to West Virginia where he resumed his Indian killing with his customary success. He went down the river again in 1799, was captured by Indians near the mouth of the Ohio and was ransomed by a friend. He went on to New Orleans, perhaps as legend has it seeking the Spaniard who had betrayed him to Spanish law earlier, but probably did not find him. Upon his return he accompanied John Madison, brother of President James Madison on a surveying trip through the Kanawha region of West Virginia where Madison was killed by Indians, Wetzel bringing the body in to Wheeling. It was reported Wetzel was invited to join the Lewis and Clark Expedition but returned after four months when he found it not exciting enough; the story no doubt is apocryphal, there is no record that Wetzel ever accompanied the party or even joined it, although he was acquainted with Patrick Gass, one of its best-known members, He descended the Mississippi again and at Natchez, Mississippi, Wetzel contracted fever and died at the age of 44. He was buried near Natchez, his remains disinterred in 1942 and removed to McCreary Cemetery near Big Wheeling Creek, Moundsville, West Virginia. He was in his prime 5 feet, 10 inches tall, strongly made, a swift runner with piercing black eyes and black hair that reached his knees when combed out. Attractive to women, red or white, he never married but had a series of affairs. A deadly marksman, he also played the fiddle tolerably well for his society. He was uneducated, with a pock-marked face, was sometimes morose but usually he was polite and well-spoken. He claimed never to have killed a white man, nor a woman or child of any color. Literature about him is fairly voluminous.

C.B. Allman, *Lewis Wetzel, Indian Fighter.* N.Y., Devin-Adair Co., 1961; Cecil B. Hartley, *Life and Adventures of Lewis Wetzel, The Virginia Ranger.* Phila., G.G. Evans, 1860.

Wetzel, Martin, Indian fighter (1757-Oct. 1829). B. in Rockingham County, Virginia, he was an older brother of Lewis Wetzel and like him an accomplished frontiersman; he was said to have been a master with a tomahawk. He served with frontier militia against Indians in September 1777, by his wits escaped a massacre of 21 men and helped rout the Indians. In 1780 he was one of Colonel Daniel

Brodhead's command against the Indian towns along the Coshocton River, Ohio, taking part in the execution of some captured Indians. He murdered a peace emissary, never receiving punishment or reprimand for his murderous activities, so long as they were directed against Indians. Later Martin Wetzel himself was captured by Ohio Indians, adopted into the unspecified tribe but soon killed three Indians and escaped. Dressed as an Indian he was almost assassinated at the first settlement he entered, but was identified by Daniel Boone, and released. He assisted in the defense of Fort Henry at Wheeling, present West Virginia September 11, 1782, scouted for another fort in Marshall County and with his brother, Lewis, was credited with saving the post from Indian entry. With Lewis he escaped the ambush slaying of his father and brother George in June 1786 on the Ohio River. Martin Wetzel died at the old Wetzel homestead on Big Wheeling Creek, Virginia, and was buried at McCreary Cemetery, near Moundsville.

C.B. Allman, *Lewis Wetzel, Indian Fighter.* N.Y., Devin-Adair Co., 1961.

Weyman, Edward A., adventurer (May 6, 1821-c. 1905). B. at New Rochelle, New York, he became a U.S. Navy midshipman at 15, serving aboard the *Boston* of which Edwin Ward Moore was commander; when Moore became commodore of the Texas Navy, Weyman followed him into that service, serving three years and being sailing master of the flagship when Tabasco in Yucatan was captured in 1842. Leaving the Navy, Weyman settled at Brownsville, Texas. He became an organizer of a bizarre scheme to capture California for Texas or, if Texas should refuse to annex it, for an independent state. Weyman was to take the sea force (consisting of the old brig, *Jim Bowie,* nee *Worton*) around Cape Horn, while Dr. William M. Shepherd a Texas Army surgeon, was to go west with land forces, the two elements to meet at San Francisco, assault that city as the start of their "conquest." Fortunately the scheme, which could scarcely have amounted to anything, was aborted by Houston. Weyman went to South America, to Europe, and returned to settle at Brownsville, becoming the first sheriff of the Rio Grande country with headquarters at Corpus Christi, after Texas was admitted to the U.S. He "rid the country of some of its most desperate characters..., was in numerous shootings...(but) never was wounded." Once in a shootout with desperado Bill Williams, in which six men were slain, Weyman had his horse killed under him. Leaving Texas, Weyman located at Durango, Mexico, was a scalp hunter for a time, in one battle killing 38 Apaches and having 18 of his own men wounded. He went to the California gold fields about 1849, remaining two years, then visited Panama and returned to Mexico, living first at Victoria and from about 1858 at Jalisco. He continued his adventurous career amid Mexican civil strife until an advanced age. He married twice and fathered children.

Hunter Anderson, "Texan Plotted Conquest of California." *Frontier Times,* Vol. 4, No. 1 (Oct. 1926), 1-3.

Wham, Joseph Washington, army officer (Jan. 18, 1840-Dec. 21, 1908). B. in Marion County, Illinois, he enlisted in the 21st Illinois Infantry June 10, 1861, was commissioned a second lieutenant July 28, 1865, and was mustered out December 16. He was commissioned a second lieutenant in the 35th U.S. Infantry May 22, 1867, and discharged January 1, 1871, at his own request. On March 3, 1877, he was commissioned major and an army paymaster. On May 11, 1889, Wham was taking $28,345.10 in gold and silver coins from Fort Grant to pay soldiers at Forts Thomas and Apache and at San Carlos, Arizona. He had a white clerk and an escort of 11 black soldiers in two mule-drawn conveyances. The party was ambushed near Cedar Springs, the robbers protected by several improvised rock shelters; nine soldiers were wounded, one, Sergeant William Brown, Company C, 24th Infantry, seriously, the others in varying degrees but indications were that the desperadoes did not intend to kill anyone if they could help it. Wham and his clerk, neither armed, ran for cover and the robbers made away with the payroll in one of the most celebrated crimes in southwestern history. Seven members of a Mormon colony along the nearby Gila River were indicted but after a 35-day trial were acquitted although some had been identified by Wham (who may not have been in a position to identify anyone). Many at the time and later thought that this was a case of miscarried justice. However Bert Cooley (see biography) reported in a 1981 article that he, his side-kick Charley Gross

and others had pulled off the job and frittered away the money; Cooley was killed about 1891 in Idaho having told his story to his sister, a newspaperwoman who retained the manuscript until her death in 1942 when it was retrieved by another and at last was published. If authentic, this might clear up the matter which does not seem likely to be solved in any other way at this late date. Wham was held accountable by the army for the lost payroll although several years later Congress in a special act relieved him of the burden. He retired May 3, 1901, because of failing eyesight. He dropped dead on the sidewalk at Washington, D.C. Wham married but had no children. He was 5 feet, 10 inches in height and had blue eyes and auburn hair.

Wham pension file, NARS; *Chronological List;* Lee E. Echols, "The Baffling Major Wham Paymaster Robbery." *Arizona* (Sunday magazine of *Arizona Republic*), Mar. 30, 1980; Bert Cooley, "Robbing an Army Mud Wagon." *True West,* Vol. 28, No. 3 (Jan.-Feb. 1981), 42-47.

Wharfield, Harold B., army officer, writer (Aug. 29, 1894-Apr. 16, 1972). B. at Marshfield, Wisconsin, he joined the 10th Cavalry in 1917, was posted to Fort Apache, Arizona, and became associated with Apache scouts. He transferred to the Army Air Corps (later the U.S. Sir Force), and served through both World Wars, attaining the rank of colonel. He wrote *With Scouts and Cavalry at Fort Apache* (Tucson, Arizona Pioneers' Historical Society, 1965), and several monographs, published privately: *Apache Indian Scouts* (1964); *10th Cavalry & Border Fights* (1965); *Cooley: Army Scout, Arizona pioneer, Wayside host, Apache friend* (1966); *Fort Yuma on the Colorado River* (1968); *Alchesay: Scout with General Crook, Sierra Blanca Apache chief, Friend of Fort Apache whites* (1969); *Cibicu Creek Fight in Arizona: 1881* (1971). All are honest, personally researched, and have value. Wharfield died at El Cajon, California, and is buried there.

Wheat, Carl Irving, historical cartographer (Dec. 5, 1892-June 23, 1966). B. at Holliston, Massachusetts, he was raised in California, graduated from Pomona (California) College and served in World War I in the Ambulance Service and with the Army Air Corps. Subsequently he received a law degree from Harvard and practiced at Los Angeles and

San Francisco. Wheat became interested in historical research and writing, partly through the influence of Henry R. Wagner, became a director of the California Historical Society and edited its publication for seven years. He was fascinated by old maps of the West, and it was in pursuing that interest that he made his greatest contribution to frontier history. In 1957 he founded the Institute of Historical Geography to publish important products of his research. Wheat died at Menlo Park, California. His significant publications included, as editor: *California in 1851; The Letters of Dame Shirley* (1933); as author: *The Maps of the California Gold Region, 1848-1857* (1942); *The Pioneer Press of California* (1948); *Books of the California Gold Rush: A Centennial Selection* (1949); with Dale L. Morgan, *Jedediah Smith and His Maps of the American West* (1954); *Mapping the American West, 1540-1857: A Preliminary Study* (1954), and his greatest contribution, *Mapping the Transmississippi West, 1540-1861*, 5 volumes (1957-1963).

James Shebl, "Carl Irving Wheat: 1892-1966." *Arizona and the West*, Vol. 25, No. 1 (Spring 1983), 1-4.

Wheat, Granville, lawman (1829-c. 1909). B. in Kentucky he went to California in 1849 and to Arizona in 1859 as a teamster in the Tucson area. He was the first sheriff of Pima County and was sheriff at the time of the 1871 Camp Grant Massacre, which he attended. He removed to Florence and became a supervisor of Pinal County.

Farish, VI.

Wheaton, Frank, army officer (May 8, 1833-June 18, 1903). B. at Providence, Rhode Island, he was selected at 17 by John Russell Bartlett (see entry) as a "chain bearer and station-marker" for the famed Mexican Boundary Commission, and served with it five years in the Southwest. He was commissioned a first lieutenant in the 1st Cavalry March 3, 1855 and was engaged in quelling Kansas border troubles out of Fort Leavenworth for a year. He was involved in an action with Cheyenne Indians on Wood River, near Fort Kearny, Nebraska, in August 1855 and was on a Cheyenne expedition in July 1857. Wheaton helped organize the Utah Expedition but accompanied it only as far as Council Grove, then was assigned to Indian Territory where

he served at several posts and assisted in construction of Fort Cobb. He became a captain March 1, 1861. Wheaton emerged from the Civil War during which his services were in eastern theatres a Brigadier General of Volunteers and brevet Major General both of Volunteers and the Army. He was a lieutenant colonel of the 39th Infantry in 1866, transferred to the 21st Infantry in 1869 and became colonel of the 2nd Infantry in 1874. While with the 21st Wheaton commanded the District of the Lakes with headquarters at Camp Warner, southern Oregon and as such directed initial military operations during the Modoc War of 1872-73 in northwestern California. It was frustrating. After the first Battle of the Stronghold, a reverse for the military, Wheaton was relieved from command of military operations, retaining that of his District of the Lakes; Gillem, his successor in command of the Modoc operation did not last long, either. Wheaton was restored to nominal command, but actual command was assumed by Colonel Jefferson C. Davis, who had succeeded Canby as commander of the Department of the Columbia. Wheaton oversaw the court-martial of Jack and three other Modocs and their subsequent execution, visiting the condemned Indians the day before their deaths to inform them that President Grant would not commute the sentences. Wheaton became a Brigadier General in 1892 and a Major General in 1897 preceding his retirement just before the Spanish American War. He died at Washington, D.C.

Heitman; Powell; Jeff C. Riddle, *The Indian History of the Modoc War.* Medford, Ore., Pine Cone Pub., 1973; Keith A. Murray, *The Modocs and Their War.* Norman, Univ. of Okla. Press, 1965; Odie B. Faulk, *Too Far North...Too Far South.* Los Angeles, Westernlore Press, 1967.

Wheeler, Ben F. (Ben F. Burton, Ben Robertson), desperado, lawman (1854-Apr. 30, 1884). B. at Rockdale, Milam County, Texas, he was a brother of the one-time general land agent of Texas. In a shooting scrape he severely wounded a man and left Texas in 1878, went to Cheyenne, then to Nebraska and finally to Caldwell, Kansas, where he became assistant city marshal to Henry Brown. With Brown he attempted to rob a Medicine Lodge, Kansas, bank in which attempt he killed cashier George Geppert.

Brown was killed in an escape attempt and Wheeler with two others were lynched. Wheeler was large, powerfully built, dark and with an open countenance. He reportedly left a wife and four children in Texas, another wife at Indianola, Nebraska.

Nyle H. Miller, Joseph W. Snell, *Great Gunfighters of the Kansas Cowtowns, 1867-1886.* Lincoln, Univ. of Nebr. Press, 1967.

Wheeler, Edward Lytton, writer (c. 1854-c. 1885). B. in Avoca, New York, and raised in Pennsylvania, Wheeler became a dime novelist and in 1877 created the character Deadwood Dick, although he had never been to Deadwood or perhaps the West. He wrote 33 dime novels with his Deadwood Dick as hero, although he was based on no actual person. The series was immensely popular however, and led Wheeler to also attempt a play, "Deadwood Dick, a Road Agent, A Drama of the Gold Mines," which had a limited success. Wheeler died concurrently with his hero.

Wayne Gard, "The Myth of Deadwood Dick." *Frontier Times,* Vol. 43, No. 6 (Oct.-Nov. 1969), 10-11, 48-50.

Wheeler, George Montague, army officer (Oct. 9, 1842-May 3, 1905). B. at Hopkinton, Massachusetts, he was commissioned from West Point a second lieutenant of Engineers June 18, 1866, becoming a first lieutenant March 7 of the following year. Initially he was employed on surveying duty in California and the southwest. In 1868 he named the Colorado Plateau, and the following year worked in southeastern Nevada and western Utah. His experiences and findings were described in his *Preliminary Report Upon a Reconnaissance through Southern and Southeastern Nevada, Made in 1869* (1875), prepared with Daniel Wright Lockwood. In 1871 Wheeler was placed in charge of the exploration "of those portions of the United States Territory lying south of the Central Pacific Railroad, embracing parts of Eastern Nevada and Arizona," with a primary function to prepare accurate maps of the region, while studying its Indians, natural history, mineral resources, climate and other features. He was authorized to hire up to ten specialists in these fields to assist him, a figure later considerably expanded. Wheeler launched his expedition from near Elko, Nevada, and worked 72,250

square miles in Nevada, California, Utah and Arizona that season. He now envisioned mapping the entire west beyond the 100th meridian. The plan was approved in 1872 and entitled the United States Geographical Surveys West of the One Hundredth Meridian. By 1874 his survey had become "thorough, painstaking and methodical," and large-scale and scientific in tone; from 1871 onward there were always more than 50 officers and assistants in the field each season, and from 1875 the work was carried out in two divisions, the California and Colorado sections. The field work continued through 1879, including 14 expeditions of varying length. As it developed, reports on one portion or another appeared in 41 volumes and the definitive *Report upon United States Geographical Surveys West of the One Hundredth Meridian* appeared between 1875 and 1889 in ten volumes, including a topographical atlas and a geological atlas together including 164 maps. Wheeler became a captain March 4, 1879. Civilians leading rival surveys, Powell, Hayden and others, eventually were instrumental in terminating the army's topographical work (which they considered competitive) about two years short of its objective of compiling a "reasonably accurate" map of 1.5 million square miles of what had been desert and wilderness at an overall cost of around $2 million. Completion of its task has not yet been accomplished by the Geological Survey, which took over Wheeler's work. "In trying to save money... Congress therefore literally threw away all the sound work that had been accomplished by Wheeler.... Congress prevented the completion of a good, useful, overall map of the West and dismantled Wheeler's organization." Wheeler was on sick leave from 1880-84 but during this time was the War Department's delegate to the Third Geographical Congress at Venice in 1881, publishing a report of it. He also wrote more than 20 technical reports on his western work, a list included in "Bibliography of the Writings of Graduates," *Centennial of the United States Military Academy at West Point,* New York, Volume II. Wheeler retired for reasons of health June 15, 1888. By an 1890 act of Congress he was promoted to major with rank and pay retroactive to July 23, 1888. He lived in New York City in retirement and died there. He was married.

Heitman; Cullum; Wheeler, *Preliminary Report upon a Reconnaissance through Southern and Southeastern Nevada, made in 1869.* Wash., Govt Printing Office, 1875; Richard A. Bartlett, *Great Surveys of the American West.* Norman, Univ. of Okla. Press, 1962; William H. Goetzmann, *Exploration & Empire.* N.Y., Vintage Books, 1972.

Wheeler, Harry C., lawman (c. 1875-Dec. 17, 1925). B. Harry Cornell Williams at Gainesville, Florida, his father died before he was 1 and Harry was adopted by his stepfather, William B. Wheeler, taking his surname. William Wheeler was a West Point graduate and career Army officer; Harry Wheeler was said to have been rejected by the Military Academy because of his short stature. Harry Wheeler joined the 1st Oklahoma Cavalry for service in the Spanish-American War, but was injured when a horse kicked him, and was forced to retire from the military. He reached Arizona in 1900, settling at Bisbee. In July 1903, he enlisted in the Arizona Rangers, rising steadily in its ranks until he became its last captain, serving from March 22, 1907, until the Rangers' disbandment February 15, 1909. In 1907 Wheeler shot and killed a man named Bostwick in Tucson and wounded mortally J.A. Tracy in a second gunfight at Benson, Arizona. With Deputy Sheriff George Humm, Wheeler killed George O. Arnett May 6, 1908, near Lowell, Arizona. Wheeler was a fine shot, and one of the best Ranger officers on record. In September 1909 he was appointed deputy U.S. marshal for Tucson, then became a line rider for the customs service, working out of Douglas, Arizona. He was elected sheriff of Cochise County in 1912 and served until he enlisted in the army during World War I. He was commissioned a captain and sailed for France in March 1918, being assigned to the Signal Corps of the Aviation Division, although he preferred to serve in a combat capacity. Three months later Wheeler was ordered back to this country because of charges against him for his part in suppressing IWW activities in the Bisbee area. The hundreds of defendants were found not guilty. Wheeler worked as a trick shooter in a carnival, and traveled with the 101 Wild West Show to Europe, giving a command performance before George V of England. He died at Bisbee of pneumonia.

AHS archives; Joseph Miller, ed., *The Arizona Rangers.* N.Y., Hastings House, 1972.

Wheeler, Henry M., physician (1857-Oct. 28, 1929). As a 19-year-old medical student on vacation from the University of Michigan, Wheeler was at Northfield, Minnesota, September 7, 1876, when the James-Younger gang attempted their famous bank robbery; using a borrowed firearm Wheeler killed Clell Miller and wounded Bob Younger in the elbow. He obtained permission to take the bodies of Miller and desperado Bill Chadwell (William Stiles), also killed in the affair, to his university for anatomical research. He and a classmate, Clarence E. Persons dug up the two corpses, packed them in kegs with salt and delivered them to Ann Arbor, Michigan. After some dissection and considerable time, the Missouri father of Miller demanded and secured the remains of his son, returning them to his home for burial. Wheeler retained the skeleton of Chadwell. Wheeler practiced medicine initially at Grand Forks, North Dakota, and later in life at Beeville, and Skidmore, Texas.

Colin Rickards, "Bones of the Northfield Robbers." *Real West,* Vol. 22, No. 161 (Jan. 1979), 28-31, 60.

Wheeler, Homer Webster, army officer, writer (May 13, 1848-Apr. 11, 1930). B. at Montgomery, Vermont, he moved with his parents to Minnesota, returned to Vermont, attended business college in New York state and in June 1868, went to Fort Wallace, Kansas, where he became acquainted with Will Comstock, scout, and took several plains trips with him, Cody and Hickok. In September he accompanied Bankhead's expedition which rescued Forsyth's scouts from Beecher Island. Wheeler went on other scouts as a civilian volunteer. He accompanied Henely in the Sappa Creek fight April 23, 1875, was commended for good judgment and conspicuous gallantry and upon the recommendation of Pope, appointed a second lieutenant in the 5th Cavalry on October 15, joining his company December 12 at Fort Lyon, Colorado. He was transferred to Fort Robinson, Nebraska, in July 1876, engaged in the skirmish at Chadron Creek, Nebraska, and in November took part in Mackenzie's expedition against Dull Knife's Cheyenne village in the Big Horn Mountains of Wyoming. Wheeler participated peripherally in the Nez Percé campaign of 1877, then served at Fort McPherson, Nebraska, Fort Washakie, Wyoming, from where in late 1879 he captured the remnant of the Bannock hostiles, and served later at Nebraska posts. He was made first lieutenant in 1883 and captain in 1893, served in Puerto Rico in the Spanish American War and became major of the 9th Cavalry in 1902. He transferred to the 11th Cavalry that year, serving in the Philippines, 1902-1904, Cuba from 1906-1909, and Hawaii, 1910-11. Wheeler became a colonel in March of 1911 and retired in September, making his home at Los Angeles, where he died. He wrote *The Frontier Trail* (1923) and *Buffalo Days* (1925).

Price, *Fifth Cavalry; Who Was Who; Battle of Beecher Island,* ed. by Simon E. Matson. Wray, Colo., Beecher Island Battle Mem. Assn., 1960; information from David Perry Perrine.

Whelan, William (Uncle Billy), pioneer (Feb. 11, 1872-July 31, 1975). B. at Tucson, he was moved to Willcox, Arizona, as an infant and lived the rest of his life in its vicinity. He became a cowboy, rancher, stagecoach escort and chased bronco Apache Indians in his youth, being a competent horseman until his mid-nineties. Married to a Mayo Indian, he was the father of nine sons, five of whom survived him. He died at Willcox.

Tucson, Ariz., *Citizen,* Aug. 2, 1975.

Whipple, Amiel Weeks, army officer, explorer (Oct. 21, 1817-May 7, 1863). B. at Concord, Masssachusetts, he attended Amherst College, was graduated from West Point in 1841, in September was assigned to the Topographical Engineers and carried out assignments in the east and south until 1844 when he was given charge of instrument work for the Northeastern Boundary Survey. In 1849 Whipple was assigned to help survey the boundary between the United States and Mexico and that year, with the "ill-starred Weller Boundary Commission," he made observations near the junction of the Gila and Colorado rivers. The next year Whipple joined the John Russell Bartlett party undertaking the joint endeavor to mark the boundary between this country and Mexico, initially being engaged in astronomical surveys and erecting an observatory at San Eleazorio, Texas, and another north of El Paso. Whipple performed important duties on the survey, although William H. Emory was chief surveyor. The expedition

reached San Diego in January 1852. Whipple Barracks (later Fort Whipple) at Prescott, Arizona, and Fort Whipple, Virginia, were named for him. Whipple next was assigned to carry out the Pacific Railroad Survey from Fort Smith, Arkansas, to the coast generally along the 35th parallel. His journal of the trip has been published and is of primary historical importance and interest. Whipple's report attracted considerable interest in this country and in Europe, Baron Alexander von Humboldt becoming interested in it and corresponding voluminously with Whipple for several years. Upon completion of the survey, Whipple was assigned to Detroit with the mission of improving navigation on the Great Lakes, and by the start of the Civil War he was a captain. As chief topographical engineer, he took part in the first engagement at Bull Run, but his principle duty initially was to oversee preparation of maps of northern Virginia, then imperfect and in very short supply, and this involved conducting armed reconnaissances to collect the necessary topographical details, a very hazardous duty accomplished successfully. Whipple became chief topographical engineer for McDowell's Army of the Potomac. By April 14, 1862, he had become Brigadier General of Volunteers and was commanding a division. Whipple took part in the Battle of Fredericksburg, and was wounded mortally at the Battle of Chancellorsville, dying at Washington. His funeral was attended by President Lincoln "as a friend of the family and not as President of the United States," the two having become intimately acquainted during operations for the defense of Washington, D.C. Just prior to his death, Whipple was commissioned by Lincoln Major General of Volunteers. Lincoln appointed Whipple's son to West Point after the death of his father, and left a note asking that his successor appoint another son to Annapolis, which was done by President Johnson. Many of Whipple's papers, sketches surveys, books and other data were donated ultimately to the Oklahoma Historical Society.

Francis R. Stoddard, "Amiel Weeks Whipple." *Chronicles of Okla.,*Vol. XXVIII, No. 3 (Autumn 1950), 226-34; *A Pathfinder in the Southwest: The Itinerary of Lieutenant A.W. Whipple During His Explorations for a Railway Route from Fort Smith to Los Angeles in the Years 1853-1854,* ed. by Grant Foreman. Norman, Univ. of Okla. Press, 1941.

Whipple, Henry Benjamin, Episcopal churchman (Feb. 15, 1822-Sept. 16, 1901). B. at Adams, New York, Whipple was 24 before he decided to enter the Episcopal priesthood. He was ordained in 1850, served pastorates at Rome, New York, and Chicago, and in 1859 was consecrated first bishop of Minnesota, then a new state, and inhabited by up to 20,000 Indians with whom the prelate quickly came into sympathetic touch. "I resolved that it should never be said that the first bishop of Minnesota turned his back upon the heathen at his door," he recalled. Whipple corresponded with a series of Presidents about Indian problems, urging reforms and that regulations be made more practicable for a paternal solicitude for Indian welfare. Many of his suggestions ultimately were adopted. He settled at Faribault, Minnesota, in May 1860, and here he developed Seabury Divinity School and related institutions. Whipple did what he could on the fringes of the great Sioux uprising of 1862, which he had predicted because of abuses of the Indians, even assisting to care for the wounded, and when the danger was past worked assiduously to mitigate the vengeance-fever of the whites and make sure that executions of those alleged to be leaders among the hostiles were as few as possible. In an article he argued that everyone knew that "the Indian Department is the most corrupt in the government . . . characterized by inefficiency and fraud. The nation, knowing this, has winked at it. . . . Who is guilty of the causes which desolated our border? At whose door is the blood of these innocent victims?" He took a petition signed by many of his fellow bishops to Washington, met Lincoln through intercession of Whipple's cousin, Major General Henry Wager Halleck, Lincoln recalling that Whipple had "talked to me about the rascality of this Indian business until I felt it down to my boots. If . . . I live, this Indian system shall be reformed." In the spring, against savage frontier opposition, Whipple cared for families of Sioux, some of whom had enlisted as scouts with Sibley for operations against the still-hostile tribesmen in the Dakotas. Whipple worked hard also among the Chippewas to the north, where the sale of white pine from Indian lands without their permission had provoked much resentment and retaliation. The bishop did a great deal to allay this normal hostility and even succeeded in halting the sale of some timber. Following

the Custer fight in 1876 Whipple was sent to the Black Hills to argue Sioux into accepting a home in Indian Territory; he did his best against much hostility, but the agreement which resulted was never ratified. Whipple made countless trips to Washington on behalf of Indian rights and became personally acquainted with all Presidents from Van Buren to McKinley, asking "only justice for a wronged and neglected race," but he was never as soft-headed as he was soft-hearted, ever insisting upon Indian obligation as well as Indian rights. Whipple made numerous trips abroad, became the friend of many great and titled persons, but never forgot his primary charge. His first wife died in 1890 after nearly 50 years of marriage; in 1896 the bishop married again. One of his sons was mysteriously shot and the body left floating in the Ohio River, and once the bishop disarmed an attempted assassin of himself. Whipple came finally to be considered "by force of his personality a bishop of the church universal." He died at Faribault.

Henry B. Whipple, *Lights and Shadows of a Long Episcopate.* N.Y., Macmillan Co., 1899; Joan C. Kyllo, "Bishop H.B. Whipple — Apostle to the Indians." *The West,* Vol. 10, No. 5 (Apr. 1969), 26-27, 54-59; DAB.

Whipple, Stephen Girard, army officer (1840-Oct. 21, 1895). B. in Vermont, he reached California before the Civil War and may have been the Captain Whipple leading a volunteer force who was seriously wounded during an Indian scuffle in Plumas or Siskiyou County in 1851. In 1858 he established and edited *The Northern Californian* at Union (Arcata) California, later publishing the *Humboldt Times.* He was elected to the Legislature by the Union Party. In May 1863 as a lieutenant colonel of Volunteers Whipple organized the 1st Battalion of Montaineers in Humboldt County, California. Its purpose was to fight Indians of southern Oregon and northern California who had become restless in the turmoil created by the eastern war. The battalion was mounted and included six companies. Whipple, who was breveted colonel, was stationed at Forts Humboldt and Gaston and commanded Fort Humboldt during the war; he was mustered out June 13, 1865. He became captain of the 32nd U.S. Infantry in 1867, served in Arizona and was transferred to the 1st Cavalry in 1870. He was

Indian agent at Hoopa Valley, California, from April 1870 until March 1871, returning then with his regiment to Arizona where he served until January 1873. From 1875 until 1878 he was on duty in Washington Territory. July 11, 1877, Howard sent Whipple with two companies to arrest Chief Looking Glass, camped on the Clearwater River of Idaho. Howard suspecting him of leaning toward the hostiles who had severely defeated troops to open the Nez Perce War. Whipple failed to arrest Looking Glass; firing commenced between the Indians and volunteers who had accompanied Whipple and soon became general. Whipple won a brevet for his role in the Battle of the Clearwater, but his action served to drive Looking Glass, who had been neutral, into the camp of the hostiles with far-reaching consequences. He was in the Bannock and Paiute campaigns of 1878. In 1881 Whipple was commanding at Fort Klamath, Oregon, and spent the remainder of his active duty in the Department of the Columbia. He retired in 1884 and died at Eureka, California. He was married and fathered a son. Whipple was described in middle life as "a large man, an even six feet in height and weighing about 200 pounds; he had blue eyes, black hair and wore a long beard, also black..."

Heitman; John D. McDermott, *Forlorn Hope: The Battle of White Bird Canyon and the Beginning of the Nez Perce War.* Boise, Ida. State Hist. Soc., 1978; Bancroft, *California,* VII; Jeff C. Riddle, *The Indian History of the Modoc War.* Medford, Ore., Pine Cone Pubrs., 1973.

Whistler, Joseph Nelson Garland, army officer (Oct. 19, 1822-Apr. 22, 1899). B. at Green Bay, Wisconsin, he was sent to West Point from Florida and graduated in 1846, joining the 8th Infantry briefly, then the 3rd Infantry with which he fought in the Mexican War, winning a brevet for gallantry in two actions. He was captured by Confederates in Texas at the opening of the Civil War, was made a captain, became a colonel of Volunteers in the conflict (and was breveted to Brigadier General). By his retirement in 1886 he had moved from major through several transfers to colonel of the 15th Infantry. Whistler in 1876 brought reinforcements up the Missouri to Terry, established winter quarters at the mouth of the Tongue River since Sheridan was determined to occupy the Yellowstone River valley in the face of Sioux hostility.

Don Russell, *The Lives and Legends of Buffalo Bill.* Norman, Univ. of Okla. Press, 1960; *Who Was Who.*

Whitam, Nat., frontiersman (d. c. 1890). Described as "an old government guide and packer," Whitam, it is said, "had gone through half a dozen Indian campaigns in the wars with the Sioux, Cheyennes and Comanches." He lived alone in a cabin on Blue River, between Clifton and Springerville, Arizona, and was shot in the doorway of his home, presumably by the Apache Kid.

William Sparks, *The Apache Kid, a Bear Fight.* Los Angeles, Skelton Pub. Co., 1926.

Whitcomb, Elias W. (Pappy), cattleman (c. 1838-1908). B. in Virginia, Whitcomb whacked bulls across the Plains in 1857, reaching Santa Fe, New Mexico. In the spring of 1858 he worked for Russell, Majors and Waddell handling their work cattle at Fort Laramie, Wyoming. The following year he commenced building up a herd of his own, trading emigrants for their trailworn stock; about 1866 he bought Texas cattle driven north and acquired six four-yoke teams he worked for the government at Fort Laramie at $10 a day each. His cattle constituted the first resident herd in southern Wyoming. Whitcomb established a homestead near Cheyenne and in 1878 entered a partnership to run ranges in western Nebraska, also operating a dry goods business at Cheyenne. Toward the end of the 1880s cattle boom he sold his ranch holdings to Swan Land and Cattle Company for a reputed $250,000. Whitcomb was reported by Smith to have had a role in the Johnson County War of 1892, being the oldest of the "Invaders," or big cattlemen. His last ranch was in the vicinity of Devil's Tower, Wyoming, and it was here that he was struck by lightning, he and the horse he was riding being killed instantly. He had married a half-French, half-Indian woman and fathered a daughter.

Casper (Wyo.) *Star-Tribune,* Apr. 29, 1971; Helena Huntington Smith, *The War on Powder River.* N.Y., McGraw-Hill Book Co., 1966; information from the Western History Research Center, University of Wyo.

White, Andrew, Jesuit missionary (1579-Dec. 27, 1656). B. at London, England, he became a priest, was ordained at Douai in France about 1605, volunteered for Catholic sub rosa missions in England, was captured and banished under threat of death if he returned. He became a Jesuit in 1609 and interested himself in the George Calvert (Lord Baltimore) plan for colonization in the New World, reaching Chesapeake Bay in 1634. For a decade he worked among white colonists and with Indians of the Conoy and Powhatan tribes and their subdivisions; he and others compiled a grammar, dictionary and catechism in the local tongues. In the 1644 insurrection of William Claiborne, White and two others were shipped in irons to England and tried for treason, White being banished again. He slipped back into England once more and became chaplain to a family in Hampshire. He died in London.

Thwaites, JR, XXXVI, 244n28, DAB; DNB.

White, Benjamin, pioneer (Nov. 17, 1814-Aug. 13, 1868). B. in Smyth County, Virginia, he moved to Wisconsin and August 24, 1843, at Belmont he married Mary Goode (b. Sept. 11, 1828 at Fort Osage, Missouri; d. post 1900). They became parents of 10 children, among them Sarah White who became an Indian captive. Benjamin White and family moved to Cloud County, Kansas, where they took up a farm. While putting up hay Benjamin was killed by Cheyenne raiders and his daughter was seized. He was buried August 15, 1868, on the Dempsey Taylor homestead near Lake Sibley; the body later was moved to Concordia Cemetery, Pleasant Hill, and still later to Pleasant View Cemetery, Fairview, Kansas.

Manuscript by Martin Adams White, St. Helen's Ore., Dec. 14, 1933; *Concordia* (Kan.) *Empire,* Sept. 1, 1898.

White, David, army chaplain (May 18, 1818-Oct. 25, 1901). B. in Bledsoe County, Tennessee, he was ordained a Methodist Episcopal minister in 1845. White enlisted in the 107th Illinois Infantry August 2, 1862, and became chaplain of the regiment in 1864, remaining in the Army after the war. He was assigned to Fort Riley, then to Fort Phil Kearny and Fort Reno, Wyoming Territory, from May 15, 1866. He was with a military wagon train enroute to his posts when it was attacked by Sioux, White interrupting the prayers of some with the remark that "there is a time for praying and a time for fighting, and this is the time to fight." On July 21, he was wounded slightly at Crazy Woman's Fork when with an enlisted volunteer he cleared a ravine of enemy and reported killing one of them. With another enlisted volunteer White then made a "magnificent" ride through Sioux-ridden country for help. At Fort Phil Kearny on December 26, 1866, in a mass service he presided over the burial of 81 men killed in the Fetterman fight; he continually buried victims of the Indians while at this post and was said to have buried more men killed by hostiles than any other chaplain. He once prevented the assassination of nine Cheyennes who visited the post under permission of its commander, Henry B. Carrington. White was stationed at Camp Verde, Arizona, from 1870 to 1872. He approved of part at least of Vincent Colyer's peace-seeking tour of the southwest, and, since Coyler was in disrepute with most Army authorities, thus came afoul of the military command structure. When he officially complained about drunkenness and gambling on the sabbath at Verde, his removal was recommended by the post commander, Captain C.C.C. Carr, and approved by Crook with the remark that White "is obnoxious to the officers and men at the post," and ought to be sent anywhere else where "he might be of service." One anonymous endorsement on a White communication urged that he be sent to Alaska. White served at a variety of posts until his retirement at age 64 on June 30, 1882. He was something of a scholar in Latin, Greek and Hebrew, and after his retirement he settled near the University of Kansas at Lawrence, "where he was considered an authority on these subjects." He was married, 5 feet, 7 inches tall, dark-complected with grey eyes. He died at Lawrence, Kansas.

Information from Lt. Col. Earl F. Stover, U.S. Army; Heitman; Dee, Brown, *Fort Phil Kearny: An American Saga,* N.Y., G.P. Putman's Sons, 1962.

White, Elijah, Indian agent, physician (c. 1805-Mar. 1879). B. in Tompkins County, New York, he became a physician and in 1837 sailed from Boston around Cape Horn with others for Oregon to reinforce the Methodist mission in the Willamette Valley. White at the time was described as of light complexion, blue eyes with dark hair, an "elastic frame" and with manners of "that obliging and flattering kind which made him popular, especially among women, but which men often called sycophantish and insincere." White was accompanied by his wife and two children. He served the mission for about four years, then after a disagreement with the superintendent, returned east. At Washington he receeived an appointment as the first Indian agent, indeed the first United States official, for Oregon. There he vigorously opposed the liquor traffic among the Indians and attempted with considerable success to mediate difficulties between whites and Indians, his work of substantial importance. But he came to cross-purposes with many settlers because of the stern principles he attempted to enforce and they prevented his reappointment although he returned to Washington to further his cause. He went once more to Oregon and in 1861 was named by Lincoln a "special Indian agent," again with undefined mission and responsibilities. Eventually he removed to San Francisco where he commenced a medical practice near Bancroft's Library where he frequently visited and where he dictated much material of use to the historian. He died at San Francisco.

Thwaites, EWT, XXIX, 20n.; Bancroft, *Oregon,* 2 vols.; Clifford M. Drury, *Marcus and Narcissa Whitman and the Opening of Old Oregon,* 2 vols. Glendale, Calif., Arthur H. Clark Co., 1973.

White, Fred, lawman (c. 1849-Oct. 28, 1880). B. in New York he was a onetime soldier who was appointed, in January 1880, the first city marshal of Tombstone, Arizona. When cowboys were roistering in the town, it is said White informally deputized Virgil Earp; in attempting to disarm Curly Bill Brocius, the cowboy's pistol accidentally discharged, mortally wounding White, who cleared Bill before he died. The report that Earp had killed White to get his job was baseless.

Ed Bartholomew, *Wyatt Earp: The Man & The Myth.* Toyahvale, Tex., Frontier Book Co., 1964.

White, James, militia officer (1747-Aug. 14, 1821). B. in Rowan (later Iredell) County, North Carolina, he served as militia captain late in the Revolution, explored eastern Tennessee, remained a year at Fort Chiswell (Chissel) on the New River in western North Carolina and in 1786 settled at the site of the present Knoxville, Tennessee. He became an officer in the county militia, directed defense of the town during Indian troubles in 1793, entered politics and was a factor in the early

history of Tennessee, being a friend of John Sevier and William Blount, also architects of the new state. White played an important role throughout his life in Indian affairs and as a Brigadier General of militia took part in the Creek War of 1813-14 in Alabama, being nominally under command of Andrew Jackson but more immediately under that of his friend, Militia Major General John Cocke. This sometimes led to confusion and misadventure. November 5, 1813, commanding 1,000 men he reported to Jackson from Turkeytown, Alabama, and was directed to march to Fort Strother on the Coosa River where wounded and survivors of recent actions had been collected, White instructed to support and defend that point against hostile Creeks. He started but received orders enroute from Cocke to join him at the mouth of the Chattanooga and he chose to obey that command of Tennessee forces in Alabama; jealousy between troops of East Tennessee and West Tennessee doubtless was a factor in White's decision. On November 18, 1813, White rashly attacked the Hillabee towns of Creeks although these Indians had agreed to surrender to Jackson and were awaiting his terms. White's engagement there was termed a massacre with 60 Indians being killed and 250 taken prisoner; it had the long-term effect of enraging the Hillabees against what they considered Jackson's treachery, and forced them to become among the most bitter of the Creeks fighting Americans. The blundering White then burned two largely vacated towns elsewhere in northern Alabama. White donated the land upon which the University of Tennessee ultimately was built, and died at Knoxville.

Albert James Pickett, *History of Alabama.* Birmingham Book and Mag. Co., 1962; H.S. Halbert, T.H. Ball, *The Creek War of 1813 and 1814.* Univ. of Ala. Press, 1969; DAB.

White, Joel, Mormon pioneer (fl. 1857-76). White, a resident of Cedar City, Utah, may have been with William C. Stewart when two emigrants seeking relief for the beleaguered Fancher wagon train at Mountain Meadows were accosted and murdered. White admitted at John D. Lee's second trial in 1876, that he had been present at the massacre on September 11, 1857.

William Wise, *Massacre at Mountain Meadows.* N.Y., Thomas Y. Crowell Co., 1976; Juanita Brooks, *John D. Lee.* Glendale, Calif., Arthur H. Clark Co., 1962.

White, John, artist, administrator (c. 1545-c. May 1606). B. perhaps at Truro, Cornwall and probably within the 1540-50 decade, he may have had a twin brother, Robert, but nothing is known with certainty of John White until 1580 when he belonged to a London guild of arts craftsmen and was a limner, a miniaturist or perhaps an illustrator. White probably shipped with Martin Frobisher's 1577 expedition to Baffin Land, two of his extant pictures of Eskimo subjects appearing to reflect that voyage. There is evidence he accompanied the Philip Amadas-Arthur Barlowe expedition sent by Sir Walter Raleigh to explore the North American coast; their glowing report of Roanoke Island, North Carolina, led to the famed 1585 colonizing effort. White was recruited as artist for this party, with Thomas Harriot (see entry) as scientific observor and Joachim Ganz, metallurgist. They shipped aboard the *Tiger,* flagship of Sir Richard Grenville's flotilla of seven vessels, leaving Plymouth April 9 and reaching the Carolina outer banks June 26, going on to Roanoke Island. There, with Ralph Lane as governor, the 108-man colony constructed Fort Raleigh. White and Harriot wintered among Indians of Chesapeake Bay to further ethnological studies. The colony was unsuccessful and the party returned to Portsmouth, England, July 28, 1586, with Sir Francis Drake, who had called at Roanoke. White's precise map-making and drawings of Indian life and natural history subjects, together with Harriot's notes "provide a remarkable insight. . .into the lifestyle of the Indian tribes they contacted (and) achieve(d) a new level of ethnological recording." Upon his return White was named governor for a 1587 expedition to Roanoke, designed to relieve a holding party Grenville had left, he visiting the abandoned site shortly after Drake had brought off the original settlers. One of White's chief assistants was Ananias Dare, married to White's daughter, Eleanor (Ellinor) who August 16 would give birth to Virginia Dare, first white child known to have been born within the future United States. White and Simon Fernandez, master of the *Lion,* came into dispute and the party was landed on Roanoke without exploring Chesapeake Bay as Raleigh had directed. No certain trace of the Grenville people was found, they presumably driven away by Indian hostility. White, at urging of the settlers, returned to England to bring out fresh supplies. He reached Southampton November 8. Raleigh pledged a new expedition under Grenville, but the Spanish Armada episode intervened. An abortive small expedition ultimately was dispatched (White accompanying it) in April 1588 but it turned back after a disastrous privateering diversion in which White was wounded. Nothing further was done until March 1590 when a relief party embarked on what White asserted was his fifth voyage to America. It weathered many adventures before arriving in mid-August off Roanoke. The settlement had vanished, legends carved on trees indicating the colonists had joined the Croatoan Indians, a friendly tribe, taking most of their possessions with them. Mishaps prevented further search and the expedition returned to Plymouth October 24. White is not positively known to have made another effort to succor the colony's remnants. The final certain report of him is a February 4, 1593, letter he wrote from his home at Newtown, County Kilmore, Cork, Ireland. It is possible that he voyaged with Martin Pring in 1601 for a last search, the goal frustrated by an unruly crew. Brigit White, sister of a John White, "late of parts beyond the seas," was appointed administratrix of his estate in May 1606; there is no positive evidence that this was the John White of Roanoke Colony, although he may well have been. Of White's great collection of accomplished art works, 76 watercolors remain, all in the British Museum. Engravings of 23 of these, plus five non-Indian subjects, were included in Theodor de Bry's edition of Harriot's *A Briefe and True Report of the New Found Land of Virginia* (1590). A definitive edition of White's work, including color reproductions of all his surviving paintings, plus the De Bry engravings and a learned discussion of White's life and works by Paul Hulton, retired deputy keeper in the Department of Prints and Drawings of the British Museum, was published in 1984. This volume included a sketch of Theodor de Bry and his part in perpetuating the work of White and Harriot. White was the first Englishman and second European, after Jacques de Morgues Le Moyne (see entry) to picture the American Indian; White had worked with Le Moyne briefly.

Thomas Harriot, *A Briefe and True Report of the New Found Land of Virginia,* Frankfurt-am-main,

Theodor de Bry, 1590 (repr. in facsimile, N.Y., Dover Publns., Inc., 1972; Paul Hulton, *America 1585: The Complete Drawings of John White.* Chapel Hill, Univ. of No. Car. Press and British Mus. Pubns., 1984; DNB.

White, John, prospector (d. Dec. 1863). White and John McGavin reached Montana from the Idaho placers in 1862 and on July 28 discovered gold on Willard Creek, which they named Grasshopper Creek. The site of the discovery was about midway between present-day Armistead and Dillon, and proved to be Montana's first significant strike, leading to the foundation of Bannack. On another prospecting trip, he and Rudolph Dorsett rescued one, Charles Kelly, snowed in and starving. Later White and Dorsett learned that Kelly had stolen livestock and set out to apprehend him. Apparently they captured Kelly, tied him up, but he worked loose and killed both White and Dorsett, then escaped; the killings occurred on the road between Virginia City and Helena. White's will, probated April 39, 1864, revealed him to be virtually broke.

Dorothy M. Johnson, *The Bloody Bozeman.* N.Y., McGraw-Hill book Co., 1971.

White, Jonathan (Buffalo Chips; Charley, Frank, James), scout (c. 1841-Sept. 9, 1876). A southerner who had ridden with the Confederate cavalry leader J.E.B. Stuart in the Civil War, a good rifle shot and excellent horseman, White came to the army hospital at Fort McPherson, Nebraska, to be treated for an injured leg but was rejected until Buffalo Bill Cody intervened and offered to pay White's bill. After his injury was healed he attached himself to Cody and became his inseparable partner. King wrote that "He copied Bill's dress, his gait, his carriage, his speech — everything he could copy; he let his long yellow hair fall low upon his shoulders in wistful admiration of Bill's glossy brown curls. He took more care of Bill's guns and horses than he did of his own." Thus he came to be called Buffalo Chips, so named by sardonic First Lieutenant Alfred Morton of the 9th Infantry. Finerty described White as "tall, stout, fair-complexioned, long-haired, pock-marked." King, who first met him in 1871, wrote that "A simpler-minded, gentler frontiersman never lived. He was modesty and courtesy itself, conspicuous mainly because of

...unusual traits for his class — he never drank, I never heard him swear, and no man ever heard him lie." When Cody went east in mid-1876 to pursue his drama career, White continued as scout for Crook on the Big Horn and Yellowstone expedition. At Slim Buttes, Dakota Territory, he was shot through the heart while stalking hostile Sioux in a ravine.

Don Russell, *The Lives and Legends of Buffalo Bill.* Norman, Univ. of Okla. Press, 1960; John F. Finerty, *War-Path and Bivouac.* Lincoln, Univ. of Nebr. Press, 1955; Charles King, *Campaigning with Crook.* Norman, 1964, 106-09.

White, Luke George, Cibecue Apache chief (c. 1850-c. 1935). White, of the Cibecue Apaches, told Lutheran missionary Arnold Nieman late in life that he had fired the first shot in the celebrated action on Cibecue Creek, Arizona, August 30, 1881, virtually the only recorded occasion when Apache scouts mutinied against the troops. It is not certain that White was a scout, and probably he was not; in the action Captain Edmund C. Hentig, 6th Cavalry and half a dozen soldiers were killed. White eventually fathered two sons who became well educated. He was "a friendly man," and occasionally served as interpreter for mission or government purposes. He died near Cibecue in the 1930s when he was in his 80s according to Nieman, who was well acquainted with White.

Correspondence with Arnold Nieman, Feb. 11, Mar. 2, 1983.

White, Owen Payne, writer (June 9, 1879-Dec. 7, 1946). White claimed to have been the first Anglo baby to be born at El Paso, Texas; at any rate he was one of the first. He attended the University of Texas and New York University, but never graduated, served in World War I in the medical corps, and returned to El Paso where he wrote *Out of the Desert* (1923), his first book. He then joined the *New York Times,* the *Brooklyn Eagle* and *Collier's Magazine* successively. His books included *Trigger Fingers, Them Was the Days,* an *Autobiography of a Durable Sinner* and the unfinished, *The Old Trails West of the Mississippi,* the manuscript held by Texas Western University. He died of cancer.

Password, Vol. X, No. 2 (Summer 1965), 53-56.

White, Samuel O., Mormon pioneer (fl. 1857-58). White took part in the Mountain

Meadows Massacre of September 11, 1857, and the following year was one of 23 signers of a statement seeking to clear William H. Dame of responsibility for it.

Juanita Brooks, *Mountain Meadows Massacre.* Norman, Univ. of Okla. Press, 1966.

White (Brooks), Sarah Catherine, captive (Dec. 10, 1850-May 11, 1939). B. at North Elk Grove, Lafayette County, Wisconsin, she was taken by her parents, Benjamin and Mary White, to Cloud County, Kansas, where they settled on a farm. On August 13, 1868, her father was killed and Sarah was captured by Cheyenne Indian raiders. She suffered great hardships, including having both feet severely frost-bitten the following winter. During the bitter season Sarah and another white captive, Anna Morgan, fled the Indian camp, making for the Arkansas River, but were overtaken, punished, and returned to captivity. In March 1869, the Cheyenne camp was come upon by Custer and the 7th Cavalry, and the 19th Kansas Cavalry; in persistent, intelligent and well-engineered negotiations Custer secured release of Sarah and Mrs. Morgan, and they were returned to their Kansas homes. Miss White taught school for a time near Clyde, Kansas, then married E.O. Brooks, a Civil War veteran; they became parents of six daughters and one son. She spent her declining years with her son, Walter, only a mile from the spot where she had been captured, but she rarely discussed the affair, and even more seldom the treatment she received from her captors.

George A. Custer, *My Life on the Plains,* ed. by Milo M. Quaife. Lincoln, Univ. of Nebr. Press, 1966; *Concordia* (Kan.) *Empire,* Sept. 1, 1898 (the most complete account of the raid in which she was seized); *Concordia* (Kan.) *Blade Empire,* Mar. 7, 1934; manuscript by Martin Adams White (the only account of the raid by an eye-witness), St. Helen's, Oreg., Dec. 14, 1933,

White, Stewart Edward, writer (Mar. 12, 1873-Sept. 18, 1946). B. at Grand Rapids, Michigan, he was graduated from the University of Michigan. He prospected in the Black Hills in 1895-96, from his experiences writing *The Claim Jumpers,* in 1900, the first of more than 40 novels, the most successful one being *The Blazed Trail,* 1902. Although his father was a millionaire, White preferred to live on the proceeds from his writings,

which were very profitable. Among them were *The Long Rifle,* a trilogy of the frontier west and early California, *Arizona Nights* and *The Gray Dawn,* about San Francisco in the gold rush days. A great traveler, White wrote always about places he knew firsthand, from the Yukon to Africa. Although a mild appearing man, when past 50 he choked to death an African leopard to save two natives. The Royal Geographical Society made him a fellow for his work in mapping German East Africa (Tanzania) in 1913. The Association for the Advancement of Science honored him for his writings on bird life. After the death April 5, 1939, of his wife Elizabeth, whom he had married in 1904, he turned his attention to communication with the departed and life after death, writing several books of considerable popularity on those subjects. White was one of the more effective writers on frontier subjects, his works generally trustworthy and more truly revealing of the life and times which concern them than many nonfiction works. He died at San Francisco.

Literature abundant.

White, William, frontiersman (c. 1748-Mar. 8, 1782). B. in Frederick County, Virginia, his birth year is conjecture; by 1768 he bore the title of "captain," and by it was known throughout the trans-Allegheny country where he became a pre-eminent scout. He was a friend of Colonel William Crawford, famed victim of the Shawnees, "and White was identified with many expeditions conducted by that famous officer against the Indians." He was in the battle of Point Pleasant, in Lord Dunmore's War of 1774, shortly before which he had been imprisoned for killing a peaceful Indian, but freed by "an armed mob of his infuriated friends." White's schooling was "savage, and he proved an apt scholar." He had settled in the Buckhannon country of Lewis County, Virginia, by about 1770, and became "the recognized head scout of the colony." He had a prominent role in the massacre of the peaceful Captain Bull settlement of Delaware Indians, was captured by Indians on the Little Kanawha River, but escaped, and perhaps became a lieutenant in Jackson's company of militia late in the Revolution. "Under no circumstances was Captain White ever known to show mercy to an Indian," and he killed many of them. His reputation may have led to his death, purportedly arranged by the renegade, Timothy Dorman, but brought about by Indians near Buckhannon Fort. He was buried at Heavner Cemetery, Buckhannon next to the grave of another victim of the Indians, John Fink, one monument serving both.

Lucullus V. McWhorter, *The Border Settlers of Northwestern Virginia.* Hamilton, O., Republican Pub. Co., 1915.

White Antelope (Wokai-hwo-ko-mas), Cheyenne chief (c. 1789-Nov. 29, 1864). White Antelope was one of the chief men of the Crooked Lance Society of the Cheyennes at the time of the 1838 battle of Wolf Creek with the Kiowas, an action in which he proved himself one of "the bravest." He was foremost in opting for a general peace in 1840 with the Kiowas, Kiowa-Apaches and Comanches, a lasting agreement to the benefit of all tribes concerned. Grinnell reports that White Antelope and two other Cheyennes were among the Indian chiefs taken to Washington, D.C., following the Laramie Treaty of 1851 in which White Antelope's Indian name, or anything close to it does not appear as signatory, although he attended the council. His name does appear on the Fort Wise Treaty of 1861, but White Antelope declared that agreement a swindle and said he had never signed it nor authorized his name to be added to it. With Black Kettle and others he conferred with Governor Evans and Chivington at Denver in the autumn of 1864 seeking a formal peace with the whites; the peace was not officially granted them but they were told to camp with their people on Sand Creek, 40 miles northeast of Fort Lyon, Colorado. They did so in good faith, and here at dawn November 29, 1864, their camp was attacked by nearly 1,000 Colorado Volunteers under Chivington. White Antelope, facing the troops with arms folded and singing his death song, was shot down along with more than 100 of his people, mostly women and children. White Antelope's body was mutilated by the whites, as were most of the others.

George Bird Grinnell, *The Fighting Cheyennes.* Norman, Univ. of Okla. Press, 1956; George E. Hyde, *Life of George Bent.* Norman, 1968; Stan Hoig, *The Western Odyssey of John Simpson Smith.* Glendale, Calif., Arthur H. Clark Co., 1974.

White Bird (Peopeo Kiskiok Hihih: White Goose), Nez Perce chief (c. 1807-c. 1882). McWhorter's informants believed White Bird was born "about 70 years" before the Nez Perce War of 1877. White Bird was the oldest of the five non-treaty Nez Perce chiefs, having refused to sign the 1863 treaty by which most of the Nez Perce lands were taken away and the tribe was to be confined upon a modest Idaho reservation. He was just under 6 feet in height, well proportioned with an outstanding physique and stately bearing. A medicine man who ever carried with him the wing of a white goose as symbol of his status, he also was a buffalo hunter with long experience in tribal warfare, and was intently listened to and much respected. White Bird was mild in temper and speech, never an advocate of war. He took little part in fighting during the 1877 events although he headed the Lamtama Band, second in size to Joseph's and including about 50 able-bodied men. Unlike many of the Nez Perce, White Bird was not a Christian and spoke harshly of that faith as represented by white so-called Christians in his country. In May 1877 he rejected an ultimatum from Howard that the non-treaties move onto the reservation with their stock within 30 days, a time span he knew impossible since their far-ranging stock could not be gathered in so brief a time. Meanwhile, young men conducted forays against white settlers and this led to open hostilities, which none of the five non-treaty chiefs favored. White Bird felt that war would only result in disaster for the Indians, but he became a leader in council and management of the exodus as befit his rank. White Bird's role in the Battle of Whitebird Canyon which initiated open warfare is indistinct and probably was not major; though opposed to war, he would not run. He also had no part in the action at Clearwater in July. His was a rallying cry at the Battle of Big Hole and he may have done much to inspire successful resistance to the surprise soldier attack, although his role as a warrior is not clear. At the decisive Battle of Bear Paw Mountains Joseph determined to surrender, but Looking Glass and White Bird reiterated that they would never give up "to a deceitful white chief." Looking Glass was killed soon thereafter, but White Bird and one-third of the Nez Perce, or around 200 followers escaped and made their way safely into Canada, being received warmly by Sitting

Bull and other Sioux also residing in the Canadian sanctuary. White Bird remained in Canada about five years. On one occasion First Lieutenant George Baird of the 5th Infantry was sent to interview him about returning to the United States. Distrustful of any U.S. Army officer, White Bird asked two British officers to monitor the conversation. Baird told him that if he would surrender, Joseph would be returned to his people in Idaho from Oklahoma exile. White Bird countered: "You bring Chief Joseph to Idaho. I will hear of it. Do this, and I promise to surrender. I will come to Idaho if I have to come afoot." Baird said he could not agree to that, and White Bird said then that he would remain in Canada. White Bird, as a medicine man was accused by another Nez Perce of being instrumental in the sickening and death of two of his sons, so this individual, Hasenahmakikt shot and killed White Bird near Fort McLeod in keeping with the customs of the tribe. There was no retaliation from the Indians, although rumor has it that the British sentenced Hasenahmakikt to life imprisonment and he died in a penitentiary in British Columbia.

McWhorter, *Hear Me;* Dockstader; Alvin M. Josephy Jr., *The Nez Perce Indians and the Opening of the Northwest.* New Haven, Yale Univ. Press, 1965.

White Bull (Ice, Ice Bear), Northern Cheyenne (1834-1921). A noted Northern Cheyenne chief and medicine man, White Bull sometimes told Grinnell of magical events of his past life. It was he who made the famous war bonnet for Roman Nose which protected the latter until its charm was broken just before the battle of Beecher Island where Roman Nose was killed. He was in the fight at the Platte River Bridge in which Caspar Collins was killed. White Bull was present at an 1875 council with Sitting Bull on Tongue River in which the Sioux predicted his coming victory over Custer. White Bull observed Crook's fight on the Rosebud from a distance, but did not get into it although he was in the Custer fight later, his exact role not determined although possibly more important than he revealed to Camp. In 1877 White Bull with others of the Northern Cheyennes surrendered to Miles in Montana, was accepted as a hostage for the remainder of the hostile Cheyennes, was the first to be enlisted

as a scout by Miles, and was a key figure in the engagement at Little Muddy Creek, Montana, at which the Sioux, Lame Deer, was killed. He retained his influence over his people into an advanced age, being a tribal judge for many years.

George Bird Grinnell, *The Cheyenne Indians,* 2 vols. Lincoln, Univ. of Nebr. Press, 1972; Grinnell, *The Fighting Cheyennes.* Norman, Univ. of Okla. Press, 1956; *Custer in '76: Walter Camp's Notes on the Custer Fight.* Provo, Brigham Young Univ. Press, 1976; information from the Mus. of the Amer. Indian.

White Calf (Onistai Pokuh), Piegan chief (c. 1835-Jan. 29, 1903). While still a young man he became noted for bravery, intelligence and charity to the old and helpless of his people. He signed the Blackfoot Treaty No. 7 on the Bow River, Canada, September 22, 1877. After the death of Big Lake in 1873 he was unanimously elected the last head chief of the south Piegan nation. His principal rival was Three Suns, equally intelligent and able, who headed the heathen, conservative faction on the Blackfoot Reservation, while White Calf led the Christian, progressive faction. Three Suns, as famous writer, was almost equally powerful, and some thought his faction larger than White Calf's. White Calf died at Washingon, D.C., where he had gone in connection with tribal affairs. His body as returned to be buried on Cut Bank Creek, on the reservation.

Montana Contributions, Vol. X, 1940, 262; John C. Ewers, *The Blackfeet: Raiders on the Northwestern Plains.* Norman, Univ. of Okla. Press, 1958.

White Eagle, Gros Ventre chief (c. 1820-Feb. 9, 1881). The son of Eagle Chief, White Eagle was second to Sitting Woman as head chief of his tribe. White Eagle signed the treaties of October 17, 1855, November 16, 1865, July 13, and September 1, 1868, and had been a chief for about 20 years when he died at Clagett, Montana. Eagle Chief met I.I. Stevens August 23, 1853, near the Milk River, Montana.

Montana Contributions, Vol. X, 1940, 272, 276.

White Eyes (Koquethagechton), Delaware chief (c. 1730-Nov. 1778). Probably b. in western Pennsylvania, he was recognized as chief about 1776 but even before had given evidence of his friendliness to whites, including the Moravian missionaries, while in

1774 he had declined to help the Shawnees in the conflict known as Lord Dunmore's War. He also refused to follow Iroquois requests that he align with the British during the Revolution, preferring neutrality or the American cause. If the Delaware were determined to go to war, he said, he would march at the head of them so he would be killed first and thus avoid witnessing the utter destruction of the tribe. He finally joined Laughlin McIntosh's force as a scout in their march on Sandusky, Ohio. Dockstader said he was shot by American soldiers for obscure reasons along the way; Hodge reports that he died of smallpox at Pittsburgh but Dockstader said that was a ploy by the Americans to avoid responsibility for the death of this noted chief.

Hodge, HAI; Dockstader.

White Horse (Wo-po-ham), Cheyenne Dog Soldier chief (fl. 1845-1875). With his fellow Dog Soldier chiefs, Bull Bear and Tall Bull, White Horse was prominent in Indian hostilities on the central Plains from around 1845 until 1875 after which he fades from view, the war days over. For about 20 years before the Sand Creek Massacre of 1864 the Dog Soldiers had ranged between the Platte and Republican rivers, rarely as far south as the Arkansas. The senseless Colorado Volunteer attack on Cheyenne villages in the spring and summer of 1864 stirred them up. White Horse probably took part in hostilities along the emigrant trails in 1865 although there is no confirmation. In April 1867 he and other prominent Cheyennes met with Hancock near Fort Larned, Kansas; when the officer insisted upon approaching the Indian villages with troops the Cheyennes fled. White Horse, with his peers, Tall Bull and Bull Bear reluctantly signed the Medicine Lodge Treaty of October 1867, convinced that such pacts did no good since the whites did not intend to abide by them. White Horse was in the Battle of Beecher's Island, and with Bull Bear persuaded Roman Nose, important Cheyenne warrior, to lead his fatal charge and contacted him when he returned with his mortal wound. After Tall Bull was killed at Summit Springs in July 1869, White Horse led his people to live with the Northern Cheyennes in the Wind River country, but then drifted south again to the reservation provided for them by the Medicine Lodge

Treaty, in Indian Territory. White Horse participated in the 1874 Red River war and was in the battle of Palo Duro Canyon in the Staked Plains of Texas, but surrendered October 20, 1874 at the Indian Territory agency once more. From then onward he remained at peace.

Donald J. Berthrong, *The Southern Cheyennes.* Norman, Univ. of Okla. Press, 1963; George E. Hyde, *Life of George Bent.* Norman, 1968; George B. Grinnell, *The Fighting Cheyennes.* Norman, 1956.

White Man Runs Him, Crow scout (c. 1855-June 2, 1929). A Crow Indian, White Man was enlisted by Lieutenant James Bradley April 10, 1876, for his detachment of Indian scouts serving with the 7th Infantry. He was on detached service with the 7th Cavalry from June 21, but withdrew from the Custer column about 3:15 p.m. June 25 and eventually returned to the Crow Agency. The story of his experiences with Custer is found in Graham, 21-24, with another version in Camp, 178-79. He died at Lodgegrass, Montana, and was buried at the Custer Battlefield National Cemetery.

W.A. Graham, *The Custer Myth.* Harrisburg, Pa., Stackpole Co., 1953; *Custer in '76: Walter Camp's Notes on the Custer Fight,* ed. by Kenneth Hammer. Provo, Brigham Young Univ. Press, 1976.

Whitehill, Harvey H., lawman (Sept. 2, 1837-Sept. 8, 1906). B. in Ohio, he was educated there, went to California in 1852, and was one of the original discoverers of the placer mines in California Gulch where Leadville, Colorado, later was located. In the summer of 1860 he took $15,000 out of his claim. Whitehill removed to New Mexico in 1861, was a freighter and miner until 1869. He reached the Silver City, New Mexico, area in 1870, helped build the first house in town, took out some of the first silver from there, and mined "more or less" for many years thereafter. He was elected sheriff in 1874, held the office until 1882 when he was elected to the upper house of the territorial Legislature. In 1884 he assisted in capturing the Kit Joy band of train robbers. In the fall of 1888 he again was elected sheriff of Grant County for two years, engaging also in farming and cattle raising. In 1891 he was indicted for allowing a prisoner to escape, embezzlement and sundry other charges;

disposition unknown. Whitehill "had many fights with Indians and helped bury many men who fell victims of the Apache," and was sheriff "When it required a brave man to fill the position and had many narrow escapes from being killed both by Indians and desperadoes." He died at Deming, New Mexico, and was buried at Silver City.

Bancroft Library archives; Deming, N.M., *Graphic*, Sept. 13, 1906; Silver City, N.M., *Enterprise*, Sept. 14, 1906.

Whitehouse, Joseph, frontiersman (b. 1775). B. probably in Fairfax County, Virginia his family moved to Kentucky in 1784. He enlisted in Daniel Bissell's company of the 1st Infantry and from it joined the Lewis and Clark Expedition January 1, 1804, accompanying it to the Pacific. He kept a journal (published by Thwaites, 1904-1905, 1959), one version of which is at the Newberry Library, Chicago. The date and circumstances of his death are not reported.

Clarke, *Lewis and Clark.*

Whiteley, Simeon, Indian agent (Mar. 18, 1831-Jan. 13, 1890). B. at Huddersfield, Yorkshire, England he arrived with his parents at Racine, Wisconsin, August 29, 1842, being raised at Dover, Racine County, and at St. Charles, Elgin and Geneva, Illinois. He became a journeyman printer, worked on papers at Watertown and Madison, Wisconsin, and Aurora, Illinois, where he became prominently anti-slavery and switched from Democratic to Republican parties to support Lincoln. When Lincoln was elected President, Whiteley worked for the War Department at Washington. In 1862 he went to Colorado, ostensibly as agent for the Ute Indians in Middle Park (the "question of (his) total lack of experience in Indian affairs was apparently never raised"), but actually to work for the admission of Colorado into the Union as a free state to strengthen Lincoln's support in Congress. He did spend a brief period with his charges but soon returned to Denver complaining that for nine months of the year snow prevented his work at the agency, and settled to newspaper publishing and editing (while steadily drawing his salary as Indian "agent"). September 28, 1864, Whiteley at Camp Weld, near Denver, was recorder for the important conference Governor John Evans had with Black Kettle, Neva and other

Cheyenne and Arapaho chiefs, preliminary to the Sand Creek massacre. John Smith was interpreter and Whiteley said the interpretation was sometimes held up to be sure he got every word correctly, although his transcript was short of verbatim. "Much of the dispute surrounding the Sand Creek affair today arises from Whiteley's incomplete and inaccurate report of the Camp Weld conference." His control of the Denver *Commonwealth* during this period was less than a journalistic triumph and in 1865 he left Colorado, having contributed to its emergence toward statehood but very little to management of its Indian problems. He became an insurance man at Racine, Wisconsin, having a somewhat successful career. He died at Racine and is buried there.

History of Racine and Kenosha Counties, Wisc. Chicago, Western Historical Co., 1879; information from the Racine County Hist. Mus.; *Sand Creek Massacre;* Harry Kelsey, "Background to Sand Creek." *Colo. Mag.,* Vol. XLV, No. 4 (Fall 1968), 259-300.

Whitlock, James H., army officer (May 15, 1829-post 1898). B. in Union County, Illinois, he left Fort Leavenworth May 4, 1850, for California, reaching Salt Lake City with a worn out train, no guide and virtually destitute. He and others proceeded on foot, hiring a Mormon guide who deserted them when well out on the desert, but Whitlock and the others arrived at Hangtown (Placerville), California, August 24, he claiming to have lost 60 pounds on the trip. He mined with varying luck and many adventures. In November 1854 Whitlock was elected Plumas County surveyor, remaining in office until 1861 when he raised what became Company F, 5th California Infantry. The outfit left Sacramento February 2, 1862, established Camp Drum (later Drum Barracks), California, and went from there into Arizona. Whitlock was commanding officer at Tucson until April 1863, then proceeded into New Mexico where he was stationed in the heart of the Mimbres Apache country, taking part in activities against those Indians. Some of the operations became highly controversial, the natives alleging treachery, the whites offering the excuse that the Apaches were inveterately hostile. February 12, 1864, Whitlock and 24 enlisted men fought Apaches at Pinos Altos and reported killing 13 while capturing a

Mexican woman who had been their prisoner 15 years, returning her to her family. On the 24th Whitlock with half of Company F, left Camp Mimbres on a scout, the next day at 5 p.m. attacking 19 Indians and again killing 13, wounding the others. April 7, 1864, Whitlock with First Lieutenant George A. Burkett and a command of 56 enlisted men attacked a purported 250 Indians near Mount Grey, or Sierra Bonita (the Graham Mountains), Arizona, killing 21, wounding many and capturing 45 horses and mules. In June Whitlock and 23 enlisted men had a skirmish with hostiles in southern New Mexico, killing two and capturing one. September 8, 1864, on a scout he had a fight, losing his guide and an enlisted man wounded, the Indian loss being unknown. Company F was mustered out November 30, 1864, at Las Cruces, New Mexico, Whitlock joining the 1st Battalion, Veteran Infantry, California Volunteers. He commanded at Fort Selden, near Las Cruces and then was stationed at Fort Garland, Colorado, under Kit Carson where he served until his discharge December 5, 1866, having been promoted to major. He returned to Plumas County, California, in April 1867, ran unsuccessfully for Surveyor General of California and engaged in merchandising at Taylorville and Greenville until 1876 when he visited the Philadelphia Sesquicentennial exhibition, on his return stopping off at Warren, Illinois, to wed Mary H. Baldwin (Sept. 27, 1852-Sept. 29, 1890), by whom he had a son. Whitlock was elected to the California State Legislature in which he served one term and on October 28, 1878, was appointed postmaster at Quincy, Plumas County. On January 1, 1898, according to court house records Whitlock was engaged in mining with several partners, although whether this was his only occupation is unknown.

Orton; AHS, Hayden file; *History of Plumas, Lassen & Sierra Counties, California,* (Fariss and Smith, pub. 1882), and Berkeley, Calif., Howell-North Books, 1974; information from Linda Brennan, Plumas County Mus., Quincy, Calif.

Whitlock, John Marmaduke, physician, victim, (d. Nov. 5, 1862). B. in Kentucky, he was related to such well-known families as the Pendletons, Marmadukes, and Morgans of Virginia and Kentucky. In the early 1840's he migrated to New Mexico, settled at Las

Vegas, married Mrs. Josefita Lucero (d. 1891) and moved to the Agua Negra valley in San Miguel County. With the Civil War he was commissioned a surgeon for the First New Mexico Volunteers, commanded by Kit Carson; he had served as surgeon under Carson earlier and now followed him south from Fort Union. In the pages of the *Santa Fe Gazette* he had charged Captain James (Paddy) Graydon with murdering Mescalero chiefs Manuelito and José Largo and some of their followers after luring them into his camp and getting them drunk (Carson was then operating against the Mescaleros in pursuance of Colonel James H. Carleton's orders). Graydon challenged Whitlock to a duel near Fort Stanton. The Kentuckian accepted and in the resulting fight Graydon was wounded mortally and Whitlock slightly. Graydon's men, however, shot down Whitlock. The story that each man of Graydon's Company H, New Mexico Volunteers ritually fired into Whitlock's corpse was false, but the body did have 20 bullet wounds plus others from Lieutenant Philip Morris's shotgun. Carson, in a towering rage at the murder of his doctor friend, threatened to punish every man of the company, but cooler heads prevailed. Three supposed ringleaders, including Morris, were arrested, sent to Santa Fe for trial for murder; Morris and another escaped from the jail January 1, 1863 but were recaptured by Carleton on the Jornada del Muerto late that month. Whitlock had fathered two children, John M., Jr., who became a Presbyterian minister and served in New Mexico for 35 years, and a daughter.

Lawrence Kelly, *Navajo Roundup.* Boulder, Colo., Pruett Pub. Co., 1970; "A Pioneer Story: The Tragical Death of Doctor J.M. Whitlock." *New Mex. Hist. Rev.,* Vol. XVI, No. 1 (Jan. 1941), 104-06; William A. Keleher, *Turmoil in New Mexico 1846-1868.* Santa Fe, Rydal Press, 1952; *Legacy of Honor: The Life of Rafael Chacón,* ed. by Jacqueline Dorgan Meketa   Albuquerque, Univ. of New Mex. Press, 1986.

Whitman, Marcus, missionary, frontier statesman (Sept. 4, 1802-Nov. 29, 1847). B. at Rushville, New York, he secured a medical degree in 1832 from the Fairfield (New York) Medical school, and began a country practice near Wheeler, New York. Here, in November 1834, he heard the Rev. Samuel Parker, just returned from Oregon, tell of the need for missionaries in the northwest territory. The next year Whitman, who was of Congregational backround and was to be supported jointly by that and the Presbyterian denomination, visited Oregon with Parker to investigate. They joined Lucien Fontenelle's fur brigade for the journey west, being treated contemptuously by hardy trappers until a cholera invasion brought down many and only Whitman's medical skill saved trapper lives; from then on he was respected and accepted. Satisfied that the need described by Parker existed, Whitman determined to go as a missionary (or "assistant missionary" at first, since he was not ordained); as the implementing agency, the American Board of Commissioners for Foreign Missions, however, would send only married couples, so he and Narcissa Prentiss (1808-47), who was equally dedicated, were wed. They set out with the Rev. and Mrs. Henry Harmon Spalding, joined a Thomas Fitzpatrick brigade and crossed the Rockies, the two wives, the first white women to cross the Rocky Mountains, thus demonstrating that the way to Oregon was feasible for couples and families. Whitman established a mission at Waiilatpu, near the present Walla Walla, Washington, and now a National Historical Site, while the Spaldings settled at Lapwai, near present Lewiston, Idaho. The work was laborious, difficult and conducted under political handicaps, since the area was in dispute between Britain and the U.S. The missionaries themselves had something of a falling out and support from the eastern Board proved always miniscule or lacking entirely. In the winter of 1842-43, one of the most severe on record, Whitman made an arduous trip east by way of Fort Hall, Taos and St. Louis, visited Washington, New York and Boston. He straightened out the mission affairs and, of immense importance for the future of Oregon, urged by every means emigration to that territory whose future, he realized, would be determined by population, rather than by diplomacy or military presence. Thus to some extent he inspired the "great emigration" of 1843, by which 1,000 or more settlers journeyed by wagon and other contrivances to Fort Hall. From there, guided by Whitman, they constituted the first party to take wagons in any number into Oregon, reaching the Willamette Valley where they settled; their pathway the Oregon Trail, with the Waiilatpu Mission an important way-

station, to be followed by countless thousands and the future of the Northwest, as an American possession, assured by their numbers, since British emigration could not hope to match it. Whitman's "legend" as "the man who saved Oregon," therefore rests on some solid ground despite detractors' assertions that as originally propounded it was myth only. Without his efforts the political sovereignty would have remained in doubt for some time. Whitman's work continued, a combination of religious evangelism, linguistic labors, medical practice and pioneering, and gradually his prospects improved. The neighboring Cayuse Indians, never very friendly, remained generally aloof from Christianity, however, and a measles epidemic accentuated their latent hostility until they rose and massacred Whitman, his wife and a dozen others; the Whitmans had realized that something of the sort was imminent, but had carried on their work nonetheless. More than 40 other whites, taken prisoner by the Cayuses, were ransomed by John McLoughlin at Fort Vancouver. Whitman's contribution to the spiritual, pioneering and political development of the Pacific Northwest can scarcely be overstated, and he was true to his deepest calling until his final breath. News of his death helped in passing in 1848 the bill that made Oregon a formal territory of the U.S., and in that way his contribution continued. Whitman County and Whitman College, Washington, were named for him.

Clifford M. Drury, *Marcus and Narcissa Whitman and the Opening of Old Oregon,* 2 vols. Glendale, Calif., Arthur H. Clark Co., 1973.

Whitman, Narcissa Prentiss, missionary (Mar. 14, 1808-Nov. 29, 1847). The wife of Dr. Marcus Whitman, pioneer physician and missionary to the Pacific Northwest, Narcissa was born at Prattsburg, New York, At school she met Henry Harmon Spalding, and rejected his proposal of marriage; later the two worked in the Northwest Mission, and difficulties between Spalding and Narcissa's husband may probably be traced in part to her earlier rejection of the former. When Samuel Parker, in November 1834, spoke at her small church at Amity, New York, of the need for missionaries in the Oregon country, he struck a responsive spark in the girl. Marcus Whitman, hearing of her interest in a missionary career, proposed marriage and after returning from his first trip to the Rockies they were married, in February 1836. Thereafter she shared his life. Narcissa and Eliza Spalding were the first two white women to cross the Rockies, demonstrating the way to Oregon practicable for families. On her 29th birthday, in 1837, she gave birth to her only child, a daughter, Alice Clarissa, who was drowned June 23, 1839, but the Whitmans took waifs into their mission station at Waiilatpu until they had collected 11 to be raised; among them was Helen Mar, a halfbreed daughter of mountain man Joe Meek. Narcissa, a much-beloved Oregon country pioneer, wrote voluminously; most of the 126 letters and diaries which have survived have been published. According to the Whitmans' primary biographer, she was "vivacious, attractive, gregarious, idealistic, and sentimentally religious." She was killed in the Cayuse uprising which also cost the lives of her husband and a dozen others.

Clifford M. Drury, *Marcus and Narcissa Whitman and the Opening of Old Oregon,* 2 vols. Glendale, Calif., Arthur H. Clark Co., 1973.

Whitman, Royal Emerson, army officer, saddler (May 11, 1833-Feb. 12, 1913). B. on a family farm at Turner, Maine, he was married by 20 to a third cousin by whom he had six children; he subsequently married twice more. He joined the 23rd Maine Infantry in 1862 and by war's end had risen to colonel of the 30th Maine, having been wounded and winning a brevet at the Battle of Sabine Crossroads, Louisiana, April 8, 1864. Whitman joined the 3rd Cavalry as a second lieutenant in 1867, partly through intercession of Brigadier General Oliver Otis Howard, also from Maine and a relative by marriage whom Whitman had known before. Whitman was promoted to first lieutenant in 1869 and retired March 20, 1879; he was made captain on the retired list in 1904. On joining the 3rd Cavalry, Whitman was posted to Fort Sumner, New Mexico, initially, then to other stations, occasionally scouting for hostiles, but with no real combats recorded. Eventually as a first lieutenant he was assigned to Camp Grant, Arizona, then in an area of almost unremitting Apache hostilities or depredations; there had seemed no solution for the Indian problem. In February 1871, five old Apache women were sent into Camp Grant bearing a truce flag, and Whitman fed them, gradually luring their people in with food and good treatment until he had the bulk of the Aravaipa Apaches camped at peace, five miles from the post. This settlement of Apaches supposed to have been hostile proved too great a temptation for turbulent elements at Tucson who collected 92 Papagoes, 42 Mexicans and 6 Anglos, 140 men in all, and attacked the rancheria, perpetrating the so-called Camp Grant Massacre on April 30, 1871, in which perhaps 125 Indians, mostly women, children and aged, were killed with no loss to the attackers. Because they were "Whitman's Indians," the officer came in for much censure and became the object of scorn and loathing on the part of many Tucsonans; Crook, who became department commander, listened to these elements and without properly assessing the evidence, came equally to detest Whitman, who was a fairly innocent victim of the situation. Several court-martials ensued, none on substantial grounds, and Whitman was cleared in all, or not completely convicted; Howard visited Camp Grant in pursuance of his peace mission, talked at length and cordially with Whitman which incurred Crook's wrath anew, the department commander being unaware of the previous contact between the two and its origin. Posted to Fort D.A. Russell, Wyoming, Whitman took part in the Newton-Jenney geological expedition to the Black Hills in the summer of 1875 and engaged in some scouting activities in western Nebraska, but chronic illness kept him out of the field much of the time. He requested retirement because of the state of his health. Early in his retirement he invented a saddle tree which became the basis for the "Whitman Saddles," which achieved great popularity and made the inventor a comfortable fortune. Whitman moved to Washington about 1885, living there the remainder of his life. He died of cancer of the stomach. He was described by an acquaintance at Washington as "I think ... about the last type of man that anybody who knew him would conceivably regard as a liar. He was quite as frank about anything to his own detriment as he was in stating facts to the detriment of any one else, and decidedly scrupulous in matters of justice and fair dealing even with the most insignificant persons." Whitman was a man with whom history has dealt unfairly.

Dan L. Thrapp, *The Conquest of Apacheria.*

Norman, Univ. of Okla. Press, 1967; Barry C. Johnson, "Whitman of Camp Grant." *10th Anniv. Publn.,* English Westerners' Soc., 1964, 53-68.

Whitney, Chauncey Belden, lawman (Mar. 31, 1842-Aug. 18, 1873). B. in New York State, he may have served as an enlisted man in the Union Army during the Civil War. In August 1867, he was elected constable of Ellsworth, Kansas, ran unsuccessfully for sheriff in November, and in August 1868, was one of about 50 scouts with Forsyth's expedition which came to grief on Beecher's Island at the hands of Roman Nose's Cheyennes. By the end of the year he again was constable and under sheriff at Ellsworth. In July 1869, he was called to active duty in the Kansas State Militia, to serve against Indians. Released in November, he was named marshal of Ellsworth July 27, 1871, and may have been elected sheriff November 7, the record being unclear. He resigned as marshal April 3, 1872, and on August 15, 1873, he was shot and wounded mortally while unarmed by Billy Thompson, brother of Ben Thompson, purportedly by accident, Billy being drunk at the time. Ben charged Billy with having shot "our best friend," his brother retorting he would have shot "if it had been Jesus Christ!" Whitney was given a Masonic burial in the Episcopal church yard.

Nyle H. Miller, Joseph W. Snell, *Great Gunfighters of the Kansas Cowtowns, 1967-1886.* Lincoln, Univ. of Nebr. Press, 1967; Kan. State Hist. Soc. records.

Whitney, Robert H., scout (Jan. 9, 1840-Oct. 24, 1871). B. in New York City, Whitney made his way to Arizona. He was described by Bourke as "one of the handsomest man I ever saw; with a face deeply tanned by exposure to Arizona's sun, the rich color mantling his cheek was well set off by an abundance of fine glossy black hair and a pair of very expressive hazel eyes." He was of upper medium height, finely proportioned, "a good horseman and very daring scout," who had often been wounded by bullet or arrow. Whitney was killed in an action in Chiricahua Pass, southeastern Arizona, in which Captain Gerald Russell of the 3rd Cavalry was lured into an ambush, but was unable to dislodge the Chiricahua Apaches, and was forced to withdraw. Barney believed the leader of the

Apaches was Cochise, but from his description it more likely was Juh. Whitney was buried at Camp Bowie on October 26 "with military honors."

"Bourke on the Southwest, II," ed. by Lansing B. Bloom. *New Mex. Hist. Rev.,* Vol. IX, No I (Jan. 1943), 67-68; James M. Barney, *Tales of Apache Warfare.*p.p., 1933, 22-24.

Whitside, Samuel Marmaduke, army officer (Jan. 9, 1839-Dec. 15, 1904). B. at Toronto, Ontario, he enlisted in the 6th Cavalry in 1858 and by the start of the Civil War was sergeant major. Commissioned a second lieutenant on November 1, 1861, he ended the war a first lieutenant. He became a captain in 1866 and 11 years later, with two troops of the 6th, established Fort Huachuca, Arizona, remaining there two years while the establishment became a permanent post. Whitside transferred to the 7th Cavalry in 1885. He captured the Sioux, Big Foot and his warriors, and the following day, as a major commanding four troops of the 7th and part of the 1st Artillery, had a central role in the Wounded Knee affair against the Brulé Sioux. This was in 1890. He commanded at Fort Riley, Jefferson Barracks and Fort Sam Houston, Texas. Whitside transferred to the 3rd Cavalry and the 5th Cavalry in 1895. In the Spanish-American War he transferred to the 10th Cavalry, taking to Cuba in 1899. He retired as a Brigadier General and died at Washington, D.C.

Heitman; Robet M. Utley, *The Last Days of the Sioux Nation.* New Haven, Yale Univ. Press, 1963; Ft. Huachuca archives; *Who Was Who.*

Wickenburg, Henry, prospector (Nov. 21, 1819-c. May 10, 1905). B. as Johannes Henricus Wickenburg at Holsterhausen, near Essen, Germany, Wickenburg and a brother were accused of illegally mining coal on their farm property, and "disappeared." A skeleton supposed to be that of his brother was found some time later in a mine shaft; Henry reportedly reached New York in 1847, and San Francisco in 1853. In 1862, it is said, he arrived in Arizona from California, a prospector, but the preserved "facts" are very contradictory. In October 1863, he discovered what became the Vulture Mine near the present town of Wickenburg (named for him), which has produced from $30 million to $50 million in gold, one of the richest in Arizona history, though Wickenburg profited little from it. Unable to finance the major operations necessary to extract the ore, he sold out in 1866 to a New York company; it is reported that two others had joined him in prospecting for the Vulture. He denied them any rights in it, and extended litigation followed. After sale of the Vulture, Wickenburg retired to the site of the present community of Wickenburg and engaged in farming. A flood damaged his property in 1890, but he survived. He apparently owned real estate of some value in the growing town. He was found with a bullet from his 1848 Colt through his brain and the weapon beside him; whether it was murder or suicide was never determined. The date of death as given is conjecture; obituary articles appeared in the *Arizona Gazette* for May 15, 1905, and the *Arizona Journal Miner* May 16.

Farish, II, 211-15; Carolyn Goff, "R.I.P., Henry Wickenburg." *True West,* Vol. 23, No. 5 (May-June 1976), 28-31, 54.

Wickliffe, Charles, army officer (c. 1820-Apr. 27, 1862). B. at Bardsville, Kentucky, his year of birth is conjecture. He was graduated from West Point in 1839 and became a second lieutenant of the 1st Dragoons at Fort Leavenworth. He took part in an expedition to the Grand River in 1839-40, then was transferred to Indian Territory where he served at Fort Wayne and Fort Gibson. He became involved with Amanda, the Anglo-Cherokee wife of a white civilian, Robert Wilkins, and in a resulting dispute shot Wilkins fatally in the back with a shotgun, claiming it was self-defense. Wickliffe was confined to Fort Gibson on honor parole, but January 28 escaped, reached Fort Wayne, 60 miles distant, the next day, then went on to freedom. He was dropped from the army April 12, 1842, having "disobeyed the order of a superior officer, broken his arrest, and deserted his post." Wickliffe was a counsellor at law and farmer at Blandville, Kentucky, from 1843-7. He became captain of the 16th Infantry April 9, 1847 and was promoted to major in February 1848, receiving an honorable discharge July 22 that year, resuming his Blandville, Kentucky, law practice from 1848 to 1861, serving one term in 1850 as a member of the state house of representatives, and as commonwealth attorney from 1851-55. He was mortally

wounded as a Confederate colonel April 7, 1862, at the battle of Shiloh.

Cullum; Heitman; Aurora Hunt, *Major General James Henry Carleton . . . Western Frontier Dragoon.* Glendale, Calif., Arthur H. Clark Co., 1958.

Widenmann, Robert A., adventurer (Jan. 24, 1852-Apr. 15, 1930). B. at Ann Arbor, Michigan, the son of a Bavarian consul, he was bilingual and studied at Biberach, Germany, then at Stuttgart and returned to this country in the 1870s. He roamed about in Colorado before reaching Lincoln County, New Mexico, where in 1877 he became associated with Tunstall whom he had met at Santa Fe; he clerked in the Tunstall store and worked at his ranch. Through his father's acquaintance with Interior Secretary Carl Schurz, Widenmann was named deputy U.S. marshal, but was removed April 1, 1878. In February 1878, Widenmann had been with the Tunstall party when Tunstall was murdered. Widenmann believed there "was dynamite in any true account of the Lincoln County War," and Fulton felt him justified in believing so. Widenmann left Lincoln County in September 1878. He went to England and stayed for a time with the Tunstall family, then settled in New York "fearing for many years (according to family tradition) for his life." He was married at Philadelphia November 23, 1881, and eventually entered business with his father at Ann Arbor. During World War I he dropped the second "n" from his name. He was more than 6 feet in height, well built, not heavy, with a fine appearance and had "an exceptionally winning manner." He held a high opinion of himself, was possessed of strong family ties; McSween however considered him lazy, indiscrete, "nosey" and pompous. He died at Haverstraw, New York.

Robert N. Mullin notes; "Frank Warner Angel's Notes on New Mexico Territory 1878," ed. by Lee Scott Theisen. *Arizona and the West,* Vol. 18, No. 4 (Winter 1976).

Wiggins, Ben, black partisan (fl. 1836). Wiggins was "probably the most active Negro partisan of the whites in the early days of the Seminole War," according to Porter. He was a mulatto, denied that he had any Indian blood although he was reared with Florida Seminoles and was equally at home with whites, being a free man. He was of great usefulness to the whites and sometimes rode express, a dangerous occupation in Indian country. At the Battle of Dunlawton, at a plantation below St. Augustine on January 18, 1836, Wiggins killed three Indians and was himself seriously wounded, but recovered. He last was reported around March or April of 1836.

Kenneth W. Porter, "*Negro Guides and Interpreters in the Early Stages of the Seminole War,*" Jour. of Negro Hist., Vol. XXXV, No. 2 (Apr. 1950), 174-82.

Wiggins, Oliver Perry, yarn spinner (c. July 23, 1823-Nov. 30, 1913). B. somewhere in the east, he became the source of much misinformation about Kit Carson and mountain man-frontier days; very little of what he said at various times can be substantiated, although his "testimony" was accepted unquestioningly by numerous writers, including some historians. At St. Louis on April 28, 1850, he joined the Chalmers party enroute for California. He left it June 11 in the vicinity of Scottsbluff, Nebraska. He married Martha Wardell (d. Oct. 16, 1895). Wiggins was a guide for five days, November 1-5, 1863, for Lieutenant Jesse Akin, 7th Iowa Cavalry, at Post Alkali, Nebraska, and was appointed first postmaster at Byers, Colorado, February 27, 1873. The next year he was on the credentials committee of the Colorado Republican Territorial Convention. He died, presumably at Denver. The above are virtually all the significant facts about his life and career now extant, but by his numerous interviews and preposterous claims and statements, especially during his latter life, he ranked with William Drannan. The damage he did to the historical record was considerable.

Lorene and Kenneth Englert, *Oliver Perry Wiggins: Fantastic, Bombastic, Frontiersman.* Palmer Lake, Colo., Filter Press, 1968.

Wilbur, Reuben Augustine, physician, Indian agent (July 7, 1840-July 10, 1882). B. at Plympton, Massachusetts, he was admitted to Harvard Medical School at 20, graduated in three years and for the next two practiced at Taunton, Massachusetts. In 1865 he went to San Francisco and from there to Arizona with its future governor, A.P.K. Safford and others. He was appointed physician for the Arizona Mining Company which operated the Heintzelman (or Cerro Colorado) Mine northwest of Tubac, Arizona, remaining until 1870 when he was named physician for the Pima and Maricopa Indians and six months later for the Papago, as well. In 1871 he also opened a private practice at Tucson. Wilbur appears to have been an earnest and dedicated agent to his Indians, seeking their betterment (and perhaps his own) in a number of ways, and being in some degree responsible for establishment of the Papago Reservation, created in June 1874. He assisted General Howard in his peace mission among Arizona Indians and assiduously attempted to have children who had been kidnapped from Apaches during the Camp Grant Massacre returned to their parents. In the spring of 1873 Wilbur was named temporary agent for the Apaches at San Carlos Reservation, his appointment intended to bridge the gap between departure of Agent George Stevens and the arrival of Major Charles F. Larrabee. Wilbur's assignment to San Carlos overlapped with Larrabee's and coincided with the murder by Apaches of young First Lieutenant Jacob Almy and a period of particular unrest among the Indians there, much of which an official Board of Investigation decided had been instigated by Wilbur whom it characterized as "a thoroughly bad man." Testimony before the board indicts Wilbur not only for Apache hostilities then generated, but for apparent corruption and malfeasance and even more serious matters. He was however exonerated in October 1873 by a U.S. Grand Jury of seemingly political orientation. Shortly after the Grand Jury rendered its opinion, Wilbur was married to Rafaela Salazar, member of a leading Sonora family, and they became parents of several children. Wilbur, although not himself a Catholic initially was a friend of Roman Catholic Bishop John B. Salpointe but they came to a parting over matters connected with creation of a school for Indian children at San Xavier, south of Tucson, and again there were allegations of misconduct on Wilbur's part and a case of suspiciously missing records. The two men became hopelessly at odds. Their dispute extended to matters of control and authority over the Papago Indian Agency and Wilbur was succeeded in 1875 by John W. Cornyn, the agency soon combined with that for the Pima and Maricopa Indians. Wilbur later was reappointed physician for the Papagoes. He also acquired a ranch near Arivaca, Arizona, where he raised beef and horses. Apparently for reasons of failing health he returned east and died at Plymouth, Massachusetts, of consumption and heart disease.

Information from the Reverend Francis J. Fox. S.J.; Dan L. Thrapp, *The Conquest of Apacheria.* Norman, Univ. of Okla. Press, 1967.

Wilcox, Charles F., Chief of Indian Police (c. 1844-post 1883). B. in Michigan, he was appointed October 21, 1882, Chief of Indian Police at the San Carlos, Arizona agency, resigning January 3, 1883.

Record of Employees, San Carlos Agency, Vols, 9, 10, RG 75, Nat. Archives.

Wild Bill (Nebraska): *see* Mortimer N. Kress

Wild Horse Annie: *see* Velma B. Johnston

Wildcat: *see* Coacoochee

Wilden, Alexander, Mormon pioneer (fl. 1857-1892). Wilden, a resident of Cedar City, Utah, was placed by *Mormonism Unveiled* at the Mountain Meadows Massacre of September 11, 1857, either participating in or consenting to the tragedy. The volume made no mention of his death at the time it was published.

Mormonism Unveiled, 380.

Wilden, Elliott, Mormon pioneer (fl. 1857-1876). A resident of Cedar City, Utah, Wilden was placed by *Mormonism Unveiled* at the Mountain Meadows Massacre of September 11, 1857, either participating in or consenting to the tragedy. He was indicted with others for the crime, but was not tried.

Mormonism Unveiled, 380; Juanita Brooks, *John D. Lee.* Glendale, Calif, Arthur H. Clark Co., 1962.

Wiley, (Wylie), Robert, Mormon pioneer (fl. 1854-1892). A man of this name was placed by *Mormonism Unveiled* at the Mountain Meadows Massacre of September 11, 1857, either participating in or consenting to the tragedy. The *Journal of the Southern Indian Mission* spells the name Wylie. Wise, who uses the variant Wiley, said that John D. Lee in his Confessions recalled that this individual "of the High Council" of Cedar City, had participated in the slaughter. *Mormonism*

Unveiled believed him to be still alive when the book was published.

Mormonism Unveiled, 380; William Wise, *Massacre at Mountain Meadows.* N.Y., Thomas Y. Crowell Co., 1976; *Journal of the Southern Indian Mission,* ed. by Juanita Brooks. Logan, Utah State Univ. Press, 1972.

Wilkins, Caleb (Cale), mountain man (July 10, 1810-Oct. 5, 1890). B. at Zanesville, Ohio, he was a brother-in-law of Joe Meek. He joined Nathaniel Wyeth at Fort Hall in 1835, already a seasoned trapper, but soon quit to join Bridger as a free trapper. He, Meek and others drove the first wagons from Fort Hall to Walla Walla in 1840, continuing on to the Willamette River, where Wilkins settled to become an important Oregon pioneer. He had married a Nez Perce woman in the mountains, fathering seven children. When she died in 1848, he married a white woman, producing additional offspring.

Harvey E. Tobie article, MM, Vol. III.

Wilkinson, James, army officer (1757-Dec. 28, 1825). B. in Calvert County, Maryland, his career of intrigue at best and treason at worst has only peripheral frontier interest. He went to medical school at 17 and in 1775 prepared to launch a practice in Maryland, but was enamored of the army and when the Revolution broke out, after some service in a Pennsylvania volunteer unit he was commissioned a captain in the 2nd Continental Infantry in March 1776 to rank from September 9, 1775. He served under Washington at Bunker Hill, on Greene's staff until April and was aide to Benedict Arnold June 2 to July 17, 1776, in the Quebec operation. He was several times in personal difficulties, and unsavory allegations were made against him, but he emerged from each unscathed and ended the Revolutionary War a Brigadier General of Pennsylvania troops though forced to resign his brevet Brigadier General commission in the Continental Army. He moved to Kentucky in 1784, becoming a leader in separation agitation in that region at the time. He wrote two broadsides in 1785 urging immediate separation from Virginia and then seems to have gotten the notion of turning dissatisfaction on the part of Kentuckians to his own financial gain. He became a pivotal figure in the Spanish Conspiracy: a plan to sever the southwestern part of the United States, east of the Mississippi, and form a separate nation allied to Spain. It was reported he had taken an oath of allegiance to Spain in return for an annual pension of $2,000, shortly raised to $4,000. A trader, much of his trade was from the fringes of United States western settlement down the rivers to New Orleans and Spanish markets. October 22, 1791, Wilkinson, whose intrigues never had surfaced fully nor been completely credited in the east, was commissioned a lieutenant colonel and commandant of the 2nd U.S. Infantry; he became a Brigadier General March 5, 1792. He was stationed initially at Fort Washington at Cincinnati, but President Washington would not appoint him to command the Northwest Indian operation seeking to undo the havoc wrought by St. Clair's defeat and instead named Anthony Wayne to the post, Wilkinson serving under him. He was present at the battle of Fallen Timbers August 20, 1794. Wayne's suspicions were aroused against him at this time, notifying the Secretary of War about them. Wilkinson apparently had renewed his dallying with the Spanish and "there has survived sufficient evidence . . . to convict the general of highly irregular conduct, if not open treason." Nevertheless, Wilkinson was named commanding head of the army in 1797 and his activities in the west increased. Perhaps to cover up his own machinations he proposed that he march against New Orleans. When the Spanish turned Louisiana over to the French and the French over to the United States as the Louisiana Purchase, Wilkinson was present with a small command. In 1805 he was appointed governor of Upper Louisiana with headquarters at St. Louis and soon it was reported that he was deeply involved in the so-called Burr Conspiracy. People in the west believed that war with Spain was likely and according to one view, Burr wished to exploit such an eventuality but within the framework of the Union; the more generally accepted version has it that he wished to detach the Old Southwest to the profit of himself and his co-conspirators. Wilkinson seems to have been at first involved in the plan, but when he saw it losing momentum cooled toward it and at last warned the capital of Burr's "treasonous" designs. Wilkinson was the foremost witness for the prosecution at Burr's trial, though almost indicted himself as evidence was produced by the defense linking him with the plot; again he escaped unscathed, however. Wilkinson was made a Major General March 2, 1813, but his campaign to seize Montreal failed and he was relieved of command; once more an official inquiry cleared him. After the war and the failure of a cotton plantation in Mississippi, he went to Mexico in search of a major land grant, but fell ill at Mexico City, where he died.

Literature abundant.

Wilkinson, Melville Carey, army officer (Nov. 14, 1835-Oct. 5, 1898). B. at Scottsburg, New York, he was commissioned a first lieutenant in the 123rd New York Infantry May 16, 1861, and became a captain the next year of the 107the New York Infantry. After the war he served from second lieutenant in the 42nd, 6th and 3rd Infantry regiments. He was aide to O.O. Howard from April 1, 1871, to August 21, 1878, and during this period accompanied the General on one of his missions to the southwest, seeking peace with the Apaches, and on the 1877 Nez Perce campaign. He won a brevet in the battle of Clearwater, Idaho, July 11-12, and at Kamiah, Idaho, July 13. Wilkinson became a captain in 1886. He was killed by Chippewa Indians in the battle of Leech Lake, Minnesota, the last U.S. serviceman slain by hostile Indians during the conquest of a continent.

Heitman; Dan L. Thrapp, *Victorio and the Mimbres Apaches.* Norman, Univ. of Okla. Press, 1974.

Willard, Alexander Hamilton, frontiersman (Aug. 24, 1778-Mar. 6, 1865). B. at Charlestown, New Hampshire, he enlisted in Captain Amos Stoddard's artillery unit and from there joined the Lewis and Clark Expedition January 1, 1804. He was remarked upon as a blacksmith and a good hunter. After his return from the Pacific he married and worked as a blacksmith, serving in the War of 1812. From 1824-52 he lived in Wisconsin, then went to California where he died and is buried at Franklin, near Sacramento. He is the only member of the Lewis and Clark Expedition of whom a photograph is known; it is reproduced by Wheeler and by Clarke.

History of the Expedition Under the Command of Lewis and Clark, ed. by Elliott Coues. N.Y., Dover Pubns., 1965; Clarke, *Lewis and Clark;* Olin D. Wheeler, *The Trail of Lewis and Clark 1804-1904,* 2 vols. N.Y., G.P. Putnam's Sons, 1904.

Willcox, Elon Farnsworth, army officer (Nov. 6, 1855-July 12, 1910). The son of Orlando B. Willcox, he was b. at Detroit and after graduation from West Point in 1878 was commissioned a second lieutenant in the 12th Infantry, transferring to the 6th Cavalry in 1882, becoming a first lieutenant in 1886 and a captain in 1897. Willcox served continuously in Arizona and New Mexico from 1878 until October 1886, the first four years as aide-de-camp to his father, the department commander. He served under Price in the aftermath of the Cibecue affair in 1881 and the Chiricahua campaign following; Willcox reported that he accompanied Crook into Mexico in 1883, but confirmation is lacking. He operated against Geronimo in 1885-86. Willcox had a minor role in the military's settling of the Powder River War in 1892 in Wyoming. He was acting superintendent of Yosemite National Park in 1898-99, served in the Far East, including China, intermittently from 1901 to 1906, retiring in that year. He died at Los Angeles.

Cullum; Powell; Heitman.

Wil(l)cox, Joseph M., army officer (c. 1791-Jan. 15, 1814). B. in Connecticut the son of a Revolutionary War officer, he was graduated from West Point in 1812 and commissioned a first lieutenant in the 3rd Infantry. Willcox was in the 1813-14 campaign under Jackson against the Creek Indians and after two desperate fights with hostiles he was engaged on the Alabama River where he was tomahawked, slain and scalped, aged 23. "No person, under the same circumstances... could have exhibited more skill, judgment, activity or determined courage. Such blood was spilt at Thermopolae." An Alabama county was named for him, but spelled Wilcox, instead of Willcox.

Cullum.

Willcox, Orlando Bolivar, army officer (Apr. 16, 1823-May 10, 1907). B. at Detroit, he was graduated from West Point and commissioned a second lieutenant in the 4th Artillery July 1, 1847, becoming a first lieutenant April 30, 1850, and taking part in the final Seminole War in Florida. Having completed the study of law he was admitted to the Michigan bar, resigned his commission September 10, 1857, and practiced at Detroit until the Civil War when he became a colonel of the 1st Michigan Infantry May 1, 1861. He emerged from the war a brevet Major General with a Medal of Honor for gallantry at Bull Run, July 21, 1861, where he was wounded and captured but exchanged after 15 months. Willcox became colonel of the 29th U.S. Infantry July 28, 1866, and transferred to the 12th Infantry March 15, 1869, which he long commanded in Arizona and the southwest. He succeeded Kautz as commander of the Department of Arizona from March 1878 until September 1882 when he was replaced by Crook. Willcox was a diligent and honest administrator but his Arizona tenure came at a time of growing Apache unrest and one outbreak after another until his superiors decided upon Crook. Willcox protested the removal, but to no avail. He then commanded Madison Barracks, New York, until October 13, 1886, when he became Brigadier General and assumed command of the Department of the Missouri, where he remained until his retirement, April 16, 1887. He resided for a time at Washington, D.C., and in 1905 moved to Coburg, Ontario, where he died. Willcox married twice and fathered six children. He wrote an artillery manual and two novels published under the name, Walter March, neither memorable.

Army and Navy Jour., May 18, 1907; *Annual Reunion, Graduates of West Point,* June 13, 1907; Cullum; Heitman; *Detroit Free Press,* May 11, 1907; Dan L. Thrapp, *General Crook and the Sierra Madre Adventure.* Norman, Univ. of Okla. Press, 1972.

Willett, Thomas, trader, colonial leader (Aug. 1605-Aug. 4, 1674). B. at Barley, Hertfordshire, England, he went to Holland to live with the Puritans, and emigrated to Plymouth Colony, Massachusetts, about 1630, "an honest younge man." He was agent on the Kennebec River, Maine, a center for trade with the Indians, from 1629-34, and agent for a trading post on the Penobscot River, Maine, in 1635. In 1649 he was one of five men to whom the Kennebec trade was leased for three years. Willett leaned toward the Jesuit, Druillettes' suggestion of an alliance with the French against the Iroquois, proposed in 1650 and 1651 and, Druillettes wrote, "spoke to the governor in advocacy of my negotiation." The priest described Willett as "greatly attached to the Abnaquois, with whom he has been acquainted...for several years." As a prominent trader and shipowner, Willett obtained considerable property in New Amsterdam and assisted in settling boundary questions between it and the English colonies; he accompanied an English expedition against New Amsterdam in 1664, and helped secure surrender of what became New York City, being appointed in 1665 its first English mayor, and again named to the post in 1667. When the Dutch recaptured the place briefly in 1673, Willett's property was confiscated. He died at Swansea, Massachusets.

Thwaites, JR, XXXVI, 91, 99, 242; George F. Willison, *Saints and Strangers*. N.Y., Reynal & Hitchcock, 1945; EA.

Williams, Charles Andrews, army officer (Apr. 3, 1852-July 4, 1926). B. in Virginia he went to West Point from Missouri and was commissioned a second lieutenant in the 21st Infantry June 17, 1874. He was on frontier duty at Forts Vancouver and Townsend, Washington, 1874-75, and at Fort Wrangell, Alaska, in 1875-76. He was severely wounded in the battle of Clearwater, Idaho, July 11, 1877 while serving with Howard's forces in the Nez Perce campaign, earning a brevet. Williams was in the field June 14 to August 11, 1878, during the Bannock War and then was stationed at Fort Lapwai, Idaho. He became a captain November 14, 1890. In the Spanish American War he served in Cuba and the Philippines and retired as colonel of the 21st Infantry April 3, 1911. He died at Washington, D.C.

Heitman; Powell; Cullum.

Williams, Constant, army officer (May 25, 1843-Apr. 20, 1922). B. at Pittsburgh, Pennsylvania, he enlisted in the 31st Pennsylvania Infantry in 1861 and was commissioned a second lieutenant in the 7th U.S. Infantry June 29, 1863. He became a first lieutenant January 1, 1864, and a captain May 10, 1873. Williams was with Gibbon in the Nez Perce campaign and at the Battle of Big Hole, Montana, August 9-10, 1877, was twice wounded and won a brevet to major for gallant service. Williams became a major January 28, 1897. By July 12, 1904, he was a Brigadier General and retired May 25, 1907, by reason of age. He lived in retirement at Schenectady, New York.

Heitman; *Who Was Who;* Helen Addison Howard, Dan L. McGrath, *War Chief Joseph.* Lincoln, Univ. of Nebr. Press, 1964.

Williams, Eleazar, Mohawk preacher, claimant (May 1788-Aug. 28, 1858). B. on the shore of Lake George, New York, he became a preacher and missionary who at length claimed to be the Lost Dauphin of France. He was a scout during the War of 1812, was wounded at Plattesburg and was elected a sachem at Caughnawaga, Ontario, by the Iroquois Council. A remarkable orator, he had great success in preaching to Indians and converted many, but he also came into a key position to manipulate the sale of lands, becoming involved at length in a scheme to move the Indians west of Lake Michigan where an Iroquois empire was to be set up, no doubt with Williams as emperor. He forged signatures to approve aspects of the transaction though the scheme finally collapsed in 1827 with only some of the Oneida moving west. Williams abandoned public activity for some years, but appeared again in 1852 when he claimed to be the Lost Dauphin of France, saying his father was Louis XVI and his mother Marie Antoinette (in fact, his father was Tehoragwanegen, a Mohawk war chief and grandson of Eunice Williams, erstwhile captive (see entry), and his mother was Konwatewenteta, or Mary Ann Rice Williams). He claimed he had been kidnapped in France, imprisoned and at length secretly carried to Canada; he found many willing believers, although most in time became disillusioned. Williams died on the St. Regis Reservation near Hogansburg, New York, neglected and in great destitution.

Hodge, HAI.

Williams, Eunice, captive (Sept. 17, 1696-c. Nov. 25, 1785). B. at Deerfield, Massachusetts, she was 7 when Indians and French on February 29, 1704, raided the town at dawn, killed two of her siblings among 47 townspeople slaughtered, and captured her father and mother, the Reverend John Williams and his wife, Eunice (for whom the daughter was named), and four of her brothers and sisters. They were driven on the toilsome trail to Quebec, Eunice's mother being murdered enroute. Young Eunice was taken to Sault Saint-Louis and instructed in Catholicism by priests and religious teachers. Once her father, still in captivity, visited her with Governor de Vaudreuil, but her captor refused to part with her, failing even to honor a bargain to release Eunice if an Indian girl of her age was substituted. The Indian who "owned" her was unwilling to lose her because she was "a pritty girl," and although he agreed from time to time to let her go, he never did. Gradually the story circulated that Eunice herself refused to return, and the Indian to force her to do so. By 1713 Eunice had been baptized under the name of Marguerite and was married to "a young Indian," a priest reporting he had married them reluctantly after they insisted upon it. Her husband's name was Franciscus Xaverius Arosen ("arosen" meaning squirrel in Mohawk). She did see her father in 1714 again. He had arrived at Montreal February 9 but it was not until May 13 that he was permitted to visit her, and then she adamantly refused to go home with him. Eunice promised to "goe & see her Father" once peace was proclaimed between French and English, but did not do it until 1740, after her father was dead. Eunice, by now one of the most celebrated captives of the French and Indian wars, came four times to New England in all. In 1740 at Albany she and her husband met her brothers, Stephen and Eliezer and Esther's husband. Eunice returned to New England each of the following two years, attended a Prostestant church but rejected entreaties from all sides that she live among her people. June 30, 1761, she and her husband returned once more to New England, remaining ten days. But she never visited Deerfield where she was born and of which she must have retained bitter memories. Her last letter to any member of the family was to her brother, Stephen in 1781 when she was very aged. Her husband had died January 22, 1765, and Eunice herself was buried November 26, 1785. She had mothered at least three children and has many descendants.

Coleman, *Captives*, II, 54-63.

Williams, Ezekiel, frontiersman (c. 1775-Dec. 24, 1844). B. in Kentucky, he received some education, reportedly married and fathered a son, and reached St. Louis by 1807, ascending the Missouri River as a free trapper that year. He joined Lisa men in constructing Fort Raymond at the confluence of the Big Horn and Yellowstone rivers, trapped the Three Forks country and returned to St. Louis with Lisa in 1808. In 1809 he probably accompanied a St. Louis Missouri Fur Company group and probably worked out of Fort Mandan above the mouth of the Knife River that winter. He trapped the next season on the upper Arkansas River, later joined the Arapaho Indians, may have spent the 1812-13 period in New Mexico and by December 15, 1814, was back at St. Louis. He served as a ranger briefly during the War of 1812, then returned to the South Plains, where his career is uncertain. He was accused of the murder of Jean Baptiste Champlain and theft of his furs, perhaps unjustly. Williams married a widow about 1814, farmed near Franklin, Missouri. He may have visited Santa Fe in 1822, but proof is lacking. In 1823 he settled near Boonville, Missouri. He guided a trading party to Santa Fe in 1827. About 1831 he removed to the later Benton County, Missouri, where he died.

Frederic E. Voelker article, MM, Vol. IX; David J. Weber, *The Taos Trappers.* Norman, Univ. of Okla. Press, 1971.

Williams, George Calvin (Parson), Mormon leader (Feb. 27, 1836-Nov. 7, 1916). B. near Chattanooga, Tennessee, he was living in north Texas at the outbreak of the Civil War but because of Union sympaties elected to fight Indians rather than Yankees. After the conflict he became a Baptist preacher in northwest Arkansas and about 1875 went to Arizona settling successively in St. Johns, Round Valley, and Bush Valley (Alpine), moving in the early 1880s to near Glenwood, New Mexico, where he founded the community of Pleasanton. Williams became interested in Mormonism, was baptized into that faith October 16, 1881, and was ordained a bishop November 18, 1883, by Brigham Young Jr. In the latter year he became a polygamist, taking a 15-year-old second wife. Threatened with lynching for this the Parson (so-called because of his former Baptist ministry) in 1885 and other polygamous Mormons headed south, establishing in Chihuahua the first Mormon colony of Mexico. After settling briefly at various Chihuahua sites, Williams in cooperation with John C. Naegle about 1889 moved over to the Rio Bavispe region of Sonora, settling by 1892 at what was called Colonia Oaxaca, on land purchased from Emilio Kosterlitzky and Colonel Juan Fenochio. The colony flourished initially, but financial troubles and other difficulties arose and Williams became disenchanted not only with the colony but with the church, having learned that the body had "fellowshipped" men involved in the Mountain Meadows Massacre of 1857 in which Williams claimed 13 of his relatives had been murdered. Since members of the doomed wagon train came largely from Arkansas this could well have been true. He drifted off into the mountains prospecting and was excommunicated for apostasy. He returned to the Chihuahua colonies, to New Mexico, to Arkansas, then went back to Arizona, was reinstated in the church and died at Miramonte, Arizona. He had married three times, the second and third wives divorcing him and his first dying in 1903.

Thomas H. Naylor, "The Mormons Colonize Sonora: Early Trials at Colonia Oaxaca." *Arizona and the West,* Vol. 20, No. 4 (Winter 1978), 325-42; information from Historical Dept., Church of Jesus Christ of Latter-day Saints; Andrew Jenson, *Latter-day Saint Biographical Encyclopedia,* Vol. 4. Salt Lake City, Andrew Jenson Meml. Assn., 1936, 598.

Williams, Isaac, frontiersman (July 16, 1737-Sept. 25, 1820). B. in Chester County, Pennsylvania, the family moved while he was yet young to Winchester, Virginia, where he became accomplished at frontier skills. At 18 the colonial government hired him as ranger, or scout, against Indians, and Williams served as such under Braddock. He accompanied the pack outfit that brought the first convoy of provisions to Fort Duquesne in 1758. In 1769 he settled on Buffalo Creek (West Liberty), Brooke County, Virginia. He explored the country around the present Wheeling with Ebenezer and Jonathan Zane that year, and took part in several extended hunting and trapping expeditions into the western wilds. Williams explored down the Ohio to the Mississippi and up it to the Missouri as early as 1770, trapping beaver in the latter's tributaries. Once, nearly frozen, he and his party were snowbound and forced to eat the furs they had taken, burning off the hair and boiling the hides into a kind of soup. As a scout he accompanied Lord Dunmore in his 1774 operations. Williams took part in the heavy fighting around Wheeling in 1777 and during the early Revolutionary years, and was a friend of and sometimes operated with the Wetzels. He moved to the vicinity of Fort Harmar, Ohio, about 1786. He ever was generous with less fortunate neighbors during times of hardship. Williams enjoyed hunting and woodland roving all his life; during the Indian war of 1791-95, he remained un-molested in his cabin, although hostiles operated all about. He was somewhat taciturn, never a rowdy, was moderate in speech and language. Many years before his death he liberated his six to eight slaves and by his will left valuable tokens of love and good feeling "for the oppressed and despised African." He was of "middle size," and erect.

Samuel Prescott Hildreth, *Biographical and Historical Memories of the Early Pioneer Settlers of Ohio.* Cincinnati, H.W. Derby & Co., 1852.

Williams, Isaac, frontiersman (1799-1856). B. in Pennsylvania, he left Fort Smith, Arkansas, in May 1830, with the Bean-Sinclair trapping party for the Rocky Mountains, in 1831 at Taos joining the Ewing Young California trapping group. They reached Los Angeles April 14, 1832, Williams remaining in southern California. In 1843 he received a land grant near the later Chino, California, adjacent to one of his father-in-law, Antonio Maria Lugo, a cattleman. Williams was captured briefly by Californians during the Mexican War. A prominent pioneer, he died at his Chino home.

Joseph S. Wood article, MM, Vol. VII; *Los Angeles Times,* Nov. 24, 1957.

Williams, Jack: *see* George Shanks

Williams, James, frontiersman, vigilante (Jan. 9, 1832-Feb. 21, 1887). B. at Greensburg, Westmoreland County, Pennsylvania (the *Register* says in 1834), he went in 1855 to Rock Island, Illinois, for two years, spent a year in Kansas where he took an active part in the 1857-58 Border troubles as a Free State man. He went to Pike's Peak (Colorado) in the fall of 1858 for the gold rush of 1858-59. He then went by wagon train to Montana (acquiring the title of "captain" enroute) and on the journey having a run-in with Joseph Slade (who as a vigilante he later would hang) over the captaincy of the train, Williams winning out. Slade then became his lieutenant and Williams conceded that "I never had a man with me that I got along with better." The party arrived either at Alder Gulch (Virginia City) June 20, 1863, or at Bannack on that date (according to Birney), then going on to Virginia City. Williams established a corral and livery business in Nevada City nearby and eventually a ranch on Williams Creek, about five miles southwest of Virginia City. For a time he ran a pack train from Elk City, Idaho, to Virginia City, charging $1 a pound for freight; he married and raised seven children. Described as "sensitive, shy, self effacing," and "uneducated, inarticulate, reticent," he was most unlikely as a choice to head the famed Montana Vigilantes. But he could also be ruthless, and he became their effective leader, although Sanders was given the credit for master-minding the operation and John X. Beidler is generally supposed to have been among the most active. Williams was first to sign the "Vigilante Oath" as executive officer of the Alder Gulch committee though he was in effect the executive of the entire activity which resulted in the executions of more than a score (some put it as high as 34) desperadoes, suspected desperadoes and other unsavory elements, and thoroughly cleaned up the Montana gold camps which until that time had been plagued by thieves, murderers, road agents and ruffians headed by the sheriff of Beaverhead County, Henry Plummer, himself among those hanged. Williams was elected county commissioner of Madison County in 1870 and ran unsuccessfully for sheriff twice. In 1885 he was vice president of the Montana Historical Society. His name is not mentioned in Dimsdale's *Vigilantes of Montana* because, according to Lew L. Callaway, onetime justice of Montana's Supreme Court who knew Williams in later life, Williams and Dimsdale had had a falling out, and the former gave "explicit orders that it should not appear." Birney explains that Jim Williams "refused to make a five hundred dollar contribution" which Dimsdale sought to defray the costs of publishing his book. Williams in his later years, explaining why he was selected to head the vigilantes, said laconically, "They had an idea I had some leather in me, I guess." His best-known portrait (Pace prints another, p. 53) has been described as showing "one of the saddest most haunted faces that any man ever wore." His frozen body was found in a creek bottom thicket on his ranch, with an empty laudanum bottle nearby; some believed him a suicide, others a murder victim. He reportedly had been having financial and domestic problems. Callaway who as a youngster had lived with the Williams family for an extended period, said Williams had "mild blue-gray eyes" that turned jet black when he was

angered. He reported that Williams never talked much about his vigilante activities except when drunk when he might become briefly loquacious. Williams, he added was 5 feet, 10 1/2 inches tall and weighed 190 pounds.

Langford; Hoffman Birney, *Vigilantes.* Phila., Penn Pub. Co., 1929; Robert G. Bailey, *River of No Return.* Lewiston, Ida., R.G. Bailey Printing Co., 1947, 121 & n.; Dick Pace, *Golden Gulch,* 2nd ed. Virginia City, Mont., p.p., 1970; *Register;* Llewellyn Link Callaway, *Two True Tales of the Wild West* (I. The Life and Death of Captain James Williams; II, The Life and Death of Joseph Alfred Slade). Oakland, Calif., Maud Gonne Press, 1973.

Williams, James Monroe, army officer (Sept. 12, 1833-Feb. 15, 1907). B. at Lowville, New York, he entered the army as a captain of the 5th Kansas Cavalry July 12, 1861, became a lieutenant colonel of the 79th U.S. Colored Infantry January 13, 1863, and colonel May 2 and ended the Civil War a brevet Brigadier General of Volunteers. He had participated in eight engagements, had three horses shot under him and was wounded four times. Williams became captain of the 8th Cavalry July 28, 1866, and was posted to Arizona where he had some hard fights along the Verde River, in the Yampa Valley and at Music Mountain where he was twice wounded by arrows; for three of his fights he earned a brevet. He resigned from the army March 29, 1873, probably as a result of incapacity due to his wounds. Williams died at Washington, D.C.

Heitman; Dan L. Thrapp, *The Conquest of Apacheria.* Norman, Univ. of Okla. Press, 1967.

Williams , J(ames) R(obert), cartoonist (Mar. 20, 1888-June 17, 1957). B. at Halifax, Nova Scotia, he was brought up in Michigan. He quit school at 15 and wandered to the southwest where he became a cowboy, camp cook and muleskinner, spending 11 years in New Mexico and Arizona. At 26 he returned to Chicago, later taking a correspondence course in cartooning. At various times he also was a machinist, policeman, served a hitch in the U.S.. Cavalry and was a railroad fireman. He worked as a cartoonist for motion pictures and on February 27, 1922 Williams' cartoon-panel, "Out Our Way," was taken up by the

Newspaper Enterprise Association syndicate of Cleveland, ultimately appearing in 700 newspapers with a combined readership of 32 million and bringing him an annual salary of around $65,000. His cartoons were of rotating themes, two of them, of cowboys or cavalrymen, appearing once or twice a week. For a decade from 1932 Williams lived on his 45,000 acre K-4 Arizona ranch, then moved to San Marino, California. His consistently funny cartoons about Arizona cowboys were true to the range life Williams knew so well, and earned the praise of J. Frank Dobie and other knowledgeable people, as did his cavalrymen. Williams became an institution in his field, all of his works notable for "humor, spice and life." He was married and fathered two children.

Gordon West, "James R. Williams: Cowboy Cartoonist," *Frontier Times*, Vol. 45, No. 1 (Dec.-Jan. 1971), 26-27, 46; *Who Was Who.*

Williams, John, Congregational clergyman, captive (Dec. 10, 1664-June 12, 1729). B. at Roxbury, Massachusetts, he was graduated from Harvard in 1683, taught school for two years, commenced to preach at 22 and when a church was organized at Deerfield, Massachusetts, was ordained as its first pastor October 17, 1688. The year before he had married Eunice, grand-daughter of Richard Mather; they had eight children. Deerfield was a frontier community, constantly threatened and sometimes attacked during French-British hostilities by French-led Indians. February 29, 1704 it was sacked by a party of French and Indians, 47 people were killed, most of the remainder herded out on the wilderness trail to Quebec. Williams wrote: "They (the enemy) came to my house at the beginning. (Twenty) with painted faces and hideous acclamations" broke in, killing Jerusha, 6 weeks old, John, 6 years, and a black woman servant, Parthena. Williams, his wife and five children, Samuel, Esther, Stephen, Eunice and Warham, and a black servant, Frank, were taken prisoner and sent north; the other Williams son, Eliezer, 15, was away at school. Williams' wife, Eunice on the second day told her husband she was dying and he "made my last farewell of my dear wife, the desire of my eyes and companion in many mercies and afflictions." Shortly afterward she was dispatched by an Indian hatchet "at one stroke." Williams himself was not mistreated.

Samuel (b. January 1690) reached Canada with his father, learned French and was forced to submit to baptism and some Catholic teaching, but returned to Massachusetts in 1706 with his father, later served as a lieutenant in the armed forces and died June 30, 1713. Esther (b. April 1691), reached Canada, was the first of the family to be redeemed, returned home by way of Albany in 1705 and in 1715 married the Reverend Joseph Meacham of Coventry, Connecticut. Stephen (b. May 1693) was with a party separated from the main force but reached Canada after great hardships; here he was hidden from the French by his Indians who feared he would be taken from them. He was returned to Massachusetts, however, in November 1705 and became a minister at Longmeadow, Massachusetts, where he served for many years, was a chaplain on the Louisburg expedition of 1758, and died in 1782. He was married twice. Eunice remained in Canada, returning rarely south of the border (see entry). Warham (b. September 1699) reached Canada, learned French so well that he forgot his English but quickly recovered it, became a minister at Watertown, Massachusetts, married and died in 1751. John Williams so sternly repulsed priestly attempts to convert him to Catholicism or adopt Catholic practices that they were glad to see him go. After two years his release was effected and he returned to Boston November 21, 1706 (the Sewall editor says October 25). He preached in a number of churches his experiences and with Cotton Mather's help produced *The Redeemed Captive Returning to Zion* (1707), a widely-read book, one of the most popular of the captivity narratives, it relating his fortitude against "Popish poisons." Williams returned to his Deerfield pulpit despite the exposed situation of the town and evident peril. He contributed to rebuilding the burned out community. He was prominent in Congregational circles, deplored the religious indifference of the age and preached against it, and died at Deerfield, survived by his second wife and their five children, as well as six children of his first marriage.

Coleman, *Captives,* II, 44-64; *Diary of Samuel Sewall 1674-1729,* ed. by M. Halsey Thomas, 2 vols. N.Y., Farrer, Straus and Girous, 1973; EB, 11th ed.; DAB; CE.

Williams, John, army officer (Jan. 29, 1778-Aug. 10, 1837). B. in Surry County, North Carolina, he was commissioned a first lieutenant in the 2nd North Carolina Volunteers September 1, 1795, became a captain in the 6th U.S. Infantry April 23, 1799, and was honorably discharged June 15, 1800. He read law at Salisbury, North Carolina, and was admitted to the bar of Knox County, Tennessee, in 1803, practicing at Knoxville. Williams was a colonel of Tennessee mounted volunteers from December 1812 to March 1813. Commanding 250 Tennesseeans he reached the Florida border eager to fight Indians and with a detachment of United States regulars drove into Spanish Florida. In a three-week campaign launched February 7, 1813, Williams burned several hundred Indian houses, destroyed crops and drove off much livestock, but inflicted only minor losses on the Seminole warriors. Williams became colonel of the 39th U.S. Infantry June 18, 1813. He served under Jackson against the Creek Indians in Alabama during the Indian war of 1813-14, and took part in the Battle of Horseshoe Bend, March 27, 1813, a decisive defeat for the Creeks which virtually ended the war. Williams served in the U.S. Senate until 1823, represented the nation in Central America in 1825-26 and returned to hold various state offices in Tennessee. He died near Knoxville.

BDAC; Heitman; Edwin C. McReynolds, *The Seminoles.* Norman, Univ. of Okla. Press, 1967; John K. Mahon, *The History of the Second Seminole War.* Gainesville, Univ. of Fla. Press, 1967.

Williams, John Lee, pioneer (1775-Nov. 7, 1856). B. at Salem, Massachusetts, he was raised in New York State, educated at Hamilton-Oneida College, Clinton, read law and moved to Virginia. He speculated in western land and in 1820 moved again, this time to Pensacola, Florida. He practiced law, by 1823 was a justice of the peace, and occasionally explored parts of Florida; in 1823 he explored the region between the Ochlockonee and St. Marks rivers and with Dr. William H. Simmons selected the site for Tallahassee, the future capital. By the middle 1820s Williams had relocated again, this time in central Florida, and by 1830 he was at St. Augustine; in 1832 he was assistant adjutant general of the 2nd Brigade of Florida Militia

under Joseph Hernandez. In 1834 Williams moved to Picolata on the St. Johns River. He wrote *A View of West Florida* (1827) and *The Territory of Florida* (1837), both widely circulated and authoritative volumes for their era. Williams died at Picolata.

John Lee Williams, *The Territory of Florida.* N.Y., A.T. Goodrich, 1837 (fac. ed., Gainesville, Univ. of Fla. Press, 1962); information from the Fla. Div. of Archives and Hist., Tallahassee.

Williams, Marshall, express agent (c. 1852-post 1882). B. in New York state, Williams became agent for Wells Fargo and for the H.C. Walker stage line, at Tombstone, Arizona, about 1880. He became aligned with the Earp faction in Tombstone's troublesome period, was suspected of skimming and otherwise profiteering on bullion shipments by stage and perhaps of complicity in stage holdups by informing bandits which stages carried valuables. By early 1882 he had "fled" Tombstone for Brooklyn, where he "seemed well supplied with money."

Ed Bartholomew, *Wyatt Earp: The Man & the Myth.* Toyahvale, Tex., Frontier Book Co., 1964; 1880 Census of Arizona.

Williams, Mike (W.?), victim (d. Oct. 5, 1871). From Kansas City, he may have been a onetime bar-keeper, but in October 1871, he was a special deputy hired by the Novelty Theater at Abilene, Kansas, to keep order, and a good friend of James Butler (Wild Bill) Hickok. During a shootout with Phil Coe at the Alamo Saloon October 5, Williams, seeking to assist Hickok, burst into the line of fire and was killed instantly by his friend. Hickok paid expenses for the burial at Kansas City.

Joseph G. Rosa, *They Called Him Wild Bill,* 2nd ed. Norman, Univ. of Okla. Press, 1974.

Williams, Oscar Waldo, lawyer, surveyor, writer (Mar. 17, 1853-Oct. 29, 1946). B. at Mt. Vernon, Kentucky, his family took him to Carthage, Illinois. He attended various colleges and graduated in law from Harvard University in 1876. The next spring he moved to Dallas, Texas, partly for health reasons. Failing to become established in law, he became a surveyor, locating land in West Texas, then beyond the frontier. He pursued this occupation for several years, keeping a diary much of the time and using it to refresh his memory when writing the later articles, "papers," and pamphlets which he produced in some profusion. They, along with his letters to family and friends, constitute an invaluable record of the natural history, frontier events, historical matters, travels and pioneer experiences Williams met with and absorbed in his 93 years of life. He had a fine mind, a superb memory, was thoroughly honest, objective, incisive, and above all interested in what he saw and experienced and recording it; the record he has left is virtually unrivaled in its delineation of an interesting border region that otherwise would be scarcely known or remembered at best fragmentarily. Williams gives a description of a buffalo stampede on the Staked Plains which he experienced that remains one of the best accounts of its kind; his narrative of Old Tascosa on the eve of one of its bloody gun battles is interesting, as are his remarks on Anton Chico and Carbonate-ville, New Mexico, where he remained briefly. In 1880 he began mining at Shakespeare, New Mexico, arriving there April 17. His writings of that camp and matters of historical interest in its vicinity are primary and generally dependable source material. His assessments of the colorful individuals of the settlement are generous and always sound. He removed to Silver City late in 1880, and lived there for some months, later writing of it extensively. On March 15, 1881, he was an official witness to the hanging of Richard Remine for murder; his account of it and related circumstances is vivid and unforgettable. He became deputy postmaster of Silver City and simultaneously held a position in the District Clerk's office, continuing his active interests in the community and among its characters. He married at Dallas December 15, 1881, bringing his wife to New Mexico. They remained at Silver City until October 1882, when they returned to Texas. Williams worked in East Texas pine lands for two years, but in December 1884, settled at Fort Stockton, Texas, where he made his home the last 50 years of his life. In addition to surveying, he was named in 1886 county judge of Pecos County, serving off and on for a decade. He tried farming unsuccessfully. In 1901-1902, Williams worked with the Texas State Mineral Survey and the U.S Geological Survey in the Big Bend area of Texas, then wild and little known. Again his special talents were evidenced in the articles and pamphlets he wrote about his experiences.

His recitals of the engaging tales of Natividad Luján have entered the mainstream of southwestern folklore. In March 1902, Williams returned to Fort Stockton to establish the law practice which lasted until 1935. His numerous pamphlets are virtually all now collectors' items; he also penned long and illuminating letters to his children describing his earlier adventures, as well as articles for newspapers and historical publications. He died at Pecos and was buried at East Hill Cemetery, Fort Stockton. His was a most useful life.

Oscar Williams; HT.

Williams, Thomas, Mormon pioneer (d.c. Apr. 1, 1860). An early convert to Mormonism, he was a city policeman at Nauvoo, Illinois, and as second sergeant, Company D, Mormon Battalion, "distinguished himself for bravery and resourcefulness." He contributed sizable sums for Mormon work, but became bitter when told he must not expect to be reimbursed; as an attorney he defended men in claims against the church. He left Utah early in 1857, returning in 1858. April 5, 1860, John D. Lee reported that a "T.S. Williams," who might have been this Williams, was killed by Indians at Bitter Springs, below Las Vegas, Nevada.

Juanita Brooks, ed., *Journal of the Southern Indian Mission.* Logan, Utah State Univ. Press, 1972.

Williams, William Sherley (Old Bill), mountain man (June 3, 1787-Mar. 21, 1849). B. in Rutherford County, North Carolina, he was educated and with the family moved to Missouri, settling near St. Louis in 1795. At 16 Bill moved among the Osage with Big Hill's band, married, fathered two daughters, and may have trapped southern Rockies rivers as early as 1807. Early in the War of 1812 he served as sergeant and scout with Company C, Mounted Rangers, along the Mississippi. Williams was interpreter at Fort Osage in 1817-18 and later at a post on the Marias des Cygnes River. He was instrumental in compiling an Osage-English dictionary for United Foreign Missionary Society people, but was not in print credited for his efforts at the time. He eventually declined to interpret the missionaries' sermons into Osage, and they "dared not preach without his approval." Williams eventually became a trader on the

Arkansas River among Osages and Kickapoos. In the fall of 1824 he headed for the Rocky Mountains, reaching a Hudson's Bay Company post on Clark's Fork of the Columbia; as a free trapper he worked with Jedediah Smith and other Ashley men, skirmishing with Blackfeet, killing some of them, acquiring the soubriquet "Old Bill" (he was then 37), and by 1825 was back with the Osages. In August he signed on a government expedition to chart the Santa Fe Trail, reaching Taos October 30. He trapped the Rio Grande, and perhaps the Gila that winter, then returned to the upper Rockies, trapped, skirmished some more with Blackfeet, and returned to New Mexico in the summer of 1826. Bill worked the Gila that winter, was robbed by Apaches, succored by the Zuñis, spent some time among the Navahos and returned to Taos. He trapped the upper Rockies again, returning to Taos about May 23, 1832, roamed the middle Rockies and Ute country, then, in 1832, trapped the southern Plains rivers. He again trapped the north country, then roamed the western New Mexico and Arizona regions, visiting the petrified forest and Grand Canyon, wintered in 1834-35 near what became known as Bill Williams Mountain, reached the Colorado and went north to Salt Lake, and resumed trapping the upper Rockies. In 1837 Williams explored what became known as Bill Williams Fork of Colorado, reached the 1838 rendezvous on the Popo Agie, spent several years among the Utes, and took part in the great 1840 horse raid on southern California ranchos. Bill spent 1841-42 in Missouri, returned to the Rockies, fought Blackfeet again, traded with the Shoshone and went back to Taos. Bill visited Oregon in 1843, went to California from Taos in 1844, fought the Modocs, guided Fremont (with Kit Carson) in 1845, roamed the Rockies some more, joined Major William W. Reynolds of the 3rd regiment, Missouri Mounted Rifles, for a military campaign against Utes and Plains Apaches, and was badly wounded in the arm. In November 1848, he was hired by Fremont for his fourth expedition at The Pueblo, on the Arkansas River, and after warning him that winter was no time to cross the Rockies, went with him anyway. He had a role in rescuing the expedition from disaster; with Dr. Benjamin J. Kern, the expedition's physician, Williams left Taos in February of 1849 to recover expedition property but the two were killed east of the Rio Grande and southwest of Mt. Blanca; their slayers probably were Utes with possible Mexican connivance. Williams was 6 feet, 1 inch in height, sinewy, of considerable power, his eyes blue and his hair red. He considered himself a "master trapper," and deserved the claim. He was probably the greatest character among the mountain men (made permanently famous by Ruxton), shot "plumb center" with a "double wobble," was slightly stooped, tireless, ever alert, wily, survivor of countless scrapes and adventures, and as well traveled and acquainted with the West as any man. He married or lived with a considerable succession of women, had a high-pitched, cracked voice, was an "impressive speaker," something of an actor, had a superior intelligence with a knowledge of Greek, Latin and comparative religion, and possessed a lively sense of humor. He prepared an account of his experiences among southwestern Indians, attempted water color sketching, but nothing save his Osage primer is known to have survived. He was twice painted by Edward M. Kern, neither work surviving. Bill loved children, was generous with his extensive knowledge, and in all things was a true mountain great.

Alpheus H. Favour, *Old Bill Williams: Mountain Man.* Norman, Univ. of Okla. Press, 1962; Robert V. Hine, *Edward Kern and American Expansion.* New Haven, Yale Univ. Presss, 1962; George Frederick Ruxton, *Life in the Far West.* Norman, Univ. of Okla. Press, 1951; Frederic E. Voelker article, MM, Vol. VIII.

Williamson, David, militia officer (1752-1814). B. near Carlisle, Pennsylvania, he moved beyond the Alleghenies as a boy and settled in Washington County southwest of Pittsburgh. He served in Dunmore's Division in Lord Dunmore's War, probably took part in the important affair at Point Pleasant, October 10, 1774, and by 1777 at 25 was a captain of county militia. Five years later he was a lieutenant colonel. Moravian missionaries had established several colonies of Christian Indians on the Muskingum River in eastern Ohio, the principal village being Gnadenhutten. Western Pennsylvania frontiersmen, suspecting these natives of border depredations, determined to break these colonies up. Late in 1781 Williamson led two companies of militia to the towns, captured some inhabitants and conveyed them to Fort Pitt where the Indians were detained briefly, then sent home. Williamson was criticized by frontier firebrands for his "leniency" in taking captives, this possibly affecting his judgment the following March. Between the Fort Pitt incident and late winter several fresh depredations were reported, arousing fury among some whites, although there was no evidence that Moravian Indians were responsible. In early March 1782 Williamson led 80 or 90 frontiersmen from Mingo Bottom to destroy the Moravian towns. It was, wrote Roosevelt, "just such an expedition as most attracted the brutal, the vicious and the ruffianly; but a few decent men, to their shame, went along." Within three days the whites seized Gnadenhutten, collecting there also a few Indians from nearby Salem although those of a third town, Schoenbrunn, escaped. The 96 bound prisoners were confined in two houses while a vote was taken as to their fate. The majority decreed death, though 18 voted against this, demanding that the Indian lives be spared and when overruled, withdrew, "calling God to witness that they were innocent of the crime about to be committed." Learning of white intentions, the Indians requested a short delay in which to prepare themselves for death. They prayed, asked forgiveness of each other for any wrongs they may have done and joined in hymns of hope and praise to God, when the butchery began. All 35 men, 27 women and 34 children were tomahawked, bludgeoned, scalped and burned as the houses were fired. Williamson was credited for the March 8 massacre by frontier Indian haters, and blamed by the more numerous decent folk. Roosevelt wrote that he was "physically a fairly brave officer and not naturally cruel; but he was weak and ambitious, ready to yield to any popular demand." Doddridge believed that had he possessed the authority of an army officer "I do not believe that a single Moravian Indian would have lost his life; but he possessed no such authority. He was only a militia officer, who could advise but not command." May 25, 1782, about 480 men, 320 of them from Washington County were mustered for a second expedition against the Ohio Indians, Williamson losing command to Colonel William Crawford (see entry) by a mere five votes. On the Sandusky River a

series of sharp actions with hostiles ensued, Crawford was captured to be burned at the stake in partial retaliation for the Gnadenhutten massacre for which he was in no way responsible, and Williamson brought the remnants of the command back to Mingo Bottom and the settlements. In 1785 he became a full colonel of militia and that year received most votes submitted to the state's Supreme Executive Council for judge of Donegal Township of Washington County, but was passed over because of "character defects." In 1787 he was elected sheriff of Washington County, and re-elected in 1789. In his advanced years he came on hard times, failed in business, died in poverty, and was buried in a cemetery on North Main Street, Washington, Pennsylvania, though "no stone marks the spot." Married, he had fathered four sons and four daughters.

Joseph Doddridge, *Notes on the Settlement and Indian Wars* (1912) reprint by McClain Printing Co., Parsons, W. Va., 1960; Theodore Roosevelt, *The Winning of the West.* N.Y., G.P. Putman's Sons, 1900, III; Consul W. Butterfield, *History of the Girtys.* Cincinnati, Robert Clarke & Co., 1890; Butterfield, *An Historical Account of the Expedition Against Sandusky Under Col. William Crawford in 1782.* Cincinnati, Clarke, 1873.

Williamson, Edward (Ned), scout (c. 1827-post 1876). B. in Pennsylvania, he was a civilian employee with Johnston's command in the so-called Mormon War of 1857 and guided Ficklin and ten men to the Bitterroot Valley of Montana that year in their effort to purchase beef, an endeavor which failed. Williamson spent the winter at Fort Owen. In 1860 he was at Walla Walla, Washington, and accompanied Maillet from there to Hell Gate (near present Missoula), Montana with a pack string of supplies. He became an expressman for Mullan, making important winter journeys to the Bitterroot Valley and later to Salt Lake City, revealing much ingenuity and hardiness in fulfilling his duties. In 1861 he was transporting whiskey to Fort Benton for the Indian trade and the next year joined a futile rush to the Marias River, Montana. In 1876 he was a trusted scout with Gibbon's column in the Sioux campaign, where he performed worthily several hazardous missions.

Montana Contributions, I, 1876, 40; II, 1896; III, 1900; IV, 1903; Granville Stuart, *Forty Years on the*

Frontier. Glendale, Calif., Arthur H. Clark Co., 1925; George F. Weisel, *Men and Trade on the Northwest Frontier.* Missoula, Mont. State Univ. Press, 1955.

Williamson, John, soldier (b. 1843). B. at Frederick, Maryland, he enlisted January 19, 1869, at Laramie, Wyoming, and was of the military escort accompanying the 1870 Washburn Yellowstone expedition. He was picked to accompany Warren Gillette and Charles Moore on a final search for the lost Truman Everts south of Lake Yellowstone. Williamson did not re-enlist.

Aubrey L. Haines, *Yellowstone National Park: Its Exploration and Establishment.* Wash., Nat. Park Service, 1974.

Williamson, Thomas S., missionary (Mar. 1800-June 24, 1879). B. in the Union District of South Carolina his father moved the family to Adams County, Ohio in 1805. Thomas was graduated from Jefferson College, Canonsburg, Pennsylvania, in 1820 and received a degree in medicine in 1824 from Yale, practicing for eight years at Ripley, Ohio. In 1833 he commenced the study of theology and was licensed to preach by the Presbytery of Chillicothe. He was appointed by the Foreign Mission Board of the Presbyterian Church to "proceed on an exploring tour among the Indians of the Upper Mississippi, with special reference to the Sacs and Foxes, but also to collect what information he could in reference to the Sioux, Winnebagos and other Indians." He reached Fort Snelling, Minnesota, in 1834 and there met Samuel and Gideon Pond, Indian missionaries. Williamson returned to Ohio and September 18, 1834, was ordained as an Indian missionary. The following spring he returned with his family to Fort Snelling, organizing there a Presbyterian church of 22 members and July 9 establishing a mission on the north side of the Minnesota River near Lac-qui-Parle. In 1839 he went to Cincinnati to superintend the printing of the Gospel of Mark in the Dakota language, later extending the work to other portions of the Bible. Williamson was invited in 1846 to establish a mission among the Sioux at Kaposia, Minnesota, four miles below St. Paul; these were Little Crow's people, the chief asking the agent for a missionary to curb evil tendencies among his followers. After the important treaty of 1851 Williamson established a mission at Yellow Medicine, in the upper Minnesota Valley, laboring there until the great Sioux war of 1862 when he escaped only with difficulty from the general massacre. Williamson then spent two years among the imprisoned Sioux at Davenport, Iowa. In 1866 he followed the Sioux to tne Missouri River, superintending establishment of missions and spending his last years in translating Scripture for the Indians; he lived to read proofs of the entire Bible in Dakota, although it was published after his death.

Edward Duffield Neill, *The History of Minnesota.* Minneapolis, Minn. Hist. Co., 1882.

Willie Boy, Morongo Indian (c. 1880-Oct. 14, 1909). B. in Nevada, Willie was of the Morongo band of Shoshone Indians called Serranos and settled with his family in a Southern California area now covered by the Joshua Tree National Monument. He worked as a cowboy, was a good baseball player and roamed a wide area of desert California. Because of infatuation with a daughter of Old Mike, a distant relative, Willie shot Mike on September 26, 1909, and kidnapped the daughter; he was followed in a somewhat spectacular pursuit by Indian and white posses; on September 30 he shot the girl and finally, after fleeing afoot an estimated 500 miles without being seen by his pursuers, shot himself on Ruby Mountain. He was 5 feet, 8 inches tall, weighed 150 pounds and had a scar on his chin where he had been shot about 1906 in an unremembered incident.

Rosemary Evans, "California's Last 'Old West' Manhunt." *True West,* Vol. 28, No. 4 (Mar.-Apr. 1981), 52-53.

Willis, Edward Banker, army officer (Jan. 9, 1831-Dec. 7, 1879). B. at New York City he went to California in 1850. August 24, 1861, he was mustered in as first lieutenant, Company A, 1st California Infantry, being promoted to captain September 5 and major May 5, 1863. He left San Diego with his company March 30, 1862, reaching Tucson June 6. Willis was sent with a detachment June 7 to the Mowry silver mine at Patagonia, Arizona, the officer assisting in the arrest of Mowry who was suspected of sedition tendencies; the detachment returned to Tucson July 2, 1862. By April 1863 Willis was at Las Cruces, New Mexico. He led a scout against the Navaho Indians in September. He was a member of the board named by Carleton to locate a site for the future Fort Whipple, Arizona. He left Fort Wingate November 7, 1863, arriving at the Little Chino Valley north of the present Prescott, Arizona, on December 23; Whipple was established initially in the valley but was relocated May 11, 1864, at its present site near Prescott. Willis had a fight with Apaches near the Salt River, Arizona, June 30, 1864. He was mustered out at Santa Fe September 5, 1864, the next day becoming a major in the 1st New Mexico Infantry, and a lieutenant colonel February 3, 1865. In January 1866 word was received by Willis, commanding Fort Selden, New Mexico, that a large band of Apaches had taken Janos, Chihuahua and Willis determined upon its relief. He organized an expedition of 50 infantrymen and 25 picked cavalrymen of Company M, 1st California Cavalry under Captain R.H. Orton. On the tenth day of forced marching the expedition reached the town at daylight, learning that the Indians, forewarned, had fled to the mountains. Citizens feted the troops for two days. Willis was honorably discharged at Santa Fe November 1, 1866. He became a civil engineer working in New Mexico, Arizona, California, Oregon and Washington Territory before removing to Omaha, Nebraska. He died at Fontenelle, Adair County, Iowa. Willis had married, but had no children.

AHS, Hayden File; Orton.

Willis, William Wesley, Mormon pioneer (Aug. 16, 1811-Apr. 8, 1872). B. in Hamilton County, Illinois, he early joined the Mormon church. He became third lieutenant of Company A, Mormon Battalion, being assigned to escort a contingent of ill men and being characterized as "heartless" in this endeavor. He reached the Salt Lake valley July 29, 1847, and settled with his family at Big Cottonwood.. In 1855 he was directed south to strengthen the Southern Indian Mission; he served one term as mayor of Cedar City, Utah, and died at Beaver, Utah.

Frank Esshom, *Pioneers and Prominent Men of Utah.* Salt Lake City, Western Epics, 1966; Juanita Brooks, ed., *Journal of the Southern Indian Mission.* Logan, Utah State Univ. Press, 1972.

Willson, Roscoe G., forest supervisor, columnist (July 13, 1879-Aug. 25, 1976). B. in Yellow Medicine County, Minnesota, the son of a country newspaper editor, he moved with his family to Grand Forks, Dakota Territory, in 1881. Willson went to Mexico and Guatemala in 1899, to Arizona in 1902 where he became supervisor of the Prescott, Coronado and Tonto National Forests in that territory and state, to Montana to become supervisor of the Madison National Forest. He was in the livestock commission field "for a couple of years" in Arizona and raised sheep briefly. After his retirement he commenced writing an historical column for the *Arizona Republic* where his work appeared from 1947 until his death. He published *No Place for Angels* (1958), a collection of his columns, and two pamphlet-volumes, *Pioneer and Well Known Cattlemen of Arizona* (1951, 1956), for the Valley National Bank of Phoenix, collections of brief biographies which earlier had appeared in the monthly magazine, *Cattlelog* of the Arizona Cattle Growers' Association.

Tucson Daily Citizen, Aug. 25, 1976.

Wilson, Benjamin David, adventurer, settler (Dec. 1, 1811-Mar. 11, 1878). B. at Nashville, Tennessee, he traded with the Choctaw and Chickasaw Indians from 15 at Yazoo City, Mississippi, then crossed the plains with the Rocky Mountain Fur Co., and reached Santa Fe in 1833. He trapped along the Gila and in Apache country for beaver in a company commanded by James Kirker; on a second trip with his own party, he was about 30 miles from the camp of Juan José Compá, when that Apache chief was assassinated, with a number of his people, by scalp hunters, loosing an Indian war upon all whites in the vicinity. Wilson's party was captured by Mangas Coloradas' Mimbres Apaches, but released, gaining Santa Fe where he learned details of the massacre resulting from the scalp hunters' blunder. Wilson narrowly missed slaughter in an 1837 revolt at Santa Fe in which Albino Perez, governor, was killed. In September 1841, he left for California in a company headed by John Rowland and William Workman, arriving at Los Angeles in November. He intended to go to China, but after three trips to San Francisco seeking a ship, abandoned that idea, purchasing a ranch on the site of present-day Riverside. In 1844 he married Ramona Yorba, daughter of Bernardo Yorba, an owner of the Santa Ana Ranch. He was seriously mauled by a grizzly bear, but recovered. On an expedition against Indians into the San Bernardino Mountains he and his vaqueros found a lake whose shores were "alive with bear," lassoed and strangled 11 of them, and named the body of water Big Bear Lake, which it still retains. On this expedition he and a hostile named Joaquin dueled, each was wounded, the Indian later killed and Wilson receiving a poisoned arrow in the shoulder. On a second expedition, near Agua Caliente, two purported renegades were killed at his instigation. On a third expedition he attacked a village of what turned out to be runaway Mission Indians; several were killed, while Wilson lost one man dead and another seriously wounded. He was involved in the Manuel Micheltorena disturbance of 1845, resulting in the Mexican General's departure for his homeland which left Wilson and his colleagues "perfectly satisfied with the result." As alcalde of his community Wilson was ordered to raise men to fight the Americans in 1846, but declined, never having become a citizen of Mexico. He was imprisoned during the operations coincident to the occupation of southern California. He moved north to Sutter's Fort, then returned to Los Angeles, engaged in merchandising, became the first clerk of Los Angeles County and the first mayor of Los Angeles. He later served as a state senator. He assembled a 1,200-acre fruit and vineyard ranch in the vicinity of present-day San Marino, deeding half of it to his first daughter in 1869.

Benjamin David Wilson's Observations on Early Days in California and New Mexico, foreword and notes by Arthur Woodward. Hist. Soc. of So. Calif. Ann. Pubn., 1934 (Vol. 16, No. 1) 74-150; Edwin H. Carpenter, "San Marino Rancho." Los Angeles Westerners *Branding Iron,* No. 110 (June 1973), 1, 4-5.

Wilson, Clarendon J.L., army officer (c. 1825-Feb. 21, 1853). B. near Leesburg, Virginia, he was graduated from West Point and became a brevet second lieutenant of the 1st Dragoons July 1, 1846, and a second lieutenant December 6. He won a brevet for gallantry at the skirmish at Embudo, New Mexico, January 19, 1847, and the assault on Taos February 4, 1847. Wilson performed frontier duty in California from 1848-50, then served under Captain Richard Stoddert (Baldy) Ewell at Las Lunas, New Mexico. Ewell commented privately that Wilson was "when

sober, an excellent officer, but unfortunately is a confirmed sot and sets such an example to my men that my trouble is doubled when he is present." Wilson died in New Mexico, aged 28.

Heitman, Cullum; *The Making of a Soldier: Letters of General R.S. Ewell,* ed. by Percy Gatling Hamlin. Richmond, Va., Whittet & Shepperson, 1935, 76.

Wilson, Jack: *see* Wovoka

Wilson, John, frontiersman (c. 1836-c. July 23, 1861). A Missourian, Wilson was hired by James Tevis, manager of the Apache Pass Overland Mail Company station. He may be the John Wilson listed in the 1860 Arizona census as b. in Canada and a sailor by profession until he reached the Southwest. José, a Mexican boy-captive of Cochise, was put up to assailing Wilson with a pistol, the instigator, according to Tevis, being Cochise himself. Wilson killed José. Wilson was of a party of seven headed by Freeman Thomas (in many histories called the Free Thompson party), who were trapped a mile west of Cooke's Spring, New Mexico, by Apaches led by Mangas Coloradas and perhaps Cochise; in a three-day fight, all of the whites were killed. Three men had sought to escape from their barricade, apparently toward the end of the siege. Thomas and Champion died within 60 yards of the shelter. Wilson reached 150 yards distance, badly wounded, "his course around the hill could be traced by the blood that flowed from his wounds."

James H. Tevis, *Arizona in the '50's.* Albuquerque, Univ. of New Mex. Press, 1954; Ray Brandes, "Mangas Coloradas: King Philip of the Apache Nation." *Troopers West,* San Diego, Frontier Heritage Press, 1970; W.W. Mills, *Forty Years in El Paso,* Rex Strickland, ed. El Paso, Carl Hertzog, 1962.

Wilson, John B. (Squire, Green), justice of the peace (c. 1821-post 1880). B. in Tennessee he served in the 1st Illinois Infantry in the Mexican War and from 1849 onward lived in New Mexico; he moved to Lincoln County, New Mexico, in 1873 and by 1876 was justice of the peace for Lincoln town. His "original" and unorthodox procedures made him a laughing stock, although he was honest and unbiased. Wilson was illegally deposed as justice of the peace on March 9, 1878, by

Governor Axtell at the behest of James J. Dolan. April 1, 1878, while working in his garden he was struck by a stray bullet during the killing of Sheriff William Brady. Wilson was sent by Governor Wallace to contact Billy the Kid regarding the proposal that the outlaw turn state's evidence. Wallace interviewed the Kid at Wilson's home on March 17, 1879. On May 7, 1880 Wilson and Billy the Kid were charged with horse theft at Albuquerque, but the charges were dismissed.

Robert N. Mullin notes; "Frank Warner Angel's Notes on New Mexico Territory 1878," ed. by Lee Scott Theisen. *Arizona and the West*, Vol. 18, No. 4 (Winter 1976), 333-70.

Wilson, Lemuel T. (Muddy), scout (c. 1843-post 1878). It is not certain that Lemuel T. and "Muddy" Wilson were the same man, but they might have been. Lemuel T. Wilson was one of a company of "Delawares and scouts" that accompanied 5th Infantry Captain Frank D. Baldwin in the 1874 Miles' operation that culminated in the so-called Battle of Lyman's Wagon Train; little is known of him otherwise to this writer. Muddy Wilson encountered the Oscar Williams surveying party near present Lubbock, Texas, on the Staked Plains in 1878, driving an ox team, speaking perfect English, explaining that he was a buffalo hunter enroute for Omaha since the big southern herd had been wiped out or fragmented to the point where it was unprofitable to hide hunt in that region. Since he was feeling poorly, he was doctored by G.H. Kent, of the Williams party, an amateur physician. The hunter gave an exhibition of his superb skill with a Sharps buffalo rifle; he said he had been born in the northeastern part of the Indian Territory, and probably was Delaware or, it may be, part-Delaware: Williams did not recollect clearly what people he was from. Wilson and a sister had been sent to Oberlin College, Ohio, she moving on to marry a naval officer then stationed at Portsmouth, New Hampshire, while Wilson had left the school, returned west, served as scout for the army "at some of the posts in Kansas," then had become a buffalo hunter and had made his headquarters for the past two years at Fort Concho (San Angelo, Texas), where he associated with Charlie Vroman. Wilson later gave another demonstration of his skill with a buffalo stand, inadvertently broken up by Kent to Wilson's

towering ire. A month later a postmaster at a frontier station told Williams there was a $1,500 reward out for Wilson for having killed two black soldiers at a Kansas army post some time earlier, but Williams never saw Wilson again. Williams was an honest, excellent observer and may be depended upon.

Nelson A. Miles, *Personal Recollections and Observations.* Chicago, Riverside Pub. Co., 1897, 164-80; G. Derek West, "Baldwin's Ride and the Battle of Lyman's Wagon Train." *10th Anniv. Pubn.,* London, English Westerners' Soc., 1964; Oscar Williams, 52-60.

Wilson, Luther, army officer (fl. 1860-1865). B. in Pennsylvania, he reached Colorado from Omaha in 1860 and the following August enlisted in the 1st Colorado Infantry (Cavalry), shortly being commissioned a second lieutenant and later becoming captain after service in the New Mexico campaigns. His only Indian fight was at Sand Creek, Colorado, November 29, 1864, when he was a battalion commander and was wounded early in the action. His deposition for a panel studying the massacre appears to be factual. *Sand Creek Massacre.*

Wilson, Richard, pioneer (c. 1830-Sept. 11, 1857). From Marion County, Arkansas, Wilson joined the Fancher emigrant wagon train at Fort Smith, Arkansas; it left in March 1857, and was destroyed by Mormons and Mormon-led Indians at Mountain Meadows, Utah, Wilson and all adults and children above the age of cognizance being murdered.

William Wise, *Massacre at Mountain Meadows.* N.Y., Thomas Y. Crowell Co., 1976.

Wilson, Robert Phillips, army officer (July 25, 1841-Mar. 21, 1926). B. at Philadelphia, Wilson was commissioned a lieutenant in the 3rd Pennsylvania Cavalry early in 1862. Later he was commissioned in the 5th U.S. Cavalry. At Brandy Station on August 1, 1863, he was wounded, captured, held in various Confederate prisons and was exchanged after seven months. He then contracted typhoid and pneumonia and was ill for six months, during which he reportedly developed an abcess of the left lung. He rejoined the 5th Cavalry and served with it to captain in Arizona and on the upper Plains, being characterized by Charles King as "an errant coward," who avoided "rough duty in Arizona by three successive leaves of absence, obtained Heaven only knows how," and sought to avoid what he construed to be dangerous Plains service said another "by swallowing blood from a self-induced nose bleed and then spitting it up to represent hemorrhaging of the lungs. The surgeons detected the deception, and Wilson's resignation was submitted as an alternative to facing charges of malingering." He resigned July 29, 1876, and when an attempt was made in 1880 to restore his commission, the facts came out in the *Army and Navy Journal* as penned by officers of the 5th, headed by Merritt, and with the endorsement of Crook and Sheridan. Wilson reported in a notarized statement in 1885 that he was "totally disabled" as a result of his illness, and was awarded a pension. He was married and fathered a daughter. He was 6 feet tall, dark complexioned, and was brevetted twice for Civil War actions.

Wilson military and pension records, Nat. Archives; Harry H. Anderson, "Charles King's *Campaigning with Crook.*" Chicago Corral of Westerners, *Brand Book,* Vol. XXXII, No. 9, (Jan. 1976), 65-67, 70-72.

Wilson, Sid, bronc rider (Aug. 21, 1879-Oct. 11, 1981). A onetime bronc rider with Buffalo Bill's Wild West Show, Wilson moved to Arizona in 1898 and except for seven years spent with Cody lived at Tombstone. He said he had once taken part in a command performance for Queen Victoria of England. Wilson owned a stagecoach line for a time near Tombstone and was mayor of the town in 1957-58. After 1977 his birthday was marked by a municipal event each year. Wilson died at 102 at Tombstone, being survived by his widow, a daughter and grand-children.

Arizona Daily Star, Oct. 14, 1981.

Wilson, Vernon Coke (Vic), lawman (May 1, 1857-Sept. 13, 1892). B. at Petersburg, Virginia, he enlisted as a private in the Texas Rangers in 1875. The following year he fought and killed "Seeley" Harris, a notorious cattle thief, being wounded twice in the leg in the process. Wilson was appointed chief of mounted inspectors for the district of Arizona and New Mexico by President Cleveland in 1885 and served a full four-year term. He was appointed special officer for the Southern Pacific Railway company April 1, 1880. Wilson was killed while attempting to capture train robbers Evans and Sontag at Sampton's Flats, Fresno County, California.

AHS archives.

Wilson, William (Billy), partisan (Nov. 23, 1861-c. 1911). B. in Trumbull County, Ohio, he became a cowboy in Texas and when 18 went to Lincoln County, New Mexico, where he bought a livery stable. Several months later he sold it to a man named West who paid him with four new $100 bills, Wilson cashing some of them before they were discovered counterfeit. Wilson then hid out in the Pecos River country eventually joining Billy the Kid and his partisans. He was arrested at least once for murder. He was arrested again at Stinking Springs December 23, 1880, turning over his new .44 to Pat Garrett who reportedly used that weapon later to kill Billy the Kid. Wilson was accused of passing counterfeit money; he was jailed at Santa Fe, convicted by a jury in Judge L. Bradford Prince's court and sentenced to 25 years. He escaped "following time-honored custom," and went to Texas where he became David L. Anderson, married, raised two children and was a respectable citizen. He was appointed a mounted inspector of the United States Customs Service August 1, 1891, at Langtry, Texas. His true identity shortly was discovered and it appeared he would be returned to New Mexico to serve out his time. William T. Thornton, who had been Wilson's attorney now was governor of New Mexico (1893-97) however, and he filed a petition with the U.S Attorney General seeking a Presidential pardon, supporting the request with about 25 letters on Wilson's behalf, including pleas from James J. Dolan (who had cashed the first of the spurious $100 bills), Pat Garrett and others. The pardon was granted July 24, 1896. Eventually Wilson became sheriff of Terrell County, Texas, and while unarmed was said to have been killed by a drunken cowboy. Wilson was buried at Bracketville, Texas. He had been described as of light complexion with light hair and bluish-grey eyes.

William A. Keleher, *Violence in Lincoln County.* Albuquerque, Univ. of New Mex. Press, 1957; Robert N. Mullin notes.

Wilson, William, scout (d. Sept. 17, 1868). Wilson on August 19, 1868, enlisted at Hays City, Kansas, in the "First Independent Company of Kansas State Militia," but soon left to join George A. Forsyth's command of about 50 scouts which engaged hostile Cheyennes and other Indians in the battle of Beecher Island near the present Wray, Colorado. Wilson was killed on the first day of the fight. He was buried on the island; when in December recovery of the bodies for reburial at Fort Wallace, Kansas, was attempted, Wilson's already had been removed, presumably by Indians, and was not relocated.

Blanie Burkey, *Custer, Come at Once!* Hays, Kan., Thomas More Prep, 1976; Simon E. Matson, ed., *The Battle of Beecher Island.* Wray, Colo., Beecher Island Battle Mem. Assn., 1960.

Wilson, William J., trail driver (1843-post 1920). B. on White River, Washington County, Arkansas, into a large family, he moved with his people in 1860 to Palo Pinto County, Texas, settling near Graford. While there Billy lost his right arm in a threshing machine accident, earning thereby the lasting soubriquet, One-armed Billy Wilson. He went to work for cattleman Charles Goodnight. In 1867 Goodnight and Oliver Loving with a longhorn herd started for Fort Sumner, New Mexico, where there was a beef market at the Bosque Redondo Navaho Reservation. Loving and Wilson went ahead of the herd to make firm the contract at Fort Sumner, but along the Pecos River they were jumped by Indians. Loving was shot in the arm and side, and believing the wound mortal, demanded Wilson return to the herd so it would be known what had become of him. Wilson, leaving most of his clothing concealed in order to float downstream past the Indians, eventually clambered out of the stream course and, barefoot, he struck out over the one hundred miles to where he believed he would find the herd. Goodnight at last discovered him, nearly dead from hardships and fatigue but able to give a coherent report. Loving meanwhile had been picked up by Mexican travelers and taken to Fort Sumner where he died of gangrene three weeks later. Wilson's account of this adventure appears in *Trail Drivers of Texas,* II, 908-13. He apparently still was living when the book was published in 1920.

Hunter TDT; E.A. Garner, "Bill Wilson's Getaway." *Frontier Times,* Vol. 42, No. 2 (Feb.-Mar. 1968), 21, 45-46.

Wilson, William J. (Buffalo Bill), assassin (d. Dec. 10, 1875). Reportedly a Texan, he reached Lincoln County, New Mexico, where on August 2, 1875, he assassinated, perhaps for pay, cattleman Robert Casey, from Mason County, Texas, who had criticized the Murphy organization. It was supposed that Casey's political enemies directed the killing. Wilson was the first individual legally hanged in Lincoln County, and it was a "ghastly bungle." Wilson was reportedly "about to accuse Murphy of instigating the Casey killing" when the trap was kicked from under him and he dropped. Believed dead, he was placed in a casket when signs of life were observed, whereupon he was hanged again, this time fatally; the incident thereafter was referred to as the "double hanging."

Robert N. Mullin notes; William A. Keleher, *Violence in Lincoln County.* Albuquerque, Univ. of New Mex. Press, 1957.

Winchell, Newton Horace, geologist, archeologist (Dec. 17, 1839-May 2, 1914). B. at Northeast, New York, he was graduated from the University of Michigan in 1866; he worked for the state geological survey of Michigan, 1869-70, and of Ohio,, 1870-72. He then was appointed state geologist of Minnesota where he served until 1900. His interests extended beyond his primary field to encompass botany, ethnology and archeology, and he was professor of geology at the University of Minnesota from 1874 until 1900. Winchell was an honest, very competent geologist, unafraid of controversy. In 1874 he was geologist for Custer's Black Hills expedition, serving under William Ludlow. His report, September 8, described the Black Hills geologically. While believing the area of future value, Winchell took reports from the expedition's prospectors of large amounts of gold "with a large grain of allowance." Asked to examine from a geologist's viewpoint the controversial Kensington Stone inscription of a purported Viking penetration of Minnesota in the 14th century, Winchell headed a committee of professionals that determined the runic inscription indeed appeared to be of ancient origin, perhaps 500 years old, and that there was no reason to question the veracity of the stone's discoverer as to the circumstances under which it was found. On this question Winchell's testimony is not to be lightly dismissed. The most valuable of his many geological and other investigations was said to be a study of the recession of the falls of St. Anthony at Minneapolis. Winchell believed because of his glacial and archeological findings that man had lived on the American continent during the most recent Ice Age, and perhaps much earlier, a view that did not win general acceptance for three quarters of a century, but now is more widely held. Winchell was a founder of the American Geological Society, and of its periodical, the *American Geologist,* which for a time he edited. In addition he wrote *Catalogue of the Plants of the State of Michigan* (1861); *The Iron Ores of Minnesota* (1891) with his son, Horace Vaughn Winchell, also a geologist, and *The Aborigines of Minnesota* (1911). He died at Minneapolis.

Who Was Who; DAB; EA; Minn. Hist. Soc. Archives, St. Paul; *Minn. Hist. Soc. Collecs.,* Vol. XV, 1915.

Winders, Robert Jackways, miner (c. 1822-post 1882). Winders was a prospector and miner who settled at Tombstone, Arizona, and became a partner of Wyatt, Virgil and James Earp in several mining and claim ventures about 1881.

Great Register of Cochise County, Ariz., 1881.

Windolph, Charles, soldier (Dec. 9, 1851-Mar. 11, 1950). B. at Bergen, Germany, he apparently enlisted in the 2nd Infantry, deserted, and at Brooklyn, New York, or Nashville, Tennessee, enlisted in the 7th Cavalry under the name of Charles Wrangel in July 1872, with Captain F.W. Benteen the enlistment officer. His enlistment was cancelled when his earlier service was revealed, but it seems he enlisted again in the 7th Cavalry. Windolph was on the Custer 1874 Black Hills expedition and in the Sioux campaign from May to September 1876. In this he won a Medal of Honor at Reno Hill during the Custer affair when "with three comrades, during the entire engagement (he) courageously held a position that secured water for the command." He also was wounded in this fight. Windolph was in the Nez Perce 1877 campaign. He was discharged March 21, 1883, as first sergeant of Troop H, 7th Cavalry. He worked for the Homestake Mining Company at Lead, South Dakota, for 49 years. He was buried in the Black Hills National Cemetery; Windolph

was married and survived by a son and two daughters. He was 5 feet, 6 inches, in height, with brown hair and eyes and a dark complexion.

No. Dak. Hist., Vol. 16, No. 2 (Apr. 1949). 76n3; BHB.

Windsor, Richard, soldier (fl. 1804-post 1829). He enlisted from Kentucky January 1, 1804, in the Lewis and Clark Expedition, previously having been a soldier. Windsor was a dependable man whose life incidentally was saved June 7, 1805 by Lewis when Windsor had become trapped on a slippery precipice and the captain coolly "talked" him to safety. Windsor settled for a time after the expedition in Missouri but soon moved to Illinois from where he served in the War of 1812 in the ranger company of Captain James B. Moore; whether he saw action is not known. Later he enlisted in the regular army where he served until 1819. From 1825 to 1829 according to Clarke he was living in the Sangamon River valley of Illinois. He does not appear to have taken part in the Black Hawk War of 1832, but when and where he died is unknown.

History of the Expedition Under the Command of Lewis and Clark, ed. by Elliott Coues. N.Y., Dover Pubns., 1965; Clarke, *Lewis and Clark; Trans. of Ill. State Hist. Soc. (1904),* 190-95.

Winema: *see* Tobey Riddle

Winnemucca, Chief (Old Winnemucca, Mubetawaka, Po-i-to), Northern Paiute (c. 1805-Oct. 21, 1882). B. near Humboldt Lake in the present Nevada, Winnemucca became chief of the Paviotso, or Northern Paiute Indians who at the time held the western half of Nevada. He was not the son of Captain Truckee (although Sarah Winnemucca believed he was), and the two were contemporaries, although Chief Winnemucca counted among his several wives a daughter of Truckee, it was reported. Little is known of his early life, although he became a figure of prominence as emigrant traffic developed across territory his people claimed in the middle 19th century. Winnemucca traveled among the Bannocks to the north and on one occasion was camped near the gold camp of Bannack, Montana when an attack upon his community by unruly whites was averted narrowly; he had laid an ambush for them if they launched the assault and might have accounted for many of them. In the spring of 1863 he went on his first buffalo hunt with the Bannocks onto the northern plains; the James Stuart party met him and the Bannocks near the Ruby River on their return. Despite uncounted provocations he remained persistently for peace with the whites and generally was regarded as non-warlike and trustworthy by them. Winnemucca became involved to some extent in the ghost dance movement of the late 1870s and may have helped it spread into Idaho, but he never was an ardent participant. Winnemucca attributed his final illness to being bewitched by a young wife, and a few days after his demise she and her 3-year-old child were stoned to death by the tribe as punishment. Winnemucca died at Coppersmith Station, Nevada.

Robert F. Heizer, "Notes on Some Paviotso Personalities." Carson City, Nev., *Nevada State Mus. Anthropol. Papers No. 2,* Jan. 1960; Jack D. Forbes, *Nevada Indians Speak.* Reno, Univ. of Nev. Press, 1967; *Montana, Contributions,* I (1876), 154-56.

Winnemucca, Sarah, Paiute woman (1844-Oct. 16, 1891). Of the Paiute (Paviotso) tribe of western Nevada, she was b. in the vicinity of Humboldt Lake. She claimed that her father was Chief Winnemucca, although this is disputed; if she was the granddaughter of Fremont's Chief Truckee as she said, she could not have been daughter of Winnemucca since the two were contemporaries and so far as is known there was no relationship between them. The band in which Sarah grew up was centered around Humboldt and Pyramid lakes, and sometimes was known as Winnemucca's Band. In 1860 Sarah and her sister entered a Catholic school at San Jose, California, remaining only a few weeks because of prejudice against Indian children and returning to the band which in 1864 was confined nominally to a reservation around Pyramid Lake. In 1865 the family lived at Dayton, Nevada, and about this time Sarah's mother and sister died. Sarah, who spoke excellent English and had some knowledge of reading and writing, about 1868 acted as interpreter for an Indian agent to the Shoshone and later became interpreter and messenger for O.O. Howard during the Paiute and Bannock hostilities of 1877-78 when no man could be found to negotiate with the Indian belligerents. She was instrumental in bringing Chief Winnemucca's band out of the hostile camp in Oregon. January 26, 1880, Sarah became interpreter at the Malheur Agency of Oregon but remained less than a year, in 1881 starting a school for Indian children at Vancouver Barracks, Washington. Sarah had visited Washington, D.C., in 1879-80 with Chief Winnemucca who sought permission for his people to return from Washington Territory to the Malheur Reservation; this was granted by the Secretary of the Interior but thwarted by the Yakima agent. In 1881-82 Sarah again went east, lecturing at Boston and elsewhere, condemning the practices of Indian agents and winning sympathy for her people and indignation over the injustices done them. To further this endeavor she wrote *Life Among the Piutes: Their Wrongs and Claims* (1883). She had married Edward Bartlett, a lieutenant (perhaps the Edward Courtney Bartlett of the 1st Calvary who had resigned his commission in 1871), but the couple separated after a year and she married a Paiute man. This marriage too failed and she married a Lieutenant Lambert H. Hopkins, probably a volunteers officer who assisted in the writing of her book. Her attacks against Indian agents and exploiters of her people were met by savage counter-charges against her character, but these were refuted by Howard and other distinguished officers for whom she had bravely worked in the field. With aid received during her eastern tours lands were purchased near Lovelock, Nevada, and an Indian school established which she operated for three years. Here her husband died of tuberculosis in 1886 and was buried in the Lone Mountain cemetery. Sarah thereupon left the school and went to live with a sister at Monida, Montana, where she died. She was afflicted with failing mental and physical powers late in her life.

Hodge, HAI; Virginia Cole Trenholm, Maurine Carley, *The Shoshonis.* Norman, Univ. of Okla. Press, 1964.

Winship, George Parker, bibliographer, historian (July 29, 1871-June 22, 1952). B. at Bridgewater, Massachusetts, he was educated at Harvard and as an undergraduate became interested in the Coronado expedition into the southwest. He came under the influence of Professor Edward Channing in the Seminar of American History; Channing suggested the subject, provided "constant guidance and inspiration, and his persistent refusal to consent to any abandoning of the work before the results had been expressed in a manner worthy of the university" kept Winship diligently at his project. It was published in 1896 by the Bureau of American Ethnology and remains today a definitive collection of primary sources on Coronado's endeavor. Even before its BAE appearance it had been accepted for publication by the Department of History at Harvard. Winship became best known as a bibliographer and specialist in rare books. He catalogued the private collection of the John Carter Brown Library of Brown University. Later he was librarian of the Widener Collection at Harvard and still later assistant librarian at Harvard in the field of rare books. Among his numerous publications, those of frontier interest include: *Coronado's Journey to New Mexico and the Great Plains* (1894, 1908, 1911); *Some Facts About John and Sebastian Cabot* (1900); *Sailors' Narratives of Voyages Along the New England Coast, 1524-1624* (1905); the *Eliot Indian Tracts* (1923) and *The First American Bible* (1929).

New York Times, June 24, 1952; Winship, *The Coronado Expedition, 1540-1542*. BAE, 14th Ann. Rep., Wash., Govt. Printing Office, 1896.

Winslow, Edward, pilgrim leader, frontiersman (Oct. 18, 1595-May 8, 1655). B. at Droitwich, Worcestershire, England, he reached America on the *Mayflower* in 1620 and was a founder of Plymouth Colony. He aided in the first explorations of the surrounding wilderness, was the pilgrim envoy in meeting Massasoit in the spring of 1621 and made the colonists' first treaty with that Wampanoag chief, becoming his trusted friend; at one time he probably saved Massasoit's life. The initial contact between the great Indian and the colonials, each side fearful of the other's intent, was made on Winslow's initiative and successfully concluded. Within two years of his arrival in Massachusetts, Winslow sent to England four narratives of his dealings with Indians and his explorations, published as *A Relation or Journal of the beginning and proceedings of the English Plantation setled at Plimoth in New England* (1922). He made a trip to England in 1623, returning with the first cattle to be introduced into the Massachusetts region. In 1624 he returned to England again

as agent for the colony, writing *Good News from New England...* (1625), a promotional tract designed to encourage emigration to that colony. In 1627 he and others assumed the new settlement's debts in return for trading privileges, Winslow often thereafter undertaking trading expeditions to the Penobscot and Kennebec rivers in Maine. Knowing the wilderness better than any other white man of his time, he was said to have been the first Englishman to visit Connecticut and traded on the Connecticut River. In 1629 he became the colony's agent and in this capacity made several trips to England, sometimes defending colonial interests in court; at one time he was imprisoned for four months for presumed civil infractions, but this fate was shared by many another who somehow fell afoul of the complicated and often unfair laws of the time. Winslow was governor of Massachusetts for three terms and aided in formation of the New Englnd Confederation. He returned to England once more in 1646 and remained there, among other things laboring for the civilization and conversion of the Indians. His 1649 publication, *The Glorious Progress of the Gospel among the Indians in New England* led largely to establishment of the important Society for the Propagation of the Gospel in New England, in which Winslow was an incorporator. This organization supported missions, printed Bibles and other books in an Indian language, and maintained schools for them. In 1654 Oliver Cromwell named Winslow chairman of a commission to investigate damages to English vessels by the Dutch in Denmark. Late that year he was appointed chief of three commissions to capture the Spanish West Indies, the fleet seizing Jamaica. On the return voyage Winslow died of fever and was buried at sea.

Literature abundant; Thwaites, JR, XXXVI, 238-39n8; George F. Willison, *Saints and Strangers*. N.Y., Reynal & Hitchcock, 1945.

Winslow, John, trader, colonist (1597-1674). B. at Droitwich, Worcestershire, England, he was Edward Winslow's second brother and reached America in November 1621, being married there six years later to Mary Chilton. In 1651 he became agent, or Indian trader, at Kennebec, in Maine, remaining in that position until 1654. During this period he was host and warmly befriended the Jesuit, Gabriel Druillettes and his sometimes colleague, the Montagnais chief Noel Taga-bamat, who came to the English colonies from Canada in 1650-51 seeking assistance for the French in their struggle against the Mohawks. Although Winslow personally favored the endeavor, it was not pursued by the English colonials. Winslow supported the Jesuit's missionary work among the Kennebec Abenaki since he was "not at all inclined to trade" but rather to convert the Indians and he "admired his courage." More than a year later the natives of Norridgewock, Maine, com-plained that although the priest had urged temperance upon them, as quickly as he left the English brought in brandy again for trade purposes, and they complained to Winslow about it. In 1655 or 1656 Winslow settled in Boston, where he died, prominent as a merchant and ship owner. He had fathered 10 children.

Thwaites, JR, XXXI, 189, 205-207; XXXVI, 85-99, 238n7; XXXVIII, 35-37; George F. Willison, *Saints and Strangers.* N.Y., Reynal & Hitchcock, 1945.

Winters, William Henry, army officer (c. 1843-June 12, 1880). B. in Ohio, he enlisted in the 6th Ohio Infantry in 1861, was commis-sioned promptly and became a captain in 1862, when he resigned and enlisted in Company I, 1st Cavalry; he was commis-sioned a second lieutenant in March 1865, rising to captain by 1873. In 1866 Winters was in charge of Camp Wallen, Arizona, in the center of hostile Chiricahua county. He led a scout after Apaches who had depredated near Santa Cruz, overtook them on December 14 and killed some; Winters was "highly commended" by McDowell for this action. He was frequently engaged in scouts after hostiles. When Chiricahuas presumably under Cochise killed several stagecoach passengers in October 1869 and stole more than 200 cattle from a Texas herd nearby, Winters led the pursuit, recovering the cattle, killing a dozen enemy and reportedly wounding Cochise. In 1870 he was married to Mrs. Kate E. Walker of Washington, D.C., at Tucson, Bourke describing the affair with his customary droll urbanity. The next year, after five years in Arizona, Winters and his wife went east, where he was on recruiting duty at Cleveland for some time. As a captain Winters took part in Howard's Nez Perce campaign, having a role in the battle of the Clearwater although he

apparently did not make the arduous trip over the Lolo Trail in pursuit of the hostiles. He also was involved in the Bannock War of 1878.

AHS archives; Lansing B. Bloom, editor, "Bourke on the Southwest." *New Mex. Hist. Rev.,* Vol. IX, No. 1 (Jan. 1934), 73; Helen Addison Howard, Dan L. McGrath, *War Chief Joseph.* Lincoln, Univ. of Nebr. Press, 1964; Prescott, *Arizona Miner,* July 13, 1867.

Winther, Oscar Osburn, historian (Dec. 22, 1903-May 22, 1970). B. in eastern Nebraska he was taken at 9 by his Danish parents to Eugene, Oregon, in 1925 was graduated from the University of Oregon and in 1928 earned a master's degree from Harvard. He received his doctorate from Stanford University in 1934. Winther was curator for a year of the San Francisco Wells Fargo Bank historical collection and in 1937 moved to the University of Indiana, specializing in the history of the trans-Mississippi west. By 1965 he was honored with the designation of University Professor. During summers he taught at a variety of universities and colleges from Alaska to Birmingham, England, served as president of the Western History Association and was managing editor of the *Mississippi Valley Historical Review* and *The Journal of American History* from 1963 to 1966. He died of cancer. Among his many publications were: *Express and Stagecoach Days in California: From the Gold Rush to the Civil War* (1936); *The Trans-Mississippi West: A Guide to Its Periodical Literature (1811-1938)* (1942); *Via Western Express & Stagecoach* (1945); *The Great Northwest: A History* (1947); *The Old Oregon Country: A History of Frontier Trade, Transportation, and Travel* (1950), and *The Transportation Frontier: Trans-Mississippi West, 1865-1890* (1964).

Dwight L. Smith, "Oscar Osburn Winther: 1903-1970." *Arizona and the West,* Vol. 14, No. 3 (Autumn 1972), 211-14.

Winthrop, John, governor (Jan. 12, 1588-Mar. 26, 1649). B. at Edwardstone, Suffolk, England, he was graduated from Cambridge, practiced law, developed Puritan interests and in 1630 arrived at Salem, Massachusetts, aboard the *Arbell,* shortly founding a settlement which became Boston. He served as governor of the Massachusetts Bay Colony for about a dozen one-year terms. The frontier interest in his career is minimal after the early years, but "the force of his influence on the history of Massachusetts was enormous." He was one of the originators of the New England Confederation. Winthrop was a man of high intelligence, good breeding, integrity and compassion, although he had little faith in democracy and believed that officials, once chosen, "should govern according to their own best judgment." He was married three times, his first wife dying in 1615, the second in 1617 and the third in 1647.

Literature abundant.

Winthrop, John, colonial leader (Feb. 12, 1606-Apr. 5, 1676). B. at Groton, Suffolk, England, he was the son of John Winthrop (1588-1649) who was many times governor of Massachusetts, and himself frequently chosen governor of Connecticut. Like his father, Winthrop studied and practiced law, but his wide interests were focused more upon medicine and science. He was a member of the Duke of Buckingham's unsuccessful expedition against La Rochelle, France, in 1627, then migrated to Massachusetts where he arrived in November 1631. He represented the settlements in England in 1634 and returned the following year as governor of a new colony in the Connecticut valley, centered upon a fort built at Saybrook. Winthrop's distinguished career thereafter had little frontier orientation. He attempted to found such industries as iron works and believed that the future of New England lay in manufacturing and commerce rather than in agriculture. Winthrop was "probably the most versatile" New Englander of his day, "one of the ablest and most interesting of his own generation," was popular and generally respected.

Literature abundant.

Wister, Owen, writer (July 14, 1860-July 21, 1938). B. in Germantown, Pennsylvania, of intellectual parents, he was well educated, had traveled and studied abroad and was graduated from Harvard in 1882, determined upon a musical career. To improve his health however he traveled to the West in 1885, spending time at a Buffalo, Wyoming, ranch and summers in the region for many years thereafter; from this custom came the material for his western writings. The first of these, a short story called "Hank's Woman," appeared about 1891. He published a collection of stories, *Red Men and White* (1896), *Lin*

McLean 1898), the *Jimmyjohn Boss* (1900) and his most famous work, *The Virginian,* in 1902, it becoming "a model and a high-water mark in cowboy fiction," and helping establish the cowboy as a folk hero, a legend which has endured to the present. It was set in Wyoming and was said to be based in part on the Powder River War. This was his last western novel, although *When West Was West,* another collection of short pieces, was published in 1928. His other writing continued productively as did his sometimes angry public career. In 1939 a peak in the Teton Range of Wyoming was named for him. He died at North Kingstown, Rhode Island, and was buried at Philadelphia.

Literature abundant: DAB; CE.

Wittick, Ben photographer (Jan. 1, 1845-Aug. 30, 1903). B. at Huntingdon, Pennsylvania, his family moved in 1854 to Moline, Illinois, and in 1861, though only 16, he enlisted in the 1st Minnesota Volunteers at Fort Snelling, Minnesota; later he saw action against the Sioux on the North Plains. Wittick learned photography from a local practitioner of the art at Moline, Illinois, and soon went into business for himself. When the Atlantic and Pacific Railroad needed a photographer, Wittick was hired and in 1878 was at Santa Fe, New Mexico; later he formed a partnership with Charles P. Russell and settled down briefly, made a tour of Mexico, then returned to Santa Fe. He became interested in recording Indians, photographed the Hopi Snake Dance, was a member of the Stevenson Expedition and photographed the Grand Canyon. He was an early explorer of the Supai Canyon and was said to be the first to photograph the Havasupai Indians. About 1885 he photographed Manuelito, a Navaho chief, later took pictures, he said, of many Apaches and set up a studio at Fort Wingate, New Mexico. He died of snake bite. He was an important photographer, but not above lifting as his own the work of others. Richard Rudisill, of the Museum of New Mexico at Santa Fe, an authority on Wittick's work, said Wittick copied and claimed the work of other photographers; for example, the famous picture of Geronimo kneeling and holding his rifle, claimed by Wittick, was made by Randall, and others of the same background were similarly mis-attributed. Randall had visited San Carlos when the pictures were made.

Roland J. Cesarini, "Ben Wittick: Adventurer with a Camera." *Arizoniana*, Vol. II, No. 2 (Summer 1961), 21-22; Angie Debo, *Geronimo*. Norman, Univ. of Okla. Press, 1976, 211n.

Wiwurna, (Waourene, Ouaourene, Sheepscot John), Abenaki chief (c. 1671-post 1738). A "warm friend" of the French, Wiwurna was termed "shrewd and sagacious" by Thwaites, "an unschooled Talleyrand" by Sylvester and "mannerly" by Parkman, all descriptions apparently containing a measure of truth. He was spokesman for the Norridgewock band of his people in meetings with the English and French, largely over encroachments by the former into Abenaki territory in Maine, and the English right or lack of justification for building forts and settlements there. The Jesuit, Sebastian Rale naturally supported Wiwurna at all points; the English opposed him. Wiwurna may have been active in a "war" between his people and the English in 1722 and the next year during a visit to Quebec, Governor Vaudreuil presented him with a lace cap in recognition of his services to the French. He at length granted the English some rights on lands he regarded as his people's, and ratified a peace with them in 1727. He visited Boston in July 1738 when he addressed the council and drank the king's health.

Thwaites, JR, LXVII, 334n12; Sylvester, III, 182; Parkman, *A Half Century of Conflict*, 225-28; DCB, II.

Wolcott, Francis Edwin (Frank), army officer, partisan (Dec. 13, 1840-Mar. 30, 1910). B. at Canandaigua, New York, he enlisted as a private in the 2nd Ohio Infantry in April 1861, was commissioned the following year and was mustered out in 1866 a major and judge advocate, U.S. Volunteers. He lived at Covington, Kentucky, until March 1870 when he moved to Cheyenne, Wyoming, where he became receiver of the U.S. Land Office; in 1872 he became U.S. marshal for Wyoming. He served until 1875 when he was removed, Governor John M. Thayer explaining Wolcott had become "offensive to almost the whole people." The next year Wolcott moved to Tolland, Wyoming, where he operated the Scottish-owned VR Ranch on a tributary of the North Platte. Tension rose in the late 1880s between owners and operators of small and big cattle operations, with the latter alleging wholesale rustling by the nesters, little

of which was ever documented. On July 4, 1891, Wolcott proposed to cattleman John Clay "a lynching bee," in a plan "so bold and open" that Clay asked that he be spared involvement. Wolcott was in the forefront of planning the so-called Johnson County "Invasion," and was its nominal leader, although actual leadership usually devolved upon Frank Canton,, a woolier man, and W.C. Irvine. Wolcott, whom Smith calls "the bloodthirsty little rooster" (he was 5 feet, 6 inches tall), went to Denver to meet and bring to Wyoming 22 Texas gunmen to form the backbone of the invading forces which pulled out of Cheyenne April 5, 1892. Wolcott had been chosen commander "for no visible reason" except for his military record of 25 years earlier and "the violence of his opinions." "He was temperamentally unfit to lead men, and his stubbornness and bad judgment...doomed the expedition to failure." After the debacle of the open invasion, Wolcott continued his efforts to swamp out the Johnson County opponents by martial law, massive indictments or other schemes, but all failed. Wolcott lived at Douglas and Sheridan, Wyoming, until 1894, then moved to Nebraska where he became a general agent at the Omaha Stockyards from 1894. He lived at Grand Island and Lincoln, Nebraska, from 1900 until his death at Denver when he was described as a "merchant." Wolcott had married in 1880 and fathered a daughter who, with his widow, survived him. He was slight of build with brown hair that turned grey in later years, brown eyes and dark complexion.

Wolcott pension record, Nat. Archives; Helena Huntington Smith, *War on Powder River*. N.Y., McGraw-Hill Book Co., 1966.

Wolfskill, John Reid, frontiersman (c. 1805-June 1897). B. in Madison County, Kentucky, Wolfskill moved with his family to Boone's Lick, and about 1828 went with his brother, William Wolfskill, to Santa Fe, spending most of his life in the southwest. He returned to Missouri in 1833, but after two years re-entered the Santa Fe trade; by 1836 he was in Sonora, working for a time as money guard between major north Mexico cities. At Oposura (Moctezuma) where he had gone on a mule-purchasing expedition with Charles Ames, he became acquainted with John Johnson and with him left there on April 3,

1837, on a plundering expedition against Apache camps to the north. On April 22, at Juan José Compá's rancheria in the Animas Mountains of today's New Mexico, the Johnson people by treachery killed a reported 20 Indians, wounding others, and touching off a prolonged series of Apache hostilities; the whites were run out of the mountains by the aroused Apaches. Wolfskill left Santa Fe October 17, 1837, with a 33-man party and on February 14 reached Los Angeles. He became acquainted with Jonathan Trumbull Warner, and once saved his life in a political disorder. In 1840 Wolfskill journeyed to northern California in search of agricultural land; ultimately he was responsible for William Wolfskill's acquiring a 17,754 acre grant on Putah Creek (obtainable because William was a citizen of Mexico; John was not), and eventually received half of that estate, where he followed agricultural pursuits until his death. He had become "one of the leading citizens of the Sacramento Valley region" by that time.

Iris Higbie Wilson, *William Wolfskill.* Glendale, Calif., Arthur H. Clark Co., 1965; Bancroft, *Pioneer Register;* Rex Strickland, "The Birth and Death of a Legend: The Johnson 'Massacre' of 1837." *Arizona and the West,* Vol. 18, No. 3 (Autumn 1976), 257-86.

Wolfskill, William, mountain man, pioneer (Mar. 20, 1798-Oct. 3, 1866). B. in Madison County, Kentucky, he was taken to Missouri by his parents, but returned to Kentucky for schooling in 1815. In 1822 he and others joined William Becknell for the journey to Santa Fe, Wolfskill trapping through the southwest until late in 1824 when he purchased horses and mules in Chihuahua, eventually selling them in Alabama. He reached Missouri again in 1826. He returned to New Mexico with Ewing Young that summer, trapped along the Gila, then drove horses from Sonora to Independence, Missouri. He returned to Taos, applied for Mexican citizenship in 1830, and took a party of trappers to California in September, reaching Los Angeles in February 1831, charting the so-called Old Spanish Trail in doing so. He endeavored unsuccessfully to hunt sea otter, using for that purpose a schooner he and Joseph Chapman had built. Wolfskill then settled in the Los Angeles area, experimented with fruit culture, vineyards, helping develop a cattle ranch in central California. He became a

factor in the economic development of the region. He died at Los Angeles.

Iris Higbie Wilson article, MM, Vol. II; Bancroft, *Pioneer Register;* Wilson, *William Wolfskill.* Glendale, Calif., Arthur H. Clark Co, 1965.

Woll, Adrian, soldier of fortune (1795-1875). B. at Saint Germain, Paris, France, he reached Baltimore in 1816 bearing an introduction to General Winfield Scott, but since no opening existed in the American Army, he went to Mexico in 1817 with the Francisco Xavier Mina expedition which sought to win independence for that country but ended in Mina's execution at Mexico City. With Mexico's later achievement of independence, however, Woll became naturalized and joined the fledgling army. By 1832 he had become a colonel, and after successful operations in Mexican civil strife was named Brigadier General on December 25 of that year. He became a friend and supporter of Santa Anna. He was sent to the San Jacinto battlefield after the engagement to learn particulars of it, was captured by Texans, then released. In September 1842, he invaded Texas with 1,000 men, capturing San Antonio, but suffered a repulse at the battle of the Salado east of that city, and withdrew to Mexico. Woll took part in the Mexican War, returned to France, but came back to Mexico to become governor of Tamaulipas and its military commander from 1853 to 1855. In 1863 he was one of the commission which offered the throne of Mexico to the Archduke Maximilian; with the fall of that regime, Woll returned to France, where he died.

HT; *Porrua.*

Wood, Abraham, militia officer, explorer (c. 1608-c. 1681). His exact date of b. is unknown as is its place, but he may have come to Virginia from England in 1620 as an indentured servant and remained in the vicinity of Jamestown for at least five years. Eventually he became one of the major landholders of the colony and held occasional political office, being a member of the House of Burgesses for Henrico County, 1644-46. In 1646 he became captain of militia at Fort Henry (Petersburg), obtaining in return the fort and 600 acres of land; a decade later he was colonel of the Charles City and Henrico regiment, actively engaged in Indian fighting. In 1671 he became a Major General. Despite military and political activities he was primarily a frontier trader and as such not only undertook explorations himself, but sent small parties into the wilderness. August 27, 1650 Wood was of a group that left Fort Henry to reach the Tuscarora settlements in the present North Carolina, and in 1652 he secured Assembly permission to explore areas "where no English have ever been and discovered." In 1671 he sent out Thomas Batts and Robert Fallam to seek "the waters on the other side of the Mountains in order to discover of the South Sea." It is generally believed that they crossed the Blue Ridge and reached Peters' Falls in the present Giles County, southwestern Virginia, land drained by the Mississippi. They carved their initials on trees, but found they were not the first to do so; they discovered the initials MA and NI carved on another tree on a branch of the New River, a tributary to the Ohio, so they were not the first of the English to touch upon the Mississippi Valley though no one knows who preceded them; Batts and Fallam at least were first of record. In 1673 Wood sent out James Needham of South Carolina and Gabriel Arthur, probably a servant indentured to Wood. They went south to the Yadkin, then west to the headwaters of the Tennessee reaching a village of the Tomahitan Cherokee, who already had muskets obtained from the Spanish to the south. Needham returned to Fort Henry while Arthur remained to learn the Cherokee language; Needham again was sent out by Wood but was killed in January 1674 by a Cherokee; Arthur was captured, taken as far north as the Ohio, wounded by an arrow, cured by the Shawnees as is supposed, probably traversed the Cumberland Gap (the first white man to do so), wandered down the Tennessee and eventually gained Virginia again. Unfortunately he was illiterate and what is known of his rambles is what he remembered and later told. Wood continued his interest in the frontier country as long as he lived. In March 1680 he conducted negotiations with Indians that threatened to become hostile and it is believed he died "shortly after this time."

Harriette Simpson Arnow, *Seedtime on the Cumberland*. N.Y., Macmillan Co., 1960; Douglas L. Rights, *The American Indian in North Carolina*. Winston-Salem, No. Car., John F. Blair, 1957; Clarence W. Alvord, Lee Bidgood, *First Explorations of the Trans-Alleghany Regions by the Virginians*. Cleveland, Arthur H. Clark Co., 1912; DAB; REAW; John R. Swanton, *The Indians of the Southeastern United States*. Wash., BAE Bull. 137, 1946.

Wood, Charles Erskine Scott, army officer, writer (Feb. 20, 1852-Jan. 22, 1944). B. at Erie, Pennsylvania, he was graduated from West Point in 1874 and commissioned a second lieutenant in the 21st Infantry, being assigned to Fort Bidwell, California, and then to Fort Vancouver, Washington. Wood became aide-de-camp and sometimes secretary to Howard in the Nez Perce War and was present at the climactic battle at the Bear Paw Mountains of Montana where Wood personally took down Chief Joseph's moving surrender speech as translated for him. Being of an intellectual and literary turn of mind it is possible he edited or "improved" it somewhat before it appeared in Howard's official report. McWhorter reproduces Wood's description of the scene as written to him in a 1936 letter. Wood continued to serve Howard as aide in the Bannock and Paiute campaigns of 1878 (becoming a first lieutenant that year) although he was "bitterly opposed to the corruption of the Indian Ring of Washington," and came to feel he was supporting an unworthy cause. When Howard was transferred to West Point, Wood, by now married, accompanied him and served as adjutant at the Point from February to September 1881 and librarian from July 1881 to August 1882. In 1881 he enrolled at Columbia University, the next year securing a leave to attend classes full time, earned a law degree in 1883, resigned from the army in 1884 and settled at Portland, Oregon. He commenced a law practice, became an expert in maritime and corporation law and sometimes practiced before the United States Supreme Court. He also was a crusader for justice, supporting the causes of Tom Mooney and Sacco and Vanzetti, and became known as a "philosophical anarchist." He wrote historical and other articles for popular magazines and became an accomplished painter with exhibits in the larger cities. He separated from his wife who refused him a divorce and lived at San Francisco with Sara Bard Field, a poet much younger than he (whom he married after his first wife died, late in his life). He wrote much poetry and prose, the only product of frontier interest being *A Book of Tales: Being Some Myths of the*

North American Indians (1901). He died near Los Gatos, California; his papers are at the Huntington Library, San Marino, California.

Cullum; Heitman; McWhorter, *Hear Me; Who Was Who;* DAB.

Wood, George, Mormon pioneer (fl. 1853-1865). A farmer near Cedar City, Utah, Wood in 1853 was captain of Cavalry Company E, Nauvoo Legion. It is not clear whether he participated in the Mountain Meadows Massacre of September 11, 1857. Some time afterward an Olive Coombs, a widow with two daughters, set up a school at Cedar City. She became interested in the massacre asked questions about it, and came to be considered "a wolf in sheep's clothing," intent upon collecting evidence and publishing it, although there was no proof of this. Wood, while drunk, heard that his son was interested in Mrs. Coombs' 13-year-old daughter and became incensed over this plus rumors that Coombs was digging up the sordid past, and shot and killed her. He was found guilty of murder, sentenced to life, but pardoned March 8, 1865, by non-Mormon Governor James Duane Doty.

Juanita Brooks, *The Mountain Meadows Massacre.* Norman, Univ. of Okla. Press, 1966; Brooks, ed., *Journal of the Southern Indian Mission.* Logan, Utah State Univ. Press, 1972.

Wood, Henry Clay, army officer (May 26, 1832-Aug. 30, 1918). B. in Maine, he "read medicine" in 1854 and studied law, passing his bar examination at Augusta in 1856. He was commissioned a second lieutenant in the 1st Infantry June 27, 1856, becoming a first lieutenant in 1861 and having engaged in frontier service since entering the army. His Civil War record was creditable, Wood emerging a major and assistant adjutant general with two brevets. In 1876 he was assistant adjutant general for the Military Department of the Columbia and made an exhaustive study of the difficulties of the Nez Perce who did not wish to leave the Wallowa Valley of northeastern Oregon, as demanded by the government. His sympathies were with Joseph and his followers, and he found no legal basis for removing them; legalities however rarely bothered the government in a case of this kind. Wood published, *The Status of Young Joseph and His Band of Nez Perce Indians* (Portland, AAG's office, 1876) detailing his findings. Howard, then command-

ing the department, endorsed Wood's views. Wood became a lieutenant colonel in 1887 and a colonel in 1893, retiring May 29, 1896; he was promoted to Brigadier General on the retired list in 1904.

Heitman; McWhorter, *Hear Me;* J.P. Dunn Jr., *Massacres of the Mountains.* N.Y., Archer House, (1958).

Wood, Leonard, army officer (Oct. 9, 1860-Aug. 7, 1927). B. at Winchester, New Hampshire, he was graduated from Harvard Medical School in 1884 and shortly joined the Army Medical Corps, being sent to Fort Huachuca, Arizona, in 1886, as the final campaign against Geronimo was underway. Wood asked for and received a line company command in an infantry regiment. He was actively engaged in a search for the hostiles in Sonora with Captain Henry W. Lawton, Tom Horn being their chief of scouts. Although they performed arduous service, it was unrewarding in that they could not find the enemy who was tracked down by Lieutenant Charles B. Gatewood with Indian scouts after reports that Geronimo had sent women into Fronteras to negotiate a surrender, perhaps as a ruse. Wood received a Medal of Honor for his Mexico service, which was worthy but by no means outstanding, while officers of greater and more effective work were not similarly honored. After his Arizona service Wood became White House physician in 1895 to President McKinley, established a friendship with Theodore Roosevelt, and as a colonel commanded the First U.S. Volunteer Cavalry, the Rough Riders. By San Juan Hill he commanded also units of the regular cavalry, winning a battlefield promotion to Brigadier General. He eventually was named military governor of Cuba, vastly improving the physical conditions on the island and winning the lasting respect of the Cubans. In 1903 he put down a rebellion on the island of Mindanao in the Philippines. His rise in the Army continued. He was chief of staff from 1910 to 1914. A man of principle, if of strongly conservative ideas, he refused to compromise and was by-passed in favor of Warren Harding for the Republican nomination in 1920. After the election Harding appointed him governor general of the Philippines. He died of a brain tumor.

Literature abundant; Herman Hagedorn, *Leonard Wood: A Biography,* 2 vols. N.Y.,

Harper & Co., 1931; *Chasing Geronimo: The Journal of Leonard Wood May-September 1886,* ed. with intro. and epilog. by Jack C. Lane. Albuquerque, Univ. of New Mex. Press, 1970.

Wood, Solomon R., pioneer (c. 1819-Sept. 11, 1857). Wood, from Marion County, Arkansas, with his wife, Martha (c. 1818-1857) and sons James, 18 and John H., 11, joined the Fancher emigrant wagon company at Fort Smith, Arkansas, bound for California. They left late in March 1857. The company was destroyed at Mountain Meadows, Utah, by Mormons and Mormon-led Indians.

William Wise, *Massacre at Mountain Meadows.* N.Y., Thomas Y. Crowell Co., 1976.

Wood, William, pioneer (c. 1823-Sept. 11, 1857). Wood, from Marion County, Arkansas, his wife Malinda (c. 1824-1857), and their children, including Thomas Benton Wood, 10; Sylvester, 9 and James Irvine Wood, 8, joined the Fancher emigrant wagon train at Fort Smith, Arkansas, bound for California. Leaving late in March 1857, the company was destroyed by Mormons and Mormon-led Indians at Mountain Meadows, Utah, and all above the age of infancy slain.

Willim Wise, *Massacre at Mountain Meadows.* N.Y., Thomas Crowell Co., 1976.

Wood, William Rhodes, pioneer (Sept. 26, 1846-Nov. 18, 1933). B. in Yorkshire, England, Wood was a cousin of Cecil Rhodes of South Africa fame and emigrated to the United States, settling in Minnesota. He was a civilian member of Custer's 1874 expedition to the Black Hills and wrote a brief account of the expedition, the manuscript held by the Minnesota Historical Society. In 1875 he married Rhoda Squire, who with her missionary parents had emigrated from England in 1873 to take advantage of the Northern Pacific railroad's colonization program. Wood became a mechanical engineer for the Minneapolis and St. Paul railroad, designing a hydraulic lift for locomotives among other devices. He fathered two children, including a son who as a soldier died at Manila, P.I., from malaria in 1898. Wood died at Van Nuys. California.

Herbert Krause, Gary D. Olson, *Prelude to Glory.* Sioux Falls, S.D., Brevet Press, 1974; information, 1975, from John F. Goeschl, Woodland Hills, Calif., a grandson.

Woodall, Zachariah T., soldier (c. 1850-Sept. 12, 1899). B. at Alexandria, Virginia, he gave his profession as blacksmith when he enlisted at Carlisle Barracks, Pennsylvania, January 24, 1871, in company I, 6th Cavalry, to serve under Captain Adna Romanza Chaffee for many years. He shortly became a sergeant and September 12, 1874, commanded a six man detachment (two of them civilian scouts) besieged by 125 Kiowa and perhaps Comanche Indians in the famous buffalo wallow fight near the Washita River, Texas. The vivid narrative of the engagement makes no mention of his outstanding leadership which saved the party, although Woodall was seriously injured, shot through the groin. He and the others on direct application of Miles received Medals of Honor for this fight. Woodall became a noted marksman in army circles. In August 1879 he won the "grand prize for the highest score" at The Presidio, San Francisco, presented with "an elegant medal and pin, which is a musket from which is hung a Maltese cross and an ivory bull's eye. On the reverse is the engraving: Score, 82 per cent." Woodall was at the Battle of Big Dry Wash, July 17, 1882, against Arizona Apaches. Tom Horn who with Al Sieber fought by his side called Woodall "a famous shot" and gave him credit for some very effective marksmanship in the affair; by this time Woodall was first sergeant of I Company. Julius Schulz said that following his enlistment in I Company in August 1882 an initial assignment was to box the sergeant of the outfit, to emphasize the company pecking order. Schulz whipped the sergeant, so Woodall took him on and Schulz laid out the first sergeant, terminating the "lesson," Woodall and Schulz thereafter becoming friends. Woodall continued to re-enlist regularly, rendering "many years of valuable service as first sergeant" under Chaffee, including duty in the 1890-91 Sioux campaign. Later he was ordnance sergeant, an office he held at his death at Havana, Cuba, during the American occupation. William Harding Carter spoke of the esteem with which the soldier was held, recalling "the impression made upon (me) and all the younger officers and men whenever Sergeant Woodall appeared in full uniform wearing the Medal of Honor." He was described by one who knew him well as "a powerfully built, short, stocky man, with clear blue eyes, and absolutely fearless. Strict on duty, but held in high esteem by the officers and men of his troop."

Woodall enlistment records, NARS; *The Indian Campaign on the Staked Plains, 1874-1875*, ed. by Joe F. Taylor. Canyon, Tex, Panhandle-Plains Hist. Soc., 1962; MH; *Deeds of Valor*, II; Prescott, *Arizona Miner*, Aug. 29, 1879; *Life of Tom Horn Written by Himself.* Denver, Louthan Book Co., 1904, 108; Julius Schulz narrative, author's possession; *Frontier Times*, Vol. 10, No. 1 (Oct. 1932), 6, No. 3 (Dec. 1932), 103; William Harding Carter, *The Life of Lieutenant General Chaffee.* Chicago, Univ. of Chicago Press, 1917.

Woodbridge, Francis, army officer (Jan. 23, 1853-Apr. 22, 1891). B. in Michigan he enlisted as a private in the general service May 11, 1869, and was commissioned a second lieutenant in the 7th Infantry February 1, 1876, being sent to Montana. In July 1877 Captain Rawn directed Woodbridge and some enlisted men up the Lolo Trail into the Bitterroot Mountains to reconnoiter and detect the approach of the Nez Perce hostiles under Chief Joseph. Woodbridge carried out his mission satisfactorily, but the Indians could not be stopped from entering Montana with the limited means at Rawn's disposal. Woodbridge was in the Battle of Big Hole, Montana, August 9-10, earning a brevet for gallantry in action on the 9th. He became a first lieutenant February 23, 1883, and retired February 20, 1891, dying two months later at Ann Arbor, Michigan at the age of 38.

Heitman; McWhorter, *Hear Me*; John M. Carroll, Byron Price, *Roll Call on the Little Big Horn, 28 June 1876.* Fort Collins, Colo., Old Army Press, 1974.

Wooden Lance: *see* Feathered Lance

Wooden Leg (Kummok'quiviokta), Northern Cheyenne leader (1858-1940). B. on the Cheyenne River in South Dakota he grew to a height of 6 feet, 2 inches, and weight of 235 pounds, his name coming from his great endurance and because his legs never tired. He was in the Powder River camp attacked March 17, 1876. His eye-witness account makes plain it was a largely Cheyenne village, with few Sioux lodges, and not Crazy Horse's camp as first reported hit by the Reynolds-Crook operation. Wooden Leg escaped to Sitting Bull's encampment and was in the action against Crook on the Rosebud June 17,

1876. He was with Sitting Bull when Custer attacked the Little Bighorn hostiles. It is in connection with that fight that Wooden Leg's testimony has its greatest interest, and is most controversial although he seems an honest and faithful witness. He told of hard fighting and then, in one company of soldiers (perhaps A.E. Smith's company), "all of the white men went crazy. Instead of shooting us, they turned their guns upon themselves... They killed themselves." Again, speaking of Keogh's or Tom Custer's troops, "all this band of soldiers went crazy and fired their guns at each other's heads and breasts or at their own heads and breasts" in an orgy of self-destruction. And once again of still another part of the action, "All of the Indians were saying these soldiers went crazy and killed themselves... I believe they did so." Wooden Leg thought that if the troops had not committed suicide the Indians would have abandoned the fight. He had been in the Reno fight in the valley, then joined the Custer action. He returned on the second night to scout the Reno positions but took no active part in any fighting on that hill. One of Wooden Leg's convictions was that a number of soldier canteens contained not water but whiskey, and he thought perhaps drunkenness contributed to the wave of self-destruction; many authorities contest this as indeed, most of Wooden Leg's testimony on other matters. With the other Northern Cheyennes, Wooden Leg was exiled to Indian Territory subsequently but disliked it there. He did not join the Dull Knife/Little Wolf exodus toward their Montana homeland but went with other Northern Cheyennes later allowed to return home. For a time he was an army scout. He was slightly involved in the Ghost Dance enthusiasm of 1890. He became a judge of the Indian Court and at 50 was baptized into the Christian faith in company with his wife and two daughters. He became something of a tribal historian and at his death on the Northern Cheyenne Reservation was widely respected. His autobiography was written by Thomas B. Marquis (see entry).

Thomas B. Marquis, *Wooden Leg: A Warrior Who Fought Custer.* Lincoln, Univ. of Nebr. Press, 1974; W.A. Graham, *The Custer Myth.* Harrisburg, Pa., Stackpole Co., 1953; Dockstader.

Woodruff, Charles Albert, army officer (Apr. 26, 1845-Aug. 13, 1920). B. in Vermont he enlisted in 1862 in the 10th Vermont Infantry and served through the Civil War in the Army of the Potomac, was wounded three times at Cold Harbor, was captured, but escaped. A fourth wound was serious and caused his discharge for disability in 1865 just as he had been commissioned a second lieutenant although because of his wounds he was not mustered. Recovered, he went to West Point, being commissioned a second lieutenant in the 7th Infantry June 12, 1871. He served in Montana and the northwest until October 30, 1877. Woodruff was in command of a mounted detachment with a scouting mission in the Judith Basin, Montana, in 1875, and was on a reconnaissance through northern Idaho, eastern Washington and western Montana in 1876 when he also served on the Yellowstone expedition. In 1877 under Gibbon he fought at the Battle of Big Hole, being three times severely wounded August 9 and that date being promoted to first lieutenant and winning a brevet. Thereafter he served largely in a commissary capacity, being stationed at various periods in the west and in the Philippines during and after the Spanish American War. He retired a Brigadier General in 1903, lived in California in retirement when he fulfilled a number of civilian occupations, and died at Berkeley.

Heitman; Powell; Cullum.

Woods, Peter, reindeer herder (Mar. 18, 1886-Nov. 16, 1946). B. at Kobuk, Alaska, he and his brother Tom were Eskimo or part Eskimo and became expert reindeer herders and Arctic travelers. On Christmas Day 1929, Woods, under the leadership of Andrew Bahr, commenced a saga: the driving of about 3,000 reindeer from Kotzebue Sound in western Alaska to Canada launching the Dominion's own reindeer industry. The Woods brothers "used skis to start off with, and back packs," until they reached Point Barrow where their wives joined them. "From Barrow we walked for three years to Canada; on the way I had a baby girl," recalled Nellie Woods, Peter's wife; the child was reported to have died enroute and to have been buried on the tundra. "When we made it to Mackenzie we stayed there five months to train the people how to keep the herd," then returned to Barrow by ship, remaining a year, and finally coming back to Kobuk. Peter Woods died at Noatak, Alaska.

Information from Nellie Woods to author, Oct. 6, 1976; New York Times, c. Mar. 27, 1935.

Woods, Tom, reindeer manager (d. Sept. 20, 1945). B. at Kobuk, Alaska, he was Eskimo or part Eskimo, and with his brother, Peter Woods, assisted in the monumental drive of 3,000 reindeer from Kotzebue Sound, western Alaska, around the Arctic coast to the Canadian tundra to start Canada's reindeer industry. The saga, managed by Andrew Bahr, required about five years to complete, from 1929 to 1935. The drive was endangered by intense cold, blizzards, wolves, losses to wild caribou and in many other ways, but somehow it continued. At one point Tom was lost for three days in the winter night and "was sure he was going to die.... When he could go no further he fell down into the snow and began to pray.... A long distance off he thought he saw a person in the storm... He stumbled on toward the person...a white woman. She was standing in front of an igloo. She turned out to be a trapper's wife, who had just gone outside for a minute to study the storm...." The two Eskimos requested that their wives join them at Point Barrow in order to rebuild their tattered clothing; the wives continued with them three years, the rest of the way to the Mackenzie River delta. This was crossed on the ice and the deer turned over to Canadians who were taught to manage them. "These boys admitted afterward that never in their lives had they gone through anything like their great trek," Bahr later reported. Tom Woods and his wife died at Kotzebue, Alaska.

Information from Nellie Woods, Peter Wood's wife, Oct. 6, 1976; New York Times, c. Mar. 27, 1935.

Woodson, Albert Emmett, army officer (c. 1841-Aug. 7, 1903). B. in Kentucky, he went in 1859 to Washington Territory where he became private secretary to the governor. Woodson enlisted May 27, 1862, in the 1st Washington Volunteers, serving as hospital steward where he learned pharmacy, was commissioned a second lieutenant in 1863, and served at Forts Walla Walla and Vancouver. He worked as a druggist in civil life, but August 5, 1867, was named a first lieutenant in the 36th Infantry, serving Forts Sanders, Bridger and Douglas. In 1868 he was on escort duty for engineers constructing the

Union Pacific railroad. December 15, 1870, he joined the 5th Cavalry at Fort McPherson, Nebraska, being transferred to Arizona where he was stationed at Camp Verde and took part in Crook's offensive against hostile Indians. In March 1873, he reported killing 15 warriors in the Tonto Basin; he took part in several such actions. Woodson participated in the Big Horn and Yellowstone expedition against the Sioux as a captain, and was in the Slim Buttes fight in September 1876. The next year he took part in the Wind River expedition against the Nez Percés and had a passive role against the Utes in 1879. Woodson became major of the 9th Cavalry in 1896 and colonel of the 3rd Cavalry in 1901, served in the Philippines and was promoted to Brigadier General the day before his retirement in 1903. Charles King, also a 5th Cavalry officer, wrote disparagingly of Woodson in letters home; how much his attitude was based upon professional jealousy is uncertain. Woodson died at Paola, Kansas, and was buried at Arlington national Cemetery.

Heitman; Price, *Fifth Cavalry,* 451-53; Harry H. Anderson, "Charles King's *Campaigning with Crook,"* Chicago Westerners, *Brand Book,* Vol. XXXII, No. 9 (Jan. 1976), 67.

Woodward, Absalom, pioneer mail contractor (d. Nov. 1851). Woodward and George Chorpenning contracted for $14,000 annually, to deliver a mail monthly each way between Sacramento, California, and Salt Lake City, the first leaving the western city May 1, 1851, traversing heavy Sierra Nevada snows, encountering other difficulties and reaching its destination June 5. Each trip required great endurance. In November Woodward and two employees were killed by Indians at Stone House Station, just west of the Malad River, Utah.

LeRoy R. Hafen, *The Overland Mail 1849-1869.* Cleveland, Arthur H. Clark Co., 1926.

Woodward, Arthur A., historian, archeologist (Apr. 18, 1898-Jan. 24, 1986). B. at Des Moines, Iowa, his family moved to San Francisco in 1907. Woodward served in the infantry in World War I, then entered the University of California at Berkeley but left after two years for a three-year stint as a newsman on the New York *Evening Journal.* In 1925 he joined the Museum of the American Indian at New York, but in the same year became curator of history and archeology at the Los Angeles County Museum where he remained until his 1953 retirement. He had excavated prehistoric sites from Arizona to Polynesia with a World War II leave to serve as a naval intelligence officer in the South Pacific. In retirement Woodward lived at Patagonia, Arizona, served as historical consultant for the Arizona State and Tubac museums, and built a book collection to more than 24,000 volumes, the oldest a 1599 dictionary of English and Spanish. His extended writings included: *Apache Scouts* (1935); *A Brief History of Navajo Silversmithing* (1946); *Feud on the Colorado* (1955); ed., *Journal of Lt. Thomas W. Sweeny 1849-1853* (1956); ed., *Man of the West: Reminiscences of George Washington Oaks 1840-1917* (1956); ed., *On the Bloody Trail of Geronimo* (John Bigelow Jr. account) (1958). He also wrote many shorter pieces for periodicals and other outlets. Woodward was married (his wife predeceased him), and was survived by a daughter.

Arizona Daily Star, Jan. 27, 1986; Andrew Wallace, *Sources and Readings in Arizona History.* Tucson, Ariz. Pioneers' Hist. Soc., 1965; Lori Davisson information, Ariz. Hist. Soc.

Woody, Clara Thompson, historian (Dec. 2, 1885-Apr. 5, 1981). B. at Belleville, Kansas, she was raised at Clay Center and moved with her parents to El Paso and Albuquerque, New Mexico, at 16, to Colorado Springs at 17, returned to Albuquerque at 20 and was graduated from New Mexico State College at Las Cruces. She taught school in New Mexico and after a period at Los Angeles moved to Globe, Arizona, in 1917 when she was 31; there she married Clarence Woody, a first lieutenant of the 17th Cavalry. Clara Woody entered business and ran an insurance company for a decade. She became interested in central Arizona history in 1938 and two years later became intrigued by the noted Pleasant Valley War to which she devoted 35 years of intense research in court records, interviews with old timers who had some memories of it, newspaper files and other sources. "I found nobody ever did much real research on it before," she said. She also headed the Gila County Historical Society, delivered radio talks on history and answered hundreds, perhaps thousands of queries from around the world on central Arizona's turbulent past about which she became one of the best informed and most generous authorities. Few writers who concerned themselves with the annals of that area and period were not in her debt for guidance and assistance. Her projected book on the Pleasant Valley War, in which she intended to radically revise the impressions left by Forrest and others, could not be completed by herself, but was incorporated into a volume based upon her labors in general and covering other areas of interest. *Globe, Arizona* (1977) by Clara T. Woody and Milton L. Schwartz, incorporated much editorial assistance by C.L. Sonnichsen and was published by the Arizona Historical Society. Most of her papers were deposited at the Arizona Historical Society, Tucson, and sometime, it is hoped, someone will delve into them and emerge with the book she originally planned. Mrs. Woody died at Globe. In 1987 Clara Woody was inducted into the Arizona Hall of Fame.

Author's notes.

Woody, Franklin H., pioneer (Dec. 10, 1833-Dec. 16, 1916). B. at Chatham, North Carolina, he went to Fort Leavenworth in 1855 and was hired by John Waddell to accompany a supply train to Salt Lake City. He quit the train before it arrived, but continued to Utah anyway. In 1856 he accompanied a Van Etten freight train to Fort Owen in the Bitterroot Valley of Montana. He worked around Fort Owen for more than two years, then became a pioneer resident of Hell Gate, on the site of the future Missoula, Montana, leaving to visit the new mining camps of Bannack, Virginia City and Gold Creek, Montana, but returning to reside at Hell Gate/Missoula the rest of his life. He studied law, was admitted to the bar in 1877, eventually became an attorney for the Northern Pacific Railroad and Montana State Judge for the 4th District. He married, fathered children, and died at Missoula.

Montana, Contributions, II (1896); VII (1910); VIII (1917); George F. Weisel, *Men and Trade on the Northwest Frontier.* Missoula, Mont. State Univ. Press, 1955.

Woolsey, Charles, frontiersman (fl. 1837). Woosley was one of 18 whites who treacherously attacked the Mimbres Apaches leader, Juan José Compá on April 22, 1837, in the Animas Mountains of present New Mexico, slaying 20 and setting off extended Apache-white hostilities

Rex W. Strickland, "The Birth and Death of a Legend: The Johnson 'Massacre' of 1837." *Arizona and the West,* Vol. 18, No. 3 (Autumn 1976), 257-86.

Woolsey, King S., frontiersman (c. 1832-June 30, 1879). B. in Alabama, he probably was raised in Louisiana and was fairly well educated. According to legend he took part in a filibustering expedition to Cuba, was jailed briefly until freed through efforts of the British consul when he boarded a British ship for California, arriving in 1849. Woolsey is supposed to have spent a decade as a miner in Calaveras County and reached Fort Yuma in 1860 with Calvin Jackson (c. 1827-1880) and Albert C. Benedict (1830-1880), both of whom became prominent Arizona pioneers. Woolsey worked as a teamster in the Yuma area of Arizona, apparently joined Albert Sidney Johnston's group marching up the Gila enroute to joining the Confederacy but left at Maricopa Wells and eventually purchased into the Agua Caliente Ranch in western Maricopa County, Arizona. From here, although Southern in sympathies, he profited greatly providing hay and other supplies to the California Column of Union troops which entered Arizona and garrisoned many points within the Territory during the Civil War. Woolsey appears to have accompanied the Walker gold-hunting party to the Prescott area and in 1863 established his Agua Fria Ranch near the present town of Dewy, Arizona. Here he engaged in ranching, farming and mining and being on the eastward fringe of settlement, was most exposed to Indian attacks and led several expeditions hunting and killing Indians. In the Bradshaw Mountains on one occasion he caused a little strychnine to be mixed with pinole for visiting Indians, the incident later becoming confused with one of his major expeditions on which no poison was used. Woolsey led three locally famed Indian-hunting and exploring expeditions in 1864. In January Indian stock thefts led to organization of a party of whites and Maricopa Indians which journeyed eastward and encountered wild Indians in Fish Creek Canyon, a dozen miles from the Salt River Canyon where Woolsey, by treachery, caused the slaying of around 20 Yavapais or Tonto Apaches for a loss of one white killed and several wounded. In the spring Woolsey led another expedition eastward, a rancheria was attacked at a place called Squaw Canyon and 14 Indians killed for no white losses. The third expedition in the ensuing summer resulted in no significant Indian fighting but much prospecting and exploration of the Verde River country. Because of losses in mining ventures Woolsey had undertaken in partnership with Governor John N. Goodwin and Secretary of State Robert C. McCormick, Woolsey was forced to sell his Agua Fria Ranch and turned to business ventures in the Salt River Valley. He became a major land owner, sold salt, and with two others organized the Phoenix Flour Mills. He prospered greatly, was five times elected to the Territorial Council, ran in 1878 for Delegate to Congress, but was defeated, and by his early death from apoplexy was regarded by many as the leading citizen of the Territory. He left an estate of $37,400 and debts of about two-thirds of that amount. Woolsey had been "married" to an Indian woman shortly after reaching Arizona, and later married a white woman from Georgia, being survived by his widow and three children.

John S. Goff, *King S. Woolsey*. Cave Creek, Ariz., Black Mountain Press, 1981; Clara T. Woody, "The Woolsey Expeditions of 1864. *Arizona and the West*, Vol. 4, No. 2 (Summer 1962), 157-76; Dan L. Thrapp, *The Conquest of Apacheria*. Norman, Univ. of Okla. Press, 1967.

Wootton, Richens Lacy (Dick), frontiersman (May 6, 1816-Aug. 22, 1893). B. in Mecklenburg County, Virginia, he hired out to Bent and St. Vrain at Independence, Missouri, in 1836, being sent from Bent's Fort on the Arkansas to trade with the Sioux, then visited Taos. In 1837 he had a fight with the Pawnees, commenced trapping in the Rockies and engaged in a fight with the Snakes. In 1838 he trapped across the Rockies to the Columbia, progressed to California, then trapped through Arizona and back to Bent's Fort. He engaged in various pioneering activities near Bent's Fort, Old Pueblo, Colorado, and other places, missed the Taos massacre, scouted for Doniphan and guided military operations against the Navahos. Wootton traded, settled at Taos for a time, visited St. Louis in 1851, and in 1852 claimed to have driven 9,000 sheep from New Mexico to California. Wootton engaged in a variety of pioneering activities, and associated with numerous

prominent figures of the southwest. He settled in Denver for a time, then built his famed toll road over Raton Pass in 1865, operating it for 13 years. "He was about the only Mountain Man who defended Chivington's action at Sand Creek," never being partial to Indians; he displayed a hot temper at times, once killing a Mexican for irritating him. Wootton married four times, his first three wives preceding him in death, was operated on successfully for cataracts at Chicago late in life and held various public positions. He died near Trinidad, Colorado.

Literature abundant; Howard Louis Conard, *"Uncle Dick" Wootton*. Chicago, W.E. Dibble Co., 1890; DAB; Harvey L. Carter article, MM, Vol. III; *Denver Republican*, Aug. 23, 1893.

Worcester, Samuel Austin, missionary (Jan. 19, 1798-Apr. 20, 1859). B. at Worcester, Massachusetts, he was raised in Vermont, graduated from its university and the Theological Seminary at Andover, and was ordained a Congregational minister in 1825. He went to the Brainard Mission among the Cherokees of Tennessee, directing the creation of type faces for the Sequoyah alphabet and, removed to New Echota, Georgia, translated portions of the Bible into Cherokee. He helped establish a Cherokee newspaper and did much job printing for that people. Arrested, he was sentenced to four years imprisonment for violating a Georgia law prohibiting a white from living among the Indians, but the Supreme Court ruled the law unconstitutional. Worcester then moved west of the Mississippi, continuing his work among the Cherokees and establishing the Park Hill Mission, "the largest and most important institution of its kind in the Indian Territory." He resumed printing literature for the Cherokees in their own tongue, using the Sequoyah alphabet and urging the Indians to learn and use it. Worcester married twice and was buried at Park Hill.

DAB; "Forerunners," *Presbyterian Life,* Vol. 5, No. 17 (Sept. 6, 1952), 11-13; Grant Foreman, *The Five Civilized Tribes*. Norman, Univ. of Okla. Press, 1934; Grace Steele Woodward, *The Cherokees*. Norman, 1963.

Worden, Francis Lyman, pioneer (1830-Feb. 5, 1887). B. in Vermont and educated in New York State he went at 22 to San Francisco. From there he traveled south to Panama and north to Oregon, where he mined for a time. He fought in the 1855 Indian war in Oregon and clerked for Governor Isaac Stevens in the Indian Department office at The Dalles. Worden settled at Walla Walla, Washington, opening a store there. He was present during the 1858 Indian war in Washington Territory. In 1860 he formed a partnership with Christopher P. Higgins and packed supplies to Montana from Walla Walla. The partners opened a trading post at Hell Gate Ronde, about four miles below the present Missoula, Montana, which they founded. Upon discovery of gold at Gold Creek they established a store there in 1862, and the next year another at LaBarge City (Deer Lodge). In 1864 they moved the post from Hell Gate Ronde to the present site of Missoula which first was known as Wordensville until Worden insisted the name be changed. Worden and Higgins constructed a grist mill almost at the same time as the first such mill was built at Bozeman by Thomas Cover and Perry McAdow. In 1868 the several Worden-Higgins mercantile establishments were withdrawn to Missoula. Worden held many public offices. He married and fathered seven children. Worden died at Missoula.

William F. Sanders, "Francis Lyman Worden." *Montana Contributions,* Vol. II (1896), 362-64.

Wordsworth, William C., pioneer (c. 1828-c. Aug. 5, 1861). B. in Mississippi, Wordsworth moved to Madison, the later Orange, Texas, before 1848, where he married Esther Cox Delano at Beaumont. The couple joined the Ake party which left Fort Smith, Arkansas, in 1853 for California; the Wordsworths and the Akes moved to Arizona in 1856, settling in the Sonoita valley. In 1860 Lewis S. Owings, the provisional governor of Arizona (which was not formally organized into a territory for three more years) named Wordsworth Major General of militia. A lawyer, he was admitted to the bar in that year. His home was burned by Indians in February 1861. In the summer, the Wordsworths with the Akes and others to the number of 70 including women and children, left Tucson with Moses Carson, Kit's half-brother, for New Mexico. Between August 1 and 10 they were ambushed in Cooke's Canyon, New Mexico, and Wordsworth and several others were killed. Benjamin Sacks believed the Indians were Mimbres led by José Mangus, the son of Mangas Coloradas.

Oscar W. Williams, "An Old Timer's Reminiscences of Grant County, New Mexico," ann. by Samuel D. Myres. *Password,* Vol. X, No. 2 (Summer 1965), 43-52; Constance Wynn Altshuler, *Latest from Arizona! The Hesperian Letters, 1859-1861.* Tucson, Ariz. Pioneers' Hist. Soc., 1969.

Work, John, pioneer (c. 1792-Dec. 1861). Work, "an important man in the Hudson's Bay Company," joined the organization in 1814 and reached the Oregon country in 1823. His journals are informative and valuable records. Work went to Oregon with Peter Skene Ogden, spent the winter of 1823-24 at Spokane House and in the fall of 1824 led a party to trade with the Flatheads, then transferred Hudson's Bay operations from Spokane to Fort Colville on the Columbia. He married a Spokan woman, Josette Legace, fathering 11 children. In 1830 Work succeeded Ogden as head of the Snake River brigade, leading trapping parties in the upper mountains and to the Sacramento River, California. Blackfeet kept his brigade out of their country after skirmishes in 1832. His Sacramento expedition also was less than successful, although he contacted both Spanish and Russian settlements. Work followed Ogden in charge of the coastal trade in 1834, in 1846 succeeded McLoughlin as chief factor and in 1849 became a member of the board of management for the Columbia District, concentrating his attention thenceforth on British Columbia, where he became prominent. He died on Vancouver Island.

Ray M. Reeder article, MM, Vol. II; Gloria Griffen Cline, *Peter Skene Ogden and the Hudson's Bay Company.* Norman, Univ. of Okla. Press, 1974.

Workman, William, frontiersman (1800-May 17, 1876). B. in Westmoreland County, England, he arrived in the U.S. probably in the early 1820s, and reached Santa Fe July 8, 1825. By 1827 he had become a trapper and Taos trader. He joined James Ohio Pattie and George Yount for a Gila River trapping expedition in 1827, returning to Taos where he concentrated on trading. Workman was suspected of taking part in an 1837 New Mexico insurrection, but his exact role is not known. Suspected also of participating in some way with the Texas Santa Fe Expedition of 1841, Workman and John Rowland in September of that year led a group of emigrants from New Mexico to California, the pair obtaining a 48,000 acre land grant in the La Puente area. Workman became a prominent pioneer. Having suffered financial reverses, he shot himself.

David J. Weber article, MM, Vol. VII; Bancroft, *Pioneer Register.*

Worth, William Jenkins, army officer (Mar. 1, 1794-May 7, 1849). B. at Hudson, New York, he was a merchant until commissioned a first lieutenant of the 23rd Infantry March 19, 1813, and became an aide to Winfield Scott which did no harm to his career. He was promoted to captain August 19, 1814, and ended the War of 1812 with a brevet of major and a gallant record. Worth served in the 2nd Infantry and transferred to the 1st Infantry June 1, 1821. He had become commandant at West Point in 1820, serving as such until 1828. He became major of ordnance May 30, 1832, served inconspicuously in the Black Hawk War of that year and was made colonel of the 8th Infantry July 7, 1838. In November 1840 he arrived in Florida with a mission to end the protracted Second Seminole War and bursting with ideas on how to do it. None worked to specification; the war dragged on, army units finding it virtually impossible to bring the elusive enemy to decisive battle and the southern Florida wilderness almost untraversable save with Indian or black guides. Worth collected many Seminole prisoners and from time to time shipped them to Indian Territory, but a hard core remained nearly inviolate in the recesses of the Everglades. In February 1842 Worth informed Washington he had shipped 230 Seminoles west, that about 300 remained in Florida who could not be brought in by force and he recommended that they be permitted to remain, the army reduced to a peace-keeping force. His suggestion was rejected. April 19, 1842, southeast of Pelikalkaha near Lake Ahapopka Worth directed his only personal engagement against the Seminoles. It was not much of a fight, with about 400 men of four regiments attacking an Indian camp of unknown strength at a cost of one killed and three wounded for uncertain Indian losses, if any. It was however the last action of the Florida War which "might be called a battle." Worth on August 14 declared the seven-year-war at an end, although in fact it dragged on for some time with minor depredations and incidents from time to time. But those Seminoles secluded in the south were not further disturbed by organized military attacks. Worth was brevetted Brigadier General for his Florida service, went on to greater things in the war with Mexico, came into dispute with various of his colleagues over minor matters, and died of cholera in Texas.

John K. Mahon, *The History of the Second Seminole War.* Gainesville, Univ. of Fla. Press, 1967; *Black Hawk War,* Vol. II, Pts. 1, 2; DAB.

Wortley, Samuel, hotelkeeper (c. 1832-Apr. 28, 1907). B. in New York, Sam Wortley reached Lincoln, New Mexico, where he became manager of the Wortley Hotel, built in 1874 to house the construction crew erecting the Murphy-Dolan store. Wortley became a strong supporter of the Murphy-Dolan faction in the Lincoln County War, and his hotel was field headquarters for that element during the celebrated July 1878 attack on the McSween House of the opposing party. Later the hotel was owned for a time by Pat Garrett. Wortley died at Capitan, New Mexico. The hotel accidentally burned in 1925, was reconstructed in 1960 by the Old Lincoln County Memorial Commission and today is a New Mexico State Monument, still operated as a hotel.

Robert N. Mullin notes; Francis L. Fugate, "The Wortley Hotel: Lincoln, New Mexico." *Amer. West,* Vol. XXI, No. 2 (Mar./Apr. 1984), 10.

Wovoka (Jack Wilson, Wanekia), Paiute medicine man (c. 1856-Sept. 20, 1932). B. in the Mason Valley of western Nevada, he was a full-blood Paiute, the son of Tavibo, also a medicine man and mystic, and after the father's death Wovoka was taken into the David Wilson white rancher's family who named him Jack Wilson, as he was commonly known among the whites. He was noted as the originator of the ghost dance among his people, from whom it swiftly spread to many tribes, although in fact it was but the most widely known manifestation of a movement that for 20 years or more had periodically swept through numerous bands of western Indians. Wovoka was an industrious and good workman and continued as an employee of David Wilson for many years. In about 1887 he said he had had a vision of passing "up to the other world," in which he met God who instructed him to return and teach his people that they must love one another, live in peace with the whites, must work and not lie or steal, put away war practices and at last they would come to their friends in the other world where there would be no more death, sickness or old age. He was then given a dance which he was to bring back to his people to be performed at intervals for five consecutive days which would hasten the event of their emerging into a more pleasant realm. God gave him control over the elements so he could manage the weather and appointed him his deputy to govern Wovoka's region. From a neighboring ranchman Mooney learned that shortly before the prophet began to preach he had been stricken with a severe fever and while ill there occurred an eclipse of the sun causing great alarm and excitement among the Paiutes during which Wovoka suffered a delirium leading, it was believed, to his trance, or vision. Wovoka however was honest and completely sincere in his narration of what had happened to him, Mooney was convinced. Wovoka's teachings were accepted by Indians as distant as the Plains tribes where they were somewhat distorted occasionally in practice. The most famous result was the Wounded Knee massacre in 1891 in South Dakota when many Sioux were slain by troops as was Sitting Bull in a related incident. Wovoka was depressed by the tragedies which had occurred in part through his teachings of a non-violent revival among the Indians. He never renounced his vision, but advocated reconciliation with the whites. He died at Schurz on the Walker River Reservation in Nevada and was buried in its cemetery. He was married but once, fathered three daughters and a son who died in his teens.

James Mooney, *The Ghost-Dance Religion and the Sioux Outbreak of 1890,* ed. by Anthony F.C. Wallace. Chicago, Univ. of Chicago Press, 1965 (originally published as Part 2 of *14th Ann Rep.,* BAE, 1892-93, Wash., Govt., Printing Office, 1896); Dockstader.

Wozencraft, Oliver Meredith, Indian agent, expansionist (1814-Nov. 22, 1887). B. in Ohio, he attended medical school at Bardstown, Kentucky, practiced in Tennessee and at New Orleans and started for California in 1848, but paused at Brownsville, Texas, to treat victims of a cholera epidemic. He continued to California by the southern route and practiced medicine at Stockton shortly after his arrival, in 1849. He attended as a delegate the California constitutional convention at Monterey in September 1849. Late in 1851 he was appointed one of three Indian commissioners for California and brought his family out from New Orleans, settling them at San Francisco. Wozencraft and the other two commissioners, Redick McKee and George Barbour, headed into Indian country in February 1851 to make what treaties were possible. March 19 the first treaty was negotiated with six bands of Mountain and Merced Indians, as they were described. By May 1 the commissioners had divided California between them, Wozencraft to handle the territory up the Sacramento Valley and including the Pit River country. He continued to work out treaties with such bands as he could contact, his work made difficult by white excesses and consequent Indian hostility. Barbour resigned believing his efforts futile, and Wozencraft took over his duties, extending his charge to the southern part of the state. He went to San Diego late in 1851, helped quell a native uprising, and concluded several new treaties. In March 1852 Edward F. Beale was appointed first Indian superintendent for California, and friction quickly developed between him, Wozencraft and McKee. Wozencraft was discouraged by the monumental task of avoiding Indian-white hostilities while securing justice for the Indians, and in the absense of strong support from Beale resigned late in 1852 or early the following year. He turned to politics and expansionism. He strongly supported construction of a railroad to the Pacific coast, and was convinced that irrigation with Colorado River water could make a garden out of the Imperial Valley in southern California. In 1858 he moved to San Bernardino, California, and pushed his irrigation scheme in every avenue from California to Washington D.C., though without avail. He was involved in an obscure gunplay incident at San Bernardino in 1862 and was wounded while also wounding his assailant. From 1870-73 he was acting physician and surgeon aboard a Pacific Mail Steamship line vessel between San Francisco and China, performing heroically when cholera broke out aboard, and working on an invention or two in his spare time. He continued meanwhile to promote his notions of irrigating the southern California desert; his ideas were very sound, and an immense agricultural empire ultimately would develop from them, but he was before his time and died with his great dream unrealized. He succumbed at 73 at Washington, D.C., unheralded but the true father of the future vast California reclamation projects.

William B. Secrest, "Wozencraft." *Real West,* Vol. 24, Nos. 180, 181 (Oct., Dec. 1981), 6-13, 56; 36-40, 54.

Wratten, George Medhurst, interpreter (Jan. 31, 1865-June 23, 1912). B. at Sonoma, California, of English parentage, his family took him at 14 to Florence, Arizona. Wratten became associated with Apaches at the San Carlos Reservation and learned to speak their language fluently. In 1881 he was named a chief of scouts, doubling as interpreter, and also served at times as superintendent of pack trains as did other chiefs of scouts; he learned "all the Apache dialects" as well as several other languages, and "gained the supreme confidence of the Apaches," according to his son. In 1886 Wratten was interpreter for Gatewood during the crucial meetings with Geronimo. Wratten volunteered to go east with the Chiricahuas being exiled to Florida, and remained with them the rest of his life. While at Mount Vernon, Alabama, with them, he married Nah-goy-yah-kizn, or "Tomboy," a Chiricahua orphan aged 17 or 18; they had two daughters, Amy (Oct. 4, 1890-Sept. 28, 1956) and Blossom, born in 1894 and still living in the 1970s. The couple were divorced in 1894 while still in Alabama. In 1889 while stationed at Fort Sill, Oklahoma, Wratten married Julia Cannon, daughter of a prominent Mobile County (Alabama) business family, and fathered three sons and two daughters (one daughter died in 1951 at Santa Fe; the other children were living in 1970). Wratten several times visited Washington, D.C., on behalf of the Apaches, but a serious back ailment late in life limited his activity. To some extent he was controversial; Geronimo came to distrust him and refused to allow Wratten to interpret for him, and there were said to be other Chiricahuas who felt similarly, although the majority seemed to trust his interpretive ability. Wratten is buried at Fort Sill, Oklahoma; his widow died a decade later at Mobile. Upon his death the government had awarded her a land allotment in Oklahoma "as an expression of gratitude for his long service with the Apaches."

Information from Albert E. Wratten, a son of George Wratten; Albert E. Wratten, "George Wratten: Friend of the Apaches," *Jour. of Ariz Hist.,* Vol. 26, No. 1 (Spring 1986).

Wren, William R., cattleman, partisan (fl. 1877). A Lampasas County, Texas, rancher, Wren was involved on the side of Pink Higgins in several shootouts in 1877 between the feuding Horrell-Higgins factions. He was said to have taken part in the ambush of Tom and Mart Horrell, March 26 in which the Higgins people were routed after wounding the two Horrells. June 14 Wren was in the Lampasas town square shootout between the parties, being wounded, though not dangerously. He was also in the siege in July of the Horrell ranchhouse, a battle which ended with no important results. Later Wren was reported to have been a county sheriff in Texas, but whether of Lampasas County is not stated.

O'Neal, *Gunfighters;* Bill O'Neal, "The Horrell Brothers of Lampasas." *Frontier Times,* Vol. 54, No. 3 (Apr.-May 1980), 6-7, 42-45; Walter Prescott Webb, *The Texas Rangers.* Boston, Houghton Mifflin Co., 1935.

Wright, Benjamin, Indian killer (Apr. 7, 1828-Feb. 22, 1856). The man deemed by many as the original cause of the sanguinary Modoc War of 1872-73 was b. at Milton, Wayne County, Indiana, the eldest son of a Presbyterian minister. The family moved to Madison County, Indiana, in 1835. Ben's mother died in 1847 and after leaving home he sought to learn the blacksmith's trade but had a fight with his employer and went to Leavenworth, Kansas, where he joined a wagon train for Oregon. Enroute he fell in love with Ruth Arnot, a comely 17-year-old, but she was killed during a brief Indian raid, the only victim of the attack. Wright swore eternal vengeance against all Indians. At Oregon City he volunteered in the company of Major H.A.G. Lee for Columbia River service following the massacre of Whitman and others in Washington. Stationed at The Dalles, Wright frequently joined scouting parties and "his fearlessness and ability... soon won for him an enviable reputation." Following this service he became a hunter-trapper finally settling at Cottonwood about

20 miles from Yreka, California. Here he continued "hunting, trapping or shooting Indians; living in fact like the Indians themselves, dressed in buckskin, and his glossy black hair reached his waist. It is said he took pride in acting like an Indian..., scalping the dead, and committing other barbarities, such as cutting off the ears, nose and fingers of the wounded." By 23 he was "the acknowledged champion Indian fighter in northern California." That summer of 1851 Modocs were stealing stock in the Shasta valley, in one raid near Butteville sweeping off 46 horses and mules. Settlers raised a volunteer company and sent for Ben Wright to lead it; he refused to captain the organization, although going along as guide and scout. The pursuers covered a 115-mile route to the northeast to Clear Lake, near the present Malin, Oregon. They rode through a suspect Modoc village as though uninterested in it, camped a few miles distant and during the night laid attack plans, carrying them out at dawn when an undetermined number of Indians were slain and others, mainly women and children were captured. In May 1852 Wright and a party from Yreka rescued a six-wagon train under Modoc siege at Bloody Point, where the emigrant road reached Tule Lake, again some hostiles being killed. Several emigrant trains were attacked with white losses in the Tule Lake vicinity, the number of victims only conjectured. Wright operated in the area in the summer of 1852, reporting that he found 22 victims of Modoc raids and buried them; the total may have reached 35 in all. He camped at Tule Lake until late autumn, trying to repossess plundered equipment and rescue captives from the Indians, and by some treachery to make a good kill for the sake of vengeance. At one time, according to persistent reports, he sought to obtain strychnine or arsenic to further his dark designs. At last Wright courageously penetrated a Modoc village alone, shot down a leading man and escaped while his followers slew 41 of the 46 male inhabitants. When they returned to Yreka dangling their trophy scalps they were hailed as heroes, but the Modocs never forgot. Wright continued his activities as the premier Indian fighter of the region, and usually the most successful, although he became a heavy drinker and this led him into excesses. He was appointed by Joel Palmer, Indian superin-

tendent for Oregon, the agent in charge of all tribes south of Coos Bay, Oregon, and in January 1856 moved his headquarters to the lower Rogue River, Oregon. Here his overall effect seemed to be almost that of a peacemaker between the races, his metamorphosis from an Indian slayer to Indian preserver appearing complete. Wright employed a half-breed, Enos, who had been one of Fremont's guides and was considered a "very brave and daring Indian" to serve as informant in the event of possible unrest or plotting in native villages. Enos and his wife however were the key elements in a plot to murder Wright, an act Enos performed with an axe (Murray dates the incident as February 25) near Whaleshead at the mouth of the Rogue. Wright's heart was reported cut out and partly eaten by an Indian woman whom he had mistreated. In a subsequent uprising at least 46 whites were killed. Enos was arrested on the Grande Ronde Reservation in northeastern Oregon, returned to Port Orford, Oregon, and lynched by miners April 12, 1856. Beckman reproduces a photograph of Wright, p. 102.

Don C. Fisher, "Ben Wright," typewritten manuscript at the Lava Beds Nat. Monument, Tulelake, Calif.; Keith A. Murray, *The Modocs and Their War.* Norman, Univ. of Okla. Press, 1965; Jeff C. Riddle, *The Indian History of the Modoc War,* Medford, Ore., Pine Cone Pubrs., 1973; Stephen Dow Beckham, *Requiem for a People.* Norman, Univ. of Okla. Press, 1971.

Wright, George, army officer (Oct. 21, 1801 [or 1803]-July 30, 1865). B. at Norwich, Connecticut, he was graduated from West Point and became a second lieutenant in the 3rd Infantry in 1822. He won a brevet as major for service against the Florida Seminoles and two brevets for Mexican War service. Wright became colonel of the 9th Infantry in 1855, moving early the next year to Washington Territory where he commanded the District of the Columbia amid serious and almost continuous Indian unrest. Wright's operations were extensive, frustrating and only rarely could the Yakimas and other tribes be brought to battle, then most often with inconclusive results. He was unsuccessful in an attempt to attack hostiles who had launched an assault on settlements on the lower Columbia in March 1856; in September 1858, he reported actions against Indians of eastern Washington, most of which were temporarily subdued, largely through summary executions of captured natives. Wright's operations had mixed results; they were not as decisive as the army claimed, nor as meaningless as opposition voices alleged, but they were in no sense major or definitive. Wright was named to command the District of Oregon and Washington and later succeeded Harney as commander of the Department of Oregon, which shortly was merged into the Department of the Pacific. With the Civil War Wright was promoted to Brigadier General of Volunteers and named in October 1861 to command the Department of the Pacific, a post he held until July 1, 1864. After the war he was named to command the Department of the Columbia, but was drowned in the wreck of the ship, *Brother Jonathan* off northern California. His body was recovered six weeks later and he was buried at Sacramento.

Ezra J. Warner, *Generals in Blue: Lives of the Union Commanders.* Baton Rouge, La State Univ. Press, 1964; Bancroft, *Washington, Idaho & Montana, Oregon,* II, *California* VII; Heitman.

Wright, Henry Haviland, army officer (Nov. 6, 1850-July 9, 1916). B. at Washington, D.C., he was commissioned second lieutenant of the 9th Cavalry on December 12, 1872, and saw much frontier duty with his black command against Apaches, Sioux, and with Navaho scouts, commanded from 1876-79. He fought the Mimbres Apache Victorio on the Rio Cuchillo Negro, New Mexico, September 2, 1876, to the displeasure of Agent John M. Shaw who said the attack was made "without cause or provocation of any kind." On January 24, 1877, Wright had a clash with Chiricahua Apaches under "Imp," in the Florida Mountains, New Mexico; he had tried to talk them into surrender, but found himself surrounded, fought free, killing five Apaches. On May 3 he had another fight with Warm Springs Apaches near Ojo Caliente, New Mexico, and on October 9 still another near the Luera Mountains, New Mexico. With 19 Navaho scouts Wright joined Captain Henry Carroll in the summer of 1878 for an operation against the Mescalero Apaches in southern New Mexico and Texas, had an action with hostiles in Alamo Canyon, Sacramento Mountains, New Mexico, on July 29, and on August 5 a repeat action

against Mescaleros in Dog Canyon of the Sacramentos. Wright reported an action against Victorio May 29, 1879, in the San Francisco Mountains of New Mexico, and on September 18 was in a very hard fight with Victorio and Nana on the Las Animas River, New Mexico. Wright was in another engagement with Victorio September 29 and 30 in the Mimbres Mountains, and near Hillsboro, New Mexico, he had still another fight on March 21, 1880. On December 30, 1890, Wright was in the Drexel Mission fight on the Pine Ridge Agency of South Dakota, an aftermath of the Wounded Knee affair. He had been promoted to first lieutenant March 18, 1880, to captain December 12, 1890; he would become major February 2, 1901, and retire October 29, 1902. Wright won a brevet for three of his Apache actions. He died at San Francisco.

Heitman; Powell; Dan L. Thrapp, *Victorio and the Mimbres Apaches.* Norman, Univ. of Okla. Press, 1974; William H. Leckie, *The Buffalo Soldiers.* Norman, 1967.

Wright, Irene Aloha, historian (Dec. 19, 1879-Apr. 6, 1972). B. at Lake City, Colorado, she was graduated from Virginia College in 1898 and studied at Stanford University until 1904. She went to Havana, where she worked on the *Havana Post* two years and the *Havana Telegraph* from 1905-1907 where she became city editor. She was owner and editor of the *Cuba Magazine* from 1908 until 1914. She had become interested in the history of the Caribbean and at Seville "she found her true vocation in researching source material on the early Spanish explorers," becoming convinced that the records of Spanish soldiers, traders and priests "are as much our history as Spain's." Her final work in Spain centered on the career of Hernando De Soto at the behest of John R. Swanton, then compiling his monumental *Final Report of the De Soto Expedition Commission,* Miss Wright providing "many crucial transcripts and copies of documents." She was "the most important" of the specialists who assisted Swanton. Her published works were mainly focused on the Caribbean area, but included *Spanish Policy Toward Virginia 1606-1612* (1920). The results of her researches, during which, she once said, she became "the boon companion of every pirate who sailed the Spanish Main," were published by learned societies in

England, the Netherlands and Cuba. Miss Wright represented the Library of Congress in Spain from 1932-36, was associate archivist of the National Archives from 1936-38, then became a foreign affairs specialist for the State Department. She died at New Rochelle, New York, and was buried at Pueblo, Colorado.

New York Times, Apr. 8, 1972.

Wright, Robert, pioneer (Sept. 2, 1840-Jan. 4, 1915). B. at Bladensburg, Maryland, he went to Missouri in 1856, worked near St. Louis three years, then traveled by ox team to Denver. He was a freighter, hay and wood cutter, and post trader at Fort Dodge, Kansas, as early as 1867. In company with Charles Rath he operated businesses as far south as Fort Griffin, Texas, and Old Mobeetie, Texas. Wright served as a civilian scout for the Army during the Dull Knife operation in 1878. At Dodge City, he became a farmer, cattleman, businessman and first mayor of the community, and held numerous county positions besides being a state legislator, elected four times. He died at Dodge City.

Ed Bartholomew, *Wyatt Earp: The Untold Story.* Toyahvale, Tex., Frontier Book Co., 1963; Kan. State Hist. Soc. archives; Robert M. Wright, *Dodge City, The Cowboy Capital.* (Wichita, 1913).

Wright, Thomas Forster, army officer (c. Dec. 1830-Apr. 26, 1873). The son of Brigadier General George Wright who was drowned while in command of the Division of the Pacific, Thomas Wright was b. in Missouri and in 1848 from California went to West Point where he remained more than a year but did not graduate. He was commissioned a first lieutenant of the 2nd California Cavalry October 2, 1861, resigning in January 1863 to become major of the 6th California Infantry; he transferred to the 2nd California Infantry in October 1864, becoming lieutenant colonel in November and colonel January 6, 1865. With a detachment from the regiment on January 21, 1866 he had an engagement with Apaches east of Fort Grant, Arizona, in which 13 Indians were killed and six taken prisoner. He was mustered out of the volunteer service a brevet Brigadier General in April 1866. Wright was commissioned a first lieutenant of the 32nd U.S. Infantry July 28, 1866, and joined the 12th Infantry January 31, 1870,

being sent with it in early 1873 to the Lava Beds of northeastern California for service in the Modoc War. During protracted and futile peace negotiations with Captain Jack and the hostiles, Wright testily claimed that he and Lieutenant Charles Eagan could round up the enemy in 15 minutes if given the opportunity; of course they were not. On April 15, 1873, he and Eagan were in the second Battle of the Stronghold which ended as disastrously as the first, with Eagan wounded and out of action along with numerous enlisted men, although Wright's company suffered no casualties. April 26, 1873, Wright's company, with troops led by Captain Evan Thomas fell into a trap laid by Scarface Charley, an able Modoc warrior-leader. Wright was slain along with Thomas. About half of the command was killed or wounded.

Heitman; Orton; Keith A. Murray, *The Modocs and Their War.* Norman, Univ. of Okla. Press, 1965; Richard Dillon, *Burnt-Out Fires.* Englewood Cliffs, N.J., Prentice-Hall, 1973.

Wyatt, Nelson Ellsworth (Zip, Dick Yeager), desperado (1863-Sept. 7, 1895). B. in Indiana, he came to Oklahoma Territory in 1889 with his family, settling east of Guthrie. He was married, a fine horseman, expert shot, and wild. Driven out of the Territory following a shooting, he went to Kansas, killed a deputy sheriff, Andy Balfour, at Pryor's Grove, was arrested in Indiana, and returned to Oklahoma for the original charge. He escaped jail, soon becoming associated with Bill Doolin in outlawry. He was with Doolin in the April 3, 1895, train robbery at Dover, Oklahoma, and robbed a post office at Winview, Oklahoma, July 26. He was surrounded in a timber grove near Canton-ment, wounded but escaped, and was mortally wounded later near Sheridan, Oklahoma.

Bailey C. Hanes, *Bill Doolin, Outlaw O.T.* Norman, Univ. of Okla. Press, 1968; William A. Pinkerton, *Train Robberies and Train Robbers.* Fort Davis, Tex., Frontier Book Co., 1968; Glenn Shirley, *Toughest of Them All.* Albuquerque, Univ. of New Mex. Press, 1953.

Wyeth, Nathaniel Jarvis, fur trader (Jan. 29, 1802-Aug. 31, 1856). B. near Cambridge, Massachusetts, he was primarily associated all his life with the New England ice trade, which his inventiveness largely built and developed.

He came under the influence of Hall Jackson Kelley, a Boston enthusiast for the development of Oregon and about 1831 embarked upon his five-year fur trading expedition to the northwest. He carefully planned the project to include a number of innovations, most of which did not work out. Wyeth reached St. Louis with his party, which he joined to a Robert Campbell-William Sublette caravan, the combined group leaving Independence May 12, 1832, for the Rocky Mountains. The Pierre's Hole rendezvous was reached after some hardships on July 8, those of Wyeth's party willing to continue toward the far northwest now reduced to 11 men; these joined a Milton Sublette-Henry Fraeb brigade and on July 18 engaged in the celebrated battle against the Gros Ventres, although the role of Wyeth's party in the incident was very slight. Wyeth and his group, after amateurish and unsuccessful attempts to trap beaver, reached Fort Vancouver in October where Wyeth learned of the loss at sea of his principal supply ship, and his initial venture dissolved with the withdrawal of his remaining men. Wyeth, however, returned to the northern Rockies, seeking an arrangement with the Hudson's Bay Company for supplies, Wyeth and his contract-trappers to work south of the Columbia and turn over their catch to HBC posts. The plan ultimately was rejected. Later he approached Bonneville with a somewhat similar suggestion, but little came of it. Finally he agreed with the Rocky Mountain Fur Company to supply it with goods at the rendezvous of 1834, and to receive payment in beaver. Wyeth then hurried down the Missouri River in a pirogue, accompanied by two Indians, one of whom he took to Boston. He arranged for fresh shipments of goods to go by sea to the Oregon coast, hurried back to Missouri to acquire supplies for the overland part of his latest scheme, and left Independence April 28. But he lost a race with William Sublette to the rendezvous, and arrived there to find no market. Furious at what he regarded as false dealing, Wyeth swore revenge and in July at the junction of the Snake and Portneuf rivers, built Fort Hall, designed to attract a fur trade monopoly, which it never did. He then continued to Fort Vancouver, arriving September 14, 1834. His ship had been delayed, reaching the coast too late for the salmon run; Wyeth sent it to Hawaii on a trading mission, and built Fort William at the mouth of the Willamette River. He spent the

winter trapping south of the Columbia, suffered a disappointment the following season with regard to his salmon project, packing in barrels for shipment to Boston only half a cargo, attempted ineffectually to make a new deal with the HBC at Fort Vancouver and finally gave up and returned to St. Louis, out $20,000 and five years. Although devoting himself to the ice and refrigeration business in New England thereafter, he retained a lively enthusiasm for the west and Oregon, promoted public attention in that direction, and was a continuing factor in implementing their development. Despite his economic reverses in Oregon and his naivete, he was an important influence on the region and in securing it for the nation.

Literature abundant: Bernard DeVoto, *Across the Wide Missouri*. Boston, Houghton Mifflin Co., 1947; William R. Samson article, MM, Vol. V.

Wyeth, Newell Convers, artist (Oct. 22, 1882-Oct. 19, 1945). B. at Needham, Massachusetts, he studied art in Boston and with artists Howard Pyle and C.W. Reed and as an illustrator "produced some of his best works for national periodicals." He also illustrated about twenty juvenile classics, including an edition of Parkman's *The Oregon Trail*. His works included murals in some of the best-known buildings of the east, including the headquarters of the National Geographic Society. Western subjects brought Wyeth his first commission and he made three important study trips west starting in 1904 when he visited Denver and the Colorado Hashknife ranch where he worked as a cowboy and participated in a roundup, also visiting New Mexico and Arizona and sketching and photographing the Navaho. His illustrations appeared in many major magazines, but his "ardor for the West" cooled by 1910 and most of his later work concerned other subjects.

Colo. Hist. Soc., *Mountain & Plain History Notes*, Vol. 17, No. 11/12 (Nov./Dec. 1980); *Who Was Who*.

Wyllys, Rufus Kay, historian (Jan. 30, 1898-Apr. 15, 1955). B. at Cambria, Michigan, he served briefly in the army during World War I, received his master's degree in history from the University of Michigan and a doctorate from the University of California at Berkeley under Bolton. He joined the faculty of what became Arizona State University at Tempe in

1929. He published widely in historical journals though he is best known for his still useful *Arizona: The History of a Frontier State* (1950). Others of his book-length writings include *The French in Sonora (1850-1854): The Story of French Adventurers from California Into Mexico* (1932) and *Pioneer Padre: The Life and Times of Eusebio Francisco Kino* (1935).

Paul Hubbard, "A Dedication to the Memory of Rufus Kay Wyllys." *Arizona and the West*, Vol. 22, No. 2 (Summer 1980), 104-08.

Wynkoop, Edward Wanshear, army officer (June 19, 1836-Sept. 11, 1891). B. in Pennsylvania he reached Leavenworth, Kansas, in 1858 and was appointed by his friend Governor James W. Denver sheriff for Arapahoe County in what would become Colorado, Wynkoop joining a party that would found the community of Denver. In December he journeyed back to Omaha and eastern Kansas (freezing both feet enroute), relating exaggerated tales of the gold wealth of the new communities springing up before the Rocky Mountains. He took a wagon train of emigrants who paid $100 each for passage to the mines which by new discoveries managed to about equal his earlier yarns of great wealth. As sheriff he attempted to halt a duel October 9, 1859, between his friend, William Park McClure and Richard E. Whitsitt, but the latter seriously wounded McClure. Attempting to still another fight he was even less fortunate, an innocent black bystander was killed. Occasionally he presided at a hanging. When two companies of militia were organized in 1860, Wynkoop joined both, becoming first lieutenant of the Denver Cavalry and a second lieutenant of the Jefferson Rangers, continuing meanwhile his law supporting activities except when he was a participant in a duel, either as principal or second. At one time he became involved as a witness and near-principal in a saloon killing by another. In 1861 he married a professional actress, Louise Wakely, a successful union which produced eight children. March 31, 1861, Wynkoop was commissioned a second lieutenant in the 1st Colorado Infantry, shortly becoming captain of Company A. He was prominent in the defeat of the Confederates at Glorieta Pass, New Mexico, March 26, 1862, and in the Pigeon Ranch fight two days later, becoming a major. In June 1863 he led

five companies on an eventless Ute campaign south of North Park, Colorado; the Indians were not contacted. May 8, 1864, he came into command of Fort Lyon, eastern Colorado, directing his men on various hunts for marauding Plains Indians. September 3 soldiers brought in three Cheyennes to see Wynkoop, the Indians desirous of peace. Wynkoop with escort accompanied the prisoners to the Smoky Hill River when he conferred with some 600 warriors of the Cheyenne and Arapaho tribes, including Black Kettle and other noted chiefs. A delegation of seven chiefs accompanied Wynkoop back to Fort Lyon with white captives they had released to the troops. Although no pledge of peace was given them, the Indians understood they were under government protection and were assigned by Major Scott Anthony, who on November 2, 1864, succeeded Wynkoop as Fort Lyon commander, to camp on Sand Creek. Wynkoop left Fort Lyon November 26 to report to the District of the Upper Arkansas commander at Fort Riley, Kansas, and was shocked to learn that two days after his departure Chivington had launched his notorious attack on the encamped Sand Creek Indians. He was ordered back to Fort Lyon to investigate the affair, the first of a series of investigations in each of which Wynkoop's actions were approved and praised. He became hated in Colorado Territory where most of the citizenry approved Chivington's action, "but his fearless testimony won the respect of military officers and federal officials who repudiated Chivington's brutality." Wynkoop became commander of the Veteran Battalion of Colorado Cavalry and on June 17, 1865, was made chief of cavalry for the District of the Upper Arkansas. He commanded the escort for the commissioners in the fall of 1865 concluding a treaty with the Cheyennes by whom Wynkoop was considered something of a hero for this position against Chivington. He resigned his commission in July 1866 and became agent to the Cheyenne, Arapaho and Plains Apache, establishing his agency at Fort Larned, Kansas. His good work was interrupted by the inept Hancock expedition of 1867 which raised suspicions among the southern Plains Indians, frightened many away from the agency and brought renewed hostilities. Wynkoop and Hancock engaged in a lengthy correspondence battle over the resumption of conflict. His Indians had become scattered and when some did come in it was obvious that the more militant would not; Wynkoop's life was even threatened by Roman Nose. He resigned as agent November 29, 1868, and returned to Pennsylvania from where he renewed his attacks on Chivington and Hancock. He tried unsuccessfully to become Commissioner of Indian affairs and in 1873 to obtain the agency to the Navahos, but here failed, too. He joined the Black Hills gold rush, reaching Custer, Dakota Territory, in March 1876, skirmishing with Sioux enroute. He organized the Black Hills Rangers, becoming captain with his second in command Jack Crawford, the so-called poet scout. Wynkoop shortly returned to Pennsylvania. In 1882 he became special timber agent for the United States land office at Denver and in 1883 removed to Santa Fe where he held a like office for three years. When the Republicans returned to power in 1889 Wynkoop became adjutant general of the New Mexico Territorial Militia, later becoming warden of the territorial penitentiary. He died of Bright's Disease.

Thomas D. Isern, "The Controversial Career of Edward W. Wynkoop." *Colo. Mag,* Vol. 56, Nos. 1, 2 (Winter-Spring 1979), 1-18.

Y

Yager, Erastus (Red), desperado (c. 1833-Jan. 4, 1864). B. probably in West Liberty, Iowa, he was briefly a classmate at 10 or 11 of James and Granville Stuart at a country school near the Iowa town, although the Stuarts did not see him for 20 years afterward. Yager meanwhile had visited gold fields on various frontiers and in Idaho had turned to a life of crime. He was an important member of Henry Plummer's gang of Montana desperadoes when picked up by vigilantes early in January 1864, was "tried," convicted and sentenced to hang. Before his execution Yager, who faced death with intrepidity and resignation, and seemed to his captors a "perfect gentleman," told them he approved of what they were about and gave them as complete a list as his memory permitted of the Plummer gang members and their functions within that criminal organization; with this the liquidation of the desperado outfit was assured. Red was hanged with George W. Brown, another Plummer outlaw in the Stinkingwater Valley near Virginia City. Red conceded that he had "merited it long ago," and added that "no poor country was ever cursed with a more bloodthirsty or meaner pack of villains." He shook hands with his executioners, his final words being, "Good-by, boys. You're on a good undertaking. God bless you all." After his body was cut down, letters in his pockets showed him to have been the Stuarts' childhood playmate. Dimsdale described Yager as "a light and wiry built man about five feet five inches high, with red hair and red whiskers."

Langford; Dimsdale; Granville Stuart, *Prospecting for Gold.* Lincoln, Univ. of Nebr. Press, 1977, 29-30.

Yantis, Ollie (Ol), outlaw (c. 1869-Nov. 29, 1892). B. in Kentucky, he was lanky, sallow, with prominent upper teeth and was a cotton farmer near Orlando, Oklahoma, when not pursuing lawless activities. He became associated with the Daltons and Bill Doolin, helping the latter hold up a train at Caney, Oklahoma, October 14, 1892, and a bank at Spearville, Kansas, November 1, 1892. He was shot by law officers on the ranch of his sister, Mrs. Hugh McGinn, south of Orlando, and died in a nearby doctor's office, game to the end.

Bailey C. Hanes, *Bill Doolin, Outlaw O.T.* Norman, Univ. of Okla. Press, 1968.

Yates, George Walter, army officer (Feb. 26, 1843-June 25, 1876). B. at Albany, New York, he enlisted June 20, 1861, in the 4th Michigan Infantry, was commissioned a first lieutenant September 26, 1862, joined the 45th Missouri Infantry August 24, 1864, and became a captain of the 13th Missouri Cavalry September 22, 1864, emerging from the Civil War a brevet lieutenant colonel of Volunteers. He was commissioned a second lieutenant of the 2nd Cavalry March 26, 1866, and a captain of the 7th Cavalry June 12, 1867. Yates commanded Company F in Custer's Battle of the Washita in November 1868 and was on Custer's Black Hills Expedition of 1874. Yates and Tom Custer were sent to Standing Rock Agency, North Dakota, by George Custer to arrest Rain in the Face late in 1875 after the Indian reportedly had boasted of killing two whites in Montana in 1873; little evidence against the Sioux could be obtained and the matter was dropped, but the incident led to Rain in the Face's reported (and never verified) grudge against the Custers. Yates accompanied Custer's 1876 Sioux expedition as a battalion commander and was killed on Custer Hill, not far from the commander, although separated somewhat from his own Company F. He was survived by his widow and three children. Yates was buried on the battlefield, his remains exhumed the following year and reinterred at the Fort Leavenworth National Cemetery. The post at Standing Rock Sioux Agency, North Dakota, was named Fort Yates December 30, 1878.

Heitman; BHB; Edgar I. Stewart, *Custer's Luck.* Norman, Univ. of Okla. Press, 1955.

Ybarbo, Antonio Gill, frontiersman (1729-1809). B. at Los Adaes (near the present Robeline) Louisiana, of Spanish parentage. When the colonists were removed in accordance with Rubí's recommendation tightening the frontier line of New Spain, Ybarbo led resistance to the resettlement. In 1774 the settlers were permitted to return as far as the Trinity River, Texas, where they founded Bucareli in today's Waller County; when Bucareli was abandoned after a disastrous Comanche raid in 1779, Ybarbo led in reconstruction of Nacogdoches and was a prominent resident of it. The government gave him the titles of lieutenant governor, captain of militia and judge of contraband, which meant the authority to control smuggling, but there were complaints that he was "contrabanding" himself and this led to his resignation as governor in 1790. The next year he was accused not only of smuggling, but trading with Indians for horses rustled from the Spanish; he was cleared but forbidden to return to Nacogdoches though permitted to live in Louisiana. However in a few years he did return to Nacogdoches and died on his ranch near there. He married twice, his first wife dying in 1794. Ybarbo lost most of his property through litigation before his death.

Noel M. Loomis, Abraham P. Nasatir, *Pedro Vial and the Roads to Santa Fe.* Norman, Univ. of Okla. Press, 1967; HT; Herbert Eugene Bolton, *Texas in the Middle Eighteenth Century.* Austin, Univ. of Tex. Press, 1916, 1970.

Yeaton, Franklin, army officer (c. 1848-Aug. 17, 1872). B. at St. John's, New Brunswick, he lived at Naples, Cumberland County, Maine, until he went to West Point, being commissioned a second lieutenant of the 3rd Cavalry June 15, 1869. His superior officer in F Company was Howard Bass Cushing, and with Cushing Yeaton took part in a pursuit and attack on Mescalero Apaches in the Guadalupe Mountains of west Texas in October 1869. On December 26, 1869, he and Cushing were in another hard fight with red stock thieves in the Guadalupe Mountains, Yeaton being severely wounded in the chest and arm. His wounds never properly healed. He was transferred to West Point where on November 14, 1871, he was retired with rank of captain. He died at the home of Dr. Sam F. Perley at Naples, Maine, the cause stated as "consumption hastened by a gunshot wound."

Cullum; Heitman; Donald N. Bentz, "Sword of

Revenge." *Golden West,* Vol. 8, No. 2 (Jan. 1972), 39-43, 66; Andrew Wallace, "Duty in New Mexico: A Military Memoir." *New Mex. Hist. Rev.,* Vol. L, No. 3 (July 1975), 231-62.

Yellow Hand (Yellow Hair, Hay-o-wei), Cheyenne war leader (c. 1850-July 17, 1876). His name, Hay-o-wei, was translated by scout Baptiste Garnier as Yellow Hand but more properly it is Yellow Hair referring to a scalp he once had taken. He was the son of Cut Nose, a Cheyenne chief. His celebrated fight with Cody occurred on Hat Creek, near present Montrose, Nebraska. The two, Cody and Yellow Hand, met by surprise, almost face to face. Each fired at the other, the Indian missing, Cody's bullet piercing the Indian's leg and killing his horse. Cody dismounted and each fired again, the Indian once more missing and Cody's bullet killing Yellow Hand whom he then scalped. The incident, picked up by dime novelists and psuedo historical writers has been magnified considerably beyond the facts. It was a "duel" only insofar as each started shooting at about the same time and continued firing until the affair was settled. But the fight, however distorted, became a sterling achievement for Cody, assisting in projecting an heroic image to the American public.

Don Russell, *The Lives and Legends of Buffalo Bill.* Norman, Univ. of Okla. Press, 1960; Dockstader.

Yellow Head (Yellow Hair, Sartair, Kitcheepone-istah), Piegan (fl. 1853-1856). He was hired by Lieutenant Donelson of Stevens' expedition in September 1853, as a guide in exploration of Cadotte's Pass. He signed the Fort Benton treaty of October 17, 1855, and was the first friendly Blackfoot to visit the Flathead country thereafter, reaching Fort Owen May 1, 1856, and leaving May 11 with a letter from Owen to Fort Benton.

Montana, Contributions, Vol. X, 1940, 277.

Yellow Serpent, Walla Walla chief: see *Peu-peu-mox-mox*

Yellow Shield (Ehyo-vohi-va-heh), Cheyenne chief (d. Nov. 29, 1864). A prominent leader of the Southern Cheyennes, he was killed in the Chivington attack on a peaceful village at Sand Creek, Colorado.

George Bird Grinnell, *The Fighting Cheyennes.* Norman, Univ. of Okla. Press, 1956.

Yellow Thunder (Wa-kun-cha-koo-kah), Winnebago chief (1774-Feb. 1874). Before 1840 the Winnebago inhabited country around Lake Winnebago and Green Bay, Wisconsin. When it was decided to move the Indians to a reservation in southeastern Minnesota and northeastern Iowa, Yellow Thunder and some others were invited to Washington, D.C., where on November 1, 1837, they were persuaded to sign a treaty ceding their lands east of the Mississippi and calling for their removal within eight months. They claimed that they had been misled, that they were told the time period was eight years. Troops were sent to Portage, Wisconsin,. to remove them. Yellow Thunder was falsely accused of plotting revolt and was chained, but soon released and the removal was effected. Not liking the new reservation, Yellow Thunder and his wife within a year returned and homesteaded a 40-acre tract on the Wisconsin River above Portage; here they remained until his death. He was respected by his people, an able counselor, industrious, temperate and a zealous Catholic. A monument to him was erected July 27, 1909, north of Baraboo, Wisconsin.

Hodge, HAI.

Yellow Wolf, Cheyenne chief (c. 1779-Nov. 29, 864). Yellow Wolf, leader of the Cheyenne Hevhaitano, or Hairy Clan, already was a chief in 1826 when he led a successful raid against Kiowa-Comanche horse herds on the North Fork of the Red River. In 1828 he led a war party of Cheyennes and Arapahoes against Comanches under Bull Hump, the action starting about 40 miles north of old Fort Lyon in eastern Colorado; it was a Cheyenne triumph. Yellow Wolf recommended to Bent where he should locate the famous Bent's Fort in order to be most advantageously situated for the Indian trade, and his advice was followed. George Bent said Yellow Wolf, "a small man, and light on his feet," was one of the most famous chiefs of the old days "and the whites considered him head chief of the Southern Cheyennes." About 1833 he led the Cheyennes in a victory over the Kiowas, and in other triumphs over Plains enemies in 1835 and 1838. Although noted as a warrior, Yellow Wolf in 1846 expressed to Second Lieutenant J. W. Abert a willingness to settle down. "He is a man of considerable influence," wrote Abert, "of enlarged views and gifted with more

foresight than any other man in his tribe. He frequently talks of the diminishing number of his people, and the decrease of the once abundant buffalo. He says that . . . the Indians. . . will have to adopt the habits of the white people," and proposed to pay in mules if a fort would be built for them and the Cheyennes taught how to cultivate the ground and raise cattle. In March 1863 Yellow Wolf was among a delegation of Plains chiefs who visited Washington, D.C. and met with Lincoln and later with P.T. Barnum in New York City. Yellow Wolf apparently did not attend the important council with Governor Evans of Colorado at Denver in late September 1864, but he was at Sand Creek with Black Kettle when Chivington attacked the peaceful camp at dawn November 29, 1864, and was killed along with 100 to 300 of the Indians, most of whom were women and children. He was 85 years old, according to George Bent.

George E. Hyde, *Life of George Bent.* Norman, Univ. of Okla. Press, 1968; Stan Hoig, *The Western Odyssey of John Simpson Smith.* Glendale, Calif., Arthur H. Clark Co., 1974; George Bird Grinnell, *The Fighting Cheyennes.* Norman, 1956; Grinnell, *The Cheyenne Indians,* 2 vols. Lincoln, Univ. of Nebr. Press, 1972.

Yellow Wolf (Heinmot Hihhih, White Thunder, Hemene Moxmox), Nez Perce warrior (c. 1856-Aug. 21, 1935). B. in the Wallowa Valley of northeastern Oregon, he was a second cousin to Chief Joseph and was raised as a Nez Perce warrior and noted horseman. Yellow Wolf had a role in the preliminaries to the 1877 Nez Perce "war," or more properly, hegira, and was in the initial engagment, the Battle of White Bird Canyon. He was among the Indians who wiped out the Lieutenant Sevier Rains party of ten enlisted men and a white scout on the Cottonwood Ranch on the Clearwater River, Idaho, July 3. Yellow Wolf was in the Battle of Clearwater July 11-12, 1877, and was twice wounded, the Indians suffering four killed and six wounded; the whites fifteen killed or wounded mortally and 25 wounded. At the important Battle of Big Hole, Montana, August 9-10, Yellow Wolf was in the thick of heavy fighting, killed one man with a war club and seized his weapons and shot down several soldiers and retrieved their arms which he distributed to other warriors, some of whom had been armed only with bows or clubs. Yellow Wolf's version of the engagement is dramatic and truthful. At Camas Meadows, Idaho, Yellow Wolf was with the raiders who stole horses and most of the mules from a soldier encampment August 20. He was one of two Nez Perce who captured John Shively, forcing him to guide the Indians toward Clark's Fork of the Yellowstone so they could find their way to Crow country and the buffalo plains. In Yellowstone Park Yellow Wolf was among the warriors who captured a party of tourists. Neither he nor his companions harmed them, although with some young warriors he did fire upon other whites during transit of the park, and there were casualties. Yellow Wolf was in the affairs of Canyon Creek, September 13 and Cow Creek Canyon, September 23 and the climactic Battle of Bear Paw Mountains, September 30-October 5, 1877. He was "perhaps the last Nez Perce warrior to leave the Bear Paw field," being sent by Chief Joseph October 5 to find the chief's daughter and Yellow Wolf's mother. He located the two with 40 or 50 other Nez Perce and accompanied them to Canada where they found sanctuary among Sitting Bull's Sioux. Yellow Wolf remained in Canada almost a year, but around June 1878 he and 28 other Nez Perce recrossed the border and made their way to Idaho, taking what horses and cattle they required for transportation or food, skirmishing on the Lolo trail with soldiers, and gaining the Lapwai Reservation, Idaho. Yellow Wolf and some of the others surrendered at the agency. He was treated fairly well, but sent to Indian Territory to rejoin Joseph's band. In 1885 he and the others were taken northwest once more, Yellow Wolf accompanying Joseph and many others to the Colville Reservation in Washington State. McWhorter met Yellow Wolf on the Colville Reservation in October 1908. "He stood 5 feet, 10 1/2 inches in his moccasins, and his weight was 187 1/2 pounds. Well built, he had been very athletic, and was quick and accurate in movement. Tragedy was written in every lineament of his face; his laughter was infrequent." His land allotment was not provided with irrigation, and he supported his family principally by fishing and hunting, although in his declining years he was recipient of considerable government aid. He died at his home on the reservation and was buried at Nespelem, near

the grave of Chief Joseph. His life story was gathered by McWhorter during nearly 30 years of interviews, conversations and correspondence. It is virtually the only narrative in existence giving the Indian side of the Nez Perce campaign, a detailed, obviously honest account, accurate from the point of view of one man and what he did, saw and heard from his peers. It is a valuable document and has been widely used by historians and others writing of the Nez Perce and their 1877 hegira.

Lucullus, V. McWhorter, *Yellow Wolf: His Own Story.* Caldwell, Ida., Caxton Printers, 1940; McWhorter, *Hear Me.*

York, Ben (?), slave, explorer (b. c. 1770). Ferris said that York was "about the same age as William Clark or possibly younger," and was born a slave, willed to Clark by his father on July 24, 1799. York was a large-sized man of prodigious strength who accompanied the memorable Lewis and Clark Expedition to the Pacific and return. Of great good humor, York was popular with Indians as with whites and in Coues' view "was evidently a wag." After the expedition's return to St. Louis York was freed (Clark freed all his slaves in 1811); fond of drink his tales grew taller and more robust with each glass, and he never lacked listeners. He returned to Louisville, Kentucky, married, was furnished a dray and six horses by Clark and engaged in the hauling business between Nashville, Tennessee, and Richmond, Kentucky, although his enterprise did not prosper. Ferris wrote that York was "apparently on his way back to join Clark at St. Louis when he fell ill with cholera and died at an unknown date somewhere in Tennessee."

History of the Expedition Under the Command of Lewis and Clark, ed. by Elliott Coues. N.Y., Dover Pubns., 1965; Robert G. Ferris, ed., *Lewis and Clark.* Wash., Nat. Park Service, 1975.

Young, Brigham, empire builder, churchman (June 1, 1801-Aug. 29, 1877). B. at Whitingham, Vermont, into a Methodist family, his formal education was limited but by 16 he had become a carpenter, joiner, painter and glazier, his early skill as a craftsman evident in the still-standing houses he constructed with his own hands. At 21 he joined the Methodist church and soon became a local preacher, in 1824 moving with his first wife to western New York. In about 1830 he came across a

Book of Mormon near Mendon, New York, left by a younger brother of Joseph Smith, the prophet of what became the Church of Jesus Christ of Latter-day Saints. Young was impressed, studied the faith and was baptized into it April 14, 1832, being ordained an elder the same evening. His first meeting with Smith was in the fall of 1834 when he visited Kirtland, Ohio; he was sent on a proselytizing mission to Canada. By now a widower, Young married his second wife. Smith, it is said, prophesied that Brigham Young would one day preside over the church. February 14, 1835, he was chosen one of the Twelve Apostles, the council second in authority in the Mormon church. He entered upon its full-time service, traveling, exhorting, collecting funds for construction of the temple at Kirtland and purchase of lands in Missouri, where converts rapidly were settling. When opposition to the sect broke out in Ohio, Young stood staunchly with Smith, sometimes at the peril of his own life, but eventually animosity grew too strong and the headquarters was moved from Ohio. At Far West, Missouri, in 1838 Young succeeded to the presidency of the Twelve, and in the absence of the first presidency of the church, directed the move of 12,000 to 15,000 Mormons, again under duress, from Missouri to Nauvoo, Illinois, where it appeared they had found a hospitable homeland at last. In 1840 Young and others began a mission to Europe, landing at Liverpool April 6, on Mormonism's tenth anniversary. He remained in Britain more than a year, with his associates baptizing more than 7,000 and starting branches of the church in many cities of the United Kingdom, firmly establishing the British work as the initial and most important foreign mission of the church. "Soon after his return from abroad, (Young) was taught by the Prophet the principle of celestial, or plural marriage, which he practiced as did others while at Nauvoo," said a Mormon publication. He married from time to time among others, several of Smith's widows, and in all had about 27 wives (the precise number is not known) by whom he fathered about 57 children. Young was in the east promoting the candidacy of Joseph Smith for President of the United States when the prophet and his brother, Hyrum were murdered in a Carthage, Illinois, jail June 27, 1844. Without Smith's hand, the church fell into disorder and

schisms were threatened. Most of the Mormons sustained Brigham Young in his position that in the absence of the first presidency, the Twelve Apostles must lead the church, and he was president of that body (although he did not take the title as head of the church for two more years). It was evident that the people must abandon Nauvoo and in February 1846 they crossed the frozen Mississippi into Iowa, halting at the Missouri River where in the summer of 1846 they supplied 500 men (the Mormon Battalion) to take part in the war with Mexico, much of the funds they earned from their pay financing the exodus of the membership to the west. Winter quarters were established at Florence, Nebraska, and from here in April 1847 Young with a company of 143 men, 3 women and 2 children started west once again, this time entering the desert valley of Great Salt Lake where on July 24, tradition says, Brigham Young struck the ground with his staff, proclaiming, "This is the place!" Here the Mormons founded Salt Lake City, and nearby all the other communities of the Salt Lake Valley, the work done under direction of Brigham Young and the theocracy he sought to establish. Under his aegis was organized the provisional State of Deseret with Young elected governor March 12, 1849. And under his supervision explorations were carried out, settlements begun and farming developed wherever water for irrigation made it possible. The only branch of industry not encouraged was mining. "We can not eat gold or silver," said Young, urging development of agriculture instead for "we need bread and clothing first. Neither do we want to bring in here a roving, reckless, frontier population to drive us again from our hard-earned homes." The Territory of Utah was organized September 9, 1850, by Congress, and President Fillmore named Young governor. He served two terms until succeeded in 1858 by the non-Mormon Alfred Cumming in the wake of the so-called Mormon War. That affair probably had its origins in the various disturbances which forced the Mormons to withdraw first from Ohio, then from Missouri, and finally from Illinois, in each case because of what they conceived as pressure and persecution by "gentiles," or non-Mormons. Their removal to distant Utah and establishment of a viable and growing commonwealth did not still the antagonism toward them of

people in the States, and the public pro-
nouncement of Orson Pratt, a prominent
Mormon leader, in an 1852 speech of the
existence of polygamy and the leadership
acceptance of it in Mormon practice added to
public clamor against them. Convinced that
Mormons were guilty of lawlessness and
plotting rebellion, President Buchanan in
1857 sent a military expedition commanded
by Colonel Albert Sidney Johnston, and
removed Young as governor. There was no
open warfare save for raids by Mormon Lot
Smith on supply caravans, but an atrocious
spin-off of the "war" was the infamous
Mountain Meadows Massacre in southwest
Utah by which about 140 emigrants bound for
California were massacred. Young was too
intelligent and pragmatic to have orderd such
a deed, but he may have condoned it and
assuredly protected the perpetrators after the
event until an apparent arrangement was
arrived at with the United States to sacrifice
John D. Lee, a leader in the affair in exchange
for federal dropping of charges against other
individuals. This incident was the darkest stain
on the otherwise admirable and at times
magnificent career of Young. His stamp is to
be seen everywhere in the Utah of today and
there can be no doubt it will last as long as the
vigorous, growing faith endures. Young early
had sent families to found colonies in Idaho,
Nevada and California but called many in
when hostilities threatened in 1857 and it
appeared the Mormons might have to battle
to hold their bastion in the wilderness.
Afterward expansion resumed, but more
slowly and in a more orderly fashion. The
growth continues today. By the time of
Brigham Young's death more than 360
communities had been established in Utah,
Idaho, Nevada, California and Arizona;
where Young in 1847 had commenced the
settlement of the Great Basin with 148 people,
by 1877 the population was more than
100,000, most of them Mormons, and a great
part of this growth was due to policies
initiated or carried out by Young, one of the
few first-rank empire builders in American
history. Prominent Mormon historian,
Leonard J. Arrington said that Young died of
"peritonitis following an acute attack of
appendicitis." A recent book by Samuel
Woolley and Samuel W. Taylor, grandson of
Mormon President John Taylor (the volume
based in part upon research in church

archives not previously open to researchers)
reported that Brigham Young may have died
of arsenic poisoning, perpetrator unknown.

Frank Esshom, *Pioneers and Prominent Men of
Utah.* Salt Lake City, Western Epics, 1966;
Church of Jesus Christ of Latter-day Saints Public
Relations Dept.; Samuel W. Taylor, Samuel
Woolley, *The Kingdom or Nothing: The Life of
John Taylor, Militant Mormon.* N.Y., Macmillan
Co., 1976 (reviewed in *Frontier Times,* Vol. 51, No.
2 (Jan.-Mar. 1977), p. 1; several articles by Leonard
J. Arrington, REAW; CE.

**Young, Code (Bob Harris, Tom Harris, Cole
Estes),** desperado (c. 1872-Oct. 2, 1896). B. in
Texas, he was a cowboy around Roswell, New
Mexico, working for the Diamond A ranch and
others, and becoming a friend of George
Musgrave, embarked into deviltry with him.
The pair joined the Black Jack Christian outlaw
gang (see William Christian biography for
details), and was killed in the holdup of a train
at Rio Puerco, New Mexico, by deputy U.S.
marshal Will Loomis.

Jeff Burton, *Black Jack Christian: Outlaw.*
Santa Fe, Press of Territorian, 1967.

Young, Ewing, mountain man, pioneer (c.
1792-Feb. 1841). B. near Jonesboro, Tennessee, he received some education and training
as a carpenter. By 1822 he was in Missouri;
that year he joined William Becknell as a
minor partner for a trip to Santa Fe, the first
time wagons were taken there from Missouri.
Young and Wolfskill trapped the Pecos River
in the fall of 1822, the San Juan River in 1824;
Young then made two or three trips back to
Missouri, trading produce from the states in
the Mexican city and mules from Santa Fe in
Missouri. In the late summer of 1826 he
organized a trapping party which grew by
merger with others including three survivors
of a Robidoux-Pattie group whose defeat by
Papagos was avenged by Young. He led his
people up the Colorado, skirmishing occasionally with the Mohaves, then apparently
circled through the Rockies and descended
upon Santa Fe again, having cached some furs
enroute. Young was jailed although he had
been properly licensed to trap, and probably
earned little or nothing from his extensive
expedition. He procured a U.S. passport and
applied for Mexican citizenship in 1828, and
opened a Taos store with Wolfskill. The next
year he led a trapping party, including young

Kit Carson, to the Salt River, and proceeded to San Gabriel, California, trapping then up the central valley of the future state until contact was made with Peter Skene Ogden. Young's men retraced their steps to New Mexico, regaining Taos by April 1831. In October he set out again for California, heading a group of 36 trappers which reached Los Angeles February 10, 1832, then hunted sea otters unsuccessfully. He may have returned to Taos that summer, but was back in California for a trapping expedition through its northern part in the fall of 1833. Influenced by Hall J. Kelley, Young journeyed to Oregon, reaching Fort Vancouver in October 1834. He had been joined enroute by nine men with 56 apparently stolen horses, and was himself accused of horse theft in a letter from California Governor José Figueroa to John McLoughlin, thus found himself out of favor with McLoughlin upon his arrival. This created lasting difficulties for him, although the accusastion against Young probably was unjust. Young settled in the Chehalem Valley, Oregon, began a sawmill and a distillery although abandoning the latter project upon protests of a temperance group. In 1837 he was elected to return to California and buy cattle, bringing back to Oregon about 630 head of which 135 belonged to himself; this launched Young into ranching. He also continued in the fur trade and with lumbering, becoming an outstanding pioneer of Oregon, one of its most useful figures. He died apparently from an ulcer of the stomach. Young's pioneering influence was long lasting, in addition to his having become one of the greatest of the mountain men.

Keneth L. Holmes, *Ewing Young: Master Trapper.* Portland, Ore., Binfords & Mort, 1967; Harvey L. Carter article, MM, Vol. II.

Young, Granville, desperado (d. Oct. 29, 1845). A member of a bandit gang operating along the Mississippi River, Young with John and Aaron Long was accused of the torture murder July 4, 1845, of George Davenport, noted frontiersman and pioneer. With the Longs, Young was hanged at the Rock Island County (Illinois) Courthouse. He was buried locally, although the location of his grave is not known at present.

Information from Will Leinicke, Hauberg Indian Museum, Rock Island, Ill.; *Arizona Daily Star,* July 14, 1978; Edward Bonney, *Banditti of the Prairies.* Norman, Univ. of Okla. Press, 1963.

Young, John, cowboy (Feb. 12, 1856-Nov. 18, 1932). The man of whom J. Frank Dobie wrote his first book, *Vaquero of the Brush Country,* was b. at Lockhart, Texas, and raised in Bee and Refugio counties, Texas, becoming a cowboy, or brush-popper, and going up the trail with longhorn herds five times with Goodnight and others. Young claimed he had swum every river from the Rio Grande to the Platte and almost lost his life when crossing the Colorado River of Texas with a herd in 1880. Intrepid, he didn't mind shooting to solve a situation and in words of one who knew him well, he would "charge hell with a bucket of water." He died at Alpine, Texas.

Frontier Times, Vol. 10, No. 4 (Jan. 1933), 179-80.

Young, Samuel Baldwin Marks, army officer (Jan. 9, 1840-Sept. 1, 1924). B. near Pittsburgh, Pennsylvania, he enlisted in the 12th Pennsylvania Infantry April 25, 1861, transferred to the 4th Pennsylvania Cavalry September 6, being commissioned a captain and ended the Civil War a colonel and brevet Brigadier General of Volunteers. He was commissioned a second lieutenant of the 12th U.S. Infantry May 11, 1866 and a captain of the 8th Cavalry July 28, being assigned to Arizona and stationed at Fort Mojave on the Colorado River. Young took a prominent part in the Hualapais War of 1866-68, commanding his troopers in the only considerable action of the conflict January 15, 1868, in the Cerbat Mountains. He also had had a fight April 24, 1866, in which five Indians were killed and as many wounded. January 25, 1869, he had an enlisted man killed in a fight in the Juniper Mountains, Arizona, and June 27 another skirmish, also in northwestern Arizona. Assigned to West Texas in 1875 a detachment under Young was reported defeated by Mescaleros near San Carlos on October 28, 1877, but Wellman gives no details nor further identifies the site. In November 1877 Young with two 8th Cavalry and one 10th Cavalry companies and First Lieutenant John L. Bullis and his Seminole scouts left Texas on a long scout to the south and after a vigorous march surprised hostile Indians in the Carmen Mountains, 200 miles deep into Mexico. Not much damage was done but a few animals were taken and the Indians "dispersed." Young remained on the Rio Grande for four more years, being detailed in November 1881 for duty as an instructor at the Fort Leavenworth Infantry and Cavalry School where he remained four years. He became major of the 3rd Cavalry April 2, 1883, lieutenant colonel of the 4th Cavalry in 1892 and colonel of the 3rd Cavalry in 1897. Young became a Brigadier General in 1900 and a Major General the following year and after Philippine service on August 8, 1903, became Lieutenant General and commanding general of the army; when that office was abolished in 1903 he became the first Chief of Staff until he was retired at 64 on January 9, 1904. He was president of the court of inquiry which investigated the Brownsville, Texas, incident of 1906 in which black soldiers were alleged to have mutinied. Eventually Young moved to Helena, Montana where he died of pneumonia.

Heitman; NCAB, XIII, 313; Dan L. Thrapp, *The Conquest of Apacheria*. Norman, Univ. of Okla. Press, 1967; Barry C. Johnson, "Young's Fight on Thanksgiving Day." English Westerners Soc., *Brand Book*, Vol. 16, No. 3-4 (Apr.-July 1974); Paul I. Wellman, *The Indian Wars of the West*. Garden City, N.Y., Doubleday & Co., 1947

Young, Samuel Hall, missionary (Sept. 12, 1847-Sept. 2, 1927). B. at Butler, Pennsylvania, though plagued with ill health he was graduated from Western Seminary, Allegheny, Pennsylvania, and ordained a Presbyterian minister in 1878. He was influenced by Sheldon Jackson, volunteered for the Alaska mission field and began work that summer among the Stickeen Indians near Fort Wrangell. He married Fannie E. Kellogg, another missionary, and organized the first American church in Alaska at Wrangell. With naturalist John Muir he explored Glacier Bay, discovered Muir Glacier and with Muir the next year explored further in Alaska, the naturalist naming another glacier after Young. Young was influential in the granting by Congress of territorial status to Alaska. He left Alaska in 1888 after seeing mission work commenced among all southern Alaska tribes. The Klondike gold rush brought him back to the North; he organized a church at Dawson, Yukon Territory, in 1897, and in 1899 settled at Nome, caring for typhoid victims, contracting the disease himself. He became general missionary for his church in Alaska, remaining

until 1910 and returning after a year at New York to spend his efforts beyond the Yukon River until 1913, retaining his interest and occasional participation in Alaskan work until his retirement in 1924. He was killed by a streetcar near Clarksburg, West Virginia. He published *Alaska Days with John Muir* (1915); *The Klondike Clan* (1916); *Adventures in Alaska* (1919), and *Hall Young of Alaska* (1927), an autobiography.

Who Was Who; New York Times, Sept. 4, 1927; DAB; "Into the Far Corners." *Presbyterian Life,* Vol. 5, No. 17 (Sept. 6, 1952), 21-22.

Young, William, Mormon pioneer (fl. 1854-1857). A man of this name, resident of Cedar City, Utah, was placed by *Mormonism Unveiled* at the Mountain Meadows Massacre of September 11, 1857, either a participant in or consenting to the tragedy. *Journal of the Southern Indian Mission* cites him several times as counsellor to the local bishop and active in Mormon affairs in 1854. Brooks reports him involved in matters immediately preceding the fatal event. Young apparently had died before 1892. There were other individuals named William Young in Utah of the mid-19th century however who were in no way implicated in the massacre.

Mormonism Unveiled, 380; Juanita Brooks, ed., *Journal of the Southern Indian Mission.* Logan, Utah State Univ. Press, 1972; Brooks, *John Doyle Lee.* Glendale, Calif., Arthur H. Clark Co., 1962.

Young Man Afraid of His Horses (Tasunka-kokipapi), Oglala Sioux chief (c. 1830-c. 1900). B. probably in Nebraska or Dakota, his name properly translated means: Young Man Whose Enemies Fear Even His Horses. He became by inheritance a chief of the Oglala Sioux (his father was Old Man Afraid of His Horses), a noted warrior and a lieutenant of sorts under Red Cloud who was not a hereditary chief. He fought in the 1865-66 wars with Red Cloud and occasionally apart. Young Man was at the Platte Bridge fight of July 25-26, 1865 and in the engagements along the Bozeman Trail in 1866, culminating with the annihilation of the Fetterman command, December 21, 1866. He with Red Cloud agreed to the peace of 1868 and thereafter Young Man ceased his war actions. He took no hostile part in the wars of 1876 but sought to work out difficulties with the whites and live at peace in the ways prescribed. He was a leader of the posse sent to arrest the great war leader, Crazy Horse, in 1877. While he sided with McGillicuddy (and was a chief agent in McGillicuddy's control of his Sioux) he adamantly opposed further sales of Sioux lands to the government. During his later period he was installed by the whites as president of the Pine Ridge Indian Council and was taken on several trips to Washington, D.C. He opposed the ghost dance fervor of the late 19th century, warning his people that it could lead only to disaster for them. He realized that hostility could no longer benefit the Sioux and tried to win as favorable consideration as possible from the whites for them, being only partially successful. He died on the Pine Ridge Reservation of South Dakota.

Hodge, HAI; Dockstader; James C. Olson, *Red Cloud and the Sioux Problem.* Lincoln, Univ. of Nebr. Press, 1965.

Younger, James, desperado (Jan. 15, 1848-Oct. 19, 1902). Probably born at Harrisonville, Jackson County, Missouri, he became a guerilla with Quantrill at least by 1864, and may have accompanied his chieftain on the fatal incursion into Kentucky. Jim Younger probably took part in the Liberty, Missouri, bank robbery February 14, 1866, with the James brothers, the first such affair reported. At Monegaw Springs, St. Clair County, Missouri, in March 1874, he and his brother, John, became involved with two Pinkerton detectives and Edwin B. Daniel, onetime lawman. John was killed, Jim Younger killed Daniel and perhaps helped John kill Louis J. Hull, one of the Pinkertons. Jim was a regular with the James-Younger band until the September 7, 1876, attempt to rob a bank at Northfield, Minnesota, in flight from which James was wounded seriously and captured. With most of his upper jaw shot away he was thought to be dying, but survived to be imprisoned until July 10, 1901. Paroled, he continued to decline in health, was disappointed in a love affair, and shot himself.

See Thomas Coleman Younger for references.

Younger, John, desperado (1846?-Mar. 16, 1874). Probably born at Harrisonville, Jackson County, Missouri, there is no record that John Younger took any part in the Civil War, but he went with his brothers to Texas afterward, and in January 1871, murdered Charles H. Nichols, acting sheriff of Dallas County, who had been his friend. John was believed involved in the Kansas City Fair holdup September 26, 1872. He no doubt participated in other crimes, including train robbery, with the James-Younger band. He was killed in a fight with detectives, mortally wounding his opponent after being fatally shot himself. This was at Monegaw Springs, St. Clair County, Missouri.

See Thomas Coleman Younger for details.

Younger, Robert, desperado (Dec. 1853?-Sept. 16, 1889). Probably born at Harrisonville, Jackson County, Missouri. Too young to join other Youngers as a Civil War guerilla, Bob lived in Texas with his brothers for a time after the conflict. He probably took part in an Otterville, Missouri, train robbery July 7, 1876, and no doubt much other outlawry, though he never was as prominent as his brothers or the Jameses. Wounded, he was captured after the attempted Northfield, Minnesota, bank robbery September 7, 1876, sentenced to life imprisonment, and died of tuberculosis in the penitentiary at Stillwater.

See Thomas Coleman Younger for references.

Younger, Thomas Coleman (Cole), desperado (Jan. 15, 1844-Mar. 21, 1916). B. near Lee's Summit, Missouri, he joined William Clarke Quantrill's guerillas by early 1862, in the developing Civil War after his father, a pro-Union man, was killed by federal militiamen. He took part in the raid on Lawrence, Kansas, August 21, 1863. He joined the regular army, was assigned to a recruiting detail in New Mexico, and was in California by 1864. He led the robbery of a stagecoach near Hot Springs, Arkansas, in 1874, and in January of that year may have helped rob a train at Gads Hill, Missouri, 100 miles south of St. Louis, an incident in which the James boys may have figured. Cole and his two younger brothers were active off and on with Jesse and Frank James for several years, until the disastrous attempt to rob a bank at Northfield, Minnesota, September 7, 1876, following which the Youngers, all wounded, were captured, pleaded guilty, and were sentenced to life terms at Stillwater Penitentiary. Bob Younger died in prison September 16, 1889, and Cole and Jim were paroled July 10, 1901. Cole was pardoned at length and in February

1903, returned to Missouri. He lived at Lee's Summit until his death, at times lecturing on "Crime Does Not Pay," or "What Life Has Taught Me," and once appearing in a Wild West show with Frank James. He purportedly wrote a book, *The Story of Cole Younger By Himself.*

William A. Settle Jr., *Jesse James Was His Name.* Columbia, Univ. of Mo. Press, 1966; EA.

Yount, George C., frontiersman (May 4, 1794-Oct. 5, 1865). B. in Burke County, North Carolina, he was brought by his family to Cape Girardeau, then to the White River, Missouri, took some part in the War of 1812 and farmed. He reached Santa Fe in 1826, perhaps in the caravan that Kit Carson accompanied as a runaway. Yount joined a Ewing Young trapping party to work the Salt and Gila rivers; it reached the Colorado, trapped up it for some distance, explored the Virgin River, and regained Taos by 1828. The next season he trapped the middle Rockies, wintering in Bear Valley above Great Salt Lake, then returned to Taos. In the fall of 1830 he joined the Wolfskill trapping party, reaching California by the Old Spanish Trail. He engaged in sea otter hunting off Santa Barbara, trapped for beaver, visited central California and secured a land grant in the upper Napa Valley, where he became a prominent pioneer. He died at his ranch.

Charles L. Camp article, MM, Vol. IX; *The Chronicles of George C. Yount,* ed. by Charles L. Camp. Denver, Old West Pub. Co., 1966.

Yount, Robert E., soldier, jurist (Apr. 23, 1909-Jan. 5, 1977). B. at Prescott, Arizona, the son of a regimental surgeon of the 1st Arizona Infantry, Robert Yount served in reserve training with the 10th, 8th and 7th Cavalry regiments but transferred to the Air Force in 1941 and ended World War II as inspector general under General LeMay in the 29th Air Force, seeing considerable service in the Pacific. Afterward he served to colonel of reserves in the armored cavalry, then the armor. He had commenced the practice of law in 1939, in 1954 was appointed superior court judge of Maricopa County, Arizona, and later became chief juvenile court referee of the county. Yount was a founder and one of the prime movers in the organization of the Council on Abandoned Military Posts (CAMP), an organization oriented toward the identification and protection of abandoned military posts of frontier and other interest, and to him belongs much of the credit for the organization's early growth and influence. He was its president from 1974 to 1976. After his death the name of the organization was changed to Council on America's Military Past, a title Yount would have opposed.

Interview, author with Yount, Nov. 19, 1975.

Ysopete (Sopete), Indian slave, guide (fl. 1540-1542). Probably a Wichita, he was from Quivira. Hernando de Alvarado picked him up with The Turk, a probable Pawnee, at Cicúique (Pecos) Pueblo, New Mexico, in 1540, both of them slaves of the community. They were taken by Alvarado as guides on his exploration of the buffalo plains that summer, and both accompanied Coronado on his journey to Quivira in 1541. The two Indians were mutually antagonistic, Ysopete insisting The Turk was a liar and was misleading the Spanish (which was true), and was delighted when Coronado finally had The Turk executed. In recompense for his faithfulness, Ysopete was left by Coronado among his people at Quivira, rewarded with presents and returned the favor with a promise to serve Coronado further should he return the following year, which the leader intended but failed to do.

George Parker Winship, *The Coronado Expedition, 1540-1542.* BAE 14th Ann. Rept., Wash., Govt. Printing Office, 1896; Herbert Eugene Bolton, *Coronado: Knight of Pueblo and Plains.* Albuquerque, Univ. of New Mex. Press, 1964; A. Grove Day, *Coronado's Quest.* Berkeley, Univ. of Calif. Press, 1964.

Z

Zachary, Bob, desperado (d. Jan. 26, 1864). Zachary became a roadster, or holdup specialist in the notorious Henry Plummer desperado band of southwestern Montana. It is said however that he declined to take part in the murder of the Magruder party in the fall of 1863 in the Bitterroot Mountains, although he once attempted to shoot Pete Daly, being thwarted only by his weapon's misfiring. Zachary was implicated in various robberies. He was taken at "Baron" Cornelius C. O'Keefe's place in the Deer Lodge Valley, but execution was delayed until Zachary had had a good breakfast since, O'Keefe reportedly insisted, it would be wrong to hang a man on an empty stomach. Zachary dictated a letter to his mother, sisters and brothers warning against drinking, card-playing and bad company which he conceded had brought him to the gallows. On the scaffold he prayed God to forgive the vigilantes for their action, while conceding it was the only way to clear the country of evil-doers. Zachary got a good drop.

Langford; Dimsdale; Edith Toole Oberley, "The Baron C.C. O'Keefe: The Legend and the Legacy." *Mont. Mag. of West. Hist.,* Vol. XXIII, No. 3 (July 1973), 23.

Zahn, William Presly, soldier, frontiersman (Oct. 25, 1849-Sept. 2, 1936). B. at Pyrmont, Indiana, he enlisted in the 17th Infantry August 22, 1869, was ordered to the Grand River Indian agency, South Dakota, then helped establish Fort Yates and the Standing Rock Indian Agency, North Dakota, in 1873. He was one of the escort for the Stanley Yellowstone expedition that year and in 1874 kept a diary on the Custer Black Hills expedition; his account is extant. Discharged from the army in 1875, Zahn served as interpreter and engaged in freighting with bull teams between Bismarck and the Black Hills. In 1879 he married Winyan-Waste, a Sioux woman, fathering two sons. After the death of his wife, he married in 1887 another Sioux woman, Kizewin, a relative of Sitting Bull, fathering three boys and six daughters. Zahn knew Sitting Bull intimately as well as Rain in

the Face and other Sioux leading men, and traveled at times with the Buffalo Bill Wild West Show as interpreter. "Zahn came into the Redman's midst as enemy soldier and remained to be the Sioux's neighbor, friend and counselor for over half a century." He instructed them in farming and other white ways. Zahn died at Fort Yates, North Dakota.

Bismarck Tribune, Sept. 2, 1936; files of the State Hist. Soc. of No. Dak.; Herbert Krause, Gary D. Olson, *Prelude to Glory.* Sioux Falls, S.D., Brevet Press, 1974.

Zaldívar, Juan de, military officer (fl. 1540-1544). From Guadalajara, Spain, he was a captain under Coronado, joining the famous expedition to Cibola early. He accompanied Melchior Diaz on a reconnaissance as far as the Gila Valley in Arizona to learn what they could of Cibola, whose marvels had been reported by Marcos de Niza, and Zaldívar carried Diaz's report and his own back to Viceroy Antonio de Mendoza at Mexico City, then returned north to rejoin Coronado. He arrived after the conquest of Háwikuh, the first pueblo, southwest of Zuñi on the Arizona line. From there he went with Coronado to Tiguex, on the Rio Grande near the present Bernalillo, New Mexico, where winter quarters were established late in 1540. Zaldívar was in the assault on Arenal in the Tiguex War early in 1541 and was wounded in the head three times so severely he took a month to recuperate. Zaldívar recovered in time to become one of the select group to accompany Coronado to Quivira, in central Kansas later in 1541 and when The Turk's promises of great quantities of gold at Quivira turned out to be chimeras, Zaldívar was among those most heatedly arguing that The Turk be executed. The hapless Indian was garroted in Zaldívar's tent. It was Zaldívar's Indian woman who escaped from the Coronado party as they neared Tiguex on their return and fled eastward onto the Plains; it was reported that she alone of the western exploration party made contact with De Soto's Spaniards of the eastern exploration party, somewhere west of the Mississippi River. In 1544 Zaldívar was alcalde of Guadalajara, Nueva Galicia. Juan de Zaldívar was the father of Juan de Zaldívar who was killed at Acoma in 1599 while a captain under Oñate, and of Vicente de Zaldívar who avenged his brother.

George Parker Winship, *The Coronado Expedition, 1540-1542.* BAE, 14th Ann. Rep., Wash., Govt. Printing Office, 1896; Herbert Eugene Bolton, *Coronado: Knight of Pueblos and Plains.* Albuquerque, Univ. of New Mex. Press, 1964.

Zaldívar, Juan de, military officer (d. Dec. 4, 1598). The son of Juan de Zaldívar who had been a captain with Coronado, Juan de Zaldívar the younger was one of four brothers accompanying Juan de Oñate, colonizer and conqueror of New Mexico, and was Oñate's nephew. Zaldívar was *maestre de campo,* or field commander of the expedition which left Santa Barbara, Nueva Vizcaya, January 20, 1598, reached the Rio Grande April 30, the site of El Paso May 4, and by July was at the Pueblo of San Juan north of the present Santa Fe, near where headquarters were established at a new town called San Gabriel. While Oñate explored in various directions, he left Zaldívar in command at San Gabriel. When Oñate visited the Moqui towns intending to explore further west he sent word to Juan de Zaldívar to turn over command of San Gabriel to his brother, Vicente de Zaldívar who should shortly return from a trip to the buffalo plains, and come on to join Oñate, bringing reinforcements. Zaldívar approached Acoma December 1 where a chief, Zutucapan, known as an intelligent and perceptive man, had organized resistance to the Spaniards but carefully hid his design. Zaldívar brought along 20 or 30 men and was persuaded to delay at Acoma while corn was prepared for provisions for his men. He waited three days, left his nearby camp with 16 armored men and entered the village, ostensibly to obtain the food; oral history reports that some of the soldiers who entered homes at Acoma to pick up corn may have molested some of the women they encountered, though Spanish records say nothing of this. With warclubs, darts, spears and stones the Acoma warriors killed Zaldívar and all but five of his men, one of whom perished in leaping over a cliff.

Twitchell, *Leading Facts;* Herbert Eugene Bolton,

Spanish Exploration in the Southwest, 1542-1706. N.Y., Charles Scribner's Sons, 1916; *Handbook of Indians,* 9.

Zaldívar Mendoza, Vicente de, military officer (fl. 1595-1604). A son of the Juan de Zaldívar who was captain under Coronado, he was a brother of Juan de Zaldívar the younger and *sargento mayor* (a commissioned rank) and recruiting officer in the 1595 organization of the expedition of Juan de Oñate (his uncle), the conqueror and colonizer of New Mexico. The expedition started in 1598 and by August had reached San Juan pueblo north of the present Santa Fe, establishing headquarters at the new town of San Gabriel nearby. September 10 Zaldívar was sent on an exploring journey to the buffalo plains eastward, returning November 8. He discovered some traces of the ill-fated expedition of Humaña in that region earlier, but aside from exciting buffalo hunts found little noteworthy of report, except futile efforts to capture buffalo alive. A huge corral was built with extensive wings, but when it was tried to drive the buffalo into the trap, the animals reversed direction and charged back through their pursuers, while attempts to capture calves alive were equally unavailing. Nor could any such efforts succeed, Zaldívar concluded, until the "cattle become tamer than they now are." November 18 Vicente's brother Juan, leaving Vicente in command at San Gabriel, left for the west to join Oñate on an exploration endeavor, but Juan was killed with some of his men December 4 at Acoma, the "Sky city" of the pueblos. Oñate returned to San Gabriel December 21 and decided to send Vicente de Zaldívar to Acoma to avenge the death of his brother. He left San Gabriel January 12, 1599, with 70 men and reached Acoma the 21st. The three-day fight began January 22; Zaldívar gained the summit of the mesa supporting the settlement by a ruse, cannon were dragged up and the third day the ruins were set ablaze. The *Handbook of North American Indians* estimates the Acoma population at that time as around 6,000, a figure difficult to accept. In February a "trial" under Spanish law arrived at "sentences": all Acoma males over 25 years of age were condemned to have one foot cut off and serve 20 years of personal service, or slavery; all males 12 to 25 were to give 20 years personal service as were all females above 12 years of age. Two Indian men who had been visiting Acoma were to have their right hands cut off and be sent to their own pueblos as a warning to those who would resist the Spanish. In the summer of 1601 Zaldívar was *sargento mayor* and *maestro de campo,* or field commander for Oñate's expedition toward Quivira, in central Kansas. The party left San Gabriel June 23, Zaldívar occasionally leading side expeditions "with the lucky star that ever guides him," and eventually they reached a heavily populated region which Bolton believes was near the present Wichita, Kansas. Zaldívar was almost cut off on one excursion but "like a good soldier" retreated in competent fashion. A major battle erupted with the Escanjaques (Kaw, or Kansa Indians) who attacked with a force of some 1,500 warriors, according to Spanish accounts. Nearly all of the Spaniards were wounded (one report says that 30 were wounded) and by the time the story was recounted in Mexico some time later it had magnified enemy losses to 1,000 slain: the true figure is unknown, but the Spanish withdrew under fire, releasing to appease the enemy several women they had captured earlier. San Gabriel was regained November 24. Oñate found the place almost deserted, most of the settlers and friars withdrawn to Mexico. He sent Vicente de Zaldívar to take letters and reports to Mexico and send back those deserters he could apprehend. Apparently Zaldívar acted with considerable imperiousness, or "great cruelty" according to the friars, but managed to send back many colonists and a number of missionaries. Early in 1602 he appeared before the audiencia in Mexico urging continued support for Oñate's effort in New Mexico and presenting an *expediente* or dossier to support his case. From Mexico he went to Spain to lay the matter before the King, but the results of his effort are not clear although it appears that the Mexico authorities were directed to supply some, if not all the reinforcements Oñate had requested. Zaldívar returned from Spain around 1604 and perhaps went again to New Mexico. There is one dubious reference to him from 1618.

Herbert Eugene Bolton, ed., *Spanish Exploration in the Southwest, 1542-1706,* N.Y., Charles Scribner's Sons, 1916; Twitchell, *Leading Facts,* I; Bancroft, *Arizona and New Mexico; Handbook of Indians,* 9.

Zane, Ebenezer, frontiersman (Oct. 7, 1747-Nov. 19, 1812). B. in Berkeley County, Virginia, of Danish ancestry, at 23 he set out with only a dog and a gun for the wilderness, built a cabin above the confluence of Wheeling Creek and the Ohio River and after a season brought his family and some friends to the site. The settlement which arose in 1773 became Wheeling, West Virginia. Zane married Elizabeth McColloch, sister to famed borderers, and fathered 13 children, four dying in infancy. He became a noted frontiersman, was disbursing officer under Lord Dunmore, believed in fair dealing with the Indians, and was described as "a plain blunt man, rude of speech but true of heart." He and others were besieged in a cabin hard by Wheeling when British-led Indians attacked September 11-13, 1782, the last skirmish where the British flag was flown in the trans-Allegheny during the Revolution. The Indians were repulsed without loss. He was hired by the government in 1796-97 to open a road from Wheeling to Limestone (Maysville), Kentucky, being granted valuable lands in payment. He died of jaundice. Zane held the rank, perhaps honorary, of colonel, and was dark with black eyes, huge brows and a prominent nose; he was of medium height and athletic, a noted shot and runner. His temperament was described as "nervous-bilious — quick, impetuous, and hard to restrain when excited," but he was just, generous, honest, brave.

De Hass, Wills, *History of the Early Settlement and Indian Wars of Western Virginia,* 1851, reprint by McClain Printing Co., Parsons, W.Va., 1960; Lucullus V. McWhorter, *The Border Settlers of Northwestern Virginia.* Hamilton, O., Republican Pub. Co., 1915.

Zarcillos Largos, Navaho peace leader and chief (c. 1800-c. Oct. 20, 1860). B. in the Navaho country, he was known as Naat'aalee (Peace Chanter), and Ke'Ntsaa (Big Feet), and early became a medicine man. By 1843 he was a chief, even then inclined toward peace and signed the November 22, 1846, Bear Spring treaty with Colonel A.W. Doniphan. Colonel E.W.B. Newby negotiated another treaty with Zarcillos Largos and other chiefs May 20, 1848, to halt slave raiding; it kept peace for a short time. By 1852 Zarcillos Largos was "the most influential chief" of the Navahos, becoming a major cooperator with the whites, and visited Fort Defiance in January and August that year. His niece married agent Henry Linn Dodge, a man generally respected among the Navahos. Zarcillos Largos met with Governor David Meriwether at Santa Fe in November 1853. On July 17, 1855, Zarcillos Largos abruptly resigned as chief, asserting he was "too old" to fulfill that office, and Manuelito succeeded him; Zarcillos Largos' real motives were that he disapproved of a treaty being negotiated to trim 20 million acres from the lands of his people; yet he was the 26th chief to mark the treaty when it was signed. The treaty never was ratified by the Senate. Zarcillos Largos frequently was instrumental in returning stolen stock or captives to the whites. In June 1858, he was a pivotal leader convincing the Navahos at a Canyon de Chelly conference, to opt for peace rather than war with the Anglos. Yet incidents mounted, and in September 1858, Zarcillos Largos finally engaged in a skirmish with troops after abuses he could no longer tolerate; he was wounded, but recovered. Again he assumed his role as a peace advocate, though he saw the inevitability of ultimate conflict, predicting nothing but disaster as a result for his people, although he did not live to see it. He struggled for viable relations as long as he lived. Zarcillos Largos was killed while returning to his Oak Springs home from a visit to the Hopi country. Near Sagebrush Spring, south of Klagetoh, he ran into an ambush of Mexicans and Zunis; although he killed four, he himself was slain. His influence is beneficially felt to this day.

David M. Brugge, *Zarcillos Largos, Courageous Advocate of Peace*. Window Rock, Ariz., Navajo Hist. Pubns: Biogr. Ser. No. 2, Navajo Parks and Recreation Dept., 1970.

Zeisberger, David, Moravian missionary (Apr. 11, 1721-Nov. 17, 1808). B. at Zauchtenthal, Moravia, he migrated to Georgia in 1737, leaving there in 1739 for Pennsylvania. With Christian Frederick Post he went in 1745 to live with the Iroquois to learn their language; they were arrested in anti-German unrest, but released and joined in treaty negotiations with the Onondaga which allied the Iroquois with the English in troubles pending with the French. For more than 60 years Zeisberger was involved in frontier affairs, his linguistic abilities useful to the whites, but his heart and soul devoted to Indian welfare and civilization, and he headed Moravian work among the Indians. He became intimate with the Iroquois and was well accepted by them. In 1763 he went to live with the Delawares, seeking to better their lot and their relations with whites and Iroquois, leading them through several removals until he founded Schoenbrunn in the Tuscarawas Valley, Ohio, and later Gnadenhutten and other communities of Christian Indians. Pressures associated with the Revolutionary struggle made things difficult, however. In 1781 Zeisberger was taken with Heckewelder prisoner by English-allied Indians, ultimately reaching Detroit. The missionaries were released eventually, but Gnadenhutten had been destroyed by border ruffians, and the other communities largely dispersed. Zeisberger founded a new Gnadenhutten in Michigan, later overseeing settlements at New Salem, Ohio, and Fairfield, Ontario. He settled at Goshen, Ohio, married at 60 but fathered no children. "When he died he had lived among the red men for 62 years, and... acquired not only their speech, but also their taciturnity and their habits of thought and action." He wrote several valuable linguistic works in addition to translations of religious literature and a *History of the Indians*, which was published in 1910. Zeisberger, a major border figure, was completely fluent in Onondaga, Delaware, Mahican and Objibway.

Paul A.W. Wallace, *Thirty Thousand Miles with John Heckewelder*. Univ. of Pittsburgh Press, 1958; DAB.

Zele (Gil-lee, Zee-lay, etc.), Chiricahua leading man (1822-1896). A noted warrior and perhaps a sub-chief as Britton Davis supposed, he never was a full chief, as others believed, though among the most prominent of Chiricahua Apaches. He participated in half a century of hostile activity, details for the most part lost. Zele during the latter hostile days associated with Benito, Chatto and Naiche. Davis characterized him and Chatto with being "as fine types of men. morally and physically as it would be possible to find in any race." Zele would not go out with Geronimo in 1885 but "remained true to his pledge of peace with the Whites and was an important influence in preventing other Indians from leaving with Geronimo." Nonetheless he was sent into exile with the captured hostiles. He died at Fort Sill,

Oklahoma, and is buried in the main Apache cemetery there. A photograph of Zele and his wife appears in Lockwood's *The Apache Indians* (1938) facing p. 274.

Griswold (Zele listed as Gil-lee); Britton Davis, *The Truth About Geronimo*, ed. by Milo Quaife, Chicago, Lakeside Press, 1951, Intro.; Davis communication, copy in author's collection.

Zephyr, Recontre, interpreter (b.c. 1800). B. in Missouri, he became a clerk and trader at Pierre, Dakota, in 1830, and in 1837 married a Yankton woman who, with her daughter, was killed by other Sioux near Fort Lookout in 1851. Zephyr was interpreter at various posts and Indian agencies; he was said to have been intelligent and faithful.

Montana, Contributions, Vol. X, 1940, 290; *Journal of Rudolph Friederich Kurz.* Lincoln, Univ. of Nebr. Press, 1970.

Zi(e)gler, Eli, scout (Oct. 1852-Apr. 3, 1916). B. in Iowa, he early migrated to Saline Valley, Kansas. Here he became at 17 the youngest of the 50 scouts and frontiersmen enlisted to serve under George A. Forsyth, and with them took part in the celebrated battle of Beecher Island in eastern Colorado in September 1868. An acquaintance later wrote in *Battle of Beecher Island,* p. 81, that Zigler, "though only a boy in years had established so fine a record in the Saline Valley for coolness and daring and for skill with the rifle that Jack Peate had no hesitancy in choosing him as a member of this band of picked men; and he made no mistake... (for none) displayed a higher order of courage and fortitude..." Zigler's extended version of the affair, as graphic as any, was published in *Beecher Island,* pp. 33-37. He died at Salem, Oregon, having been a resident of that state for some 18 years, his occupation listed as "farmer."

Simon E. Matson, ed., *The Battle of Beecher Island.* Wray, Colo., Beecher Island Battle Meml. Assn., 1960; Ziegler death certificate.

Zinzendorf, Count Nicolaus Ludwig von, Moravian churchman (May 26, 1700-May 9, 1760). A leader of the Moravian Church, he was b. at Dresden and for 13 months directed the affairs of his church in America, being of importance in the development of its missionary thrust among the Indians. Zinzendorf reached New York December 2,

1741, devoted himself initially to unity efforts among the members of his faith, and in 1742 took three journeys in the interests of Moravian missions among the Indians in Pennsylvania and New York. He left New York January 9, 1743; he died near Bertelsdorf, Saxony. Zinzendorf was among the most important influences through which the Moravian sect, minute in size, is perhaps the most mission-minded, and the most effective in mission fields, of all Christian churches.

Literature abundant: CE; DAB.

Zogbaum, Rufus Fairchild, illustrator (Aug. 28, 1849-Oct. 22, 1925). B. at Charleston, South Carolina, he studied art at New York and abroad and specialized in military and naval illustrations, traveling widely and insisting upon meticulous accuracy in his work, producing oils as well as watercolors and pen and ink sketches. He visited Montana, Indian Territory and other western locations for research purposes, and wrote many magzine articles as well as three books, one of which, *Horse, Foot, and Dragoons* (1888) was devoted to Army life. His work was considered by contemporaries second only to Remington, but his interests and talents were more diverse than Remington's and his work differed in focus and intent. He died at New York, survived by his widow and four children.

Robert Taft, *Artists and Illustrators of the Old West: 1850-1900.* N.Y., Charles Scribner's Sons, 1953; DAB.

Zontam, Paul (Pone-audle-tone, Snake Head), Kiowa artist/missionary (1853-Apr. 27, 1913). Snake Head was an active warrior before 1875; on August 19, 1874, he and five other Kiowas killed and scalped a white man at Signal Mountain, Indian Territory, and no doubt took part in other depredations. He surrendered in 1875 and with other late hostiles was sent to Fort Marion, Florida where he got over his initial unruliness and became a talented painter of Indian life and scenes. In 1878 he went to New York State to pursue his art training near Utica. Here he became an Episcopalian and was sponsored for study for the ministry. He was ordained a deacon June 7, 1881, and sent to Indian Territory to open a Kiowa mission, which he found not to be an easy task. Because of his lack of Episcopal decorum he was dropped as a missionary and in 1894 lost his position as deacon. He then joined a local Baptist congregation, but this too failed to meet his specifications and he quit that to enter the Native American Church. He progressed meanwhile in his art work and supported himself largely from it. He died at 60 in Oklahoma. He had been married three times, divorced twice, and was survived by his widow and several children.

Dockstader; W.S. Nye, *Carbine & Lance.* Norman, Univ. of Okla. Press, 1951.

Zutacapan, Acoma pueblo chief (fl. 1598). Described as a highly intelligent and resourceful man, he was a leading warrior referred to as chief of the New Mexico pueblo of Acoma, the "sky city." He was inveterately opposed to Spanish domination of his people. October 27, 1598, he tried to entrap and assassinate Oñate, who became suspicious and failed to accept the bait; then he attempted to take the poet-soldier Gaspar de Villagrá, but failed to lure him into a trap, either. December 1, 1598, Juan de Zaldívar reached the pueblo with a small force; he was lured into it and with 11 of his men killed on December 4, Villagrá said by Zutacapan himself who slew the Spaniard with a war club; this could be poetic whimsy, since no eye-witness to the climactic little battle has reported its details. Juan's brother, Vicente de Zaldívar was sent to avenge the slayings and January 22-25 killed hundreds of defenders, razed and burned the pueblo, and harshly punished the survivors. The fate of Zutacapan is not reported, but if he survived the battle he may well have been executed afterward.

Handbook of Indians, 9; Twitchell, *Leading Facts;* Bancroft, *Arizona and New Mexico.*

Supplemental Index

Supplemental Index

Since formal entries in this encyclopedia are arranged alphabetically, they are rarely listed in the Supplemental Index. Rather, this calls attention to names and subjects appearing incidentally, to supplement the biographies. The Index also includes names of numerous individuals not given formal attention in the body of the work, while the subject listings may assist the rounding out of information about significant or interesting incidents, themes or activities.

Aaron, Sam: 273
Abbadie de St. Castin: Abenaki chief, 1
Abbott, Grafton: 1124
Abeel, John: father of Cornplanter, 323, 324
Abel, Hannah: 1439
Abercrombie, James: British officer, 499
Abercromby, Sir Ralph: 1234
Abernathy, Jack R: wolfer, 195
Abert, James W: army engineer, 176, 496, 631, 1609
Abraham: Seminole chief, 209, 210, 660, 754, 1140
Accault, Michel: French explorer, 647-48
Acoma pueblo (New Mexico): 19, 482, 1040, 1083, 1472-73, 1486, 1618-19, 1622
Adair, James: writer, 1198
Adair, John C., Cornelia: 570
Adair, Lewis D: 527
Adam, Emil: army officer, 1213
Adams, Charles Francis: 1022
Adams, Herbert Baxter: historian, 1448
Adams, J.C: 781
Adams, James: Sand Creek veteran, 1217
Adams, John Quincy: President: 121, 870
Adams, Margaret: *see* Margaret Fitzpatrick
Adams, Ramon F: writer, 17, 295, 730, 1372, 1462
Adams, Thomas: 197
Adamson, Carl: 541-42, 655
Adario (The Rat): Iroquois, 387
Addington, Ann: 1024
Aden, William: victim, 38, 1369
Adobe Walls (Texas), battle of: (Nov.1864), 234, 758, 891, 1384
Adobe Walls, battle of: (June 27, 1874), 98, 227-28, 252, 357, 406-407, 708, 869, 955, 1058, 1077-78, 1113, 1193
Agreda, María de Jesús de: mystic, 1261
Aguinaldo, Emilio: 524
Ah-we-lak: Eskimo explorer, 471
Aiken, Tom: 1232
Aikens, Frank: 20
Ainza, Filomena: 334
Ake, William: 1597
Akin, Jesse: 1563
Alamo (San Antonio, Tex.), battle of: (March 6, 1836), 46, 54, 57, 73, 292, 327, 329, 346, 399,

403, 468, 474-75, 503, 510, 538, 570-71, 622, 626, 632, 669, 682, 722, 772, 781, 783, 908, 934, 947, 989, 991, 1036, 1048, 1095, 1156, 1210, 1241, 1265, 1283, 1325, 1439-40, 1463, 1498, 1513-14
Alarcón, Hernando de: explorer, 402, 932
Albanel, Charles: Jesuit, 1400
Alchisay: White Mountain Apache, 402, 1128-29
Alden, John, Priscilla: 83, 1353
Alderdice, Thomas: 1527
Aldrich, Mark: Tucson mayor, 1514
Alexander (No Horses): Pend d'Oreille chief, 13, 1075
Alexander, Andrew J: army officer, 758
Alexander, Ella Serena: 1128
Alexander, Hartley Burt: professor, 23
Allard, Charles P: rancher, 1101, 1504
Allen, Ethan: 870, 879
Allen, George: *see* Caralambo
Allen, John: gunman, 881
Allen, Joseph: partisan, 283
Allen, William Francis: historian, 1448
Alligator: Seminole chief, 16-17, 245, 726, 754
Allison, Clay: 448, 1430
Allison, Dave: 282
Allouz, Claude: Jesuit, 582, 1055
Almy, Jacob M: army officer, 180, 467, 487, 815, 869, 1213, 1521, 1563
Alsate (Arzate): Mescalero Apache chief, 18-19
Alters, Lewis Jacob: 1128
Altman, Perry: 833-34
Altshuler, Constance Wynn: historian, 1098
Alvarado, Hernando de: explorer, 325, 1102, 1447, 1616
Alvarado, J.B: 1339
Alvarado, Juan B: insurgent against Micheltorena, 1518
Alvarado, Juan de: explorer, 1023
Alvarado, Juan Batista: Calif. governor, 1361
Alvarado, Pedro de: conquistador, 19, 209, 939-40, 1023
Alvarez, Nicolas: 20
Alvord, Burt: outlaw, 992
Amache Ochinee: Cheyenne woman, 1177
Amadas, Philip: discoverer, 1551
Ambrister, Robert: suspected spy, 33, 714, 908

Carleton, James H: army officer, 36, 48, 75, 219, 298, 343, 378, 381, 512, 608, 696, 723, 891, 935, 939, 951, 1030, 1070, 1182, 1228, 1231, 1297, 1362, 1507, 1535, 1558, 1577
Carling, Elias Brown: 142
Carlisle Kid: Apache, 1037
Carlisle, Robert S: Calif. rancher, 783
Carlyle, James: lawman, 91, 1248
Carmona, Alonso de: 534
Carnegie, Andrew: 669
Carondelet, Francisco Luis Hector de: Spanish governor of Louisiana, 302, 426, 1060
Carpenter, Bill: mountain man, 228, 492, 1399
Carpenter, Christopher: 177, 1067
Carpenter, Jeremiah: 228
Carpenter, Louis H: army officer, 493-95, 1127, 1507
Carpenter, Nicholas: 298, 690
Carr, B.P. (Bat): lawman, 176
Carr, Camillo Casatti Cadmus: army officer, 1549
Carr, Eugene Asa: army officer, 64, 103, 237, 293, 304, 352, 491, 506, 594, 596, 633, 649, 895, 907, 1061-62, 1175, 1190, 1366, 1399-1400, 1491, 1499, 1527
Carranza, Venustiano: revolutionary, 672, 1216
Carrington, Henry B: army officer, 116-17, 175, 257, 489, 522, 595, 1549
Carrington, Robert: 127
Carroll, Bill: 480
Carroll, Henry: army officer, 308, 919, 1326, 1602
Carroll, Matt: Montana freighter, 1422
Carron, Thomas: 1432
Carson, Adaline: daughter of Kit, 1309
Carson, Alexander: 738
Carson, Bob: 204
Carson, Joe: lawman, 957
Carson, Joseph: in Creek War, 1399
Carson, Kit: mountain man, guide, 35, 63, 75-76, 95, 165-67, 226-27, 232, 302, 372, 378, 423, 496, 519-20, 535, 539, 567, 579, 584, 651, 658, 663-64, 693, 758, 784, 785, 801, 891, 961, 1090, 1094, 1099, 1193, 1202, 1274, 1309, 1341, 1384, 1426, 1503, 1518, 1558, 1563, 1574, 1613, 1616
Carson, Moses: mountain man, 1412, 1597
Carter, Alex: desperado, 319-20, 644, 710
Carter, Robert G: army officer, 257, 383, 729, 890, 915, 918, 1371, 1442
Carter, William Harding: 94, 1591
Cartier, Jacques: discoverer, 181
Cartwright, John: chaplain, 1521
Cartwright, Joseph L: 743
Carver, Frank: marksman, 1425
Carver, John: of Plymouth colony, 156
Carver, Jonathan: frontier traveler, 1235
Carver, Will: desperado, 167, 189, 485, 781, 823, 872, 880, 1111, 1325
Casa Calvo, Marquis de: 1060
Case, Leland: co-founder of Westerners, 1520
Casey, James P: 1065-66
Casey, Mike: 850

Casey, Robert: assassinated, 1581
Casey, Silas: army officer, 239, 627
Cashesegra: Osage chief, 1121
Cashman, Nellie: 748, 1324
Cashner, John: 781
Cass, Jonathan: 542
Cass, Lewis: governor of Mich., Indian dealer, 419, 696, 913, 1011, 1092, 1108, 1276
Cassels, Major: 999
Cassidy, Butch: desperado, 189, 239, 358, 405, 612, 780, 823, 866-67, 872, 1148-49, 1272, 1309
Cassidy, Jack: 1370
Cassidy, Mike: 1110
Casson, Francois Dollier de: 816
Castañeda, Pedro de: explorer, chronicler, 470, 529
Castaño de Sosa, Caspar: explorer, 1017
Castello, Joe: 957
Castillo, Diego del: explorer, 595, 948
Castillo, Domingo: pilot, 12
Castro, José: 599
Castro, Manuel de Jesus: rose against Micheltorena, 1518
Catholics, Roman: see also Capuchins, Dominicans, Franciscans, Jesuits, Recollets, Sulpitians): 10, 36, 88, 101, 124, 148, 160, 164, 187, 240, 250, 286, 316, 378, 391-93, 411, 426, 512, 533, 544, 650, 663, 670, 697-98, 710, 757, 760, 772-73, 777, 813, 819, 842-43, 845, 922, 969, 972-73, 997, 1003, 1006, 1035, 1044, 1047, 1065, 1106, 1207-08, 1212, 1216, 1225, 1239-40, 1245, 1254, 1258, 1283-84, 1299, 1338, 1343, 1380, 1430, 1432, 1490, 1563, 1567-68, 1571, 1583, 1609
Catití, Alonso: Pueblo leader, 413
Catlin, George: artist, 132, 255, 289, 385, 410, 420, 696, 798, 958, 1046, 1091, 1198, 1264, 1355, 1398, 1410, 1493
Catlin, Polly Sutton: 244
Catron, Thomas B: attorney, 26, 411, 421, 1035, 1222
Cattle Annie: see Annie McDougal
Cattle drives: 7, 51, 195, 216, 223, 263, 282-83, 300-301, 312, 356, 377, 443-44, 450, 461, 614, 620, 652, 673, 768, 795, 870, 881, 894, 958, 1079, 1080-81, 1143-44, 1165-66, 1177, 1268, 1320, 1374-75, 1583, 1613
Caughey, John Walton: historian, 904
Cavallo, John (John Horse): Seminole chief, 15, 245
Cavendish, Thomas: sea captain, 748, 1489
Cayetanito: Navaho leader, 245
Cayetano: Navaho chief, 245, 939
Cazneau, William Leslie: 785
Cecil, George R: 94
Céleron de Blainville, Pierre: French military officer, 135, 803
Chacón: Jicarilla chief: 378
Chacón, Augustin: outlaw, 20, 1027
Chacon, Juan: 1156, 1442
Chadwell, Bill: see William Stiles

Ewell, Richard Stoddert: army officer, 1357, 1390, 1578

Ewers, Ezra P: 693

Ewers, John C: ethnologist, 393, 419, 1476

Ewing, W. C., G. W: 165

Explorers (also *see* Polar explorers): 5, 10-12, 19, 23-24, 32-33, 37-39, 43, 47, 72, 91, 118, 131, 141, 144, 151, 181-84, 198, 208-09, 238, 241-44, 255-56, 272, 276-78, 310-12, 325-26, 360, 391, 394-95, 397-99, 402-03, 406, 412-13, 418, 429-30, 456-57, 465-66, 468-69, 474, 477, 488, 491, 519-20, 526-29, 529-31, 544-45, 562, 568-69, 586-87, 589, 591-92, 595, 619, 647-48, 657, 687-88, 692, 702, 710, 719-20, 723, 736-37, 747-49, 751, 770-71, 773-75, 811-14, 816-17, 820, 828-30, 841, 843-46, 852-53, 875-77, 931-34, 939-41, 948, 966, 970-71, 983, 1023-24, 1026, 1028, 1032, 1042-43, 1046-47, 1055-56, 1066, 1075-76, 1083-84, 1092, 1107-09, 1133-34, 1146, 1157-58, 1164, 1169, 1178, 1308, 1340, 1420-21, 1431, 1434-35, 1437-38, 1447, 1456, 1473-74, 1478-82, 1487, 1489, 1500-01, 1502, 1516, 1521-22, 1551, 1572, 1584, 1588-89

Faber, Charles: lawman, 17

Fabry de La Bruére, Andre: 934

Fages, Pedro: first Calif. governor, 1224

Fain, James C: 478

Fairbanks, Myra: 454

Fairchild, John B: 1071

Fairfield, John: 1239

Fairweather, Bill: prospector, 330, 453, 1089, 1232, 1309, 1394

Faison, John Miller: 479

Fall, Albert B: politician, 282, 296, 502, 513, 926

Fallam, Robert: explorer, 1589

Fallen Timbers (Ohio), battle of: (Aug. 20, 1794), 130, 271, 277, 331, 519, 542, 561, 622, 772, 852, 862, 1146, 1164, 1280, 1403, 1522-23, 1532, 1565

Fallon, Thomas: 480

Fambo, Robert: 231

Fancher, Alexander: 481

Fancher, Hampton Bynum: 481

Fancher wagon train (destroyed at Mountain Meadows, Utah): (Sept. 11, 1857), 9, 38, 55, 57, 72, 92, 214, 335, 396, 431, 480-81, 508, 609, 630, 633, 687-88, 713, 733, 741, 744, 783, 811, 833, 911, 922, 988, 995, 1017, 1021, 1173, 1213, 1249, 1278, 1281-82, 1327, 1367, 1369, 1397, 1550, 1579, 1591

Fannin, James Walker: Tex. colonel, 455, 564, 1463

Farfán de los Godos, Marcos: explorer, 1083

Farish, Thomas Edwin: historian, 951

Farley, Louis: at Beecher Island, 618, 1008, 1128

Farquhar, Francis P: Calif. writer, 166-67

Farr, Edward J: lawman, 776, 1325

Farrington, Rufus E: 1128

Farris, William: 313

Fast, Christian: 561

Faver, Juan: 486

Faver, William: 581

Favour, Alpheus H: attorney, writer, 567

Febre, Luis, 521

Feliz, Jesus: 728

Feliz, Reyes: 79

Fellows, Charles: 396

Ferguson, William: 83

Fergusson, David: army officer, 1095

Fernandez, Alvaro, Benito: explorers, 488, 545-46

Fernandez, Santiago: 1481

Fernandez, Simon: Roanoke colony, 1551

Fero, David: beheaded in Mexico, 77, 316

Ferrelo (Ferrer), Bartolome: 209

Ferris, Robert G: writer, 1610

Fetherstun, John: 1495

Fetterman, William J., and fight (Wyo.): (Dec. 21, 1866), 22, 114, 116-17, 153, 175, 194, 231, 341, 374, 522, 581, 595, 692-93, 862, 1104, 1122, 1140, 1188, 1191, 1265, 1315, 1379, 1549, 1614

Feuille, Louis: 521

Fewkes, Jesse: ethnologist, zoologist, 1538

Ficklin, Benjamin F: mail contractor, 1318, 1517, 1575

Field, Edward: 361

Field, Sara Bard: poet, 1589

Fields, Richard: Cherokee chief, 78, 108, 150, 696

Figueroa, José: Calif. governor, 1613

Filibusters: 90, 125, 150-51, 166, 326, 333-34, 908, 965, 980, 1129, 1411

Filson, John: explorer, historian, 493

Finch, Ephraim S: 198

Findlay, Polly: 346

Finerty, John F: newsman, writer, 377, 593, 744, 929, 969, 1303-04, 1376, 1492, 1552

Fink, John: Virginia borderer, 1554

Fink, Mike: keelboat man, 228, 501, 1399

Finley, Eliza: 994

Finley, John: Kentucky explorer, 137, 155

Finn, Bill: cowboy, 1539

Finn, Robert: desperado, 1292, 1477-78

Finnbogi: Iceland merchant, 521, 541

Fire Body: Nez Perce, 742

First Seminole War (southeast): (1817-18), 4, 44, 128, 149, 370, 463, 525, 575, 664, 714, 754, 924-25, 1046, 1050, 1422, 1451-52

Fischel, Samuel: 197

Fisher, Don C: 464

Fisher, Helen, 1114

Fisher, King: gunman, 606, 1309-10, 1420, 1424

Fisher, Stanton G: scout, 558, 1456

Fisher, William S: 345

Fisk, James L: wagon train to Mont., 504, 701, 811

FitzGerald, Jenkins Augustus: 483

Fitzgerald, John S: 564-65

Fitzgerald, Mike: 731

Fitzpatrick, Thomas: mountain man, 167, 233-34, 287, 495-96, 505, 515, 522, 538, 550, 1154, 1177, 1229, 1330-31, 1333, 1369, 1385, 1559

Gon-shay-ee: Bronco Apache, 1194
Gonzales, Juan: 1372
Gonzáles, José María Elías: Mexican military officer, 573
Gonzales, Rafael Elías: 759
Good, John H: feudist, 834
Good, Walter: 834, 1222
Good Bear: Cheyenne, 779
Goodall, Henry: 715
Goode, Mary: wed Benjamin White, 1549
Goodhue, George: 1386
Goodlet, William (Dutchy): 763
Goodman, H.L: 88
Goodnight, Charles: cattleman, 3, 7, 17, 37, 881, 1397, 1581, 1613
Goodrich, Benjamin Briggs: 570-71
Goodrich, Mary E: 503
Goodwin, Grenville: ethnologist, 94, 401, 466, 518, 1063
Goodwin, John: Ariz. governor, 831, 1337. 1516, 1596
Goodwin, Millard Fillmore: army officer, 296
Goodwin, Neil: television producer, 571
Gookin, Daniel: colonist, magistrate, 1024
Gordillo, Francisco: 47
Gordon, Jack: renegade, 1065, 1363
Gordon, James: victim, 658, 890
Gordon, John: 332
Gordon, John Brown: Confederate officer, 890
Gordon, Mike: 670
Gore, Sir St. George: game shooter, 157, 258, 1474
Gorges, Ferdinando: colony promoter, 395, 1022, 1332
Gorman, Willis A: Minn. governor, 859
Gossan, Thomas: 850
Goupil, René: Jesuit, 329, 575
Graham, Carson: 680
Graham, E.B: physician, 312
Graham, Felix: 1158
Graham, George Wallace: military officer, 1190
Graham, H.G: 834
Graham, Isaac: mountain man, Calif. pioneer, 88, 1038
Graham, James Duncan: 1161
Graham, Jesse (George Davis): outlaw, 473
Graham, William A: Custer student, 693, 1556
Graham, William: Mont. pioneer, 889
Graham, William Hicks: dueled Wm. Walker, 1503
Grahams, The: Ariz. partisans, 126-28, 318-19, 576-78, 681, 901, 1227, 1412-14
Grand Canyon: 526-27, 876, 970, 1026, 1169, 1371, 1437
Grand Duke Alexis Plains hunt: (1872), 14, 39, 294, 454, 1192, 1209, 1349
Grand Teton mountain: 1367
Granger, Gordon: army officer, 291, 461, 1451
Grant, Hiram P: military officer, 947
Grant, James: British military officer, 6, 605, 1073, 1159
Grant, Joe: 113
Grant, John: 931

Grant, Susan: 909
Grant, Ulysses S: President, 36, 304-05, 363-64, 385, 427, 580, 588, 601, 633, 635, 683, 928, 939, 963, 1009, 1109, 1136, 1295-97, 1402
Grapp, Francois: 490
Gratiot, Henry: Black Hawk War (1832), 1493
Grattan, John L., massacre (Wyo.): (Aug. 19, 1854), 139, 309, 499, 618, 861, 883, 1196, 1209, 1261, 1348
Graves family (Donner party): 906, 1200
Graves, Alfred: 1372
Graves, Mary: Donner party, 511, 1358
Graves, W.C: 1357
Graves, William (Whiskey Bill): desperado, 794
Gravier, Jacques: Jesuit, 5, 18, 143, 697-98, 842, 1189, 1245
Gray, Alfred Gilliat: 582
Gray, Andrew Belcher: surveyor, 69, 158, 1277
Gray, Dixie Lee: 811
Gray, John S: historian, 1020
Gray, G.W: 852
Gray, Mike: 583
Gray, Robert: sea captain, 770-71, 966
Gray Beard: Cheyenne chief, 547, 1096
Graydon, James (Paddy): military officer, 75, 1558
Graymont, Barbara: historian, 1388
Grayson, Watt: Creek Indian, 1359
Great Smoky Mountains National Park: 600
Great Swamp Fight (Rhode Island):(Dec. 19, 1675), 929, 1039, 1407
Greathouse, James (Whiskey Jim): 228
Greeley, Horace: newsman, 770, 1401
Greely, Adolphus W: army officer, Arctic explorer, 193, 537, 635
Green, John: army officer, 68, 436, 626, 716, 769, 1391
Green, Patrick: 1200
Green, Samuel: 1246
Greene, William C: copper magnate, 195, 502, 558, 1002
Greenville (Ohio), treaty of: (Aug. 3, 1795), 130, 185, 333, 862, 1403
Greenwood, Caleb: mountain man, 767
Gregg, John Irvin: army officer, 665, 900
Gregg, Josiah: Santa Fe trader, writer, 151, 750
Gregg, P.P: 869
Gregg, Tom: 315
Gregory, Joseph: 1170
Greiner, John: Indian agent, editor, 1390
Grenville, Sir Richard: British sea captain, 1551
Grey, Zane: writer, 313, 422, 740, 1328
Griego, Francisco: 17
Grierson, Benjamin H: army officer, 322, 493, 501, 827, 1059, 1485
Griffin, Coke: 283
Griffin, Jesse: 908
Grigsby, George: 637
Grijalva, Merejildo, Francisco: captives, interpreters, 290, 590*
Grimes, A.W: lawman, 64, 71, 716, 1034
Grimes, Arly: lawman, 1439

1576; *Shasta*: 348, 1362; *Shawnee*: 6, 38, 57, 129-30, 138, 143, 150, 188, 200, 228, 241, 298, 340, 374-75, 424-25, 432, 461, 553, 558-62, 605, 614, 622, 662, 668, 738, 741, 763, 772, 792, 803, 835, 867, 870, 897, 924, 998-99, 1047, 1146, 1159, 1172, 1176, 1180, 1197, 1277, 1280, 1284, 1298, 1307, 1322, 1329, 1339, 1346, 1406-07, 1410, 1494, 1502, 1522, 1556, 1589; *Shoshone* (Snake): 13, 57, 168, 284, 308, 322, 348-49, 374, 496, 505, 508, 522, 589, 608, 613, 621, 649, 660, 797, 839, 895, 902, 911, 931, 968, 994, 1098, 1117, 1135, 1169, 1173, 1177, 1191, 1201, 1257, 1297, 1314, 1362, 1402, 1455, 1478, 1497, 1500, 1515-16,1574, 1576, 1583, 1596; *Sinkiuse-Columbia*: 1025.

Sioux: 39, 43-44, 49, 54, 56, 63-65, 84, 98, 117, 120-21, 123, 138-39, 146-47, 153, 156-57, 172-73, 175, 178, 181, 193-94, 199, 226, 230-31, 238, 241, 247-48, 255, 261, 266, 268, 278, 286, 291, 321, 322, 332, 341-42, 345-46, 349-51, 357, 359, 363-65, 374, 376, 381-82, 387, 397, 403-05, 407, 409, 418, 427-30, 471-72, 474, 476, 484, 486, 489, 491, 496, 497-98, 506, 511, 513, 515, 527-28, 530-31, 536-38, 543, 546, 549, 569, 584, 592-93, 597, 604, 607, 610, 618, 624, 636, 638, 642, 645, 647-50, 656, 667-69, 685, 699-700, 703-05, 719, 725, 745, 759, 762, 764, 766, 768, 772-73, 777-79, 781-82, 801, 805, 816, 823, 825-26, 837-40, 842, 849, 859-60, 862, 868-69, 873, 877, 881, 883, 892, 900, 916-17, 928, 933, 937, 941, 944, 947, 960, 969, 971, 977, 981, 985, 992-93, 999, 1009, 1011-12, 1014, 1021, 1030, 1049, 1055-56, 1059, 1061-62, 1074, 1092-94, 1104, 1115, 1126, 1134, 1139-40, 1143, 1145-46, 1150, 1157-58, 1164, 1167-68, 1173, 1175, 1179, 1182-83, 1186, 1188, 1191-92, 1196-97, 1199, 1204, 1207-08, 1209-10, 1212-14, 1227, 1229, 1236-37, 1240, 1251, 1260, 1264-65, 1274, 1281-82, 1296, 1302, 1303-1304, 1305, 1314-15, 1324, 1336, 1338, 1348-50, 1352, 1366-67, 1375-76, 1381-82, 1388-89, 1391, 1402, 1408, 1410-11, 1422, 1432-33, 1435, 1447, 1453-55, 1469, 1471, 1473, 1479, 1490, 1501-02, 1510, 1513, 1515, 1521, 1547-49, 1552, 1555, 1561, 1575-76, 1582, 1586, 1591-92, 1594, 1596, 1599, 1602, 1606-07, 1610, 1614-15, 1621; *Sioux Brulé*: 236, 239, 309, 509, 618, 671-72, 861, 1049, 1062, 1104, 1245, 1261, 1301, 1323, 1348-50, 1456, 1471, 1561; *Sioux Hunkpapa*: 22, 297, 527-28, 1188, 1314-15; *Sioux Mdewekanton*: 5, 859-60, 1161-62, 1172, 1199, 1510; *Sioux Miniconjou*: 309, 499, 538, 581, 691-92; *Sioux Oglala*: 21-22, 73, 236, 530, 604, 722, 905, 1008-09, 1048-49, 1070, 1104, 1122, 1196-97, 1213-14, 1315, 1453-54, 1614-15; *Sioux Santee*: 450, 703, 859, 1510; *Sioux Sisseton*: 703, 1208; *Sioux Teton*: 1199, 1442; *Sioux Wahpeton*: 1092-93; *Sioux Wakpekute* (Wahpekute):

703-704; *Sioux Yankton*: 530, 546, 574, 700, 703, 1052, 1158, 1509, 1621.

S'klallam: see *Clallam; Snake*: see *Shoshone; Snohomish*: 813; *Sokokis*: 103, 652, 1350; *Sokulk*: 1338; *Spokan(e)*: 332, 425, 483, 1001, 1025, 1086, 1114, 1348, 1456, 1497; *Stickeen*: see *Tlingit; Suquamish*: 1283-84, 1367; *Susquehanna*: see *Conestoga; Tamaroas*: 101, 187, 512, 998, 1003, 1147; *Tano*: see *Tewa; Taovaya*: see *Tawehash: Tarentines* (Tarrateens): 103; *Tawehash* (Taovaya): 941, 1060, 1117, 1481; *Tejas* (Teyas, possible Apache): 243, 932, 948, 953; *Tewa* (Pueblos): 692, 1040, 1160-61, 1472-73; *Timucuan*: 210; *Tionontati* (Tobacco): 539, 728; *Tlingit*: 1614; *Tobacco*: see *Tionontati; Tomahitan*: see *Yuchi; Tonkawa*: 257, 729, 741, 777, 835, 896-97, 1048, 1117, 1285; *Tualatin* (Atfalati): 233; *Tunica*: 378, 399, 1003; *Tuscarora*: 65, 386, 789, 821, 1006, 1589; *Ucita*: see *Pohoy; Umatilla*: 153, 243-44, 253, 526, 1079, 1132, 1515-16; *Ute*: 35-36, 48-49, 84, 95, 107, 168, 186, 239, 247, 302, 452, 491, 494, 520, 537, 565, 597, 607, 628, 750, 758, 773-74, 788, 797, 805, 821, 823, 848, 873, 928, 936, 961, 967, 968-69, 976-77, 991, 1019, 1040, 1049, 1161, 1172, 1177, 1196, 1212, 1260, 1304, 1368, 1371, 1384, 1390, 1409, 1416, 1425-26, 1438, 1456, 1464, 1468, 1487, 1490, 1496-97, 1518, 1594, 1605; *Ute Capote*: 700; *Ute Mouache*: 700, 758; *Ute Tabeguache*: 1094; *Ute Uncompaghre*: 963, 967, 1094; *Ute Wiminuche*: 699-700, 1156, 1165, 1442, 1534, 1557, 1574.

Waco: 1069; *Waicuri* (Baja California): 656; *Walla Walla*: 153, 639-40, 1114, 1137-38, 1367; *Wampanoag*: 27, 221, 270-71, 694, 953-54, 978-79, 1166, 1246, 1267, 1269-70, 1350-51, 1509, 1537; *Wappinger*: 995, 1057; *Warm Springs* (Oregon): 911; *Wateree*: 1107; *Watlala* (Cascade): 1295; *Wawenock*: 103; *Waxhaw*: 38; *Wea* (subdivision of Miami, which see); *Wenatchee*: 1025; *Wichita*: 19-20, 119, 218, 244, 263, 326, 443, 708, 755, 855, 919, 951, 1103, 1262, 1447, 1468, 1470, 1616; *Winnebago*: 41, 121, 241, 762, 1046, 1055, 1168, 1178, 1195, 1202, 1258, 1290, 1308, 1474, 1493, 1576, 1609; *Wintun*: 1103; *Wyandot* (Huron): 57, 200, 241, 340, 560, 561, 616, 1005, 1403, 1499, 1522; *Xarame* (Charame), San Antonio region (Texas): 1464; *Yahi*: 709; *Yakima*: 15, 44, 118, 348, 441, 608, 627, 757, 926, 1059, 1137, 1295, 1367, 1583, 1601; *Yamasee*: 65, 754, 1011; *Yana*: 709; *Yaqui*: 534; *Yavapai*: 109, 304, 432, 542, 704, 831, 878, 891, 1001, 1014, 1026, 1071, 1279, 1306, 1339, 1366, 1595; *Yazoo*: 427, 998, 1341; *Yokut*: 1414; *Yuchi* (Tomahitan): 38, 47, 151, 1046-47; *Yuma*: 11, 24-25, 66, 402-03, 477, 534, 564, 1014, 1050, 1070, 1071, 1224, 1374; *Zuñi*: 62, 68, 361, 443, 469, 1041, 1355, 1367, 1437, 1472, 1574, 1620

969, 971, 974-75, 979, 989, 1003, 1012, 1014, 1027, 1047, 1055, 1064, 1084, 1096-97, 1106, 1133-34, 1145, 1147, 1154, 1157, 1164, 1166-67, 1178, 1182, 1185-87, 1189, 1193, 1195, 1205, 1245, 1260-61, 1283-84, 1286-87, 1308, 1341, 1400, 1403, 1408, 1414, 1428, 1447-48, 1467-68, 1476-77, 1487-89, 1491, 1519, 1536, 1549, 1566, 1584-85, 1587
Jesuit Martyrs: canonized in 1930; eight Jesuits slain by Indians course of duties were Jean de Brebeuf, 164; Gabriel Lalemant, 164; Antoine Daniel, 374; Noel Chabanel, 246, René Goupil, 575; Charles Garnier, 539; Jean de Lande (donne), 806; Isaac Jogues, 728-29; martyrs not canonized as such: Paul Du Poisson, 434; Antoine Senat, 1286. Oct. 16, 1940, Pope Pius XII proclaimed the eight canonized Jesuits patron saints of Canada.
Jesup, Thomas Sidney: army officer, 212, 245, 288-89, 353, 557, 651, 754, 980, 1091, 1101, 1175, 1517
Jett, William Bladen: soldier, 758
Jim Boy: Creek leader, 999
Jironza Pétriz de Cruzate, Domingo: New Mex. governor, 413
Jogues, Isaac: Jesuit, 144, 329, 539, 575, 728-29, 779-80, 806, 843, 969, 1084, 1195, 1468
Johnny-Behind-the-Deuce: see O'Rourke
Johnson, Albert: lawman, 1475
Johnson, Albert M: 1282-83
Johnson, Arkansas: desperado, 1462
Johnson, Bill: victim, 1375-76
Johnson, Bill (Kid): desperado, 992, 1148, 1272, 1508
Johnson, Carl P: 428
Johnson, Carter Page: army officer, 1344
Johnson, David: lawman, 1151
Johnson, Dorothy Marie: writer, 718
Johnson, Edwin C: stockman, 1391-92
Johnson, Francis W: Texas military officer, 1325
Johnson, Guy: British Indian official, 161
Johnson, Ishmael: 732
Johnson, James: pearl fisher, 1230
Johnson, John J: scalp hunter, 22, 25, 44, 88, 385, 731, 749-50, 788, 792-93, 824, 939, 1161, 1255, 1587-88
Johnson, Julian: 732
Johnson, Lewis: army officer, 468, 784
Johnson, Manuel: 732
Johnson, Nathaniel: South Carolina governor, 1010
Johnson, Patrick: gunman, 1172
Johnson, R.A: lawyer, 1231
Johnson, Ricardo: 732
Johnson, Richard Mentor: shot Tecumseh, politician, 623, 1407
Johnson, Tom (Dick): train robber, 964
Johnson, W.D: lawman, 1273
Johnson, Sir William: British Iroquois specialist, 6, 160-62, 187, 200, 347, 563-64, 647, 730-31, 788-89, 1004, 1057, 1159-60, 1528-29
Johnson, William Harrison: 86

Johnson, William M: of Donner party, 511, 1035, 1444
Johnson, William Weber: writer, 1436
Johnson County (Powder River) War (Wyoming): (1892), 27, 47, 62, 174, 216, 222, 249, 286, 297, 382, 433, 505, 540, 543, 655, 706, 738, 743, 771, 838, 974-75, 1110, 1130-31, 1195, 1300, 1337, 1392, 1431, 1471, 1504, 1520, 1530, 1534, 1548, 1566, 1586-87
Johnston, Albert Sidney: military officer, 65-66, 168, 355, 384, 489, 508, 618, 620, 637, 722, 758, 1049, 1312, 1334, 1374, 1378, 1381-82, 1531, 1575, 1595, 1612
Johnston, John: Mohawk Valley raider (1780), 200
Jolliet, Louis: explorer, 523, 736-37, 816, 943, 1012
Joncaire, Louis-Thomas Chabert de: Indian specialist, 1005
Jones, Ben: Johnson County War figure, 216, 1503-04
Jones, Benjamin: trapper, 232-33, 1304
Jones, Calico: pseudonym, 1215
Jones, Charles Jesse (Buffalo Jones): 14, 422, 527, 1101
Jones, Charles O: 742-43
Jones, Charley: desperado, 359
Jones, David: clergyman, Shawnee language student, 559
Jones, E.A: Arizona rancher, 676
Jones, Frank: Texas Ranger, 788, 1096
Jones, Ida: 942
Jones, John A: Lincoln County War gunman, 86, 113
Jones, John B: Texas Ranger, 37, 316, 556, 662, 678, 680, 708, 854, 870, 996, 1034, 1051
Jones, John S: freighter, 177, 237, 1253
Jones, Oakah L. Jr: historian, 1077
Jones, Orley E. (Ranger Jones): victim, 222, 655
Jones, Sam: see Arpeika
Jones, Thomas: lynched in Nebraska, 1405
Jones, William H: dueled John Nugent, 1065
Jones, William Heiskell: New Mexico pioneer, 741
Josanie (Ulzana): Chiricahua raider, 207, 262, 303, 513, 928, 1031
José, Largo: Mescalero chief, 75, 584, 1558
Joseph, Chief: see Chief
Josephy, Alvin Jr: historian, 425, 604-05, 1138
Josh: Apache scout, 1063, 1118
Joutel, Henri: explorer with LaSalle, diarist, 813, 817
Joy, Kit: desperado, 830, 1397, 1556
Joyce, Marcellus E: justice of the peace, 307, 748, 1033
Joyce, Milt: Tombstone saloonist, 88, 670
Juan Chivaria: Maricopa chief, 109
Juan José Compá: see Compá
Juana Maria: castaway, 1056-57
Juchereau de St. Denys, Charles: entrepreneur, 976
Juchereau de St. Denys, Louis: explorer, 390
Judah, Henry Moses: army officer, 627
Judd, Neil M: archeologist, 355

Lucas, Elmer (Chicken): 313
Lucas, S.D: 415
Luce, Jason: 191
Lucero, Josefita: 1558
Lucero, Juan: 1481
Luckey, Bass: 313
Ludlow, William: army engineer, 590, 1209, 1581
Lugo, Antonio María: cattleman, 1569
Luján, Natividad: 18-19, 1573
Luján, Rosa Elena: wed B. Traven, 1436
Lumholtz, Carl: 686
Lummis, Charles F: Southwest intellectual, writer, 810, 899, 1203-04
Lumpkins, Tom: 1332
Lumsden, Francis Asbury: 770
Luna, Bernardino de: 469
Luna, Ramon: 1263
Lupton, Lancaster P: trader, 785, 979, 1258, 1431, 1511
Lushbaugh, Benjamin F: 1061
Lutherans: 969, 972-73, 1124, 1552
Luttig, John C: 1257
Lux, Charles: Calif. cattleman, 987-88
Lux, Odile Delor: 258
Luxan, Diego Pérez de: 469
Luxan, Caspar de: 886
Lyman, Amasa: 1213
Lyman: Jack, Marjorie, 891
Lyman, Wyllys: army officer, 1579
Lynch, James: 852
Lynde, Isaac: army officer, 74
Lynn, Wiley: shot Tilghman, 1430
Lyon, Nathaniel: military officer, 1030
Lyons, Hayes: desperado, 406, 794, 1327, 1371
Lyttleton, William Henry: So. Car. governor, 6, 1073

McAdow, Perry: Mont. pioneer, 125, 330, 578, 1597
McAdow, William: 889
McAlester, J.J: 623
McAllister, Harry: 317
McArthur, Daniel D: 1017
McArthur, Neil: trader, 172, 930-31
McAteer, Pat: 75
McBride, Jack: 578
McBride, John R: 898
McCall, Jack: killed Hickok, 190, 220, 659
McCanles, David: in Hickok fight, 658, 783, 1054, 1303
McCann, Bill: 174
McCann, Lloyd E: 1261
McCarty, Bridget: 112
McCarty, Henry: see Billy the Kid
McCarty, Joseph: 112
McCarty: Patrick, Catherine D, 112
McCarty, T.L: 957
McCarty, Tom: 1110
McCleave, William: army officer, 109
McClellan, George B: army officer, 363, 941, 1147-48

McClellan, Robert: fur trader, 350, 988
McClintock, James Harvey: historian, 467, 667, 1441
McCloskey, William: of Lincoln County War, 56
McClure, William Park: duelist, 1605
McColloch, Elizabeth: 1619
McCollum, Margaret Adams: 1007
McComas, Charlie: captured by Apaches, 259
McComas, Hamilton Calhoun: lawyer, killed by Apaches, 259
McConnell, Andrew: 1335-36
McCook, Alexander McDowell: army officer, 468
McCool, Lon: 222
McCoon, Perry C: 416
McCorkle, Emily: 495
McCormick, John: bandit, 898
McCormick, Richard C: Arizona governor, 1596
McCormick, W.J: 1097
McCoy, Joseph G: pioneer cattleman, 652
McCubbin, Robert G: writer, 614-15
McCue, John: 204
McCulloch, Ben: Tex. Ranger, 212, 658, 770, 1095, 1248
McCusker, Philip: scout, Comanche interpreter, 596
McCutchen, William: 1356; Mrs. William, 511
McDaniel, David: 898
McDaniel, John: desperado, 178, 260
McDermott, James: 852
McDermott, John D: historian, 1116
McDonald, Angus: fur trader, 574, 1075
McDonald, H.B: 898
McDonald, John: victim, 1213
MacDonald, Philip: 919
McDonald, W.H: supposed rustler, 1080-81
McDonald, William G: 275
McDonald, William Jesse (Bill): lawman, Tex. Ranger, 851
McDougal, Annie (Cattle Annie): 1430
McDougall, Charles: 900
McDougall, Duncan: fur trader, 305
McDougall, Thomas M: army officer, 759, 1207
McDowell, Irvin: army officer, 665, 1546, 1585
McElroy, William (William Blair): bandit, 573
McFadden, George: 1294
McFadden, Joseph: Pawnee Scouts captain, 1061
McFadden, W.H: Okla. oilman, hunter, 856
McFadden, William T: 901
McFarland, David F: 901-02
McFarlane, John: 902
McGavin, John: 1552
McGaw, William C: writer, 750, 824
McGillicuddy, Valentine T: Sioux agent, 1192, 1197, 1615
McGillivray, Alexander: Creek chief, 53, 323, 437, 986, 998-99, 1106, 1398, 1524
McGillivray, Farquhar: 903
McGillivray, Lachlan: southeast trader, 437, 903
McGillivray, Panton: 1398
McGillivray, Sehoy: daughter of Alexander, 1398
McGillivray (Durant), Sophia: 437

Maillet, Louis: Mont. frontiersman, 959, 1575
Majors, Alexander: Great Plains freighter, 293, 1253, 1312, 1435
Majors, Benjamin: 1304
Majors, Robert Darwin: 292
Maldanado, Alonso del Castillo: with Cabeza de Vaca, 208, 418, 470, 1043
Maldonado, Rodrigo: friend of Coronado, 326, 601
Mallet: Paul, Pierre, Frenchmen who contacted Santa Fe, 184, 521, 933-34
Malott, Catherine: captured by Girty, married him, 560-61
Man, John: 235
Man Afraid of His Horse: Brulé Sioux chief, 581
Mancos Jim: Ute leader, 1156
Maney, George: 934
Maney, James A: scouts commander, 438, 952, 1111-12
Maney, M.E. (Mike Manning): 1118
Mangas Coloradas: Apache chief, 227, 290-91, 298, 305-06, 308, 315, 343, 352, 388, 547, 613, 769, 865, 891, 990-91, 1037, 1042, 1261, 1394-95, 1406, 1412, 1418, 1483, 1485, 1500, 1535, 1577-78, 1597
Mangus: Mimbres Apache, son of Mangas Coloradas, 319, 368, 936, 1038, 1597
Mangus, Frank: 936
Manhattan Purchase: 995
Manhead: Indian hunter, 663
Manigault, Gabriel H: 41
Manion, James M: 299
Mannings, The: Tex. gunmen, 215, 355, 605, 1375-76
Manning, Jake: 1360
Mansker, Kaspar: Kentucky long hunter, 422
Manuelito: Mescalero chief, 75, 584, 1558
Manuelito Grande: Navaho leader, 199, 245, 687, 1041, 1586, 1620
Many Wounds: Nez Perce, 1155
Mappen, Joel: 1301
Mar, Helen: daughter of Joe Meek, 1560
Marble, Dannie: 1239
Marcelo: Mimbres Apache, 732, 750
Marchand, Sehoy: mother of Alexander McGillivray, 903-04
Marco Banjek: 672
Marcos de Niza: Franciscan friar, discoverer, 325, 402, 470, 529, 1617
Marcus, Henry: 446
Marcus, Josephine Sarah: married Wyatt Earp, 88, 445-49
Marcy, Randolph B: army officer, traveler, 57, 622, 1048, 1311
Mares, José: Texas trail blazer, 1481, 1482
Marest, Jesuits: Joseph Jacques, 942; Pierre Gabriel, 114
Marguerie, Francois: 566
María, José: 675
Marias, Anselmo: 487
Mariposa Indian War (Calif.):(1850-51), 1269
Marion, John H: newsman, editor, 983

Marlows, The: hard-cases, 730, 942-43
Marmaduke, Meredith: 1385
Marquette, Jacques: Jesuit, 367, 523, 737, 1012, 1145
Marquis, Thomas B: historical writer, 357, 527, 1314, 1592
Marsh, Grant: steamboat captain, 357
Marsh, James B: 1240
Marsh, John S: military officer, 1183
Marsh, Josiah F: military officer, 944
Marsh, Othniel C: paleontologist, 321, 590, 1061
Marshall, George: editor, 945-46
Marshall, H.H: 1023
Marshall, James W: struck gold in Calif. 1248
Marshall, John: U.S. chief justice, 376, 673, 1242
Marshall, Louis Henry: 1131
Marshall, Miles: 1273
Marshall, William Rainey: army officer, 175, 498
Marshe, Witham: 1006
Marshland, Stephen: desperado, 710, 794, 1495
Martín, Alejandro: 941
Martin, Dan: 948
Martín, Francisco: garroted The Turk, 1447
Martín, Hernán: explorer, 243, 595
Martin, Jim: 965
Martin, John: Custer trumpeter, 363
Martin, Joseph: 1168
Martin, Hurricane Minnie: 948-49
Martin, William A. (Hurricane Bill): hard-case, 448
Martinez, Antanacio: 102
Martinez, Curley: 1346
Martinez, Ignacio: Mexican Calif. official, 1216
Martinez, Jesus(a): mother of Mickey Free: 518
Martinez, Juan: Lincoln, New Mex. lawman, 602, 677, 1514
Martinez, Mariano: Navaho chief, 1517
Marx, Karl: political theorist, 804
Maryland, colonization of; 213-14
Mason, Charles G: 1388
Mason, Charlie: wed Anna Wetherill, 1538
Mason, David M: 1517
Mason, Edwin C: army officer, 356, 717, 1316
Mason, George: Constitution signatory, 951
Mason, Joe: 445
Mason, John: military officer, King Philip's War, 575, 1461
Mason, John Sanford: army officer, 1507
Mason, Julius: army officer, 1213
Mason, William: 898
Mason County (Tex.) Feud (Hoodoo War): (1875-76), 742
Massai: Apache, 1210, 1530
Massanet, Damian: missionary, 845-46
Massasoit: Wampanoag chief, 27, 395, 978, 1262, 1351, 1353, 1509, 1584
Massé, Enemond: Jesuit, 104, 439, 817, 848, 1182
Masterson, Edward J: lawman, 71, 299, 955, 1195, 1495
Masterson, James P: lawman, 448, 954, 956, 1058, 1525

Peacock, A.J: Dodge City gunman, 956
Peacock, George C: 1119
Peak, June: Tex. Ranger, 651, 729, 1148
Peale, Charles Willson: 1125
Peale, Titian: painter, 1270
Pearson, Ballard: 274
Peary, Robert A: polar explorer, 11, 69-70, 311, 649, 796, 922, 1073
Pease, F.D: 650
Pease, William B: 56
Peate, James J: Beecher Island scout, 1324, 1444, 1621
Peck, Edmund G: scout, prospector, 88, 1078, 1340
Peck, Sarah A: 495
Peckham, Howard H: historian, 1159-60
Pedraza, Juana: 825
Pedro, White Mountain Apache chief: 316, 402, 466-67, 983
Peel, B.L: 693
Peel, Ben: 794
Peeples, Abraham H: prospector, 919, 1525
Pelly: Kootenai Indian, 1348
Peña, José Enrique de la: 346
Pengra, Byron J: 769
Penn, William: founder of Penna., 1050, 1400, 1534
Pennington, Eli: Arizona frontiersman, 1103
Pennington, James: 1130
Pennington, Jim: bush pilot, 1459
Pennington, John L: So. Dak. governor, 190
Pennington, John P. (Jack): 1130
Penrose, Charles B: physician, 62, 216
Pepoon, Joseph B: 1131
Peppin, George W: Lincoln County lawman, 152, 321, 925, 957, 1240
Pequod War: (1637), 221, 270, 950, 979, 1353, 1373, 1461
Peralta, Miguel: of mine myth, 1509, 1529
Peralta, Pedro de: 1084
Peraltas, The: 1132, 1509
Peré, Jean: 737
Perez, Albino: New Mex. governor, 1041
Perez, Geneviva Hinajosa: 785
Perez, Juan: Spanish ship's officer, explorer, 344, 657, 949
Perez del Castillo, Sebastian: 748
Perico: Apache, 700
Perkins, George: 610
Perley, Sam F: physician, 1608
Perrine, George: gunman, 848
Perrine, Henry Bratt: army officer, 1156
Perrot, Nicolas: explorer, fur trader, 18, 376, 849, 941
Perrot, Nicolas (Jolycoeur): soldier, 1134
Perry, Cicero R.(Rufe): Indian fighter, Tex. Ranger, 15, 316, 854, 1307
Perry, Cis: 313
Perry, David: army officer, 742, 798, 1116, 1441, 1444, 1455
Perry, Frank W: army officer, missioner to Cochise, 291, 400, 612

Perry, John S: 1136
Perry, Matthew Calbraith: navy commodore, 1232
Perry, Oliver Hazard: naval officer, 347
Perry, W.I: 88
Pershing, John J: army officer, 207, 423, 1485-86
Persons, Clarence E: medical student, 1545
Peshine, John H.H: 94
Pesquiera, Ignacio: Sonora politician, 334, 651
Peta Nocona: Comanche chief, 356, 570, 1113-14, 1243
Pete Owl Child: Piegan Indian, 280
Peter: Indian guide in Philip's War, 271
Peter Joe: 9
Peters, Augusta: 1223
Peters, De Witt Clinton: 234
Peterson Charles S: historian, 1303
Peterson, William: 504
Petillon, W.F: 1302
Petone Sageski: Apache subchief, 12, 983, 1128-29
Peu-peu-mox-mox (Yellow serpent): Walla Walla chief, 639, 664
Pfouts, Paris S: vigilante, Mont. pioneer, 1067, 1152, 1505
Phelps, Frederick E: 1531
Phelps, Jesse: 1250
Phelps, John E: 1097
Phelps, Louis G., Eugene: 89
Phillips, John (Portugee): Wyo. frontiersman, 216, 522, 772
Phillips, Paul C: historian, 1380
Phillips, Samuel: 230
Phillips, Wendell: lawyer, reformer, 1401
Phillips, William K. (Butch Cassidy?): 1111
Philpot, Bud: stagecoach driver, 446, 449, 670, 1121
Phipps, William: 1137
Phips, William: Mass. governor, 134, 845
Photographers: 67, 81, 89, 116-17, 198, 237-38, 360, 503, 535, 662, 688-89, 701, 718, 794, 1021-22, 1036, 1151, 1191, 1241-42, 1342, 1586
Phy, Joe: 368
Pickett, Albert James: Ala. historian, 924, 993
Pickett, Tom: partisan, 147, 1248
Pico, Andres: 763
Pico, Pio: Calif. governor, 392, 922-23
Pico, Salomon: 79, 487
Picotte, Charles: 1143
Picotte, Honore: 354
Pierce, Abel (Shanghai): cattleman, 1145
Pierce, Charley: desperado, 1052, 1430
Pierce, Francis E: army officer, 30
Pierce, Michael: King Philip's War, 1039
Pierce, William: Creek War, 1399
Piernas, Pedro: 1224
Pierre's Hole fight: (1832), trappers and Blackfeet, 45, 60, 115, 137, 167, 216, 496, 514-15, 568, 576, 636, 822, 846, 967, 1052, 1056, 1225, 1229, 1313, 1385, 1386, 1411, 1469, 1604
Pijart, Jesuits: Claude, 1195; Pierre, 971
Pike, William: Donner party, 511, 1200

Vasquez, Louis: mountain man, trader, 87, 167, 1385

Vaudreuil, Rigaud de: *see* Rigaud de Vaudreuil

Vaughan, Alfred J: Blackfoot agent, 574, 629, 860

Vaughn, J.F: 334

Vaughn, Jesse Wendel: writer, historian, 349, 766, 1210, 1215, 1455

Vavasour, Mervin: 1076

Vedder, John: 1151

Velasco, Luis de: Viceroy, 1477

Vélez de Escalante, Francisco Silvestre: 466

Velo, Jacques: 521

Venard, Stephen: lawman, 1292

Venavides, Mariano: 386

Veramendi, Ursula Maria de: 148

Verdugo, Juan: 946

Verdun, Trinidad: last captive of hostile Apaches, 1128

Verendryes, The: 44, 246, 322, 544, 805, 855, 960, 1478-80

Verhulst, Willem: 995

Vestal, Stanley: writer, 397, 1314-15

Vial, Pedro: plains traveler, explorer, 941

Viana, Francisco: 519

Victor: Flathead chief, 256

Victor, Henry Clay: 1482-83

Victor, Orville: 1482

Victoria, Manuel: Calif. governor, 1361

Victorio: Mimbres Apache chief, 36, 60, 72, 74, 85, 94, 103, 128, 186, 203, 215, 230, 232, 237, 261, 263, 291, 317-18, 339, 352, 381, 383-85, 432, 438, 493, 501, 513, 520, 543, 548-49, 556, 565, 588, 613, 629, 684, 687, 744-45, 753, 761, 764, 827, 863, 865, 919, 936, 952, 976, 991, 1007, 1019, 1038, 1051, 1059, 1065, 1078, 1109, 1111-12, 1114, 1135, 1179, 1303, 1326, 1363, 1378-79, 1416, 1429, 1432, 1446-47, 1485, 1491, 1493, 1505, 1602

Vigilantes: 116, 139, 175, 191, 197, 322, 330, 367, 378, 392, 406, 423, 476, 487, 515, 528, 644-45, 685, 695, 710, 730, 744, 794, 811, 815, 878-79, 888, 947, 972, 1017, 1065-67, 1077, 1121, 1138-39, 1149, 1152-53, 1182, 1195, 1249, 1252, 1262, 1285, 1293, 1301, 1316, 1318-19, 1328, 1330-31, 1347, 1371, 1379-80, 1381, 1405, 1435, 1495, 1505, 1514, 1569-70, 1607, 1617

Villa, Francisco (Pancho): 672, 1216

Villagra, Gaspar de: Spanish poet-historian, 1622

Villanueva, José Vicente: Pedro Vial companion, 1482

Villasur, Pedro de: 1720 expedition of exploration, 814, 1040, 1468

Villegas, Juan de: precipitated Tiguex uprising, 876

Villereal, Enrique: 785

Villiers de Jumonville, Joseph Coulon de: killed by George Washington command, 328

Vincent, Frederick R: 107, 317

Viola, Herman J: writer, 913

Virgin Mary: *see* Mary Brown

Vizcaino, Sebastian: Spanish seaman, discoverer, 10, 209

Vizcarra, José Antonio: 750, 1042

Vollum, Edward P: 187

Volney, Constantin: 862

Von Schmidt, Eric: 1491

Voorhees, Luke: 320

Vroman, Charlie: 1579

Waddell, John C: merchant, freighter, 1595

Waddell, William B: Plains freighter, 293, 1253

Wade, Kid: outlaw, 198

Wade, Mason: historian, writer, 1115-16

Waden, Jean Etienne: 1158

Wadsworth, Samuel: 171-72

Waggoner, Dan: cattleman, 870

Wagner, Henry R: historian, writer, 500, 940, 1543

Wagner, Jack: 954

Wagner, Dutch John: desperado, 685

Wahmangopath: Little Turtle daughter, 1532

Wahoo Swamp (Fla.), battle of: (Nov. 17-21, 1836), 212, 727, 998

Wakely, Louise: 1605

Waldron, Richard: New Hamp. colonial, 1536

Waightman, George (Red Buck): desperado, 417, 851, 929

Waldo, Samuel: colonial entrepreneur, 1536

Waldo, William: 1120

Walkara: Ute chief, 86-87, 936, 1336, 1426

Walker, Alf M: 954

Walker, Elkanah: missionary to Spokans, 1232

Walker, Felix: a founder of Boonesboro, 1498

Walker, Fergus: army officer, 332

Walker, Francis A: 1192

Walker, Francis Marion: 1498

Walker, H.C: stagecoach operator, 1572

Walker, Henry P: historian, 1339

Walker, James T: nephew of Joseph R., 1501

Walker, John Hobart: military officer, 1131

Walker, John G: military officer, 230

Walker, John Grimes: naval officer, 1498

Walker, Joseph Reddeford: mountain man, 62, 136, 308, 336, 480, 515, 526, 636, 846, 935, 958, 967, 977, 1038, 1056, 1304, 1394-95, 1497-98, 1535, 1595

Walker, Joseph Rutherford Jr: lawman, 410

Walker, Kate E: 1585

Walker, Lucien: 1499

Walker, Sam: 140

Walker, Samuel: army officer, 297, 308-09, 1236

Walker, Samuel H: Tex. Ranger, 303

Walker, Thomas: 1168

Walker, Wayne T: writer, 1462

Walker, William: filibuster, 90, 125, 247, 334, 512, 578, 620, 637, 785, 1065, 1088, 1231, 1255, 1411

Walker, William W. (Bill): of Johnson County War, 174, 185, 216, 738, 1494

Walking Coyote, Samuel: Pend d'Oreille, buffalo conservor, 14, 1101

Webster, Daniel: statesman, 785, 935
Webster, John L: 1352
Webster, Theophilus C: 747, 830
Weedon, Frederick: 1092
Wee-no-sheik: Winnebago, 1168
Weichel(1), Mrs. George: 362
Weightman, Richard H: military officer, hard-case, 43, 1182
Weikert, Andrew: 405
Weippert, George: 624
Weir, Anthony: 217
Weir, Thomas Benton: army officer, 567
Weisel, George F: historian, writer, 1001
Weisenburg, Catherine: wed Sir William Johnson, 162, 730-31, 734
Weiser, Conrad: interpreter, 1003, 1006, 1299
Weiser, Jacob: prospector, 1132, 1508-09
Weium (William) Faithful: Modoc, 122
Weller, John B: surveyor, 1546
Wellman, Paul I: writer, 953, 1613
Wells, Daniel H: 1213
Wells, Edmund: writer, 389
Wells, L.B: 992
Wells, William: partisan of Indians, served whites, 862
Wells, Yelberton: William Wells' son, 1533
Welsh Indians: 474
Wesendorff, Max: army officer, 1438
Weslager, C.A: historian, writer, 395
Wesley, John: missionary, 176
West, Benjamin: artist, 149
West, Edgar: 955
West, James (James Love): shot by Mather, 957
West, Joseph R: military officer, 389, 935, 1069
Westbrook, John: farmer, 1536
Westbrook, Thomas: colonial officer, 820
Westerners, The: 1520
Weston, Edward: photographer, 1436
Weston, Thomas: 1022
Wetamoo: Wampanoag woman sachem, 1246
Wetherill, Anna: 1537
Wetherill, (Benjamin) Alfred: archeologist, 1538-39
Wetherill, Clayton: lay archeologist, 1537-38
Wetherill, John: trader, lay archeologist, 422, 1156, 1537-39
Wetherill, Louisa: John's wife, 1156, 1538
Wetherill, Richard: archeologist, trader, 493, 1537
Wetherill, Winslow: lay archeologist, 1537
Wetzels, The: 57, 159, 542, 688, 1540-41, 1569
Weyman, Edward: 1294
Wham, John W: Sioux agent, 1191-92
Wham, Joseph Washington: army paymaster, 315, 964
Wharfield, Harold B: historical writer, 1063
Wharfield, John C.A: army sergeant, 362
Wharton, Clifton W: army officer, 226, 385
Wharton, John A: 74
Wheat, Carl Irving: map historian, 579, 1015
Wheat, Mary Givens: 1499
Wheaton, Frank: army officer, 1273

Wheeler, Ben F: lawman, desperado, 176, 671
Wheeler, Bruce: 730
Wheeler, George M: topographical engineer, 321, 877, 946, 1345
Wheeler, Harry C: Ariz. Ranger, 778, 1070
Wheeler, Henry M: 1370
Wheeler, Homer W: army officer, writer, 591, 647, 1134
Wheeler, William Almon: 511
Wheeler, William B: army officer, 1545
Wheelock, Eleazar: 161
Whipple, Amiel W: army officer, 69, 704, 710, 848, 1353
Whipple, Stephen Girard: army officer, 128, 511, 874, 1198
Whirlwind: Cheyenne chief, 861
Whistler: Oglala Sioux chief, 192, 796
Whitcomb, Elias W: Wyo. rancher, 538
White, Andrew: 19
White, Benjamin, Mary: Kan. pioneers, 1553
White, Bill: 666-67
White, Blossom: 613
White, Brigit: sister of John White, 1551
White, Charlie: 670
White, Elijah: agent to Nez Perce, 461, 480, 822, 1234, 1252
White, Elizabeth: wed to Stewart E. White, 1553
White, Fred: lawman, 171, 448, 611, 1194
White, J.M. family: victims, 89, 95, 848
White, James: Volunteers officer, 392
White, James C: 1119
White, Joel: Mormon, 37-38
White, John: Roanoke colony, 619, 1176
White, John: California Ranger, 728
White, John, Joan: Massachusetts pioneers, 1246
White, John: Montana prospector, 766
White, Sarah: captive, 858, 1014, 1150, 1549
White, Sarah Gilbert: 1323
White, William: Virginia borderer, 187, 491, 1553-54
White Antelope: Cheyenne chief, 122, 265, 693, 1217, 1258, 1333
White Bird: Nez Perce chief, 54, 745-46, 874, 1000, 1059, 1194
White Bird Canyon (Idaho) battle of: (June 17, 1877) 53, 497, 874, 1079, 1116-17, 1135, 1187, 1415, 1441, 1444, 1455, 1554, 1609-10
White Buffalo Bull: Cheyenne, 1236
White Buffalo Woman: 1400
White Calf: Blackfoot Piegan chief, 109
White Eagle: Gros Ventre chief, 1315, 1555
White Eyes: Delaware chief, 1050
White Horse: Cheyenne leader, 1399
White Horse: Kiowa leader, 107
White Mountain Apache Reservation: 127
White Owl (Ookoonekah): Cherokee chief, 42, 422
White River (Colo.) fight: (Sept.-Oct. 1879), 302
White Stone Hill (No. Dak.), battle of : (Sept. 3, 1863), 1057, 1388
Whitehill, Harvey: lawman, 112, 688, 747, 1378, 1392, 1411, 1443, 1508